International Encyclopedia of
Business and Management

International Encyclopedia of Business and Management

Second edition

Edited by
Malcolm Warner

THOMSON
™
LEARNING

Australia • Canada • Mexico • Singapore • Spain • United Kingdom • United States

THOMSON
LEARNING

International Encylcopedia of Business and Management – Second Edition

British Library Cataloguing-in-Publication Data
A catalogue record for this book is available from the British Library

IEBM website http://www.iebm.com
IEBM Online http://www.iebm-online.com

ISBN: 1-86152-161-8 (set)
ISBN: 1-86152-985-6 (volume 1)
ISBN: 1-86152-986-4 (volume 2)
ISBN: 1-86152-987-2 (volume 3)
ISBN: 1-86152-950-3 (volume 4)
ISBN: 1-86152-951-1 (volume 5)
ISBN: 1-86152-952-X (volume 6)
ISBN: 1-86152-953-8 (volume 7)
ISBN: 1-86152-954-6 (volume 8)

First edition published in 1996 by Routledge, London

Typeset by HWA Text and Data Management, Tunbridge Wells

Printed in Great Britain by TJ International, Padstow, Cornwall

Using the encyclopedia

The *International Encyclopedia of Business and Management* is designed for ease of use. The following notes outline its organization and editorial approach and explain the ways of locating material. This will help users to make the most of the encyclopedia.

Sequence of entries

The encyclopedia contains 750 entries arranged in a single, alphabetical sequence through seven volumes. Entries are listed in alphabetical order. Note that the sequence follows the order of words rather than that of letter, and that the words *and, in, of* and *the* in entry titles are disregarded. A complete alphabetical list of entries is given in Volume 8 (the Index Volume).

The Index Volume

Volume 8 is devoted to a comprehensive index of the key terms, concepts, countries and names covered in Volumes 1 to 7, allowing users to reap maximum benefit from the encyclopedia. A guide to the index can be found at the beginning of the index. The Index Volume also includes permission acknowledgements, listed in alphabetical entry order.

Cross-references

The encyclopedia has been extensively cross-referenced in order to signpost other entries that are likely to be of interest. There are three types of cross-reference in the encyclopedia:

'See' cross-references

Throughout the alphabetical sequence of entry titles, there are cross-references which direct the user to the entry where a particular topic is discussed either under a different entry title or as part of a larger entry. For example:

Corporate taxation: see TAXATION, CORPORATE

Ethics: see BUSINESS ETHICS; MARKETING ETHICS

'See' cross-references within an entry

Cross-references within an entry direct the user to other entries closely related to the theme under discussion. These other entries will normally give a fuller explanation of the specific theme. These cross-references appear in small capital letters.

'See also' cross-references

At the very end of each entry, 'See also' cross-references guide the user to other entries of related interest, such as more specialized entries, biographical entries and geographical entries, as well as related entries in other disciplines. These cross-references appear in small capital letters in alphabetical order.

Structure of entries

A numbered contents list at the beginning of each entry in the encyclopedia gives the headings of its main sections. The scope and structure of the entry can thus be reviewed and sections of particular interest easily located.

Thematic entries begin with an 'Overview' section that serves as a brief introduction to the topic and a useful summary of the entry's contents. Biographical entries begin with a summary of the significant dates and events in the life of the subject and a list of his or her major works. Every entry is followed by a 'Further reading' section (see below).

Authors

The name of the author or authors is given at the end of each entry. A full list of contributors, showing their affiliation at the time of writing and the titles of the entries they have written, can be found in Volume 8.

Further reading

Each entry has a 'Further reading' section which gives details of all the references cited in the text. Additional suggestions for reading are also provided for those who wish to delve deeper into a particular subject. References cited in the text are preceded with an asterisk (*).

The Further reading list is arranged alphabetically by author/editor and chronologically under the authors'/editors' names. Publications with joint authors are listed under the name of the first author and are listed after any individual publications of that author. Where publications have been issued by an institution, the name of the institution is given as the author. English translations of publications in other languages have been given wherever possible.

Items in the Further reading list have been annotated with a brief description of the level, importance and usefulness of the publication listed.

References and suggestions for further reading are given in the Harvard style. The authors and editors have attempted to provide bibliographic data in the fullest possible detail.

Editorial style

Spelling and punctuation in the encyclopedia have been standardized to follow British English usage. The use of italics has been kept to a minimum and is normally restricted to foreign words and book or journal titles. Abbreviations and acronyms are spelled out in full on their first appearance in an entry. Chinese names have been westernized (i.e. Chen Derong becomes Derong Chen or Chen, D.). In alphabetical lists of names, *Mc* and *Mac* are treated as *Mac* and the next letter in the name determines the position of the entry.

Singapore, management in

1 Multicultural society and
   management
2 Western and Japanese management
   practices
3 The influence of Confucian values
4 The role of government and related
   agencies
5 Cross-border/transnational
   management
6 Future directions

Overview

Management practices and styles of business
organizations often reflect the culture of the
society in which these organizations exist. In
Singapore, there is a variety of management
practices and styles which can be attributed to
two major factors. The first factor is Singapore's multicultural immigrant origins. The
second factor is Singapore's open, pragmatic
and pro-business policies of attracting foreign
investors and multinational companies. These
two factors contribute to the array and richness of management practices and styles in
Singapore.

As Singapore experiences change and modernization, existing management practices and
styles are also transformed and modernized.
Changes in management are inevitable in order
that business organizations in Singapore,
whether they are small and medium enterprises
or multinational companies, may continue to
be competitive in the increasingly competitive
global business environment.

In this entry, four areas of management in
Singapore are examined: multicultural management, multinational management, the influence of Confucian values, and the role of
the government and related agencies.

1 Multicultural society and
management

Since its founding in 1819, Singapore has been
open to a wide variety of cultural influences.

As an immigrant society involving various ethnic groups and as a trading society involving
traders from both East and West, different peoples lived and traded with one another in the
city state. As the meeting point between East
and West, Singapore has always been a society
continually undergoing rapid socioeconomic
changes. It is therefore not surprising that Singapore has remained a culturally fluid society
until today (Chong 1987). The cultural fluidity
helps to explain the pragmatic adoption and
assimilation of new and foreign values and
practices into the existing management of business organizations in Singapore.

Multicultural management is a unique characteristic of Singapore's business organizations (see BUSINESS CULTURES, ASIAN
PACIFIC). Many foreign business organizations
operate in Singapore and they transfer some aspects of their own management cultures here.
Not only do these organizations bring to Singapore their own management values and practices, they also adopt and adapt some values
and practices of other business organizations in
Singapore. It is common for foreign business
organizations to adopt local practices, especially in the areas of human resource management and labour–management relations. The
local business organizations also adopt and
adapt some of the managerial values and practices of foreign businesses. The foreign and the
local are therefore intertwined in the management culture of many business organizations.
The existence of a multicultural mix of management values and practices is an indisputable
facet of Singaporean management.

2 Western and Japanese
management practices

Successful foreign management styles and
practices are viewed as an integral component
of Singapore's industrialization drive and
economic modernization strategy. By encouraging multinational businesses from both East
and West to operate and invest in Singapore,

the government has succeeded in linking up with multinational businesses and gaining much sought after foreign managerial expertise, in addition to capital investments, technology and foreign markets.

The use of US management concepts and the adoption of US management practices are common, especially among the larger local companies in Singapore. The government also helps to encourage certain types of foreign management, such as the open appraisal system used by Shell.

With the ascent of Japan as an economic power, Singapore, like other countries in the West and in the region (see, for instance, Malaysia's 'Look East' policy), has adopted Japanese management practices such as 'open offices', 'house unions' and 'quality control circles'. Japanese management practices have been accepted and become part of the management systems of both the local and foreign companies operating in Singapore (see JAPAN, MANAGEMENT IN; MALAYSIA, MANAGEMENT IN).

The adoption of foreign management practices and policies in Singapore is an outcome not only of the large number of foreign businesses in Singapore, but also of Singapore's desire to learn from the successful management practices of developed countries, such as the USA and Japan, in order to maintain its competitive edge in international business. Indeed, this policy of adopting the best management practices of both East and West has helped Singapore to remain competitive over the years, as Singapore continues to be ranked among the most competitive economies in the World Competitiveness Yearbook (2000).

Another contributing factor is modern Western-type education, particularly business and management education at both the undergraduate and MBA levels (see MANAGEMENT EDUCATION IN ASIA PACIFIC). Singaporeans who have studied and have been trained in the USA, for instance, find themselves fitting in very easily into the management culture of US multinational companies in Singapore. Singaporeans who set up their own businesses will also implement some aspects of the management practices they have studied overseas.

The survival motive

There is a compelling reason why management in Singapore is so pragmatic and open to new and foreign influences. This is inherent in the people's need for economic survival. With a total area of 639 square kilometres (247 square miles), it is a speck on the world map. With no natural resources to depend on, Singapore has to rely on its people for its continued survival and economic prosperity. This human capital has to be continually expanded and improved with the best management practices from other countries because international trade is the lifeblood of the city state.

The openness of Singapore's economy makes it necessary to compete with businesses from all over the world as well as with local businesses. Therefore business firms in Singapore need to be highly efficient and competitive. Acquiring the strengths of others, especially in the management of business, is considered a necessity.

Workers in Singapore are called on periodically by the government and related agencies to continually upgrade and improve their skills by training and retraining in order to maintain their competitiveness. According to the 1994 OECD (Organization for Economic Cooperation and Development) report, Singapore will be classified as a developed economy in 1996. As Singapore's economy matures, Singapore is moving towards higher value-added industries.

3 The influence of Confucian values

Singapore's small and medium business environment is dominated by people of Chinese descent, who comprise almost 80 per cent of the population. Singaporean Chinese retain many of their cultural characteristics. The mind-set of the Singaporean Chinese is still shaped largely by the teachings of Confucius. The basic tenets of Confucianism are obedience to and respect for superiors and parents, duty to family, loyalty to friends, humility, sincerity and courtesy (see CHINA, MANAGEMENT IN).

It is interesting to note that these values are also shared by the other ethnic groups in Singapore such as the Malays and the Indians. In many ways, Singaporeans place greater emphasis on the family than on the individual. They view themselves more as parts of the family unit than as free individuals, in sharp contrast to the Western emphasis on individualism. The strong impact of the family institution on the management of small and medium enterprises (SMEs) is not surprising, as a high proportion of SMEs are family businesses or family-orientated businesses. Thong (1987) highlights this point in his study of the management of Chinese small businesses in Malaysia.

The Chinese in Singapore favour increased modernization and a continuous improvement in living standards. They look to the West for new ideas concerning technology and business management. Western influences may have caused some traditional values to erode but the basic tenets of Confucian behaviour can still be observed.

The importance of close personal connections, or *guanxi*, is a vital element of business in Singapore, as in China, Taiwan and Hong Kong. Little or no distinction is made between business and personal relationships. Any successful businessperson in Singapore will belong to a network of personal friends, relatives and associates with common interests. The importance of personal connections has its roots in the traditional concept of family. For the Chinese, individuals are parts of the collective family whole. In Singapore, executives and entrepreneurs work constantly to maintain and expand their networks of connections. For Chinese entrepreneurs, networking is inherent in their tradition and culture.

Most owners (or managers) are paternalistic toward their employees and feel responsible for their well-being, which is very much like the responsibility felt by most heads of families toward members of their own households. The paternalistic attitudes of management and the family atmosphere are clearly demonstrated in the management of many SMEs in Singapore. Chong (1987) sums up the management style of the typical Chinese small business in Singapore as 'paternalistic'

and 'authoritarian', with the manager behaving as the 'patriarch' of a family.

With the rapid development of Singapore's economy and the modernization of Singapore's society, the family system is also being transformed. Traditional small businesses in Singapore have been affected by the changes in society, particularly in the family system. A generation gap has developed between the older owners (or managers) and the younger family members or relatives (employees) in terms of perceptions, values and management practices. Change seems to be the only solution for continued survival in a fast-changing business environment. Chong *et al.* (1983) provide an illuminating analysis of the traditional coffee shops in Singapore and show how this traditional Chinese small business has to change and modernize to keep in step with the changes taking place in Singapore.

4 The role of government and related agencies

The government in Singapore has always adopted a pro-business stance and played a leading role by setting examples through its civil service departments, statutory boards and government-owned companies. The Economic Development Board (EDB) and Trade Development Board (TDB) have played key roles in promoting business and trade in Singapore and helped Singaporean companies and entrepreneurs expand into overseas markets. Certain types of management practice are encouraged, such as the open appraisal system, quality control circles and harmonious labour–management relations. Management courses are conducted by various government agencies such as the Productivity and Standards Board (PSB). There is also provision of financial support for training through the Skills Development Fund (SDF).

All these demonstrate the pragmatism of Singapore's government. Pragmatism is seen in the modernization of traditional small businesses, as well as in the adoption of foreign management practices by local firms and the adoption of local practices by foreign firms. Pragmatism and openness to change and adaptation are therefore common characteristics of Singaporean management. Indeed,

Singaporean companies are continually exhorted to adapt and to anticipate changes in order to survive and remain competitive in the global business environment.

Supplementing the government's efforts, private educational institutions and professional bodies such as the Singapore Institute of Management (SIM) also conduct regular management and management-related courses.

5 Cross-border/transnational management

In 1993, a group of Singaporean companies signed a joint-venture agreement with provincial leaders in Suzhou, China. The plan is to develop a self-contained industrial, commercial and residential estate modelled on Singapore itself. Dubbed the 'Second Singapore' development project, it will see the transfer of Singapore's managerial expertise and success to Chinese partners.

As part of its regionalization drive, Singapore's government is actively promoting investments in the rapidly growing markets of the region, such as China, India, Vietnam, the Philippines and Malaysia. Singapore has a pivotal role to play by promoting cross-border, transnational regional economic development with its neighbours and other countries in Asia. This is clearly evident in the transfer of managerial expertise to the other economies in the region (see ASIA PACIFIC, MANAGEMENT IN).

An illustration of this transfer of managerial expertise by Singaporean companies can be seen in the economic collaboration between Singapore and its neighbours, Malaysia and Indonesia, in what is termed the 'Growth Triangle'. The promotion of the Growth Triangle is part of Singapore's regionalization drive. In this agreement, Singapore has a venture with Malaysia and Indonesia to move some of its low-end production offshore to the adjacent areas of Johore (a southern state in Malaysia) and Batam (an Indonesian island located close to Singapore). Under the agreement, Singapore will provide the management expertise while Malaysia and Indonesia will provide cheap labour and land for labour-intensive industries such as electronics assembly.

6 Future directions

With the maturing of Singapore's economy, a larger entrepreneurial base is necessary as the private sector is expected to become the engine of growth in the economy in the 1990s and beyond. The move to encourage greater entrepreneurial participation is also part of a counter-strategy to ensure Singapore's survival and competitiveness.

The push for entrepreneurism will have an impact on the evolution of Singapore's management culture and style. Even as the best management practices of the East and West are adapted and assimilated, local entrepreneurs and managers will increasingly have to understand the diverse cultures and business environments in the region. This new breed of managers, with a new mind-set orientated towards the region, will have to develop the necessary skills and competences to manage a different cultural workforce in a different cultural workplace. Managing employees in Vietnam, Burma, the Philippines or China will be different from managing employees in Singapore. In view of the fact that more Singaporean companies are investing and setting up joint-venture operations in the region (as they 'fly the nest'), cross-cultural management will become an increasingly important aspect of Singapore's transnational management development.

The promotion of entrepreneurism will contribute to the development of business management in Singapore. As the management culture evolves, the best management practices and policies of both West and East will continue to be adapted and assimilated into the management of Singapore's businesses. The success of Singapore's business management style and expertise in moving across borders, for instance in the Singapore–Suzhou project, will depend on how well Singapore management assimilates the local business culture and environment in China, or for that matter, other countries in the region in which Singaporean companies have invested and will invest in the future.

The multicultural and multinational mix of management practices and styles will continue to be a characteristic of management in Singapore due to Singapore's pro-business policies, pragmatism and open economy.

The financial crisis that was precipitated by the devaluation of the Thai baht in July 1997 was a wake-up call to Singapore. Singapore is one of the few countries in the Asia Pacific region to escape the titanic financial meltdown that engulfed the region. Singapore has strong and sound financial institutions, and a prudent economic management which has resulted in yearly budget surpluses. However, Singapore has not been unscathed by the financial maelstrom. The drive towards greater regionalization and the increase in intra-ASEAN (Association of South East Asian Nations) trade between Singapore and her major trading partners in the region, notably Indonesia and Malaysia, have made Singapore vulnerable to the vagaries and violent changes in the financial systems of the neighbouring countries. The economic slowdown experienced by the region as a whole also affected Singapore's economic growth. However, Singapore remains the most competitive economy, maintaining her open market economic systems and taking decisive action to reduce business costs. In spite of the slower pace of economic growth, Singapore's economy continues to be robust and resilient.

JOO-SENG TAN
NANYANG TECHNOLOGICAL UNIVERSITY

Further reading

(References cited in the text marked *)

Chew, S.B. (1988) *Small Firms in Singapore*, Singapore: Oxford University Press. (Examines the nature and economic contribution of small firms in Singapore.)

Chiu, S.W.K., Ho, K. and Liu, T.K. (1998) *City-States in the Global Economy: Industrial Restructuring in Hong Kong and Singapore*, Boulder, CO: Westview Press. (Comparative study of two dynamic Asian city-states that are emerging as key regional – indeed global – cities. Providing both historical comparisons and analyses of contemporary issues, the authors consider the patterns, strategies, and consequences of industrial restructuring.)

* Chong, L.C. (1987) 'History and managerial culture in Singapore: "pragmatism", "openness" and "paternalism"', *Asia Pacific Journal of Management* 4 (3): 133–43. (Examines the historical evolution of culture and management in Singapore.)

Chong, A. (ed.) (1997) *Business Guide to Singapore*, Oxford: Butterworth Heinemann. (Part of the *Business Guide to Asia* series, provides detailed information on setting up and running business ventures in Singapore.)

* Chong, L.C., Kau, A.K. and Tan, T.S. (1983) 'Management adaptation to environmental change: the coffee shop industry in Singapore', *Proceedings of the 10th International Small Business Congress*, Singapore: Applied Research Corp, 277–82. (Analyses the modernization of the traditional coffee shop business in Singapore.)

ENDEC (Entrepreneurial Development Centre) 'Contribution to Entrepreneurship and Small Business Development Research' 1994, special issue of *Journal of Small Business and Entrepreneurship* 10 (3). (Focuses on various aspects of the development of small business entrepreneurship and management.)

Hansen, H.L. (1989) 'Harvard Business School theory in foreign cultures with special reference to east and south east Asia', in *Management Development of Small and Medium-Sized Enterprises in Asia*, proceedings of the 2nd Tokyo conference of the Foundation for Asian Management Development, Tokyo: Foundation for Asian Management Development. (Elaborates on the importance of cultural sensitivity in Western-style management training on Asian economies.)

Koh, J.K., Tan, T.S. and Goh, Y.T. (1989) 'Singapore', in *Management Development of Small and Medium-Sized Enterprises in Asia*, proceedings of the 2nd Tokyo conference of the Foundation for Asian Management Development, Tokyo: Foundation for Asian Management Development, 161–77. (Elaborates on the upgrading of management skills of SMEs in Singapore.)

Lee, K.Y. (2000) *From Third World to First: The Singapore Story 1965–2000*, New York: HarperCollins. (Singapore's founding father and senior minister's memoirs documents key moments in Singapore's history including its separation from Malaysia as a separate nation to the Asian financial crisis of the late 1990s.)

Low, P.S. (1984) 'Singapore-based subsidiaries of US multinationals and Singaporean firms: a comparative management study', *Asia Pacific Journal of Management* 1: 29–39. (A comparative study of various aspects of US and Singaporean management.)

McKendrick, D., Doner, R.F. and Haggard, S. (2000) *From Silicon Valley to Singapore: Location and Competitive Advantage in the Hard Drive Industry*, Stanford, CA: Stanford University Press. (Examines how decisions to locate manufacturing in Southeast Asia (predominantly Singapore) have contributed to the global dominance of US firms in the hard disk drive industry.)

Putti, J.M., Chong, F.H. and Thomas, J. (1985) 'American and Japanese management practices in their Singapore subsidiaries', *Asia Pacific Journal of Management* 2 (2): 106–14. (Analyses the extent of the transfer and implementation of US and Japanese management practices in their subsidiaries operating in Singapore.)

Stening, B.W., Everett, J.E. and Longton, P.A. (1983) 'Managerial stereotypes in Singaporean subsidiaries of multinational corporations', *Asia Pacific Journal of Management* 1 (3): 56–64. (Examines various managerial stereotypes held by local and expatriate managers.)

* Thong, T.S.G. (1987) 'The management of Chinese small-business enterprises in Malaysia', *Asia Pacific Journal of Management* 4 (3): 178–86. (Traces the development of Chinese business enterprises in Malaysia.)

* *World Competitiveness Yearbook* (2000) Lausanne, Switzerland: International Institute for Management Development. (Useful annual report ranking the various economies in terms of competitiveness.)

See also: ASIA PACIFIC, MANAGEMENT IN; BUSINESS CULTURES, ASIAN PACIFIC; CHINA, MANAGEMENT IN; CULTURE, CROSS-NATIONAL; HOFSTEDE, G.; HONG KONG, MANAGEMENT IN; HUMAN RESOURCE MANAGEMENT IN ASIA PACIFIC; JAPAN, MANAGEMENT IN; MALAYSIA, MANAGEMENT IN; ORGANIZATION CULTURE; TAIWAN, MANAGEMENT IN

Skill formation systems

1 Overview
2 The governance of skill formation systems
3 Conclusion: systems and cases

1 Overview

The formation of vocationally relevant skills is problematic: although skills are used within the market, there are frequently difficulties in producing them through pure market means. A diversity of mechanisms for resolving this problem have been devised, producing a diversity of skill formation systems.

Individuals must make many decisions about acquiring skills when very young, and often neither the individuals nor their parents have the knowledge about the future required to make decisions in an economically rational manner. There are major time lags and risks. Education is expensive and can take many years to complete before there is any return; it is an investment decision. Then, chances of entry into the chosen occupation can be difficult to predict. The skill requirements of occupations also change, further increasing risk. The situation is also problematic for employers. Skills have something of the character of public goods. A firm which trains its employees may find that other firms which do not do so simply recruit the workers it has trained – in the worst case attracting them with higher salaries made possible by the fact that the 'poaching' firms have not borne training costs. Interest therefore focuses on mechanisms which might resolve these information, investment and public goods problems. Research has here been able to draw on a more general literature concerning different forms of governance of economies (Crouch *et al.* 1999).

2 The governance of skill formation systems

According to governance theory, economic transactions are nested in a wider institutional context which provides sanctions to encourage certain kinds of behaviour rather than others. The main types of governance have been identified as a) market, b) hierarchy, c) state, d) association, and e) community. We shall here examine each of these governance institutions, but only in so far as they relate to the question of skill formation.

Market

Within a pure market, decisions over and expenditure on the acquisition of all education would be left entirely in the hands of young people and their parents. In practice this is rarely done; in all but the poorest countries we find state education systems which are both free of charge and compulsory up to a certain age level. Parents might lack the incentive to pay for the education of their children, and might prefer to send them to work to supplement the family income. They could also experience difficulties in assessing the quality of the education their children were receiving. However, in some countries (e.g. the United Kingdom) the market governs general education for the children of wealthy families. The parents of these children are not only rich enough to pay the high costs and to discount the long time horizons of financing their children's education, but also themselves usually come from educated backgrounds and understand in some detail the uses of education.

An alternative mode of relying on the market for the provision of education would be for potential employers to provide and/or fund education for children from a very early age, in the expectation that the children would later work for them. However, firms would have no guarantee that the children, once educated, would in fact supply their future labour to them. As investors in education, employers would also have to accept the risk of supporting a child's education long before they had knowledge of his or her capabilities. There are again some exceptions that show that the model of pure market provision is not absurd. Some large Swedish firms have recently taken an interest in the development of company schools, which would provide normal secondary education as well as specific skill formation (Crouch *et al.* 1999: 123). These are usually firms in a labour monopoly position and therefore at less risk from poaching than others; and under the Swedish scheme the state subsidizes the project (see SWEDEN, MANAGEMENT IN).

The market becomes really important at later stages, when vocational skill formation takes over from general education. The role of parents becomes smaller, time horizons become shorter, and it becomes easier to determine the aptitudes of the young people concerned. The factors that handicapped the market as a provider of general education diminish, and it becomes easier to envisage it as a major influence on the provision of education.

In a classic contribution, Becker (1962, 1975) argued that in fact the market was all that was necessary for skill formation, because skills consisted of two components: a general one and a firm-specific one. If public provision deals with the former, firms have adequate incentive to provide the latter. The poaching argument does not apply, since by definition a firm-specific skill cannot be transferred to another employer. Therefore, provided firms can pay trainees low enough wages to make the cost of the training worth while, there is no problem of vocational skill formation that the market, building on a public general system, cannot solve (see TRAINING).

According to Stevens (1995), Becker's argument ignored the existence of an intermediate kind of skill: those that were too specific to particular work contexts to be provided through general education, but which, even if provided within the framework of an individual firm's working procedures, could be transferred from one firm to another. She called these skills 'transferable', and identified them as a case of market failure. Further, Becker oversimplified the question by focussing on it as the poaching issue alone. There are also problems in inducing young people to bear or share the costs of their skill formation, whether by directly paying fees or by accepting low wages during the training period. The issue is not absolute: many examples can be found of training markets operating in this way, but these are usually explicable in terms of some factor which reduces either the transferable cost problem or the problems of ignorance and uncertainty facing the individuals.

For example, in many countries young people (mainly young women) pay fees to commercial institutions that equip them with office skills. The skills concerned are highly transferable, reducing the willingness of employers to provide them, but the job opportunities that they make available are sufficiently widespread and predictable to give young women the incentive to pay for the courses.

A very different example is provided by certain new high-technology sectors, primarily computing software. Here individuals are regularly responsible for providing their own training, which, in contrast to the acquisition of office skills, can be very expensive. These are well-informed investors, with strong expectations that their investment will pay off after a short time lag. They are already knowledgeable in the field and therefore accurately understand their training needs. The firms for which they work are usually grouped geographically close to each other – as in the Silicon Valley case which has become paradigmatic for this kind of activity – so there is high interaction among both firms and individuals (Saxenian 1994). Knowledge of the labour market, firms' requirements and individuals' capacities are therefore high on all sides. Knowledge of this kind reduces risk, especially in a sector which to date has known only constant expansion. It has even been argued that in this field the usual theories about poaching are reversed, and that the movement of personnel from one firm to another helps advance technical creativity.

Whether the market can operate in this way in sectors lacking these distinctive characteristics is more doubtful. As we shall also see in the later discussion of community governance, it may in fact be argued that the Silicon Valley phenomenon is so underwritten by specific institutional characteristics that it does not constitute a pure market.

Lazonick and O'Sullivan (2000) have criticised Becker's model more profoundly, by questioning the very existence of many 'firm-specific' skills. Their review of the literature on firm-specific human capital found that those characteristics that make skills 'firm specific' have still not been identified, almost four decades after Becker wrote his seminal work. They point out that in Japan skilled manual workers are usually described as 'multiskilled', which is very different from training in distinct 'craft skills' (as has historically been the case for example with British workers) (see JAPAN, MANAGEMENT IN). In recent years, German training schemes too have stressed 'polyvalent' skills and adaptability (see GERMANY, MANAGEMENT IN). More generally, argue Lazonick and O'Sullivan, given extensive in-house training and long-term employment relations, it may well be the social tie between employer and employee rather than skill per se which is 'specific'. The Beckerian model assumes that, whether skill is 'general' or 'specific', the only tie between employer and employee is an economic one. At the same time, the social tie may have positive productivity consequences if workers are engaged in a cumulative and collective learning process. This, they point out, is also excluded from the Becker model: there is no theory of why skills, be they 'general' or 'specific', are productive; the Beckerian theory, like neo-classical theory more generally, is about who pays for investment in skills, and even then is inconclusive, both theoretically and empirically.

Hierarchy

As has long been recognized by the theory of the firm, corporations, especially large ones, do not operate by market transactions alone, but also through internal relations of authority, or hierarchy. Sometimes a hierarchy can extend beyond the boundary of the firm itself. Inter-firm hierarchy occurs where large firms develop long-running relations with subcontractors that are not liable to be disrupted by market fluctuations. Customer firms, for example, may sustain long-term relations with suppliers, or a manufacturing firm with distributors. It is a pattern particularly associated with the Japanese economy.

The hierarchy model is very important for skills provision (Crouch *et al.* 1999: chapter 7). Large corporations are frequently labour monopsonists. Such firms are however unlikely to pay lower wages than those in competitive labour markets, as conventional monopsony theory would suggest. Indeed, their cumulated competitive advantages enable them to pay wages to workers in local labour markets that are *above* the competitive market wages. These high wages can in turn elicit greater productivity from employees that can sustain the higher wages of these employees over time. In that case they have little fear of poaching and may well provide extensive training services. The skills transmitted may in principle be transferable, but the firm's position makes them equivalent to specific skills. Sometimes there will be small firms in the area, which will depend parasitically on recruiting persons trained by the large firm. However, provided these other firms are small enough and few enough, it is of little concern to the large firm, constituting merely a trickle of waste and not a challenge to its dominance. Sometimes these small firms may be suppliers to the large one, in which case the latter positively gains from the fact that the former are using staff which it had trained. In the case of the large firm with stable relationships with suppliers or distributors, it may even organize such training as part of its means of sustaining quality within its value chain.

This model solves most of the normal problems of vocational training (see TRAINING, ECONOMICS OF). The collective goods aspects which cause problems for market provision either become private goods within the enterprise or club goods within the supplier or distributor chain. As such, it is a model found very widely wherever there are large firms. The Japanese case is exceptional, in that so much industrial production is based on firms of this type. It is notable that the Japanese formal education system has virtually no vocational component at all. Young people leave either high school or higher education with an entirely general formation. Firms recruit them on the basis of their examination achievements (as well as some informal personal criteria), and then train them, and subsequently retrain them over the years, for vocational tasks. But these Japanese employees are usually deemed to be 'multiskilled' rather than trained for specific vocational or craft functions. However, this does not make these firms vulnerable to the loss of workers to whom they have imparted transferable skills, as identified by Stevens (1995), because there is almost no transfer among the large Japanese firms; skilled individuals at all levels rarely leave the firm with whom they started their careers. Similar examples may be found, though less frequently than in Japan, among large firms in virtually all countries which cultivate long-term identities and corporate cultures linked to long-service employment. Although Becker's model seems to follow the rationale of pure markets, it in fact seems more applicable within the hierarchy model.

Hierarchy is of course of little help in sectors dominated by small firms, unless these work for customer firms which integrate suppliers. It therefore flourishes in situations of imperfect competition. While neo-classical economic theory has difficulty in accounting for dynamism and efficiency in firms having these characteristics, studies of business management in the Schumpeterian tradition have identified many ways in which such firms do in fact pursue growth paths that establish new standards of efficiency – their capacity to invest strongly in skill formation being an important aspect of this (Lazonick 1991; Lazonick and O'Sullivan 2000). (See DYNAMIC CAPABILITIES, PENROSE, E.T., SCHUMPETER, J.)

State

The most straightforward answer found in advanced societies to the problem of collective goods is provision by the state, which can use its authority either to provide them directly (funding them by taxation or other levies) or to require their provision by other entities. Not surprisingly, the state has played a major role in the provision of skill formation. In the purest cases (found, for example, in France and Sweden), vocationally relevant courses are provided as branches of the state education system (Crouch *et al.* 1999: chapter 4). Most state education systems provide general education for the majority of children until the end of the compulsory stage (nowadays around 15 or 16), with continuing general (or academic) education for those likely to proceed to higher education or enter occupations requiring advanced literacy and numerical skills. Under a system of state-provided vocational skill formation a far higher proportion of the age range continues within the school system until about age 18, but taking a diversity of vocationally related courses rather than general ones. More generally, state provision also exists for certain occupations in systems that are not generally dominated by the model: for example, the training of medical practitioners.

Direct state provision is in some respects the mirror image of market provision: they have opposite advantages and defects. If public provision scores over the market in its unproblematic solution of collective goods problems, it loses in often being remote from firms' needs. There is a constant need to bridge the gap between teachers in the training schools and employers. One solution, found very generally but particularly evident in the case of Sweden, is to have representatives of the industry concerned on the bodies which amend curriculum, set standards and regulate examinations. A second possibility is to have young people spend part of their training time working in firms (a French system known as *alternance*). Such solutions still have defects. One is the problem of deciding with which firms the public system should cooperate, to put representatives on boards or to provide placements; errors in selection based on lack of knowledge of the leading firms could lead to training being based on inadequate models.

A further issue concerns the difference between initial and further training. This distinction was not a problem in the pure hierarchy case, where, once one can assume stable long-term employment and supplier relations, it is in the large firm's interests to sustain levels of competence in the long run. Within the market form it presents the same problems as does initial training. The state can provide some good solutions to initial training, but has particular problems with further training. Further training needs are often firm-specific, but even if they are not it is difficult for public authorities to provide courses for skills upgrading for people already with careers.

The state has certain means for tackling the problem. Institutions such as distance-learning universities have been extremely useful for people seeking a change of career. Another device, again pioneered in France, is to provide a system of training levies (Aventur and Brochier 1996). Firms pay a compulsory charge which finances a state system of adult courses but can avoid the levy by providing courses themselves. Clearly they have an incentive to do the latter, since in that way they can provide courses devised by themselves. The French government has found this mechanism useful in securing an upgrading of the skills of the existing work force. There are however disadvantages: how does a government agency know which skills it is worth developing? How does it evaluate the quality of internal training provided primarily to avoid paying a levy?

Association

A mechanism that has one foot in the collective-good capacity of public authority and the other close to firm's needs is a skill formation system based on associations of firms. If an association has authority over its members it acquires something of the stature of the state. If it remains close to its members it solves the problem of remoteness common to public agencies. Associational systems can function alongside state provision: for example, one solution to the problem of recruiting employer representatives to assist public agencies is to delegate the task to associations.

Associational governance is particularly suited to the management of apprenticeships, one of the most prominent forms of skill formation (Crouch *et al.* 1999: chapter 5). Emerging out of medieval systems of craft training, it has adapted to the growth of large-scale industry and a growing diversity of services. It requires detailed co-operation between the public education system and associations which manage the contribution of firms without simply seeking advantages for individual companies, for instance the case where the state seeks direct partnerships with

corporations rather than representative bodies.

Apprenticeship systems exist for various occupations in many countries, especially for highly skilled manual crafts. In Germany, Austria, and a small number of other countries it is more extensive and has become the main system of skill formation. In Germany and Austria these associations are not straightforward private organizations of employers but official chambers. These are representative bodies, democratically accountable to their member firms, but having public status. Membership in these associations is compulsory and they are financed through compulsory levies. They therefore exist in a space between the state and private associations. As such, they can have public tasks delegated to them. Many of the successes in German industry have been attributed to its apprenticeship system, though in recent years it has come under some strain (Backes-Gellner 1996; Büchtemann and Verdier 1998; Wagner 1998). It is a high-cost system, and German employers complain that they are suffering from a burden not carried by their competitors in countries which neglect skills provision and that the officers of some chambers are not close enough linked to industry at a time of rapid change. Finally, although the system has demonstrated its capacity to move into many services sectors, it can be slow to adopt new activities.

To date, these problems have not undermined the apprenticeship system as such, but they have been important at a different point. Like the state skill formation systems with which they are in fact integrated, apprenticeship schemes operate at the initial training stage. In principle they could be extended into partnerships between chambers and the formal education system at further training levels, but in practice this has never been the case (Sauter 1996). Now that further training has become so important, firms have taken the opportunity to stress their determination to place it outside the framework of apprenticeship. Instead it operates through corporate hierarchies, mainly therefore among large firms only. This could have the consequence of leaving the apprenticeship model to deal only with a static initial training, while all innovation is dealt with within firms at a higher training level.

Community

Claims that formal associations might lose touch with firms have directed attention to a final possible form of governance, the informal local community. Under the community model informal relations of reciprocity and the possibilities for behaviour control afforded by a local community enforces a production of collective goods on small and medium-sized enterprises (SMEs) (Crouch *et al*. 1999: chapter 6).

Within an advanced economy, relations of this kind are found only in specialized areas and sectors. Localities may have pre-existing traditions of cooperation and solidarity. These in turn will have made possible local production systems, where many SMEs sharing similar specializations are concentrated. These thrive in an advanced economy in sectors where there are competitive gains from interaction, mainly because of a capacity to advance knowledge ahead of its codification (so-called tacit knowledge). These include those where innovative design is required to stay abreast of fashion (clothing, footwear, jewellery), those which benefit from close relations between customers and suppliers (both supplier chains and specialized machinery producers), and those dependent on scientific advance (computer software, high-tech science industries), or other forms of knowledge (financial sector, publishing).

The most closely studied cases of this phenomenon are the local production systems of central and north-east Italy (Becattini 2000). A similar outcome can however be generated by other means. For example, in Germany, and parts of the UK and the USA, research oriented universities and research centres, rather than traditional communities, can provide the focus for concentration on specialisms. Interfirm interaction will develop from this, though it is unlikely that a community as such will emerge; the research centre or university remains the focal point for collective goods provision.

Skill formation can be among the collective goods provided in such an environment, since the required control mechanisms exist. However, with the exception of university-based systems, the training provided is often highly informal, uncertified, possibly even unnoticed. There will also be little recognizable distinction between initial and subsequent training. Indeed, in all knowledge- and innovation-based industries, including those based on university research, it becomes impossible to distinguish between further training and simply doing the job. A dress designer or applied scientist is constantly expanding her knowledge base, simply by working.

The creative community therefore represents a skill formation system where most of the distinctions that are normally crucial to the discussion of this topic break down: if the community is strong enough, the distinction between collective and private goods breaks down; distinctions between levels of training disappear; even that between training and the job itself, and therefore that between the school and the market. This has the advantages of extreme flexibility. However, as with the other systems, the strengths of the form are also its weaknesses. The Italian districts mentioned have difficulty in progressing to more advanced kinds of skill and applications of technology. Levels of formal education among Italian entrepreneurs are low. Indeed, measured by formal qualifications the prosperous districts of central Italy are considerably 'behind' the economically backward south of the country. Small enterprises employ young people who leave the education system without completing courses, and train them in vocationally relevant skills. This provides a disincentive to young people in these regions to remain in education, limiting the country's ability to excel in high-tech industries.

But this case raises a fundamental issue. Central and north-eastern Italy continue to do well in those sectors where the flexible, informal knowledge they have brings advantages. Is this a defect? From the point of view of the methodology of skill formation research, the answer is 'yes'. The starting point of this research is always formal educational qualifications. Informally acquired knowledge, however rich, counts for nothing. In terms of the value of knowledge for economic innovation, this is clearly false. This is true, not only for a Tuscan entrepreneur successfully designing shoes, but also for a Silicon Valley software specialist whose PhD tells us little about his most recent achievements in knowledge and skill acquisition. Meanwhile, many young people are today extending their formal education but finding that this does not necessarily help them find work (Béduwé and Espinasse 1995).

3 Conclusion: systems and cases

The five forms of skill formation system outlined above should not be regarded as a series of empty boxes to which individual national or other examples can be assigned. 'Does Germany count as statist or associationist?' is not a sensible question. Empirical examples, certainly if these are examined at national levels, will almost always comprise mixes. We can see that this is likely to be true when we consider that each theoretical form has weaknesses that are the obverse of its strengths. It is through the balancing of characteristics from a mix of types that it is possible to avoid the consequences of this. This should not be interpreted in a functionalist way: there is no necessary reason why actors in a particular system will have produced an optimal mix; and in any case the strengths and weaknesses of particular forms and mixes of forms will vary with time and circumstance.

But the fact of empirical mixing remains important. Very few of the cases which have been referred to above are absolute, even though they are cited because they provide clear examples of specific forms. High-tech districts such as Silicon Valley are a combination of market- and community-driven forms. The Swedish state system draws on both large-firm hierarchy and associations. Although the German system makes particularly strong use of associations, they are associations of a statist kind. The Italian industrial districts are increasingly using the hierarchy of the large firm's supplier chain to keep abreast of product innovation and marketing.

The fact that the various types of system appear in varied combinations produces considerable diversity at national and other levels. These differences in turn are likely to be asso-

ciated with different performance capabilities at the level of products, markets, sizes of firm and forms of organization (Lazonick and O'Sullivan 2000; Juergens 2000; Freyssenet *et al.* 1998).

COLIN CROUCH
EUROPEAN UNIVERSITY INSTITUTE

Further reading

(References cited in the text marked *)

* Aventur, F. and Brochier, D. (1996), 'Continuing vocational training in France' in J. Brandsma *et al.* (eds), *Continuing Vocational Training: Europe, Japan and the US*, Utrecht: Uitgeverij Lemma. (Discussion of French approaches to the issue of further training.)

* Becattini, G. (2000) *Il Distretto Industriale*, Turin: Rosenberg and Sellier. (A state of the art account of the Italian industrial district model by one of its leading analysts.)

* Backes-Gellner, U. (1996) *Betriebliche Bildungs- und Wettbewerbungsstrategien im deutsch-britischen Vergleich*, Munich: Rainer Ham. (Comparison of British, German and some other skill-formation systems from an institutional economics perspective.)

* Becker, G. S. (1962, 1975) *Human Capital: A Theoretical and Empirical Analysis, with Special Reference to Education*, 1st edn 1962, 2nd edn 1975, New York: Columbia University Press. (A locus classicus for a neo-classical account of skills.)

* Béduwé, C. and Espinasse, J.-M. (1995), 'France: politique éducative, amélioration des competences et absorption des diplômés par l'économie', *Sociologie du Travail* 37 (4): 527–54. (Account of problems faced by young French people following a major expansion of education.)

* Brandsma, J., Kessler, F. and Münch, J. (eds) (1996) *Continuing Vocational Training: Europe, Japan and the US*, Utrecht: Uitgeverij Lemma. (A country-by-country survey of further training in major industrial economies.)

* Büchtemann, C.F. and Verdier, E. (1998) 'Education and training regimes', *Revue de l'économie politique* 108 (3): 291–320. (A major analysis of contrasts between French and German skill formation systems.)

* Crouch, C., Finegold, D. and Sako, M. (1999) *Are Skills the Answer? The Political Economy of Skill Creation in Advanced Industrial Countries*, Oxford: Oxford University Press. (An

analysis of forms of governance of skill creation systems in seven industrial countries.)

* Freyssenet, M., Mair, A., Shimizu, K. and Volpato, G. (eds) (1998) *One Best Way?: Trajectories and Industrial Models of the World's Automobile Producers*, Oxford: Oxford University Press. (An important study of comparative work organization.)

* Juergens, U. (ed.) (2000) *New Product Development and Production Networks*, Frankfurt-am-Main: Springer. (An important study of comparative work organization.)

* Lazonick, W. (1991) *Business Organization and the Myth of the Market Economy*, Cambridge: Cambridge University Press. (A critique of the deficiencies of neo-classical theory in the analysis of empirical business organizations.)

* Lazonick, W. and O'Sullivan, M. (2000) *Perspectives on Corporate Governance, Innovation, and Economic Performance*, Report to the European Commission, DGXII, Fontainebleau: INSEAD. (A critical survey of existing models of relations between forms of economic organization and performance, including analyses of skill formation systems.)

Prais, S.J. (1991) 'Vocational qualifications in Britain and Europe: theory and practice', *National Institute Economic Review* 136. (A comparative study by one of the pioneers of research on skills and training.)

Regini, M. (ed.) (1996) *La Produzione Sociale delle Risorse Humane*, Bologna: Il Mulino. (Study of skill formation in SMEs in four key European regional economies.)

* Sauter, E. (1996) 'Continuing vocational training in Germany' in J. Brandsma *et al.* (eds), *Continuing Vocational Training: Europe, Japan and the US*, Utrecht: Uitgeverij Lemma. (Discussion of French approaches to the issue of further training.)

* Saxenian, A. (1994) *Regional Advantage: Culture and Competition in Silicon Valley and Route 128*, Cambridge, MA: Harvard University Press. (A study of advanced technology districts in the US economy.)

Shavit, Y. and Müller, W. (eds) (1997) *From School to Work*, Oxford: Clarendon Press. (A country-by-country statistical analysis of transitions from education to employment in a number of advanced economies).

* Stevens, M. (1995) 'Transferable training and poaching externalities' in *Acquiring Skills: Market Failures, Their Symptoms and Policy Responses*, Cambridge: The Centre for Economic Policy Research. (A critique of the neo-classical model of skill formation.)

* Wagner, K. (1998) 'Costs and other challenges to the dual system' in D. Finegold and P. Culpeper (eds), *The German Skills Machine in Comparative Perspective*, Oxford: Berghahn Books. (An account of recent problems of the German training system.)

See also: AEROSPACE INDUSTRY; AUTOMOBILES INDUSTRY; CORPORATE CONTROL; DEVELOPMENT AND DIFFUSION OF TECHNOLOGY; DIVISION OF LABOUR; ETHNIC AND GENDER; DYNAMIC CAPABILITIES; EAST ASIAN ECONOMIES; ECONOMIC GROWTH; ECONOMY OF JAPAN; EMPLOYMENT RELATIONS; GLOBAL MACHINE TOOLS INDUSTRY; GROWTH OF THE FIRM AND NETWORKING; GROWTH THEORY; INDUSTRAL RELATIONS SYSTEMS; INNOVATION; LABOUR MARKETS; MARSHALL, A.; MARX, K.; SMITH, A.; TRUST; VEBLEN, T.; WORKFARE

Skills: see CAREERS; COMMUNICATION; EMPLOYEE DEVELOPMENT; INTERPERSONAL SKILLS; JOB DESIGN; ENTRIES LISTED UNDER MANAGEMENT EDUCATION; NEGOTIATION SKILLS; TRAINING; TRAINING, ECONOMICS OF

Sloan, Alfred Pritchard, Jr (1875–1966)

Personal background

- born 23 May 1875 in New Haven, Connecticut
- eldest of four sons of a New Haven tea, coffee and cigar wholesaler and retailer
- grew up in Brooklyn, New York, from the age of 10
- graduated with degree in electrical engineering from Massachusetts Institute of Technology in 1895
- began career with Hyatt Roller Bearing Company, New Jersey, in 1895, becoming its president at the age of 26
- after Hyatt was acquired by General Motors (GM) he became vice-president and a member of its executive committee in 1918, then its operating vice-president in 1920, then its president and chief executive officer in 1923
- reorganized GM from an untidy group of largely separate businesses into a widely emulated model of rational organization
- divided GM into five different divisions, each with its make of car in a different price range
- decentralized production while centralizing administration
- built up GM to surpass Ford's car sales in the USA in the late 1920s, and to become the largest company in the world
- funded several charities named after him, a centre for the advanced study of engineering and the prestigious Sloan School of Management at the Massachusetts Institute of Technology

Major works

Adventures of a White Collar Man (with B. Sparkes) (1941)
My Years with General Motors (1964)

Summary

Alfred P. Sloan, Jr (1875–1966) was an administrative genius who, with Henry Ford, brought the modern car industry into being. His successes followed Ford's with the Model-T Ford, which was becoming increasingly obsolescent as General Motors (GM) (see GENERAL MOTORS CORPORATION) began developing a wider range of cars. His very successful reorganization and development of GM along federal lines and evolving elaborate decentralization was and is imitated all over the world. Sloan used cost accounting, market analysis and internal competition as strong frameworks for a philosophy and style of management which were relatively fair, open, informal and democratic. Sloan joined GM in 1918 and retired in 1956, and was its chief executive officer (CEO) from 1923 to 1946.

Sloan's flexible and innovative approach to very large-scale organization and management was extremely successful, but elements of complacency and fear of change were apparent in GM by the 1960s. Habits of undue emphasis on economy and rather stereotyped approaches to marketing, as well as a decreasing emphasis on technical innovation, combined with foreign competition to give the company problems from the 1970s onwards. Nevertheless, most of the main elements of Sloan's philosophy are still widely praised for their administrative, economic, moral, political, psychological and social logic.

1 Introduction

Sloan is generally recognized as an organizational genius and, to a lesser extent, a marketing genius, who unified the efforts of a varied group of car manufacturing companies into the world's largest and most successful maker of cars. His achievements brought the car industry to its early maturity and were massively influential on other companies and in other sectors, and on the understanding and study of management (see CORPORATE CONTROL; UNITED STATES OF AMERICA, MANAGEMENT IN THE).

The principles of decentralization and of the use of staff services in senior management developed under Sloan were not new, but he and Pierre Du Pont (of Du Pont Chemicals), his helper and collaborator, applied and elaborated them extensively in large-scale private-sector manufacturing for the first time. He was also responsible for influential developments in consumer marketing, for innovations in the use of specialist expertise in management, and for numerous developments in ways of obtaining, presenting and using data needed by decision-makers.

The above achievements of Sloan have been built upon but not genuinely superseded, in spite of criticisms based on their somewhat inward-looking character. They were inward-looking in so far as they were strongly focused on GM's internal or immediate commercial concerns, and because GM faced little seriously effective competition during the 1920s, when its mould was made. They were sometimes described as being important building blocks for a democratic capitalist social order and then criticized for their narrowness, for the failure of GM executives to think beyond the corporation's relations with its suppliers, dealers and customers to its role in the wider society. However, Sloan's emphasis on fairness, on cooperation and competition used creatively in management, and on decision-making based on rational discussion of facts, all within a very large, diverse, widespread and productive organization, continues to point the way forward for students and practitioners of management, industry and business, and for their roles in society (see ORGANIZATION BEHAVIOUR; ORGANIZATION BEHAVIOUR, HISTORY OF).

2 Biographical data

Alfred P. Sloan, Jr, was born into a middle-class business and professional family in New Haven, Connecticut, on 23 May 1875. The family moved to Brooklyn in New York City when he was 10, and in 1895 he graduated from the Massachusetts Institute of Technology with a degree in electrical engineering. In the same year he began work for the Hyatt Roller Bearing Company of Harrison, New Jersey, which made tapered roller bearings, as a $10 per week draughtsman. After a short while Sloan left Hyatt to work for a firm which made one of the first electrical refrigerators, but after two years he returned to Hyatt, which was about to go out of business. However, the company was loaned $5000 by Sloan's father and some friends while Sloan and a young bookkeeper, Peter Steenstrup, tried to change its fortunes. Steenstrup looked after Hyatt's finances and Sloan looked after design, engineering, production and sales, learning much about business management and something about mass production in the process. The latter occurred because when Sloan took Hyatt over the car industry was the main buyer of its products, and its demands were constantly growing and changing. Two particular lessons concerned the ever-growing precision of the parts used in cars and the demand for price concessions from major buyers, which impressed on Sloan the need to look continually for lower costs and better methods, and thus the full value of systematic accounting, research and planning.

In 1916 the first major architect of General Motors, William C. Durant, then of the currently forming United Motors, suggested that Hyatt be sold to it. After some thought Sloan saw that because the future of Hyatt lay with large mass producers like Ford and GM it was dependent on mass production and could only be profitable as long as it was selling to mass producers. Because Ford and GM were both capable of making their own roller bearings, the Durant proposal was accepted. Sloan became president of United Motors, which GM bought in 1918, when he also became a vice-president of GM. At the same time the General Motors Company became the General Motors Corporation. This ended Chevrolet control of GM, with Chevrolet remaining a major part of the new corporation. William C. Durant, the founder of GM, had foreseen, around 1900, the brilliant prospects for big vertically integrated companies making a variety of cars. GM was first founded in 1908 from Buick, Cadillac, Oakland (to become Pontiac) and Oldsmobile. Durant made two attempts to buy Ford at a time when Ford's great successes were imminent or starting, with Ford's responses making it hard to believe that he was doing any more than flirting with the idea of joining the corporation which was to overtake his company to become the USA's and the world's number one car producer from the mid-1920s onwards.

Durant had a whirlwind approach to business growth. He joined forces with Louis Chevrolet in 1911 to produce, around 1915, a popular car to challenge the rise of Ford's all-conquering Model T. Durant had lost control of GM and he began to try to recover it with the help of the Du Pont family, which was making a great deal of money manufacturing chemicals during the First World War and which saw a potentially very good investment in the motor industry. The bankers' trust that controlled GM expired in 1916 and Durant returned to power, along with the Chevrolet company as the tail wagging the GM dog.

During the First World War and for most of the following decade until 1928, Ford's enormous success with the Model T swept almost all before it (see FORD, H.). Most cars apart

from the Model T, however, were becoming more complicated and expensive to make, and newcomers to the industry found survival increasingly difficult. The First World War had given a big impetus to the mass production of motor vehicles. In 1919 Ford produced about 50 per cent and GM about 20 per cent of the cars made in the USA, and the prospects for the industry seemed very bright. However, the depression of 1920–1 began with most car manufacturers overextended and led to major reorganizations in the industry which had long-term effects on its future structure. In 1919 the General Motors Acceptance Corporation was founded to help dealers with the finance of loans to customers and with handling used car sales. Dealers were thus supported through difficult periods by what was a very forward-looking measure for its time. However, while Durant was a very dynamic salesman and promoter with considerable energy, integrity and managerial ability, his management of so large and complex an organization as GM tended to be too single-handed and impulsive.

Unlike Walter Chrysler, then head of Buick, Sloan did not quarrel with Durant about the effects of the latter's style of management. However, Sloan reacted to it by producing a plan for the reorganization of GM which Durant approved but then did nothing to implement. The plan offered decentralization and delegation of authority to counteract the administrative chaos of Durant's approach to management. In 1920 Sloan saw that GM needed to cut its prices from wartime to peacetime levels. The ever-optimistic Durant could not see this and feared that price-cutting could put at risk his attempts to support GM on the stock market. Sloan saw this as an example of Durant's overemphasis on financing operations through the stock market and relative neglect of more mundane but important matters.

Sloan took a month's leave of absence in Europe to consider his future, as he could foresee ruin for GM. When he returned it was to find Durant gone. The Du Pont company had bought Durant's GM shares, paid off his obligations and secured his resignation from the presidency of GM. Sloan and other executives got Pierre Du Pont to take over as president of GM to reassure the public about the com-

tional planning had to be both undertaken and balanced, and considerable attention had to be paid to the selection and development of all kinds of staff, at all levels and for almost every purpose. In the 1930s and 1940s GM consisted of three major product groups: cars and trucks; accessories and spare parts (also refrigerators); and non-automotive (diesel and aircraft) engines. These businesses were organized into around thirty divisions, some very large, such as Chevrolet cars, and some small single-plant ones with fewer than 1000 employees.

Each division was organized and managed as an autonomous business unit, and the three largest were represented at the most senior level of GM by their own top managers. The others were represented at that level of GM by individuals drawn from product-based groups. As part of GM's central management and side by side with the product management organization, functional service staffs with their own vice-presidents (manufacturing, engineering, sales, research, personnel, finance, public relations, legal affairs and so on) advised both divisional (line managers) and central management, liaised between the divisions and formulated corporate policies. The line or manufacturing organization of GM was headed by the president and two executive vice-presidents, and the staff one was headed by the chairman of the board of directors, who was also the chief executive officer (CEO) of GM, and by the vice-chairman of the board.

These five formed a team that worked with and through two major committees, the administration and policy ones. These two committees were the 'government' of GM, the 'central organ[s] of co-ordination, decision and control' (Drucker 1946: 43). They were the final courts of appeal for disagreements about policy in GM. All the most senior people in GM and representatives of its major shareholders belonged to them, and they combined all sorts of experiences and backgrounds into one policy. They were kept fully informed about all general and staff and line issues and decisions facing GM, and their role was to discuss and decide about them.

Numerous much smaller subcommittees formed from these members dealt with mainly functional matters on a regular basis, feeding information and recommendations upwards to the two main committees. GM had up to 500 senior executives and 250,000 employees (double the latter number in the Second World War). Strong financial control had become one of the main ways of keeping divisional managements in line while encouraging them to have the prestige and to exercise the power of real bosses. Central management needed to know even minor details of divisional management, but divisional managers needed to have real authority and standing, too. Drucker (1946: 47) called GM 'an essay in federalism', which successfully combined the highest levels of corporate unity with divisional autonomy and responsibility. Decentralization at GM under Sloan was far more than a division of labour. It was a philosophy of management and a system of local self-government which extended down to include the level of first-line supervision and externally to relations with business partners (especially car dealers) (see MANAGERIAL BEHAVIOUR).

The benefits of Sloan's system of decentralization appear to have included clear and reasonably quick decision making (see DECISION MAKING), a relative lack of internal conflict, an atmosphere of fairness, democracy and informality, a sense of management being a large-scale activity shared among many, a plentiful supply of experienced and able leaders, the early detection and timely resolution of problems and an absence of management by edict. Central policies were unified and coherent, and set clear goals and gave clear guidance to divisions. Central management acted as eyes and ears for the whole of GM, and it planned and governed the long-term future of the divisions. It obtained their capital and it handled many of their financial, legal and accounting tasks, as well as most trade union negotiations and contracts. Central management's services staff also kept divisions up to date with developments in engineering, marketing, accounting and other specialist areas. Divisional managements were in complete charge of production and sales, almost all staffing, of engineering, investment planning, advertising, public relations, buying and relations with dealers and so on (see ADVERTISING

CAMPAIGNS; PUBLIC RELATIONS; STRATEGY AND BUYER–SUPPLIER RELATIONSHIPS).

About 95 per cent of all division-level decisions were taken by divisional managers who were virtually in complete control of their own businesses. They operated a system of bonuses which gave them considerable independence within centrally determined limits designed to curb excesses of favouritism and spitefulness. There were many open and informal devices designed to maintain a two-way flow of information between the highest levels of central management and the lowest levels of the divisions' management. Twice a year, at the GM headquarters in Detroit, between 200 and 300 senior managers from all over GM met, so as to ensure that all senior managers got to know something about the whole GM picture. Also, members of GM's central management regularly visited divisions for several days at a time.

GM's relations with car dealers were a further significant element in the decentralized approach. Dealers were often locally prominent businessmen, who were nonetheless tied to GM and its fortunes. They had little control over their own costs, or over the price of cars or the manner of their sale. Also, while GM was mainly interested in dealers' new car sales, dealers got most of their profits from the sales of used ones. GM applied the philosophy of enlightened self-interest to support dealers through difficult times and to protect them against financial pressures from sales staff. GM established a Dealers' Council in the mid-1930s, with nearly fifty members representing a geographical cross-section of GM's USA car dealers. It discussed such issues as the nature of GM's franchise, car design and advertising techniques. The less well-known Motor Holdings Division financially supported and encouraged about 300 good and improving dealers from the late 1930s onwards. GM–dealer relations typified GM's management policies through their emphasis on harmony, mutual self-interest and stability (see MARKETING; MARKETING, FOUNDATIONS OF; MARKETING STRATEGY).

Managers at all levels were encouraged to criticize GM policies and practices. Criticisms were not penalized: they were taken seriously (see MANAGERIAL BEHAVIOUR).

Persuasion and rational arguments were used at virtually all times. However, central management was the boss. There was a mixture of freedom and order; open management tended to ensure that issues, ideas, problems and decisions were discussed and decided upon thoroughly. Cost accounting and market analysis provided the necessary objective and impersonal background and framework for all this, with base pricing and competitive market standing, respectively, the main indices in use. Efficiency was thus measured and debated thoroughly, with all measurements and discussions being related to production planning. The style of management mixed the informal and the impersonal, and was based on the strong respect for facts which Sloan encouraged perhaps more than anything else.

When Sloan ceased to be GM's CEO in 1946, he had used decentralization to manage and develop GM very effectively for a quarter of a century. Henry Ford II had just taken over his grandfather's ramshackle empire and was unashamedly copying GM's methods of organization. Sloan's methods were flexible and strongly entrenched enough to handle all but the most unusual and special problems which face very large companies. However, the experience of government control in the Second World War had shown how decentralization within GM could be threatened, not just by the centralizing tendencies of government contracts and demands, but also by other external forces such as *one* very big and powerful trade union or the US motor industry becoming a cartel.

Sloan's main contribution to the practice and understanding of business and management was to demonstrate how to balance the conflicting interests of the central and the local in a very large and diverse company. He also made a major contribution to the development of the car industry through his recognition of the growing, if structured, diversity of its market. His organizational methods and some of his other innovations were copied widely, notably by the General Electric Company as well as by Ford in the USA, by Imperial Chemical Industries in the UK, and in the USSR, Japan and western Europe (see MULTINATIONAL CORPORATIONS, ORGANIZATION STRUCTURE IN).

4 Evaluation

From the 1930s to the 1960s many GM managers saw GM as something of a model for a capitalist society's industrial and social order. A very diverse and large enterprise had practised diversity through decentralization, using many different kinds of training, team building, internal representation of interests, decentralization within its constituent divisions, various forms of autonomous group working, and so on. GM's management under Sloan was a good compromise between efficiency and personal freedom and development. Performance was measured objectively and improved by a reasonable mixture of discussion, persuasion and coercion. Decentralization under Sloan meant respect for small scale and to some extent, implementation of the belief that small is beautiful (see SCHUMACHER, E.F.). Certainly a significantly higher proportion of GM's top executives than might be expected tended to come from its smaller divisions.

During the years from when Sloan, after the Second World War, was largely part of GM's past, through the year of his death in 1966 and until the 1970s and the rise of serious foreign competition, GM continued to prosper. From the 1960s to the 1980s at least, so-called liberal criticism of big US business grew louder and more strident. GM had been very effective at developing its expert management, but since the 1920s it had also been more of a managed than a truly innovating company, and in almost every respect a domestic, US one rather than a true multinational, at least until long after 1945. By the 1970s it was no longer an unequivocal source of pride for most Americans, just as car ownership no longer symbolized their personal achievements. Decentralization had been a very positive thing, but GM and other large US organizations increasingly needed to work with the US and other governments, and with international agencies and with each other, in an internationalizing and ever more interdependent world.

There is a real if rather unfair sense, using hindsight, in which Sloan's policy of decentralization looks like one of insularity. In his book *My Years with General Motors* (1964)

Sloan tells his story in a highly impersonal way, and focuses almost entirely on the internal management and organization of GM. By writing in such a way Sloan was clearly trying to set a strong example of his ideal of 'professionalism' in management. In one sense this was odd because Sloan was a very human and people-centred person. However, while he was very democratic in a typically demotic, ebullient and even slightly folksy American way, and while GM was a more or less unequivocal major success from the 1920s until the 1970s, it was increasingly under attack and out of touch with the views of many people from the 1960s onwards.

In many important respects GM was a prisoner of its own success. The affluence that it had played a big part in creating gave people the time and other resources to criticize the hands that were feeding them. Sloan appreciated business very well as a source of work, jobs, wealth, security and so on, but less well in terms of its wider roles as a source of power and influence, within communities and within society in general. He understood its economic, technical, psychological, commercial and financial aspects both imaginatively and in great detail, but, at least as far as GM and his own work was concerned, his historical, political and sociological imagination was rather limited from a later twentieth-century vantage point. However, they were far from limited from the appropriate one, that of the early to mid-twentieth century, a far less affluent period in which the scale of international economic cooperation and interdependence was much smaller than it is now (see ECONOMIC INTEGRATION, INTERNATIONAL; GLOBALIZATION).

Sloan has long been a hero figure in GM as much for the atmosphere that he encouraged as for anything else (Kanter 1985: 347). Dale described him as 'the great empiricist … a complex personality and a tireless worker who made GM his all-embracing interest' (Dale 1971: 86). According to Kennedy, Sloan was very much 'the type that does well with a big organization, provided that big organization is supplied for him' (Kennedy 1941: 157, 158). He had been helped by being 'an accessory man, not an automobile man' in his big task of 'keeping peace among the various heads of the General Motors manufacturing divisions'. Until Sloan had the authority to do this, the very sound policy of each of the five car divisions being virtually independent was hampered by all attempts at control from head office. Sloan was very much a second-generation car-industry leader, more of a team leader than an individualist, more pragmatic than romantic, more of a manager than an innovator (see LEADERSHIP).

Even so, Sloan's organization and management of GM were original in several respects through their very strong emphasis on facts, cooperation and 'system', in particular through the coordination and control of staff services. The line–staff distinction came from the military, and decentralization to partly autonomous sub-units had been practised by the Roman Catholic church for centuries when Sloan came to power in GM. But it was his dynamic combination of them in a commercial context (simultaneously taking place at Du Pont Chemicals) which was new, along with the presentation and continued adaptation of his flexible 'framework of "decentralized operations and co-ordinated control"' (Dale 1971: 106), mainly through oral tradition among Sloan and other GM founder members, over several decades. Sloan and his team were also innovative in marketing policy: their aim to offer 'a car for every purse and purpose' (Chandler 1964: 16), to reach every sector of the market, effectively superseded Ford's concentration on one model. Regular developments in the performance and styling of GM's cars and energetic advertising helped the company to expand market share. Sloan's policy of financing both its car dealers and customers was also highly innovative in its day, and also the opposite of Ford's policies.

Sloan and GM's other top managers of the 1920s and 1930s had to innovate because their company, their industry and the scale of their operations were all new. As a consequence, and while most of their ideas have stood the test of time, some elements have a dated quality. Their early success probably helped to curtail consideration of alternatives and to engender a certain conservatism. This tendency was discussed by Rothschild at some length in her discussion of 'Sloanism, or GM's variety marketing' (1973: 37–40). She noted how the

company focused on sales techniques in the 1930s, at the expense of technical innovation. GM stimulated and developed the cyclical trading of used cars as down payments on new ones, so that 'USA auto marketing became a worldwide model for the selling of expensive consumer goods, showing businesses how to create and nourish demand' (Rothschild 1973: 40). However, while the US car industry 'led the expansion of consumer demand at the end of the Second World War' (Rothschild 1973: 41), the increasingly saturated car market became more and more jaded.

On the technical side, the industry was no longer a new one and GM's investment levels had fallen from around 25 per cent of total sales value from 1918 to 1920, to about 4 per cent in the early 1970s. Capital investment was increasingly seen as a 'regrettable necessity' (Rothschild 1973: 49), not as an exciting adventure, as it was viewed previously. Marketing techniques and cost-cutting had increasingly been the main preoccupations of large USA car-company head offices, at the expense of technical innovation. Also, ever-increasing 'Fordist regimentation' (Rothschild 1973: 33) of car production, aimed at cost-cutting, had long been alienating the workforce. Customers were often alienated, too, by the perpetual upgrading of the product – generally marginal at best and expensively cosmetic at worst. For Rothschild (1973: 247), cars were the definitive US product, just as railways had been for the UK and as televisions and other electronic consumer goods were for Japan.

5 Conclusion

The main achievements of Sloan's work were: (1) the stabilization, restoration and very successful expansion of the fortunes of the major grouping of companies in a major industry; (2) the solution of many problems of very large-scale and diverse commercial management through elaborate and flexible systems of decentralization; (3) influential developments in techniques of consumer marketing; (4) the development of numerous techniques and structures for providing top managers with facts needed for making strategic policy and operational decisions; and (5) the dissemination of his experiences and achievements through example and informal education programmes, influencing management and organizational practices across the world.

Sloan's main achievement was to make the practice of management more sophisticated and to show how management could be a broadly responsible and socially benign activity. Affluence, the internationalization of production and markets, and foreign competition all eventually eroded Sloan's success at GM, but others have continued to emulate and build on them for many years, both there and elsewhere.

IAN GLOVER
UNIVERSITY OF STIRLING

Further reading

(References cited in the text marked *)

Baughmar, J.P. (ed.) (1969) *The History of American Management: Selections from the Business History Review*, Englewood Cliffs, NJ: Prentice Hall. (Contains varied accounts of the development of US organizations and management which help to explain the influence of Sloan and GM in US industrial history.)

* Chandler, A.D. Jr (ed.) (1964) *Giant Enterprise: Ford, General Motors and the Automobile Industry: Sources and Readings*, New York: Harcourt, Brace & World. (Mainly consists of readings and discussions of their relevance, concerned with the development of GM and Ford from 1900 to the 1950s; excellent on GM's innovations in management and marketing.)

* Dale, E. (1971) *The Great Organizers*, New York: McGraw-Hill. (On the development of systematic organization in US management: particularly stories on the contributions of Sloan and GM.)

* Drucker, P.F. (1946) *The Concept of the Corporation*, New York: John Day. (Considers the problems of large-scale capitalist organization and industry in the USA using GM under Sloan as its main source of evidence.)

* Kanter, R.M. (1985) *The Change Masters: Corporatist Entrepreneurs at Work*, Hemel Hempstead: Unwin. (Contains a chapter on GM's problems of the 1970s and 1980s, which includes a useful account of Sloan's legacy.)

* Kennedy, E.D. (1941) *The Coming of Age of Capitalism's Favourite Child*, New York: Reynal & Hitchcock. (Covers the period 1890 to 1940; rather descriptive but useful for understanding the roles of Sloan and GM in the US car industry in the years when it was established.)

Rae, J.B. (1959) *American Automobile Manufacturers: The First Forty Years*, Philadelphia: Chilton. (Excellent, balanced account of the history of the industry's companies until the mid-1930s; contains many useful comparisons between GM and its rivals.)

Rae, J.B. (1965) *The American Automobile: A Brief History*, Chicago, IL: University of Chicago Press. (Covers the industry from the 1890s to the 1960s; includes a balanced account of the roles of Sloan and GM.)

* Rothschild, E. (1973) *Paradise Lost: The Decline of the Auto-Industrial Age*, New York: Random House. (On the problems of the US car industry in the early to mid-1970s, facing public scepticism, market saturation and foreign competition; excellent on the growing conservatism of GM.)

* Schnapp, J.B. (1979) *Corporate Strategies of the Automotive Manufacturers*, Lexington, MA: D.C. Heath & Co. (Covers the strategies of four American, one German and three major Japanese car companies in the mid- to late 1970s; GM and its history are compared usefully with the others.)

* Sloan, A.P. Jr (1964) *My Years with General Motors*, New York: Doubleday. (Impressively professional account of General Motors' story under Sloan, of the 'logic of management in relation to the events of the automobile industry' [p. xxiii].)

* Sloan, A.P. Jr and Sparkes, B. (1941) *Adventures of a White Collar Man*, New York: Books for Libraries. (Ebullient and endearing account of most of Sloan's life which offers much evidence of his integrity, enthusiasm, imagination and middle-class American folksiness.)

Stewart, T.A., Taylor III, A., Petre, P. and Schendler, B. (1999) 'Henry Ford, Alfred P. Sloan, Tom Watson Jr., Bill Gates: the businessman of the century', *Fortune* 22 November, 64–76. (A highly accessible article which documents the lives and achievements of each of these great [American] businessmen.)

Further resources

The Alfred P. Sloan Foundation
http://www.sloan.org
Sloan Museum
http://www.sloanmuseum.com
MIT Sloan School of Management
http://www.mitsloan.mit.edu./index.html
General Motors
http://www.gm.com

See also: CHANDLER, A.D.; CORPORATE STRA-
TEGIC CHANGE; FORD, H.; GLOBALIZATION;
MANUFACTURING STRATEGY; MULTINA-
TIONAL CORPORATIONS, ORGANIZATION
STRUCTURE IN; ORGANIZATION BEHAV-
IOUR; ORGANIZATION BEHAVIOUR, HIS-
TORY OF; ORGANIZATION STRUCTURE;
STRATEGIC CHOICE; STRATEGY, CONCEPT
OF; WILLIAMSON, O.E.

Small business finance

1 **Definition of small business**
2 **Unique features of small businesses**
3 **Finance and stages of the business**
4 **Potential external constraints**
5 **Potential internal constraints**
6 **Consequences of constraints**
7 **Solutions to perceived constraints**

Overview

Small businesses dominate enterprise numbers in the economy and make significant contributions to employment and income. They are not just scaled-down versions of larger businesses and their financing has unique features. These include a primary reliance on bank debt as a source of funding, higher failure rates with associated higher lending margins, and the potential for internal and external constraints on funding in both the debt and equity markets. Such funding 'gaps' are due to informational asymmetries, scale economies in the provision of funds and the greater market power of large businesses over small. Government small firm policies have been largely directed at rectifying these perceived market failures, in particular to obviating funding gaps. However, the empirical evidence suggests that market failures are less widespread than is commonly thought.

1 Definition of small business

In this article, 'small business' is taken to mean a business that satisfies the following criteria. First, the business has no significant power to control the prices of the products it buys and sells and the credit it gives and receives. In other words, it is a price taker rather than a price maker in these markets. Second, the business is managed by its owners who also control the business (for example, by majority shareholdings) (see SMALL BUSINESS STRATEGY).

A small business will most likely be a sole trader or a partnership but may also be a limited company. It will typically have fewer than 20 employees, but may have as few as one (the owner-manager) or as many as 500. The business (in the case of limited companies) may have its shareholdings concentrated in one person (the owner-manager) or it may be about to float its shares on the stock exchange of a major industrialized country.

2 Unique features of small businesses

Some of the unique features of small businesses from the point of view of finance are as follows (Ang 1991).

1 The business's securities are not publicly traded. There is no ready market for the shares of small businesses so that the valuation of a small business is a much more subjective affair than that of large businesses.
2 Business owners have undiversified personal portfolios. The owner's investment in the business constitutes a major portion of their personal wealth, so that an owner-manager's portfolio is highly risky, as compared with one spread over many different investments ('diversified').
3 Limited liability is absent or ineffective. The provision of limited liability formally implies that the owner's liability for the debts of a business is limited to the amount of their shareholding in the business. However, limited liability is legally prohibited in the case of sole traders and partnerships and is often vitiated through the requirement by lenders to provide personal guarantees for loans.
4 The business management team is incomplete. The business may depend on a few key individuals and is thus subject to severe disruption if some become ill or leave; it may have no succession plan in the event of the death of the family head and owner, creating problems of continuity; it is likely, especially at an early stage, to have an

incomplete management team, lacking management skills in finance, marketing, production, etc.

5 The business is potentially subject to various constraints, both internal and external, on borrowing, equity participation by outsiders and on the scale and growth of the business. These constraints arise due to the smallness of the business relative to other market participants (banks, big firms), the psychology of the management team, the information the business makes available to the market, the information the business is able to acquire itself, and so on (see EN-TREPRENEURIAL STRATEGIES; ENTREPRENEURSHIP).

3 Finance and stages of the business

We can distinguish the finance required by a business according to the stage the business has reached (Hutchinson and Ray 1986). Most businesses will never go beyond the first or second stages, while a small minority will traverse all the stages to flotation in rapid succession (see Table 1).

Start-up finance

To understand the financing of start-ups it is necessary to identify some of the parameters of the start-up business. In the UK, some two-thirds of boom period start-ups are sole traders, a further one-fifth are partnerships and

only one in eight are limited companies. The proportion of limited companies rises to about a quarter in a recession-based sample. Other European countries such as Italy are more likely to use the cooperative legal format. In the USA, the proportion of limited companies appears to be slightly higher than in Europe.

Start-up businesses typically employ only one or two staff including the proprietors. They are mainly located in the retailing, construction and service industries. Initial premises are likely to be one of the owners' homes or leased premises, rather than bought premises. Turnover and employment grows over the first few years until the business reaches minimum viable scale. Smaller start-ups tend to grow faster than large ones over this initial period (Cressy 1993).

Recent work in Europe and the USA (Cressy 1993; ENSR 1993; Dunkelberg and Cooper 1989) has identified the empirical characteristics of start-up financing and the financing of early growth. These are as follows.

Sources of finance used

Not all start-ups even use finance to commence business. (The classic case is of the start-up window cleaner who already possesses his ladder, bucket and cloth/squeegee.) Of those that do, the predominant source is personal finance (owner savings, redundancy money, etc.), either alone (35 per cent of businesses) or in conjunction with bank finance (another 14 per cent of businesses). Money from friends and relatives is used by

Table 1 The financial life-cycle of the firm

Stage	Source of finance	Potential stress factors
Inception	Owners' resources	Under-capitalization
Growth I	As above, plus retained profits, trade credit, bank loans and overdrafts, hire purchase, leasing	'Overtrading', liquidity crises
Growth II	As above, plus longer-term finance from financial institutions	Finance gap
Growth III	As above, plus New Issue Market	Loss of control
Maturity	All sources available	Maintaining ROI*
Decline	Withdrawal of finance, firm taken over, share repurchase, liquidation	Falling ROI*

*ROI = return on investment

Source: Hutchinson and Ray (1986)

some 5–10 per cent of businesses and government funds for somewhat less. Money from other banks, finance houses (hire purchase), etc. plays only a very small role at start-up. In the USA, the use of informal venture capital (supplied by individuals outside the family) is widespread. Its importance rises with the size of the start-up. Formal (that is, institutional) venture capital financed start-ups occur in only 1 or 2 per cent of cases, and venture capital is important for hi-tech, fast-growth businesses. In such businesses research and development (R&D) costs may result in losses in the early years despite the huge future earnings potential of the firm. Bank lending under these circumstances is usually inadequate and limited to whatever security the firm can provide, which may be small.

Bank borrowing over time

To examine the trend in borrowing from the start-up stage it is crucial to remember that small businesses are highly cessation-prone. US start-ups have larger injections of capital than their European counterparts (see Dunkelberg and Cooper 1989 and Cressy 1993 for data on start-up finance in the USA and UK respectively). Their survival rates are however similar. Tables 2 and 3 show that typical four-year survival rates in Europe are around 60 per cent; Table 3 shows that in a similar timeframe US businesses have survival rates of 63 per cent. (The latter table also shows the interdependence of growth and survival: faster growth businesses are more likely to survive than slower growth businesses.)

The following discussion relates to the surviving businesses over a three and a half year timeframe (Cressy 1993). About one-third of start-ups appear to borrow from their banks at inception, rising to one-half after three and a half years' trading. Borrowing is mainly on overdraft (revolving credit) and is therefore of short-term duration, depending on the average period of trade credit extended (see below for European data on trade credit). It is used mainly to finance working capital requirements (that is, business cash flow) (see CAPITAL, COST OF). The average amount borrowed at the business minimum viable scale has increased by some two-thirds over initial amounts as a result of developing working capital needs to fund a larger scale of operations.

After the minimum scale has been reached, and in some cases before, fixed investment may require term lending. However, term lending is only used by half the number of businesses that use overdraft borrowing three and a half years into trading. This is perhaps because a significant proportion of businesses do not expand sufficiently to purchase premises, manufacturing machinery, etc., because a high proportion of start-ups are in services and because many businesses start from home. Hence their requirements for fixed investment are minimal. Furthermore, such investment as occurs may

Table 2 Survival rates in 1989 for new firms born in 1985 in selected EU member states

Denmark	France	Germany	Ireland	The Netherlands	UK
58.0	48.0	63.0	57.9	64.0	59.0

Source: ENSR (1993)

Table 3 Two-year, four-year and six-year business failure rates (%) in the USA, 1989

Years since business was founded	All firms	Growing firms*	Non-growing firms
2	23.7	8.0	29.5
4	51.7	19.1	65.5
6	62.7	35.7	72.5

*Firms adding at least one job during each of the respective periods

Source: US Small Business Administration, Office of Advocacy, Small Business Database USELM file, version 9, November 1987

be financed from retained profits because of fear of 'control' by the banks (see below).

Expansion finance

Surveys of small businesses suggest that only a minority wish to grow (Gray 1991). Businesses that do wish to grow face the problem of finding funds with which to do so. It is clear in general that the larger the business the greater the range of financial instruments used. Thus access to finance house funds, additional banks (possibly specialist merchant banks), venture capital, and so on, is made as business scale increases. Accumulated profits from trading can also be employed to fund expansion plans. This appears to be in fact the main source of funds for all but the fastest growing companies.

Stock market flotation

Fast-growing companies tend to make more use of debt, particularly long-term debt to finance expansion (see CAPITAL STRUCTURE). They also tend to have low liquidity matched by high profitability (Hutchinson and Ray 1986). Businesses that reach a sufficient scale of operation, have substantial growth potential and a convincing track record, may wish to go for a public flotation of their shares. The advantages of such a flotation are that the business will find that it has more continuous access to cheaper equity finance, a lower debt–equity ratio for a given project (implying less risk) and a ready market for its shares. The ready market for shares helps expansion plans by providing the possibility of issuing more shares at a later time, and provides an exit route for early-stage investors should they wish to capitalize their gains. The disadvantage of flotation is its cost. This is both financial and in terms of loss of control by the original owners, since outside investors will take substantial tranches of the firm's equity.

4 Potential external constraints

The absence of growth in a large proportion of small businesses, the tendency of banks to ration credit under certain circumstances and the reliance of banks on collateral rather than business prospects in lending decisions, has led theorists to posit the existence of capital market imperfections (see EFFICIENT MARKET HYPOTHESIS).

A market imperfection is said to exist if the equilibrium values of the market (price, quantity, etc.) deviate from those of a perfect market. The operation of the latter presupposes, among other things, large numbers of buyers and sellers, price-taking behaviour, full information about all relevant parameters and frictionless transactions. Under such conditions market outcomes are said to be economically optimal. Very roughly, this implies that everyone in the market is as well-off as they can be, given the initial allocation of resources.

Financial market imperfections

Three kinds of financial market imperfections impinge on the small firm: informational asymmetries, credit market power and government regulation. We will now examine each of these in turn.

Informational asymmetries

In practice, information is not costless, so that an optimal, rather than unlimited information will be acquired. The presence of imperfect information does not, however, necessarily create an economic problem. But, if some parties to a transaction (for example, a lending contract) have more information about facts relevant to the terms of the contract than others, the informational asymmetry can lead to sub-optimal outcomes. These phenomena are known as adverse selection and moral hazard.

Adverse selection can be illustrated as follows. Assume two potential borrowers (firms) have different chances of loan repayment and each knows this better than the lender (bank). The 'bad' borrower (lower repayment probability) will have an incentive to pretend to be a 'good' borrower (higher repayment probability) to get more favourable loan conditions (lower margins, larger loan amount). (Thus they may present a falsely optimistic view of the firm's projects for which money is required.) If the bank cannot distinguish between the two types of borrower, the good borrower's more favourable contract will not, in competitive banking conditions, break-even for the bank because of dissembling by bad borrowers. (The applicant pool is more risky than the bank thinks.) In order to eliminate the incentive for the bad borrower to dissemble, the bank may, for example, raise the collateral level required from the good borrower, imposing an unfair cost on them. This is a market imperfection, since under perfect information, each borrower would receive a contract that simply reflected their own risk (higher risks getting higher margins), not the need for others to tell the truth. The logic of this argument is that, if information to the less informed party (the bank) were increased at a sufficiently low cost, then both lender and borrower could be made better off.

Moral hazard can be illustrated in a similar way. Assume now that the borrower's success probability can be influenced by effort: more effort increases the chances of success. If borrower effort cannot be observed by the lender, then the borrower may have an incentive to choose a lower level of effort than is socially optimal. (Optimality would mean equating the firm's marginal returns to borrowing to its marginal cost.) Then, the bank will find that the lending contract will have to be designed to induce more effort. Again this can be achieved by requesting more collateral to be posted by the 'delinquent' borrower. Since this increases the bank's expected return and collateral is lost by the borrower only if the borrower defaults, the latter will put in more effort to avoid default occurring. However, the collateral posted is unnecessary in a perfectly informed world where lending will in general be greater. Hence, the contract under moral hazard is 'sub-optimal'.

Credit market power

Market power consists of the ability to act as a price maker rather than a price taker. More generally, it means a market participant can influence the parameters of the transaction: price, quantity, security levels of loans, etc. There are two obvious forms such influence can take in the credit market: large banks can influence the lending terms offered to small business customers, and large purchasers of small business products can influence the terms of trade credit. These are discussed in turn.

In its dealings with its bank, the small firm will find limited or no scope for bargaining over margins, charges, security requirements, etc. These are usually 'imposed from above', particularly in recessionary environments when the bank may be under pressure to improve profitability.

Smaller firms tend to have the terms of trade credit dictated to them by their larger trading partners who can obtain supplies from a range of alternative independent producers. Thus a large buyer of the firm's product will decide (within the parameters dictated by the market, that is, the urgency of other suppliers) how long it will take to pay him. Trade credit conditions for small firms, like bank lending conditions, worsen in a recessionary environment as large debtors squeeze their suppliers to improve profits.

Government regulation

There are economies of scale in form-filling and in the preparation of accounts. The paperwork done by a large firm will have a much less disruptive effect on its operations than on a small firm since it cannot so economically employ specialists to do the work. Likewise financial reporting requirements (the need for audited accounts, etc.) are a heavier burden on the small business.

5 Potential internal constraints

Control aversion

Small businesses are jealous of their independence. Indeed this is what motivates a significant proportion of entrepreneurs to enter business in the first place (see ENTREPRENEURSHIP). The UK Bolton Committee (Bolton 1971) found that many firms did not borrow from their banks for fear of outside control. Loss of voting control is perceived as an even greater infringement of owner independence. Yet studies have shown that fast-growth firms are characterized by higher levels of borrowing than slow- or non-growth firms. It is also known that European and North American venture capitalists usually require a board member in the firm as a condition of providing finance (Murray and Lott 1993). Thus in both these areas of finance (debt and equity), businesses may fail to grow because of the control aversion of the owners. Recent theoretical work has attempted to integrate the concept control aversion with the traditional economic theory of the firm (Cressy 1995).

Poor management skills

Many businesses fail to grow because their owners have poor management skills (see MANAGERIAL BEHAVIOUR). For example, the stress of delegating first tasks and then responsibility may be too great for them. They may be poorly educated and have a narrow experience of the market. These deficiencies have been highlighted by studies of the characteristics of managers in high- and low-growth firms (see MANAGERIAL THEORIES OF THE FIRM). For example, a recent UK study of small firms found that founders of fast-growth firms are better educated and have had more experience across a broad range of industries than founders of low-growth firms. In addition these founders were more likely to have had recent management experience (Storey *et al.* 1989).

Ignorance of the market

Businesses that wish to succeed will be aware of alternative sources of finance and choose the best value for money at any one time. Failure to do so may, especially in recessionary environments, cause the destruction of the business. Small businesses, however, often fail to spend time becoming aware of the market alternatives.

6 Consequences of constraints

Sub-optimal dependence on external finance

Retained earnings (profits minus dividends and taxes) are essential for a business to survive and prosper. However, most small businesses, for reasons of internal and external constraints, feel they have to rely on retained earnings to fund expansion, whereas their larger counterparts are much more likely to

use external finance. In the USA, for example, small firms rely on retained earnings for more than half their capital. This percentage declines progressively with business size, to about one-third for the largest firms (Walker 1989).

Collateral-based bank lending the norm

Banks have tended to adopt an arm's length relationship with the small firm. Such firms are regarded as having little growth prospects and being highly risky. The strategy adopted has therefore been to lend only to businesses perceived as viable (thus avoiding bank capital losses) but at the same time requiring high levels of security for loans. The security ratio is often of the order of two or three times the amount lent.

Moral hazard: asset switching by borrowers

Small businesses, because of a lack of substantial amounts of collateral for bank lending, tend to rely on short-term finance for their needs. Collateral for working capital-based lending can often be found in the sales ledger (invoices), whereas collateral for fixed investment tends to be in the form of buildings and plant. Thus businesses frustrated by bank collateral requirements will sometimes use bank finance intended for working capital to fund fixed investment, an example of moral hazard in operation. This increases the risk of the bank's portfolio of loans and the bank can do little about it.

Asymmetric information: banks have little knowledge of the small business

Because of the low returns from the small firm, and their numerical predominance, banks have, as we have seen, traditionally regarded an in-depth knowledge of their customers as unimportant. Recent studies in Europe have confirmed that this is still generally the case (for example, Cowling *et al.* 1991), although in Germany, banks have always been much more involved with their business customers than elsewhere.

Banks do not help to run small businesses

With the exception of Germany in Europe, banks rarely take shares in the small businesses to whom they lend. This is partly the effect of collateral-based lending as noted above, and a lack of industrial experience of bankers, but is also a function of the control aversion of the businesses themselves. For example, only a quarter of UK firms surveyed in Cowling *et al.* (1991) had ever considered equity as a source of long-term funding and two-thirds of surveyed firms indicated that they would object to a bank holding an equity stake in the business.

Debt rationing

The practice of debt rationing of smaller firms by the banks, particularly in economic downturns, has been in evidence in Europe and the UK for some time. Rationing consists of the banks, in the face of 'excess' demand, simply refusing certain types of firms' loans, rather than raising the interest rate to choke off demand. Finance theorists have explained this market imperfection in terms of adverse selection (see Stiglitz and Weiss 1981). In the USA and the UK today credit rationing among smaller firms does not, however, seem to be an important phenomenon (Berger and Udell 1992; Cressy 1994b) – excessive credit availability has recently been a much more serious preoccupation in Europe and the USA.

High lending margins to small borrowers

Margins for small firm lending are considerably higher than those offered to larger firms, ranging in the UK from 2 per cent to 9 per cent (for start-ups) above the base (prime) rate, with an average of some 3–4 per cent for the typical small business (ENSR 1993; Cressy 1994a). This reflects three things: higher riskiness, higher unit costs and lower bargaining power of the small firm.

First, where security for a loan is deemed by the bank as inadequate, but the business prospect is perceived as viable, margins are usually raised to compensate for the extra risk. This is more likely to occur with small business lending where collateral is less available. Second, the higher margins of smaller firms reflect the higher cost of administering smaller loans. For example, higher unit costs are associated with 'perfecting' security (making sure security is adequate) for a smaller loan since the total legal costs vary little with the volume of credit. Third, higher margins reflect the smaller bargaining power of the small firm with the bank.

Although we have discussed interest rates as the primary cost of borrowing, it is important to include bank charges in the equation. These are also a very important cost of borrowing, particularly for smaller firms. Here too there are obvious economies of scale, both in setting up the loan and in its monitoring. However, the smaller firm has little chance to negotiate these charges or, quite often, even lacks an awareness that negotiation is possible.

High cost of trade credit to small firms

Trade credit represents a significant proportion of outstanding commercial debt in a majority of developed economies. In France, the UK and the Netherlands, for example, trade credit represents one-third of current assets in manufacturing (see Table 4) whereas for large firms the same ratio is only about a quarter. Small firms are disadvantaged in that they seem to receive less credit from their suppliers than they extend to their customers. Because they are more reliant upon a smaller customer base, to maintain their loyalty they are willing to extend longer lines of credit. The market power exercised by large firms is evidenced in the shorter credit lines extended by them to small firms by comparison with their smaller counterparts.

Venture capital is under-utilized

The fact that banks are willing to lend only on collateral implies that fast-growing businesses, with few assets and with worth highly dependent on future earnings, may have to sell equity to grow. This will often mean the use of venture capital. However, once again there are economies of scale in this area. The provision of venture capital requires, due to

Table 4 Trade credit terms in the EU, 1991

	Average credit terms (agreed days to payment)	Average debtor days (actual days to payment)	Average excess debtor days*
Belgium	30	75	45
Denmark	30	50	20
France	60	108	48
Germany	30	48	18
Italy	60	90	30
The Netherlands	30	52	22
UK	30	78	48

*excess debtor day = debtor day minus credit terms

Source: Institute of Directors (1993)

its riskiness, monitoring of the investments. However, unit monitoring costs are higher for smaller investments. Thus small firms may find they have insufficient funds from this source also. This is particularly true of early-stage financing where risks are greatest.

There are significant differences in the role of venture capital *vis-à-vis* the financing of small firms between Europe and the USA. In the USA, 32 per cent of the total amount of venture capital dispersed in 1991 was in the form of seed, start-up or early stage financing, whereas in only three EC countries did the proportion exceed 20 per cent of total dispersements. For European small firms this effectively limits their ability to raise external finance at crucial stages in their development.

Innovation may be stifled

In the UK and Europe there has been a consistent downward trend in technology-related venture capital investments over the 1980s. These figures are in marked contrast to the USA where venture capital activity has been defined with a technology focus.

7 Solutions to perceived constraints

Market solutions

Sometimes the market may, independent of government action, step into a perceived gap and provide a solution. We outline some examples of where this has occurred.

Mutual guarantee schemes

For business start-ups the lack of a track record is an additional risk factor which tends to induce credit rationing from financial institutions. Such behaviour gave rise to the development of a number of mutual guarantee schemes (MGSs), most notably in France and Italy. MGSs consist of joint action by a number of independent firms with the aim of providing one another with security cover when borrowing from commercial sources (see INDUSTRIAL STRATEGY). Functionally, an MGS has three main effects: first, it spreads risk over a larger number of firms, thus effectively presenting a more balanced spread to financial institutions; second, it tends to focus on viability of proposals rather than the collateral-based lending techniques preferred by banks; third, an MGS can improve the negotiating position of firms *vis-à-vis* banks, thus addressing the issue of market power in the relationship.

Government solutions

Governments have long recognized the potential disadvantage conferred by smallness in the credit market. Policies have therefore been designed to combat a number of the market imperfections identified above.

Government loan guarantee schemes

Governments and other agencies in a number of countries, notably the UK, France, Germany, Kenya and the USA, initiated credit guarantee schemes, the aim being to encourage financial institutions, primarily commercial banks, to lend to small firms with viable projects where security or collateral requirements cannot be met. Such schemes, either explicitly or implicitly, seek to address the problem of capital market gaps (see above) at the small firm level. This is achieved by the government providing security to the bank for a specified proportion (say, 75 per cent) of the loan. Security is provided at some cost to the borrower who pays a percentage risk premium (say, 2 per cent) in addition to the interest rate on the loan. This premium is paid to the government rather than the bank to defray some of the costs of default.

Start-up lump sums/income supplements

Capital constraints on start-up businesses have been identified in the USA and other countries (Evans and Jovanovic 1989). Furthermore, the social security system may in some countries militate against start-ups, for example, if starting a business entails losing entitlement to unemployment benefits. To facilitate the move into self-employment many governments, particularly in European countries, have initiated schemes which subsidize individuals wishing to switch into self-employment. One such scheme is the Enterprise Allowance Scheme (EAS) in the UK which provides previously unemployed individuals with a weekly income for up to 66 weeks in addition to the income that the business generates through trading. A study of the scheme (Cowling and Mitchell 1994) has found that it exerted a significant and positive effect on UK self-employment rates in the 1980s.

Picking the winners

Some government policies, recognizing the difficulties fast-growth firms may encounter in obtaining finance, have aimed to identify fast-growth firms and foster their development. Technology awards are one such example.

It is often argued that small high-technology firms face great difficulties in raising finance for innovation. This is attributed in part to the large 'front-end' loading of product development costs and the time-lag before the product is manufactured, reaches the marketplace and generates revenues. There are greater risks to potential lenders in such cases where the bulk of revenues attributable to the product are generated in the distant future. Governments in Belgium, the Netherlands and the UK have sought to redress this financing problem by grants or subsidies to smaller hi-tech firms. In the UK for instance, there are two technology awards, SMART and SPUR, which aim to stimulate highly innovative and highly marketable technology by contributing directly towards development costs of new products and processes.

Seed capital funds

In response to the apparent risk averseness of European venture capitalists the European Commission has instigated a number of initiatives to support seed capital funding of new technology-based firms (Murray 1993).

ROBERT CRESSY

MARC COWLING
WARWICK BUSINESS SCHOOL

Further reading

(References cited in the text marked *)

* Ang, J.S. (1991) 'Small business uniqueness and the theory of financial management', *Small Business Finance* 1 (1): 1–14. (Non-technical overview of some of the main issues in small business finance.)
* Berger, A.N. and Udell, G.F. (1992) 'Some evidence on the empirical significance of credit rationing', *Journal of Political Economy* 100 (5): 1047–77. (A technical, statistical study of the importance of credit rationing phenomena in the US economy.)

Berle, A.A. and Means, G. (1932) *The Modern Corporation and Private Property*, New York: Macmillan. (An early classic in the analysis of the divorce of ownership from control in large corporations.)

* Bolton, Sir J. (Chairman) (1971) *Committee of Enquiry into Small Firms*, London: HMSO. (A seminal report and for many years virtually the sole source of information on UK small firms.)

Brock, W.A. and Evans, D.S. (1986) *The Economics of Small Businesses*, New York: Holmes & Meier. (A good US-based text on small firms, combining theory and statistical analysis.)

* Commission of the European Communities (1991) *The Role of Mutual Guarantee Systems in the Financing of SMEs in the European Community*, Brussels: CEC. (Non-technical summary of the role of MGSs in the European Community.)

* Cowling, M. and Mitchell, P. (1994) 'Self-employment trends in the 1980s', occasional paper, Coventry: Centre for Small and Medium-Sized Enterprises, University of Warwick.

* Cowling, M., Samuels, J. and Sugden, R. (1991) 'Small firms and clearing banks', report to Association of British Chambers of Commerce, London. (Report of a survey into the relationship of small firms to their banks in the UK.)

* Cressy, R.C. (1993) 'The startup tracking exercise: third year report', prepared for National Westminster Bank. (Major study of start-up financing. Examines using bank-supplied data, business and proprietor background characteristics and their influence on borrowing, growth and survival of a cohort of UK start-ups.)

* Cressy, R.C. (1994a) 'Overdraft lending and business starts: an empirical investigation on UK data', in M. Chittenden, M. Robertson and D. Watkins (eds), *Small Firms: Recession and Recovery*, London: Paul Chapman. (A study of the financing of start-up businesses in the UK. First to use a combination of data on background characteristics of firms and entrepreneurs and bank-supplied data on lending.)

* Cressy, R.C. (1994b) 'Are startups debt-rationed?', working paper 20, Coventry: Warwick Business School. (Tests for credit rationing on UK start-up businesses. Concludes that human rather than financial capital is the prime constraint.)

* Cressy, R.C. (1995) 'Borrowing and control: a theory of business types', *Small Business Economics* 7: 1–10. (Develops a theory of small business borrowing under control aversion.)

* Dunkelberg, W. and Cooper, A.C. (1989) 'Enterprise and capital diversity in the small enterprise', in R. Yazdipour (ed.), *Advances in Small Business Finance*, London: Kluwer. (Significant study of the financing of US start-up businesses. Uses comparable data to Cressy 1994.)

Dunne, T., Roberts, M.J. and Samuelson, L. (1989) 'The growth and failure of US manufacturing plants', *Quarterly Journal of Economics* 104 (November): 671–98. (Important semi-technical statistical study of the growth and failure of US firms, large and small.)

* ENSR (1993) 'The European Observatory for SMEs: first annual report', Zoetermeer, The Netherlands: EIM. (Major European study of every aspect of small businesses. Chapter 7 on financing is particularly relevant.)

* Evans, D. and Jovanovic, B. (1989) 'An estimated model of entrepreneurial choice under liquidity constraints', *Journal of Political Economy* 97 (4): 808–27. (Important study that examines the capital constraints on US start-up businesses.)

* Gray, C. (1991) 'Stages of growth and entrepreneurial career motivation', paper presented at the Small Firms Policy and Research Conference, Southampton University. (Examines the relationship between growth of businesses and motivation of the owners.)

* Hutchinson, P. and Ray, G. (1986) 'Surviving the financial stress of small enterprise growth', in J. Curran, J. Stanworth and M. Watkins (eds), *The Survival of the Small Firm*, vol. 1, Aldershot: Gower. (Outlines the stages of firm financing and analyses factors distinguishing fast- from slow-growth firms.)

* Institute of Directors (1993) *Late Payment of Debt*, London: Institute of Directors. (Study of the issues of late payment to the small firm in the UK with European comparisons and policy suggestions.)

Mason, C. and Harrison, R. (1994) 'Closing the regional equity gap: the role of informal venture capital', paper presented at the ESRC Regional Economics Conference, University of Paisley. (Study of the regional dimensions of informal venture capital in the UK.)

* Murray, G. (1993) 'Third party equity support for new technology based firms in the UK and continental Europe', paper presented at the Institute for Management, Innovation and Technology, Brussels. (A European study of venture capital provision for new, high-tech firms.)

* Murray, G. and Lott, J. (1993) 'Have UK venture capital firms a bias against investment in new technology-based firms?', working paper series, Coventry: Warwick Business School, Marketing and Strategic Management Group. (Useful preliminary analysis of the role of the

UK venture capital industry in financing high-tech UK businesses.)

* Stiglitz, J.E. and Weiss, A. (1981) 'Credit rationing in markets with imperfect information', *American Economic Review* 71 (3): 393–410. (Classic technical, theoretically-based paper on the role of asymmetric information in lending contracts.)

Storey, D., Keasey, K., Watson, R. and Wynarzyck, P. (1987) *The Performance of Small Firms*, Beckenham: Croom Helm. (Well-written and well-researched study of some 600 small UK firms with particular reference to their financial characteristics, survival and growth.)

* Storey, D.J., Watson, R. and Wynarczyk, P. (1989) 'Fast growth small businesses', research paper 67, London: Department of Employment.

(Good empirical study of UK fast-growth businesses, including their financing.)

* US Small Business Administration (1989) 'The state of small business', report to the President, Washington, DC: Small Business Administration. (Valuable statistical data – with interpretation – provided on an annual basis on small businesses.)

* Walker, D.A. (1989) 'Financing the small firm', *Small Business Economics* 1 (4): 285–96. (A non-technical, statistical overview, from a US perspective, of the financing of small firms.)

See also: CAPITAL STRUCTURE; ENTREPRENEURSHIP; INDUSTRIAL STRATEGY; SMALL BUSINESS MARKETING; SMALL BUSINESS STRATEGY

Small business marketing

1 **The growth of the small firms sector**
2 **The management characteristics of small firms**
3 **Explaining small firm survival**
4 **Marketing and small firms**
5 **Improving the marketing capabilities of small firms**

Overview

In the past two decades small firms have been the subject of much interest from governments throughout the world, keen to stimulate both the cultural endowments of entrepreneurship and the job creating potential of small firms. During the same period, there has been a substantial growth in the small firms sector of many countries, both numerically and in employment share.

This entry considers the growth in size and importance of the small firms and self-employment sector and the characteristics of small businesses. It then assesses the relative advantages and disadvantages of management within small firms, concentrating in particular on the marketing function. Finally, a proposition is presented which is designed to improve the marketing capabilities of small firms.

1 The growth of the small firms sector

Although small firms are now almost universally regarded as a vital element of prospering economies, this view is of fairly recent origin. In the 'big is best' era from the late 1930s to the early 1970s, small firms were regarded with only peripheral interest by economists and business analysts who tended to view them as a form of business anachronism, a structural apology for inefficiency and lack of growth. During this period the decline of the small business sector was seen as a sign of economic progress: '…as industrial societies matured, it was asserted, the small business

sector gradually withered before the advance of the super-efficient large firms enjoying ever-increasing economies of scale' (Curran and Blackburn 1991: 1). The evolution in the way that small businesses were viewed occurred as a result of changes in the broader orientations of economic theory, especially where these changes permeated popular perceptions, as occurred following the international oil crisis of 1972 and after the publication of popular and pioneering works such as *Small is Beautiful* (Schumacher 1973). This evolution was supported by a better research understanding of the characteristics of small firms, and reinforced by the associated decline in Europe and North America in both popular and governmental confidence in the integrity and capacity of large-scale business structures to sustain growth, employment and wealth.

The last two decades have seen an expansion in the number of small firms in many advanced economies, stimulated by changes in the industrial infrastructure and the commitment of various governments to encouraging new forms of economic enterprise. Throughout the 1980s there was a widespread increase in confidence in the potential of small firms to contribute to economic regeneration, encompassed by the ideological formulation of the 'enterprise culture'. Small firms are now regarded as an important element in attempts to increase the rate of job creation, improve competitiveness and exploit new technologies. It is also likely that the number of small firms will continue to grow: 'At the empirical level, statistic after statistic supports the various restructuring theses in their emphasis on the resurgence of small scale economic activities and an increasingly idiosyncratic consumer' (Curran 1991: xiv).

In the UK, interest in the small business sector essentially dates from the publication in 1971 of the Report of the Committee of Inquiry on Small Firms under the chairmanship of John Bolton. The Bolton Report (Bolton 1971) presented for the first time an assessment of the statistical profile of the small firms sector from a number of perspectives and was a significant turning point in contemporary understanding of small businesses. The rate of new firm formation rose during the economic boom of the 1980s, but was sustained even through the ensuing recession; between 1987 and 1990 the total net number of new businesses rose by 420,000 or 33 per cent (Westhead and Birley 1994). Similarly, by 1990, self-employment reached 11.7 per cent of the total UK labour force, 'very nearly double the level of twenty-five years earlier' (Storey 1994: 28).

There are, however, quite wide discrepancies between the genders with regard to self employment. A recent study showed that between 1979 and 1997 the number of self-employed women increased by 163 per cent from 319,000 to 840,000. In the same period the number of self-employed males increased by 67 per cent from 1,449,000 to 2,421,000. Although female self-employment has increased at a much faster rate, women only constitute 26 per cent of the total self-employed in the UK (Labour Force Survey 1997).

While the small firm sector in the UK has demonstrated a pattern of clear and consistent growth since the 1970s, the situation in other countries has shown more variable trends. In the USA, the number of small businesses varies between 5 and 20 million (depending on how they are defined) and the number of new businesses grows at a rate of about 2 per cent per year, nearly the same as the rate of growth of the population. In addition, the small business share of US employment is also growing. In the ten year period to 1987, small businesses increased their share of private sector employment by over 4 per cent, accounting for 11.3 million of the 16.5 million net new jobs (SBA 1992). As the US Small Business Administration points out, 'all of the small-business-dominated industries grow in employment faster than large-business-dominated industries' (SBA 1992: 55). This growth rate has continued its healthy trend throughout the 1990s. In the period 1990–5 3.1 million new jobs were created in the US from the small firm sector. New business formation reached another record level in 1998. An estimated 898,000 new firms started trading – the most ever recorded in one year and a 1.5 per cent increase over the record 885,000 in 1997 (SBA1999).

In Europe, research from the European Commission suggests that the growth in the number of small and medium sized enterprises (SMEs) throughout the European Community in the 1980s was 3.6 million or 25 per cent (Cambridge Small Business Centre 1992). This aggregated figure, however, masks different patterns within the member states. In France, the employment share of small firms increased from 39 per cent in 1971 to 46.2 per cent in 1985, and in Italy, small firms' employment share increased from 61.6 per cent in 1971 to 69.3 per cent in 1981 (Storey 1994). By contrast, the German small business sector shows less marked increases; small manufacturing enterprises increased their share of employment from 14 per cent in 1963 to just 16.2 per cent in 1984 (Storey 1994).

By contrast, the employment share figures for Japan do not demonstrate clear and continuous patterns of growth. Between 1971 and 1985, the employment share of small firms remained comparatively stable (at about 55 per cent), although some increase was seen in the small and medium sized sector (0–299 employees). Neither do the data on manufacturing enterprises demonstrate growth in the small business sector. Between 1979 and 1983, small manufacturing employment declined from 49 per cent to 47 per cent, while the small and medium sized sector's share of manufacturing employment grew from 65 per cent in 1975 to 67 per cent in 1983. As Storey (1994: 29) concludes: 'Insofar as a comparison can be made, it appears that small enterprises in Japan were relatively more important during the 1949–55 period than at any time either previously or subsequently'. Data from Switzerland also show that there has been very little change in the relative importance of small firms in the past thirty years. In 1965, small firms in Switzerland accounted for 45.4 per cent of all employment; this figure had increased to 46.3 per cent by 1985.

These figures demonstrate that the small business and self-employment sector has not shown a universal trend towards growth, even among developed economies. While some countries have experienced growth in this sector, others, notably Japan, have declined. Storey (1994) notes that the pattern of earlier decline followed by the growing importance of the small firms sector which has been apparent in the UK since the 1960s appears to predate changes in other countries during later periods. As he warns, however, it would be unwise to assume that patterns observable in the UK will necessarily be repeated in other countries at later times.

2 The management characteristics of small firms

Irrespective of the relative size and importance of each country's small business sector, the main management characteristics of small firms remain very similar regardless of nationality. Researchers have consistently noted that small firms play an important role in new product and process innovation and are characterized by their product specialization (Rothwell 1986). Research has also suggested that these firms are often undercapitalized, product-led, family owned concerns in which the management function is confined to one person or a few key individuals (Carson 1990; Scase and Goffee 1980). Moreover, small firms operating in different industrial sectors also share many common features. Some propositions about small firm management characteristics include a loose and informal management task structure, a short-term planning horizon (see SHORT-

TERMISM), a limited knowledge of the business environment and informal communications and control systems (see ENTREPRENEURIAL MARKETING).

A central characteristic of small firms is that of owner-management. Owner-management influences small firm performance through the way that owner-managers often concentrate on tasks that they value personally, through their leadership style (see LEADERSHIP) and orientation, previous career and experience, psychological and physiological characteristics and state of health, social orientation in the community, and through family influence on shareholder structure, succession, opportunities for non-family managers and recruitment. In addition, owner-management often influences the corporate objectives of small firms, which may be personalized and subject to the individual preferences of the owner. Finally, the owner-manager's income and standard of living is directly related to his or her decision making (see ENTREPRENEURSHIP; MANAGERIAL BEHAVIOUR). The management differences between small and large firms are summarized in Table 1.

3 Explaining small firm survival

A number of theories have been advanced to explain the survival and development of the small firms sector. Industrial sociologists normally approach the survival of small scale capitalism in one of three ways: 'First, as "separate" and "removed" from the two major

Table 1 Management differences between small and large firms

Small	Large
Short-term planning horizon	Long-term planning horizon
React to environment	Develop environmental strategy
Limited knowledge of environment	Environmental assessments
Personalized company objectives	Corporate strategy
Communication informal	Formal and structured communication
Informal control systems	Formalized control systems
Loose and informal task structure	Job descriptions
Wide range of management skills	High specialist/technical skills demanded
Income directly at risk in decision making	Income derived from wider performance base
Personal motivations directly affect company performance	Broader based company performance

classes of capitalist society. Secondly, as part and parcel of an emerging "post-industrial" or "service" society. Finally, as a legacy of an earlier or pre-capitalist stage of production' (Scase and Goffee 1986: 140). It is now commonly accepted that survival is best explained by the view that the small business stratum is separate and highly distinctive. Increasingly, research has shown that the petite bourgeoisie possess a well-developed class ideology, including possession of a shared set of values, ideals and opinions, which sets them apart from other social strata. In their efforts to provide empirical support for this view, small business scholars have emphasized that self-employment is an important individual and family ideology which can be passed through successive generations (Litvak and Maule 1974; Mancuso 1984). The inheritance of a tradition of self-employment can be seen both in the succession of a family member and in the creation of new firms by the offspring of self-employed parents.

Management theorists (see MANAGERIAL THEORIES OF THE FIRM) generally explain the survival of the individual small firm by emphasizing either cost-based or specialization arguments. Cost-based explanations emphasize that small firms benefit from the optimum use of scale in production, low unit costs, reduced overheads and cheap, often family, labour (see WORK SYSTEMS). An alternative theory, increasingly favoured in academic and policy circles, is that small firms survive through specialization and participation in segmented or niche markets where they can provide usually high value added, sophisticated and customized products or services. There has been some considerable debate about which is the most likely explanation for small firms survival, a debate which has yet to reach a satisfactory conclusion. While some marketing experts believe that differentiation, specialization and a strategy (see MARKETING STRATEGY) of moving away from large-firm competition is an important competitive advantage for small firms, others believe that small firm success, particularly in the manufacturing sector, is more evident when they are able to compete with larger firms in usually larger markets. This theory was supported by a study of employment growth in new independent owner-managed firms in the UK which found that manufacturing firms which developed a strategy of competing 'head on' with larger competitors rather than adopting a niche market position recorded significantly higher levels of employment growth (Westhead and Birley 1993).

The crux of this debate is concerned with market size and relative market share and whether it is a more appropriate strategy for a small firm to have a large share of a small niche market or a small share of a large volume market. It is likely that firms operating in different sectors of the economy must pursue different competitive strategies in order both to survive and to optimize their levels of success. It is worth noting that for many small firms, survival and growth are ensured by using a combination of both cost-based and specialization strategies. Small firms are adept at exploiting niche markets and at forming their own unique cost-cutting strategies in order to optimize survival.

In recent years there has been growing interest in the more individual strategies used by small firms to aid survival and growth. In particular, the use of networks (see NETWORKS AND ORGANIZATIONS; NETWORKING) has proved beneficial for many firms. Inter-firm collaboration takes many forms, from relatively loose associations to more structured networks, but the overriding goal is to achieve certain economies of scale through collaboration which could not be achieved at the enterprise level. The hotel sector provides an obvious example of an industry where independent operators, often competing in the same geographical markets, collaborate through bookings syndicates and marketing consortia. Similar approaches have been observed where structured networking has allowed apparently competing small firms to benefit from collaboration. Notable examples of small business networking have come from northern Italy and Scandinavia (Bellandi 1991; Johannisson et al. 1994).

4 Marketing and small firms

Inherent in the study of small firms is the idea of growth and development from the original state of a new start-up firm to that of mature enterprise capable of creating and sustaining wealth and employment. Marketing (see MARKETING) is now an accepted and central tool in the development of small firms into mature enterprises. However, scholars have noted that for many small firms, marketing is perceived as being at best peripheral to the management function. Carson (1993) identified two common factors which led to an under-utilization of marketing in small firms: first, small firms use marketing in such a general, wasteful and inappropriate way that it does not appear to have any significant impact on performance and as a result is not perceived as being useful, and second, small firms often grow without formal and planned marketing effort and, as a result, owner-managers feel it is unnecessary to invest time and effort in formal marketing planning. In these circumstances a 'credibility gap' occurs between the satisfactory growth performance experienced by a firm and the theoretical and hypothetical performance which might occur with the use of planned marketing. In addition, Carson (1993) points out that there are major functional differences between the management and decision-making approaches of entrepreneurs (in this case owner-managers) and marketing professionals, which is manifested in a dichotomy between marketing planning decisions and entrepreneurial marketing decisions (see ENTREPRENEURIAL MARKETING; ENTREPRENEURIAL STRATEGIES; ENTREPRENEURSHIP). As he points out:

> Entrepreneurial decisions are inherently informal whereas marketing decisions are inherently formal; entrepreneurial decisions are haphazard, creative, opportunistic and reactive, whereas marketing decisions are sequential, systems orientated, disciplined and structured; and entrepreneurs decision time span is short term whereas marketing time spans are both short term, medium term and long term.
>
> (Carson 1993: 192)

If, as Carson suggests, marketing is not perceived as being a central concern of small firms, then questions must be posed in considering what types of markets they participate in and how well they perform. One of the largest studies of small firms performance analysed over 2,000 UK companies (Cambridge Small Business Centre 1992). The size of firms included in the study ranged from fewer than 5 employees (microenterprises) to those employing up to 500 people (large SMEs). This research showed that small firms, being inherently heterogeneous, sell their products into a wide variety of markets and that their main customers (in order of importance) are manufacturers, other firms, retailers and wholesalers. In general, however, small firms depend on very few customers and this dependence is particularly apparent among the micro and very small enterprises where nearly half of these firms relied on one customer to provide 25 per cent or more of their sales.

Similarly, dependence on a limited number of customers was seen among those firms that operate within segmented product markets. This type of niche market firm was also characterized by low levels of competitors. Nearly half of all the surveyed firms believed that they had fewer than five serious competitors and 6 per cent, mostly service firms, stated that they had none. The study also found that sub-contracting is a major feature in the work of many small firms, especially in the service sector; again, this trend is most noticeable among very small firms.

Although the Cambridge study was based on UK companies, many of its main conclusions can be applied to small firms in other countries (see INTERNATIONAL BUSINESS, FUTURE TRENDS). The main competitive advantage of small firms was believed to be the personal attention to client needs, although established reputation, the provision of specialized expertise and product quality were also found to be important factors. In contrast, factors such as product design, cost advantage and price were of lesser importance, although product-related factors such as design and quality were more important among export-orientated firms. Collaboration and cooperation are important features of the small firm sector; nearly one-third of all firms surveyed had entered into either a formal or an informal partnership with other organizations in the three years preceding the study. Mostly, these relationships were formed with supply chain partners, suppliers and customers. The motivation for entering into collaborative arrangements varied, with expansion of product range and expertise and development of specialized services and products, the two most frequently cited reasons. Additional motivations for collaboration were market related and included increased access to new domestic and overseas markets (see INTERNATIONAL MARKETING), improving financial and market credibility and to keep current customers. Finally, for many small firms, participation in segmented or niche markets which emphasize quality and reputation over price and cost factors is of growing importance.

The performance of small firms within markets is perhaps more difficult to quantify. While the conventional financial measures of business performance such as turnover, sales growth and profitability are normally applied to measure business performance, in the case of the small firms sector additional measures are required. New job creation and export performance are also used as important indicators of performance, not least because of the importance various governments have placed on the sector, and the number of policies introduced to expand it.

The Cambridge study also sheds some light on the relative performance of the sector in relation to larger firms. The study found that employment growth (in percentage terms) was highest in microenterprises, with a median growth rate six times higher than for larger SMEs (those employing between 100 and 500 people). However, the study also pointed out that the greatest contribution to employment generation by the sector did not come from the additional jobs created in each enterprise, but that the sector's potential significance in employment generation came from the absolute numbers of small firms compared to larger firms.

The use of export performance as a measure of small business success also shows disparities within the sector. Although traditionally older firms, and medium and larger firms, are more likely to be established exporters, export to sales ratios are highest among micro and newer exporting firms. It is apparent that when new and small firms do export, their relatively high export intensity implies an early degree of export specialization in their strategies (see EXPORTING).

The advent of the new technology offered by the Internet has enabled many small firms to bypass the traditional internationalization process, whereby they would have gradually become accustomed to dealing in the export environment. The Internet has meant that many small firms, especially those dealing in the high technology sector, are global from day one. These firms perceive their markets as worldwide from the outset and may well be operating a niche strategy but at a global level. Where many small firms have faced difficulties is in their eagerness to establish a website and trade on the Internet, they have not fully appreciated the wider implications of this medium. This has resulted in many small firms attempting to service markets in several countries, without the internal infrastructure and secure resource base to deal with such orders. Customers will be expecting all the firm's product literature to be in the required language and delivery and distribution channels to be already established. Like customers in the domestic markets, they will expect to receive the same amount of after sales service and backup. Although the Internet does provide small firms with access to a wider international market, the resultant changes required in-house need to be fully appreciated in planning this step (see E-MARKETING).

Notwithstanding some of these problems, many small firms, especially in the niche markets of food and drink and tourism related products, have successfully become exporters in a very short space of time. Many have entered into collaborative arrangements with local tourism websites in order to benefit from those potential customers accessing a country's site. This collaboration has enabled many small firms to provide a level of sophistication on their web based promotions, which individually would have been prohibitive from a cost perspective.

5 Improving the marketing capabilities of small firms

For marketing scholars the key concern is how to overcome the apparent schism between the characteristics of the small firm owner-managers' approaches to decision making (see DECISION MAKING) and formal marketing decision making as employed by marketing professionals. This concern goes beyond the issue of the psychological characteristics of entrepreneurs and takes into consideration how marketing should be undertaken in firms where there are limited resources. Carson (1993) suggests that this should be approached from a position of compromise and matching of formal marketing to small firm's marketing requirements and capabilities. He proposes three approaches to developing a better understanding of small firms needs and the improvement of the utilization of marketing within small firms. The first is concerned with *adapting* formal marketing to suit the characteristics of entrepreneurs, whereby entrepreneurs can benefit from the integrity of the marketing process (see ENTREPRENEURIAL MARKETING; MARKETING PLANNING) but remain unburdened by the rigours of the technique. An example of this is given in Table 2, where an entrepreneur can follow a market planning approach but in a way which is compatible with his or her characteristics.

The second approach is based on accepting that small firms are characterized by their growth and development and, moreover, that small firms mature in an evolutionary way. Small firms marketing should be matched with this *evolutionary* process (see ORGANIZATIONAL EVOLUTION) and be phased in over four separate and distinct stages, from the first stages of simply reacting to customer demands to the final stage of employing a marketing professional. The final approach is that of encouraging entrepreneurs to move away from the poor implementation of overly generalized marketing concepts and engage in *situation-specific* marketing. The main point of this approach is that small firms must be matched to specific marketing which is unique to the entrepreneur and their firm. Adopting an entrepreneurial marketing approach in small firms will enable them to harness the benefits of a structured approach to marketing, but within a context and in a format which is best suited to the entrepreneurial small firm (see ENTREPRENEURIAL MARKETING).

SARA CARTER

ELAINE COLLINSON
UNIVERSITY OF STRATHCLYDE

Further reading

(References cited in the text marked *)

* Bellandi, M. (1991) 'The role of small firms in the development of Italian manufacturing industry', in E. Goodman and J. Bamford (eds), *Small Firms and Industrial Districts in Italy*, London: Routledge. (Much of the present interest in networks originates from the experience of small firms in Italian manufacturing industry.)
* Bolton, J. (1971) *Report on the Committee of Enquiry on Small Firms*, London: HMSO. (Also known as the Bolton Report, this is a summary of the findings of a UK government committee of enquiry into the small business sector conducted from 1969–71.)

Table 2 Adapted marketing planning process

External considerations	Internal considerations
Those issues concerned with all aspects outside the firm's influence and control	Those issues that are within the firm's control
For example:	For example:
Market environment	Internal environment
Market information	Market variables
Market knowledge	Marketing variables
Market segments	Marketing system
Market opportunities	Marketing strategies
Competition	Marketing plans

Source: Carson (1993)

* Cambridge Small Business Centre (1992) *The State of British Enterprise*, Cambridge: Department of Applied Economics, University of Cambridge. (An empirical study of the British small firms sector.)
* Carson, D. (1990) 'Some exploratory models for assessing small firm marketing performance', *European Journal of Marketing* 24 (11): 5–51. (A useful summary of marketing theory in small firms.)
* Carson, D. (1993) 'A philosophy for marketing education in small firms', *Journal of Marketing Management* 9 (2): 189–204. (In this article the author argues that marketing practice should be tailored to the small firm and offers suggestions as to how this can be achieved.)
* Curran, J. (1991) 'Foreword', in R. Burrows (ed.), *Deciphering the Enterprise Culture: Entrepreneurship, Petty Capitalism and the Restructuring of Britain*, London: Routledge. (A brief introduction to this book provides a useful summary of the reasons why small firms remain an important element of the economy.)
* Curran, J. and Blackburn, R. (1991) *Paths of Enterprise: The Future of the Small Business*, London: Routledge. (A well-argued view of the future importance of the small firm sector.)
* Johannisson, B., Alexanderson, O., Nowicki, K. and Senneseth, K. (1994) 'Beyond anarchy and organization: entrepreneurs in contextual networks', *Entrepreneurship and Regional Development* 6 (4): 329–56. (A view of how entrepreneurs use networks.)
* Labour Force Survey (1997) UK Labour Force Statistics on Self Employed
* Litvak, I.A. and Maule, C.J. (1974) 'Profiles of technical entrepreneurs', *Business Quarterly* 39 (2): 40–9. (Like the Mancuso article cited below, this gives a now dated, but still relevant, insight into the potential inheritance of an entrepreneurial tradition.)
* Mancuso, J.R. (1984) 'What drives the entrepreneur?', *Across the Board* 21: 7–8, 43–7. (Gives a now dated, but still relevant, insight into the potential inheritance of an entrepreneurial tradition.)
* Rothwell, R. (1986) 'The role of small firms in technological innovation', in J. Curran, J. Stanworth and D. Watkins (eds), *The Survival of the Small Firm*, Aldershot: Gower. (An account of the role of small firms in technological innovation, by the leading researcher in the field.)
* SBA (Small Business Administration) (1992) *The State of Small Business: A Report of the President*, Washington, DC: United States Government Printing Office. (An annual report on the American small business sector.)
* SBA (Small Business Adminstration), (1999) *The Facts About Small Business 1999*, US Small business Adminstration Office of Advocacy.
* Scase, R. and Goffee, R. (1980) *The Real World of the Small Business Owner*, London: Croom Helm. (A seminal account of the lives, occupations and ambitions of small firm owners.)
* Scase, R. and Goffee, R. (1986) 'Class analysis and the entrepreneurial middle class', in J. Curran, J. Stanworth and D. Watkins (eds), *The Survival of the Small Firm*, Aldershot: Gower. (A sociological examination of the small firms sector.)
* Schumacher, E.F. (1973) *Small is Beautiful*, London: Abacus. (At the time of publication, this book was an important influence in regenerating interest in small firms. Some parallels may be drawn between the broad philosophy outlined here and the more recent concepts of communitarianism.)
* Storey, D.J. (1994) *Understanding the Small Business Sector*, London: Routledge. (A summary of the main issues affecting small firms. International comparisons are included in many of the chapters.)
* Westhead, P. and Birley, S. (1993) 'Employment growth in new independent owner-managed firms in Great Britain', paper presented to the Research in Enterpreneurship (RENT VII) Conference, Budapest, 25–6 November. (A research paper which contributes to the small firms employment debate.)
* Westhead, P. and Birley, S. (1994) 'Environments for business deregistrations in the United Kingdom, 1987–1990', *Entrepreneurship and Regional Development* 6 (1): 29–62. (A research paper examining small business 'deaths' – failure.)

See also: EMPLOYMENT AND UNEMPLOYMENT, ECONOMICS OF; EXPORTING; ENTREPRENEURIAL MARKETING; MARKETING; MARKETING, GREEN ISSUES IN; MARKETING ENVIRONMENT; MARKETING PLANNING; NETWORKING; RELATIONSHIP MARKETING; SMALL BUSINESS FINANCE; SMALL BUSINESS STRATEGY; WORK SYSTEMS

Small business strategy

Overview

Approaches to business strategy are well developed for large businesses and organizations. Until recently, these contributions to business strategy appeared unsuited to small businesses, but some recent thinking suggests a convergence, though there are inherent limitations on how far this can be taken. Thinking on small business strategy has developed separately with its own models to suggest, for example, the typical path small businesses follow as they develop and grow. Other approaches make the entrepreneur's psychological characteristics and vision central. Finally, there are empirically based models which attempt to isolate factors statistically associated with small business development. There is also much practical advice available to small business owners on developing a business strategy.

1 Role of the small business in modern economies

The importance of small businesses in modern economies is now widely accepted. In advanced industrial societies this importance was lost sight of for much of the twentieth century, with small businesses often seen as disappearing remnants of earlier stages of the development of the economy. The large enterprise was seen as superseding small businesses and as an indicator of economic progress. By the end of the century, however, this view was increasingly recognized as mistaken (see INDUSTRIAL STRATEGY).

One reason for the above change of view was the resurgence of small businesses in many industrial societies from the 1970s onwards. For instance, in the United Kingdom, there were about 2.4 million firms in 1980 but by 1998 this total had risen to 3.7 million (Department of Trade and Industry 1999). Most of these additional enterprises were small. Small businesses, therefore, comprise the great majority of all small businesses in the United Kingdom, with well over 95 per cent of all businesses having fewer than 20 employees. Other advanced industrial societies, ranging from the United States to Japan to Germany, offer similar profiles.

Of course, although most businesses are small, larger businesses are proportionately more important in national production and employment. However, small businesses are still significant. In the United Kingdom, by the 1990s, for instance, businesses with under 50 employees were responsible for almost 45 per cent of private sector jobs (Department of Trade and Industry 1999). Elsewhere in Europe, businesses with under 10 employees provided almost a third of all jobs in the European Union (Eurostat 1998). In the USA, often seen as the home of the giant corporation, a similar pattern occurred (The State of Small Business 1997). In Japan, official data suggested that 75 per cent of all jobs were in small and medium-sized enterprises with fewer than 300 employees (Whittaker 1997: 3).

A similar picture holds in many developing countries. A high proportion of economic activities are in small enterprises, particularly in agriculture. Often these small enterprises exist outside or at the margins of the formal economy, unrecorded in official statistics. Transactions are often in cash or even by barter but the importance of such activities should not be discounted simply because they do not appear in the national accounts of the particular countries. Many larger businesses in these countries started small as a result of the activities of indigenous entrepreneurs.

In the transitional economies of former communist countries, there has been a re-emergence of small-scale economic activities. Some result from privatization while others are new businesses arising from the entrepreneurial initiatives of individuals. Many have seen this as the 'inverted pyramid' of the typical command economy (large state-owned enterprises dominating the whole economy with little or no small-scale enterprise) being reversed. Increasingly, they are expected to come to resemble the conventional pyramid distributions of older market economies in which very large numbers of smaller businesses coexist with a relative handful of large businesses (see RUSSIA, MANAGEMENT IN; EASTERN EUROPE, MANAGEMENT IN). In virtually every economy, therefore, regardless of its development or political character, small-scale enterprise is important. In many also, for a wide variety of reasons, the last part of the twentieth century saw a considerable growth of small businesses likely to continue in this century.

It is usual to stress that it is from the ranks of small businesses of today that the large enterprises – national and multinational – of tomorrow come. In practice, relatively few small firms grow to any size, as the highly skewed size distributions of businesses in most economies demonstrate. For instance, Storey (1994) reviewed the histories of a sample of firms set up in the United Kingdom between 1965 and 1978. By 1978, of the 774 surviving firms, only 1 per cent employed more than 100 workers. Other recent research has reached similar conclusions.

The main focus in examining business strategy and small businesses has been on strategies underlying the growth process (see STRATEGY, CONCEPT OF). Given also the relative rarity of substantial growth by the typical small business, academics, management experts and governments in many countries have been keen to discover how best small business growth can be encouraged. What kinds of strategies do successful small businesses use to grow and, conversely, what constraints prevent growth? Attention to the rather more mundane issue of the strategies adopted to ensure continuity and survival has been very much less, despite the fact that this is what commonly occurs in the great majority of small businesses.

2 Business strategy and planning

Business strategy and planning generally have received much attention in management theorizing and research. Businesses and public sector organizations are seen as needing a strategy or plan to guide the future of the enterprise. Without such an approach, it is argued, success is unlikely. It is also needed to demonstrate to shareholders (or taxpayers for public sector organizations) that the enterprise has clear goals and that resources are being managed effectively. Once a broad strategy for the future has been articulated, operational policies need to be developed to achieve the strategy's aims. The overall strategy will have to be reappraised from time to time to take account of changed circumstances and, especially, unpredictable events. Operational policies realizing the strategy will require a more frequent, even continuous, monitoring to ensure they are meeting the long-term goals of the enterprise.

Business strategy thinking has developed most clearly in relation to larger enterprises. In the oldest and best known approach (exemplified by the highly influential work of Ansoff (1965)) the emphasis was an explicit, highly rational, long-term planning process aimed at the development and growth of the business. The approach was based on a wide range of techniques to aid decision making, such as check lists, analytical exercises, the use of diagrams and other aids in what often emerged as a very complex approach overall. A number of similar models were developed by other writers and the approach became highly influential both in business schools and among managers of large enterprises.

However, the applicability of the above business strategy and planning models to small businesses was questionable on a number of grounds. First, few small business owners have the time, skills or inclination to use these kinds of business planning techniques. Owner-managers, even those with business partners, often suffer from managerial overload. They are responsible for all the major functions of the business, production, marketing, finance and human resource management. Often because the business is small, it cannot afford professional salaried managerial support. One result of managerial overload is short time horizons. Much research shows that small firm owner-managers are so busy coping with the immediate management of the enterprise that they have little or no time to plan ahead. Second, small business owners have less need to take others into account. Typically, they own the enterprise outright or are the dominant shareholders and therefore there is less need to demonstrate to others a long-term strategy for the business. (There are exceptions, however, as where a business plan is required to secure outside finance, an issue discussed further below.)

Even if they had the time to adopt highly systematic approaches to business strategy and planning, the skills barrier would remain. Small business owners rarely have any formal management training. One reason is again lack of time; another is that most formal management training is aimed at the executive in the larger enterprise (see MANAGEMENT DEVELOPMENT). This makes it less attractive to the small business owner-manager since its relevance to the smaller enterprise may not be apparent. For instance, many formal business strategy models stress adopting plans and policies to manipulate the environment in which the business operates, but small business owners may feel this is unrealistic because they typically face very risky environments and have little power to influence them.

Finally, there is the psychological profile of the small business owner. Research on the outlooks, motivational patterns and goals of small business owners suggests several factors which make adoption of highly formal planning approaches unlikely (Chell *et al.* 1991; Gibb 2000) (see MOTIVATION AND SATISFACTION). A high proportion of small business owners believe in an instinctive, flexible management style which they feel helps them to be highly responsive to customers and market opportunities. Another reason why so few small businesses ever reach any substantial size is that growth is not a main priority of the typical owner-manager (Storey 1994). A common motivation of small business owners, for example, is a strong desire for autonomy and independence expressed through running the business.

Substantial or rapid growth can easily threaten owner-manager independence. Growth, for example, can easily lead to feelings of loss of control over what is happening to the business. Growth may require additional management resources and delegation which again may easily produce feelings of loss of control. Growth may also need additional finance from outside the enterprise. External finance will normally only be forthcoming if those offering the finance can share in the major decisions guiding the business or, at the least, can veto decisions which they feel put their investment at risk.

Later thinking on business strategy and planning for the larger enterprise has been highly critical of early approaches and suggested alternatives which may have more relevance to the small business. Whittington (1993) and Mintzberg (1994), for instance, argued that earlier models did not reflect the actual strategy and business planning practices of larger businesses. Mintzberg, in particular, argued that the evidence for the effectiveness of earlier models was far from robust. Both reviewed a range of alternative models which they felt came closer to the reality of business strategy and planning processes in larger enterprises.

Mintzberg, for instance, distinguished between *deliberate* strategies formalized in a plan of some kind and *realized* strategies. Deliberate strategies are highly explicit plans formulated for some future time 't'. Realized strategies are the actual outcomes at the future time 't'. Realized strategies, in other words, are the outcome of a mix of aims from the original plan and responses to unexpected events such as those arising from new technology that have occurred over the period of the plan. Businesses typically develop *emergent* strategies to cope with unexpected events and modify the original plan or, alternatively, develop a strategy on a step-by-step basis. For instance, a business may take decisions to diversify one by one, in effect testing the market at each decision. Some are abandoned while others, deemed more successful, are consolidated by further decisions which, *ex post facto*, can be seen as adding up to a strategy.

In the real world, argued Mintzberg, few strategies are entirely deliberate or purely emergent. Entirely deliberate strategies, rigidly adhered to, means that the business cannot respond to unforeseen threats and opportunities. Entirely emergent strategies imply that the business is just drifting with the tide. Whittington (1993) offered a somewhat similar view in his isolation of *evolutionary* and *processual* approaches to planning in which the business survives and grows by learning and adjusting to new influences and events as they occur without necessarily having any real long-term goals beyond survival. A more recent review (Geroski 2000) argues that study after study of businesses shows that growth, usually a main aim of strategy, follows what is called a 'random walk' pattern. That is, it follows an erratic, unpredictable course which, while not entirely dictated by chance, is only partly influenced by declared strategy. More generally, thinking on large enterprises (Domagalski 1999) has argued that conventional approaches to business organizations over-emphasize rationality and greatly under-emphasize the extent to which their processes are 'saturated with emotions'.

Models of business strategy and planning which allow it to be much less explicitly rational and to flexibly respond to events as they occur, are seemingly much easier to apply to the small business owner. They appear to recognize and accommodate the lack of control over the environment by the small business and the psychological attributes of small business owners. Strategy is much less of a conscious process based on detailed prescriptive models or sophisticated techniques and more of an instinctive, flexible approach to survival consistent with the owner's broad personal and business goals.

3 Approaches to small business strategy

Although mainstream thinking on business strategy and planning has been largely generated from a large enterprise perspective, those concerned with the small enterprise have also focused on how small firms develop. There

have been two main ways in which the problems have been tackled. First are extraneous models which define a pattern which it is alleged small firms must follow if successful growth is to be achieved. The processes involved are seen as mainly externally dictated with the owner-manager constrained by these external forces. Owner-managers can undermine the processes by poor decision making and success occurs where their behaviour and decisions fit the demands of external forces. Second are entrepreneurial models of small business strategy and planning which make the owner-manager/entrepreneur's vision central. All decisions revolve around the entrepreneur with little reliance on formal planning techniques except where these are harnessed to the entrepreneur's vision. Owner-manager decisions can be swift, opportunistic, instinctive and bold and are rarely committed to paper, but can impact on the environment, even changing it fundamentally through their innovativeness and boldness.

Extraneous models

Extraneous models come in several forms but by far the most common are *stage models* which suggest that the small firm passes through identifiable stages to reach maturity or achieve successful growth. Typically the models offer three to five main stages though some offer up to ten. A well-known example by Churchill and Lewis (1983) offered a five-stage model (as shown in Figure 1). The authors argued that although small firms vary enormously, it is nevertheless possible to generate a model covering '... a corner dry-cleaning establishment with two or three minimum-wage employees to a $20 million-a-year computer software company experiencing a 40 per cent annual rate of growth' (1983: 30). They were careful to avoid any assumption that all small firms must pass through all stages or fail in the attempt. Such an assumption would be absurd given that so many small firms never grow beyond a very small size and yet survive prosperously, often for very long periods.

The first stage in the model, *existence*, is essentially the attempt to reach viability suffi-

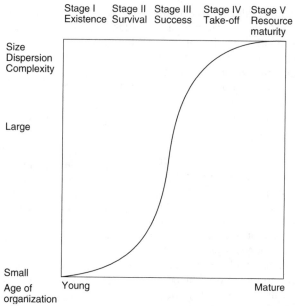

Figure 1 Growth stages of the small business

cient to survive. The second stage, *survival*, is where the firm generates an economic return on its assets. The organization remains simple, with most decisions still taken by the owner-manager(s). Many businesses will stick at this stage, just surviving, or decline, eventually going out of business.

The third stage, *success*, has two sub-stages – either the owners use the firm as a platform for growth or they keep the firm stable and profitable enough to pursue alternative activities. Organizationally, the business is big enough to need and afford added management capacity. The *success-disengagement* sub-stage, in which the firm remains in business but does not experience serious further growth, allows the owner-managers to do other things, perhaps start other businesses. Growth may also be inhibited by external factors such as limited market opportunities. Alternatively, there is the *success-growth* sub-stage where the owners attempt strong growth. This requires much more attention to organizational matters, management development and explicit planning. If the strategy is unsuccessful the firm may revert to the *success-disengagement* sub-stage and stabilize, but it can also slip back a stage or two, or even fail.

Take-off is the penultimate stage where there are key problems associated with rapid growth. Owner-managers, for instance, need to delegate. They must also accept a high debt–equity ratio to finance growth. If these changes are managed successfully, the result can be a large successful enterprise. Again, however, failure can occur. Owners may refuse to delegate or the firm may run out of finance and collapse. It may also slip back to earlier stages or it could be sold.

Finally, Churchill and Lewis proffer the *resource-maturity* stage which consolidates the fourth stage, stabilizing the firm's structure and procedures. It can now enjoy the advantages of size and success. If it retains its entrepreneurial drive it will continue to be a force in the market but, equally, it may ossify, seeking a risk-free comfortable existence. Eventually, it may fail, for example because it has lost its ability to cope with change and seize new opportunities.

The Churchill–Lewis model is typical of stage models of small business growth, albeit developing some aspects of the alleged processes in more detail. In an earlier article, Stanworth and Curran (1976) criticized stage models of small business growth on a number of epistemological and empirical grounds and the Churchill–Lewis model illustrates a number of their criticisms. First, as Churchill and Lewis admit, many small firms do not pass through the postulated stages. Their model contains several implicit hypotheses of the form the small enterprise will do (a) or (b) or (c) where (a), (b) and (c) cover all possible outcomes. For instance, at the third stage (success) the business may go for strong growth, stabilize, revert back to a previous stage or fail. Non-testable hypotheses of this kind are not helpful in developing a robust model of how small firms develop or fail to develop.

Second, there are few or no well-researched, methodologically adequate studies of good-sized samples of small businesses passing through the postulated stages. Churchill and Lewis claimed that their model was based, in part, on data from owners of 83 firms but these respondents offered their views only *after* reading an article on the proposed five-stage model. Other objections are that such models implicitly assume relatively unchanging motivations on the part of owner-managers. In reality, it is quite plausible that owner-managers' outlooks and ambitions will change as they develop their businesses, gain experience and find new markets or other opportunities for the business to change over time. Stanworth and Curran (1976) offered a social action model of small business development based on the notion of changing motivations on the part of owner-managers. As the business changes, so will owner-managers' outlooks. Personal circumstances also change. For example, as owner-managers age it might be expected that their ambitions for growth might well change also.

In terms of the kinds of large business strategy and planning models which dominate management writing discussed earlier, it can be seen that stage models of small business growth offer a different picture. First, they impose a framework which constrains the range of strategies that can be adopted. Small business strategies for growth have to fall within the boundaries set by the stages or the business will stagnate, or worse, fail. The planning processes only come to resemble classic large enterprise models in the later stages, if at all. Emergent and processual models, on the other hand, are much more consistent with the stage

models but again only within the constraints of the stages the small firms are argued to have to follow.

Entrepreneurial models

Entrepreneurial models of small business growth are much less well formulated than stage models (Chell *et al.* 1991; Gibb 2000). One reason for this is that the notion of 'entrepreneurship' is not easy to define clearly and therefore the behaviour associated with it is equally ill-defined. In some definitions it is simply a synonym for small business ownership. In others, emphasis is placed on risk taking and significant or radical innovation. The latter seems a better use of the term 'entrepreneur' to demarcate those who are genuinely breaking new ground economically from small business owners generally. Much of the literature on entrepreneurship consists of anecdotal biographies of particular entrepreneurs, sometimes purporting to reveal the 'secrets' of their business success strategy. Often these emerge as *ex post facto* rationalizations of the individual's behaviour with little obvious generalizability. One reason for this lack of theorization is that, by definition, entrepreneurs are often portrayed as economic revolutionaries who break with accepted practice and textbook approaches. It is hard to generate a theory of the one-off situation which others can systematically put into practice as a well-defined strategy (see ENTREPRENEURSHIP).

Psychologists have made a number of attempts to identify the key characteristics of the entrepreneurial personality on the assumption that, if this were possible, it would show what personal characteristics produce the successful high-growth small business. A well-known example is that of McClelland (1961, 1965), based on the notion that the key to entrepreneurial behaviour is achievement motivation, that is, the drive to excel or achieve goals (see MCCLELLAND, D.C.) The need to achieve, 'nAch', is unevenly spread through the population but can be raised through appropriate socialization and training. Several programmes to increase nAch and entrepreneurial attitudes were introduced in developing countries based on McClelland's ideas.

His ideas have been subject to considerable refinement by later theorists but have also been criticized by other psychologists.

Assessments of these approaches (Chell *et al.* 1991, especially Ch. 3) have suggested that little progress has been made in isolating what characteristics or traits distinguish the entrepreneur from others in society. A key criticism of personality-based approaches is that they often ignore the context of the enterprise – its organizational, human-resource and market situations. The development of the small firm is more realistically seen as the outcome of a complex set of interactions between the person (the entrepreneur) and these contextual influences.

This is not to deny that an individual with a brilliant idea for a new product or a new way of delivering goods or services to the market, who has drive and dedication, a willingness to take risks and work long hours, can build a major business enterprise starting from scratch. But this is not the same as a theory of small business strategy and growth. Sometimes attempts are made to combine psychological and contextual elements to overcome these problems but usually they add up to little more than marrying psychological trait approaches to some variety of stage theory, with the weaknesses of both remaining.

Descriptive models

Descriptive models represent an empirically based, less theorized alternative to the stage and entrepreneurial models discussed above. They use quantitative data from samples of small firms to isolate those factors which appear statistically associated with growth and success. This highly empirical approach to small business strategy was reviewed well by Storey (1994). He acknowledged that most owner-managers have no developed plans or strong desires for growth but pointed out that it is the very smallest firms which are most likely be in this group. Owners of larger small firms, those employing say ten or more people already, tend to display more positive attitudes. Rather more small business owners state that they are actively seeking growth than actually achieve growth, but this is to be expected. Some may well be giving lip service

to growth or saying what they feel people expect to hear. Others may be constrained by external factors such as lack of finance.

Yet, of course, some small firms do grow and how they accomplish this can be tracked empirically. Storey rejected stage models of the kind offered by Churchill and Lewis and offered a widely cited example of an alternative, empirically grounded approach. He argues that the growing small firm may be conceptualized in terms of three components:

- the starting resources of the entrepreneur(s);
- the firm;
- strategy.

The three components should not be seen as independent influences but rather as overlapping or interconnecting. Each component can be broken down into different elements. For instance, the entrepreneur/resources component has fifteen elements ranging from motivation to gender. The firm is seen as having six elements (age, sector, legal form, location, size and ownership) and strategy is given fourteen elements ranging from workforce training to exporting (see Table 1). The elements of the entrepreneur/resources component can be identified before the business is set up and each can, in principle, be measured. The elements which constitute the firm are attributes and can again be identified unambiguously. Of the final component he wrote:

> It is perhaps the elements within the third factor – strategy – that are of prime interest. To some extent 'strategy' in this context can be considered as asking the question – given the characteristics of the entrepreneur(s) and the firm – what managerial actions, once the firm has started, are likely to be associated with more rapid rates of growth?
>
> (Storey 1994: 124–5)

Storey then reviewed a number of empirical studies producing quantitative data undertaken mainly in the United Kingdom and the United States (see UNITED KINGDOM, MANAGEMENT IN THE; UNITED STATES OF AMERICA, MANAGEMENT IN THE). As he pointed out, it would be preferable to use only studies us-

Table 1 Factors influencing growth in a small firm

The entrepreneurs/resources	The firm	Strategy
1 Motivation	1 Age	1 Workforce training
2 Unemployment	2 Sector	2 Management training
3 Education	3 Legal form	3 External equity
4 Management experience	4 Location	4 Technological sophistication
5 Number of founders	5 Size	5 Market positioning
6 Prior self-employment	6 Ownership	6 Market adjustments
7 Family history		7 Planning
8 Social marginality		8 New products
9 Functional skills		9 Management recruitment
10 Training		10 State support
11 Age		11 Customer concentration
12 Prior business failure		12 Competition
13 Prior sector experience		13 Information and advice
14 Prior firm size experience		14 Exporting
15 Gender		

Source: Storey (1994: 123)

ing multivariate analysis incorporating more than one factor since relations are often complex, requiring more than one element to be held constant, but there are few such studies and it is necessary to draw upon univariate studies also. Because the studies were conducted independently of each other there are also frequent problems in comparing findings. Research methods also varied, as did the size of samples. 'Growth' also needs to be defined carefully and most studies use employment creation as a measure of growth. There is also the time period to be covered since clearly the results are likely to differ if, for example, ten years is chosen but another study takes only three years. Pooling results from different countries with their different economies may also be suspect. Finally there is a further time period issue of whether the study was conducted under conditions of recession or economic expansion. Storey was, therefore, well aware of the problems of such an empirical approach to studying small business strategy but nevertheless argued that there are useful generalizations to be drawn from the results.

Having reviewed a large number of studies covering the thirty-five elements categorized under the three main components, Storey concluded:

> The elements which appear to be associated with growth in the entrepreneur/resources factor are: motivation, education, having more than a single owner and having business owners in middle age. Amongst the firm-related elements, smaller and younger firms grow quicker, as do limited companies. There are also sectoral and locational differences. Finally, amongst the strategy variables, a willingness to share ownership, the ability to identify niches, the introduction of new products and the ability to create teams of managers are generally related to growth.
> (Storey 1994: 158)

There are also identifiable constraints on growth. The studies reviewed suggest that such constraints may be related to finance (particularly the availability of external funding), human resources and markets for the firms' goods and services. These will vary also with the external conditions faced by firms, such as whether the economy is expanding or in recession and the sectors in which the businesses are located.

Empirical approaches to small business strategy might be said to be at a fairly primitive stage to date. The predictive power of these approaches is limited by the fact that they deal in the characteristics of *populations* of businesses, not individual businesses. Nor is the empirical base very secure, because of the limitations resulting from problems linked to sample selection and sample size, sectoral coverage, time period covered, point in the economic cycle at which the study was undertaken, the economic mix, the extent and importance of restructuring of the economy in which the enterprise is situated and the methodologies employed to collect data. However, over time it might be expected that the quality and coverage of research of this kind will improve, leading to more powerful generalizations, though the extent to which these will ever be applicable to individual firms may remain limited.

4 Practical approaches to small business strategy

Academic reservations about progress towards developing theories of small business strategy have not prevented the emergence of a large literature offering practical advice on strategy to the small business owner. At its worst, this literature reflects the opinions and prejudices of the author(s) concerned who may never have managed a small business or even had much contact with small businesses or any knowledge of the relevant research. Other authors offer advice and strategy recipes based on their experiences in larger enterprises which they feel can be adapted to help the small firm although, given the differences between small and large firms, this may not as be helpful to the small firm as they hope.

More useful are 'how-to-do-it' texts by authors with a good knowledge of the relevant theoretical and research literatures who then translate this into more concrete advice for small business owners or those involved in counselling small business owners. There are rather fewer works of this kind but this literature is growing. An example is Stokes (1998), a text aimed at students and support providers. Inevitably, any translation of research and theorizing into a text and practical advice means some of the qualifications academic researchers would want to include are lost. Another example, aimed at providing practical advice on small enterprise business plan preparation, the basis of any written business strategy, is Barrow *et al.* (1998).

A further problem with these more practical approaches to small business strategy is the extent to which small business owners are likely to accept and implement the advice offered (Gibb 2000). The evidence on the psychological profiles of small business owners discussed earlier indicated that small business owners are often very sceptical of systematic approaches to planning the future of their businesses. For example, there is wide agreement among academics and those providing practical support for small business owners about the value of a business plan. This is to all intents and purposes a strategy statement intended to guide the development of the business. Yet there is considerable research to indicate that small business owners themselves are very doubtful about having a business plan and will often generate a plan simply to please the bank or other external source of support but not use it thereafter as a management aid. They prefer an instinctive management approach which they argue allows them to react quickly to the environment and maintain market advantage. Growth, should it be desired, will follow if the business is flexible, responsive, attentive to customer wants and on the lookout for opportunities.

Thinking and research on small business strategy, therefore, differs sharply from the approaches developed for the large enterprise which constitute the conventional treatment of business strategy and planning in the mainstream business and management literature. While contributions to the latter, particularly those emphasizing an emergent or processual approach, could be applied to small businesses, there is a case for arguing that the importance of the small enterprise in economic life deserves an approach developed to meet its special and distinctive characteristics.

JAMES CURRAN
SMALL BUSINESS RESEARCH CENTRE
KINGSTON UNIVERSITY

Further reading

(References cited in the text marked *)

* Ansoff, H.I. (1965) *Corporate Strategy*, New York: McGraw-Hill. (A very influential book on strategy updated by the author in further editions, e.g. *The New Corporate Strategy*, New York: Wiley, 1988, and in numerous other publications.)

* Barrow, C., Barrow, P. and Brown, R. (1998) *The Business Plan Workbook*, London: Kogan Page. (A down-to-earth analysis and review of the issues involved in developing, writing and presenting business plans, the foundation of a written business strategy. It offers a step-by-step guide to advisers and small business owners covering the key areas of the business which need to be included in the plan.)

* Chell, E., Haworth, J. and Brearley, S. (1991) *The Entrepreneurial Personality, Concepts, Cases and Categories*, London: Routledge. (A detailed examination of theories of the entrepreneurial personality together with an ambitious attempt to use the notion of neural networks in developing thinking on the topic.)

* Churchill, N.C. and Lewis, V.L. (1983) 'The five stages of small business growth', *Harvard Business Review* 61 (3): 30–50. (Widely cited, above average example of a stage model of small business growth.)

Curran, J. (1999) *The Role of the Small Firm in the UK Economy: Hot Stereotypes and Cool Assessments*, Milton Keynes, England: Small Business Research Trust/The Open University, May. (A critical review of widely accepted assumptions and explanations about the role and the importance of the small enterprise in the UK economy suggesting a need to be sceptical about many of the highly positive and ideologically charged assertions offered.)

* Department of Trade and Industry (1999) *Small and Medium Enterprise (SME) Statistics for the United Kingdom, 1998*, Sheffield: SME Statistics Unit, August. (Accurate statistics on small businesses in modern economies are often difficult to assemble. This is a detailed and careful set of estimates of the numbers of small and medium enterprises in the main sectors of the UK economy. The equivalent official statistic units in other countries should be consulted to ascertain whether similar data is available.)

* Domagalski, T. A. (1999) 'Emotion and organizations: main currents', *Human Relations* 52 (6): 833–52. (Review article discussing the role and importance of emotion in social relations and the main functions of the larger organization, including leadership and decision making. It provides a counterbalance to the strong emphasis on rationality in business organization processes central to many approaches to business strategy.)

* Eurostat (1998) *Enterprise in Europe, Fifth Report, SME Project*, Luxembourg: Eurostat. (The European Union commissions the collection of data to provide a detailed overview of small and medium enterprises in the member states. Reports are normally published annually.)

Georgellis, Y., Joyce, P. and Woods, A. (2000) 'Entrepreneurial action, innovation and business performance: the small independent business', *Journal of Small Business and Enterprise Development* 7 (1): 7–17. (A good example of a carefully conducted quantitative study of small business owners' propensity to plan ahead, innovate and take risks and how these are related to growth. The conclusions offer a well-balanced view of the processes involved.)

* Geroski, P.A. (2000) 'Growth of firms in theory and practice', in N. Foss and V. Malinke (eds), *New Directions in Economic Strategy Research*, Oxford: Oxford University Press. (Examines competing theories on business growth such as life cycle and core competency approaches and argues that it is difficult to square these with empirical observation. An alternative is offered stressing innovation and the way firms innovate erratically which, in turn, leads to erratic growth and development of the firm.)

* Gibb, A.A. (2000) 'SME policy, academic resarch and the growth of ignorance: mythical concepts, myths, assumptions, rituals and confusions', *International Small Business Journal* 18 (3): 13–35. (A wide-ranging examination of entrepreneurship, small enterprise development and policy initiatives aimed at promoting smaller businesses and their growth. It includes a critical consideration of the role of planning.)

Goffee, R. and Scase, R. (1995) *Corporate Realities, The Dynamics of Large and Small Organizations*, London: Routledge. (A highly accessible text examining management and business strategy practices in small and large organizations which brings out very well the differences and similarities significant in comparing different-sized organizations in relation to these issues.)

* McClelland, D.C. (1961) *The Achieving Society*, Princeton, NJ: Van Nostrand. (Very well-known contribution to psychological explanations of entrepreneurial behaviour which has inspired much further work but also been the subject of much criticism.)

* McClelland, D.C. (1965) 'Achievement motivation can be developed', *Harvard Business Review* 43: 6–24 and 178. (Describes how the need to achieve, nAch, the claimed key motivational element in entrepreneurship, can be developed through appropriate programmes.)

* Mintzberg, H. (1994) *The Rise and Fall of Strategic Planning*, Hemel Hempstead: Prentice-Hall International. (Critique of established business strategy and planning models by a distinguished contributor to thinking on the topics with suggestions for developing more adequate approaches.)

Perren, L., Berry, A. and Partridge, M. (1999) 'The evolution of management information, control and decision making processes in small growth-oriented service sector businesses: exploratory lessons from four cases of success', *Journal of Small Business and Enterprise Development* 5 (4): 351–61. (A qualitative study exploring longitudinally how small business owners handle information provision and decision making. It suggests a shift from informal to formal systems as firms develop but that this occurs highly variably due to the complex interplay of a wide range of influences. The authors argue, therefore, that the processes involved cannot be reduced to the 'universal banality' of simple models of business strategy.)

* Stanworth, M.J.K. and Curran, J. (1976) 'Growth and the small firm – an alternative view', *Journal of Management Studies* 13 (2): 95–110 and reprinted in D.J. Storey (ed.) (2000) *Small Business: Critical Perspectives*, London: Routledge. (A widely cited, critical examination of a range of models and theories of small business growth offering an alternative social action-based model.)

* Stokes, D. (1998) *Small Business Management, A Case Study Approach*, 3rd edn, London: Letts International. (A sound, well-structured introduction to starting and developing a small business. There are many texts of this type published, particularly in the United States, but the quality is highly variable and more than one should be consulted.)

* Storey, D.J. (1994) *Understanding the Small Business Sector*, London: Routledge. (A broad, highly informed and well-argued review of the situation of the small business in advanced industrial economies, concentrating especially on the United Kingdom.)

* The State of Small Business (1997) *The State of Small Business: A Report to the President*, Washington, DC: US Government Printing Office. (A very detailed report prepared by the US Small Business Administration which provides data and a commentary on the role of the small business in the US economy. It is normally published annually.)

* Whittaker, D.H. (1997) *Small Firms in the Japanese Economy*, Cambridge: Cambridge University Press. (A well-researched overview of the small firm in the Japanese economy which challenges older, stereotypical views.)

* Whittington, R. (1993) *What is Strategy and Does it Matter?*, London: Routledge. (A careful and critical review of established approaches to strategic management and planning in the large organization with suggestions for refining thinking on the topics.)

See also: ENTREPRENEURSHIP; INDUSTRIAL STRATEGY; MANAGEMENT DEVELOPMENT; SMALL BUSINESS FINANCE STRATEGY, CONCEPT OF; SMALL BUSINESS MARKETING; SMALL AND MEDIUM-SIZED ENTERPRISES

Small and medium sized enterprises

Overview

Small business has been classified by the United States Small Business Administration as enterprises with 500 or fewer employees. While this definition is arbitrary, it has generally been accepted as the definition for small- and medium-sized firms in the USA and most other developed countries.

The role that small firms play in economics has evolved considerably since the Second World War. This article seeks to document how and why small business plays a very different role in industrial organization research today than they did some three decades ago.

The most important development in the field of small business economics has been a shift in the framework for analysing small business. While there were always a few studies around analysing small business through a dynamic lens, a much more profound and comprehensive shift in the literature began in the later 1980s and early 1990s. The most salient characteristic feature of this literature was the introduction of a dynamic or evolutionary framework.

In the second section of this entry, the view of small business emerging from the static framework of the post-war analysis is described. This view identifies small business as being sub-optimal in terms of scale of production. The resulting impact on performance is negative, in terms of productivity and wages. The policy implication is that, at least in terms of economic efficiency, small business exerts a drag on economic welfare.

In the third section, the view of small business emerging from the dynamic framework of the last decade is introduced. This view provides a striking contrast to the role and contribution of small business. When viewed through the lens of a dynamic framework, small businesses are seen as *agents of change*. The empirical evidence supporting this dynamic view of small business is presented in the fourth section. The implications for public policy towards business are presented in the fifth section. In particular, we find that the role of public policy towards business has shifted from constraining the power of large corporations to enabling the creation and commercialization of knowledge, particularly by small business.

1 Introduction

As recently as a decade ago, there were serious concerns about the ability of the USA to withstand competition in the global economy, create jobs and continue to develop. Lester Thurow (1985) bemoaned that the USA was 'losing the economic race,' because:

> Today it's very hard to find an industrial corporation in America that isn't in really serious trouble basically because of trade problems. ... The systematic erosion of our competitiveness comes from having lower rates of growth of manufacturing productivity year after year, as compared with the rest of the world.
>
> (Thurow 1985: 23)

W.W. Restow (1987) predicted a revolution in economic policy, concluding that, 'The United States is entering a new political era, one in which it will be preoccupied by increased economic competition from abroad and will need better cooperation at home to deal with this challenge.'

In the influential study, *Made in America*, directed by the leaders of the MIT Commission on Industrial Productivity, Michael L. Dertouzos, Richard K. Lester and Robert M. Solow, a team of 23 scholars, spanning a broad range of disciplines and backgrounds, reached the conclusion that for the USA to restore its international competitiveness, it had to adapt the types of policies targeting the leading corporations prevalent in Japan and Germany.

The last decade has seen a re-emergence of competitiveness, innovative activity and job generation in the United States. Not only was this economic turnaround largely unanticipated by many scholars and members of the policy community, but what was even more surprising than the resurgence itself was the primary source – small firms. As scholars began the arduous task of documenting the crucial role played by small and medium sized enterprises (SMEs) in the United States as a driving engine of growth, job creation and competitiveness in global markets (Audretsch, 1995), policy makers responded with a bipartisan emphasis on policies to promote SMEs (see *U.S. News and World Report* 1993). For example, in his 1993 State of the Union Address to the country, President Bill Clinton proposed, 'Because small business has created such a high percentage of all the new jobs in our nation over the last 10 or 15 years, our plan includes the boldest targeted incentives for small business in history. We propose a permanent investment tax credit for the small firms in this country (quoted in Davis *et al.* 1996: 298). The Republican response to Clinton was, 'We agree with the President that we have to put more people to work, but remember this: 80 to 85 percent of the new jobs in this country are created by small business. So the climate for starting and expanding businesses must be enhanced with tax incentives and deregulation, rather than imposing higher taxes and more governmental mandates' (Representative Robert Michel, House Minority Leader, in the Republican Response to the 1993 State of the Union Address, quoted in Davis *et al.* 1996: 298).

One of the puzzles posed by the important contribution of small firms to the resurgence of the American economy is that their share of economic activity, measured in terms of share of total establishments, employment, or output, has not dramatically increased over the last 20 years (Acs and Audretsch 1993). In fact, a meticulous comparison documenting the role of SMEs across a broad spectrum of

countries revealed that the share of economic activity accounted for by SMEs is considerably less than in Japan, Germany, the UK, Italy, the Netherlands and other European countries.

If SMEs are so important to the US economy, how come they account for such a small share of economic activity, at least relative to other economies? The answer to this question lies in a crucial distinction between the static role of SMEs and the dynamic role. In the second section of this entry we contrast the static and dynamic role of SMEs.

2 The static view

The starting point for the analysis of SMEs is the theory of the firm (see GROWTH OF THE FIRM AND NETWORKING). The field of economics that focuses the most on links between the organization of firms in industries and the resulting economic performance has been industrial organization. The ascendancy of industrial organization in the post-war period as an important and valued field of economics came from the recognition not only by scholars but also by policy makers that industrial organization matters. The widespread fear *vis-à-vis* the Soviet Union pervasive throughout the United States at the end of the 1950s and early 1960s was not just that the Soviets might bury the Americans because they were the first into space with the launching of the *Sputnik*, but that the superior organization of industry facilitated by centralized planning was generating greater rates of growth in the Soviet Union. After all, the nations of Eastern Europe, and the Soviet Union in particular, had a 'luxury' inherent in their systems of centralized planning – a concentration of economic assets on a scale beyond anything imaginable in the West, where the commitment to democracy seemingly imposed a concomitant commitment to economic decentralization.

Although there may have been considerable debate about what to do about the perceived Soviet threat some three decades ago, there was little doubt at that time that the manner in which enterprises and entire industries were organized mattered. And even more striking, when one reviews the literature of the day, there seemed to be near unanimity about the way in which industrial organization mattered. It is no doubt an irony of history that a remarkably similar version of the giantism embedded in Soviet doctrine, fuelled by the writings of Marx and ultimately implemented by the iron fist of Stalin, was also prevalent throughout the West (see MARX, K.). This was the era of mass production when economies of scale seemed to be the decisive factor in dictating efficiency. This was the world so colourfully described by John Kenneth Galbraith (1956) in his theory of countervailing power, in which the power of big business was held in check by big labour and by big government (see GALBRAITH, J.K.).

It became the task of the industrial organization scholars to sort out the issues involving this perceived tradeoff between economic efficiency on the one hand and political and economic decentralization on the other. The scholars of industrial organization responded by producing a massive literature focusing on essentially three issues:

1 What are the economic gains to size and large-scale production?
2 What are the economic welfare implications of having an oligopolistic market structure, i.e. is economic performance promoted or reduced in an industry with just a handful of large-scale firms?
3 Given the overwhelming evidence from (2) that large-scale production resulting in economic concentration is associated with increased efficiency, what are the public policy implications?

A fundamental characteristic of the industrial organization literature was not only that it was obsessed with the oligopoly question but that it was essentially static in nature. There was considerable concern about what to do about the existing firms and industrial structure, but little attention was paid to where they came from and where they were going. Oliver Williamson's classic 1968 article in the *American Economic Review*, 'Economies as an antitrust defense: the welfare tradeoffs', became something of a final statement demonstrating this seemingly inevitable tradeoff between the gains in productive efficiency that could be obtained through increased concentration and

gains in terms of competition that could be achieved through decentralizing economic policies, such as antitrust. But it did not seem possible to have both, certainly not in Williamson's completely static model (see WILLIAMSON, O.E.).

One of the most striking findings emerging in this static view of industrial organization is that small firms generally operate at a level of output that is too small to sufficiently exhaust scale economies, even when the standard definition of a small firm employing fewer than 500 employees is applied. A large number of studies found that because the minimum efficient scale (MES) of output, or the lowest level of output where the minimum average cost is attained, large-scale production is typically required to exhaust scale economies in manufacturing. Any enterprise or establishment that was smaller than required by the MES was branded as being *sub-optimal* or inefficient, in that it produced, at average, costs in excess of more efficient larger firms. Weiss (in Audretsch and Yamawaki 1991: 403) assumed that 'The term "suboptimal" capacity describes a condition in which some plants are too small to be efficient'.

The importance of scale economies in the typical manufacturing industry relegated most small firms to being classified as suboptimal. For example, Weiss (1979) found that sub-optimal plants accounted for about 52.8 percent of industry value-ofshipments, Scherer (1976) found that 58.2 per cent of value-of-shipments emanated from the suboptimal plants in 12 industries, and Pratten (1971) identified the sub-optimal scale establishments accounting for 47.9 per cent of industry shipments. After reviewing the literature on the extent of sub-optimal firms, Weiss (in Audretsch and Yamawaki 1991: xiv) concluded that, 'In most industries the great majority of firms is suboptimal. In a typical industry there are, let's say, one hundred firms. Typically only about five to ten of them will be operating at the MES level of output, or anything like it.'

What are the economic welfare implications? Weiss (1979: 1137) argued that the existence of small firms which are sub-optimal represented a loss in economic efficiency and therefore advocated any public policy which 'creates social gains in the form of less sub-optimal capacity.' Empirical evidence suggested that the price umbrella provided by monopoly power encouraged the existence of sub-optimal capacity firms. Weiss (1979) went so far as to argue that the largest inefficiency associated with market power was not the higher prices charged to consumers but rather that it facilitated the existence of sub-optimal scale small firms.

Wages and productivity would be expected to reflect the degree to which small firms are less efficient than their larger counterparts. There is a large body of empirical evidence spanning a broad range of samples, time periods and even countries that has consistently found wages (and non-wage compensation as well) to be positively related to firm size. Probably the most cited study is that of Brown *et al.* (1990: 88–9), who conclude that 'Workers in large firms earn higher wages, and this fact cannot be explained completely by differences in labor quality industry, working conditions, or union status. Workers in large firms enjoy better benefits and greater security than their counterparts in small firms. When these factors are added together, it appears that workers in large firms do have a superior employment package' (see COLLECTIVE BARGAINING; EMPLOYEE RELATIONS, MANAGEMENT OF).

Seen through the static lens provided by traditional industrial organization and labour economics, the economic welfare implications of the recent shift in economic activity away from large firms and towards small enterprises is unequivocal – overall economic welfare is decreased since productivity and wages will be lower in small than in large firms. As Weiss (1979) argued in terms of efficiency and Brown *et al.* (1990) in terms of employee compensation, the implication for public policy is to implement policies to shift economic activity away from small firms and towards larger enterprises. However, the view that small firms are sub-optimal was the result of an analytical framework that is static in nature, a framework in which innovation and growth play no role (Sylos-Labini 1992). As the next section shows, incorporating the role that innovation and growth play in SMEs leads to a radically different view of SMEs

that challenges the inference that they are somehow sub-optimal.

3 The dynamic view

Coase (1937) was awarded a Nobel Prize for explaining why a firm should exist (see COASE, R.). But why should more than one firm exist in an industry? One answer is provided by the traditional economics literature focusing on industrial organization. An excess level of profitability induces entry into the industry. And this is why the entry of new firms is interesting and important – because the new firms provide an equilibrating function in the market, in that the levels of price and profit are restored to the competitive levels. The new firms are about business as usual – they simply equilibrate the market by providing more of it.

An alternative explanation for the entry of new firms was provided by Audretsch (1995), who suggests that new firms are not founded to be smaller clones of the larger incumbents but rather to serve as *agents of change* through innovative activity.

The starting point for most theories of innovation is the firm. In such theories the firms are exogenous and their performance in generating technological change is endogenous. For example, in the most prevalent model found in the literature of technological change, the model of the *knowledge production function*, formalized by Zvi Griliches (1979), firms exist exogenously and then engage in the pursuit of new economic knowledge as an input into the process of generating innovative activity.

The most decisive input in the knowledge production function is new economic knowledge. And as Cohen and Klepper (1991 and 1992) conclude, the greatest source generating new economic knowledge is generally considered to be R&D. Certainly a large body of empirical work has found a strong and positive relationship between knowledge inputs, such as R&D, on the one hand, and innovative outputs on the other hand.

The knowledge production function has been found to hold most strongly at broader levels of aggregation. The most innovative countries are those with the greatest investments in R&D. Little innovative output is associated with less developed countries, which are characterized by a paucity of production of new economic knowledge. Similarly, the most innovative industries also tend to be characterized by considerable investments in R&D and new economic knowledge. Not only are industries such as computers, pharmaceuticals and instruments high in R&D inputs that generate new economic knowledge, but also in terms of innovative outputs (Audretsch 1995). By contrast, industries with little R&D, such as wood products, textiles and paper, also tend to produce only a negligible amount of innovative output. Thus, the knowledge production model linking knowledge generating inputs to outputs certainly holds at the more aggregated levels of economic activity.

Where the relationship becomes less compelling is at the disaggregated microeconomic level of the enterprise, establishment or even line of business. For example, while Acs and Audretsch (1990) found that the simple correlation between R&D inputs and innovative output was 0.84 for four-digit standard industrial classification (SIC) manufacturing industries in the USA, it was only about half, 0.40, among the largest US corporations.

The model of the knowledge production function becomes even less compelling in view of the recent wave of studies revealing that small enterprises serve as the engine of innovative activity in certain industries. These results are startling, because as Scherer (1991) observes, the bulk of industrial R&D is undertaken in the largest corporations; small enterprises account only for a minor share of R&D inputs. Thus the knowledge production function seemingly implies that, as the *Schumpeterian Hypothesis* predicts, innovative activity favours those organizations with access to knowledge-producing inputs – the large incumbent organization. The more recent evidence identifying the strong innovative activity raises the question, 'Where do new and small firms get the innovation producing inputs, that is, the knowledge?' (see SCHUMPTER, J.)

One answer, proposed by Audretsch (1995), is that, although the model of the knowledge production function may still be

valid, the implicitly assumed unit of observation – at the level of the firm – may be less valid. The reason why the knowledge production function holds more closely for more aggregated degrees of observation may be that investment in R&D and other sources of new knowledge spills over for economic exploitation by third-party firms.

A large literature has emerged focusing on what has become known as the *appropriability problem*. The underlying issue revolves around how firms which invest in the creation of new economic knowledge can best appropriate the economic returns from that knowledge (Arrow 1962). Audretsch (1995) proposes shifting the unit of observation away from exogenously assumed firms to individuals – agents with endowments of new economic knowledge. But when the lens is shifted away from focusing upon the firm as the relevant unit of observation to individuals, the relevant question becomes 'How can economic agents with a given endowment of new knowledge best appropriate the returns from that knowledge?'

The appropriability problem confronting the individual may converge with that confronting the firm. Economic agents can and do work for firms, and even if they do not, they can potentially be employed by an incumbent firm. In fact, in a model of perfect information with no agency costs, any positive economies of scale or scope will ensure that the appropriability problems of the firm and individual converge. If an agent has an idea for doing something different than is currently being practised by the incumbent enterprises – both in terms of a new product or process and in terms of organization – the idea, which can be termed as an innovation, will be presented to the incumbent enterprise. Because of the assumption of perfect knowledge, both the firm and the agent would agree upon the expected value of the innovation. But to the degree that any economies of scale or scope exist, the expected value of implementing the innovation within the incumbent enterprise will exceed that of taking the innovation outside of the incumbent firm to start a new enterprise. Thus, the incumbent firm and the inventor of the idea would be expected to reach a bargain, splitting the value added to the firm contributed by the innovation. The payment to the inventor – either in terms of a higher wage or some other means of remuneration – would be bounded between the expected value of the innovation if it were implemented by the incumbent enterprise on the upper end, and by the return that the agent could expect to earn if he used it to launch a new enterprise on the lower end.

Penrose (1959) argued that the distinguishing characteristic of an enterprise is the knowledge embedded in the firm (see PENROSE, E.). Because, 'The productive activities of a firm are governed by what we shall call its "productive opportunity," which comprises all of the productive possibilities that its entrepreneurs see and can take advantage of. ... It is clear that this opportunity will be restricted to the extent to which a firm does not see opportunities for expansion, is unwilling to act upon them, or is unable to respond to them.'

Thus, each economic agent would choose how to best appropriate the value of his endowment of economic knowledge by comparing the wage he would earn if he remains employed by an incumbent enterprise, w, to the expected net present discounted value of the profits accruing from starting a new firm, π. If these two values are relatively close, the probability that he would choose to appropriate the value of his knowledge through an external mechanism such as starting a new firm, $\Pr(e)$, would be relatively low. On the other hand, as the gap between w and π becomes larger, the likelihood of an agent choosing to appropriate the value of his knowledge externally through starting a new enterprise becomes greater, or

$$\Pr(e) = f(\pi - w)$$

Shifting the unit of observation to the individual, and the model of entrepreneurial choice depicted in the equation does not imply that the innovation process is solely individual rather than collective. The history of industrial enterprise lends considerable support to the argument that the innovation process is collective both in terms of interactive learning and the expectations of participants in sharing in the gains from enterprise (Chandler 1990; Teece 1993; and Teece et al.1994). Rather, it

does suggest that individuals will make decisions about which contexts of their endowments of knowledge and experience are the most valuable. In most cases, this means remaining with an incumbent firm. In some cases, it will mean creating a new context, either by moving to a different firm or creating a new enterprise. However, even when an individual decides to start a new firm it is almost never in an isolated context cut off from the collective process. More typically, entrepreneurs starting new firms are 'standing on the shoulders of giants' by applying knowledge they learned in one context to a different one. In any case, new-firm startups typically belong to collective networks and groups of firms. Thus, the model of entrepreneurial choice suggests that while each individual makes a choice about how best to apply his or her endowment of knowledge and experience, that choice is crucially shaped by and dependent upon other individuals, teams and groups, other firms, and a whole range of social, political and economic institutions.

The model proposed by Audretsch (1995) refocuses the unit of observation away from firms deciding whether to increase their output from a level of zero to some positive amount in a new industry, to individual agents in possession of new knowledge that, due to uncertainty, may or may not have some positive economic value. It is the uncertainty inherent in new economic knowledge, combined with asymmetries between the agent possessing that knowledge and the decision-making vertical hierarchy of the incumbent organization with respect to its expected value that potentially leads to a gap in the valuation of that knowledge between the agent and the decision-making hierarchy.

How the economic agent chooses to appropriate the value of his or her knowledge, that is either within an incumbent firm or by starting or joining a new enterprise, will be shaped by the knowledge conditions underlying the industry. Under the routinized technological regime the agent will tend to appropriate the value of his or her new ideas within the boundaries of incumbent firms. Thus, the propensity for new firms to be started should be relatively low in industries characterized by the routinized technological regime.

By contrast, under the entrepreneurial regime the agent will tend to appropriate the value of his or her new ideas outside of the boundaries of incumbent firms by starting a new enterprise. Thus, the propensity for new firms to enter should be relatively high in industries characterized by the entrepreneurial regime.

Audretsch (1995) suggests that divergences in the expected value regarding new knowledge will, under certain conditions, lead an agent to exercise what Albert O. Hirschman (1970) has termed as *exit* rather than *voice*, and depart from an incumbent enterprise to launch a new firm. But who is right, the departing agents or those agents remaining in the organizational decision-making hierarchy who, by assigning the new idea a relatively low value, have effectively driven the agent with the potential innovation away? *Ex post* the answer may not be too difficult. But given the uncertainty inherent in new knowledge, the answer is anything but trivial *a priori*.

Thus, when a new firm is launched, its prospects are shrouded in uncertainty. If the new firm is built around a new idea, i.e. potential innovation, it is uncertain whether there is sufficient demand for the new idea or if some competitor will have the same or even a superior idea. Even if the new firm is formed to be an exact replica of a successful incumbent enterprise, it is uncertain whether sufficient demand for a new clone, or even for the existing incumbent, will prevail in the future. Tastes can change, and new ideas emerging from other firms will certainly influence those tastes.

Finally, an additional layer of uncertainty pervades a new enterprise. It is not known how competent the new firm really is, in terms of management, organization and workforce. At least incumbent enterprises know something about their underlying competencies from past experience. Which is to say that a new enterprise is burdened with uncertainty as to whether it can produce and market the intended product as well as sell it. In both cases the degree of uncertainty will typically exceed that confronting incumbent enterprises.

This initial condition of not just uncertainty, but a greater degree of uncertainty *vis*-*à-vis* incumbent enterprises in the industry is captured in the theory of firm selection and industry evolution proposed by Boyan Jovanovic (1982). Jovanovic presents a model in which the new firms, which he terms *entrepreneurs*, face costs that are not only random but also differ across firms. A central feature of the model is that a new firm does not know what its cost function is, that is its relative efficiency, but rather discovers this through the process of learning from its actual post-entry performance. In particular, Jovanovic (1982) assumes that entrepreneurs are unsure about their ability to manage a new firm start-up and therefore their prospects for success. Although entrepreneurs may launch a new firm based on a vague sense of expected post-entry performance, they only discover their true ability – in terms of managerial competence and of having based the firm on an idea that is viable on the market – once their business is established. Those entrepreneurs who discover that their ability exceeds their expectations expand the scale of their business, whereas those discovering that their post-entry performance is less than commensurate with their expectations will contact the scale of output and possibly exit from the industry. Thus, Jovanovic's model is a theory of *noisy selection*, where efficient firms grow and survive and inefficient firms decline and fail.

The role of learning in the selection process has been the subject of considerable debate. On the one hand, the argument can be made that those new firms that are the most flexible and adaptable will be the most successful in adjusting to whatever the demands of the market are. As Nelson and Winter (1982: 11) point out, 'Many kinds of organizations commit resources to learning; organizations seek to copy the forms of their most successful competitors'.

On the other hand, one can argue that the role of learning is restricted to discovering if the firm has the *right stuff* in terms of the goods it is producing as well as the way they are being produced. Under this interpretation the new enterprise is not necessarily able to adapt or adjust to market conditions, but receives information based on its market performance with respect to its *fitness* in terms of meeting demand most efficiently *vis-à-vis* rivals. The theory of organizational ecology proposed by Michael T. Hannan and John Freeman (1989) most pointedly adheres to the notion that, 'We assume that individual organizations are characterized by relative inertia in structure'. That is, firms learn not in the sense that they adjust their actions as reflected by their fundamental identity and purpose, but in the sense of their perception. What is then learned is whether or not the firm has the right stuff, but not how to change that stuff.

The theory of firm selection is particularly appealing in view of the rather startling size of most new firms. For example, the mean size of more than 11,000 new-firm start-ups in the manufacturing sector in the USA was found to be fewer than eight workers per firm (Audretsch, 1995). While the MES varies substantially across industries, and even to some degree across various product classes within any given industry, the observed size of most new firms is sufficiently small to ensure that the bulk of new firms will be operating at a sub-optimal scale of output. Why would an entrepreneur start a new firm that would immediately be confronted by scale disadvantages?

An implication of the theory of firm selection is that new firms may begin at a small, even sub-optimal, scale of output, and then if merited by subsequent performance expand. Those new firms that are successful will grow, whereas those that are not successful will remain small and may ultimately be forced to exit from the industry if they are operating at a sub-optimal scale of output.

Subsequent to entering an industry, an entrepreneur must decide whether to maintain expand, or contract its output, or exit. Two different strands of literature have identified several major influences shaping the decision to exit an industry. The first, and most obvious strand of literature suggests that the probability of a business exiting will tend to increase as the gap between its level of output and the MES level of output increases. The second strand of literature points to the role that the technological environment plays in shaping the decision to exit. As Dosi (1988) and Arrow (1962) argue, an environment characterized by more frequent innovation may also be associated with a greater amount of uncertainty regarding not only the technical nature of the product but also the demand for that product. As technological uncertainty increases, particularly under the entrepreneurial regime, the likelihood that the business will be able to produce a viable product and ultimately be able to survive decreases.

An important implication of the dynamic process of firm selection and industry evolution is that new firms are more likely to be operating at a sub-optimal scale of output if the underlying technological conditions are such that there is a greater chance of making an innovation, that is under the entrepreneurial regime. If new firms successfully learn and adapt, or are just plain lucky, they grow into viably sized enterprises. If not, they stagnate and may ultimately exit from the industry. This dynamic perspective suggests, that entry and the start-up of new firms may not be greatly deterred in the presence of scale economies. As long as entrepreneurs perceive that there is some prospect for growth and ultimately survival, such entry will occur. Thus, in industries where the MES is high, it follows from the observed general small size of new-firm start-ups that the growth rate of the surviving firms would presumably be relatively high.

At the same time, those new firms not able to grow and attain the MES level of output would presumably be forced to exit from the industry, resulting in a relatively low likelihood of survival. In industries characterized by a low MES, neither the need for growth, nor the consequences of its absence are as severe, so that relatively lower growth rates but higher survival rates would be expected. Similarly, in industries where the probability of innovating is greater, more entrepreneurs may actually take a chance that they will succeed by growing into a viably sized enterprise. In such industries, one would expect that the growth of successful enterprises would be greater, but that the likelihood of survival would be correspondingly lower.

4 The empirical evidence

Not only was the large corporation thought to have superior productive efficiency, but conventional wisdom also held the large corporation to serve as the engine of technological change and innovative activity. After all, Schumpeter (1942: 106) concluded that: 'What we have got to accept is that the large-scale establishment has come to be the most powerful engine of progress'. A few years later, John Kenneth Galbraith (1956: 86) echoed Schumpeter's sentiment when he lamented: 'There is no more pleasant fiction than that technological change is the product of the matchless ingenuity of the small man forced by competition to employ his wits to better his neighbor. Unhappily, it is a fiction'.

Knowledge regarding both the determinants and the impact of technological change has been largely shaped by measurement. Measures of technological change have typically involved one of the three major aspects of the innovative process: (1) a measure of inputs into the process, such as R&D expenditures, or the share of the labour force accounted for by employees involved in R&D activities; (2) an intermediate output, such as the number of inventions that have been patented; or (3) a direct measure of innovative output.

The earliest sources of data, R&D measured, indicated that virtually all of the innovative activity was undertaken by large corporations. As patent measures became available, the general qualitative conclusions did not change, although it became clear that small firms were more involved with patent activity than with R&D. The development of direct measures of innovative activity, such as databases measuring new product and process introductions in the market, indicated something quite different. In a series of studies, Acs and Audretsch (1988, 1990) found that while large firms in manufacturing introduced a slightly greater number of significant new innovations than small firms, small-firm employment was only about half as great as large-firm employment, yielding an average small-firm innovation rate in manufacturing of 0.309, compared to a large-firm innovation rate of 0.202. The relative innovative advantage of small and large firms was found to vary considerably across industries. In some industries, such as computers and process control instruments, small firms provide the engine of innovative activity. In other industries, such

as pharmaceutical products and aircraft, large firms generate most of the innovative activity. Knowledge regarding both the determinants and the impact of technological change has largely been shaped by measurement.

Acs and Audretsch (1988, 1990) concluded that some industries are more conducive to small-firm innovation while others foster the innovative activity of large corporations, corresponding to the notion of distinct technological regimes – the routinized and entrepreneurial technological regimes.

Empirical evidence in support of the traditional model of entry, which focuses on the role of excess profits as the major incentive to enter, has been ambiguous at best, leading Geroski (1991: 282) to conclude, 'Right from the start, scholars have had some trouble in reconciling the stories told about entry in standard textbooks with the substance of what they have found in their data. Very few have emerged from their work feeling that they have answered half as many questions as they have raised, much less that they have answered most of the interesting ones'.

Perhaps one reason for this trouble is the inherently static model used to capture an inherently dynamic process. Manfred Neumann (1993) has criticized this traditional model of entry, as found in the individual country studies contained in Geroski and Schwalbach (1991), because they

are predicated on the adoption of a basically static framework. It is assumed that startups enter a given market where they are facing incumbents which naturally try to fend off entry. Since the impact of entry on the performance of incumbents seems to be only slight, the question arises whether the costs of entry are worthwhile, given the high rate of exit associated with entry. Geroski appears to be rather skeptical about that. I submit that adopting a static framework is misleading. ... In fact, generally, an entrant can only hope to succeed if he employs either a new technology or offers a new product, or both. Just imitating incumbents is almost certainly doomed to failure. If the process of entry is looked upon from this perspective the high correlation between gross entry and exit reflects the inherent risks of innovating activities. ... Obviously it is rather difficult to break loose from the inherited mode of reasoning within the static framework. It is not without merit, to be sure, but it needs to be enlarged by putting it into a dynamic setting.

(Manfred Neumann 1993: 593–4)

Still, one of the most startling results that has emerged in empirical studies is that entry by firms into an industry is apparently not substantially deterred or even deterred at all in capital-intensive industries in which scale economies play an important role (Audretsch 1995). While studies have generally produced considerable ambiguity concerning the impact of scale economies and other measures traditionally thought to represent a *barrier to entry*, Audretsch (1995) found conclusive evidence linking the technological regime to start-up activity. New firm start-up activity tends to be substantially more prevalent under the entrepreneurial regime, or where small enterprises account for the bulk of the innovative activity, than under the routinized regime, or where the large incumbent enterprises account for most of the innovative activity. These findings are consistent with the view that differences in beliefs about the expected value of new ideas are not constant across industries but rather depend on the knowledge conditions inherent in the underlying technological regime. They also correspond to the conditions described by Christensen (2000) where large incumbent corporations experience an innovative disadvantage in some, but not all, industries, depending upon the underlying knowledge conditions.

Geroski (1995) and Audretsch (1995) point out that one of the major conclusions from studies about entry is that the process of entry does not end with entry itself. Rather, it is what happens to new firms subsequent to entering that sheds considerable light on industry dynamics. The early studies (Mansfield 1962; Hall 1987; Dunne *et al.* 1989; and Audretsch 1991) established not only that the likelihood of a new entrant surviving is quite low, but that the likelihood of survival is positively related to firm size and age. More recently, a wave of studies have confirmed these findings for diverse coun-

tries, including Portugal (Mata *et al.* 1995; Mata 1994), Germany (Wagner 1994) and Canada (Baldwin and Gorecki 1991; Baldwin 1995; Baldwin and Rafiquzzaman 1995).

Audretsch (1991) and Audretsch and Mahmood (1995) shifted the relevant question away from 'Why does the likelihood of survival vary systematically across firms?' to 'Why does the propensity for firms to survive vary systematically across industries?' The answer to this question suggests that what had previously been considered to pose a barrier to entry may, in fact, constitute not an entry barrier but rather a barrier to survival.

What has become known as *Gibrat's Law*, or the assumption that growth rates are invariant to firm size, has been subject to numerous empirical tests. Studies linking firm size and age to growth have also produced a number of stylized facts (Wagner 1992). For small and new firms there is substantial evidence suggesting that growth is negatively related to firm size and age (Hall 1987; Wagner 1992, 1994; Mata 1994; Audretsch 1995). However, for larger firms, particularly those having attained the minimum efficient scale (MES) level of output, the evidence suggests that firm growth is unrelated to size and age.

An important finding of Audretsch (1991, 1995) and Audretsch and Mahmood (1995) is that although entry may still occur in industries characterized by a high degree of scale economies, the likelihood of survival is considerably less. People will start new firms in an attempt to appropriate the expected value of their new ideas, or potential innovations, particularly under the entrepreneurial regime. As entrepreneurs gain experience in the market they learn in at least two ways. First, they discover whether they possess the *right stuff*, in terms of producing goods and offering services for which sufficient demand exists, as well as whether they can produce that good more efficiently than their rivals. Second, they learn whether they can adapt to market conditions as well as to strategies engaged in by rival firms. In terms of the first type of learning, entrepreneurs who discover that they have a viable firm will tend to expand and ultimately survive. But what about those entrepreneurs who discover that they are either not efficient or not offering a product for which their is a viable demand? The answer is that it depends – on the extent of scale economies as well as on conditions of demand. The consequences of not being able to grow will depend, to a large degree, on the extent of scale economies. Thus, in markets with only negligible scale economies, firms have a considerably greater likelihood of survival. However, where scale economies play an important role the consequences of not growing are substantially more severe, as evidenced by a lower likelihood of survival.

What emerges from the new evolutionary theories and empirical evidence on the economic role of new and small firms is that markets are in motion, with a lot of new firms entering the industry and a lot of firms exiting out of the industry. But is this motion horizontal, in that the bulk of firms exiting are comprised of firms that had entered relatively recently, or vertical, in that a significant share of the exiting firms had been established incumbents that were displaced by younger firms? In trying to shed some light on this question, Audretsch (1995) proposes two different models of the evolutionary process of industries over time. Some industries can be best characterized by the model of the revolving door, where new businesses enter, but where there is a high propensity to subsequently exit from the market. Other industries may be better characterized by the metaphor of the forest, where incumbent establishments are displaced by new entrants. Which view is more applicable apparently depends on three major factors – the underlying technological conditions, scale economies, and demand. Where scale economies play an important role, the model of the revolving door seems to be more applicable. While the rather startling result discussed above that the start-up and entry of new businesses is apparently not deterred by the presence of high scale economies, a process of firm selection analogous to a revolving door ensures that only those establishments successful enough to grow will be able to survive beyond more than a few years. Thus the bulk of new entrants that are not so successful ultimately exit within a few years subsequent to entry.

There is at least some evidence also suggesting that the underlying technological regime influences the process of firm selection and therefore the type of firm with a higher propensity to exit (Malerba and Orsenigo 1993; Dosi *et al.* 1995). Under the entrepreneurial regime new entrants have a greater likelihood of making an innovation. Thus, they are less likely to decide to exit from the industry, even in the face of negative profits. By contrast, under the routinized regime the incumbent businesses tend to have the innovative advantage, so that a higher portion of exiting businesses tend to be new entrants. Thus, the model of the revolving door is more applicable under technological conditions consistent with the routinized regime, and the metaphor of the forest, where the new entrants displace the incumbents, is more applicable to the entrepreneurial regime.

The general shape of the firm-size distribution is not only strikingly similar across virtually every industry – that is, skewed with only a few large enterprises and numerous small ones – but has persisted with tenacity across developed countries over a long period of time. The evolutionary view of the process of industry evolution is that new firms typically start at a very small scale of output. They are motivated by the desire to appropriate the expected value of new economic knowledge. But, depending upon the extent of scale economies in the industry, the firm may not be able to remain viable indefinitely at its start-up size. Rather, if scale economies are anything other than negligible, the new firm is likely to have to grow to survive. The temporary survival of new firms is presumably supported through the deployment of a strategy of compensating factor differentials that enables the firm to discover whether or not it has a viable product.

The empirical evidence supports such an evolutionary view of the role of new firms in manufacturing, because the post-entry growth of firms that survive tends to be spurred by the extent to which there is a gap between the MES level of output and the size of the firm. However, the likelihood of any particular new firm surviving tends to decrease as this gap increases. Such new sub-optimal scale firms are apparently engaged in the selection process. Only those firms offering a viable product that can be produced efficiently will grow and ultimately approach or attain the MES level of output. The remainder will stagnate, and depending upon the severity of the other selection mechanism – the extent of scale economies – may ultimately be forced to exit out of the industry. Thus, the persistence of an asymmetric firm-size distribution biased towards small-scale enterprise reflects the continuing process of the entry of new firms into industries and not necessarily the permanence of such small and sub-optimal enterprises over the long run. Although the skewed size distribution of firms persists with remarkable stability over long periods of time, a constant set of small and sub-optimal scale firms does not appear to be responsible for this skewed distribution. Rather, by serving as agents of change, new firms provide an essential source of new ideas and experimentation that otherwise would remain untapped in the economy.

5 The public policy response

The policy response to this new view of the knowledge production function has been to shift away from targeting outputs to inputs. In particular, this involves the creation and commercialization of knowledge. Examples include the promotion of joint R&D programmes, education and training programmes, and policies to encourage people to start new firms. As Saxenian (1985: 102) points out, 'Attracting high-tech has become the only development game of the 1980s.' Justman (1995) and Justman and Teubal (1986) show how investment in infrastructure provide an important source of growth.

The provision of venture and informal capital to facilitate the creation and growth of new firms has replaced concern about the market power of existing ones in policy debates (Hughes 1997; Mason and Harrison 1997). The lack of finance capital for new ventures has been blamed for the inability of Germany and France to shift economic activity into new industries that generate high-wage employment. One of the most repeated phrases on the pages of the business news over the last few years has been 'Put Bill Gates in Europe and it just wouldn't have worked out' (see *Newsweek* 1994).

Policy efforts to address the most pressing contemporary economic problems have fo-
cused on enablement rather than constraint. Emphasis on enabling firms and individuals to create and commercialize new knowledge is not restricted to any single country or set of countries. Laura Tyson (Tyson *et al.* 1994), former chair of the Council of Economic Advisers in the Clinton Administration, recently emphasized the importance of government policies to promote entrepreneurship and new firm start-ups in the former Soviet Union. Similarly, as unemployment in Germany surpassed four million, and stood at nearly 11 per cent of the labour force, it is not surprising that Chancellor Helmut Kohl should undertake action to spur the creation of new jobs. What is more surprising is the main emphasis announced by the Chancellor in the *Initiatives for Investment and Employment* in 1996 on new and small firms (this was announced as the Aktionsprogramm für Investitionen und Arbeitsplätze ('Soziale Einschnitte und Steuerreform sollen Wirtschaftswachstum anregen: Bundesregierung beschliesst Aktionsprogramm für Investitionen und Arbeitsplätze') *Der Tagesspiegel* 31 January: 1). The first and main point of the Chancellor's Programme consists of a commitment to the 'creation of new innovative firms'. (The original text of the *Aktionsprogramm* states, 'Offensive für unternehmerische Selbständigkeit und Innovationsfähigkeit' ('Ein Kraftakt zu Rettung des Standorts Deutschland') *Frankfurter Allgemeine* 31 January 1996: 11). The rationale underlying this policy approach by the Chancellor is stated in the Program: 'New jobs are created mainly in new firms and in small- and medium-sized enterprises' (the original text reads: 'Neue Arbeitsplätze entstehen zumeist in neugegründeten Unternehmen und im Mittelstand', see 'Ein Kraftakt zu Rettung des Standorts Deutschland', *Frankfurter Allgemeine* 31 January 1996: 11).

Audretsch and Feldman (1996) argue that industrial policies targeting the production and commercialization of new economic knowledge will have a greater impact on particular regions and not diffuse rapidly across geographic space. They point out that knowledge spillovers are a key source of new knowledge generating innovative activity, but due to the tacit nature of that knowledge, knowledge flows tend to be geographically bounded. Although the cost of transmitting information has become invariant to distance, the cost of transmitting knowledge, and especially tacit knowledge, rises with distance. By creating regions of knowledge-based economic activities, government policies can generate highly concentrated innovative clusters.

As long as the major policy issue was restricting large, oligopolistic firms in command of considerable market power, a federal or national locus of control was appropriate. This is because the benefits and costs derived from that market power are asymmetric between the local region where the firm is located and the national market, where the firm sells its product. Not only was production concentrated in one or just several regions, but the workers along with the ancillary suppliers also tended to be located in the same regions. These workers as well as the community at large share the fruits accruing from monopoly power. Systematic empirical evidence (Weiss 1966) shows that wages are positively related to the degree of market power held by a firm, even after controlling for the degree of unionization. Higher profits resulting from market power are shared by labour. Workers and firms in the region have the same interest.

As Olson (1982) shows, relatively small coalitions of economic agents benefiting from some collective action tend to prevail over a large group of dispersed economic agents each incurring a small cost from that action. The costs of organizing and influencing policy are relatively low for the small coalition enjoying the benefits but large for the group of dispersed economic agents. Government policies to control large oligopolistic firms with substantial market power are not likely to be successful if implemented on the local level. Rather, as Olson (1982) predicts, a regional locus of policy towards business tends to result in the capture of policy by the coalition of local interests benefiting from that policy. Only by shifting the locus of policy away from the region to the national level can the capture of policy by special interest groups be minimized. The negative effects of market power in the form of higher prices are spread throughout the national market while the benefits accruing from that power are locally concentrated. Lazonick (1991) argues that historically encompassing organizations are often more important and enduring than Olson considered, and distributional coalitions appear in context where the key players do not have sufficient collective organization. Ferleger and Lazonick (1993) provide the compelling example of the role of the state in developing US agriculture.

Starting in the Carter administration in the late 1970s and continuing into the administrations of presidents Reagan, Bush and Clinton, antitrust has been de-emphasized and a twenty-year wave of deregulation has led to a downsizing and even closure of a number of the former regulatory agencies.

Many economists interpret the downsizing of the federal agencies charged with the regulation of business as the eclipse of government intervention. But to interpret the retreat of the federal government as the end of public intervention is to confuse the downsizing of government with a shifting of the locus of government policy away from the federal to the local level. The last decade has seen the emergence of a set of enabling policy initiatives at the local level. This new type of industrial policy is decentralized and regional in nature. As Sternberg (1996) emphasizes in his review of successful technology policies in the four leading technological countries, the most important industrial policies in the last decades have been local, not national. They have occurred in locations such as Research Triangle (Link 1995), Austin, Texas and Cambridge (UK). Sternberg (1996) shows how the success of a number of different high-technology clusters spanning the four most technologically advanced countries is the direct result of enabling policies undertaken at the regional level.

Eisinger (1990) asks the question, 'Do the American States do industrial policy?' in a 1990 article published in the *British Journal of Political Science*. Lowery and Gray (1990) confirm Eisinger's affirmative answer by analysing the impact of state industrial policy in the USA. They develop a new data set on gross state product and a new measure of state industrial policy activism. Their results suggest that the implementation of industrial policy at the state level tends to promote growth.

For example, Feller (1997: 289) points out that 'in theory and implementation, state technology development programs – as in Texas, Ohio, New York, New Jersey, and Pennsylvania – may be viewed as bands on a wide spectrum from basic research to product development, with the ends reflecting quite divergent state strategies'. The Advanced Research Program in Texas has provided support for basic research and the strengthening of the university infrastructure, which played a central role in recruiting MCC and Sematech and developing a high-tech cluster around Austin. The Thomas Edison Centers in Ohio, the Advanced Technology Centers in New Jersey and the Centers for Advanced Technology at Case Western Reserve University, Rutgers University and the University of Rochester have supported generic, precompetitive research. This support has generally provided diversified technology development involving a mix of activities encompassing generic research, applied research and manufacturing modernization through a broad spectrum of industrial collaborators spanning technology-intensive multinational corporations, regional manufactures and new firm start-ups.

This shift in the locus of policy is the result of two factors. First, because the source of comparative advantage is knowledge, which tends to be localized in regional clusters, public policy requires an understanding of region-specific characteristics and idiosyncrasies. As Sternberg (1996) concludes, regional strengths provide the major source of innovative clusters. The second factor is that the motivation underlying government policy is now growth and the creation of (high-paying) jobs, largely through the creation of new firms. These new firms are typically small and pose no oligopolistic threat in national or international markets. There are no external costs imposed on consumers in the national economy in the form of higher prices as in the case of a large oligopolistic corporation in possession of market power. There is no reason that the promotion of local economies imposes a cost on consumers in the national economy, so that localized industrial policy is justified and does not result in any particular loss incurred by agents outside of the region.

6 Conclusions

While traditional theories suggest that entrepreneurship will retard economic growth, new theories suggest exactly the opposite – that entrepreneurship will stimulate and generate growth. The reason for these theoretical discrepancies lies in the context of the underlying theory. In the traditional theory, new knowledge plays no role; rather, static efficiency, determined largely by the ability to exhaust scale economies, dictates growth. By contrast, the new theories are dynamic in nature and emphasize the role that knowledge plays. Because knowledge is inherently uncertain, asymmetric and associated with high costs of transactions, divergences emerge concerning the expected value of new ideas. Economic agents therefore have an incentive to leave an incumbent firm and start a new firm in an attempt to commercialize the perceived value of their knowledge. Entrepreneurship is the vehicle by which (the most radical) new ideas are sometimes implemented.

While this policy emphasis on small and new firms as engines of dynamic efficiency may seem startling after decades of looking at the corporate giants to bestow efficiency, it is anything but new. Before the United States was even half a century old, Alexis de Tocqueville, in 1835, reported, 'What astonishes me in the United States is not so much the marvellous grandeur of some undertakings as the innumerable multitude of small ones'.

DAVID AUDRETSCH
INDIANA UNIVERSITY

Further reading

(References cited in the text marked *)

* Acs, Zoltan J. and David B. Audretsch (1988) 'Innovation in large and small firms: an empirical analysis', *American Economic Review* 78 (4): 678–90. (Documents the innovative strengths and weaknesses of small firms.)
* Acs, Zoltan J. and David B. Audretsch (1990) *Innovation and Small Firms*, Cambridge: MIT Press. (Analyses the determinants of small-firm innovative activity.)
* Arrow, Kenneth J. (1962) 'Economic welfare and the allocation of resources for invention', in R.R. Nelson (ed.) *The Rate and Direction of In-*

ventive Activity, Princeton: Princeton University Press. (Develops a theoretical framework for knowledge-based economic activity.)

* Audretsch, David B. (1991) 'New firm survival and the technological regime', *Review of Economics and Statistics* 73 (3): 441–50. (Shows how the likelihood of small-firm survival is lower in innovative industries than in non-innovative industries.)

* Audretsch, David B. (1995) *Innovation and Industry Evolution*, Cambridge: MIT Press. (Develops theory and empirical analyses of the impact of entrepreneurship on industry evolution.)

* Audretsch, David B. and Talat Mahmood (1995) 'New-firm survival: new results using a hazard function', *Review of Economics and Statistics* 77 (1): 97–103. (Shows how the survival of start-ups are shaped by the industry environment.)

* Audretsch, David B. and Maryann P. Feldman (1996) 'R&D spillovers and the geography of innovation and production', *American Economic Review* 86 (3): 630–40. (Links geographic clustering of innovation and production to the importance of knolwedge.)

Audretsch, David B. and Paula E. Stephan (1996) 'Company-scientist locational links: the case of biotechnology', *American Economic Review* 86 (3): 641–52. (Shows how the geographic links between scientists and biotechnology companies are shaped by the role the scientist plays in bringing knowledge to the firm.)

Audretsch, David B. and Roy Thruik (1999) *Innovation, Industry Evolution, and Employment*, Cambridge: Cambridge University Press. (Links job creation and wage performance to industry evolution and entrepreneurial activity.)

* Baldwin, John R. (1995) *The Dynamics of Industrial Competition*, Cambridge: Cambridge University Press. (Analysis of industry dynamics, such as entry, growth and turbulence.)

* Baldwin, John R. and M. Rafiquzzaman (1995) 'Selection versus evolutionary adaptation: learning and post-entry performance', *International Journal of Industrial Organization* 13 (4): 501–23. (Tests whether selection or adaptation drives industry evolution.)

* Baldwin, John R. and Paul K. Gorecki (1991) 'Entry, exit, and production growth', in P. Geroski and J. Schwalbach, (eds) *Entry and Market Contestability: An International Comparison*, Oxford: Basil Blackwell. (Provides links between entry, exit and firm growth.)

Best, Michael (1990) *The New Competition: Institutions of Industrial Restructuring*, Cambridge: Harvard University Press. (Shows how globalization is triggering industrial restructuring.)

* Brown, Charles, James Hamilton and James Medoff (1990) *Employers Large and Small*, Cambridge: Cambridge University Press. (Documents that wages are systematically and positively related to firm size.)

Carrol, Paul (1993) *Big Blues: The Unmaking of IBM*, New York: Crown Publishers. (Documents the difficulties IBM had in innovating in the 1980s.)

Caves, Richard E. (1998) 'Industrial organization and new findings on the turnover and mobility of firms', *Journal of Economic Literature* 36 (4): 1947–82. (Literature synthesis and review of firm and industry dynamics.)

Chandler, Alfred D. (1977) *The Visible Hand: The Managerial Revolution in American Business*, Cambridge: Harvard University Press. (Documents the emergence of the modern corporation.)

* Chandler, Alfred D. (1990) *Scale and Scope: The Dynamics of Industrial Capitalism*, Cambridge: Harvard University Press. (Documents the role of scale and scope in shaping the modern corporation.)

* Christensen, Clatton M. (2000) *The Inventor's Dilemma: When New Technologies Cause Great Firms to Fail*, New York: HarperCollins. (Documents the difficulties large corporations have in inventing.)

* Coase, R.H. (1937) 'The nature of the firm', *Economica* 4 (4): 386–405. (Basis for transactions cost economics.)

* Cohen, W.M. and Klepper, S. (1991) 'The tradeoff between firm size and diversity for technological progress', *Journal of Small Business Economics*, December.

* Cohen, W.M. and Klepper, S. (1992) 'The anatomy of R&D intensity distributions', *American Economic Review* 82(4): 773–9. (This, and the above article consider the economics of technological change.)

Cringley, Robert X. (1993) *Accidental Empires*, New York: Harper Business. (Provides anecdotal description of Silicon Valley.)

* Davis, S.J., Haltiwanger, J.C. and Schuh, S. (1996) *Job Creation and Destruction*, Cambridge, MA: MIT Press. (Research on employment flows in US manufacturing.)

* Dertouzos, M.L., Lester, R.K. and Solow, R.M. (1989) *Made in America: Regaining the Productive Edge*, Cambridge, MA: MIT Press. (Seen as the 'definitive' account of how America works.)

Dosi, Giovanni (1982) 'Technological paradigms and technological trajectories: a suggested interpretation of the determinants and directions of technical change', *Research Policy* 13 (1): 3–

20. (Introduces the concept of technological trajectories.)

* Dosi, Giovanni (1988) 'Sources, procedures, and microeconomic effects of innovation', *Journal of Economic Literature* 26 (3): 1120–71. (Literature review of microfoundations of innovation.)

* Dosi, Govianni, Oriettta Marsili, Luigi Orsenigo and Roberta Salvatore (1995) 'Learning, market selection and the evolution of industrial structures', *Small Business Economics* 7 (6): 411–36. (Simulation models linking small business to industry evolution.)

* Dunne, T., M.J. Roberts and L. Samuelson (1989) 'The growth and failure of U.S. manufacturing plants', *Quarterly Journal of Economics* 104: 671–98. (Empirical documentation of entry, growth and failure.)

* Eisinger, Peter (1990) 'Do the American States do industrial policy?' *British Journal of Political Science* 20: 509–35. (Examines state policy to promote small business and economic development.)

* Feller, Irwin (1997) 'Federal and State Government roles in science and technology,' *Economic Development Quarterly* 11 (4): 283–96. (Shows how states play a crucial role in science and technology policy.)

* Ferleger, Louis and William Lazonick (1993) 'The managerial revolution and the developmental state: the case of US agriculture', *Business and Economic History* 22 (2): 67–98. (Shows how the government engaged in policies to develop US agriculture.)

* Galbraith, John Kenneth (1956) *American Capitalism*, Boston: Houghton Mifflin. (Describes major US economic and social institutions and their functioning.)

* Geroski, Paul A. (1991) 'Some data-driven reflections on the entry process', in Paul Georski and Joachin Schwalbach (eds) *Entry and Market Contestability: An International Comparison*, Oxford: Basil Blackwell. (Reviews and interprets entry literature.)

* Geroski, Paul A. (1995) 'What do we know about entry', *International Journal of Industrial Organization* (Special Issue on *The Post Entry Performance of Firms*, D.B. Audretsch and J. Mata, eds) 13 (4). (Reviews and interprets literature on the post-entry performance of firms.)

* Geroski, Paul A. and Joachim Schwalbach (eds) (1991) *Entry and Market Contestability: An International Comparison* Oxford: Basil Blackwell. (Contains a collection of empirical studies identifying determinants of entry in different countries.)

* Griliches, Zvi (1979) 'Issues in assessing the contribution of R&D to productivity growth', *Bell Journal of Economics* 10 (Spring): 92–116. (Introduces the knowledge production function model.)

* Hall, Bronwyn H. (1987) 'The relationship between firm size and firm growth in the US manufacturing sector', *Journal of Industrial Economics* 35 (June): 583–605. (Links firm growth to firm size and age.)

* Hannan, Michael T. and John Freeman (1989) *Organizational Ecology*, Cambridge, MA: Harvard University Press. (Treats firm demography as an ecological phenomenon.)

* Hirschman, Albert O. (1970) *Exit, Voice, and Loyalty*, Cambridge: Harvard University Press. (Provides the theoretical framework for decisions to remain in a situation or change.)

Holtz-Eakin, Harvey S. Rosen, and Robert Weathers (2000) 'Horatio Alger meets the mobility tables', *Small Business Economics* 14 (4): 243–74. (Links entrepreneurship to income mobility.)

* Hughes, Alan (1997) 'Finance for SMEs: A U.K. perspective', *Small Business Economics* 9 (2): 151–66. (Documents financing sources of SMEs in the United Kingdom.)

Ijiri, Yuji and Herbert A. Simon (1977) *Skew Distributions and Sizes of Business Firms*, Amsterdam: North Holland. (Documents that the firm-size distribution is skewed and consists mostly of SMEs.)

* Jovanovic, Boyan (1982) 'Selection and evolution of industry,' *Econometrica* 50 (2): 649–70. (Introduces a theory of selection based on entrepreneurial learning.)

* Justman, M. and M. Teubal (1986) 'Innovation policy in an open economy: a normative framework to strategic and tactical issues', *Research Policy* 15: 121–38. (Analyses innovation policies.)

* Justman, M., (1995) 'Infrastructure, growth and the two dimensions of industrial policy', *Review of Economic Studies* 62 (1): 131–57. (Links industrial policy to growth.)

Knight, Frank H. (1921) *Risk, Uncertainty and Profit*, New York: Houghton Mifflin. (Analyses role of uncertainty in decision making.)

* Lazonick, William (1991) *Business Organization and the Myth of the Market Economy*, Cambridge: Cambridge University Press. (Shows how business organization preempts the market economy.)

* Link, Al (1995) *A Generosity of Spirit*, Durham, NC: Duke University Press. (Documents the formation of Research Triangle.)

* Lowery, D. And Gray, V. (1990) 'The corporatist foundation of state industrial policy', *Social Science Quarterly* 71 (March): 3–24. (Analyses

the impact of state industrial poilicy in the USA.)

* Malerba, F. and L. Orsenigo (1993) 'Technological regimes and firm behaviour', *Industrial and Corporate Change* 2 (1): 74–89. (Links technological regimes to firm behaviour.)

* Mansfield, Edwin (1962) 'Entry, Gibrat's Law, innovation, and the growth of firms', *American Economic Review* 52 (5): 1023–51. (Analyses the entry and growth of firms.)

* Mata, Jose (1994) 'Firm growth during infancy', *Small Business Economics* 6 (1): 27–40. (Analyses the growth patterns of start-ups.)

Mata, Jose and Pedro Portugal (1994) 'Life duration of new firms', *Journal of Industrial Economics* 27 (3): 227–46. (Analyses survival patterns of start-ups.)

* Mata, Jose, Pedro Portugal and Paulo Guimaraes (1995) 'The survival of new plants: start-up conditions and post-entry evolution', *International Journal of Industrial Organization* 13 (4): 459–82. (Analyses the post-entry performance of start-ups in Portugal.)

Moore, John H. (1992) 'Measuring Soviet economic growth: old problems and new complications', *Journal of Institutional and Theoretical Economics* 148 (1): 72–92.

* Nelson, Richard R. and Sidney G. Winter (1982) *An Evolutionary Theory of Economic Change*, Cambridge: Harvard University Press. (Revisits the Soviet growth controversy.)

* Neumann, Manfred (1993) 'Review of entry and market contestability: an international comparison', *International Journal of Industrial Organization* 11 (4): 5934. (Reviews a book on entry and provides critical comments on the static framework.)

* *Newsweek* (1994) 'Where's the venture capital?' 31 October: 44. (A similar sentiment was expressed by Joschka Fischer, parliamentary leader of the Green Party in Germany, who lamented: 'A company like Microsoft would never have a chance in Germany' ('Those German banks and their industrial treasures', *The Economist*, 21 January 1994: 778).)

O'Sullivan (2000) *Contests for Corporate Control: Corporate Governance and Economic Performance in the United States and Germany*, Oxford: Oxford University Press. (Links corporate governance to firm performance in Germany and the USA.)

Palfreman, Jon and Doron Swade (1991) *The Dream Machine: Exploring the Computer Age*, London: BBC Books. (Documents the development of the computer industry.)

* Penrose, Edith T. (1959) *The Theory of the Growth of the Firm*, Oxford: Basil Blackwell. (Provides a framework for analysing firm growth.)

* Pratten, C.F. (1971) *Economies of Scale in Manufacturing Industry*, Cambridge: Cambridge University Press. (Provides estimates of the importance of scale economies.)

* Restow, W.W. (1987) 'Here comes a new political chapter in America', *International Herald Tribune*, 2 January.

Saxenian, Annalee, (1990) 'Regional networks and the resurgence of Silicon Valley', *California Management Review* 33 (1): 89–111. (Documents the role of networks in Silicon Valley.)

Scherer, F.M. (1976) 'Industrial structure, scale economies, and worker alienation', in Robert T. Masson and P. David Qualls (eds) *Essays on Industrial Organization in Honor of Joe S. Bain*, Cambridge: Ballinger, pp. 105–22. (Links worker alienation to large corporations.)

* Scherer, F.M. (1991) 'Changing perspectives on the firm size problem', in Z.J. Acs and D.B. Audretsch (eds), *Innovation and Technological Change. An International Comparison*, Ann Arbor: University of Michigan Press. (Describes how the conventional wisdom about small firms has evolved over time.)

Schumpeter, Joseph A. (1911) *Theorie der wirtschaftlichen Entwicklung. Eine Untersuchung über Unternehmergewinn, Kapital, Kredit, Zins und den Konjunkturzyklus*, Berlin: Duncker und Humblot. (Provides theory of creative destruction.)

* Schumpeter, Joseph A. (1942) *Capitalism, Socialism and Democracy*, New York: Harper and Row. (Suggests large corporations are more innovative than small firms.)

Simon, Herbert A. and Charles P. Bonini (1958) 'The size distribution of business firms', *American Economic Review* 48 (4): 607–17. (Documents a skewed size distribution.)

* Sternberg, Rolf (1996) 'Technology policies and the growth of regions', *Small Business Economics* 8 (2): 75–86. (Analyses technology policies in a number of countries and links them to regional growth.)

Sutton, John (1997) 'Gibrat's Legacy', *Journal of Economic Literature* 35 (1): 40–59. (Reviews literature testing Gibrat's Law, which posits that firm growth is invariant to firm size.)

* Sylos-Labini, Paolo (1992) 'Capitalism, socialism, and democracy and large-scale firms', in F.M. Scherer and Mark Perlman (eds) *Entrepreneurship, Technological Innovation, and Economic Growth*, Ann Arbor: University of Michigan, 55–64. (Notes that firms are getting larger over time and small business is disappearing.)

* Teece, David J. (1993) 'The dynamics of industrial capitalism: perspectives on Alfred Chandler's scale and scope', *Journal of Economic Literature* 31: 199–225. (Provides an interpretation of Chandler's work.)

* Teece, David, Richard Rumult, Giovanni Dosi and Sidney Winter (1994) 'Understanding corporate coherence: theory and evidence', *Journal of Economic Behavior and Organization* 23 (1): 1–30. (Explains why large corporations may have difficulties innovating.)

* Thurow, Lester (1984) 'Losing the economic race', *New York Review of Books* September: 29–31.

* Tyson, Laura d'Andrea, Tea Petrin and Halsey Rogers (1994) 'Promoting entrepreneurship in Eastern Europe', *Small Business Economics* 6 (3): 165–84. (Suggests that entrepreneurship is key to reviving Eastern Europe.)

* *U.S. News and World Report* (1993) 'What do Bill Clinton, George Bush and Bob Dole have in common? All have uttered one of the most enduring homilies in American political discourse: That small businesses create most of the nation's jobs', *U.S. News and World Report* 16 August.

* Wagner, Joachim (1992) 'Firm size, firm growth, and persistence of chance: testing Gibrat's law with establishment data from Lower Saxony. 1978–1989', *Small Business Economics* 4 (2): 125–31. (Tests Gibrat's Law for Germany.)

* Wagner, Joachim (1994) 'Small firm entry in manufacturing industries: Lower Saxony, 1979–1989', *Small Business Economics* 6 (3): 211–24. (Analyses the entry on Germany.)

* Weiss, Leonard W. (1979) 'The structure–performance paradigm and antitrust', *University of Pennsylvania Law Review* 127 (April): 1104–40. (Suggests that a cost of allowing oligopoly is that it enables inefficient sub-optimal scale SMEs to survive.)

* Williamson, Oliver E. (1968) 'Economies as an antitrust defense: the welfare tradeoffs', *American Economic Review* 58 (1): 18–36. (Argues that a tradeoff exists between corporate size and efficiency, on the one hand, and less efficiency with decentralization on the other hand.)

Williamson, Oliver E. (1975) *Markets and Hierarchies: Antitrust Analysis and Implications*, New York: The Free Press. (Transactions cost analysis.)

Winter, Sidney G. (1984) 'Schumpeterian competition in alternative technological regimes', *Journal of Economic Behavior and Organization*, 5 (September–December): 287–320. (Argues for the existence of two distinct technological regimes, one dominated by SMEs, the other by large corporations.)

See also: COOPERATION AND COMPETITION; DYNAMIC CAPABILITIES; ECONOMIES OF SCALE AND SCOPE; GALBRAITH, J.K.; GROWTH OF THE FIRM AND NETWORKING; INDUSTRIAL AGGLOMERATIONS; INDUSTRIAL DYNAMICS; INNOVATION; MARSHALL, A.; MARX, K.; MEANS, G.; OWNERSHIP, TYPES OF; PENROSE, E.T.; RESOURCE ALLOCATION; SCHUMACHER, E.; SCHUMPETER, J.; SMITH, A.; WILLIAMSON, O.E.

Smart cards

Overview

Smart cards have been in use for over two decades, primarily for storing small amounts of money for specialized purposes. People carry them to pay for telephone calls, transportation, photocopying in libraries and the like. These cards are very popular in Europe and Asia. Recently, the use of smart cards has expanded considerably through the use of microprocessor chips. For example, in several countries smart cards are used as identification cards in applications from checking health status and insurance to payment of retirement benefits.

The latest development in smart cards technology is in Internet-related applications, principally in support of electronic commerce payment systems and security. There are many benefits in using smart cards that will ultimately translate into savings for businesses and consumers.

1 What are smart cards?

Two types of cards are classified under the generic term 'smart card'. The first is a memory card, built with a magnetic stripe. The second type is an intelligent smart card, which contains a memory chip. Both are usually a standard-sized plastic card that looks similar to a credit card.

Conventional smart cards, or memory cards, have been in use for over two decades, primarily in Europe and Asia. Roland Moreno, a Frenchman, developed and patented the technology in 1974. Memory cards basically store monetary value which the user can 'spend' in pay phones, retail vending, or related transactions. These cards have matured over the past 20 years into intelligent smart cards, which today can store and process data.

By the end of the 1990s, it was estimated that almost 1 billion smart cards were produced worldwide, still with high concentrated use in Europe and Asia. As smart card technologies are maturing, there has been a shift in use to other parts of the world. The Smart Card Industry Association has researched and published many statistics about the use of smart cards worldwide. Both Table 1 and Table 2 were obtained from this association's website. See www.scia.org for additional information regarding smart card usage worldwide.

Since smart cards were developed in Europe, this part of the world had been the primary user of this technology. As the technology has matured, newer applications are being developed which address issues in other parts of the world, resulting in a shift in usage of smart cards.

Intelligent smart cards are embedded with either a microprocessor/memory chip combination – also referred to as an integrated circuit chip – or only a memory chip with nonprogrammable logic. A memory-chip card can only undertake a predefined operation or rely on the card-accepting device for processing. The integrated circuit chip makes a smart card much more versatile than the memory card. It has the ability to store and secure information, offers a 'read/write' capability, allows protection of the information from damage or theft, and can be used to make decisions as required by the application needs. As a result, these applications can include transactional elements to be used later for further processing (see E-COMMERCE).

Table 1 Where smart cards are used (percentage)

Region	1996	2000
North America	3%	12%
South America	11%	10%
Western Europe	70%	40%
Asia	10%	30%
Rest of the world	6%	9%

Table 2 Areas where smart cards are used

Card application	1996 (000)	2000 (000)	Avg. annual growth (%)
Pay phone	605	1,500	29
GSM* (wireless communications	20	45	25
Health care	70	120	14
Banking	40	250	105
Identity/access	20	300	280
Transportation	15	200	247
Pay TV	15	75	80
Gaming	5	200	780
Metering/ vending	10	80	140
Retail/loyalty	5	75	280

* GSM is an abbreviation for Global Systems for Mobile Communications

2 Smart cards in use

Many industries are adopting the use of smart cards to benefit their customers. In 1996, approximately 805 million smart cards were issued, with an estimated 2.8 billion to be distributed in 2000 (see Table 2). Smart cards are an effective way of ensuring secure access to open interactive systems, such as encryption key mobility, secure single sign-on and electronic digital signatures. As an access-control device, smart cards make personal and business data available only to the appropriate users. These benefits are what will drive the triple digit growth of these cards in certain markets. Another Internet site focused on smart development, the Smart Card Forum, has additional information regarding these benefits. See *www.smartcardforum.org*.

Compared with European and Asian countries, adoption and use of smart cards within the United States has been rather slow. Recently there have been a number of pilot projects, with one of the biggest occurring in Atlanta during the 1996 summer Olympic Games. Table 3 lists various pilot smart card projects taking place around the world.

A more in-depth description of actual smart card application uses include the following.

Replacing cash

In Singapore, the CashCard is a smart card that acts as an electronic purse. In fact, it replaces coins and bank notes for everyday purchases such as movies, parking, gas, telephones, vending machines, retail outlets and fast food restaurants. The CashCard is available in several different initial values of $20, $50 and $100 and can be reloaded. People will use 'electronic money' for several reasons, such as convenience, reduction in the cost of cash handling, and fraud protection.

While credit cards are commonplace in developed countries, especially the United States, they remain uncommon in other countries, particularly those with undeveloped credit markets and developing economies. But, even with credit cards, cash transactions have consistently accounted for more than half of total global personal expenditures. As documented in a 1996 *Financial Times* article 'Smart Cards: A technology whose time has come', in 1993 alone, cash transactions accounted for $8.1 trillion of $14 trillion in global personal spending. The new system of digitized commerce can be seen as market expansion for credit card companies. People who use only cash by choice, or cannot qualify for a credit card because they have yet to build a credit history, are ideal candidates for smart 'cash' cards.

Streamlining health care services

Smart cards are increasing the quality of service in health care and reducing its cost by improving the efficiency of handling medical and administrative information. They are useful in a wide range of situations in the medical field. The advantages are outlined in Table 4.

In the United States, Oklahoma City has a smart card system called MediCard, available since 1994. Designed by health care professionals, this smart card is able to selectively control access to a patient's medical history, which is recorded on his/her MediCard. However, essential information, including family physician and close relative contact, is available to emergency personnel in extreme circumstances.

Smart card readers are installed at hospitals, pharmacies, ambulance services, physician's offices, and even with the fire

Table 3 Pilot smart card projects

Program (location)	The players	No. of cards/status	Date begun/description
Stored value/ electronic purse	*Over two dozen projects in operation around the world with several having hit the 1-million-card level*		*Most in the pilot stage*
Mondex (worldwide)	Shares in Mondex International held by MasterCard (51%) and major banks on five continents	50,000 in various pilots around the world	1992: anonymous cash scheme which allows peer-to-peer transfers and handles up to six currencies; was launched by NatWest, two-tier ownership, with international and country licences established in 1996.
Danmont (Denmark)	Danmont, major banks, Danish phone company	1 million in continuous operation	1993: the first broad-scale electronic purse system uses disposable cards, but a reloadable function is planned.
Proton, Cash, ChipKnip (worldwide)	Belgian, Canadian, Swiss, Dutch, and other banks, plus American Express	2 million in 1996; 12 million in 1997	1994: system designed by Belgium banks and since licensed to banks in Switzerland, Holland, Brazil, Australia, Sweden and Canada for their programmes, but under different names in each country; American Express licensed for worldwide use.
Visa Cash (worldwide)	Visa member banks	2,000,000 in several parts of the world	1996: pilot at Atlanta Olympic Games, programs are being initiated in over a dozen nations using disposable and reloadable cards.
Clip (pan-European)	Europay member banks	50,000 in pilot	1996: pilots for Clip, Europay's electronic purse scheme, began in Austria, Iceland, and the Czech Republic, with other existing national programmes announcing intent to incorporate Clip.
New York City pilot	Chase Manhattan and Citibank	50,000 pilot launch in late 1997	1997: programme will be the first to accept both Visa Cash (Citibank) and Mondex (Chase Manhattan) stored-value schemes at same terminals
Other financial uses	*Wide variety, including credit/debit card security, bank account information, and corporate cash management security.*		
Group Carte Bancaire (France)	Major French banks	24 million ongoing	1992: since this year, every bankcard in France has contained a chip for cardholder ID and transaction authorization.
Taiwan Financial Services Card	14 Taiwanese banks and Financial Information service centres	700,000 in 1995	1993: system uses smart cards and point-of-sale terminals to deliver financial services to banking customers nationwide.
Zolotaya Korana (Russia)	Over 100 Russian banks	150,000 at roll-out; 400,000 now	1994–95: debit/credit smart cards for use with automatic teller machines (ATMs) and terminals, support varied banking applications, including electronic purse.
US Treasury Electronic Certification Program	US Treasury	5000 ongoing	Early 1990s: smart card identifies disbursing officers at Federal agencies that send payment information to Treasury Financial Centers that execute transactions.

Source: Be Miller, Card Tech/Secur Tech Inc.

Table 4 Advantages of smart cards

Medical cards	Advantages
Health insurance card	Reduces rotine paperwork
	Eliminates error and fraud
	Speeds up payment and claim process
	Inexpensive equipment setup
Medical file access card	Patient controls doctors' access to information
	Patient's medical history readily available using a single process
	Pharmacist has access to prescription information only
	Allows automatic check for medication compatibility

department, allowing the MediCard to be used in both ordinary and emergency circumstances. Gemplus, a leader in smart card production, has published many articles related to industry-specific usage of smart cards. See www.gemplus.com for more information.

Smart cards and the Internet

Today, Internet payments can be made by using electronic cheques, electronic credit cards, electronic cash or electronic debit cards, all of which have advantages and limitations. Most of the limitations can be removed by using smart cards (see INTERNET). With a recent report by International Data Corporation showing that e-commerce will increase from $2.6 billion in 1996 to more than $220 billion in 2001, online buyers will need better online payment options.

Therefore, several companies are developing smart cards that can be used for Internet shopping. These cards slip into a smart-card reader that is a stand-alone unit, or installed in the PC, dubbed 'Plug and Pay'. In the UK, Visa is testing its 'electronic purse' card for Internet purchases. In France, the Banque Nationale de Paris, Gemplus and others are working to develop a secured way to purchase goods and services over the Internet through smart cards. In the USA, Verifone demonstrated in mid-1997 its Personal ATM system, which is designed to support downloading of virtual cash from your bank account into a smart card.

Smart card readers are inexpensive, low-power devices that can be easily added to existing computers. The additional cost of build-ing them into future computers or peripherals is extremely low. Many computer manufacturers are planning to include these devices as standard equipment.

The recently debuted WebTV includes a smart card reader. WebTV is an Internet service provider that aims to capture a large part of what will be the mass-market future of the Internet, including bank-originated electronic commerce.

3 Smart card application benefits

Smart card advocates contend substantial advantages like cheaper administration, better fraud protection, multiple financial services support through the electronic channel, better prospects of data mining and an interest-free loan to the bank from the cardholder. These all represent good reasons for card issuers to adopt smart cards. Such benefits can be observed in the following.

Transaction savings

Smart cards enable customers to make payments without requiring communication between the merchants and a centralized credit card information network or ATM clearing system (see INFORMATION TECHNOLOGY). They avoid the high costs of physical cheque clearing and, unlike cheques, entail no credit risk. Therefore, smart cards offer the convenience of cash without collection risks.

Another advantage is that interest could be paid on smart card account balances. Since the chip within the card costlessly keeps track of the timing and amounts of transfers, smart card banks could share several financial benefits with cardholders, like the cost savings from avoiding cleared-cheque processing and interest earned on the money while 'stored' on the card.

Security applications

Smart cards have advantages over software implementations for security by providing tamper-proof devices that users can carry with them to protect corporate data and communications. On a corporate level, it looks to be somewhat simpler to add smart cards to a security system than with consumer-banking-type applications. Smart cards are the attractive option for remote corporate users because private cryptographic keys, certificates, profiles, and other user data are held apart from the enabling device, and if a computer is lost or stolen, encrypted files and data will be protected.

Fraud protection

The best way to appeal to the user's mind is to appeal to his (her) commonsense self-interest, and stress smart cards' strong fraud protection. Since preventing fraud is in everyone's best interests, offering it should prove a strong selling proposition.

With credit card fraud topping over $1 billion annually in the USA alone, the need for enhanced authentication mechanisms are the main catalyst of the search for alternative solutions. In France, the use of smart cards with a personal identity number cut the costs of fraud from around $4–$5 per card in 1992 to almost nothing in 1996.

Cash error handling

Similar in nature to fraud is cash pilferage from industries like restaurants, hotels, parking lots and tolls. Traditional cash-management practices attempt to reduce pilferage, shortages and overages, which inevitably occur with currency in cash handling with the help of a physical and perpetual inventory of cash. With smart cards, and their digital cash transactions, these problems should be

eliminated along with the time-consuming accounting, auditing and adjustment activities. A 1996 article by Sheel and Leverer in the *Cornell Hotel and Restaurant Administration Quarterly* addressed many of these specific issues.

4 Implementation issues

In the ongoing use of smart cards in future applications there are a number of issues which need to be addressed. Among these are the following.

General security

In a report released in February 1997, the Computer Security Institute (CSI) and the FBI revealed that 47 per cent of the 563 US organizations surveyed had been attacked through the Internet, up from 37 per cent reported in a 1996 CSI–FBI survey. The survey also contradicts the conventional wisdom that the vast majority of attacks come from within the organizations. While 43 per cent of respondents reported attacks from within, 47 per cent said they experienced external attacks. Smart cards are tools that, if used properly, can provide a high level of security. Hewlett-Packard broadened its security offerings in May 1997, with two smart-card solutions that include the cards, readers to scan the information stored on the processor embedded in the cards and a management system. Also included is a developer's toolkit to let third-party vendors build hooks into applications that can then use the smart-card authentication capability.

Securing privacy

One of the unknown elements in smart card technology is how much data mining will be built into smart card applications. Most people are very protective about privacy and issues relating to their rights to privacy. Chairman of the US Federal Reserve System's Board of Governors Alan Greenspan said, 'Since privacy is such an evident value in our society, where technology threatens the value, entrepreneurs can be counted on to seek means to defend it.' If we wish to foster innovation, we must be careful not to impose rules that inhibit it. To develop new forms of payment, the private sector will need the flexibility to experiment without broad interference by the government.

Alan Westin, a Columbia University researcher of privacy issues, cited a 1996 Louis Harris & Associates survey that found 83 per cent of consumers believe they have lost control of how information about them is gathered and used. That figure was up from 80 per cent only a year earlier. If smart cards are going to become ubiquitous in our society, consumers are going to demand that the issues of privacy be addressed right up front.

Legal issues

As scores of banks and businesses charge onto the Internet, cyber-commerce and electronic cash, or e-cash, transactions are creating a myriad of untested legal issues (see WORLD WIDE WEB (WWW)). One urgent issue: is e-cash really cash and legally recognized currency? After months of study and debate, David Loundy published his article in the *Chicago Daily Law Bulletin* which stated that lawyers from Silicon Valley to Capitol Hill seem to be saying that e-cash is not a legal tender, like paper money and coins. That conclusion will have vast implications for future consumer protection and banking regulations. E-cash is not real cash but an obligation that an issuer has created to pay a monetary amount at some future date. Unlike cash, which by law a merchant is obligated to accept, a merchant can refuse a payment from a stored-value card. Transactions conducted with real money are overseen by a range of state and federal laws and government agencies. Bank deposits, for example, are federally insured up to $100 000. What about insuring e-cash contacted on a stored-value smart card?

Other related legal issues include: Who is liable if a smart card is lost or stolen? What kind of contract is best for all parties, including banks, merchants and consumers? Will e-cash be affected by state civil and criminal laws on the Internet? Should e-cash be regulated by federal laws and policies? Or should the federal government let the cybermarket police itself?

5 The next steps

Smart card incentives

Since cash has been a good medium of exchange for thousands of years, the adoption process for smart cards may not be so easy. In order to 'jump start' this process, incentive programmes may be needed to induce consumers to change. Vendors realize that convenience is not enough. The 1996 Olympic Games in Atlanta was a test-bed for smart cards. Wells Fargo is developing and testing a number of financial and technology incentive programmes for paying for fast food. To find out how much incentive it will take to wean consumers off cash, about 900 Wells Fargo employees are using the cards with 22 selected merchants near their downtown San Francisco headquarters.

Banking and stock trading

Web users who bank, shop and trade stocks online via the Internet will be able to use cryptography-enabled smart cards for authentication, to access restricted areas, and to sign documents. Several pilot tests of cryptographic smart cards are under way in the corporate environment, and applications for intranets and business-to-business networks are expected to begin rolling out soon. The advantages to stock traders in using smart cards relate to security. If you have the card and know what that encrypted password on the card is, a more secure environment can be created.

Multi-application cards

Although most current smart cards can only handle single applications, future versions will be able to hold and process multiple applications. Sun Microsystems Inc. introduced in 1996 the Java Card APIs (application programming interfaces), and Gemplus and Schlumberger have licensed the APIs for use in developing an interoperable smart-card operating system. The Java APIs are expected to allow multiple applications to be loaded and upgraded in a single card. Schlumberger introduced a Java-based smart card in May 1997 called CyberFlex, which includes support for Secure Electronic Transaction (SET).

Early adopters should beware. Until smart-card solutions are widely available, it may be difficult to piece together best-of-breed and standards-based cards, applications and software infrastructure. It's like the chicken and the egg, the standards won't be established until enough people start to deploy the technology. But, multi-application capability is seen as necessary for the widespread adoption of smart card technology. A typical smart card should be able to handle cash, access to financial services, mass transit, medical information, and also provide credit card capabilities.

6 Summary and conclusion

In reviewing smart card advancements, it is apparent that there are compelling reasons to use this technology to provide new solutions in business. Smart cards offer clear advantages to card issuers, merchants and customers. They reduce cash handling expenses, reduce losses due to fraud, expedite customer transactions and enhance customer convenience. In addition, new services will begin to evolve and payment mechanisms for existing services will change. For example, through the use of smart cards, software could be paid for on a per use basis instead of through a licence fee, or journalism could be bought by the article. Many companies will be able to set up online businesses and begin to receive revenue.

Managers need to take a close look at their markets and products to determine what their best strategies are regarding smart card technologies. Companies must evaluate whether to utilize smart cards in their infancy or wait for a mature market. But for some, if significant product and service benefits can be gained, the future may be now. In the near future, you can count on mass acceptance of smart card systems.

DEBBIE MCELROY
CALIFORNIA STATE UNIVERSITY

EFRAIM TURBAN
CALIFORNIA STATE UNIVERSITY

Further reading

(References cited in the text marked *)

Allen, C.A. (1996) *Smart Cards: Seizing Strategic Business Opportunities: The Smart Card Forum*, Irwin Professional Publishing. (Brings readers face to face with the potential impact of the smart card and provides insights on implementing new technologies.)

Fox, J. (1996) 'Cyberbunk: what's new about digital cash', *Fortune* 30 September: 50. (Provides information about the use of this new technology.)

Hendry, M. (1997) *Smart Card Security Applications*, Artech House. (A solid overview of the benefits and limitations of smart cards for secure applications.)

Jones, C. (1997) 'Special news report; sizing up smart cards', *Info World* 10 March: 1. (Covers the pros and cons of smart card usage.)

Loshin, P. and Murphy, P. (1997) *Electronic Commerce: On-Line Ordering and Digital Money*, Charles River Media. (Addresses the present state of Internet-based commerce and its promise for the future.)

* Loundy, D. (1997) 'Congress scrambles to address encryption', *Chicago Daily Law Bulletin*, March: 5. (Addresses specific legal questions regarding electronic commerce.)

Monk, J.T. (1997) *Smart Cards: A Guide to Building and Managing Smart Card Applications*, John Wiley & Sons. (A complete guide to the major technology of the emerging 'cashless society'.)

Rankl, W. (1997) *Smart Card Handbook*, John Wiley & Sons. (Provides an overview of the technology from information processing through design and operation of the applications.)

* Sheel, A. and Levever, M. (December 1996) 'The implications of digital cash for hotels and restaurants', *Cornell Hotel and Restaurant Administration Quarterly* December: 92. (Covers specific industry-related issues in the use of digital cash.)

Vartanian, T.P., Ledig, R.H. and Brueau, L.N. (1998) *21st Century Money, Banking, & Commerce*, Fried, Frank, Harris, Shriver & Jacobson. (Provides a comprehensive analysis of electronic financial projects and services and electronic commerce.)

See also: E-BUSINESS; E-COMMERCE; INFORMATION TECHNOLOGY; INTERNET; INTERNET BANKING; WORLD WIDE WEB

Smith, Adam (1723–90)

Personal background

- born before 5 June 1723 in Kirkcaldy, Fife, Scotland, the son of a customs official
- educated at University of Glasgow, 1737–40
- Snell Exhibitioner, Balliol College, Oxford, 1740–6
- professor at University of Glasgow, 1751–64
- tutor to the Duke of Buccleuch, 1764–6
- Commissioner of Customs, 1778
- died in Edinburgh on 17 July 1790 of stomach cancer

Major works

The Theory of Moral Sentiments (1759)
Lectures on Jurisprudence (1762–3; first published 1978)
The Wealth of Nations (1776)

Summary

Adam Smith (1723–90), the leading figure in the classical school of economics and prominent in the Scottish Enlightenment, is one of the few economists to be credited with founding economics. In his compendious work, *The Wealth of Nations*, he integrated the information and ideas provided by historical and contemporary authors to explain how an economy operates and how it can grow. He set out a system of natural liberty for an economy, justified free trade and inspired subsequent value and distribution theories. Both socialist and libertarian economists look to him as a precursor.

1 Introduction

Adam Smith was born into a prosperous Scottish family and baptised on 5 June 1723. His father, the Clerk of the Court Martial and Comptroller of Customs at Kirkcaldy, died before his only son was born. Smith was educated at the local burgh school then entered the University of Glasgow in 1737 to study Latin, Greek, Logic, Moral Philosophy, Mathematics and Natural Philosophy for an MA degree. In 1740, without graduating, he left Glasgow when he was awarded a Snell Exhibition at Balliol College, Oxford. This minor scholarship was intended to enable young men to train for the ministry in the Church of England. Disgusted by the poor quality of the teaching at the University of Oxford, Smith embarked on an extensive course of self-education. Smith returned to Scotland in 1746, resigning the exhibition in 1749.

He had no intention of entering the church's ministry so he looked for a career in the law or elsewhere. Encouraged by the Lord Advocate, he gave private lectures in Edinburgh for three winters on rhetoric, *belles-lettres* and philosophy. Anticipating his later views, Smith told his audience: 'Little else is required to carry a state to the highest degree of opulence from the lowest barbarism, but peace, easy taxes, and a tolerable administration of justice; all the rest being brought about by the natural course of things' (Smith 1983).

In 1751 he was appointed Professor of Logic at Glasgow; in 1752 he was translated to the Chair of Moral Philosophy. He interpreted his academic remit widely to lecture on rhetoric, ethics, jurisprudence and economics. From reconstructions of students' lecture notes, it is possible to see the breadth of Smith's erudition. He was an enthusiastic teacher, lecturing eight hours weekly and involved in university administration, being Dean of the Faculty 1760–2. The University of Glasgow conferred the LLD degree on him in 1762. Residence in Glasgow enabled Smith to gain a detailed knowledge of the views and methods of merchants, putting that knowledge to use in his later economic writings.

The publication of *The Theory of Moral Sentiments* in 1759 brought him considerable fame. Charles Townshend, Secretary of State and stepfather of the eighteen-year-old Duke of Buccleuch, was sufficiently impressed by the book to invite Smith to leave the University of Glasgow to accompany the duke on a grand tour of Europe. Smith was given a life pension of £300 per annum, the same amount as his previous academic earnings. From January 1764 to November 1766 Smith travelled with the duke and his younger brother to Paris, Toulouse and Geneva, meeting François Quesnay (1694–1774) and other leading physiocrats, as well as Voltaire. The death of the duke's younger brother in Paris ended Smith's only journey beyond Britain.

Smith spent the winter of 1766–7 in London working on a revision of *The Theory of Moral Sentiments*, as well as advising Townshend, then Chancellor of the Exchequer, on the sinking fund. For six years to 1773, Smith stayed at his mother's home in Kirkcaldy gathering information for and preparing drafts of *The Wealth of Nations*. From 1773 to 1777 he resided in London, with a nine-month break in Scotland in 1776 to visit his dying friend David Hume and his ageing mother. In 1773 he was elected to the Royal Society. In London his opinions were eagerly sought. However, his view that the problem of the American colonies should be solved by a union of the colonies with Britain, with American representatives in the House of Commons, was rejected; later it was used as a model for the union with Ireland in 1800. *The Wealth of Nations* was published on 9 March 1776 to the immediate acclaim of contemporary thinkers. He received a flat fee of about £500 from his publishers.

He was appointed Commissioner of Customs at a salary of £600 in 1778, diligently attending board meetings at the Royal Exchange (now the City Chambers) of Edinburgh and residing at Panmure House, Canongate. It was strange for the apostle of free trade to administer a protectionist trade policy but it had no effect on his revisions to *The Wealth of Nations*. In his last years he revised his major works and took an active part in the social life of the city, becoming famous for his Sunday night supper parties. He died of stomach cancer. His personal papers were burnt, on his orders, by his executors but his personal library substantially survives at Edinburgh University and in Tokyo. His grave in Canongate kirkyard, Edinburgh, has attracted respectful visitors from numerous countries.

2 Main contribution to economics

At the outset of his writing career, Smith wrote on moral philosophy. In *The Theory of Moral Sentiments* he set out to show that nature is a cosmic harmony and society is bound together by sympathy. Also, he introduced ideas which were to be central to *The Wealth of Nations*. He recognized that human behaviour is motivated by self-interest, but also by the contemplation of a grand and harmonious design for society. Nevertheless, there is an optimistic tone to the book. In his discussion of income distribution he states:

> The rich only select from the heap what is most precious and agreeable. They consume little more than the poor… They are led by an invisible hand to make nearly the same distribution of the necessaries of life which would have been made, had the earth been divided into equal portions among all its inhabitants, and thus without intending it, without knowing it, advance the interest of the society and afford means to the multiplication.
>
> (Smith [1759] 1976: 184)

This passage is typical of the whole book. The underlying principles influencing society, including the idea of the 'invisible hand', are set out with economic mechanisms suggested but not discussed in detail.

As a professor of moral philosophy, he lectured on jurisprudence. Jurisprudence was regarded by Smith as including the study of trade, commerce, agriculture and manufactures as the police had the task of regulating markets. A copy of his lectures to the jurisprudence class for the winter of 1762–3 survives. It provides a clear insight into his early economic thinking. The influence of Francis Hutcheson (1694–1746), who had taught

Smith in the 1730s at Glasgow, is strong but there is also a preview of Smith's later theories. Already there is a critique of the mercantilist policies of prohibiting the export of bullion and maintaining a favourable balance of trade. He uses a four-stage theory of economic development with human history divided into the four ages of hunters, shepherds, agriculture and commerce. He sets out the important principle of the division of labour and distinguishes natural price from market price. But in his theory of value he uses a straightforward notion of scarcity to explain paradoxes such as water being necessary but cheap and jewels with an immense price but little usefulness: 'cheapness is a necessary consequence of plenty' (Smith [1762–3] 1978: 333).

Smith's visit to France enabled him to have discussions on economics with the Physiocrats, the French school of economics which believed that agriculture was the only productive sector of an economy and that government regulation of economic life should be minimal. Subsequently Smith diligently collected information from numerous sources to write a detailed survey of economics. The full title of Smith's magnum opus, *An Inquiry into the Nature and Causes of the Wealth of Nations of 1776* indicates clearly that he wanted to analyse the nature of economic growth. At the outset he stated that the welfare of a state is measured by the ratio of produce to population, similar to the modern measure of economic welfare, per capita gross domestic product. Smith attributes growth to the 'skill, dexterity and judgment with which its labour is generally applied' (Smith [1776] 1976: 10) and, less importantly, to the ratio of productive to unproductive labour.

The Wealth of Nations is divided into five books but has a continuous argument. Smith begins with determinants of productivity (see PRODUCTIVITY) and income distribution then considers how capital is employed. He surveys the growth record of other nations, the diversity of economic systems and the activities of states in taxing and spending. The major themes are economic growth, value and distribution, the working of markets, international trade and the relationship between the state and the individual (see INTERNATIONAL MARKETING).

The human motive which starts an economy on a growth path is 'the desire of bettering our condition' (Smith [1776] 1976: 341) which prompts saving; the saving is invested to provide a capital fund which will make possible the employment of the labour force and the division of labour. Division of labour is a fundamental principle, the consequence of 'a certain propensity in human nature … the propensity to truck, barter, and exchange one thing for another' (Smith [1776] 1976: 25). Using the example of pin-making, he explains that by dividing the tasks of human labour into its component parts, the dexterity of the worker increases, the time lost in one piece of work to another is saved and machinery can be invented as a consequence of analysing work into its sub-operations. However, Smith did appreciate that economic growth has its costs. The effect of the division of labour is to make a person who spends his life on a few simple operations 'as stupid and ignorant as it is possible for a human creature to become' (Smith [1776] 1976: 782).

Again, in this work Smith makes use of his 'four stages' theory to explain how value is determined and the national product is distributed among the landlord, the capitalist and the labourer. The determination of value changes as the economy has progressed from its earliest stage to a commercial society. It is only in the most primitive of human societies, the age of the hunters, that goods (beavers and deer) are exchanged according to the quantities of labour required to obtain the goods. Only then do labourers obtain the whole produce of their labour. With population growth and the accumulation of capital, land becomes private property and the landlord receives a share of the national produce as rent and the capitalist profits. Like Aristotle before him, Smith distinguishes 'value in use' from 'value in exchange'. He also contrasts market prices and natural prices. The proportion between supply and demand determines the market price but the natural price is 'the central price to which the prices of all commodities are continually gravitating' (Smith [1776] 1976: 75). This natural price is brought about by free competition and can be regarded as a long-run equilibrium price equal to the costs of production in the form of rent, profits and wages.

Smith's concept of the market mechanism is clear in his celebrated account of how in labour and capital markets (see LABOUR MARKETS; CAPITAL MARKETS, REGULATION OF) there will be equilibrating flows in response to differentials: 'The whole of the advantages and disadvantages of the different employments of labour and stock must, in the same neighbourhood, be either perfectly equal or continually tending to equality' (Smith [1776] 1976: 116). But he was aware, too, of market imperfections. In product markets, businesses are constantly trying to engage in collusive oligopoly: 'People of the same trade seldom meet together, even for merriment and diversion, but the conversation ends in a conspiracy against the public, or in some contrivance to raise prices' (Smith [1776] 1976: 145).

In the labour market there is, according to Smith, unequal bargaining. Smith states that the workmen desire to get as much, the masters to give as little as possible. The masters, being fewer in number, can combine much more easily. Moreover, the law authorizes, or at least does not prohibit, their combinations, while it prohibits those of the workmen (Smith [1776] 1976: 84–5)

After his discussion of the domestic economy, Smith turns his attention to different economic systems and to international trade. Having argued that the division of labour is the desirable course for the domestic economy, he justifies free trade in terms of the efficiency and productivity gains arising from a similar specialization internationally:

The tailor does not attempt to make his own shoes...All of them find it for their interest to employ their whole industry in a way in which they have some advantage over their neighbours and to purchase with a part of its produce ... whatever else they have occasion for ... What is prudence in the conduct of every private family, can scarce be folly in that of a great kingdom...Would it be a reasonable law to prohibit the importation of all foreign wines, merely to encourage the making of claret and burgundy in Scotland?

(Smith [1776] 1976: 456–8)

This trade theory based on 'absolute advantage' was part of Smith's attack on mercantilism. He also criticized the mercantilists for identifying wealth with gold and silver, not goods; also, for putting the interest of the producer above that of the consumer.

Smith disapproved of state intervention as subsidization of industry would divert economic activity away from its natural course. He saw the only justification for public institutions as being the benefits they conferred on society and the impossibility of the beneficiaries paying for them. Defence, law and order, the expenses of the sovereign and some public institutions were all that he recommended. As far as possible expenditure on the infrastructure was to be directly financed, for example, by tolls on roads and fees for education. Some taxation was necessary to finance this minimal state. The taxation should be according to ability to pay, certain, payable at the time of receipt of income and collected at minimum cost.

When faced with particular economic problems, Smith was willing to accept some departures from *laissez-faire*. Regulations on the issue of paper currency, support for the Navigation Acts which ruled that English trade be carried in English ships, and a maximum interest rate of five per cent are all advocated. But the individual was more important than the government in economic life. At the heart of his analysis Smith maintained the beneficial effects of the pursuit of self-interest:

By directing that industry in such a manner as its produce may be of the greatest value, he intends only his own gain, and he is in this, as in many other cases, led by an invisible hand to promote an end which was no part of his intention.

(Smith [1776] 1976: 456)

3 Conclusions

Schumpeter, in a celebrated criticism of Smith, noted that Smith's admirers praised *The Wealth of Nations* for the policies it advocated and for the fact that it contained 'no really novel ideas' but was a feat of coordination of previous economic writings. Also commended were Smith's accessible style and the fact that he 'was thoroughly in sympathy with the humours of his time' and 'advocated the things that were in the offing' (Schumpeter 1954: 185).

Gray, too, admitted that Smith was not a pioneer and could be confused, especially on value, but that he has the greatest name in the history of economics. He stated that 'before Adam Smith there had been much economic discussion; with him we reach the stage of discussing economics' (Gray 1980: 110). A more recent commentator on Smith, Hollander, sees in *The Wealth of Nations* 'not merely … the extraordinary range of topics treated, but also … Smith's demonstration of a high degree of interdependence between apparently unrelated variables culminating in his development of a more or less consistent 'model' of value and distribution' (Hollander 1973: 305).

Although Smith's method of economic exposition is literary, twentieth-century mathematical economists award him high marks. Samuelson (see SAMUELSON, P.A.) has written a strong defence of Smith and praises him for anticipating general equilibrium theory. The breadth of economic life discussed by Smith makes his work relevant to the discussion of modern business life: monetary economics, joint stock companies and entrepreneurship all commanded his attention (Laidler 1981; Anderson and Tollison 1982; Pesciarelli 1989). Smith's genius has been recognized throughout the world, with both ardent free marketers and socialists, even Lenin, acknowledging their debt to him (Mizuta and Sugiyama 1993).

DONALD RUTHERFORD
UNIVERSITY OF EDINBURGH

Further reading

(References cited in the text marked *)

* Anderson, G.M. and Tollison, R.D. (1982) 'Adam Smith's analysis of joint stock companies', *Journal of Political Economy* 90 (6): 1237–56. (An exposition of how corporations survive under competition through superior efficiency.)

Campbell, R.H. and Skinner, A.S. (1982) *Adam Smith*, London: Croom Helm. (A precise biographical summary of his life, principal lecture courses and books.)

* Gray, A. (1931, 1980 with A.E. Thompson) *The Development of Economic Doctrine*, London:

Longman. (A stimulating general survey of economics placing Smith in the context of other leading economists.)

* Hollander, S. (1973) *The Economics of Adam Smith*, Toronto: University of Toronto Press. (Smith's analysis of the price mechanism and economic development in its historical context.)

* Laidler, D. (1981) 'Adam Smith as a monetary economist', *Canadian Journal of Economics* 14 (2): 185–200. (An explanation of how Smith integrated his banking theory into his theory of economic development.)

* Mizuta, H. and Sugiyama, C. (eds) (1993) *Adam Smith: International Perspectives*, London: Macmillan. (International symposium papers which trace Smith's past and present influence.)

* Pesciarelli, E. (1989) 'Smith, Bentham and the development of contrasting ideas of entrepreneurship', *History of Political Economy* 21 (3): 521–36. (Smith's view of the entrepreneur as a risk taker, planner and organizer of productive forces.)

Samuelson, P.A. (1977) 'A modern theorist's vindication of Adam Smith', *American Economic Review* 67: 42–9. (A mathematical proof that Smith's economic model survives the attacks of Ricardo and Marx.)

* Schumpeter, J.A. (1954) *History of Economic Analysis*, London: George Allen and Unwin. (A monumental study of how economic analysis developed from its earliest beginnings.)

Skinner, A. and Wilson, T. (1975) *Essays on Adam Smith*, Oxford: Clarendon Press. (A collection of articles which demonstrate the relevance of Smith to modern economic discussions.)

* Smith, A. (1759) *The Theory of Moral Sentiments*, ed. D.D. Raphael and A.L. MacFie, Oxford: Oxford University Press, 1976. (Smith's first book which established his position as a leading thinker. This system of ethics is based on the principle of sympathy. He introduces the concept of the 'invisible hand' in his discussion of income distribution.)

* Smith, A. (1762–3) *Lectures on Jurisprudence*, ed. R.L. Meek, D.D. Raphael and P.G. Stein, Oxford: Oxford University Press, 1978. (A transcript of his lectures of 1762–3 and 1766. In the section on the police he provides his early thinking on the division of labour, price and monetary theories.)

* Smith, A. (1776) *An Inquiry into the Nature and Causes of the Wealth of Nations*, ed. R.H. Campbell and A.S. Skinner, Oxford: Oxford University Press, 1976. (His principles of economics which begins with an account of the role of the division of labour in economic growth

then presents theories of value, prices and distribution. Also he studies the relative opulence of nations, analyses mercantilism and physiocracy, argues for free trade, as well as discussing the role of the state and the nature of taxation.)

Smith, A. (1795) *Essays on Philosophical Subjects*, ed. I.S. Ross, Oxford: Oxford University Press, 1980. (Smith's views on astronomy, ancient logic and metaphysics, external senses, imitative arts, together with his contributions to the *Edinburgh Review* of 1755–6.)

Smith, A. (1977; 1987) *The Correspondence of Adam Smith*, ed. E.C. Mosner and I.S. Ross, Oxford: Oxford University Press. (Important letters with other leading philosophers of the day, including Hume and Bentham.)

* Smith, A. (1983) *Lectures on Rhetoric and Belles-Lettres*, ed. J.C. Bryce, Oxford: Oxford University Press. (Smith's first teaching in Glasgow 1762–3, which attempts to change the nature of rhetoric by introducing a Newtonian approach to the study of literature.)

See also: BUSINESS ECONOMICS; CAPITAL MARKETS, REGULATION OF; DURKHEIM, E.; INTERNATIONAL MARKETING; INTERNATIONAL TRADE AND FOREIGN DIRECT INVESTMENT; LABOUR MARKETS; PRODUCTIVITY; SAMUELSON, P.A.

Social and environmental accounting and reporting

Overview

Social and environmental accounting and reporting (SEEAR) is an extension of and a reminder of the limitations of conventional corporate reporting. It reflects a growing concern over environmental and social issues and a consensus that organizations should be more accountable for, and aware of, the results of their activities. SEAAR is an extensive field which is undergoing rapid and widespread development and experimentation – it involves corporations, governments, supranational bodies, non-governmental organizations, practitioners and academics in accounting and other disciplines. Some flavour of this diversity is given in what follows – and further reading is suggested – but the main aim of this entry is to consider the intrinsic nature of SEAAR, the rationale behind it and its fundamental importance.

1 Introduction and scope of SEAAR

Social and environmental accounting and reporting (SEEAR) encompasses diverse areas of accounting practice with some core features in common. First, SEAAR is founded on the belief that each organization should be accountable for its actions to a variety of individuals and groups who are external to, but who have an interest in, that organization (see ORGANIZATION BEHAVIOUR). These individuals and groups are called stakeholders and are defined as being those who affect – or who are affected by – an organization. This definition means that an organization will have a large number of actual and potential stakeholders. Stakeholders include: providers of capital (such as owners and banks), suppliers (including Third World supplier communities), customers, employees and trade unions, communities in which organizations physically exist, non-governmental organizations (who have an interest in, for example, the environment and how the organization impacts on the environment) and society in general (including future generations). In this respect, SEAAR differs from traditional accounting practice, which focuses on providing accounts to the financial stakeholders (shareholders and creditors) of the organization.

Second, while the types of accounts produced under traditional accounting practice focus on the economic performance of the organization (measured in financial terms), accounts provided by SEAAR focus on social and environmental events which are related to the economic activities of an organization (see ACCOUNTING). Further, while these events may be measured and communicated in financial terms, it is more likely that information will be conveyed in non-monetary quantified terms or in qualititative terms. The image of an organization which is created from the production of SEAAR accounts, therefore, differs from that produced under conventional accounting practice. With a greater variety of ways of expressing events, SEAAR helps provide a fuller picture of the impacts of an organization.

In summary, Gray *et al*. define corporate social reporting (a name which is often used to describe SEAAR) as

the process of communicating the social and environmental effects of organizations' economic actions to particular interest groups within society and to society at large. As such, it involves extending the accountability of organizations (particularly companies), beyond the traditional role of providing a financial account to the owners of capital, in particular, shareholders. Such an extension is predicated upon the assumption that companies do have wider responsibilities than simply to make money for their shareholders.

(1996: 3)

This last aspect of SEAAR (extending the responsibilities of corporations) is the reason why SEAAR is, potentially, a controversial area of accounting theory and practice. Further, changing expectations of corporate responsibilities will affect the development of SEAAR practice. This can be seen from a review of the history of the area.

2 A brief history of SEAAR

Debates in the 1970s over the responsibilities of business underlay what is usually thought of as being the first era of SEAAR (concerns about corporate social responsibility, however, existed well before this time). While corporate responses to these debates were not widespread, some organizations experimented with both social and environmental accounts as a way of representing and accounting for their interactions with society, and thereby suggesting that they took their social and environmental responsibilities seriously (see ENVIRONMENTAL MANAGEMENT).

In addition to these *ad hoc* experiments by organizations, both the accounting profession and governments in a variety of countries contributed to debates in this area and mandated for the reporting of some aspects of social and environmental information. For example, data about charitable and political donations is currently required by UK companies legislation. This information could be seen to reflect corporate philanthropic attitudes and may also indicate how (in particular) companies seek to influence the political environment. Data on the numbers and pay rates of women and racial minorities employed can also be found in company annual reports, especially in the USA, where equality issues have had a high priority since the 1960s (see GENDER AND ACCOUNTING; GENDER AND ORGANIZATIONS).

Likewise, during the 1980s it was common to find in corporate annual reports data about employment practices adopted in South Africa by corporations which had operations in that country. In this phase of SEAAR, environmental information was found in annual reports but this type of information generally took second place to employment disclosures.

Interest in SEAAR waned during the 1980s as much of the West moved towards the right on the political spectrum. At this time the belief that, in generating profits, organizations were fully discharging their accountability to society, seemed to dominate the business and political agenda. As a result, the consideration of social and environmental factors was largely seen as irrelevant and attention generally switched away from SEAAR (ironically provision of information on SEAAR themes did continue to grow – in company annual reports if nowhere else). In this climate, it tended to be newer uses of SEAAR that attracted attention. The most popular (in terms of numbers of reports produced) was the value-added statement. In this statement the conventional profit and loss account was restated to show who received the 'value added' by the firm. Employee costs, therefore, became a distribution of value added rather than being an expense. This, in itself, reflected the idea that employees are stakeholders in the financial success of an organization. This era also coincided with the closure of many manufacturing plants, particularly in the UK, which spawned another type of social account: the plant closure audit (see DOWNSIZING). What these audits sought to demonstrate was that while it may be financially advantageous to close a particular plant, such an action has a negative impact upon the local area in terms of a rise in unemployment (and the need for the government to pay various benefits as a result), loss of business to local suppliers (with the potential knock on effect of these suppliers going out of business) and social costs which arise from the likes of the preceding impacts (such as increased family breakdown and higher levels of illness of various types). The idea behind plant closure audits was to highlight the wider impacts of plant closure decisions and, especially, to demonstrate how these decisions incurred costs for local and national governments.

When SEAAR re-emerged in the 1990s it was the environmental impact of corporate activity which was the main area of concern. The growth of environmental accounting and reporting continued for much of the 1990s but towards the end of this period social issues were once again recognized as being an area of concern when evaluating corporate behaviour. Social issues have also been reintroduced by virtue of the fact that sustainable development has become an important issue for corporations, amongst others (see below for likely future trends and developments).

In summary, this very brief historical review has provided a glimpse of the array of subject areas of SEAAR. Further, the point has been made that the prevailing political climate in any particular country will help define those areas of SEAAR which are found to be popular at any particular point in time.

3 Current issues in SEAAR

SEAAR can be seen to cover a very wide spectrum of information and activities. The area is currently dominated by environmental accounting. In this section the elements of environmental accounting will be briefly reviewed before turning to look at emerging areas in social accounting.

Environmental accounting

Environmental accounting can be thought of as comprising four sub-areas. First, conventional accounting has had to incorporate situations where environmental issues impact upon items in the financial accounts. For example, identification of contingent liabilities (most often for possible future land remediation costs), the extent to which environmental concerns affect asset value or reduce assets' useful lives and the separate disclosure of material items arising from environmental factors have exercised the accounting profession. Further, the financial auditor's job is affected by the environmental agenda. For example, auditors have to be able to assess the extent to which environmental problems cause going concern problems for an entity.

Auditors also have to assess whether or not environmental provisions, for example, are properly established.

Second, management accounting practices have been modified to enable organizations to be more sensitive to environmental concerns. Accounting information is used by organizations as they make decisions about how best to achieve their objectives. The environmental agenda places demands on organizations which they have to identify and manage. Accounting techniques, therefore, also need to be sensitive to environmental elements. For example, investment appraisal techniques may require modification in order to ensure that likely environmental costs and benefits from various options are incorporated into decisions. Budgeting processes may need to be amended to ensure environmental improvements sought are adequately funded and supported. Product costing procedures may also be used to ensure that products bear the full costs of, for example, waste disposal related to them. Further, organizations have developed environmental reviews and audits to assess their environmental impacts and their exposure to financial risk arising from the environmental agenda. All these types of environmental accounting are designed to ensure that an organization can identify issues which may impact upon its operations.

The third area of environmental accounting activity involves environmental reporting (see ENVIRONMENTAL MANAGEMENT). In this area, organizations provide information about their impacts on the environment in stand-alone environmental reports or as part of the annual report and accounts package. Some countries have made environmental reporting mandatory. For example, Australia, Denmark, the Netherlands, Spain and Sweden all have some form of mandatory reporting for large corporate entities. In other countries, for example the UK, there are increasing levels of voluntary environmental reporting. The development of environmental reporting in the UK has been supported by an environmental reporting awards scheme (run by the Association of Chartered Certified Accountants, one of the UK's accountancy bodies) and similar schemes now operate across a number of European countries. A number of the largest companies worldwide produce environmental reports of some sort with the motivation and ability to produce such a report being linked in many minds to an ability to maintain effective control of an organization's activities.

Finally, accounting for sustainable development is usually included as a subset of environmental accounting. It is, however, in this area that social and environmental concerns combine and this area will be discussed in the likely future trends and development section. See Gray and Bebbington (2000) for more detail on how companies have sought to develop environmental accounting.

Social accounting

In addition to the above environmental accounting activities, social accounting activities appear to comprise three main areas which are of particular interest at the moment. First, of major interest is the practice of ethical investment. An investment could be said to be ethical where there is some social and/or environmental criteria applied as part of the investment screening process or where the shareholder actively engages with investee companies to encourage better social and environmental performance. Corporations which are involved in tobacco or alcohol manufacture, who make arms or who publish pornography are usually excluded from ethical funds as their products are seen to be socially harmful. Likewise, companies which have poor social or environmental records are likely to be shunned. Poor social records, for example, could related to treatment of customers, suppliers and employees. That is, organizations' interactions with their stakeholders will impact upon their desirability from an ethical investment point of view. Some ethical investors may not avoid poorly performing companies, *per se*, but will seek to help those organizations deal with their shortcomings in social and environmental performance (see ORGANIZATIONAL PERFORMANCE). Social (and environmental) reporting is an important source of information for these ethical investors.

The second broad area of social accounting involves the design, implementation and operation of social bookkeeping and social audit

systems. In a similar manner to other information systems, these information systems collect social data about an organization's activities and this helps evaluate the quality of the organization's interactions with its stakeholders (see Gray *et al.*, (1997) for a summary of the major innovations in this area). This area is in an early stage of development but is gaining ground rapidly as organizations attempt to understand what their social responsibilities really involve.

Finally, as with environmental reporting, there has been a long history of social disclosures in company annual reports (see also the history of SEAAR section). More recently, stand-alone social reports are being produced by large corporations who are, it would appear, seeking to be transparent about how they interact with their stakeholders. Information from social bookkeeping systems and/or data produced from some sort of social audit can be used to produce social reports. This is an area, along with that of accounting for sustainable development, which is likely to develop significantly in the future.

When thinking about SEAAR it is useful to distinguish between who prepares the relevant information and for whose consumption it is prepared. Table 1 illustrates the various combinations of preparers and consumers which exist. Clearly the reliability and credibility of the data produced will vary according to the preparer, the intended consumer and whether there is independent assurance on that information (some social and environmental data will be auditable while some may be very subjective). Further information on any area listed in Table 1 can be found in Gray *et al.* (1996), which is the core text in this area.

4 Likely future trends and developments

SEAAR practice has always been affected by shifts in societal attitudes and priorities. For example, the pattern of development of SEAAR noted in the brief history of the area reflected political changes taking place over time. It should be no surprise that as a result of the swing to the political right during the 1980s, SEAAR largely disappeared from view. Likewise, when global concern for the

Table 1 Different approaches to SEAAR

Report for the consumption of	Report compiled by	
	Internal participants	*External participants*
Internal participants	• Social accounts • Programme evaluation • Attitudes audit • Indicators • Compliance audit • Environmental audit and accounting	• Quango Reports e.g. Health and Safety Her Majesty's Inspectorate of Pollution Environmental Protection Agency Water pollution regulators • Environmental consultants • Waste and energy audits
External participants	• Social accounts • Social reports Narrative Quantitative Qualitative Financial • Compliance audit • Mission statements • Environmental performance report	• Social Audit Ltd • Counter Information Services • New Consumer • Consumers Association • Friends of the Earth • Greenpeace • Journalists • Ethical investment/Ethical Information Research • Information Service • Social audits

Source: Extracted from Gray *et al.* (1996)

state of the environment began to develop in the early 1990s environmental accounting came to the fore. Likely future trends and developments, therefore, will be dictated by changing political and social priorities. Of particular importance currently, and likely to dominate the policy agenda in the future, is the issue of sustainable development. It is this area on which this section concentrates. A focus on sustainable development includes social accounting, auditing and reporting, and also reinforces the importance of environmental accounting and reporting.

The Brundtland Report (United Nations World Commission on Environment and Development 1987) first brought sustainable development to worldwide media attention. Sustainable development was defined as 'development which meets the needs of the present without compromising the ability of future generations to meet their own needs' (1987: 8). Sustainable development was also at the core of the Earth Summit in Rio in 1992 and is

currently believed to be the key to resolving the current environmental difficulties which the globe faces (see ACCOUNTING IN THE EMERGING COUNTRIES).

Sustainable development is not only concerned with environmental security. Implicit within the above definition of sustainable development is the need to meet the needs of all people alive today (as well as their descendants). At present this is not happening worldwide, so consideration of social issues and economic arrangements are also important when considering sustainable development.

SEAAR could be thought of as addressing itself to the concerns of sustainable development: environmental security (also known as eco-efficiency) and social justice (also known as eco-justice). It is impossible, however, to split social and environmental outcomes of business activity from the economic performance of an entity. This is because economic activity drives the social and environmental outcomes of organizations. Conventional ac-

Table 2 Roles of SEAAR in accounting for the pursuit of sustainability

Improvement within current economic orthodoxy (reducing unsustainability/'weak' sustainability)

Eco-efficiency issues	*Eco-justice issues*
• European Management and Audit Scheme accounting – for wastes, efficiency, energy, pollution etc. ('Pollution Prevention Pays') • Reworking investment appraisal methods • Contingent liabilities, asset revaluations and other financial reporting issues • Tellus Institute methodology • Basic environmental reporting	• Employee and employment reporting, information for collective bargaining • Value-added statements • Bilan Social (a French employee account) • Community reporting • Stakeholder analysis

Recognition of the demands of sustainability ('strong' sustainability)

Eco-efficient issues	*Eco-justice issues*
• Sustainable cost calculation and reporting • Full cost accounting (European Commission's Fifth Action Programme): • Advanced environmental and sustainability reporting (including Life Cycle Assessment and Okobilanz) – accountability and transparency	• Full social reporting and social bookkeeping systems • External social audits • Transparency on transfer pricing and resource aquisition issues • Accountability and transparency

counting depicts the economic outcomes of an organization's activities and along with SEAAR may provide a glimpse of the extent to which an organization is moving towards or away from sustainable development. This idea of three accounts (economic, social and environmental) is behind Elkington's (1997) 'triple bottom line' for business as they seek to tackle the concerns of sustainable development.

Table 2 outlines how SEAAR could be seen to be contributing to sustainable development. The split in the table reflects two ends of a possible spectrum of views on sustainable development. One of the problems in assessing the extent to which sustainable development has been achieved is that no one knows what sustainable development would entail. What we do know, however, is that current operations are not sustainable. The 'weak'/'strong' continuum is designed to address this inherent uncertainty. The top tier describes a 'weak' sustainability position. This is where social and environmental problems are seen to be of concern but are assumed to be able to be resolved relatively easily. In contrast, a 'strong' sustainability position sees the prob-lems as being of a more fundamental nature (see Bebbington and Thomson (1996) for a greater analysis of this distinction).

The elements listed here are various social and environmental techniques. Some of these were specifically discussed in section 3 above. Other techniques are newer and more experi-mental SEAAR techniques which started to be developed late in the 1990s. One such area is full cost accounting (FCA).

FCA is an attempt to identify costs associ-ated with a particular product, process or en-tity which are not fully reflected in the accounts of that entity. Rather, these costs are external to that organization. These costs, however, are real and fall either on the envi-ronment or on individuals and groups other than the company which generated the im-pacts. A lack of information about the full cost implications of economic activities has re-sulted in negative impacts of those activities being excluded from the decision-making process within the organization. Environ-mentally and socially bad outcomes are not accounted for at the point where these bad out-comes are generated. As a result, we experi-ence the current social and environmental problems which led to the idea of sustainable development being important. FCA attempts to remedy this by linking external costs to business activities. This area is very much in a fledgling stage of development but much work is being, and is likely to continue to be, done. FCA does not, as of the year 2000, encompass the social issues of sustainable development, and in this area innovative work is urgently needed.

5 Conclusion

SEAAR is often described as being the mirror image of conventional accounting practice in that it is concerned with areas of corporate impact (social and environmental) that conventional accounting fails to capture or fails to capture completely. Further, SEAAR is directed not only at financial stakeholders but also at other stakeholders. In communicating with these stakeholders, an organization implicitly accepts that it has an accountability relationship with those stakeholders and is responsible for its impacts on those stakeholders. SEAAR, therefore, plays a role in determining how society defines its relationship with corporate entities and in influencing behaviour both inside and outside such entities.

JAN BEBBINGTON
UNIVERSITY OF ABERDEEN

DAVID COLLISON
UNIVERSITY OF DUNDEE

ROB GRAY
UNIVERSITY OF GLASGOW

Further reading

(References cited in the text marked *)

* Bebbington, Jan and Thomson, Ian (1996) *Business Conceptions of Sustainable Development and the Implications for Accountancy*, London: Association of Chartered Certified Accountants. (This research report introduces the background to accounting and sustainable development.)
* Elkington, John (1997) *Cannibals with Forks: The Triple Bottom Line of 21st Century Business,* Oxford: Capstone. (A book which sets out the crucial elements for business to consider with respect to sustainable development.)

Gray, Rob (forthcoming) 'The social accounting project and accounting organizations and society: privileging engagement, imaginings, new accountings and pragmatism over critque?', *Accounting, Organizations and Society.* (An academically oriented review of the social accounting literature from 1975 until 2000 along with an evaluation of what may be learned from such work.)
* Gray, Rob and Bebbington, Jan (2000) *Accounting for the Environment*, 2nd edn, London: Sage. (Examines how accountants and the tools of accountancy can be used to assist organizations' response to the environmental agenda.)
Gray, Rob, Collison, David and Bebbington, Jan (1998) 'Environmental and social accounting and reporting', in *Financial Reporting Today: Current and Emerging Issues*, London: Institute of Chartered Accountants in England and Wales. (A summary of SEAAR for accounting practitioners.)
* Gray, Rob, Owen, David and Adams, Carol (1996) *Accounting and Accountability: Changes and Challenges in Corporate Social and Environmental Reporting*, London: Prentice Hall. (A theoretical and practical book examining the history and current developments in social accounting and reporting practice.)
* Gray, Rob, Dey, Colin, Owen, Dave, Evans, Richard and Zadek, Simon (1997) 'Struggling with the praxis of social accounting: stakeholders, accountability, audits and procedures', *Accounting, Auditing and Accountability Journal* 10 (3): 325–64. (An academic paper which reviews social accounting and social auditing practice and problems.)
* United Nations World Commission on Environment and Development (1987) *Our Common Future (The Brundtland Report)*, Oxford: Oxford University Press. (A report which summarizes the concerns which lead to the sustainable development policy goal and a consideration of what sustainable development requires.)

Further resources

Centre for Social and Environmental Accounting Research, Department of Accountancy and Finance, University of Glasgow, 65–71 Southpark Avenue, Glasgow, G12 8LE, Scotland. (Important contact in the area.)

See also: ACCOUNTING; ACCOUNTING IN THE EMERGING COUNTRIES; BUSINESS ETHICS; DOWNSIZING; ENVIRONMENTAL MANAGEMENT; GENDER AND ACCOUNTANCY; GEN-

DER AND ORGANIZATIONS; GENDER DIVERSITY IN ORGANIZATIONS; GLOBALIZATION; GLOBALIZATION AND SOCIETY; INTERNATIONAL MONETARY FUND; MULTINATIONAL CORPORATIONS; ORGANIZATION BEHAVIOUR; ORGANIZATIONAL PERFORMANCE; WORLD BANK; WORLD TRADE ORGANIZATION

Society: see GLOBALIZATION AND SOCIETY

Solow, Robert M. (1924–)

1 Biographical data
2 Main contributions
3 Assessment

Personal background

- born 24 August 1924, in New York City
- 1940–2 and 1945–50 studied at Harvard University (BA, 1947; MA, 1949; PhD 1951)
- 1942–5 military service in US Army
- 1950–8 Assistant and then Associate Professor of Statistics, Massachusetts Institute of Technology
- from 1958 Professor and then Institute Professor of Economics, Massachusetts Institute of Technology
- 1987, Nobel Prize for Economics

Major works

'A contribution to the theory of economic growth' (1956)
'Technical progress and the aggregate production function' (1957)
Linear Programming and Economic Analysis (with R. Dorfman and P.A. Samuelson) (1958)
'Analytical aspects of anti-inflation policy' (with P.A. Samuelson) (1960)
Capital Theory and the Rate of Return (1963)
'Output, employment and wages in the short run', *Quarterly Journal of Economics* (with J. Stiglitz) (1968)
Growth Theory: An Exposition (1970)

Summary

Though he has been involved in a variety of contributions to economics, Solow's most influential work has been on the theory of economic growth. Within this field, he has made three main contributions. The first is the formulation of the neo-classical growth model. His paper, 'A contribution to the theory of economic growth' (1956) is one of the most widely cited articles of all time. The following year he published pioneering work on estimating the rate of technical progress – the so-called Solow residual. He was also a major participant in the 'two Cambridges' controversy over the measurement of capital and the logical coherence of the concept of the aggregate production function. In recent years he has been a staunch defender of Keynesian economics, becoming involved in the attempt to construct a theory of unemployment that has respectable microeconomic foundations.

1 Biographical data

Solow describes himself as the last of the generation of economists that became interested in the subject because of what happened during the 1930s. As he puts it, 'everyone in Brooklyn in the 1930s was interested in economics' (1990: 182). He went to Harvard as an undergraduate, and after three years in the US army was introduced to mathematical economics by Wassily Leontief. His Ph.D. thesis involved modelling the size-distribution of incomes as the result of a stochastic process involving movements into and out of employment. Having taken courses in mathematical statistics at Columbia, given by Abraham Wald, he obtained a position teaching statistics at MIT in 1950. While there he taught courses in business cycles, from which he was led into macroeconomics and the theory of economic growth, in which his major contributions to economics lie.

In 1960, following Kennedy's election as President, Solow was invited to join the Council of Economic Advisers. He was one of the authors of the 1962 *Economic Report* by the Council, which advocated, among other measures, a sustained fiscal expansion to bring the economy up to full employment. This Keynesian position was also found in a widely-read paper Solow wrote together with Paul Samuelson in 1960, which established the idea of the Phillips curve as a stable trade-off between inflation and unemployment that could be used as the basis for macroeconomic policy making: policy makers had to choose, on the basis of political or other criteria, between low unemployment and low inflation (see SAMUELSON, P.A.). In recent work Solow has continued to defend Keynesian economics and maintains a sceptical attitude towards the theoretical purism of the new classical macroeconomics.

2 Main contributions

The neo-classical growth model

Prior to Solow's work the standard model of economic growth was the Harrod–Domar model. This had three key variables: the savings ratio (s); the capital–output ratio (v) and the growth rate of the labour force adjusted for technical progress (n). It is easy to show that in equilibrium $n = s/v$. The problem this was seen to create was that these three variables are determined by completely different factors – saving depends on households' attitudes towards present and future consumption; the capital–output ratio on technology, and the rate of growth of population on a range of mostly non-economic factors. There was thus no reason why the Harrod–Domar equation should be satisfied.

Solow's solution to this problem (independently discovered by Trevor Swan) was to argue that the capital–output ratio would depend on relative factor prices – the ratio of the cost of capital to the cost of labour (see CAPITAL, COST OF; HUMAN CAPITAL; LABOUR MARKETS). If the population were growing faster than the capital stock, capital would become scarce, and the price of capital would rise relative to the price of labour. Firms would adopt less capital-intensive techniques and the capital–output ratio would fall. On the other hand, if the rate of population growth were too low, labour would become scarce, the price of labour would rise, and the capital–output ratio would rise. In short, the price mechanism, operating through supply and demand, would ensure that the economy converged on a balanced growth path.

There are a number of reasons why Solow's growth model was so successful:

1 The model could be summarized with a simple, elegant diagram that could easily be taught to students. Once the diagram was understood, various policy issues could be analysed simply by shifting curves in the diagram.

2 More important, the model provided a wealth of possibilities for theoretical research. The model could be extended to two sectors (producing capital goods and consumption goods); government spending and money could be added; the savings ratio could be explained in terms of intertemporal optimization by households; the possibility of unemployment in the short run could be introduced; and the assumptions concerning technical progress and technology could be changed. It thus provided the basis for an entire research programme, one of the reasons why Solow's article has been so widely cited.

3 Solow, as explained below, linked the model to a simple way of measuring technical progress.

4 The fundamental reason for the model's success, however, was that it was a miniature general equilibrium model. Though the model was simple in that there was only one product and two homogeneous factors of production (labour and capital), it none the less bore a family resemblance to the more general models made popular by Hicks, and analysed more rigorously by Samuelson, Arrow, Debreu and others. General competitive equilibrium was becoming the generally accepted organizing principle for economic theory, and the Solow growth model fitted into that framework. It soon became, for many economists, the 'obvious' way to think of the problem of economic growth (see ARROW, K.J.; HICKS, J.R.; SAMUELSON, P.A.).

Measuring technical progress

One of the key questions concerning economic growth is the extent to which the observed growth in output per head is caused by capital accumulation, and how much is due to technical progress. Solow answered this question using the aggregate production function that was central to the neo-classical growth model. This can be written $Q = A(t)f(K, L)$ where Q is the quantity of output, K the quantity of capital, L the quantity of labour and t is time. A is a multiplicative constant, assumed to increase over time and the function f exhibits positive but diminishing marginal products. It captures the idea that over time the quantity of output that can be obtained from given inputs of capital and labour increases, the main reason for this being technical progress. Given this framework, the growth of output can be divided into three components: the contributions of capital and labour and the rise in A.

Solow's method for calculating the growth rate of A involved estimating the contributions of capital and labour to the growth of output, and then subtracting these from the overall growth of output. To do this he observed that, given perfect competition, the prices of capital and labour will equal their marginal products. For example, the wage rate will equal the marginal product of labour – the increase in output that would occur if one extra unit of labour were employed – otherwise firms would have an incentive either to hire more labour (if the marginal product exceeded the wage) or to lay off labour (if it were less than the wage). Given this, it follows that:

$$\frac{\dot{Q}}{Q} = \frac{\dot{A}}{A} + w_k \frac{\dot{K}}{K} + w_L \frac{\dot{L}}{L}$$

where w_L and w_K are the shares of profits and wages in output. All the variables in this equation apart from $\dot{A}/A$ are observable, which means that $\dot{A}/A$ can be calculated as the residual – as what is left over when the contributions of capital and labour are deducted from the growth rate of output.

Given that the shares of the two factors must amount to one, this equation can be rewritten as:

$$\frac{\dot{q}}{q} = \frac{\dot{A}}{A} + w_K \frac{\dot{k}}{k}$$

where $q = Q/L$ is output per worker (labour productivity) and $k = K/L$ is capital per worker. This shows that the growth of labour productivity can be decomposed into two elements: the part due to increased capital per worker, and the part due to outward shifts in the production function. Applying this framework to US data for the period 1909–49, Solow came to the conclusion that, of the doubling of labour productivity that had taken place during this period, 80 per cent was due to outward shifts in the production function (technical progress) and only 20 per cent was due to capital accumulation. Though Solow recognized that technical progress might be linked to capital accumulation (new techniques have to be 'embodied' in new capital goods) this was a surprisingly low figure for the contribution of capital accumulation to economic growth.

Solow's approach has become the standard method for estimating technical progress, the most elaborate application being that of Edward Dennison and his associates. The 'Solow residual', otherwise known as 'multi-factor' or 'total-factor' productivity, has been used, for example, to make sense of the productivity shocks of the 1970s when rising energy prices were believed to have reduced the growth rate of productivity. Though it has become the standard method and an invaluable tool for analysing productivity growth, however, Solow's residual has been strongly criticized on a number of grounds.

1 It is a residual, and as such includes not only technical progress but changes in utilization rates, measurement errors and a range of other factors. These problems are particularly severe in the short run.
2 The use of factor shares as weights presumes perfect competition. If product markets are not perfectly competitive, wage and profit rates will not measure marginal products, and the estimates of the contributions of capital and labour will be incorrect.
3 The concept of a production function, on which Solow's approach relies, has been questioned on theoretical grounds, the subject of the next section.

The 'two Cambridges' controversy

In 1953, Joan Robinson threw down a challenge to the economics profession. She argued that the concept of a production function relating output to inputs of capital and labour was incoherent. The quantity of capital, K, was required simultaneously to perform two functions: it was a measure of the physical stock of capital goods, and it was a measure of the value of capital goods on which profit rates were calculated. Robinson argued that no index could perform these two functions, for if the stock of capital goods were unchanged, changes in the rate of profit (or the wage rate) would cause changes in relative prices that would, in general, lead to changes in the value of the capital stock. Although Robinson's target was marginal productivity theories such as found in J.R. Hicks' *The Theory of Wages* (1933), Solow's neo-classical growth model was clearly vulnerable to such criticism. Solow, in a series of articles in the 1950s and early 1960s, sought to respond to this critique, with its destructive implications for much economic theory. One of his most imaginative attempts to find a way round Robinson's argument was contained in *Capital Theory and the Rate of Return* (1963). Here he argued that the neo-classical theory could be developed without mention of a quantity of capital: the rate of profit could be derived as a rate of return on *investment*. This involves comparing the cost of investment (the consumption that has to be given up in order to undertake it) with the additional consumption that can be obtained if the investment is undertaken. It was soon shown, however, that this reformulation of the question, illuminating as it was, did not circumvent Robinson's challenge.

Solow's attitude in this controversy provides a good illustration of his attitude towards economic theory. While not spurning theoretical rigour, Solow has always been more concerned to construct simple models that capture the essence of important problems. There might be theoretical problems with the concept of capital or with the Solow residual as a measure of technical progress, but they can none the less be useful, shedding light on important economic problems.

Other contributions

Though his major contributions lie in the theory of economic growth and technical progress, he has made important contributions, often with colleagues, in other areas. His article, with Samuelson (1960), on the Phillips curve has already been mentioned. In 1968, with Joseph Stiglitz, Solow published a pioneering work on the determination of output and employment in the short run. This paper took as its starting point the observation that prices and wages respond slowly to changes in demand and supply, and that as a result markets will typically not be in equilibrium. Out of equilibrium, output and employment will be the minimum of supply and demand, and in such a system an economy may well get stuck in a position of less than full employment (see EMPLOYMENT AND UNEMPLOYMENT, ECONOMICS OF). Though such models were, for a while, fashionable, this paper 'fell with a dull thud' (Solow 1990: 195). More widely recognized is Solow's earlier work on the theory of production. *Linear Programming and Economic Analysis* (1958), written with Robert Dorfman and Paul Samuelson, showed how many economic problems, notably the theory of production, could be analysed using techniques of linear programming (see LINEAR PROGRAMMING). In a paper with K.J. Arrow, H.B. Chenery and B.S. Minhas (1961), Solow developed the widely used constantelasticity-of-substitution production function (sometimes known as the ACMS production function).

3 Assessment

The major criticism of Solow's work on economic growth is that it fails to say much about the key questions concerning productivity growth: Why do some countries grow faster than others? What causes high growth rates? His 1956 model shows how an economy might, given competitive markets, adjust to a given growth rate, not what determines that growth rate. His work on technical progress provides a system of growth accounting, not an explanation of productivity growth. His work has, however, provided the conceptual framework within which a generation of economists has sought to analyse the problem.

Solow has distinguished between two categories of economist, system-builders and puzzle-solvers, placing himself squarely in the latter category. Though primarily an economic theorist, he has shown a preference for simple theories that can readily be related to clearly-identifiable real work problems. It is because it has proved useful, not because it can be derived rigorously using formal aggregation theorems, that he defends work using aggregate production functions. He defends models in which prices and wages are inflexible on the grounds that they capture important aspects of real-world macroeconomic problems, even though they lack the rigorous microeconomic foundations that have recently become fashionable. He adopts what he describes as an 'opportunistic' approach towards doing economics, in the sense that he is 'unwilling to sacrifice potentially useful insights on the altar of methodological purity' (Solow 1992: 273).

ROGER BACKHOUSE
UNIVERSITY OF BIRMINGHAM

Further reading

(References cited in the text marked *)

* Arrow, K.J., Chenery, H.B., Minhas, B.S. and Solow, R.M. (1961) 'Capital–labor substitution and economic efficiency', *Review of Economics and Statistics* 43: 225–50. (The paper that first put forward the constant elasticity of substitution production function.)
* Dorfman, R., Samuelson, P.A. and Solow R.M. (1958) *Linear Programming and Economic Analysis*, New York: McGraw-Hill. (Shows how many economic problems can be analysed using techniques of linear programming.)
* Hicks, J.R. (1933) *The Theory of Wages*, London: Macmillan. (Analysis of income distribution in terms of an aggregate production function and marginal productivity.)
* Samuelson, P.A. and Solow, R.M. (1960) 'Analytical aspects of anti-inflation policy', *American Economic Review* 50 (Papers and proceedings): 177–94. (Posed the problem of unemployment and inflation policy in terms of the Phillips curve tradeoff.)
* Solow, R.M. (1956) 'A contribution to the theory of economic growth', *Quarterly Journal of Economics* 70: 65–94. (Article from which the modern neo-classical theory of economic growth descends.)
  Solow, R.M. (1957) 'Technical progress and the aggregate production function', *Review of Economics and Statistics* 39: 312–20. (Article that is the source of the literature on growth accounting, concerned with estimating the contributions of various factors to economic growth.)
* Solow, R.M. (1963) *Capital Theory and the Rate of Return*, Amsterdam: North Holland. (Possibly his most creative contribution to the 'two Cambridges' controversy.)
  Solow, R.M. (1970) *Growth Theory: An Exposition*, Oxford: Oxford University Press. (Series of lectures in which Solow provided an exposition of the theory of economic growth as it had developed since his original article on the subject.)
* Solow, R.M. (1990) 'My evolution as an economist', in W. Breit and R.W. Spencer (eds), *Lives of the Laureates: Ten Nobel Economists*, 2nd edn, Cambridge, MA and London: MIT Press. (Solow's (very readable) autobiography.)
* Solow, R.M. (1992) 'Notes on coping', in M. Szenberg (ed.) *Eminent Economists: Their Life Philosophies*, Cambridge: Cambridge University Press. (This very short piece reveals something of Solow's attitude towards his work.)
* Solow, R.M. and Stiglitz, J. (1968) 'Output, employment and wages in the short run', *Quarterly Journal of Economics* 82: 537–60. (Pioneering work on the determination of output and employment in the short run.)

See also: ARROW, K.J.; BUSINESS CYCLES; HICKS, J.R.; KEYNES, J.M.; MARKET STRUCTURE AND CONDUCT; NEO-CLASSICAL ECONOMICS; SAMUELSON, P.A.

Soros, George (1930–)

Personal background

- born 1930 in Budapest, Hungary, to Tiviador Soros, a Jewish lawyer who survived internment in Siberia from 1917 to 1921
- fled communist Hungary in 1947 when he was 17 and made his way to Paris; worked as a farm hand, house painter and railway porter
- began his studies in 1949 at the London School of Economics (LSE)
- graduated with a BS in Economics in 1952
- worked at the Singer and Friedlander merchant bank in London
- moved to New York in 1956; his parents followed him in 1957 and he supported them after their Coney Island coffee shop failed
- began as a Wall Street researcher and worked his way up to international money manager
- in 1963, became vice-president of Arnhold and S. Bleichroeder, specializing in foreign securities and investments
- in 1969, formed a business partnership with James B. Rogers, Jr, which became Soros Fund Management in 1973; Rogers left the business in 1981
- in 1973, became president of Soros Fund Management
- in 1998, left day-to-day management of his funds to focus on philanthropy

Major works

The Alchemy of Finance (1987)
Underwriting Democracy (1991)
Soros on Soros: Ahead of the Curve (1995)
Open Society: From Global Capitalism to Global Democracy (2000)

1 Introduction

The Soros family was Jewish and survived the Nazi regime in Budapest during the Second World War by using false names and identity papers. As a student at the LSE George Soros 'was influenced by the British philosopher Karl Popper, who argued that Communism and Fascism were philosophically linked and who championed the open, democratic system' (Hedges 1990).

Soros is active on a number of boards, including Fairchild Industries, Helsinki Watch, Americas Watch, the International League for Human Rights, the Brookings Council, and AIESEC (Cuff 1987; *PR Newswire* 1987). 'His philanthropies include the Open Society Inc., The Soros Foundation, the Fund for Reform and Opening of China, Inc. and the Glasnost Foundation Inc.' (*PR Newswire* 1987). He has received honorary doctoral degrees from the New School for Social Research, the University of Oxford, the Budapest University of Economics and Yale University. In addition, he was awarded the Laruea Honoris Causa by the University of Bologna for his global efforts to promote democratic societies (*http://www.soros.com* 1998).

Soros is 'an intellectual who could discuss finances in five languages while turning his clients' investments into fortunes' (Scardino 1987). He enjoys playing chess and philosophical debates. He has three children with his first wife, whom he broke up with in 1978 and divorced in 1981. His philanthropic activities began after his 1981 divorce. In 1983, he married Susan Weber, an art historian who is twenty-five years younger than him. The couple have two sons and maintain homes in Manhattan, Long Island and Bedford, New York, as well as London, England (Lycett 1993; Crowley 1994; Hawthorne *et al.* 1994; Smith 1996).

2 Main contribution

Soros spends 'two-thirds of his time and half of his annual income on promoting democracy abroad and a more tolerant society in the United States' (Miller 1997). In 1992 Soros contributed $100 million to support scientists and scientific research in Russia and the former Soviet countries. The donation was made by Soros in an attempt to slow the 'brain drain' which has occurred since the break-up of the Soviet Union and to create what he hopes will become the equivalent of the National Science Foundation in the United States (Southerland and Brown 1992). Also in 1992, Soros provided Bosnian civilians with $50 million to help alleviate their suffering (Miller 1997). 'Soros now runs foundations in 18 central and east European countries that support educational, cultural and economic activities' (Southerland and Brown 1992). His contributions have 'funded Oxford scholarships for Hungarian, Polish and Soviet students' (Hedges 1990). Worldwide, his philanthropic efforts in 1997 employed 1300 people in twenty-four countries coordinated by regional headquarters in New York and Budapest (Miller 1997). Soros is listed as the 'most generous American' according to *Worth Magazine* stating that he has donated $2.62 billion to '… various causes around the world' (Bell 2000).

In 1993, he was the highest-paid executive on Wall Street, earning $1.1 billion or more (*Chicago Tribune* 1994). 'For years he has been a hugely successful money manager and investor, but the $1 billion that he reportedly made in just a few days ... by betting against the British pound [1992] has turned him into a guru – and his investments are mimicked across the world' (Uchitelle 1993). He is, however, not immune to failures: 'George Soros lost $600 million on Feb. 14 [1994] when the yen took a jump he had bet against ... Soros' Quantum Group said the loss took almost 5% of the fund group's $12 billion in assets' (Joy 1994). However, $10,000 invested in Soros's Quantum Fund in 1969 was worth more than $21 million in 1994 (Crowley 1994). 'He [Soros] stepped away from day to day management of his fund company in 1998 to focus on Philanthropy' (Kirkpatrick, 2000). The Soros funds reached a peak value of $22 billion in August, 1998 (Hakim 2000). In April 2000 after the Soros' Quantum fund lost $3 billion in six weeks, he announced that

'…his days of large 'macro' bets were over and he will focus on lower risk strategies' (Cave 2000). 'He warned investors who stick with him to expect lower returns' (Hakim 2000). Soros plans to retire completely from investment management once he has determined that his funds no longer need his guidance (Paterson 2000). There may be a few minor exceptions such as the Clinton Administration selection of Soros to manage a $150 million business development fund for the Balkan region (Phillips 2000).

Soros is an active author. In 1987, Soros published a book on his financial philosophies titled *The Alchemy of Finance*. In this book, he explains his 'theory of reflexivity', which is based on his belief that stock prices are not based on facts but on the attitudes of investors. After incorrectly predicting the 'disintegration of the global capitalist system' in his 1998 book *The Crisis of Global Capitalism: Open Society Endangered*, Soros has responded with a new book *Open Society: From Global Capitalism to Global Democracy* (Kirkpatrick, 2000).

3 Evaluation

According to *Institutional Investor Magazine*, George Soros is 'The World's Greatest Money Manager' (Cuff 1987). Soros also has his share of critics of his approach to both money management and philanthropy. There are some who claim that there is a conflict of interest when Soros invests in countries where he is giving money (Lycett 1993; Miller 1997). A French magistrate has ordered Soros to stand trial in 2001 on charges of insider-trading of Société Générale bank shares in 1988 (*The New York Times* 2000).

Even after the market turmoil that hit the Soros funds, he is personally still worth $5 billion (Crawshaw 2000). In terms of his philanthropy, 'Some say it is too impulsive and mercurial, too arrogant and micromanaged' (Miller 1997). According to Shawcross (1997), 'Soros deliberately courts controversy and publicity, trying to build a platform from which to propagate his views'.

In 1990, Soros stated that his biggest failure was in China, where his multimillion-dollar donations did not stimulate the democratic movement: 'The foundation itself [in China] had become an organ of the security police, ... I thought that I could apply the thinking that I used in Hungary, but the Chinese society has not reached that stage' (Hedges 1990).

He has not let that experience dampen his interest in helping emerging democracies around the globe. For example, in Russia alone, 'His foundation ... spent $25.8 million in 1994 printing textbooks, helping Russian journalists, helping libraries and carrying out other reforms' (Gordon 1995). Over the past decade, Soros 'has spent more than a billion dollars promoting a free press and political pluralism abroad' (Miller 1997). He says, 'I never have regrets about having spent a lot of money trying to make things better' (Miller 1997). Soros plans to spend all of his money by his 80th birthday in 2010 (Crawshaw, 2000). Soros considers himself to be more of a 'philosopher than a money manager' (Scardino 1987).

STEPHEN J. HAVLOVIC
UNIVERSITY OF WISCONSIN – WHITEWATER

Further reading

(References cited in the text marked *)

* Bell, Diane (2000) 'Givers who keep on giving and giving ...', *The San Diego Union-Tribune*, 11 April: B1–2. (Article on top American givers to charity including four from San Diego County.)
* Cave, Andrew (2000) 'Top Soros man Bessent quits to start hedge fund', *The Daily Telegraph*, 9 June: 35. (Article reviews changes affecting the Soros' funds.)
* Crawshaw, Steve (2000) 'George Soros: Who wants to be a billionaire?', *The Independent*, 3 December: Features 6–8. (An interview with Soros that discusses his new book, investments, and philanthropy.)
* *Chicago Tribune* (1994) 'George Soros 1993's highest-paid Wall Street exec, at $1.1 billion', *Chicago Tribune*, Business Section, 16 June: 3. (Discusses the salaries of investment managers.)
* Crowley, Lyle (1994) 'George Soros', *New York Times*, Section 6, 3 April: 26. (Examines his philanthropy, business activities and personal life.)
* Cuff, Daniel F. (1987) 'Top fund manager overcame '81 loss', *New York Times*, Section D, 13 July: 2. (Reviews Soros's money management successes.)
* Gordon, Michael R. (1995) '"Cautiously pessimistic", but investing in Russia', *New York Times*, Section D, 22 December: 1. (Review of George's efforts to stimulate Russian democracy.)
* Hakim, Danny (2000) 'Huge losses move Soros to revamp empire', *The New York Times*, 29 April: A1. (A review of the recent market turmoil and Soros' decision to abandon aggressive investment strategies.)
* Hawthorne, Fran, Carroll, Michael, Conger, Lucy, Cooper, Wendy, Davis, Stephen, Muehring, Kevin, Peltz, Michael and Picker, Ida (1994) 'Why George Soros is Bedford-bound', *Institutional Investor*, April: 13. (Announces his new weekend estate.)
* Hedges, Chris (1990) 'Honoring investing that paid', *New York Times*, Section A, 15 October: 3. (Reviews Soros's investments to support emerging democracies.)
* *http://www.soros.com* (1998) 'About George Soros'. (Provides biographical information.)
* Kirkpatrick, David D. (2000) ''I goofed' on global collapse: Soros', *The Toronto Star*, Section WAB, 13 August. (A review of his 1998 and 2000 books.)
* Joy, Pattie (1994) 'Dow drop', *USA Today*, Money Section, 28 February: 1B. (Announces Soros's loss when he bet against the yen.)
* Lycett, Andrew (1993) 'Soros: Midas or Machiavelli?', *Accountancy* 112, July: 36–40. (Reviews Soros's business ventures and personal life.)
* Miller, Judith (1997) 'A promoter of democracy angers the authoritarians', *New York Times*, Section 1, 12 July: 1. (Examines conflicts between governments in former Soviet states and Soros's foundations.)
* Paterson, Lea (2000) 'Euro has turned the corner, says Soros', *The Times*, 8 December: Business Section. (An interview with Soros on the Euro and the US economy.)
* Phillips, Michael M. (2000) 'U.S. chooses Soros to run Balkans fund', *The New York Times*, 26 July: A16. (Bank abstract information from *The Wall Street Journal*.)
* *PR Newswire* (1987) 'Fairchild elects Soros to board', *PR Newswire*, 10 July. (News release.)
* *Reuters Financial Service* (1996) 'Vinik could team up with George Soros', *Reuters Financial Service*, 1 August. (News release.)
* Scardino, Albert (1987) 'Market turmoil', *New York Times*, Section D, 28 October: 1. (Analyses losses to Soros's Quantum Fund and his investment theories.)

* Shawcross, William (1997) 'Turning dollars into change', *Time Magazine* 150 (9), 1 September. (Discusses Soros's philanthropy.)
* Smith, Dinitia (1996) 'At home with: Susan Soros', *New York Times*, Section C, 7 March: 1. (Interviews George's wife Susan.)
* Soros, George (1987) *The Alchemy of Finance*, Simon & Schuster. (Discusses his theory of the markets and finance.)
* Soros, George (1991) *Underwriting Democracy*, Free Press. (Give his personal perspective on creating democratic societies).
* Soros, George (1995) *Soros on Soros: Ahead of the Curve*, J. Wiley. (Presents his observations on life, politicians and philosophy).
* Soros, G. (2000) *Open Society: From Global Capitalism to Global Democracy*, New York: Little, Brown & Company. (Updated version of his earlier works, but now offering a much more upbeat vision of the future of the global economy.)
* Southerland, Dan and Brown, David (1992) 'Former Soviet Union to get science aid', *Washington Post*, Financial Section, 10 December: B11. (Discusses Soros's philanthropy and personal history.)
* *The New York Times* (2000) 'French trial reportedly ordered for Soros', 23 December: C3. (Associated Press news release on Soros being ordered to stand trial in France for insider-trading.)
* Uchitelle, Louis (1993) 'Europe's currency crisis', *New York Times*, Section D, 2 August: 1. (Examines his influence and leadership as a money manager.)

Further resources

Soros' home page *http://www.soros.com*

See also: BANKING CRISES; EASTERN EUROPE, MANAGEMENT IN; GOLOBALIZATION; RUSSIA, MANAGEMENT IN

South Africa, management in

1 Introduction
2 Context
3 Specific features
4 Conclusion

Overview

South Africa's re-entry into competitive global markets in the 1990s created new managerial challenges. The legacy of apartheid is systematically being eroded, with some 30 per cent of South African managers who are black. Employment discrimination is being replaced by policies and practices aimed at recruiting and developing black managers. Management development, changes in corporate culture and black advancement have become more prominent. Legislation such as the Employment Equity Act (1998) and Promotion of Equality Bill (1999) require employers of more than fifty people to develop an employment equity plan with specific measures to remove discriminatory employment practices.

Following Western approaches to management there is an emphasis on general management at middle to senior levels. These skills are acquired through career path planning experiences such as job rotation, project assignments and cross-functional appointments. General management education programmes such as an MBA or a shorter executive development programme, either at one or more of South Africa's seven business schools, or through international business schools which have recently entered the management education market, are popular. Management consulting firms also play an important role.

Decades of economic isolation have created tough but inward-looking managers in South Africa who are hands-on and results oriented. Managers tend to be individualistic and directive in their styles, with a masculine orientation. Other than in the retail sector, fewer than 20 per cent of managerial jobs are held by women. Managers are appointed to such positions following 5–10 years work experience in a functional discipline or occupation such as engineering. With affirmative action and the impact of external factors, such as globalization, new technology and intense competition, this internal focus has begun to make way for greater internationalization, an export orientation and an opening of business practices to international best practice

1 Introduction

Management work in South Africa has, since the 1990s, been influenced by a fluid and sometimes uncertain political climate (see AFRICA, MANAGEMENT IN). Complexity and change have become standard features of the decision-making process now that simple 'right or wrong' responses of the past no longer work. In the latter 1990s however, greater stability has prevailed and democracy has also been accompanied by higher economic growth, predicted to be around 3 per cent per annum in the early part of the twenty-first century.

There are certain watershed events which have shaped management practices in South Africa since 1970. These include the 1973 Natal strikes for improved working conditions and trade union recognition, the Soweto riots of 1976, the legalization of industrial relations rights and the impact of sanctions and disinvestment in the 1980s. The state of emergency introduced in 1986 created a siege economic strategy with inward-looking managerial practices, and further isolated South African business from international competition and new technology. This mindset made re-entry into world markets in the post apartheid era more difficult, especially for the manufacturing and service sectors. However, several South African firms such as the Old Mutual insurance company, South African Breweries and SAPPI (paper and timber) have now adapted quickly to global challenges and compete successfully in international markets.

2 Context

Labour and political rights

Several factors are important in the evolution of management in South Africa. Rapid growth of the trade union movement since 1980, from less than 10 per cent to over 30 per cent and around 3,272,999 members, has changed the nature of managerial work. The changes have consisted primarily of increasing support for human resource management, fair employment practices and equitable treatment. Authoritarian managerial styles and unilateral decisions have been eroded as expectations increased as apartheid structures were gradually eaten away. Managers have faced demands in which the separability of political and workplace issues is unclear. As a result they have experienced a steep learning curve, being forced into acquiring negotiating skills and getting used to dealing with complex issues (see INDUSTRIAL RELATIONS IN THE EMERGING COUNTRIES).

Socio-economic factors

While a positive increase in economic growth has occurred since 1993, in the decade up to 1993 economic growth averaged at 1 per cent; this compared with a population growth rate of 2.5 per cent and unemployment of over 5.5 million, estimated at nearly 30 per cent of the economically active population. Whereas retrenchment in the 1980s focused primarily on blue collar employees, the 1990s and early 2000s saw job cuts at managerial and professional levels following organizational restructuring, de-layering, downsizing and outsourcing. Rising costs, poor labour and capital productivity and intense competition as South Africa re-enters global markets, coupled with poorer economies of scale and higher wage costs than the Pacific Rim economies, have led to job losses at all levels. Meanwhile, the hoped-for high level of foreign investment necessary for employment creation, has not been attained. Managerial work in South Africa is therefore influenced by a mix of socio-political and labour market factors and the prevailing organizational culture.

The labour market

A structural inequality in the skill profile exists: a shortage of occupationally and managerially skilled workers is contrasted with an excess of unskilled labour. Meanwhile fairly low economic growth and a lack of managerial skills have led to a comparatively low level of spending on training and development. The *World Competitiveness Report* (1999) has indicated, however, that organizational investment in training and development is a decisive competitive factor. In comparison to developed market economies, South Africa's per capita output is one-sixth of Switzerland's, one-fifth of that of the USA and one-quarter of Japan's. Ultimately, labour and capital productivity is a managerial function.

Whilst more than 35 per cent of managers have tertiary educational qualifications, nearly 60 per cent of formal sector employees working for them do not have a high school education. South African companies under apartheid did not invest sufficiently in human capital. This neglect has hampered successful large-scale re-entry into global markets. South Africa is still rated lowly by the World Competitive Report among emerging industrial countries in terms of human resource priorities. Socio-economic and labour market issues remain pressing managerial challenges in the transition to a post-apartheid South Africa. Recently government has relaxed legislative provision on basic conditions of employment to allow greater flexibility for small firms, and is encouraging better education and training through the Skills Development and Employment Equity Acts (1998).

Structural factors

Apartheid created a distorted labour market with economic power concentrated in a few white hands. Economic power was, until recent moves to disaggregate or unbundle large corporations such as Gencor and Barlow Rand, concentrated in eight conglomerates which controlled over 70 per cent of the share capital on the Johannesburg Stock Exchange (see MULTINATIONAL CORPORATIONS). There is also a concentration of managerial control through a system of interlocking directorates where the same person(s) serve on the boards of several corporations. This social closure has limited the upward mobility of black managers and women. However, South Africa's re-entry into the international business community has forced an awareness about its relative competitiveness in the manufacturing and services sectors. Recently, the impetus has also been towards employment equity and diversity at all levels. There have been several black directors appointed to boards of directors. Although less than 15 per cent of South Africa's company directors are black or women, this is likely to change significantly by the year 2005.

3 Specific features

Management styles

Managerial styles reflect both Western values based on individualism and meritocracy and the authoritarian legacy of apartheid (see CULTURE, CROSS-NATIONAL; ORGANIZATION CULTURE). Indigenous models of leadership have slowly begun to emerge. The concept of *ubuntu* (humaneness) underlines traditional group decision making. Transformational leadership styles are exceptional, for example Albert Koopman, former Chief Executive of Cashbuild, a building supply company, and Leon Cohen, former Chief Executive of PG Bison Ltd and Dr Mamphela Ramphele, Vice Chancellor of the University of Cape Town. Managerialism – a focus on administrative systems and risk aversion – has been reinforced by an inward-looking economy. Nonetheless, increasing globalization of markets coupled with rising costs and low productivity has resulted in reassessment of organizational strategies, restructuring and downsizing, and an experimentation with Japanese work methods such as self-directed work teams and employee empowerment through task-level participation and multiskilling. South African management now emphasizes cooperative teamwork and communal decision making, where the core is the group and not the individual. Companies such as Pick 'n Pay in retailing and SA Breweries where significant black advancement has occurred are examples of this new approach. Organizational culture

in South Africa thus reflects the co-existence of both Western and African leadership styles. A synergy of these ostensibly different leadership approaches is part of organizational development in the post-apartheid era. This is evident in black-owned insurance companies such as African Life and Metropolitan Life and in New Africa Investments Ltd (NAIL).

Unfair labour practice jurisprudence has also eroded unilateralism and ensured more participative managerial styles. While managers retain traditional rights to hire and dismiss, how they may do so has changed. Procedural and substantive fairness are a cornerstone of managerial labour relations practice reinforced by the Labour Relations Act (1995), which defines managers as 'employees' and thus entitled to fair treatment such as a proper disciplinary hearing. Traditional managerial styles are increasingly questioned by employees. However, although behavioural change has occurred in this regard, a shift in mindset is important for developing suitable styles for managing diversity.

Managerial culture

Management styles reflect organizational and national cultural patterns (see CULTURE, CROSS-NATIONAL). In South Africa, while achievement is valued, group and organizational conformity is also important. Although little research has occurred on managerial culture in South Africa, a masculine dominance across ethnic groups, is evident, underlined by individualist values and a societal culture with a relatively large power distance between groups. This is based on historical racial disparities. However, an emergent black middle class has begun to occupy decision-making positions in business and government sectors, and this class mobility is likely to have an impact on managerial culture and inform a debate about desirable values, rituals and organizational practices. Managerial ideologies also reflect unitarist ideas – the organization as a 'happy family' or team with organizational loyalty, and conflict avoidance – which are similar to the Japanese notion of industrial familism. Organizational realities in South Africa reflect diversity and pluralism and the procedural regulation of inherent conflicts. The late 1990s has, however, seen a significant move to unbundle or disaggregate large corporations to focus on their core business.

Management development

Management development programmes are run internally in larger organizations (see MANAGEMENT DEVELOPMENT). The Skills Development Act (1998) levies firms 1–1.5 per cent of their payroll cost to encourage investment in human resource development through sectoral education and training authorities (SETAS). Many organizations send managers to MBA programmes and executive development at one or more of South Africa's business schools, international business schools in South Africa, or abroad (see MANAGEMENT EDUCATION IN THE EMERGING COUNTRIES). Average expenditure on training and development is around 2 per cent of salary budgets, with a small number of companies spending around 6 per cent. Of this expenditure, 21 per cent goes on management training. Black management development has been neglected historically, but employment equity policies and programmes have now been introduced in more than 35 per cent of medium and large organizations. These policies seek to remove discriminatory policies and practices and to actively recruit and develop black managers. In terms of the Labour Relations Act (1995) discriminatory employment practices constitute an unfair labour practice.

Creating employment equity in organizations dominated by white males is an important aspect of employment equity. Black empowerment includes both advancement into positions of executive authority and the provision of equity and profit sharing. Most management development programmes set numerical goals based on workforce requirements and labour market supply of relevant occupations. Employers reject quotas in favour of a goals and timetable approach. An important lobby group, the Black Management Forum (BMF), has formulated a blueprint of management development, which stresses the process, and importance, of increasing the supply of suitable managers with requisite skills. This blueprint advocated that by the year 2000, 40 per cent of middle-management positions must be held by black people, 30 per cent of senior management posts and 20 per cent of executive directors. The Employment Equity Act requires employers of more than 50 people to submit employment equity plans with targets, timetables and measures to redress past discrimination.

Subtle discrimination still acts as a barrier to occupational mobility. This is mitigated by pressure to build non-racial organizational structures emanating from trade unions, lobby groups, foreign multinational companies and legislation. However, perceptions of black inferiority have developed a white managerial mindset, which often doubts the ability of black people to perform managerial work. Although higher economic growth coupled with a new political order may stimulate management development efforts, until significant numbers of black people have the decision-making authority to affect organizational outcomes, the corporate culture of South African organizations will change gradually. Nonetheless, a restructuring of the workforce at all levels to reflect a visible non-racial diversity is occurring, for example in parastatal organizations such as Transnet.

The historically small black managerial class is a function of a defunct political dispensation. The presence of black majority government means more emphasis is being placed on the upward mobility of black managerial staff. The questions of employment equity and black advancement are more complex in South Africa than in post-colonial African countries. The upper echelons of state bureaucracy were dominated by an Afrikaner cultural ethos: the civil service elite was predominantly male, but a rapidly increasing proportion are now held by black managers. There is concern among skilled and experienced civil servants that patronage appointments will occur. This has in fact been the case, in reverse, historically.

4 Conclusion

Participative practices are an example of a collective orientation towards motivation and work design. This is more a feature of European and Japanese organizations than the individualism of North American managerial culture. An important question is the extent to which teams with multicultural and interfunctional diversity can be fostered in South African organizations. A shift from a traditional to a flexible organization requires a move away from a command and control style towards cooperation and motivation. Managers will have to learn new principles and practices if South African organizations are to compete effectively. This is also essential because employee expectations and attitudes to work are changing; socio-political change and a workforce which is becoming more educated mean higher levels of expectations for personal growth, fair treatment and better income.

Participative practices are more successful where management has restructured to create a de-layered organization in which authority and responsibility are delegated to lower levels and where employees are empowered through information sharing, knowledge and skills, recognition and rewards, and the opportunity to influence decisions. In South Africa such approaches are increasing and include a range of organizations such as Anglogold, Cape Cabinets, Escom, SA Nylon Spinners, Pick 'n Pay retailers and the Delta Motor Corporation. Although not extensive, flexible work practices, multiskilling and performance-based pay have become issues in the field of human resource management.

There is a need to reduce racial polarization, erode a tradition of adversarialism and nurture a sense of common purpose. The latter requires the visible advancement and economic empowerment of black people in order to create employment equity and the stability necessary for economic growth. The diversity of South African organizations creates an insistent need to find common goals, shared values and foster reconciliation after the divisiveness of apartheid. Raising managerial competence in strategic management, resource utilization, negotiation and operations is vital for organizational effectiveness. Performance improvement, greater accountability and active measures to address racial and gender mixes in the occupation structure are necessary. While management development emphasizes planned interventions, informal experiences often provide meaningful learning. There is no uniform approach to management development. Differing cultural contexts imply that for management initiative to have a lasting effect, integration with corporate objectives, organizational structure and job design, reward systems and corporate culture is necessary.

FRANK M. HORWITZ
UNIVERSITY OF CAPE TOWN, SOUTH AFRICA
AND NANYANG TECHNOLOGICAL
UNIVERSITY, SINGAPORE

Further reading

(References cited in the text marked *)

Adam, H. and Moodley, E. (1993) *The Negotiated Revolution: Society and Politics in a Post-Apartheid South Africa*, Los Angeles, CA: University of California Press. (An insightful and detailed analysis of socio-political developments in South Africa, with reference to the role of business.)

Barker, F. (1999) *The South African Labour Market*, Pretoria: van Schaik. (A useful summary of relevant statistics.)

Blunt, P. and Jones, M. (1993) *Managing Organisations in Africa*, Berlin: Walter de Gruyter. (A rigorous, comprehensive comparative study of management and organizations in African countries.)

Bowmaker-Falconer, A., Horwitz, F.M. and Searll, P. (1994) 'Affirmative action and equal opportunity', *Breakwater Monitor Update* 1: 5–10. (A member publication for participating organizations in a large multisectoral national database of human resource development. The biannual survey covers one million employees.)

Bowmaker-Falconer, A., Horwitz, F., Jain, H. and Tagger, S. (1998) 'Employment equity programmes', *Industrial Relations Journal* 29 (3): 1–12. (An analysis of affirmative action and human resource trends based on a longitudinal study.)

Horwitz, F.M. (1993) 'Elements in participation, teamwork and flexibility in South Africa', *International Journal of Human Resources Management* 4 (4): 917–31. (A study of management culture and innovative human resources practices in three South African companies.)

Horwitz, F.M. (1998) 'The Employment Equality Bill', *South African Labour Bulletin* 22 (3): 80–2. (An analysis of the Bill.)

Horwitz, F.M. and Smith, D. (1998) 'Flexible work practices and human resource management: a comparison of South African and foreign owned companies', *International Journal of Human Resource Management* 9 (4): 590–607. (An empirical study of differing managerial practices.)

Horwitz, F.M., Bowmaker-Falconer, A. and Searll, P. (1995) 'Employment equity, human resource development and institution building in South Africa', *International Journal of Human Resource Management* 6 (3): 671–85. (Focuses on structural and labour market factors associated with employment equity and diversity management in South Africa, based on findings from 130 organizations.)

Human, P. and Horwitz, F.M. (1992) *On the Edge: How South African Companies Cope with Change*, Kenwyn: Juta. (A research project, written in a popular style, involving a large sample of organizations and managers.)

Visser, J. (1994) 'Why South Africa is not a winning nation', *Human Resource Management* 9 (10): 26–8. (A factual and critical look at factors hindering South Africa's international competitiveness.)

* *World Competitiveness Report* (1999) University of Lausanne: World Economic Forum and the Institute for Management Development. (Ranks countries according to various indices such as human resource development.)

See also: AFRICA, MANAGEMENT IN; CULTURE; CULTURE, CROSS-NATIONAL; INDUSTRIAL RELATIONS IN THE EMERGING COUNTRIES; MANAGEMENT EDUCATION IN THE EMERGING COUNTRIES; MULTINATIONAL CORPORATIONS; ORGANIZATION CULTURE

South Korea, management in

1 Organizational structure
2 Managerial processes
3 Human resource management
4 Competitive strategies
5 Trends in management in South Korea

Overview

The spectacular economic success of Korea in the past few decades (and now under a cloud) can be traced to a number of factors, one of which is the competitiveness of Korean companies. The Korean management system has three major sources of influence. The first is Confucianism, which was the state philosophy of Korea for more than 500 years, beginning with the Yi Dynasty in 1392 and ending in 1910 when Korea was annexed by Japan. The profound influence of Confucianism on the values, attitudes and behavioural patterns of Koreans has apparently spilled over into the Korean management system. The second and third sources, Japanese and US influences, are more recent. Korea was a Japanese colony from 1910 to 1945; after the Second World War, influences from the USA outweighed those from Japan until 1965, when Korean–Japanese relations were normalized. Since then, many Korean companies have developed close business ties with both nations. The USA is seen as a key market for exports, while Japan is relied upon as a source of intermediary products needed to manufacture those exports.

Based on these sources of influence and Korea's own historical traditions and experiences, Korean companies have developed their own management system, sometimes known as 'K-type management', that includes top-down decision making, paternalistic leadership, clan management, *inhwa* (harmony-oriented cultural values), flexible lifetime employment, personal loyalty, compensation based on seniority and merit rating, high mobility of workers and expansion through con-glomeration. In spite of various inherent problems and a constant pressure for change, the Korean management system has maintained its own uniqueness (but may be now forced to change). This entry will focus on the organizational structure of Korean companies, their common managerial processes, their competitive corporate strategies and trends towards development and change.

1 Organizational structure

Organizational structure is an important aspect of the Korean management system (see ORGANIZATION STRUCTURE). Structure in Korean terms refers to relatively stable relationships between individuals and sub-units within a given organization. In many ways, organizational structure reflects the management values of Korean culture.

Formal structure

Korean companies are often characterized by a high degree of centralization and formalization. Authority is concentrated in senior levels of managerial hierarchies, with major decisions (especially financial decisions) entailing *kyul-jae*, a formal approval from top levels of management that involves taking many *chops* (personal stamps of approval). The Samsung group in the past used a process of twenty-one *chops*, needing several months to get a project approved; upon taking over the group in 1987, Kun Hee Lee demanded that the number be cut to three (Paisley 1993). The hierarchic structure starts with the chairman, followed by the president, vice president (*busajang*), senior managing director (*junmu*), managing director (*sangmu*), department manager (*bujang*), section manager (*kwajang*) and so on down to the foreman and workers. Korean structures tend to be much more top-down and authoritarian than their counterparts in Japan, for example.

Korean companies usually have a 'tall' hierarchical structure of organization. One outstanding organizational feature of Korean companies is that they normally do not employ personal staff, with the exception of assistants for the group chairman. Other executives tend to be supported by deputies and assistants in line positions rather than as personal staff. This increases the layers of vertical hierarchies conducive to a centralized and tall organizational structure. Another outstanding feature of Korean companies is that their vertical and hierarchical control is supported by strong functional control from staff departments such as planning, finance and personnel. Korean companies attach great importance to functional specialization, allowing the planning and finance departments to exercise functional control under the leadership of the chief executive. Many *chaebols* (large industrial groups; see CHAEBOLS) have a planning and coordination office under the group chairman, that is responsible for allocating major internal resources within the group (Aguilar and Cho 1984). Therefore, many Korean companies have a combined organizational structure placing a vertical concentration of decision-making power at the senior levels of management and a horizontal concentration of functional control in staff departments.

In contrast to the centralized organizational structure and formalized functions, individual jobs are not clearly structured in many Korean companies and do not usually have clear-cut job descriptions. The responsibilities of the individual employees tend to be decided by the supervisor according to the needs of the occasion. Although poorly defined job descriptions can bring about low efficiency from ill-distributed workloads and work redundancy, the managers may also enjoy a high degree of flexibility when adjusting to changing conditions. When the high degree of centralization and formalization is combined with poorly defined work assignments, then it can be seen that the individual manager's ability to obtain the support of others is crucial to work performance.

Generally speaking, the organizational performance of Korean companies is closely related to how effectively the company can overcome the centralized and formalized structure. This can be achieved in a number of ways. Many companies depend heavily on autonomous or temporary organizations such as task teams or special committees. Others take advantage of informal interaction. Highly successful Korean companies tend to use fewer top executives and staff personnel in order to increase delegation of authority while decreasing central control (Lee 1989). Task forces and informal interactions help overcome departmental divisions and enhance organizational flexibility. Authority delegation helps simplify the organizational structure.

Informal structure

The concentration of authority results partly from the fact that ownership and management are not separated in most Korean companies. The owner and family actively participate in the management of most companies, and family and clan members dominate the management structure, as is shown in Table 1. Many Koreans are part of an extended clan or *chiban*, based on blood relationships, that provides broad-based security for family members; the larger the *chiban*, the greater the security for individual members (Song 1990). Business leaders are expected to take care not only of their own immediate family members but also of other relatives. This relationship based on kinship is called *hyul-yun* (literally meaning 'blood related').

Professional executives and managers also form an important power group in Korean companies (see Table 1). In some Korean companies the career managers, who have been promoted during their extended service with the company, can also exert powerful influence on company management through the creation of personal networks within the company and foster them over the years. Many of these managers are initially recruited through open competition from an elite group (*gong-chae*); most Korean companies have been using the *gong-chae* system since the early 1990s. With the passage of time, internally promoted career executives and managers will grow in number and power.

Common geographical and educational ties also play a strong role in the formation of

Table 1 Backgrounds of chaebol executives

	The founder and family members	Professional career managers	Others	Total
Hyundai	7	42	8	57
Samsung	2	28	11	41
LG	7	26	11	44
Daewoo	2	25	25	52
Sungung	3	21	2	26
Sangyong	2	11	8	21
Hankuk Hwayak	1	9	11	21
Total	24	162	0	0

Source: Chang 1988

management and power groups. It is common practice for owners to bring their friends from school and their home town into management. In some Korean companies, top management positions are predominantly filled by those who are from the same geographical area, such as Seoul, the south-western province of Honam, or the south-eastern province of Yeongnam. In other Korean companies, graduates from elite universities such as Seoul National or Yonsei dominate top management. In the past, a graduate with a 'K-S mark' (a degree from Kyunggi High School and Seoul National University) automatically enjoyed a better chance of getting into top management. The relationship with the owner based on geographical ties is called *ji-yun* (region-related) while the relationship with the owner based on school ties is called *hahk-yun* (school-related). Both *ji-yun* and *hahk-yun* tend to constitute a very strong factor in informal relationships, giving common identities, backgrounds and a sense of belonging.

Hyul-yun, or blood relationship, promotes career managers internally while *ji-yun* and *hahk-yun* are important not only in senior-level power group formation but also in the formation of informal cliques or groups at all levels within a Korean company. All three relationships affect the power structure and informal groupings. Family ownership based on *hyul-yun* has been the most important factor affecting the power structure of Korean companies whose ownership and management are not separated. While the power of internally promoted career managers has been increas-

ing with continued management professionalization, power based on *hyul-yun* remains predominant in Korean companies. *Ji-yun* and *hahk-yun* also significantly influence informal groupings and social interactions with these companies.

2 Managerial processes

Leadership and decision making

Owing to the strong influence of family traditions, there is a tendency for Korean corporate leaders, especially founders, to manage on the basis of principles governing the family or clan system. In the traditional Korean family, the father is the unquestioned and respected head. If he wishes, he can wield almost absolute power. The traditional Korean father also has full responsibility to feed the family and decide the future of the children. One legacy of such a family tradition for business leadership in Korean companies is the strong authoritarian style of superiors in the managerial process (see LEADERSHIP). A top-down decision-making style is fairly typical among Korean companies; usually, 80 per cent of the authority lies in the upper management level, with middle or lower management having a very limited authority (Lee and Yoo 1987a). Authoritarian leadership has been a well-accepted managerial norm under the centralized structure of Korean companies, the passive attitude of the subordinates being further conducive to this authoritarian style. The traditional decision-making style has been used more to diffuse responsibility than to reach consensus (De Mente 1991).

Nevertheless, the authoritarian style is not despotic. Corporate leadership in Korean companies is also heavily influenced by a key value of Korean behaviour, *inhwa* (harmony), which is similar to the Japanese *wa*. However, *inhwa* does not emphasize the group element as in *wa*; it emphasizes harmony between unequals in rank, power and prestige (Alston 1989). Korean managers cherish good relations with their subordinates and try to keep the needs and feelings of their subordinates in mind. Another aspect of *inhwa* is that each party has a responsibility to support the other.

This aspect of harmony is evidenced in the decision-making patterns of Korean managers, who try to maintain good relationships with subordinates even if this sometimes means they have to compromise group performance. Korean managers tend to make decisions with the consultation of subordinates. The Korean process of informal consensus formation, *sajeonhyupui*, is similar to that found in Japan (Song 1990), but Korean subordinates are usually reluctant to express their opinions. Subsequently, managers are often expected to understand the feelings of their subordinates before making appropriate decisions. Managers maintain various interactions with the subordinates on an informal basis as an important way to achieve a harmony-oriented leadership that is based on mutual trust and benevolent authoritarianism.

Motivation

Koreans are highly motivated workers and are well known for being willing to work long hours (see MOTIVATION AND SATISFACTION). The motivation of Korean employees is influenced by traditional values as well as realistic needs. The key Confucian values of diligence and harmony have contributed to a relatively strong work ethic. The instinct for survival has also been an important driving force among Koreans, who have been haunted by instability and poverty throughout most of their recent history. A strong work ethic and harmony have become the most cherished values of Korean employees.

While the specific motivations of Korean employees vary depending on the size of the company and the level of seniority, high wages and job security tend to be the most important motivational factors. According to a study conducted in 1984 by the Korean Chamber of Commerce and Industry, executives of large companies tended to cite an 'environment for voluntary participation' as the most effective incentive, while the Chief Executive Officers (CEOs) of small companies regarded the management-by-objectives system as the best way to heighten the spirit of workers. It was also reported that employees aged over sixty cited wages as the most important incentive for hard work, while new management staff aged under thirty viewed 'environment for voluntary participation' as the most effective means of motivating employees and promoting productivity (Kim and Kim 1989).

As a group, Korean employees tend to put a somewhat stronger emphasis on extrinsic factors (such as wages, working conditions and job security) than on intrinsic factors (such as creativity and a sense of achievement) for high motivation (Lee 1989). Moreover, the need for a sense of achievement and recognition tends to be satisfied within the framework of the harmony of a given group. Since harmony is a dominant value in interpersonal relationships within a group, external factors tend to be even more important motivating factors to Korean employees. Nevertheless, the trend is for more Korean companies to shift their emphasis to intrinsic motivating factors such as *changjo* (creativity), achievement and recognition.

Communication

One outstanding feature of organizational communication in Korean businesses is that formal communication is mainly handled through vertical hierarchies (Lee 1989). The organizational communication process depends heavily on hierarchical relations, which are determined by a combination of factors ranging from formal authority and informal social status to length of employment and age. In the vertical communication process, superiors are expected to give directives while subordinates are expected to understand and implement those directives. The superiors tend to prefer to issue general directives as opposed to specific and detailed instructions; and subordinates prefer using their own judgement rather than asking superiors for explanations in event of the latter's directives not being clear-cut or detailed.

Another notable feature of communication in Korean companies is that employees usually attach much greater importance to upward formal communication on horizontal interdepartmental lines. This may have resulted from the high centralization of authority in Korean companies. The strictly hierarchical structures of Korean companies tend to determine the nature of vertical and horizontal communication. For employees, vertical communication is more work-related than horizontal communication, and thus more important. Poor horizontal communication between vertically structured departments has become a major barrier to efficient organizational performance in many large Korean companies (De Mente 1991).

The preference of superiors to communicate in general terms, combined with a relatively large power distance, comprises a major source of misunderstanding in Korean companies. It is very important for subordinates to develop the ability to decipher the intentions of the superior from general directives. Good personal relations with superiors tend to help overcome hierarchical barriers to communication; blood relationships as well as school and regional ties may further enhance mutual understanding and trust, thereby contributing to more straightforward communication. Those who share good lines of communication often tend to develop an informal management clique within the company.

Many Korean employees are not good at open communication in formal meetings and have difficulty in airing their views, especially opposing ones. An openly different opinion may embarrass or antagonize one's superior, or provoke a colleague. Besides, Koreans are not culturally encouraged to share information openly with others except within close personal relationships. However, many Koreans are very good at informal communications, especially on a one-to-one basis with a superior. Sophisticated superiors will con-

stantly make available opportunities for such communication; they may for example invite subordinates to dinner at their home or at a restaurant. Subordinates can also visit their superiors at home for private talks. The use of informal occasions or settings for open communication is very important for mutual understanding and trust between superiors and employees.

3 Human resource management

Korea has a large pool of well-educated human resources (see HUMAN RESOURCE MANAGEMENT IN ASIA PACIFIC). About 98 per cent of the population is literate; more than 80 per cent of Korean teenagers finish high school studies and most high school graduates attend colleges or professional training schools. Human resource management priorities in Korea include recruiting the best candidates, operating on-the-job training programmes and instituting reward and appraisal systems.

Recruiting and training

In a general survey (Shin 1985), it was found that most large Korean corporations classify employees into three categories: core (top management), basic (permanent employees) and temporary. Most Korean companies hire employees through a combination of reference checks, tests of knowledge, common sense and proficiency in English, personal interviews and physical examinations. New college graduates or experienced professionals are preferred. Large companies recruit twice a year, in June and November, and prefer to recruit their management trainees from reputable universities such as Seoul National University, Yonsei University and Korean University. Mid-sized and small Korean companies recruit once a year. Recruitment is very competitive.

Once new employees have been recruited, the elite groups tend to be assigned to such core departments as planning and finance after an in-house training programme lasting 7–10 days. Korean companies place great emphasis on employee development, which is normally conducted through in-house training programmes; many large *chaebols* have their own employee training centres and set aside as much as 5 per cent of regular work hours for formal training . The emphasis on employee development is in conformity with traditional Korean cultural values that attach great importance to education. Traditional Korean society was ruled by the *yangban* or educated class; the greatest ambition of the promising sons of *yangban* families was to pass the civil service examination and attain a high rank in government.

Reward and promotion system

The reward and promotion systems in Korean companies are traditionally based on social seniority, but performance is becoming an increasingly important factor (Lee 1989). Korean companies have gradually combined social seniority with performance in distributing their rewards; wages may be based on seniority but bonuses are often based on performance. Generally speaking, high-growth companies tend to attach greater emphasis to performance than do low-growth companies.

Promotion is regarded as extremely important to both employees and employers. In many Korean companies, top management is actively engaged in promotion decisions. Promotion is based on a number of criteria that can include seniority, performance, personality, family ties, school and region. Many Korean companies consider not only performance but also job attitude and special ability. Many managers are unwilling to give their employees too negative an evaluation; *inhwa* emphasizes the importance of harmony among individuals who are not equal in prestige, rank and power, and superiors are required to care for the well-being of their subordinates. A negative evaluation may undermine harmonious relations. Another Korean value, *koenchanayo* (which can be loosely translated as 'that's good enough'), also hampers critical evaluation as it urges tolerance and appreciation of people's efforts. According to this tradition, one should not be excessively harsh in assessing someone else's sincere efforts.

Severance and retirement

Layoffs are a common practice in Korean companies. Whenever they encounter a business downturn, they feel free to lay off employees at all levels. Korean employees also change jobs fairly freely, although many do work in the same company until retirement; while Korean employees normally attach great importance to their companies, they would not normally feel embarrassed at accepting better offers from other companies. Skilled employees tend to change jobs more often than do the unskilled. As the concept of loyalty in Korea is often based on individual relationships, the loyalty of Korean employees is often devoted to a particular superior (Song 1990); consequently when managers change companies they often bring many of their subordinates with them.

Korean companies do not have a uniform retirement age, though many require their employees to retire at fifty-five to sixty. Retirement age is also determined by rank and senior executives and managers tend to have an extended retirement age. Korean companies do not make a distinction between resignation and retirement when calculating severance pay; most companies set aside one month's salary per year for severance or retirement (Chang 1988), while some companies will add an additional two or even three months per year when calculating the total length of service.

Trade unions

After the Korean War, US-style labour legislation was enacted, guaranteeing workers' rights to organize and bargain collectively. However, these rights never emerged in practice. The government-dominated Federation of Korean Trade Unions helped employers to control workers. In 1960, workers joined radical students in overthrowing the government of Syngman Rhee.

Through the 1960s and 1970s the government of Park Chung Hee followed a policy of growth first and distribution later, and suppressed the labour movement. The Special Act on National Security of 1971 required workers to obtain government approval prior to any labour confrontation; this law was lifted in 1981 but new restrictions were then imposed. Industry-wide national unions were banned in 1980 and replaced with 'enterprise unions' that were controlled by labour–management councils, and were required to meet on a quarterly basis to coordinate conflicts between productivity and welfare. These councils tended to favour the interests of management, as many labour representatives were appointed by the government.

The political reforms of 1987 removed government intervention in labour relations and granted workers the right to unionize. Industry-based national unions were allowed to be established, and the newly amended Trade Union Act ensured protection from unfair labour practices and allowed workers to organize, negotiate and take collective action. Since that time trade unions have been growing and have begun actively seeking wage increases and improved working conditions.

4 Competitive strategies

Manufacturing development strategies

In the early period of development, many Korean companies followed the strategy of choosing the growth/maturity stages of products (Hahn 1989), taking advantage of governmental policies promoting import substitution. Apart from the cement and fertilizer industries which were very important for Korean reconstruction and agricultural development, most manufacturing was concentrated in the labour-intensive light industrial sectors. Selecting products in the growth/maturity stage decreased the risks for Korean companies, while from the government's perspective the development of labour-intensive and consumer-product industries provided employment for the large pool of unskilled workers and conserved badly needed foreign currency. Protected by governmental industrial policies, Korean manufacturing companies developed quickly into strong competitors in international markets.

There have been two basic types of technology transfer into Korea. The large intermediate goods manufacturers in sectors such as chemicals, cement and fertilizer adopted an apprenticing policy and relied heavily on foreign assistance in the form of turnkey plants, consultants and licensing. On-the-job training under the direction of foreign suppliers and off-the-job training at foreign sites provided Korean engineers and technicians with the basics of production expertise. Small manufacturing companies, which lacked the financial resources to negotiate with suppliers of foreign technology, upgraded their products and production technologies through reverse engineering of locally available foreign products (Kim and Kim 1989). This informal approach was prevalent in the early period of technology transfer; Korean Steel Pipe, for example, successfully duplicated and improved the Japanese model through imitation.

Other commonly used manufacturing strategies were concerned with the project implementation process, during which many Korean companies tried to minimize the total project completion period. There are a number of competitive advantages to be gained thus: cash flow can be generated much earlier, interest and overhead costs can be reduced significantly, and huge profits and market share can be achieved by early entry into growth markets. Samsung, for example, completed its first 64K DRAM chip manufacturing facility in just six months, as compared to an average of eighteen months for a similar project in the USA (Hahn 1989).

Diversification strategies

Diversification strategies are important for growth in any business. In Korea, large business groups, or *chaebols*, have been pursuing diversification strategies for the last three decades; in fact, diversification strategies have been widely advocated by the Korean government as part of the national economic policy. The Korean government has also favoured the development of world-class large business that can compete successfully in the international market. With the support of government, the *chaebols* have successfully implemented an 'octopus arm' diversification strategy and expanded their role in the Korean economy. Major *chaebols* such as Samsung, Hyundai, Lucky-Goldstar (now the LG Group) and Daewoo have become mainstays of the economy. Diversification has also been facilitated by strong Korean entrepreneurship; many Korean business leaders have an attitude of 'get the order first and figure out how to do it later' (Kang 1989: 67).

Generally speaking, diversification can be classified into seven categories: single, vertical, dominant-constrained, dominant-linked, related-constrained, related-linked and unrelated. The largest *chaebols* have tended to follow a strategy of unrelated product diversification. Samsung, for example, entered into sugar and wood textiles in the 1950s, electronics, fertilizer and paper production in the 1960s, construction, electronics components, heavy industry, synthetic textiles, petrochemicals and shipbuilding in the 1970s, and aircraft, bioengineering and semiconductors in the 1980s. Smaller companies generally pursue a strategy related to a single or dominant product structure. Medium-sized companies tend to fit in between these two extremes, typically following a strategy of related product diversification. The latter seems to be the most important strategy followed in terms of numbers, but, given that the ten largest *chaebols* own more than 200 companies, it can be seen that unrelated product diversification has been an important strategy and has greatly facilitated the rapid growth of Korean business (see Table 2).

The types and degrees of diversification strategies vary substantially from industry to industry, mirroring the differences in their nature. Vertical diversification, for example, is most often used by manufacturers in textile and garment industries because a continuous supply of raw materials and market outlets is critical to the maintenance of a company's competitive edge. A related-constrained strategy is more prevalent among companies in the food and beverage industries, which tend to produce goods closely related to each other in terms of the use of raw materials and distribution channels. In the metal and non-metal manufacturing industries, dominant-constrained strategies seem to be popular as they enable management to focus on a few dominant product lines while using the same organizational resources.

5 Trends in management in South Korea

The business environment in South Korea is undergoing rapid change, especially after the Asian financial crisis. Traditional managerial values and organizational systems are under growing pressure to change accordingly. In many companies changes have already taken place; examples include shifts from seniority-based reward systems to more balanced systems combining seniority and performance, a shift from strict family control to an increased role for career managers, a move from over-centralized functional control to decentralized horizontal cooperation, a shift of cultural emphasis from *inhwa* to the encouragement of *changjo*, and a shift in emphasis from non-material rewards to a balance of the material and the non-material. There are also signs of a shift in attitude by the Korean government towards the *chaebols*, particularly over the issue of ownership.

With the continued internationalization of Korean companies, the trend towards professionalization will increase in strength. However, whether Korean management will continue to maintain its uniqueness, based on the country's general cultural and social envi-

Table 2 Growth strategies of *chaebols*

Business group	Single	Dominant	Related	Unrelated	Total
10 largest (213)	0	1 (10%)	1 (10%)	8 (80%)	10
11–20 largest (123)	0	2 (20%)	3 (30%)	5 (50%)	10
21–50 largest (206)	0	9 (30%)	14 (47%)	7 (23%)	30
51–108 largest (248)	12 (21%)	21 (36%)	19 (36%)	6 (10%)	58
108 largest (788)	12 (11%)	33 (31%)	37 (34%)	26 (34%)	108

Source: Chung (1989), based on Jung (1987); reprinted with permission of Greenwood Publishing Group, Westport, CJ, Copyright 1989

ronment, in the wake of the changes in the Asia-Pacific economic environment remains to be seen.

MIN CHEN
THUNDERBIRD – THE AMERICAN GRADUATE
SCHOOL OF INTERNATIONAL MANAGEMENT

Further reading

(References cited in the text marked *)

* Aguilar, F. and Cho, D.S. (1984) 'Daewoo Group', Harvard Business School Cases 385–014, Cambridge, MA: Harvard Business School Press. (Pioneering case study on Korean *chaebol*, very informative on the early development of Daewoo.)
* Alston, J.P. (1989) '*Wa, guanxi* and *inhwa*: managerial principles in Japan, China and Korea', *Business Horizons*, March–April: 26–31. (Concise cultural introduction to the differences and similarities of the three related cultural values: *Wa* (Japanese), *Guanxi* (Chinese), and *Inhwa* (Korean).)
* Chang, C.S. (1988) '*Chaebol*: the South Korean conglomerates', *Business Horizons* 31 (2): 26–31. (General introduction to large Korean business conglomerates, *chaebol*, covering their organizational structure, cultural values and historical evolution.)
Chang, C.S. (1989) 'Human resource management', in K.H. Chung and H.C. Lee (eds), *Korean Managerial Dynamics*, New York: Praeger. (Intensive discussion on various aspects of Korean human resource management.)
Choi, Sung-No (1995/1996/1997/1998/1999) *HanKook-eui Daekumo Kieopjipdan* [The Korean big business groups], Jayu Kieop Centre. (Presents a quantitative analysis of Korean *chaebol* groups from the point of view of the national economy.)
Chung, K.H. and Lee, H.C. (1989) *Korean Managerial Dynamics*, New York: Praeger. (This is so far the most comprehensive edited volume on Korean management.)
* De Mente, B. (1991) *Korean Etiquette and Ethics in Business*, Lincolnwood, IL: NTC Publications. (Well-written cultural handbook on how to do business in Korea.)
Fair Trade Commission (2000) *2000 nyun-do daekymo-jipdan* [Large Scale Business Groups in 2000]. (Gives detailed statistics of major *chaebol* groups.)
* Hahn, C.K. (1989) 'Korean manufacturing strategy', in K.H. Chung and H.C. Lee (eds), *Korean Managerial Dynamics*, New York: Praeger. (Explains the major strategies that Korean manufacturing companies have used in their period of rapid growth.)
Jung, K.H. (1987) *Growth Strategy and Management Structure of Korean Business*, Seoul: Korean Chamber of Commerce and Industry. (Provides one of the most authoritative explanations on the growth and management of Korean businesses during the first three decades.)
* Kang, T.W. (1989) *Is Korea the Next Japan?*, New York: The Free Press. (Very informative book on Korea's overall competitiveness, written in a straightforward and simple style.)
* Kim, D.K. and Kim, C.W. (1989) 'Korean value systems and managerial practices', in K.H. Chung and H.C. Lee (eds), *Korean Managerial Dynamics*, New York: Praeger. (Good conceptual discussion on the influence of the Korean cultural value system on managerial practices.)
* Lee, H.K. (1989) 'Managerial characteristics of Korean firms', in K.H. Chung and H.C. Lee (eds), *Korean Managerial Dynamics*, New York: Praeger. (Detailed discussion on unique Korean managerial features, using a cultural approach.)
* Lee, S.M. and Yoo, S. (1987a) 'Management style and practice of Korean *chaebols*', *California Management Review* 29 (4): 95–110. (Short, simple but very interesting discussion on the management style and practices of large Korean business conglomerates.)
Lee, S.M. and Yoo, S. (1987b) 'The K-type management: a driving force of Korean prosperity', *Management International Review* 27 (4): 67–8. (There are many similarities between this article and their earlier one, although this article tries to develop a conceptual framework for the understanding of Korean management style and practices.)
* Paisley, E. (1993) 'Innovate, not imitate', *Far Eastern Economic Review* 13 May: 64–9. (Updated, journalistic description of recent reforms among *chaebol*, especially the Samsung Group.)
* Shin, Y. (1985) *Characteristics and Problems in Korean Enterprise*, Seoul: Seoul National University Press. (Good critique of Korean management style and practices by a Korean scholar.)
* Song, B. (1990) *The Rise of the Korean Economy*, New York: Oxford University Press. (Concise but interesting introduction to the economic miracle of Korea for those who know little about the country.)

See also: ASIA PACIFIC, MANAGEMENT IN; BANKING CRISES; CHAEBOLS; HUMAN RE-SOURCE MANAGEMENT IN ASIA PACIFIC; JAPAN, MANAGEMENT IN; LEADERSHIP; MANAGEMENT EDUCATION IN ASIA PA-CIFIC; MOTIVATION AND SATISFACTION; NORTH KOREA, MANAGEMENT IN; ORGANI-ZATION STRUCTURE

Spain, management in

Overview

In structural and strategic terms, Spanish management is relatively fragmented. It has had to evolve in an economic, social and political environment that has witnessed phases of discontinuous and uneven development. In recent years, accelerated levels of economic growth and economic internationalization have exacerbated the degree of fragmentation within capital and management structures. In addition, there are within the country competing management styles and practices. The unifying characteristic, if anything, is an attempt to cope with certain types of external, state and industrial relations regulation. This has been achieved to some extent through both the use of traditionalist, paternalist organizational and employment methods and the copying of modern (some would say 'postmodern') managerial styles and practices. This is an intriguing characteristic due to the way modern bureaucratic forms of regulation were developed under the Francoist dictatorship (1939–75) and during recent modernization projects of a partially 'social democratic' nature.

Another important factor is that management in Spain has had to work within a historic legacy whereby business elites have been unable to develop national projects and state relations that are popular in political terms. That is to say, the failure of the Spanish Right and its reliance until recently on militarist elites at moments of social and political crisis has undermined the attempt within organizations to develop long-term, modern and participative forms of management practice: hence, a more paternalistic model of management relations has tended to prevail. Given the degree of political stability in recent years and the process of internationalization, external points of reference have been sought regarding management practice. Such a transformation in management finds its origins in the Francoist regime's renovation programme of the late 1950s that opened Spain up to more international economic influence and moved the emphasis of policy making to a new range of business elites. Such contextual factors are central to any analysis of the nature and orientation of management in Spain.

1 Economic context

The economic development of Spain in the last 30 years of the twentieth century has been spectacular. Its growth rates have been amongst some of the highest in the developed world. From what was principally an agrarian economy, a substantial manufacturing and service industry has developed. Spain is now the fifth largest producer of automobiles in the world. Its service sector, especially tourism and hospitality, has seen a significant development in both quantitative and qualitative terms. The sheer innovation of the country and its marketing capacity have intrigued many external observers. At the centre of these developments have been two key factors: international capital and the State. Given the problems of national capital historically (see below), these two factors have been central to developing the productive capacity of the country and its service sector. Such dynamic economic growth was due to the internationalization of capital coupled with what were previously protected national product markets.

Such economic growth has had its down side, however. First, the benefits of economic growth have not been distributed across the whole country. Regional differences are still substantial. Second, the rushed and labour-intensive form of development made the restructuring of the late 1970s and 1980s particularly difficult in both political and social terms (Fina 1987). This in turn meant that technologically the country was dependent and relatively backward. Third, the workforce was highly segmented, with low labour market penetration rates in relation to the overall population, a core of protected male workers in key sectors and a periphery of unprotected workers in a range of other sectors such as textiles and footwear. Fourth, and more generally, the rate of external dependency in investment terms in key sectors such as car manufacturing (even if it is the fifth producer in terms of scale) has increased dramatically in the last 15 years in the form of direct and indirect investment.

These factors have influenced the character of employers and management in Spain, contributing to certain uneven and diverse practices within organizations. Such problems also accentuated the traditionalist bureaucratic character of Spanish management in place until the 1970s, as did the Francoist political context which did not allow for strategic and complex management styles, in particular in the area of labour management.

2 The fragmented character of management and capital in Spain

It is important to recall that capital and management are not homogeneous entities. It is always tempting to try to racially, nationally and socially typecast management without paying due regard to the structural factors and complex relations that underpin them.

In the case of Spain, there are a range of complex factors that contribute to the nature and strategic orientation of management. First, there are regional differences due to the internal geopolitical character of the country. Rates of development both politically and economically have varied enormously. The relatively modernist, liberal characteristics of areas such as Catalonia have not always been reproduced in other regions.

Second, there have been uneven rates of development in sectoral terms. Within manufacturing, significant differences existed between the electronic and car-manufacturing areas in terms of their development. Of particular importance here is the strength of the Spanish banking sector, which through systematic restructuring in recent years and the gradual incorporation of international capital has been one of the dominant poles of Spanish capital. The dominance of finance capital in both economic and political terms is also significant, particularly given its increasing concentration in terms of ownership.

Third, there are differences between national and international capital. Multinationals in Spain tend to be less directly involved in national employers' organizations and local regulatory apparatus. Strategic decisions regarding production and broad management strategy are made beyond the frontier of the country, with only the question of implementation being left to local management elites. One should not underestimate the presence of multinational capital in key manufacturing sectors in Spain and the way these have been located in Spain within international production structures (although Spain tends to remain at the periphery of most of these integrated production processes).

Fourth, there are significant differences in terms of scale. A large number of Spanish employers and employees are concentrated in small and medium-sized firms. This tends to accentuate the regionalist factors outlined above and gives rise to more paternalistic methods within employment and organizational behaviour (Aguar et al. 1999). That is not to say that these firms are not regulated legally or through collective bargaining mechanisms, but that these sometimes become formal modes of regulation and are not always effective in reality, especially with smaller firms. Within this context paternalistic practices are common.

Finally, given this pattern of development and the complexity of relationships, the State's industrial agents have played a key role in development; both indirectly and directly. During the Francoist regime, the State established a range of directly managed core infrastructure and manufacturing industries. Its Instituto Nacional de Industria (INI) was a major vehicle of development and until recently it has remained the core cluster of nationally led manufacturing concerns and interests. This has been a modernizing feature of the country, although during the 1980s its restructuring – considered necessary by various governments owing to its labour-intensive nature and bureaucratic management system – was a complex and politicized national issue. The real and quasi-privatization of such concerns has given rise to a new nucleus of national corporate interests which have begun to develop export and international growth strategies. These entities have emerged as key players and articulators of new management styles. In fact, their presence within national employers' organizations has become more prominent. For many observers this quasi-public and newly-privatized constituency is the most organized and strategically-orientated of large-scale Spanish capital. The role of Spain's telephone company, Telefonica, and its petroleum companies have been central to the emergence of a genuinely Spanish multinational capital.

Whilst there has been a broad democratization and modernization of management and employers (Perez Diaz 1984), one should not underestimate the fragmented nature of capital in Spain which in turn gives rise to competing management styles and projects. Within each management constituency, very different management practices and styles exist. This diversity has been accentuated by the social background of management in Spain which is only now beginning to see serious intellectual enquiry. Traditionalist career routes were worked through familial or religious networks. Modern career paths have been structured through legal and economic studies. The rigidity of the Spanish education system has meant that beyond informal processes, which are extensive, private universities and in particular Catholic institutions have intervened directly in the organization of business and management education. Beyond the public sector, to some extent this has created a nexus of private sector and political interests around management education elites. These have not been slow to innovate in the face of change but it has meant that traditional social elites continue to dominate Spanish management at the higher levels. The process of privatization and new forms of economic development have accentuated the issue of informal relations as witnessed in the political uncertainty of stock options amongst leading corporate directors. Research on this issue remains relatively undeveloped and unpopular.

3 In search of an effective management strategy

The bureaucratic and historically paternalistic traits of management are being exposed to new intellectual changes from the more innovative of US and Japanese producers in Spain. While the general orientation has been one of attempting to negotiate complex and politicized external regulatory processes (for example, the legal apparatus and industrial relations structures) on the one hand, and continue to develop economically on the other, the new historic task added to this has been the search for new managerial discourses and organizational cultures. The aim of this has been to increase competitiveness, essential given the emergence of new competitors for foreign investment (the Far East and eastern Europe) and the increasing cost of labour (cheaper labour having been one of the attractive aspects of Spain previously, although the myth of excessive labour cost increases in recent years must be questioned).

Consequently, there are a range of key 'projects' within Spanish management. First, one of the ways in which the question of employer fragmentation, diverse management approaches and deteriorating external environments have been tackled is through the discourse of 'free' labour markets (Martinez Lucio 1991). The main Spanish employer federations have lobbied against the increasing role of the State and in particular the supposedly tight nature of the Spanish labour market with its restrictions on dismissals (although many have argued that increasing numerical flexibility has more than compensated for this – in 1999, one-third of the workforce was still on temporary contracts – as has the individualizing of collective redundancies through state agencies which bypass judicial processes). However, the question of labour market flexibility in Spain has been a central obsession of the policy and management debate, resulting in a reactive outlook at the expense of broader approaches to the question of human resources.

Second, there has been an increasing amount of what can be termed 'submerged' economic activity. The extent of undeclared economic activity has reinforced highly paternalistic practices amongst smaller firms who have bypassed regulatory processes. This has contributed to the increasing use of casual labour, but has meant that highly informal, social and less strategic types of managerial activity continue to prevail in certain sectors. This can undermine the long-term and strategic orientation of management which focuses purely on short-term costs, not long-term investment. It has also contributed to the labour market developments noted above, namely an emergent 'free-market' and anti-State management culture which finds itself at odds with the regulatory culture that still persists.

Third, regardless of these more reactive qualities within management, there is an increasing attempt in certain key sectors and within certain education circuits to construct alternative, pro-active managerial cultures that may fuse with some of the more innovative economic and organizational activity that has already been seen in Spain. The growing interest in new human resource management techniques and quality discourses is a central point on the agenda of larger scale capital, both public and recently privatized. It is difficult to establish whether such attempts at engagement with new developments are part of the modernization of Spanish industry, a genuine attempt to construct customer-orientated and high-participation organizations within the economy, or whether they are merely new points of reference and certainty within what can be described as an increasingly competitive and open market economy with uneven social relationships in the labour market and society generally. Furthermore, it is hard to judge the extent to which such an engagement actually constitutes part of the managerial tradition in Spain of trying to negotiate and bypass external regulations, especially in industrial relations. Some therefore see new innovations in the workplace as uneven with the primary form of employment management based on a dualist approach which divides protected core workers from those on the periphery (Martin Artiles 1999; Perez Diaz and Rodriguez 1995).

None the less, these developments in renovating management strategy and education can be intellectually located within the general 'project' to cope with what are perceived politically by employers and certain managers to be the cost and burden of external regulatory processes. By making income contingent on economic success and viability, by making firms more numerically flexible and less dependent on legal processes for dismissing workers, and by developing new forms of involvement that bypass industrial relations structures that are considered by some employers to be politicized, the role of such new management approaches is seen by some as valid to any future regeneration. It is here where the issue of industrial relations becomes an important environmental factor.

4 Industrial relations in Spain

Industrial relations in Spain have provided employers with a set of interesting challenges (see INDUSTRIAL RELATIONS IN EUROPE). Autonomous and liberal democratic features within industrial relations began to emerge during the latter years of the Francoist dictatorship (1960–75). Both independent worker representatives and 'enlightened' employers began to a certain extent to negotiate in a democratic and formal manner regardless of the dictatorial context. Hence the industrial relations system had achieved a certain type of regularity by the 1980s. However, it was, and to a great extent remains, politicized (Miguelez and Prieto 1991). Actors within industrial relations – both unions and employers' organizations – tend to have very strong political relationships and motives. It may be argued, though, that this is inevitable and that this development plays an organizing role politically in a country with weak traditions within civil society. In addition, although there may not have been broad national tripartite agreement between labour, capital and the State since the 1984–6 Social and Economic Agreement (which covered a range of issues such as pay and economic intervention), the role of unions and employers' organizations in state bodies has been steadily increasing. With the election of the *Partido Popular* Conservative government in 1996 came the irony of a new phase of state–labour relations. A new set of tripartite and bipartite agreements on specific social and industrial relations issues underpinned this new wave of dialogue which involved the government, trade unions and employers (in some cases the agreements were bipartite but overall it was based on a three way, albeit complex, relation). Furthermore, a new type of participation within the state was being developed. Together with employers the unions were to act as overseers of discreet and separate areas of state intervention. Initially suspicious of such developments, the main employer bodies realized this would provide unions with a limited, albeit symbolically important role, within areas of the state, apart from areas such as lifelong learning and health and safety where union participation has developed.

Industrial relations may appear to be constituted by unions with low levels of trade union membership (15–20 per cent density rates on average), but the actual presence of the union through legally elected trade union delegates and works' councils is substantial. This is also true of the collective bargaining system with smaller, in practice unorganized, workplaces being covered by regional sectoral or national sectoral collective agreements that address basic issues and conditions.

Thus the formal presence and the political role of the union is, in theory, quite significant. However, these regulatory structures in areas of industrial relations such as bargaining (both macro and micro) are not always highly developed in the way they actually influence the employment relationship and the behaviour of employers and managers. While active in certain areas of work such as pay, these structures are not as constraining as they may appear. A certain mythology regarding dismissals has emerged, but this is not generally true. Where industrial relations appears to provide employers and managers with challenges, it is also fragmented in terms of the competing union organizations (although managers have sometimes utilized these divisions) and in the way broader political considerations have been at certain moments woven into the politics of the employment relationship. Levels of conflict have also remained some of the highest in Europe, although recent evidence suggests that this high level should not be attributed to the lack of legal reforms (Milner 1995). The real problem for employers is probably the low levels of trust that exist within the workplace between management and labour and even between different tiers of management; the introduction of new management practices such as teamworking have been problematical and limited in countries such as Spain for exactly this reason (Andersen Consulting 1995) (see HUMAN RESOURCE MANAGEMENT IN EUROPE). Involvement strategies have been met not so much by union opposition but by traditionalist management structures and groups, the archaic role of the supervisor and management use of numerical flexibility (for example, temporary contracting) which is not always compatible with company-orientated high-commitment strategies (Blyton and Morris 1992). In this respect, in Spain functional flexibility (the way workers are used within production processes) has been seriously undermined by the extent of numerical flexibility. Informal economic and institutional activity does not provide management with a suitable basis for innovations regarding worker involvement and effectiveness: short-termism prevails instead.

Recent developments on national negotiations between the Conservative government elected in 1996, employers' organizations and the main union confederations have pointed to an attempt at resolving some of the key labour market issues. Agreements on facilitating a certain amount of flexibility with regards to redundancies, along with the introduction of new types of employment contracts of a more subtle nature for new employees, have emerged. However, their development has to date been limited and the fundamental problems of a fragmented and dual workforce remain. The stability of the new industrial relations processes will depend on the extent to which such issues of fragmentation are dealt with.

5 Conclusion

Since the 1960s, Spain has experienced impressive economic growth rates, its economy has become increasingly export-orientated and an innovative and publicly led external marketing programme has been successful in giving the country wider recognition within the international economic community. However, the development of management in Spain has had to occur at a time when economic problems and structural transformations have coincided with increasing social and economic pressures and expectations from both state and society. Negotiating demands for greater regulatory consistency on the one hand and increasing demands for economic flexibility and change on the other have forced Spanish management to seek new organizational models. This has been underpinned by developments in management education and ownership structures which have been facilitative but which have not solved the problem of high dispersity, decentralization and 'disorganization' (Lash and Urry 1987: Aguar *et al.* 1999) within the Spanish economy, let alone the role of informality. The major issue of diversity and informality in management structures beyond the core internationalized and neo-public sector/privatized monopoly part of Spanish industry remains a central characteristic.

The above reasons mean that coping with external regulatory processes is key to the agenda of Spanish management and employers. The attraction for management of new organizational panaceas which purport to provide a basis for the managerial prerogative is therefore important. Research has shown that Spanish enterprises are in certain instances highly efficient and cost-effective (Andersen Consulting 1995). However, the very economic social and political structures discussed may make such engagements problematic for a range of reasons. As the traditional advantages of Spain decline in the world economy (for example, the cost of labour and the limits being reached in product markets), management will be forced to seek alternative models. This may prove unsuitable or difficult to adapt to, as in the case of the high-trust, high-regulation north European model. The situation may be further complicated by the possibility or an unwillingness among management to adapt, a consequence of the political changes within the country since the mid-1990s. Yet without a consistent and long-term industrial and economic policy

(and polity), management may be forced to focus on micro-level solutions in an increasingly decentred environment.

MIGUEL MARTINEZ LUCIO
UNIVERSITY OF LEEDS

Further reading

(References cited in the text marked *)

* Aguar, M.J., Casademunt, A., and Molins, J.M. (1999) 'Las organizaciones empresariales en la etapa de la consolidacíon democratica (1986–1997)' in Miguelez, F. and Prieto, C. (eds) *Las Relaciones de Empleo en España*, Madrid: Siglo Veintiuno. (An update of the earlier edition outlined below (Miguelez and Prieto, 1991) and considered to be the most significant text in the subject of Spanish industrial relations.)

* Andersen Consulting (1995) *Worldwide Manufacturing Competitiveness Study*, London: Arthur Andersen. (A short report on the adoption of new managerial practices in a range of countries. The results on Spain are intriguing.)

* Blyton, P. and Morris, J. (1992) 'HRM and the limits of flexibility', in Blyton, P. and Turnbull, P. (eds), *Reassessing Human Resource Management*, London: Sage Publications. (An academic piece that clearly outlines the contradiction between numerical flexibility and HRM practices. The book itself is an interesting evaluation of HRM.)

* Fina, L. (1987) 'Unemployment in Spain', *Labour* 1: 1. (One of the best pieces to cover the background to a very high level of unemployment, a good piece of economic and political history.)

* Lash, S. and Urry, J. (1987) *The End of Organized Capitalism*, Oxford: Blackwell. (A classic account of the changes taking place within capitalism in terms of the move away from the postwar model.)

* Martín Artiles, A. (1999) 'Organización del trabajo y nuevas formas de gestión laboral', in F. Miguelez and C. Prieto (eds), *Las Relaciones de Empleo en España*, Madrid: Siglo Veintiuno. (An update of the earlier edition outlined below (Miguelez and Prieto, 1991) and considered to be the most significant text in the subject of Spanish industrial relations.)

* Martinez Lucio, M. (1991) 'Employer identity and the politics of the labour market in Spain', *West European Politics* January. (Looks at the way the politics of dismissal have become central to employer identity and debates regarding flexibility in Spain.)

* Miguelez, F. and Prieto, C. (1991) *Las relaciones laborales en Espana* (Industrial Relations in Spain), Madrid: Siglo Veintiuno. (The key text available for understanding Spanish industrial relations; covers a range of areas very effectively.)
* Milner, S. (1995) 'Industrial disputes and the law in Spain', working paper, London: Centre for Economic Performance, London School of Economics. (Looks at the reality of strike action in Spain and its more complex features.)
* Perez Diaz, V. (1984) *El Retorno de la Sociedad Civil*, Madrid: Instituto de Estudios Económicos. (A collection of essays covering developments in Spanish society and economy by one of the country's leading sociologists.)

Perez Diaz, V. and Rodriguez, J.C. (1995) 'Inertial choices: an overview of Spanish human resources, practices and policies', in R. Locke, T. Kochan and M. Piore (eds), *Employment Relations in a Changing World Economy*, Boston, MA: MIT. (A very insightful overview of developments in Spanish employment relationships.)

See also: BUSINESS CULTURES, EUROPEAN; EUROPE, MANAGEMENT IN; HUMAN RESOURCE MANAGEMENT IN EUROPE; INDUSTRIAL RELATIONS IN EUROPE; LATIN AMERICA, MANAGEMENT IN

SPSS

1 **Data entry, data files and data definition**
2 **Data manipulation**
3 **Statistical analysis**
4 **Syntax commands**
5 **Help systems and instructional guides**
6 **SPSS modules**

Overview

SPSS is the abbreviation for both a commercial organization and a statistical software computer package which that organization continues to develop and market. The acronym for the computer package is the *Statistical Package for the Social Sciences*. The acronym for the commercial organization stood for *Statistical Products and Service Solutions* (Fielding and Gilbert 2000) to indicate that the organization has acquired and now develops a wider range of software products. The acronym is now the name of the company. Further information about the organization and its products can be obtained from its website which is: http://spss.com. This entry is only concerned with the statistical package and not with the organization, which may be distinguished by adding Inc. after the acronym.

Introduction

SPSS is one of the most comprehensive and widely used computer programs for analysing data in the social sciences and in universities, commercial and administrative organizations (see MANAGEMENT RESEARCH, MANAGEMENT OF). The development of this package began in 1965 at Stanford University and from 1970 continued at the National Opinion Research Centre at Chicago University. In 1975 a commercial organization was established based in Chicago. Initially called SPSS (Nie *et al.* 1970, 1975), the package was known as SPSS[x] (SPSS Inc. 1983) or SPSS-X (SPSS Inc. 1988) for a number of years, the X referring to the tenth major revision or release. This package was run on large or mainframe multiuser computers using various operating systems. With the development of personal computers came versions called SPSS/PC+ (Norušis/SPSS Inc. 1986), SPSS for the Macintosh (SPSS Inc. 1990) and SPSS for Windows (Norušis/SPSS Inc. 1993). The Windows version of SPSS is very probably the most widely used format. It has had four major releases, the latest of which is Release 10 (SPSS Inc. 1999c).

The use of a computer package such as SPSS is essential for the efficient quantitative analysis of data. This entry describes the main features of the Windows version of SPSS.

1 Data entry, data files and data definition

Basically data consist of numerical values (such as age and income) or categories (such as gender and occupation). Category data are most usually and most conveniently coded as numbers (such as 1 for females and 2 for males). Both types of data are stored in a computer *file* consisting of a potentially very large number of columns and rows. Columns represent different variables (such as age and gender) and rows different units or cases (such as people, organizations or locations).

To be analysed, data needs to be entered into a spreadsheet called the *Data Editor*. If the data are already available as a computer file (such as a simple text file or Excel file), this file can be read directly into the Data Editor. Otherwise, the data need to be entered individually into the appropriate row and column of the Data Editor. Different data files can be combined. For example, two or more files can be combined containing either common variables for different samples or other variables for the same sample.

Files and variables have to be given unique names to identify them. The value of a variable which is missing for one or more units also needs to be coded as a number and this number needs to be defined as missing. The numerical codes for categories can be assigned labels. Defining aspects of data such as their names and missing values is known as data definition.

Accurate entry of data into a file is essential. The ideal procedure for doing this is for two people to enter the data separately into two files and to cross-verify the files. It is unlikely that two individuals will make the same mistake. Values that differ for a particular variable and individual indicate an error. The two values need to be checked against the data in its original form. This can be done with SPSS Data Entry Builder, which is not part of standard SPSS. At the very least, frequency analyses should be conducted for each variable to check for invalid values such as 180 for a person's age.

Tables containing frequencies for one or more variables can also be entered into the Data Editor. These contingency tables can be analysed with statistical techniques such as chi-square and log-linear analysis. Correlation matrices may be entered with syntax commands in the Syntax window and can be analysed with statistical procedures such as partial correlation, multiple regression and factor analysis.

2 Data manipulation

The data, once entered, can be manipulated in various ways. Values can be recoded. For example, age or income may need to be categorizd or grouped rather than treated as continuous variables. These recoded values are best stored as a new variable so that the original values are not lost. New variables can be computed. For instance, the values of a particular variable may be transformed to reduce their variance so that parametric statistics can be performed. The values of a set of variables may be added together to create a new index such as an attitude towards a product or company. Subsets of units from the complete data set can be selected for analysis. For example, the subset may consist of married women aged between 30 and 40 and having two children living at home aged between 4 and 16.

3 Statistical analysis

The major reason for using a statistical package such as SPSS is for the more complicated statistical procedures it offers. Tabachnick and Fidell (1996) provide useful comparisons of the features available for various statistical procedures such as multiple regression and factor analysis for the four most popular statistical packages of SPSS, BMPD, SAS and SYSTAT. Among the statistics offered by SPSS are the following:

- chi-square and associated contingency table statistics such as phi, Cramér's v, lambda, gamma and kappa
- related and unrelated t tests with Levene's test for homogeneity of variance
- multivariate analysis of variance and covariance with various post hoc tests for unrelated samples such as Bonferonni and Scheffé
- canonical correlation
- profile analysis
- Pearson, Kendall's tau-b and Spearman correlation
- Pearson partial correlation
- simple and multiple regression
- logistic regression
- log-linear analysis
- cluster analysis
- discriminant function analysis
- principal components and principal axis analysis
- Cronbach's alpha reliability
- multidimensional scaling
- various non-parametric tests for related (such as Wilcoxon and Friedman two-way analysis of variance) and unrelated samples (such as Mann-Whitney U and Kruskal-Wallis H)
- time series analysis such as exponential smoothing and Autogressive Integrated Moving Average (ARIMA) models
- survival analysis such as life tables and Kaplan-Meier survival analysis.

Structural equation modelling in the form of a separate statistical package called Amos (Arbuckle 1999) can be added, enabling such techniques as confirmatory factor analysis and path analysis with latent variables to be carried out.

4 Syntax commands

Before the development of Windows and window-like procedures, quantitative data analysis was carried out using batches of syntax commands rather than menus and dialog boxes. SPSS still offers the facility for using syntax commands although these are not as easy to learn to use as choosing from options presented visually. Options selected from menus and dialog boxes can be stored as syntax commands. This is particularly helpful when the steps are not easy to recall such as, for example, selecting units defined by a large number of characteristics. Syntax commands are also useful for writing programmes for carrying out procedures which are not available on SPSS. Cramer (1998) has presented programmes for comparing the statistical significance of correlations for unrelated and related samples.

5 Help systems and instructional guides

SPSS Inc. publishes various manuals describing how to use its statistical package, a selection of which are listed under Further reading. Because many of these contain more information than the user may need or may not present the information in the way the user is most likely to use it, an increasing number of guides have been and are being published by other individuals, some of which are cited under Further reading. SPSS also has a Help option which gives a brief description of the procedures available, tutorials to work through, some syntax commands and a Statistics Coach. The Statistics Coach suggests the kind of statistics that may be required to answer certain simple questions.

6 SPSS modules

The computer software and the manuals describing its use generally consist of the Base System (SPSS Inc. 1999c) and include the following additional optional modules:

- Regression Models, formerly called Professional Statistics (SPSS Inc./Norušis 1994b)
- Advanced Models, formerly called Advanced Statistics (SPSS Inc. 1999a)
- Tables (SPSS Inc. 1994a)
- Trends (SPSS Inc. 1999g)
- Categories (SPSS Inc. 1999d)
- Amos 4.0 (Arbuckle 1999).

The following procedures are included in these packages:

Base system: recoding values; computing new variables; selecting cases; combining data files; chi-square; *t* test; analysis of variance and covariance; *post hoc* multiple comparison procedures such as Tukey's honestly significant difference and Scheffé; scatterplots; Kendall and Spearman correlation; Pearson correlation and partial correlation; simple and multiple regression; and numerous non-parametric tests including Friedman's two-way analysis of variance, Kendall's *W* and Cochran's *Q*.

Regression models: Cronbach's alpha reliability; factor analysis; cluster analysis; multidimensional scaling; and discriminant analysis.

Advanced models: multivariate analysis of variance and covariance; logistic regression; log-linear analysis; probit analysis; life tables; Kaplan-Meier survival analysis; and Cox regression.

Tables: customizing tables.

Trends: AutoRegressive Integrated Moving Average (ARIMA) forecasting and time-series modelling; exponential smoothing; regression with first-order autocorrelated errors; seasonal decomposition and adjustment.

Categories: optimal scaling procedures such as non-linear principal components and non-linear canonical correlation analysis.

Amos: Linear structural relationship modelling with Amos 4.0 (Arbuckle 1999).

DUNCAN CRAMER
LOUGHBOROUGH UNIVERSITY

Further reading

(References cited in the text marked *)

* Arbuckle, J. L. (1999) *Amos Users' Guide Version 4.0*, Chicago: SPSS Inc. (The official SPSS

guide to using Amos, a linear structural equation modelling programme.)

Bryman, A. and Cramer, D. (2001) *Quantitative Data Analysis with SPSS Release 10 for Windows: A Guide for Social Scientists*, London: Routledge. (First published in 1990, this is the fifth edition of this popular, non-technical guide to SPSS.)

* Cramer, D. (1998) *Fundamental Statistics for Social Research: Step-by-Step Calculations and Computer Techniques Using SPSS for Windows*, London: Routledge. (This book shows how to compute by hand and explains many of the more basic statistics produced by SPSS.)

* Fielding, J. and Gilbert, N. (2000) *Understanding Social Statistics*, London: Sage. (A clearly laid-out guide using SPSS for Windows Release 9.)

Howitt, D. and Cramer, D. (2001) *A Guide to Computing Statistics with SPSS Release 10 for Windows*, Hemel Hempstead: Prentice Hall/Harvester Wheatsheaf. (First published in 1997, this is the third edition of probably the simplest and quickest guide to using SPSS.)

Kinnear, P. R. and Gray, C. D. (2000) *SPSS for Windows Made Simple*, 4th edn, London: Psychology Press. (The PC version was first published in 1992; this is another popular guide to SPSS.)

* Nie, N.H., Hull, C.H., Jenkins, J.G., Steinbrenner, K. and Bent, D.H. (1970) *SPSS: Statistical Package for the Social Sciences*, New York: McGraw-Hill. (The official SPSS guide to the first mainframe version of SPSS.)

* Nie, N.H., Hull, C.H., Jenkins, J.G., Steinbrenner, K. and Bent, D.H. (1975) *SPSS: Statistical Package for the Social Sciences*, 2nd edn, New York: McGraw-Hill. (The official SPSS guide to a greatly expanded mainframe version of SPSS.)

Norušis, M.J. (2000) *SPSS 10.0 Guide to Data Analysis*, Upper Saddle River, NJ: Prentice Hall. (A more user-friendly official SPSS guide to beginning data analysis.)

* Norušis, N.J./SPSS Inc. (1986) *SPSS/PC+ Base Manual*, Chicago: SPSS Inc. (The official SPSS guide to the first MS-DOS version of SPSS.)

* Norušis, N.J./SPSS Inc. (1993) *SPSS for Windows: Base System User's Guide Release 6.0*, Chicago: SPSS Inc. (The official SPSS guide to the first Windows version of SPSS.)

* SPSS Inc. (1983) *SPSSX User's Guide*, New York: McGraw-Hill. (The official SPSS guide to the tenth release of the mainframe version of SPSS.)

* SPSS Inc. (1988) *SPSS-X User's Guide*, 3rd edn, New York: McGraw-Hill. (The official SPSS guide to an expanded tenth release of the mainframe version of SPSS.)

* SPSS Inc. (1990) *SPSS for the Macintosh*, New York: McGraw-Hill. (The official SPSS guide to the first Macintosh version of SPSS.)

SPSS Inc. (1991) *SPSS Statistical Algorithms*, 2nd edn, Chicago: SPSS Inc. (The official and very useful SPSS guide to the statistical algorithms used in the SPSS software.)

* SPSS Inc. (1994a) *SPSS Tables 6.1*, Chicago, IL: SPSS Inc.

* SPSS Inc./Norušis, M. (1994b) *SPSS Professional Statistics 6.1*, Chicago, IL: SPSS Inc.

SPSS Inc. (1999a) *SPSS Advanced Models 10.0*, Upper Saddle River, NJ: Prentice Hall. (Formerly titled Advanced Statistics, this is the official SPSS guide to more advanced models such as the general linear model and survival analysis.)

SPSS Inc. (1999b) *SPSS Base 10.0 Applications Guide*, Upper Saddle River, NJ: Prentice Hall. (The official SPSS guide to more basic statistics, concentrating on explaining output.)

* SPSS Inc. (1999c) *SPSS Base 10.0 for Windows User's Guide*, Upper Saddle River, NJ: Prentice Hall. (The official SPSS guide introducing basic features of the windows' operations.)

* SPSS Inc. (1999d) *SPSS Categories 10.0*, Upper Saddle River, NJ: Prentice Hall. (The official SPSS guide to various forms of category analysis.)

* SPSS Inc. (1999e) *SPSS 10.0 Regression Models*, Upper Saddle River, NJ: Prentice Hall. (Formerly titled Professional Statistics, this is the official SPSS guide to regression models.)

SPSS Inc. (1999f) *SPSS 10.0 Syntax Reference Guide*, Upper Saddle River, NJ: Prentice Hall. (The official SPSS guide to using syntax commands for generating SPSS output.)

* SPSS Inc. (1999g) *SPSS 10.0 Trends*, Upper Saddle River, NJ: Prentice Hall. (The official SPSS guide for trend analysis such as ARIMA modelling techniques.)

Stevens, J. (1996) *Applied Multivariate Statistics for the Social Sciences*, 3rd edn, Mahwah, NJ: Lawrence Erlbaum. (First published in 1986, this is a useful but more technical guide to interpreting SPSS output.)

* Tabachnick, B.G. and Fidell, L.S. (1996) *Using Multivariate Statistics*, 3rd edn, New York: HarperCollins. (First published in 1983, this is a helpful but more technical guide to interpreting and writing up SPSS output.)

See also: INFORMATION TECHNOLOGY; MANAGEMENT RESEARCH, MANAGEMENT OF

Sraffa, Piero (1898–1983)

Personal background

- born in Turin, Italy, on 5 August 1898 into a wealthy Jewish family; his father a famous professor of commercial law
- studied law at the University of Turin, interrupted by military service
- doctoral thesis in economics under the supervision of Luigi Einaudi, later President of the Italian Republic, on inflation in Italy during and after the war
- during the Fascist era emigrated to Britain; on John Maynard Keynes' suggestion appointed to a lectureship in economics in Cambridge, 1927
- from 1930 Librarian of the Marshall Library; Fellow of Trinity College
- died 3 September 1983 in Cambridge

Major works

'Sulle relazioni fra costo e quantità prodotta' (On the relationships between cost and output) (1925)
'The laws of returns under competitive conditions' (1926)
The Works and Correspondence of David Ricardo (with M.H. Dobb) (1951–73)
Production of Commodities by Means of Commodities (1960)

Summary

Piero Sraffa (1898–1983) is known for essentially three intellectual achievements: (1) his criticism of Alfred Marshall's partial equilibrium analysis, in which he challenged the concept of the supply function and of the classification of different industries according to whether they were subject to constant, decreasing or increasing returns; (2) his masterful edition of the works and correspondence of David Ricardo, which threw new light on the 'classical' approach to economic problems, in particular to the theory of value and distribution; (3) his reformulation of the classical theory in his *magnum opus* (Sraffa 1960), placing special emphasis on the problems of joint production, fixed capital and natural resources; his book was a major point of reference of the so-called two Cambridges (that is, Cambridge, UK, and Cambridge, Massachusetts) controversy in the theory of capital in the 1960s and 1970s.

1 Introduction

Sraffa is widely seen as the initiator of a revival of the classical point of view in the theory of value and distribution from Adam Smith to David Ricardo (see SMITH, A.; RICARDO, D.). This point of view differs markedly from the one taken by later marginalist, or neo-classical, authors, including William Stanley Jevons, Léon Walras, Eugen von Böhm-Bawerk, Alfred Marshall and John Bates Clark (see MARSHALL, A.). In investigating the relationship between relative prices and the distribution of income at a given time and place, classical authors start from the following set of data: (1) the set of technical alternatives to produce the various commodities from which cost-minimizing producers can choose; (2) the size and composition of the social product; and (3) the ruling wage rates. From these data they determine, in conditions of free competition, a uniform rate of interest (or profit) on the supply price of capital goods and relative prices of the different commodities produced and used. A characteristic feature of the classical approach is the *asymmetric* treatment of wages and profits: the former being assumed to be given from outside the system of production, the latter seen as a dependent residual. The data from which marginalist theory typically begins are: (1) the initial endowments of the economy with goods and factors of production and the distribution of property rights among individual agents; (2) the preferences of consumers; and (3) the set of technical alternatives from which producers can choose. From these data marginalist economists determine the quantities produced of the different goods, the amounts of the factors of production employed and the prices of all goods, including the prices of factor services. The latter comprise the rate of interest (or profit). A characteristic feature of this approach is the *symmetric* treatment of wages and profits in terms of the supply of and the demand for the respective factor services.

Sraffa was able to show that the latter approach is logically flawed, that is, it generally cannot accomplish what it sets out to do. The reason for this is to be traced back to the notion of 'capital' entertained by the marginalist authors. In order to be compatible with the notion of a *long-period* competitive rate of return on capital invested, 'capital' could not be conceived of as a set of given *physical* endowments of produced means of production. For, if the capital endowment is given in kind, only a short-period equilibrium, characterized by differential rates of return on the supply prices of various capital goods, could be established by the forces constituting supply and demand. Thus, the formidable problem for the marginalist approach consisted of the necessity of establishing the notion of a market for 'capital', the 'quantity' of which could be expressed *independently* of, and prior to, the determination of the price of its service, that is, the rate of interest. Sraffa demonstrated that this is possible only in excessively special cases and fails in general. Hence, conventional (that is, long-period) marginalist analysis has to be abandoned.

2 Biographical data

Sraffa was born into a wealthy, liberal Jewish family on 5 August 1898 in Turin. Sraffa's father was a well-known professor of commercial law who, towards the end of the First World War, became Rector of the Luigi Bocconi Commercial University of Milan. After having finished his secondary schooling with the highest possible marks, Piero Sraffa studied Law at Turin University. He took courses in political economy; his diploma thesis on 'Inflation in Italy during and after the war' was supervised by Luigi Einaudi, who later became President of the Italian Republic. After graduation he studied at the London School of Economics (1921–2). During his first stay in England he also met Keynes who asked him to contribute an article on the Italian banking system for the *Manchester Guardian*. The article was also published in Italian and provoked fierce reactions by the Fascist Government.

In 1923 Sraffa was appointed to a lectureship in political economy and public finance at the University of Perugia. The preparation of his lecture stimulated him to write 'Sulle relazioni fra costo e quantità prodotta' (On the relationships between cost and output) (1925), which contains an analysis of the foundations of decreasing, constant and increasing returns in Alfred Marshall's theory and a critical discussion of the latter's partial equilibrium approach. Not least due to this article Sraffa obtained a full professorship at the University of Cagliari, a post he held *in absentia* to the end of his life, donating his salary to the library. Francis Y. Edgeworth's high opinion of the article led to an invitation to publish a version of it in the *Economic Journal* (see Sraffa 1926). Moreover, Sraffa was offered a lectureship in Cambridge. In October 1927 he began his teaching in Cambridge, giving courses on the theory of value and distribution and on the relationships between banks and industry in continental Europe. He was to lecture for only three years, finding the very task increasingly difficult. In 1930 Sraffa was appointed to the position of the librarian of the Marshall Library and was also placed in charge of the Cambridge programme of graduate studies in economics. He was on friendly terms with major intellectuals of this century, including Keynes and the philosopher Ludwig Wittgenstein.

Shortly after his arrival in Cambridge Sraffa showed Keynes the set of propositions which were to grow into *Production of Commodities by Means of Commodities* (Sraffa 1960). However, his work on the manuscript was overwhelmed both by the intense debate in Cambridge surrounding Keynes's *Treatise on Money*, and later, *The General Theory of Employment, Interest and Money*, and by Sraffa's assuming the editorship of the Royal Economic Society's edition of *The Works and Correspondence of David Ricardo* in 1930 (see KEYNES, J.M.). The publication of the altogether eleven volumes of Ricardo's works and correspondence began in 1951 and was accomplished in 1973 (Sraffa 1951–73). The edition, for which Sraffa was awarded the golden medal *Söderstrom* by the Swedish Royal Academy in 1961, is widely acknowledged to be a scholarly masterpiece. (The award is commonly considered equivalent to the Nobel prize in economics when the latter had not yet been established.) In the late 1950s Sraffa eventually found time to put together, revise and complete his notes on the classical approach to the theory of production and distribution which were then published as *Production of Commodities* (1960). Sraffa died on 3 September 1983 in Cambridge. He left his personal estate and his precious library, which includes several first editions of classic writings in economics, to Trinity College (see Potier 1991).

3 Main contributions

Early works

The main concern of Sraffa's early contributions (Sraffa 1925 and 1926) was with scrutinizing the validity of Marshall's partial equilibrium analysis. The central issue consists in the following: a change in the quantity produced by a variable cost industry *at the same time* entails a change in the costs of firms in *other* industries as it entails a change in the costs of firms in the industry in which the change in the quantity produced took place. A typical example is that in which the same quality of land is used to produce two different commodities, say apples and pears. An increase in the production of apples, for instance, may lead to a rise in the cost function of the producers of apples because of an increase in the rent paid for the use of land. However, this rise in rent would likewise affect the cost function of the producers of pears. The changes in costs would be of the

same order of magnitude in both industries, so that it would seem to be illegitimate to disregard the changes in the cost functions of firms outside the industry in which the quantity produced has changed (that is, pears), while taking into account the changes obtained in the cost functions of firms inside the industry only in which the variation in quantity took place (that is, apples). The necessity to take into account other industries is accentuated in the case in which these industries provide means of production to the industry in which the implications of a change in quantity is studied.

When a change in the quantity produced by a variable cost industry does not entail a change in the costs of firms in other industries, the variable costs are said to be *internal to the industry*. A typical example is that in which returns are decreasing because land is in short supply and each quality of land is specific to the production of one commodity only. If the (dis)economies responsible for variable costs are external to the firm and internal to the industry, variations in the quantity produced by one industry may affect the cost functions of the firms outside that industry only as a consequence of the change in the equilibrium price and quantity of the commodity produced by the industry in which the variation took place. This would be an effect of the second order of magnitude only, the presence of which, it could be contended, is perhaps compatible with using the *ceteris paribus* clause (see Roncaglia 1978; Kurz and Salvadori 1995).

In his 1926 paper Sraffa suggested retaining partial equilibrium analysis. This was possible, however, at the cost of abandoning the concern with the free competition form of markets only; in order to preserve the partial framework the analysis had to be limited to the study of economies *internal* to the firm. Sraffa's proposal was taken up by several authors and triggered a rich literature on market forms which bloomed during the 1930s; see, especially, Joan Robinson's *The Economics of Imperfect Competition* (1933). Apart from a contribution to the 1930 *Economic Journal* symposium on increasing returns, Sraffa did not participate further in the debate on the Marshallian theory of value. He rather focused attention on an analysis of 'the process of diffusion of profits throughout the various stages of production and of the process of forming a normal level of profits throughout all the industries of a country ... [a problem] beyond the scope of this article' (1926: 550). This problem constituted the main topic of his *magnum opus*: *Production of Commodities*.

His *magnum opus*

The basic premise that Sraffa starts from is that commodities are produced by means of commodities. For a given system of production or *technique* in use, that is, a set of methods of production to produce the different commodities (with the number of methods equal to the number of products the prices of which have to be ascertained), he shows in particular that: (1) the share of wages in net national income is inversely related to the rate of interest (profit); (2) relative prices may be complicated functions of the rate of profit; (3) the value of capital per unit of labour employed, or 'capital intensity' of production, need not fall as the rate of profit goes up; if the value of capital per unit of labour rises with the rate of profit we talk of 'reverse capital deepening'; (4) with the possibility of a choice of technique it cannot be excluded that a technique is cost-minimizing at two disconnected ranges of the rate of profit and not so in between these ranges; this phenomenon became known as the 'reswitching of techniques'. The implication of the possibility of 'reswitching' is that the direction of change in the proportions between means of production and labour cannot be related unambiguously to changes in so-called factor prices.

With the possibilities of 'reverse capital deepening' and 'reswitching' the central element of the marginalist explanation of income distribution in terms of supply and demand is revealed as defective. The demonstration that a fall in the wage rate (that is, a rise in the interest rate) may lead to the adoption of the less 'labour-intensive', that is more 'capital-intensive', of two techniques destroyed, in the minds of the critics of traditional neo-classical theory, the whole basis for the neo-classical view of *substitution in production*. Moreover, since a fall in the wage rate may cheapen some of the commodities, the production of which at a higher level of the wage rate was charac-

terized by a relatively low labour intensity, the substitution among consumption goods contemplated by the traditional theory of consumer demand may result in higher, as well as in lower, labour intensity. It follows that the principle of substitution in consumption cannot offset the breakdown of the principle of substitution in production.

This can be shown as follows. The plausibility of the supply and demand approach to the theory of distribution was felt to hinge upon the demonstration of the existence of a unique and stable equilibrium in the market for 'capital'. With the 'quantity of capital' in given supply, this, in turn, implied that a monotonically *decreasing* demand function for 'capital' in terms of the rate of interest had to be established. Since with reverse capital deepening the demand function for 'capital' would have upward sloping segments, it cannot be excluded that the single equilibrium of the economy under consideration is unstable. With free competition, conceived of, as it is in neo-classical (but not in classical) theory, as including the perfect flexibility of the distributive variables, a deviation of the rate of interest from its equilibrium level would lead to the absurd conclusion that one of the two income categories, wages and interest (that is, profits) would disappear. Hence, there would be no sensible equilibrium at all. According to the critics of traditional neo-classical theory, this result demonstrates the failure of the supply and demand approach to the explanation of normal prices and income distribution (see also Garegnani 1970; Schefold 1989; Kurz and Salvadori 1995; Kurz 2000). These findings do have implications for other parts of economic analysis; for their application to the theory of international trade, see Steedman (1979). It should also be mentioned that Sraffa tackled the issues of fixed capital, joint production and natural resources of production (land).

4 Evaluation

Sraffa launched the revival of the 'classical' approach to the theory of value and distribution and dealt a serious blow to traditional neo-classical economics, both in its partial and general equilibrium versions (see HICKS,

J.R.; SAMUELSON, P.A.). His main concern was with systems of interdependent production, that is the production of commodities by means of commodities. He rejected the widespread marginalist view of production as a one-way avenue leading from the services of 'original' factors of production to final goods as grossly misrepresenting the process of production in developed industrialized economies characterized by a sophisticated system of the division of labour (see JOB DESIGN). His view of production is thus similar to, but a good deal more general than, that entertained by input–output analysis.

The impact of Sraffa's criticism on mainstream economic teaching has so far been limited (with the possible exception of his contribution to the theory of imperfect competition). It may be conjectured that this is at least partly due to the fact that the profession is largely unwilling to face the fact that its foundations are much less consolidated than is generally believed. Sraffa's findings overthrow the received simple messages of textbook economics and deprive the applied economist of a well-entrenched pattern of thought concerning price–quantity relationships that allows him to come up with quick answers to policy questions. However, given the doubtful success of economic policy recommendations the profession might want to ask the question whether that has anything to do with the analytical core from which these recommendations are generally derived.

HEINZ D. KURZ
UNIVERSITY OF GRAZ

Further reading

(References cited in the text marked *)

* Garegnani, P. (1970) 'Heterogeneous capital, the production function and the theory of distribution', *Review of Economic Studies*, 37: 407–36. (Expounds the implications of Sraffa's work for the theory of capital and income distribution.)
* Kurz, H.D. (ed.) (2000) *Critical Essays on Piero Srafffa's Legacy in Economics*, Cambridge: Cambridge University Press. (Contains a set of essays dealing with the different themes of Sraffa's contributions.)
* Kurz, H.D. and Salvadori, N. (1995) *Theory of Production: A Long-Period Analysis*, Cambridge: Cambridge University Press. (Provides a mathematically rigorous treatment of linear economic theory post-Sraffa, including the issues of joint production, fixed capital, land and exhaustible and renewable resources.)
* Potier, J.-P. (1991) *Piero Sraffa Unorthodox Economist (1898–1983): A Biographical Essay*, London: Routledge. (Contains useful information on Sraffa's life, his training, intellectual origins and political leanings.)
* Robinson, J. (1933) *The Economics of Imperfect Competition*, London: Macmillan, 1969. (Important study of imperfect competition, following Sraffa's article 1926.)
* Roncaglia, A. (1978) *Sraffa and the Theory of Prices*, New York: Wiley. (A detailed monograph on Sraffa's contributions to economic analysis and their implications for neo-classical economics.)
  Roncaglia, A. (2000) *Piero Sraffa: His Life, Thought and Cultural Heritage*, London: Routledge. (This new book seeks to illuminate our understanding of Sraffa's work by re-examining his intellectual biography, providing a new interpretation of his main works and by bringing Italian debates on Sraffa to an English-speaking audience.)
* Schefold, B. (1989) *Mr Sraffa on Joint Production and Other Essays*, London: Unwin Hyman. (Contains a thorough discussion of Sraffa's contribution and relates it to classical, Marxist and neo-classical economics.)
* Sraffa, P. (1925) 'Sulle relazioni fra costo e quantità prodotta' (On the relationships between cost and output), *Annali di Economia*, 2: 277–328. (Contains Sraffa's criticism of Alfred Marshall's partial equilibrium analysis.)
* Sraffa, P. (1926) 'The laws of returns under competitive conditions', *The Economic Journal*, 36: 535–50. (Summarizes the argument in Sraffa (1925); it triggered the development of the analysis of imperfect competition in the 1930s.)
* Sraffa, P. (1960) *Production of Commodities by Means of Commodities: Prelude to a Critique of Economic Theory*, Cambridge: Cambridge University Press. (Sraffa's main work, aiming at the revival of the classical approach to the theory of value and distribution.)
* Sraffa, P. (ed.) with the collaboration of M.H. Dobb (1951–73) *The Works and Correspondence of David Ricardo*, Cambridge: Cambridge University Press. (Eleven volumes containing the definitive edition of Ricardo's collected works and correspondence and a general introduction by Sraffa.)
* Steedman, I. (ed.) (1979) *Fundamental Issues in Trade Theory*, London: Macmillan. (The con-

tributions to this book draw the lessons of Sraffa's main contribution for the theory of international trade.)

Wood, J.C. (1995) *Piero Sraffa: Critical Assessments*, London: Routledge. (Useful reference volumes which bring together some 115 articles of his work. Invaluable for anyone studying the development of modern economics.)

See also: GROWTH OF THE FIRM AND NETWORKING; INTERNATIONAL TRADE AND FOREIGN DIRECT INVESTMENT; KEYNES, J.M.; MARSHALL, A.; NEO-CLASSICAL ECONOMICS; RICARDO, D.; SMITH, A.

Sri Lanka, management in

1 Introduction
2 Business and management
  development
3 Conclusion

Overview

Management development in Sri Lanka has been influenced by many factors such as its history, political environment, and colonization by Western powers resulting in institutional structuring, economic/business conceptualizations, cultural traits, etc. The work ethics, organizational culture, systems development and entrepreneur/employee relationships have been shaped accordingly.

In a competitive situation, entrepreneurship, innovation, achievement, quality, etc. overtake ad hocism in management. Therein, professionalism overtakes family affiliations and the adoption of new systems/technology and scientific management embraces organizations. Thus managerial dimensions in Sri Lanka, affecting behaviour, work ethics, practices, etc. are changing fast, heading towards professionalism. Hence, future management projections will face the challenges of competition, human resources development and technology transfer with a professional outlook.

1 Introduction

Sri Lanka is a Democratic Republic with a Unitary Constitution with a population of 18.6 million living in 25,000 square miles. The demographic division of gender is equally distributed. Reduction of maternal/child deaths, 1.3 per cent population growth, per capita income of US$814 (Central Bank of Sri Lanka 1997), high literacy rates and quality of life in the South Asian context are Sri Lanka's achievements.

Its history has influenced the culture and socioeconomic environment. The *Sinhalese* (the majority race) kingdom existed up to 1815 when the British took control. Since 1505, parts of the country had been controlled by the Portuguese, Dutch or British. Economic diversification, education, physical infrastructure development, democratic governance, legal systems, administrative institutions, businesses and their practices etc. were the bases on which management systems were built. The inevitable outcome was that those systems were imprinted with the ruling management cultures, mainly the British but also with traces of the other colonial rulers.

The Constitution (1972 and 1978) conferred the status of a Republic to Sri Lanka. The 13th Amendment to the Constitution in 1987 provided for power sharing through Provincial Councils (Government of Sri Lanka 1987). Although only partly fulfilled, it is a positive response towards decentralized management. The Local Authorities supervised by the Provincial Councils are threefold – Municipal, Urban and Divisional Councils (*Pradeshiya Sabha*), engaging mostly in environmental management.

The country's economic performance was the most important influence on management. The issues of population, unemployment, local/foreign prices, the aspirations of the younger strata of the population, etc. were all problems faced by the country. Until 1956 Sri Lanka had a capitalistic welfare economy. Nationalization of private assets and businesses was carried out from 1956 to 1965. From 1965 to 1977 an attempt was made to achieve agricultural self-sufficiency, and to develop industry and tourism. An open-economic policy was implemented after 1978. Appropriate management changes accompanied these policy changes.

2 Business and management development

Since government policies are based on political philosophies, political parties are important policy determinants. Reducing public service delivery and increasing the role of the private sector highlighted public confidence in the private sector. The rule of subsidiarity (i.e. minimal government engagement in business), as accepted by the government, has helped the expansion of the private sector.

The historical development of management in Sri Lanka

Chronologically, Sri Lankan private businesses can be identified as colonial (until independence), traditional (1948–56), conservative (1957–77) and new (1978 onwards) (see INDIA, MANAGEMENT IN; PAKISTAN, MANAGEMENT IN). The main characteristics of these different forms are:

1 *Colonial business*: Controlled by domineering colonial masters; male dominated; with foreign managerial attitudes, mostly concerned with the repatriation of profits.
2 *Traditional businesses*: Small-scale businesses owned by nationals/non-nationals; male dominated; managers have less exposure to education/management concepts, and are inclined to consult relations, peers and elders for crucial decision making advice; are helpful to co-businessmen, generally honest, and consider business as a service.
3 *Conservative businesses*: In addition to some characteristics in number 2, above these are industrially inclined; ownership shifting towards nationals; somewhat innovative and risk taking; managers have some education in management; receiving government incentives, bank-financed; have less customer consideration.
4 *New businesses*: Larger organizations; diversified activities; national, foreign and even multinational ownership; few females at managerial levels; more innovative; employing new management techniques, taking more risks; technically upgraded; professionals employed; large capital investments; market oriented; spendthrift; jealous of competitors; indifferent to honesty, some engaging even in antisocial businesses.

After independence, the private sector had good access to resources and enjoyed a fa-

vourable public policy. With the changing competitive business scenario, socialist thinking began to encroach upon public policy, and the business environment also changed. Nationalization of private sector assets reduced private initiatives and aggravated the fear psychosis of business managers.

The state sector was the major employer of personnel, paid from the annual budgets of the ministries/departments or statutory authorities. Privatization reduced the expenditures on personnel of statutory authorities as they came under the purview of companies, which were floated to manage them (see PRIVATIZATION AND REGULATION). The determination of cadres, recruitment, training, retrenchment, pension payments, etc. of public officials is the responsibility of the government. The private sector has more flexibility on hiring, but less on firing, as such action is challengeable under labour laws (see INDUSTRIAL RELATIONS IN THE EMERGING COUNTRIES).

With 73 per cent of the population living in rural areas, the government was concerned about their personal and political aspirations and cultural requirements. Therefore, official language policy was changed in the mid-1950s. This has affected the performance of private sector management, as the vernacular educated joined the private sector. With more privatization, the demand for English-educated managers has increased. International schools and foreign educational opportunities have improved the situation, but have not brought about miracles.

The private sector, reluctantly, had to accept the nationalization of plantations, trade, industry, services, etc. The pressure of nationalization was relieved only after 1978 with economic liberalization, again affecting business management and development. This can be seen in the increase of commercial and development banks/branches, foreign capital transfers, the establishment of consultancy firms, a relaxation of negative policies and procedures, and the introduction of new business mechanisms such as stock exchanges, capital markets and new technologies. The passage of the Companies Act gave greater encouragement to the systematic development of companies. However, the labour rights movements were not to the liking of the private sector. The Workers' Charter, benefiting labour, has been put on hold for several years, as the government seeks to retain the private sector's goodwill.

Entrepreneurship

When considering management status, we should briefly look at entrepreneurship. One study of Sri Lankan management (Perera and Buddhadasa 1992) opines that 'entrepreneurship could be part of the solution to existing social and economic ailments'. Joseph Schumpeter has described entrepreneurs as innovators. To describe colonial or traditional Sri Lankan business managers in this way sounds unsatisfactory. However, McClelland's conclusion that power orientation is more prominent as a motivator among successful entrepreneurs has been visible in Sri Lanka.

In Sri Lanka, the need for achievement as a means of gaining social power seems to be the prime motivator of some entrepreneurs (Perera 1990). The recent intervention of the business community into the search for a solution to the ethnic crisis shows how business and social power can be extended into political power.

There have been managers and entrepreneurs, men and women, who have excelled in innovation and management acumen. The traits for success in the Sri Lankan corporate world have been identified by a leading business personality as 'boundless energy, intelligence, integrity, likeability, drive and the willingness to sacrifice' (Jayasundara 1992). This, undoubtedly, is comparable with Western thinking.

There are a number of family-centred firms controlling large businesses in Sri Lanka. In many such businesses, an ancestral entrepreneur had been positively innovative and enterprising due to extraordinary managerial capacity. Sometimes, family companies engage relations in managerial positions. Such management arrangements can be criticized as being inimical to innovation, as pointed out by Hagan (1986), who stated that 'key managerial posts given to family members may sometimes result in the employment of incompetents'. It is notable that there are some

companies having a nominal head of the family (e.g. mother) symbolically leading the firm, although the firm is really managed by the children and other managers. However, there are also businesses in Sri Lanka which have been developed and efficiently run for long periods of time by family managers, proving the sustainability of family managed businesses in Sri Lanka. Although it may be argued that those companies may have performed better given the opportunity to explore an open management system.

Management styles and the cultural environment

With increasing competition and modernization, management systems have changed, showing a shift towards recruiting non-family members. A typical life-cycle for a Sri Lankan family-owned enterprise would be: the initial stage, where the owner-entrepreneur's involvement in managerial decision making is high; the growth stage, where the number of non-related managers increases; while in matured organizations, the family's participation in managerial decision making decreases, perhaps in the belief that business achievements are not a corollary to family affiliation.

Some management theoreticians argue that the affiliation motive/need is negatively correlated with the achievement motive/need. Concurrently, achievement is considered to be correlated to risk taking. Research in Sri Lanka (Perera and Buddhdasa 1992) challenges this theory by concluding that the successful Sri Lankan entrepreneur is one who takes medium risks and is highly persevering and innovative, while the less successful entrepreneur takes medium risks, is moderately persevering, but low in innovation. Hence the significant variable in Sri Lanka is innovation, although McClelland identified risk taking as a significant factor in high achievement motivated entrepreneurs. Cultural traits in the West may have created this confusion.

Hofstede (1987) identified four cultural dimensions affecting management: individualism vs. collectivism, large vs. small power distance, strong vs. weak uncertainty avoidance and masculinity vs. femininity. Although Sri Lanka was not in his study, the dimensions are relevant for Sri Lankan management. Cultural factors show that Sri Lankan management tends to be closer to collectivism, with recognizable power distance, weak in uncertainty avoidance and with 'feminine' managerial characteristics (see ORGANIZATION CULTURE).

The collectivist approaches in Sri Lanka are not as strong as in Japan. However, group influences such as the '5-Ss' of Japanese origin are now employed by management. The influence of work values on employee involvement and the achievement of success by changing the job structures of employees have had positive effects, according to a study done in Sri Lanka (Jayawardana 1996). It is heartening to note that a few tea estates have started employing '5-Ss' to motivate workers for partnerships. A sense of belonging, group interest, tolerance of nepotism and third-party involvement of conflict resolution are some symbolic situations of collectivism.

In Sri Lanka, the issues of power distance in management are not as critical as in India. The flat managerial structures are remote, but management is reasonably accessible; age is respected; management by objectives is comparatively less in Sri Lanka. Uncertainty avoidance is reflected in weak planning in Sri Lanka. Lacking predictability, poor punctuality, minimum standardization, tolerance of deviance, etc. can all be observed in Sri Lanka, reflecting the level of uncertainty avoidance. However, planning and its importance as a management tool to maximize the use and value of limited resources, efficient management review of targets against performance, and maintenance of standards are now identified as favourable outputs of planning in Sri Lanka. The extended family relationships, people orientation, interdependence ideal, sympathy for the less fortunate, empathy, caring for employees, etc. exemplify the feministic behaviours of Sri Lankan managers (Fernando 1996).

A closeness to the Indian cultural dimensions reflects another facet of management. Many aspects of family and religious thought in Sri Lanka have been moulded by Indian influences. Conquering man had been the main cultural theme of Indian civilization. Research done on the influence of culture on

work ethics points to the reasonableness of classifying the preferences for 'being', manipulative, negative and working for social fulfilment, as the main work relevant values in Sri Lanka (Nanayakkara 1994). It is emphasized that culture cannot adequately explain the state of work ethics in Sri Lanka. Other factors, for example colonial heritage, social welfare programmes, the structure of economic organizations, etc. also influence work ethics.

Against a background of the East Asian 'Tigers' which have shown such accelerated development (although this has slowed down considerably towards the end of the 1990s), it is interesting to compare their work ethic – such as discipline, hard work, thrift, 'this worldliness', quality achievement, etc. – with the Sri Lankan work ethic (see ASIA PACIFIC, MANAGEMENT IN). A need to develop human resources to upgrade the work ethic, attitudes, capacities, etc. has been identified in Sri Lanka. Foreign investors have been expected to disseminate their 'imported' technical and technological expertise locally. Expertise accrued in the Middle East was expected to seep into the economy on the return of expatriate workers. These assumptions never materialized due to the establishment of less sophisticated industries in Sri Lanka and as most expatriate workers were engaged as housemaids, preventing any accumulation of technology. A void in knowledge and technology was therefore inevitable.

Management education

The universities, who increased their enrolments in commerce and management subjects (50 in 1966/67, to 800 in 1981/82 and 2000 by 1996/97) faced the void creatively. Postgraduate students increased from 40 (1981) to 300 (1997). Competition for admission is reflected by the increase in admission requirements, which have risen from the lowest in 1981/82 to the highest in 1996/97. Since independence, 7000 management graduates, 8000 commerce graduates and 1000 postgraduates have been produced by the universities. Private sector and/or foreign university collaborations have begun to offer MBA courses in the 1990s, with the Institute of Technological

Studies initiating one such course. Technical institutions have supported business management as seen by the increase of institutes from 8 in 1960 to 39 by 1997. The Institute of Chartered Accountants, the Chartered Institute of Management Accountants, the Chartered Institute of Marketing of Sri Lanka, the Chartered Institute of Secretaries, the Sarvodaya Management Training Institute, the Sri Lanka Institute of Marketing, the National Institute of Business Management are major private sector training organizations (Nanayakkara 1998) (see ACCOUNTING IN THE EMERGING COUNTRIES).

Entrepreneurship training is undertaken by the Industrial Development Board, Small Business Development Centre, Employment Investment and Enterprise Development Division of the Ministry of Mahaweli. The private sector has also contributed to management training, with companies such as Business Consultancy Services Ltd., Business Management Bureau, etc. One important development had been the interest shown by leading companies in demonstrating to their employees the importance of work values, and using employee involvement to motivate them to become positive managers and team workers. Those interested in quality improvement have sometimes lamented that the lack of interest at the top management level is a stumbling block to making use of quality and productivity enhancement programmes, although some top managers have utilized quality improvement programmes. The critics have described many top managers as 'theory X managers' who are 'autocratic and living in the past' (The *Sunday Leader* [paper] 22 November 1998) and explain that as the reason for negativism.

There are several problems with the training processes in Sri Lanka. The main issue is the incompatibility of graduates to the needs of employers. Employers in Sri Lanka look for analytical, adaptation, communication and team work skills and for leadership potential. A survey conducted by Nanyakkara (1998) has shown that 47.1 per cent of graduates preferred to go into teaching rather than take risks in business. Some of the major weaknesses in the system are that little publicity is given to management education, selection processes

have been found to be wanting, courses tend to have a theoretical and product orientation instead of a market orientation, and there are low levels of follow-up and weak inter-agency cooperation and coordination (Ranasinghe 1996).

Public servants have the benefit of receiving general training through Management Development Training Units and at the Sri Lanka Institute of Development Administration, for certificate courses. Even the clerical and allied grades make use of these programmes. There are many Teacher Training Colleges and a National Institute of Education to undertake major human resources development activities among educational personnel. The School of Cooperation of Sri Lanka, Institute of Cooperative Management and National Co-operative Council and its branches train cooperative employees. Sector-wise training and skill upgrading programmes are available in plantation management, textile industry, agriculture, veterinary and livestock development. With this infrastructure in place, one can satisfactorily conclude that the setting is complete for human resources development in management (see MANAGEMENT EDUCATION IN THE EMERGING COUNTRIES).

3 Conclusion

A movement towards economic success in a country has to be supported by managerial capacity. A stable private-sector oriented economic approach has become established in Sri Lanka. Hence, the issues in management should be regarded in this light.

With increased support for liberalization and commitment to the principle of subsidiarity, the role of the government will contract in the future. Power sharing exercises will create a situation where the government will undertake a more or less regulatory function, assisting and servicing business management, in addition to centralized functions such as security, foreign exchange management, immigration/emigration, customs, etc. Such contraction would automatically mean an expanded private sector, as non-governmental organizations cannot and will not fill the void.

In profit-motivated private sector development, entrepreneurship, innovation and productivity will be the key elements. The government and private sector organizations would like to see higher levels of entrepreneurship, which is in short supply in Sri Lanka. Human resources development towards the encouragement of entrepreneurship is one increasingly popular move. Supplementary support for the establishment of institutions, such as development banks, Sri Lanka Board of Investment, Export Development Board, research and training institutions, etc. are some of the positive recent developments to facilitate entrepreneurship.

The problems created by cultural factors are slowly changing due to political, international and socioeconomic influences. An interest in learning languages such as English, Japanese, Chinese and German; enthusiastic efforts to implement quality circles in the workplace; use of high technology in operations; contracting in non-related professionals; the use of consultants, etc. are all trends seen in management that can be called positive and proactive. The easing of cultural limitations against females, a preference for merit over seniority, and younger executives beginning to take the reins of management, etc. are changing scenarios which will have a positive effect on management.

Even the work ethic is slowly changing due to other integrated developments in the management field. The participatory approaches to management, power sharing with the periphery, etc. are serious activities, but are common issues related to the work ethic and productivity development. The culturally negative feeling of 'being' is changing as a work ethic, due to the competition among various organizations.

Therefore, the future projections on management will be centred on factors other than simply business. The social, cultural, political, economic and international factors will have an input to the successful management of both state and private sector businesses in Sri Lanka. Hence, identifying the proper mix of the various components has to be done carefully to avoid any pitfalls. This is the challenge before government, entrepreneurs, financiers and human resources developers in Sri Lanka.

AUSTIN FERNANDO
RESOURCES DEVELOPMENT
CONSULTANTS LTD

Further reading

(References cited in the text marked *)

* Central Bank of Sri Lanka (1997) *Annual Report*.
* Fernando, A. (1996) 'Hofstede's Cultural Dimensions – Application on Pradeshiya Sabha Management', MBA Research. (The research applies the four cultural dimensions identified by Hofstede to local government management in Sri Lanka.)
Fonseka, A.T. and Jayawardena, A.K.L. (1996) 'Self-managed teams and organisational performance: the experience of Asian Cotton Mills Ltd, Sri Lanka', *Sri Lanka Journal of Management* PIM 1 (4) October–December. (Documents the experience of Asian Cotton Mills Ltd in operating self-managed teams as a managerial innovation to meet the challenge of competition, the gains achieved in higher employee motivation, productivity and output and the lessons to be learnt from the experiences.)
Fonseka, K.B.M. (1997) 'Cost management strategies: A theoretical framework and a glimpse of Sri Lankan practice', *Sri Lanka Journal of Management,* 2 (2) April–June. (Responses obtained from a sample of 44 middle and upper level managers from the services and manufacturing sectors in Sri Lanka suggest an inclination towards 'come what may type strategies' in their organizations and the unfavourable trend that requires correction.)
* Government of Sri Lanka (1987) Constitution of the Democratic Socialist Republic of Sri Lanka.
* Hagen Everett, E. (1986) *The Economics of Development*, Homewood IL: Richard D Irwin. (This study on entrepreneurship highlights innovation as doing something new and economic innovation as doing something new in production, products and markets.)
* Hofstede, G. (1987) *Cultural Consequences* (abridged edn) Third Printing, Berkeley, CA: Sage. (The extent of influence borne by societal values and culture on managerial functions has been researched in IBM and the four major dimensions described by Hofstede are dealt with in this book.)
* Jayasundara, D.S. (1992) 'Management Leadership and the Emerging Economic Order in Sri Lanka'. (Address given at the Convocation of

the University of Sri Jayewardenepura, centred on the qualities of chief executives in the changing economic order and activities in Sri Lanka.)

* Jayawardana, A.K.L. (1996) 'Work values and employee involvement', *Sri Lanka Journal of Management* 1 (2). (Highlights the fact that the quantity and quality of work of autonomous groups was higher than the groups of hierarchical model and such positive results can be obtained when power, information, knowledge and skills are moved down to the lower levels through adequate changes in the organization structures.)

Nanayakkara, G. (1992) 'Work values: To be "imported" or "Made in Sri Lanka"?' in *Culture and management in Sri Lanka*, Colombo: PIM. (A book written to assist foreign experts in development to understand some important cultural aspects in the Sri Lankan work environment, especially in the public sector.)

* Nanayakkara, G. (1994) 'Sri Lankan cases in management', PIM. (A collection of Sri Lankan cases and a method of analysis that has been written with experience gathered in consultancies, teaching and training in real managerial and organizational situations.)

* Nanayakkara, G. (1998) 'Development of management studies in modern Sri Lanka', PIM. (Gives an overall view of management education, the gaps between demand and supply of educational outputs, resource availability, research and related issues.)

* Perera, T. and Buddhadasa, S. (1992) 'Characteristics of Sri Lankan entrepreneurs: how valid is the Schumpeterian model?' *Sri Lanka Journal of Management*. (A study on the characteristics of Sri Lankan entrepreneurs, analysed in the light of Western literature and the authors' research.)

* Perera, T. (1990) 'Social power of low-country Sinhala entrepreneurs', MBA Research. (This research has been conducted by surveying a small number of low-country Sinhala business organizations on five hypotheses postulated within a single model relating to the concepts of a collective work ethic, social power base, expansion of social power, level of achievement motivation and the growth of social power potential.)

* Ranasinghe, S. (1996) 'Entrepreneurship education and training in Sri Lanka', *Sri Lanka Journal of Management*. (Due to mixed success results obtained by the entrepreneur development programmes in Sri Lanka, the author makes a case for changing the focus, content and methodology of such programmes, taking into account the lessons learned in the past and indigenous entrepreneurial values and experiences.)

* The *Sunday Leader* (1998) 22 November, p. 19. (Discusses the difficulties faced by practitioners of quality improvement due to negative attitudes of traditional, 'old school' top managers.)

See also: INDIA, MANAGEMENT IN; INDUSTRIAL RELATIONS IN THE EMERGING COUNTRIES; INTERNATIONAL MONETARY FUND; MANAGEMENT EDUCATION IN THE EMERGING COUNTRIES; PAKISTAN, MANAGEMENT IN; PRIVATIZATION AND REGULATION; WORLD BANK; WORLD TRADE ORGANIZATION

Starbuck, William Haynes (1934–)

Personal background

- born 20 September 1934 at Portland, Indiana, USA
- graduated from Harvard University (AB Physics 1956), Carnegie Institute of Technology (M.Sc. 1959; PhD 1964), University of Stockholm (honorary PhD 1995)
- held professorships in administrative sciences and economics (Purdue 1964–67), administration and sociology (Cornell 1967–71), and business administration (Wisconsin-Milwaukee 1974–84),
- held visiting professorships at Johns Hopkins University, (1966–67), London Business School (1970–71), International Institute of Management, Berlin (1971–74), Norwegian School of Economics and Business Administration, Bergen (1977–78), Stockholm School of Economics (1977–78), Université de Versailles Saint-Quentin-en-Yvelines (1998), University of Canterbury (1999), Université de Paris IX – Dauphine (1999), University of Oregon (1999), Université de Aix-Marseille III (2000), Iona College (2001), Université de Paris I – Sorbonne (2001)
- Fellow, American Psychological Association (1975), Academy of Management (1986), Society for Industrial and Organizational Psychology (1990), American Psychological Society (1995), British Academy of Management (1998)
- developed the concepts of self-designing organizations, organizational design, environmental niches, organizational equilibria composed of antithetical processes, relativity of aspirations through time, knowledge-intensive firms
- contributed extensively to behavioural research methods and epistemology
- President, Academy of Management (1997–98)
- currently ITT Professor of Creative Management at New York University

Major works

'Organizational growth and development' in J. G. March (ed.), *Handbook of Organizations* (1965)

'Camping on seesaws: Prescriptions for a self-designing organization' (with Bo L.T. Hedberg and Paul C. Nystrom) *Administrative Science Quarterly* (1976)

Handbook of Organizational Design (two volumes, edited with Paul C. Nystrom) (1981)

More than one hundred articles to leading scientific journals including *Administrative Science Quarterly, American Sociological Review, Behavioral Science, Journal of Management Studies*

Summary

William H. Starbuck has exerted a pervasive influence on three generations of behavioural scientists and management researchers. His works, which range over many topics, are distinguished by cautious inferences and constant reflexive interrogation. They investigate decision making, organizational design, learning, cognition, interaction between rationality and ideologies, forecasting, crises, and scientific methods. They emphasize the relativity of managers' perceptions, the interactions between rationality and ideologies, the use of experimental prescriptions, and crisis management through unlearning of behavioural and cognitive patterns. His writings assume a world filled with paradoxical, contradictory and antithetical processes. He has striven to foster prescriptive organizational design, and his four edited books include the classic *Handbook of Organizational Design* with Paul Nystrom (1981). During his term as the editor of *Administrative Science Quarterly* (*ASQ*), he reoriented its focus on organization theory and enlisted an international editorial board.

1 General appraisal

'Self, career, family, organization and society tangle together. To abstract myself or my career from context would violate my scientific standards' (Starbuck 1993: 66).

William H. Starbuck's works stand among the most influential and most quoted in management sciences. Yet the range and depth of his contributions makes them difficult to describe, and the basic pattern of his research cannot be encapsulated in a single recurrent theme. His works range widely across applied mathematics and experimental psychology (1963, 1965a, 1965b, etc.), sociology and organizational theory (1974, 1983, etc.), information systems and man–machine interaction (1975, etc.), to scientific methods (1968, 1974, 1988: 73–77, 1993a, 1994; Starbuck *et al.* 1981: 9–13).

Constant self-reflection and relentless interrogation of his own assumptions and values are key attributes of Starbuck's research. His autobiographical essay (1993) expresses extreme frankness. His research creates a paradoxical feeling because it is sometimes very prescriptive – such as works on managing crises (Starbuck *et al.* 1978) – and sometimes very relativist, embodying astute wisdom and scepticism. This relativism is exemplified by the notion that organizations rely on antithetical processes that counterbalance and neutralize each other (Starbuck *et al.* 1976).

Consistent with the behaviourist school – which is more attitude than doctrine, more philosophy and epistemology than specific assumptions – Starbuck's works are deeply rooted in a constant interrogation of concrete behaviours, extracting theoretical revolutions from singulars and exemplars. Human failures and weaknesses are particularly praised by Starbuck, who integrates his own life experiences (1993a) into his theoretical constructions and his reflections on science.

2 Early aspirations

With a BA in Physics from Harvard University and three summers at IBM, Starbuck was aiming for a doctorate in applied mathematics and a career as a computer designer. Then Richard Cyert, one of his professors at the Carnegie Institute of Technology, offered him financial aid for doctoral studies in Industrial Administration and advised him to focus on behavioural sciences (see MARCH, J.G. AND CYERT, R.M.). One result of this history is that Starbuck's writings reflect a tension between determinism and relativism. He sometimes does elegant acrobatics to avoid choosing between his intransigent and mathematical logic, on one hand, and the wisdom of a behaviourist who is willing to introduce fragility and relativity in the act of research, and consequently in theory construction.

From 1957 to 1960, Cyert and March mobilized students to conduct various studies in support of their forthcoming *A Behavioral Theory of the Firm* (1963). Starbuck ran an experiment in which three people had to cooperate to achieve joint results while also pursuing somewhat divergent individual goals (Cyert *et al.* 1961). The experiment drew two conclusions: (1) Individuals modify the information they transmit to pursue the rewards they expect from alternative group actions. (2) However, in the experimental situation, these manipulations do not affect the groups' performance.

Also, as part of the *Behavioral Theory of the Firm* project, Starbuck wrote a paper about aspiration levels that built upon Simon's notions. This student paper, which eventually turned into a published article in the highly prestigious *Psychological Review* (Starbuck 1963), debunked Festinger's theory that people set their aspirations so as to maximize subjective utility. The latter regarded a level of aspiration as a point of reference for feelings of success or failure; a performance exceeding the level of aspiration is a success, a performance that fails to reach this level is a failure. Starbuck pointed out that the utility-maximization model implies that, in this case, people should set their aspirations so low that every outcome would produce feelings of success. Starbuck argued, instead, that levels of aspiration change as goals are matched or missed. He also suggested that people construct their preferences ex-post so that behaviours and preferences interact continuously. This relative treatment of preferences was later echoed by March and Olsen's work.

This theme of antithetical processes that correct themselves in the course of events has been persistent throughout Starbuck's works, borrowing different clothes and disguises as the scope and focus shifts from very small to very large units of analysis. Organizing processes generate other processes that counterbalance them ('self-designing organizations' 1975–81). Decision making becomes a continuous collision between rationality and ideologies (Starbuck *et al.* 1978). The ironies and bitter surprises of his life probably led him to study brutal and unilateral changes (such as social revolutions) and to develop a theoretical predilection for breakdowns and paradoxes that revolve and self-dissolve.

3 Organizational growth and metamorphosis

The article that first made Starbuck well known was a chapter about Organizational Growth and Development in the *Handbook of Organizations* (1965b). This chapter began by reiterating the theme that behaviours and preferences interact continuously. Starbuck analysed motives for organizational growth – self-realization, risk, prestige, executives incomes, profit, cost, monopoly, stability and survival – and then he (1965b: 465) wondered: 'Do these goals produce growth, or does growth produce these goals?' (see ORGANIZATION BEHAVIOUR; ORGANIZATION BEHAVIOUR, HISTORY OF).

He divided growth models into four categories : (a) cell-division models, which focus on growth as a change in percentage of size by adding cells and divisions; (b) metamorphosis models, which acknowledge that growth is not a regular process but incorporates abrupt changes; (c) will-o'-the-wisp models, which portray growth as the pursuit of opportunities that disappear as expansion is realized; and (d) decision–process models, which examine decision rules and decision-making procedures. Sometimes with an obvious lack of diplomacy, Starbuck unveiled brick by brick the flawed constructions of each model, picking up empirical weaknesses, shedding light on logical inconsistencies or methodological limits. He showed how cell-division models tend to concentrate on effects and to ignore causes of growth; how metamorphosis models, although describing causes and effects of change fail to show their connections; how will-o'-the wisp models frame internal processes and external factors as 'chicken and egg'; and how decision–process models become harder to understand as they become more realistic.

'One problem with most models of organizational growth', Starbuck concluded, 'is that they imply a degree of autonomy and predestination which is difficult to reconcile with one's direct observation' (1965b: 494). Thus, Starbuck (1968, 1973) sought models that would embrace the totality of the phenomenon from its emergence to its extinction. Metamorphosis models seemed promising because they left room for unforeseen and fast adjustments, gave attention to details, and allowed for non-linearity and intrinsic regulation in the course of action. Starbuck's penchant for experimentation and his abilities in mathematics led him to the works of the Russian mathematician Pontryagin. The latter demonstrated that it is far more parsimonious to describe a revolution by three distinct groups of equations, instead of trying to integrate all phenomena into a single system of equations. These three systems describe (a) the slow transformation before the revolution, (b) the fast transformation during the revolution, and (c) a slow transformation after the revolution. This analysis also convinced Starbuck (1973) that for any system capable of dramatic revolution, it is impossible to state precisely why the revolution occurs.

Starbuck's acute and cutting analyses, which leave little hope for the reviewed theories, have become as renowned as his generosity and commitment to young researchers. Starbuck's sharp scrutiny literally destroyed contingency theory ('A trip to view the elephants and rattlesnakes in the garden of

Aston' 1981). In that case and many others, he has devoted enormous effort to producing evidence contradicting widely held theories, beliefs, or methods. For instance, he has repeatedly attacked tests of statistical significance (e.g. 'On behalf of naïveté' 1994).

4 Organizational design

George Box and Norman Draper were working on improving industrial processes in the late 1960s. The classical approach was, at that time, to establish the best possible design *a priori* given the state of current and exhaustive knowledge. Unfortunately, the constant improvement of industrial processes necessitated frequent interruptions and ad hoc fine tuning, so they proposed the use of evolutionary operation (EVOP). The philosophy of this method was to manage processes so that not only products were produced, but also the necessary information to improve the manufacturing processes. Box and Draper saw an analogy between EVOP and biological evolution, with natural selection operating to improve industrial processes.

This idea of a learning derived from incremental experiments eventually led Starbuck to the concept of 'self-designing organizations' (see ORGANIZATIONAL LEARNING). But first, it influenced a project for the German Federal Health Bureau. Starbuck and Wolfgang Müller (1972) were asked to design an information system that would help the Bureau to evaluate the efficacy of medicines (1993a: 87). However, the rapid development of medical research would make any fixed system rapidly obsolete, as would the ever changing information about the efficacy and side-effects of medicines. So Starbuck and Müller proposed that the system be designed to support constant redesign. 'The central design challenge is to allow for solutions to an endlessly and rapidly evolving set of problems, taking into account changes in one's own comprehension of the problems as well as changes in the problems themselves' (1975: 219).

'Self-designing organizations' became the focus of a fruitful collaboration with Bo Hedberg and Paul Nystrom that extended over a decade and that continues to influence works on learning organizations and paradoxical change in organizations. An early statement of principles appeared as 'Camping on Seesaws: Prescriptions for a self-designing organization' (Hedberg *et al.* 1976). This article emphasized the roles of antithetical processes and contradictory prescriptions as sources of their inner balance for organizations. The deliberately prescriptive approach was itself a methodological prescription. By introducing changes in organization, they said, researchers can simultaneously generate better data, learn more about organizations' behaviour, and improve organizations.

Prevalent prescriptions for organizational design, said Starbuck *et al.*, were calling for 'organizational palaces' where specialization, clear objectives, and unequivocal structures would create differentiated yet harmonious ensembles, where rational procedures and delimited responsibilities would build rigid structures with 'refined and elegant' components. But such 'palaces' avoid experiments, praise certainties, ossify their behaviours, balk at reorientations, and intolerant despotic leaders. One method to sustain 'organizational palaces' is periodic redesign, but a procedure can itself become a routine of self-indulgent examinations and self-fulfilling prophecies. For Starbuck *et al.*, there was no reason an organization should behave more consistently than its environment. They proposed that 'organizational tents' should replace palaces. Indecisiveness can increase exploration, unlearning and re-learning. More ambiguous roles can produce flexibility.

Not only should managers live in tents, they should pitch the tents on seesaws that balance antithetical organizational forces. Six seesaws interact: consensus and dissension, contentment and discontent, resource abundance and scarcity, faith in plans and doubt, consistency and experimentation, and rationality and imperfection. 'A self-designing organization can attain dynamic balances through overlapping, unplanned, and non-rational proliferation of its processes; and these proliferating processes, collide, contest and interact with one another to generate wisdom'(Hedberg *et al.* 1976: 63).

5 Crises: reframing and unlearning

Starbuck's organizational design theories are rooted in a distinctive analysis of the interactions between ideologies and rationality. The question that originally motivated this work was why organizations or people remain in stagnating environments. Starbuck (1982) attributed this inertia to the ideologies people invent to justify their actions. Ideologies are integrated aggregates of beliefs, values, rites and symbols. Environments are both products and sources of ideologies, as decision-making unfolds and intertwines people, ideologies and rationalization of upcoming events. The conformity of organizational ideologies to societal aspirations acts as a source of reassuring legitimacy for the organization.

Starbuck drew a distinction between problem solving, which aspires to rationality, and action generating, in which people observe the results of their actions and propose either new actions or new problems to fit the available solutions (see PROBLEM SOLVING). He argued that the issue of whether problems are real or not is resolved by collective voting, in which clichés and quasi-theories play important roles. 'Organizations' characteristics create perceptual filters that strongly distort their attempts at rational analyses' (Starbuck 1982: 6). These ideas about cognition reflect the influence of Watzlawick, and colleagues who examined situations in which people invent solutions that make their problems worse. Before they can generate effective solutions, this view said that, the people must see the problems in entirely different frames. Likewise, argued Starbuck, organizations are often unable to respond appropriately to problems until they see the problems in new frames.

Starbuck's ideas on non-rational decision processes culminated in a paper of 'action generators,' which built on the writings of March and Simon (see MARCH, J.G. AND CYERT, R.M.; SIMON, H.A.). 'Organizations' activities categorize in at least two modes: a problem-solving mode in which perceived problems motivate searches for solutions, and an action-generating mode in which action taking motivates the invention of problems to justify the actions. The problem-solving mode seems to describe a very small percentage of the activity sequences that occur, and the action-generating mode a large percentage' (Starbuck 1983: 91–92).

Hence, organizations build ideologies that turn into structures, language, actions or problems, and then become themselves sources for building new ideologies (Meyer and Starbuck 1993). Past successes are interpreted as criteria for the validity and consistency of current behaviours, as in the case of NCR, where eighty years of success in mechanical cash registers fused beliefs, strategies, structures, and action programmes into a self-reinforcing ensemble. Ideology then blinds the organization to signals of dramatic change, and crises materialize while organizations act in ways that make the crises worse (Starbuck et al. 1978).

Starbuck's longitudinal case studies – the Challenger disaster, Facit, Kalmar Verkstad, NCR – have made 'unlearning' a prescription for preventing and dealing with crises (Starbuck et al. 1976: 49–54; 1978). As a prevention, unlearning counteracts the inertia of learning. Busy with applying old programmes, organizations fail to invent new behavioural patterns and they discount signs of trouble as being merely expected outcomes.

A finding of the Challenger study is that 'fine-tuning' can finally be the cause of failure because it creates sequences of experiments that test the limits of theoretical knowledge. Hence, if crises are occasions to learn, they are also occasions to discover that beliefs are failing to explain events (1983). Human and organizational flaws pervade Starbuck's theories as do behavioural programs that develop autonomously, showing his taste for relativity and indeterminateness.

6 Scientific methods

Managers are not the only people who take their objectivity for granted. Recognizing that researchers' perceptions, language and founding assumptions produce systematic interpretation biases, Starbuck turned his humble attitude towards knowledge into a life-long epistemological commitment, while he relentlessly combated theorizing that adopts a rational façade: 'Scientific rationality is a fantasy that appeals to us aesthetically, but it violates its own rules, distorts our observations, and extrapolates incomplete knowledge to ridiculous extremes' (1988b: 71).

Starbuck made such statements from experience. All of his theorizing has involved his questioning, without complacency or self-indulgence, his own epistemological assumptions. One result has been scepticism about clear-cut positions and theories presented as absolute truths. Even as he advocated the use of mathematics in social sciences, he pointed out that 'Symbolic representation can be as unspecific and as ambiguous as one chooses to make it' (1965a: 340). When James Price exhorted researchers to have more logical rigour, Starbuck protested, 'there are circumstances in which increases in logical rigor will decrease the value of a study' (1968: 135).

Instead of faking objectivity, a sincere researcher, Starbuck suggested, acknowledges the ambiguous border between prescription and prevision, between observation and interpretation. He or she does not reject paradigms, but understands their ideological nature (1974). He or she experiments and predicts in the course of experimentation, so as to surprise himself with errors (Starbuck *et al.* 1981; Starbuck and Pant 1990). He or she acknowledges with humility that observations may say more about the researcher than about observed phenomena. He or she acknowledges that time series are autocorrelated and that one progresses faster by eliminating poor hypotheses than by defending plausible ones (1994).

7 Conclusion

Starbuck's contributions pervade management. Ideas and methods that he promoted are widely used everyday – action generator, computer simulation, environmental niche, evolution, knowledge-intensive firm, mathematical models, organizational design, prescription, fine-tuning, unlearning. Contingency theory is no longer popular, and he continues to wage campaigns against multiple regression, point null hypotheses, and significance tests. His most important contribution lies perhaps in the modesty that he assigned to the research act. He showed that scientists have personal values that impact their research. Instead of adopting objective façades that look like grimaces, he invites us to constantly reconsider our descriptions with wisdom and our prescriptions with humility.

PHILIPPE BAUMARD
UNIVERSITÉ DE AIX-MARSEILLE III

Further reading

(References cited in the text marked *)

* Cyert, R.M., March, J.G. and Starbuck, W.H. (1961) 'Two experiments on bias and conflict in organizational estimation', *Management Science* 7: 254–64. (Introduces the relativity of perception in decision situations. A breakthrough implicitly announcing March and Cyert's 'bounded rationality'.)
* Hedberg, B.L.T., Nystrom, P.C. and Starbuck, W.H. (1976) 'Camping on seesaws: Prescriptions for a self-designing organization', *Administrative Science Quarterly* 21: 41–65. (A most influential and quoted paper, calling for wisdom in organizational studies. The core of the self-designing paradigm.)
Meyer, A.D. and Starbuck, W.H. (1993) 'Interactions between politics and ideologies in strategy formation', in K. Roberts (ed.), *New Challenges to Understanding Organizations*, London: Macmillan. (Based on NCR's case, this paper shows how ideologies can be collaterally stabilizers and destabilizers of organizations, impeding or fostering strategic reorientations.)
* Starbuck, W.H. (1963) 'Level of aspiration', *Psychological Review* 70: 51–60. Based on Working Paper No. 7, Carnegie Institute of Technology 1958. (Suggests that levels of aspiration may be subject to changes over time, in contradiction of Festinger's maximization assumptions.)
* Starbuck, W.H. (1965a) 'Mathematics and organization theory', in J.G. March (ed.) *Handbook of Organizations*, Rand McNally. (Explores the limits of mathematical languages and theoretical apparatus when applied to social sciences.)
* Starbuck, W.H. (1965b) 'Organizational growth and development', in J.G. March (ed.) *Handbook of Organizations*, Rand McNally. (An extensive and critical review of classical growth models, that underly their methodological pitfalls. Suggests broader and more detailed data could correct past theoretical failure.)
* Starbuck, W.H. (1968) 'Some comments, observations, and objections stimulated by design of proof in organizational research', *Administrative Science Quarterly* 13: 135–61. (An offen-

sive critique of Price's claim for logical rigour as a means of increasing the value of a study. A provocative invitation to consider small changes, idiosyncratic samples, and to resist organization research methodological clichés.)

* Starbuck, W.H. (1973) 'Tadpoles into Armageddon and Chrysler into butterflies', *Social Science Research* 2: 81–109. (Invites researchers to factor the study of large metamorphosis in time segments, and to concentrate on initial sparks rather than hazardous supposively complete understanding. A seminal paper on metamorphic changes.)

* Starbuck, W.H. (1974) 'The current state of organization theory', in J.W. McGuire (ed.) *Contemporary Management: Issues and Viewpoints*, Prentice-Hall. (A humorous invitation to broaden the scope of organization theory.)

* Starbuck, W.H. (1975) 'Information systems for organizations of the future', in E. Grochla and N. Szyperski (eds), *Information Systems and Organizational Structure*, de Gruyter. (Claims that restrained designs provide opportunities for adaptation. A true foresight on information systems two decades later.)

* Starbuck, W.H. (1982) 'Congealing oil: Inventing ideologies to justify acting ideologies out', *Journal of Management Studies* 19 (1): 3–27. (A seminal paper on the interaction of ideologies and action in organizations.)

* Starbuck, W.H. (1983) 'Organizations as action generators', *American Sociological Review* 48: 91–102. (Action rationality prevails ideologies and decision-making in organizations.)

* Starbuck, W.H. (1988) 'Surmounting our human limitations', in R. Quinn and K. Cameron (eds) *Paradox and Transformation: Toward a Theory of Change in Organization and Management*, Ballinger. (Points to the value, not the sin, of paradoxical settings in organizational research. An invitation to celebrate perceptual distortion, and to make it the ground for theoretical construction.)

Starbuck, W.H. (1992) 'Learning by knowledge-intensive firms', *Journal of Management Studies* 29 (6): 713–40. (Seminal article about the development and control of knowledge in organizations.)

* Starbuck, W.H. (1993a) ' "Watch where you step!" or Indiana Starbuck amid the perils of Academe (Rated PG)', in A. Bedeian (ed.) *Management Laureates*, volume 3, JAI Press. (Links his own experiences of brutal changes to the evolution of his research. A seminal paper on researchers' values and their influence on their practice and epistemological assumptions.)

Starbuck, W.H. (1993b) 'Keeping a butterfly and an elephant in a house of cards: The elements of exceptional success', *Journal of Management Studies* 30 (6): 885–921. (Shows the interdependence of human resources, organizational structure, strategy, and societal context. Argues that understanding exceptional performance requires case studies of unusual organizations.)

* Starbuck, W.H. (1994) 'On behalf of naiveté', in J.A.C. Baum and J.V. Singh (eds) *Evolutionary Dynamics of Organizations*, Oxford University Press. (A claim to take into account feedback into causal processes, and to carefully watch appearances of randomness in non-random process. A seminal contribution on researchers' values and influence on research process.)

Starbuck, W.H. (1996a) 'Trying to help S&Ls: How organizations with good intentions jointly enacted disaster', in Z. Shapira (ed.) *Organizational Decision Making*, Cambridge University Press, 35–60. (Attributes a national financial disaster to the interacts among interdependent organizations.)

Starbuck, W.H. (1996b) 'Unlearning ineffective or obsolete technologies', *International Journal of Technology Management* 11: 725–37. (Suggests actions managers can take to promote unlearning.)

Starbuck, W.H., Greve, A. and Hedberg, B.L.T. (1978) 'Responding to crises', *Journal of Business Administration* 9 (2): 111–37. (Suggests unlearning and reframing can prevent organizations from crises, and foster reorientations).

* Starbuck, W.H., Hedberg, B.L.T. and Nystrom, P.C. (1976) 'Camping on seesaws: Prescriptions for a self-designing organization', *Administrative Science Quarterly*, 21: 41–65.

Starbuck, W.H. and Mezias, J. (1996) 'Opening Pandora's box: studying the accuracy of managers' perceptions', *Journal of Organizational Behavior* 17 (2): 99–117. (Explains why academic researchers find it impossible to assess the accuracy of managers' perceptions.)

Starbuck, W.H. and Milliken, F. (1988a) 'Challenger: Changing the odds until something breaks', *Journal of Management Studies* 25: 319–340. (Suggests acclimatation and fine-tuning slowly degrade and impede sense-making.)

Starbuck, W.H. and Milliken, F. (1988b) 'Executives' perceptual filters: What they notice and how they make sense', in D.C. Hambrick (ed.) *The Executive Effect: Concepts and Methods for Studying Top Managers*, JAI Press. (A complete account on sense-making in organizations that set up a widely used framework in managerial cognition studies.)

* Starbuck, W.H. and Narayan Pant, P. (1990) 'Innocents in the forest: Forecasting and research methods', *Journal of Management* 16 (2): 433–60. (Least-square regression does not produce reliable findings. A call for simplicity in research and forecasting methods).

* Starbuck, W.H. and Nystrom, P.C. (eds) (1981) *Handbook of Organizational Design*, two volumes, Oxford: Oxford University Press. (Two volumes with major contributions to the management field. Installs organizational design as a new paradigm in management sciences.)

Starbuck, W.H. and Rindova, V.P. (1997a) 'Ancient Chinese theories of control', *Journal of Management Inquiry* 6: 144–59. (Describes various prescriptions about managerial practice formulated by the Chinese between 2350 BCE and 0 BCE.)

Starbuck, W.H. and Rindova, V.P. (1997b) 'Distrust in dependence: The ancient challenge of superior–subordinate relations', in T.A.R. Clark (ed.) *Advancements in Organization Behaviour: Essays in Honour of Derek Pugh*, Dartmouth, 313–36. (Discusses evidence about superior–subordinate relations from ancient China, Egypt, and Mesopotamia.)

See also: MARCH, J.G. AND CYERT, R.M.; NONAKA, I.; ORGANIZATION BEHAVIOUR; ORGANIZATION BEHAVIOUR, HISTORY OF; ORGANIZATIONAL INFORMATION AND KNOWLEDGE; ORGANIZATIONAL LEARNING; SIMON, H.A.

Statutory audit

Overview

A statutory audit refers to the verification by a professional public accountant of information in financial statements prepared by the management of an organization or enterprise. The purpose of an audit is to detect material misstatements in the information, thereby making the information more credible or believable in the eyes of financial statement users, such as shareholders and creditors. While audits are sometimes mandated by law (hence the term 'statutory audit'), an economic demand for auditing can arise whenever one party (for example, management) assumes stewardship over resources owned by another party (for example, shareholders).

The practice of auditing has ancient roots. For example, in Greco-Roman times, government agents frequently audited the records of private tax collectors. The modern audit, in which professional accountants verify financial statements prepared by management, is linked with the growth of business corporations in the twentieth century, along with the increasing dispersion of the ownership of corporate shares.

In order for an audit itself to be credible, it is important that auditors are technically knowledgeable and have strong incentives both to detect and truthfully report any material misstatements which may exist in the information they are verifying. Thus, in most jurisdictions, only professional accountants who have met certain standards of education and practical experience are licensed to perform audits. Moreover, auditors must comply with detailed professional technical standards and rules of ethical conduct. Finally, auditors are subject to being sued both by clients and third-party financial statement users if they are negligent in their work.

The audit process begins with a set of financial statements, which can be viewed as containing numerous management assertions about transactions that took place during the reporting period, and their effects on the assets, liabilities and shareholders' equity of an entity. Specifically, management asserts that transactions and their effects are valid (they actually exist) and complete (all are included in the financial statements). In addition, legal rights and obligations (for example, asset ownership) are properly recognized. Finally, valuation, along with presentation and disclosure, are in accordance with generally accepted accounting principles.

The auditor's objective is to collect the type and quantity of evidence, at an appropriate time, to support a reasonable degree of belief or assurance that the assertions in the financial statements are true, in all material respects. The concept of reasonable assurance recognizes that there is only a probability (not certainty) that assertions are true, while the concept of materiality recognizes that there is an acceptable degree of imprecision in assertions. For example, the valuation of transactions need not be exactly correct.

After completing an examination, the auditor communicates his or her beliefs to financial statement users in a formal report which contains an expression of opinion. The auditor's opinion will usually be unqualified, but may be modified to reflect a lack of sufficient appropriate evidence or because the financial statements contain an uncorrected material misstatement.

1 Demand for auditing

The demand for auditing arises because of the risk that information provided by one party to another may be incorrect, incomplete or otherwise unreliable. A major cause of information risk is that the goals of the information provider may not be congruent with the goals of the information user.

An organization's management has an incentive to use organizational resources to maximize its own utility. Maximization of management's utility will not necessarily result in utility maximization for the shareholders, creditors and others who supplied those resources. For example, management may engage in the excessive consumption of perquisites – such as luxurious office space or personal leisure facilities. Excess perquisite consumption creates an incentive to misrepresent operating results, lest such consumption be revealed. Likewise, a dishonest manager who simply steals corporate assets has an obvious incentive to conceal the theft by issuing misleading information.

In addition to the risk of intentional misrepresentation, modern organizations engage in voluminous transactions which have also become increasingly complex. Thus, there is a risk that transactions and their effects are simply unreported, or not reported properly in accordance with generally accepted accounting principles.

Finally, the risks of both deliberate and unintentional misstatements of information are exacerbated by the fact that information users are frequently remote from the organization. Thus, they have little or no first-hand knowledge of events that occur within the organization and their effects, relying instead on information provided by others. The basic purpose of a statutory audit is to reduce the information risk associated with general purpose financial statements prepared by an organization's management (see FINANCIAL REPORTING, SOCIAL THEORIES OF).

2 Auditing and the public accounting profession

Early audits of corporate records and financial statements were not performed by professional accountants. For example, the 1844 Joint Stock Companies Act in the UK required the financial statements issued by corporate directors to be audited. However, the auditor was not required to be independent of management nor a qualified accountant. In fact, most persons serving as auditors were simply shareholders in the firm.

The increasing complexity of business transactions and increasing reliance on external financing through debt and share offerings gradually led to the development of public accounting as a profession. The first professional organization of public accountants in the world was organized in Edinburgh, Scotland, in 1854. As the profession in the UK matured, it also spread to other English-speaking countries.

The crash of financial markets in 1929 and the prevalence of corporate business failures during the economic depression of the 1930s led to several auditing developments in the USA, which are still important today. Most notable were the passage of the Securities Act of 1933 and the Securities Exchange Act of 1934. The 1933 Act governs the preparation of registration statements for new public issues of securities, which are to include audited financial statements. The 1934 Act governs periodic reporting (including the issue of annual audited financial statements) by companies whose shares are publicly traded.

Among other things, the 1934 Act created the Securities and Exchange Commission (SEC), which has the legal authority to issue accounting and auditing standards in the USA. While the SEC has generally been content to allow the profession to set detailed standards, it continues to monitor and influence the development of both US and international auditing standards.

Finally, the 1933 and 1934 Acts contain explicit provisions governing the legal liability of all parties (including auditors) associated with financial information prepared pursuant to the Acts. These statutes have been instrumental in shaping the 'liability crisis' confronting US auditors in the 1990s, and thereby the worldwide public accounting profession.

Professional accountants are typically members of national professional bodies, such as the Institute of Chartered Accountants in England and Wales or the American Institute of Certified Public Accountants (AICPA). These professional bodies set rules of conduct for their members, as well as technical standards of auditing. The professional bodies are themselves organized through membership in the International Federation of Accountants (IFAC), with headquarters in New York City. Currently, professional accounting bodies from 78 countries are members of IFAC. Among other activities, IFAC technical committees formulate model education requirements, codes of conduct and international auditing standards, which can then be adopted (perhaps after modification) by the member bodies in individual countries.

Professional public accountants perform many services for their clients – most notably auditing, general management consulting and tax consulting. The vast majority of statutory audits, however, are performed by the larger public accounting firms, particularly the dominant international firms previously known as the Big Six: Arthur Andersen & Co., Coopers & Lybrand, Deloitte & Touche, Ernst & Young, KPMG Peat Marwick, and Price Waterhouse & Co., but subsequently becoming the Big Five following the merger of Price Waterhouse and Coopers & Lybrand to form PriceWaterhouseCoopers. For example, in the USA, the Big Six audit about 60 per cent of smaller publicly held companies (sales less than $25 million) and about 95 per cent of the larger corporations (sales greater than $500 million), whose shares are publicly traded.

Given the dominance of the Big Six firms in the market for audit services, it is not surprising that they have sometimes been accused of operating as a cartel to increase the price of audits artificially. Simunic (1980) investigated that allegation in the USA, using data for audits performed in the late 1970s, and found no evidence of cartel pricing. Rather, the evidence suggested that the Big Six firms performed higher quality audits (on average) than smaller firms, and also appeared to enjoy economies of scale which were at least partially passed through to their clients. Similar conclusions have emerged from numerous subsequent studies performed using data from many countries.

3 Auditing standards and other quality assurance mechanisms

The performance of an audit by a firm of professional accountants is not directly observable by users of financial statements. Even if the process were observable, most users would lack the knowledge to be able to evaluate the quality of work being performed. Thus, in order for the market for audits to be viable, there must be mechanisms in place to assure that the quality of service purchased is actually delivered. The most important of these quality assurance mechanisms are:

- professional auditing standards;
- professional ethics;
- auditors' legal liability;
- individual audit firm reputations.

Auditing standards

The concept of generally accepted auditing standards (GAAS) arose in the USA following the McKesson & Robbins fraud of the 1930s in which, among other misrepresentations, the company claimed to own millions of dollars worth of inventories that were entirely fictitious. The fictitious inventories had been recorded in McKesson & Robbins' books to cover up a theft by management.

During subsequent hearings held by the SEC, it was determined that the profession at the time had no written auditing standards, and that accepted procedures did not require an auditor actually to observe the physical existence of inventories. As a result, the SEC urged the AICPA to develop a set of broad standards governing the practice of auditing. These basic standards, which have remained essentially unchanged to the present time, require that:

1 the audit be performed by a person or persons having adequate technical training and proficiency in auditing;
2 an independent mental attitude be maintained by the auditor in all matters relating to the engagement;
3 due professional care be exercised in the performance of the audit and in the preparation of the auditor's report;

4 the audit work be adequately planned and any assistants be properly supervised;
5 an understanding of the client's internal control structure be obtained which is sufficient to plan the audit and to determine the nature, extent and timing of tests to be performed;
6 sufficient competent evidential matter be obtained through inspection, observation, inquiries and confirmations to afford a reasonable basis for an opinion regarding the presence or absence of material misstatements in the financial statements under audit (see Arens and Loebbecke 1994).

In addition to the above, the standards contain guidance on the wording of the auditor's report. This feature is discussed in a later section of this entry.

As the basic principles of auditing are so general, it has been necessary to elaborate and expand upon them. This work is carried out by both standard-setting boards and committees of the individual professional bodies. For example, the Auditing Standards Board of the AICPA issues *Statements on Auditing Standards* and the UK Auditing Practices Board issues *Auditing Guidelines*. At the international level, *International Standards on Auditing* (ISAs) are issued by the International Auditing Practices Committee (IAPC) of IFAC. The ISAs typically resemble detailed national auditing standards, and form the basis for the standards used in many countries, including Australia and the UK.

Professional ethics

The other major form of professional self-regulation governing the practice of auditing are rules of conduct and codes of professional ethics. The *Code of Ethics for Professional Accountants* (IFAC 1995), issued by the Ethics Committee of IFAC, is typical.

Probably the single most important concept contained in the ethical codes is that the auditor must be independent of an audit client, in both fact and appearance. Since independence in fact is an unobservable state of mind, specific requirements are imposed on auditors in practice. For example, auditors are prohibited from having any direct financial interest in an audit client through share ownership or loans to or from the organization. Also, they, as well as immediate family members, are prohibited from serving as a director or member of an audit client's management. Furthermore, while public accounting firms are allowed to perform multiple services, such as auditing and consulting, for the same client, they may not become involved in managerial decision making.

A second important ethical principle is the confidentiality of information obtained during the performance of an audit. Auditors are prohibited from divulging such information, except as required by law, and cannot use such information for personal gain. As discussed later in this article, the requirement of confidentiality can create a reporting dilemma if, for example, the management of an audit client is engaged in illegal activities.

Up until the 1980s, public accountants in most Western countries were prohibited by ethical rules from advertising their services and actively soliciting clients. On the whole, normal competitive business behaviour was discouraged as being unseemly for professionals and a possible threat to the quality of their work. By the 1990s, these restrictions had largely been eliminated, primarily because of pressures put on the AICPA by both the Anti-Trust Division of the US Department of Justice and the US Federal Trade Commission. During the 1980s, public accounting firms throughout the world became more aggressive and competitive. The possible effects of this increased competitiveness, particularly in pricing, are discussed in the last section of this article.

Legal liability

Perhaps the most important mechanism assuring that audits are performed to an acceptable level of quality is the legal liability of auditors. The specific details of auditor liability vary considerably across legal jurisdictions. However, in general, auditors are liable to their clients for negligent performance of duty under contract; they are liable to other parties who have not specifically (or constructively) contracted with the auditor for any deceit or fraud;

and they are liable under the terms of relevant statutes.

In common law countries such as the UK, the USA and Canada, an auditor's liability to the client for negligent performance of duty under contract is well established (see Causey 1979). There are four requisites for liability to a client:

1 A duty is owed with respect to a standard of conduct. This is defined by the terms of the contract and/or usual expectations concerning the performance of auditors.
2 There is a failure to act in accordance with the duty. This failure may take the form of ordinary negligence or, worse, gross negligence or fraud.
3 There is a causal connection between the auditor's failure to perform his or her duty and injury to the client.
4 The client suffers actual losses or damages.

The burden of proof is on the client to show that these four conditions exist.

While the basic principles are clear, exactly who can sue an auditor as the 'client' is not so clear. Technically, the client is the corporation (as a legal entity) that hired the auditor, while management and directors have the authority to act on behalf of the entity. However, in some circumstances – such as when an auditor fails to uncover a material management fraud – the interests of shareholders diverge from those of managers and directors. In that case, the shareholders themselves, acting as a body, may be deemed to constitute the 'client'.

An auditor's common law liability to other parties, such as investors and creditors with whom the auditor does not specifically contract, is much more ambiguous and fluid than liability to clients. The greatest controversy surrounds liability for ordinary negligence to persons other than the client. Depending on the legal jurisdiction, this may range from no liability at all, to liability only to those people who were foreseen (or should have been foreseen) as relying on the audited financial statements. However, it is clear that an auditor who commits a fraud or deceit is liable to all injured parties, and will most likely face criminal charges as well. Also, an auditor who commits a constructive fraud through gross negligence in the performance of duty will probably be liable to all injured parties.

The ambiguity of an auditor's common law liability to investors apparently motivated the US Congress to write specific liability rules into the 1933 and 1934 Securities Acts. Of the two laws, the 1933 Act is the more onerous. Under Section 11, a purchaser of securities registered with the SEC can sue an auditor (and other parties involved in the securities registration process) if the audited financial statements are false or misleading and the investor suffered a loss, such as a decline in share value. As a defence, the auditor must show (essentially) that the financial statements were not false or misleading or that the auditor exercised 'due diligence' in performing the audit examination. Due diligence has been taken to mean a lack of ordinary negligence. Thus, the 1933 Act holds auditors liable to investors for ordinary negligence, while also switching much of the burden of proof from investor plaintiffs to auditor defendants.

The liability provisions of the 1934 Act are less draconian. In addition to showing that the financial statements were false or misleading, investors must also show that they relied on the financial statements in making their decisions. However, the reliance may be indirect, in that false or misleading financial information can be expected to affect the market price of securities. In addition, an auditor need not prove due diligence, but simply that he or she acted 'in good faith'. This term has been interpreted to mean that there is an absence of gross negligence, rather than ordinary negligence as under the 1933 Act. The weaker liability provisions of the 1934 Act relative to the 1933 Act apparently resulted from intense lobbying. As discussed in the last section of this article, both laws have been instrumental in fuelling the American liability crisis of the 1990s.

Given legal liability, when performing an audit, an auditor can be seen as trading off the increasing out-of-pocket and opportunity costs of performing more (or better) tests, against a reduction in the risk of failing to detect material misstatements and hence expected future losses from litigation. In addition, the more (and better) tests an auditor performs, the more likely he or she will be found to have complied with generally accepted auditing standards. Thus, at some point (short of a perfect audit), additional testing will not be deemed economically desirable and the auditor will have attained reasonable (but not absolute) assurance that the financial statements are free of material misstatements.

Audit firm reputation

While auditing standards, professional ethics and legal liability support an auditor's motivation to perform audits of average quality, a specific public accounting firm (or firms) may find it economically desirable to perform even higher quality audits. A higher quality audit is generally taken to mean that the level of assurance provided to users is higher than the usual or average level. The promise to deliver a higher than average audit quality is credible to both clients and financial statement users if the audit firm has an investment in reputation, which would be damaged by a failure to perform as expected.

The demand for higher quality audits is driven by the fact that information risk may be higher in certain circumstances. For example, the motivation to deliberately misstate financial information is greater than usual if a company has high gearing and is close to violating debt covenants. Or, managers who own a small percentage of a company's shares and whose interests are not closely aligned with those of shareholders through incentive compensation arrangements may be motivated to shirk their duties or otherwise consume excessive perquisites.

Auditing researchers have performed a variety of tests of audit quality differentiation, many of which have focused on the hypothesis that Big Five firms perform higher quality audits than non-Big Five firms. For example, a study of 1484 audits of Australian public companies found that the Big Five firms were able to charge an 18–25 per cent price premium in that market.

One of the most direct tests of the hypothesis was performed by Teoh and Wong (1993). If client earnings audited by a Big Five firm are viewed by the securities market as being more believable (credible) than earnings verified by a non-Big Five firm, then the magnitude of the stock market price reaction to an earnings surprise (unexpectedly high or low earnings) should be greater in cases where a Big Five audit firm was involved. (This is true because market participants should be motivated to discount, or ignore, unusually high or low earnings that are seen as having a greater likelihood of being materially misstated.) Using data for a large sample of earnings announcements by US companies in the 1980s, where Big Five clients were matched on company size and industry to non-Big Five clients, the authors found strong evidence of a differential price effect. In short, the clients of Big Five firms got 'more stock market bang for their reported earnings buck' than did non-Big Five clients.

Another interesting piece of evidence comes from auditor litigation studies. If the average level of assurance provided by a Big Five audit is higher than the assurance provided by non-Big Five firms, then the incidence of successful lawsuits against Big Five auditors should be relatively low, other factors remaining constant. If the Big Five firms' target audit assurance level is higher than that implicitly required by generally accepted auditing standards, then the Big Five should experience lower rates of failure to detect material misstatements in financial statements (audit failure). In addition, they should be less likely to be found in violation of GAAS by a court in the event of a lawsuit. Evidence consistent with this prediction was developed by Palmrose (1988). She studied 472 legal cases filed against US audit firms during the period 1960–85, and found that 3 per cent of the publicly held clients of Big Five firms were involved in auditor litigation, while 5.1 per cent of the publicly held clients of non-Big Five firms were involved in such litigation. Note that if all cases of audit failure lead to subsequent litigation, then Big Five auditors provide, on average, a 97 per cent level of assurance, while non-Big Five auditors provide about 95 per cent assurance.

4 Materiality and audit risk

As discussed above, an auditor provides financial statement users with a level of assurance that the audited financial statements are free of material misstatement. As a result, the monetary amount of misstatement which is deemed tolerable or immaterial is a fundamental audit judgement, as is the level of assurance – or its complement, audit risk – which the auditor provides.

The larger the amount of money deemed to be immaterial (called 'materiality'), the lower the quantity and/or quality of evidence an auditor needs to obtain to provide a given level of assurance, other factors remaining constant. The lower the level of assurance the auditor chooses to provide – or, equivalently, the higher the risk of failing to detect material misstatements the auditor is willing to tolerate – the lower the quantity and/or quality of evidence an auditor needs to collect, other things remaining constant. Finally, if the quantity and quality of evidence is kept constant, then the relationship between audit risk and materiality is inverse. Increasing the amount of money deemed immaterial reduces audit risk; reducing the amount of money deemed immaterial increases audit risk. For example, if an auditor's objective is to detect only huge misstatements, audit risk will be low. But (for a given quantity and quality of evidence) if his or her objective is to find the proverbial 'needle in the haystack', audit risk will be high.

Assessing materiality

In order to plan the performance of an audit examination, the auditor must specify a level of materiality at the beginning of an engagement. Conceptually, a misstatement is immaterial if knowledge of the misstatement would not affect the investment, lending or other decisions of financial statement users. While auditing standards do not specify what the level of materiality should be, it is usually set at about 510 per cent of a company's normal income before income taxes. That is, a misstatement which (taken alone) is less than that cut-off value is deemed immaterial, while a misstatement equal to or greater than the cut-off value would be considered material. In addition, research evidence suggests that the materiality percentage becomes relatively smaller for larger clients. That is, while materiality increases in absolute (say) dollar amounts as clients increase in size, this amount is a relatively smaller percentage of income before taxes for large companies than for small companies.

When evaluating the possible materiality of misstatements actually detected during an audit, auditors also consider various qualitative factors in addition to the dollar amount. For example, even a small misstatement which arose from management's deliberate attempt to deceive would likely be deemed material. Or, if a small misstatement affected the trend line of net income or earnings per share over time, it would most likely be deemed material.

Audit risk models

Having assessed an appropriate materiality level, an auditor must consider the risks associated with an engagement, including the ultimate audit risk the auditor is willing to take. As discussed earlier, the research suggests that audit risk ranges from about 3 per cent (97 per cent assurance) for the Big Five firms to about 5 per cent (95 per cent assurance) for other public accounting firms.

The planning of modern audits very much revolves around risk assessment and analysis, through the use of audit risk models. A particular model of risk has attained wide acceptance in practice, being incorporated, for example, into US, UK, Canadian and international auditing standards. That model is:

Audit risk(AR) = Inherent risk(IR) × Control risk (CR) × Detection risk(DR)

where:

AR = probability that an undetected material misstatement exists in the audited financial statements;

IR = probability that a material misstatement will occur in the financial statements, without considering the client's internal controls;

CR = probability that the client's internal controls will fail to detect a material misstatement;

DR = probability that the auditor's tests of financial statement assertions will fail to detect a material misstatement.

Thus, audit risk is viewed as being the joint probability of a material misstatement arising, but where the client's control systems and the auditor's tests of management's assertions fail to detect the misstatement. Note that all of the risks are defined with respect to a material misstatement. An auditor must therefore assess materiality prior to using the risk model. Also, if assessed materiality changes, the risks must also change.

Operationally, when planning and performing an audit, the model would be used in a form where detection risk is a function of all of the other risks, or:

$$DR = \frac{AR}{IR \times CR}$$

Applying the model, the sequence of steps in performing an audit would be as follows:

1 Choose a desired level of audit risk. As noted above, this is largely a matter of public accounting firm policy, and audit risk could be expected to be relatively constant across all the audits performed by a particular firm.
2 Assess inherent risk for the engagement. Inherent risk is assessed at both the overall financial statement level, and with respect to specific financial statement assertions.
3 Assess control risk, again both at the overall level and with respect to specific assertions.

Having determined values or levels for the risks on the right-hand side of the equation, a value or level of required detection risk is determined. A low level of required detection risk implies that the auditor must perform relatively 'powerful' audit tests. The power of a test is increased by obtaining more evidence, and/or more persuasive types of evidence, and/or performing tests in a more timely manner (for example, at or near the balance sheet date). Conversely, a high required detection risk implies that an auditor's tests need not be very powerful. Note that for a given audit risk, 'low power' audit tests would be required if the inherent risk of material misstatement was low and/or the client had excellent internal controls in place (CR was low).

5 Audit testing and audit evidence

Auditing efficiently

To perform an audit efficiently, auditors exploit the transaction structure associated with the double-entry book-keeping system and the fact that financial statements are articulated (see FINANCIAL STATEMENT ANALYSIS). That is, the basic financial statements – balance sheet, income statement and cash flow statement (or statement of changes in financial position) – can be viewed as arising by taking differences between two balance sheets:

$$\text{Assets}^E = \text{Liabilities}^E + \text{Owners' equity}^E$$
$$- (\text{Assets}^B = \text{Liabilities}^B + \text{Owners' equity}^B)$$
$$\overline{\Delta\text{Assets} = \Delta\text{Liabilities} + \Delta\text{Owners' equity}}$$

where the superscript E denotes the ending balance sheet, B denotes the beginning balance sheet, and the symbol Δ denotes flows through these accounts.

In a continuing engagement (most audit clients retain the same public accounting firm for many years), the assertions associated with the beginning balance sheet accounts will have been verified in the previous year. Thus, verification of the assertions associated with the ending balance sheet not only directly verifies that specific financial statement, but also indirectly verifies the year-to-year changes in assets, liabilities and owners' equity. Since such changes are the components of the income statement and cash flow statement, those financial statements are indirectly verified. In addition, auditors normally perform direct tests of specific income statement accounts – such as depreciation, income taxes, repairs and maintenance, and legal fees – to determine that certain key amounts were properly calculated, transactions were appropriately classified, and to obtain information useful in performing the audit.

The essence of the audit approach described above is that audit tests are concentrated on the end-of-period balance sheet accounts. Further efficiency gains are possible if the auditor can reasonably make assumptions about management's motives with respect to intentional misstatements.

If the auditor believes that the inherent risk of an overstatement of net income is high – perhaps because management seems to lack integrity and their compensation is closely tied to reported income – then the auditor will emphasize the detection of overstated assets and/or understated liabilities. That is, the auditor will be most concerned with verifying the existence and valuation of assets, and the completeness and valuation of liabilities. The majority of audit examinations are designed from this perspective.

Alternatively, the auditor may believe that the situation involves a high inherent risk that income will be understated – perhaps because the client is a closely held company and management seeks to minimize income taxes. In that case, the risk is that assets are understated and/or liabilities are overstated. Here the auditor will be most concerned with the completeness and valuation of assets and the existence and valuation of liabilities.

Generally, the completeness assertion is the most difficult to verify, and it is easier to detect incomplete liabilities (creditors demand subsequent payment which is difficult to conceal) than to detect incomplete assets (these usually can be readily concealed). As a consequence, for example, auditors are not normally able to give an unqualified opinion on the financial statements of charities which solicit funds door-to-door, because it is not possible to verify that reported cash collections are complete.

Types of test

The tests performed during an audit can be classified by their purpose into two basic categories:

- tests of internal controls (sometimes called compliance tests);
- substantive tests of financial statement assertions.

Substantive tests can be further classified by their nature into analytical tests, tests of transactions and tests of details.

Tests of internal controls are performed when an auditor chooses to place some reliance on the client's internal control system, or, in the language of the risk model, plans to assess control risk at a level less than the maximum (100 per cent). The assessment of control risk is discussed in a subsequent section of this article.

Analytical tests involve making comparisons and contrasts between actual financial statement amounts or relationships (such as ratios) and the auditor's expectations or predictions as to what these amounts or relationships should be. Analytical testing has become increasingly popular since the 1980s, at least partially in response to competitive pressures which have motivated auditors to improve the efficiency of the audit process. Analytical procedures are discussed in more detail in a subsequent section of this article.

The majority of substantive tests performed during an audit will be tests of transactions and tests of details, in which the auditor obtains specific evidence bearing on the assertions associated with particular transactions or the details of account balances.

Hierarchy of evidence

When an auditor performs substantive tests of transactions and details, he or she recognizes that audit evidence varies considerably in quality or persuasiveness. A basic requirement for substantive tests is that financial statement amounts are supported by primary evidence in the form of the books and records of the company. During the audit examination, the mechanical accuracy and internal consistency of the client's books and records will be tested. In fact, in earlier times, a statutory audit was largely concerned with verifying the mechanical accuracy of the client's books and records. However, in the modern audit, obtaining sufficient competent supporting evidence is of fundamental importance. Supporting evidence can be rank ordered by its persuasiveness as follows:

1 Evidence obtained directly by the auditor through his or her own senses by observation or inspection.

2 Evidence obtained from a third party who is knowledgeable, unbiased or biased against the client (such as a customer or vendor):
  (a) a third-party document (confirmation) sent directly to the auditor;
  (b) a third-party document found within the client's organization;
  (c) a document that originates with the client but is validated by a third party.
3 Evidence obtained from within the client organization:
  (a) a client document not validated by a third party but produced under conditions of good internal control;
  (b) a client document produced under poor control conditions;
  (c) written responses to auditor inquiries by members of the organization;
  (d) oral responses to auditor inquiries.

While evidence obtained directly by the auditor through observation or inspection is generally the best, its persuasiveness will vary with the level of the auditor's own knowledge. For example, personal observation of an inventory of diamonds will not be too persuasive as to their grade, etc. unless the auditor is a qualified gemologist. An auditor would normally rely upon an independent expert in such circumstances. Also, evidence obtained directly by the auditor is likely to be relevant to testing the existence and perhaps the valuation assertions, but will not be likely to bear on the assertion as to legal rights and obligations.

A typical audit relies heavily on documentary evidence obtained from third parties. The rank ordering of such evidence largely reflects the extent of information coming from a third party and the ease or difficulty with which a fictitious document can be issued or the information altered. Thus, direct communication between the auditor and a third party with regard to confirmation of amounts such as cash balances and customer accounts receivable balances is best. While a client-prepared document reflects client information and may be fictitious or altered, its persuasiveness is enhanced by the (usually limited) third-party involvement. A disbursement cheque showing cancellation by the bank is an example of such a document.

The design and execution of an audit programme requires that the auditor exercise considerable professional judgement in choosing the quantity and quality of evidence to examine. In addition, a high level of professional judgement is required in aggregating evidence derived from tests of various assertions to form an overall opinion on the financial statements.

Analytical procedures

Analytical procedures involve 'auditing by exception'. There are four basic steps in the process:

1 formulating an expectation as to what some financial statement assertion, account balance or ratio should be;
2 comparing the actual unaudited value of an item to the expectation and observing or calculating a difference;
3 deciding whether the difference is sufficiently large to warrant further investigation;
4 structuring the nature, extent and/or timing of other substantive tests as a function of the difference and the outcome of any investigation performed.

An auditor can form expectations in many ways. However, expectations should be based on the auditor's knowledge of the business and derived from reliable data, such as audited amounts from the client's financial statements for previous years (for example, published industry statistics). Analytical procedures may range from simple scanning of the current year's financial statements and detailed supporting amounts, to the application of formal statistical regression models (see FORECASTING AND STATISTICAL MODELS). However, studies have shown that only very simple methods – such as scanning and ratio analysis – are used in the majority of engagements.

Analytical procedures have two basic uses – directing an auditor's attention to important areas where further testing is appropriate, and as source of assurance that an assertion is not materially misstated. In the planning stage, analytical procedures assist the auditor in understanding the client's business and assessing the inherent risk of material misstatement of various assertions. This is an attention-directing use. During the substantive testing stage of the audit, an auditor may derive assurance from performing an analytical procedure. When analytical testing is used in that way, the expectation developed by the auditor must be sufficiently precise so that a material misstatement can reasonably be detected. For example, it would not be appropriate to derive assurance from a simple scanning of data, since there the auditor's expectation would be vague and intuitive. Statistical regression analysis, on the other hand, can yield precise predictions and is appropriate for deriving assurance.

Analytical procedures are used in the final review stages of an audit as part of the formation of an overall conclusion that the financial statements as a whole are consistent with the auditor's knowledge of the organization, its business and underlying economic conditions. Again, this is an attention-directing use of analytical procedures. *International Standards on Auditing*, as well as auditing standards in the USA and other countries, mandate the use of analytical procedures in the planning and overall review stages of an audit.

Assessing inherent and control risks

In the audit risk model, inherent risk and control risk are closely related. Recall the expression for detection risk:

$$DR = \frac{AR}{IR \times CR}$$

As the formula shows, an increase in inherent risks and/or control risks reduces detection risk, thereby increasing the power of tests an auditor must perform to attain a desired audit risk. In addition, recall that inherent risk is defined in such a way as to exclude the mitigating effects of a client's internal controls. For example, when auditing a bank, an auditor is likely to assess a high inherent risk of misstatement of cash through theft. At the same time, however, a prudent management would be expected to implement exceptionally strong internal controls over cash and cash transactions in a financial institution. Thus, the product of inherent and control risk, often termed relative risk, need not be high, and it is

the product of these risks that drives the required level of detection risk. Because of this interrelationship, auditors normally assess the level of inherent and control risks for particular assertions at the same time.

An auditor typically considers several major factors when assessing inherent risk. These include:

* the nature of the client's business and industry;
* the integrity of management;
* the results of previous audits;
* the presence of related parties;
* the presence of non-routine transactions;
* the degree of judgement required to properly record transactions;
* the degree of judgement required in valuing account balances;
* the susceptibility of underlying assets to theft.

In addition, as noted in the previous section, analytical procedures may identify unusual balances or relationships which indicate that the inherent risk of misstatement is higher than normal.

The assessment of control risk is somewhat more complex. Control risk refers to the perceived effectiveness of client internal controls, which themselves consist of two parts:

1 policies, systems and procedures that are concerned with the collecting, recording, processing and reporting of information (often termed the internal control structure);
2 policies, systems and procedures that enhance the reliability of data and information.

Until about 1990, international auditing standards, as well as standards in most countries, allowed auditors to ignore completely the client's internal control system, if it was deemed economical to do so. That is, an auditor could bypass internal controls and perform an audit consisting entirely of substantive audit tests. Using this approach, an auditor was required neither to understand nor test internal control systems, and would assess control risk at the maximum level of 100 per cent.

Recently, the profession has recognized that in order to design an effective and efficient audit plan, an auditor must have at least a basic understanding of the client's accounting system and the environment in which it operates. Such knowledge enables the auditor to better predict the types of misstatements which may occur, and the probability of such misstatements occurring. Thus, international, US and Canadian auditing standards, among others, now mandate that an auditor obtain an understanding of a client's internal control structure in every engagement. After obtaining such an understanding, an auditor can still assess control risk at (or near) the maximum level. Alternatively, the auditor may elect to perform tests of controls for all or parts of the system, and plan to assess control risk at less than 100 per cent. The ultimate control risk assessment will depend upon the extent of tests of controls performed and the outcomes of those tests.

When assessing the quality of an internal control system, an auditor considers such factors as:

- competence of client personnel;
- existence of clear lines of authority and responsibility;
- segregation of duties, so that different persons are responsible for authorizing, executing and recording transactions, and these persons do not have control over related assets;
- existence of adequate documents and records;
- physical controls over assets and records;
- continuous monitoring of the system by persons such as internal auditors.

Experience has shown that internal controls are likely to be most effective in large, bureaucratic organizations. However, even small organizations require adequate records and basic controls, particularly to insure that transactions are captured and recorded as they occur. In the absence of basic internal controls, an organization may not be auditable.

Statistical sampling

The quantity of evidence an auditor requires to verify assertions is a critical audit judgement, and the auditor may use statistical methods to facilitate that decision. While auditing standards do not mandate the use of statistical methods, use of a statistical approach to testing has major advantages over a purely judgemental approach. Specifically, the auditor must think through the sampling problem and focus on the key parameters that affect sample size. Inferences from the sample to the population must be made in a logical, orderly manner. Finally, the test is likely to be better documented, and the process will be defensible.

Two basic classes of statistical methods are used by auditors in determining sample sizes for substantive tests. One class of methods relies on the assumption that the sampling distribution of the estimator is the normal distribution. The other method is monetary unit sampling, which is based on the binomial sampling distribution.

Three normal distribution-based methods are sometimes used in auditing practice. The first is the mean-per-unit estimator, which uses the average audited dollar value of items included in a sample to estimate or test a hypothesis about the true, but unknown, population value. From the central limit theorem in statistics, it is known that if repeated samples of a certain size are drawn from a population, the probability distribution (sampling distribution) of the average value of items in the sample will be normal when the sample size is sufficiently large. This is true no matter what the distribution of the population looks like. The fact that auditors do not find it economical to examine very large samples can limit the usefulness of the mean-per-unit method, since the central limit theorem may not hold. However, this problem can often be overcome if the population is stratified into relatively homogeneous (low variance) subgroups.

A second method is the difference estimator, which uses the average value of differences (audited value minus client's recorded value) for items included in a sample to estimate or test a hypothesis about the true, but unknown, population difference. Again, for larger sample sizes, the central limit theorem ensures that the distribution of sample mean differences is normal. This method can be quite efficient because the standard deviation of population differences is typically much smaller than the standard deviation of item values in a population. However, the method is not reliable if the population has a very low error rate, because it becomes very difficult to obtain a reasonable estimate of the population standard deviation in such circumstances.

The third normal distribution-based method is the ratio estimator, which uses the average of the ratio of the audited values to a client's recorded values to make an inference about the population. Again, a small sample size and a low population error rate can create difficulties in applying this method.

The essence of the monetary unit sampling method is to convert an error rate result into a conclusion about monetary value. Error rates observed in repeated samples taken from a population with some true but unknown error rate have a binomial sampling distribution, when sampling is with replacement. Thus, the sampling distribution underlying monetary unit sampling is known to be correct, no matter what the size of the sample or the magnitude of the population error rate. However, the computations used in practice to convert error rate estimates into monetary unit error estimates are somewhat arbitrary. In addition, monetary unit sampling can be ineffective in detecting understatement errors. That is, it is not useful for testing the completeness assertion. Finally, monetary unit sampling is likely to be inefficient when the population error rate is high.

To summarize, while statistical methods can be helpful in determining sample size in auditing, no single technique is likely to be suitable in all circumstances. In addition, the use of statistics does not eliminate the need for professional judgement when making this decision.

The Big Five firms have tended to adopt statistical methods in their practices to varying degrees. For example, Deloitte & Touche and the firm of KPMG Peat Marwick use quantitative approaches much more than firms such as PriceWaterhouseCoopers. In addition, there appears to have been a move-

ment away from the use of statistical methods by all firms during the 1990s.

6 Auditor's report

The outcome of an audit is the auditor's report which includes, among other things, an expression of opinion concerning the absence (or presence) of material misstatements in the audited financial statements. While the wording of audit reports used in different countries varies, the language recommended by ISA 13 is illustrative of current best practice. An auditor who had obtained sufficient competent evidence and had no reservations about the fairness of the audited financial statements would issue the following report, containing an unqualified opinion, under ISA 13:

AUDITOR'S REPORT

(Appropriate addressee, usually the shareholders):

We have audited the accompanying balance sheet of the ABC Company as of 31 December 19xx, and the related statements of income and cash flows for the year then ended. These financial statements are the responsibility of the Company's management. Our responsibility is to express an opinion on these financial statements based on our audit.

We conducted our audit in accordance with *International Standards on Auditing*. Those standards require that we plan and perform the audit to obtain reasonable assurance about whether the financial statements are free of material misstatement. An audit includes examining, on a test basis, evidence supporting the amounts and disclosures in the financial statements. An audit also includes assessing the accounting principles used and significant estimates made by management, as well as evaluating the overall financial statement presentation. We believe that our audit provides a reasonable basis for our opinion.

In our opinion, the financial statements give a true and fair view of (or, alternatively, 'present fairly in all material respects') the financial position of the company as of 31 December 19xx, and of the results of operations and its cash flows for the year then ended in accordance with international accounting standards.

AUDITOR

Date

City and country

Two situations could prevent the auditor from issuing an unqualified opinion. If the auditor was unable to obtain sufficient competent evidence with respect to a material area of the financial statements, because of a client-imposed scope restriction or because it was not possible or practicable to do so, he or she would issue a qualified opinion as to the scope of the audit, or would simply deny (disclaim) an opinion. If, on the other hand, the auditor had obtained sufficient evidence and believed that the financial statements contained a material misstatement which management refused to correct, he or she would issue either a qualified opinion as to the client's conformance with international accounting standards (or relevant domestic standards) or an adverse opinion.

The evidence suggests that the vast majority of audit opinions, particularly on financial statements issued by companies whose shares are publicly traded, are unqualified.

7 Current issues and controversies in auditing

Auditors and their reports are subject to constant scrutiny. While an audit is performed to reduce the information risk faced by shareholders and creditors, the auditor has little or no direct contact with these financial statement users. Rather, an auditor deals largely with the client's management. As a result, there is considerable room for disagreement about the auditor's role and responsibilities. These disagreements constitute an 'expectations gap' between auditors and financial statement users. In addition, a dynamic, increasingly global economy can be expected to change periodically the auditor's role, and perhaps require a rethinking of auditing methods and underlying institutional arrangements.

The litigation crisis

A major concern of auditors is the extensive, worldwide litigation – amounting to tens of billions of US dollars – faced by public accounting firms. In 1990, the then seventh-largest public accounting firm in the USA, Laventhol & Horwath, declared bankruptcy under a crush of litigation. In 1992, the financial weakness of the firm of Arthur Young & Co., arising from litigation problems associated with its audits of savings and loan associations in the USA, motivated it to merge with the firm of Ernst & Whinney.

Research evidence suggests that, because of the fear of litigation, the Big Five firms in the USA have curtailed their involvement with companies issuing new securities to the public (Clarkson and Simunic 1994). Recall that persons associated with initial public offerings, such as auditors and underwriters, are subject to the harsh liability provisions of the Securities Act of 1933.

However, the threat of liability has positive aspects. While professional regulations – such as minimum education requirements and ethical standards – are useful, the large potential penalties arising from litigation are probably needed to assure investors and creditors that audits are performed to a reasonable level of quality. Moreover, the mounting litigation may simply reflect more basic problems that need to be resolved. In fact, most litigation against auditors involves certain common issues, namely: reporting when a client faces going concern problems, detecting and reporting fraud and illegal acts, and unresolved problems with auditor independence. This article will now consider these issues.

Reporting going concern problems

Financial statements are prepared on the assumption that the organization is a going concern. This is generally taken to mean that it will continue to operate normally during the next fiscal year, and will be able to realize assets and discharge liabilities in the normal course of business. If an organization is deemed not to be a going concern, generally accepted accounting principles require that its assets be comprehensively revalued at the lower of cost or market, and its liabilities reassessed.

Accounting standards essentially require management to treat the possibility that an organization may not be a going concern as a contingency. That is, management should accrue the amount of contingent loss in the financial statements when the business failure of the organization during the next year is deemed to be likely and the amount of loss can be reasonably estimated. In the absence of these conditions, the possible losses arising from failure of the organization should be disclosed in the footnotes to the financial statements, unless failure is deemed unlikely. In that case, no loss accrual or disclosure is necessary.

International auditing standards require that the auditor give an unqualified opinion if he or she agrees with management's accounting treatment. In addition, the auditor may choose to mention the contingency in his or her report, to alert the reader to the organization's going concern problems. In some countries, such as the UK, auditors deny an opinion when an organization's going concern status is in doubt.

While reporting standards vary, there is also some question as to how well auditors are applying current standards. For example, a recent study in the UK (Citron and Taffler 1992) found that of 107 listed companies which failed during the years 1977–86, 74 per cent received an unqualified opinion from their auditor in the previous year, with no mention of going concern problems. Moreover, about one-third of these companies failed within six months of receiving an unqualified audit opinion.

A similar situation probably exists in other countries because it is highly unlikely that, in practice, an auditor would insist that losses resulting from a comprehensive revaluation of a company's assets and liabilities be accrued, unless the organization actually files for bankruptcy and goes into receivership. Most auditors would be concerned that loss accrual prior to actual bankruptcy would simply precipitate a bankruptcy (a self-fulfilling prophecy). However, failure to report losses in a timely manner encourages lawsuits. Shareholders and creditors typically argue that they would have taken defensive measures earlier, thereby reducing their losses, had they been informed of a company's problems.

The major difficulty seems to be that current disclosures of risks associated with the operations of organizations are not adequate. Rather than treating going concern problems as present or absent, it appears that accounting and auditing standards need to be revised in such a way as to require auditors to disclose and verify all relevant information known to management, which is necessary to enable financial statement users to assess an organization's future prospects.

Fraud and illegal acts

An auditor's responsibility for the detection of employee or management fraud has changed considerably in recent years. Prior to 1988, auditors argued that an audit could not be relied upon to detect the effects of even material fraud in financial statements. However, if an auditor stumbled upon a possible fraud when performing normal audit procedures, he or she was obliged to confirm or dispel these suspicions, and inform management at a sufficiently high level.

In 1988, the AICPA issued *Statement on Auditing Standards* (SAS) 53, which clearly requires an auditor to assess the inherent risk that unintentional errors and intentional irregularities may cause the financial statements to contain a material misstatement. Based on that risk assessment, the auditor should design the audit to provide reasonable assurance of detecting material misstatements from all sources. This principle has been incorporated into international auditing standards and national standards in many countries.

Auditing standards typically go on to state that the likelihood that an auditor will detect a material fraud is lower than the likelihood of detecting material, but unintentional, misstatements. This is so because a fraud is usually accompanied by acts designed to conceal its existence. Thus, the level of reasonable assurance concerning the detection of fraudulent misstatements is probably lower than the assurance that unintentional misstatements are detected.

The issues associated with an auditor's responsibility for detecting and reporting material misstatements caused by a client's illegal acts are similar in many ways to the problems of fraud detection and reporting. However, the many laws and regulations which impact on the operations of organizations complicate the situation.

Auditors are not detectives and are not interested in uncovering illegal acts per se. However, an auditor must be concerned if a client's illegal activities result in a material misstatement of the financial statements. Generally, illegal acts, if detected and confirmed by authorities, are likely to give rise to criminal penalties, as well as some form of financial liability. Thus, a failure to detect an illegal act will typically result in understated liabilities or failure to disclose a contingency.

The AICPA's SAS 54 was the first professional pronouncement in this area. Because of the large number of laws and regulations governing the operations of organizations, SAS 54 distinguishes between illegal acts that have a direct and material effect on financial statement amounts, and those that have only an indirect effect on financial statements. An example of the former are income tax laws, while environmental laws and regulations are an example of the latter.

The basic principle of SAS 54 is that a US auditor must assess the inherent risk of material misstatements arising from direct illegal acts, and design an appropriate audit. However, an auditor need not plan to detect indirect illegal acts, but should make relevant inquiries of management concerning compliance with such laws and regulations. Principles similar to those of SAS 54 are contained in international auditing standards. However, there is evidence that auditors have great difficulty distinguishing between direct and indirect illegal acts in practice. Thus, in order to resolve the expectations gap in this area, it is probably necessary to introduce auditing standards which mandate a comprehensive risk assessment, and which concern possible violations of all significant laws and regulations affecting an organization.

Auditing standards require that any fraud or illegal act detected by the auditor be reported to high levels of authority within the organization. However, disclosure of such findings to persons outside the organization is normally not a part of the auditor's responsibilities. Recall that an auditor is bound by the ethical rule of confidentiality. Information obtained during an audit is confidential and can be disclosed only to satisfy the auditor's reporting responsibilities. For example, if an illegal act is discovered, but management refuses to make adequate disclosure of a resulting material contingent liability, an auditor will qualify his or her opinion because the financial statements do not conform to generally accepted accounting principles. However, in the absence of specific legislation, an auditor could not directly inform the police or other authorities.

Price competition and auditor independence

As the practice of public accounting became more competitive during the 1980s, fears were expressed that competitive behaviour would compromise the quality of audits. In particular, it has become popular for auditors to decry the practice of 'low-balling' – where an audit firm bids to perform a new engagement for a very low fee, perhaps lower than its own initial costs.

However, low-balling can be explained on purely economic grounds (De Angelo 1981). Since audits of a client are usually performed by the same firm for many years, an incumbent auditor is likely to learn a great deal, over time, about the operations of the organization. The incumbent is therefore able eventually to earn excess profits from the engagement, as no potential new auditor can be as knowledgeable as the incumbent, hence as efficient in performing the audit. The effect is aggravated in cases where the client would incur significant direct costs by changing auditors.

A rational auditor will anticipate his or her ability to earn excess profits 'down the road'. As a result, when competing for a new client, the amount bid in early years may well be less than the auditor's initial costs. The deficiency will be recovered through excess profits in later years, assuming the client is retained. However, the need to retain a client, in order to recover early fee discounts, may compromise an auditor's independence.

Thus, price competition among auditors potentially has both a positive and negative effect. Competition is clearly beneficial to consumers – that is, to audited organizations and their owners. However, the profession must take care to maintain sufficient incentives – such as professional ethics and the risk of legal liability – to ensure that auditing continues to be a credible service.

8 Conclusion

Audits of financial statements play an important role in a market economy. By adding credibility to financial information prepared by management, auditing can lower the cost of debt and equity capital to a firm. The auditing process is technically complex and requires the exercise of a high level of professional judgement, while auditors themselves often face conflicting economic incentives – including a growing risk of litigation by shareholders and creditors. These complexities and risks have fostered the growth of the Big Five international public accounting firms, which dominate the market for audit services. Moreover, the complexities and risks add to the challenges of professional practice and make the field a fertile research area.

DAN A. SIMUNIC
UNIVERSITY OF BRITISH COLUMBIA

Further reading

(References cited in the text marked *)

* AICPA (1995) *Codification of Statements on Auditing Standards*, Chicago, IL: Commerce Clearing House. (These are the official auditing pronouncements of the American Institute of Certified Public Accountants' Auditing Standards Board.)

* Arens, A.A. and Loebbecke, J.K. (1994) *Auditing: An Integrated Approach*, 6th edn, Englewood Cliffs, NJ: Prentice Hall. (A popular and thorough introductory auditing text.)

* Causey, D.Y. Jr (1979) *Duties and Liabilities of Public Accountants*, Homewood, IL: Dow Jones–Irwin. (A complete reference work on auditor legal liability in the USA.)

* Citron, D. and Taffler, R.J. (1992) 'The audit report under going concern uncertainties: an empirical analysis', *Accounting and Business Research* 22 (88): 337–45. (An interesting British study of auditor reporting when there are going concern problems.)

* Clarkson, P.M. and Simunic, D.A. (1994) 'The association between audit quality, retained ownership, and firm-specific risk in US vs. Canadian IPO markets', *Journal of Accounting and Economics* 17 (1–2): 207–28. (An empirical study of the ramifications of different legal liability regimes in the USA and Canada on auditor involvement in new issues of securities.)

* De Angelo, L. (1981) 'Auditor independence, low-balling, and disclosure regulation', *Journal of Accounting and Economics* 3 (2): 113–27. (Classic paper analysing multi-period pricing of audit services in a competitive market.)

Guy, D.M., Carmichael, D. and Whittington, O.R. (1994) *Audit Sampling: An Introduction*, New York: Wiley. (A good overview of statistical sampling methods and uses in auditing.)

* IFAC (1995) *IFAC Handbook: Technical Pronouncements*, New York: International Federation of Accountants. (The *Handbook* contains all the pronouncements of IFAC committees, including *International Standards on Auditing* and the *Code of Ethics for Professional Accountants*.)

* Palmrose, Z. (1988) 'An analysis of auditor litigation and audit service quality', *The Accounting Review* 63 (1): 55–73. (Systematic study of auditor litigation in the USA, and its implications for the auditing market.)

* Simunic, D.A. (1980) 'The pricing of audit services: theory and evidence', *Journal of Accounting Research* 18 (1): 161–90. (A widely cited study examining the determinants of audit fees and testing for price competition among US auditors.)

* Teoh, S.H. and Wong, T.J. (1993) 'Perceived audit quality and the earnings response coefficient', *The Accounting Review* 68 (2): 346–66. (Careful empirical study of the impact of audit quality on clients' share prices.)

See also: ACCOUNTING; ACCOUNTING, INTERNATIONAL; AUDITING; FINANCIAL ACCOUNTING

Stiglitz, Joseph E. (1943–)

Personal background

- born 9 February 1943, Gary, Indiana
- BA Amherst College, 1964; PhD Massachusetts Institute of Technology (MIT), 1967
- joined faculty of MIT in 1966
- Combined careers of economic theorist and teacher, at a succession of universities, with government consulting, 1966–93 and 2000–
- research fellow at University College, Nairobi, Kenya, under Rockefeller Foundation grant, 1969–71
- received the John Bates Clark Medal in 1979, awarded biennially by the American Economic Association for the most distinguished work by an economist under the age of 40
- founding editor of the *Journal of Economic Perspectives*, 1987
- served on the United States Council of Economic Advisors as a member, 1993–95, and as chair, 1995–97
- chief economist, World Bank, 1997–99

Selected major works

'Increasing risk: I. A definition', *Journal of Economic Theory* (with M. Rothschild) (1970).

'Increasing risk: II. Its economic consequences', *Journal of Economic Theory* (with M. Rothschild) (1971).

'On the optimality of the stock market allocation of investment', *Quarterly Journal of Economics* (1972).

'Incentives and risk sharing in sharecropping', *Review of Economic Studies* (1974).

'The theory of "screening", education, and the distribution of income', *American Economic Review* (1975).

'Equilibrium in competitive insurance markets: an essay on the economics of imperfect information', *Quarterly Journal of Economics* (with M. Rothschild) (1976).

'Bargains and ripoffs: a model of monopolistically competitive price dispersion', *Review of Economic Studies* (with S. Salop) (1977).

'Monopolistic competition and optimal product diversity', *American Economic Review* (with A. Dixit) (1977).

Lectures in Public Economics (with A.B. Atkinson) (1980).

'On the impossibility of informationally efficient markets', *American Economic Review* (with S. Grossman) (1980).

'Credit rationing in markets with imperfect information', *American Economic Review* (with A. Weiss) (1981).

The Theory of Commodity Price Stabilization (with D. Newbery) (1981).

'Equilibrium unemployment as a worker discipline device', *American Economic Review* (with C. Shapiro) (1984).

'Informational imperfections in capital markets and macroeconomic fluctuations', *American Economic Review* (with B. Greenwald and A. Weiss) (1984).

'The Architecture of Economic Systems: Hierarchies and Polyarchies', *American Economic Review* (with R. Sah) (1986)

'Externalities in economics with imperfect information and incomplete markets', *Quarterly Journal of Economics* (with B. Greenwald) (1986).

'Moral hazard and non-market institutions: dysfunctional crowding out or peer monitoring', *American Economic Review* (with R. Arnott) (1991).

'Financial market imperfections and business cycles', *Quarterly Journal of Economics* (with B. Greenwald) (1993).
Whither Socialism? (1994).

Summary

Joe Stiglitz's ambition was to remake economic theory in a way that would provide insights into problems of imperfect information, the costs of communication, and innovation. In the process of realizing that ambition, he contributed to a revolutionary shift in economics from Walrasian models of the market – in which information is costless and private rationality leads as if by an 'invisible hand' to a socially rational outcome – to a post-Walrasian paradigm in which markets solve, but only imperfectly, problems of screening for hidden characteristics, providing incentives for imperfectly observed behaviours, and creating incentives for innovation.

Stiglitz's most profound insight is that if information is costly to acquire, prices have a role other than clearing the market – in particular, as screening and incentive devices. This implies that markets may not clear. This theoretical insight has helped to provide a new basis for the synthesis of Keynesian and neoclassical economics, and has brought the study of developing economies back into the mainstream. For those living and working in developing countries, where markets are not well-developed and unemployment and rationing are pervasive, pre-Stiglitzian neoclassical economics with its market-clearing predictions seemed to many irrelevant and led them to turn to neo-Keynesian, Ricardian, and Marxian perspectives. Stiglitz's work was largely responsible for attracting some of the best minds of the new generation of economists in developing countries to neoclassical economics.

Stiglitz's work includes over 300 technical papers that have proved central theorems in many fields: the theory of uncertainty and information, finance, taxation, industrial organization, development, and macroeconomics. His intense schedule of peripatetic lectures and consulting for governments means that unlike many theorists, Stiglitz brings a tremendous knowledge of institutions to his theoretical work. His modus operandi is to identify a problem in a particular market, develop a new set of tools to model the way individuals respond to that problem, and show how the interaction of their responses affects the industry and the macroeconomy. He would thus try to examine the implications of the information problem at all levels – the level of the individual and the firm, the industry, and the economy. Then he would show how that set of tools proved useful in a wide range of further applications. Finally, he would demonstrate how more realistic descriptions of the economy could be obtained by combining into a single model a combination of information problems.

Stiglitz is notable for having written not only important theoretical papers, but also provocative 'thought pieces' on broad themes. These themes include the role of the government in markets, the politics of reform, and the possibility of modeling economic behaviour in terms of a broader set of postulates than self-interest. This work clearly reflects his hope of changing the *Weltanschauung* of economists and advancing policies that he believes will improve welfare.

I Biographical data

Joe Stiglitz was the middle of three children. After the failure of an earlier business, his father became an independent insurance agent; part of his job was to find new insurers for firms whose businesses had burned down and whose insurance policies had been cancelled. An important theme throughout Joe Stiglitz's career has been the way in which the economy handles risk. Stiglitz's mother worked in the family insurance business when Stiglitz was young and later taught elementary school in a low-income inner city neighbourhood of Gary, Indiana. After she retired from elementary education, she worked in adult remedial education, where she met up with some of the same students whom she had taught as children. The role that education plays as a screening process that enables high-ability people to obtain a higher wage, partly, however, at the expense of others, was a second important early theme of Stiglitz's work.

Stiglitz's genius was recognized early. In high school, he was assigned independent study in lieu of some of the regular classes, which he had outstripped. After following his older brother at Amherst College, where he studied economics, physics, and mathematics, he obtained a Ph.D. from the Massachusetts Institute of Technology (MIT) in two years. He started teaching at MIT and then moved from university to university: Yale (1968–74), St Catherine's College, Oxford (Visiting Fellow, 1973–74), Stanford (1974–76), All Souls' College, Oxford (1976–79), the Institute of Advanced Studies at Princeton (1978–79), Princeton University (1979–88), and Stanford (1988 to date).

In 1993, Stiglitz accepted an invitation to join President Clinton's Council of Economic Advisors, of which he was chair from 1995–97. By the time he became Chief Economist of the World Bank in 1997, Stiglitz was famous, and he used his position to argue publicly against policies of the International Monetary Fund (IMF) towards the East Asian financial crisis of 1997–99 (see INTERNATIONAL MONETARY FUND; WORLD BANK). In evaluating any policy, there are judgements one has to make concerning the consequences of the policy, and tradeoffs one has to make between competing goals. Stiglitz's positions on both these points led to conflict with other officials in Washington. In November 1999, he resigned from the World Bank and returned to Stanford University. There he created an institution that, by providing training to policymakers from developing countries, was intended to increase their ability to negotiate with the IMF.

2 The economics of information

When Stiglitz began working on the economics of information, James Mirrlees had been working for a few years on the problem of how a government could design an optimal tax schedule, taking into account that government could observe incomes, but not ability and effort (Mirrlees 1971). Stiglitz's key insight was to recognize the similarities between this problem and a broad set of problems that arise in markets where the characteristics of the commodities exchanged are not known to one of the parties to the transaction. For example, insurance companies and banks want to design a menu of offers that will maximize their profits, taking into account that they know the distribution of risks but not each individual's characteristics. Employers want to design labour contracts to maximize productivity, taking into account that they can only imperfectly observe workers' ability and effort. Together with a small group of pioneers in the 1970s, and influenced in particular by Akerlof (1970) and Spence (1974), Stiglitz devised models in which these kinds of problems could be formally analysed. This work came to be called 'the economics of information'. It showed that much of what economists had believed on the basis of the Walrasian model was not robust to considerations of imperfect information.

Hidden characteristics

It is interesting to be more specific and study a famous model that introduces central themes in Stiglitz's work. Rothschild and Stiglitz (1976) constructed a simple model of the insurance market: individuals differed in their probability of having an accident, they knew that they differed, but at the time the market opened, the insurance firms knew only the distribution of risks in the population and did not know who was high risk or low risk. The results of their model were startling and confusing. Most of their argument was made by the analysis of the canonical textbook apparatus of consumer choice – budget lines and indifference curves.

Consider an individual whose situation is described by his income if he is lucky enough to avoid an accident (W_{NA}) and his income if an accident occurs (W_A). Without insurance, his income in these two states, 'no accident' and 'accident', is (W, W-d), where d represents the damages incurred in the accident. An individual purchases insurance in order to alter his pattern of income across these two states of nature.

As a benchmark case, suppose that insurance companies knew the individual's probability of accident. Given this probability of accident, let $\overline{W}$ denote the individual's expected income. Then competitive equilibrium

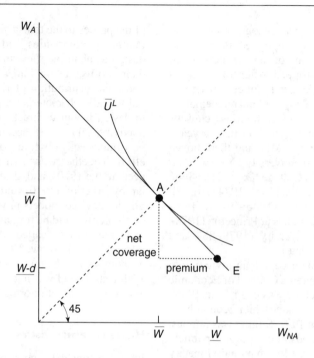

Figure 1

would be at a point A, illustrated in Figure 1, where the insurance company breaks even and the individual's indifference curve, denoted U^L, is tangent to the budget line. Since risk averse individuals who are offered a fair price for insurance will fully insure, the equilibrium is along the 45 degree line. The line that goes through the initial endowment point E and the point A is the locus of contracts at which an insurance company breaks even (which Rothshild and Stiglitz referred to as the fair-odds line).

But now suppose that individuals differ in their probability of having an accident, and that they know that they differ. Clearly, the high-risk individual has lower expected wealth, denoted by $\overline{W}$ in Figure 2. If the insurance company could observe who was low-risk and who was high-risk, then using the same reasoning as above, the equilibrium contracts would be at A and B in Figure 2: high accident probabilities give rise to a flatter indifference curve (individuals are willing to pay more, at the margin, for insurance), and also to more costly insurance (a flatter fair-odds line). If, however, the insurance firms do not know the characteristics of individuals, then clearly they cannot offer contracts A and

B (for all individuals would in that case claim they were the low-risk type and choose the contract A, and the insurance companies would not break even). Offers that survive the competitive process also cannot specify a price at which customers choose to buy all the insurance they want, because the high-risk individuals would always purchase more insurance at that price than the low-risk individuals, and the insurance firms would not break even. Offers of contracts instead consist of both a price and a quantity.

Figure 3 illustrates at point C a contract that would break even if all individuals purchased it (which Rothschild–Stiglitz called a 'pooling' contract). Is this, however, an equilibrium? Rothschild–Stiglitz pointed out that no pooling contract could be consistent with individuals' and firms' incentives. Firms would perceive that they could benefit from deviating in order to 'pick off' the low-risk individuals. Consider what would happen if one firm were to announce that it was willing to sell a contract C′ with slightly less insurance coverage than C but at a lower price per dollar of coverage, with the point C′ located in the shaded area in Figure 3 – below the high-risk individual's indifference curve, but above the

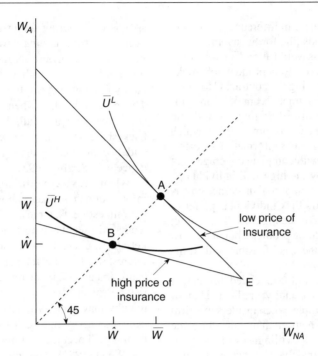

Figure 2

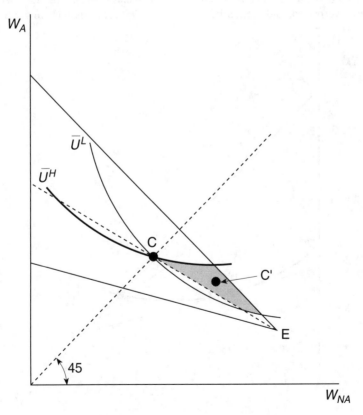

Figure 3

low risk individual's indifference curve, and above the fair-odds line for the average risk? A firm that did this would attract only the low-risk individuals as customers and would make a profit, while causing the contract C to make a loss. Thus the contract C cannot be an equilibrium. Rothschild and Stiglitz showed that the only possible equilibrium is one in which the market distinguishes information by offering a contract B with complete coverage (that will be chosen by the high-risk individuals), and a contract D with partial insurance coverage (which the low-risk individuals prefer to full insurance at B); see Figure 4. The market 'solves' the screening problem, but at the cost of foreclosing otherwise feasible and desirable exchanges.

In later work, Stiglitz extended this insight to explain puzzles in equity, credit, and labour markets. For example, when insiders in a firm have more information than outsiders, the controlling insiders' willingness to issue equity conveys a signal that says that on average the shares are overpriced, and the market re-

sponds by lowering the price. This discourages firms from issuing new shares and provides an important explanation for the observation that firms have limited access to equity (Greenwald, Stiglitz and Weiss 1984). The prediction that when firms issue new shares the share price falls, and when they buy back shares, the share price rises, has been widely confirmed (a survey of theory and evidence is in Stiglitz 1992).

When prospective borrowers have more information than lenders about the riskiness of their investments, there are situations where a lender will set his interest rate below the market-clearing rate. He will not wish to raise his interest rate to 'what the market will bear' because an increase in the rate causes the lowest risk borrowers to drop out of the market, and thereby may actually reduce the lender's expected return to lending. In this case, credit rationing will occur, as demonstrated in Stiglitz and Weiss (1981). Beginning with work in the late 1980s, discussed below, Stiglitz drew im-

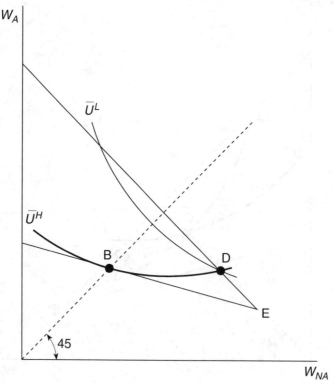

Figure 4

portant consequences for macroeconomics from the failures in equity and credit markets.

In many settings, individuals can, at a cost, provide credible information about their characteristics. What were 'hidden characteristics' become public information. Will individual choices lead to the efficient level of investment in information? Stiglitz showed that the private returns to the provision of information generally differ from the social returns. Individuals are likely to spend too much on 'hierarchical screening' – that is, on screening for characteristics that individuals value in the same way – and too little spending on 'matching screening' – on screening for characteristics that individuals value in different ways but that is valuable by permitting better matches, e.g. between workers and jobs, or investors and financial assets (Stiglitz 1974, 1982).

The fact that the investor-in-information must be able to obtain a return on average from his information-gathering activity led to a fundamental result in finance. There had long been a theory in finance, called the efficient markets theory, that the observation of prices in capital markets suffices to reveal all relevant private information (see EFFICIENT MARKET HYPOTHESIS). Grossman and Stiglitz (1980) showed that the theory was incorrect: if information is costly and markets are competitive, then there must be an 'equilibrium degree of disequilibrium' – persistent discrepancies between prices and 'fundamental values' that provide incentives for individuals to obtain information. In capital markets, prices serve two functions: besides being used in the conventional way to clear markets, they also convey information. When individuals invest in information and thereby learn that the return to a security is going to be high (or low), they bid its price up (or down), and thus the price system makes that information publicly available But if all information were publicly conveyed, there would be no incentives for individuals to invest in information. Grossman and Stiglitz's work stimulated further work in finance. Kyle (1989) showed that a number of puzzles could be resolved by assuming that the informed traders are imperfect competitors, who take into account the effect their trading has on prices. Under that assumption,

prices are never fully revealing and, therefore, a positive amount of costly private information is always obtained.

In many settings, differential information can be a source of pure economic rents. Stiglitz argued that firms recognize that fact and exploit it by actually creating information problems. For example, stores know that it is costly for customers to search, and Salop and Stiglitz's (1977) paper on 'Bargains and ripoffs' showed that stores can exploit that (by varying their prices) to extract rents from customers who have high search costs. The market equilibrium prices thus serve to discriminate (imperfectly) among individuals with different search costs. Their results overturned a standard theory called *the Law of the Single Price* (a given commodity is sold at the same price in all stores). Edlin and Stiglitz (1995) extended this idea to create a theory of *managerial entrenchment*. They argued that differential information between managers and outsiders is a source of rents to managers, and that managers may preserve their jobs and increase their rents by investing in activities for which information asymmetries are particularly large.

Hidden behaviours

Besides the problem of hidden characteristics, the problem of providing incentives for hidden behaviours also changes the way the market mechanism works. One may try to write a contract that fully specifies the desired actions, but that will require monitoring, and monitoring is costly and imperfect. Another response to the problem of hidden behaviours is to motivate the individual through an incentive contract. This is the central idea of *principal–agent* theory, in which a principal, who delegates a task to an agent, designs a contract that makes payment depend on observable circumstances (e.g. revenues) that are correlated with the desired but unobservable actions of the agent. Principal–agent theory was developed contemporaneously by Stephen Ross, James Mirrlees, and Joe Stiglitz. Stiglitz (1974) addressed a particular puzzle that had been recognized since at least Alfred Marshall – the apparent inefficiency of the institution of sharecropping, where the tenant receives only a share of the marginal return to his effort (see MARSHALL, A.). Stiglitz showed that share-cropping was advantageous to tenants and landlords because of the *savings in monitoring costs* compared to a wage system with costly monitoring, the *increases in output* compared to a wage system with imperfect monitoring, and the *reduction in risk borne by tenants* compared to a system where workers pay fixed land rents but do not have access to risk markets.

Four insights in this paper have been important for further developments in economics.

1 It is sometimes useful to take the transaction, rather than the market, as the unit of analysis.
2 There is a trade-off between incentives and insurance.
3 The extent of incentive problems in an economy depends on the distribution of wealth.
4 Agency problems are also pervasive in a complex modern economy, for example, in the relationship between the owners of a firm and the manager.

One of the most interesting developments in principal–agent theory that other economists have pursued (see Baker 2000) is the study of the dangers in focusing incentives on easily observable variables (e.g. in car repair services, the mechanic's billings), because such incentive structures divert attention from more important but more difficult to measure outcomes (e.g. careful diagnosis and correction of car malfunction).

Reputations also play an important role in providing incentives. For reputation to be an effective incentive mechanism, a firm must have something to lose. That something is income. Carl Shapiro (1983) developed a model of reputation in which, for all but the lowest possible quality goods, price exceeds marginal cost in competitive equilibrium. The price–cost margin gives the firm a future stream of rents as long as it maintains its reputation. The prospect of the loss of these rents if it 'milks' its reputation by providing less than the promised quality induces the firm to actually live up to consumers' expectations. Why doesn't competition lead to price-cutting?

Consumers come to learn that if the price is too low, firms do not have an incentive to maintain their reputation, and therefore the offer of high quality goods at a low price is not credible.

Joint work between Shapiro and Stiglitz (1984) extended this idea in a very important way to provide a model that has come to be called the 'shirking model'. Their work envisaged a setting where the firm could observe the effort of workers only randomly, and there was no fixed retirement date. The only penalty that a firm could impose on a worker for shirking was to fire him. In such a situation, an employer has an incentive to pay a wage *above* that of others. For then, if the employee loses his job, he will suffer a real loss; and thus, the employee will have an incentive not to shirk. But as all employers do that, none benefits. This would seem to be like the case where when every spectator in the stadium stands up to get a better view, no one sees any better. But unlike that case, the fact that all employers raise their wage has a real effect. It creates unemployment: at the higher wage firms hire fewer workers, but no fewer individuals seek work. Now a worker who is fired cannot immediately find another job but enters the unemployment pool. In equilibrium all firms pay the same wage above market-clearing; and unemployment, which makes job loss costly, serves the role of creating work incentives. While this role is socially valuable, the equilibrium unemployment rate will be higher than the optimum.

The 'shirking model', Grossman–Stiglitz's (1980) capital markets model, and Rothschild–Stiglitz's (1976) insurance model all illustrate central ideas developed throughout Stiglitz's work: endogenous information radically changes the way the market mechanism functions; the market mechanism can itself mitigate many problems of information (e.g. revealing hidden characteristics and creating incentives for hidden actions), but there are government interventions that could, in principle, improve upon the market outcome. For example, in the insurance model, the costs of separating low- from high-risk individuals (the limitations on insurance) may exceed the benefits. A government intervention that imposed the pooling outcome could in some cases make everyone in the economy better off. In the 'shirking model', the market outcome does not maximize aggregate income. A wage subsidy would reduce unemployment and raise total income.

3 Macroeconomics

As discussed above, Stiglitz established that informational imperfections would limit the scope of equity and credit markets. In a series of papers with Bruce Greenwald and Andy Weiss, he drew out the implications for the failures of capitalism – the marked fluctuations in output and employment that have characterized capitalism throughout its history. The argument was as follows: limitations in the scope of equity markets, combined with the assumption of significant bankruptcy costs, mean that firms behave in a risk-averse manner. They pay attention to own-risk, while traditional theory suggests that the only risk firms should care about is the correlation with the stock market. Higher levels of investment or production entail increased debt, and as debt is increased, the bankruptcy probability is increased. Firms will therefore produce and invest only up to the point where expected marginal returns equal expected marginal bankruptcy costs. This has four implications.

Amplification of small shocks

Changes in the net worth of the firm and the riskiness of the environment affect the production and investment decisions of the firm (in contrast to the standard theory). For a highly leveraged firm, small changes in demand can result in large changes in output and employment. Thus, disturbances to the economy tend to be amplified.

Persistence

If for some reason net worth is reduced at a given time, production falls in subsequent periods. Only gradually will production be restored to normal, as net worth builds up again.

Risk-averse banks

Banks are a specialized kind of firm whose production activity is making loans. A reduction in the net worth of banks and an increase in the riskiness of their environment will lead them to contract their output – i.e. to make fewer loans, which has multiplier effects throughout the economy.

Worsening of the applicant pool for loans during a recession

For any given bankruptcy cost, there is a critical net worth such that, below that net worth, firms act in a risk loving manner, above that, in a risk averse manner. If the economy moves into a recession and firms find their net worth decreases, good (i.e. risk-averse) firms reduce their loan applications, bad (i.e. risk-loving) firms increase their loan applications, and there is an increasing proportion of bad (i.e. low net worth) applicants. These effects may be so strong as to lead to a situation where the bank makes no loans at all!

During Stiglitz's tenure as Chief Economist of the World Bank, the contrast between Stiglitz's perspective on macroeconomics and the perspective based on well-functioning markets came to a head. These are two starkly different ways of looking at the world. If there are well-functioning markets, then opening up capital markets will lead to efficient outcomes. In this view, essentially adopted by the US Treasury Department and the IMF in the 1990s, the appropriate response to the 1997–98 East Asian financial crisis was to require, as a condition of IMF financial support, that the East Asian economies adopt contractionary fiscal and monetary policies. The contractionary monetary policy would raise interest rates and, at some point, reverse private capital outflows and restore the ability of the East Asian countries to repay their foreign debts (see ASIA PACIFIC, MANAGEMENT IN; EAST ASIAN ECONOMIES). Under the alternative view, taken by Stiglitz and other critics of the IMF, the increase in interest rates would seriously erode the net worth of debtors and, for reasons described above, the erosion of their net worth would lead to a recession that could not easily be reversed.

In the perfect markets view, the basic reason for the East Asian financial crisis was lack of transparency, or corruption, in the business practices of these economies, which frightened away foreign investors. However, Furman and Stiglitz (1998) argued that there was no basis for the view that a lack of transparency *caused* the crisis (although it aggravated the effects of the downturn once it began). They argued that small developing countries are financially fragile. There are pervasive externalities in banks' and firms' decisions to obtain short-term loans from abroad. Each takes the risk environment as given, and yet the aggregate set of decisions determines the risk of a financial crisis. Thus, Furman and Stiglitz argued that some limits on free capital markets were appropriate in developing countries. Stiglitz's views ultimately were very influential. But the openness of his conflict with the IMF and US Treasury frayed his relationships with many people in Washington, and hastened his departure from the World Bank.

4 Development economics

Whereas Stiglitz's work in macroeconomics is highly controversial, his work in development economics is much less so. Before 1970, there was little understanding of the imperfections in markets in developing countries (see EMERGING COUNTRIES, MANAGEMENT IN THE). Economists that tried to design policies to fit the realities of imperfect markets in developing countries generally assumed rigidities in markets, but did not explain them by reference to a choice-based perspective. Stiglitz's work in development economics played a major role in changing that. His central contributions were (1) to show that non-market institutions can be efficient responses to missing markets and high transaction costs; (2) to show that while (1) is true in partial equilibirum, it may not be true in general equilibrium; and (3) to provide models of 'development traps' created by various types of positive feedback mechanisms.

Institutions

There is a widespread intuition that institutions that have emerged out of individual actions are optimal: they are there because their benefits outweigh the costs. Stiglitz's work on sharecropping, discussed above, and on group lending (Stiglitz 1990) exemplify that approach.

But as Stiglitz has remarked, that intuition is not compelling: 'In a society that has had Jim Crow laws, how could one believe that institutions are optimal?' Stiglitz's later work showed that there is no necessity that the equilibrium set of institutions be efficient. For example, Arnott and Stiglitz (1991) examined the effects of a social institution that arises because of incomplete insurance in markets faced with moral hazard problems. They showed that informal social insurance may crowd out market insurance and lower social welfare – partly because it does not address the broader issue of information externalities. More generally, with endogenous institutions, developing countries may be caught in a vicious circle in which low levels of market development result in high levels of information imperfections, and these information imperfections give rise to institutions – for example, personalized networks of relationships – that impede the development of markets.

In work with Avishay Braverman, Stiglitz made another contribution to the debate over why some countries have failed to develop. Braverman–Stiglitz (1986) showed that when monitoring is costly and land contracts entail sharecropping, there are 'biases' in the nature of the innovations that are adopted: landlords may resist innovations that increase output but exacerbate incentive problems.

Positive feedback effects

Another strand in Stiglitz's work in development examines learning externalities that generate *positive feedback effects*. As a result of such effects, there can be multiple equilibrium behaviour patterns. Through accidents of history, one pattern comes to be entrenched as the standard. For example, in Sah and Stiglitz (1989), a high level of expenditures on R&D by one firm may have sufficiently high spillovers that it increases the marginal return to another firm of doing research. Thus there may exist one equilibrium in which R&D is low, and another where R&D is high. Socio-economic interactions may also give rise to multiple equilibria: if each individual looks to the apparent preferences of his peers to infer the appropriate behaviour, then there is a possibility of multiple self-sustaining norms. Hoff and Stiglitz (2001) termed this approach to development 'ecological economics'. The term tries to capture the idea that economies with the same deep properties (technology and preferences) can have markedly different equilibria. Innovation can encourage further innovation, just as corruption can encourage further corruption.

In a celebrated model, Dixit and Stiglitz (1977) posed a question seemingly unrelated to development that, however, turned out to provide a building block in models constructed by other economists working in the new fields of endogenous growth theory and economic geography. 'Will a market solution yield the socially optimum kinds and quantities of commodities, if there are multiple possible varieties of goods and each entails increasing returns to scale in production?' They used a trick that turned out to be very important analytically. By assuming a continuum of goods, the set-up lets the modeller respect the discrete nature of many location decisions and yet analyse the model in terms of the behaviour of continuous variables like the share of manufacturing in a particular region. That paper gave rise to development models (e.g. Rodriguez-Clare 1996) in which an economy consists of three sectors: a low-technology sector, an advanced sector, and an intermediate sector that produces an array of non-traded, i.e. domestic, goods, modeled as Dixit-Stiglitz commodities, that are inputs into the advanced sector. An expansion of the advanced sector increases the demand for these nontraded inputs, and so lowers their average costs and increases the available variety. With a greater variety of intermediate inputs, production in the advanced sector is more efficient. It can thus be the case that when all other firms enter the advanced sector, it pays the remaining firm to do so, but when all other firms remain in the traditional, low-technology sector, it pays the remaining firm to do so, too. A

low-level equilibrium can therefore be sustained even when the economy is fully open to international trade.

5 Evaluation

Stiglitz's work has proceeded by analysing models in which the implications of particular information problems can be examined in idealized settings. The high level of idealization and the very surprising (or at least counter-Walrasian) results often obtained have led his harshest critics to see in his work a predilection for the intriguing exception rather than the general rule: Granted that market failures occur, do they really matter? From a staunch admirer, Avinash Dixit, one hears the statement that a paper by Stiglitz begins with the phrase, 'Assume there are two types'. But that is not a criticism. The statement that 'there are two types' marks a radical departure from the Walrasian paradigm. Walrasian models all begin with the implicit assumption that 'there is only one type' (i.e. among commodities selling in a single market, there are no hidden characteristics about which consumers care). Stiglitz's work demonstrates that markets where there is 'one type' have properties markedly different from those with two or more types (i.e. where there is imperfect information).

Stiglitz's work has led to a re-evaluation of the market mechanism (see, especially, Stiglitz 1992). Walrasian theory both overestimates and underestimates the actual virtues of the market. It overestimates the role of prices and fails to take account of the difficulties of making the price system work. But it understates central virtues of the market: its ability to solve, though only imperfectly, problems of selection, incentives, information gathering, and innovation – problems about which the Walrasian paradigm is silent. It remains an unsettled question whether the Walrasian paradigm is so limited that it does not provide a useful overview of the economy. A challenge for future work is to determine what information assumptions are appropriate in particular circumstances. This is important because results often depend sensitively on the information assumptions employed. By the 1990s, this question had become the subject of a very active research agenda.

A source of some misunderstanding in the evaluation of Stiglitz's work is his treatment of the role of the state. Most of his work has focused on analysing how markets work. It has by and large not focused on analysing how the public sector works. His theoretical work has thus, by and large, not provided theorems as to what interventions a state, governed by rational maximizing behaviour of voters and politicians, actually would undertake. As early as 1975, Stiglitz wrote: '[T]o turn over an allocation process to the public sector is to make it subject to 'political laws' which may be no less forceful – and even less efficient – than the 'economic laws' which previously governed the allocation process' (Stiglitz 1975: 299). Those who have studied such 'positive political economy' make use of the framework of asymmetric information that Stiglitz pioneered in the market context (e.g. Laffont and Tirole 1993 and Grossman and Helpman 1994). Stiglitz's work has thus helped identify the theoretical and empirical questions on which the resolution of the debate should turn. It permits us to see the possibility of constructing models that embody as special cases the conservative, radical, and liberal worldviews. 'Conservative' economists, in arguing for a very limited role for the state, point to the enormity of *principal–agent problems* between the electorate and politicians and between politicians and bureaucrats. They posit the relative absence of such problems in the private sector. 'Radical' economists, in arguing for extensive state intervention, point to ways in which information-based imperfections in capital and labour markets make the rich richer and the poor poorer. 'Liberal' economists, in defending a moderate role for the state, argue that the government and private sectors are complements, not substitutes, because the information and agency problems they face are not the same. They argue that an imperfect government may mitigate the failures of the imperfect market.

6 Conclusion

Joe Stiglitz has played a leading role in formulating a paradigm that would be an alternative to the Walrasian paradigm, and that would explain how economies process and transmit information, select the set of goods to be produced, and innovate. His work articulates four major themes:

- Economic behaviour is not just a response to scarcity; it is also a response to information problems. A key issue is understanding interactions of individuals who know that other individuals possess private information.
- The basic theorems of Walrasian theory are not robust in the presence of imperfect or costly information. Policy analysis based on that theory is misleading.
- The failures in equity, credit, and labour markets have important consequences for macroeconomics.
- Development is primarily a problem of changes in institutions, not an automatic catch-up process of capital accumulation.
- Important areas for future advances in economics are the identification of the information assumptions appropriate in particular circumstances, and the dynamics of institutional change.

KARLA HOFF
WORLD BANK

Further Reading

(References cited in the text marked*)

* Akerlof, G. (1970) 'The market for "lemons": quality uncertainty and the market mechanism', *Quarterly Journal of Economics* 84: 488–500. (Buyers may be reluctant to purchase a product whose quality is known to the seller but not to the buyers, because they correctly fear getting stuck with a 'lemon'.)

* Baker, G. (2000) 'The use (and non-use) of distortionary performance measures', *American Economic Review* 90 (2): 415–20. (In choosing the performance measures to use to reward employees, firms need to consider the distortion of incentives that results when firms 'reward for A while hoping for B'.)

* Braverman, A. and Stiglitz, J.E. (1986) 'Landlords, tenants, and technological innovations', *Journal of Development Economics* 23: 313–32. (Landlords may wish to – and can – resist innovations that increase production but exacerbate principal–agency problems.)

* Edlin, A. and Stiglitz, J.E. (1995) 'Discouraging rivals: managerial rent-seeking and economic inefficiencies', *American Economic Review* 85 (5): 1301–12. (Managers can preserve their jobs and increase their rents by investing in activities that increase the informational asymmetries between them and rival managers, takeover artists, and boards of directors.)

* Furman, J. and Stiglitz, J.E. (1998) 'Economic crises: evidence and insights from East Asia', *Brookings Papers on Economic Activity* 2: 1–114. (Lack of transparency, or corruption, did not play a large part in causing the East Asian financial crisis.)

* Grossman, G.M. and Helpman, E. (1994) 'Protection for sale', *American Economic Review* 84 (4): 833–50. (When special-interest groups make political contributions in order to influence the state's choice of trade policy, politicians' maximizing behaviour, which depends on total contributions and the welfare of voters, leads to inefficient trade policies as a political equilibrium.)

Hoff, K., Braverman, A. and Stiglitz, J.E. (eds) (1993) *The Economics of Rural Organization: Theory, Practice, and Policy*, New York: Oxford University Press. (Information and enforcement problems can explain a wide variety of institutions in the rural sector of developing countries.)

* Hoff, K. and Stiglitz, J.E. (2001) 'Modern economic theory and development', in G. Meier and J.E. Stiglitz (eds) *The Future of Development Economics in Perspective*, Oxford: Oxford University Press, 389–459. (Theoretical advances in economists' understanding of imperfect information, coordination failures, and institutions have radically changed the focus of development economics. Development is no longer seen as a process of capital accumulation that automatically occurs under free markets, but rather as a difficult process of institutional change.)

* Kyle, A.S. (1989) 'Informed speculation with imperfect competition', *Review of Economic Studies* 56: 317–56. (When asset markets are imperfectly competitive and each trader takes into account the effect his demand has on the equilibrium price of assets, prices will not be fully informative of private information, and thus traders will have an incentive to obtain costly private information.)

* Laffont, J.-J. and Tirole, J. (1993) *A Theory of Incentives in Procurement and Regulation*, Cambridge, MA: MIT Press. (Industry regulation can be modelled as a political game.)

* Mirrlees, J. (1971) 'An exploration in the theory of optimum income taxation', *Review of Economic Studies* 38 (2): 175–208. (Assuming government does not know the income-earning skills of individuals but does know the distribution of skills within the population, there is an optimum earned-income tax schedule, and it will imply distortions in labour supply.)

* Rodriguez-Clare, A. (1996) 'The division of labour and economic development', *Journal of Development Economics* 49: 3–32. (When the modern sector of an economy depends on non-tradeable inputs produced with increasing returns to scale, multiple equilibria – some entailing modernization, some not – can be sustained.)

* Sah, R. and Stiglitz, J. E. (1989) 'Source of technological divergence between developed and less developed economies in developed and less developed countries', in G. Calvo *et al.* (eds), *Debt, Stabilizations and Development: Essays in Memory of Carlos Diaz-Alejandro*, Cambridge, MA: Basil Blackwell. (In the presence of learning externalities, an economy can have multiple equilibria.)

* Shapiro, C. (1983) 'Premiums for high quality products as returns to reputations', *Quarterly Journal of Economics* 98 (4): 659–80. (In competitive markets with imperfect information about quality, high quality items will sell at a premium above their cost, and the premium will forestall opportunistic quality-cutting by firms.)

* Spence, A.M. (1974) *Market Signaling: The Information Structure of Hiring and Related Processes*, Boston, MA: Harvard University Press. (The market value of signals, such as education, depends on the fact that the costs of signalling are correlated with hidden characteristics of individuals, such as ability.)

* Stiglitz, J.E. (1982) 'Information and capital markets', in William F. Sharpe and Cathryn Cootner (eds) *Financial Economics: Essays in Honor of Paul Cootner*, Englewood Cliffs, NJ: Prentice Hall, 118–58. (In capital markets, the private returns to information differ from the social returns.)

* Stiglitz, J.E. (1985). 'Information and economic analysis: a perspective', *Economic Journal* 95: 21–41. (Information economics shows that central assumptions of the Walrasian paradigm are indefensible, and that the main results of the Walrasian paradigm are not robust to considerations of imperfect information.)

Stiglitz, J.E. (1987) 'The causes and consequences of the dependence of quality on prices', *Journal of Economic Literature* 25: 1–48. (In markets with imperfect information, there are a very large number of forces, operating through either selection or incentive effects, that can lead an increase in price in a given market to increase the quality of the good.)

* Stiglitz, J.E. (1990) 'Peer monitoring and credit markets', *World Bank Economic Review* 4 (3) 351–66. (In group lending, such as undertaken by the Grameen Bank, the gains from improved monitoring can offset the costs of increased interdependence.)
* Stiglitz, J.E. (1992) 'Capital markets and economic fluctuations in capitalist economies', *European Economic Review* 36: 269–306. (Imperfect capital markets can explain many puzzles in macroeconomic behaviour of capitalist countries.)
* Stiglitz, J.E. (2001) 'The contributions of the economics of information to twentieth century economics', *Quarterly Journal of Economics* 115 (4): 1441–78. (Although it has roots in eighteenth and nineteenth century economics, information economics represents an intellectual revolution.)

See also: CAPITAL MARKETS; EFFICIENT MARKET HYPOTHESIS; INTERNATIONAL MONETARY FUND; KEYNES, J.M.; MARSHALL, A.; MARX, K.; RICARDO, D.; WORLD BANK

Strategic alliances, global: see GLOBAL STRATEGIC ALLIANCES

Strategic change: see CORPORATE STRATEGIC CHANGE

Strategic choice

Overview

The 'strategic choice' perspective was originally advanced as a corrective to the view that the way in which organizations are designed and structured has to be determined largely by their operational contingencies. This view overlooked the ways in which the leaders of organizations, whether private or public, were in practice able to influence organizational forms to suit their own preferences. Strategic choice drew attention to the active role of leading groups who had the power to influence the structures of their organizations through an essentially *political* process. It led to a substantial re-orientation of organizational analysis and stimulated debate on three key issues: the role of agency and choice in organizational analysis; the nature of organizational environment; and the relationship between organizational agents and the environment.

Since the intention was to redress an imbalance in organization theory, the exposition of strategic choice the time contributed to the diversity of perspectives on the subject, along with other emerging approaches such as radical organization theory. Over twenty years later, the situation has changed considerably, in that the field is now extremely diversified with a wide range of competing perspectives.

While different theoretical perspectives or paradigms may be irreconcilable in their own philosophical terms, when applied to the study of organizational phenomena they are not necessarily 'incommensurable'. It does not follow from the attachment of different meanings to the same concept that reference is being made to wholly different phenomena. Without an attempt to draw upon, and even to reconcile, the insights offered by its various perspectives, organization studies will run a serious risk of becoming little more than an arena of 'clashing cymbals' (or indeed symbols), making little real theoretical advance and having nothing useful to say for practice either.

A major contribution of strategic choice analysis today derives from its potential to integrate some of these different perspectives. This integrative potential derives from the fact that strategic choice articulates a political process, which brings agency and structure into a dynamic tension and locates them within a significant context. In so doing, it not only bridges a number of competing perspectives but also adopts a dynamic, non-deterministic position. Strategic choice analysis has been from its inception critical of determinism within organizational analysis, which derives from the adoption of an essentially mechanistic paradigm. The model of strategic choice points to the possibility of a continuing adaptive learning cycle, but within a theoretical framework that locates 'organizational learning' within the context of organizations as sociopolitical systems. Strategic choice is thus consistent with a more *evolutionary* model of organizations, in which organizational learning and adaptation proceed towards not wholly predictable outcomes within the shifting forces of organizational politics. This model finds a parallel in the new evolutionary political economy that bids to revitalize microeconomics.

The following two sections summarize the key features of the original strategic choice analysis. The third section then considers the key issues arising from this analysis and how they have been interpreted. The fourth section examines the integrative potential of strategic choice analysis within the contemporary study of organizations, with particular reference to organizational change and learning.

1 The origins of strategic choice analysis

Organization studies had by the early 1970s seen the completion of several major research programmes which investigated the components of organizational structure and their relationships with situational variables ('context') on a systematic comparative basis (for example, Blau and Schoenherr 1971; Pugh *et al.* 1968) (see ORGANIZATION BEHAVIOUR; ORGANIZATION STRUCTURE). The mode of research was cross-sectional and positivistic, involving the statistical examination of associations between phenomena which were regarded as objective in nature. The processes accounting for any statistical correlation were left to be inferred. The inferences which were being drawn reflected the predominant theoretical orientation at the time, which was one of structural determinism. This assumed that the contextual factors of environment, technology and size imposed certain constraints upon the structural choices managers could make, especially in the case of work organizations which had to achieve certain levels of performance in order to survive (see ORGANI-

ZATIONAL PERFORMANCE). The general argument was that: 'if organizational structure is not adapted to its context, then opportunities are lost, costs rise, and the maintenance of the organization is threatened' (Child 1972: 8).

Burrell and Morgan (1979) placed this theoretical orientation squarely within the 'functionalist' paradigm and there are continuities with it in several contemporary approaches, namely *the structural contingencies* perspective (Donaldson 1985, 1995), the *ecological* approach (Hannan and Freeman 1989) and the institutional perspective (Powell and DiMaggio 1991). The first stresses the importance for organizational performance of matching internal organizational capabilities to external conditions. The second considers that units which do not have organizational forms characteristic of their sector or 'niche' have a poorer chance of survival; its focus is primarily on organizational populations (see ORGANIZATIONAL POPULATIONS) and it gives little attention to how decision makers might endeavour to adapt to the environment. The institutional perspective is a rather 'broader church', but most of its adherents find common ground in the assumption that the structural forms (as well as the identities and values sustaining these) of relevant external institutions map themselves onto organizations which depend on them for legitimacy, resourcing or staffing. All of these contemporary approaches therefore regard environmental conditions as ultimately determining organizational characteristics. *They stress environmental selection rather than selection of the environment* (see ORGANIZATIONAL EVOLUTION).

Consideration of strategic choice led to the conclusion that this deterministic view was inadequate because of its failure: 'to give due attention to the agency of choice by whoever have the power to direct the organization' (Child 1972: 2). 'Strategic choice' was defined as the process whereby power holders within organizations decide upon courses of strategic action. (Such action could be directed towards different targets, although the 1972 paper focused on the design of an organization's structure.) 'Strategic choice extends to the environment within which the organization is operating, to the standards of perfor-

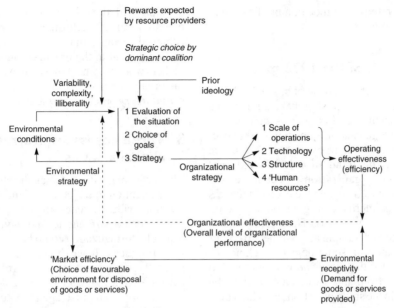

Figure 1 The role of strategic choice in organization theory
Source: Child (1972: 18)

mance against which the pressure of economic constraints has to be evaluated, and to the design of the organization's structure itself' (Child 1972: 2). Strategic choices were seen to be made through initiatives within the network of internal and external organizational relationships – through *pro-action* as well as *reaction*. It was assumed that effective strategic choice required the exercise of power and was therefore an essentially *political* phenomenon:

> Incorporation of the process whereby strategic decisions are made directs attention onto the degree of choice which can be exercised..., whereas many available models direct attention exclusively onto the constraints involved. They imply in this way that organizational behaviour can only be understood by reference to functional imperatives rather to political action.
>
> (Child 1972: 2)

This identified the need for a corrective to, rather than an outright rejection of, the prevailing paradigm. Indeed, it implied a potential synthesis between the political process and functionalist perspectives. For the power available to decision makers was seen to be

accountable in terms of the consequences for organizational performance that flowed from its exercise. It was assumed that some assessment of those consequences (albeit not necessarily well-informed or rational) would enter along with actors' prior preferences into their decisions. The model towards which strategic choice analysis led would therefore:

> direct our attention towards those who possess the power to decide upon an organization's structural rationale, towards the limits upon that power imposed by the operational context, and towards the process of assessing constraints and opportunities against values in deciding organizational strategies.
>
> (Child 1972: 13)

The 1972 paper offered the outline of a processual model under the title of 'The role of strategic choice in a theory of organization'. This model is reproduced as Figure 1. It locates strategic choice within the organizational context, and through the feedback of information to decision makers, depicts the conditions for what today some would call an *organizational learning process*. Since much of the discussion in the third section of this article will refer to the model, a brief explanation now follows.

2 Analysis of the 1972 model

In the model, the exercise of strategic choice by organizational decision makers refers to a process in which the first stage is their evaluation of the organization's position – the expectations placed on it by external resource providers, the trend of relevant external events, the organization's recent performance, how comfortable the decision makers are with its internal configuration, and so on (see DECISION MAKING). Their prior values, experience and training are assumed to colour this evaluation in some degree. A choice of objectives for the organization is assumed to follow on from this evaluation, and to be reflected in the strategic actions on which they decide. This process is, in practice, often formalized into an annual planning round and/or procedure for making capital expenditure, which appears usually to be accompanied by considerable informal lobbying and negotiation.

Externally-oriented actions may include a move into or out of given markets or areas of activity in order to try and secure a favourable demand or response that will be expressed by a high consumer valuation of the organization's products or services. They could also include attempts to negotiate the terms of acceptable organizational performance with external resource-providers or institutions holding sanction over the organization, although this possibility was not considered in the 1972 paper. Rather common examples occur when companies go to banks for a substantial loan and when they seek permission to erect a new processing facility that has an environmental impact. Internally-oriented actions may involve an attempt, within the limits of resource availability and indivisibility, to establish a configuration of personnel, technologies and work organization which is both internally consistent and compatible with the scale and nature of the operations planned. The 'goodness of fit' that is in the event achieved is seen to determine the level of efficiency expressed by output in relation to costs. The conjunction of efficiency with external demand will determine the organization's overall level of performance. Performance achieved becomes in turn a significant informational input to the organization's decision makers when they next make an evaluation of the organization's position. Thus, a *circular*, *evolutionary* process is established.

3 Three key issues in strategic choice analysis

The earlier exposition of strategic choice gave some attention to the choice of internal organization with reference to the 'contextual' parameters of size and technology; how, for example, formalization could be a response to increasing scale. It was, however, more fundamentally concerned with the relationship between agency and environment. The ability of decision makers ('agents') to make a 'choice' between policies was seen to depend ultimately upon how far they could preserve autonomy within the environment, through achieving the levels of performance expected of them. The term 'strategic' was used to signify matters of importance to an organization as a whole, particularly those bearing upon its ability to prosper within an environment where it faces competition or the need to maintain its credibility. It is closely related to the idea of 'stratagem', which is a way of attempting to accomplish an objective in interaction with, or against, others. The three key issues arising from strategic choice analysis therefore concern: (1) the nature of agency and choice; (2) the nature of environment; and (3) the nature of the relationship between organizational agents and the environment.

Agency and choice

'The problem of human agency' has had a continuing intellectual significance in the social sciences (see AGENCY, MARKETS AND HIERARCHIES). Human beings have succeeded during the course of their history in creating socially organized systems which then limit further exercise of human agency, even to the point of determining human action. Such organized constraint acts both upon individuals and organizations. The forms it takes include culture, institutionalized norms for socially approved action (often prescribed in laws), and the constricting bureaucracies of government and big business. While the derivation of each of these forms is external to any one person or group of people, cultural values and institutional norms can become internalized so that they act to constrain choice primarily through the social actor's own interpretative mechanisms rather than through constraints which are ostensibly imposed from outside. For example, the management of many organizations have banned smoking within their buildings although there is no law obliging them to do so.

Whittington (1988) developed the distinction between external and internal forms of constraint, with the intention of thereby refining strategic choice analysis. He pointed out that the initial impact of the strategic choice concept had been to encourage analysts to dichotomize perspectives on organization between those which focus on agency (the 'voluntaristic' approach) and those which emphasize determinism. The dichotomous approach tended to ignore the preconditions for exercising agency, and the possibility that actors themselves may not have sufficient capacities for exercising choice could also be overlooked. This reasoning led Whittington, following Estler (1984), to distinguish between 'environmental determinism' and 'action determinism'.

Action determinism qualifies the simple assumption that organizational actors can exercise choice once external constraints are removed. It draws attention to the mechanisms used by actors in deciding what to do. Action determinism holds that, given certain types of drive, such as an overriding intention to maximize a firm's profits, a decision maker will only select one kind of action such as keeping costs to the bare minimum. This formulation is clearly problematic as it stands, since it assumes that actors can perceive only one way of realizing their intentions. Nevertheless, the concept of action determinism does draw attention to the relevance of predetermined mind-sets for the interpretative process which takes place when strategic choice is exercised, and it accounts for how they could limit the range of choices recognized and considered. It points to the significance of managerial beliefs, and of the factors shaping them, for an understanding of the strategic choice process in organizations, a subject which has attracted a growing body of research in recent years. Spender (1989), for example, showed how managers in particular industries tend to share a common set of strategic 'recipes' – which can become embedded, to the extend of inhibiting an innovative response to changing competitive conditions. The latter phenomenon is illustrated by the difficulties which the managers of the British clothing firm, Foster Brothers, had in adjusting to a new competitive situation at the beginning of the 1980s (Johnson 1987).

The original analysis of strategic choice identified 'prior ideology' as exercising an influence over how decision makers would evaluate their organization's situation (see STRATEGY MAKING, POLITICS OF). The concept of ideology draws attention to the ways that class, occupational and national socialization may shape managerial beliefs about action choices. While its relevance has been supported by subsequent research, we are now able to understand how other factors, such as age and educational level, can also exert an influence. Age and education, although they locate people within social categories which can generate common identities and beliefs, are likely to affect action determination not only through the medium of ideology but also through competence.

The introduction of action determinism enriches the analysis of strategic choice because it focuses attention onto the characteristics of key organizational actors themselves which may foreclose the degree of choice that they exercise, even in the absence of external constraints. It complements the political process perspective, present in the original exposition of strategic choice, which assumes that limitations on action choices not arising from outside the organization derived from its internal politics. The political process perspective draws attention to what would be collectively acceptable within the 'dominant' decision making group, or acceptable to the organization's wider body of employees or members, and it allows for an internal negotiation process though which there can be a coalescence of diverse initial action preferences into an agreed policy. The notion of action determinism draws attention to the prior factors which shape the mind-sets of key actors. Its application in research promises to shed light on how firmly beliefs are held by actors as they enter into discussions and negotiations with others in the organization, and how flexible they will be in modifying their beliefs in the light of the pressures of contrary opinion and evidence.

While action determinism can lead to an unwillingness to consider information that does not fit preconceived ideas, the scarcity of information as a resource can also inhibit the range of choices considered. There are two issues to note here. The first concerns the problem of securing relevant information that is timely, in an analysable form and not prohibitively expensive. The second concerns the problem of coping with information that is ambiguous, of questionable reliability and incomplete. Decision making, especially of the non-routine kind considered within strategic choice analysis, is thus liable to be conducted with uncertainty. The degree of choice will therefore be limited not only by action determinism and the constraints of intraorganizational political process; it will also be inhibited by limited and/or ambiguous information. The three phenomena – action determinism, political process and imperfect information – are likely to react upon each other. The foreclosing of options through action determinism is one way of coping with uncertainty – the actor 'enacts' the situation in his or her terms instead and is not troubled by externalities. If this behaviour predominates, it is likely to heighten the political process, either between key actors themselves if they hold divergent beliefs and/or between closed-minded actors and the rest of the organization. A lively political process around the making of strategic organizational decisions will of itself generate greater uncertainty, at least as to how information should be interpreted.

In short, limitations to agency and choice may arise from action determinism and intraorganizational political process, and also from informational deficiencies. The identification of these limitations carries the original concept of strategic choice forward, since they highlight the constraints upon choice additional to those which are imposed by an organization's environment.

Environment

It is not possible to abstract from the environment when considering the strategic choices available to organizational actors (see CONTEXTS AND ENVIRONMENTS). This is partly because the environment presents threats and opportunities for the organization which establish the parameters of choice. It is also because the ways in which organizational actors understand the environment affect the extent to which they believe they enjoy an autonomy of choice between alternatives.

Strategic choice analysis recognizes both a pro-active and a reactive aspect in organizational decision making *vis-à-vis* the environment. Organizational agents are seen to enjoy a kind of 'bounded' autonomy. They can take external initiatives, including the choice to enter and exit environments, and also make adaptive internal arrangements. At the same time, the environment within which they are operating is seen to limit their scope for action because it imposes certain conditions for their organization to perform well. It is assumed that organizational actors will themselves have a similar understanding of the environment, because this is what experience teaches them.

Weick (1969) maintains that people in organizations 'enact' their environments. This can be interpreted in two ways. The first is that people can only be aware of a literally all-embracing concept like 'the environment' in terms of how they enact it in their minds. Organizational actors therefore necessarily respond to their own subjective definitions of the environment. This interpretation is fundamental to strategic choice analysis and indeed to any view of organizations that admits of human agency. The second interpretation is that people in organizations can enact the environment in the sense of 'making it happen as they wish'.

A very qualified form of this second interpretation informed the original description of strategic choice that could be exercised by organizational decision makers:

To an important extent, their decisions as to where the organization's operations shall be located, the clientele it shall serve, or the types of employees it shall recruit determine the limits to its environment – that is, to the environment significant for the functions which the organization performs.

(Child 1972: 10)

The possibility of environmental enactment is here limited to the selection of environments in which to operate, and even this decision cannot necessarily be entered into lightly or frequently since it many incur large entry and exit costs. Enactment in strategic choice analysis thus refers mainly to actions which bring certain environments into relevance – which introduce them onto the organizational stage. Once entered, the conditions of an environment assume an object reality which is consequential for an organization, however much they are filtered by a subjective interpretation. That interpretation will shape the actions taken within the environment, which will amount to further enactment insofar as they are able to effect intended changes in it. The level of change which the managers of an organization can effect within its environment is always liable to be limited by the countervailing powers of institutions, as telecommunication companies found under previously regulatory regimes, and/or by the possibility of new competition, as former market leaders like IBM have experienced.

This interpretative view sees the decision maker entering into interaction with people outside the organization, but it does not necessarily conceive of the two forming an identity either objectively or in the minds of organizational actors. What they are interpreting, albeit within the cognitive and informational limits discussed earlier, can exist apart from them. A person or organization does not constitute its environment; the environment consists of other actors in other organizations, and it cannot be reduced to the subjective interpretations of any one group of organizational players. Some writers, however, have pursued Weick's argument to the point of maintaining that environments are wholly enacted through the social construction of actors (for example,

Smircich and Stubbart 1985). This is to apply an extreme form of voluntarism to the concept of strategic choice. Rather, the emphasis on human agency and subjective interpretation contained in strategic choice analysis was intended to counteract the theoretical shallowness and inherent pessimism of environmental determinism, *not* to reduce either organization or environment to being simply the products of a subjective understanding. Strategic choice analysis recognizes that environments have real and consequential properties distinct from the perceptions and understandings of organizational actors, but it maintains that those perceptions and constructions are also of consequence in their own right if they contribute to determining the actions of organizations.

Strategic choice analysis thus incorporates both subjectivist and objectivist perspectives on organizational environment. This dualism does not result only from identifying organizational decision makers' subjective evaluations of the environment as a critical link between its objective features and organizational action, although that is an important element in it. It also reflects a recognition that organizational actors do not necessarily, or even typically, deal with an 'environment' at arm's length through the impersonal transactions of classical market analysis but, on the contrary, often engage in relationships with external parties that are sufficiently close and long-standing as to lend a mutually pervasive character to organization and environment. This indicates that the environment of organizations has an institutional character and, indeed, that people inside and outside the formal limits of an organization may share institutionalized norms and relationships. Examples include the members of occupational unions and professional associations. The 'environment' contains cultural and relational dimensions in addition to the 'task' and market variables identified respectively by structural contingencies and economic theories. This conception of the organizational environment as a social entity has provided useful additional insights into how companies have developed over time (for example, Smith *et al.* 1990). It also helps to clarify two long-standing issues in the relationship between organizational agents and the environment which arise from strategic choice analysis, namely: (1) whether or not the environment is constraining or enabling; and (2) how externalized the environment actually is.

Organizational agents and the environment

Whittington (1988) criticizes environmental determinism in which exogenous structural constraints are assumed necessarily to limit and regulate the actions that can be taken by organizational decision makers. This point is consistent with the strategic choice argument, which drew attention to various possibilities allowing for choice on the part of organizational actors without their incurring intolerable penalties. Whittington conceives of environment in terms of how it is socially structured and argues that this structuring can be enabling as well as constraining for strategic choice. Thus, organizational actors who are members of a professional occupation and bound by norms of appropriate conduct may thereby be externally constrained in their actions, whereas owner-managers supported by entrepreneurial ideologies and the rights of capitalist ownership may thereby be externally enabled to consider a wider range of action alternatives.

A more extended consideration of the enabling and constraining features of the environment is similarly encouraged by the sectoral concept of environment just described. This indicates how, for instance, long-standing relationships between the members of the same sector, structured within industry associations, can furnish a basis for concerted action on matters of common interest such as political lobbying (see INTEREST GROUPS). Or it may show how the sharing of sector-specific strategic recipes (Spender 1989) can facilitate the interpretation of the environment by a firm's managers. At the same time, the cultural and relational norms shared by members of a sector are likely to constrain organizational actors who seek to diverge from them. For example, divergence from normal strategic recipes may be perceived as risk by members of the capital market familiar with the sector, with the result that

they impose a premium on the cost of raising external funds. Thus, while the social nature of an organization's environment will under some circumstances act as a constraint upon action, even to the point of determining it, it can also enable action and widen the range of available strategic alternatives. It is a misleading oversimplification to treat the environment simply as an external determinant of organizational action.

The concept of an organizational environment as a social network also raises doubts about how externalized it really is from its constituent organizations (see GROWTH OF THE FIRM AND NETWORKING; NETWORKS AND ORGANIZATIONS). The distinction between organization and environment contained in the original strategic choice article (Child 1972) has to be softened by a recognition that organizational actors often create choice possibilities through their relationships with people who are formally outside the organization. They may, for example, be able to secure from officials with whom a good relationship has been developed a rather more liberal interpretation of environmental controls, especially in countries like China where the application of regulations is open to a flexible interpretation (see CHINA, MANAGEMENT IN). Organization and environment are becoming interpenetrated through collaboration between actors in such a way as to diffuse the distinction between the two entities and, incidentally, to blur the distinction between 'firm' and 'market'. With the rapid growth of collaborative relationships between organizations, in the forms of joint ventures and other strategic alliances, this interpenetration assumes a fully operational form (see GLOBAL STRATEGIC ALLIANCES). It is, of course, qualified by the terms on which the parties can agree to cooperate and by how far they can identify mutual complementarities. Such alliances can indeed be unstable, and many survive for only a limited period. Nevertheless, they constitute an increasingly important arrangement through which part of the relevant environment is internalized, often with the motive of affording greater control over, or access to, other areas of the environment (such as markets) in a bid to extend strategic choice. The recent spate of alliances between telecommunications companies, for example, has facilitated entry into markets otherwise protected by governments and they may also restore a degree of market control following the implementation of deregulation policies.

Strategic choice analysis therefore allows for the objective presence of environments, while at the same time it recognizes that organizations and environments are mutually pervasive. This pervasiveness occurs in two main ways. The first is through the interpretation of environments as being consequential for organizational action. The second is through the relationships that extend across an organization's 'boundaries'. It takes the very definition of those boundaries to be in large part the consequence of: 'the kinds of relationships which its decision makers choose to enter upon with their equivalents in other organizations, or ... the constraints which more dominant counterparts impose upon them' (Child 1972: 10). Organization and environment therefore permeate one another both cognitively and relationally – that is, both in the minds of actors and in the process of conducting relationships between the two.

The concept of strategic choice was for some time interpreted as justifying a sharp distinction between organizational agency and organizational environment, with the former emphasized by voluntaristic perspectives and the latter by deterministic approaches (see the comprehensive review by Astley and Van de Ven 1983). Strategic choice was associated with an absence of external determination, a procedure maintained even in later analyses which explored the possibility of different combinations of choice and determinism (for example, Hrebiniak and Joyce 1985). This is understandable, given the intention of the 1972 article to criticize the then prevailing dominance of determinism, but it overlooked that article's statement that organizational decision makers are in a position of response to feedback from the environment. This feedback may in turn provide them with a learning opportunity which brings to light new action choices, but the process overall was seen as an *interactive* one between organizational agents and the environment, and in effect between choice and constraint.

This interactive view is one which writers on strategic management have generally adopted, exemplified by the influential study of US firms and hospitals conducted in the 1970s by Miles and Snow (1978). They recognized how strategic choice analysis identified the ongoing relationship between organizational agents and the environment, giving rise to what they termed 'the adaptive cycle':

> The strategic-choice approach essentially argues that the effectiveness of organizational adaptation hinges on the dominant coalition's perceptions of environmental conditions and the decisions it makes concerning how the organization will cope with these conditions.
>
> (Miles and Snow 1978: 21)

From their investigation, Miles and Snow concluded that the policies which organizational agents adopted towards the environment could be placed into the four generic categories of 'defender', 'prospector', 'analyser' and 'reactor'. This categorization was an important refinement of the strategic choice concept.

Bourgeois, in similar vein, argued for a view of strategic management as a creative activity which is intrinsic to a dialectic between choice and constraint: 'So, though environmental and internal forces act as constraints, strategy making often selects and later modifies the sets of constraints' (1984: 593). Hambrick and Finkelstein (1987) developed and explored the concept of chief executive discretion, defined as 'latitude of action'. They argued that this concept reconciled popular views of organizations as either inertial or highly adaptive. Their premise was that chief executives vary in how much discretion they possess, and that variation is due to a combination of: (1) factors in the environment; (2) organizational characteristics which promote inertia (such as size, age and culture); and (3) the chief executive's own attributes. While Hambrick and Finkelstein in this way identify discrete factors rather than the processes and relationships through which choice and constraint work themselves out, they identify the influences which might enter interactively into the process.

More recently, Neergaard (1992) has developed a 'partial contingency model'. This recognizes that the nature of the environment, such as its levels of dynamism and complexity, can impact upon the internal controls systems which it is functional for an organization to adopt. At the same time, the model also recognizes that environmental management is possible through two main strategies which Neergaard (borrowing from previous writers) calls 'buffering' and 'bridging'. Through buffering, managers aim to protect their core activities from external influences – examples include stockpiling, attempts to reduce input and output fluctuations such as marketing campaigns, and public relations activities. With bridging, managers endeavour to manage their environments through various forms of negotiation, cooperation, exchange of information and other forms of reciprocity. Neergaard illustrates how environmental management has a direct bearing on the type and degree of organizational control that it is necessary to adopt. His conclusion in effect reiterates the basic strategic choice argument: 'Only by studying the interplay between environment and environmental management is it possible to gain a more full understanding of different controls [that is, internal organization]' (Neergaard 1992: 29).

Strategic choice is recognized and realized through a process whereby those with the power to make decisions for the organization interact among themselves (so constituting a shifting 'dominant coalition'), with other organizational members and with external parties. Analytical centrality is given to organizational agents' interpretations (their goals and views of the possibilities for realizing them) as they engage in these relationships. This is to say that organization, as a social order, is the subject of adjustment through negotiation on a continuing, although not necessarily continual, basis. The possibilities for this negotiation are at any one point in time framed by existing structures, both within and without the organization. The use of 'framing' here is intended to convey a sense that the issues and options open to negotiation by actors have some structured limits, although it may be possible to change the limits themselves over time through the negotiation process.

Structures within the organization include the channels through which relevant information is obtained and processed, and formalized policies which define action priorities for the organization. External structures include the configuration of competitor organizations within the organization's operating domain, that of its suppliers and customers, and the system of regulations relevant to its activities.

Strategic choice in organizational analysis thus furnishes an example of 'structuration' (Giddens 1984). That is, action is bounded by existing structures but at the same time acts upon those structures. Through their actions, agents endeavour to modify and redefine structures in ways that will admit of different possibilities for future action. The process is a continuing one. Strategic choice thus presents a dynamic rather than a static perspective on organizations and their environments. In keeping with structuration theory, it also addresses the so-called problem of levels of analysis. For, while the actions taken in the name of organizations may be individually driven, and some of this drive may be explicable at the level of the individual, they are organizational both in their representation and in the resources, relationships or other features which are activated. When these actions become a constituent element in the relations between organization and external bodies, they move into an even higher level of social process. The consequences of this process for the organization, which strategic choice analysis depicts as being transmitted to it through a feedback of information on its performance, are social in origin but may be interpreted in some circumstances by individual actors primarily in terms of their own personal values or priorities. Strategic choice analysis admits of a role for the individual organizational actor (as an entrepreneur), assumes that actors will more often constitute a collective (as in a dominant coalition), and treats the cycle of action and response as one that is environmentally and therefore socially contextualized. It does not regard the wider social arena simply as a constraining or defining context for the narrower, lower-order unit of analysis, as did, for instance, the founders of the influential Aston Programme of organizational research in their original 'conceptual framework' (Pugh *et al.* 1963) (see ASTON GROUP). Nor does it do the opposite and simply treat action as explicable in individual terms or, for that matter, as interpretable solely in terms of any one individual's understanding. Rather, its conception of agency entering into a cycle of organizational development within the environment cuts across analytical levels and in this sense helps to bridge what has sometimes been a source of division among theorists of organization.

The following section examines how these characteristics of strategic choice analysis – the interaction between agency and structure, and the cyclical nature of organizational development – can contribute to the challenge of constructively reconciling different paradigms. In so doing, the consistency of this integrative interpretation with an evolutionary learning perspective will become apparent.

4 The role of strategic choice in contemporary organization studies

It is significant that the classification of paradigms within organization studies which has attracted the most attention (Burrell and Morgan 1979) did not attempt to allocate strategic choice analysis to any of its categories (see ORGANIZATION PARADIGMS). Its authors claimed that the paradigms they identified were mutually exclusive, a claim which has contributed substantially to present divisions in the subject area. Strategic choice analysis, by contrast, cannot be contained within any one of these paradigms. Indeed, it bridges and potentially integrates them.

Burrell and Morgan placed different perspectives within four main paradigms which were defined in terms of two dimensions. The first dimension was whether the perspective regarded organizational phenomena as subjective constructs or as objective in nature. The second was whether the perspective was concerned with the possibilities, or process, of radical change or with the maintenance of the existing order ('regulation'). Burrell and Morgan argued that the four paradigms 'offer alternative views of social reality' and cannot

therefore be synthesized. Hence the claim of 'paradigm incommensurability' in organization studies.

Strategic choice analysis would actually be impossible if an assumption of paradigm incommensurability was maintained. It bridges the four paradigms identified by Burrell and Morgan. First, it is concerned *both* with the ways in which subjective constructions have objective consequences through the actions they inform, *and* with how those consequences subsequently impinge upon future actions through the subjective interpretations which are given to them. *Cash flow* would be one objective indicator of such action consequences, which is open to divergent subjective interpretations as to its sufficiency and implications. Neither a wholly subjectivist paradigm nor a wholly objectivist one could of itself provide a sufficient theoretical foundation for this process. The argument here is, in effect, that process of agency in organizations cannot be treated adequately by a perspective that does not incorporate both the subjective and objective features inherent in structuration.

Second, it is also impossible to consign strategic choice analysis to either the Burrell/Morgan paradigm of the sociology of regulation or that of radical change. For, while the original exposition of strategic choice analysis did tend to assume that dominant members of the organization would act in ways that preserve their privileged positions (an aspect of 'regulation'), it does not assume they will necessarily succeed in so doing. It therefore allows for situations in which organizational change can occur and this change could possibly be quite radical. For example, conditions of crisis occasioned by the failure of an organization to achieve a level of performance in its environment that can meet the expectations of its member groups are likely, according to strategic choice analysis, to give rise to a radical change in the composition of the 'dominant coalition' (for example, through takeover, employee buyout or election of new leaders in an association or union) with a probable consequent change in the policies and practices instituted for the organization. Strategic choice analysis draws attention to conditions under which change is likely to be activated, either by the established decision makers or by new ones. In the former case, the change will be motivated by the desire to preserve certain continuities and thus be conservative, if not regulatory, in character. In the latter case, the change may be motivated by a desire to introduce relatively radical reformulations. The mutual dependence between different groups in an organization implies, according to strategic choice analysis, that even a dominant group will have to preserve certain features valued by the others when it is endeavouring to introduce change, thus giving rise to the paradox of continuity and change in organizational life. Studies of organizational transformation have in fact noted how even apparently radical developments usually incorporate elements of continuity, at least of an ideological nature, in order to increase the acceptability of the changes among those who have to work with them (Pettigrew 1985; Child and Smith 1987).

The strategic choice perspective on organizational process thus brings agency and structure into a dynamic tension along the subjective-objective dimension. It locates this relationship within a social context which is significant to the *subjective* aspect as the source of agents' values and perceived interests towards the organization (referred to as 'ideology' in Child's article). It also locates the relationship within an economic or institutional context which is relevant to how an organization performs *objectively*; for example, in terms of its capacity to attract further resources. The level and type of performance that is achieved in relation to the expectations of those with power over an organization in turn bear upon the question of whether that organization's status quo can be maintained or not. This form of analysis draws from insights provided by each of Burrell and Morgan's four paradigms and offers a bridge between them. It is not, as the role accorded to performance might suggest, a pseudo-functionalist analysis, since it admits that the conditions for organizational survival are open to negotiation between organizational agents and external resource-holders and that the evaluation of performance can be the subject of claim and counter-claim. For example, the employees of a company may claim that the lack of opportu-

nities for further training are a mark of poor managerial performance, even though the cost savings boost profits in the short term. Like functionalism, strategic choice analysis adopts a position of contextual relativism, but it differs from it in not admitting of incontestable and overriding situational determinants.

The continuing relevance of the strategic choice perspective derives to a large extent from the way it identifies possibilities for integration between different paradigms. Its rejection of paradigm incommensurability is not intended to open the door to imperialistic claims from any particular theoretical quarter and, indeed, one should recall that the approach grew out of a critique of a then dominant paradigm in organizational analysis. In fact, its position is quite the opposite. The integrative potential of strategic choice analysis stems from the way it is conducive towards a recognition of the fundamental paradoxes in organizational life, which both paradigm incommensurability and paradigm imperialism fail to take into account. There is a tension between apparently contradictory aspects of organizational life – the subjective and objective, the conservative and innovative – that establishes a dynamic which transcends them.

This dynamic contributes to an evolutionary adaptive or 'learning' cycle (see ORGANIZATIONAL LEARNING). There is a parallel here between the strategic choice adaptive cycle and the analysis of knowledge formation advanced by Boisot (1986). Both analyses regard new circumstances as posing a potential challenge to knowledge which has been previously codified into formalized/structured organizational practices. If adaptation is to take place (which of course does not necessarily happen), this challenge will initiate a process of enquiry and search which initially brings ill-defined information specific to the new situation within the purview of organizational factors (uncodified/undiffused knowledge in Boisot's terminology). From the process of evaluating this new knowledge, proposals emerge for the definition and formalization of new actions and structures, which if acceptable and successful become standardized and hence widely applied ('diffused'). The contribution that this adaptive cycle model can offer stems largely from the fact that it bridges the subjective/objective and change/continuity dichotomies in the study of organizations. It begins to unpack the concept of structuration through suggesting how interpretation becomes objectified into structures and individual learning becomes translated into organizational practice, while it indicates that structure and practice are themselves always liable to become deconstructed in the face of external and internal changes with which they are inconsistent. Recognition that the interplay between organization and environment is mediated by the interpretation and evaluation of actors operating within the arena of organizational micropolitics also helps to resolve the paradox that change and continuity co-exist and may even by symbiotic.

Apart from the attractiveness of its integrative potential, further development of the strategic choice approach along the lines just indicated promises to offer insights into what has come to be called 'organizational learning'. This is a prominent topic within the study of organizations which, however, exhibits considerable theoretical disarray despite attracting much attention over the past twenty years. The term 'organizational learning' appears to be quite beguiling, even contradictory, in the light of the Burrell and Morgan scheme. Does it reflect a subjective or objective view of organization? Individuals can learn through a process of internalization, but what about organizations? Organizational learning implies the acquisition of new understanding and competence, but does this lead to a radical change or to new ways of maintaining the status quo in the light of different circumstances? Some of the confusion about organizational learning stems from a failure to apply to it an analysis that can incorporate these apparent contradictions within the framework of a dynamic adaptive cycle.

A great deal of the thinking about organizational learning has modelled itself on studies of individual learning, borrowing terms such as 'organizational memory'. Both cognitive and behaviourist theories of individual learning have been imported into discussions of organizational learning. A cognitive orientation is reflected in terms such as 'organizational intelligence', and a behavioural orientation in a concept such as 'organizational routines',

which are regarded as codifications of understanding and competence that the organization has acquired. A subjective–objective distinction is also present here, in that cognition is by definition subjective whereas behaviour can in principle be externally observed. Although frequently attempted, the application of individual learning models to organizations is deeply problematic. It reifies the organization into a mechanism or organism and wholly avoids the politics of agency which are integral to strategic choice analysis.

Much of the organizational learning literature fails to locate the prime movers of the process, the relevant actors – managers or other staff – within the political systems of organizations. In recognizing that there are barriers to learning, this literature explores defensiveness as a personal attribute, but usually fails to enquire into its non-psychological sources such as the organizational micro-politics which lead to much learning and innovation being contested between groups (Child and Loveridge 1990). For the actors involved in organizational learning and adaptation often belong to several groups which have different views about the desirable future path for their organization to follow. They may, for instance, be a mix of top managers, technical experts, functional managers and external consultants. Strategic choice analysis, by focusing upon a leading or initiating group operating within a political context that is both internal and external to the organization, draws attention not just to the capacity of individuals or groups to learn but equally to those people who are controlling and managing the learning process 'on behalf of' the organization. It admits the possibility that existing structures may limit learning because of the way they can close off certain options, through, for example, the absence of procedures or staff that can access certain areas of information, or because the options are too politically sensitive to consider in the light of the hierarchical privilege embedded in a organization's structure. At the same time, strategic choice analysis also allows for the possibility that such structures may offer some resources for the achievement of change.

Strategic choice analysis thus recognizes that it may be necessary to sustain certain paradoxes for learning to take place as a collective phenomenon in organizations, such as the need to achieve consensus from a diversity of views and the preservation of some continuities within the process of introducing change. In particular, it can bring an appreciation of the politics of change to bear upon the understanding of the organizational learning process. The relevance of these considerations may be illustrated by quoting just three of the conclusions drawn from a detailed study of organizational transformation in the Cadbury chocolate company.

1 A lengthy process of recognition preceded transformation. This involved a combination of symbolic and power-relevant activities, namely: (a) re-framing the definition of relevant contextual conditions and appropriate internal arrangements with (b) the ascension into powerful positions of those advocating new interpretations and solutions.
2 Competing frames of meaning and recipes for improvement were advanced by actors whose views were conditioned by their training, speciality and previous experience in the company.
3 The traditional and hitherto dominant corporate ideology was not simply a barrier to transformation. Its wide acceptance and cohesion provided a clear position against which the case for change had to be developed. This was easier because the ideology itself was malleable, stressing receptivity to new techniques and intellectual enquiry, and management had been encouraged to proceed in that mode. (Child and Smith 1987: 590).

The strategic choice perspective places the agency-structure relationship within a context. The evaluation by organizational agents of information feedback on the organization's performance in its environment, if it identifies either problems or new opportunities, encourages a learning process and provides a trigger for further action. The cycle is thus:

choice→action→outcome→
feedback→evaluation→choice

In this way, a structuration dynamic is established in which previously codified poli- cies and practices become targets for reformulation but where elements from the old structure are normally incorporated into the new. Hence the paradox of change and continuity.

5 Conclusion

This entry has highlighted the key points of strategic choice analysis within a theory of organizations. It has traced the issues which arose from the introduction of this perspective and it has considered some of the refinements of the original analysis which were indicated by subsequent criticism and deliberation.

An important corrective to some of the interpretations which others have made of strategic choice is the affirmation that it is neither a pseudo-functionalist perspective (showing organizational leaders how to run the show in a politically more sensitive manner) nor an outright rejection of the contingency strand of functionalism which it originally criticized. The strategic choice perspective transcends these distinctions which some have built up into formidable barriers within the study of organizations and it is precisely this which gives it the potential to assist future integration within the subject.

Strategic choice analysis therefore opens a door to future progress in organization studies by drawing together insights from different paradigms and locating these within a dynamic process of interplay between agency and structure, and organizations and environment.

JOHN CHILD
UNIVERSITY OF BIRMINGHAM

Note

This entry has benefited greatly from editorial advice kindly offered by Sally Heavens and Malcolm Warner.

Further reading

(References cited in the text marked *)

* Astley, W.G. and Ven, A. Van de (1983) 'Central perspectives and debates in organizational theory', *Administrative Science Quarterly* 28: 245–73. (Classifies perspectives according to

levels of organizational analysis, and deterministic versus voluntaristic assumptions.)

* Blau, P.M. and Schoenherr, R.A. (1971) *The Structure of Organizations*, New York: Basic Books. (Reports on comparative research examining organization structure and its predictors.)

* Boisot, M. (1986) 'Markets and hierarchies in a cultural perspective', *Organization Studies* 7: 135–58. (An early exposition of an influential model of the 'knowledge cycle' which is consistent with the strategic choice process.)

* Bourgeois, L.J. (1984) 'Strategic management and determinism', *Academy of Management Review* 9: 586–96. (Suggests a dialectic between free will and determinism in conceptualizations of strategic behaviour.)

* Burrell, G. and Morgan, G. (1979) *Sociological Paradigms and Organizational Analysis*, London: Heinemann. (Extremely influential division of organizational sociology into four discrete paradigms.)

* Child, J. (1972) 'Organizational structure, environment and performance: the role of strategic choice', *Sociology* 6: 1–22. (Classic exposition of the strategic choice perspective.)

* Child, J. and Loveridge, R. (1990) *Information Technology in European Services*, Oxford: Blackwell. (Considers political versus technologically-deterministic perspectives in the light of detailed cases of information technology introduction into services in six European countries.)

* Child, J. and Smith, C. (1987) 'The context and process of organizational transformation – Cadbury Limited in its sector', *Journal of Management Studies* 24: 565–93. (Application of 'firm-in-sector' analysis which incorporates the paradoxical combinations of action with constraint, and continuity with change.)

* Donaldson, L. (1985) *In Defence of Organization Theory*, Cambridge: Cambridge University Press. (Criticizes strategic choice analysis because it does not adopt a normative approach towards organizational design.)

* Donaldson, L. (1995) *American Anti-Management Theories of Organization*, Cambridge: Cambridge University Press. (Criticizes organization theories which, the author claims, do not admit the role of managers as designers of organization structure in the light of operational contingencies.)

* Estler, J. (1984) *Ulysses and the Sirens: Studies in Rationality and Irrationality*, Cambridge: Cambridge University Press. (Proposes a two-step model of human action which recognizes both exogenous constraints and those inherent in the action selection mechanisms of actors themselves.)

* Giddens, A. (1984) *The Constitution of Society*, Cambridge: Polity Press. (One of many works in which Giddens articulates 'structuration' theory.)

* Hambrick, D.C. and Finkelstein, S. (1987) 'Managerial discretion: a bridge between polar views of organizational outcomes', *Research in Organizational Behavior* 9: 369–406. (Develops and explores the concept of chief executive discretion.)

* Hannan, M.T. and Freeman, J.H. (1989) *Organizational Ecology*, Cambridge, MA: Harvard University Press. (The main source on this perspective, collecting together these authors' previous work.)

* Hrebiniak, L.G. and Joyce, W.F. (1985) 'Organizational adaptation: strategic choice and environmental determinism', *Administrative Science Quarterly* 30: 336–49. (Develops a typology of organizational adaptation based on the assumption that choice and determinism are independent variables.)

* Johnson, G. (1987) *Strategic Change and the Management Process*, Oxford: Blackwell. (Presents research exploring how managers' understandings affect their action in respect of environmental changes.)

* Miles, R.E. and Snow, C.C. (1978) *Organizational Strategy, Structure and Process*, New York: McGraw-Hill. (Develops the strategic choice perspective into an 'adaptive cycle' which identifies four generic policies adopted by managements towards their environments.)

* Neergaard, P. (1992) 'Environment, strategy and management accounting', in D. Otley and H. Lebac (eds), *Proceedings of the Second European Symposium on Information Systems*, Versailles: HEC. (Explores and illustrates the need to modify contingency approaches to management accounting through cognizance of the interplay between environment and its management. Available from the Copenhagen Business School.)

* Pettigrew, A.M. (1985) *The Awakening Giant: Continuity and Change in ICI*, Oxford: Blackwell. (Major study which traces the impact of its top management on a major UK corporation.)

* Powell, W.W. and DiMaggio, P.J. (1991) *The New Institutionalism in Organizational Analysis*, Chicago, IL: University of Chicago Press. (Exposition of the new institutionalism and a collection of the significant contributions to that approach.)

* Pugh, D.S., Hickson, D.J., Hinings, C.R., Macdonald, K.M., Turner, C. and Lupton, T. (1963) 'A conceptual scheme for organizational analysis', *Administrative Science Quarterly* 8: 289–315. (Sets out the framework for the Aston Programme of organizational studies which strategic choice analysis later critiqued.)
* Pugh, D.S., Hickson, D.J., Hinings, C.R. and Turner, C. (1968) 'Dimensions of organization structure', *Administrative Science Quarterly* 13: 65–105. (One of many publications reporting on the findings of the first study in the Aston Programme.)
* Sklair, L. (2000) *The Transnational Capitalist Class*, Oxford: Blackwell. (This book links strategy and globalization to offer a new perspective.)
* Smircich, L. and Stubbart, C. (1985) 'Strategic management in an enacted world', *Academy of Management Review* 10: 724–36. (Takes an interpretative worldview and claims that environments are enacted.)
* Smith, C., Child, J. and Rowlinson, M. (1990) *Reshaping Work: The Cadbury Experience*, Cambridge: Cambridge University Press. (Traces in detail how the senior management of a large confectionery company articulated the requirements for changes in its organization.)
* Spender, J.-C. (1989) *Industry Recipes*, Oxford: Blackwell. (Pioneering study of senior managers' mental maps for guiding their businesses.)
* Weick, K.E. (1969) *The Social Psychology of Organizing*, Reading, MA: Addison-Wesley. (Influential book which stresses the enactment of the organizing process by those involved.)
* Whittington, R. (1988) 'Environmental structure and theories of strategic choice', *Journal of Management Studies* 25: 521–36. (Argues for a more sophisticated analysis of choice and determinism, recognizing how 'action determinism' may limit the perception of choice and how the environment may enhance actors' capacities for strategic choice.)

See also: CHANDLER, A.D.; MINTZBERG, H.; ORGANIZATION BEHAVIOUR; ORGANIZATION BEHAVIOUR, HISTORY OF; STRATEGIC COMPETENCE; STRATEGY, CONCEPT OF; STRATEGY MAKING, POLITICS OF; STRATEGY AND RATIONALITY

Strategic competence

Overview

Firms compete in product markets on the basis of resources that they have either acquired externally or built up by themselves. The first kind of resources, even if not necessarily tangible, can be specified and hence bought and sold. The second kind is much more difficult to specify. It represents a slow accumulation of know-how and competences that are tacit, organization-wide, and for that reason, specific to a firm. Such competences become strategic or 'core' when they confer distinct benefits on a firm's customers and provide the firm with competitive advantages that are hard to discern and imitate.

Not all firms possess core competences, and those that do find it difficult to identify and nurture them. Their effective exploitation requires a corporate level perspective which does not always sit comfortably with the more extreme forms of decentralization to strategic business units that is sometimes associated with profit centre management.

1 Introduction

Traditional approaches to business strategy and to strategic management view competition as product-based and market-based (see STRATEGY, CONCEPT OF). Firms are regarded as collections of strategic business units (SBUs) each of which has a portfolio of products which compete with the products of the SBUs of other firms. Much strategic attention is, consequently, focused on the competitive positioning of products in markets. While these 'positioning' approaches have been fruitful in many areas, there are others in which they are more problematic. One such area concerns diversified firms. Beyond the financial logic of conglomeration, what rationale is there for diversification? In what ways can and do SBUs benefit from being part of a larger entity?

2 The resource-based view

Wernerfelt (1984) provided one answer. Rather than viewing firms from the perspective of their products and their markets – the positioning view – he suggested viewing them from the perspective of their resources. Although this proposal was not novel (Penrose 1959; Andrews 1971), it did represent a neglected approach at the time. Wernerfelt argued that looking at firms in terms of their resources led to different insights on diversified firms. First, as resources tend to be firm-based rather than SBU-based, it focused on what SBUs share by virtue of being members of the same firm. Second, it enabled a different set of strategic questions to be posed, questions which sought to identify and to exploit resources (as opposed to the products incorporating them) as a source of competitive advantage. Another strategic puzzle addressed by this perspective is the difficulty which traditional approaches have in explaining some aspects of differences in performances between firms (see CORPORATE PERFORMANCE, ANALYSIS OF). Dierickx and Cool (1989) distinguish between strategic asset stocks and strategic asset flows. Stocks of strategic assets are built up over time through a pattern of strategic asset flows, and while the flows themselves can be adjusted rapidly, the stocks cannot, since they represent the cumulative effects of flows over time. A new technology, for example, will reflect the flow of research and development (R&D) resources over a period of years. Typically, the strategic analysis of performance differences between firms has tended to compare strategic asset flows rather than the accumulation of stocks. The resource-based view redresses this imbalance. A third, and related, strategic puzzle which is solved by taking a resource-based approach is the success of firms such as Canon which have successfully managed both movement into, and rapid dominance of diversified markets. Canon's strength in these diversified markets reflects common resource strengths – strategic competences – across its SBUs, which provide it with corporate, as opposed to product-based, competitive advantages (Hamel and Prahalad 1994).

One impetus for the revival of interest in a resource-based view of the firm has been the changing structure of the competitive environment. Globalization, deregulation, rapid technological change and a concern for quality are just some of the changes which have taken place (see GLOBALIZATION). Such changes have altered the 'competitive space' in which firms operate. Increasingly, success in the marketplace depends as much on how a firm defines and positions itself in relation to future competitive spaces as on how it confronts current ones. The accumulation and exploitation of strategic competences is central to this task.

Rumelt traces the roots of the strategic competence concept to a number of areas: to the resource-based view of the firm; to the addition of a dynamic developmental dimension to prevailing notions of 'competence as a given'; to extending the idea of learning beyond the reduction of production costs; and to developments in diversification theory which focused attention on strategic resources (Rumelt 1974).

Such is the context in which the resource-based approach to strategic management has emerged. It has been put forward as a complementary rather than an alternative approach to one based on product or markets.

3 Core competences

The term which is most widely used to describe strategic resources is *core competences* (Prahalad and Hamel 1990). Other terms used in the literature include: strategic assets (Amit and Schoemaker 1993; Dierickx

and Cool 1989); firm resources (Barney 1991); intangible resources (Hall 1992) and capabilities (Stalk *et al.* 1992).

Hamel and Prahalad (1994) set five tests for a competence to be considered as a core competence. First, a core competence is more than just a bundle of skills and technologies. In a core competence these skills must be organizationally integrated in some way – a typical large firm might have no more than five or six core competencies. They are consequently neither a property of individuals nor of small teams. Second, a core competence is more than an asset as used in the accounting sense: it is the product of a learning process, incorporating both tacit and explicit knowledge, the value of which tends to appreciate rather than depreciate over time. Third, a core competence delivers a highly valued customer benefit. As an example, the authors contrast Honda's engines with the firm's dealer network. The former embodies a core competence because Honda's engines provide the firm's customers with a number of benefits which competitors cannot match. In contrast, Honda's dealer network provides no special benefit to customers over and above those offered by the firm's competitors. In process and service industries the core competence which provides a given customer benefit may, of course, not be visible to customers themselves. Fourth, a core competence must in some sense be unique and sustainable if it is to convey competitive advantage. Finally, a core competence should provide a 'gateway to new markets'. It should provide a bridge from 'what is now' in terms of market concept and definition to 'what might be' in the future. In so doing, it moves a firm beyond a 'product-centric' view of itself.

Core competences thus differ from products in a number of important ways: they are embodied in a variety of products and hence are more 'generic' than any particular product; they are typically longer-lived than products; and they provide firms with more routes to competitive advantage. Hamel and Prahalad (1994) divide core competences into three types: (1) market-access competences which bring the firm into contact with its customers; (2) integrity-related competences which enable the firm to do things better and faster, and to a higher quality than their competitors; and (3) functionally-related competences which confer distinctive customer benefits.

The Economist Intelligence Unit (1992) has produced a report on core competences in which it identifies a number of ways in which the concept could be applied. It can be used:

1 to guide diversification – it facilitates a move into new markets on the basis of established strengths;
2 to drive revitalization – it facilitates the recognition of shared competences between business areas and hence of a strategic orientation based on these;
3 to protect competitiveness – firms often realize, too late, that they have lost key skills through outsourcing or divestment;
4 to focus R&D efforts – the development and maintenance of core competences provides a rationale for the selection of R&D projects as well as a justification for R&D expenditure;
5 to choose strategic alliances – these should build on complementary core competences;
6 to balance SBU goals with company-wide objectives – core competences (as we have seen) build linkages between SBUs and promote corporate integration.

4 Managing core competences

Several elements are involved in the management of core competences. These can be grouped into identification, development, use and maintenance. Identification has two aspects. On the one hand, it may involve a firm in the recognition of existing core competences; here it is important that the firm validates its self-perception. Core competences only provide a genuine competitive advantage if they are indeed unique and sustainable so that the identification of existing competences should be tested through a benchmarking of competitor's skills in the same area. On the other hand, it may involve a selection of new core competences which the firm will need to develop in order to adopt a particular strategic orientation. In either case, identifying core competences will be, in part at least, a political process (Child 1972; Guth and Macmillan

1986). It will also call for what various commentators have labelled *industry foresight* (Hamel and Prahalad 1994; Martin and Irvine 1989), a sense of what customer benefits the firm might be required to deliver in ten to twenty years' time, and what critical skills and technologies will need to be integrated into core competences in order to deliver them. Hamel and Prahalad make much of this element. Firms 'competing for the future' will need to be more visionary. They will need the courage and the vision to reshape both the industries they compete in and themselves. The core competence approach to strategy, by focusing on the future in the way that it does, highlights the need for industry foresight.

Having identified and/or selected competences, the firm then faces the task of developing and nurturing them. Core competences take time to develop (Dierickx and Cool 1989). Firms may need to make acquisitions, enter alliances or take licenses in order to access either key aspects of a competence or the competence itself (Hamel 1994). Corporate strategy thus needs to reflect the logic of competence acquisition and development, a logic which requires a cross-SBU consensus with respect to corporate level objectives.

The third element of competence management concerns their deployment within an organization. Core competences transcend SBU boundaries and get incorporated into a range of products throughout the firm. SBUs, many of them with their own strategic agenda, must be receptive to competences flowing in from outside (however, they may not always succeed in being receptive).

Finally, firms need to protect and maintain their core competences. Firms can lose competences in various ways: they can outsource them, sell them, starve them, take them too much for granted, and so on. The corporate possession of core competences must clearly translate into the corporate – rather than the SBU – ownership of core competences if they are to flourish.

5 Some problems with the competence concept

Even though the concept of strategic competence is not new (Zelnick 1957) it has attracted a great deal of interest from firms confronting a business environment characterized by globalization and deregulation. One problem with so intuitively attractive a concept, however, is that it will often be misunderstood and handled superficially. The process of identifying core competences, for example, or of selecting and developing them, is both difficult and time consuming and firms have frequently been overly hasty in claiming to have them.

A second problem is the gap that exists between theory and practice with respect to the management of core competences. Much of the literature is normative and didactic, and as such has not always provided practitioners with an adequate blueprint for action.

A third problem concerns the longevity of a competence. Are there points beyond which a competence can become a trap for a firm? One can envisage situations in which, as Hamel and Prahalad (1994) put it, in order to 'reinvent itself' a firm should divest itself of old or even current competences in order to develop new ones. No easy task!

6 Conclusion

In spite of such problems, senior managers have found the strategic competence perspective to be of value. It provides a useful corrective to the natural tendencies shown by executives to focus unduly on the day to day competitive dynamics of current products in existing markets. It places a firm's future competitiveness firmly on the strategic agenda and does so with a degree of clarity and persuasiveness that few other management concepts have been able to match.

MAX H. BOISOT
ESCUELA SUPERIOR DE ADMINISTRACIÓN Y
DIRECCIÓN DE EMPRESAS, BARCELONA

Further reading

(References cited in the text marked *)

* Amit, R. and Schoemaker, P.J.H. (1993) 'Strategic assets and organizational rent', *Strategic Management Journal* 14: 33–46. (Treats a capability as the ability to deploy resources.)
* Andrews, K.R. (1971) *The Concept of Corporate Strategy*, Homewood, IL: Irwin. (One of the key texts of the 'positioning school' of strategic thinking.)
* Barney, J. (1991) 'Firm resources and sustained competitive advantage', *Journal of Management* 17 (1): 99–100. (Discussion, analysis and categorization of firm resources, and review of their strategic relevance.)
* Child, J.L. (1972) 'Organisational structure, environment and performance: the role of strategic choice', *Sociology* 6: 1–22. (Argues that managers are strategically autonomous agents who actively mediate the relationship between a firm and its environment.)
* Dierickx, I. and Cool, K. (1989) 'Asset stock accumulation and sustainability of competitive advantage', *Management Science* 35 (12): 1504–14. (The authors distinguish between stocks of strategic assets and the flows which create them.)
* The Economist Intelligence Unit (1992) *Building Core Competences in a Global Company*, Research report no. 1–12, New York: The Economist Intelligence Unit. (Explores why companies need core competences, how to create them, and how to apply them.)
* Guth, W.D. and Macmillan, I.C. (1986) 'Strategy implementation versus middle management self-interest', *Strategic Management Journal* 7 (4): 313–27. (Explores the tension that exists between managerial and corporate objectives.)
* Hall, R. (1992) 'The strategic analysis of intangible resources', *Strategic Management Journal* 13 (2): 135–44. (Treats part of a firm's technological assets as intangible resources.)
* Hamel, G. (1994) 'The concept of core competence', in G. Hamel and A. Heene (eds), *Competence-Based Competition*, Chichester: Wiley. (Papers from a 1992 conference on core competences. Contains some helpful contributions.)
* Hamel, G. and Prahalad, G.K. (1994) *Competing for the Future*, Boston, MA: Harvard Business School Press. (Draws together the arguments of two major contributors to the concept of core competence.)
* McGrath, R.G., MacMillan, I.C. and Venkataraman, S. (1995) 'Defining and developing competence: a strategic process paradigm', *Strategic Management Journal* 16: 251–75. (An original exploration of the antecedents of competence.)
* Martin, B. and Irvine, J. (1989) *Research Foresight*, London: Pinter Publishers. (Describes the foresight process and compares its uses in eight countries.)
* Penrose E.T. (1959) *The Theory of the Growth of the Firm*, Oxford: Blackwell. (Takes manage-

rial competence and objectives as key determinants of firm growth.)

* Prahalad, G.K. and Hamel, G. (1990) 'The core competence of the corporation', *Harvard Business Review* 68 (3): 79–91. (The article in which the concept of core competence was first outlined.)

* Rumelt, R.P. (1974) *Strategy and Economic Performance*, Boston, MA: Harvard Business School Press. (Develops a theory of diversification based on corporate strategy and structure.)

Sanchez, R., Heene, A. and Thomas, H. (eds) (1996) *Dynamics of Competence-Based Competition: Theory and Practice in the New Strategic Management*, London: Elsevier. (A useful set of readings that explore the scope of the competence concept and offer practical definitions.)

Schoemaker, P.J.H. (1992) 'How to link strategic vision to core capabilities', *Sloan Management Review* Fall: 67–81. (Proposes a methodology for identifying core capabilities and provides a worked example as illustration.)

* Stalk, G., Evans, P. and Shulman, L. (1992) 'Competing on capabilities: the new rules of corporate strategy', *Harvard Business Review* 70 (2): 57–69. (Discusses the principles of capability-based competition.)

* Wernerfelt, B. (1984) 'A resource-based view of the firm', *Strategic Management Journal* 5 (2): 171–80. (Introduces ideas about resource position barriers and describes a resource–product matrix.)

* Zelnick, P. (1957) *Leadership in Administration: A Sociological Interpretation*, New York: Harper & Row. (One of the earlier works in which the competence approach was developed.)

See also: MANAGERIAL THEORIES OF THE FIRM; ORGANIZATION BEHAVIOUR; ORGANIZATION STRUCTURE; ORGANIZATIONAL PERFORMANCE; STRATEGY AND INTERNAL MARKETING

Strategic marketing planning

1 **Strategic marketing planning**
2 **Strategic options in planning**
3 **Conclusion**

Overview

Planning consists of looking ahead and making decisions about what to do in the future. For companies, the planning process is a systematic approach to these questions: Where is the company now and how did it get there? What is the future? Where does the company want to go? How can it get there? How much will this process cost? How can progress be measured? Some attempt at planning (looking ahead to what needs to be done) is always better than improvisation or trying to cope with problems as they arise.

There is considerable debate as to how strategic marketing planning should be conceptualized. Some writers focus on developing a sequence of steps which will define strategic planning as a logical procedure; others claim there is a need to understand decision-making processes in order to deal with the problems of biased thinking, and to recognize the political nature of the strategic planning process. Finally, there are those who point out that following logical procedures and processes is not enough, commenting that doing so is analogous to focusing on the computer program and neglecting the data itself; the focus, it is argued, should be on strategy content. All of these points of view are important and have validity, and will be considered below. While there are many views of the strategy process, these can be regarded as different windows on to the problem, with some windows offering on occasions clearer views than others though none of the views are mutually exclusive (see Mintzberg, Ahlstrand and Lampel 1998).

1 Strategic marketing planning

The direction of strategic marketing planning is usually determined in the larger corporate plan, which defines where the firm will seek its markets, which strengths or competencies should be built on for competitive advantage, and which investment objectives (growth, hold/defend, harvest, turnaround) will be adopted for which product group (see STRATEGY, IMPLEMENTATION OF). Marketing can be considered as a boundary-spanning activity in that it links the organization to external groups who use, buy or sell the company's products or can influence the company's market position (see MARKETING ENVIRONMENT). Strategic marketing planning is concerned with the broad concepts of how resources are to be deployed to induce those external groups to respond favourably to the organization's offerings, and to overcome any resistance to these offerings which may be encountered.

Marketing plans are typically annual plans, although some firms tie the annual plan into five-year or other long-term plans: the annual plan becomes the detailed plan for the immediate financial year which, if successful, is the first step to achieving the long-term plan (see MARKETING PLANNING; MARKETING STRATEGY). In either case, however, it should be assumed that the strategic market planning process will be guided by objectives set at the corporate level, which will define the firm's business or businesses and determine investment objectives. The strategic marketing planning process can then be divided into eight logical steps:

1 setting tentative objectives for the market;
2 historical review and situation analysis;
3 interpretation of the data collected;
4 calculation of the planning gap (if any);
5 problem diagnosis;
6 strategic options;
7 evaluation of strategies and choice of strategy;
8 contingency planning.

This process mimics the typical steps involved in problem solving, and every organization that adopts a formal approach to planning will follow stages similar to those above. Each stage requires systematic planning, rational decision processes, political networking and, last but not least, ideas for strategy content; all of these are essential if strategic marketing planning is to be effective.

Setting tentative objectives

An organization cannot set realistic, realizable objectives until it has gathered a full range of information about its market and competitive situation (see ORGANIZATION BEHAVIOUR). However, at the outset of the planning process marketing management will first set tentative objectives, based on experience, for sales volume, market share, or other indicators which show progress towards the firm's objectives. The exact nature of these tentative goals will be influenced by subjective estimates of what is considered reasonable at the time, in relation to what resources are likely to be available. Goals should also be defined in ways that are meaningful and offer guidance to those working towards them; goals defined purely in terms of profit, for example, are inadequate as they offer too little guidance.

Historical review and situation analysis

A historical review records and orders the historical development of the company, its products or its brands, while the situation analysis focuses on the company's present position. The historical review is thus a developmental analysis, while the situation analysis is cross-sectional and ignores processes through time. In practice, the historical review and the situation analysis tend to be closely interwoven, with the aims of both being to: (1) develop a reference projection or forecast of the future (in terms of factors such as earnings and market share), assuming that current plans and practices remain unchanged; (2) identify strengths, weaknesses, opportunities and threats; and (3) determine the historical strengths, capabilities or competencies of the organization and its corresponding competitive advantages.

The nature and quantity of information collected during these analyses will depend on the specific situation and what marketers consider to be relevant and related to some definite question. Setting limits on the quantity of information to be collected is a constant concern; there is a need for a 'stopping rule' that relates to the cost and benefits of collecting information and defines when and where companies should limit collection, but no such rule is at present in general use. In terms of type, relevant information generally falls into five different categories: *external environment information, market information, customer information, competition information* and *company information* (see MARKETING ENVIRONMENT; MARKETING INFORMATION SYSTEMS; MARKETING RESEARCH).

A wide variety of external environmental factors can affect company performance. These include economic factors such as changes in gross national product (GNP) and government legislation, tax changes and interest rate changes, introduction of new technologies and demographic changes. A growth in national income brings with it a readiness to spend in new directions; an improved level of general education affects consumer tastes and responsiveness to different types of advertising; shifts in the age distribution of the population make different aggregate demands on industry. All such trends have a direct impact on markets, and need to be identified along with their likely turning points. This is not a simple process; neither the speed nor the direction of market change is easily predictable. In 1960, for example, the computer was a vastly complex and expensive machine, the use of which was limited to large and sophisticated organizations; today, in the developed world at least, computers in the home are nearly as common as televisions. This in turn has given rise to the importance of the Internet for direct marketing.

Information on market structure needs to reflect Porter's five forces: threat of entry, degree of rivalry, substitute inroads from other industries, the bargaining power of buyers and the bargaining power of suppliers (Porter 1980, 1985). Information is also needed on market growth, seasonality of sales and market share trends. Although the 'customer' could be considered under the category of 'market', customers deserve to be considered separately as they are the major players of interest. Ideally, a marketing manager would like to know everything about buyers and any others who influence the buying decision: who they are, what they seek, where they buy and use the product, when they buy and use the product and how they use the product. Just as a potter must know the behaviour of clay under different conditions, marketing managers must know the behaviour of their customers at different times and places.

Firms are seldom in a position where competition can be ignored; in nearly all markets, other companies are attempting to compete with and take market share from the firm. Accordingly, firms need to evaluate threats from competitors and to learn as much as possible about their performance in the market, their capabilities and their likely intentions. Marketers often describe their task as being to beat the competition, but they cannot do this by looking only at what the competition is doing (although this is important); they also need to understand the customer better than the competition does. Finally, the company needs to know its own strengths and weaknesses as a basis for considering a vulnerability analysis and in order to develop a competitive advantage based on the firm's core capabilities or competencies (see MARKETING STRATEGY).

Interpretation of the data collected

Once the data has been collected, it needs to be interpreted. This is a key task; how the situation is interpreted determines what strategies will appear to be most appropriate. When managers misunderstand the basic situation, even the cleverest and best developed strategies will be misdirected and will in effect be aimed at solving the wrong problem. The issue is complicated by the fact that in most situations, no final or absolutely true interpretation can be reached, and some conjecture is inevitable as facts are selected, connected and put into a plausible pattern. However, interpretations are never arbitrary but must square with the available evidence. The best interpretations are consistent with agreed facts and account for those facts in a coherent way, using the maximum number of facts and the

minimum degree of conjecture (see MARKETING RESEARCH).

Where problems occur is in reaching agreement on the meaning or significance of the facts themselves. Facts cannot be used alone; they must be selected, ordered, weighted and interpreted against some perspective or set of presuppositions. Here there is a danger of distortion. Just as those who believe that all dreams reflect secret fears and wishes will interpret dreams in that way, managers tend to select facts from the data collected that fit with their own beliefs. Such distortion can be reduced by making clear throughout the process (1) what is really known (such as actual sales or other hard data); (2) what is unclear (including competitor intentions and other factors which can never be known exactly); and (3) what is being presupposed that might be questioned (this will include key assumptions such as whether market trends will persist). Although we speak of 'weighing the evidence', the weightings are inevitably influenced by values and political considerations. Emotions are tied to these values and so enter into all decision making, even if marketing academics sometimes forget this, viewing managers as emotion-free calculating machines. The emotional is so interconnected with the cognitive that it is impossible to identify situations where deliberated decisions do not have an emotional dimension (see De Sousa, 1990 and Damasio, 1994).

What should be sought at this stage is an assessment of the firm's strengths, weaknesses, opportunities and threats, the so-called SWOT analysis. Once these four factors have been analysed they need to be matched against each other. This stage should also include a 'vulnerability analysis' which aims to identify where the firm is vulnerable, such as an overdependence on a few customers or just one industry, and a list of critical success factors. Critical success factors are those elements of the business (whether resource inputs, internal organization/processes or strategies) where high performance cannot be taken for granted yet where high performance in these elements, whether singly or in combination, is essential for success. Thus the buying of the wool is likely to be a critical success factor for a manufacturer of woollen worst-eds; low cost production is critical in the case of ball point pens, and a marketing strategy ensuring wide distribution is critical for a gasoline manufacturer.

There are a variety of techniques which can be used to order data and bring out the important implications. The best-known are probably Boston Consulting Group's growth market share matrix (the Boston Box), General Electric's business screen and the concepts developed by Porter (see PORTER, M.E.); of which there are also various quantitative techniques, all help to order and bring out the implications of the data collected. These techniques can be useful in that they provide frameworks, analogies and models that help structure problems and reduce the incidence of purely *ad hoc* analysis (see MARKETING STRATEGY). Two books of interest here with a quantitative approach are Rao and Steckel (1997) and Jagpal (1998).

Even with all the above analyses, there is no guarantee that any planning decision will turn out to be correct. Equally, it is fallacious to assume that a poor outcome implies the decision was wrong; the decision may well have been the most rational one at the time. In any case, strategies are seldom absolutely wrong or right; all have different degrees of imperfections.

Calculation of the planning gap

A further analysis which needs to be undertaken is what will happen in the future, assuming the firm does not change its current strategies. This analysis results in a reference projection which describes the future that can be expected in the absence of planned change. The reference projection is compared with a target projection, or set of tentative goals which the firm has set for itself (as described above). The difference between the target and reference projections is known as the planning gap or performance gap:

planning gap (performance gap) = target projection − reference projection

The size of the planning gap or gaps identified will depend on which performance measures are being considered. At the highest level,

these could include earnings per share, sales and market share or various financial indices such as return on investment (ROI). At the marketing level, measures might include sales, market share, costs, market penetration or various behavioural indices such as buyer attitudes.

Problem diagnosis

If the planning gap is large, then the firm is often viewed as having a problem. However, the planning gap is not in itself a problem but is rather the symptom of one. The recognition of a problem situation is not the same as identification of the actual problem; problem diagnosis points to the type of solution that is required as the first step towards developing an actual solution. Problems cannot be understood unless corresponding solutions can be understood as well, just as objectives cannot be understood unless it can also be seen what the achievement of those objectives will mean. The nature of the problem addressed will thus depend to some degree on the individual or group which is defining the problem and responsible for finding solutions. Most managers are capable of being influenced by credible arguments and so true technical expertise usually wins the day; as it should, for if the wrong problem is addressed then the wrong decisions are made, and this can be more wasteful of resources than solving the right problem in an inefficient way. But companies often do persist in clinging to failing strategies because it is such an emotional thing for them to contemplate change with its suggestion of faulty planning in the first place.

2 Strategic options in planning

The strategic options for closing the planning gap should not only fit the problematic situation and take account of trends and competition, but should also exploit the firm's core competencies and strengths. Unless the problem being solved represents a crisis, the firm should undertake a process of searching for strategic options, guided by:

- the current situation, as revealed by the performance gap;
- the perceived problem;
- the strengths, weaknesses, opportunities and threats identified in the historical review/situation analysis;
- current strategies and policies;
- existing capabilities or core competencies.

Ideally, a company should seek to build on its demonstrated competencies (core competencies) and key skills to obtain a critical advantage, that is, an advantage that is central to the function for which the product is bought but which is unique to the company itself. However, the strategy search process should always allow for the possibility of inspiration which in some cases may be superior to methodical analysis.

Strategic options come in many forms, and their relevance will depend on the specific firm, its goals and its situation. However, there are a number of generic strategies including growth, hold/defend, turnaround, harvesting and divestment. Growth strategies involve broadening the technology, customer groups or the functions served. Because all growth strategies involve one or a combination of these, talk of changing the scope of the business or going into another business is superfluous and simply misleads. Growth option categories (Ansoff 1990) are:

1 *market penetration*: selling the same products into the same markets and attempting to increase market share;
2 *market development*: selling the same products into new markets;
3 *product development*: developing new products to sell into existing markets;
4 *diversification* or *vertical integration*: developing new products and new markets.

Hold/defend strategies are common when firms see no possibility of growth or are satisfied with their current position in the market. The aim is to retain existing customers while attracting enough new entrants into the market to replace those that leave. In the most general terms, hold/defend strategies require the firm to keep abreast of competition by upgrading the firm's offering and matching whatever competitors have to offer.

Turnaround or turnabout strategies are, as the name suggests, concerned with restructuring the organization or, more simply, 'putting it on its feet' again. A firm which considers a turnaround strategy may be facing persistent decline in market share, declining profit margins and working capital, increasing debt and probably high voluntary management turnover as managers become aware that the firm is in trouble.

Harvesting is a way of winding down a business by accepting a continuing decline in market share in exchange for an increase in net cash flow. Products that suffer from low profitability may become more profitable if all promotional support is withdrawn; however, this situation may not last for long as competitors will rush in to exploit the absence of promotional support. It is not always possible to harvest a business, however, and some products or businesses continue to be a cash drain regardless of whether support expenditure is withdrawn; in such situations, a firm will try to divest the business. Divestment implies an orderly approach to exiting the market.

Porter (1985) argues that it is an industry's competitive structure, as reflected in the strength of the five forces noted above, that determines the state of competition (both the rules of competition and the strategies available for competing) and ultimately the profit potential of the industry. He claims there are just three generic strategies for coping with the five forces: overall cost leadership, differentiation and segmentation. To many marketers, however, it is not clear that these three strategies are distinct; for example, it is difficult to conceive of a product differentiation strategy that does not appeal to only a segment of the market or, if it appeals to the whole market, does not imply a price that many in the market would be unwilling to pay. In either case, differentiation implies segmentation. Porter refers to cost leadership and differentiation, but marketers might argue both are paths to segmentation in that there can be both price segments and segments based on non-price differentiation (see SEGMENTATION).

Evaluation of strategies and choice of strategy

Strategies should be evaluated both before adoption and after implementation. In either case, strategies can only be evaluated against some criteria derived implicitly or explicitly from objectives. Evaluative criteria after implementation revolve around the strategy's effectiveness and reliability; thus a strategy is effective if it achieves its goals, and it is reliable if it is able to do so consistently.

In evaluating strategies as a basis for adoption, the criteria selected should help predict a strategy's effectiveness and reliability after implementation. Every proposed strategy should be evaluated for desirability, practical feasibility and commercial viability.

Desirability

The first step in evaluation is to consider what objectives or goals are sought. How is success defined? One common error is to think about goals in insufficiently broad terms; this is because goals are typically multiple and conflicting, and there is a need to establish priorities or alternatively to set some of the goals as constraints or semi-constraints. A common reason for irreconcilable conflicts among parties to any decision lies in one party having an extremely narrow set of goals. The following questions should be asked.

1 Does the proposed strategy promote objectives? Any proposed strategy must contribute to the company's mission and goals, cohere with investment objectives and, in the case of the marketing strategy, exploit the firm's strengths and core competencies and be concerned with building customer trust and loyalty.

2 Is the degree of risk acceptable? Risk is defined as the probability of earning less than what is sought and the magnitude of possible losses. Measuring the degree of risk is generally a matter of judgment. There can never be any certainty of measurement, since the relationship between options (strategies) and outcomes (results) is never entirely clear when long-term consequences are influenced by unpredictable competitive actions and the wants and beliefs of those in the market are often fickle. In the most

general terms, it can be said that the further an organization moves away from its existing markets and core competencies, the more risky the strategy becomes.

3 Does the strategy promote portfolio balance? There is a need for a balanced mix in a firm's portfolio of products so that, for example, the firm not only has offerings in stagnant markets but is also backing future winners in growth markets.

4 Is the investment required acceptable? The investment requirement, including initial entry costs and the costs of securing market share, has to be estimated. Start-up or entry costs can usually be estimated reasonably accurately, but estimating the costs of achieving a desired market share is more problematic.

If a strategy is desirable, then there must be a fit between the strategy and behaviour in the market, between the strategy and the firm's internal capabilities and resources and, finally, between the strategy and higher level corporate plans, since the strategy will become part of the corporate hierarchy of plans. However, even if all these 'fits' are in place, this merely determines that the means suit the ends; it will also be necessary to take account of likely undesirable side effects or dysfunctional consequences.

Practical feasibility

The problem of the feasibility of proposals receives too little attention in discussions on strategy formulation. Although it is accepted that evaluating feasibility involves judgement and an imaginative analysis of the problems likely to be encountered in implementing the strategy, the importance of experience and knowledge are seldom emphasized strongly enough. In order to judge the feasibility of a marketing plan or strategy, it is necessary to know about the role of product, price, promotion and distribution and the likely behaviour of customers and competitors, and to have considerable knowledge of the specifics of the market such as distribution alternatives.

Commercial viability

Considerations of commercial viability might include the following:

1 Will the strategy yield the profit or cash flow sought? Estimates of potential pay-offs can range all the way from little more than prophecy to predictions of sales, costs and profits based on hard evidence.
2 Does the strategy contribute to the minimization of possible competitive retaliation? The selection of any strategy is accompanied by the selection of rivals with whom the firm will compete; the question must be answered as to whether the strategy minimizes the potential for these competitors to retaliate against the firm. The most basic questions in marketing are: *Why should the buyer buy from us? How are we going to compete? What do we want the brand to stand for in the mind of the buyer?* All this relates to having a competitive (preferably critical) advantage so as to position the brand in a way that captures the brand's critical points of difference from its rivals.
3 What are the impediments to achieving commercial goals? This consideration requires the firm to think about what obstacles to success may exist, and then make plans to overcome or avoid these.

Contingency planning

Managers, if asked directly, will seldom entertain the failure of any proposed strategy. It is better to ask these managers to visualize the strategy having failed and to write down what they think must have gone wrong. Behind every set of plans is a set of assumptions that need to be realized if the plans are to achieve success. Certain factors can be assumed to remain constant, such as government policy, and certain trends can be assumed to persist, such as the increasing cost of healthcare. However, many of those assumptions which relate to environmental and market factors are in constant danger of being invalidated due to the rapidity of environmental change (see MARKETING ENVIRONMENT).

Where different sets of assumptions are equally tenable, contingency plans are needed. Typically, firms assume that certain major assumptions may be invalid and thence develop alternative plans which are held in re-serve; this is also common practice in the military, where there is often a pressing need to have alternative plans available. Monitoring the assumptions behind a plan as it is put into effect can provide a major check on the plan's continuing validity; when assumptions are no longer valid, plans need to be revised or previously devised contingency plans must be put into effect. In practice, however, plans need to be continually revised. In addition, planning must be relevant to today's decisions if it is to be treated seriously by managers at the operational level, and long-term planning should be tied to guiding present decisions.

3 Conclusion

Any firm that has adopted a systematic approach to planning will have a sequence of stages similar to that discussed in this chapter. While these stages provide a useful guide, however, they cannot be simply followed like a computer program; simply working through each stage in turn will not bring forth a successful strategy. Strategy depends on data and ideas, and the key to developing an effective strategy lies not so much in following a sequence of stages (although this does help provide structure and guidance to the process), but in finding answers to the following questions:

1 what should be the content of our objectives?
2 what is the most relevant information to collect?
3 what is the correct problem diagnosis?
4 what strategies should be considered given our objectives?
5 what evidence is relevant to the evaluation of proposed strategies?

Strategic marketing planning can never be a matter of formula. Successful planning must concentrate on areas such as identifying flawed decision-making processes, finding tactics for coping with the organizational politics which will inevitably arise during the planning process (as strategic marketing planning is such a value-laden activity) and, last but not least, identifying strategic options and the market conditions that suggest when each strategy is most appropriate.

A final point. In a recent article John Kay (1999) argues that strategy is no longer about planning, visioning or forecasting but a set of analytic techniques for understanding a company's position in the market and identifying its distinctive capabilities because traditional strategic planning is based on the illusion of rationality and controls. This, taken literally, makes little sense since strategy is about the future, and future action involves planning and imaginative vision since the alternative is improvisation which, taken to extreme, makes coordinated action impossible. Also, the very phrase 'set of analytical techniques' implies rationality of rule, while talk about identifying distinctive capabilities implies forecasting that such capabilities will not be obsolete in the future. Kay also sets up a straw man in talking about the 'absurdity and irrelevance of using the blank sheet of paper approach to corporate strategy' as if any company can or does ignore constraints on its resources and capabilities, its past history and potential as it goes about strategic planning.

JOHN O'SHAUGHNESSY

THE JUDGE INSTITUTE OF MANAGEMENT
STUDIES

UNIVERSITY OF CAMBRIDGE

Further reading

(References cited in the text marked *)

* Ansoff, I. (1965) *Corporate Strategy*, New York: McGraw-Hill. (One of the classic works in this field.)

Ansoff, I. and McDonnell, E. (1990) *Implanting Strategic Management*, Englewood Cliffs, NJ: Prentice Hall. (This book offers state-of-the-art methodologies, including an interactive computer-based system for strategy formulation, to help line managers choose competitive posture for their business.)

Camillus, J.C. (1986) *Strategic Planning and Management Control: Systems for Survival and Success*, Lexington, MA: Lexington Books. (This book pulls together strategic planning and its control.)

Certo, S.C. and Peter, J.P. (1988) *Strategic Management: Concepts and Applications*, New York: Random House. (Chapters 2–4 provide a thorough treatment of the historical review, situation analysis and formulating strategies, and also identify the specific problems encountered in formulating various functional area strategies.)

Chakravarthy, B.S. and Lorange, P. (1991) *Managing the Strategy Process*, Englewood Cliffs, NJ: Prentice Hall. (This book focuses primarily on the process through which strategies are formed, and includes cases for class discussion at the end of each section.)

* Damasio, A. (1994) *Descartes' Error: Emotion, Reason and the Human Brain*, New York: A Grosset/Putnam Book.

* De Sousa, R. (1990) *The Rationality of Emotion*, Cambridge MA: The MIT Press.

Goodstein, L., Nolan, T. and Pfeiffer, J.W. (1993) *Applied Strategic Planning: How to Develop a Plan That Really Works*, New York: McGraw-Hill. (A step-by-step guide to the strategic planning process. Of particular interest is chapter 3, on culture and applied strategic planning, which recognizes that a dramatic shift in company culture may be needed in order to change to a market-driven organization.)

Hax, A.C. and Majluf, N.S. (1984) *Strategic Management: An Integrative Perspective*, Englewood Cliffs, NJ: Prentice Hall. (This well-known text covers the evolution of strategic planning thinking, concepts and tools for strategic planning, methodology for developing a corporate strategic plan and methodology for ensuring congruency between corporate structure and strategy.)

Hill, C.W.L. and Jones, G.R. (1992) *Strategic Management: An Integrated Approach*, Boston, MA: Houghton Mifflin. (Chapters 3–4 provide an in-depth discussion of analysis of the external environment and the firm's strengths, weaknesses and distinctive competencies; there is also an excellent bibliography at the end of each chapter.)

* Jagpal, S. (1998) *Marketing Strategy and Uncertainty*, Oxford and New York: Oxford University Press.

* Kay, J. (1999) 'Strategy and the delusion of grand designs', in *Mastering Strategy, Financial Times* 27 September: 1–4.

Mintzberg, H. (1994) *The Rise and Fall of Strategic Planning*, Englewood Cliffs, NJ: Prentice Hall. (A work by the foremost critic of current approaches to strategic planning.)

* Mintzberg, H., Ahistrand, B. and Lampel, J. (1998) *Strategy Safari: A guided Tour through the Wilds of Strategic Management*, New York: Free Press.

O'Shaughnessy, J. (1995) *Competitive Marketing*, 3rd edn, London: Routledge. (Chapters 2 and 3 have more information on planning models such as the GE model and the Boston Box.)

* Porter, M.E. (1980) *Competitive Strategy: Techniques for Analyzing Your Business and Competitors*, New York: The Free Press. (A classic in the literature of strategy: it is in this book that Porter first articulated the five forces mentioned in this entry along with strategies for different evolutionary stages of the product.)

* Porter, M.E. (1985) *Competitive Advantage*, New York: The Free Press. (Similar to Porter (1980) but more useful to marketers since it describes the obtaining of competitive advantage in more detail.)

* Rao, V.R. and Steckel, J.H. (1997) *Analysis for Strategic Marketing*, New York: Addison-Wesley.

Walker, O.C., Boyd, H.W. and Larreché, J.-C. (1992) *Marketing Strategy: Planning and Implementation*, Homewood, IL: Irwin. (The third section of this book deals with formulating strategies, and also offers strategies for new market entries, growth markets, mature markets, declining markets and international marketing.)

See also: CORPORATE PLANNING, PROCESS OF; MARKETING; MARKETING ENVIRONMENT; MARKETING INFORMATION SYSTEMS; MARKETING PLANNING; MARKETING STRATEGY; SEGMENTATION; STRATEGY, IMPLEMENTATION OF; STRATEGY MAKING, POLITICS OF

Strategic planning, global: see GLOBAL STRATEGIC PLANNING

Strategic turnaround

1 Studies of corporate decline and turnaround
2 A typology of turnaround situations
3 Measuring turnaround success
4 Recovery strategies
5 Conclusion

Overview

Corporate turnaround has been variously defined, from recoveries from sustained losses which threaten the company's existence, decreasing revenues resulting in negative earnings and depletion of cash reserves, declining return on investment (ROI) or loss in industry position, declines in sales or market share, to relative declines in returns in relation to corporate growth rates. This entry will discuss the measures that have been used to describe corporate decline and turnaround in the research literature, a typology of measures that can be used to classify turnaround situations, and recommended strategies for recovery.

1 Studies of corporate decline and turnaround

Corporate turnaround has been the focus of numerous doctoral dissertations and scholarly articles. The question appears to be simple: What causes a decline in performance and how can this decline be reversed? One problem plaguing researchers who attempt to find answers is equally simple: What is a turnaround? Before turnaround strategies can be examined and/or tested, one must look not only at the nature of the decline from which a company has recovered, but also at the reasons contributing to the decline.

The turnaround process is conceptually straightforward: a company experiences a decline in performance as a result of its actions or failure to act, and subsequently takes action to reverse this decline:

$$\text{action} \rightarrow \text{decline} \rightarrow \text{action}$$
$$\rightarrow \text{recovery (turnaround)}$$

However, in order to examine the actions that precipitated either the decline or recovery, one must be able to identify the decline and recovery. Definitions of decline differ in terms of the performance measures, the magnitude of decline and the length of time required for the designation 'turnaround situation'.

Table 1 lists the empirical studies that have been done by turnaround researchers (see also Hoffman 1989). This table specifies the performance measures used in each study, the magnitude or level of performance inadequacy or decline that constitutes a 'turnaround situation', and the length of time of declining or inadequate performance needed to target a firm for study.

These measures appear to be chosen for several reasons: they appear conceptually logical, they are either measurable or observable and they fit the population of firms (or the database) available for the study. In some cases, researchers have taken previously used measures as a guide, modifying them to accommodate the population studied or the feasibility of the research project.

2 A typology of turnaround situations

Table 2 presents a classification scheme for describing turnaround situations by linking suggested performance measures to the type

Table 1 The turnaround research

Author(s)	Performance measures	Definition of decline and recovery	Sample data sources	Size
Schendel *et al.* (1976)	Normalized net income	Four declining years and four increasing years	Compustat 1951–70	54
Bibeault (1982)	Net income	Not defined	US companies questionnaires and interviews	81
O'Neill (1989)	Net income (to industry)	Three declining years and two increasing years	Compustat Banks	51
Hofer (1980)	Cash flow (implied)	Decline in strategic and operating health; return to former position	Published cases	12
Hambrick and Schecter (1983)	Pre-tax ROI (net income supplied)	Two years > 10% and two years < 20% ROI	PIMS	260
Ramanujam (1984)	ROI	Four years > 5% ROI	Compustat	75
Slatter (1984)	Net income	Three years declining pre-tax income; four years improvement in six years	UK companies 1961–76 1962–79	40
Heany (1985)	ROI (Net income implied)	'Profit trouble' and unspecified improvement	PIMS	573
Sheth (1986)	Market share (implied)	Falling/recovering market share (period not specified)	Case studies	18
O'Neill (1986)	Net income (implied)	*Fortune* magazine articles	Case studies	13
Pant (1986)	Pre-tax ROI	Lowest quartile in the industry; turnaround to highest quartile	Compustat 1964–83	85
Grinyer *et al.* (1988)	ROA, ROE, sales, exports, labour, productivity	Marginal performers: below industry-wide average; 'sharply' improved performance	UK companies public information and interviews	25
Zimmerman (1989)	Shareholder concern, net income, sales	Five years negative net income; three year improvement	Case studies	9
Thain and Goldthorpe (1989)	Net income (implied)	'Decline in fortunes' and unspecified improvement	UK companies 1970–85	27
Winn (1989)	Asset productivity (utilization)	Four years >10% ROA and four years >13% ROE non-declining income three-year recovery	Compustat 1968–86	43
Gopinath (1991)	Cash flow (implied)	'Losses' unspecified performance	Case studies 1975–88	22
Pearce and Robins (1992)	ROI and ROS	Two-year decline greater than industry average; two-year increase return to pre-decline level	Case studies 1976–85 textile industry	32

Table 2 A typology of corporate decline and turnaround

	Type of performance problem				
	Imminent bankruptcy	*Declining profitability*	*Substandard performance*	*Declining market share*	*Inadequate assest productivity*
Performance measure	Severe losses liquidity ratios (debt coverage)	Declining cash flow; declining profit margins; increasing debt ratios	ROI, ROA, or net income relative to industry; non-negative cash flows	Declining sales relative to market; non-negative cash flows	ROI or ROA; sales/ employee; sales/assets; non-negative cash flows
Benchmark	Current ratio < 1; negative net worth	Negative working capital; 50–70% net income decline	Industry median; GNP growth	Decline from previous position	Industry median; 15–20% decline
Timeframe	1–2 years	3–5 years	4–5 years	3–4 years	3–5 years
	Type of successful turnaround				
	Solvency	*Profitablilty*	*Superior performance*	*Market growth*	*Efficiency*
Performance measure	Cash inflows; debt pay-off	Retained earnings; increased profits	ROI, ROA, ROE, net income relative to industry	Increasing sales relative to market	ROI, ROA and productivity improvements; non-declining asset base
Benchmark	Current ratio > 1; stable or increasing cash flow	Positive cash flows	Industry median; GNP growth	Previous or desired position	Industry median; previous position
Timeframe	1–2 years	3–5 years	4–5 years	3–4 years	3–5 years

of problem to be studied (Winn 1993) (see ORGANIZATIONAL PERFORMANCE). This typology consolidated past researchers' definitions, and groups' performance problems into five general categories: (1) pre-bankruptcy or crisis situations, consisting of firms that are facing bankruptcy within the near future (one or two years); (2) declining cash flow situations, consisting of those firms that are currently losing money, but will not fail within a year or two because of their strong asset position; (3) substandard performance situations, consisting of firms whose profits are low or stagnant, or lag behind the general economy, but who are not yet losing money; (4) market share turnaround situations, consisting of firms whose sales or market share have started to decline sharply, but whose profits are not yet substantially affected; and (5) asset productivity turnaround situations, firms whose asset productivity (efficiency) has started to decline sharply or is at inadequate levels, but whose sales and profits are not yet affected. Specific measures are recommended for examining companies in each category.

Pre-bankruptcy (crisis) situations

Companies in crisis situations face failure unless immediate action is taken. Many researchers have examined firms that did not recover from decline in order to isolate key financial indices that precede economic failure. A common thread to these studies is the relationship between cash inflows (current assets) and short-term obligations (current liabilities). Turnaround studies have defined pre-bankruptcy situations in terms of firm viability as assessed by gross profit, liquidation value, current position and capabilities, and even Z-score ratios (Altman 1968).

In order to differentiate between firms in danger of insolvency and firms with severe but controllable losses, crisis situations must be scrutinized for their ability to absorb these losses. Liquidity ratios (debt payment coverage) are helpful in making this distinction. Multiple measures are necessary since any individual ratio is not a good predictor of failure, nor is it a good measure of financial soundness.

While crisis situations usually occur after a company has already sustained several years of losses, they can be distinguished from companies that are losing money yet not in danger of insolvency by the degree of decline and the extent of unmet debt payments. A true crisis situation cannot persist for several years. When debts cannot be covered, companies must act quickly or cease to exist.

Cash flow problems

Companies with cash flow problems are prime turnaround candidates because, despite obvious profitability concerns for the company and its shareholders, their short-term survival is not in question (see CASH FLOW ACCOUNTING). These are the companies that are the subject of case studies in *Fortune* and *Business Week*. Some researchers (for example, O'Neill 1986; Zimmerman 1989) have avoided defining performance parameters for these 'traditional' turnaround candidates because their deterioration and recovery is easily observed. Obvious performance parameters include precipitous sales declines accompanied by negative operating income and decreasing shareholder returns. Bibeault's (1982) classic work examined the turnaround process in companies that had suffered severe losses, with testimonials from the managers that stepped in to turn them around. According to Bibeault's interviews with turnaround managers, declining profit margins, declining market share, increasing debt and declining working capital are the leading financial 'red flags'. Firms with severe cash flow problems may be in danger of insolvency if the situation persists to the point where

losses are irreversible and accumulated debt overwhelming.

Typically, large-scale studies of these 'traditional' turnaround firms relied on accounting net income or return on investment (ROI). However, these measures in the absence of benchmarks do not differentiate between firms with severely declining cash flow and firms with declining efficiency (see CREATIVE ACCOUNTING). This is evidenced by the fact that over 90 per cent of the 1,266 manufacturing firms listed in Standard & Poor's Compustat database between 1962 and 1979 had at least one three-year period of declining ROI (Ramanujam 1984). Despite its utility at cross-company comparisons, ROI is not a useful measure for companies with severe losses unless assets are held constant. Asset reduction strategies may be undertaken to improve ROI, but net income will only be affected by reducing costs or increasing revenues.

Companies that are trying to absorb severe losses clearly have 'cash flow' problems. Non-cash items such as credit sales and depreciation may mask the severity of these problems on a firm's income statement. Profit margins, debt increases and working capital decreases can be used in conjunction with cash flow to identify these companies. A benchmark or decline in magnitude can distinguish cash flow problems from stagnation or relative position deterioration in studies using large databases.

Although Bibeault found that more than a quarter of all publicly listed companies suffered losses (between 1967 and 1976), few companies can sustain severe losses over several years. The companies in Bibeault's turnaround population had severe earnings declines (80 per cent or more) over three to four years. Likewise, Zimmerman's (1989) turnaround population reached a point of negative net income after four years of declining profitability. These studies suggest that cash flow problems can be detected by precipitous earnings declines spanning three or four years, usually resulting in negative returns.

Substandard performance problems

Companies with 'substandard' performance are companies whose performance has chronically lagged behind their industry or the general economy. These companies have not necessarily declined from a previously stellar position; rather they have failed thus far to achieve an effective strategy for long-term growth and profitability. Grinyer *et al.*'s (1988) 'sharpbend' firms were described as excellent firms, having turned around not from a position of crisis, but rather from a position of mediocrity.

Since companies with substandard performance are performing poorly in relation to the economy or other firms in their industry, a relative measure, such as normalized net income or ROI, should be used. Grinyer *et al.* included market share and leverage.

Inadequate performance has been measured in various ways. Hambrick and Schecter (1983) and Heany (1985) differentiated inadequate performance as pre-tax ROI below 10 per cent. Ramanujam (1984) used 5 per cent after-tax ROI as his benchmark for inadequacy. Pant (1986) used industry position (lowest quartile performers) to define inadequate performance.

Median performance measures, specific to industry groups, can ensure that realistic comparisons are made. As Ramanujam and Pant point out, industry characteristics (for example, concentration, fragmentation, barriers to entry) preclude the effectiveness of certain strategies and actions. For this reason, studies of marginal performers are best done in the context of their industry with industry norms or relative returns defining the benchmark for determining poor performance. Previous research has indicated that a minimum of three years must be examined for substandard performance. Pant and Zimmerman found that two-year fluctuations in performance are common.

Market share declines

Sheth (1986) and Grinyer *et al.* (1988), examined turnarounds involving reversals in market position performance. Sheth's market share research can be differentiated from Grinyer's sharpbend population since a substantial proportion of companies in Sheth's study that had declining market share did not have declining profits.

Market share is measured in relation to a specific market segment, thereby directing the focus of this research towards firms that vie for position in common market segments with similar product lines (see MARKETING). Sheth specifically examined business units with declining market position and the strategies that they used for regaining share. Heany's (1985) turnaround study specifically examined 'low-share' businesses, as defined by the PIMS database, although Heany did not examine strategies for increasing share, but rather for increasing profitability (ROI).

Like substandard industry performance, market share is a relative measure and hence must be examined in relation to other firms in the same market. Firms that are losing money may not be losing market share, while at the same time firms that are losing market share may or may not be suffering from declining profitability. Care must be taken to restrict the research population so that share-related strategies are analysed and separated from profitability or efficiency problems.

Although market share is volatile, studies of market share declines, like declines in net income or cash flow, need to take a three- to four-year view of market trends to eliminate inclusion of firms with short-term fluctuations in market position.

Asset productivity (inefficiency) situations

Asset productivity has been the subject of increased focus during the past decade, as evidenced by the wave of asset restructuring for improved efficiency, for better shareholder returns and for increased competitiveness. Even when sales and income do not show signs of decline, a company may be experiencing a deterioration of its competitive capabilities. In the absence of sales and/or profitability declines, which are typically associated with turnaround efforts, a company may not appear to be in danger, yet inefficient asset utilization hampers long-term profitability and growth.

Many turnaround researchers have focused on asset utilization as part of the total process of achieving traditional (profitability) turnarounds (Kibel 1982; Taylor 1982). Other research has shown that firms with asset productivity problems, while not necessarily suffering from profitability declines, have increased their assets at a faster pace than their profitability, to the point where they are operating inefficiently (Winn 1989). Inefficient firms are characterized by the decline in returns relative to the growth of the firm. Typical productivity measures include return on investment (or total assets), sales revenue per dollar of total assets, and sales revenues per employee. As in the above categories, companies with marked profit declines should be excluded so that efficiency, not profitability, is the object of focus.

An examination of asset productivity declines and inadequacies over a period of two to seven years revealed that while most asset productivity declines occur in consecutive-year patterns over three years, many firms showed precipitous declines in non-consecutive years over a five-year period.

3 Measuring turnaround success

In addition to diagnosing candidates for turnaround, companies that have successfully turned around must be identified if their actions are to be differentiated from companies that did not turn around. While any upturn may be considered a sign of improvement, the length of time for investigation should be long enough to establish a pattern of success. Certainly, one year of decline or recovery is not long enough to rule out temporary market shifts, introduction of a new product, technology or manufacturing process, change in accounting methods, or chance. On the other hand, companies in crisis must take immediate action to avert insolvency. A longer period of time would be necessary to examine purposeful product/market and/or structural changes associated with strategic turnarounds.

Crisis turnarounds

Firms in danger of insolvency need immediate action to avoid bankruptcy or liquidation. Firms in crisis cannot remain in crisis for long. Companies in imminent danger of bankruptcy need to take immediate action, within a period as short as three months to a year. While the success of this action may ultimately be assessed over the long term, the turnaround

from impending insolvency will be visible as the crisis passes. This suggests that, if the turnaround action is successful, these near-bankrupt firms will show signs of recovery within two years.

Cash flow turnarounds

As in the case of 'crisis' situations, companies with cash flow problems may need immediate action before long-term strategies can be implemented. Since, by definition, these companies have declined from a previously profitable position, a sustained period of profitability, as measured by previous levels, is a reasonable benchmark for success. Schendel and Patten (1975) found that turnaround firms in their study showed an average rate of decline and recovery of 15 per cent as compared with gross national product growth.

Bibeault's analysis of the recovery process indicates that few strategic moves are accomplished in two years. Even Zimmerman's non-turnaround companies increased consistently for three years. Bibeault's and Zimmerman's successful turnarounds averaged at least four years from trough to peak.

Turnarounds from mediocrity

Turnarounds from marginal performance are evidenced by changes in position. By definition, these firms were 'inadequate' performers, and thereby need not have shifted in position. These turnarounds are not recoveries, but rather, marked improvements from previous performance. The Hambrick and Schecter, and Heany studies required at least a 20 per cent pre-tax ROI to denote a successful turnaround; Ramanujam used 5 per cent after-tax ROI as his turnaround (and decline) benchmark. No justification for these benchmarks was given.

If industry position defines inadequate performance, then it must also set the benchmark for measuring turnaround success. Pant defined turnaround as a change in return on total assets (ROA) performance from the bottom quartile to the top quartile of the industry. Robbins and Pearce's (1992) turnaround firms returned to their pre-downturn ROI and return on sales (ROS) over a two-year period at a rate greater than the industry average.

Pant found that sustainable recovery was not achieved in two years, but was evident after a four-year period. Other studies (Schendel *et al.* 1976; Ramanujam 1984) have imposed four-year timeframes for examining turnaround efforts.

Market share turnarounds

Market share measures a firm's sales relative to its competition. A turnaround in share position is, by definition, a recapturing of lost markets (Sheth 1986). As in the decline phase, a market share recovery must be evaluated against other firms in the same market, since sales increases do not necessarily represent share gains.

While market share is more volatile than profitability, sustainable gains in market share must be observed over a period of several years. Although no empirical studies of market share turnarounds have examined timeframes for assessing turnaround success, Sheth described turnarounds in market share within a four-year period.

Asset productivity turnarounds

Winn's (1989) study of asset productivity turnarounds showed that recoveries from inefficient asset utilization were accomplished in two to six years, with most firms regaining previous ROA or ROE (return on stockholders' equity) levels in three to four years. Companies that gained efficiency from previously inadequate levels typically had four or more years of increasing ROA or ROE. Most of the turnaround companies in this study had gains in consecutive years.

Winn's research suggests that recapturing previous ROA or ROE levels may be an unrealistic task for companies with ROA or ROE declines, since most of the companies in the study declined from unusually high levels. Since acceptable levels of ROA or ROE vary depending on industry norms, a benchmark should be imposed for differentiating turnarounds from non-turnarounds. Industry medians can serve as guidelines, both for inadequacy and turnaround.

4 Recovery strategies

Once a turnaround situation is observed or diagnosed, action must be taken if the decline or inadequate performance is to be reversed. Table 3 lists the questions posed, the methodology used, and the findings of the major empirical research on turnarounds.

Turnaround actions can be categorized into 'operating' changes, those actions which have short-term operational effects but do not alter the strategic thrust of the company, and 'strategic' changes, those actions which change the product mix, market positioning, technological or delivery systems in a significant way. Hofer (1980) defined inefficiency or 'operating' problems (and responses) as those which impede (boost) the company's immediate profitability, and which require revenue-increasing, cost-cutting and/or asset-reduction efforts to restore solid footing to an ordinarily healthy firm; and 'strategic' problems (and responses) that threaten (further) the effectiveness of the firm's competitive stance, and thereby require repositioning the company's existing business(es) or entering new business(es).

Turnarounds from crises

By definition, turnarounds from crises require operational changes which can bring solvency to a company in danger of bankruptcy. Because these changes require immediate actions that either increase revenues or cut costs or assets, companies in crisis frequently install new management, who do not have emotional or political ties. Schendel and Patten (1975), Schendel *et al.* (1976), O'Neill (1980), Bibeault (1982) and Thain and Goldthorpe (1989b) found that companies with net income or cash flow downturns revamped their organizational structure and/or replaced top management to facilitate cost-cutting programmes or strategic repositioning (see ORGANIZATION STRUCTURE). Only one-third of the companies that successfully recovered from asset productivity inadequacies or declines changed their organizational structure and/or replaced top management, fewer changes than in companies that did not turn around. This may reinforce the notion

Table 3 The turnaround research findings

Author(s)	Research questions	Methodology	Findings
Schendel *et al.* (1976)	Characteristics of turnarounds	Moody's, S&P, WSJ significant incident reports	Downturn: higher costs, lower demand; lower revenues; competition upturn: reorganization new management, expansion; divestiture; new product development
Bibeault (1982)	How to turn around a declining business	Questionnaires	External/internal causes of decline; need viable core business; need bridge financing; need new management; stages of turnaround process
O'Neill (1989)	Turnaround strategies for banks	Compustat banks	New structure cost controls; new business development restrict growth
Hofer (1980)	Framework for designing turnaround strategies	Theoretical; case corroboration	Strategic/operating turnarounds
Hambrick and Schecter (1983)	Strategic moves for turnaround; strategic/ operating position relation to turnaround strategy	PIMS variables 4-year period	Three gestalts: asset/cost surgery; product/ market pruning; piecemeal moves
Ramanujam (1984)	Causes of decline and turnaround	Compustat ROI	Cost reduction/debt control; asset reduction; acquisitions
Slatter (1984)	Management actions for succesful turnaround	UK firms; fifteen-year study	Need management change; assert reduction; cost reduction; financial controls
Heany (1985)	Reasons for profit trouble in low-share companies	PIMS ROI; investment, R&D	Need new management; cut costs/cut fat; reduce inventories; redefine markets; divest unprofitable units
Sheth (1986)	Actions to regain market share	Case studies	Reposition products
O'Neill (1986)	Key factors in successful turnarounds	Successful/ unsuccessful cases *Fortune* magazine 1970s	Competitive position; product life cycle; industry type/strategy group; cause of decline
Pant (1986)	Key factors in turnaround strategies	Compustat/ archives	Change management; cut costs/restructure; redefine bsuinesses
Grinyer *et al.* (1988)	Keys to success for improving performance	UK marginal performers	Reduce costs; reposition products
Zimmerman (1989)	Differences between successful/unsuccessful turnarounds	Successful/ unsuccessful cases; financial/ interview/ production data	Size not a factor success: incremental stability, consistency
Thain and Goldthorpe (1989)	Cause of decline; recovery strategies	Investment analysts' reports	New management; improved controls; divest weak units; restructure
Winn (1989)	Definition of decline; recovery strategies	Compustat/ archives	New products/markets; acquisition/ expansion; efficiency moves
Gopinath (1991)	Understand the nature of failures and turnarounds	Cases from published sources (magazines)	New management; improved controls/ monitoring at critical phase
Pearce and Robins (1992)	Understands the measures taken by textile companies for revival	Textile industry financial data questionnaires	Focused marketing; centralized management; labour productivity

that bringing in new management or restructuring operations is symbolic and necessary for companies that are in obvious financial difficulties, but not necessarily advised for companies that are engaged in longer-term strategic plans.

Cash flow or net income turnarounds

Turnarounds from cash flow or net income problems require a combination of operating and strategic moves; operating actions to stem the drain on the company's resources, and strategic actions to reposition the company for future profitability. Asset reduction or retrenchment strategies have been linked to successful net income turnarounds (Hofer 1980; Bibeault 1982; Hambrick and Schecter 1983; Heany 1985; Robbins and Pearce 1992). Like companies in crisis, these firms typically introduce new management to send strong cost-cutting and restructuring messages in order to 'stop the bleeding' before a longer-term plan can be initiated (Bibeault 1982; Gopinath 1991). Cash flow turnarounds were generally accompanied by major plant redesign and efficiency moves (Schendel and Patten 1975; Schendel *et al.* 1976), cost and budget controls (Bibeault 1982; Hofer 1980; O'Neill 1980) and increased capacity utilization (O'Neill 1980; Hambrick and Schecter 1983). Acquisition, expansion or market repositioning strategies are not likely to be undertaken until the firm is on its way to recovery.

Conventional turnaround wisdom for firms with profitability problems calls for reducing debt and divesting assets or business units in order to increase cash flow and restore profitability (Bibeault 1982; Gopinath 1991; Hambrick and Schecter 1983; Heany 1985; Hofer 1980; Thain and Goldthorpe 1989a; Robbins and Pearce 1992). Schendel *et al.* (1976) found that marketing programme changes and product diversification accompanied successful net income turnarounds. O'Neill (1980) found that turnaround banks were more likely to be engaged in diversified activities than their non-turnaround counterparts and that acquisitions of new businesses helped declining banks regain profitability by refocusing on more profitable product lines or industries. Schendel and Patten (1975), Schendel *et al.* (1976), Bibeault (1982), Hofer

(1980), and O'Neill (1980) found that divestitures were prevalent in net income or cash flow turnarounds.

Turnarounds from mediocrity

Turnarounds from mediocre performance require long-term strategic actions to reposition the company among its competition, either through existing operations or by entering new markets or industry segments. Revenue-increasing strategies are recommended for successful turnarounds for these marginal performers. Heany (1985) suggests that companies reassess past pricing policies in order to achieve gains in revenue through increased profit margins. Hambrick and Schecter (1983) found that selective product or market pruning was associated with ROI turnarounds. Heany's low-ROI companies turned around when they redefined their business scope. Hofer (1980) found that successful strategic turnarounds were often accompanied by a change in the emphasis on businesses in the portfolio and/or a refocusing of the business on more defensible product-market segments. Both Hofer (1980) and Sheth (1986) emphasized shifts in share position as successful turnaround strategies.

Market share turnarounds

As the name implies, market share turnarounds require the revamping or repositioning of existing products in order to recapture share from competitors. Sheth (1986) specifically recommended broadening product horizons and redefining markets to regain market share. Rather than entering new businesses, market share turnarounds may require the acquisition of additional capacity, or penetration of additional market segments. Thain and Goldthorpe (1989b) observed that increased market share and improved profitability from existing market segments were obtained by improving product quality, distribution channels, promotion activities and pricing policies.

Asset productivity turnarounds

Companies with asset productivity problems, while operating inefficiently, are not unprofitable by definition. Asset productivity turnarounds, those turnarounds in productivity or efficiency, require a company to focus on productive units by pruning or restructuring unproductive assets and/or acquiring or expanding efficient and effective operational units. Winn (1989) found that major increases in plant expenditures or plant capacity were not significantly associated with asset productivity turnarounds. Likewise, efficiency moves and cost controls were not found to be significantly related to asset productivity turnaround success. Decreased leverage (debt as a percentage of total assets, but not decreased debt) and increased assets were linked to asset productivity turnarounds. As companies recover from asset productivity problems, they tend to increase their assets in order to generate more income. However, successful turnaround companies altered or increased their market scope, but did not alter their product scope. Few successful companies either acquired new products or internally developed new products. While acquisition activity was high for asset productivity turnaround companies, diversification activity was low.

5 Conclusion

Effective turnaround measures depend on the severity and nature of the decline. Crisis measures – those actions taken to ensure solvency in the short term – must be addressed quickly, while operational measures – cost-cutting and sales-increasing efforts – can be engaged in to strengthen a company with cash flow or net income problems. Companies with less obvious financial problems must look towards those strategic moves – acquisition or expansion of potential growth businesses and divestiture or redirection of failing businesses – that can position the company for long-term success.

Most of the recommended interventions in turnaround situations can be categorized as operational cost-cutting (efficiency-increasing) or debt-reduction measures, operational revenue-increasing (pricing and advertising) measures, strategic asset redeployment (retrenchment or expansion), or strategic repositioning (changes in product offerings or market scope).

JOAN WINN
UNIVERSITY OF DENVER

Further reading

(References cited in the text marked *)

* Altman, E.I. (1968) 'Financial ratios, discriminant analysis, and the prediction of corporate bankruptcy', *Journal of Finance* 23: 589–609. (This is a seminal study on bankruptcy prediction.)
* Bibeault, D.B. (1982) *Corporate Turnaround: How Managers Turn Losers into Winners*, New York: McGraw-Hill. (This work, originally published in 1979 as the author's doctoral dissertation, is a comprehensive study of eighty-one turnaround firms.)
  Goodman, S.J. (1982) *How to Manage a Turnaround: A Senior Manager's Blueprint for Turning an Ailing Business Into a Winner*, New York: The Free Press. (This is a practitioner's guide to turnaround management.)
* Gopinath, C. (1991) 'Turnaround: recognizing decline and initiating intervention', *Long Range Planning* 24 (6): 96–101. (This is an examination of twenty-two firms that experienced decline and turnaround.)
* Grinyer, P.H., Mayes, D.G. and McKiernan, P. (1988) *Sharpbenders: The Secrets of Unleashing Corporate Potential*, Oxford: Blackwell. (This study examined publicly-traded UK companies who rebounded after performing poorly.)
* Hambrick, D.C. and Schecter, S.M. (1983) 'Turnaround strategies for mature industrial-product business units', *Academy of Management Journal* 26: 231–48. (This study examined turnaround actions for 260 businesses from the PIMS database that had experienced decline.)
* Heany, D.F. (1985) 'Businesses in profit trouble', *Journal of Business Strategy* 5 (4): 4–12. (This study examined turnaround actions for 573 businesses from the PIMS database that had declining ROI.)
* Hofer, C.W. (1980) 'Turnaround strategies', *Journal of Business Strategy* 1 (1): 19–31. (This paper used twelve case studies of companies which had been described as turnaround situations to classify successful and unsuccessful responses.)
* Hoffman, R.C. (1989) 'Strategies for corporate turnarounds: what do we know about them?', *Journal of General Management* 14 (3): 46–66. (This work examined the previous research on corporate turnarounds.)
* Kibel, H.R. (1982) *How to Turnaround a Financially Troubled Company*, New York: McGraw-Hill. (This is a practitioner's guide to turnaround management.)
* O'Neill, H.M. (1980) *Turnaround Strategies in the Commercial Banking Industry*, doctoral dissertation, University of Massachusetts. (This study

examined the successful turnaround strategies of fifty-one publicly traded US commercial banks.)

* O'Neill, H.M. (1986) 'Turnaround and recovery: what strategy do you need?', *Long Range Planning* 19 (1): 80–8. (This study examined nine company case studies, five of which successfully turned around.)

* Pant, L.W. (1986) *The Determinants of Corporate Turnaround*, doctoral dissertation, Boston, MA: Boston University. (This study classified and examined publicly traded US companies with poor or declining ROA performance.)

Pearce, J.A., II and Robbins, D.K. (1992) 'Toward improved theory and research on business turnaround', *Journal of Management* 19 (3): 613–36. (Reviews turnaround research and provides a conceptual model of business turnaround.)

* Ramanujam, V. (1984) *Environmental Context, Organizational Context, Strategy, and Corporate Turnaround: An Empirical Investigation*, doctoral dissertation, Pittsburgh, PA: University of Pittsburgh. (This study examined publicly traded US companies that had turned around declining ROI performance.)

* Robbins, D.K. and Pearce, J.A., II (1992) 'Turnaround: retrenchment and recovery', *Strategic Management Journal* 13 (4): 287–309. (This is a study of retrenchment as a survival strategy for firms competing in the US textile industry.)

* Schendel, D.E. and Patten, G.R. (1975) 'An empirical study of corporate stagnation and turnaround', in *Proceedings of the National Meeting of the Academy of Management* (August). (This study examined the decline and recovery patterns of fifty-four US companies experiencing turnarounds from net income problems.)

Schendel, D.E. and Patten, G.R. (1976) 'Corporate stagnation and turnaround', *Journal of Economics and Business*, 28: 236–41. (This study examined the turnaround actions of thirty-six matched pairs of US firms.)

* Schendel, D.E., Patten, G.R. and Riggs, J. (1976) 'Corporate turnaround strategies: a study of profit, decline and recovery', *Journal of General Management* 3 (3): 3–11. (This study examined the strategies that fifty-four publicly traded US companies used for successful turnaround.)

* Sheth, J.N. (1986) *Winning Back Your Markets: The Inside Stories of the Companies that Did It*, New York: Wiley. (This is a study of market-share declines and successful turnaround strategies in eighteen large companies.)

* Slatter, S. (1984) *Corporate Recovery: Successful Turnaround Strategies and their Implementation*, Harmondsworth: Penguin. (This is the report of a fifteen-year study of UK firms' successful turnaround strategies.)

* Taylor, B. (1982) 'Turnaround, recovery, and growth: the way through the crisis', *Journal of General Management* 8 (2): 5–13. (This is a turnaround manager's guide to successful turnaround.)

* Thain, D.H. and Goldthorpe, R.L. (1989a) 'Turnaround management: causes of decline', *Business Quarterly* 5 (1): 55–62. (This is the first part of a study of the decline of twenty-seven publicly traded UK firms.)

* Thain, D.H. and Goldthorpe, R.L. (1989b) 'Turnaround management: recovery strategies', *Business Quarterly* 5 (2): 7–13. (The second part of a study of twenty-seven companies, this article examines the successful turnaround strategies that these companies employed.)

* Winn, J. (1989) *Asset Productivity Turnarounds: An Exploratory Study*, doctoral dissertation, Athens, GA: University of Georgia. (This is a study of publicly traded US firms that experienced asset productivity declines.)

* Winn, J. (1993) 'Performance measures for corporate decline and turnaround', *Journal of General Management* 19 (2): 48–63. (This is a typology of turnaround situations which links performance measures to turnaround problems.)

* Zimmerman, F.M. (1989) 'Managing a successful turnaround', *Long Range Planning* 22 (3): 105–24. (Contains case studies of nine companies, six of which turned around from precipitous declines.)

See also: ACCOUNTING; CAPITAL MARKETS, REGULATION OF; CORPORATE PERFORMANCE, ANALYSIS OF; CORPORATE STRATEGIC CHANGE; FINANCE, INTERNATIONAL; MARKETING; ORGANIZATIONAL DECLINE AND FAILURE; SMALL BUSINESS STRATEGY; STRATEGIC COMPETENCE

Strategies, competitive: see COMPETITIVE STRATEGIES, DEVELOPMENT OF

Strategies, entrepreneurial: see ENTREPRENEURIAL STRATEGIES

Strategies for international expansion

Overview

This entry is about how a firm may expand its operations to other countries. There are many ways to enter foreign markets. Each presents a strategic choice to the manager. Let us suppose a company wishes to deliver a product or service to customers in a new market abroad. The first choice is whether to produce inside that country, or whether to produce the service or item in the company's existing plants and ship it to the new market. The first decision, then, is between local production and exports. Several economic and strategy criteria affect this choice. To export the item to a foreign market means additional costs of freight, customs duties, insurance, special packing and other taxes which may be avoided if the item were to be produced in the foreign country itself. On the other hand, setting up production in a foreign nation involves additional capital investment, and possibly higher production costs compared to the company's existing

facilities (especially when we take exports from the latter on a variable cost basis). The manager also has to consider the risks and organizational issues associated with setting up a new foreign investment, such as political instability, an unfamiliar environment, currency fluctuations, training a new management and staff to fit in with the company's existing procedures, hierarchy and operating specifications, and ongoing control and communication costs.

Licensing the company's expertise, patents or brands to another firm in the foreign market, and to have this firm produce the good or service for customers there, is another option. The licensee company receives training and the rights to intellectual property, and in turn pays fees and royalties to the company as licensor. This is sometimes a 'hands-off' approach to international expansion, involving less control over the foreign operation than an equity investment. Since it is the licensee company that makes the investment and assumes the risk of developing the market in their country, the royalties and technical fees they are willing to pay the licensor are often inferior to the dividends and growth in equity value the company could have earned if it had made the foreign investment by itself.

Each option involves different levels of investment, expected return, control, risk, duration, competitive threat, tax and strategy implications. There is no single optimal choice. The decision depends on the product and market in question, on the company's financial and managerial resources, its risk averseness and overall global strategy.

This entry has two major parts. First, the 'classic' foreign market entry choices of exporting, licensing and foreign direct investment are presented and compared as strategy alternatives. How a firm may choose a particular mode in developing a particular country market is shown. Reality, however, is often far more complicated. For one thing, tax, risk and strategy often call for *combining* some of the options rather than treating them as substitutes for each other. The second part of this entry describes how and why the classic strategy options are often combined in large, mature global companies. Globalization calls for treating a foreign market not as a compartmentalized operation, but as one that is integrated with the rest of the global firm's activities. For instance, foreign affiliates (equity investment) may also have received technology or intellectual property from the parent (under licence), while at the same time their inputs are supplied by an affiliate from another nation (intra-firm exports). In this example, direct equity investment, licensing and trade are not substitutes but are combined into one foreign operation. Firms beginning their international expansion are more likely to view them as substitutes. The mature globalizing firm may view them as concurrent strategies.

1 The classic strategy options

The three classic international expansion options are shown in Table 1 which indicates that cash returns under each type are likely to be very different in magnitude, timing, duration, risk and tax liability. In exporting, profit margins are earned immediately, shipment by shipment, under control of the company; risks are those associated with the exporting location, and the profits are immediately taxable in the exporting nation (see GLOBALIZATION).

In foreign direct investment (FDI) a new company is acquired or created abroad with a substantial investment, and the investing company owns its shares. If the parent company owns *all* of the foreign affiliate's shares it is called a 100%-owned subsidiary. If the shareholding is less than 100 per cent then it is still called an equity 'affiliate'. If the shareholding is above 50 per cent the affiliate may be called 'majority-owned affiliate' in some nations. If some of the affiliate's shares are held by a local partner, then it is called a 'joint venture' affiliate. In some cases, the parent's shareholding may be well below 100 per cent, but if the balance of the shares are widely held by small investors in the foreign nation, then effective control still rests with the parent.

In the term 'foreign direct investment' the word 'direct' reminds us that the investor directly controls, or has some influence over, the management of the foreign company (see INTERNATIONAL TRADE AND FOREIGN DIRECT INVESTMENT). A shareholding under 10 per cent is generally considered passive or portfolio investment. Shareholding above 10 per cent is considered 'direct investment'. The degree of control is, of course, only very loosely correlated with the percentage of shares held. By value, most international direct investment takes the form of fully-owned subsidiaries or majority (over 50 per cent shares) affiliates. The cash returns under a capital investment are usually considerably delayed compared to exporting or licensing, but all in all, they are likely to be far bigger and lead to eventual

Table 1 Classic strategy options and type of income from each

Strategy	Type of return
1. Exporting the product, that is, trading	Immediate direct profit mark-up on item sold; taxable in exporting country
2. Foreign direct investment (FDI)	Eventual profits and equity growth declared by foreign subsidiary; taxable in foreign nation
3. Licensing to independent party	Technical fees and royalties over life of the agreement; tax deductible to licensee firm

growth in equity value as well. Unlike licensing, for instance, there is usually no time-limited agreement. Capital investments do, of course, face the risk of failure and eventual termination. The investment is also subject to political and foreign exchange risk in the foreign country. Dividend returns are a partial distribution after the corporate tax bite in the country, and remittances are subject to an additional withholding tax in several nations.

In licensing the returns are under an agreement (between two more or less independent, or arm's-length firms. This is our assumption in the first part of this entry). Agreements usually have a limited life, of between three and ten years generally, unless renewed. The agreement often calls for a significant lump sum payment at the inception, plus running royalties, usually expressed as a percentage of the sales value of the licensed item in the licensee's market. Most governments (within limits) allow licensing fees and royalties to be counted as deductible expense to the payer, that is, the licensee. This means that, unlike dividends, remittance of licensing payments legally escapes the foreign country's corporate income tax altogether. This confers a marginal to significant advantage to the licensing option (see TAXATION, INTERNATIONAL).

Key decisions in international expansion: Location, Ownership and Control

Among the key variables in choosing a foreign market entry mode are location, ownership and control, as shown in Figure 1 (see GLOBAL STRATEGIC ALLIANCES; GLOBAL STRATEGIC PLANNING). The location question regards where the product is to be made, or the service created – inside the foreign nation, or made in the company's home or other production locations? The decision is affected by production cost in each place, transport costs (if the item is produced in one location and sent to another), tariffs, non-tariff barriers and other factors (see NON-TARIFF BARRIERS). Immediate cost comparisons should be modified by *long-run* forecasts of relative exchange rates when calculating import costs, just as local production cost estimates are to be tempered by forecasts of input costs of local

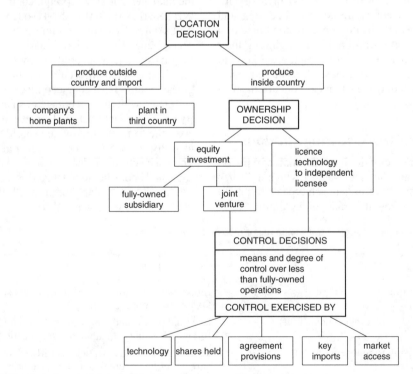

Figure 1 The three key decision domains: location, ownership and control

labour, materials and finance. Costs are sometimes not the crucial factor because marketing success may be predicated on speedy and effective delivery and quality, rather than on price. In terms of overall strategy, criteria other than simple direct cost comparisons may dominate the location decision.

If the decision is made to produce inside the foreign market, this can be done by a foreign direct investment, either fully owned, or (i) in a joint venture, or (ii) by a licensing arrangement. In the latter two cases a partner firm is involved, and designing the arrangement to exercise 'control' over the operation becomes important. In a fully-owned subsidiary, or a majority foreign affiliate, managers obey the wishes of the parent firm even if they are nationals of the country. But when other interests are involved, such as joint venture partners or licensees, their aims, methods and behaviour may not conform to the investor company's objectives. The term 'control' should not appear sinister or manipulative. In any good business arrangement involving two or more parties, mutual checks and balances should be built in. In international business this is all the more important because of economic, legal and cultural differences (see GLOBAL STRATEGIC ALLIANCES). For example, a licensee, having acquired a technology, may then want to compete with the licensor in other countries. There are several classic examples involving US firms, such as RCA, which licensed technology to Japanese companies. In the early years they provided very good income to the US licensors, but later, the Japanese became competitors outside Japan, and even in the 'home' market of the US licensors. In a joint venture one partner may want a high dividend declaration or a quick 'payout', whereas the other may have a long-term strategy preferring reinvestment of most of the joint venture's earnings in the early years. Such differences can be serious and they should be anticipated, with mutual checks and balances built into the arrangement from the beginning.

How control can be wielded

These checks and controls could be written into the agreement. For example, an agree-ment may confer the majority of seats on the Board of Directors to one partner although they hold less than 50 per cent of the shares. Some agreements give one of the partners veto power over certain key managerial appointments, or specify which production method will be used. An agreement could specify maximum and minimum dividend payouts in each year, and so on.

Control can also be wielded by means other than a written agreement, by holding out the lure of new technology or improvements which the other partner desires (see INTERNATIONAL TECHNOLOGY TRANSFER); by one partner controlling the supply of key materials, components or ingredients; by the threat of withdrawing a valuable brand; or by controlling access to international markets for the output of the joint venture or licensee. The ongoing dependence of one partner over the other would temper their behaviour in the interest of mutual gain. Some of the longest-lived strategic alliances are those where the partners continue to be mutually dependent.

In strategic alliances the two firms, while remaining separate organizations, coordinate activities for a common purpose. Beginning in the late 1980s, there has been a proliferation, not only in the common forms of strategic alliance such as joint ventures and licensing agreements, but also in other modes of cooperation between firms. Examples include research consortia, long-term supply and service agreements, joint marketing arrangements and co-production agreements. However, since much of the strategy discussion about licensing and joint ventures also applies to these other forms, we will not treat them separately here.

2 Exporting as an international strategy

Advantages of exporting

Exporting is a logical means of serving a foreign market when the exporting location has a comparative advantage, or when the foreign market is small (see EXPORTING). For an initial expansion into a foreign market, exporting from existing plants means no new investment is needed in the foreign location, with its capi-

Table 2 Pros and cons of an export strategy

Pros	Cons
No new investment (true for small orders)	Existing slack production capacity maybe used up by domestic demand
Very profitable on variable cost basis	Can face formidable 'non-tariff', transport, tariff and other barriers
Utilizes existing capacity and employees	
Economies of large-scale production	High exposure to foreign exchange risk (in long-term strategic sense)
Familiar production environment	
Very low foreign exchange risk exposure (short-term)	Just-in-time delivery and customer relations difficult

tal investment and risk. The company merely uses its slack capacity by increasing plant running hours or adding shifts. Plant managers love export orders, especially if domestic demand is slack, as they utilize existing equipment and employees. (See Table 2 for a summary of the advantages).

Assuming that the fixed costs of the plant are covered by existing domestic sales, any incremental order adds handsomely to profit, since any revenue above variable cost goes directly to profits. An export order, even at a price *less* than the domestic price, can still be profitable. (This may subject the firm to 'dumping' allegations as we will see later. The domestic price may cover all costs – fixed and variable. The export price can be lower than the domestic price if the foreign market is price sensitive, very competitive or poor. Of course, the export price can also be higher than the domestic price in other markets).

Drawbacks of exporting

The drawbacks of an export strategy are also indicated in Table 2. The additional costs of freight, insurance, special packing and customs tariffs often make the delivered or landed cost in the foreign market prohibitively high, even with costing near to the variable cost floor.

International freight costs, on average, are 5 per cent of value or below. However, this is an average with huge variation, depending on the foreign location and the ratio of transport cost to product value. Because of the coun-

try's location, Australian consumers pay a higher price for many goods. Being light in relation to value, a diamond may be mined in South Africa, cut in Israel, set in jewellery in China, and the finished piece sold in the USA – all of this without too much of a freight penalty, as a percentage of the high value of the item. Other bulk goods, however, such as construction materials, are restricted by freight costs to a certain radius around their manufacturing location. Software is exported from India to the USA at the click of a key on a computer in Bangalore. This appears to have low 'transport' cost, but this is misleading since we cannot ignore the huge outlays for satellites and transponders.

After forty years of the General Agreement on Tariffs and Trade (GATT) talks, now under the auspices of a renamed organization called the World Trade Organization (WTO), customs tariffs in the major industrialized nations are down to an average of 5 or 6 per cent (see WORLD TRADE ORGANIZATION). So on average, in the rich nations of the world at least, tariffs are not a significant obstacle to international trade, any more. Today, far more than tariffs, it is 'non-tariff barriers' that remain a principal obstacle to trade. Non-tariff barriers impede trade, not by adding on an extra tariff element, but by imposing regulations, bureaucracy, tough or unreasonable inspection requirements and quantitative restrictions on imports. Restrictive quotas have been imposed on a wide range of items from clothing to cauliflowers to cars. A government may force another to restrict its shipments, and imposes an unwritten quota. These are sometimes called 'Voluntary Trade Restraints', but the restriction is far from voluntary and was undertaken because of strong, behind-thescenes pressure. Another tactic is to impose such tough inspection rules and certification requirements for certain items as to preclude their import. A 'buy local' mentality in some nations may produce a similar *de facto* limitation on imports. Many markets simply cannot be served by exports because of such 'non-tariff' restrictions (see NON-TARIFF BARRIERS).

An exporting strategy faces other problems. By definition, exporting means doing business (or at least the production) at a distance. This means 'just-in-time' delivery and customer relations are more difficult, compared with the option of being present within the foreign market.

Another limitation to exporting is that while utilizing existing spare capacity is desirable, that argument can only be carried up to the capacity limit of the factory. Up to a point the company can handle foreign demand by adding second or third shifts. After that, if foreign demand is bigger still, how does the firm handle further growth? Even adding shifts escalates costs: on night shifts workers have to be paid higher wages, quality is often poorer and the reject rate higher. The time comes when the company will have to contemplate adding another factory or line, which requires additional capital investment. Then the firm can no longer treat its incremental export sales on a variable cost basis. Additional capital investment means additional fixed costs, which then have to be covered from the export price.

Exporting as an evolutionary stage

At this stage in the evolution of a company's international business, when another plant must be added because of growing foreign demand, some companies conclude that they may as well build a plant inside the foreign market (see MULTINATIONAL CORPORATIONS). This would eliminate transport costs and customs duties, reduce non-tariff barriers and logistics, shorten delivery times and improve customer contacts. This is how firms most often make their first overseas investment.

Of course, in some cases, companies may conclude that the foreign market is too small or uncertain, or the required capital investment too massive to justify such a step. Such companies must then restrict their international business to a level based on available capacity or consider the licensing option.

Foreign exchange risks in exporting

Each shipment can usually be hedged against foreign exchange risk. The easiest approach is for exporters to ask for payment in their own currency (see FOREIGN EXCHANGE RISK, MANAGEMENT OF). However, this does not eliminate the exchange risk but transfers it to the importer. So this approach can work at the risk of annoying the buyer. It depends on whether it is the buyer or seller that holds the dominant negotiating position. At any rate, for major currencies (such as the US dollar, Japanese Yen, Euro or Sterling in which most exports are denominated), forward cover is easily obtained, whereby a bank commits, in advance, the foreign exchange rate on shipment. Or an 'option' can be bought. Thus, each shipment can be hedged and the exchange rate made certain.

However, forward cover and options extend out only a year at most into the future. Moreover, while the exchange rate for each shipment can be fixed in advance, the forward rate itself will move over time with the spot rate for a currency (appreciation or devaluation). Hence in the long run, with repeated future shipments, there is no escape from foreign exchange risks associated with exporting.

Plants dedicated to export markets are therefore fundamentally exposed to shifts in the exchange rate over the long term. Consider a Japanese plant selling cameras to the USA. What if the yen moves from a rate of Yen 140 = \$1, to say Yen 100 = \$1 over three years? If the camera price is kept the same in dollars, the company loses, as one dollar would earn it only Yen 100 instead of Yen 140. One possible solution for the Japanese firm would be to increase the dollar price for their cameras by 40 per cent, so as to retain the same yen reve-

Table 3 Scale economies in video game production

Quantity	Variable total cost	Fixed cost	Total costs	Average cost
10000	90000	2200000	2290000	$229
100000	900000	2200000	3100000	$31
200000	1800000	2200000	4000000	$20
210000	1890000	2200000	4090000	$19.48
250000	2250000	2200000	4450000	$17.8

Variable cost per unit	= $9
Domestic sales Q	= 200000 games per year
Trial export order	= 10000 games
Domestic wholesale price	= $22 (10 per cent above average cost)
Maximum factory capacity	= 250000 games per year

nue per camera. However, this may not work. Because of intense competition in the US market for cameras (aided by the open market policies of the US government) the dollar unit price of cameras cannot be raised significantly. As a result, the last time the dollar weakened (same as the Yen strengthened) Japanese exporters of cameras could not increase their dollar prices by much. They saw, not just their profits eliminated, but their gross yen revenues dramatically reduced. A calamitous situation for Japanese companies was a happy situation for the US consumer. Thus, while exporting has minimal exchange risk in the short term (shipment by shipment), this strategy leaves the company exposed in the long term.

A numerical case study

The numerical example below illustrates the concepts of: (1) variable and average cost pricing; (2) economies of scale; (3) tariff barriers; and (4) transfer pricing and 'dumping', which enter into export pricing decisions.

A US video game manufacturer sells 200,000 units of a video game to a mature domestic US market. Variable cost per game is $9 each and fixed costs amount to $2,200,000 per year. The game is sold in the US at a wholesale price of $22 each, involving a profit mark-up of 10 per cent – or $2 over the average cost of $20 per game. Maximum capacity of the factory is 250,000 video games per year. We see in Table 3 that there are strong economies of scale – from a prohibitively high cost

of $229 per unit for a volume of 10,000 units, to a reasonable $20 per unit at a volume of 200,000 games.

Let us suppose that the company receives a letter one day, indicating that there may be a nascent demand for the video game in a foreign market. Would the company please quote for a trial export shipment of 10,000 units, on a 'landed cost' basis (meaning that the exporter bears all costs including freight, insurance and import tariff), to the foreign market? Investigation reveals freight and insurance costs to be $1 per game, and the tariff will be 50 per cent on the 'Free on board' (FOB) value. (FOB in international trade refers to the exporter bearing the cost of goods, including delivery and loading on board a vessel or aircraft in the exporter's port.)

The most common reaction of small US exporters is to reason thus: 'We charge $22 to our domestic customers. Why should we treat our foreign clients any better or worse? We will charge them the same $22 plus whatever freight and tariff costs are incurred – that is their responsibility.' This is quote No. 3 in Table 4, which amounts to a landed cost of $34 in the foreign market. Quote No. 2 is similar, with only a slight difference. Since the export order adds to domestic volume, making the total 210,000 units, this lowers average cost to $19.48 (in Table 3). Add to $19.48 the customary $2 profit margin, and we get $21.48 as the FOB value. This makes for a landed cost of $33.22 in the foreign market, as shown in Table 4.

Table 4 Possible export quotations for video game (delivered to foreign market)

Quote	FOB US port	Freight and insurance	Customs duty at 50% on FOB	Total landed cost in foreign market
1	$ 9.00	+ 1	+ 0.50(9)	= $14.5
2	$21.48	+ 1	+ 0.50(21.48)	= $33.22
3	$22.00	+ 1	+ 0.50(22)	= $34
4	$38.00	+ 1	+ 0.50(38)	= $58

However, both quotes 2 and 3 may be wildly off the mark. Foreign markets are likely to be very different from the domestic market in tastes, income, product cycle maturity, competition and price elasticity. To make an export quote based on the domestic price is nothing more than a shot in the dark. Unfortunately, this is what many exporters do (particularly small ones), either because of ignorance, or because the costs of overseas market research are too high. The foreign market may be able to sustain a price much *higher* than the domestic price. Customers there might be affluent, or the video game, being new, might attract a coterie of fanatics willing to pay a high price. Alternatively, the foreign market may only be able to sustain a price much *lower* than the domestic US price, because income levels are low or because the culture does not appreciate video games, or because of intense competition. What the manager needs to do is to calculate a minimum and a maximum.

What is the minimum? If fixed costs are said to be covered by domestic US sales, any quote above the $9 variable cost floor would make some contribution towards profit. Quote No. 1 in Table 4 constitutes the absolute *minimum* price. It corresponds to a landed cost of $14.50 in the foreign nation – useful if the market is poor or very competitive.

What is the maximum price? (This is useful to compute as a reminder that the foreign market may be affluent.) Here we cannot work upwards from FOB cost, but must work downwards from whatever price the market can bear. Let us suppose in this scenario that the market is affluent, and competition is weak, and that 10,000 video games can be sold to teenage fanatics at a wholesale price of $58 each (quote No. 4 in Table 4). The export ex-

ecutive, works backwards from the expression:

$$X + 1 + 0.50X = 58.00, \text{ i.e. } X = 38.$$

This calculation derives an FOB value of $38 which is much higher than the US price of $22. If a foreign market can bear a higher price, it would be foolish for the company not to charge it. (As long as conditions in the foreign market allow higher prices, and the company itself is not using monopolistic tactics to reduce competition, its higher price is generally considered legal.)

Profit maximization in global marketing

The essential point is that the price charged in one territory (domestic) often has little bearing on the price to be charged in another territory (export). This is especially true in international business when the territories are separated by borders, oceans, and cultural and income differences. In international business, to maximize its global total profit, the company should charge a different price in different nations – even for the exact same product. Global price discrimination is a simple but profound fact in international marketing, and is legal. If the company can get away with it, it should have different prices in different nations.

The 'grey market'

Even if legal, such a policy is not always workable. The item may be easily moved, and encounter low tariffs. In that case, unauthorized parties may buy the item in the cheaper price location and ship it to a higher price nation, thus undercutting the company's own distribution channels and undermining its price discrimination policy. Companies respond to this 'grey market' by attempting to differentiate products, using different designs, packaging or warranties for different nations. The same consumer electronic – say a video player – may be given different model numbers, or a different colour, and in some cases a few extra control buttons may be added, or a few features disabled, to make it look different. But it is the same product. However, sometimes this is costly to the company and may not work for commodity items. Thus, there are such things as globally standard prices for copper, wheat and oil. The price variation across countries for small, easily transported items like watch batteries also tends to be lower. Pan-European regulatory scrutiny of drug prices has reduced price disparities for drugs in the European Union (EU). However, the vast majority of manufactured goods and services are not standardized, but remain differentiated – by design, technology, brand names and the uses they are put to in different nations. So the 'grey market' problem affects some industries, but not others.

Other reactions to global price discrimination

Besides the grey market, other adverse reactions to a company's price discrimination policy include (i) governments forcing down prices for so-called essential products such as pharmaceuticals; (ii) large global buyers who have discovered the price differences across nations and now demand that the supplier quote one 'global price' to all their subsidiaries worldwide; (iii) adverse public reaction from a public that increasingly travels abroad and learns about prices in different nations; (iv) accusations of 'dumping'.

E-commerce, the euro, and eventual price convergence ?

The introduction of e-commerce and a common currency such as the euro will, over time, reduce price disparities, as gaps in price across countries become more obvious to buyers (see E-COMMERCE). But transport costs, tariffs, taxes, delivery times, the desire for quick gratification, buyer search costs, and other impediments will prevent complete price

convergence, except in items close to being generic or being commodities. Moreover, price is far from always being the principal motivator to purchase decisions. Indeed, in many sectors, ranging from garments to electronics, customers lately seem to value speed and variety over low price. Hence mass production, in some sectors, is being replaced by mass-customization, flexible production, and smaller but varied batches.

The overall conclusion is nevertheless that for the foreseeable future, the world will remain a fragmented marketing landscape for a majority of items sold. There is therefore currently no need, and moreover it is globally sub-optimal, for a company to charge identical prices in the different countries it sells in. The very attempt is foolish and doomed in a world of floating exchange rates. Apart from the euro or the US dollar which cover less than one-tenth of mankind, the rest of the world comprisens nations with distinct currencies which float against each other. Even if prices were set equal in two different countries, they would soon drift apart as the rate of exchange varied.

Dumping and international trade

Historically, the Japanese were the first to digest this important lesson and apply its potential. In competitive markets they showed flexibility by setting prices low (a bit above variable cost – quote No. 1 in Table 4), but below average cost (quote No. 2). A company cannot sell at low prices in all countries, because it would go bankrupt if average costs were not covered over all territories taken together. However, the 'below-global-average-cost' price in competitive territories can be made up by charging 'above-global-average-cost' prices in other countries where the market can sustain a high price (quote No. 4).

But charging low prices can invite accusations of 'dumping.' The question of 'dumping' products has been an especially sensitive issue in the US. The US has relatively open policies towards imports. But the US is also one of the most price competitive markets in the world for many industries, in part because of its openness. Foreign producers exporting a product to the USA are often forced to accept very low prices. They make up for this by charging higher prices for the same item in 'other countries'. The 'other country' is often the company's own home market. Japanese consumers often pay higher prices than their US counterparts for a wide range of items, although as Japan opens itself to imports, this trend is diminishing.

The same 'boom box' (an AM/FM stereo radio, plus cassette recorder) sold in Manhattan for $150 may cost a Japanese teenager the yen equivalent of $250. There are thousands of similar examples, in many nations. The explanation is that the US is an open, low-tariff, fiercely competitive market for consumer electronics. Companies from all over the world try to sell their products. Other countries, by contrast, may have a sheltered market and the competition is generally among fewer companies who then set a higher price.

The US public at large does not understand this aspect of dumping. Most consider dumping nasty and predatory. Looking at it one way, the teenager in Tokyo is subsidizing the teenager in Manhattan. If the Manhattan buyer understood this fact of international business they would probably say, 'If this is dumping, then dump more products on me at a low price.' Unfortunately, things are not so simple or neat. The US consumer's gain is offset by the loss of jobs, in perhaps Ohio or Michigan, if not in Manhattan itself. The importing society must balance the consumer gain against possible losses to the domestic producer, and their employees and shareholders.

Transfer pricing in exporting

The observant reader may have found something curious going on in Table 4. Notice that the customs duty is not constant. It varies depending on the FOB price. Who sets the FOB price? The exporting company, of course. The customs official will look at the FOB figure typed on the manufacturer's invoice and compute the duty owed, at 50 per cent of the FOB figure. In quote No. 1, it would amount to $0.50(9) = \$4.50$. If quote No. 4 were used instead, the duty would be $0.50(38) = \$19.00$. This is a huge variation.

Let us change our story a little, just to make a point. Instead of an independent US exporter and an independent foreign importer at 'arm's-

length' to each other, let us consider two scenarios:

Scenario A, where the importer and exporter collude with each other
Scenario B, where the US company exports to its own sales office abroad – the importer and exporter are one company.

In the above two scenarios, there is a strong temptation to declare (type) a lower FOB price on the invoice, in order to pay less duty. Remember that the landed cost abroad is a wholesale price. The ultimate retail customer would pay the same price, regardless. The gain from a lower customs duty would be pocketed by the company in scenario B or shared between the importer and exporter in scenario A, with an illegal 'kickback' or extra under-the-table payment.

This can be illegal! If the customs authorities can prove an intent to defraud by 'under-invoicing', that is, deliberately putting a lower price on the invoice, that is clearly illegal. Regrettably, this is a widespread practice, especially in some developing nations. There are countries whose total figure as reported in International Monetary Fund (IMF) statistics is suspect. We have no option but to consider such practices reprehensible.

Alas, things are not always so clear cut. Suppose the foreign market for the video games was very competitive and our company set a low FOB price *for that reason*, merely to penetrate the market. If customs authorities investigated, they would find the company selling the game for $22 in the USA, but at a lower price in their country. They may accuse the company of under-invoicing and cheating – even although the FOB price was not set low in order to cheat, but because business conditions required it. International company executives have to be vigilant about the possibility that, even although their motives are honest, their company could be accused of under-invoicing, dumping and price discrimination.

The evolution from exporting to foreign direct investment

In our video game example in Table 3, the US factory has a maximum production capacity of 250,000 video games. With US domestic sales of 200,000 units, the most that can be

Table 5 Strategy Motivations for Foreign Direct Investment (FDI)

Market driven investment

- To develop a ripe or untapped foreign market based on differentiated product or proprietary firm technology
- Oliogopolistic or defensive counter-moves
- Overcoming trade barriers

Natural resource-seeking investment

- Multinational company efficiency in exploration, extraction, refining, global distribution

Global rationalization and cost reduction

- Access to cheapest sources of inputs and resources
- Vertically integrated investments
- Production-sharing
- Economies of global scale

Risk diversification

- Taking advantage of non-synchronous business cycles
- Reduction in foreign exchange risk
- Reduction in total political risk exposure

produced for exports is an additional 50,000. Although the foreign demand for this particular video game is only 10,000 units at present, in time it could be as great as the US sales of 200,000 units. Another factory will be needed to serve mature foreign demand. If so, it may as well be established there. This will avoid the cost of freight and the tariff. For these reasons many companies decide to make a foreign direct investment near their foreign customers, despite the uncertainties of operating in a strange environment. Thus exporting may evolve, over time, to a foreign direct investment strategy (see INTERNATIONAL TRADE AND FOREIGN DIRECT INVESTMENT).

3 Foreign direct investment

For the world as a whole, foreign direct investment (FDI) is a far more important means of serving foreign customers than exporting to them, or licensing firms in their nations. For example, in 1995 (the latest year for which comparable figures are available), the sales made by the foreign affiliates of US-based multinationals were worth approximately $2,140 billion. By contrast, US exports or goods and services totalled only about $794 billion (Contractor 1999). This means a for-

eign customer was more than two and a half times more likely to receive a so-called 'American' product or service from a US firm operating in the customer's nation, than receiving a made-in-America product via import (see UNITED STATES OF AMERICA, MANAGEMENT IN). The reasons for investing abroad and the advantages which accrue to a multinational firm are shown in Table 5.

Market-seeking investments

By far the most common motivation for foreign investment is to exploit an untapped potential market. Through its past research, product development and advertising expenditures, the firm may possess a distinctive technology, product and brand equity which local companies in the country may not have. US computer companies' international dominance is based on proprietary high technology. But there are humbler products than computers that have led their firms to develop untapped foreign markets. Kellogg's corn flakes and other breakfast cereals are not high technology products, but the company has made several investments in Europe, Japan, Australia, South Africa and some developing countries. Dietary habits among the middle and upper classes in those countries were changing, or could be changed by advertising. Attractively packaged cereal boxes and the internationally recognized Kellogg brand name meant that buyers were enjoying not just the cereal but also identifying themselves with new ideas.

Natural resource investments

In natural resource investments, global firms are most sensitive to criticism that they are exploiting the country's natural 'patrimony'. However, large multinational firms often offer proprietary expertise in all stages from exploration to extraction to distribution. These advantages cannot be easily replicated by local companies in one nation.

An example of the global network advantage that the major oil companies possess is found in their quantitative production scheduling models. Crude oil, being an organic substance, is found in an astonishing variety of specific gravities, hydrocarbon mixes, impurities, etc. No two wells produce the same crude. Refineries have different capabilities. Some can handle light crudes, others heavy. Some can tolerate a sulphur content, others not, and so on. Furthermore, within each refinery, the company can take the same crude oil and decide what kind of refined petroleum product it needs, depending on market demand, price and inventory. In some cases, they may want more aviation fuel, or heating oil or kerosene. The operating cost, scale and capacities of refineries vary, of course. The final set of variables relate to transport and tariff costs. They arise from the location of the wells in n countries, with oil tankers going to p refineries, from which the finished products are shipped to m markets. Additionally, the price paid by the company for the crude, and the price it gets for each refined product vary over time and have a bearing on the optimal plant allocation decision. This makes for a gigantic, global optimization problem.

The problem is insoluble in its detailed form, even using the best analysts and computers. But algorithms exist inside the large companies, and are used. The fact that the major oil companies have this flexibility to route their crude from many sources to refineries worldwide gives them a considerable cost ad-

vantage over purely national or smaller oil firms. On some occasions a global oil company may have scores of vessels in mid-ocean which can be redirected to different ports, as prices, inventories and demand change in different markets. This global network advantage cannot be replicated by a one-nation firm.

Global rationalization

In fact, the oil companies are using some of the concepts listed in Table 5 under global rationalization and cost reduction. Compared to purely national firms, the global firm has access to the cheapest sources, not just for resources like oil, but also for capital and personnel. There is widespread borrowing by companies in international financial markets (see INTERNATIONAL FINANCIAL SYSTEMS). (Even a domestic company can do the same, but it is less likely to do so, and its information is likely to be poorer.) Some international shipping companies or hotel chains make it a point to recruit in nations like Egypt or India, where skilled, French and English-speaking staff are available at modest salaries. Immigration laws do not easily allow foreign personnel to enter other nations to work. However, several nations do allow such skilled workers, especially when there is a labour shortage in their countries. Global firms are constantly asking governments to permit the entry of specialist managerial and technical personnel. Regional integration, such as the EU, necessarily involves the relaxation of barriers to expatriate employment (see EUROPEAN UNION).

The concepts of vertical integration, 'production rationalization' and scale economies are separate, but intertwined in many global operations. If an automobile company designs a car for sale in many countries, it need not then produce all the components in each market. By combining duplicative facilities – for example, by producing the transmission/axle sub-assembly in only three locations instead of ten, the company gains in two ways. First, there is a saving in moving production to the lower-cost global locations, that is, eliminating the more expensive locations. Second, there is an additional cost saving because the scale of operation in the remaining locations is now larger. The plants are vertically integrated with the assembly operations and the markets. However, this means that the company must now undertake a far larger volume of shipments of components and sub-assemblies across national borders. This increases transport cost and risk since the plants are now more interdependent on each other. If something went wrong in the transmission plant, it would affect assembly in many countries. However, such risks, extra transport costs and increased coordination and logistics costs must be outweighed by the overall cost savings in the automobile industry which is moving towards a greater degree of global integration (see GLOBALIZATION).

Risk-reducing investments

There are obvious political and foreign exchange risks in making direct investments abroad (see FOREIGN EXHANGE RISK, MANAGEMENT OF; POLITICAL RISK). How can an investment *reduce* the company's risk? One method is to channel investment into product areas and countries where the business cycle is 'out-of-phase' with the company's existing operations – the principle underlying diversification, in short. While Europe may still be in a recession, North America may be in an expansionary stage, or vice versa.

The concept is also applicable in currencies. If a company believes the US dollar and Japanese yen will fluctuate against each other substantially, then it may wish to locate its operations in both sets of countries, since the net exposure in their cash flows and accounts can be greatly reduced by carefully structuring their liabilities and assets in the two currencies. This is not to say that investments are made purely for risk-reduction reasons, but these could be important *secondary* considerations.

When it comes to reducing so-called 'political' risk, Japanese car companies provided a good illustration. Giving an industry protection by imposing quotas or tariffs has economic consequences, but it is essentially a political act. If Honda and Toyota hedge their bets by having assembly operations in the USA and the EU as well as importing cars to those markets, they are less vulnerable to future shifts in US or EU policy, compared to other firms which do not yet have this multiple

source capability. This also gives them the flexibility to switch output from one location to another as the yen goes up or down against the euro or dollar. Transport costs in automobiles have also been reduced with special ships specifically designed to bulk-carry cars. The cost of shipping an automobile across the Pacific to California is no higher than sending a car from Detroit to California.

4 Licensing

The third 'classic' foreign market strategy is licensing to an independent local firm in the other country. Instead of undertaking to manufacture or sell on its own, the licensor firm transfers that capability to a licensee company which pays it lump sum fees and royalties. Usually the licensee has exclusive rights to their market for the duration of the agreement.

How does licensing compare with the other two international strategy options? In choosing any option, the manager must balance its advantages and drawbacks *vis-à-vis* the alternatives. This balance is described in Table 6.

Of the strategy alternatives, licensing has unquestionably the highest return on incremental investment (ROI), that is, if we consider the research and development (R&D) costs of a particular product as 'sunk' or already expended. Then the *incremental* costs of negotiating an agreement, transferring blueprints and specifications, and training the licensee's personnel can be very small – in the region of a few hundred thousand dollars at the most – compared with the millions needed for a capital investment in factories, buildings and personnel. This investment and its risks are borne by the licensee. Once the agreement is signed and the licensee trained, subsequent licensing income is pure profit to the licensor. One study shows that over the life of international agreements, more than 90 per cent of licensing income earned by US companies goes directly to the 'bottom line' – that is to say, costs of executing the agreement average well below 10 per cent of revenues, a fabulous ROI indeed. Moreover, if the product is patented and foreign markets can be segmented by strong patents in each nation, territorial limits placed on each licensee, or products hard to ship from one country to another, in theory the

Table 6 Licensing compared with other strategies

Advantages	Drawbacks
• Very high ROI (if R&D costs neglected)	• Often lower NPV compared with other strategies
• No new capital investment	• Royalties alone may be a poor income source (unless other income types included in agreement)
• Low negotiation/implementation costs	• Agreements may have a limited life (unless renewed)
• Most income goes directly to profits	• Lack of control over licensee's quality may hurt licensor's reputation
• Low cyclical fluctuation in income (compared to dividends)	• Licensee can become a competitor after agreement expires, or even before
• Very low political risk	
• Could have lower tax rate to licensor if licensing income treated as return on capital	
• Company can license in many worthwhile markets closed to exports or investment	
• Quicker way to enter foreign market compared to investment	
• Licensee may be used as a guinea pig to test market	
• Return of technical information from licensee	

company could sign separate agreements in each worthwhile foreign market, thus increasing total global licensing income.

While ROI from licensing is very high, net present value (NPV) is usually lower compared with the other strategies of direct investment or exporting. After all, companies are not in the business of maximizing ROI, but NPV. This is perhaps the main drawback to licensing – inadequate total income from royalties. By tradition, if not theory, most royalty rates are less than 8 or 10 per cent of the licensee's sales, and the average is perhaps 4 per cent. Considering how little was spent to implement the agreement and transfer the technology this is attractive. But if the company were to invest in the foreign nation and sell the product itself, the total income could be much higher (except in mature or very competitive industries where return on capital investment is low already). That is to say, foreign direct investment (FDI), for all its risks and high investment costs, can also yield a much higher absolute magnitude of total profit.

When comparing licensing with other alternatives, one cannot overlook the fact that agreements have a limited life, ranging from three to twelve years typically, although they are frequently renewed because the licensee still depends on, and benefits from, the link. By contrast an investment has a theoretically unlimited life, and the company at least hopes that it will continue to earn dividends on its foreign investment indefinitely.

Another possible advantage accruing to licensing is that whereas dividends declared by foreign direct investment affiliates are subject to tax in the parent nation at the regular corporate income tax rate, royalty income may attract a lower, capital returns rate of tax. Although licensing (to independent foreign parties) runs a distant third as an overseas strategy in the minds of many executives, in recent years its use has been growing faster than FDI. Of course, for smaller companies, for many multinational firms based outside the USA and for mature industries, licensing can be an important global strategy.

Another factor that powerfully affects any strategy choice is the relative risk of the two options. For the same projected cash flow, the lower the risk, the lower the discount rate, and the higher the consequent net present value calculation. Licensing has inherently lower risks compared to a company's own investment because:

1 Royalties are usually a percentage of sales. Sales fluctuate over a business cycle or recession much less than FDI dividends, which are declared out of profits, if any. In a bad year there may be no foreign dividends; however, a licensee still pays the royalty.
2 There is no 'political' risk in licensing. Agreements are almost always honoured by all governments.
3 The licensee is the guinea pig, making the investment and testing the waters of the marketplace. (There have been instances where a successful licensee has been brushed aside by a more powerful licensor, once the agreement has expired.)

On the other hand, licensees may become so successful and entrenched that they may become competitors with the original licensor not only in that country, but other countries as well. In the worst scenario the foreign licensee comes back to compete in the licensor's home market. Several Japanese licensees of US firms have done exactly that. A classic example involves RCA, which licensed colour television technology to Japanese companies, only to find them competing with RCA in the US market itself. However, in the majority of cases, the licensee remains, to some degree, technologically and organizationally inferior, and sometimes dependent on the licensor for materials or trademarks. In most cases the licensee is bound under the purview of the agreement to the assigned territory. On average, executives do not show an excessive concern with the issue of licensee competitiveness in third markets. In specific industries, however, such as semiconductors, biosciences and some chemical processes, the consideration is so dominant as to preclude licensing to non-affiliated firms (see INTERNATIONAL TECHNOLOGY TRANSFER).

In an increasingly risky environment for direct investment, firms can no longer afford a policy which ignores the option of licensing. That licensing in many selected situations is not only very profitable, but superior in a net risk-adjusted comparison with alternatives, is an idea gaining ground. Some of the largest companies already have far more global licensees than subsidiaries; and cases exist where the more stable licensing income from royalties related to licensee sales has helped to smooth out the greater volatility of foreign dividend income, since profits are, by definition, more variable than output volume.

5 Comparing the three classic strategy options

Table 7 and Figure 2 list the principal factors affecting the choice of strategy. Although such generalizations cannot possibly apply to all companies or all countries, these concepts are useful for a manager to consider when choosing an appropriate strategy for their firm.

Direct investment in majority controlled or fully-owned investment generally yields the highest total net returns despite the high investment of capital and personnel. This is because the firm internalizes its advantages in technology, organizational learning, intangible proprietary assets such as patents or trademarks, and an international scope of operation. These give it control of strategy, as opposed to sharing decisions with other parties who may later become competitors. However, the risks are also greatest in such a strategy. Besides ordinary commercial risk of business failure, there is political risk in that the host nation government policies may go against the interests of foreign investors.

Exporting can be highly profitable at very low risk, but this is only true if the company uses existing plants' slack capacity for exports. Assuming domestic or existing sales cover fixed costs, the incremental contribution of exports, over the variable costs thereof, is substantial. Risks and costs are much higher, however, if a factory is built especially for exports.

Licensing involves negligible costs of execution compared with the revenues earned from licensing agreements. Over 90 per cent

Table 7 Factors involved in choosing a strategy

	Majority/fully-owned investment	Exporting	Licensing
Total returns	High	Moderate	Moderate to low
Financial resource costs	High	Low	Negligible
Managerial resource costs	High	Moderate	Small
Control over foreign operation	High	High	Low
Ordinary commercial risk	High	Low	Almost zero
Political risk	High (depends on country)	Low	Zero
Foreign exchange or convertibility risk	High (depends on country)	Low	Lowest
Effective tax rate	High	Highest	Lower
Threat of creating competition	Very low	Low	Can be high

of licensing revenues are pure profit (in an incremental sense, ignoring sunk R&D costs). However, the absolute profit from licensing is generally, although not necessarily, smaller than profit which could be earned from direct investment or export sales – but then, the risks are generally far lower also. There is little investment of financial or managerial resources, and commercial risk is borne by the licensee. Assuming that the global market is segmented by patents, tariffs, or by territorial agreement provisions, so that each country is a separate territory, then a licensing agreement can be signed in every viable market. This would make global total revenue from licensing very worthwhile. By comparison, even the largest of companies find it impossible to make an investment in every worthwhile foreign market. In selected cases, licensing has the drawback of creating a competitor in the licensee.

The effective tax rate is likely to be highest in exporting since profit margins on export sales go directly to that year's reportable income in the exporting nation (unless sheltered through a foreign sales corporation). The income of foreign affiliates and subsidiaries may be reinvested indefinitely, postponing the parent nation tax bite, if not taxes in the country of operation. It is not until foreign affiliates' dividends are actually repatriated to the parent that additional tax is owed. Even then, the taxes paid to the foreign nation can be used as a credit against parent firm tax lia-

bility. If a licensing agreement is properly structured, royalty and licensing income can be treated as a return on past R&D investment. This is taxed at a far lower rate than ordinary corporate income, in the licensor's nation.

Before making the decision as to how to earn income in a foreign territory, the strategist needs to consider all the factors of potential income, financial and managerial resource cost, commercial, political and foreign exchange risk, the effective tax rate and the potential for creating or reducing international competition.

In conclusion, Figure 2 shows a spectrum of choices, from contractual or licensing-type arrangements to increasing equity investment at the other end. As a generalization, expected return and control increase as the firm increases its equity strike. However, the risk also increases. For each product/market combination, the strategist must decide which modal choice provides the optimum combination of return, control and risk in the foreign market.

6 Combining international strategies

So far in this entry we have examined how contractual methods such as licensing versus exporting or direct investment in the foreign market may be looked upon as substitute methods for serving the foreign customer. We

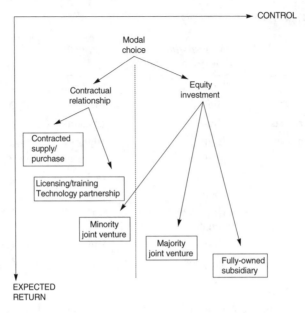

Control versus return mapping of modal choices

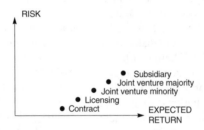

Risk versus return map of alternatives

Figure 2 Levels of control, risk and return
Source: Contractor and Narayanan, 'Integrating Strategic Planning with Technology Management in the Global Firm,' in Tayeb, M. (ed.), *International Business: Theories, Policies and Practices* (London: Pearson, 2000).

next look at what some mature global companies are actually doing, which is combining the benefits of the foreign market entry modes, by using them simultaneously for strategy and tax reasons. Let us begin by seeing how trade and direct investment (FDI) are not just substitutes, but complement each other as well.

Exporting and foreign direct investment as complementary strategies

One-third of the exports of the US economy, as well as those of many major industrialized countries, are from a company to its own foreign equity affiliates acting as importers. Exporting then, is not a pure substitute for foreign direct investment, but the two are intermingled strategies. The trade deficit that the USA suffers against the rest of the world (particularly China and Japan) has been the source of much concern to the public and breast-beating in American politics. But perhaps, to look at trade *only*, is to look at only half the overall international business picture. Some scholars argue that trade deficits should not cause concern because they are offset by the fact that US firms produce more abroad than

Table 8 Combining trade and foreign direct investment ('Lies, damn lies and statistics' in trade and investment figures)

For a particular year let us suppose that:
- **Exports from USA to Fredonia – Exports from Fredonia to USA = (US suffers a trade deficit of)**

25.6	–	*56.8*	=	*31.2*

- But from the consumer's perspective in each country, combining Trade and FDI figures shows,

The Fredonian market for US items		vs	The US market for Fredonian items	
Exports from USA to Fredonia	+ US company production in Fredonia	vs	Exports from Fredonia to USA	+ Fredonian company production in USA
[A]	**[B]**	vs	**[C]**	**[D]**
(25.6	+ *43.0)*		*(56.8*	+ *12.8)*
	= 69.5	vs		*= 69.6*

Some additional comments

1. The 'Job Balance': *[43.9 = 56.8] vs [25.6 + 12.8]*

2. *Some double counting:*

   (i)   Some sales in Fredonia by US affiliates have inputs from US exports. That is to say, some value is added in [B] with [A] inputs

   (ii)   Similarly, some value is added in [D] from [C] inputs

   (iii) Part of [B] shows up in [C], that is, Fredonian production by US affiliates is exported back to the USA

   (iv) Part of [D] is similarly exported from USA to Fredonia and shows up in [A]

3. Items produced in Fredonia under licence from US firms also substitute for both US FDI in Fredonia as well as US exports to Fredonia

Source: Adapted from Ohmae (1987)

the affiliates of non-US firms produce in the USA.

Table 8 examines the case of a hypothetical nation called Fredonia, against which the US suffers a large trade deficit of $31.2 billion. However, adding exports from the USA to Fredonia (A) to US company production in Fredonia (B), the total comes to $69.5 billion. This is almost exactly equal to exports from Fredonia to the USA (C), plus Fredonian company production in the US (D) which comes to $69.6 billion. After all, whether a Fredonian product is imported or made in the US by Fredonian firms, they are still labelled by the consumer as 'Fredonian' products. Similarly, Fredonian customers buy US imports directly, as well as indirectly, from the production by US FDI affiliates in Fredonia. In terms of US 'product presence' in Fredonia, this is almost exactly equal to Fredonian 'product presence'

in the USA, in the Table 8 illustration. This despite an alarming trade deficit.

Local production by foreign investment affiliates substitutes for imports into a nation. Therefore from a 'jobs' and employment perspective, the US position *vis-à-vis* Fredonia is even worse than that suggested by the trade statistics. (See comment No.1 in Table 8.) There are other flaws and omissions in the logic, with a lot of double counting. Sales in Fredonia by US affiliates have components imported from their US parents. Consequently part of [A] is double counted in B. Similarly, part of the value of Fredonian company production in the USA (D), is accounted for by part of [C], which is the exports from Fredonia to the USA. To compound the statistical spaghetti-mix, on the output side, part of B shows up in C. That is to say, some US company production in Fredonia is exported back to the USA, just as Fredonian affiliates may export part of their production in the USA (D), back to Fredonia (A).

Because of the complementary way in which global companies use exports and direct investment simultaneously, these statistics did not give a complete or accurate picture.

Finally, even the labels 'US firm' or 'Fredonian firm' or 'Japanese firm' will become inaccurate in the future. With large global firms having sales in many nations, their home market sales may have fallen below half of the global total. Can they be any longer identified with their 'home base' from which the company started? A large part of the global sales of so-called 'Japanese' companies like Honda already take place in the US market, with over 60 per cent value-added in the US for many models. A significant part of Honda's R&D and design operations are in the USA. The company exported US-made cars back to Japan, some components in the cars having made a ten thousand mile round trip back to Japan, while many of the other parts are US or Mexican. Already, a fraction of the shares of many Japanese companies is owned by US and European investors, a fraction that will grow in the future.

At any rate, the purpose of the foregoing discussion was to show how trade and foreign direct investment are at once substitutes, as well as complements, to each other, in rather complex ways. Moreover, country-of-origin labels, already suspect, may mean even less in the future.

Direct investment and licensing in combination

Most governments allow licensing fees and royalties to be considered a deductible expense, even when a fully-owned subsidiary is paying its own parent. Governments offer this tax concession (illustrated in Table 9) in order to induce the transfer of technology and intellectual property to their countries. From the point of view of foreign investors, many of them would have transferred the expertise and intellectual property to their majority equity affiliates anyway, even without this concession, but governments have no way of distinguishing those that would have transferred the technology without the tax incentive, from companies that would not have done so. Hence the concession is offered to all. As illustrated in Table 9, a Japanese subsidiary has established a fully-owned subsidiary in the US. In the first column there is no licensing agreement between the Japanese parent and its US affiliate. In the second, a licensing agreement is introduced whereby the US subsidiary has to pay a 5 per cent royalty to its own Japanese parent. Because US law (and the laws of most nations) allows the deduction of reasonable royalties as a deductible expense item to the payer (in this case the US licensee firm), the remittance of royalty to the foreign (Japanese) parent legally escapes US corporate income tax altogether. The total tax liability to the US government is lowered in the second column of Table 9. Therefore, the after-tax profit remitted to Japan increases from 210 in the left-hand column to 225 in the rightmost column. And

Table 9 Tax effect on intra-firm royalty payment

• Sales by Japanese subsidiary in USA	1000	• Sales by Japanese subsidiary in USA	1000
• Total costs (no royalties involved)	700	• Royalty (at 5% on sales)	50
• Profit before tax	300	• Total costs (excluding royalties)	700
• US tax (at 30%)	90	• Profit before tax	250
• Profit after tax	210	• US tax (at 30%)	75
		• Profit after US tax	175
		• Royalty remittance to Japanese parent	50
		• Total remittance to parent	225

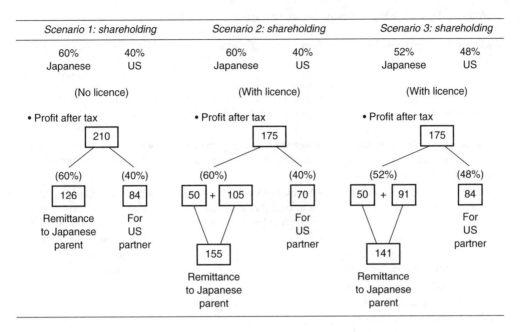

Figure 3 What if the above affiliate was a joint venture?

this is legal. But there is a temptation to channel more and more of the remittance via the royalty channel, even if that means less is remitted under the 'profit after local tax' category, because the *total* of the two cash flow channels is higher than after-tax profits alone. Some companies may indeed divert 'too much' of their intra-corporate funds via the royalty and intellectual property payments categories in order to minimize tax liability in a nation. The royalty rate may be *un*reasonable and considered by the tax authority to be 'too high'. Then tax authorities' audits ask the company to justify the intra-corporate charge. But who is to say whether a 10 per cent royalty is unreasonable, where a 5 per cent royalty is reasonable? That depends on the value of the technology, the market, the R&D cost and several complicated factors. What is an appropriate charge for global overheads levied against a subsidiary in another nation? What fee should a parent charge an affiliate for introducing a brand into the country? The valuation of intangibles and intellectual property, especially in international transactions, remains among the critical management and accounting issues of our day (Contractor 2000).

The fact remains however, that as a consequence of the deductibility of such intracorporate payments, two-thirds to three-quarters of the royalty and licensing fees remitted across national borders are between foreign majority affiliates and parents. Only a third or less are between unrelated or quasi-arm's-length licensors and licensees (Contractor 1999) (see TAXATION, INTERNATIONAL).

Licensing is only one form of corporate alliance. Others include equity joint venture (two or more firms jointly holding the shares of another company). Figure 3 indicates the effects of a licensing agreement cum joint venture. This is a common arrangement in international business. To extend the case from Table 9, let us suppose that, instead of a 100 per cent subsidiary, the US company is a joint venture where 60 per cent of shares are held by a Japanese partner and 40 per cent held by a US company. Distribution of the $210 after-tax profit, proportional to the shareholding, would earn $126 for the Japanese and $84 for the US partner in scenario 1. With the introduction of 5 per cent royalties payable to the Japanese partner by the joint venture corpora-

Table 10 Strategic advantages of multiple cash flow types

Lump-sum fees and royalties	Dividends/equity share	Margins on components or product traded with affiliate or licensee
• Lump-sum fee provides immediate cash return	• Direct share in future success, growth and profits of affiliate	• Margins can be high on proprietary, high-tech, or branded items
• Royalties are inherently less volatile compared to dividends paid out of uncertain profits	• More valuable as years pass than fixed percentage royalties	• Less affected by cyclical fluctuations compared to dividends
• Royalties earned even if affiliate/licensee's profits are zero	• No expiration (by comparison, a licensing or material supply agreement may terminate)	• Profit margins earned outside affiliate/licensee country jurisdiction, i.e., no convertibility risk
• Licensing income legally escapes the local tax in the payer's nation		• Transfer pricing advantages
• Also possible lower tax to the licensor (compared to dividends)		
• All royalties kept by licensor (dividends have to be shared with an equity joint venture partner)		

tion in scenario 2, the Japanese partner's take (legally) jumps to $155. The US partner's after-tax distribution declines somewhat to $70. As a negotiating demand therefore, the US partner may demand an increased 48 per cent shareholding in scenario 3 in order to accommodate the Japanese partner's desire for a licensing agreement. The 48 per cent shareholding of the US partner restores their share to $84 in scenario 3, while still leaving the Japanese partner better off than in scenario 1 with a total take of $141.

Why companies should consider combining strategies for global integration

It has been shown in this entry that licensing, foreign direct investment and exporting are used in many cases as substitute methods for serving foreign markets. This is appropriate for all firms expanding into a new foreign nation, and in particular, for smaller companies who are beginning their internationalization process. But for a large global company seeking global optimization and efficiency, an integrated strategy would combine the meth-

ods to achieve higher income and control, lower taxes, and reduce risk. Table 10 summarizes the advantages.

Agreement-defined fees and royalties have the tax advantage described above. The payer, whether an independent licensee, or an affiliate of the licensor, gets to deduct royalties paid as a deductible expense. The remittance of these fees then legally escapes the corporate income tax of the nation of the licensee. In addition, in some nations, there are also preferential tax advantages in the licensor's country for receipts of licensing income versus receipt of foreign affiliate dividends. An obvious but critical factor in joint ventures is that while profits are shared, one of the partners, as licensor, gets all of the royalties and fees. Lump sum fees paid on signing the agreement provide immediate and certain returns, in contrast with distant and uncertain dividends. Royalties are payable even if the venture's profits are zero. Moreover, a royalty linked to sales is axiomatically more stable over the business cycle than dividends. In recessions, many firms have found that royalties come in at almost the normal level, even when profits on their equity investment have disappeared.

On the other hand there is no denying the fact that an equity stake is a direct claim on the future success and profits of a venture, and this is likely to be far more valuable, in the long run, than royalties which are usually capped at a fixed percentage of sales, and eventually expire. (Licensing agreements should be continued indefinitely to take advantage of legal tax concessions. However, in the case of a joint venture, the local partners may be unwilling to renew the joint venture's licensing agreement with the international company, because it reduces their share of dividends. They may feel that once they have learned the technology and business from their partner and paid royalties for several years, there is no need to keep paying – unless new technology or knowledge is to be transferred.)

Finally, there are significant advantages in setting up an intra-corporate trading relationship for the purchase of components or sale of finished products between the global firm and its affiliates in each nation. There are, of course, strategic imperatives in many businesses for this setting up of a trading or supply relationship between the companies. There are other advantages. Margins on the supply of components, being linked to production, are a more stable profit flow to a global firm, compared to volatile dividends. Moreover, mark-ups can be high on proprietary, hightechnology or branded items, and these markups are earned outside the tax jurisdiction of the country. (There is often a very thin line between the above strategy prescription and conscious tax evasion by transfer pricing abuses. The latter is illegal and immoral.)

Transfer pricing revisited

Figure 4 provides a simple example of transfer pricing. An affiliate A supplies 1,000 widgets per year to affiliate B, initially at $1 each, in scenario 1. The tax rate in A is 30 per cent, and in country B it is 50 per cent, with pre-tax profit levels in each affiliate as shown in Figure 3. There is therefore an obvious temptation to declare less profit in the high-tax location B, and to declare more profit in the lower-tax country A. This is done in scenario 2 by raising the unit transfer price to, say,

$1.50 per widget. In scenario 2 (compared with scenario 1) after-tax profits in B decline less than the amount by which after-tax profits in A increase. Consequently the global total, after-tax profit of the global company as a whole increases from $9,000 in scenario 1, to $9,100 in scenario 2.

However, this results in paying $250 less tax to country B, which is illegal if the intent was to evade taxes. In the long run, no company or individual can survive or prosper on such a basis without being discovered. An honest company will attempt to follow 'arm's-length pricing', based on an estimation of what the transfer price would be if companies A and B were independent, arm's-length firms. Alas, things are not always so clear-cut, since there are no 'arm's-length equivalents' for much of the intra-corporate trade within global firms which is based on products and services which are highly differentiated, partially assembled or even unique. In many cases there is no similar item on the market. Consider another scenario. What if affiliate A has undertaken costly R&D to develop a new model, and for that legitimate reason wishes to raise the transfer price to $1.50 per unit? This illustrates how, even with honest motives, a company can be accused of cheating.

This form of transfer pricing manipulation is not likely to be widespread. Notice how, in Figure 3, even with a fairly wide differential in tax rates between the nations, and although the unit transfer price was raised by as much as 50 per cent, the total after-tax profit of the global firm increased by a measly $100 or 1.1 per cent. With converging tax rates in the major Organization for Economic Cooperation and Development (OECD) nations, the incentive is even less. Far more important is the fact that the intra-corporate trade was set up between affiliates A and B in the first place. Suppose that in years past B was sourcing this widget locally. Now A supplies B, in scenario 1. That means that as much as $1,000 is being transferred to a lower tax jurisdiction – and perfectly legally. Unit price manipulation therefore is of far less consequence than the fact that after-tax global rationalization calls for (legally) setting up internal intra-corporate trade in components and finished products.

S C E N A	1000 widgets per year at $1 each		
R I O 1	(A) $\longleftarrow$ $1,000 payment (B)		

	(tax rate: 30%)		(tax rate: 50%)		total profit
	pretax profit	10,000	pretax profit	4,000	after taxes
	tax (30%)	3,000	tax (50%)	2,000	7,000 + 2,000
	aftertax profit	7,000	aftertax profit	2,000	= 9,000

S C E N A	1000 widgets per year at $1.50 each		
R I O 2	(A) $\longleftarrow$ $1,500 payment (B)		

	(tax rate: 30%)		(tax rate: 50%)		total profit
	pretax profit	10,500	pretax profit	3,500	after taxes
	tax (30%)	3,150	tax (50%)	1,750	7,350 + 1,750
	aftertax profit	7,350	aftertax profit	1,750	= 9,100

Figure 4

7 Conclusion

For many companies beginning their international expansion into a foreign market, the strategy options include exporting, foreign direct investment and contractual arrangements (of which the most notable is the licensing of expertise and intellectual property to a firm in the foreign market). This entry discussed the pros and cons of each, and enumerated several criteria whereby a firm may choose between the foreign market entry methods. The choice of method will depend on the firm, the product and the foreign market in question. There is no one optimum. Some of the important criteria influencing the choice include expected returns, intended duration of the strategy and product cycle, required degree of managerial control, the risk appetite of the company, availability of financial and managerial resources, applicable tax rules, political and foreign exchange risk, and the risk of future competition from former licensees and strategic allies.

In the second part of this entry it was shown that as firms mature, and integrate globally, they will not treat foreign market entry methods as merely separate options, but consider combining these methods, and have a trading and a licensing relationship with their affiliates and equity partners abroad. Exports, licensing and foreign direct investment, in this view, are alternate channels for income extraction, as much as they are market-serving strategies. Moreover, this combined approach lowers volatility and risk, increases control and strengthens ties with partners (if any) in the other nation. With increased globalization of business this trend will become even more important in the future.

FAROK J. CONTRACTOR
RUTGERS UNIVERSITY

Further reading

(References cited in the text marked *)

Bach, C.L (1997) 'U.S. international transactions, First Quarter 1997', *Survey of Current Business*, July. (Statistics on US Investment and Trade.)

Contractor, F.J. (1986) *Licensing In International Strategy: A Guide for Planning and Negotiations*, Westport, CT: Quorum Books. (A comprehensive volume on the role of licensing in the international strategies of companies. The book contains considerable empirical data drawn from firms directly, as well as from secondary sources. Several cases illustrate what companies are doing.)

Contractor, F.J. (1990) 'Ownership patterns of US joint ventures abroad and the liberalization of foreign government regulations in the 1980s: evidence from the benchmark surveys', *Journal of International Business Studies* (1): 55–74.

(An empirical analysis of the variation across countries in equity ownership by US companies in foreign joint ventures. The paper also traces the liberalization in foreign investment rules in forty-six nations.)

* Contractor, F.J. (1999) 'Strategic perspectives for international licensing managers: The complementary roles of licensing, investment and trade in global operations', *Journal of the Licensing Executives Society* June: 1–12. (This article provides a comprehensive comparison between FDI, trade, and licensing statistics for the US and the world, and also traces their strategic significance. The article also provides insights into the intra-firm nature of trade and licensing, as combined with FDI because of tax, transfer pricing, risk reduction and other strategy considerations.)

Contractor, F.J. (2000) 'Integrating strategic planning with technology management in the global firm', in M. Tayeb (ed.), *International Business: Theories, Policies and Practices*, London: Pearson. (Describes how technology management can be integrated into multinational strategy.)

Contractor, F.J. (2000) 'Valuing intangible assets in alliance negotiations', in F. Contractor (ed.), *The Valuation of Intangible Assets in Global Operations*, Cheltenham, UK: Edward Elgar, forthcoming. (Treats the issue of setting a price for technology and corporate knowledge.)

Gomes-Casseres, B. (1989) 'Ownership structures of foreign subsidiaries: theory and evidence', *Journal of Economic Behavior and Organization* 11: 1–25. (This paper traces the percentage equity of foreign affiliates held by parent firms in global companies. Ownership and strategic control are contrasted.)

Hill, C., Hwang, P. and Kim, W.-C. (1990) 'An eclectic theory of the choice of international entry mode', *Strategic Management Journal* 11: 117–28. (An analysis of the choice between licensing, joint ventures and wholly-owned subsidiaries as a function of strategy factors.)

Kim, W.-C. and Hwang, P. (1992) 'Global strategy and multinationals' entry mode choice', *Journal of International Business Studies* (1): 29–53. (An empirical analysis of the choice between licensing, joint ventures and wholly-owned subsidiaries as a function of factors such as industry concentration, transnational synergies, country risk, competition and firm-specific know-how.)

Lowe, J. and Mataloni, R. (1991) 'US direct investment abroad: 1989 benchmark survey results', *Survey of Current Business* October: 29–55. (A summary of results from the monumental survey of 2,300 US-based multinationals.)

Ohmae, K. (1987) 'Companies without countries', *The McKinsey Quarterly* Autumn: 49–63. (The author questions conventional wisdom about global companies.)

Reich, R. (1990) 'Who is Us?' *Harvard Business Review* January–February: 53–64. (The author describes how the affiliation of companies with their national or home base is becoming weaker.)

Reilly, R. (1995) 'Economic evaluation techniques', *Les Nouvelles: Journal of the Licensing Executives Society*: 53–58. (Benchmarks for valuing intangible assets.)

UNCTAD (1993) *World Investment Report 1993: Transnational Corporations and Integrated International Production,* New York: United Nations. (The 1993 annual report issued by the United Nations Conference on Trade and Development focuses on integration of economic activity across national borders.)

United Nations (1999) *World Investment Report 1999,* New York: United Nations. (Digest of information gleaned from UN sources.)

US Department of Commerce (BEA) (1997) *U.S.Direct Investment Abroad: Operations of U.S. Parent Companies and their Foreign Affiliates*, Washington, DC: US Government Printing Office. (Official statistics from US government sources.)

See also: CROSS-CULTURAL COMMUNICATION; E-COMMERCE; EUROPEAN UNION; EXPORTING; FOREIGN EXCHANGE RISK, MANAGEMENT OF; GLOBAL STRATEGIC ALLIANCES; GLOBAL STRATEGIC PLANNING; GLOBALIZATION; INTERNATIONAL TECHNOLOGY TRANSFER; INTERNATIONAL TRADE AND FOREIGN DIRECT INVESTMENT; POLITICAL RISK; TAXATION, INTERNATIONAL; WORLD TRADE ORGANIZATION

Strategy, concept of

Overview

The concept of strategy applied to business and management is of relatively recent origin. Modern research in the area largely stems from Chandler's study of strategy and structure. Two approaches have typically been adopted to the concept of strategy. The first involves a consideration of the components or dimensions of strategy. The second involves the development of typologies of strategies or what are often called generic strategies.

Much of the writing in the area of strategy is overly rational and has a strong tendency to be prescriptive. It is also disproportionally dependent upon case studies rather than comparative research. There has been a lack of overarching or integrating theoretical perspectives, with theoretical ideas being borrowed from a variety of different subject areas. Strategy typically involves a determination of strategic objectives which often have only a limited relationship to official organizational goals and missions. The making of strategy is normally a senior management function, but many others may have an involvement depending on the nature of the company or organization in question.

The main components of strategy relate to strategic objectives, the definition of scope or domain, competitive advantage, synergy, resource deployment and organizational structure. A variety of typologies have been developed by writers in the strategy area. The best known of these stems from the work of Porter, who suggested just three generic strategies, namely a cost leadership strategy, a differentiation strategy and a focus strategy.

1 Introduction

Surprisingly, the systematic study of strategy in business and management is of relatively recent origin. The concept first gained currency in the area of military activity and was associated with the planning of wars, campaigns and battles (see MILITARY MANAGEMENT). It only began to be widely applied in business and management after the publication of Chandler's book on strategy and structure in 1962 (see CHANDLER, ALFRED DUPONT, JR (1918-)). Since then there has been a very large amount of research and writing relating to the concept of strategy. This writing has encompassed theoretical approaches and empirical studies and the subject has developed rapidly during the last thirty years, so that it is now virtually always a key core course in the business school curriculum (see BUSINESS SCHOOLS).

In this period of rapid development our understanding of strategy has increased significantly, but it is now realized to be a much more complex phenomenon than the early work suggested. Research and understanding in the area have suffered from both the diversity and lack of completeness of conceptualizations of strategy that have appeared in the literature and guided different streams of research (see STRATEGIC CHOICE).

At the same time as our understanding of the issues has increased, so the overt application of strategic planning and corporate strategy has become significantly more widespread. Initially this development was most noticeable in the private sector in industrial and commercial companies, but the ideas are now commonly applied in the public sector and not-for-profit organizations (see NOT-FOR-PROFIT MANAGEMENT). The belief in the necessity of strategic planning has now reached the point where individuals setting up new companies or trying to obtain finance for small businesses are almost always required to develop and present a strategic plan in order to convince those who provide funding, whether in terms of debt or equity, to part with their money.

It is now the case that in most business schools worldwide, strategy or strategic management is a core course in the curriculum. As such, it is regularly seen as a course which brings together or integrates the teaching relating to specific disciplines relevant to management or to particular functional areas. However, such courses are often strongly normative and based on case studies of particular organizations. Examination of such cases tends to indicate a strong bias towards marketing or finance, with some attention being given to issues of the management style of senior executives. These same biases are reflected to some extent in the research literature.

2 Past developments

The idea of strategy applied to business and management really stems from the work of Alfred Chandler (1962) (see CHANDLER, A.D.). Chandler was a business historian whose major work was a study of the history of the largest business enterprises in the USA. The results of this study demonstrated quite clearly the importance of the concept of strategy in attempts to understand the behaviour, and particularly the growth, of business firms. It also raised the critical issue of the relationship between company strategy and organizational design or structure. Although Chandler emphasized the importance of the relationship between companies and the marketplace, his descriptions of the reality of strategy formulation and implementation made it completely obvious that these relationships were immensely more complex than earlier approaches had suggested.

Hofer and Schendel (1978) in their book on analytical concepts in the strategy area have reviewed the concept's short history since Chandler's work was published. They suggested that it was only in the mid-1960s with the publication of books by Andrews (1965) and Ansoff (1965) that the formal study of strategy in the business arena could genuinely be said to have started. Since then the topic has been widely studied, and even more widely written about. However, much of the writing in the area has been normative and the empirical research that has been conducted has often tended to examine either very limited aspects of strategy, such as acquisitions or portfolios of business interests, or has been of a descriptive case study sort.

In both the research literature and in textbooks it would seem that there has been a strong tendency to prescribe what should be done in strategy formulation and implementation based largely on either armchair theorizing or the description of individual cases. There has been little work of an empirical nature which presents the results of large-scale comparative research.

Although there has been some recognition of the political nature of the strategy-making process (see STRATEGY MAKING, POLITICS OF) writing in the area has tended to concentrate on the rational approach to the subject. Indeed, much of the work on strategy might be criticized as being overly rational and failing to take sufficient account of the many factors which in reality limit any given senior management's ability to develop and implement strategy in a wholly rational manner. In particular, there is a strong tendency to underestimate the effects of uncertainty in the environment with which the organization in question is confronted. This remains true, despite the fact that nearly all work in the area mentions the problems involved in working in an uncertain situation. All too often, having mentioned the problem, writers then go on to ignore it. These criticisms have validity despite the early work of writers such as Simon (1949) who suggested that, at best, strategic decision making could only achieve 'bounded rationality'. This, he argued, was because of the variety of political pressures, incomplete information and general uncertainty. Also Lindblom (1959), in a very well-known article suggested that the reality of strategic decision making was typically a variety of disjointed incrementalism, which he called 'the science of muddling through'. It must be noted that Lindblom argued that not only was this method prevalent in practice, but also that it is the one that should be used. More radical and rational approaches of the sort that are commonly suggested by many other writers, he dismissed on the grounds that they are 'of course impossible'.

Much of the very considerable quantity of recent research relating to the concept of strategy has examined particular aspects of strategy or the strategy formulation and implementation processes. In so doing the full complexity of the topic has begun to be revealed, but conceptual approaches to encompass this complexity have not been developed to a sufficient extent.

One of the difficulties that clearly underlies the failure to develop conceptual approaches sufficiently is the lack of any clear indication of where an approach to establish theoretical foundations should come from. Though different writers on strategy have tried to adapt approaches from a variety of different social science areas, there is little, if any, logic for one rather than another. The obvious partial exception to this is the work of Michael Porter (1980) (see PORTER, M.E.) whose theoretical approach to strategy has been largely formulated on the basis of extensions of economic theory and ideas. The remainder of theoretical ideas have been gleaned from a large number of different starting points with apparent difficulty.

Taking strategy as a general concept, two somewhat different approaches have characterized writings of a theoretical sort over the years. The first of these approaches characteristically tries to examine the concept of strategy in terms of its component parts or dimensions. The second approach was essentially typological and looked for particular types of strategies, often referred to as generic strategies. Without doubt this latter approach was massively publicized in advance by Michael Porter (1980) (see PORTER, M.E.).

3 The state of the art

There would seem to be a general consensus that strategy formulation is normally the business of top management in any organization. In terms of the ultimate sanctioning of new or different strategies this must inevitably be true owing to the hierarchical nature of organizations. However, as Mintzberg (1987) (see MINTZBERG, H.) has pointed out, the strategy-making process should not necessarily be seen as a carefully planned process orchestrated or carried out by top management with, on certain occasions, the assistance of specialist staff. He suggests, realistically, that strategy need not always be deliberate but that it can emerge or develop in all kinds of strange ways. It is also clear, from his work, that many people at lower levels in organizations, or indeed outside them, may have inputs of a valuable nature to the strategy-setting process. None the less, at the end of the day, strategic decision making in organizations amounts to 'top decisions' (Hickson *et al.* 1986).

It generally seems to be agreed that strategy should involve the integration of ideas from all the different sub-disciplines of management studies and from all functional areas. In the introduction to a collection of readings on the subject, Ansoff (1969) (see ANSOFF, H.I.) suggests that business strategy consists of a set of management guidelines which specify the firm's product market position, the direction in which the firm seeks to grow and change, the competitive tools it will employ, the means by which it will enter new markets, the manner in which it will configure its resources, the strengths it will seek to exploit, and conversely the weaknesses it will seek to avoid. Strategy is a concept of the firm's business which provides a unifying theme for all its activities.

There are inevitably many different versions of the stages in the overall strategy formulation and implementation processes. However, there would seem to be a fair degree of commonality in these. The main stages would seem to involve:

1 the evaluation of the present state of a company, or more generally organization, particularly examining its strengths and weaknesses;
2 scanning the environment, particularly with a view to identifying opportunities and threats;
3 the development of some set of basic strategic objectives;
4 the development of a strategic plan;
5 communication of the plan to relevant personnel;
6 implementation of the strategic plan;
7 evaluation of the progress of the implementation of the plan;
8 periodic reassessment of the various stages.

Much of the literature in the area concentrates on providing a series of techniques for carrying out the various stages of the process described above. This is particularly true of works designed for managerial audiences. Such techniques are described for different types and sizes of company and other types of organization. In this literature, there has frequently been a bias towards consideration of the problems of large companies, particularly multinationals and conglomerates. However, recently this imbalance has been to some extent redressed, with increasing numbers of books and articles being devoted to the problems of small companies and new business start-ups. The development and elucidation of techniques is particularly pronounced in the area of corporate planning (see CORPORATE PLANNING, PROCESS OF), which is usually seen as a central part of the overall strategy-making and implementation process. This, no doubt, reflects the apparently increased formal role of corporate planning in many organizations. It is also associated with the increasing development of an occupational group of corporate planners. What is perhaps worrying is the apparent lack of a solid theoretical basis, or relevant systematic empirical research, upon which the various prescriptions or techniques are based.

The other principle area of attention in the literature focuses upon the variety of possible strategies or components of strategies which are possible. Thus, there are books and articles on growth strategies, turnaround or recovery strategies, diversification, territorial expansion, portfolio analysis, innovation strategies, acquisition strategies, market entry strategies and so on. What tends to be lacking is a theoretical rationale for deciding which type of strategy or mixture of types should be adopted in particular circumstances. It is also to be noted that there tends to be a bias in much of the literature towards problems relating either to markets or to capital acquisition and ownership and away from problems relating to production, personnel and labour relations. However, in this latter area, the advent of human resource management as a concept has begun to change the nature of the literature with human resource issues becoming much more likely to be considered as a strategic matter.

The breadth of the concept

Hofer and Schendel (1978), in their book on analytical concepts in the strategy area, examined the early perspectives developed by Andrews (1965) and Ansoff (1965) and suggested that their ideas concerning the concept of strategy differed markedly on three main points. The first of these involved the breadth of the concept; the second questioned whether the means of achieving organizational aims or goals can be analytically subdivided into components or dimensions; the third questioned whether goal setting is part of the strategy formulation process. On the first of these issues Hofer and Schendel (1978: 17) wrote 'here the question was whether the concept included both the aims – goals and objectives – an organization wishes to achieve and the means that we use to achieve them (Andrew's view) or whether it included only the means (Ansoff's view)'. They go on to conclude from their examination of most of the major subsequent contributions to the field that this issue continues to be debated and is probably the greatest point of disagreement amongst recent writers. It is worthy of note that this debate has continued since Hofer and Schendel wrote their book, and it is still a major issue to be considered.

This issue relates to, and reflects, general discussions relating to the nature of the strategic objectives formulated by senior managers (see MANAGERIAL BEHAVIOUR). Clearly such objectives are likely to effect the development of strategy. However, it must be acknowledged that these do not always bear any particular clear relationship to the official goals or mission of the organization in question. The matter is complicated by the plethora of different terms and concepts which are employed in this area.

Organizational goals

The study of the goals of organizations has a lengthy history but the research that has been conducted in this area has been very limited. Examination of this literature suggests that two types of organizational goals have been identified (Perrow 1961) (see ORGANIZATION BEHAVIOUR; ORGANIZATION BEHAVIOUR, HISTORY OF). These are official or charter goals and operational goals. The official or charter goals are often stated or defined in constitutional documents relating to the organization as a whole. The precise nature and legal implications of such constitutional documents varies considerably by type of organization and by country as they often emanate from aspects of the legal system of that country. However, the examination of such documents suggests that official or charter goals are often too vague and general to be capable of any precise translation into strategic objectives. It must also be noted that very often official goals remain constant over very extended periods of time, while strategic objectives are likely to change, in some cases rapidly and frequently. In many cases it can be argued that the official goals do little more than define the nature of the organization in the most general of terms or delimit the legitimate area of activity of the organization.

The operating or operational goals of an organization can normally only be deduced from the decision-making outcomes of key actors, normally senior management. For this reason they often bear a close resemblance to strategic objectives, but may have no separate existence from them.

Missions and mission statements

Over recent years it has become increasingly common for organizations to define their mission and issue mission statements encapsulating the aspirations of the organization or its senior management. Such mission statements usually relate to the official goals of the organization but regularly encompass a selection of means, as well as these goals, and are typically designed to be a public statement for employees and others of some of the key policies of the organizations. It has to be noted that mission statements often have a strong public relations element and rarely relate in any direct way to strategic objectives. Also, mission statements are normally designed to have a lengthy life and do not, therefore, change as frequently as strategic objectives.

Johnson and Scholes (1993) suggest that the characteristics of missions and mission statements are that they are general, visionary and central, and overriding. They also suggest that they are often unwritten. This latter char-

acteristic is substantially less true than it used to be with the increasing numbers of organizations, of all types, defining their mission statements for public promulgation. Coupled to this, they are increasingly publicized in written form to a variety of audiences.

Strategic directions

Many senior managements have opted to make statements of strategic directions for their organization rather than publicly define strategic objectives. As the nomenclature suggests, strategic directions define the way in which the organization is intended to progress and develop but do not define specific time scales or targets. As such, they provide a way of laying out the bare bones or driving forces of strategy without the attendant problems of giving clear hostages to fortune which may alienate employees and other stakeholders by their apparent difficulty, or after the event by giving a clear indication of failures to accomplish objectives. Although they may be altered relatively frequently, they have the virtue of providing guidance to operational decision making (see DECISION MAKING) and a vision for employees of a relatively precise nature.

Strategic objectives

Not all organizations establish strategic objectives, even where they have a fairly well-articulated strategy (see STRATEGIC CHOICE; STRATEGY AND RATIONALITY). To be meaningful, strategic objectives must be capable of definition against a particular time scale and post hoc assessment as to whether they have been achieved or not. One reason why strategic objectives may not be set is to avoid the possibility of failure. Very often the failure to set such objectives is a consequence of the assessment of the level of uncertainty surrounding the organization's activities in the future and therefore the difficulty of establishing such precision.

It can be seen that the setting of organizational goals, missions, strategic directions and strategic objectives involves a variety of decision-making processes normally dominated by senior management. However, the extent to which other employees and other stake-holders are involved can be very variable. The publication and/or advertisement of goals, mission statements, strategic directions and strategic objectives serves a number of purposes for an organization, but may have associated with it certain potential problems particularly in a politically sensitive or highly competitive environment. Although it has become increasingly common for strategic plans to be published, many organizations choose to keep them relatively secret in order to avoid providing hostages to fortune or information to competitors or potentially hostile stake-holders. In some cases the publication of strategic objectives and/or detailed strategic plans may be helpful in assisting in their accomplishment in that they provide a clear way forward for employees and others and may provide a source of employee commitment and motivation. However, there is a risk that in certain circumstances, the very publication of strategic plans and objectives may make their accomplishment more difficult. In any case, it is difficult to divorce the establishment of strategic objectives from the development of strategy itself, and in this sense it seems that any concept of strategy must involve a consideration of ends as well as means.

The second point of disagreement between Andrews' position and that of Ansoff, noted by Hofer and Schendel, relates to the issue concerning whether the means of achieving organizational aims or goals can be analytically subdivided into components or dimensions. Andrews argued against this. On the other hand, Ansoff and many later writers have suggested a number of main components of strategy. Ansoff divided strategy into four components. The first of these he referred to as 'product/market scope', by which he meant the delineation of the variety of products a firm makes and the markets into which it sells. The second component was the 'growth vector', indicating the intended or planned future changes in the scope of the organization's activities. Third, he suggested the concept of 'competitive advantage', referring to those aspects of the product or marketing approach which particularly enhanced the firm's competitive position relative to its main competitors or the market generally. Finally, Ansoff

suggested the notion of 'synergy', relating to the extent to which the firm's activities taken together are potentially stronger and more competitive than the sum of the parts. Hofer and Schendel themselves suggested an approach which is relatively close to Ansoff's position on this issue, also subdividing the concept of strategy into four components. Of these, three, namely scope or domain, competitive advantage and synergy, are the same or similar to those components identified by Ansoff. Their fourth component, resource deployment, is rather different.

The third point of divergence between the conceptualizations of strategy developed by Andrews and Ansoff might be regarded as the processual equivalent of the first divergence they note. This they described as 'the question whether the goal setting is part of the strategy formulation process or whether it is a separate process' (Hofer and Schendel 1978: 17). As with the first point of difference, the issue is probably not of great consequence in one sense, although it is hard to divorce fully the processes of setting goals or strategic objectives from the process of developing a notion of the means by which they are to be accomplished. Clearly the setting of official or charter goals is often significantly divorced from the process of establishing strategy and strategic objectives. However, as has been noted above, official goals only set the broadest constraints on strategy, they do not determine it.

On the basis of this discussion, it can be suggested that the strategy of an organization may be regarded as the more or less planned collective predisposition of senior management to make particular decisions regarding the task of the organization and its relationships with its environment. Some organizations have a highly formalized procedure for the formulation of strategy, whereas others leave this somewhat vague. At one extreme, organizations may have a clearly documented and publicized strategy which will tend to guide operational decision making in a close and well-defined manner. At the other extreme there is little strategic guidance for individual operational decisions, which may be taken on a largely ad hoc basis with little consistency in overall direction.

Levels of strategy

Conceptually, it is possible to distinguish between corporate strategy, business strategy and functional area strategy. In the small firm there will be little, if any, difference between these different concepts. However, in the large multinational, multiproduct company or other organization the differences may be significant and correspond to clearly defined strategic levels, which in turn are likely to relate to hierarchical levels within the overall structure of the organization.

Clearly, it is possible for the management of any organizational system or sub-system to develop its own strategy. Hence, when one considers corporate strategy one is referring to a strategy developed by and for the overall or complete organization. Business strategies refer to particular identifiable businesses where business is defined in terms of a particular product-market arena. In some organizations there is only one business, whereas in others there may be multiple businesses. In this latter case the corporate strategy must be more than an amalgam of the different business strategies but must also establish the interrelation between them and possibly the different levels of priority which they are accorded. In some organizational systems different businesses are conducted by different business units which are clearly differentiated within the structure of the organization. In others this is not the case and either there is no differentiation into business units or product-market groups, or the structural differentiation is less finely tuned than the strategic differentiation of businesses. Equally, strategies may be developed to cover particular functional areas. Again these may correspond to structurally differentiated units within the organization or not, as the case may be.

There is also a processual element to these distinctions. In one approach the development of business strategies or functional area strategies may be largely or solely a product of the managers' governing those particular businesses or functional areas. At the other extreme, the organization may determine centrally the strategy for each of its different businesses or functional areas with, or without, consultation with those with direct managerial responsibility for them.

It can be seen, therefore, that in the large multi-business organization there may well be a series of strategies nested within the overall corporate strategy, which may directly correspond to structural differentiations or not. Most commonly, the reality of strategy formulation and implementation depends on the structure of the organization in question and particularly on the extent to which the component parts are differentiated. Some indication of the variety may be illustrated by comparing two hypothetical examples. In one company, each business area may be the responsibility of a separate division which has significant devolved power to conduct the business subject only to central control in terms of return on investment. Under such a system, the strategy for each business is almost exclusively the responsibility of divisional management, and corporate strategy relates to the approach to the allocation of resources between divisions and little more. In the second company the central administration may develop strategies for carrying out each of the businesses, and the divisions would only have responsibility for implementing the strategies so formulated. In the first company, business strategies are separated to a considerable extent from corporate strategy, while in the second they are clearly components of an overall corporate strategy. This suggests that organizational design must itself be regarded as a component of strategy, created as a consequence of strategic decision making. In other words, structure cannot just be seen as one of the factors which will affect strategy, but as part of the same concept.

Generic strategies

Up to the present, attention has been given to considerations of the different components or dimensions of strategy. An alternative approach is to develop a typology or classification of strategies or the identification of generic strategies. Although earlier writers had discussed possible typologies of strategies, it was the publication of a book on competitive strategy by Michael Porter (1980) which first suggested the clear importance of this approach to the study and execution of strategies. Porter, coming from a theoretical position strongly influenced by economics, argued that there were only three fundamental ways in which firms could achieve a sustainable competitive advantage. The first of these is a cost-leadership strategy, where a firm seeks to reduce its costs such that it may underprice its competitors. The second is a differentiation strategy, where a firm seeks to be unique in some way which is valued by buyers and may be associated with the ability to charge a premium price. The third strategy Porter defined as a focus strategy, where a firm selects a segment or group of segments in an industry which it may dominate to the exclusion of others. He argued that such a strategy could be based on cost advantage or strong differentiation.

Since Porter's work there has been considerable debate about his specific ideas and also about the extent to which other generic strategies may be possible. Mintzberg (1988) (see MINTZBERG, H.) identified five groups of generic strategies relating to locating the core business, distinguishing the core business, elaborating the core business, extending the core business and reconceiving the core business. Clearly this latter approach is based on a notion of organizations which have a clearly defined core business from which any other business interests emanate or to which other businesses are related. In reality this approach may not correspond to the reality of strategy in businesses which clearly have a variety of equally important businesses, such as Unilever. Nevertheless it does suggest a logical approach to the strategic consideration of the relationship between businesses which is almost certainly applicable to the majority of the companies. It clearly relates well to the prescription advanced by Peters and Waterman (1982) on the basis of their study of excellent companies in the USA which suggests that companies should stick to businesses they know well and in which their senior management has competence (see PETERS, T.J.).

Overall picture

It is clear from the foregoing discussion and the large variety of literature written on the topic of strategy that there is no clear logic that has so far been advanced to a consideration of strategy in organizations. Definitions of strategy are many and various and are probably of little help, at this stage, in deciding the way forward for a theoretical understanding of strategy or for practical strategy-making in organizations. As Chandler (1962) suggested in the introduction to his famous book on strategy and structure, 'strategic decisions are concerned with the long term health of the enterprise'. As such they may clearly take a wide variety of forms covering a wide variety of components or be developed into a logically consistent generic strategy. The nature and variety of those components or the logic of the generic strategy can be almost infinitively variable.

None the less, the notion of strategy is of considerable value in alerting commentators and managers alike to the need for organizations to develop a position relative to their particular environment which guides their decision making and operations in a consistent manner.

4 Theoretical aspects

As has been indicated above, the study of strategy has suffered from a lack of any clear theoretical perspective. To be fair, it is possibly more correct to say there has been a lack of any overarching or integrating theoretical perspective. Indeed, in much of the writing on strategy it has been very unclear as to the direction from which such a theoretical perspective might come. Perhaps the most obvious partial exception to this is the work of Michael Porter (1980), which has been largely derived from extensions of economic theory. It must be noted that Porter defined strategy in a way which limits his attention to what most would regard as a subset of the issues, particularly those relating to diversification and competitive advantage. It can also be argued that some of Porter's conclusions, particularly those relating to generic strategies, may in some respects be simplistic. However, despite these reservations and criticisms which have been widely made since Porter's work was published, it none the less remains true that his work is perhaps the closest yet to a theoretical approach to the concept of strategy and the development of strategies. It must also be noted that although his work tends to have a bias towards issues emanating from the market in which firms sell their products or services, he has covered a wider range of other issues in his writings concerning strategy than many writers. Perhaps the greatest criticism of Porter's work has stemmed from his particular argument relating to generic strategies and particularly his suggestion that there were only three strategies which would achieve sustainable competitive advantage. Perhaps such criticisms of these conclusions may have detracted from a more balanced appreciation of Porter's overall theoretical contribution to the development of the study of strategy.

Mansfield (1986) suggested that an ecological theoretical perspective might have merit in providing an overall basis within which theories of strategy could be developed. In particular he attempted to use his ecological perspective to understand the linkage between strategy and structure. It is worth noting that he also suggested a number of generic strategies, although he did not use the term. His suggestion was that organizations might choose between competitive, cooperative, innovative and retrenchment strategies. Unfortunately his work did not sufficiently examine the full complexities of strategies and the strategy formulation process in the modern industrial firm.

Most other theoretical approaches to the study of strategy have tended to import theoretical ideas from other disciplines or functional areas into the study of strategy in a partial way in order to examine some particular aspect of strategy or implications of strategic decision making. Without doubt such contributions have been very useful. However, until they can be in some sense integrated, their contribution does not necessarily help clarify the overall concept of strategy or help us to design a theoretical model which would assist in the development and implementation of particular strategies in particular firms. Given the notion of strategy as the integrating influence in an organization, it must almost certainly be true that an integrated theory of strategy must include elements from such diverse social sciences as economics, sociology, psychology and political science. It is also virtually certain that it must include elements from the theories developed within the quasi sub-disciplines of management relating to the different functional areas of the typical enterprise, such as marketing, production, personnel, finance, purchasing, and research and development.

It may well be that the difficulties in developing theories relating to the concept of strategy stem from a failure to have a clear definition of the concept in the first place. However, it would be completely wrong to conclude from the various shortcomings of theoretical approaches to this area that there is no relevant theory or knowledge which helps our understanding of the processes and can help practitioners in carrying them out. Our knowledge of the subject has increased enormously in the last thirty years and it would not be unreasonable to predict that an additional thirty years' progress at that rate would create a very much more sophisticated theoretical perspective and knowledge base to guide both researchers and practitioners.

5 Practical applications

Reading a wide variety of textbooks and casebooks on strategy would without doubt convince the normal reader that the study of strategy has enormous practical applications. However, it is rather less obvious that the conceptualization of strategy and theories of strategy will generally assist in the practice of management or, more specifically, of strategic management. For those who are capable of learning by example, the quantity, quality and range of case studies provide a valuable aid to managers confronted with a wide variety of issues. More theoretical approaches to the concept of strategy, and its formulation and implementation, may be of considerable use to those who read them with care both as a guide to what can be done and as a warning against some of the suggested panaceas designed to solve management's problems in the strategic area.

In concluding a consideration of practical applications of the concept of strategy it must be necessary to state that on the basis of the empirical research conducted in this area almost all propositions relating to strategy are problematic. It is not obvious from the research evidence that the formulation of strategy is necessarily helpful or that any of the various processes that contribute to the formulation of the strategy are guaranteed to assist. These cautionary remarks are made because the evidence is insufficient, rather than because it is compellingly negative. However, this is clearly an area where caution might well be advocated in the interpretation of research conclusions and even more so of prescriptive writings.

6 Future development and conclusions

The study of strategy has a fairly obvious and relatively close link to the practice of strategy. This makes it particularly difficult to see what directions research will take. However, it is clear that there is a high rate of research activity in this area at the present time and there are no signs that it will slow down in the future. Clearly, given the potentially integrative nature of the concept of strategy, its future development will depend greatly on developments in almost every area covered by this encyclopedia.

At the present time, the beginning of the twenty-first century, strategy and strategic plans seem to be highly fashionable in most parts of the world. It seems likely that a more cynical approach may begin to be adopted as a reaction to the present enthusiasm. If such a development occurred, it would in all probability lead to a more critical variety of research being conducted and possibly the creation of a more theoretical and rigorous approach to the study and application of strategy.

ROGER MANSFIELD
CARDIFF BUSINESS SCHOOL

Further reading

(References cited in the text marked *)

* Andrews, K. (1965) *Business Policy: Tests and Cases*, Homewood, IL: Irwin. (A pioneering work setting out an approach to strategy in business firms, illustrated with cases.)
* Ansoff, I. (1965) *Corporate Strategy*, Harmondsworth: Penguin. (Another of the pioneering works in the field setting out a conceptual approach to corporate strategy.)
* Ansoff, I. (1969) *Business Strategy*, Harmondsworth: Penguin. (A further development of Ansoff's ideas on business strategy.)
* Chandler, A. (1962) *Strategy and Structure*, Cambridge, MA: MIT Press. (A starting point for modern thinking on strategy based on a study of the fifty largest corporations in the USA.)
* Hickson, D.J., Butler, R.J., Grey, D., Mallory, G.R. and Wilson, D.C. (1986) *Top Decisions*, Oxford: Blackwell. (An empirical study of strategic decision making in a large number of organizations.)
* Hofer, C.W. and Schendel, D. (1978) *Strategy Formulation: Analytical Concepts*, St Paul, MN: West Publishing Co. (A strongly analytical approach to the concept of strategy and its application.)
* Johnson, G. and Scholes, K. (1993) *Exploring Corporate Strategy*, 3rd edn, London: Prentice Hall. (A textbook on strategy which includes some original ideas on the topic.)
* Lindblom, C.E. (1959) 'The science of muddling through', *Public Administrative Review* 19 (1): 79–88. (An important article casting doubt on the rational approaches to strategy formulation.)
* Mansfield, R. (1986) *Company Strategy and Organizational Design*, London: Croom Helm. (An attempt to develop an ecological framework for the analysis of strategy and structure.)
* Mintzberg, H. (1987) 'Five Ps for strategy', *California Management Review* 30 (1): 44–53. (A consideration of strategy as plan, ploy, pattern, position and perspective.)
* Mintzberg, H. (1988) 'Generic strategies: towards a comprehensive framework', in R. Lamb (ed.), *Advances in Strategic Management*, vol. 5, Greenwich, CT: JAI Press. (An analysis of generic strategies based on the concept of the core business.)
* Perrow, C. (1961) 'The analysis of goals in complex organizations', *American Sociological Review* 26 (4): 854–66. (A sociological analysis of the concept of goals in organizations.)
* Peters, T.J. and Waterman, R.H. (1982) *In Search of Excellence*, New York: Harper & Row. (A prescriptive book on corporate management based on studies of successful US companies.)
* Porter, M. (1980) *Competitive Strategy*, New York: Free Press. (An analytical but prescriptive book on strategy based on the development of economic theory.)
* Simon, H. (1949) *Administrative Behaviour*, New York: Free Press. (An early work of a strongly analytical type on management and administration.)

See also: ANSOFF, H.I.; CHANDLER, A.D.;
MINTZBERG, H.; PORTER, M.E.; STRATEGIC
CHOICE; STRATEGIC COMPETENCE; STRATE-
GIC MARKETING PLANNING; STRATEGIC
TURNAROUND; STRATEGY, IMPLEMENTA-
TION OF; STRATEGY AND BUYER–SUPPLIER
RELATIONSHIPS; STRATEGY AND INTERNAL
MARKETING; STRATEGY MAKING, POLITICS
OF; STRATEGY AND TECHNOLOGICAL DE-
VELOPMENT

Strategy, implementation of

Overview

This entry reviews strategy implementation in the context of strategy formulation, strategic planning systems, problems of organization change and strategic evaluation and control systems. It is argued that traditional approaches to implementation contribute to a damaging dichotomy between strategy formulation and implementation. In turn, that dichotomy has many implications for managerial motivation, the effectiveness of the strategy formulation process and subsequent implementation problems in organizations.

Implementation barriers are discussed in terms of a strategic gap analysis technique. In addition, common implementation issues are related to a typology of approaches for overcoming resistance to change in an organization and developing required management execution skills. These approaches may be useful in considering how to solve implementation problems which have been identified. The entry concludes with a broader agenda of process issues relevant to avoiding the barriers arising from the strategy 'formulation–implementation dichotomy' including participation, developing strategic understanding in the organization, identifying champions and leaders, shaping the strategy process, moving towards the 'learning organization', the use of liaison units, and the development of career paths and the design of management development programmes to enhance implementation capabilities. Lastly, a force field analogy is used to provide a practical management agenda and structure for improving strategy implementation.

1   Introduction

It is now some years since Bernard Taylor wrote about corporate planning and the 'strategy that stays on paper' and noted that 'The most important New Frontier is *implementation*' (Taylor 1986). Yet until the 1970s, the term 'implementation' and its related issues were hardly part of the standard vocabulary of the analytical managerial disciplines, let alone part of the research agenda they addressed. Since then, there have been many theoretical and prescriptive contributions to the debate about strategy implementation, though less has been achieved in the way of systematic conclusions which can be placed before managers as the basis for action (see STRATEGY, CONCEPT OF).

At its simplest, the implementation problem has been described as 'the all too frequent failure to create change after seemingly viable plans have been developed' (Nutt 1983: 600). Such views lead to the common theoretical perspective that implementation involves actors, intents and 'a procedure directed by a manager to install planned change in an organization' (Nutt 1986: 233). While providing a useful starting point, there are substantial problems with this view of implementation as part of a rational, logical and sequential flow of missions, goals, strategies and tactics which are then implemented (see Figure 1 below).

In more practical terms, the managerial view of implementation is commonly stated as 'making strategy work' by evaluating what is required to achieve strategic goals in a specific organizational environment (Cespedes

1991; Piercy 1985, 1992). This environment is one where individuals and groups 'use gesture, delay, and obstruction to contain or block change attempts they find threatening or merely disagreeable' (Nutt 1986: 230).

2 Traditional approaches to implementation

The traditional approach to implementation characteristically treats it as an activity which follows on from strategy formulation, and emphasizes organization design and the manipulation of systems and structures around strategic goals (Bourgeois and Brodwin 1984). In this approach, managers ultimately rely on their authority to adjust the organization's structural framework as a means of enacting strategic decisions. In turn, this emphasis on structure and control systems follows from the assumption that, when clearly articulated, strategic goals will be viewed as desirable and widely supported in the organization (see ORGANIZATION BEHAVIOUR). Conventional approaches to implementation thus focus on the following types of issues:

1 Strategy and structure. Much work has focused on the 'fit' between organizational structure and strategic choices. At the simplest level, this view holds that 'strategy drives structure'; new strategic directions require the development of new structures and administrative mechanisms. There is, however, a danger of underestimating the effect on those strategic choices of the pressure towards the status quo and the preferences represented by existing organizational frameworks. As Corey and Star point out:

> It must be recognized, as well, that the direction of strategy is certainly a function, in part, of the kind of organization which produces it and the balance of power within the structure. Today's organization is an important influence in molding tomorrow's strategy which, in turn, shapes tomorrow's organization.
>
> (Corey and Star 1971: 51)

2 Budgeting and resource allocation. Similarly, budgeting and resource allocation decisions represent the distribution of the people and money needed to put strategies into effect, and also provide signals about the strategic direction chosen and the priorities for managers. However, this view also cautions us to bear in mind that this form of communication is fraught with political risk and the planning intents of resource allocators may be ignored or subverted (Piercy 1987) (see CAPITAL, COST OF).

3 Executive style and leadership (see LEADERSHIP). Another perspective frequently associated with implementation is the matching of management style with the strategy to be pursued, both in a technical sense and in terms of requisite 'vision' and leadership in the desired direction.

4 Goals, missions and control systems. Other issues conventionally considered are the translation of strategies into statements of organizational goals and missions as a way of communicating requirements, though it has been noted that this is problematic and frequently poorly done in practice (Piercy 1992; Piercy and Morgan 1994) (see STRATEGIC CHOICE). Moreover, the ever tighter controls required to monitor progress are themselves an implementation barrier in many circumstances.

Limitations of traditional approaches to implementation

Perhaps the most fundamental underlying assumption behind such conventional approaches is that strategic decisions are well understood and widely agreed upon within the organization. Evidence suggests that this is frequently – indeed, usually – not true. As well as the often divergent preferences of politically powerful players for alternative strategic directions or the status quo, managers are frequently not trained or prepared for the execution of plans, being generally 'strategy-sophisticated and implementation-bound' (Bonoma 1985: 17).

For such reasons as these, there has been some movement towards analysing implementation in terms of process within organizations, rather than (or in addition to) constituting a matter of structural realignment and administrative direction. This in turn reveals a fundamental problem in the separation of implementation issues from the process of formulating strategies: the formulation–implementation dichotomy.

3 The strategy formulation–implementation dichotomy

Many of the difficulties associated with implementation in practice appear to arise not simply because of practical problems in management action, but because conventional approaches to the formulation of strategies have taken the view that strategy development and implementation are distinct and sequential activities. Where it exists, this dichotomy is fraught with dangers.

First, this separation ignores (or at least underestimates) the interaction between the process of strategy formulation and an organization's unique implementation capabilities and constraints, and reduces the ability of an organization to establish a strategy which draws on its core competencies, that is, what it is best at in a particular market or industry (Hamel and Prahalad 1989). The dichotomy also risks divorcing the plans produced from the changing realities of the inner workings of the organization, as well as encouraging the establishment of 'professional planners' and the risk of the consequent 'uncoupling' of strategy from operating plans (Piercy 1992; Hobbs and Heaney 1977).

In addition, the traditional approach may rely too heavily on the rational–analytical belief that strategies are direct and are chosen by top management, rather than being emergent and growing from the experiences and preferences of the organization and its members (Mintzberg 1987; Hart 1992). Indeed, this view implicitly assumes that strategies are problematic and execution is not, which is the reverse of much managerial experience: knowing what to do is relatively easy compared to actually doing it (see MINTZBERG, H.).

Further, a dichotomized view of strategy formulation and implementation takes no account of the need for effective strategies to span internal boundaries between functional and organizational interest groups (see INTER-

EST GROUPS). It risks also underestimating the significance of the political and negotiating infrastructure within the organization, and its impact on the process of gaining the commitment of organizational members at all levels. Further, the conventional approach largely ignores the potential for middle management 'counter-implementation' efforts (Guth and MacMillan 1986). Indeed, separating formation and implementation can generate increasing opportunity costs for firms, as 'time-based' strategies place a premium on a firm's ability to implement plans more quickly than in previous stages of competition; for similar reasons the formulation–implementation dichotomy can prevent a firm from realizing important first-mover or pioneer advantages as product life cycles become shorter (Cespedes 1994; von Braun 1990).

Finally, it has been suggested that the inherent advantage of any given strategy itself is now subject to a shorter 'window of opportunity', as global competition, rapid diffusion of technology and information systems make imitation of successful strategies easier and quicker (Hamel and Prahalad 1989). This in turn means that competitive advantage is increasingly a function of a firm's ability to execute effectively a succession of appropriate but increasingly short-lived strategic initiatives (see INFORMATION TECHNOLOGY).

The conclusions suggested by these arguments seem to be threefold. First, there is a need to pay proactive attention to the process of how strategy formulation and implementation are linked within the organization. Second, strategy implementation needs to be viewed in the broader context of organizational change and the sources of potential resistance to change from different parts of the organization. Third, the management of implementation may involve quite different mixes of skills and abilities from the formulation of plans and strategies, which has implications for training and development, task allocation and the linking of strategy formulation and implementation.

Figure 1 summarizes the main points underpinning this argument. In the conventional view of strategic decision making, issues are handled sequentially and implementation is concerned with putting prior decisions into

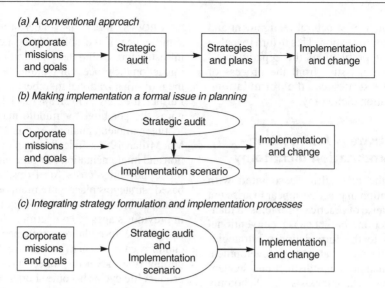

Figure 1 The strategy formulation–implementation dichotomy

effect. The second model in Figure 1 is where implementation is at least made a formal issue in planning; that is, when strategies are formulated, attention is given to analysing their implementation requirements and barriers. The third model is one where there is integration between the processes of strategy formulation and implementation.

4   Identifying the sources of implementation problems

Before considering the development of implementation strategies and tactics, the types and sources of execution problems faced in a particular situation need to be made clear. A useful approach is provided by strategic gap analysis, the underlying principle of which is shown in Figure 2. The goal is to contrast 'intended' with 'realized' strategies (Mintzberg 1988), and to isolate the gaps between them. A company example can be found in Piercy (1994).

The procedure involves four stages. First, it is necessary to identify the strategy in question and its parameters (such as which parts of the organization and which markets are involved) and summarize that strategy in a few words. Next, the strategy must be translated into its operational requirements, or what must be achieved in operational terms for this

strategy to be real and effective; in other words, the strategic intent.

Third, the strategic reality (what the firm has actually achieved) must be evaluated with the input of significant individuals and groups inside (and possibly outside) the organization. Fourth, it is then possible to identify and interpret the strategic gaps (the differences between strategic intent and strategic reality), in order to uncover what insights they may reveal into the implementation barriers inherent in this strategy.

The gaps identified through this analysis are likely to vary considerably in their seriousness, source and cause, suggesting that appropriate managerial responses may be diverse. Initially, strategic gaps that are identified may include the inability of key members of top

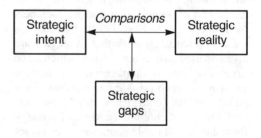

Figure 2 Strategic gap analysis
Source: Adapted from Piercy (1992: 120)

management to identify with or articulate clearly their strategy, or the inability of managers in the organization to recognize that the strategic intent may reflect problems of internal communications or, more covertly, the rejection via deliberate 'misunderstanding' of that strategy. Indeed, the inability of planners or top management to translate their strategy into operational requirements may reflect poor strategic thinking, which in turn adversely affects implementation.

It may be that the operational requirements for the strategy are simply unattainable for reasons of capabilities, resources, external constraints or the lack of relevant execution skills. However, strategic gaps may also exist because there are too many internal barriers and obstacles, reflecting not simply overt issues like skills and resource shortages or inappropriate structures and procedures, but also more covert issues like resistance to change and political manoeuvring. For example, strategic gaps may exist because line managers and operatives do not accept the validity of the strategic intent. Figure 3 suggests some basic questions to be addressed in considering such problems. However, the usefulness of this analysis and its interpretation may be enhanced by a more detailed examination of the underlying reasons for implementation barriers.

5 Understanding the sources of strategy implementation problems

As noted above, some implementation barriers are relatively overt and identifiable. However, it is often necessary to pursue more covert issues that help explain why a strategy that apparently 'fits' the organization's capabilities and is coherent and complete may still fail in implementation.

One view is that organizations, and the units within them, differ systematically in two implementation-related characteristics: the perception that there is a strategic problem and consensus about the nature of that problem, and a willingness and capability to change (Piercy 1992). This observation underpins the model in Figure 4, which suggests that organizational responses may fall into one of four categories:

1 receptive (there is consensus about the problems that have to be solved and a willingness and capability for change);
2 immobile (there is no real perception of significant problems to be solved, though there are no particular barriers to change as such);
3 recalcitrant (there is agreement that there are strategic problems that require change, but no willingness or ability to change);

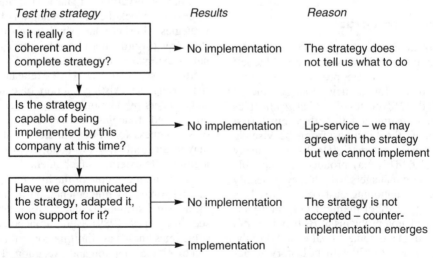

Figure 3 Testing strategies
Source: Piercy (1992: 332)

Strategic problem
perception/consensus

		High	Low
Willingness/ capability to change	High	I Receptive	II Immobile
	Low	III Recalcitrant	IV Intractable

Figure 4 Strategic problems and change
Source: Adapted from Piercy (1992: 326)

4 intractable (there is neither perception of strategic problems, nor the ability to change).

It is useful for managers to identify where their business units fall within this model, and then to compare their views with others in the organization. There are many reasons which may explain a wide divergence in perceptions of the strategic 'imperatives' and organizational 'reality' facing a firm. Such issues can be organized for discussion into the following categories: organizational inertia, organizational myopia, active resistance to change in the organization, political interests in the organization, designed error in the organization, and information flows, measurement systems and time horizons (see BUSINESS ECONOMICS).

Organizational inertia

Organizational history provides an implementation barrier in so far as the residue left from previous strategies provides an inappropriate context for the new strategy, since it may be that 'advocates of bold new strategies have not recognized that they must first "uncouple" the functions from the viselike grip of past strategies' (Hobbs and Heany 1977: 119). This may produce incompatible demands on managers, which they generally resolve by continuing past behaviours. In a similar way, Wernham (1984) analyses implementation problems at British Telecom in terms of the 'organizational validity' of the strategy, that is, its 'fit' with the history of success or failure of similar developments in the past.

A related factor concerns the impact of 'organizational routines' (Nelson and Winter 1982) or functional 'thought worlds' (Dougherty 1992) on the implementation of strategic initiatives. Different units within the same firm (such as marketing, manufacturing, sales or service) typically adopt routines or standard operating procedures that accelerate the performance of their own subset of strategy implementation responsibilities. Provided these routines are coherently synchronized, and the use of those procedures with the highest potential for customer satisfaction is supported, this specialization is advantageous; but in most busy organizations, the routines themselves soon are treated as fixed. The result can be a series of 'competency traps' (Levitt and March 1988) in which each organizational unit is unwittingly executing tactics that are incompatible with the tactics of other units in the firm and often relevant only to a previous stage of product–market competition. Further, each unit's established procedures can keep the firm from gaining valuable experience with new procedures; other alignments may be appropriate to changing market conditions and more necessary for effective implementation, but 'competency' is associated with established organizational routines and implementation procedures. Cespedes (1993a) provides examples from firms in contemporary consumer goods industries.

Other observations emphasize the 'inertial forces' that block the implementation of new strategies (Ginsberg and Abrahamson 1991). Pressures towards inertia can be either internal or external to the organization. External inertial forces are reflected in the reluctance to risk losing the existing support of external stakeholders by adopting new, different and unexpected strategies. In this sense, the lack of willingness to implement new strategies may result from efforts to continue to appear legitimate to external stakeholders.

A common example of the impact of such inertial forces on implementation occurs in the area of distribution strategy (for examples see Corey et al. 1989). Here, a phenomenon sometimes known as 'limiting commitments' can block the adoption and execution of new channel arrangements in the face of market changes. When a market is entered or a new product introduced, elements of a firm's distribution strategy tend to cohere around the particular market circumstances and strategic goals held at the time. Further, both the supplier and resellers must make mutual commitments of capital, time and other resources in order to establish the original distribution arrangements. As markets evolve, buyer criteria change and new channel strategies are typically required; but each dimension of the existing arrangement tends to cement established patterns, making it difficult for the supplier to alter its channel strategy.

In practice, management often seeks to invest in existing channels, as the short-term incremental cost of utilizing existing arrangements is often lower than the start-up costs of a new channel. In addition, current distribution arrangements have often been in place for years and may account for a large share of company or divisional revenues and profits. Hence, while the firm may maximize long-term profits from adopting a different distribution strategy, individual profit centre managers will see their performance decline in the short term and may thus block or resist the implementation of the new strategy.

More attention has been devoted to inertial forces which are internal to the organization. These can be summarized as follows:

1 organizational myths and ideologies tend to endure and have the effect of reinforcing past behaviour and encouraging its extension into the future;
2 programmes, goals and expectations grow up around the preferences and skills of the powerful in the organization, and are likely to favour the continuation of those preferences and skills in the future;
3 to change strategic direction may involve the admission of failure and the weakening of a political base for some managers, as well as undermining the position of employees.

In short, it is necessary to examine the past and the pressures which may encourage the organization and its people to favour the status quo.

Organizational myopia

Another reason for implementation problems lies in the development of what Hobbs and Heany (1977) called 'faulty perspectives', where the perspectives of individual departments and specialists in the organization foster perceptions which are quite different from the broader view of the environment adopted in planning strategies. This may be manifested as a dogged belief by many in the organization that strategic planning is not 'practical' but is just the head office 'field of dreams', to which they feel little commitment or loyalty.

Ginsberg and Abrahamson (1991) link such problems to the 'cognitive biases' of individuals and groups (see COGNITION). These include such factors as the tendency among managers to seek out and give credibility only to information that confirms their preconceptions, and the parallel tendency to discount, criticize or ignore information that conflicts with those preconceptions. At the level of the group, such biases and resistance are illustrated by the Janis (1972) study of 'group think', where group processes were observed to result in self-validating pressures towards conformity and narrow group responses to critical external issues. Such managerial biases have been widely observed, and linked to a highly imperfect and biased process of 'environmental enactment' (Weick 1969).

Tendencies such as those described here may be approached through techniques of strategic issue identification and improved environmental scanning rather than more direct managerial intervention. However, it is also wise to bear in mind the possibility that when implementation is blocked by those who have made a different assessment of the situation being faced, those persons may be right, even though 'this likelihood is not obvious to some managers who assume that resistance is always bad and therefore always fight it' (Kotter and Schlesinger 1979: 113).

Active resistance to change in the organization

Resistance to change by individuals and groups in organizations is a well-documented and analysed topic, a useful summary of which is provided by Stanislao and Stanislao (1983). The authors distinguish between resistance to change by those with the authority to accept or reject an innovation, and resistance by the individual who has no formal voice in the acceptance or rejection decision. Their analysis identifies the following sources of change resistance by those having veto power:

1 inertia, or preference for the status quo, even if it is known to be inferior;
2 uncertainty and fear of the unknown;
3 insecurity and fear of failure;
4 ignorance (lack of understanding of the innovation can produce cautiousness, resentment and rejection);
5 obsolescence (changes that make previously highly valued skills obsolete may be resisted);
6 personality, particularly interpersonal conflicts which may influence the implementation of change;
7 'not invented here' (external change agents may be resented and their programmes undermined and resisted);
8 resentment of criticism or implied criticism of past practices;
9 distrust or lack of trust in the proposers of change.

Similarly, Stanislao and Stanislao list the reasons for resistance to change associated with those who have no veto power over the decision:

1 surprise (change which is unexpected, sudden and radical may be resisted because people have no time to evaluate and adjust);
2 lack of information about how the change will affect an individual's position;
3 lack of training, which in turn produces lack of understanding;
4 lack of real understanding, which produces misconceptions and resistance;
5 loss of job status, so that reduced skill requirements and responsibilities produce insecurity for the employee or manager;
6 peer pressure (ingrained work group practices may produce rigidities in individual behaviour);
7 loss of security or threats to job tenure;

8 loss of known work group and changes to social relationships within the workplace;
9 personality conflicts, particularly antagonism and hostility towards the sponsors of change;
10 poor timing.

There is little that is profound or unusual in these lists, or that would not be expected by most managers. However, the success of strategic change is often contingent on whether and how such issues are managed.

Middle management resistance and political behaviour

The use of political power by managers to resolve conflicts of interest is contingent on uncertainty, power differences and disagreement about goals and cause-and-effect relationships. If these contingencies surround a strategy – as they often do – then the use of political force is anticipated. This may be difficult to identify, since political effectiveness involves skills in obscuring the use of power and rationalizing and legitimizing the course of action favoured. Kotter and Schlesinger (1979) evaluate this factor as 'parochial self-interest', involving change avoidance by public conflict or subtler, more covert, behaviour (see POWER; STRATEGY MAKING, POLITICS OF).

Guth and MacMillan (1986) have studied middle management 'self interest' in the context of strategy implementation and suggest that:

> a particular strategy sponsored by general management can have predicted outcomes with low desirability to a substantial number of middle-level managers, and/or can have outcome predictions with which a significant number of middle-level managers do not agree ... This lack of commitment may not result only in passive compliance. Instead it could result in significant 'upward' intervention by the middle managers either during the strategy formulation process, or during the implementation of the strategy.
>
> (Guth and MacMillan 1986: 313–14)

The widely observed resistance of middle management to corporate re-engineering efforts is a current example of this (see Hammer and Champy 1993 for case examples).

Guth and MacMillan state further that this type of middle management intervention may be either active or passive. Active intervention by middle managers to protect their political and vested interests may include: (1) mounting campaigns of 'persuasion' in meetings and in written media against the sponsored strategy; (2) seeking to form alliances and coalitions with other members of the organization who will agree also to oppose the strategy; (3) deliberately taking (or not preventing) ineffective action in implementation, or creating 'roadblocks'; and (4) outright sabotage of the implementation to 'prove' that the strategy was poorly constructed in the first place. Passive intervention by middle managers may involve giving low priority to the implementation of the strategy compared to other activities, or creating delays unnecessarily in order to compromise the quality of the implementation or postpone it beyond the time that it is likely to be effective.

Piercy (1992) provides a list of 'counter-implementation' strategies which may be adopted by organizational members to prevent the implementation of strategies which threaten their own interests in various ways. These include:

1 deflecting goals, or manipulating objectives and goals to avoid change;
2 diverting resources, so that money and people disappear to other projects, never to return to this one;
3 dissipating energies, as hostility and aggression can reduce people's drive for change;
4 delaying decisions, to the point where prospects for implementation are reduced;
5 destroying credibility, by undermining the position of the change sponsors;
6 deflating excitement, or 'taking the fun out of things', to slow implementation down;
7 'depth charge' (if all else fails, outright conflict and attack may work, particularly if unpredicted);

8 defiance (say 'no' as long as you can, and maybe even longer if there is no one who can stop you).

These managerial actions may be the hidden reasons for implementation problems which are apparently explained by other more rational or legitimate reasons. If so, it is important that such behaviour is not simply denied because it is perceived to be 'irrational'. The reality is that such behaviour places major constraints on what management can in fact 'decide' and implement.

Designed error in the organization

Argyris (1985) argues that many implementation failures occur 'by design', which arises because organizations develop routines for implementing strategy which are taken for granted and rarely challenged (see ARGYRIS, C.). Although line management and strategic planners might question how well each side understands the 'real' problems, they avoid the embarrassment and threat associated with discussing these differences; and then cover up that avoidance, reflecting an organizational defensive routine, defined as 'any policy, practice, or action that prevents the people involved from being embarrassed or threatened, and, at the same time, prevents them from learning how to reduce the causes of the embarrassment or threat' (Argyris 1985: 7). Organizational defensive routines are over-protective and anti-learning, and favour the retention of the status quo. Argyris also suggests that people in organizations develop programmed responses to deal with embarrassment and threat, where the rules are: (1) bypass embarrassment and threat wherever possible; (2) act as though you are not bypassing them; (3) do not discuss steps 1 and 2 while they are happening; and (4) do not discuss the undiscussability of the undiscussable.

A more sweeping perspective on designed error in organizations has been suggested by Hannan and Freeman (1989). They postulate an inherent limitation on any one firm's ability to integrate its organizational units and thus effectively implement a chosen strategy. Their argument runs as follows: as integration among internal units occurs, differences between these units diminish and behaviours across each group tend to converge. The result is that the organization exhibits greater reliability in performing its current activities, but the diversity of beliefs and behaviours necessary for further adaptation to market forces is lessened or eliminated. In this view, organizational capabilities are akin to ecological niches, and the forces that permit an organization to thrive in one set of circumstances inhibit its ability to thrive or survive in an altered environment.

Implementation problems resulting from conditions such as those discussed above may be difficult to identify and understand in practice. Nevertheless, they should form part of our understanding of why implementation may be ineffective, and suggest that strategic approaches to the implementation process may involve broader issues of organizational development, not simply tactical responses and formal implementation programmes around particular strategies.

Information flows, measurement systems, and time horizons

Other implementation barriers often reside in the information, measurement and career path infrastructure of firms. In most companies, execution of strategy typically encompasses at least three groups: those who manage the firm's product offerings, those who manage the sales channels and those responsible for customer services of various kinds. In a field study, Cespedes (1993b) found that these units differed in terms of: (1) information priorities and, hence, the types of data tracked by each unit; (2) the role and use of the data that was tracked; and (3) hardware and software systems used to disseminate information within and between these groups. Product managers viewed data about pertinent products and markets (defined as segments across geographical boundaries) as their highest information priorities. Sales managers sought data about geographically defined markets and specific accounts and resellers within those markets. Service managers needed data about both products and accounts, but in different terms from the data categories most salient to product and sales units. Figure 5

summarizes these and other differences that often affect the success and failure of implementation efforts.

Among other things, these differing information flows mean that product, sales and service managers often meet to discuss strategic goals and tactics on a reactive rather than proactive basis. Furthermore, each group tends to arrive at such meetings with ideas based on different data sources and with different assumptions about what is happening in the market. In practice, it is difficult to integrate these perspectives and provide effective implementation responses under such circumstances. Moreover, in most companies, accounting systems track costs and other financial information primarily by product categories rather than customer or channel categories, with the result that there is often a gap between the aggregate data most meaningful to product planning activities and the disaggregated data essential to specific account or region implementation activities.

The organizational units most directly involved in field implementation of strategy also often differ in terms of their measurement systems and time horizons. Sales personnel are most often measured according to sales volume. In the setting of quotas, performance appraisals and incentive pay, the focus of sales metrics in most firms is primarily on sales volume rather than profit contribution or activities and tasks performed. Product management measures exhibit more variance, but profit responsibility or forms of return-on-assets measures are usually more prominent. Customer service metrics also vary, but sales volume is rarely a prominent component while service responsiveness, cost efficiencies and (in recent years) 'customer satisfaction' indices often loom large in service evaluations. These groups share many customer contact activities, but their differing measurement systems can generate conflicts in the implementation of different aspects of joint tasks.

Similarly, these units also differ in terms of their members' time horizons. In consumer goods firms, career paths in brand management have traditionally emphasized frequent rotation among product groups and an 'up or out' promotion philosophy that puts a pre-

Product management	Field sales	Customer service
ROLES AND RESPONSIBILITIES:		
Operate across geographical territories with specific product responsibilities	Operate within geographical territories, with specific account assignments	Operate within geographical territories, with multiple product/ account assignments
TIME HORIZONS DRIVEN BY:		
Product development and introduction cycles Internal planning and budgeting processes	Selling cycles at multiple accounts External buying processes	Product installation/ maintenance cycles Field sevice processes
KEY PERFORMANCE CRITERIA:		
Performance measures based on profit and loss and market share metrics	Measures based primarily on annual, quarterly or monthly sales volume	Measures vary, but typically 'customer satisfaction' and cost efficiencies
INFORMATION FLOWS:		
Data priorities: Aggregate data about products and markets (defined in terms of user segments)	*Data priorities:* Disaggregated data about geographical markets, specific accounts, and resellers	*Data priorities:* Disaggregated data about product usage at accounts
Key data uses: Roles of data makes compatibility with internal planning and budgeting categories a criterion of useful information	*Key data uses:* Roles of data makes compatibility with internal buyers' categories important; 'timely' data as a function of varied selling cycles at assigned accounts	*Key data uses:* Role of data makes compatibility with relevent technical vocabularies a criterion of useful information
Information systems: Often incompatible with sales and service systems	*Information systems:* Often incompatible with product and service systems	*Information systems:* Often incompatible with product and sales systems

Figure 5 Implementation differences between groups
Source: Cespedes (1993b: 29)

mium on individual brand managers' performance during their initial years with the firm. Meanwhile, salespeople at these firms typically stay much longer in a given territory with their assigned accounts. Promotion from sales representative to unit manager to district manager often takes a decade or more and does not entail 'switching' accounts in the same manner that the brand manager switches product assignments. Hence, each group approaches joint activities with different time lines in mind, and each may inhibit implementation efforts because the requisite payoff from the strategy may not mesh with that group's temporal perspective.

Time horizons also differ along another important implementation dimension, namely where each group concentrates in the firm's value chain. Especially in industrial firms, product management usually has product development issues as a key concern and any one product group must often compete with others for the firm's available R&D resources. Such a situation provides an incentive for individual product managers to 'stretch' a proposed product's applicability across multiple customer segments in order to justify budget requests and drive development and production resources in their direction (see Cespedes 1995 for case examples). The most common method for doing so is for product management to use information selectively, for example, crafting segmentation schemes that highlight current or potential product leadership, choosing particular time periods for analysis and projections, or simply focusing on data favourable to product proposals and omitting less favourable data.

Cespedes (1995) uses the term 'hierarchies of attention' to refer to these differences in information flows, measurement systems and time horizons among the groups typically responsible for field implementation of strategic plans. These are differences in what each group takes for granted as part of its daily work versus what it considers as 'nice to have' or discretionary in its allocation of attention and effort. One result in many companies is explicit conflict or confusion in strategy implementation due to implicit disagreements about what constitutes 'success' in performing joint activities. Managers in each group may well agree that success is ultimately defined by 'the customer'. But these hierarchies of attention mean that the groups that are jointly responsible for field implementation and customer satisfaction perceive the customer differently.

6 Implementation tactics and strategies

The brief review above indicates that the sources of implementation problems may vary both in source and seriousness, and it is within this varied context that management and strategic planners must operate. This variation suggests in turn that different types of responses may be most appropriate in developing programmes and processes to address the implementation problems identified in a particular situation. Discussed below are implementation tactics, meeting resistance to change, management execution skills and implementation strategy.

Implementation tactics

Implementation tactics are concerned primarily (though not exclusively) with actions managers take to achieve the strategies they have chosen. In his analysis of planned change, Ansoff (1984) identified four procedures: the entrepreneurial, exploration, control and implementation sub-processes (see ANSOFF, H.I.). From that administrative perspective, it has been noted that:

> implementation can be viewed as a planned change process that lays out steps taken to entice stakeholders to support changes. A coherent set of steps becomes a tactic used by managers to elicit the support, cooperation, or acquiescence needed to ensure compliance with planned changes. Tactics should capture the arranging and maneuvering steps that managers take to deal with social and political issues provoked by change attempts.
>
> (Nutt 1986: 234)

This approach follows the logic of the conventional views outlined earlier. Tactics provide a framework for organizing and focusing implementation approaches such as structural change, incentives and budgeting, rewards and sanctions, leadership selection and delegation. Figure 6 summarizes a number of approaches to classifying implementation tactics and strategies, which differ primarily in their relative emphasis on problem solution as opposed to problem avoidance in implementation.

Nutt (1983) suggests that implementation techniques can be unilateral, manipulative or delegated. *Unilateral tactics* rely on the use of power by the implementor, who announces the change overtly and prescribes the expected behaviour. Typically this starts with an 'official edict' by memorandum, presentation or instruction. If problems ensue, edict is followed by demonstration to show the reluctant that the plan 'works' and that acceptance is required. Further problems are countered by a replacement approach to move or remove those blocking implementation, and then a structural change to place those likely to implement the strategy in question in key positions.

Using *manipulative tactics*, implementation can be viewed as a game (Bardach 1977) or an 'unfreeze–refreeze' process (Schein 1961). The 'freeze' analogy refers to three stages: unfreezing (attempts to reduce the strength of existing patterns of behaviour),

Types of implementation approach (Nutt, 1983)	Implementation process models (Bourgeois and Brodwin, 1984)	Implementation tactics observed (Nutt, 1986)	Tactics to gain commitment (MacMillan, 1978)	Emphasis of approach to implementation
Unilateral Official edict Demonstration Replacement Structural change	**Commander model** How do I formulate the optimum strategy?	**Edict** Orders are given	**Coercion** Use of management sanctions	Solving implementation problems by short-term action
	Change model I have a strategy, now how do I implement it?	**Intervention** Managers are given authority to make changes	**Persuasion** Demonstrate benefits to those affected	↑
Manipulative Games Unfreeze– refreeze	**Collaborative model** How do I involve management to get staff commitment?	**Persuasion** 'Experts' must sell strategies to management	**Inducement** Build in extra payoffs	
	Cultural model How do I involve the whole organization in implementation?		**Obligation** Trade on old favours owed	
Delegative Cooptation Participation	**Crescive model** How do I encourage managers to come forward as champions of sound strategies?	**Participation** Delegation and cooptation		↓ Developing the strategy process to integrate formulation and implementation

Figure 6 Implementation tactics and strategies

changing (introducing the new skills and behaviour required) and refreezing (reinforcing the new patterns). Bardach suggests assessing implementation scenarios which involve six steps:

1. state the plan and its objectives;
2. inventory the affected parties;
3. identify areas of compromise that lower resistance and identify implementing units that are compatible;
4. determine if resistance is likely to stem from low effort games (delay), resource diversion games, objective modification games, evasion games or incomplete adoption;
5. identify the players and the stakes in each likely game, find natural allies and whether they are likely to be supportive of the plan, and measure prospects for success by determining who must be confronted and their power;
6. fix the game by offering incentives to participate that create a manageable coalition supportive of the plan (or its modification).

Delegative tactics aim at coopting those involved in the change by involving them in various ways. In broad terms, unilateral tactics follow the administrative assumptions discussed earlier, manipulative tactics are based on political approaches and delegative tactics are more concerned with process strategy issues.

Bourgeois and Brodwin (1984) have identified five process approaches to strategy implementation:

1. The commander model. This model reflects a normative bias towards centralized direction, using conventional analytical techniques to select strategic direction. The chief executive is a rational actor, and the key question is: 'What is the optimum strategy?' The model works best under conditions where: (1) the CEO wields much power and can command implementation, or where the strategy poses little threat to organizational members, so implementation can be achieved easily; (2) accurate and timely information is

available to make decisions, or the environment is changing slowly to allow good information to be assimilated; (3) the strategist is isolated from personal biases and political pressures which might influence the content of the plan; and (4) there are no motivational problems arising from splitting the firm into 'thinkers and doers'. In spite of the limitations imposed by those conditions, this model persists among consultants and managers because it offers the CEO a strategic insight (even though potentially limited by implementability), it simplifies things for the general manager, it enhances the power of the strategic planner and it fits the rational–analytical paradigm of management 'objectivity' (see LEADERSHIP; MANAGERIAL BEHAVIOUR).

2   The change model. Here, the chief executive is an 'architect' whose major tools are:

* the use of structure and staffing decisions to communicate the organization's new priorities and focus attention on desired areas;
* altered systems for planning, performance measurement, and/or incentive compensation to produce the behaviour required; and
* cultural adaptation techniques to introduce organization-wide changes in behaviour and practices (see ORGANIZATION DEVELOPMENT).

3   The collaborative model. Here the chief executive acts as coordinator and the emphasis is on team building at a senior level in the organization, in different forms. This may overcome the informational problems and cognitive limits of the commander model by involving line management, and may improve commitment through participative decision making. However, this approach may substitute a politically feasible 'negotiated' strategy for an optimal one, with subsequent costs in the marketplace (see GROUPS AND TEAMS).

4   The cultural model. Here the emphasis is on implementing strategy through the infusion of a new corporate culture throughout the organization, with the chief executive cast mainly as 'coach'. This approach comes out of the 'human relations' school of the 1960s and the rejuvenation of those

approaches in interpretations of the Japanese management systems of the 1970s and 1980s. The underlying principle is that, with an organizational ethos in place, the implementation problem is mostly solved, although possibly at the cost of much time in consensus decision making and culture-building activities. This model assumes the availability of: (1) informed and intelligent people throughout the organization; (2) mechanisms for maintaining the focus of the culture on key issues while combating the tendency of strong culture to foster homogeneity, stability, inbreeding and conformity; and (3) time and resources (see ORGANIZATION CULTURE).

5   The crescive model. Here the emphasis is on the process of 'growing' strategy within the organization by drawing on the abilities of managers who run the business to create new strategies for that business. The chief executive functions as premise-setter and judge, and the key question is: 'How do I encourage managers to come forward as champions of sound strategies?' The crescive model emphasizes maintaining the openness of the organization to new information, manipulating systems and structures in very general ways to encourage bottom-up strategy formation, intervening in the logical incrementalist way described by Quinn (1981) and adjusting structure and staffing to minimize problems (for case examples see Kotter 1990).

These process models can be seen as points on an important continuum. At one end of this scale, we are seeking appropriate tactics to drive through a chosen strategy; at the other end, we are seeking to integrate the processes of strategy formulation and strategy implementation (see Figure 1 above). This corresponds to what Wernham (1984) describes in the context of British Telecom's experience as the difference between *solving* the implementation problem once it exists, and *avoiding* the implementation problem in the first place.

More specific to the question of management commitment or motivation, Guth and MacMillan (1986) suggest that there are three primary sources of low managerial commitment to implementing a particular strategy:

low perceived ability to perform successfully in implementing the strategy, low perceived probability that the proposed outcomes will result even if individual performance is effective, and low capacity of the outcome to satisfy individual goals and needs. Guth and MacMillan propose that, in managing implementation, each strategy requires a different approach. First, if the problem is that managers perceive an inability to execute the strategy, this may be countered by: training and development, support resources, and formal and informal encouragement. Second, if the problem is that managers do not believe the strategy will work, approaches should include investigating middle management positions on the strategy in order to understand clearly the basis for disagreement and then use this as a basis for focusing on what strategy is appropriate rather than whose strategy wins, and fully identifying the risks associated with the strategy and making explicit the cause/effect theories in use by different parties in order to achieve 'a more careful consideration of what is the right strategy rather than whose strategy is right' (Guth and MacMillan 1986: 325).

Third, if the problem is that managers perceive that strategy outcomes will not satisfy individual goals, then there are four approaches open to management (MacMillan 1978):

1 inducement (build in additional payoffs to the strategy to win over low commitment managers);
2 persuasion (help managers to perceive payoffs they had not seen before);
3 coercion (use sanctions to change the perceptions of payoffs and risks in the implementation of the strategy);
4 obligation (connect implementation of the strategy to past favours owed).

Meeting resistance to change

The literature of resistance to change has grown in large part from the 'human relations' school of thought and thus reflects many of the underlying premises of that style of analysis (see HUMAN RELATIONS). At one level, the major conclusions of this perspective may seem obvious, though no less valuable for

that. For example, Stanislao and Stanislao (1983) recommend that implementors (1) explain better the need for change; (2) facilitate participation or the feeling of consultation; (3) use a tactful approach to avoid implying criticism of past practices; (4) make the change in stages to avoid disruption; (5) plant the idea of change; and (6) demonstrate management support for the change. Such approaches are frequently characterized by consultation and consensus-building activities.

A widely quoted and systematic approach to dealing with resistance to change, which provides a useful link between the strategy implementation process and change resistance, is provided by Kotter and Schlesinger (1979). They proposed a continuum of approaches, as shown in Figure 7.

The *education and communication* approach is designed to help people see the need and logic for change. The assumption is that, once persuaded, commitment to change will be high, though at the cost of time (see COMMUNICATION). On the other hand, *participation and involvement* means sharing some of the design and implementation of change with potential resistors, which is appropriate where the initiators do not have all the information they need to design the change and where others have considerable power to resist. The gain is commitment from those who participate and access to their information, but at the cost of time and correcting inappropriate choices by participators (see INDUSTRIAL DEMOCRACY).

The *facilitation and support* approach involves providing resources, encouragement and supportiveness to change resistors when people are resisting because of adjustment problems. However, this approach can be time-consuming and expensive, and can still fail. On the other hand, *negotiation and agreement* means offering incentives to active or potential resistors when an individual or group will lose as a result of the change and has power to resist. It may mitigate major resistance, but can also encourage others to bargain.

Manipulation and cooptation involve attempts to influence through selective information and by giving key roles to individuals or

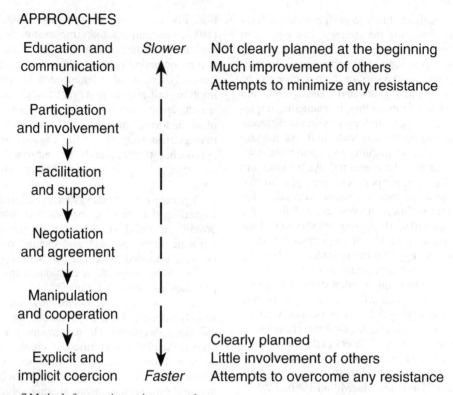

APPROACHES

Education and   *Slower*   Not clearly planned at the beginning
communication   Much improvement of others
                                 Attempts to minimize any resistance

Participation
and involvement

Facilitation
and support

Negotiation
and agreement

Manipulation
and cooperation

                                 Clearly planned
Explicit and   Little involvement of others
implicit coercion   *Faster*   Attempts to overcome any resistance

Figure 7 Methods for meeting resistance to change
Source: Adapted from Kotter and Schlesinger (1979: 111–12)

groups to gain their visible endorsement of the change. It can be quick and relatively inexpensive, but people may feel manipulated. Lastly, *explicit and implicit coercion* involves forcing the change through threat or use of sanctions and is used most effectively where speed is essential and the change initiators have considerable power. The advantage is speed, but it may leave bad feelings for the future.

This typology emphasizes: (1) the amount and type of resistance that is anticipated; (2) the position of the initiator relative to the resistors, particularly with regard to power; (3) who has the relevant information; (4) who has the energy and time for the project; and (5) the stakes involved.

Management execution skills

As well as the development of tactics and actions to secure adoption of strategies, there remains the reality that the way in which the strategy implementation process is managed

at an interpersonal level may be a critical determinant of implementation success, and may even represent the substitution of personal skills for formal structures and policies. Bonoma (1984) has argued that managers need four critical execution skills: interacting, allocating, monitoring and organizing. Interacting skills refer to the manager's behavioural style and influence over other people's behaviour, including leadership by example and role model, the use of power and negotiating and bargaining (see LEADERSHIP; MANAGERIAL BEHAVIOUR). Allocating skills involve approaches taken to budgeting time, money and people in order to achieve implementation of the high priority items. Monitoring skills involve developing and using feedback mechanisms that focus on the critical issues for success (which may not be the information provided by formal systems), while organizing skills are concerned with a manager's 'networking' behaviour that may involve going around the formal structure to achieve strategy implementation. Bonoma observes that managers who are effective implementors 'customize their informal organization to facilitate good execution. Often, their organization and the formal one have little in common' (Bonoma 1984: 75).

The force of this argument comes from the observation that formal structures and systems are often inadequate and inappropriate for implementing new strategies. This is particularly true when external change rates and task complexity are high. The role of management execution skills is therefore to bridge the gap between strategy and structure until new systems and structures (which take time to develop) are instituted in the firm.

Strategy implementation process

Attention turns now to the broader questions of avoiding the emergence of implementation problems in the way described by the cultural and crescive models of strategy process. Although this is not a well-structured area of knowledge, the following issues can be considered:

- participation in the strategy process
- strategic understanding in the organization
- champions and leaders
- shaping the strategy process
- the learning organization
- liaison units
- career paths and management development programmes

Participation of line management and other employees in planning has been advocated as a way of achieving the commitment of line managers to the implementation of plans and their 'ownership' of the problems of execution. If successful, this route would provide a basis for removing the formulation–implementation dichotomy discussed earlier. Different forms of participation were discussed by Nutt (1987) as tactics for coopting the powerful and influential and lessening their resistance to strategic change. However, participation in planning process in the fuller sense discussed by Bourgeois and Brodwin (1984), or more recently by Giles (1991), is a

broader process-related question more relevant to building a longer-term strategy for organizational change and strategy implementation. This may be compared to 'organizational socialization' of various types, in which people learn and internalize organizational goals and values pertinent to the strategy implementation process.

Strategic understanding in the organization is concerned with the perception by organizational members of the environment which they face and the strategic assumptions they make. This is partly a cultural issue, which reflects not 'the way we do things here', but rather 'the way we look at things here'. It may involve sharing processes such as environmental scanning and strategic issue analysis with those in the organization who will be affected by the strategic changes implied and whose commitment to change is most important. Indeed, it has been suggested that some 'corporations have created a world in which managers not only cannot see what is salient in their markets, they have gradually become impervious to learning', and a critical skill becomes 'unlearning' the past (Brown 1991: 107) (see ORGANIZATIONAL LEARNING). In a longitudinal study focused on field implementation of strategy in a fast-changing, high-technology environment, Cespedes (1990) identifies a key tension facing companies in strategy implementation: how to embed new skills in the organization with minimal disruption to the efforts and attention required to maintain current sources of revenue. His study indicates how organizational structures and reorganizations can simultaneously be an impediment to learning and a necessary means of 'unlearning' accrued skills and habits.

Champions and leaders may be critical to implementation and yet actively discouraged by the organization. Change agents of this type have been variously described as 'monomaniacs with a mission', 'change masters' or 'corporate entrepreneurs' (Kanter 1983), 'mavericks' or 'rebels' (Sathe 1988), 'fixers' (Peters and Austin 1986), or 'subversives' (Bonoma 1985). The key question would seem to be the degree to which an organization is able to facilitate and nurture the development of such players and to build its longer term implementation capabilities while still

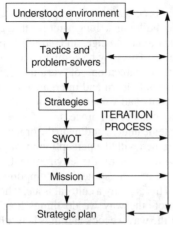

Figure 8 Reconfiguring planning process
Source: Piercy (1992: 277)

retaining the necessary questioning and flexibility in the organization. This extends beyond the issue of individual project execution tactics in the short term. Examples include the massive shift in strategic focus and culture at British Petroleum and the drive for customer focus in companies such as Avis and DEC.

Shaping the strategy process is concerned with the operation of the process of strategy formulation in the organization and the ways in which this may be designed to avoid implementation problems. Figure 8 illustrates one such approach; more detailed descriptions can be found in Giles (1991) and Piercy (1992). The underlying proposal is that planning should start with the understanding of the environment held by line management and work back to generate strategies for the future. This relies on an iterative approach, and typically involves sacrificing sophistication in plans for commitment and enthusiasm in planning and execution.

The learning organization and the use of organizational development techniques to avoid implementation issues is discussed by Argyris (1985, 1989) (see ORGANIZATIONAL LEARNING). In the later work, Argyris describes a form of organizational development programme where managers and their subordinates work together in a training environment to produce a strategy, a definition of some of the human problems that occur during implementation, the formulation of steps to overcome these problems and the monitoring

of implementation. The role of planning in the 'learning organization' is not well understood at present (Slater and Narver 1994), but it seems probable that the knowledge development function (information acquisition, information dissemination and shared interpretation) and the growth of 'generative learning' will offer some new approaches to avoiding the formulation–implementation dichotomy in the strategy process in organizations of the future.

In order to help address the differences in information flows and measurement systems that often impede implementation efforts, some firms have established formal liaison units focused on various dimensions of strategy implementation. Many companies have long had headquarters units whose ostensible responsibility has been to coordinate implementation activities among various functional groups. However, as integration requirements have increased in many industries, some companies have reorganized these groups and expanded the scope of their responsibilities (see Cespedes 1995 for specific examples).

One benefit of establishing such units is that they clearly signal the importance of cross-functional collaboration in companies where product, sales and customer service activities have long resided in separate departments, each with its own measurement systems, career paths and operating procedures. Usually staffed by personnel from these various departments, these units help to integrate divergent information flows. They also provide a specific decision-making mechanism in an environment where important trade-offs and implementation decisions increasingly reside at the interface between functional groups rather than within each group's traditional domain of expertise. One study of the operations of such groups stresses the analogy with quality initiatives: such units, as one manager commented, help 'to make visible issues that cut across product and sales groups, just as quality circles helped to build our awareness of the cross-functional requirements of total quality management' (Cespedes 1993a: 50).

A key to building the skills and capabilities required for implementation is a set of human resource management (HRM) initiatives that broaden perspectives, build inter-unit experience and establish relationships that encourage and support appropriate behaviour (see HUMAN RESOURCE MANAGEMENT). Some companies have revised HRM policies with these aims in mind. According to Cespedes (1995), they have found that these initiatives do not simply adapt implementation tactics to established structural and information characteristics of these firms. Rather, two aspects of HRM policy – career pathing and training and development activities – are especially important in determining whether and how the organizational systems required for implementation are used, maintained and kept up to date.

Some firms have altered traditional career paths with implementation efficiencies in mind, and may for example provide assignments in both sales and product management positions. Others have expanded the length and type of field sales exposure required for personnel in product development or production. In addition, new positions in many firms focus managers explicitly on joint cross-functional issues and activities. One benefit of these career path initiatives is increased awareness of another organizational unit's operating conditions, constraints and contributions. Managers with both product management and sales experience, for example, are more likely to develop strategies and implementation programmes with an awareness of the reciprocal requirements. Such assignments also help to build what Kotter calls the 'thick informal networks one finds wherever multiple leadership initiatives work in harmony. … Too often these networks are highly fragmented: a tight network exists inside the marketing group and inside R&D, but not across the two departments' (Kotter 1990: 107).

Other companies have altered the form and content of their management development programmes (see MANAGEMENT DEVELOPMENT). These firms use redesigned programmes as a way to build recognition of the need for implementation linkages, develop a shared understanding of each area's contribution to customer satisfaction and broaden the individual relationships that are needed for effective field execution of strategies. Cespedes (1995) cites the following characteristics of successful initiatives in this area. First, these programmes are typically defined and designed as company-specific endeavours intended to promote a change in attitudes and orientation as well as in the skill sets of individual managers. The line between cultural transformation and traditional management education blurs, and customization of programme content becomes essential. Second, while top management attended, these programmes typically included managers at various levels of the firms involved; indeed, a major benefit is often the education of top managers by front-line managers about changing implementation requirements. Third, these programmes usually complemented traditional classroom and case study instruction with actual projects dealing with implementation issues at the firm. Often billed as exercises in 'action learning', these programmes were influenced by total quality management (TQM) doctrine and its emphasis on the 'plan, do, check, act' cycle required for systematic problem solving (see TOTAL QUALITY MANAGEMENT). The assumption is that an effective learning programme for strategy implementation must develop both skills and shared awareness in the context of meaningful business issues; either alone is inadequate.

A development initiative illustrating these characteristics is the WorkOut programmes begun at General Electric in 1989. Company-specific in focus, cross-functional in the composition of participants and project-driven in agenda, these sessions deal with various issues within GE's many business units. Many WorkOut programmes involve the need for better integration of product, sales and service units in the context of global competition, lower-priced alternatives and flat or shrinking headcounts in many GE businesses. Chairman John Welch has been explicit about the implementation challenge facing his firm: 'even in a horizontal structure you'll still have product managers, still need accountability. But the lines [between various functional units] will blur' (Stewart 1991: 61). Hence, many WorkOut programmes at GE concern the development of cross-functional implementation programmes with customers, in the context of

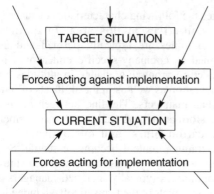

Figure 9 A force field analysis for
implementations
Source: Piercy (1989: 21)

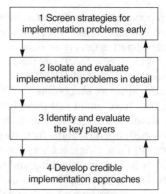

Figure 10 Screening strategies form
implementation problems
Source: Piercy (1989: 22)

a corporation with a heritage of autonomous, functionally-orientated product, sales and service units.

7 Developing implementation programmes

This section presents a framework for managers to use in addressing tactical and strategic issues in implementation. This framework works at two levels: the development of effective implementation approaches where this is possible, and the evaluation of the impact of implementation barriers on the feasibility and attractiveness of different strategies as an integral part of the planning process. The approach used is a force field analysis as shown in Figure 9. The procedure requires the enumeration and evaluation of the forces favouring the implementation of the strategy in question and the forces which are believed to act against implementation, and then using this evaluation as a basis for developing implementation approaches. This logic suggests the four stages shown in Figure 10.

1. Screen strategies for implementation problems early. At the earliest stage possible, strategy possibilities should be screened for implementation barriers and the acceptability of the strategy in question to the organization concerned. This suggests the possibilities in Figure 11: (1) 'loser strategies', which are low in priority and low in acceptability to the company, and which will probably not be pursued; (2) 'winner strategies', which are high in priority and acceptability, and promise few implementation problems; (3) 'low risk/low pay-off strategies' which are acceptable to the company but low in priority for the plan; and (4) 'conflict strategies', which are high in priority for the plan but low in acceptability to the company, and to which most of management's attention will probably be given. The earlier this task is undertaken, the less wasteful the planning process is likely to be: if there is an absolute barrier, and a strategy is not capable of being implemented, it can be abandoned, postponed, or adapted, before it has used up scarce management time and effort; also, if problems can be identified early enough, there is more time to develop appropriate responses.

2. Isolate and evaluate implementation problems. For each strategy item which has a high priority, implementation problems should be made explicit and evaluated in terms of their seriousness and their underlying causes, as far as these can be determined.

3. Identify and evaluate the key players. There is also value in being specific about the people, departments, committees or other decision-making units offering support or opposition for the strategy in question. One style of analysis is shown in Figure 12. This model suggests that we may be able to identify (1) influential supporters, where the goal will be to use this support to facilitate strategy implementa-

Acceptability to the company

	High	Low
High	Winner strategies	Low risk/ low payoff strategies
Priority in the plan		
Low	Conflict strategies	Loser strategies

Figure 11 Strategy priority and acceptability
Source: Piercy (1989: 26)

Decision making influence

	High	Low
High	Influential supporters	Non-involved supporters
Support for the strategy		
Low	Influential antagonists	Non-involved antagonists

Figure 12 Key player analysis
Source: Piercy (1989: 31)

tion; (2) influential antagonists, where issues may include the potential for winning their support (perhaps by bargaining or persuasion) or reducing their influence over the critical decision; (3) non-involved supporters, where the goal may be to increase their involvement in the decision-making process; and (4) non-involved antagonists, who are a potential threat to be watched.

4 Develop credible implementation approaches. This analysis should focus on what has to change and what has to be done if strategies are to be effectively executed. It should make explicit exactly what is required and what it will cost in resources. Evaluation of the likelihood of success should enable informed choices to be made about which strategies can be pursued (and what the organizational change costs are likely to be) and which strategies are unlikely to succeed in this organization at this time.

This structure provides a systematic approach to uncovering and evaluating specific implementation issues relating to a specific strategy set. It can help managers make informed choices early in the strategy process. In this way it provides a framework for applying the insights into implementation barriers and tactics as they have been discussed in this entry. The emphasis in this approach is on developing solutions to the implementation problems of predetermined strategies; however, it is also a means to bring closer together the processes of strategy formulation and implementation (see Figure 1) and thus how to

manage the strategy process to avoid the emergence of implementation problems of the type discussed here.

8 Conclusion

There are no 'quick fixes' available to remove the implementation issue from the management agenda. Similarly, there are no unified, simplifying models which capture the issue in a holistic way.

This entry has attempted to highlight the major sources and types of implementation problems and what is known about the development of appropriate managerial responses. To facilitate the use of these insights, techniques such as strategic gap analysis and a structured approach to evaluating implementation issues as part of the strategy formulation process have been suggested.

Underlying the approach here is the argument that one of the fundamental problems faced is the organizational and managerial separation of strategy generation and execution processes, the formulation–implementation dichotomy. Another conclusion is that it is efforts to reduce or remove this dichotomy which will ultimately hold the key to the implementation problem.

FRANK V. CESPEDES
THE CENTER FOR EXECUTIVE DEVELOPMENT,
CAMBRIDGE, MA

NIGEL PIERCY
ASTON BUSINESS SCHOOL

Further reading

(References cited in the text marked *)

* Ansoff, H.I. (1984) *Implanting Strategic Management*, Englewood Cliffs, NJ: Prentice Hall. (An overall treatment of strategic management issues by one of the original writers in this field, covering formulation and implementation of strategy from a rational–analytical viewpoint.)

* Argyris, C. (1985) *Strategy, Change, and Defensive Routines*, New York: Ballinger-Harper & Row. (Original analysis of some of the most covert and pervasive barriers to organizational change and strategy implementation.)

* Argyris, C. (1989) 'Strategy implementation: an experience in learning', *Organizational Dynamics* 17 (2): 5–15. (Considers defensive routines and organizational development programmes.)

* Bardach, E. (1977) *The Implementation Game*, Cambridge, MA: MIT Press. (A now classic analysis of the types of political behaviour found in implementation situations, adopting a game-based framework and identifying counters for management.)

* Bonoma, T.V. (1984) 'Making your marketing strategy work', *Harvard Business Review* 62 (March–April): 69–76. (A short review of research into management execution skills in successful implementation.)

* Bonoma, T.V. (1985) *The Marketing Edge: Making Strategies Work*, New York: The Free Press. (Starts from the marketing/sales area to develop a general management approach to implementation, firmly grounded in case research.)

* Bourgeois, L.J. and Brodwin, D.R. (1984) 'Strategic implementation: five approaches to an elusive phenomenon', *Strategic Management Journal* 5 (2): 241–64. (An original analysis of process models in strategy implementation which distinguishes problem solution and problem avoidance.)

* Braun, C.F. von (1990) 'The acceleration trap', *Sloan Management Review* 31 (2): 49–58. (Provides data and discussion of shortening product life cycles in consumer and industrial markets.)

* Brown, J.S. (1991) 'Research that reinvents the organization', *Harvard Business Review* 69 (January–February): 102–11. (Encapsulates the views of a senior manager concerned with implementation and change at Xerox.)

* Cespedes, F.V. (1990) 'Agendas, incubators, and marketing organization', *California Management Review* 33 (3): 27–53. (Discusses how companies attempt to meet dual marketing requirements of growing future business with minimal disruption to current revenue-generating routines.)

* Cespedes, F.V. (1991) *Organizing and Implementing the Marketing Effort*, Reading, MA: Addison-Wesley. (Offers a broad perspective on the strategy formulation–implementation dichotomy, then applies this to the marketing area.)

* Cespedes, F.V. (1993a) 'Coordinating sales and marketing in consumer goods firms', *Journal of Consumer Marketing* 10 (1): 37–55. (Discusses the relationship of brand and sales groups in implementing consumer marketing strategies.)

* Cespedes, F.V. (1993b) 'Market research and marketing dialects', *Marketing Research* 5: 26–34. (Outlines key differences in the information needs of product, sales and service managers.)

* Cespedes, F.V. (1994) 'Industrial marketing: managing new requirements', *Sloan Management Review* 35: 45–60. (Discusses factors affecting field implementation tasks in business-to-business markets.)

* Cespedes, F.V. (1995) *Concurrent Marketing: Integrating Product, Sales, and Service*, Boston, MA: Harvard Business School Press. (Discusses how the requirements of strategy implementation are changing, the organizational implications and what some companies are doing to manage new implementation requirements.)

* Corey, E.R., Cespedes, F.V. and Rangan, V.K. (1989) *Going to Market: Distribution Systems for Industrial Products*, Boston, MA: Harvard Business School Press. (A study of industrial channel design and channel management practices, including case histories of major companies.)

* Corey, E.R. and Star, S.H. (1971) *Organization Strategy: A Marketing Approach*, Boston, MA: Harvard Business School Division of Research. (A seminal study of strategy–structure relationships with a focus on marketing organization, including case histories of major companies.)

* Dougherty, D. (1992) 'Interpretive barriers to successful product innovation in large firms', *Organization Science* 3: 179–202. (Discusses the different 'thought worlds' that characterize different functional groups.)

* Giles, W.D. (1991) 'Making strategy work', *Long Range Planning* 24 (5): 75–91. (An original and highly practical view of managing planning process to enhance commitment, ownership, and hence strategy implementation success.)

* Ginsberg, A. and Abrahamson, E. (1991) 'Champions of change and strategic shifts: the role of internal and external change advocates', *Journal of Management Studies* 28 (2): 173–90. (A

thorough and systematic study of the role and impact of 'champions' in strategy implementation and organizational change.)

* Guth, W.D. and MacMillan, I.C. (1986) 'Strategy implementation versus middle management self-interest', *Strategic Management Journal* 7 (4): 313–27. (A systematic analysis of the sources, causes and counters to managerial resistance to strategic change.)

* Hamel, G. and Prahalad, C.K. (1989) 'Strategic intent', *Harvard Business Review* 67 (May–June): 63–76. (Widely cited study of strategic goals and corporate competences.)

* Hammer, M. and Champy, C. (1993) *Re-engineering the Corporation*, London: Brealey. (A widely cited managerial treatment of managing fundamental organizational change, with examples of resistance problems.)

* Hannan, M.T. and Freeman, J. (1989) *Organizational Ecology*, Cambridge, MA: Harvard University Press. (A provocative discussion of the life cycle of organizations and the implications for adapting to new environments.)

* Hart, S.L. (1992) 'An integrative framework for strategy-making processes', *Academy of Management Review* 17 (4): 327–51. (A review of conventional concepts of decision-making processes at a strategic level.)

* Hobbs, J.M. and Heany, D.F. (1977) 'Coupling strategy to operating plans', *Harvard Business Review* 55 (May–June): 119–26. (An early but very readable statement of the organizational and planning systems problems in driving strategic intentions through to operational plans and budgets.)

* Janis, I.L. (1972) *Victims of Groupthink*, Boston, MA: Houghton Mifflin. (An original and highly quoted study of the constraining effects of groups on decision maker responses to change.)

* Kanter, R.M. (1983) *The Change Masters: Corporate Entrepreneurs at Work*, London: Unwin Hyman. (A now-famous study of managers who create and manage change processes in organizations.)

* Kotter, J.P. (1990) *A Force for Change*, New York: The Free Press. (Discusses the leadership issues that are relevant in change management initiatives.)

* Kotter, J.P. and Schlesinger, L.A. (1979) 'Choosing strategies for change', *Harvard Business Review* 57 (March–April): 106–14. (A widely cited, influential and highly readable analysis of barriers to organizational change and appropriate counter-strategies in different contingencies.)

* Levitt, B. and J.G. March (1988) 'Organizational learning', *Annual Review of Sociology* 14: 319–40. (A review of the growing literature on organizational learning.)

* MacMillan, I.C. (1978) *Strategy Formulation: Political Concepts*, St Paul, MN: West. (One of the few texts in the strategic management field which develops frameworks for managing in a political context.)

* Mintzberg, H. (1987) 'Crafting strategy', *Harvard Business Review* 65 (September–October): 66–75. (An original and influential view of the processes of strategy formulation.)

* Mintzberg, H. (1988) 'Opening up the definition of strategy', in J.B. Quinn, H. Mintzberg and R.M. James (eds), *The Strategy Process*, London: Prentice Hall. (A review of the alternative perspectives that can be adopted in strategy formulation, and their implications.)

* Nelson, R. and Winter, S. (1982) *An Evolutionary Theory of Economic Change*, Cambridge, MA: Harvard University Press. (This discussion of organizational routines as the 'genes' of company capabilities and constraints is influential and enlightening.)

* Nutt, P.C. (1983) 'Implementation approaches for project planning', *Academy of Management Review* 8 (4): 600–11. (An early review of implementation issues at the level of project planning.)

* Nutt, P.C. (1986) 'Tactics of implementation', *Academy of Management Journal* 29 (2): 230–61. (A widely cited study of the tactics and programmes used by managers to achieve strategy implementation.)

* Nutt, P.C. (1987) 'Identifying and appraising how managers install strategy', *Strategic Management Journal* 8 (1): 1–14. (Examines successful approaches to strategy implementation.)

* Peters, T. and Austin, N. (1986) *A Passion for Excellence*, New York: Random House. (A polemic with many insights into how managers get things done, in the spirit of the search for 'excellence'.)

* Piercy, N.F. (1985) *Marketing Organization: Analysis of Information Processing, Power and Politics*, London: Unwin Hyman. (Examines organizational issues from the perspective of structure, information and political behaviour.)

* Piercy, N.F. (1987) 'The marketing budgeting process', *Journal of Marketing* 51 (3): 45–59. (An analysis of resource allocation from a process perspective.)

* Piercy, N.F. (1989) 'Diagnosing and solving implementation problems in strategic planning', *Journal of General Management* 15 (1): 19–38. (Provides a structured approach to developing implementation strategies at a practical level, with worksheets for manager use.)

* Piercy, N.F. (1992) *Market-Led Strategic Change*, Oxford: Butterworth Heinemann. (Provides a focus on implementation strategy development and the link to internal marketing, in the context of organizational change to respond to market needs.)
* Piercy, N.F. (1994) 'Marketing implementation and internal marketing strategy', in M.J. Baker (ed.), *The Marketing Book*, Oxford: Butterworth Heinemann. (Reviews internal marketing as an approach to solving implementation problems, including a worked example of strategic gap analysis.)
* Piercy, N.F. and Morgan, N.A. (1994) 'Mission analysis: an operational approach', *Journal of General Management* 19 (3): 1–19. (Develops a structure for analysing mission statements to confront their credibility and chances of impacting on corporate behaviour.)
* Quinn, J.B. (1981) 'Formulating strategy one step at a time', *Journal of Business Strategy* 1 (3): 42–63. (A now-classic presentation of the concept of 'logical incrementalism' to describe progress towards corporate goals.)
* Sathe, V. (1988) *Culture and Related Corporate Realities*, Homewood, IL: Irwin. (A thought-provoking study of the corporate environment with many potential insights for those concerned with implementation barriers and solutions.)
* Schein, E.H. (1961) *Coercive Persuasion*, New York: Norton. (A classic review of the processes of attitude and behaviour change.)
* Slater, S.F. and Narver, J.C. (1994) *Market Oriented Isn't Enough: Build A Learning Organization*, Cambridge, MA: Marketing Science Institute. (A systematic conceptual evaluation of the facets of the 'learning organization' with valuable insights for the manager seeking a longer term approach to reducing strategy implementation barriers.)
* Stanislao, J. and Stanislao, B.C. (1983) 'Dealing with resistance to change', *Business Horizons* 30 (July–August): 74–8. (An easily accessible listing of the sources of change resistance and possible managerial remedies.)
* Stewart, T.A. (1991) 'GE keeps those ideas coming', *Fortune* (12 August): 58–64. (Discussion of management development and strategy implementation initiatives at GE.)
* Taylor, B. (1986) 'Corporate planning for the 1990s', *Long Range Planning* 19 (6): 117–27. (A review of the future of corporate planning, identifying implementation issues as paramount.)
* Weick, K.E. (1969) *The Social Psychology of Organizing*, Reading, MA: Addison-Wesley. (An analysis of organizations that presents the powerful concept of environmental enactment to describe how the environment is understood.)
* Wernham, R. (1984) 'Bridging the awful gap between strategy and action', *Long Range Planning* 17 (6): 34–42. (Looks at implementation problems in strategic planning at British Telecom.)

See also: COMPETITIVE STRATEGIES, DEVELOPMENT OF; CORPORATE STRATEGIC CHANGE; HUMAN RESOURCE MANAGEMENT; INTERNAL CONTEXTS AND EXTERNAL ENVIRONMENTS; MANAGERIAL BEHAVIOUR; MINTZBERG, H.; ORGANIZATION BEHAVIOUR; ORGANIZATION DEVELOPMENT; STRATEGIC CHOICE; STRATEGIC COMPETENCE; STRATEGY, CONCEPT OF; STRATEGY AND INFORMATION TECHNOLOGY; STRATEGY AND INTERNAL MARKETING; STRATEGY MAKING, POLITICS OF; STRATEGY AND RATIONALITY; TECHNOLOGY STRATEGY, INTERNATIONAL

Strategy, industrial: see INDUSTRIAL STRATEGY

Strategy in Asia Pacific

Overview

Strategy in the Asia Pacific generally differs significantly from that practised in the West. In the Asia Pacific, national differences surface among managerial cadres, and strategies evolve with interactions, and over time, as they do in the West; yet researchers and managers have identified at least three indigenous styles of strategic management – that of the Overseas Chinese, Overseas Indians and Japanese. These three business groupings' cultures differ on companies' characteristics, concepts of loyalty, and understandings and expectations of commercial trust, which differentiate their strategies. Companies' relations with public sectors and regional governments, as well as a lack of high-quality market information, greatly influence strategy in the Asia Pacific. Research also reveals that in their strategies, the regional, family-owned, Overseas Chinese and Overseas Indian companies emphasize hands-on experience, lateral transfers of knowledge, qualitative information, holistic information-processing, action-driven decision making and emergent planning. The indigenous companies' strategies strongly affect their competitors' business environments in the Asia Pacific and should influence Western multinational corporations' strategic plans and responses for effective management.

1 Introduction

For Western companies, the Asia Pacific (broadly defined to include primarily Asia and the Pacific) represents a strategic opportunity and a threat. Western efforts to capitalize on Asia's potential have often led to failure; many of these failures have arisen from faulty assumptions about strategic behaviours. Many Western managers believe in Western management concepts' universal acceptability and applicability; strategy in the Asia Pacific requires novel assumptions and new lenses. The Overseas Chinese and Overseas Indians that dominate business operations in Asia and constitute major investors in the Pacific present two distinct strategic-management styles; similarly, the Japanese do another. This chapter on strategy in the Asia Pacific surveys some of the diverse managerial styles and practices in the region (see ASIA PACIFIC, MANAGEMENT IN).

The first section reviews historical influences on business structures and strategies among the Overseas Chinese and the Overseas Indians, the next analyses cultural differences that explain some variance in Overseas Chinese, Overseas Indian and Japanese strategies. The ensuing section crystallizes research to identify a distinctive style of strategic management in the Asia Pacific. The final section explores implications for strategies by Western multinational corporations (MNCs) operating in the Asia Pacific. A concluding note and annotated bibliography indicate further readings on strategies in the Asia Pacific.

2 Historical influences on business structures and strategies in Asia

Successful Asian companies' structures diverge significantly from their Western counterparts (see UNTIED STATES OF AMERICA, MANAGEMENT IN THE). For example, Haley, G.T. (1997) and Haley, G.T. and Haley, U.C.V. (1998) indicated that for successful Overseas Chinese and Overseas Indian companies operating in South and Southeast Asia: (1) little differentiation exists between the controlling families and the companies; (2) the companies have very strong familial and informal networks; (3) the companies exhibit good relationships with the often enormous public sectors in these countries; and (4) the companies appear highly diversified often undertaking unrelated diversification, thereby contravening mainstream, Western theoretical notions.

The major differences in Asian strategic decision making, as reflected in their companies' structures, stem from the information that Asian managers have and desire: this information often differs greatly from that used by Western managers and strategic planners. Haley, G.T. and Tan (1996) categorized Asia as an informational void relative to the amount of information available in industrialized economies. This section explores some of the historical influences that have bolstered the informational void in Asia.

Historically, three major business clusters have dominated Asia: government-linked corporations (GLCs), either wholly or partly controlled by regional governments; family-owned businesses; and manufacturing-based MNCs. In South and Southeast Asia, the Indians, Overseas Indians and Overseas Chinese have generally controlled family-owned businesses. Historically, none of the three clusters in Asia have desired local market information, and all have generally adapted their strategies to their information-poor environments.

GLCs usually began as suppliers of products and services in protected, domestic markets. For GLCs, strategic planning synchronized with governmental plans for economic growth and development. Market information rarely comprised a critical success factor; hence, information gathering did not assume top priority. Although MNCs first entered Asia over two centuries ago, those in manufacturing had the greatest impact and entered primarily after the Second World War; this latter group invested mainly to rationalize

manufacturing costs for products intended for Japan and the West. Not seeking to serve local markets, the manufacturing-based MNCs neither needed nor sought more local market information (see MULTINATIONAL CORPORATIONS).

The Overseas Chinese probably constitute the single, most dominant, private business grouping in Asia outside China, Japan, South Korea and South Asia. The Overseas Chinese form 3.5 per cent of Indonesia's population, 29 per cent of Malaysia's, 2 per cent of the Philippines', 10 per cent of Thailand's, and 77 per cent of Singapore's – yet control respectively 73 per cent, 69 per cent, 50–60 per cent, 81 per cent and 81 per cent of listed companies by market capitalization in these countries (Vatikiotis 1998). Many Overseas Chinese started as merchants and traders who moved into property-related businesses, and then into any business deemed profitable. Their companies generally exhibit an entrepreneurial, intuitive and fast decision-making style, and paternalistic management (Haley, G.T. et al. 1998). The founders of the Overseas Chinese companies generally had little formal education and even less formal, Western-style business education (Chan and Chiang 1994).

Today, the Overseas Indians form an extremely viable business force in Asia. For example, Indian businessmen account for one-tenth of Hong Kong's exports, even though they comprise less than 1 per cent of its population (Cragg 1996). Yet systematic efforts to understand the Overseas Indians' business structures and strategies often fail. Few from this business grouping assume prominent or high-profile public positions, often preferring to operate behind the scenes. Also, where the business climate allows, Overseas Indians tend not to report specifically their companies' structures. Almost all Indian émigrés arrived in their new homelands with few material assets. Often beginning as traders or retailers, they formed close communities for support and to create natural markets for goods and services (Haley, G.T. and Haley 1998). Like the Overseas Chinese, the Overseas Indians also generally adopt an entrepreneurial and fast decision-making style (Gidoomal and Porter 1997). Frequently, the Overseas Indians decide to invest, expand and compete mainly on business sense, experience and individual propensity for risk (Piramal 1996, Shigematsu 1994). Protected competitive environments and the informational void in which these companies operate have bolstered the Overseas Indians' decision-making propensities.

With difficult business decisions, when additional information seems necessary, the Overseas Chinese and Overseas Indians usually depend upon their webs of friends and government officials for information. Trust and loyalty form central concerns for these business groupings. Desired information often reflects subjective views or beliefs that raise the managers' confidence in their decisions (Haley, G.T. and Haley 1998).

The local business groupings' somewhat holistic, intuitive, decision-making styles conform well to information-scarce environments including those providing poor quality market survey data; these styles concurrently serve to exclude new entrants without the established communities' experiences and webs of contacts. For instance, many Asian banks have historically served particular communities or networks, not geographic areas; these community bases persist today. The Overseas Indians often prefer to use internal labyrinths of business contacts over outside sources of funding to finance their ventures. When borrowing from these internal contacts, interest rates competitive with prevailing banks' rates accrue. The business contacts issue *hoondies* or bills of exchange that constitute private financial circles' instruments to control and to honour debts. Each *hoondie* has a payment and maturity date. Despite bypassing traditional banking systems, the *hoondie* system, based on honour and reputation, appears functional and continues in South Asia and wherever Overseas Indians operate.

Many researchers and managers attribute the rapid growth of the local business groupings in South and Southeast Asia to their unique processing and channelling of information (see Haley, G.T. *et al.* 1998). Chu and MacMurray (1993) argued that in Southeast Asia, decision-making speed and control of information constitute primary competitive advantages for the Overseas Chinese, aiding them in seizing major business opportunities

across industries; similar advantages accrue to the Overseas Indians (Piramal 1996). Thus, the informational void in Asia exists because of historical business practices and participants' goals. The next section focuses on culture and strategy in the Asia Pacific.

3 Cultural influences on strategy in Asia Pacific

This section elaborates on the region-specific characteristics that differentiate the Overseas Chinese and Overseas Indians' cultures from their Japanese competitors' and from each other. The cultural differences explain some variance in strategic styles and practices in the Asia Pacific (see BUSINESS CULTURES, ASIAN PACIFIC; CULTURE, CROSS-NATIONAL; ORGANIZATION CULTURE).

Like the Japanese, most of the managed Asian economies have depended primarily on export-led growth. Japanese companies have always formed Japan's principal source of exports; until recently, Japanese exports focused mainly on North America and Europe. Alternatively, except for South Korea, manufacturing-based MNCs have formed the non-Japanese Asian nations' principal sources of exports to Western nations; local companies have concentrated on the local markets that Western MNCs now perceive as so important (Haley, G.T. and Tan 1996). Companies from most Asian nations, outside Japan, have built their size and managerial expertise within the informational void described in the previous section – rather than in competition with Western MNCs as Japanese companies did. Table 1 summarizes some significant cultural differences between the Chinese, Indians and Japanese; these cultural differences have influenced the strategic management of local companies, their concepts of loyalty as well as the bases for commercial trust in business dealings with them.

Company-related attributes

Merchants
The Japanese, Chinese, and Indian cultures exhibit divergent attitudes towards merchants. The Japanese culture incorporates an

Table 1 Cultural similarities and differences between the Chinese, Indians and Japanese

Attributes	Chinese	Indian	Japanese
Company			
Merchants	Reviled	Specialized	Exalted
Primogeniture	None	Very strong	Strong
Company's life-span	Short	Medium	Long
Loyalty			
Family definition	Blood	Blood	Role
Focus	Individual	Group	Institution
Intensity	Low	High	High
Filial piety vs. patriotism	Opposed	No relationship	Equivalent
Commercial trust			
Ethical foundation	5 relationships and social harmony	Dharma	Mutual self-interest
Ethical focus	The Way	Family	Service to father figure
Expectations of benefits	Immediate and up-front	Immediate and up-front	Long-term and delayed

Source: Haley, G.T. And Haley, U.C.V. (1998: 308)

economic philosophy of growth that exalts merchants. A major influence on the Overseas Chinese, the Confucian culture, incorporates a subsistence-based economic philosophy that exalts peasants and reviles and persecutes merchants. Confucian philosophers frowned upon merchants whom they perceived as excessively concerned with profits rather than the 'Way' (Lau 1995, Waley 1996); the philosophers also saw merchants as mobile, and therefore unreliable supporters of rulers (see CHINA, MANAGEMENT IN; INDIA, MANAGEMENT IN; JAPAN, MANAGEMENT IN).

Alternatively, since ancient times, Indian cultures have encouraged and provided specialized places for thriving merchant classes. Many Overseas Indians come from the *Vaisya* or *Jain* merchant castes that encouraged business within the broad Hindu system. Others emanate from small, highly-prosperous, niche, non-Hindu communities, such as the *Parsis*, whom local rulers protected and encouraged. Several Overseas Indians, such as the Shah brothers from Palanpur, in the Western state of Gujarat, have parlayed their traditional occupations, in their case that of diamond merchants, into major multinational operations: today, the

Shah brothers rank among the world's largest diamond dealers with operations in Belgium, Thailand and India.

Primogeniture and companies' life-spans
Another difference between Chinese, Japanese and Indian customs revolves around primogeniture or the emphasis on single heirs, usually the oldest sons. These customs have influenced companies' life-spans. Confucian customs emphasize large families and ban primogeniture; consequently, an ancient Chinese saying prophesies that 'No fortune survives the third generation'. Most of today's major Overseas Chinese companies have survived only as far as the second generation of managers (Chu and MacMurray 1993). Alternatively, Japanese customs emphasize primogeniture; however, according to customs, the oldest sons need not necessarily inherit regardless of competence, and consequently, the Japanese companies have built concentrated and continued wealth. Japanese companies, especially large ones such as Mitsubishi, have survived for a considerable time in some form. Some of Japan's major companies began hundreds of years ago as family compa-

nies which have evolved through growth into the Japanese *keiretsu* conglomerates.

The Indians emphasize primogeniture even more than the Japanese. Many Overseas Indian companies have evolved from traditional, small, family businesses into third or fourth-generation family-controlled conglomerates (*Business Today* 1998). The oldest sons often succeed their fathers as the family companies' heads, regardless of their competence or aptitudes, thereby debilitating top-management cadres and increasing the need for professionalization. Consequently, Gidoomal and Porter (1997) noted that succession forms a major concern among the Overseas Indian companies.

Loyalty-related attributes

Family, focus and intensity

In Japanese cultures, loyalties, though very strong, have institutional bases: family members owe filial loyalties to the bread-winners, not to the actual fathers (see JAPAN, MANAGEMENT IN). Conversely, in both Chinese and Indian cultures, family members owe filial loyalties to the fathers, regardless of who actually constitute the bread-winners; members of the cultures share highly personalized, as opposed to institutional, bases for loyalties. The Indian cultures glorify loyalties that members may transfer to groups within the extended families and their businesses. In the Chinese cultures, however, loyalties accrue to individuals; members often do not transfer loyalties to friends or employers and hence employees' loyalties do not survive individual managers.

Patriotism

The relationships that the Japanese, Chinese and Indians perceive between individuals and societies also differ; these associations affect the ways in which the Overseas Chinese and Overseas Indians contribute to their adopted and native countries. A Japanese adage posits that 'To be a good patriot is to be a good son'. Alternatively, the equivalent adage in China argues that 'One cannot be both a good patriot and a good son'. In Indian cultures, no relationship exists between patriotism and filial piety.

Trust-related attributes

Ethical foundations

Concepts of ethics differ significantly between the three cultures (Haley, G.T. and Haley 1998) affecting the bases of commercial trust (see BUSINESS ETHICS). Although the Japanese view contractual duties as binding and familial and friendship ties as helpful, ties of personal and corporate self-interest prove paramount; trust in commercial relationships derives from perceived, mutual self-interest. Hence, numerous social gatherings occur in which potential business associates seek out similarities in outlooks, perspectives and values.

In Confucianism, the major ethical influence on the Overseas Chinese, five relationships define ethical duty:

1 sovereign and minister;
2 father and son;
3 husband and wife;
4 brother and younger brother;
5 friends.

If relationships fall outside the above categories, then Confucian necessities to maintain social harmony, rather than normative ethical desires, regulate relationships. Without familial or established friendship ties, trust rarely exists in commercial relationships with the Overseas Chinese: to work well with them, foreign business associates must build non-commercial ties of friendship or family.

Dharma

Loosely translating from the Sanskrit to the Natural Law and incorporating duty, *Dharma* assumes centrality for many South Asian communities including the Overseas Indians. *Dharma* covers duties to families, to business partners and to societies. Many Overseas Indians view succeeding financially as a familial duty, especially for the oldest sons. This association with familial duty transforms success into religious obligation; among South Asians, financial rewards from business success provide overtones of personal virtue for successful people.

Ethical focus
The three cultures' ethics demonstrate different normative focal points. To the Overseas Chinese influenced by Confucian philosophies, individuals should behave in manners appropriate to their stations within the five relationships' frameworks; the Confucian philosophers refer to these collectively appropriate behaviours as the 'Way'. To the Japanese, individuals should serve their superiors (their father figures), and through their superiors, patriotically, their emperors. But, to South Asians including the Overseas Indians, families should provide the central concerns: codes of *Dharma* regulate the duties of individuals to their families.

Expectations of benefits
The Overseas Indians and Overseas Chinese differ from the Japanese in their expectations of benefits from contractual relationships. Among the Overseas Indians, legal principles and the rule of law appear to mould trust in commercial relationships. However, neither the Overseas Indians nor the Overseas Chinese will enter or maintain contractual relationships without minimal benefits and the expectations of making profits: when the benefits and expectations fade, so do contractual duties for the most part. Unlike the Japanese, although the Overseas Chinese and the Overseas Indians will invest time, money and effort, they expect to see tangible benefits up front (Redding 1996, Shigematsu 1994). Because of unfavourable experiences that include persecution in foreign lands, both groups emphasize earning fairly immediate, tangible returns and maintaining substantial holdings of liquid assets.

Although familial and friendship ties oil commercial relationships in Indian cultures, most Overseas Indians view contractual duties in commercial relationships as ethically binding as Westerners do. Thus, commercial partners with signed contracts can have some confidence that the Overseas Indians will follow the contracts' terms. However, with the Overseas Chinese, signed contracts may often begin, rather than end, negotiations (Haley, G.T. and Tan 1996); consequently, commercial partners should expect some quibbling over the contracts' terms.

Lasserre and Schütte (1995) provide a more complete discussion of Japanese culture and strategies in the *keiretsu*. However, Japan's recent economic problems, and the major restructuring of corporate and governmental institutions, are rapidly changing business practices (Haley, U.C.V. 2000; Haley, U.C.V. and Richter 2001; Sapsford 1998). The next section elaborates on some unique characteristics of the Overseas Chinese and Overseas Indians' strategic-management styles that continue greatly unaltered in most of the Asia Pacific.

4 The Overseas Chinese and Overseas Indians' strategic management styles

Drawing on their observations and study of Asian top managers, Haley, G.T. and Tan (1996) and Haley, G.T. and Haley (1998) posited that the following characteristics seem common to Overseas Chinese and Overseas Indians' strategic management practices and styles:

1 hands-on experience;
2 lateral transfers of knowledge;
3 reliance on qualitative information;
4 holistic information processing;
5 action-driven decision making;
6 emergent planning.

This section elaborates on and identifies distinctive facets of Asian managers' strategic management styles and practices.

Hands-on experience
To make decisions quickly, without detailed analyses of hard data, successful Asian managers must approximate hands-on, line managers who know the companies' work routines and processes as well as the products, markets, business environments and industries first hand. This level of experience and involvement contributes to making the right decisions without the supporting information most Western managers would desire.

Lateral transfers of knowledge
To succeed in industries in which they have no prior experiences, and to engage in frequent unrelated diversification, Asian managers

must generalize from past experiences in other industries, and apply those generalizations in the new contexts. The ability to tackle new problems in different situations involves conceptualization skills different from analytical skills (Haley, U.C.V. 1997; Haley, U.C.V. and Stumpf 1989).

Qualitative information

The Asian managers almost always use external sources of information in making strategic decisions. However, the managers rarely seek published information, generally preferring qualitative, even subjective information supplied by friends, business associates, government officials, and others in whose judgement and character they trust. They prefer to visit localities personally to check information rather than to rely on secondary information. Their local contacts can often supply up-to-date, accurate, unpublished information superior to available, published or traditional, primary, research alternatives.

Holistic information processing

With experience-based intuitive models, the Asian managers take general approaches to problems, define parameters intuitively, and explore solutions holistically: Such approaches resemble Asian thinking and learning. The intuitive models provide alternative modes of decision making that frequently work well, especially in those markets where they evolved: the models reduce risk, not through formal data collection and analyses, but through the collection of subjective information and incremental approaches to investments (Haley, G.T. *et al.* 1998).

Action-driven decision making

Speed constitutes a key characteristic of decision making in Asian business. This speed reflects the managers' empowerment and accountability. The decision-making models used by Asian managers reflect authoritative management. However, when responsibility coincides with authority, projects often progress faster in emerging and rapidly-developing markets.

Emergent planning

Asian managers appear to engage in what Mintzberg (1987) termed emergent planning (Haley, G.T. *et al.* 1998). Strategies bubble-up through individual companies and also collectively through networks (Piramal 1996). Typically, news, rumors or insider information will reach the managers and create interest. The managers will then seek confirming evidence, gauge available resources, make and implement decisions. As further information becomes available, the managers will modify strategies. The companies' strategies emerge from the managers' and the companies' learned business behaviours. If managers feel they need strategic partners, they seek them out, preferably within their respective networks; the potential partners' decisions to join hinge largely on their confidence in the proposing managers' judgement and abilities.

5 Implications for Western multinational corporations

As discussed in previous sections, Overseas Chinese and Overseas Indian companies exhibit great speed in decision making. Unlike Japanese companies, which sometimes seem to move glacially, other successful Asian companies move quickly and expect rapid decisions from their potential partners; MNCs following standard operating procedures will probably lose several good opportunities. To move rapidly however, MNCs' managers cannot wait until they perceive potential opportunities to research markets; they must have the knowledge substantially on hand and leverage to beat the odds. This section first highlights some general implications for MNCs' strategic success in the Asia Pacific; it then hones in on implications for MNCs' successful human-resource strategies (see HUMAN RESOURCE MANAGEMENT, INTERNATIONAL).

General implications

To succeed in Asia, Western MNCs must develop flexible corporate cultures that can respond to regional distinctions, promote cultural sensitivity and seek out home/host similarities. Managers must have close links in each Asia Pacific country to speed decision making and have ready access to the highest levels of corporate management. Using more locals with strong local connections, and building trust-based relationships are some of the ways to establish stronger links to local information.

Western MNCs operating in Asia should institute experience-based training programmes and staff Asian operations with line managers rather than people who have risen through staff functions. Line managers can better understand their senior counterparts at most Asian companies, as they will have had many of the same operational experiences. Line-management experiences will also help top managers to build local information links more rapidly: the senior Asian managers with whom they will interact should relate to line managers more as equals than they do with staff managers.

Finally, managers should learn to recognize how Asian relationships evolve. Unlike many other networks around the world, individuals enjoy flexible acceptance within Overseas Chinese networks (Haley, G.T. *et al.* 1998). Acceptance stems from situations in which the individuals interact within the networks. Western managers do not have total freedom to undertake some behaviours that may cement their positions with Overseas Chinese and Overseas Indian networks. (This concerns their freedom to act independently and to involve their families in business relationships as completely as the Asian managers often do). Consequently, Western managers must learn to recognize the cues given by Asian managers to indicate the state of the relationship.

Implications for human resource practices
Many Western MNCs' practices of rotating managers in foreign postings every two or three years appear counterproductive in the Asia Pacific. First, the rotations diminish the MNCs' abilities to employ emergent regional strategies: the managers fail to gain intimate knowledge of the markets and cannot recognize the emerging patterns in environments or in local operations. Consequently, the managers cannot generate effective strategies. Second, MNCs do not build contacts, their employees do. When MNCs rotate employees, they lose the employees' contacts. The

damage may prove minimal because in the short period of two or three years, the employees could not have built substantial numbers of influential contacts. However, if after three years the managers could socialize with the local business communities effectively and build contacts, the MNCs were probably only starting to get substantial returns from those managers. As discussed in the previous section, many Asians ascribe loyalty and trust to individuals, not companies. Additionally, many Asians view trust and loyalty as nontransferable. The incoming managers will not receive the good will built by their predecessors. These two reasons appear especially valid when the MNCs operate in Asia without local partners.

Asian companies' strategies also offer opportunities to MNCs to augment their talent pool. Bright, non-family managers working for Overseas Chinese companies often wish they worked for someone else, providing occasions for MNCs to acquire experienced local executives. Recent surveys have shown that local Hong Kong companies' executives feel uncomfortable and dissatisfied with their jobs; most would prefer to work for companies where they could contribute to corporate strategy and to aspire to top managerial positions (*The Economist* 1996). However, many Overseas Chinese companies buy their managers' loyalties through substantial annual performance bonuses and generous retirement schemes, practices some Western companies follow also.

USHA C. V. HALEY
COLLEGE OF BUSINESS ADMINISTRATION
UNIVERSITY OF TENNESSEE, KNOXVILLE

Note

For a more complete discussion of (1) the Overseas Chinese and their strategies, see Haley, G.T. *et al.* (1998) and the East Asia Analytical Unit (1995); (2) the Overseas Indians and their strategies, see Haley, G.T. and Haley (1998) and Shigematsu (1994); (3) local companies', governments' and MNCs' strategic management in the Asia Pacific, see Haley, U.C.V. (2000) and Lasserre and Schütte (1995).

Further reading

(References cited in the text marked *)

* *Business Today* (1998) 'India's business families: Can they survive?', 6th anniversary issue, January/February. (Detailed survey of India's largest family-owned companies including their strategies and network ties.)
* Chan, K.B. and Chiang, C. (1994) *Stepping Out: The Making Of Chinese Entrepreneurs*, Singapore: Prentice Hall. (Case histories of Singaporean Chinese entrepreneurs, including interviews and archival research.)
* Chu, T.C., and MacMurray, T. (1993) 'The road ahead for Asia's leading conglomerates', *McKinsey Quarterly* 3: 117–26. (Analysis of Overseas Chinese business strategies.)
* Cragg, C. (1996) *The New Maharajas: The Commercial Princes of India, Pakistan and Bangladesh*, London: Random House. (Directory of who's who in the Overseas Indian business grouping.)
* East Asia Analytical Unit (1995) *Overseas Chinese Business Networks*, Canberra, Australia: AGPS Press, Department of Foreign Affairs and Trade. (Extremely detailed, meticulous study of the Overseas Chinese networks drawing on research and surveys conducted in Australia and Asia.)
* *The Economist* (1996) 'A survey of business in Asia', 9 March (Review of business groupings and environments in Asia.)
* Gidoomal, R., and Porter, D. (1997) *The UK Maharajahs: Inside the South Asian Success Story*, London: Nicholas Brealey Publishing. (Anecdotal histories and network ties of some successful Overseas Indian companies in the UK.)
* Haley, G.T. (1997) 'The values Asia needs', *Business Times* (Singapore), Editorial and Opinion Section, 24 December: 6. (Newspaper article on how Asian values and strategic styles might have hurt Asian economies.)
* Haley, G.T. and Haley, U.C.V. (1998) 'Boxing with shadows: competing effectively with the Overseas Chinese and Overseas Indian business networks in the Asian arena', *Journal of Organizational Change Management* 11 (4), Special Issue on 'Strategic dimensions of organizational change and restructuring in the Asia Pacific: Part I, strategies for foreign investors': 301–20. (Theoretical framework highlighting and differentiating Overseas Chinese, Overseas Indians' and Japanese strategic decision-making styles, with implications for Western collaborators and competitors.)

* Haley, G.T. and Tan, C.T. (1996) 'The black hole of Southeast Asia: strategic decision making in an informational void', *Management Decision* 34: 37–48. (Study of how the Overseas Chinese make strategic decisions with implications for businesses and governments in the Asia Pacific.)
* Haley, G.T., Tan, C.T. and Haley, U.C.V. (1998) *New Asian Emperors: The Overseas Chinese, Their Strategies and Competitive Advantages*, Oxford: Butterworth-Heinemann. (Extremely detailed analyses based on interviews with Asian Chief Executive Officers of the Overseas Chinese strategic styles, and the implications of their strategies for Western competitors and collaborators.)
* Haley, U.C.V. (1997) 'The Myers-Briggs Type Indicator and decision-making styles: identifying and managing cognitive trails in strategic decision making', in Fitzgerald, C. and Kirby, L. (eds), *Developing Leaders: Research and Applications in Psychological Type and Leadership Development*, Palo Alto, CA: Consulting Psychologists Press: 187–223. (Review and analysis of connected heuristics and biases, or cognitive trails, in international strategic decisions.)
Haley, U.C.V. (1998) 'Virtual Singapores: shaping international competitive environments through business–government partnerships', *Journal of Organizational Change Management* 11 (4), Special Issue on 'Strategic dimensions of organizational change and restructuring in the Asia Pacific: Part I, strategies for foreign investors': 338–56. (Analysis and business implications of Singapore's industrial parks and the government's strategies in the developing Asian economies.)
* Haley, U.C.V. (ed.) (2000) *Strategic Management in the Asia Pacific: Harnessing Regional and Organizational Change for Competitive Advantage*, Oxford: Butterworth-Heinemann. (Experts' research, analyses and commentaries, identifying patterns of continuity and discontinuity in strategic management in the Asia Pacific before, through and after the Asian financial crisis.)
Haley, U.C.V. and Low, L. (1998) 'Crafted culture: Governmental sculpting of modern Singapore and effects on business environments', *Journal of Organizational Change Management* 11 (6), Special Issue on 'Strategic dimensions of organizational change and restructuring in the Asia Pacific: Part II, concerns of local stakeholders': 530–53. (Study of how and why the Singaporean government has shaped Singaporean cul-

ture with implications for multinational corporations' operations.)

Haley, U.C.V., Low, L. and Toh, M.H. (1996) 'Singapore Incorporated: reinterpreting Singapore's business environments through a corporate metaphor', *Management Decision* 34 (9), Special Issue on 'Strategic management in the Asia Pacific': 17–28. (Theoretical framework identifying the important stakeholders in Singapore's business environments – the Singapore government later used the metaphor Singapore Inc. to market itself and to explain policies.)

* Haley, U.C.V. and Richter, F.-J. (2001) *Asian Post-crisis Management: Corporate and Governmental Strategies for Sustainable Competitive Advantage*, London: Macmillan/Palgrave. (Strategies for corporations and governments in the new business environments of post-crisis Asia).

* Haley, U.C.V. and Stumpf, S.A. (1989) 'Cognitive trails in strategic decision making: linking theories of personalities and cognitions', *Journal of Management Studies* 26: 477–97. (Model of cognitive trails or systematic heuristics and biases that one can identify in managers' strategic styles through the Myers-Briggs Type Instrument.)

* Lasserre, P. and Schütte, H. (1995) *Strategies for Asia Pacific*, London: Macmillan Business. (Country-specific strategies for Western multinational corporations in the Asia Pacific prior to the Asian financial crisis and restructuring.)

* Lau, D.C. (1995) *Mencius Says*, Singapore: Federal Publications Pte. Ltd. (Commentary and translation of ancient Chinese philosopher Mencius' discourses.)

* Mintzberg, H. (1987) 'Crafting strategy', *Harvard Business Review* July/August: 66–75. (Theoretical analysis of how managers engage in strategic planning.)

* Piramal, G. (1996) *Business Maharajas*, India: Viking Penguin India. (Detailed case studies and interviews of India's major business families covering business and managerial strategies.)

* Redding, S.G. (1996) 'Weak organization and strong linkages: managerial ideology and Chinese family business networks', in Hamilton,

G.G. (ed.), *Asian Business Networks*, Berlin, New York: Walter de Gruyter, pp. 27–42. (Study of Chinese families' distinguishing characteristics.)

* Sapsford, J. (1998) 'The right model for Asia?' *The Wall Street Journal Interactive*, 26 October. (Newspaper article identifying chronic problems with and recasting of Japanese management styles and strategies.)

* Shigematsu, S. (1994) 'The study of Overseas South Asians: Retrospect and prospect', Working paper Graduate School of International Development, Nagoya University, Japan. (Sociological and historical account of the Overseas Indians.)

* Vatikiotis, M. (1998) 'The Chinese way', *Far Eastern Economic Review* 26 February: 45. (Discussion of Overseas Chinese business strategies for adapting to changed Asian business conditions.)

* Waley, A. (1996) *Confucius: The Analects*, Ware, Hertfordshire, UK: Wordsworth Editions Ltd. (Commentary and translation of ancient Chinese philosopher Confucius' discourses and sayings.)

Further resources

Asia-Pacific.com – experts, resources and data for effective strategic management: *http://www.asia-pacific.com*

See also: ASIA PACIFIC, MANAGEMENT IN; BUSINESS CULTURES, ASIAN PACIFIC; CHINA, MANAGEMENT IN; COMPETITIVE STRATEGIES; CULTURE, CROSS-NATIONAL; GLOBALIZATION; HONG KONG, MANAGEMENT IN; INDIA, MANAGEMENT IN; JAPAN, MANAGEMENT IN; SINGAPORE, MANAGEMENT IN; SOUTH KOREA, MANAGEMENT IN; STRATEGY, CONCEPT OF; STRATEGY IN EUROPE; STRATEGY IN NORTH AMERICA; STRATEGY IN THE EMERGING COUNTRIES; TAIWAN, MANAGEMENT IN; WORLD TRADE ORGANIZATION

Strategy and buyer–supplier relationships

Overview

This entry contains a review of the application of strategy within buyer–supplier relationships and logistics. The importance of strategy in this area is demonstrated by its use by state of the art companies such as Toyota, as well as in the fact that the average company spends more on bought-in resources than on those employed within its four walls.

The author has attempted to summarize the history of the subject since the early days when purchasing was not even given operation status. A number of early cases, where suppliers have yielded competitive advantage to their customers, are presented as well as the early key works in the subject. More recent modelling and work concerning the strategic role of the buyer–supplier relationship is presented. The majority of this work suffered from the fact that the causality relationships were not discussed, with the implication that a close or partnership relationship is possible simply by improving one or other feature of the relationship such as trust, length, number of suppliers or asset specificity.

A review of the state of the art situation, including a summary of the position taken by Toyota and their suppliers, shows that the creation of very close relations is a far more complex matter. A ten-point model called network sourcing, summarizing the key features of this relationship, is presented. Further analysis reveals that there are two primary features which are seen to cause the type of relationships demonstrated by Toyota, namely supplier coordination and supplier development.

The other features of network sourcing are partly or mainly effects of supplier coordination and development.

In order to understand how these two features can be reproduced outside Japan, a discussion of the Western version of the *kyoryoku kai* or supplier association is undertaken, centred mainly around the ongoing work with Calsonic Llanelli Radiators. This successful early work has led to a number of important policy implications for British companies, professional institutes and government agencies alike. The future direction of work in this area is shown to be likely to centre around broader and deeper application of the *kyoryoku kai* as well as the search for other appropriate tools. A number of practical conclusions are presented which highlight the need for further research and practical application of state of the art methods within this important strategic area.

1 Introduction

Three key strategic tasks (see STRATEGY, CONCEPT OF) have been set for management by the authors of *The Machine that Changed the World* (Womack *et al.* 1990). These tasks are: the management of processes, the management of relationships and the management of change. Evidence compiled through comparative research in Japan and Europe (Storhagen 1993) has revealed that although the knowledge is available in the former area of management, it is not widespread in the latter two areas (see EUROPE, MAMAGEMENT IN; JAPAN, MANAGEMENT IN). It is an understanding and application of all three areas that is required by Western organizations in order to help them to compete with the pioneering Japanese companies.

The key role for the management of inter-company relationships is revealed in the fact that the bought-in content of the typical manufacturing company in the West ranges from 50 to 70 per cent of the value of the final product and is therefore central to the pursuit of competitive advantage. As a result, the recent elevation of the purchasing and logistics function to a strategic level within leading Western companies is therefore no coincidence. The subject area that logistics covers is the complete flow of materials throughout the value stream from raw material source to point of consumption and back through to final disposal. However, this entry will primarily concentrate on an exploration of the development of strategies within the inter-company relationships. This will be undertaken from both a theoretical and practical viewpoint.

2 Past developments

It is only in the last twenty years that purchasing and logistics has started to gain a place within the strategic direction of leading Western companies (see PURCHASING; LOGISTICS AND PHYSICAL DISTRIBUTION). Indeed, in the majority of companies even today it is still regarded as being of only operational or tactical importance, with its work subsumed within other departments such as finance or manufacturing.

This having been said, there are a few isolated early examples of a more strategic role for purchasing. In the nineteenth century when Isambard Kingdom Brunel, the engineer responsible for the Great Western Railway and the steamship SS Great Britain, required a supplier capable of manufacturing timber bridges he was faced with a position where no such company existed. As a result he had to create strategic alliances with wooden shipbuilders and develop them into the type of companies that he required (Baily and Farmer 1986). A similar example quoted by Chandler (1962) refers to Duke, the first mechanized US cigarette maker. The problem faced by Duke was that he could not obtain sufficient tobacco of the required quality to satisfy his machines. The strategy that he pursued to remedy this problem was to buy the complete output of farmers and to work with them to ensure that they harvested the leaf of the quality that he required. In effect, Duke developed the first quality and supply assured purchasing strategy. The result of this was a very successful business enterprise.

A similar example from the early twentieth century is that of Lord Nuffield and Morris Motors (Baily and Farmer 1986). Lord Nuffield, in contrast to his competitors, undertook a strategy of buying in the components required for his Morris cars rather than making such parts. As part of this strategy he helped his suppliers in their production planning but was exacting in his quality and delivery requirements. The close relations with suppliers involved co-design and what might today be called design for manufacture (DFM) and parts standardization. This work was undertaken with a range of small companies including Lucas and Smiths.

These three examples show that close relations between buyers and suppliers were undertaken by a few early companies and in these cases with considerable success. Each of them sought to achieve competitive advantage in the marketplace by working with suppliers to mutual advantage while setting tough standards with regard to price, quality and delivery. As a result total costs were reduced and competitive advantage obtained. These individuals and their respective companies thought in a strategic way, outside of traditional functional boundaries and with close links to customers and suppliers alike.

However, these isolated examples were far from the norm and indeed, purchasing was not included in any texts on business or management until after the first world war. One of the earliest references to purchasing was in the *Handbook of Business Administration* produced by the American Management Association in 1931. In this text purchasing was referred to as an essentially clerical or transactional task with six major aspects: administration, ordering, payment, economics, inspection and salvage. The key principles of purchasing were defined as: centralization, coordination, standardization, aggressive fair play and the employment of honest, able and calm people.

It was not until the 1960s that the first texts specifically on purchasing appeared. These included the influential *Purchasing and Supply Management* (Baily 1963). This was the first serious attempt to put purchasing on the map as a key function within organizations. While much of the text is concerned with tactical and operational issues (such as materials coding, operating stores, the legal aspects of purchasing) it did start to address the role of purchasing at a strategic level, including the role of purchasing research. However, although a chapter is devoted to choosing and dealing with suppliers, the emphasis is less strategic and more on issues of reciprocity, ethical behaviour and possible conflicts of interest.

During the 1970s purchasing continued to gain momentum, at least as a function within organizations. Work carried out by Farmer in the early 1970s showed that there was a growing awareness of the role of purchasing as part of corporate activity within multinational organizations (Baily and Farmer 1986). However, from a literature point of view purchasing and marketing were still being kept firmly separate. As a result, the purchasing texts of the time were filled with examples of how the active buyer could gain control over the passive sales representative (Lee and Dobler 1971). At the same time, marketing texts were adapting traditional consumer marketing concepts to industrial marketing (Kotler 1976). The assumption of this marketing literature was that the active supplier found ways to sell to the passive buyer.

At this time, the strategic importance of buyer and supplier working together within an ongoing relationship went largely unnoticed, with the exception of the classic article 'Vertical quasi-integration' by Blois, written in 1972. This paper explores the possibility of creating relationships between companies that would gain from the advantages of vertical integration, while giving the flexibility of the market conditions. The evidence that Blois presents, drawn largely from the automotive industry, was useful in suggesting this important middle ground between the vertical integration and market economics which forms the basis of the later transaction cost economics (Williamson 1985).

Although this shortcoming of both purchasing and marketing literature was partially resolved with passing references to relationships in newer editions of both marketing and purchasing texts (Baily and Farmer 1986), it was not until the 1980s that the true strategic value of buyer–supplier relationships was be-

ing discussed in any depth. One of the first to do this was the Industrial Marketing and Purchasing (IMP) Group, an international collection of university-based academics. The IMP Group developed an interaction approach based on the premise that both buyer and seller played an active role in transactions. The IMP Group stress the importance of both short-term interactions or episodes, as well as the longer-term relationship (Ford 1980).

Within these long-term relationships, Ford notes that there is an institutionalization of expectations and contact patterns, with adaptations made by each partner to propagate the relationship. The degree and extent of these adaptations are shown to grow with the length of the relationship, ultimately leading to mutually beneficial cost savings.

A key text in the development of strategic inter-company relationship literature was *Beyond Negotiation* by Carlisle and Parker (1989). This book moves the focus from a traditional win–lose relationship based on the location of power between the bargaining positions of the two parties, to a scenario where a win–win relationship can be created. The vehicle suggested to attain such a relationship is the mandate team, with members drawn from both buyer and seller organizations. The advantages of creating a win–win scenario or purchasing partnership have been defined within management, technology and financial spheres and have been summarized by Ellram (1991: 2) and are reproduced in Figure 1. This partnership is defined by Ellram as: 'an agreement between a buyer and a seller that involves a commitment over an extended time period, and includes the sharing of information along with a sharing of the risks and rewards of the relationship.'

A further development of this theme is that of supply chain management (Macbeth *et al.* 1989) and pipeline management (Farmer and Ploos van Amstel 1990) (see SUPPLY CHAIN). Both of these areas take the relationship further, towards end consumers and raw materials sources, and are primarily concerned with optimizing the complete value chain by creating the correct balances, work allocation and relationship type at each company between raw material and end consumption. In order to aid this process, Macbeth *et al.* (1990) have

Management

1 Reduced supplier base is easier to manage
2 Increased mutual dependence lowers risk of losing supply source and creates greater stability through increased supplier loyalty
3 Reduced time looking for new suppliers/gathering competitive bids
4 Allows for joint planning and information sharing based on mutual trust and benefit
5 Loyalty may increase supplier attention and customer service in areas such as:
  • Lead time reliability
  • Priority in times of scarcity
  • Increased attention when problems arise
6 Greater cooperation from suppliers to support the firm's strategy

Technology

1 Partners may be more willing to share/give access to technology
2 Partners may be more willing and capable of participating in product design based on knowledge and commitment to the other partner
3 Supplier knowledge/involvement in design may:
  • Improve quality
  • Reduce time to market for new products/design changes

Financial

1 May share business risks through:
  • Joint investment
  • Joint research and development
  • Sharing of financial risks associated with market shifts
2 Information sharing/forecasting may reduce inventory levels
3 Long-term commitment of a partnership may lead to more stable supply prices

Figure 1 Potential advantages from Japanese style sub-contracting
Source: Ellram (1991)

developed a measurement or positioning tool designed to assess the relationship by gauging the degree to which the different elements of the relationship have been optimized.

Sako (1992) brings together different aspects of relationship strategy based on comparative research between Japan and the UK. The focus of her thesis revolves around trust and the achievement of mutual benefit through long-term relationships. In describing the types of relationships achieved between companies, a spectrum scale has been developed between arm's length contract relations and obligational contract relations (ACR-OCR). The scale ranges from very poor relations at the ACR end to very close at the OCR end. Her detailed research work highlights the benefits of the OCR relationship, which was found to be characteristic of the majority of Japanese electronics firms surveyed, but largely absent in British firms from the same industrial sector.

The most recent important work on relationships is the lean supply model developed by Lamming (1993), largely during his work on the International Motor Vehicle Programme (Womack *et al.* 1990). The lean supply model is designed to capture the present position of the leading manufacturing and assembly companies in the automotive industry and, like the work of Sako, draws heavily on the recent Japanese experience (see MANUFACTURING STRATEGY; JAPANIZATION). Within the lean supply model Lamming shows that it is not the individual abilities or strategies of buyer or seller that are important, but it is the mutual relationship between the two that is the key to their joint strategy. The key elements to this relationship are given as the organizational structure, the communications mechanisms, the business goals and the culture. In order to achieve true lean supply, Lamming (1993: 252) notes that: 'the people working in the relationship are more concerned with their immediate working environment (the relationship) than with that of the customer or the supplier (either of which might be legally their employer)'.

3 State of the art

Peter Drucker (1982: 17) (see DRUCKER, P.F.) commented on the potential advantage through working closely with suppliers: 'Nowhere in business is there greater potential for benefiting from ... interdependency than between customer firms and their suppliers. This is the largest remaining frontier for gaining competitive advantage – and nowhere has such a frontier been more neglected'. Added to this are the views of Carlisle and Parker (1989: 5) who state that: 'cooperation between industrial users and sellers is a far more powerful strategy for making them both more profitable in the long term than any adversarial approach yet devised'.

However, the question remains whether any organization has truly reaped the full benefits of the competitive advantage available by creating this type of interdependent relationship. The answer to this is probably no, but a number of companies, particularly in the Japanese automotive and electronics industries, have come close. These organizations may therefore be regarded as the present state of the art and indeed, are in most cases ahead of the present understanding level of Western observers. As a result this section will briefly highlight the position taken by one such organization, Toyota, and go on to develop a new explanatory model of what state of the art relationships look like with Toyota and similar organizations.

Toyota's state of the art model

Toyota's basic philosophy towards suppliers is one of mutual cooperation and mutual benefit (see TOYODA FAMILY). This is enshrined in four operating principles:

1 long-term stable transactions;
2 stabilization and reinforcement of cooperative relations with suppliers;
3 multiple sourcing of parts;
4 creating and maintaining an optimal ratio between in-house manufacturing and bought-in goods, often weighted towards the latter.

In order to improve the abilities of their suppliers, Toyota organizes a number of different supplier associations or *kyoryoku kai*. Such associations are designed to coordinate the activities of suppliers, as well as to provide a forum for strategy sharing and mutual development. The first such group was started by eighteen Toyota suppliers in 1939 mainly for wartime reasons, but was used in the 1950s and 1960s largely as a teaching medium for suppliers. In recent years Toyota has moved further towards a coordinating and trust building role within this *kyohokai* group, rather than a teaching role. The reason for this is that the majority of its direct suppliers have achieved a high degree of excellence in quality, cost, delivery and new product development. In some respects the main supplier development activities can be seen to be focused at lower tier levels within the Toyota supplier network, as very low tier suppliers still need assistance. However, this assistance is provided not by Toyota directly but by the lower tier supplier's own customers within similar supplier associations.

However, the guiding principles imparted by Toyota at the top of the network are cascaded through the system. A major focus of this process at present is in the responsiveness of the management of the supplier companies in adjusting to the rapidly changing market conditions. The main area of development within the supplier network is consequently cost reduction, quality improvement and technology development as illustrated in Figure 2.

The various supplier associations are key to this process and, as stated above, play a particularly important coordinating role. It will be useful to look at how this occurs in greater detail. As shown diagrammatically in Table 1, there are a number of administrative layers within the *kyohokai*. At the top is the general assembly with an elected board. This general assembly meets yearly to discuss the general type of activities that should take place within the *kyohokai* as well as authorizing the necessary budget allocations. The layer below the general assembly is the board meeting. These meetings take place six times a year and include reports made by Toyota executives, as well as requests from these people for activities to take place within the associations. These suggestions are then taken up by the president and vice president of the *kyohokai*

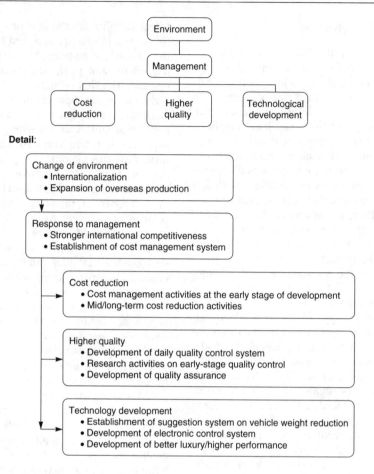

Figure 2 Toyota: focusing of the supplier network

for subsequent implementation. However, there is another important ingredient in the activities of the association. This is the twice yearly meetings with the suppliers' top managers. These meetings help to maintain close relations between Toyota and its suppliers as well as giving the suppliers an opportunity to express their opinions about the future direction of the *kyohokai*. For further details of Toyota's approach in Japan see Hine and Rich (1998).

This type of close relationship, where the customer offers free of charge assistance, is at the heart of the closest buyer–supplier relationships. As yet, this has not been seen very widely outside Japan although it is in Toyota's overseas operations that the nearest Western approximation is to be found. As Jim Robinson, then General Manager, Pur-

chasing Division of Toyota Motor Manufacturing (UK) Limited noted in 1991: 'The development of Toyota's Production System and Human Resources policy has not just been contained to its own boundaries, but has extended into every aspect of Toyota's relationships with its suppliers in an effort to strive for ultimate satisfaction and mutual prosperity' (Robinson 1991: 2). He regards the following as crucial in the development of such relationships:

- honesty and openness
- trust
- effort
- teamwork
- understanding
- desire to improve

Table 1 Outline activities of Toyota's *Tokai kyohokai*

Activites	Frequency	Description of activities
General assembly	1/year	Election of board members
		Activites/budget authorization
Board meeting	6/year	Report/request from TMC top management, etc.
Meeting with suppliers' top management	2/year	Development of close communication between suppliers' top management and TMC top management
Committee Cost, quality, safety/sanitation	1/month	Improvement of suppliers' management level through concrete, substantial study on cost, safety/sanitation
Sectional meeting number 1 – number 3 sectional	1/month	Improvement/development of communication/management level among suppliers
Others		Publication of *Kyoho News*
		Sports activites, etc.

At the same time as setting these targets Toyota have stated in the UK that they will assist their suppliers through education and training and by setting up supplier associations, as happened earlier at their Kentucky site in the USA. The stated aim of these groups is: 'to bring suppliers in all areas of manufacturing together, to exchange views and experiences which will help them in their pursuit of technical excellence in all aspects of their business' (Robinson 1991: 4). Toyota started such an approach in 1993 in the UK through a pioneering venture with Cardiff Business School and the Welsh Development Agency to run an association for their Wales-based suppliers, with Toyota playing an observatory role in the group.

While Toyota and their network of suppliers exhibit the closest relations as a group, their type of relationship is not unique and is found in other discrete parts industries in Japan, particularly in the automotive and electronics industries. Studies carried out in Japan between 1991 and 1993 (Hines 1994) have demonstrated that there are ten key features to the resulting relationships:

1 supplier tiering structure;
2 few suppliers but reliance on multiple sources;
3 high asset specificity;
4 low value added ratios;
5 bilateral design;
6 high degree of supplier innovation;
7 close high trust long-term supplier relations;
8 supplier grading and self-certification;
9 supplier coordination;
10 supplier development.

It should be noted that it is very difficult to separate these individual features and indeed, it is their very interactions that embody the unique relationships found in Japan. However, it should be noted that in Japan it is the active and prolonged use of the *kyoryoku kai* that has led to these features.

Network sourcing

The complete relationship system has been termed *network sourcing* (Hines 1994) (see NETWORKS AND ORGANIZATIONS) as, although it involves many tiers of supply, it does not rely on a simple supply chain or pipeline but rather the close relationships formed between a customer and their suppliers, between these suppliers and also between firms at each subsequent tier of the supply structure. As a result, a highly cohesive and stable relationship structure is formed.

The first notable feature is that of the many tiers within the system, with each company operating a maximum buy strategy within the framework of a maximum make strategy within the stable supply network. Due to the highly tiered structure, there is a considerable reliance on small firms for a high percentage of the value of the final assembled product. Coupled with this tiering structure, each customer typically has a very restricted number of suppliers in total, with a company such as Toyota having only about 250 direct parts suppliers. These suppliers would typically only have about twenty-five to thirty sources, with the latter only having between six and ten suppliers. As a result of this narrow supplier base, Western observers have often concluded that Japanese companies single source their parts. This is in fact untrue, as there are usually two or even three actual or potential sources for each part. However, what is more common is the single sourcing by part number but multiple sourcing by part type. This hybrid sourcing method helps to encourage close relations between customer and supplier, while allowing for active competition between suppliers.

The third feature of network sourcing is the high rates of asset specificity. Asset specificity is concerned with the degree to which suppliers make specific investments concerned with their ability to supply any one particular customer. These asset investments are found in four areas: physical assets (specific dies, moulds and tooling), dedicated assets (production capacity and capital equipment), human assets (specifically trained personnel) and site assets (physical proximity to customers' premises). These high asset specificity rates are signs of the investment that suppliers have made in the relationship. These types of specific investments are found at each tier of the supplier network structure with each firm concentrating on core activities and subcontracting other tasks outside of its specialist range. As a result, generally, high bought-in content rates pertain at each tier. Such bought-in rates in the automotive industry, for instance, typically range between 70 and 85 per cent meaning that customers are highly reliant on the abilities and expertise of their suppliers, and so close relationships are essential.

These close relations are also exhibited in the design process where the customer is again often highly reliant on their suppliers. For instance, Mazda are only responsible for 30 per cent of the design of their cars. This shared design process is coupled with a high rate of innovation within the suppliers themselves. This type of innovation is concerned with both new product development as well as the improvement of quality, cost and delivery processes.

As noted above, the relationships formed between companies are very close and tend to result in a high level of trust between companies. This trust has been categorized by Sako (1992) to be of three types: competence trust (that each trading partner is capable of fulfilling its promises), contractual trust (that each trading partner will honour its promises) and most important, goodwill trust (that each partner will go beyond the call of duty in their relationship). This last feature is the most important one and is rare outside Japan, although it is of a similar nature to the term 'exceeding customer requirements' used in the West. However, crucially, goodwill trust is not a one-way process flowing from supplier to customer, but a multi-way process running also from customer to supplier and even between suppliers. Such high trust relationships tend to result in close long-term business beneficial to all parties involved. Indeed, such mutuality has led to a reduction in the need for negotiation, with prices fixed by joint disaggregation of the end consumers' requirement, with any resulting gap between cost and price narrowed by active value engineering and value analysis between customers and suppliers throughout the supplier network.

In order to focus improvement efforts, customers have traditionally operated supplier grading systems focusing on quality, cost reduction and delivery performance. However, with increasing competency levels (towards 100 per cent on time delivery and zero defects) in the supplier networks, increasingly suppliers are becoming self-certified, removing the need for additional grading.

The last two major features of network sourcing are the high degree of investment made in supplier coordination and development, mainly through the use of the *kyoryoku kai*. In this context, supplier coordination may be defined as the activities made by a customer to mould their suppliers into a common way of working so that competitive advantage can be gained, particularly by removing intercompany waste. Examples would include the use of common quality standards, transport and electronic data interchange (EDI) systems. Supplier development may be defined as the activities made by a customer to help improve the strategies, tools and techniques employed by suppliers to improve their competitive advantage, particularly by removing intra-company waste. Examples would include the communication of customer strategies so that suppliers could plan their processes more effectively, as well as customers offering specific assistance to the suppliers in areas such as factory layout, set-up time reduction and the operation of *kanban* systems (card-based inventory pull systems).

Supplier coordination by its very nature is most effectively achieved when a group of companies are brought together for regular meetings, as happens within the *kyoryoku kai* structure. Supplier development can be undertaken either *en masse* through joint education and exchange forums or through individual one-to-one development activities. However, although the latter are very widespread they are primarily successful because the high levels of trust and openness have already been created by the regular attendance of customer and supplier alike at *kyoryoku kai* meetings. Thus, when the customer visits a supplier's plant there is an anticipation of joint problem solving and improvement and not posturing and lip service.

The foregoing discussion has centred on the state of the art buyer–supplier relationship as exhibited by firms such as Toyota in Japan. The following section will attempt to model how this state of the art system operates, as well as exploring its causality and potential outside Japan.

4 Theoretical aspects

Corporate strategy according to Andrews (1984) refers to the pattern of decisions in a company that:

1 determines and reveals its goals and objectives;
2 produces the principal policies and plans for achieving those goals;
3 defines the range of business the company is to pursue, the kind of economic and human organization it is or intends to be,

and the nature of the economic and non-economic contribution it intends to make to its shareholders, employees, customers and communities.

Watts *et al.* note the following:

> In the centre of corporate strategy is the organization's competitive strategy. The competitive strategy is a combination of the goals for which the company is striving and the means by which it will compete in the marketplace. The purchasing strategy can be viewed as the pattern of decisions related to acquiring materials and services to support operations activities that are consistent with the overall corporate competitive strategy.
>
> (1992: 5)

When reviewing the strategies of the leading lean producers in Japan, it is apparent that profit maximization is not at the top of their list of objectives. During recent research tours in Japan this question was posed to managers of ten large discrete parts assemblers from the automotive, electronics and machine tools industries. While they were not unanimous in their answer, the satisfaction of consumer requirements ranked higher than profit maximization in all cases. Thus, total quality is given as the primary aim, with profit a key supporting feature, not the other way around.

A wider survey summarized by Dimancescu (1992) into Japanese Deming (see DEMING, W.E.) prizewinners (the prizes are for the best quality firms in Japan) found that the implementation of this successful strategy involved the use of cross-functional teams. He found that of the eighty-two Deming prize-winners, sixty-one were concerned with cross-functional cost reduction, fifty-nine with cross-functional quality improvement, fifty-nine with the cross-functional delivery process and twenty-two with the cross-functional design process. However, when these successful companies are viewed more closely, we can see that they typically buy in 70 per cent of their end product, and their excellent position could not have been gained without working very closely with their suppliers, and indeed with close relations between lower tier suppliers. In fact, a complete

Raw material	Supplier chain	Inbound logistics	Operations	Outbound logistics	Customer chain	Consumer

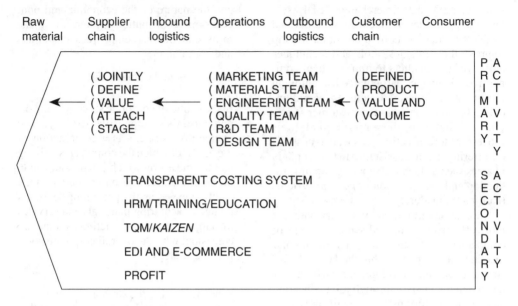

Figure 3 The integrated materials value pipeline

cross-company teaming scenario must have been set up. Figure 3 attempts to capture what this cross-company teaming looks like.

Figure 3 presents a simple depiction of the integration of the key processes across company boundaries. The integrated materials value pipeline is designed to show how these intra-company processes can be effectively spread along the supply pipeline to involve the suppliers and unlock the potential competitive advantages that they hold to the benefit of consumer, customer and supplier alike. As Newman and Rhee comment on the NUMMI Toyota/General Motors factory in California:

> A supplier becomes part of the team and, in turn, is responsible for structuring its operation to meet team requirements. Crossing traditional organization boundaries is acceptable because these boundaries really do not exist. Traditional functional responsibility has given way to responsibility for improvement and information flow. ... Compartmentalization creates waste by requiring the same message to be repeated to several people.
>
> (1990: 19)

This situation is in stark contrast to the familiar Porter (see PORTER, M.E.) value chain/system (Porter 1985) which, although capturing the Western manufacturing *push* philosophy, does little to point the way for companies seeking excellence. Three major problems are apparent in the Porter value chain. The first is that the primary company driving force is its own margin and profitability rather than customer satisfaction. Second, although Porter concedes that integration is important, his models demonstrate the true functional barriers all too common in Western companies. Third, there is little or no integration across company barriers, meaning that each company is operating as an island without sharing a strategic direction with its customers and suppliers alike.

The integrated materials value chain is a *pull* model designed to correct these problems and point the way to how companies linked by the common supply of the end customer can achieve excellence in the key processes of quality, cost, new product development and delivery. The first feature of the new model that is noteworthy is that it has the consumer as the starting point for all intra- and inter-company activities. Indeed, the consumer under the pull philosophy is responsible for defining the quality (defect rates, reliability, features and functionality) of a product, the cost they are prepared to pay, the type of product and the timing of its appearance on the market and at the retailer convenient to the consumer. Thus, the collective consumer base defines the product value and volume it is willing to pay for and buy.

This value and volume is translated or deployed throughout the integrated materials value pipeline through the use of teams cutting across the traditional functional and company boundaries. Thus, the building into the product of quality, the optimization of cost, the incorporation of correct features and the delivery when required is the responsibility of all members of the companies in the network of supply. The key team members in the four processes are defined in the model as marketing, materials, engineering, quality, research and development and design as all have a significant part to play. For further discussion of these key cross-functional and cross-company processes see Dimancescu *et al.* (1997).

As the integrated materials value chain has a number of secondary or support activities associated with it concerned with supply chain cohesion, intercompany integration can be readily facilitated. The first of these mechanisms is a transparent costing system, such that costing information is available across the supply network so that sensible value engineering, value analysis and industrial engineering decisions can be made to maximize the potential competitive advantage of the whole network. This cost transparency is necessary within any target/*kaizen* costing environment and hence means that suppliers have to adjust to the fact that their customers will want them to be open with their cost information.

The second intercompany integration mechanism is the area of human resource policies, training and education (see HUMAN RESOURCE MANAGEMENT). For companies who purchase 60 or 70 per cent of the value of their final products, to pay no attention to the levels of knowledge and skills in their suppliers' strategies in management process implementation is obviously nonsensical. Thus a coordinated approach to developing these abilities

in their suppliers is only logical given the necessity for long-term relationships inherent in any stable system. Coupled to this is a shared view of the importance of the end customer and hence a translation of the total quality management and *kaizen* philosophies down the pipeline is essential.

In order to reduce the paperwork flows and cut down on the cost of inter-company communication, meetings with suppliers can be carried out *en masse*. Meetings between customer and supplier on an individual basis can be confined to the resolution of individual problems and potential for continuous improvement. In addition, EDI and other e-commerce can be employed between companies to cut down on the wasteful and time consuming paperwork sent between firms such as purchase orders, confirmation orders, production schedules and so on.

The last secondary activity that runs along the supply pipeline (see SUPPLY CHAIN) is that of profit. It is obviously essential for all companies to make a reasonable profit as a return on shareholder investment and source of future investment funds. However, with this new open system with open book accounting practices, it becomes readily apparent as to the profitability of each firm in the supply pipeline. As a result, firms can both be controlled from making excessive profit and given a partial safety net when profit levels fall too low. It should be noted that the level of profit made collectively in the supply of goods is the result of reducing collective costs of production below the price the consumers are willing to pay for the products that they have defined are required. The skill that the Japanese have learnt is not to fight with customers and suppliers alike over the apportionment of turnover and profit. Instead, by close adherence to the consumers' requirements, they compete as supply networks one against another to gain greater market share and hence increase the sizes of their mutual turnover and profits. A major nexus for this inter-company cooperation and development is the *kyoryoku kai* or supplier association. This situation is neatly summarized by Womack *et al.*:

By contrast (to Western counterparts), suppliers to a lean producer know that as long as they make a good-faith effort to perform as they should, the assembler will ensure that they make a reasonable return on their investment. So sharing with other group members means that the performance of the whole group will improve and every member will benefit. In other words, active participation in mutual problem-solving through the supplier group (supplier association) is an act of simple self-interest.

(1990: 153–4)

The question that arises from this modelling is, how is this closer state of relationship achieved? In order to understand this, it is necessary to review the features of network sourcing and attempt to explore the causality flows. This has been done in a simple way in Figure 4. For each feature of network sourcing an attempt has been made to gauge the causality of all the other features by reference to the author's observations of the operation of network sourcing in Japan. Thus for supplier tiering (first row in Figure 4) the degree to which the other features have affected this feature and led to its creation is plotted. A strong causal relationship is marked with a circle within a circle and a weak relation with a circle. This process has then been repeated for each feature to check their causalities. For a strong relationship a score of three points is given and for a weak relation a score of one point is awarded.

The degree to which any one feature is a cause of the others is ascertained by summing the causations as shown on the bottom row of Figure 4. The cause scores are seen to range from five to twenty-three, where five shows that the feature (supplier grading) has only a small affect on the others and where twenty-three shows that the feature (supplier coordination) has a considerable effect on the other features. In a similar way the effect scores are given by the sum of the rows and are seen to range from two to nineteen. The two score (supplier coordination) shows that this feature is only slightly affected by the other features whereas the nineteen score (close high trust relations) shows this feature is considerably affected by the other features.

In order to gain a net cause and effect score the latter score is subtracted from the former

and given in the last column in Figure 4. These scores are then ranked and reproduced in Table 2. The net causality scores are seen to range from twenty-one (supplier coordination) to minus ten (close high trust relations). Although it is obvious that each of the ten features is a partial cause and a partial effect, it is possible to group the end results into three distinctive sets. The first set consisting of supplier coordination and supplier development can be seen to be primarily causes with reasonable positive scores. A second group consisting of low added value ratios and close high trust relations can be seen to be primarily effects with reasonable positive scores. The other six features fall between the two extremes and can be seen to be partly cause and partly effect although the effect scores are seen to predominate.

The implication from these causality scores is that in order to create the presently exhibited network sourcing pattern in Japan, some features have been given more precedence than others, with some features largely being the effects of work in other areas. In this respect it is attention to supplier coordination and development that are the primary cause factors of the type of relationships exhibited today. As a result, if Western organizations are to seek to emulate such close buyer–supplier relations then attention should be paid to these two areas while creating an environment where the mixed causality factors are encouraged. The primary mechanism with which to do this and the one employed by the lean assemblers and parts makers in Japan is the *kyoryoku kai* or supplier association. The method by which this can be implemented in a Western environment is given in Figure 5. How this can be undertaken and what particular practical modifications will be required to use this Japanese tool in the West will be discussed in the next section.

5 Practical aspects

When Japanese companies set up overseas they often find that the most difficult problem they face is the creation of the network sourcing style relations they are accustomed to in their homeland. As Mr Negishi, European Director of the Electronic Industries Association of Japan, reports: 'local components are

A \ B	Supplier tiering	Few suppliers	High asset specificity	Low value added ratio	Bilateral design	Supplier innovation	Close high trust relations	Supplier grading	Supplier coordination	Supplier development	Factor A affected by sum of Factor Bs — EFFECT SCORE	C/E SCORE — CAUSE/EFFECT SCORE
Supplier tiering		○		●		○	○		●	○	10	(2)
Few suppliers	●		●		○			○	●	○	12	(4)
High asset specificity	○	○			●	○	●		○	●	13	(4)
Low value added	●				●	●	○	○	●	●	17	(7)
Bilateral design		○	○	○		●	○	○	●	○	12	0
Supplier innovation		●	○	○	○		○		○	●	11	(2)
Close high trust relations	○	○	●	●	●	○		○	●	●	19	(10)
Supplier grading							○		●	●	7	(2)
Supplier coordination				○	○						2	21
Supplier development		○	○	○			○	○	●		8	10
Factor B affects sum of Factor As — CAUSE SCORE	8	8	9	10	12	9	9	5	23	18		

● Strong Cause (3 points)
○ Weak Cause (1 point)

Figure 4 Network sourcing causality matrix

our most serious problem in manufacturing in the UK' (Trevor and Christie 1988: 1). This is not surprising given that the network sourcing system has taken over fifty years to develop in Japan and no equivalent causation factor is prevalent in the West to create the closeness of relations seen in Japan. Indeed, the situation may be worse as there is not as yet a widespread understanding in the West that close long-term cooperative relations are an effect rather than a cause factor. It is therefore imperative that a Westernized *kyoryoku kai* or other similar mechanism be used if the same type of competitive advantage forming relations are to be achieved outside Japan.

However, at present there are only about 60 examples of *kyoryoku kai* outside Japan.

There are three main reasons why there is only a limited number of such groups outside Japan. First, such groups may be considered by the Japanese to be part of their 'crown jewels' and something they are not keen to share with Western competitors. Second, the type of inter-company relationships presently exhibited in the West, namely arm's length or adversarial, do not make the setting up of such groups easy or even possible due to high levels of mistrust. The third reason is that Japanese inward investors do not regard local suppliers as being developed enough to benefit from supplier associations and that they lack sufficient Japanese staff trained and capable of setting up these groups. Whatever the individual reason, without outside assistance it is to be

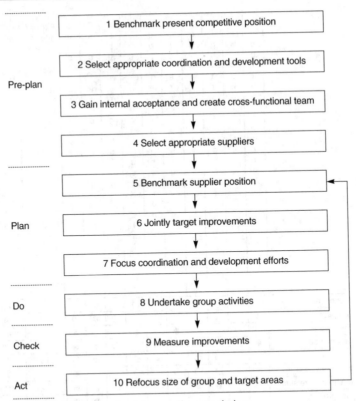

Figure 5 A generic model for the creation of a supplier association

Table 2 Network sourcing causality scores

Cause	CIE score	
Supplier coordination	21	Primarily causes
Supplier development	10	
Bilateral design	0	Mixed cause and effect
Supplier innovation	(2)	
Supplier tiering	(2)	
Supplier grading	(2)	
High asset specificity	(4)	
Few suppliers	(4)	
Low added value ration	(7)	Primarily effects
Close high trust relations	(10)	

expected that such groups will only develop slowly and will mainly be associated with Japanese-owned companies.

A Welsh example

In order to increase the number of these beneficial groups in the British environment and test the necessary localization required, work at Cardiff Business School has centred on facilitating the creation of a number of such groups within different industrial sectors, supply tiers and nationalities of customer companies. This work has been undertaken in collaboration with the Welsh Development Agency and has resulted in about fifty supplier associations involving Welsh companies. The first of these groups was centred around Calsonic Llanelli Radiators, a Japanese-owned automotive cooling system manufacturer. Subsequent groups have been formed at retail, assembler and first tier level in the electronics, furniture, telecommunication, defence, office equipment and food retailing industries with Japanese, British, French, German and North American-owned companies.

As noted above, the spread of *kyoryoku kai* outside Japan (and Korea) has been slow. Indeed with the exception of those groups directly or indirectly facilitated by the author, there are only a few other known examples. These include Toyota (Kentucky, USA), NUMMI (California), Canon (France) and Crosfield Electronics (UK).

The work carried out by the author in Japan, the USA and Europe has shown that various degrees of localization are required for successful application outside Japan. The following main adaptations are generally recommended.

1 Membership should not be limited to direct suppliers as in Japan, as active development and networking with some indirect suppliers was felt to be critical.
2 The inclusion of service companies, particularly those that constitute the outward face of the customer firm's quality. Such firms would include specialist design houses and transport firms.
3 The size should be kept small, at least in the first months, so that customer and suppliers could learn the technique together. An initial maximum size of twelve firms was felt to be necessary.
4 A modification of the traditional Japanese paternalistic relationship whereby suppliers are dominated. It was felt that a more equal and democratic forum would be more applicable in the West.
5 To start the group, a benchmarking of each supplier is to be undertaken which can act as the focus for deciding future events as well as a measuring tool for development success.
6 Outside facilitation was felt to be necessary, particularly as the technique is very new outside Japan and involves considerable administrative support, especially in the setting up stages.

In many respects, therefore, the British experience of supplier associations has been a localized version of the Japanese *kyoryoku kai*, taking advantage of western tools but adapted to the European environment. The first of these, Calsonic Llanelli Radiators Supplier Association was set up in 1991 around the automotive cooling system manufacturer.

It is not the intention of this entry to relate the detailed experiences of each British group but rather to give an understanding of the application of the *kyoryoku kai* technique outside Japan. However, it will be useful to review the first Welsh example, particularly the early stages, as these are the most critical to the success of the association. (A fuller account of this work can be found in Hines [1994] and Hines and Rich [1998].) As mentioned above, the Calsonic Llanelli Radiators Supplier Association was set up in 1991 as a pilot scheme to test the applicability of the *kyoryoku kai* to the UK. The work was undertaken by the author and Calsonic Llanelli Radiator staff with financial assistance from the Welsh Development Agency.

The first group of firms involved totalled nine in number, five of which were indirect suppliers particularly relating to design and tool making. The concept was explained in detail to each of these firms and all companies contacted agreed to take part, although two indirect suppliers later withdrew. In order to gain a closer understanding of the firms a detailed questionnaire was completed on a face-to-face basis. Subsequently a benchmarking assessment was made of all the companies, including Calsonic Llanelli Radiators, in order to understand their absolute and relative development positions across a range of relevant attributes.

This information was then presented to the collected suppliers at the first official meeting in September 1991. This was used as the basis for deciding the future direction and priorities of the group in terms of mutual development. This direction would revolve around the following areas seen as key to future development:

- employee involvement schemes
- machine downtime analysis and improvement schemes
- value analysis
- integrated design

- external relations with suppliers and customers.

It was also decided that seminar meetings for senior staff would be held quarterly with workshops on specific tools for 'operational' staff to be held between each seminar. More recently Calsonic Llanelli Radiators have started a second similar group, with a third planned for later in 1994, which will bring 30 per cent of suppliers and over 90 per cent of purchasing spend within the associations. The importance of this supplier association and its later Western emulators is that it provides a practical method of developing towards a true network sourcing relationship. While it does not provide the only possible route, its early success in around sixty UK-based customer organizations has proved that it is a viable route to the creation of the type of relationships found in state of the art organizations.

The result of this work is a higher degree of sharing between customer and supplier, but also between the different suppliers themselves. This system also helps build mutual trust and increases the unity of the customer and its group of direct suppliers. As a result, this mechanism not only provides a more efficient mechanism for teaching suppliers about new tools and techniques, but it also helps the companies share strategies and direction, and hence remove inter-company waste. The combination of this intra- and inter-company waste removal results in significant competitive advantage. In this context Lamming (1993: 96–7) comments: 'As has been seen from the discussion of ... Japanese *keiretsu* and *kyoryoku kai* in the automotive industry, there may be many potential benefits from this type of collaboration beyond those traditionally expected.'

6 Policy implications

There are a number of policy implications of the foregoing discussion. At the micro level these implications are for customers, their purchasing staff and their suppliers, and at the macro level for the various professional bodies as well as national and regional government organizations. These implications will be briefly reviewed in the sections below.

At the customer level there are three major implications for customer companies:

1 If the world's best manufacturing companies are achieving significant competitive advantage through the application of network sourcing, can any customer company afford not to adopt a similar approach?
2 If the basics of network sourcing have been transferred from company to company in Japan by close networking between leading edge companies, can any Western company who wishes to achieve world class status afford to follow a different route?
3 If the key to facilitating network sourcing is the coordination and development of suppliers, primarily through the use of the *kyoryoku kai*, can leading Western companies enjoy the benefits of strategic partnerships without investing in their suppliers in a similar way?

A number of implications are apparent for purchasing staff within these organizations. Nishiguchi comments on these implications:

An important repercussion of the foregoing change was that purchasing agents were no longer merely downstream price negotiators but evaluators of subcontractor performance and coordinators of various intra- and inter-firm functions. Whether or not purchasing agents were engineers by profession, sound technical knowledge became part of their essential job requirements so that they could evaluate their subcontractors' technical capabilities on their own. At Toyota, for example, every purchasing agent became technically trained so that whether or not the person was an engineer by profession they were able first-hand to evaluate subcontractors' technical competence and teach them the principles of the Toyota Production System in the office and in the factory.

(1989: 220)

This new role for purchasing staff includes:

1 The coordination of all activities between buyer and seller including activities undertaken by other functions such as production, quality, design and production engineering.
2 Purchasing's role in seeking new areas and sources of competitive advantage from the supplier network and formulating

strategies to maximize this advantage for the benefit of buyer and seller alike.

3 A role as consultant in coordinating the cascade of developmental assistance to suppliers from the different internal departments through the use of a supplier association.

4 A pivotal role in the two-way dissemination of strategic information between buyer and supplier. This dissemination would involve keeping the suppliers fully aware of developments in the marketplace so that they can respond to the needs of the end consumer as well as adopt the best technologies and operating methods. It would also involve the formulation of joint strategies with the supplier association membership.

5 A role in targeting and measuring the improvement of suppliers as they seek either collectively or individually to develop continuously.

There are a number of implications for suppliers as a result of their customers' moves towards network sourcing. These include:

1 Are they willing and able to enter into the type of relationship that their customers are seeking?

2 Have they started to select the customers they wish to deal with and developed a preferred customer policy?

3 Have they developed links with at least one leading edge customer who will demand rapid improvement in all areas of the suppliers' process deliverables and will offer both coordination and development assistance?

4 Are they as demanding of their suppliers as their customers are of them?

5 Are they willing and capable of replicating Network Sourcing with their own suppliers?

The new directions that customers need to take with their suppliers as a result of the potential competitive advantages exhibited by the Japanese have obvious implications for the various professional bodies in Europe and the USA. These implications include:

1 Are these professional bodies attuned to the new network sourcing methodology

and are they encouraging their members to follow a similar route?

2 Does the literature and periodicals they produce reflect this new focus?

3 Do their education and training courses align with the approaches of network sourcing or are they still reinforcing traditional Western arm's length buyer–supplier approaches?

4 What do they need to do to change if the answers to the above questions are not to their liking?

The last set of implications refers to the various government agencies and includes:

1 Are these organizations encouraging companies to develop the types of benefits inherent in network sourcing?

2 Are such bodies encouraging and even funding customer companies to set up mechanisms such as supplier associations to gain competitive advantage for the local and national economies?

3 What more could these organizations do to help?

7 Future developments

There are three areas where future developments are likely to be felt; strategy, buyer–supplier relationships and logistics. The first of these is further exploration of the existing examples of the application of *kyoryoku kai* in the West. At the time of writing there are a number of programmes being run that will address this localization by testing the concept in a wide range of industries in several European countries. It will be of great significance to test whether the network sourcing type of relationships can be produced in the process or service industries where there has perhaps been less progress made in Japan. It will also be of interest to ascertain and test the type of localization the *kyoryoku kai* will require when it is used in other European countries.

The second area from which future developments will spring is the more widespread use of the *kyoryoku kai* in the industries and companies where it is already being employed. This work will help in gaining a better understanding of the cost benefit economics of its use, the payback period, as well as the industry specificity of the mechanism. It will also be possible to measure the full range of network sourcing features against Japanese benchmarks to gauge whether the *kyoryoku kai* in the West are creating the same, an inferior or a superior system.

The third area of future developments regards the use of other mechanisms designed to create a similar type of close relationship that has resulted from the application of the *kyoryoku kai*. Such mechanisms may be drawn from Japan and may be complementary to the *kyoryoku kai*, or may originate in the West.

8 Conclusion

This entry has reviewed the existing position of strategic application within buyer–supplier relationships. The importance of strategy in this area has been demonstrated in its use by state of the art companies such as Toyota as well as in the simple fact that the average company spends more on bought-in resources than on those employed within its four walls.

The author has attempted to summarize the history of the subject since the early days when purchasing was not even given operation status. A number of early cases were presented where suppliers have yielded competitive advantage to their customers, as was a summary of the early key works in the subject. More recent modelling and work concerning the strategic role of the buyer–supplier relationship was also presented. The majority of this work was seen to suffer from the fact that the causality relationships were not discussed, with the implication that a close or partnership relationship is possible simply by improving one or other feature of the relationship such as trust, length, number of suppliers or asset specificity.

A review of the state of the art situation, including a summary of the position taken by Toyota and their suppliers, showed that the creation of very close relations is a far more complex matter. A ten-point model called network sourcing, summarizing the key features of this relationship was reported. Further analysis was undertaken and this revealed that there were two primary features which were seen to cause the type of relationships demonstrated by Toyota, namely supplier coordination and supplier development. The other features are partly or mainly effects of supplier coordination and development.

In order to understand how these two features can be reproduced outside Japan a discussion of the Western version of the *kyoryoku kai* was undertaken, centred mainly around the ongoing work with Calsonic Llanelli Radiators. This successful early work has led to a number of important policy implication for British companies, professional institutes and government agencies alike. The future direction of work in this area is likely to centre around broader and deeper application of the *kyoryoku kai* as well as the search for other appropriate tools.

The main conclusions from the work are:

1 The strategic role of the buyer–supplier relationship has only recently been understood at an academic level.
2 The present day state of the art situation as demonstrated by companies such as Toyota is ahead of the present conceptualization of academics.
3 The state of the art situation within this subject area at present lies in Japan.
4 That in order to create these state of the art relationships Japanese customers were seen to invest in their supplier network particularly through the use of their *kyoryoku kai* or supplier associations.
5 As yet the mechanisms by which these state of the art relationships function are poorly understood and replication and localization in the West has only just begun.
6 That if rapid progress is not made by Western companies in this important strategic area they are likely to fall further behind their Japanese counterparts in the race for sustainable competitive advantage.

PROFESSOR PETER HINES
CARDIFF BUSINESS SCHOOL

Further reading

(References cited in the text marked *)

* American Management Association (1931) *Handbook of Business Administration*, New York: American Management Association. (Classic text on purchasing which first gave practical information on the function.)

* Andrews, K.R. (1984) *The Concept of Corporate Strategy*, Homewood, IL: Irwin. (Useful text discussing the range and scope of corporate strategy.)

* Baily, P. (1963) *Purchasing and Supply Management*, 1st edn, London: Chapman and Hall. (First British text specifically on purchasing primarily concentrating on operational matters.)

* Baily, P. and Farmer, D. (1986) *Purchasing Principles and Management*, 5th edn, London: Pitman. (Fifth edition of the most successful and popular British student text.)

* Blois, K.J. (1972) 'Vertical quasi-integration', *Journal of Industrial Economics* 20 (3): 253–72. (First academic paper discussing the possibility of close relationships outside of joint ownership.)

* Carlisle, J.A. and Parker, R.C. (1989) *Beyond Negotiation: Redeeming Customer–Supplier Relationships*, Chichester: Wiley. (Pioneering work written in consultancy style, showing how buyer–supplier relationships can be revolutionized.)

* Chandler, D.A. (1962) *Strategy and Structure*, Cambridge, MA: MIT Press. (Classic text on strategy involving discussion of causality within strategy and structure.)

* Dimancescu, D. (1992) *The Seamless Enterprise: Making Cross Functional Management Work*, New York: Harper Business. (Easy to read text on cross-functional management particularly relating to new product development.)

*Dimancescu, D., Hines, P. and Rich, N. (1997) *The Lean Enterprise: Designing and Managing Strategic Processes for Customer Winning Performance*, New York: Amacom. (Application of process based thinking.)

* Drucker, P.F. (1982) *The Changing World of the Executive*, London: Heinemann. (Consultancy style book including discussion of key role of suppliers in corporate improvement.)

* Ellram, L.M. (1991) 'A managerial guideline for the development and implementation of purchasing partnerships', *International Journal of Purchasing and Materials Management* 27 (3): 2–8. (Academic article describing partnership relationships and how they may be achieved.)

* Farmer, D.H. and Ploos van Amstel, R. (1990) *Effective Pipeline Management: How To Manage Integrated Logistics*, Aldershot: Gower. (Describes the strategic movement of goods in terms of a pipeline flow analogy.)

* Ford, I.D. (1980) 'The development of buyer–supplier relationships in industrial markets', *European Journal of Marketing* 14 (5/6): 339–53. (Classic early work of the IMP Group viewing buyer–supplier relationships within complex networks.)

* Hines, P.A. (1994) *Creating World Class Suppliers: Unlocking Mutual Competitive Advantage*, London: Pitman. (Easy to read text on supplier development and supply chain improvement involving supplier associations.)

* Hines, P. and Rich, N. (1998) 'Outsourcing competitive advantage: the use of suppliers associations', International *Journal of Physical Distribution and Logistics Management* 28 (7): 524–46. (Academic paper demonstrating the original Japanese and later Western versions of supplier associations; shows how competitive advantage stems from their use.)

* Kotler, P. (1976) *Marketing Management, Analysis, Planning and Control*, 3rd edn, Englewood Cliffs, NJ: Prentice Hall. (Classic marketing text involving discussion of industrial buyer–supplier relationships from a marketing viewpoint.)

* Lamming, R. (1993) *Beyond Partnership: Strategies for Innovation and Lean Supply*, Hemel Hempstead: Prentice Hall. (Automotive related discussion of how firms may employ lean supply.)

* Lee, L., Jr and Dobler, D.W. (1971) *Purchasing and Materials Management: Text and Cases*, 2nd edn, New York: McGraw-Hill. (Classic early US textbook on purchasing and materials management.)

* Macbeth, D.K., Baxter, L.F., Ferguson, N. and Neil, G.C. (1989) 'Not purchasing but supply chain management', *Purchasing and Supply Management* November: 30–2. (Early discussion in practitioner journal of the supply chain management concept.)

* Macbeth, D.K., Baxter, L.F., Ferguson, N. and Neil, G.C. (1990) *Customer–Supplier Relationship Audit*, Kempston: IFS. (Consultancy approach to auditing the buyer–supplier relationship.)

* Newman, R. and Rhee, K. (1990) 'A case study of NUMMI and its suppliers', *Journal of Purchasing and Materials Management*, 26 (4): 15–20. (Academic discussion and case showing buyer–supplier relationship at NUMMI in California.)

* Nishiguchi, T. (1989) 'Strategic dualism: an alternative in industrial societies', PhD thesis, Oxford University. (Academic text providing history of Japanese sub-contracting and buyer–supplier relationships.)

* Porter, M. (1985) *Competitive Advantage: Creating and Sustaining Superior Performance*, New York: The Free Press. (Classic discussion

of how competitive advantage is achieved, including the use of the value chain.)

* Robinson, J. (1991) 'The importance of customer/supplier partnerships', *Proceedings of the Institute of Materials Management Annual Conference*, Solihull, 29–30 October, Institute of Materials Management, Cranfield School of Management. (Practitioner paper describing buyer–supplier relationships involving Toyota in the UK.)

* Sako, M. (1992) *Prices, Quality and Trust: Inter-Firm Relations in Britain & Japan*, Cambridge: Cambridge University Press. (Easy-to-read comparison of the buyer–supplier relationship in the UK and Japanese electronics industries.)

* Storhagen, N.G. (1993) 'Just-in-time in Japan – conditions and possibilities for implementation in Western countries', *Proceedings of the International Symposium on Logistics*, Nottingham University, 6–7 July. (Academic study of just-in-time implementation in Sweden and Japan and success criteria involved.)

* Trevor, M. and Christie, I. (1988) *Manufacturers & Suppliers in Britain & Japan*, London: Policy Studies Institute. (Easy-to-read comparative study of buyer–supplier relationships in the UK and Japan.)

* Watts, C.A., Kim, K.Y. and Hahn C.K. (1992) 'Linking purchasing to corporate competitive strategy', *International Journal of Purchasing and Materials Management* 28 (4): 2–8. (Academic paper linking purchasing with the wider corporate strategy process showing the key value of purchasing.)

* Williamson, O.E. (1985) *The Economic Institutions of Capitalism*, New York: The Free Press. (Classic text on transaction cost economics, very hard to read.)

* Womack, J.P., Jones, D.T. and Roos, D. (1990) *The Machine That Changed The World*, New York: Rawson. (Popular text on lean production summarizing studies on worldwide automotive assemblers.)

See also: EUROPE, MANAGEMENT IN; JAPAN, MANAGEMENT IN; LOGISTICS AND PHYSICAL DISTRIBUTION; STRATEGY, CONCEPT OF; SUPPLY CHAIN MANAGEMENT

Strategy in the emerging countries

Overview

Many of the developing countries of Asia and Africa with large and increasing populations have been at very low levels of economic development. They are characterized by abysmally low income levels, poor infrastructure, poor health facilities, etc. But these countries represent potentially large markets for consumer as well as industrial products. Several developing nations in these two continents are in the process of implementing large scale economic reforms as a result of which their economies are in the process of transformation from a tightly controlled one to an economy based on market forces.

In this entry we explore the broad characteristics of the emerging environment of business and competitive strategies being pursued by firms in the emerging countries of south Asia and Africa.

1 Emerging environment of business

Geographically the two regions are large and have huge populations. Most countries in the two regions have had turbulent political histories for long periods, except for India which has had a relatively more stable political situation. On the whole countries in the two regions are economically poor and poverty is rampant.

The countries themselves are characterized by large agricultural sectors and relatively smaller industry and service sectors. Productivity growth in general has been low to moderate across sectors and countries in the two regions. The role of the government in the running of the economy has been highly signifi-

cant and the public sectors in these countries are large and inefficient. Several countries in these two regions are in the process of implementing major macroeconomic reform programmes under the guidance of the World Bank and International Monetary Fund (IMF) which are expected to bring about positive changes in the business environment (see INTERNATIONAL MONETARY FUND; WORLD BANK).

Far reaching economic reforms were instituted by the Indian government in the middle of 1991. These reforms included cutting the overall government deficit, an increase in the subsidized fertilizer price, a reduction in defence spending, steps for attracting investments from non-resident Indians (NRIs), major changes in the industrial licensing policy and policy on foreign collaborations. As part of the reform programme a new industrial policy was also initiated with the objective of maintaining sustained growth in productivity and gainful employment; encouraging the growth of entrepreneurship and upgrading technology to achieve international competitiveness. With the opening up of the Indian economy to foreign competition many foreign firms have entered different sectors of the Indian economy thereby increasing the intensity of competition.

Bangladesh announced a new industrial policy in mid-1991. One of its objectives was to encourage foreign and local investment in the private sector. Specific measures included steps to remove the distinctions between local and foreign investors and to reduce the state's role in the economy, tax exemptions to exporters and permission for foreign investors to set up 100 per cent owned ventures anywhere in the country (Far Eastern Economic Review *Asia 1992*).

In 1991 Pakistan adopted a package of reforms aimed at increasing the rate of privatization and deregulation. Plans were made to disinvest over 200 public sector enterprises and steps were taken to make the local currency fully convertible. As in the case of India the pace of reforms in Bangladesh and Pakistan has varied after their inauguration due to uncertain political conditions (Far Eastern Economic Review *Asia 1992*).

Many African countries have undertaken structural adjustment programmes to accelerate economic growth. A World Bank report (World Bank 1994) points out that in the African countries that have undertaken and sustained major policy reforms, adjustment is working; however a number of countries have yet to introduce the reforms required to restore growth. No African country has yet achieved a sound macroeconomic policy profile (inflation under 10 per cent, very low budget deficit and competitive exchange rate). On the positive side the reforms have improved external competitiveness. Increased access to imports required for growth has been achieved and also the reduced taxation of agriculture has encouraged production and exports.

Reforms of agricultural pricing and marketing systems are in progress across the African continent. Almost all countries are attempting to ensure better prices for their major agricultural exports. In some cases they have abolished state marketing boards and have allowed the private sector to compete with them. Some countries have adopted pricing formulas linked to world market prices and there has been a major withdrawal of government from food crop marketing. There has also been a move to deregulate prices and markets in other sectors. In many countries commodities like rice, sugar and tea can now be imported freely by the private sector. Monopolies continue in important sectors such as petroleum, wheat and fertilizer and infrastructure services.

2 Using technology for competitive advantage

The importance of the role of technology in bringing about economic transformation is being realized increasingly in the emerging countries. One of the objectives of the reform programmes initiated by emerging countries has been to attract foreign direct investments which would enable them to upgrade their industries technologically.

With the adoption of the new economic policy in India the use of technology as a competitive weapon has gained prominence. For example, with the entry of new multinational companies (MNCs) in the passenger car industry (Daewoo, Ford, Mercedes-Benz, etc.) the existing players Maruti-Suzuki, Premier Automobiles and Hindustan Motors have signed new collaboration agreements with foreign car manufacturers to acquire new technologies for improving existing products and also to introduce new models. As a related development several auto ancillary manufacturers have also signed up foreign collaboration agreements for upgrading technology for component manufacture (see MULTINATIONAL CORPORATIONS).

With the adoption of a new industrial policy as part of the reform programme by India the increasing trend in the number of foreign collaborations seen during the 1980s has been maintained. From 976 collaborations signed in 1991 the figure went up to 1854 during 1994. During the 1980s and 1990s there was also an increase in the number of collaboration agreements with foreign equity. For the period 1948–96 foreign investments formed about 30 per cent of the total number of collaborations. In 1994, 57 per cent of the collaborations were with foreign equity (Chaudhuri 1997).

In the post-reform period there are three sectors that stand out: chemicals, electricals and electronics, and consultancy and other services. The chemicals sector attracted around 14 per cent; electricals and electronics about 15 per cent; consultancy and other services about 14 per cent of all collaborations. The increase in collaborative activity between Indian companies and foreign ones is a good augury, but it is posing new managerial challenges. A significant number of joint ventures (JVs) have broken up because of the foreign partners' insistence on hiking up their equity control after the establishment of the JVs. The challenge for Indian firms would be to improve their own skills through continuous learning from their partners as well as through their own R&D activities in order to continue to be wanted as JV partners by their foreign collaborators.

On an overall basis it is evident that the USA has been the most significant provider of technology to Indian firms during the period 1981–94 with an average of 20.84 per cent of the total number of approvals. Germany and the UK follow in the same order accounting for 16.15 and 13.89 per cent of the total. During the period 1991–94 companies from countries other than those traditionally known as technology suppliers became active in this field. For example Mauritius became an important source indicating the importance of tax considerations in technology transfer.

Some of the other countries in south Asia have also been attempting to upgrade their industries by acquiring new technology through foreign collaborations. As mentioned previously, Bangladesh launched its new industrial policy in 1991 and one of the features was the attraction of foreign investors who would bring in much needed foreign exchange as well as new technology. Some positive results seem to have followed from this. During the period 1995–96 Bangladesh received US$100 million in foreign investment of which US$20 million was in the form of direct investment. During the period 1997–98 Bangladesh made significant progress in attracting foreign direct investment in the energy sector (Far Eastern Economic Review *Asia 1997, Asia 1998*).

Pakistan too has been giving prominence to securing foreign investment and technology. For example, Singapore and Malaysia agreed to finance three power generation projects in Pakistan, while Malaysia offered to put up a US$100 million oil terminal near Karachi during 1996–97 (Far Eastern Economic Review *Asia 1997*: 187).

Major industries in Africa are dominated by multinational companies which are the sources of new technologies. For example, the chemical and petrochemical industries in Africa are characterized by the presence of all the major multinationals. The mining industry also has been dominated by foreign companies but due to a break down in the rule of law in several countries new foreign investments have not been forthcoming. South Africa is struggling to keep its mining industry competitive while other countries are in the process of making changes in their mineral legislation, fiscal and foreign exchange regimes which could make their industries attractive exploration prospects. Canadian companies have been in the forefront of exploration and mining ventures in the recent past.

3 Competitive strategies

The overall cost leadership and focus strategies (Porter 1980) have been quite common in the emerging countries characterized by the predominance of natural resource based industries. However, the increasing competitiveness of the business environment in India during the last few years has seen a surge in the use of differentiation as a competitive strategy. We examine below how some companies in different industries in India are trying to achieve differentiation.

Brand building

Currently most software companies in India earn more than 90 per cent of their revenues from consultancy and projects. On average, less than 8–10 per cent of their revenues come from generic software products. However, the scenario is likely to change fast. Indian companies are now considering introducing branded software packages to boost their bottom lines. Their brand presence is expected to generate loyalty among users and strengthen long-term business prospects. Tata Consultancy Services (TCS), the leading infotech company in the country launched five branded products during 1998. Infosys, another significant IT company, launched two branded products during the same period (*Financial Express* 1998: 1).

Time to market: the emerging competitive edge

Rapid product development and market launch is an important way to score over competitors. This has been seen to be true in the TRIAD countries (USA, Europe and Japan) for a long time. However, the emerging competitive scenario in India is pointing toward the need for pre-emptive launches to exploit first mover advantage. Nestlé (India) like its multinational parent has used this strategy for its products ranging from macaroni snacks to chocolates and soups. In mid-1997 Dabur launched its Homemade Cooking Pastes ahead of Kissan's launch of a similar product. Hindustan Lever, the Indian subsidiary of Unilever, the Anglo-Dutch multinational, launched Clinic All Clear, a new anti-dandruff shampoo ahead of Procter and Gamble's launch of the world famous Head and Shoulders (*Financial Express* 1998: 2). With the progress of economic reforms in the emerging countries the intensity of competition is likely to increase, thus paving the way for firms to shift from a predominant use of cost leadership to differentiation as the source of competitive advantage.

Efficiency improvement through organizational restructuring

The pressure of competition is likely to bring about a radical change in the thinking of industry leaders. In India the advent of global competition has already made a dramatic impact on the thinking of corporate leaders in India. Whereas unrelated diversification propelled by industrial licensing norms and other governmental regulations was the norm during the pre-liberalization era, large multiproduct and multi-divisional firms are now rethinking their strategic approaches. During the last few years larger firms have been pursuing complex strategies, at the heart of which is the objective of building on a few core competencies. A small number of Indian examples will illustrate this process.

Foseco India
Foseco India is the market leader in speciality foundry chemicals and steel fluxes and was born as a joint venture between Greaves Cotton Limited and Foseco International in 1964. In 1992 the Thapar group as a part of their long-term strategy divested the shares of Greaves Cotton in Greaves Foseco International and brought about organizational changes that included creating strategic business units to focus on the different markets and product lines and delayering to bring down the number of managerial layers (All India Management Association (AIMA) 1995: 43).

Tata Refractories (TRL)
Tata Refractories (TRL), the market leader in the Indian refractory market was set up by Tata Steel in technical collaboration with Didier of Germany (see TATA, J.R.). In the late 1980s TRL discontinued its range of low-quality alumina bricks due to competition from smaller players and decline in profitability. In 1992 TRL diversified into high-technology products and to meet the competitive challenge it reorganized its operations into strategic business units focusing on its dolomite, mag carbon and range of speciality products. In 1994–95 TRL sold off its loss-making companies, and was planning to prune its product range and make best use of tax benefits by merging with a sister company (AIMA 1995: 45).

The RP Goenka Group
The RP Goenka Group, a large, multiproduct company (sales turnover: Rs 64,000 million) is in the midst of a complex restructuring and refocusing exercise. Recently it sold off its stake in a five-year old joint venture with Goodyear Tyres of the USA. During the last few months it divested itself of or diluted its shareholding in several JVs operating in diverse business. The new parameters that are guiding the company's entry into a business line are: competitiveness, leadership and sustained profitability. The group is currently involved in a globalization effort with JVs in Saudi Arabia, Lebanon, Malaysia and Vietnam and is exploring the possibility of a JV in China for carbon black business (*Economic Times* 1998: 1).

Public ownership as strategic constraint

Improved efficiency has been emphasized by most African governments but their efforts have at best been only moderately successful (see AFRICA, MANAGEMENT IN). Almost all countries have halted the increase in the number of public enterprises, and some have reduced the number. A number of governments have signed performance contracts with key enterprises but available evidence shows that they have mostly failed in improving enterprise efficiency. Most of the divestiture of government shareholdings has occurred in the small and medium-sized public enterprises. The larger ones – airlines, railroads, mining, utilities – have generally not been privatized. The experience of India, Pakistan and Bangladesh parallels that of African countries in many ways. Public sector corporations account for a major part of their respective economies.

State owned undertakings in the emerging countries are a legacy of the past. They were created at a time and stage of development of the country when private enterprise was not forthcoming due to ideological reasons. Though they played a useful role there is now an increasing need to revamp them. However, their turnaround is being impeded by government ownership which has made managers of the enterprises vulnerable to the bureaucracy or their political bosses. Political interference has also often led to financial irregularities and profligacy which these corporations can ill afford.

Despite the difficulties associated with public ownership there are some well-run public enterprises. Bharat Heavy Electricals Limited and Gujarat Narmada Valley Fertilizer Corporation in India have performed well over relatively long periods. Strategic autonomy and a high degree of professionalism of their management have contributed to their success.

4 Internationalization

Export promotion has been a major plank of the reform programmes initiated by some of the emerging countries. Major exports of the emerging countries are natural-resource based. For example, India's major exports during 1997–98 were textiles, gems and jewellery, agriculture and allied products and engineering goods. Low labour costs is one of the most important sources of competitive advantage in these industries. But there are some emerging areas, for example computer software and pharmaceuticals, which are becoming increasingly important in India's export basket. Software and pharmaceuticals are competitive not only because of low labour costs, but also due to technological competence, for example in developing software for principals based in the USA and by

developing alternative technical routes to bulk-produce drugs.

An exploratory study of the internationalization process by ten of the larger Indian firms that cut across several industries revealed some interesting facts. These firms' internationalization efforts were characterized by:

1 a fairly rapid rate of internationalization;
2 a long-term orientation to their planning;
3 a global mindset;
4 a strategy of creating beach-heads in critical markets other than the TRIAD – Europe, USA and Japan;
5 a strong emphasis on quality;
6 creation of global scale plants;
7 an emphasis on building on distinctive capabilities;
8 an international perspective on funds mobilization;
9 a willingness to change the existing product portfolio when necessary;
10 a strategy of backward integration for better quality when necessary (Chaudhuri *et al.* 1996: 35).

Pakistan's major exports are cotton yarn, cotton cloth, synthetic textiles, cotton, rice, leather, fish, carpets and rugs, petroleum products and footwear. The export industries in Pakistan are basically geared towards pursuing a cost leadership strategy targeted towards the low end of international markets.

Though the above description of Pakistan's industries does not portray a rosy picture there are some silver linings as evidenced by the relative success of the surgical instrument industry, which has emerged in the provincial town of Sialkot. Around 300 small and medium-sized enterprises (SMEs) located in Sialkot have made Pakistan a global player in the manufacture of stainless steel medical, dental and surgical instruments. Since the mid-1980s export growth in real terms for the industry has averaged approximately 10 per cent per year. Total exports sales exceeded US$100 million in 1997. Eighty-five per cent of exports were to North America and Western Europe. Pakistan's share of the world market in this industry was 20 per cent (Far Eastern Economic Review *Asia 1998*; Nadvi 1997). The success of this industry illustrates the concept of the national diamond of competitiveness as well as the working of industrial clusters (Porter 1990).

Bangladesh's major export industries are ready-made garments, jute textiles, leather products, processed fish and seafood and tea. Available evidence suggests that exporting firms are pursuing a cost leadership strategy targeting low end customers based on low wage advantage. The ready-made garment industry has expanded quite rapidly in recent years. The small industry sector seems to have shown some amount of dynamism. Within the small industry sector, industries that have experienced significant growth are bakeries, oil mills, ready-made garments, hosiery, wooden furniture and fixtures, printing and publishing, industrial chemicals, lime products, soap, cosmetics and perfumery, light engineering, automobile servicing and repairing, steel furniture and jewellery (Far Eastern Economic Review *Asia 1998*; Quibria, 1997). All these industries are labour intensive. Bangladesh, with a vast population has comparative advantage in these labour intensive industries which exporting firms are exploiting.

Sri Lanka's major exports include tea, rubber, coconuts, textiles and garments, petroleum, gems – all characterized by labour intensive technologies (Far Eastern Economic Review *Asia 1998*).

5 Conclusion

The emerging countries of south Asia and Africa are in a state of transition. Having been subjected to strong regulatory influence of their respective governments over long periods in the past there was negligible pressure on firms to be competitive or responsive to customer demand. However, these economies are now in flux. Many of them are in the process of implementing wide-ranging economic reforms which have resulted in a competitive industrial environment in several countries. Firms in south Asia and Africa are now under pressure to (i) improve operational efficiency and (ii) respond to customers' needs in a more flexible manner. The changing business environment has resulted in several firms experimenting with new strategic approaches. Differentiation, organizational restructuring

and internationalization are strategies that are likely to become more common in the near future at least in south Asia. Africa, however, seems to be slow in responding; though there have been some improvements. The presence of a large public sector in the economies of most African nations and south Asian countries is posing a challenge to their desire for improving operational effectiveness and efficiency. Future progress on the economic front in India as well as on the sub-continent would depend on improvement in the governance processes. Political stability would be a key to further reforms and in turn industrial resurgence. Africa is going to face a very major challenge in the process of industrial development as the political situation there is far more complex with widespread armed internecine conflicts.

SHEKHAR CHAUDHURI
INDIAN INSTITUTE OF MANAGEMENT
AHMEDABAD

Further reading

(References cited in the text marked *)

* All India Management Association (1995) *Restructuring to Change*, New Delhi: AIMA. (This book contains articles describing the process of organizational restructuring and strategic refocusing in eight large companies in India.)
* Chaudhuri, S. (1997) 'International transfer of technology to India: problems, prospects and policy issues', Indian Institute of Management, Ahmedabad: WP No.1384.
* Chaudhuri, S. and Shah, N. (1996) 'Some aspects of internationalization by larger Indian firms: evidence from ten case studies', Indian Institute of Management, Ahmedabad, WP No.1299, March. (This paper describes briefly the internationalization strategies adopted by ten of the larger Indian firms and analyses the key aspects of the internationalization process.)
  Colletta, N.J., Kostner, M. and Wiederhofer, I. (1996) *The Transition from War to Peace in Sub-Saharan Africa*, Washington, DC: The World Bank. (This book describes the complex political, economic and cultural transitions many countries in sub-Saharan Africa are currently facing.)
* *Economic Times* (1998) 'Dossier', May 8–14. (The *Economic Times* is one of the top business newspapers in India. It brings out a special feature called Dossier that publishes stories about

interesting developments and strategies being pursued by Indian as well as international firms operating in India.)

* Far Eastern Economic Review (1998) *Asia 1998*. (This book provides brief sketches of the political, economic, social and cultural aspects of Asian countries on an annual basis.)

* *Financial Express* (1998) 'Brand Wagon', September 8. (Brand Wagon is a special feature of the *Financial Express*, a business newspaper in India. It brings out stories about new developments in the field of brand management in Indian industry).

Meier, G.M. and Steel, W.F. (eds) (1989) *Industrial Adjustment in Sub-Saharan Africa*, Washington, DC: Oxford University Press. (This book presents a collection of papers on various aspects of industrial development in sub-Saharan Africa. Topics covered include the business environment, small scale entrepreneurs, financial intermediation, technology and public sector management.)

* Nadvi, K. (1997) 'The cutting edge: collective efficiency and international competitiveness in Pakistan', Institute of Development Studies, Discussion Paper, July. (This paper explores how a cluster of predominantly small firms have made Pakistan a global player in the world market for stainless steel surgical instruments.)

Pigato, M., Farah, C., Itakura, K., Jun, K., Martin, W., Murrell, K. and Srinivasan, T.G. (1997) *South Asia's Integration into the World Economy*, Washington, DC: The World Bank. (This study takes a comprehensive look at the process of integration of South Asia's economy with the world economy and explores the implications of the Uruguay Round on clothing and textiles.)

* Porter, M.E. (1980) *Competitive Strategy: Techniques for Analyzing Industries and Competitors*, New York: The Free Press. (This book was a landmark work on competitive strategy at the time of its publication. It provides techniques for industry and competitor analysis and discusses concepts to help firms design effective strategies to fight competition.)

* Porter, M.E. (1990) *The Competitive Advantage of Nations*, London: Macmillan Press. (This book builds on Porter's earlier work on competitive strategy to explore what makes a nation's firms and industries competitive in global markets.)

* Quibria, M.G. (1997) *The Bangladesh Economy in Transition*, Delhi: Oxford University Press. (This volume is a collection of papers presented on different aspects of Bangladesh's economy at a conference organized by The Asian Development Bank.)

* World Bank (1994) *Adjustment in Africa: Reforms, Results and the Road Ahead*, New York: Oxford University Press. (This book provides comprehensive data on policy changes in sub-Saharan Africa and analyses whether reforms are paying off.)

World Bank (1995) *Claiming the Future: Choosing Prosperity*, Washington, DC. (This book explores the causes of the poor economic performance of countries in the Middle East and North Africa and recommends that the MENA countries must carry out reforms in the political and economic spheres to improve the lot of the people in the region.)

Websites

http://www.mbendi.co.za/indy/ming /mingaf.htm#Overview 'An MBendi Profile: The African Mining Industry'.

http://www.mbendi.co.za/indy/chem /chemaf.htm#Overview 'An MBendi Profile – African Chemical Industry'.

http://www.mbendi.co.za/afoi.htm#Overview 'An MBbendi Profile: The African Oil Industry'.

See also: AFRICA, MANAGEMENT IN; GLOBALIZATION; MULTINATIONAL CORPORATIONS; STRATEGY, CONCEPT OF; STRATEGY IN EUROPE; STRATEGY IN LATIN AMERICA; STRATEGY IN NORTH AMERICA; WORLD TRADE ORGANIZATION

Strategy in Europe

1 Introduction
2 Managing diversity
3 Managing stakeholders
4 Competitive advantages across
  borders
5 Post-merger integration
6 Future developments

Overview

Given the relatively small size of their respective domestic markets, European firms are driven to international business. As soon as Europeans cross borders they face a great diversity of markets, production factors and norms of behaviour in the workplace. Variety is being slowly reduced by institutional changes and global competition, however European firms (and foreign firms in Europe) still have to manage diversity, reconcile differentiation and integration and adopt transnational strategies. Profit has become the universal business value, however European firms, particularly on the continent, have inherited social responsibilities that require a stakeholders' approach. In order to cope with North American and Asian competitors European firms also have to achieve integration: enhance competitive advantage through learning across borders, exploit the synergies from the unprecedented wave of mergers, acquisitions and alliances of the 1990s, and build business links from the Atlantic to the Urals.

1 Introduction

The last decade of the twentieth century has witnessed unique European events: the opening of Eastern Europe to market economy, the integration of twelve countries into a Single Market (1993) and the formation of the European Union (EU) with fifteen member states. In this institutional context many European firms came to consider the EU as their domestic market and their home base for world-wide

expansion strategies; many contributed to the accelerated globalization of industries (see EUROPEAN UNION).

However convergence is slow. In the 1990s, European markets, production factors and business systems are still diverse (Calori and Lawrence 1991). As a consequence (and compared to other large domestic markets such as the USA or Japan) the principal strategic challenge for European firms (and foreign firms in Europe) is to manage diversity.

Most European executives welcomed deregulation, however they are still concerned with social responsibility, particularly on the continent. This is partly due to social constraints exercised by governments and social partners. As a consequence European enterprises have to adopt a 'stakeholders' approach in strategy making so as to reconcile sometimes conflicting interests.

As far as competitive advantage is concerned it is hard to find a common denominator across Europe. There are significant differences between the UK and the continent, and between the rest of northern Europe and southern Europe. The challenge is to combine the resources of European nations so as to compete successfully against Japanese and North American rivals (see EUROPE, MANAGEMENT IN).

In order to catch up with the US in terms of economies of scale and market power, European firms get actively involved in mergers, acquisitions (M&As) and alliances. The target keeps moving ahead as US firms also are actively merging (sometimes with European partners). As a consequence strategy making is much concerned with choosing partners, making the deal and managing post-merger integration across borders.

The following pages address the above four main strategic challenges which are particularly marked in Europe: managing diversity, managing stakeholders, reciprocal learning across borders, and managing international acquisitions. These issues converge toward the common theme of *integration*. In the economic battle between Japan, Europe and America, who will own the twenty-first century? As Lester Thurow (1991) put it, Europe can be the winner *if* the Europeans (governments and businesses) complete the *integration* of Western European countries and allow much of middle and Eastern Europe to join the House.

2 Managing diversity

Diversity is the most fundamental characteristic of Europe. The European business community is concerned with several layers of diversity: diverse markets, diverse sets of production factors, and diverse norms of behaviour in the workplace. The East–West segmentation is clear enough (see for instance Child and Czeglédy 1996); here we will focus on the segmentation of the western part of the continent.

In many industries customers' behaviour and distribution channels (markets) vary greatly from one country (or region) to the other. For instance at the beginning of the 1990s the European retail banking industry looked like a mosaic: the Germans believed in universal banks linked with insurance companies, the French believed in multi-specialization, Italy was underbanked whereas Great Britain was overbanked (Calori and Lawrence 1991). The competitors (such as the Deutsche Bank) who expanded across borders, had to manage diversity: acquire or swap networks, or make reciprocal international agreements so as to preserve local responsiveness.

For instance, in their study of the domestic appliance industry, Baden-Fuller and Stopford (1991) showed steep differences in market factors (physical features of products, prices, retail distribution) across Europe. Such diversity allowed the coexistence of national players and international players, and forced the latter to expand through international acquisitions and adopt dual brand strategies (a few international brands on top of many local brands). In the same industry, the case of Electrolux acquiring Zanussi (Ghoshal and Haspeslagh 1990) has become a classic in transnational management. It describes how a company with international ambitions in Eu-

rope has to reconcile integration and differentiation in designing marketing strategies and organizational structures. The marketing challenge of the 1990s and beyond is to exploit standardization opportunities while being responsive to specific local demands (Quelch *et al.* 1991).

Production factors still vary across European countries. The most important variation concerns the unit cost of labour, higher in the north than in the south. For instance a study completed in the car industry by the PSA Group (unpublished) showed that, in 1995, the cost of labour by unit of added value was 50 per cent higher in Sweden than in Spain. In labour intensive industries such as footwear the difference was more significant (from 1 to 3), as a consequence, since the end of the 1970s, the manufacturing of footwear moved to the south – Italy, Spain, Portugal – and manufacturers from the north had to relocate their production (in the late 1980s a second wave of relocation moved manufacturing to Asia). Differences also are significant between Western and Eastern Europe, thus many western footwear manufacturers are tempted to outsource or relocate production in Romania or in Poland. As compared to low-cost Asian countries for instance, Eastern Europe has the advantage of shorter distance, that is lower freight costs and faster reaction time. Production factors (labour, capital and access to supply) contribute to a nation's competitive advantage (Porter 1990) which also includes its knowledge base, its customers and its strengths in related industries. Indeed the different nations within Europe have different national competitive advantages. The strategic challenge for a firm with international ambitions is to tap the sources of competitive advantage wherever they are, often in different countries. Strategy making in Europe deals with decisions about where to locate manufacturing, research and development and logistical assets, in other words how to exploit the diversity of competitive advantages. To a large extent this is a well-known aspect of global strategizing (Porter 1986) (see PORTER, M.E.); the particularity of Europe is that diversity is concentrated in a relatively small geographic area.

European managers have to conduct their businesses in multicultural settings. A number of studies agree that Europe is composed of several business cultures or systems roughly delineated by national or regional frontiers: the UK, Germanic countries, Scandinavian countries, and Latin countries (Hofstede 1980; Whitley 1992). There is less agreement about the segmentation of business cultures in Central and Eastern Europe, but the impression of a mosaic is confirmed. The UK is viewed as an exception in Europe, British businesses tend to have a short-term and shareholder orientation, a relatively high turnover of managers and relatively high management freedom *vis-à-vis* the workers and the government. Northern European businesses (in Germanic countries and Scandinavia) are characterized by the participation of workers in decisions through the system of co-determination and/or through works councils, social controls more than hierarchical controls, the loyalty of employees, and the importance of in-house training. Management in the south is characterized by a strong hierarchy, intuitive management, a bias toward state intervention and protectionism. A study conducted for the European Round Table of Industrialists (ERT) (Calori and De Woot 1994) also reveals a cluster of 'small countries' (including the Netherlands, Switzerland, Belgium, Luxembourg and Scandinavian countries) characterized by international openness and transnational structures, decision by compromise, modesty, pragmatism, informality, reduced hierarchy and a dual ethic of hard work and quality of life.

Such differences affect the strategy process in European firms. In general the headquarters tend to respect some diversity and accept negotiations with country subsidiaries or regional area managers within Europe. When European headquarters coordinate regional strategies instead of centralizing the formulation of a single Euroglobal strategy, the strategy content is affected: some aspects of business strategies are standardized *and* some other aspects are differentiated across geographic areas (see GLOBALIZATION).

The subtle mix of integration and differentiation responds to the three sources of diversity: markets, production factors and norms of behaviour in the workplace. Bartlett and Ghoshal (1989) called this formula 'the transnational solution'. The transnational is described as an asymmetrical integrated network composed of a centre and a number of geographical units. The centre does not overdominate the foreign sites, some of the sites act as competence centres for the rest of the corporation and integration is achieved by intense knowledge flows between the units in the network. The study for the ERT (Calori and De Woot 1994) shows that the transnational model is viewed as typically European. More precisely it is considered as typical of the small countries. Indeed many companies considered as transnationals originate from small European countries: Asea Brown Boweri (Swedish–Swiss), Philips (the Netherlands), Nestlé (Switzerland). The Anglo-Dutch Unilever represents the transnational archetype (Maljers 1992). Concerning competitive strategy *stricto sensu* the transnational is characterized by: the coexistence of global brands, regional brands and local brands, the concentration of some elements of the value chain in order to exploit economies of scale and the dispersion of other elements (coordinated across borders), the combination of competitive advantages from diverse locations and their transfer throughout the organization. Transnational European strategies also flourish in service industries that require local networks grouped in regional hubs. For instance in the late 1990s several leading European road transport companies started to combine local differentiation with Europe-wide integration, the alliance between THL (Germany), Mory (France), Schier-Otten (Austria), and Stifte Berti (Italy) was a good example.

Institutional harmonization and firms' integrative strategies contribute to reduce diversity, however the convergence process is slow. At the end of the 1990s, in many industries European firms still have to manage diversity and reconcile differentiation and integration.

3 Managing stakeholders

In spite of the deregulation achieved by the European Union in the 1990s, for instance in banking (1990, 1993, 1999), insurance (1994), telecommunications, airlines (1997), etc. and privatizations, European firms are still dependent on industrial policies defined at the level of nation-states *and* at the European level (see PRIVATIZATION AND REGULATION). To some extent lobbying at Brussels has complemented local lobbying. Strong trade unions and/or works councils have maintained the need for social dialogue, particularly on the continent. In other words the 'social market economy' (in the German way) and the '*économie concertée*' (*à la Française*) have not been totally upset by the wave of liberalism in the 1990s. Moreover, even if profit has become the main corporate goal, many European executives do not want to give up their social responsibilities. As the Vice President in charge of Personnel at Siemens put it:

> For important issues, the Chancellor invites the heads of the most important firms to a meeting – let us say Daimler-Benz, Siemens, Thyssen, Hoechst, BASF, etc., – The Presidents of the BDA [the body of employers], the Presidents of the BDI [The German Association of Industries], the heads of the most powerful labour unions: DGB, IG Metall, etc. We discuss important issues which require concerted effort and agreement; we manage by Round Table.
> (Calori and De Woot 1994: 35)

European executives have to negotiate a lot and convince multiple stakeholders when they formulate their strategies. Of course this phenomenon is not exclusively European, however it is particularly marked in this continent, and many North American managers find it difficult to play the European stakeholders' game: 'being wound up in political things', 'getting support from governments', 'going through endless debates' (Turcq 1994). The European Round Table of Industrialists, a think tank of about 40 chairmen and/or chief executives of large European companies, is trying to gain more freedom of action for businesses, but not at the expense of social responsibility. At the sectoral level strategies have emerged from the dialogue between businesses and the corresponding divisions and programmes of the European Community. The EU launched a number of technology

programmes that framed firms' strategies, for instance the European strategic programme for Research and development in Advanced Communications technologies for Europe (RACE), Biotechnological Research for Innovation Development and Growth in Europe (BRIDGE), etc. Such policies influenced business strategies and fostered inter-firm cooperation, for instance in telecommunications.

Stakeholders may also become a constraint that hinders necessary strategic moves. For instance the case of Air France at the end of the 1990s showed that the power of the State (majority shareholder) and trade unions can delay restructuring. In this domain the relative freedom that British companies enjoy (as compared to their continental counterparts) proves to be beneficial. For instance since its privatization as early as 1987 British Airways regained flexibility and competitive advantages and became the European leading airline, ten years after they could fully exploit the opportunities offered by European deregulation.

4 Competitive advantages across borders

European enterprises tend to adopt differentiation strategies, particularly when they expand across borders. This is not surprising given the relatively high cost of labour and capital and the limited potential of scale economies in small local markets. In particular German and Scandinavian firms are known for their bias towards quality, for instance in making automobiles or machine tools (see GERMANY, MANAGEMENT IN; SWEDEN, MANAGEMENT IN). However this does not mean that European firms are customer oriented, they are not, at least in the eyes of US and Japanese executives (Calori and De Woot 1994). European enterprises are product oriented, they rely on their brilliant engineers who design wonderful products (the UK is viewed as an exception to this rule). In other words, continental Europe is driven by technique more than by marketing. Beyond this general competitive characteristic, each country or region enjoys specific competitive advantages (Porter 1990). For instance Germany is strong in automobiles, electromechanics and chemicals, the UK has skills in trading and finance, France has competitive advantages in luxury goods and distribution, Italy has strengths in design, central and Eastern Europe have low-cost manpower. European firms with international ambitions should be able to exploit the knowledge base and the demand potential of *several* European countries. In the 1990s, Ferrero, an Italian family business, joined the top five multinationals in the chocolate and confectionery industry. They got the idea of their Kinder Egg surprise from an Italian tradition, they chose to make light products, they strengthened their product marketing and boosted their sales in Germany, they learned to deal with French distribution channels, then, based on their European experience, they ventured into other continents. Learning across borders is a major strategic opportunity for European firms, indeed within a range of 2000 kilometres firms and managers can find and exploit a variety of technical and managerial competitive advantages. Of course the development of an international knowledge base has to be managed. More and more firms set up transnational project groups to develop new products, and organize international technical data bases, and international working groups, particularly after a merger (e.g. Lafarge Coppée, Atamer *et al.* 1994) (see COMPETITIVE STRATEGIES, DEVELOPMENT OF).

5 Post-merger integration

The sixth and seventh waves of mergers and acquisitions, respectively at the end of the 1980s and in the late 1990s, were world-wide phenomena; what was specific to Europe was the international character of these mergers which raises specific agency problems. At the beginning of the 1980s, the European industry was still fragmented as compared to North America. There were exceptions, for instance chemicals, but the rule was that each nation-state had its national champions. The car industry provides a good example. At the beginning of the 1980s the two leading car manufacturers were North American (General Motors [GM] and Ford), the number three and the number four were Japanese (Toyota and Nissan), the Volkswagen Group (Volkswagen and Audi) was number five and four times smaller than GM. Fifteen years later the Volkswagen group had doubled its sales through organic growth and a number of international acquisitions in order to complete the range of models and reach a critical size: Seat (Spain), Skoda (Czech Republic) and Rolls-Royce (UK).

Mergers allow economies of scale and synergies in research and development (it costs about one billion Euros to develop a new model) and manufacturing based on common platforms. The Volkswagen Group had to grow through acquisitions to catch up with foreign competition. When faced with the cultural diversity of firms like Seat, Skoda and Rolls-Royce they adopted a 'transnational' organization (see MULTINATIONAL CORPORATIONS). The acquisition of Rover by BMW, the (failed) alliance between Renault and Volvo, the acquisition of Chrysler by Mercedes, show that European firms have to merge when they compete in global industries. The joint European Ariane project was the only way to compete with the USA. The Airbus consortium between France's Aerospatiale, Daimler Benz Aerospace and British Aerospace (major shareholders) was the only way to fight the hegemony of the American Boeing in the civilian aircraft industry. When Europeans took the initiative of international M&As they sometimes achieved world-wide leadership positions as in the case of Alcatel Cables in the cable industry, or ICI and Akzo Nobel in the paint industry. International mergers and acquisitions are followed by rationalization strategies, some plants are closed and logistical systems are reorganized. Indeed European companies went through a lot of re-structuring in the 1990s, and more re-structuring is expected in the future.

6 Future developments

European strategies are moving to the East. A study in four industries – cables, paint, chocolate and footwear – (Calori *et al.* 1999) shows that European firms are looking for growth in Asia and in central and Eastern Europe. Central and Eastern Europe including Russia represent a reservoir of new consumers and low-cost manpower, German and Scandinavian companies led the flow of foreign direct investments, others followed. These long-term strategies went through a first stage of reciprocal learning, from the Eastern side (see for instance Child and Czeglédy 1996) and also from the Western side. The next stage is expected to bring more significant economic results.

The Euro is a great historical project. Political expectations on the positive stimulative impact of European Monetary Union are high but several economists voice severe concerns (*World Link* 1998). The low labour mobility in Europe, because of language barriers and cultural diversity, will not help solve regional problems in a monetary union. In other words, the Euro will make business easier for many companies but the risks of regional unemployment will be high. This is a typically European paradox in which firms are involved: on the one hand there is a need to harmonize social policies across Europe, on the other hand decentralization in wage formation is a condition of reducing the risk of unemployment.

Under the combined effects of slow institutional changes (for instance Europe is still missing a common legal form of enterprise), global competitive pressures, and firms' competitive actions across borders, European diversity will be slowly reduced: the turn of the century is an epoch of transnational integration. However integration within Europe and worldwide will not rub off diversity; indeed a creative tension between integration and differentiation should be maintained in order to preserve flexibility.

ROLAND CALORI
LYON MANAGEMENT SCHOOL

Further reading

(References cited in the text marked *)

* Atamer, T., Nunes, P. and Berthelier, M. (1994) 'Integrating diversity: case studies', in Calori, R. and de Woot, P. (eds), *A European Management Model, Beyond Diversity*, 197–235, London: Prentice Hall. (Discusses six case studies of cross border integration: Lafarge Coppée, Pilkington, Fiat, Petrofina, Unilever, and Hoffmann-La Roche.)
* Baden-Fuller, C.W.F. and Stopford, J.M. (1991) 'Globalization frustated: the case of white goods', *Strategic Management Journal* 12 (7): 493–507. (Shows how forces driving local responsiveness leave room for differentiation strategies.)
* Bartlett, C.A. and Ghoshal, S. (1989) *Managing Across Borders, the Transnational Solution*, Boston MA: Harvard Business School Press. (Describes transnational strategies and organizations that reconcile global integration and local responsiveness.)
* Calori, R. and Lawrence, P. (1991) *The Business of Europe, Managing Change*, London: Sage Publications. (Analyses the dynamics of four European markets: retail banking, car manufacturing, book publishing and brewing.)
* Calori, R. and De Woot, P. (1994) *A European Management Model, Beyond Diversity*, London: Prentice Hall. (Gives an overview of management and strategy style across borders with a particular emphasis on European integration.)
* Calori, R., Atamer, T. and Nunes, P. (1999) *The Dynamics of International Competition*, London: Sage Publications. (Explains the development of international business in four industries: cables, chocolate and confectionery, paint and footwear.)
* Child, J. and Czeglédy, A.P. (eds) (1996) 'Managerial learning in the transformation of Eastern Europe', *Organization Studies* 17 (2), Special Issue: 167–341. (A selection of research papers on learning in Eastern European businesses.)
* Ghoshal, S. and Haspeslagh, P. (1990) 'The acquisition and integration of Zanussi by Electrolux: A case study', *European Management Journal* 8 (4): 414–33. (Describes the strategic and organizational challenges following an international acquisition in Europe.)
* Hofstede, G. (1980) *Culture's Consequences*, London: Sage. (Presents four dimensions of cultural distances between nations and discusses their consequences for management.)
* Maljers, F.A. (1992) 'Inside Unilever: the evolving transnational company', *Harvard Business Review* September–October: 46–50. (Gives insights into the transnational strategy of a major European company.)
* Porter, M.E. (ed.) (1986) *Competition in Global Industries*, Boston MA: Harvard Business School Press. (Provides a framework to analyse international strategies, particularly the international configuration of value chain activities.)
* Porter, M.E. (1990) *The Competitive Advantage of Nations*, New York: Macmillan. (Gives a framework to understand how a nation may create and sustain specific competitive advantages.)

* Quelch, J.A., Buzzell, R.D. and Salama, E.R. (eds) (1991) *The Marketing Challenge of 1992*, New York: Addison Wesley. (Gives an overview of European marketing strategies and diverse case studies in the context of the Single European Market.)
* Thurow, L. (1991) *Head to Head*, Cambridge, MA: MIT Press. (Analyses the strengths and weaknesses of North America, Europe and Japan in the global economic battle.)
* Turcq, D. (1994) 'Is there a US style in Europe ?', in Calori, R. and de Woot, P. (eds), *A European Management Model, Beyond Diversity*, 82–111, London: Prentice Hall. (Analyses the strategies of several North American multinationals in Europe.)
* Whitley, R. (ed.) (1992) *European Business Systems, Firms and Markets in their National Contexts*, London: Sage Publications. (This book of readings provides a theoretical framework – institutional systems – to understand cross national differences in management.)
* *World Link* (1988) March–April, London: World Link Publications Ltd. (Gives an overview of the debates in the World Economic Forum of 1998.)

See also: EUROPEAN UNION; GLOBALIZATION; STRATEGY IN ASIA PACIFIC; STRATEGY IN THE EMERGING COUNTRIES; STRATEGY IN NORTH AMERICA; WORLD BANK

Strategy and internal marketing

Overview

This entry seeks to broaden and deepen the understanding of the internal marketing concept with particular reference to the role of internal marketing in influencing business performance outcomes through the various organizational processes associated with the formulation and implementation of strategies designed to deliver desired organizational objectives. In pursuit of this demanding objective the entry will: examine the various disciplinary conceptualizations and definitions of internal marketing in a review of the extant literature; develop a conceptual model of propositions concerning internal marketing grounded in the existing literatures of a number of disciplines with appropriate theoretical underpinnings, develop and illustrate the role of the internal marketing concept in the formulation and implementation of organizational strategy; and finally, expand on the potential avenues of future developments for both researchers and managers in the internal marketing paradigm.

1 Introduction

Although the concept of internal marketing has a relatively short history in its explicit form, both the theoretical underpinnings in the academic literature and the implicit management activity in practice have a considerably longer and richer past (see MARKETING). The explicit study of internal marketing began in the late 1970s, and grew rapidly in the early 1980s in the emerging services marketing field in the USA and Scandinavia (Berry 1981; Gronroos 1981). New impetus to the development of internal marketing has been evidenced from the quality management, human resource management, organization theory and strategic management disciplines (see HUMAN RESOURCE MANAGEMENT; ORGANIZATION PARADIGMS; STRATEGIC COMPETENCE; TOTAL QUALITY MANAGEMENT). While researchers from different disciplinary perspectives have ascribed different meanings to the internal marketing concept, an implicit paradigm is emerging which views organizations as having internal as well as external marketplaces, made up of internal and external customers, to whom internal marketing programmes and strategies, as well as external marketing programmes and strategies are (either explicitly or implicitly) delivered, in an attempt to achieve desired organizational goals.

While the empirical evidence is sparse, there is widespread agreement in the literature and among practising managers that the internal marketing concept has a potentially vital role to play in effecting desired external customer outcomes, and hence business performance (see ORGANIZATIONAL PERFORMANCE). The limited empirical evidence that exists in the literature (for example, Tansuhaj *et al.* 1987; Piercy and Morgan 1991) supports the potential impact that internal marketing can have upon such important precursors to improved business performance as customer satisfaction levels and marketing plan credibility and utilization.

2 Past developments

The history of the development of the internal marketing concept is relatively short. However, while the concept in its explicit form is relatively young, the diversity of disciplinary perspectives that have characterized the literature provide a surprisingly rich and varied mix of conceptual developments. This diversity is characterized by the numerous definitions of the internal marketing concept that have been proposed. These have included:

1 'Internal marketing is the philosophy of treating employees as customers … and it is the strategy of shaping job-products to fit human needs' (Berry and Parasuraman 1991).
2 '… the internal marketing concept states that the internal market of employees is best motivated for service-mindedness and a customer-oriented behaviour by an active marketing-like approach, where marketing activities are used internally' (George 1990).
3 'What may be called "strategic internal marketing" has the goal of developing a marketing programme aimed at the internal marketplace in the company, that parallels and matches the marketing programme aimed at the external marketplace of customers and competitors' (Piercy and Morgan 1991: 83).

However, a wider reading of the literature would suggest that there are five major sources of the development of the internal marketing concept. While these sources of development are discussed here separately, there are obviously various degrees of interconnection between them. The five sources that may be identified are: services marketing, human resource management, quality management, organization structure and design, and planning and strategy implementation.

Services marketing origins

The term 'internal marketing' is believed to have been used explicitly for the first time in the services marketing literature that began developing an identity distinct from the wider marketing literature in the late 1970s (see MARKETING). One of the earliest differentiating characteristics of marketing services to be discussed was the influence of the service provider over the service 'product' that was delivered to customers. The importance of service providers in affecting customer-based outcomes, and hence business performance, was recognized as both a problem and an opportunity. The problem potential was clear,

as in most service businesses the service delivered to customers is largely determined by the person who is delivering the service. Since most service businesses need to have more than one service provider in order to be able to meet demand satisfactorily, quality control becomes more problematic because service providers are bound to be heterogeneous.

It was also realized that immediate customer-based marketing objectives such as customer satisfaction and perceived quality were more directly influenced by service providers in a service business than by the business unit's marketing managers. This realization led to the initial identification of the need for internal marketing in service businesses, suggesting that service providers who are happy with the service company for which they work are more likely to establish positive customer-based outcomes than service providers who are unhappy.

From this relatively simplistic logic in the late 1970s the internal marketing paradigm began explicit development. First, service marketers began to conceptualize the goal of service provider employee satisfaction in terms of an explicit marketing framework, which began to be labelled 'internal marketing' (see SERVICES, MARKETING OF). In this early conceptualization, service provision employees were viewed as internal customers, and the goal of producing satisfied internal customers was seen as being best achieved through the creation of 'internal job products' that were built around the jobs and wider role within the organization that could be marketed to employees.

Second, services marketers began to reassess the role that service provision and other customer contact staff in service businesses played in the marketing effort of the firm. Recognizing the influence of service provision staff in achieving customer-based outcomes such as satisfaction and future purchase intention, services marketers began to attempt to include service provision and customer contact personnel (who were not employed in the marketing department) in the implementation of marketing strategy. For marketers and service business senior managers it made little sense to continue to focus on the use of marketing models which ignored the vital role of service provision and customer contact employees. Similarly, once the influential role of service provision and customer contact employees had been identified, it made little sense to leave this route to achieving customer-based outcomes implicit, largely unplanned, uncoordinated and unmanaged.

This new approach to marketing in the services sector quickly developed to embrace particular business and marketing strategies, that were founded upon the improvement of levels of customer service and perceived service quality as a basis for non-price-based competition. Since this was seen to involve changing the way service provision and customer contact personnel viewed their interaction with customers, and introduce a new 'part-time' marketer element to their role, the extension of the internal marketing framework to this particular application seemed a natural development. In this context, services marketing analysts began increasingly to cast internal marketing in an expanded role which included the creation of a customer orientation throughout the service business by the attraction, training, retention and satisfaction of customer-orientated and 'service minded' employees.

Human resource management extensions

Given the essential thrust of much of the early services marketing work on internal marketing, in terms of satisfying employees through the creation of job 'products', it would be surprising if the implications for human resource management practice had been ignored (see HUMAN RESOURCE MANAGEMENT). However, while many human resource managers may argue that the whole area of human resource and personnel management is implicitly grounded in an internal marketing paradigm, much of the impetus for exploring the explicit implications of the internal marketing framework for human resource management has come from the marketing discipline, where the human resource management function has been criticized for being frequently 'oriented towards control and administrative activities

rather than the alignment of human resources towards achieving strategic organizational purposes and goals' (Collins and Payne 1991: 263).

It has been suggested that the implications of internal marketing for human resource management are twofold. First, it is proposed that human resource managers could utilize marketing and 'marketing-like' approaches and techniques in the execution of their role within the organization. Particular attention has been drawn to the role that marketing communication skills externally can play in the attraction of staff (or potential internal customers) to jobs where customer service may be important. In this important human resource management function, marketing skills such as market research, media planning, message and copy creation, etc. can help to attract high quality candidates for important roles (see MARKETING RESEARCH). A further focus of attention has been upon how human resource managers communicate with employees on matters of importance within the organization. Technological developments and their allied cost implications over the past decade have allowed a much greater choice of media with which managers can now communicate with staff, including video, electronic mail, video-conferencing, satellite TV hook-ups, etc. (see INFORMATION TECHNOLOGY). Similarly, the development of desktop publishing systems has brought internal newspapers, newsletters, brochures, etc. within the reach of most organizations. With this broadening range of media, marketing communication skills have become more applicable and important to the human resource function.

Second, in light of criticisms of the role of the human resource function within organizations in the past, it has been suggested that human resource and personnel functions should treat the organization in which they operate as much more of an internal market, and employees as internal customers with needs for which the human resource function is largely responsible for satisfying. The rationale is that an internally market-orientated human resource function is much more likely to contribute to the success of the organization both by demonstrating the potential utility of the human resources department and by better matching recruitment, training and reward systems and practices to the twin needs of the internal customers and the organization's strategies, goals and objectives.

In this conceptualization, the human resource function has both internal and external customer marketplaces including: employees within the company, senior managers within the organization, external interest groups and regulatory bodies such as the government and the trade unions, and the external labour market made up of potential future internal employee customers. These various customer marketplaces may be researched, have new 'products' developed for them, require communication and the 'selling' and distribution of 'products' in line with conventional marketing models.

The impact of quality management

Chronologically paralleling the development of the internal marketing framework in the services marketing literature was the rapid rise in so-called 'total' approaches to quality management in the operations, and subsequently the broader, management literatures. 'Total' approaches to quality management were positioned as having a strategic focus in contrast to the operational nature of 'traditional' quality control, and as being cross-functional in implementation, in comparison with the operations/engineering discipline focus of earlier quality control and quality assurance approaches. The total quality management (TQM) approach views quality as a vital strategic and competitive weapon that is best managed by the following methods: by taking a customer-orientated rather than a product-orientated perspective in the setting of product/service specifications; by improving conformance to these specifications both through the design of the product/service itself and also through the design and management of the processes by which the product/service is produced and delivered; and by the involvement of all employees, staff and management in coordinated programmes of activities and approaches designed to both ensure and improve upon product/service quality levels (see TOTAL QUALITY MANAGEMENT).

It is in the area of cross-functional management and organization-wide employee involvement that TQM both breaks significantly with traditional approaches to quality management and enters the world of internal marketing. The central notion in many models of TQM is the so-called 'chain of quality'. The rationale is as follows. If quality improvements are to deliver significant competitive advantage then they have to meet customer needs and requirements and also be recognized as improvements relative to competing goods and services by the end customer. It therefore follows that in this broader conceptualization of product/service quality a much greater number of employees, and a wider functional area than simply operations/production and quality control, have the ability and skills to alter at least one of the following: the product/service delivered to customers, the interaction between the customer and the seller organization, and the perceptions of both product/service and interaction in the mind of the customer. Hence the TQM model conceptualizes a series of interrelationships, working backwards from the end-user customer, through the seller organization, stretching back to the suppliers of raw materials. This series of relationships represents the 'chain of quality', since each link influences the eventual outcome of quality improvement efforts in the customers' eyes.

The TQM conceptual model suggests that all internal customer-supplier marketing relationships would benefit from formal marketing research and communication to establish the exact and precise requirements of each next 'customer' in the chain, and from formal feedback to ensure that each subsequent customer in the chain (including the final end-user external customer) is consistently satisfied with what is being delivered. As with the services marketing approach, the TQM conceptualization ties internal marketing directly with the achievement of customer-based performance outcomes (again mainly discussed in terms of customer satisfaction and customer perceived quality), through all employees and personnel who either interface directly with the external customer or who, through their actions and activities, can influence what is delivered to and experienced by the external customer.

The major contributions to the development of the internal marketing concept made by the TQM approach may be viewed as three-fold:

1 TQM was developed originally in the manufacturing sector and thus takes internal marketing outside of the sphere of the services sector, where much of the early development within the marketing literature had been anchored.

2 The TQM conceptualization has extended the scope of the boundaries and composition of the internal marketplaces within organizations, identifying multiple sets of interdependent internal customers and suppliers, each of whom had the potential, either directly or indirectly, to influence customer-based performance goals.

3 TQM as a popular movement which gained intense management interest around the world in the middle of the 1980s has popularized the existence and language of the basic internal marketing framework among managers and personnel, who often had little or no knowledge or experience of the traditional external marketing framework.

Organization theory contributions

From an organization design perspective, the ability to maintain both sufficient flexibility and integration to respond appropriately to changing external markets and environments is one of the central problems and challenges faced by large organizations (see ORGANIZATION BEHAVIOUR; ORGANIZATION STRUCTURE). While large organizations have often used multi-divisionalization, matrix structures and strategic planning processes to cope with some of these conflicting demands, all of these solutions can be both difficult to manage and lead to excessive administrative control and 'red tape'. One mechanism that has been suggested as an alternative to the problems associated with traditional solutions such as those listed above, is the creation of an 'internal market' mechanism. This approach has been termed 'intrapreneurship' in the organization theory literature.

The intrapreneurship model suggests that activities that are not directly related to an organization's central mission can effectively be organized into semi-autonomous entities that operate within an internal market inside the organization. It is suggested that this allows these units to innovate, develop and test-market new and improved services within the organization, in a way that is almost impossible within the confines of normal administrative, planning and coordinating mechanisms (which by necessity concentrate primarily on areas that are central to the organization's strategy). This internal marketing or intrapreneurship approach may allow secondary activities within the organization to deliver the flexibility/innovation and integration required by the organization's primary activities.

In the practical setting this theoretic approach may be used to explain the growing phenomenon of 'outsourcing' non-core services in many businesses, and the growth of large companies specializing in providing such outsourced services (such as ARA in the USA and BET in the UK). This theory has also been extended in practice by the UK government in its reform of the National Health Service, through the creation of separate organizational units of buyers and suppliers of health services (see HEALTH MANAGEMENT).

Planning and strategy implementation considerations

Much of the concern in the early conceptualizations of internal marketing in the services marketing literature concerned the implementation of customer service improvement strategies through the recruitment and retention of 'customer and service minded' employees and service providers. Similarly, the conceptual model that emerged from the quality management literature concerned the effective implementation of quality improvement strategies and approaches. In the late 1980s, however, marketing strategists and writers in the wider strategic management and planning literatures began to extend the internal marketing framework to the development and effective implementation of strategies of any kind.

Analysts of strategy formulation and implementation at functional, business and corporate level had become increasingly aware that many plans and strategies were ineffective in terms of delivering desired outcomes, not because they were necessarily poor strategies but because they were not implemented in anything like the form that the planners had originally envisaged (see STRATEGY, IMPLEMENTATION OF). However, while the issue of implementation had been highlighted as an area of particular concern, and there had been numerous calls in the literature for further research, there was little progress evident in the form of conceptualizations or approaches to overcoming strategy implementation problems that were readily accessible to managers.

One of the problems associated with the interface between business academics and managers in this important and problematic area has been the relative lack of a common frame of reference. While research into the causes of implementation failures was (and still is) relatively sparse, there was some emerging agreement that many of the problems encountered in implementing plans and strategies were concerned with resistance to change among managers and employees within the organization. The overwhelming emphasis in most planning and strategy formulation systems and processes is upon the analysis of the external environment in which the organization operates. Since the weight of available evidence suggests that the external environments faced by organizations of all kinds are becoming increasingly complex and dynamic, it is not surprising that, in order to maintain a match between an organization and the environment in which it operates, most marketing and strategic plans require some degree of change within the organization if they are to be effectively implemented. Thus, the resistance to change, which seems to be a facet of individuals and groups in most organizations, forms a substantive and substantial barrier to the implementation of many strategies and plans.

In the context of such implementation problems it has been proposed that the internal marketing paradigm can provide both a conceptual framework and a management tool for working on strategy implementation issues. In this adaptation of internal marketing the classic 'four Ps' (product, price, place, promotion) framework is adopted to constitute an internal marketing programme where:

1 the core product component relates to the strategy or plan that has been formulated;
2 the price component relates to what it costs people within the organization to 'buy into' the strategy (for example, other opportunities, ideas, etc. that they have to give up);
3 communications relates to the messages sent out in the internal marketplace relating to 'product' and 'price' issues;
4 distribution concerns the media and venues through which the plan is communicated and delivered in the internal marketplace.

This internal marketing programme is aimed at the key segments and individuals within the organization whose agreement, approval, cooperation and support is needed for the effective implementation of the strategy in question.

This conceptualization is similar in many ways to the practice of 'policy deployment' operated in many Japanese companies. In essence, policy deployment is a form of collective strategic decision making where senior managers set yearly objectives related to relatively consistent strategic 'milestones'. These are communicated to groups of managers and workers in a downward flow of meetings where all groups are then involved in contributing to a tactical plan to detail how they may best achieve the objectives to which they may contribute. This system of short-term planning has a long history at many Japanese manufacturing companies such as Toyota and Mitsubishi (see JAPAN, MANAGEMENT IN; TOYODA FAMILY).

One of the most useful attributes of this extension of the internal marketing concept as a tool for planning implementation strategies in organizations is the intuitive appeal of the framework to managers. Working on strategy implementation issues is frequently difficult due to the pervasive influence of organizational power and political structures, processes and outcomes on the ability of an organization to implement strategies effectively, even if they are well conceived and planned. Such covert issues obviously need to be addressed in planning implementation strategies, yet are frequently difficult for managers to articulate formally and discuss in the context of strategy formulation and implementation, which is widely regarded as requiring the rigid maintenance of rational objectivity at all times. While sociotechnical terminology and frameworks from the organization theory and strategic management literatures relating to structure, process, culture, information, etc. address largely the same issues, the language and concepts are widely seen by managers as academic and technical rather than managerial and practical. The internal marketing framework however provides both a neutral language for addressing these problematic and emotive covert power and political issues, and utilises a 'four Ps' model that is recognized and widely viewed as both 'user-friendly' and practical.

Thus, in the context of strategy implementation two different types of internal marketing mix have been identified as useful to managers; covert and overt. The 'overt' marketing mix concerns the rational elements associated with strategy implementation, as described above. The second 'covert' facet concerns the internal power and political aspects of the internal marketing mix associated with a particular strategy.

In the covert internal marketing mix, the 'product' element relates primarily to the changes that are explicitly and implicitly required of individuals and groups, in order for the plan/strategy that has been formulated to be effectively implemented. The 'price' element relates to the individual and group psychological, power and political costs associated with the changes required for effective strategy implementation. The 'communication' element relates to the approach taken to communicate the required changes for effective implementation to the key customers and segments in the internal market. This may include personal selling, promotion/sponsorship by key players internally, and even the creation of a broader image around the plan/strategy. The 'distribution' element relates to the range of covert mechanisms within the organization that exist to deliver the new requirements and changes necessary to implement the desired strategy/plan effectively. These may include changing company 'rules' and policies, informal communications and social interaction between senior managers and key internal market targets. The overt and covert aspects of the internal marketing mix are summarized in Table 1.

The covert level of internal marketing is conceptually similar to the *ringisei* form of decision making by consensus, evident in many Japanese companies, which usually involves circulating documents and proposals to groups and individuals within the firm who may have some concern or interest in the implementation of the proposals. Typically the process in-

Table 1 Internal marketing programme

Internal marketing mix	Overt	Covert
1 Product	Plan or strategy	Changes and conditions required for effective implementation of overt 'product'
2 Price	Opportunities given up by internal customers	'Cost' to individuals and groups in the internal marketplace of changing and meeting the conditions required for effective 'product' implementation
3 Communications	Messages and approaches to communicating overt 'product' and 'price' issues to the internal customers	Messages and approaches to communicating covert 'product' and 'price' issues to internal customers
4 Distribution	Media and venues through which the overt 'product' is delivered to internal customers	Media and venues through which the covert 'product' is delivered to internal customers

volves four stages: proposal, circulation, approval and record. The effect of such decision making approaches is to modify proposals (the internal product) in the light of concerns and ideas from those affected (target internal customer segments), in order to make the proposal acceptable to those concerned (successfully completing an internal sale to the satisfaction of the internal customer), and helping to lower internal implementation barriers. While this approach may be criticized in terms of speed of decision making, the potential to achieve substantially improved implementation has meant that companies such as IBM have tried to adopt similar approaches built around group meetings and presentations, as well as through the use of internal communication channels such as the 'NOS' global e-mail system and the 'THINK' employee publication.

3 State of the art

Our emerging knowledge from the multiple disciplinary perspectives discussed suggests that there are a number of areas in which 'state-of-the-art' propositions, constituting a broadly based model of internal marketing, may be identified.

Internal marketplaces exist within organizations

The state of the art reflected in the diverse disciplines that have been discussed here is overwhelmingly supportive of the existence of 'internal customers' as an appropriate, insightful and potentially useful conceptualization of the individuals, groups and departments that constitute the inner workings of organizations. Not only can these various internal customers and segments be identified but the exchanges and transactions between them create a true internal marketplace. These exchanges can be both explicit (for example, the contract of employment between an employee and the organization) and implicit (the informal sharing of information between departments).

The literature suggests that internal marketplaces can be identified in a very wide range of organizations, including service businesses, manufacturing businesses, large multi-divisional organizations and not-for-profit organizations. Thus, the conceptual framework may be useful in a large number of different types of organizational contexts.

Internal marketplaces and external marketplaces are interdependent

One of the earliest basic tenets of internal marketing, and one of the basic reasons for the development of the concept in the context of service businesses, was the explicit recognition that internal customers within the organization can affect external customers and influence external customer-based outcomes (satisfaction, loyalty, market share, price sensitivity, etc.), and ultimately, therefore, impact upon business performance outcomes. However, this recognition now extends beyond the service sector context and recognizes that it is not only customer contact personnel, but also other internal customers who influence customer-based outcomes.

The internal marketplace can be viewed as a series of exchange relationships between internal customers and internal suppliers at many different levels: individual to individual, group to group, function to function, department to department, employee to manager, etc. Each of these exchange relationships can directly or indirectly affect the organization's ability to achieve its external customer-based goals. Furthermore, since the achievement of external customer-based goals is fundamental to future business performance, the content and the process of the exchanges between internal suppliers and internal customers are to a large degree dictated by the needs and requirements of the external customer in organizations who successfully achieve their customer-based goals. It is therefore obvious that internal and external marketplaces are, and should be, interdependent in most organizations and marketplaces.

Many external marketing approaches may be adapted for use in the internal marketplace context

Once the existence of an internal marketplace, consisting of individuals and groups of internal customers engaged in a variety of exchange relationships, is recognized, then it has been suggested that this opens up the possibil-

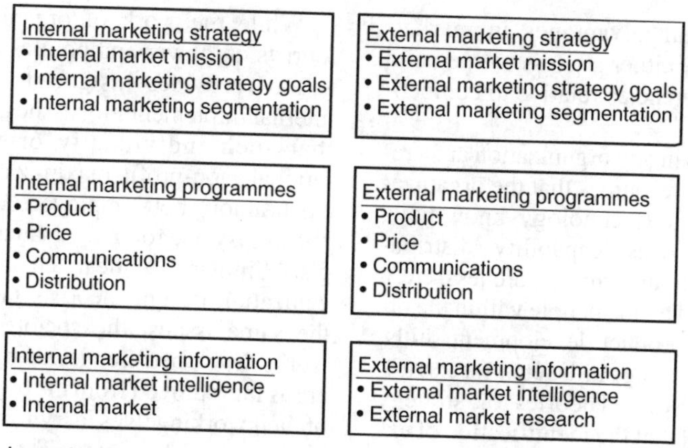

Internal marketing strategy	External marketing strategy
• Internal market mission • Internal marketing strategy goals • Internal marketing segmentation	• External market mission • External marketing strategy goals • External marketing segmentation

Internal marketing programmes	External marketing programmes
• Product • Price • Communications • Distribution	• Product • Price • Communications • Distribution

Internal marketing information	External marketing information
• Internal market intelligence • Internal market	• External market intelligence • External market research

Figure 1 A holistic marketing framework
Source: Adapted from Piercy (1992)

ity of using many different tools, techniques, models and approaches that have already been developed for external marketing. Those external marketing approaches that have been either identified in the literature or developed for use in practice include:

1 internal communications mix planning and implementation (advertising, personal selling, public relations, sponsorship, etc.);
2 internal market research (employee surveys, skills audits, etc.) among internal customers;
3 diffusion of innovation models of consumer behaviour (identifying opinion leaders within the internal marketplace to target as primary customers for new internal 'products') (see COMMUNICATION; INNOVATION AND CHANGE; MARKETING RESEARCH).

In fact, it is possible to conceive a framework for internal marketing that entirely parallels that of external marketing. For example, if we take a recent model developed to frame external marketing it is relatively simple to adapt this to the development of an internal marketing framework (Figure 1).

Different levels of internal marketing can be identified

As Figure 1 suggests, it is possible to differentiate between strategic and operational levels of internal marketing. Strategic level internal marketing is distinguished by its ability to influence the match achieved between the organization and its external customer environment, and also to affect the formulation and/or achievement of competitive strategy and external marketing strategy goals. Operational level internal marketing, by contrast, concerns short-term actions taken to achieve short-term objectives that neither directly affect the achievement of strategic goals, nor directly influence the match an organization achieves between itself and its external customer environment.

Strategic internal marketing is directly connected to the formulation and implementation of the competitive strategy pursued by the organization, and therefore concerns activities such as designing planning processes for strategy formulation, pre-testing plan/strategy ideas on key internal customer segments, aligning hiring, training and reward systems with the business strategy, communicating strategy/plan rationale to employees, etc.

Internal marketplaces should be an important focus of attention in strategy formulation

Strategy is widely seen to be concerned with the formulation of organizational goals, the means the organization chooses to pursue its objectives and the match that the organization achieves with the environment in which it operates. A fundamental tenet of conceptualizations of strategy is that an organization needs to allocate resources and attempt to achieve positional advantages in market-places where they either possess or can build distinctive competencies relative to competi-tors.

Competencies in any organization are a re-sult of the mix of resources that the organiza-tion has within it (technology know-how, manufacturing process capability, distribu-tion penetration, brand name awareness, etc.), and the skills held by the people within the or-ganization (new product development skills, R&D skills, marketing skills, etc.) (see STRA-TEGIC COMPETENCE). Theories of strategy therefore suggest that the identification of ex-isting competencies, the enhancement of ex-isting competencies and the development of new competencies is a fundamental process in strategy formation. All of this relates to the in-ternal marketplace that constitutes the inner workings of the organization. By highlighting the appropriateness and utility of a number of different internal market intelligence and re-search approaches, tools and techniques, the internal marketing concept enhances the abil-ity of strategy makers to undertake the internal analysis that is an integral part of strategy for-mulation processes.

Internal marketing is critical to achieving effective strategy implementation

In essence, strategy implementation may be viewed as the creation of the appropriate inter-nal marketplace, structures and processes to deliver the desired strategy into the target marketplace. Almost all strategies, since they are grounded in the analysis of dynamic exter-nal marketplaces and environments, require some degree of change in the internal work-ings of the organization if it is to remain in alignment with the needs and requirements of its external environment. It is in creating this changed internal environment that many plans and strategies encounter implementation problems. Once this problem area has been identified, then managers require some plan-ning approach that enables them to formulate internal implementation strategies, to enable externally orientated competitive strategies to be delivered effectively.

While the work of organization behav-iourists on power and politics within organi-zations provides insights to exactly these internal implementation issues, the admission that such individually orientated, non-rational, non-profit maximization behaviour exists among both employees and managers is not an easy one for many managers and strate-gists. Similarly, while much of the work of or-ganization design theorists tackles many of the same issues, the sociotechnical frame-works developed are viewed by many manag-ers as far removed from the day-to-day reality of their working lives in trying to get plans and strategies implemented. The major intuitive attraction of the internal marketing concept in this situation is that it provides a user-friendly managerial framework, couched in familiar management terminology which, by recog-nizing both overt and covert facets of internal marketing, deals with both the rational and power/political aspects of strategy implemen-tation.

It is only by explicitly addressing the re-quired changes in the internal marketplace, recognizing the barriers to achieving these changes among key groups, individuals and departments, and designing ways to lower re-sistance and overcome internal marketplace obstacles, that strategists can ensure the effec-tive implementation of plans and strategies. The internal marketing framework provides a tool that forces managers to confront these is-sues and gives them a technique to plan imple-mentation strategies pro-actively. While many managers may already do some of this implicitly, experience suggests that it is only when this element of the planning activity is made explicit that successful implementation strategies can be developed, rather than the re-liance upon ad hoc implementation tactics which is evidenced in most organizations.

Internal marketing has a cost associated with it

Any management activity incurs a cost to the organization, even if it is only the cost of the management time involved (see MANAGERIAL BEHAVIOUR). Explicit internal marketing planning can add significantly to the time and resources consumed in the planning activity, whether the planning activity has a dedicated budget or not. Similarly, many of the elements of the internal marketing programme that may be delivered within the internal marketplace will have cost implications.

The meetings, reports, training sessions, report-back sessions, presentations, reward system changes, planning workshops, etc. which are all integral to many overt internal marketing programmes can have quite significant costs associated with them. On the covert side of internal marketing the time taken by key senior managers in 'off the record' meetings, dinners, golf days, etc., and the deals that may need to be done to obtain support or tacit approval from important individuals and groups, also have significant budget implications when 'costed out'. Even greater costs are associated with internal marketing planning, which concludes that the strategy proposed for external delivery is simply not capable of being effectively delivered because the obstacles to achieving the required internal marketplace conditions are too big to overcome. This then requires the development of a new external strategy, necessitating significant further investments in strategy formulation.

There is a difference between internal marketing and internal selling

In the theory and practice of external marketing a clearly defined difference is evident between marketing and selling activities. Marketing activities focus on the needs of the customer while selling activities focus on the needs of the seller. Marketing is a long-term process, while selling is an activity that occurs towards the end of the marketing process once market intelligence and research have been translated into need-satisfying products and services, whose benefits and costs have been communicated to the target market. This distinction also holds true within the sphere of the internal marketplace.

Internal marketing therefore requires the development of a product (the plan or strategy to be delivered into the external marketplace) which reflects the needs and wants of key internal customers. Internal selling, on the other hand, concentrates upon persuading and cajoling the internal customers to buy into a plan/strategy product which has typically been developed with little or no focus upon internal customer needs and requirements. Internal selling has become evident in many organizations where senior managers have tried to improve implementation by finding a greater range of ways to coerce managers and employees to facilitate changes in the internal marketplace, rather than formulating strategy products with an eye towards the needs of internal as well as external customers.

While internal selling may be an improvement over the old fashioned military style 'I'm the boss, you'll do what you are told' approach to strategy implementation, it still lacks the ability to build effective implementation strategies in a range of organizational contexts. Superior strategy execution seems to be associated with the degree of commitment and ownership felt by those internal customers who will have to comply with, and be affected by, required changes in the internal marketplaces in order to achieve effective external strategy implementation. Internal selling approaches, while superior to straightforward coercion, do not seem to be capable of building commitment and ownership among key internal customer groups in the internal marketplace.

4 Theoretical underpinnings

The state-of-the-art propositions presented here as a broadly based model of the internal marketing framework have substantial theoretical support in a number of areas. Three major substantive areas of theory may be viewed as particularly important underpinnings for the internal marketing model: contingency theory, the theory of marketing and resource models of strategic management. Each of these theoretical underpinnings will be examined in turn.

Contingency theory

In essence, contingency theory suggests that organizations can be viewed as complex open systems facing environmental uncertainty, in which decision makers are bound by some basic rationality criteria in making and implementing decision choices (see ORGANIZATION

BEHAVIOUR; ORGANIZATION STRUCTURE; STRATEGIC CHOICE). As a result of this, organizations develop different structures, strategies and decision processes to cope with different environmental problems, threats and opportunities. The essential thesis is that organizations can achieve the same performance outcomes in different ways, depending upon the environments in which they operate.

Thus, implicit in contingency theory approaches is the notion of congruency or 'fit'. This refers to the idea that organizational effectiveness is broadly determined by the fit or congruency between the characteristics and processes of the organization, its strategy and the environment in which it operates. There is broad support for the underlying proposition that the co-alignment between organization strategy and (1) external environmental conditions and (2) internal organizational and management characteristics, has significant positive implications for performance.

Contingency theory and the notion of co-alignment as a source of competitive advantage supports the internal marketing framework at a basic level by demonstrating, theoretically and empirically, that competitive strategies are unlikely to deliver superior performance unless they match both the external environmental contingencies (customers, competitors, technology, complexity, dynamism, etc.), and internal organizational and management characteristics and processes (centralization, specialization, planning comprehensiveness, management style, decision making process, etc.). A competitive strategy that 'fits' the external environment but not the internal organizational characteristics is unlikely to affect business performance positively, as the strategy is likely to experience significant implementation difficulties due to the inappropriate organization design and management decision processes required to implement the strategy effectively. Conversely, a competitive strategy which has an appropriate 'fit' with the internal organization and management characteristics is more likely to be effectively implemented. However, unless the strategy implemented is able to achieve an appropriate 'fit' with the external environment then it is unlikely to achieve the positional advantages in the marketplace that are required to deliver business performance advantages.

Within this general contingency theory, internal marketing may be viewed as an integrating framework that attempts to ensure that strategies formulated within organizations have sufficient fit with the internal organization and management characteristics to be implemented effectively and efficiently. Thus, internal marketing provides the vital link in planning processes which examines the internal organizational co-alignment issues associated with strategy formulation and implementation, in the same way that traditional strategic management tools and techniques focus upon formulated strategies that are co-aligned with external environmental characteristics.

The theory of marketing

There is broad agreement that the fundamental building block of any theory of marketing is the concept of exchange. Much of the focus of attention of marketers has been concerned with how wide the definition of exchange can be, while still concerning marketing rather than any other social science discipline (see MARKETING).

Exchanges obviously take place within organizations as well as between the organization and external individuals, constituencies and bodies. The underlying thesis in marketing theory is that mutually satisfying long-term exchanges (increasingly being referred to as 'relationships', to emphasize the lengthening time horizons that are viewed as important) are essential to the achievement of organizational goals. While these long-term relationships are usually discussed in terms of external customers, and increasingly also suppliers and channel members, this rationale can also be extended to include internal customers and internal suppliers within the organization.

Thus, the essential thesis of marketing theory may be viewed as directly supportive of the internal marketing concept, when this same thesis is extended to include the internal as well as the external marketplace. Hence the extended theory of marketing suggests that long-term mutually satisfying relationships, built through multiple exchanges between the supplier organization and the external customer, are an outcome of achieving long-term mutually satisfying relationships between the organization and its internal customers, built through multiple exchange.

Resource-based models of strategic management

The resource-based models of strategic management which emerged in the 1980s took an internal perspective on the creation of positional advantages in the marketplace, suggesting that these arose not simply from external industry conditions but from the 'distinctive competencies' (the resources and skills held within the organization) that allow one organization to better achieve a particular positional advantage in a marketplace than competing suppliers. These competencies are generally not viewed as simply having been created in supplier organizations due to some process of gradual adaptation to marketplace and industry demands. Rather, the models suggested that managers may consciously and systematically attempt to achieve and reinforce particular distinctive competencies in order to pursue mid- and longer-term competitive strategies.

Thus, the resource-based view strongly suggests that senior managers and those involved in strategy formulation and implementation need to analyse not only the external environment to spot opportunities and threats, but also to analyse the organization's internal environment to identify existing and potential areas of distinctive competence within the organization that may be deployed in the marketplace, to take advantage of the opportunities and minimize the threats identified in the external environment. This both supports the need for, and highlights the utility of, the internal marketing concept in providing a conceptual model for understanding much of the internal 'environment' within the organization, and a practical framework for applying external marketing tools to the analysis of internal customers and suppliers and the relationships between them as existing and potential sources of distinctive competency within the organization.

These three widely recognized and acknowledged areas of management theory may be seen as providing both a broadly based and a substantive body of theory, which directly and indirectly supports the validity and potential utility of the internal marketing framework. Furthermore, it is strongly suggestive of the role of internal marketing in effective strategy *formulation* as well as in the more widely accepted role of ensuring the effective and efficient *implementation* of strategies and plans.

5 Practical aspects

One of the major strengths of the internal marketing concept is its strong and readily identifiable practical implications and utility to managers. These will be considered here in terms of both strategy formulation and strategy implementation.

Strategy formulation

Managers and strategists receive more than adequate guidance in analysing the external environment in which their business operates, as part of the strategic audit stage that is essential in any explicit strategic planning exercise. However, in attempting to analyse the internal environment inside the organization itself as a vital component part of the strategic auditing process, managers are rarely given anything more than the 'strengths' and 'weaknesses' boxes of a SWOT (strengths, weaknesses, opportunities and threats) analysis as guidance, tool and framework for analysing the internal environment. Therefore, it is hardly surprising that planning processes in organizations tend to be externally focused in terms of collecting and analysing information. Furthermore, the internal information used tends only to be that which relates directly to the external environment (for example, sales data, inventory data, customer satisfaction ratings, etc.).

Internal marketing provides a counterbalance to this by providing managers with a conceptualization of the internal environment with which they are comfortable and which seems intuitively appealing (that is, as an internal marketplace made up of internal customers and internal suppliers involved in long-term exchange relationships). Furthermore, it both provides strategists with a series of logical guiding questions, and suggests appropriate techniques for analysing the internal marketplace in relation to the organization's competitive strategy needs, which are largely determined and driven by the external marketplace. By focusing attention on the internal marketplace, internal marketing forces strategists to consider the following vital questions:

1 Who are the key internal customers and suppliers who affect what this organization delivers to our external customers?
2 What internal marketplace segments or coalitions can be identified and what are their needs, requirements and fears concerning the external competitive strategy that we wish to deliver in future?
3 In what areas do our internal customers and suppliers have skills and/or resources that could be deployed to gain positional advantage over competitors in this marketplace?
4 In what areas do our internal customers and internal suppliers exhibit weaknesses, in relation to what we are able to deliver to our external customers, that our competitors may be able to take advantage of?

Thus, the internal marketing approach produces a much clearer agenda of issues for managers and strategists to consider in conducting an internal analysis as part of the strategic audit process than the traditional and often highly simplistic SWOT framework. Additionally, the internal marketing framework suggests appropriate intelligence and research tools that may be adapted from external marketing for use in the internal marketplace.

For example, in the formulation of competitive strategies some companies have now started to make use of market research techniques, such as semi-structured interviews, employee surveys and even qualitative internal focus groups, in order to find out how various stakeholder groups and internal coalitions of various kinds in the internal marketplace perceive the company's resources and skills relative to competitors. This would appear to be a much better way of evaluating the organization's true distinctive competencies and po-

tential, rather than simply asking a planning team what should go in the top half of the SWOT 2 x 2 matrix. Similarly, at a covert level this kind of market research can be used to uncover the 'hidden agendas' of the dominant coalitions in the organization. For this reason, it is sometimes appropriate to use external consultants, market researchers or internal individuals who are viewed as outside the 'power plays' within the business.

Gaining an understanding of the implicit agendas of the various coalitions and stakeholder groups in the organization is a critical part of any strategy formulation process. By using market research approaches and couching questions and answers in terms of relationships between important internal customers and internal suppliers within the internal marketplace, it is possible to learn a good deal about the reality of the power and political infrastructure of any organization. This is vital information to incorporate in formulating strategies that are successfully executed. With this information, managers and strategists have a much better idea about which key individuals and groups will support various strategy options. Strategy options can also be modified, radically altered or even dumped depending upon the strategists' estimates of the likely acceptability to the key customer and supplier segments in the internal marketplace.

Strategy implementation

Once one or a number of outlined strategy options has been agreed by the planners using the analyses of both the external environment and the internal marketplace, then strategists should begin to evaluate the imperatives for the implementation strategy required to deliver the strategy options effectively into the customer marketplace. At this stage the use of the two-stage internal marketing programme framework is appropriate.

First, managers should work at the overt internal marketing programme by identifying what each outline strategy option means for the various important internal customer and supplier segments in the marketplace. The best starting point for this is the identification of the appropriate strategic internal marketing gaps, that is, the gaps between the conditions, systems, processes, structures, personnel, resources, skills, etc. required for the effective implementation of the critical component parts of the proposed strategy, and the reality of those same variables at that time in the organization.

Once these strategic internal marketing gaps for effective implementation are identified, then managers can begin the process of identifying how each and every gap-closing action plan (the core content of any implementation strategy) will affect, and be perceived by, each of the core customer and supplier segments and coalitions in the internal marketplace. The overt level marketing programme is useful here in conceptualizing this process – each gap-closing action can itself be viewed as a product, and each internal coalition can be looked at in turn to evaluate the 'price' that they would have to pay to support this gap-closing action. Appropriate communication messages and media for each group and internal coalition can then be assessed. In parallel with the overt internal marketing programme assessment, managers involved in strategy formulation also need to assess the covert internal marketing programme implications for each of the key internal coalitions/groups.

Having used the internal marketing mix framework to identify sources of likely implementation difficulties, strategy makers are in a strong position to design an implementation strategy, since they have identified which specific gap-closing actions are likely to encounter implementation obstacles, and they will also know which individuals/groups, etc. are opposed to which actions, and have some idea as to the reason for the opposition. At this stage, the question becomes one of altering, modifying and re-packaging the strategy itself and its associated gap-closing requirements to make it more acceptable to the key groups of customers and suppliers in the internal marketplace. Any implementation obstacles that cannot be overcome by minor modifications or repackaging of the strategy may require more radical alterations to the strategy itself. On some occasions this may make a particular strategy unfeasible, and strategists have to go back to the formulation process and design a

strategy that has a better chance of appealing to the internal marketplace, even if it does not do such a good job of taking advantage of the opportunities and minimizing the threats identified in the external environment. The logic is, that a sub-optimal external strategy that is well executed is likely to deliver more benefits to the organization than an optimal external strategy which is not effectively implemented at all.

Other types of external marketing approach may also become important and appropriate at both strategic and operational levels of internal marketing during implementation. One of the most important of these can be the diffusion of innovation models which propose that in external marketplaces, innovations and new products are purchased by different groups and types of people over time, suggesting that markets can be segmented by their willingness to try something new and different. Of particular importance in these models are 'opinion leaders', who are both the first to try new products and services, and important role models and sources of information for other more risk averse segments in the marketplace.

These models also appear to hold true in internal marketplaces where certain individuals and groups have a much greater propensity to embrace and accept change and new ways of doing things than others. This may involve specific individuals, small teams, individual product groups or even whole offices or regions of a business. What they have in common is that they try new things faster and more eagerly than anybody else, and that if they are successful other people in the internal market tend to follow them.

6 Policy implications

Perhaps the biggest and most obvious policy implications for managers arising from the internal marketing framework concern the processes by which organizations attempt to formulate and implement strategies and plans. In essence, internal marketing is a potential solution to two fundamental problems that appear endemic in the planning processes evidenced in most organizations.

The first problem concerns an imbalance between the analysis of the external environment and the internal workings of the organization in formulating plans and strategies. The 'tools and techniques' associated with planning activities have not changed dramatically in essence for many years. Managers' toolkits are full of 2 x 2 and 3 x 3 matrices, checklists, frameworks and models for analysing broad environmental trends, customer value-chains, market attractiveness, business position assessment, etc. This is the core of what we expect our planners and strategists to do as they go through the planning process, and the basis on which we teach executives about strategy on MBA programmes.

The 'technology' of planning in this sense is almost wholly externally orientated. While this external orientation is entirely appropriate in the dynamic and complex marketplaces that now emerge in even the 'sleepiest' industries, this has to be balanced with tools for analysing and identifying existing and potential sources of distinctive competencies within the organization. Without distinctive competencies, organizations will simply not have the skills and resources that they require for deployment in external marketplaces in order to achieve the positional advantages relative to competitors that will ultimately deliver enhanced business performance.

While our theoretical and anecdotal knowledge of the nature of distinctive competencies has developed rapidly over the past few years, planning technology in terms of the tools and techniques available to planners has not kept pace. The internal marketing framework can help to plug this gap. Using the internal marketing approach, managers must be encouraged to visualize an internal marketplace, use market research techniques and approaches to identify internal customers and suppliers, analyse the skills, resources, strengths and weaknesses evidenced in these internal customer-internal supplier relationships, and consider these findings in the context of what the organization does, and can, deliver to external customers. While this may not represent a particularly sophisticated tool or approach, it is a significant advance on the internal analyses undertaken by many planners at present.

The second problem endemic in most organizations' planning processes is an imbalance between senior management's time and attention spent on formulating strategies and planning implementation. Although it may be conceptually useful to distinguish between formulation and implementation in the context of strategy for the purposes of research, writing and teaching, this is a dangerous conceptualization to apply to planning processes in organizations. While differentiating between planners and implementers may have been a reasonable way to deal with strategy in the past in large, centralized, stable organizations dealing with munificent and static environments, these conditions have now largely disappeared for most organizations.

In the world of contemporary organizations, splitting planning process participation along the lines of planners versus implementers is often the precursor to ineffective execution of strategy and the failure of the strategy as implemented to deliver required organizational goals. The converse of this, getting everybody in the organization involved in the planning process as well as in the implementation process, is obviously a practical impossibility and may even be undesirable anyway. However, internal marketing encourages planners to identify key internal customer groups and to use market research approaches to ensure that their views are fed into and reflected in the planning process. The internal marketing framework built upon (1) the identification of key internal customers, suppliers and segments, (2) the development of overt marketing mix programmes as a conceptualization of rational implementation requirements of strategy options, (3) the development of covert marketing mix programmes as a conceptualization of the 'irrational' likely sources of opposition to various strategy elements and options, and (4) the repackaging, modification or complete redesign of a preferred strategy in response to this, provides those involved in the planning process with a basic framework for both formulating implementable strategies and designing specific detailed implementation plans to ensure effective execution.

7 Future developments

Managerial interest in the internal marketing framework is great and growing. At present, this is still largely fuelled by the growing recognition that implementation failures in strategy are commonplace and expensive. While, as presently constituted, the internal marketing framework provides a good conceptual model and adequate planning tool, further developments and refinements are obviously required. However, it seems almost certain that the internal marketing model will become rapidly absorbed into the mainstream textbook models of strategy process, and further refinements will result from this process.

While major interest and development is presently driven by strategy implementation problems, it is entirely possible that the greatest contribution of the internal marketing framework lies in the area of strategy formulation and has largely yet to be realized. The need for managers and strategists to analyse the internal workings of their organizations, in the search for existing and potential sources of distinctive competence that may be capable of being deployed in the marketplace to build positional advantages, is becoming much more widely recognized. The internal marketing framework as both a conceptual model and management tool has the potential to deliver an operational version of the theoretical models of distinctive competence that are becoming so influential in the academic and management literatures.

8 Conclusion

This entry set out to broaden and deepen the reader's understanding of the concept of internal marketing by pulling together the various strands of literature into a propositional model of internal marketing, that was both underpinned by strong theoretical foundations, and practical in its application to the management task of formulating and implementing strategy. In the context of the relative lack of specific treatments of internal marketing in the literature (particularly at the strategic level) this has proven a difficult and challenging task. However, the richness of the various disciplinary perspectives, the magnitude of the problems faced by planners, strategists and general managers and the almost limitless conceptual insight that can be gained through the conceptualizations of internal marketplaces within organizations, serve to allow the development of a very practical and wonderfully flexible management tool. With the modifications, extensions and refinements that are bound to occur, the internal marketing framework looks set to establish itself as one of the core tools of the emerging new approaches to formulating and implementing strategy in complex organizations facing increasingly hostile environments.

NEIL A. MORGAN
JUDGE INSTITUTE OF MANAGEMENT STUDIES,
UNIVERSITY OF CAMBRIDGE

Further reading

(References cited in the text marked *)

Barnes, J.G. (1989) 'The role of internal marketing: if the staff won't buy it, why should the customer?', *Irish Marketing Review* 4 (2): 11–21. (Useful and interesting expansion of the individual components in the internal marketing mix.)

* Berry, L.L. (1981) 'The employee as customer', *Journal of Retail Banking* 3 (1): 33–40. (Classic treatment of internal marketing from the services perspective, often quoted and rarely bettered.)

* Berry, L.L. and Parasuraman, A. (1991) *Marketing Services: Competing Through Quality*, New York: The Free Press. (Managerial treatment of services marketing from a quality perspective with explication of the role of internal marketing in supporting such efforts.)

* Collins, B. and Payne, A. (1991) 'Internal marketing: a new perspective for HRM', *European Management Journal* 9 (3): 261–70. (Illuminating extension of the internal marketing framework to the human resource management function, exploring the implications for organizations and human resource professionals.)

* George, W.R. (1990) 'Internal marketing and organizational behavior: a partnership in developing customer-conscious employees at every level', *Journal of Business Research* 20 (January): 63–70. (Brings together much of George's earlier work, which has been influential in the development of the internal marketing concept.)

* Gronroos, C. (1981) 'Internal marketing – an integral part of marketing theory', in J.H. Donnelly

and W.R. George (eds), *Marketing of Services*, Chicago, IL: American Marketing Association. (Classic conceptual development with particular attention to differences between strategic and tactical levels of internal marketing.)

Gronroos, C. (1990) 'Relationship approach to marketing in service contexts: the marketing and organizational behavior interface', *Journal of Business Research* 20 (January): 3–11. (Further development of the internal marketing model in the broader framework of relationship marketing.)

Neilson, R.P., Peters, M.P. and Hirsch, R.D. (1985) 'Intrapreneurship strategy for internal markets – corporate, non-profit and government institution cases', *Strategic Management Journal* 6 (2): 181–9. (Good explanation of the organization design perspective on the existence and utility of the concept of internal markets; includes examples.)

* Piercy, N.F. (1992) *Market-Led Strategic Change*, Oxford: Butterworth-Heinemann. (Managerial treatment considering market-led change in organizations, with some attention to the role of internal marketing in strategy implementation.)

Piercy, N.F. and Morgan, N.A. (1990) 'Strategic internal marketing: managerial frameworks and empirical evidence', in *Proceedings of the AMA Summer Educators' Conference*, Chicago, IL: American Marketing Association. (Overview of strategic-level internal marketing and the results of a study showing the relationship between internal marketing and marketing plan credibility and utilization.)

* Piercy, N.F. and Morgan, N.A. (1991) 'Internal marketing – the missing half of the marketing programme', *Long Range Planning* 24 (2): 82–93. (An overview of the concept of and need for internal marketing in strategy implementation; includes two case examples.)

Richardson, B.A. and Grant Robinson, C. (1986) 'The impact of internal marketing on customer service in a retail bank', *International Journal of Bank Marketing* 4 (5): 3–30. (Results of a study in a bank relating internal marketing activities to the achievement of external customer strategies based on service quality perceptions.)

* Tansuhaj, P., Wong, J. and McCullough, J. (1987) 'Internal and external marketing: effects on customer satisfaction in banks in Thailand', *International Journal of Bank Marketing* 5 (3): 73–83. (Reports on an empirical study suggesting relationships between internal marketing activities and external customer satisfaction.)

See also: HUMAN RESOURCE MANAGEMENT; MARKETING; MARKETING, FOUNDATIONS OF; ORGANIZATION BEHAVIOUR; ORGANIZATIONAL PERFORMANCE; STRATEGY, CONCEPT OF

Strategy in Latin America

Overview

Strategy in Latin America has, until fairly recently, been dominated by political and/or macroeconomic strategy. Business strategy, such as it is, has been dominated by political considerations. Tendencies towards client-ilism and corporatism, coupled with a short-termism that has roots both in Latin American business culture and the chronic political and economic instability of most Latin American countries, has meant that, until recently, strategy making has been of comparatively little importance for most Latin American businesses. Effectively, most strategic decisions were out of their hands.

More recently, with trends towards economic and political liberalization, businesses have been given a freer hand to compete, both domestically and internationally. Latin American businesses now have to face the task of making and implementing strategies, often with little or no experience in this field. In the decade to come, the clear winners among Latin American businesses will be those that are capable of defining and grasping their strategic imperatives and working out ways of reaching their goals.

1 Introduction

Business strategy in Latin America is closely linked to and dominated by macroeconomic and political strategies, perhaps more closely than in any other region of the world. Historically, since the Second World War at least, the business communities of Latin America have been weak and have seen their interests subordinated to those of the political élites. As Peralta-Ramos (1993) has pointed out, traditionally, conflict and competition in Latin America have been conducted in the political sphere, and corporatism and state control have been the dominant models in business. Sheahan (1987), among others, makes the point that the political and business spheres are closely tied; this remains largely true, even after a decade of liberalization across the region.

Any discussion of business strategy in Latin America, therefore, must be largely a discussion of the existing limits to strategic thinking. Many of the Latin American economies remain highly insular; this, coupled with political and economic instability, means that short-termism is the order of the day. Even though the political situation is now much more stable in most countries, the roller-coaster ride taken by the major Latin American economies (notably Brazil, Mexico and Argentina) since 1990 makes the process of strategy formulation difficult.

Nevertheless, there are signs of more sophisticated strategic blueprints emerging at company level in some countries (notably Mexico). Companies could survive, though not necessarily prosper, under corporatism and state control. Economic liberalization and political security have brought the cold winds of commercial competition sweeping through the region. Just as the smaller economies of the region are growing more dependent on the larger ones, so the smaller companies are finding themselves vulnerable; ambitious acquisition programmes by both foreign and local firms are already under way. Latin American companies are in a weak competitive position; their strategic imperative must be to find a way forward, exploiting regional and national competitive advantage and creating a distinctive economic force.

2 Political, economic and business strategy

As noted, business, economic and political strategy are almost inseparable in most of Latin America. Although some countries in the region (notably Argentina) had successful free market economies in the early part of the twentieth century, by mid-century political instability had all but killed these off. Left-wing political movements emerged in nearly every country of the region, sometimes taking the form of armed insurrection. Between 1950 and 1980, nearly every democratic government in the region was overthrown, sometimes by leftist revolutionaries (Cuba, Nicaragua), but more commonly by right-wing political and military elements seeking to crush the leftists (Argentina, Chile, Brazil, Uruguay, Paraguay, Peru, Bolivia, El Salvador, Guatemala). These military governments were rarely stable; Bolivia, for example, once suffered three changes of government in 48 hours. This trend culminated in the 'lost decades' of the 1970s and 1980s, with 'dirty wars' conducted against left-wing elements in the population by the military governments of Chile, Argentina, Paraguay, Guatemala and El Salvador. Although political instability has declined notably since the restoration of democracy beginning in the 1980s, there remain active insurgent forces in Mexico, Peru and Colombia, while Ecuador and Peru have only just resolved a long-standing state of war between them.

In this environment, two business models have developed. The first, communism (or variants on it), relies on state control of industrial and landed capital and the business sector. This model has been employed in Cuba, and a highly modified form was instituted in Nicaragua under the Sandinistas (and has since been partly dismantled). The Allende government in Chile was moving towards such a model before it was overthrown by the armed forces in 1973. In such models, strategy making is the exclusive preserve of the state. Right-wing ideologies, however, have also advocated state control, at least in key sectors such as telecommunications and transport (one reason being that, in the event of war or a state of emergency, these state-controlled firms can be more easily put at the disposal of the armed forces).

The other model, corporatism, has been widespread. In Argentina, for example, business interests were often represented by large industrial associations; these, along with the major trade unions, worked in close cooperation with the government and the central bank to set economic policy (although in practice, the government tended to issue orders which the unions and associations obeyed). Thus a strong central planning element remains present.

Large corporations themselves were often formed on similar models. Aubey (1979) describes the dominant form of large business in Mexico, the investment group, structured around a core bank or financial institution, then with subsidiary financial institutions, these latter controlling a tertiary layer of industrial and commercial business units. However, these businesses, while individually powerful, seldom accounted for more than a very small proportion of any Latin American economy. The bulk of economic activity remains in the hands of small, often very small firms; these latter are often family owned and managed, particularly in areas where agriculture is the dominant activity.

Strategy making, therefore, has tended to focus on centralizing power and control on a small élite core (as Aubey (1979) and Moran (1979) point out, this is a key cultural characteristic of business in Latin America). Political strategy often dominated business and economic strategy; thus the need to crush political dissent would often override economic and business needs. Crushing dissent often involved seeking outside assistance (notably from the USA), and the *quid pro quo* sometimes involved opening up opportunities for US business interests, accepting economic policies which fit with US strategic aims, or both (Sheahan 1987; Bartell and Payne 1995). Strategy as a firm-specific activity was therefore extremely limited in scope. To some extent, many of these constraints remain in force.

3 Limits on strategy

Any discussion of strategy in Latin America must take into account the limits – political, cultural and economic – on strategy making (see STRATEGY, CONCEPT OF). The focus of the discussion here is on business strategy, but many of the same constraints apply to other fields. The limits on strategy described here have been identified by Sheahan (1987), Bartell and Payne (1995), Galal and Shirley (1994) and Peralta-Ramos (1993), among others.

The key limiting factors can be described as follows:

- *Economic and political instability.* As noted above, although political instability has reduced significantly in most countries, economic instability continues, as witnessed by the January 1999 crash of the Brazilian currency. Currency fluctuations, high interest rates, shortages of domestic capital, flight of foreign capital and inflation all combined to create a highly uncertain business environment, where forward planning becomes difficult if not impossible.
- *Insularity of economies.* The economies of Latin America have opened up significantly in the past decade, with Mexico joining the North American Free Trade Association (NAFTA), and other regional associations have been established; restrictions on foreign investment have also eased (see MEXICO, MANAGEMENT IN; NORTH AMERICAN FREE TRADE AGREEMENT). Nonetheless, many of the smaller economies of Latin America, such as Ecuador and Paraguay, remain insular in focus, with domestic firms paying little attention to outside investment. There are obvious limits to expansion within such small markets. Additionally, as noted, many of the smaller markets remain heavily dependent on agriculture; the events of 1997–8, when El Niño-related storms and Hurricane Mitch badly damaged crops in a number of countries, show how fragile these economies often are.
- *Foreign influences.* As noted above, external political pressures can have unforeseen consequences for Latin American economies, although here too the situation is becoming more stable. The Latin American economies also remain highly vulnerable to external economic shocks. Mexico and Brazil are widely regarded as the bellwether countries of Latin America, and when their economies go into crisis, other economies in the region tend to suffer as well.
- *Remnants of corporatism.* Despite a decade of economic liberalization, corporatist modes of thinking remain strong in many countries. Corporatist structures are weaker than previously in some countries (notably Argentina and Chile) but remain strong in others. In terms of state divestment from the economy, Argentina, Chile and Mexico have made considerable strides, and in July 1997, Brazil launched Latin America's largest privatization, that of the telecommunications company Telebrás (75 per cent of shares were bought by foreign investors) (Economist Intelligence Unit 1998).
- *Tendency towards clientelism and patriarchy.* These are social trends, noted by Moran (1979) and Aubey (1979), which tend to encourage dependency on the part of firms and managers. Within firms, managerial responsibility tends to be devolved towards the top; between firms, there is a tendency for small firms to develop clientelist relations with larger ones, either informally or formally through structures such as investment groups, thus surrendering control of strategy making. Business strategy has in the past been concentrated in the hands of a relatively few powerful business leaders. This situation is changing, more quickly in some countries than in others.
- *Societal needs.* With their recent violent history of left-wing rebellion and right-wing repression, the political and social needs of Latin American countries impinge heavily on business and economic strategy. Economic strategy across the region remains primarily focused on development and on improving standards of living. Businesses are not always free to act solely in their own self-interest.

- *Short-termist culture*. Finally, as Moran (1979) and Aubey (1979) have noted, Latin American business culture tends to have a strong short-termist orientation. All of the factors above of course represent pressures towards short-termism, but beyond these, it is safe to say that long-term forward planning and clear goal identification have never been hallmarks of Latin American culture. Time horizons tend to be short, and strategies are often aimed at immediate goals.

4 Competitive positions

Strategically, most of the economies of Latin America are in a position of considerable competitive weakness. Their key strengths remain a ready supply of agricultural, mineral and petrochemical resources coupled with relatively low-cost industrial bases. The key weaknesses, however, are mirror images of those strengths: the economies are over-reliant on commodities, and the industrial bases have suffered from decades of under-investment, shortage of capital goods, high interest rates and high inflation.

Of all the Latin American economies, only Mexico and Brazil have achieved any kind of significant international profile; but again, such is the paradox of Latin American economies that these have also been two of the most volatile economies, and their economic troubles have threatened the entire region. Both countries have large and well-developed industrial sectors – Brazil, indeed, is usually counted as the world's eighth-largest economy – and during the 1980s both became prime sites for multinational companies wishing to locate new manufacturing facilities; Mexico was particularly attractive to its NAFTA partners, while Brazil attracted firms from Europe and East Asia. However, both countries suffer from the effects of having what are in effect two economies: a modern industrial economy based around the main urban centres, and a rural economy based predominantly on agriculture or resource extraction. This dual structure tends to make for lack of focus in economic policy terms, and the two sectors have quite different and

sometimes conflicting strategic goals and needs.

Continuing economic mismanagement in both countries means economic stability has been hard to achieve. Of the two countries, Mexico looks most likely to reach a stable position first, thanks largely to NAFTA; in recent months, falling oil prices have been offset by rises in exports in other sectors. By diversifying its industrial bases, Mexico is managing to insulate itself from the worst shocks. Brazil, by contrast, has whipsawed from one economic extreme to the other. In 1993, inflation was running at 2000 per cent. Stabilization measures were successful for a time, but by 1998 a new crisis was emerging, with interest rates soaring as the government attempted to defend the currency and got the worst of both worlds; foreign capital flight continued unabated, at one point reaching almost £2 billion per day, while lack of investment and shortage of capital goods hampered industry at a critical time. Although the crisis has since subsided, Brazil's economy remains acutely vulnerable to shocks.

Argentina and Chile, by contrast, have achieved greater stability, though both remain vulnerable to shocks from their larger neighbours. It is here that economic reform has perhaps been most extensive, with strong privatization programmes removing much of the burden from the state. Bartell and Payne (1995: 91) have noted the emergence of a new breed of entrepreneur in Chile, one exhibiting fewer of the standard traits of Latin American business culture and more likely to look to the long term and develop strategic responses to business problems. While this is true, Chile's economy remains small, with insufficient critical mass to compete on its own, either in the region or globally. In addition, Argentina remains fatally hampered by the lack of high-quality management education (see MANAGEMENT EDUCATION IN LATIN AMERICA).

Many of the smaller countries of Latin America remain highly conservative in outlook. Uruguay, governed by a long-standing coalition of its centrist parties, has been slow to undertake reform; a referendum proposing widespread privatization was rejected by a large majority in 1992. In Ecuador, the election of Jamil Mahuad as president in 1998 with a mandate to launch economic reforms means change may at last begin there. In the meantime, however, both countries remain almost entirely dependent on primary sector industries such as agriculture. Venezuela, with much of its economy dependent on its oil reserves, has been similarly conservative and slow to carry out reforms.

In summary, then, the nations of Latin America have potential strengths in terms of their resource bases and, in some cases, developed or developing industrial sectors. There are also powerful weaknesses, notably an over-reliance on commodities, continuing economic mismanagement and failure to reform. Economies remain too insular, and are neither sufficiently specialized nor sufficiently diversified; there are no signs of emerging clusters based on special advantages, and few signs of strategic moves towards diversification, except in Mexico. Weakness on the part of economies means weakness on the part of firms, and increasingly, small and mid-sized companies in Latin America are either being forced aside by international competitors, or taken over by them. (Interestingly, Mexico is the home of a number of such predators; Telemex, for example, has been embarking on an ambitious programme of acquisitions throughout the region, causing some resentment as it does so [Latin Trade Online 1999].)

5 Strategic choices

Although clear problems remain, and although some countries remain reluctant to take the economic medicine needed for a full recovery from the turmoils of the past 50 years, it can be generally said that Latin America has made a key strategic choice about the nature and shape of its economies. This has not been without pain: Sheahan (1987) has noted how Argentina and Brazil have swung from early industrialization to violent reaction, Chile has gone from Marxism to monetarism, and violent revolutions have shaken Cuba and Peru. With the exception of Cuba, nearly all of Latin America is now moving into the centre ground. Policies are almost without exception oriented towards free market economies, integrated to some extent with others in the region, and with development remaining a key goal.

Evidence of this comes in the growing power and influence of transnational economic bodies. The most powerful of these is Mercosur (Brazil, Argentina, Uruguay and Paraguay; Chile and Bolivia are associate members), which has already established a customs union and is making progress towards integrating the economies of its members. The Andean Union (Colombia, Venezuela, Peru and Ecuador) is less advanced, as is the Central American Common Market (Costa Rica, El Salvador, Guatemala, Honduras and Nicaragua). Cooperation within and between these organizations is likely to increase, and all three are gradually drawing closer to NAFTA.

With the old barriers to strategy making and implementation declining, the new businesses of Latin America now have more freedom to develop their own strategies for competition within and beyond national borders. The immediate need is for companies to develop their strategic capabilities. This means first, learning how to do strategy, and second, defining and learning how to exploit their own strategic advantages. They need to explore new possibilities for enhancing their strength, for example linkages and joint ventures with other domestic or foreign firms, but as partners rather than clients.

Another immediate strategic priority in nearly every country in Latin America is enhancing skills bases and creating or expanding the élite pools of managers and skilled workers. This in turn needs investment in education and training, both by firms and by governments. Terragno (1988) has already set out this need in some detail, along with policy prescriptions; so far, however, there has been little progress towards this goal, and only in Chile and Mexico can any sizeable population of 'new' managers and business leaders be found to have emerged.

At the same time, human and social issues cannot be ignored in strategy making. Sheahan (1987) has listed the following issues as being of prime importance in the growth and future of Latin America: poverty, employment, economic growth, exporting, industrialization, inflation, debt, land ownership and capital ownership. As Chile has already discovered, strict monetarist policies are insufficient for dealing with these issues. It seems likely that businesses will have to develop social strategies as well as commercial strategies if the long-term future of Latin America is to be assured. To put it another way, 50 years of state intervention have come close to ruining many Latin American countries; business is probably the only institution left with the ability – or the credibility – to manage recovery.

MORGEN WITZEL
LONDON BUSINESS SCHOOL

Further reading

(References cited in the text marked *)

* Aubey, R.T. (1979) 'Private sector capital mobilization: family control of business in Latin America', in D.R. Shea, F.W. Swacker, R.J. Radway and S.T. Stairs (eds), *Reference Manual on Doing Business in Latin America*, Milwaukee, WI: University of Wisconsin Press. (Describes two key types of private sector organization, the family business and the investment group.)
* Bartell, E.A. and Payne, L.A. (eds) (1995) *Business and Democracy in Latin America*, Pittsburgh: University of Pittsburgh Press. (Valuable work on the relationships between business and government strategy, with chapters on Chile, Bolivia, Peru, Mexico and Brazil and a useful summary.)
  Business International Corporation (1991) *Developing Strategic Partnerships and Joint Ventures in Latin America*, New York: Business International Corporation. (Primarily a guide for foreign companies wishing to set up joint ventures.)
* Economist Intelligence Unit (1998) *EIU Country Reports*, London: Economist Intelligence Unit. (Quarterly reports in a valuable series on political and economic events: *Country Reports* drawn on for this article include those for Venezuela, Mexico, Costa Rica, Cuba, Bolivia, Ecuador, Uruguay, Paraguay, Argentina, Brazil and Chile.)
* Galal, A. and Shirley, M. (eds) (1994) *Does Privatization Deliver? Highlights from a World Bank Conference*, Washington, DC: World Bank. (Includes a number of case studies, notably Mexico and Chile.)
  Inter-American Development Bank (1994) *Economic and Social Progress in Latin America*, New York: Inter-American Development Bank. (General description of the economic state of Latin America in 1993, when the crisis of the early 1990s was having a serious impact.)
* 'Latin Trade Online: January 1999 Panorama', at *http://www.latintrade.com/current/html/panorama.html*. (Useful bullet-point survey of current issues in Latin American business. The related 'Trade Talk' website is also useful.)
* Moran, R.T. (1979) 'Cross-cultural dimensions of doing business in Latin America', in D.R. Shea, F.W. Swacker, R.J. Radway and S.T. Stairs (eds), *Reference Manual on Doing Business in Latin America*, Milwaukee, WI: University of Wisconsin Press. (Useful chapter on culture, including its impacts on planning and decision making, in an otherwise dated text.)
* Peralta-Ramos, M. (1993) *The Political Economy of Argentina*, Boulder, CO: Westview Press. (Largely historical account of how Argentina's political and economic position has developed; the author is a strong critic of President Menem.)
* Sheahan, J. (1987) *Patterns of Development in Latin America*, Princeton, NJ: Princeton University Press. (Dated, but still a good summary of key strategic issues.)
* Terragno, R.H. (1988) *The Challenge of Real Development: Argentina in the Twenty-First Century*, Boulder, CO: Lynne Rienner. (The author, a minister in the Alfonsin government, argues that Argentina needs to develop its science and knowledge bases in order to compete; sets out the framework of the philosophy known as *terragnismo*.)

See also: ARGENTINA, MANAGEMENT IN; BRAZIL, MANAGEMENT IN; CHILE, MANAGEMENT IN; GLOBALIZATION; MEXICO, MANAGEMENT IN; NORTH AMERICAN FREE TRADE AGREEMENT; STRATEGY, CONCEPT OF; STRATEGY IN ASIA PACIFIC; STRATEGY IN THE EMERGING COUNTRIES; STRATEGY IN EUROPE; STRATEGY IN NORTH AMERICA; WORLD BANK; WORLD TRADE ORGANIZATION

Strategy making, politics of

Overview

The politics of strategy making is one of the core areas of management theory and practice. This centrality derives from the way the subject has emerged from among the specialist research on strategy, decision making and corporate politics. Consequently, an understanding of the politics of strategy formation leads to an appreciation of the more general development of the strategy and organization fields.

Political analysts of strategy have drawn attention to the varieties of power exercised from within and outside the organization and their impact on decision making. They have uncovered an array of sources of power and, in particular, the problems of those decision makers who endure 'powerlessness'. The subject has produced some potent frameworks for understanding the politics of strategy, especially in the case of unobtrusive power and the management of meaning.

The strength of the literature lies in the way scholars have taken seriously the processual dimension of strategy. Leading exponents have been responsible for major advances in comprehending the more subjective or interpretative aspects of strategic activity. In so doing, they have forged strong links with other theories of management. The limitations of the field arise from its qualities; it is questionable, for example, how far the hidden political features of strategy are recognized. Equally, the practical relevance of academic work on power and strategy still has not been fully demonstrated to practitioners.

1 Introduction

Power, according to some, is the organization's last dirty secret (see POWER). Equally, politics is regarded as somehow illegitimate and destructive in nature. However, as most managers and employees have instinctively reacted to politics in this negative way, academics have expended considerable effort to expose and explore the problem. The result has been to produce one of the most challenging and conceptually rich fields of management research.

The distinctive character of the subject derives from its synthetic quality. In other words, the politics of strategy making brings together specialist interests in the three areas of strategy, decision making (see DECISION MAKING) and politics. Business strategy and strategic management have been at the heart of the expansion of teaching, research and commentary on management since the 1970s. The breadth of this flow of scholarship has encompassed not only the orthodox, rationalist understandings of strategy seen as planning; it has also covered those who explain strategic management as an incremental process or who relate it to given contexts. Others have used cognitive, ecological or visionary perspectives. It is clear that the political dimension has proved to be one of the more robust approaches. In many ways, those who make power an essential component of their appreciation of strategy have had a profound impact on the area. The work of Pfeffer or Schwenk (Pfeffer 1992; Schwenk 1989), for example, has been critical to both the theoretical growth of strategy studies and its empirical coverage.

Running in parallel to these events has been the sustained attention devoted to decision making. The foundation provided by the Carnegie school in the 1960s and 1970s has been built upon subsequently by organization analysts. The result has been a refined knowledge of not just the cycles and patterns of such processes but an awareness of the less rational character of the links between problems and decisions. The emergent nature of many strategic decisions – where managers constantly interpret signals from the environment in the light of cultural and group norms, for example – has led many writers to question the original precepts of Ansoff or Chandler (Ansoff 1965; Chandler 1962) (see ANSOFF, H.I.; CHANDLER, A.D.). Strategy making can no longer be regarded as an advanced form of planning and resource allocation.

If decision making experts questioned certain core assumptions of the strategy world, then political analysts have been responsible for a frontal assault. Interestingly, those who trained outside of the management discipline demonstrate that the process and outcomes of strategic decision making is often only distantly related to commercial or technical logics. Path-breaking studies by Mintzberg (see MINTZBERG, H.) and Pettigrew point to the way individuals or departments use power to control resources, secure advancement and define problems and policies. Above all, they show how strategic goals are by definition disruptive of vested interests. The consequences are never trivial.

The results of this combination from three specialist areas (strategy, decision making and organizational politics) have been impressive. Three aspects stand out. First, strategy making is now understood as conditioned by a host of potential influences; these originate from both within and outside the organization, involving diverse stakeholders. Second, the sources of power are equally varied. Power may derive from expertise or the ability to control information. The converse is equally true. Third, sophisticated accounts of power demonstrate how it is mobilized to legitimate courses of action through the management of meaning. Power is frequently unobtrusive within organizations; it is only manifest in social action.

Overall, the political aspects of strategy are vital to any understanding of strategic management. Power and strategy making as a research problem have illuminated much of the less than rational behaviour of managers. How far this exposure has travelled is open to question. Equally, the transfer of such insights to practical advice remains incomplete in many respects. However, the future of the topic will

consequently be dominated by attempts to fill such gaps. The opportunity also exists for engagement with other specialists, coming from recent advances in sociology for instance. New empirical areas of inquiry also beckon, notably in the public sector in Europe. From a consideration of academic research, therefore, the negative connotations of corporate politics may be productively overturned.

2 Origins and context

Although well established as a core subject in management, the politics of strategy making arose as a research problem from the linkages between three scholarly traditions: the strategy school, decision making experts and political analysts. The connections across the three streams of work have been extensive. However, in order to aid exposition separate attention should be given to each before going on to examine the combined results (see ORGANIZATION BEHAVIOUR; ORGANIZATION BEHAVIOUR, HISTORY OF).

Strategy making is by no means short of academic commentators. Indeed, what has become a hallmark of the subject is the way that different emphases are evident among writers internationally. Fundamental agreement has existed, though, among mainstream scholars as to the point and purpose of strategy. According to Schendel and Hofer (1979: 11), its essential features are entrepreneurial. In their terms, strategy should be about organizational renewal and growth via the appropriate use of a firm's resources. Strategies are made with the purpose of ensuring an organization's survival in a world of competitive rivalry.

The evolution of the subject bears out the strength of this orthodoxy. In the 1960s, strategy making and planning were like Siamese twins. Creating a strategy involved assessing the environment of the firm, forecasting future trends and evaluating the necessary adjustments to be made to internal structures and resources. Successive generations of strategy models were erected on this platform of a knowable environment and adjustable organization. Examples include the Boston Box product portfolio matrix of the 1970s, the 'generic strategies' of cost leadership and differentiation a decade later, or the notion of 'strategic intent' offered for the 1990s.

The spinal connection which joins such orthodoxies together over the years has been neo-classical economics. Through training in economics, or by emulating its techniques, many leading writers rely on a rational deductive notion of problem-solving informing the conduct of strategy formation. The impression given is of a firm speaking with a single voice, through well-informed leaders who are able to choose between clearly articulated alternatives. Those who have followed Chandler (1962) have emphasized therefore that strategies are formed via an analytical and intentional process.

The trajectory of the decision making specialism at first matched the objective view of the strategists. In time, subsequent research raised important issues for the conventional rationalist view. March and Simon (1958) pointed to the way that people's 'bounded rationality' and 'satisficing' behaviour limit their ability to engage in straightforward rational choices. Cyert and March (1963) sustained the idea of the organization as equivalent in decision making terms to an individual. They emphasized the firm's concern with goal attainment through efficiency and learning. While they noted conflict as routine, the framework to explore the political dimension of decision making was undeveloped (see MARCH, J.G. AND CYERT, R.M.; SIMON, H.A.).

It was not until the research of March and Olsen (1976) that such progressive, rationalist hopes for mastering the decision-making process were questioned. In one of the more colourful metaphors of the genre, the 'garbage can' was produced. The keynotes of this theory emphasized the partial comprehension of others' interests by members of an organization, the shifting population of contributors to a decision process, and the way solutions are produced yet unrelated to official problems. Rationality does not inform action, rather preferences arise from action.

While many were content to associate the garbage-can approach to decision making with the educational organizations which its proponents researched, others recoiled from its full anarchic force. Writers, such as Quinn in the 1970s, argued that strategic decisions (largely on the basis of private-sector examples) are reached via intentional processes of formulation. Strategies are constantly modified during development in response to environmental signals. This process of strategic decision making became known as logical incrementalism. Emphasis is placed on informal channels of information and the sensing of opportunities by non-specialists. The result is a logically managed flow of experiment, partial implementation and reassessment. Analysis, assessment and refinement are cyclical and the advantages of the organization are retained in a context of low risk.

The third group to contribute to the politics of strategy making has been the political analysts. In broad terms, it is widely accepted that power is the potential ability to influence behaviour, to alter events, to overcome resistance and make people do things they would not otherwise do. Politics and influence concern the actions and behaviours through which power is realized and used (Pfeffer 1992). Others have referred to power as the ability to control premises of actions, and hence the difficulty in observing power straightforwardly. It has been pointed out that such subtleties are routinely ignored in practice: those on the receiving end of power are abundantly clear about who possesses it (Salancik and Pfeffer 1977).

However, while debate has continued over definitions, researching strategic formation as a political process has paid sizeable dividends. Appreciating organizations as political systems has proved extremely useful in understanding the forces which help or inhibit strategy making (Pettigrew 1977). Interest groups form around strategic issues, exhibit contrasting rationalities and compete for space and resources. Such relationships between groups (often formed around the traditional expertise of accounting, personnel, engineering or planning) exhibit shifting balances of power. Organizations are dominated at certain epochs in their development by the power of specialist groups. Yet it is precisely around the episodes of change which strategy making addresses, that power relations receive their sharpest expression.

The earlier understanding of power as a means of securing preferred outcomes was important for drawing attention to the way strategy making was connected to the majority in an organization, not just to senior management. This resource-based conception of power and strategy has been extended though by the view of politics as the management of meaning. The emphasis is on the way power is mobilized. The benefit came in research twenty years ago which demonstrated the way actions around strategic decisions could be legitimated or their relevance undermined (Pettigrew 1977). The key means to establishing such legitimacy may come through the combined shaping of language and values, together with the construction of supporting symbols and myths. In process terms, the political analysts have shed light on both the overt and less visible aspects of strategy making. In other words, confrontation, negotiation and bargaining between interest groups or coalitions openly occurs as they seek to establish their preferred strategic option. At the same time, their representatives may well have worked as hard to establish a conducive reception for their ideas: by the prior construction of key terminology, the recognition of specialist logics and the generation of stories about the organization which reinforce their world view.

The development of the strategy field has benefitted greatly from the long-term contribution of the decision making and political specialists. In truth, the subject of strategy has been transformed by their inputs. The result is an agreement that strategic decisions are those that make use of a firm's threats and opportunities to improve its future prospects. Strategic decisions are by their nature, therefore, interconnected to other problems, exhibiting uncertainty and ambiguity and involving conflicting trade-offs between solutions (Rajagopalan *et al.* 1993). It is also noticeable that such richness in the characteristics of strategy has led scholars to apply widely differing theoretical perspectives to different parts of the problem (including for example, implementation). Given such activity it would be appropriate to look more closely at the results of research into the politics of strategy making and, by so doing, evaluate the findings against the backdrop of the wider strategy field.

3 Analysis

The outcomes of the study of the political dimension of strategy formation may be usefully considered around four main topics: the effects of internal and external influences, the sources of power, the unobtrusive nature of politics and, lastly, the empirical areas where new light has been shed on the political process.

The identification of both internal and external power influences on strategy making is one of the strongest conclusions produced by researchers. In the internal sphere, the 'strategic contingencies model' (Hickson *et al.* 1971) has become well established. Groups (see GROUPS AND TEAMS) in organizations may derive power from five main, often overlapping, influences. The first is dependency, where a department may control resources which other departments require. The second, financial resources, relates to the ability of individuals or coalitions to generate dependency because of their determination of financial allocation. Centrality, the third influence, reflects on actors' roles in the primary activity of the organization and how far their work affects the final output. Non-substitutability is the fourth aspect and refers to the way the function of a group cannot be performed by others. Non-substitutability increases power. Coping with uncertainty is the fifth feature. Those in an organization who can cope with the unpredictable effects of the environment and reduce the impact on others have been shown to enhance their power.

Clearly the interior world of the organization produces major influences on how power may be acquired in relation to strategic decisions. Yet while these influences may appear the most directly relevant, one ignores external factors at one's peril. Dependency is a critical component of the situation. Firms, or their equivalents, face pressures from a variety of stakeholders (see CORPORATE GOVERNANCE). Organizations tend to comply with such demands to the extent that they are dependent on these groups. Stakeholders are understood as any group or individual who can affect, or is affected by, the achievement of the organization's objectives. Mintzberg summarized the different types of stakeholders (Mintzberg

1983) which might influence strategic management. They include: owners of the organization, associates who transact with it, collectives which represent employees, and the variety of publics which are related to an organization.

Although this range of potential influences on strategy formation is well documented, it is the operation of such power which is all-important (see INTEREST GROUPS; TRADE UNIONS). It must be remembered that the direction of the influence is seldom one-way. Organizations affect and are affected by their stakeholders – internal and external – through a mutual influence process. The extent to which management responds to such influence is conditional upon the organization's dependency on these groups. Yet the influence is never constant, nor is it easily perpetuated across decisions. It is the unpredictability of this dialectic process which produces the context where specific groups may augment their political position within strategy making. In short, 'boundary-spanners', or those who resolve issues between the organization and its environment, are able to achieve the highest levels of political influence over strategy formation. It may not necessarily be senior managers who enjoy such roles; specialist departments or professional experts may well fulfil the need.

These types of influence on strategy making provide strong clues as to the precise sources of power which actors may, or may not, enjoy in the process. The answers provided by academics are often surprising. Resource and position power runs through the forms of influence described already. Expert power is a similar source. Yet it is the manner in which such power is exercised which is critical to its impact on strategic management. It is one thing to possess a resource or expertise, it is quite a different accomplishment to utilize such capacities in the uncertain process of strategy making. Those who technically depend on an expert or a well-positioned department (such as finance) may be able to rise above that dependency by other means. Filtering of external information to reinforce the strategic priorities of the supposedly dependent group (such as manufacturing, say) is one means. Equally, operating parts of the organization's systems in order to constrict information can help to legitimize the preferences of otherwise politically weak actors.

Moreover, personal sources of power serve to complicate the pattern of political influence on strategy. Personal attributes (articulateness or social adroitness for example), the effect of charisma and a matching of personal style and skill may well overcome established dependency relations. Research on the politics of strategy formation as a process points to the way results are linked to the intersection of such influences and sources. A member of an organization will impact on the decision process in relation to the nexus of formal position and resource-based power allied to personal reputation and performance.

It is this combined appreciation of power in use that led Kanter (1979) to further telling insights. In her thinking, a person's power within organizational processes rested on the person's maintenance of three types of connection with other parts of the organization. These are termed lines of supply, lines of information and lines of support. The first summarizes a person (or group's) adeptness at bringing in relevant resources; the second overlaps with the notions of information as a key means of producing others' dependency on you; and the third expresses the unit's capacity to protect allies or sponsor key projects.

It may be relatively easy, in the light of previous work, to see how the three lines notion encapsulates a composite idea of power around strategy making. What marks out the three-point approach though is the way it has been used to demonstrate those who are 'powerless'. Indeed, Kanter's experience of North American corporations led her to suggest that top executives could easily find themselves lacking power to shape strategy. The core of the problem was found to be uncontrollable lines of supply owing to environmental upheaval, blocked lines of information, often about other levels in the organization, and weak lines of support arising from the volatility of stakeholder behaviour.

The third area which stands out in the unfolding of the analysis of the politics of strategy creation is also the most subtle in character. It was noted earlier that political scholars of organizations developed the ideas of legitimacy as a vital quality which could be secured by managing meaning. This orientation to power emphasizes the often covert manipulation of symbols, language and beliefs in order to legitimate preferred decision outcomes. Work in this tradition has revealed the unobtrusive nature of politics amongst managers (Hardy 1985). The argument is that visible conflict is not a necessary precondition for the exercise of power. Power may be used by actors to prevent conflict and ensure opposing groups do not attempt to challenge key decisions or the direction of strategic thinking. The mechanisms for sustaining unobtrusive power seek to institutionalize existing power in structures and cultures which protect groups from unwanted change. Strategic and other processes are deliberately mystified by the construction of beliefs in, for example, inevitable market pressures or unavoidable technological advances. Procedures, precedents, rules and symbols are used to prevent challenges to orthodoxy by restricting access to strategic decision arenas. Potential opponents are scripted out of the accepted narratives of organizational events and performance. The identification of such unobtrusive power has been invaluable in opening up a distinct area of study beyond the established interest in overt sources and means of political influence in the strategy process.

The breakthrough has been paralleled by developments which produced a fourth core area of analysis – the political characteristics of the industry or sector. An understanding of unobtrusive power has proved extremely helpful. At one level it has been possible to see how the content of given strategies has been directed at the competitive power relations of an industry. Uncertainty caused by competitors or the need for formal interdependence with suppliers, creditors and customers has led to well-known, overt strategic responses. These include joint ventures, interlocking directorates and the appeal for regulation.

More challenging as an approach to the politics of strategy making has been the exposing of the nuances of power and influence found across the idea systems of whole industries. The creation or adjustment of a firm's strategy may well be deeply influenced by both overt power relations with rivals and the less obtrusive influences of dominant recipes or reputation effects. Often, attempts to change business strategy within a firm are thwarted by the lack of ideological and political shifts at the sector level. The commercial power of the original dominant corporations in both the early computing and airline sectors was clearly used to crush competitive advances. What was less commented on at the time was the immense power of companies such as IBM and DEC to proscribe alternative ways of conceiving of strategic options. Huff (1982) and subsequent industry analysts have argued that sectors exhibit collective managerial cognitive structures. If they stabilize they can become interpretive frames which help actors to make sense of their firm's environment. As these frames mature, strategic paradigms emerge which condition the way executives consider their strategic options. The opportunities for influencing such frames and paradigms in a political way are legion. Research in Scandinavia supplies sharp examples of the insidious yet successful impact of the Wallenberg family in Sweden; in creating an 'industrial wisdom' or the less well-known but equally important 'quasi-boards' or informal networks of executives which join certain industries. Work on the sector concept itself has shown the limits to the operation of market economics provided by the combination of institutional arrangements which embody both commercial, social and political networks (Rasanen and Whipp 1992).

4 Evaluation

It is evident that the politics of strategy making embraces a rich mixture of approaches. Any evaluation of the area is obliged to recognize the undoubted strengths that have grown from lead authorities' skill in excavating the political dimension right to the core of strategic management. Inevitably, such advances raise questions about how far the project still has to travel and, in addition, to what extent the practical relevance of academic findings has been made clear.

The most striking achievement made by scholars of the politics of strategy formation is one of integration. In one respect, the understanding of politics as both resource-based, contingent on multiple stakeholders and involving the management of meaning has been liberating. The conjunction of these key perspectives has not only re-invigorated the political specialists, it has also enabled them to find common cause with experts from other areas, such as organizational culture.

It is apparent that the major accounts of politics related to the strategic decision making process discussed here have been decisive in building an alternative perspective of the strategy concept. Revealing the role of political influence on all phases of the process has helped to build an understanding wholly distinct from the orthodox rationalist planning school. Power relations have demonstrated how strategies are as much the product of cognition as contest in spite of the attempts to evaluate and plan in a manner which fits an organization's environment. Indeed, the so-called 'interpretive' perspective on strategic management would be nowhere without the advances made by political analysts. It is now established, therefore, that the dominant culture and paradigm of an organization offer a framework of ideas and values. These frameworks provide a means of interpretation for dealing with the complexity generated by the environment. Issues of power and influence are the very lifeblood of such frames of reference.

Furthermore, attention paid to politics has produced large dividends for the appreciation of strategy making as a process. Going beyond technical imperatives, it emerges that the process of strategy formation takes its shape, pace and temporal pattern from an amalgam of forces. The efforts to exploit dependency or the attempts to construct the legitimacy of specialist interests are the very motor which drives decision making processes. The uneven, iterative, sometimes highly irrational course of strategy formation is inexplicable without recognizing the contribution of politics (Pettigrew and Whipp 1991).

The second major attraction of the field of politics and strategy making arises from its abundant linkages with other aspects of organizations and management. Those who have tried to capture the range of possibilities have been daunted by the potential connections. Thorough reviews (Rajagopalan *et al.* 1993)

have been forced to simplify the linkages down to four. None the less, the breadth of relationships involved under each main link is wide. Organizational factors extend from past strategies to top-management characteristics; environmental issues encompass the vast potential sources of uncertainty; process outcomes include such features as decision quality and learning effects; and lastly, economic outcomes cover a host of possible indicators and ratios.

While the scope of the connections between political decision making within strategy formation is huge, a word of caution is required. There still remains an equally daunting task to synthesize these patterns. An example drawn from one area of linkage with strategic change will illustrate the point. At the level of process theory one may distinguish between perspectives based on strategic choice, structural contingency, natural selection and collective action. It is apparent that political analysis has entered these domains very unevenly. Consequently, only the collective action view of change uses politics to understand change as a conflictual process of mutual adjustment and coercion among interest groups with pluralistic power bases. Similar weaknesses exist within the proponents of process theories of strategic change. Otherwise sophisticated appreciations of the process which include a political perspective employ rather dated versions; they rely heavily on resource-based notions of power rather than the cognitive and unobtrusive models discussed earlier.

It is possible also to raise a third main point of evaluation which extends the relevance of the covert nature of strategic politics. Experts on organizational politics maintain that, in practice, it is easier to talk about money or sex than openly to discuss power. As we noted at the outset this has spurred some academics to uncover the hidden character of politics and its unobtrusive qualities. In spite of this effort two problems loom large. First, the subtleties of the concepts of unobtrusiveness have not been widely accepted in strategy studies. It may be that the emphasis on power used to exclude issues or prevent people from even thinking of opposing given courses of action is regarded with suspicion, not least because of its implicit denial of human agency or its over emphasis of personal or collective quiescence. There is a need for a new generation of research which investigates the ideological structures of contemporary or post-industrial societies and their connection with the mobilization of bias by dominant groups within and outside the organization.

Perhaps the strongest criticism of the academic literature on politics and strategy making is its limited impact on practitioners. As the research has grown conceptually advanced, few authors have addressed the practical questions of how to apply such frameworks. Pfeffer (1992) is one of the exceptions in that he addresses the issue head-on in the form of a question: what does it mean to manage with power? His answer is constructed around the action points of: diagnosing relevant interest groups; appreciating the views of individuals and sub-units on issues which concern one as a manager; recognizing sources of power and seeking to obtain them; and developing an understanding of the means by which power is generated within an organization. What these prescriptions do not cover though are the specific implications for the strategy-making process. Any evaluation of the politics of strategy making will dwell upon the advantages of its linkages with all aspects of the strategy field; it will also be forced to recognize the areas which it has left untouched. Judgements of this kind point to a challenging future for current experts and future users of their work.

5 Conclusion

Overall, the politics of strategy making deserves its position as one of a central subject within management. This status is appropriate to a subject which has matured over the second half of the twentieth century. While the body of writing has evolved through resource-based or contingent theories of power to more recent interpretive approaches, leading exponents have at the same time pushed forward the reputation of management research itself. The political dimension of strategy making contains a robust set of theoretical props which are sensitive to both the internal and external influences on the process, the way

power is used and the requirement to follow its covert and indirect features of operation. The health of the subject can be gauged from the way its limitations are to do with the opportunities for extending the existing frameworks and their relevance even further, rather than being associated with major internal contradictions.

The future of the area will almost certainly involve the maintenance of the tradition of engagement with diverse areas of the social sciences. High on the agenda must be some kind of rapprochement with the burgeoning literature on postmodernism and organizations. The critical disposition of both sets of writers and the joint awareness of power as a salient feature of corporate and societal forms promise an outstanding new phase of research. The empirical and practical subjects to be investigated are certainly not in short supply; they extend from the impact of the grand-scale fragmentation of established economic and commercial structures on strategy formulation, to the micro-level outcomes of the information revolution on managerial power. In the case of strategy, therefore, there will be little reason to continue seeing power as the organization's last dirty secret.

RICHARD WHIPP
CARDIFF BUSINESS SCHOOL

Further reading

(References cited in the text marked *)

* Ansoff, H. (1965) *Corporate Strategy*, New York: McGraw-Hill. (One of the earliest and influential conceptions of strategy as an analytical and intentional process. Provided the basis for subsequent prescriptive literature.)

* Chandler, A. (1962) *Strategy and Structure: Chapters in the History of American Industrial Enterprise*, Cambridge, MA: MIT Press. (Probably the classic text on strategy as a rational planning process.)

* Cyert, R. and March, J. (1963) *A Behavioural Theory of the Firm*, Englewood Cliffs, NJ: Prentice Hall. (Foundation account of human action within organizations which first identified conflict as an essential component of behaviour.)

* Hardy, C. (1985) 'The nature of unobtrusive power', *Journal of Management Studies* 22 (4): 384–99. (Closely-argued review of the covert

operation of political processes with particular emphasis on the pre-emptive use of power.)

* Hickson, D., Hinings, C., Lee, C., Schneck, R. and Pennings, J. (1971) 'A strategic contingencies' theory of intraorganizational power', *Administrative Science Quarterly* 16: 216–29. (One of the original and clearest expositions of the range of internal sources of power and the circumstances in which they are relevant.)

* Huff, A. (1982) 'Industry influences on strategy-formulation', *Strategic Management Journal* 3: 119–30. (Compelling analysis of the cognitive character of industries and the implications of the collective assumptions and perceptions of managers on their strategic choices.)

* Kanter, R. (1979) 'Power failure in management circuits', *Harvard Business Review* (July–August): 65–75. (Intriguing use of contingency approach to power in organizations to demonstrate how senior executives and others can lose political influence.)

* March, J. and Olsen, J. (1976) *Ambiguity and Choice in Organisations*, Bergen: Universitetsförlaget. (Seminal argument developed here which questions the exclusively rational basis of decision making and, in turn, constructs an appreciation of the way preferences arise from action with often anarchic results.)

* March, J. and Simon, H. (1958) *Organisations*, New York: Wiley. (Path-breaking text which helped the reputation of the Carnegie School to grow by creating the core concepts of bounded rationality and satisficing.)

* Mintzberg, H. (1983) *Power In and Around Organizations*, Englewood Cliffs, NJ: Prentice Hall. (Engaging exploration of both the sources of power around organizations and, most importantly, their interrelations.)

* Pettigrew, A. (1977) 'Strategy formulation as a political process', *International Studies of Management and Organisation* 7 (2): 78–87. (Leading example of the conception of politics as the management of meaning. Here it is applied directly to strategy formulation.)

* Pettigrew, A. and Whipp, R. (1991) *Managing Change for Competitive Success*, Oxford: Blackwell. (Covers research on the impact of political, analytical and educational forces within the firm on strategic change and the outcomes for competitive performance across manufacturing and service sectors.)

* Pfeffer, J. (1992) *Managing with Power*, Boston, MA: Harvard Business School Press. (Mature reflections on the contingency/resource-based view of power with a set of prescriptive observations for managers.)

* Rajagopalan, N., Rasheed, A. and Datta, D. (1993) 'Strategic decision processes: an integrative framework and future directions', in P. Lorange, R. Chakravarthy, J. Roos and A. Van de Ven (eds) *Implementing Strategic Processes*, Oxford: Blackwell. (Thought-provoking review of extensive range of relevant studies with a much-needed framework which summarizes the key research objects to date and identifies consequent gaps.)

* Rasanen, K. and Whipp, R. (1992) 'National business recipes: a sector perspective', in R. Whitley (ed.) *European Business Systems*, London: Sage Publications. (Examination of the way industries operate through joint economic and social relationships, and the political outcomes for individual firms.)

* Salancik, G. and Pfeffer, J. (1977) 'Who gets power and how they hold on to it', *Organisational Dynamics* 5: 3–21. (Sharp explanation of the way power is not just acquired through resource control but, more importantly, how it is used and maximized.)

* Schendel, D. and Hofer, C. (1979) *Strategic Management: A New View of Business Policy and Planning*, Boston, MA: Little, Brown & Co. (Clear example of the way Chandler's thinking was applied and augmented as the instruments of strategic analysis and business policy multiplied in the 1970s.)

* Schwenk, C. (1989) 'Linking cognitive, organizational and political factors in explaining strategic change', *Journal of Management Studies* 26 (2): 177–88. (An overview of strategic decision research using the classification of cognitive, organizational and political perspectives. The account culminates in an integrative model of strategic change based on the three-fold framework.)

See also: DECISION MAKING; INDUSTRIAL STRATEGY; ORGANIZATION BEHAVIOUR; ORGANIZATION CULTURE; POWER; STRATEGY, CONCEPT OF

Strategy and manufacturing: see MANUFACTURING STRATEGY

Strategy in North America

Overview

Business strategy is a comparatively new business discipline, and emerged in the 1960s in response to largely historical examinations of the success of North American businesses around the world. Concluding that this success was largely due to the superior organizational forms of these businesses, the pioneers of business strategy constructed models of strategy which focused on organizational fit and convergence with strategic goals, and on goal formulation as being largely a matter of responding to challenges from the external environment. This model was itself increasingly challenged from the 1980s onwards in response to perceived strategic failures by US businesses, first by Porter and the economics approach to strategy, and then by radical thinkers calling for responsibility for strategy to be devolved downward within the organization and for an end to the separation between strategy formulation and strategy implementation. At present, business strategy is in a state of some disarray, preoccupied by arguments between opposing camps, while business strategy as practised by firms has a tendency to be ad hoc, reactive and conservative, focusing on often negative organizational responses. A coherent strategic model which is both comprehensive in nature and proactive in outlook is now required.

1 Introduction

Business strategy is generally defined as the setting of long-term business aims and goals and determining the best method of reaching those goals (more commonly referred to as strategy formulation and strategy implementation, respectively). Somewhat surprisingly, given their pioneering efforts in other business-related disciplines, North American businesses have come late to the concepts of strategic thinking. The pioneering efforts of Chandler and Ansoff in the 1960s resulted in a mainstream approach to strategy that concentrates on its relationship to structure and organization. In the 1970s, Miles and Snow (1978) would articulate this as the concept of 'fit' between an organization's shape and structure on the one hand, and its strategic needs on the other.

Other approaches to strategy exist, notably Michael Porter's (1980) economics-based models and the 'emergent strategy' route pioneered by Mintzberg (1994) and taken still further in recent years by Hamel and Prahalad (1994) (see HAMEL, G. AND PRAHALAD, C.K.; MINTZBERG, H.; PORTER, M.E.). While mainstream strategy generally sees strategy formulation and implementation as tasks carried out at the top of the organization and then imposed downwards through command and control structures, the Mintzberg–Hamel and Prahalad approach sees it as very much a bottom-up process. Mintzberg has argued that most managers are reactive in their approaches to strategy, using ad hoc methods to make and implement strategic decisions. Hamel and Prahalad have called for this 'ad hocracy' to be deliberately adopted by companies, referring to a process of 'democratic strategy' whereby everyone in the firm generates strategic ideas and top management's primary role is to manage the various strategic ideas as they emerge from below.

The debate between these approaches is a vigorous one, and the stakes are high. Although there is dispute over how far academic approaches to strategy are reflected in actual business practices, there is no arguing the strategic challenges facing North American businesses. Globalization and free trade are having a profound impact on countries whose balance of payments deficits increase yearly (see GLOBALIZATION) . North American companies are still among the largest and most successful in the world, but they face challenges not only in their international markets but also increasingly at home. Technology strategy is also an issue of critical importance as companies face the need to adapt both product and process technologies in order to become more efficient and improve their offerings. To some extent, the current debates in business strategy risk making the discipline irrelevant, unless the discipline itself can change with the times. While this entry discusses some of the strategic challenges facing North American businesses, the primary focus is on the origins of strategic thinking and the current divergences between orthodox and heterodox thought and practice.

2 The origins of strategy in North America

Business strategy, or business policy as it was sometimes formerly known, has only recently begun to be considered as a business issue in its own right. Before about 1960, strategic thinking in North American businesses was usually considered to be part of the generic task of top management. Such intellectual and conceptual frameworks as existed were largely drawn from military strategy, which exercised considerable influence on management thinking right into the 1950s. The same was largely true in Japan and Europe, where in both cases a large corpus of literature on military strategy has been built up over centuries. This had not happened in the USA or Canada, and North American top managers accordingly looked to Europe for their models. At General Motors, for example, a firm later identified by Chandler (1962) as being a stra-

tegic success story in the decades before the Second World War, strategy originated at the top and was one of the primary activities of GM's charismatic leader, Alfred P. Sloan (see SLOAN, A.P.). Sloan's vice-president and *eminence grise*, James Mooney, drew his strategic thinking from European history, primarily from the examples of the military and the monasteries.

Strategy was seen as part of the task of administration or management. Indeed, Lindblom (1959) famously argued that strategy was *not* a discipline or a science but was a largely intuitive and even reactive approach to business problems. Lindblom called this form of business thinking 'the science of muddling through' (this view was to return to prominence in the 1980s with the work of Mintzberg). Support for this concept came from writers on organization behaviour and psychology, who took note of Simon's (1947) writings on bounded rationality and took the view that, in view of the fact that strategy making was nearly always carried out in conditions of incomplete knowledge, a coherent science of strategy was therefore impossible. Peter Drucker (1954), representing the non-scientific approach to management, concurred; his view was that strategy was ingrained in the managerial task. Although in his later writings Drucker did take account of strategy as a separate discipline, he never deviated from the view of its central position among top management's basic functions.

This view predominated during what was arguably the 'golden age' of North American business. Rapid growth and expansion into global markets brought unprecedented prosperity, for firms, employees and the nation as a whole. The period of post-war reconstruction saw American business thinking exported to its old rivals, Europe and Japan. The American system seemed utterly dominant. The first academic explorations of the concept of strategy in the early 1960s, then, need to be seen against this background. Strategy as a discipline grew out of an investigation, not of what had gone wrong, but of what had gone right.

3 Stages in strategic thinking

The first North American work that identifies business strategy as an issue in its own right is generally agreed to be Alfred Chandler's *Strategy and Structure* (1962). Chandler's perspective was and remains historical; he sought to determine why US firms in particular had been so successful in the period of unprecedented growth since 1900. Studying successful firms such as General Motors and DuPont, Chandler came to the conclusion that one generic factor that appeared to lead to success was the adoption by successful firms of the multi-divisional (M-form) structure. In M-form firms, individual divisions took responsibility for operations, while head office focused on strategy and coordinated the activities of the divisions towards reaching the overall corporate goals. It was this M-form structure, with its explicit origins in military command structures, which had been adopted almost universally by large American firms.

In Chandler's view, strategy and structure are inexplicably linked. A firm's ability to succeed in its strategic aims depends on the structure it adopts to meet those aims. The model is very much one of challenge and response, with firms determining what the future holds for them, then mustering resources and putting plans into action. Chandler made explicit the link between strategy formulation and strategy implementation, going so far in some cases as to see them as separate tasks. His early work in this field was quickly followed up by Andrews (1965) and more famously by Ansoff (1965).

Although Chandler determined the bounds of the inquiry, it was Ansoff who made the greatest contribution to conceptualizing strategy and making it into a concept that managers could easily understand. Ansoff continued, however, very much in the structure approach and continued to see strategy as an organizational response to external challenges. Ansoff's strategic success paradigm (explored in detail in Ansoff 1984) is built on responses to environmental turbulence and the ability of top management to respond to change. Ansoff is also notable for his straightforward dealing with the concept of strategic uncertainty and for the various tools he developed to help managers cope with uncertainty and define and implement strategy (see ANSOFF, H.I.).

This approach became the foundation to the mainstream approach to strategy, an approach that has persisted to the present day. Numerous refinements have taken place and there have been notable contributions from eminent scholars. Miles and Snow (1978) articulated the concept of organizational 'fit' and the need to ensure that the organization and its goals were correctly aligned (see MILES, R.E. AND SNOW, C.C.). From an organization behaviour perspective, Argyris (1985) made a notable contribution to the study of strategy implementation, discussing barriers to change within organizations (see ARGYRIS, C.). W. Edwards Deming can be regarded on one level as the father of technology strategy, and Alvin Toffler's work on futures had important impacts on organizations' forecasting methods. In the 1990s, the business process re-engineering movement emerged as a powerful force in North American business, reaffirming many of the precepts of the structure approach to strategy (see DEMING, W.E.; TOFFLER, A.).

Alternative approaches to strategy were slow to develop, but by the 1980s several critiques of traditional strategy were under way. The origins of these critiques lie at least partially in the gathering economic crisis in both the USA and Canada. The old certainties of the golden age were gone, and North American firms were under siege in both their domestic and foreign markets as rising costs coupled with cheaper imports left them vulnerable to foreign competition. This was the background against which Michael Porter (1980) produced his economics approach to strategy (see PORTER, M.E.). In Porter's view, the key determinant of a firm's strategic approach must be its competitive position. It follows, therefore, that how a firm is organized is less important than how it competes. Simple concepts like the five-forces model and the value chain made clear the relationship between competition and strategy, and encouraged firms to take a more market-based approach, based on their competitive advantages more generally and not just on their organization and structure.

More radical and challenging approaches were already beginning to emerge. In particular, the 'emergent strategy' approach challenged the whole notion that strategy should be formulated at the top and implemented downwards. Also challenged was the notion that strategy was a coherent discipline in its own right. Leading the challenge to the mainstream view was the Canadian academic Henry Mintzberg, whose early studies of how managers actually did strategy (as opposed to how academics said they should) convinced him that most strategy making was ad hoc and improvised rather than planned and rigidly controlled. That is, managers were far more flexible in their approaches than doctrine said they should be. Mintzberg argued that this approach was correct. He has famously defined strategy as a craft or an art rather than a science, and has called for an end to the separation of strategy formulation and strategy implementation, an inflexible system which he believes can lead to disaster. His most radical work on this issue is Mintzberg (1994) (see MINTZBERG, H.).

Mintzberg's influence can be seen over a number of later writers on strategy and organizations. His views on a softer, less bureaucratic approach to strategy emerged at about the same time as Tom Peters (1992) began calling for a less hierarchical, more inspirational approach. Echoes of both can be seen in the approaches of Kanter (1989) and Senge (1990), for example, both of whom from varying perspectives call for organizations to become more fluid, flexible and integrated and for strategy to be developed from within the organization on a wider basis rather than simply imposed from the top (see KANTER, R.M.; PETERS, T.; SENGE, P.).

The most radical approach to date is probably that of Hamel and Prahalad (1994). In their work, 'emergent strategy' becomes 'democratic strategy'; strategy becomes the property of every member of the firm. Rejecting the confines of standard business disciplines, they see strategy as a revolutionary process extending throughout the organization. Top management no longer formulates strategy, but rather, manages the various strategic options that rise from the ferment of strategic activity going on at lower levels in the firm. This view has been widely acclaimed, and Hamel and Prahalad have the distinction of writing on this subject the best-selling management book to date. Ironically, Hamel and Prahalad's work shows strong influences of both Japanese and European strategic thinking (see HAMEL, G. AND PRAHALAD, C.K.).

4 Key issues in business strategy

Most writing on business strategy concentrates on one or more of the various stages of strategy development and implementation, including assessing the company's own resources and capabilities, environmental scanning, setting strategic goals, strategic planning, strategy implementation, and evaluation of the success of any strategy (see STRATEGY, CONCEPT OF). These can be regarded as the basic building blocks of strategy. Both within and beyond these, however, there exist a number of issues of strategic concern which preoccupy both managers making strategy and academics writing about it.

Who makes strategy?

Despite nearly two decades of challenge from the 'emergent strategy' school, there is little evidence that US and Canadian firms are changing the way they make strategy, in particular that any more than a handful of firms are successfully devolving strategy down from the top level. Concepts of the 'virtual organization', now widely discussed, may have the unintentional effect of devolving strategy downwards, but it remains to be seen how widely this will happen. What is happening more frequently, however, is that as strategic alliances and other forms of collaborative behaviour gain in popularity (see below), more individuals and organizations outside the firm are having input into both strategy formulation and strategy implementation. This itself is having an unexpected impact on how firms think about strategy, and in general strategic thinking is becoming more tolerant of collaborative options. In this respect, Canadian strategic thinking is a little ahead of that in the USA, though still far behind that of Europe or Japan.

Strategy and structure/form

The interventions of Porter and others using the economics approach have ameliorated the strictly disciplinarian aspects of the structure approach, but North American firms continue to see strategy primarily in terms of challenge and response, and the most common responses are structural in nature. The most talked-about and commonly used strategic options over the past two decades have been largely structural in nature: reorganization, downsizing, delayering, divestment, business process re-engineering, to name just a few. More progressive and proactive strategic options such as the virtual corporation, mentioned above, have been developed but their impact has so far been limited. Looking at North American business activity over the past two decades, it is hard to avoid the conclusion that most strategic thinking is ad hoc and reactive. Unfortunately, this does not seem to have resulted in widespread diffusion of the hoped-for benefits of this approach, such as flexibility, proactivity or strategic democracy.

Strategy and technology

Technology strategy has within the past decade become recognized as a branch of strategy in its own right. Technology strategy aims to take account of the impacts of new technology both on a firm's production processes (will new technology make the firm more efficient?) and on its product/service offerings (will new technology make the firm more effective?). Key branches of the discipline include technology forecasting, technology acquisition and technology integration. Technology forecasting seeks to predict future technological developments and determine what the firm's technology needs will be in the future. Technology acquisition is primarily an investment strategy, which commits the firm's resources to acquiring new technology in line with wider strategic needs. Technology implementation aims to ensure that new technologies are successfully integrated into the firm's products/operations. Technology strategy can thus be seen to be largely derived from the challenge and response model, but it does tend to be focused on specifics. Current evidence shows that firms are planning and implementing formal technology strategies on a wide scale.

Globalization

Large North American firms probably have more experience of global operations than either their Japanese or European counter-

parts, but for emerging newer firms the process can still be painful. The strategic choices to be made when going global concern not only the choice of markets to enter but also the method of entry (with options including agency relationships, joint ventures and so on) and also brand/product decisions such as standardization or localization. In the past, globalization has tended to be a proactive step; secure in their domestic markets, US and Canadian firms could move overseas when they were fully prepared and ready. In the past few decades, however, foreign competition has cut into many domestic markets, and many firms have woken up to the fact that they are players in a global game, even though they have not left home. As a result, strategic choices associated with globalization are now having to be made even by firms that do not operate overseas.

Core competencies and intangible resources

Increasingly, a firm's core competencies have begun to be regarded as synonymous with, or at least deriving from, its stock of intangible capital. The latter, referred to variously as 'organizational capital', 'human capital' or 'knowledge capital', can be generically defined as the collected knowledge, information and skills embedded in a firm's mechanical and human assets. The management, acquisition and direction of these intangible resources are becoming a major strategic concern for many companies. As a result, there is an increasing convergence between disciplines such as technology management, information management and human resource management, and all these are having an effect on strategy. Firms that recognize this allow for direct input into the strategic process by, for example, the firm's human resources function.

Strategic relationships

As noted above, North American businesses are becoming more receptive to the idea of alliances, both within North America and with firms in other parts of the world. Traditionally, North American legal and philosophical thinking on business has drawn little distinction between collaboration and corruption. However, the increasing uncertainty associated with rapid technological change and globalization is making alliances an attractive means of augmenting core competencies and spreading risk. The increasing popularity of joint ventures is a good example of this (though it should be noted that most joint ventures with a US partner do in fact fail, in large part because of inexperience at managing this kind of organization).

The formulation/implementation dichotomy

As discussed in the previous section, there is a large body of work on this issue. The debate over whether formulation and implementation are properly separated or united has not so far been resolved. However, so long as the challenge and response model continues to dominate, it seems unlikely that the separation will disappear. The progression from defining a challenge to defining a solution to implementing a solution has sound scientific roots, and is ingrained in much of current strategic thinking. More proactive strategy making holds out the prospect for less separation; but as we have also noted, there are few signs of this becoming the norm.

Strategic turnaround

One final issue deserving of mention is strategic turnaround. Turnaround began to become a major issue in the late 1970s and early 1980s with the decline of many sectors of North American industry, and again there is a large body of literature on this subject. Current thinking on strategic turnaround owes much to Porter and the economics approach to strategy, although the structure approach has also had a strong impact. The debate over whether firms seeking to arrest an otherwise terminal decline should focus their strategic thinking on their market position or on their organization and structure has not been entirely resolved, although Peters and Kanter, for example, have attempted to do so; the bias in both cases has been towards making companies more responsive to their markets, but it is accepted that structural changes may be required to enable this.

5 The future of strategy

One widely recognized problem with strategic thinking in North America is that though there is no shortage of theories, too few of these have been studied and validated with reference to actual business experience. The military strategy models in use up to the 1950s at least had the advantage of offering examples for study, and if business and warfare are not entirely analogous, there are enough similarities to at least enable study of which strategic options work and under what conditions. Business strategy, however, has no accumulated bank of experience and therefore has not been properly tested.

This weakness lays business strategy open to the attacks of Mintzberg and others who have gone so far as to assert that business strategy is dead as a discipline. Yet, as studies of technology strategy have shown, there is value in attempting to capture generic strategic principles, and there is probably even value in attempting to conceptualize these in purely business terms, rather than in terms of some alien activity.

To remain credible, however, business strategy as a discipline needs to do a little strategic thinking of its own. It seems clear that decentralized models of management such as the virtual corporation will become increasingly popular (as much for their ability to reduce costs as for any inherent virtues they may possess), and that current trends such as globalization and technology change will continue. In light of these, strategy needs to find some way of harmonizing the competing needs of top management for control over strategy and demands of other ranks within the organization to have a say in both the formulation and implementation of strategy. The real strategic gap in North America at the moment is between the competing schools of thought. An acceptable, coherent and understandable model of strategy that addresses the future needs of North American companies must go to the top of the academic agenda.

MORGEN WITZEL
LONDON BUSINESS SCHOOL

Further reading

* Andrews (1965) *Business Policy: Texts and Cases*, Homewood, IL: Irwin. (An early casebook in business strategy, important but overshadowed since by Ansoff [1965].)

* Ansoff, H.I. (1965) *Corporate Strategy*, New York: McGraw-Hill. (One of the first conceptual approaches to business strategy. Ansoff's work, since refined, remains influential.)

* Ansoff, H.I. (1984) *Implementing Strategic Management*, Englewood Cliffs, NJ: Prentice Hall. (Advances from Ansoff's original concepts of strategy, looking at how strategic decisions can be implemented.)

* Argyris, C. (1985) *Strategy, Change, and Defensive Routines*, New York: Ballinger. (Analysis of barriers to change from an organization behaviour perspective.)

  Beerel, A. (1998) *Lead Through Strategic Planning*, London: ITBP. (A global perspective on leadership and strategy.)

* Chandler, A.D. (1962) *Strategy and Structure*, Cambridge, MA: MIT Press. (The first book on strategy, which effectively launched the strategy movement of the 1960s.)

* Drucker, P.F. (1954) *The Practice of Management*, London: Heinemann. (Drucker's first work concentrating on management, laying the ground for his later and more famous works.)

  Gulick, L.H. (1948) *Administrative Reflections from World War II*, University, AL: University of Alabama Press. (Lessons for management and administration drawn from a study of the organization of the USA's war effort.)

* Hamel, G. and Prahalad, G.K. (1994) *Competing for the Future*, Boston, MA: Harvard Business School Press. (The major work to date on core competences.)

* Kanter, R.M. (1989) *When Giants Learn to Dance: Mastering the Challenge of Stategy, Management and Careers in the 1990s*, New York: Simon & Schuster. (Kanter's views on strategy tend more towards the 'emergent strategy' model.)

* Lindblom, C.E. (1959) 'The science of muddling through', *Public Administration Review* 19 (1): 79–88. (Another approach to strategy from the perspective of administration, rejecting rational or formal approaches and calling for an intuitive approach.)

* Miles, R.E. and Snow, C.C. (1978) *Organizational Strategy, Structure and Process*, New York: McGraw-Hill. (Develops a typology of organizational strategies.)

* Mintzberg, H. (1994) *The Rise and Fall of Strategic Planning*, New York: The Free Press. (Mintzberg's most polemical work, in which he controversially demolishes the concept of strategic planning.)

* Peters, T. (1992) *Liberation Management: Necessary Disorganization for the Nanosecond Nineties*, New York: Knopf. (One of the more radical expositions of Peters' views.)

* Porter, M. (1980) *Competitive Strategy: Techniques for Analyzing Industries and Competitors*, New York: Free Press. (An economics-based approach to strategy.)

* Senge, P.M. (1990) *The Fifth Disciple: The Art and Practice of the Learning Organization*, New York: Doubleday. (Includes a discussion of business strategy in the context of the learning organization.)

* Simon, H.A. (1947) *Administrative Behavior: A Study of Decision Making Processes in Administrative Organization*, New York: The Free Press. (Introduced the concept (and problem) of bounded rationality, of considerable importance for strategy makers then and now.)

See also: CHANDLER, A.; GLOBALIZATION; HAMEL, G. AND PRAHALAD, C.K.; INTERNATIONAL MONETARY FUND; KANTER, R.M.; MILES, R.E. AND SNOW, C.C.; MINTZBERG, H.; MULTINATIONAL CORPORATIONS; PORTER, M.E.; SENGE, P.; STRATEGY IN ASIA PACIFIC; STRATEGY IN THE EMERGING COUNTRIES; STRATEGY IN EUROPE; STRATEGY IN LATIN AMERICA; WORLD BANK

Strategy and rationality

Overview

In strategic management (strategy) the term 'rational model' is normally associated with the use of formal strategic plans. However, the term 'rationality' itself has many meanings, for there are many distinctive forms of rationality. Each form corresponds closely in meaning with some well-documented concept within the field of strategy. The general theory of rationality involves meta-rational relations and criteria that lend a complex structure to the set of rationalities. This theory also illuminates the interface relationships between corresponding strategy concepts. In addition, there are many new types of strategic entity and rational agent made possible by technological change.

1 Introduction

Rationality and strategy are both very active areas of research, so any account of their interrelationship must remain open to subsequent revision or extension. The general theory of rationality incorporates many diverse but distinctive forms of rationality, together with their meta-rational relationships. 'Rationality', thus conceived, is not a single idea, but an elaborate and interwoven fabric of principles and prescriptions for cognition and behaviour; but so too is strategy. Inevitably, from time to time, the two fields have been compared (for example, Hogarth and Makridakis 1981; Bryman 1984; Singer 1992, 1994). However, one important distinction between strategy and rationality pertains to the diverse nature of strategic entities (for example, organization, alliance, network, etc.) versus the nature of

rational agents (individuals, or other proper subjects of the general theory). Nevertheless, it has been argued (Levi 1984; Singer 1992; Cudd 1993) that this distinction has been rather overplayed.

2 The rational model

In mainstream strategy (for example, Mintzberg and Quinn 1991), any references to rationality are usually in the context of assessing the contributions from economic theory. Accordingly, rationality is often contrasted with the political and psychological orientations of organization theory. The rational model of strategic planning (see NEO-CLASSICAL ECONOMICS), associated with decision analysis (see DECISION MAKING), refers specifically to a comprehensive, formal and possibly iterative process of planning, with implementation, including: (1) the setting of explicit objectives; (2) the gathering of facts (for example, about the competitive environment, etc.); (3) the generation of a set of strategic options; and (4) a process of strategic choice, that is, selecting or choosing from among well-defined courses of action (see STRATEGIC CHOICE).

This model suffers from a variety of limitations, including the implicit assumption of a command and control hierarchy, the tenuous and difficult relationship between formulation and implementation (that is, plans gather dust) and the unspecified manner in which the various strategic options are to be described. On the latter point, the rational model is conspicuously silent about appropriate levels of detail, the reliability of predictions, as well as the choice of language employed to describe the various objects of choice (that is, strategic options).

To the extent that any particular forms of rationality are explicitly described in the strategy literature, these are usually the rational utility maximizing form or else the bounded form. In the latter, costs of information search and cognitive limitations are recognized.

3 Rationality set and strategy set

In some accounts, this so-called 'rational model' of strategy has been extended, so that it refers to a larger set of *economic* rationalities (Table 1). Each form of rationality listed in Table 1 is the foundation of a theoretical structure within economics (see BUSINESS ECONOMICS). Yet each form of rationality listed there also represents a rather simple 'strategy' prescription (see STRATEGY, CONCEPT OF). For example, Elster's strategic rationality – which simply refers to an entity taking account of the fact that the environment is made up of other actors and that it is part of their environment – is definitive to the theory of games and industrial organization (I/O) economics, yet it is also an elemental concept of strategic management. In contrast, the analytically derived theorems of the formal economic theories have had minimal impact, if any, on strategy.

Many other linkages between concepts of strategy and forms of rationality reflect a much larger rationality set, or *plural* rationality, of which the economic rationality set is merely a subset. Each element of plural rationality is explicitly defined and studied somewhere within the wider social and cognitive sciences, but not necessarily within economics. Table 2 lists a few of these forms of ratio-

nality, together with their corresponding strategy concepts.

4 Correspondences

Apart from the correspondences listed in the tables, several others are noteworthy. With regard to belief-orientated forms, *parametric* rationality, like myopic plans, refers to the treatment of the environment as a set of parameters (for example, cash flow forecasts) that are input to some calculated decision process. It is associated with the scientific and intensive forms of rationality in which explicit formal models are used to shape expectations. These, in turn, may be distinguished from the open and natural forms of belief rationality. In the former, the entity takes corrective measures to revise its beliefs in response to all of its past mistakes. In the latter, the entity's beliefs converge towards validity as experience leads to piecemeal revision. Linking belief-orientated and means-orientated forms, the concept of *minimal* rationality refers to an entity activating (accessing or using) some of its relevant beliefs, having the ability to detect some inconsistencies and to make some appropriate inferences. Strategy case studies, in turn, point to many failures to act rationally, in this sense.

The means-orientated forms include not only maximization, bounded and adaptive rationality (Table 2), but also the notions of pre-commitment and weakness of will, in which an entity takes costly actions, such as irreversible moves, promises and deals, with the in-

Table 1 Economic rationalities and strategy prescriptions

Branch of economic theory	Form(s) of rationality	General prescription for management practice Managers should...
Transaction cost	bounded, weak	take into account the costs of information search and processing (indecisions about strategy and structure).
I/O and game theoretic	strategic	consider the reactions of other entities to your moves and others' moves. Hence, take into account reputations, beliefs, signals, etc.
Evolutionary	systemic, adaptive	learn from past mistakes. Discover rules in the environment. Utilize experience to continually refine beliefs.
x–efficiency	selective, adaptive	seek motivational devices that improve capabilities and develop the full potential of the firm. Allow for organizational inertia, or status quo bias
Behavioural	cognitive, quasi	take into account sysematic biases, heuristic use, costs of search and processing for self (that is *meta*-congnition) and for others.

Table 2 Some strategy–rationality correspondences

Strategy concept	Rationality concept	Meanings and features
1 Perspectives or expectations as beliefs:		
Perspectives, dominant logic expectations	*Belief, cognitive (substantive, epistemic)*	The degree of objectivity, validity or veracity of the entity's beliefs and expectations. Integrity of the knowledge-base.
Competitor-analysis ploys	*Strategic*	The entity's beliefs and expectations take into account the anticipated responses and interactions of other entities.
Extrapolation historic data	*Extensive*	The entity's expectations are formed by extrapolating historical data.
2 Strategic-decision as means-rationalities:		
Means-ends planning logic	*Instrumental (zweickrationalist)*	The entity selects the best means to achieve current known goals, given current beliefs.
Bounded and *Quasi*-rat (organization)	*Bounded*	The entity allocates cognitive resources efficiently or optimally, attends selectively to information, satisfies with respect to goals and uses heuristics.
	Quasi	The entity makes choices that are consistent with empirically supported variants of SEU models, for example, prospect theory, transaction utility theory.
Adaptive-search planning method experiential-learning	*Adaptive*	The entity uses decision rules and heuristics iteratively over time, as further information becomes available or as experience accumulates.
3 Strategic behaviour as action-rationality:		
Logical incrementalism	*Action-rationality, practical-rationality*	Rational action to achieve a desired goal involves selective attention to content and process, within a responsive or reactive environment.
Signals, symbolic acts (position)	*Expressive, communicative acts*	In a social system, actions are primarily symbolic (carrying meaning for others to interpret and respond to) rather than instrumental. Therefore, a rational entity builds identity and reputation.
4 Historical-process as backward-looking-rationalities:		
Forward-in reverse planning logic	*Systemic*	Knowledge, goals, behavioural rules and capabilities accumulate and must be developed by the entity, over time.
Emergent vision implicit goals	*Posterior*	The entity's goals (values, preferences) are the products of its actions. Goals emerge and crystallize through processes of deliberation, reflection and dissonance.
Strategic persistence (completion of plans)	*Resolute*	An entity should persist with very long-standing missions or plans rather than abandon them in favour of a fleeting opportunity or preference. It is worthwhile to develop habits (or traditions) of task-completion.
5 Strategic-goals as ends-rationalities:		
Objectives, goals	*Value, substantive, (wertrationalist)*	For any entity, some goals (values, preferences) are better, or more rational, than others.
Stakeholder approach	*Extended*	A rational entity has other goals, oriented towards the wider society or the interests of other entities, in addition to self-interest.
Not-for-profit service ethos	*Commitment (altruism)*	A rational entity can make genuinely counterpreferential choices, sacrificing utility for the sake of other entities.
6 Ethical reasoning as rational-morality:		
Social cost-benefit analysis	*Utilitarianism*	An entity should choose the action that will bring about the greatest good (variously defined as wealth, happiness, harmony, freedom etc.) for the greatest number, as in social cost-benefit analysis.
Fairness-goals rights-policies	*Contractarianism*	An entity should act so as to promote fairness and justice.

tention of preventing its own future deviations from its current mission. One must also be mindful here of excess of will in rational choice, which corresponds with the idea of deliberate versus emergent strategy and warns us that some types of desired outcome (for example, self-respect, laughter or possibly a company's profit and its market share) can only be achieved indirectly, as by-products of intentions and actions that are consciously directed elsewhere (see below).

In reviewing belief-orientated and means-orientated forms one must not overlook postmodern thinking. The term *contextual* rationality has been used in several ways, including the notion of achieving consensus: a rational entity arrives at its intentions and its beliefs through processes of conversation and the clashing of meanings. To achieve rationality in this sense, power relations must be held in abeyance. Contextual also refers to cognitive and backward-looking dimensions of rationality: an entity's attention is directed to particular problem attributes, as determined by the social and historical context. This corresponds closely with the notion of a dominant logic in organizational strategy. In addition, contextual rationality has also been defined in ways that sweep in institutions. A rational entity is one that acts in ways orientated towards the creation and maintenance of those institutions that symbolize a good life with others.

The interwoven fabric of rationality and strategy also covers ends (such as goals, values, missions and purposes) together with their related processes. Expressive rationality (the idea that actions simply express values) also sees that the processes of goal formation (ambiguity reduction) are of ultimate value in their own right, that is, independently of any particular outcomes. This idea finds substance in the *ringi* method, a participative process of decision making used to achieve (real or apparent) consensus about strategy in some Japanese organizations (see JAPAN, MANAGEMENT IN). The process itself contributes to a crucial sense of self-management, identity or autonomy, as a by-product.

The contrast between expressive and utility maximization forms is important for business policy and strategy. It is often said that the primary purpose of a company is to create shareholder value. This goal is ultimately derived from considerations of utility maximization placed within a carefully specified market mechanism, and further justified with reference to a somewhat pessimistic assessment of human nature. Expressive rationality, in contrast, suggests that the primary purpose of any strategic entity is to provide an arena for autonomous human growth and development. This is a very different understanding of human nature and purpose. Meta-rational and meta-ethical theory is such that neither viewpoint can be entirely dismissed.

The fabric of rationality also wraps up much of business ethics. Plural forms of ethical reasoning, such as utilitarianism, contractarianism and deontology, correspond to the 'strategies' of social cost-benefit analysis, promotion of fairness and justice, respect for rights or fulfilment of duties (see BUSINESS ETHICS). Finally, the idea of rationality has also been considered by many as being something 'in the eye of the beholder' (that is, interactive) just as strategy may be defined as a pattern in a stream of decisions. Structural rationality, a term used in systems theory, refers to the determination of an entity's best structure and configuration for decision making.

In summary, the concepts of strategy and rationality are extensionally all but equivalent. It has been suggested (Singer 1992, 1994) that the two fields really are one and the same. Certainly, both sets of concepts have emerged together over time, from countless empirical and reflective studies of behaviour, decision making, cognition and action set in a wide range of economic and social (that is, strategic) contexts.

5 Meta-relations and isomorphism

In Table 2, the partitioning of the rationality set, hence also the strategy concepts, with reference to belief-, means- or ends-orientation, is but one example of a classificatory meta-rational criterion. More generally, this term meta-rationality refers to criteria and relationships, expressed in natural language or in mathematical language, that together lend a complex and evolving structure to the rationality set. The most basic of such meta-rational relations are merely sketched out in Figure 1. They are:

1 'r_i is a form of r_j' (where r represents an element of the rationality set). For example: sympathy is a form of extended ends rationality.
2 'r_k has significant common properties with r_l'. For example: expressive rationality (which concerns communicative action like signalling) has significant common properties with Elster's strategic belief rationality (which is concerned with game-theoretic interdependencies).

Similar relationships also pertain among corresponding elements of the strategy set, as follows:

1 Stakeholders as constraints is a form of organizational goal system.
2 Positioning is an ingredient of organizational strategy. This strategy concept has significant common properties with signalling behaviour.

In addition to these basic meta-rational relationships, the general theory also includes various relational meta-rational arguments, covering questions such as capture of Rational Utility Maximization (RUM) and belief-ends relations; *classificatory* meta-rational criteria, such as aggregate versus agent orientation, temporal orientation; with *evaluative* meta-rational criteria, such as the universalizability, globality and self-supportability of any given form of rationality.

These meta-rational relationships and criteria, in turn, appear to provide a corresponding way of characterizing, locating and evaluating the elemental concepts of strategic management. It has been argued on pragmatic grounds (Singer 1992) that the general relationship between 'strategy' and 'rationality' is one of *isomorphism* (that is, same structure) so that it is useful to regard all strategy interfaces (that is, relations between concepts of strategy) as directly reflecting the meta-rational relationships.

For example, the strategy concept of 'stakeholders viewed as constraints' corresponds to rational sympathy (Sen 1977); but meta-rationality locates the latter as agent-orientated, RUM-captured, forward-looking, local, non-universalizable and self-defeating.

Therefore any prescription, such as 'strategic managers should view stakeholders as constraints' (that is, on profit maximization) may be explicitly qualified, by the very same criteria.

More generally, to the extent that strategy and rationality are understood to be the same subject, any advances in the one, directly inform the other. Certainly, a great many examples of such interplays, or cross-fertilization of ideas, may be found throughout the extensive literature on strategic decision processes, business ethics, meta-modelling and competitive strategy.

6 Entities and agents

As mentioned at the outset, questions as to whose strategy is to be managed, or whose competitive advantage is to be sought, are being asked with increasing regularity and urgency. Similar unresolved questions pertain to the general theory of rationality, as well as related issues arising in decision theory and moral philosophy. Far from being resolved, the question of the nature of strategic entities and rational agents seems certain to grow in complexity and importance in coming decades, because technological changes (for example, distributed cognition, inter-organizational systems, etc.) are rapidly creating new types of strategic entity (for example, virtual corporation, networked industry, etc.) (see STRATEGY, CONCEPT OF). These entities are often quite different from the originally assumed units of analysis in strategy (that is, firms) and in rationality (that is, individuals) (see NETWORKS AND ORGANIZATIONS).

Other technological changes (for example, genetic engineering, artificial intelligence, microchip implants, etc.) have also come to represent challenges to long-standing notions of individuality and identity. Therefore, there are now many types of entity that could be regarded, pragmatically, as worthy subjects for the theories of strategy and rationality. Indeed, it is highly likely that future developments in these fields will be crafted with an ever-expanding entity set in mind.

ALAN E. SINGER
UNIVERSITY OF CANTERBURY,
CHRISTCHURCH

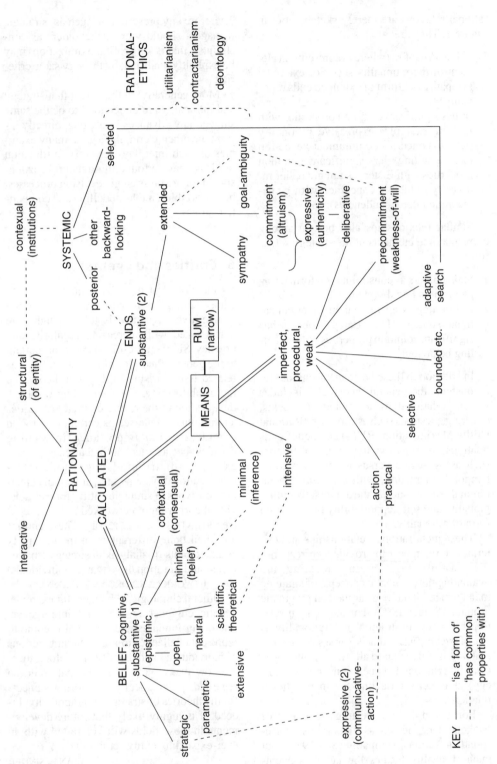

Figure 1 A partly constructed rationality set

Further reading

(References cited in the text marked *)

* Bryman, A. (1984) 'Organizational studies and the concept of rationality', *Journal of Management Studies* 19 (1): 29–44. (Organization theory: rejection of rationality concepts was premature because the former were changing.)

Calori, R. (1998) 'Philosophizing on strategic management models', *Organisation Studies* 19 (2): 281–306. (This article offers an epistemological critique of orthodox models of strategic management, based upon various important philosophiocal works on the subjects of knowledge and action.)

Cherniak, C. (1986) *Minimal Rationality*, Cambridge, MA: MIT Press. (Cognitive science: formal analysis of knowledge activation and the making of inferences.)

* Cudd, A.E. (1993) 'Game theory and the history of ideas about rationality', *Economics & Philosophy* 9: 101–33. (Article linking game theory and rationality.)

* Elster, J. (1989) *Solomnic Judgements: Studies in the Limitations of Rationality*, Cambridge: Cambridge University Press. (Philosophy: rationality and ethics in social problems. Builds on several other major works on rationality by the same author.)

Etzioni, A. (1988) *The Moral Dimension: Towards a New Economics*, New York: The Free Press. (Sociology: constructive critique of RUM and the hidden curriculum in economics education.)

Hamlin, A.P. (1986) *Ethics, Economics and the State*, Brighton: Wheatsheaf. (Political science: discussion of forms of rationality.)

Hargreaves-Heap, S. (1989) *Rationality in Economics*, Oxford: Blackwell. (Economics: compares expressive with instrumental forms.)

* Hogarth, R.M. and Makridakis, S. (1981) 'Forecasting and planning: an evaluation', *Management Science* 27 (2): 115–37. (Behavioural decision theory: remarks upon some parallels between the fields of human cognition and organizational strategy.)

* Levi, I. (1984) *Hard Choices: Decision-Making Under Unresolved Conflict*, Cambridge: Cambridge University Press. (Decision theory: places value conflict, rather than consistent preference, at the centre of a new formal theory of rationality.)

* Mintzberg, H. and Quinn, J. (eds) (1991) *The Strategy Process: Concepts, Context, Cases*, Englewood Cliffs, NJ: Prentice Hall. (A collection of definitive articles on strategic management, with a North American orientation.)

* Sen, A.K. (1977) 'Rational fools: a critique of the behavioural foundations of economic theory', *Philosophy and Public Affairs* 6: 317–44. (Article looking at concepts such as rational empathy, described in this entry.)

Sen, A.K. (1987) *On Ethics and Economics*, Oxford: Blackwell. (One of a series of books and articles by Sen that show why decisions must involve more than utility.)

Simon, H.A. (1987) 'Rationality in psychology and economics', in R.M. Hogarth and M.W. Reder (eds), *Rational Choice*, Chicago, IL: University of Chicago Press. (Simon continues his classic works on bounded rationality in economics, emphasizing procedural means-orientated forms versus substantive belief-orientated forms.)

* Singer, A.E. (1992) 'Strategy as rationality', *Human Systems Management* 11 (1): 7–22. (Strategy and the general theory of rationality are the same subject.)

* Singer, A.E. (1994) 'Strategy as moral philosophy', *Strategic Management Journal* 15 (3): 191–213. (Strategic management and business ethics are the same subject. Article includes the source references for many of the elements of the rationality set.)

White, S.K. (1988) *The Recent Work of Jürgen Habermas: Reason, Justice and Modernity*, Cambridge: Cambridge University Press. (Discusses communicative action, with the role of institutions.)

See also: DECISION MAKING; NEO-CLASSICAL ECONOMICS; ORGANIZATION BEHAVIOUR; SIMON, H.A.; STRATEGIC COMPETENCE; STRATEGY, CONCEPT OF

Strategy and technological development

Overview

Technological change is both an outcome and an important driver of competition. As technological developments lead to shorter life cycles and as the degree of national and international competition increases the ability to develop, introduce and commercialize new products and services quickly, as well as the capacity to rationalize, administrative and production processes become a prominent prerequisite of economic success. Thus, the anticipation of and participation in technological changes are crucial elements in the process of establishing and securing competitive advantages.

Technology can be defined as the entire set of capabilities, the theoretical knowledge, practical know-how and equipment, that is used to develop, produce and deliver products and services. Since tangible or intangible technological assets are incorporated in virtually everything which is done by firms, technological change can influence industry structures as well as corporate competitiveness through its impact upon almost any activity. Therefore, technological change is not merely a question which only concerns the management of research and development (R&D). Rather, the competition-induced compulsion to renew technology bases and add to them is an issue calling for overall strategic guidance and cross-functional collaboration.

Technological change can have a significant impact on the formation of strategies. In the following section, the important linkages between technological change and strategic decision making will be analysed.

1 Technological change as a multi-level phenomenon

The challenge of competition rests on the fact that existing products are superseded by new or improved products or services and that production techniques are rendered inefficient and obsolete over time; hence, the continuous introduction of new products, renewal of existing product lines, improvement of processes and refinement of support or service technologies are important prerequisites to safeguarding economic success (see TECHNOLOGY AND ORGANIZATIONS). This implies that long-term competitive performance depends on the ability to produce sequences of innovations which generate and maintain advantageous competitive differences, and that technological change has to be treated as an evolving flow of innovations rather than as a discrete event (Metcalfe and Gibbons 1989) (see INNOVATION AND CHANGE).

The level of investment in technologies is an important determinant of this ability and subsequent competitive performance. However, for companies, it is not possible to operate on the frontiers of all technologies relevant to their operations; resource constraints put a limit on the number of technological developments which can be pursued internally. Furthermore, depending on societal values, government policies, industry characteristics and the evolution of customers' preferences, the inherent value of technological options and the return on investments in certain technologies may be quite different.

In order to acquire, develop and deploy technological capabilities most effectively, companies have to address a broad array of issues. Simply allocating resources to technical functions is not enough. Particularly, a strategic approach to the management of technology involves:

1 identifying the sources of technological change in the external environment;
2 anticipating the general nature of this change and appraising the potentials, that is, threats and opportunities arising from new technologies;
3 assessing how the conditions for successful operations will or can be altered as a result;
4 identifying the firm's distinctive technological capabilities and core competencies;
5 determining their mission and objectives as well as the related posture towards technology;
6 conceptualizing their technology strategy within the context of an overall strategy;
7 formulating policies concerning the management of technology;
8 deciding on the levels and foci of investments in technologies;

9 choosing the appropriate means of technology acquisition (for example, internal research and development (R&D), contracted-out research, licensing or horizontal cooperation);
10 deciding on the timing and means of technology exploitation (for example, internal use, licensing or contracted-out marketing).

This agenda suggests that technological change is a multi-faceted and multi-dimensional phenomenon which can be treated at several levels. In order to capture the interaction between technological developments and business decisions, three conceptual levels can be distinguished (Adler 1989): the general level of the external environment and technological changes taking place within the environment, the level of individual firms operating in certain environments, and the level of innovation projects which are elements of the firms' entire innovation endeavour.

Figure 1 depicts a framework for analysing the technology dimension at these different

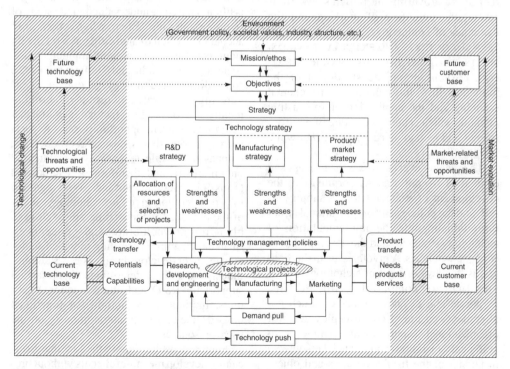

Figure 1 Linkages between technological change and strategy

levels, and offers some indications concerning the interactions between them, both between the external environment and the individual firm, and within the firm.

Since technology is a fundamental, yet multi-faceted determinant of successful operations, it is not possible to draft unambiguous and clear-cut conceptions for such complex problems as the integration of technology into strategic decision making. Frameworks such as the one presented in Figure 1 might bear little relation to the actual formulation processes within firms. Nevertheless, from a normative point of view the framework highlights the cross-functional nature of technology strategies and shows that the interrelatedness of the different levels should be taken into account in the process of shaping the firm's mission, objectives and strategy.

The first level concerns the dynamics of the external environment. In order to conceptualize strategic options *vis-à-vis* the environment, it is essential to gain an understanding of the interplay between technology dynamics, the development of societal values, the direction of government policies (Welfens 1998), the evolution of markets and the dynamics of competitive behaviour (see INTERNAL CONTEXTS AND EXTERNAL ENVIRONMENTS; ORGANIZATION BEHAVIOUR; STRATEGIC CHOICE). From the standpoint of the individual firm, this calls for environmental scanning and the application of forecasting methods which capture the nature of environmental and technological changes (Brownlie 1992).

The second level addresses the process and content of overall strategy formulation, the development of strategies for technology itself, and the policies and organizational structures which guide the implementation of technology strategies and the development of core competencies. A pivotal issue in this context is the development of technology strategies that are compatible with, or 'fit', corporate and business strategies. Such co-alignments ensure effective deployments of organizational resources (for example, technological capabilities and financial resources) in pursuit of the firm's missions and objectives (Cooper 2000).

Finally, the third level focuses on the management of the R&D function and specific innovation projects, that is, the linkages between strategy and R&D project selection and management (Danila 1989) (see INNOVATION MANAGEMENT).

It is fairly obvious that corporate decision making should be guided by an integrated view on each of these levels and that a strategic perspective can help to achieve such an integration. This is because it reaches out to the environment, and down to specific innovation projects.

2 Strategic management of technology

Strategic management is concerned with strategic choices which match the organization's capabilities (strengths and weaknesses) with environmental characteristics and developments (opportunities and threats) to achieve long-term objectives (see STRATEGIC CHOICE; STRATEGIC COMPETENCE). Although most business scholars would agree on this definition, the key strategic parameter, technology, is often ignored or undervalued in the study of firms' strategies. Even when taken into account it is often treated either as a relatively static construct or as a mere implementation issue, or both (Itami and Numagami 1992). Accordingly, technology is conceived as entering the strategy formation process mainly as a constraining factor or as a tool that determines current opportunity sets. Aspects such as market shares, costs and products are emphasized, while technology is addressed only implicitly and, therefore, downgraded in terms of its overall importance. With regard to the consideration given to technology, many of the proposed models come pretty close to blunt top-down hierarchical concepts of financial planning, according to which senior management develops business goals autonomously, and then determines the financial support for R&D and other functional sub-units. Implicit is the notion that functional units decide relatively autonomously on the use of resources.

Such approaches ignore the fact that firms cannot develop meaningful goals without previously analysing their technological profile and the existing paths for improving their technological capabilities. Technologies and associated strategic issues often evolve too rapidly in order to maintain the top-down planning mode without running the risk of losing their competitive edge. A coherent approach or successful innovations cannot be expected unless the activities of R&D and other functional activities are coupled. For these reasons, simple hierarchical approaches can easily lead to strategies, disregarding the implications of technological assets and the dynamics of technological change.

Four major conclusions can be drawn from these assertions. First, it may be helpful to conceptualize technology both as an independent variable that enters the process of strategy formulation and as an outcome of intended and unintended strategies. Such an approach allows one to address the dynamic interaction between technology and strategy (Goodman and Lawless 1994). Second, the starting point of the strategy formation process should be an analysis of threats and opportunities associated with strategic technology areas, and an analysis of the firm's capabilities and its developmental potentials (Macharzina and Fisch 1999). Hence, the definition of technology-related business goals should not be treated as a discrete activity (Adler 1989). Third, effective technology management necessitates regular top-down and bottom-up communication. At best, functional managers actively participate in the corporation's strategy development process. Fourth, especially with regard to the management of technology it is necessary to take into account interdependencies between functional and business units. Responsiveness to internal client and external customer needs requires interfunctional communication and collaboration.

3 Types of technological change and technology forecasting

Developing strategic concepts of technology involves monitoring new technologies that are beginning to manifest their competitive potentials and those that are just emerging. Not attempting to anticipate new technological potentials is a major cause for strategic failure. This is true not only for new, emerging industries but also for mature industries, which are likely to face technological threats from outside their sphere of activity. The anticipation of threats and opportunities which are rooted in changes in the technological environment necessitates forecasts of technological developments as well as predictions of social, political and economic changes (Sundbo 1988). This raises the question, whether it is indeed possible to foresee the path technological progress may follow (see MODELLING AND FORECASTING).

A salient feature of industrial innovation is that both markets and technologies are continually (evolutionarily) and sometimes radically (revolutionarily) changing (Freeman 1982). The differentiation between incremental, order-creating and drastic, order-breaking technological changes points to the existence of different types of technology dynamics which may be captured by the notion of technology hierarchies (Clark 1985), or the concept of technological paradigms (Nelson and Winter 1982). The latter embraces the idea that technologies can be structured into paradigms or regimes. Within a paradigm, technology develops along a fairly well-defined trajectory towards some technological frontier, while a paradigm shift involves completely new designs or problem solving routines. Obviously, revolutionary technological breakthroughs are far more difficult to forecast, analyse and plan than evolutionary technological changes. Since revolutionary technological changes transform products and processes at an increasing pace, the task of technology forecasting has become more difficult.

In order to anticipate technological changes, several forecasting techniques can be employed (Ayres 1969). Quantitative methods are based on the extrapolation of past trends or on econometric models. However, one severe shortcoming of these forecasting methods is the lack of consideration given to qualitative factors. In order to take these 'soft' factors into account the application of quantitative techniques can be supplemented by qualitative methods. These methods may also allow one to envisage technological discontinuities. Among the tools available for the identification of future technology generations and their likely development are patent analyses, expert enquiries (for example, Delphi method) and scenario techniques. Scenarios in particular are considered to be a useful tool for anticipating discontinuous technological developments. This is because scenario methods allow for holistically incorporating a set of coherent hypotheses concerning technological developments and the future activities of a multiplicity of relevant actors (for example, government, competitors, customers). They can be used to generate several possible futures in a simulation process, thereby allowing firms actively to take steps towards the creation of a desired future. Their weakness, as with other forecasting methods that are applied to explore the nature of long-term technological change, is that they are speculative and, hence, inevitably inaccurate. Moreover, predicting the effects of changes in terms of threats and opportunities is even more difficult than forecasting the primary changes themselves.

4 Life cycle models of technological change and strategic planning

Several models can be employed in order to discern at least some empirical regularities of technological change. Most prominent are the product life cycle, the technological life cycle and the technological S-curve. It should be noted, however, that these models are mechanistic in nature, leaving only limited space for pro-active behaviour of firms. To view the future as being predetermined imposes a reactive doctrine that overlooks the potential every firm has to influence developments. For this reason these concepts are more useful as planning tools which characterize typical options and challenges, than as forecasting tools or as methods pushing firms towards pro-active or collaborative behaviour.

The product life cycle describes the evolution of sales and profits in an industry. According to this concept the opportunity space and the courses for effective action are coupled to the stage in the evolution of product sales. Because of this linkage, the product life cycle may be considered a useful tool for the development of strategies at the corporate and business unit level. At the latter level, the product life cycle provides some indication of the formation of business strategies which in turn determine the relative importance and focus of functional activities. For example, a business strategy for a growing market may require major support from R&D, while required R&D support may be considerably less for units competing in mature markets.

At the corporate strategy level, product life cycles can be employed to determine a balanced portfolio of business units. A balanced portfolio consists of companies operating at different stages of a product life cycle. The notion of product life cycles is implicit in the portfolio concepts of companies like the Boston Consulting Group and General Electric, and forms a separate dimension in the A.D. Little matrix (Patel and Younger 1978).

The product life cycle concept's units of analysis are products or classes of products. For this reason, product life cycles are usually constructed at the level of the relevant industry, which can be defined as the aggregation of all businesses within a specified field of activity. Focusing on business units rather than on product-related sales and profits in the entire industry allows for highlighting the interdependence between product characteristics and the production process used.

This interdependence is the predominant issue in the technology life cycle concept which models the relationship between product and process innovations in a business unit (Abernathy and Utterback 1982). According to this model, product and process innovations proceed at different rates, and the time contingent focus of competition in an industry can have significant implications for the required mix of product and process innovations at the level of the business unit (Figure 2).

In the beginning of a technology life cycle, procedures are not fixed; the processes are 'fluid'. During the initial fluid stage the primary form of innovation is product innovation. Due to the emergence of a dominant design in the marketplace, the rate of product innovations is assumed to decline monotonously throughout the life cycle. As products become more standardized, efficiency becomes a critical success factor. The emphasis

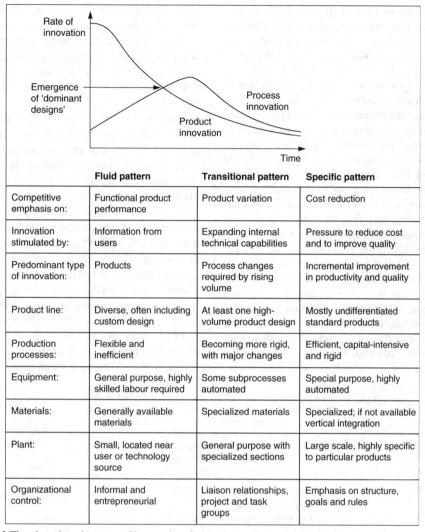

	Fluid pattern	Transitional pattern	Specific pattern
Competitive emphasis on:	Functional product performance	Product variation	Cost reduction
Innovation stimulated by:	Information from users	Expanding internal technical capabilities	Pressure to reduce cost and to improve quality
Predominant type of innovation:	Products	Process changes required by rising volume	Incremental improvement in productivity and quality
Product line:	Diverse, often including custom design	At least one high-volume product design	Mostly undifferentiated standard products
Production processes:	Flexible and inefficient	Becoming more rigid, with major changes	Efficient, capital-intensive and rigid
Equipment:	General purpose, highly skilled labour required	Some subprocesses automated	Special purpose, highly automated
Materials:	Generally available materials	Specialized materials	Specialized; if not available vertical integration
Plant:	Small, located near user or technology source	General purpose with specialized sections	Large scale, highly specific to particular products
Organizational control:	Informal and entrepreneurial	Liaison relationships, project and task groups	Emphasis on structure, goals and rules

Figure 2 The changing character of innovation during the technology life cycle
Source: Adapted from Abernathy and Utterbuck (1982)

shifts from product to process innovations. Process innovations are supported by learning effects related to increased volumes which in turn allow for automation. At the end of a technology life cycle, only incremental innovations will occur. The latter assumption, however, has been criticized on several grounds. It is argued in particular that processes of technological de-maturation are enhanced by increasing international competition. The result of such technological transformations and the globalization of markets is that even in low-growth, mature industries, competitiveness can often be maintained only by means of continuous technological improvements and the cost advantages arising from such innovations. Getting access to global sources of technology through international R&D networks (Granstrand *et al.* 1992) and the internalization of technologies by means of contractual research, inter-company collaboration or acquisitions are possible means by which to de-mature technologically mature business units (Moenaert *et al.* 1990).

Besides analysing the situation at the level of the industry or the business unit, it is possible to assess the future development and limits of technologies themselves. For this purpose, the concept of technological S-curves can be applied. The technological S-curve reflects a hypothesis concerning the relationship between invested R&D resources and performance capabilities of a specific technology. According to this concept, the trajectories of technological regimes follow the shape of an S-curve, which comprises three stages (Figure 3). During the emergence stage of a technology, initial efforts only result in a marginal performance improvement. Once a critical mass of knowledge has been accumulated a rapid performance growth takes place. Due to technological and economic causes technological developments slow down and reach their limits during the maturity stage.

From a managerial perspective the concept of technological S-curves leaves some important issues unresolved. For example, no conclusions can be drawn regarding: (1) which emergent technologies will in fact 'take off'; (2) how many resources will be needed to move along the curve; and (3) at which point in time the growth or the maturity stage will be reached (Adler 1989). However, these uncer-

tainties translate into technological risks. The level of technological risk corresponds to technological maturity insofar as new technologies imply higher risks. Technological S-curves can therefore be used for technological risk assessment. Furthermore, inventorying technological assets and classifying technologies according to their S-curve status allow for drawing some strategic conclusions. Technological S-curves can provide an indication when to switch to new, promising technology areas and how to allocate R&D resources. Furthermore, technological S-curves can be used for an overall diagnosis of the firm's technological situation and technological options. For this purpose technology portfolios can be applied which conceptually use the S-curve hypothesis. As an off-shoot of 'conventional' business portfolios, technology portfolios have been developed, for instance, by Booz, Allen and Hamilton (Harris *et al.* 1984) and McKinsey (Foster 1988). The application of these portfolios is most useful when a firm is confronted with many technological op-

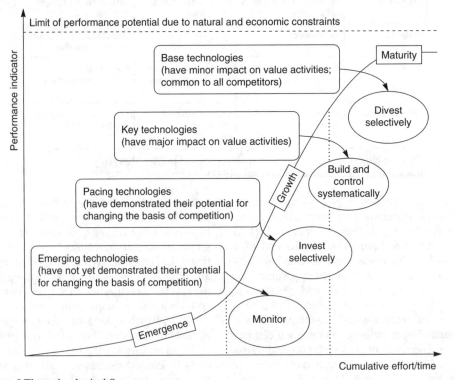

Figure 3 The technological S-curve

tions among which resources are to be allocated.

5 Technology and the formulation of missions, objectives, strategies and policies

Identifying technological trends, monitoring the sources and driving forces of technological change and appraising the potentials and limits of new technologies are essential elements in the process of strategy formation. Along with shared values, this information forms the basis for establishing the firm's mission or purpose. Technology has been recognized as a factor shaping the business mission of companies by constituting a principal dimension of the business domains in which firms plan to operate. Technological change, therefore, implies a dynamic character of the task of defining the business mission (Abell 1980).

Mission statements should be translated into objectives. To the greatest extent possible, the latter should be stated in quantitative terms in order to be most helpful in the process of planning, implementation and control. Unfortunately, the extent and range of firms' technology objectives is not well documented in the literature.

Besides missions and objectives, firms need to formulate a set of guiding principles which indicate how the stated mission will be fulfilled and in what way the goals planned ought to be achieved. These guiding principles are referred to as strategies. A technology strategy is a subset of the broader strategy making of the firm, defining the role technology should play in gaining competitive advantage. With respect to technology several strategy typologies are discussed in the literature.

Porter (1983) identifies leadership and followership as technology strategies, and proposes potentially critical points of technological leverage in the value chain which are suited to achieve cost leadership or differentiation (see LEADERSHIP). Other authors (for example, Maidique and Patch 1982) follow and extend the typology developed by Ansoff and Stewart (1967) who distinguish between first-to-market, follow-the-leader, application-engineering and me-too-low-cost strategies. Within the framework of these strategies firms have to decide on the mix of resources assigned to basic, exploratory and applied research, development and engineering (Brockhoff 1997), whether they should follow a path of incremental or radical innovation (Ettlie *et al.* 1984), whether they should concentrate on demand-pull or technology-push innovations, and whether they should balance, or focus on, service, product or process innovations.

The implementation of technology strategies requires their operationalization. The operationalized substance of technology strategies is referred to as technology policies. Technology policies may cover a broad range of issues which can be assigned to three areas. First, policies for processes such as the recruitment, development and evaluation of personnel, selection, termination and management of projects, and quality assurance. Second, policies which concern the management of a company's resources, which include intellectual properties, the firm's equipment and financial resources. The third area covers policies which regulate the management of internal and external linkages (Adler *et al.* 1992).

The latter policy field is, in particular, of critical importance. Successful innovations depend upon the contributions of experts in diverse fields such as R&D, marketing or production. A lack of internal cross-functional collaboration can delay or even thwart the successful development and application of new technologies. Technology choices and other functional decisions are usually interdependent, and potential synergies between product, process and support technologies have to be taken into account. Consequently, the technology strategy of a business unit should not be the sole property of any particular function. Rather, firms need policies which foster downstream coupling (Ansoff and Stewart 1967) and the joint elaboration and implementation of technology strategies. Similarly, potential synergies between technological developments of business units argue for joint efforts to devise and implement technology strategies at the corporate level.

Besides the management of intra-organizational interfaces, the management of external commercial relations has become a policy field of growing concern. The nature of technological change itself has been one of the driving forces for this development. While technological change and the increasing inter-dependence of different technologies have induced a sharp increase in R&D costs, the accelerating pace of technological changes is continuously reducing the length of product life cycles. Since many technological fields are advancing so rapidly and advancements in many technological areas require enormous financial commitments, even financially powerful corporations often neither have the time nor the resources to investigate all of the technologies which are potentially relevant in their business domain. Not only the task of technology generation, but also technology exploitation has become more difficult in many industries. Again, a new class of challenges arose from changes in the technological environment and the intensified competition induced by the internationalization of markets (see GLOBALIZATION). Basically, in many industries firms are now confronted with the requirement to commercialize rapidly new products, processes and services on a global scale. These developments have enhanced the evolution of collaborative arrangements that involve the development or commercialization of new technologies (Hagedoorn 1993). Hence the effective management of external linkages has become an important source of technological progress and commercial success. Collaborative arrangements for acquiring and exploiting technological capabilities include joint ventures, strategic alliances, research consortia, and joint developments with universities or government laboratories (Vedovello 1998).

In addition to collaborative arrangements, feedback information from the users of products and services can be applied as a source for refining technology bases. Intermediaries and customers may also provide product ideas, which can contribute to the innovation process (von Hippel 1988). The earlier the dialogue with customers is begun and the more intense it is, the more efficiently one can use its findings to refine existing technologies and select the most promising new technologies at an early stage.

6 Strategic issues in the management of technological projects

Technological projects contribute to and enlarge knowledge bases of firms. The desired evolution of these knowledge bases is mapped by technology objectives and strategies. Vice versa strategic maps are refined or even altered by experiences gained from technical projects. Specific project activities can lead to emergent strategies. According to the concept of absorptive capacity, the acquisition of technological knowledge is a self-enforcing and path-dependent process (Cohen and Levinthal 1990). Those firms in particular which pursue a leadership strategy in hi-tech industries often emphasize the initial development of specific capabilities which in turn offer strategic windows, rather than formulating elaborated and quantified objectives and plans in advance (Itami and Numagami 1992). Hence, the strategic management of technological projects involves more than the mere application of formal instruments of control and supervision. There are strong links between project management and strategy, and the ability to align mutually project activities with mission, objectives and strategies is a critical success factor (Adler 1989).

Linkages between strategy and individual projects can be traced at all phases of the innovation cycle. First, the *raison d'être* of the pre-project phase in which priorities are established and potential technologies for future projects are identified is to break down strategies to an operational level. Second, the application of technology policies during the process of project execution embraces elements of strategic concern. For example, allowing for adjustment processes through feedback loops from direct project experience to strategy formation enhances the ability to take advantage of opportunities that emerge spontaneously outside of the scope of current strategies. On the contrary, an adequate recognition of new findings is prevented if there is poor bottom-up communication between those directly involved in R&D projects and those who shape strategy formation processes. Finally, the organizational learning which takes place in the post-project phase is an issue of strategic concern (Itami and Numagami 1992). Such organizational learning relates to the ability to learn from one project to the next, to assess the effectiveness of the approaches employed, and to make improvements which translate into distinct, strategically relevant technological capabilities, for example, the general ability to plan and implement effectively projects or technological core competencies as intangible assets which emerge from the entire set of the organization's project experiences (Metcalfe and Gibbons 1989).

7 Conclusions

Shorter life cycles, the internationalization of markets and rising development costs have boosted the necessity to thoroughly incorporate technology into corporate and business planning and strategy formulation processes. Given the inherent complexity of the links between technological change and strategy, a multi-level and multi-function concept of technology strategy can help to gain a more adequate understanding of the features of successful and unsuccessful strategic approaches to the management of technology. In particular, multi-level approaches mean that the process and content of strategy formulation are intertwined. Many factors influence the design of technology strategies (for example, industry structure or financial situation). Among the contextual factors that influence the content of technology strategies, the process of strategy formulation seems to be a very important one. For these reasons, universal formulae for the formation and implementation of technology strategies are neither available at the moment nor can be expected in the future.

KLAUS MACHARZINA

DIETMAR BRODEL
UNIVERSITY OF HOHENHEIM, STUTTGART

Further reading

(References cited in the text marked *)

* Abell, D. (1980) *Defining the Business: The Starting Point of Strategic Planning*, Englewood Cliffs, NJ: Prentice Hall. (Presents a framework for defining business domains using the concepts of customer groups, customer functions and technologies.)
* Abernathy, W.J. and Utterback, J.M. (1982) 'Patterns of industrial innovation', in M.L. Tushman and W.L. Moore (eds), *Readings in the Management of Innovation*, Boston, MA: Pitman. (Suggests a model of the changing character of innovation during the evolution of successful enterprises.)
* Adler, P.S. (1989) 'Technology strategy: a guide to the literatures', in R.S. Bosenbloom and R.A. Burgelman (eds), *Research on Technological Innovation, Management and Policy*, vol. 4, Greenwich, CT: JAI Press Inc. (An introduction to technology strategy and an overview of the literature on the strategic implications of technological change.)
* Adler, P.S., McDonald, D.W. and MacDonald, F. (1992) 'Strategic management of technical functions', *Sloan Management Review* 33 (2): 19–37. (Contains a framework for the assessment and strategic development of technical functions.)
* Ansoff, I.H. and Stewart, J.M. (1967) 'Strategies for a technology-based business', *Harvard Business Review* 45 (6): 71–83. (Examines characteristic parameters of technically intensive businesses and the strategic implications of technological profiles for competitive postures.)
* Ayres, R.U. (1969) *Technological Forecasting and Long Range Planning*, New York: McGraw-Hill. (Analyses the fundamental problems associated with and the techniques of technological forecasting.)
* Brockhoff, K. (1997) *Industrial Research for Future Competitiveness*, Berlin *et al.*: Springer. (Investigates the potentials of research in the private sector.)
* Brownlie, D.T. (1992) 'The role of technology forecasting and planning: formulating business strategy', *Industrial Management & Data Systems* 92 (2): 3–16. (A short overview of the linkages between technology forecasting and strategic planning.)
* Clark, K.B. (1985) 'The interaction of design hierarchies and market concepts in technological evolution', *Research Policy* 14 (5): 235–51.

(Explores the nature and strategic implications of different types of innovation.)

* Cohen, W.M. and Levinthal, D.A. (1990) 'Absorptive capacity: a new perspective on learning and innovation', *Administrative Science Quarterly* 35 (1): 128–52. (Presents a model of firm investment in R&D.)

* Cooper, R.G. (2000) 'Product innovation and technology strategy', *Research Technology Management* 43 (1): 38–41. (Proposes strategic cornerstones of new product development.)

* Danila, N. (1989) 'Strategic evaluation and selection of R&D projects', *R&D Management* 19 (1): 47–62. (Reviews techniques for R&D project evaluation and selection.)

* Ettlie, J.E., Bridges, W.P. and O'Keefe, R.D. (1984) 'Organization strategy and structural differences for radical versus incremental innovation', *Management Science* 30 (6): 682–95. (Analysis of the relationship between strategic and organizational characteristics and technological change patterns.)

* Foster, R.N. (1988) 'Linking R&D to strategy', in R.A. Burgelman and M.A. Maidique (eds), *Strategic Management of Technology and Innovation*, Homewood, IL: Irwin. (Presents a portfolio concept for the strategic management of technology.)

* Freeman, C. (1982) *The Economics of Industrial Innovation*, London: Frances Pinter. (Explores the economic role and different types of industrial R&D.)

* Goodman, R.A. and Lawless, M.W. (1994) *Technology and Strategy – Conceptual Models and Diagnostics*, Oxford et al.: Oxford University Press. (Presents ways to find successful technology strategies.)

* Granstrand, O., Håkanson, L. and Sjölander, S. (eds) (1992) *Technology Management and International Business. Internationalization of R&D and Technology*, Chichester: Wiley. (Collection of articles analysing the determinants, location and management of international R&D operations in multinational corporations.)

* Hagedoorn, J. (1993) 'Understanding the rationale of strategic technology partnering: interorganizational modes of cooperation and sectoral differences', *Strategic Management Journal* 14 (5): 371–85. (An overview of the literature on the motives for inter-firm technology cooperation and an analysis of interorganizational modes of strategic technology collaboration.)

* Harris, J.M., Shaw, R.W. and Sommers, W.P. (1984) 'The strategic management of technology', in R.B. Lamb (ed.), *Competitive Strategic Management*, Englewood Cliffs, NJ: Prentice

Hall, 530–55. (Presents a portfolio concept for the strategic management of technology.)

* Hippel, E.A. von (1988) *The Sources of Innovation*, New York: Oxford University Press. (Discussion of management and marketing instruments geared to benefit from customer groups yielding commercially useful novel product concepts or attributes.)

* Itami, H. and Numagami, T. (1992) 'Dynamic interaction between strategy and technology', *Strategic Management Journal*, 13 (6): 119–35. (Discussion of alternative interaction modes between strategy formation and technological development over time.)

* Macharzina, K. and Fisch, J.H. (1999) 'Management of technology in Europe', in M. Warner (ed.), *Regional Encyclopedia of Business and Management*, London: Thomson Learning. (Explores technology management in Europe as compared to other regions.)

* Maidique, M.A. and Patch, P. (1982) 'Corporate strategy and technological policy', in M.L. Tushman and W.L. Moore (eds), *Readings in the Management of Innovation*, Boston, MA: Pitman. (Develops configurations of corporate and technological strategies.)

* Metcalfe, J.S. and Gibbons, M. (1989) 'Technology, variety and organization: a systematic perspective on the competitive process', in R.S. Rosenbloom and R.A. Burgelman (eds), *Research on Technological Innovation, Management and Policy*, vol. 4, Greenwich, CT: JAI Press Inc. (Develops an evolutionary framework of the interaction between technological advancement and organizational performance.)

* Moenaert, R., Barbé, D., Deschoolmeester, D. and De Meyer, A. (1990) 'Turnaround strategies for strategic business units with an ageing technology', in R. Loverige and M. Pitt (eds), *The Strategic Management of Technological Innovation*, Chichester: Wiley. (Identifies stages of appropriating the benefits of new technologies by mature business units.)

* Nelson, R.R. and Winter, S.G. (1982) *An Evolutionary Theory of Economic Change*, Cambridge, MA: Harvard University Press. (Analysis of organizational capabilities and routines, the dynamics of competition and technological change as drivers of economic change within an evolutionary framework.)

* Patel, P. and Younger, M. (1978) 'A frame of reference for strategy development', *Long Range Planning* 11 (April): 6–12. (Presents a portfolio-concept using the industry life cycle as a separate dimension.)

* Porter, M.E. (1983) 'The technological dimension of competitive strategy', in R.S. Rosenbloom

and R.A. Burgelman (eds), *Research on Technological Innovation, Management and Policy*, vol. 1, Greenwich, CT: JAI Press Inc. (Offers a framework concerning the interaction between technological change and industrial evolution and proposes a framework for determining the choice of generic technology strategies.)

Preece, D.A. (ed.) (2000) *New Technology and Innovation – Critical Perspectives on Business and Management*, New York: Routledge. (Collection of 75 papers previously published on technology management.)

* Sundbo, J. (1998) *The Theory of Innovation – Entrepreneurs, Technology and Strategy*, Cheltenham, UK/Northampton, MA: Elgar. (Searches for explanations of technological change.)

* Vedovello, C. (1998) 'Firms' R&D activity and intensity and the university-enterprise partnerships', *Technological Forecasting and Social Change*, 58 (Special Issue): 215–26. (Analyses the interaction between private and public research organizations.)

* Welfens, P.J.J., Audretsch, D., Addison, J.T. and Grupp, H. (1998) *Technological Competition, Employment and Innovation Policies in OECD Countries*, Berlin *et al.*: Springer. (Discusses corporate R&D in the context of economic policy.)

See also: INTERNAL CONTEXTS AND EXTERNAL ENVIRONMENTS; GLOBALIZATION; ORGANIZATION BEHAVIOUR; TECHNOLOGY AND ORGANIZATIONS

Strategy and technology, international: see
TECHNOLOGY STRATEGY, INTERNATIONAL

Strauss, George (1923–)

1 Biographical data
2 *Personnel: the Human Problems of Management*
3 *The Local Union* and trade union government
4 Conclusions

Personal background

- born 23 June 1923 at Manhattan, New York
- served in US Army in Second World War
- graduated from Massachusetts Institute of Technology (1951)
- Research Associate, New York State School of Industrial and Labor Relations, Cornell (1951–4)
- Assistant Professor, latterly Professor, School of Business, University of Buffalo (1954–61)
- Professor of Business Administration, University of California-Berkeley (latterly Emeritus) (1962 onwards)
- Editor, *Industrial Relations*, for twelve years during the period 1964–95
- President, Industrial Relations Research Association (1993)
- developed ideas on industrial relations, organizational behaviour, personnel management, and human resource management

Major works

The Local Union: Its Place in the Industrial Plant (with L.R. Sayles) (1953)
Personnel: The Human Problems of Management (with L.R. Sayles) (1960)

Human Behavior in Organizations (with L.R. Sayles) (1966)
Managing Human Resources (with L.R. Sayles) (1977)
The State of the Unions (with D. Gallagher and J. Fiorito) (1991)
Researching the World of Work. Strategies and Methods in Studying Industrial Relations (with K. Whitfield) (1998)
Organizational Participation, Myth and Reality (with F. Heller, E. Pusic and B. Wilpert) (1998)

Summary

George Strauss is a leading scholar in the fields of industrial relations and personnel management. In an academic career spanning more than 45 years, he has written numerous scholarly books and articles. Strauss has made an important contribution to thinking on trade union government, shaping understanding of local union organization, leadership and participation. He has also co-authored comprehensive textbooks integrating knowledge on personnel management, human resource management and organizational behaviour, including one of the first organizational behaviour textbooks published. Strauss has continued to influence thinking and research, particularly on industrial relations, through an extensive body of review articles on many topics including union government, comparative industrial relations, worker participation, human resource management in the United States (USA), collective bargaining and industrial relations theory.

1 Biographical data

George Strauss was born in 1923 and spent his childhood in Staten Island, New York. His mother was Belgian, the daughter of a longshoreman who had been an active socialist. His father, a chemical engineer, was the son of a lawyer, later a judge in Pennsylvania (Strauss 1992). In 1940, Strauss embarked on a college education in economics and political science at Swarthmore. His studies were interrupted by three years' service in the US Army, beginning in February 1943.

After graduating from Swarthmore in 1947, Strauss enrolled as a graduate student in the Department of Economics and Social Sciences at Massachusetts Institute of Technology (MIT), Cambridge. Among Strauss's fellow students in the industrial relations stream was Leonard Sayles with whom Strauss subsequently collaborated on a series of projects, including four books and numerous articles on trade unionism. At MIT, Strauss was taught by scholars who were, or subsequently became, leading figures in economics, industrial relations and human resource management. These included John Dunlop, Bob Livernash, Douglas McGregor, Charles Myers, Paul Pigors and Paul Samuelson. It was at MIT that Strauss's ethnographic research skills were developed, as was his optimistic view that social science research can generate answers to most societal problems. The influence of MIT can also be seen in Strauss's interest in the development and dynamics of groups, formal and informal, which has characterized much of his scholarly work (see ORGANIZATION BEHAVIOUR; ORGANIZATION BEHAVIOUR, HISTORY OF). In 1951, Strauss completed his dissertation, a study of the determinants of leadership and participation in a local union. This work was further developed in *The Local Union* Strauss's first book which he later wrote with Sayles.

His graduate studies finished, Strauss joined a research project on human relations in unions at the School of Industrial and Labor Relations, Cornell. William Foot Whyte, a leading human relations scholar, was the project's director and Sayles another researcher on the project (see HUMAN RESOURCE MANAGEMENT). Whyte's work had had a major influence on Strauss's dissertation, with its stress on the way in which attitudes and behaviour at work are affected by the objective conditions of work. At Cornell, Strauss and Sayles wrote *The Local Union*, for which the Society for the Psychological Study of Social Issues awarded them the Marrow Prize in September 1952 for best contribution to 'scientific understanding of labour–management relations'. Strauss also wrote scholarly articles on the internal life of trade unions in this period, and contributed to Whyte's study of economic incentives and human relations, *Money and Motivation* (1953) (see INCENTIVES: MOTIVATION AND SATISFACTION).

In 1954, Strauss was appointed to the Business School at the University of Buffalo. There he taught labour relations, labour history and labour law, human relations, wage administration and personnel administration. In 1955, Strauss and Sayles began their collaboration on the textbook *Personnel: The Human Problem of Management*. Strauss married in Buffalo in 1957. Three years later, he completed *Personnel* with Sayles. In 1960, Strauss also accepted a visiting appointment for one year at the University of California-Berkeley. In 1962, he was appointed Professor of Business Administration in the School of Business at Berkeley. He has remained there ever since, with the exception of one year as a Fulbright Scholar in Australia in 1979 and one year as Visiting Professor and Head of the Department of Industrial Relations at the University of Sydney, Australia, in 1986.

In the 1960s, Strauss researched and published on subjects as diverse as apprenticeship systems, professional associations, and industrial relations change in the USA, as well as completing *Human Behavior in Organizations* with Sayles. Organizational behaviour had emerged as a new field in the late 1950s and early 1960s, and this textbook was one of the first to comprehensively document the main elements of the field. At Berkeley, Strauss's teaching spanned the full range of organizational behaviour courses and he developed a popular Masters of Business Administration course on negotiation and conflict resolution. Strauss co-founded the Organizational Behavior Teaching Society in 1973. His administrative and other professional responsibilities also grew. These included appointments as Editor of the journal *Industrial Relations*, for twelve years during the period 1964–95. Strauss was also Director of the Institute of Industrial Relations at the University of California-Berkeley in the years 1984–88, Associate Dean of the Business School, member and chairperson of the City of Berkeley Personnel Board for 5 years, and President of the Industrial Relations Research Association in 1993.

Since the 1970s, Strauss has collaborated with Sayles on their third textbook, *Managing Human Resources*, and the fourth edition of their first textbook, *Personnel* has been published. Human resource management had emerged in the US as a field of study and practice in the 1960s, following the application of organizational behaviour research to traditional personnel problems. In *Managing Human Resources*, Strauss and Sayles documented the main elements of human resource management, as they had done with personnel management seventeen years earlier (see HUMAN RESOURCE MANAGEMENT). However, Strauss's work has increasingly focused on industrial relations rather than personnel or human resource management. He has written numerous review articles which summarize and critically evaluate knowledge on such matters as union government, comparative industrial relations, worker participation and industrial relations theory.

Three contributions are of particular importance. First, his collaboration with Frank Heller, Eugen Pusic and Bernhard Wilpert on *Organizational Participation, Myth and Reality* (1998) provided a comprehensive discussion of how participation is conceptualized, changing forms and character of participation, and the conditions for effectiveness. Second, in *Researching the World of Work* (1998) Strauss collaborated with Keith Whitfield to explore whether the field of industrial relations could emerge from its state of flux at the turn of the century through a judicious use of traditional and innovative research methods. Third, Strauss was Guest Editor of *Industrial Relations* for its 1998 Symposium issue on regional studies of comparative international industrial relations. As guest editor, Strauss stressed the importance of extending the study of comparative industrial relations to include developing countries and highlighted the variety of analytic methods available.

While Strauss has continued to influence thinking and research in the fields of industrial relations, organizational behaviour and human resource management, this contribution will consider Strauss's early seminal contribution to these fields, *Personnel: The Human Problems of Management* and *The Local Union*, and his continuing work on union government.

2 Personnel: The Human Problems of Management

Personnel: The Human Problems of Management was the textbook which first made Strauss's reputation in personnel management and the field of organizational behaviour which had emerged in the late 1950s. This was the second book on which Strauss and Sayles had collaborated. They began writing *Personnel* in 1955 to assist their teaching in the fields of personnel management and organizational behaviour. At that time textbooks in these fields typically described practices and formal procedures, and treated personnel problems as clinical cases which managers could and should solve. The textbooks gave little attention to underlying organizational forces, behavioural science research or the politics of implementation. *Personnel* was the first textbook to comprehensively integrate these issues. The authors argued that managers needed analytical tools that went beyond the transitory practices of specific firms at specific times, to provide an enduring understanding of personnel management.

Personnel consisted of 31 chapters, divided into 7 parts. These included the nature of the personnel problem, supervisory functions, managerial skills, organizational structure, manpower and employee development, incentives for effective performance, and managerial responsibilities. Strauss and Sayles wove three threads through these chapters: an exploration of managerial techniques, consideration of the power relationships between management and union representatives, and an emphasis on relationships experienced by first-line supervisors, whose task it was to implement personnel techniques in the workplace.

This emphasis on the supervisor was unusual. Textbooks had previously concentrated on the role of specialist personnel departments. In contrast, Strauss and Sayles highlighted the staff administrative aspects of personnel management, the day-to-day responsibility of line managers for applying personnel policy and eliciting work group performance. Also unusual was the extent to which Strauss and Sayles made reference to empirical research in the behavioural and social sciences, including works by Hawthorne, Lewin, McGregor and Whyte, and such sociologists as Blau, Gouldner and Bendix. *Personnel* also included case problems at the end of many chapters, a device which subsequently became common to organizational behaviour and human resource management textbooks. An additional novel feature of *Personnel* was its emphasis on the politics of implementing personnel practices in complex organizations. This included study of the impact of such elements as hierarchical structures, trade unions and informal organization on the function of line management and methods for countering problems in order to effectively apply personnel practices. For Strauss and Sayles, an understanding of the problems associated with application and implementation was critical to effective personnel management. Strauss (1992) later said that when writing *Personnel*, he and Sayles had 'viewed implementation as a political process requiring endless accommodation' (see PERSONNEL MANAGEMENT).

In subsequent years, Strauss and Sayles published two other textbooks which drew on and extended the themes of *Personnel*, while also charting the main elements of the younger and increasingly popular fields of organizational behaviour and human resource management. The first was *Human Behavior in Organizations* (1966). As one of the first textbooks to comprehensively canvass the concerns of organizational behaviour, this book placed Strauss and Sayles as leading commentators in the field. The other textbook was *Managing Human Resources* (1977) which integrated material on both human resource management and organizational behaviour. While US universities had continued to teach personnel management, human resource management had emerged as an increasingly popular field of study from the mid 1960s, built on the basis of the application of organizational behaviour research to traditional personnel practices. These two textbooks which Strauss co-authored with Sayles were unusual, like the earlier *Personnel*, because they applied and evaluated empirical research from a variety of disciplinary fields, emphasized the politics of implementation, and were exhaustively comprehensive.

Since writing *Managing Human Resources*, Strauss has continued to comment on human resource management in the USA. He has remained critical of most textbooks in the field. In 1989, Strauss wrote that most were too 'cookbooky', paid little attention to the problems of implementation and poorly integrated the various parts of the field. Strauss (1989) also lamented what he considered a continuing paucity of research on how to effectively implement human resource management techniques, the narrow psychological focus of the field and the concentration on staff specialists to the neglect of line managers.

3 *The Local Union* and Trade Union Government

With *The Local Union: Its Place in the Industrial Plant*, Strauss gained prominence as a leading scholar on trade union government, a subject on which he has continued to write throughout his career (see INDUSTRIAL AND LABOUR RELATIONS; TRADE UNIONS). Co-authored with Sayles, *The Local Union* was Strauss's first book. It was the first major study of the role of the local industrial union in the US labour movement. As such, it provided a richly detailed ethnographic study of life, leadership and participation in local unions. The book highlighted the importance of studying the 'local' for evaluating trade union democracy. In the process, it provided one of the earliest analyses of the factors which determine participation in local unions, the conditions for union democracy, and the involvement of women and minority groups in trade unions (see INDUSTRIAL DEMOCRACY).

The Local Union was based on a study of 20 local unions primarily in the manufacturing sector. Over 16 chapters the book documented the role and function of the local union. Early chapters examined the role of union officers in the grievance process, the demands and pressures which they confront within the process and how they respond. The middle chapters of the book studied the personalities of union officers, their orientations to the role, and how they are selected. Strauss and Sayles classified shop stewards and local-wide officials, identifying three types of steward (social leaders, active unionists, self-seekers) and two types of local official (administrators and social leaders).

The last part of *The Local Union* was concerned with the problems of union democracy: the functions and problems of local meetings, patterns of participation, involvement of women and minority groups, employee attitudes towards unions and the conditions for democratic unionism. In explaining the differing participation patterns of work groups, Strauss and Sayles argued that groups participate because they obtain benefits from unions, and continued participation is linked to union success. They identified four factors affecting the success of groups in union activity; the homogeneity of the group, its status or prestige in the plant, strategic position in the company, and the nature of the job. Strauss and Sayles found that work groups which are socially united, have high status within the plant community, a strategic position in the production line, and some free time usually obtain greater satisfaction from participation and are the more likely to participate in the 'local'. Another essential condition they identified is the existence of respected leaders within the group who are interested in taking on union activity.

In the final chapter, Strauss and Sayles discussed the meaning of the term 'union democracy', what makes locals democratic, and why some local unions are more democratic than others. In the process, they argued that many commonly used indicators of democracy are of limited value, including the union's constitutional structure, numbers of election candidates, turnover of officials, existence of organized parties and attendance at meetings.

Strauss and Sayles suggested a more useful measure to be responsiveness of officers to demands of the membership. Their thesis was that local unions were typically more democratic than national bodies because participation and communication were easier at local level, leading to greater official responsiveness to members' concerns.

Finally, Strauss and Sayles identified three main reasons why some local unions are more democratic than others. These factors are the locus of control over collective bargaining, the history and organization of the union, and the collective bargaining relationship (or the degree of industrial peace). In a later edition of *The Local Union*, Strauss and Sayles extended this list to include geographical location and the character of work groups. They concluded that participation is greater in smaller local unions, in smaller urban centres, and when collective bargaining is relatively decentralized, there is a tradition of union democracy and the membership enjoys a sense of occupational community.

As the first comprehensive empirical study on local unionism, *The Local Union* had an immediate influence on academic research on union government, including Spinrad (1960) and Barbash (1967). It formed part of the body of early US literature on union government which focused on the informal life of unions, combining the concerns of human relations and industrial relations. The book also provided an early analysis of the influence of occupational community and technology on union behaviour, and employee attitudes towards unionism, the latter subsequently becoming the subject of extensive union instrumentality studies. Some aspects of the book were overlooked in later scholarly work, including Strauss and Sayles's discussion of the impact of sex and ethnicity on participation rates.

Strauss has continued to comment on union government issues throughout his career. In 1977, he co-edited (with Malcolm Warner) 'Research on Union Government', a symposium edition of the journal *Industrial Relations*. The intention behind the symposium was to publish and spur interest in behavioural research on trade unions. Strauss contributed an article, 'Union Government in the US: Research Past and Present', which documented the history of empirical research on union government, reviewed literature on union behaviour published since 1960 and suggested a future research agenda. In the process, Strauss developed some of the ideas explored in *The Local Union*. In particular, he proposed a more systematic classification of the determinants of local union democracy, identifying three categories; legal, behavioural, and responsiveness and control.

In 1991, Strauss co-edited *The State of the Unions* with Daniel Gallagher and Jack Fiorito. He also contributed chapters on participation and union democracy to the book. In his chapter on union democracy, Strauss extended the historical account of research on union government he had written in the 1977 symposium, and critically reviewed knowledge on the function and measurement of union democracy. Strauss began by asking why union democracy is important, a question to which most treatments of the topic give little attention. He followed by evaluating the findings of numerous studies conducted since the 1950s, in the process reaffirming many of the conclusions of *The Local Union*. In particular, he restated the central place of responsiveness as a criteria of democracy. Strauss also referred again to the factors which determine participation in local unions. He stressed the importance of occupational community in facilitating participation and the role of the activist core who undertake much of a union's work and can check the power of the leadership. Finally, Strauss discussed the factors which account for variations in participation, including occupational community, status, size of local, structure, degree of centralization, and history, tradition and ideology. In an important departure from his earlier writings, Strauss argued that while homogeneity may contribute to greater responsiveness in local unions, diversity may also foster democracy by engendering disagreement, electoral competition and officer turnover.

4 Conclusions

Strauss is one of the few early scholars of personnel management who has also had a continuing prominence in the field of industrial relations. He is also a leading commentator on organizational behaviour and human resource management. In his scholarly works, Strauss has provided an unusually sensitive blend of the concerns and insights of these fields. He has highlighted the importance of understanding unions and workplace politics in human resource management, for example, and of examining informal organization, leadership and attitudes in studies of union behaviour. Strauss's textbooks have played a significant role in defining the expanding fields of organizational behaviour and human resource management and his early and continuing work on union government has an enduring importance. Strauss has remained a leading commentator on industrial relations, his writings vigorously documenting the state of knowledge in the field and conveying his unceasing interest in the day-to-day realities of industrial life. Increasingly, Strauss has pointed to research needs and agendas, to encourage future scholars to expand the frontiers of knowledge in industrial relations and human resource management.

LOUISE THORNTHWAITE
UNIVERSITY OF WOLLONGONG, AUSTRALIA

Further reading

(References cited in the text marked *)

* Barbash, J. (1967) *American Unions: Structure, Government and Politics*, New York: Random House. (A large US study of trade unions which examines union participation and government.)
* Gallagher, D., Fiorito, J. and Strauss, G. (eds) (1991) *The State of the Unions*, Madison, Wisconsin: Industrial Relations Research Association. (A wide-ranging book which discusses union membership, growth and governance, and the tasks and challenges facing unions in the late twentieth century.)
* Heller, F., Pusic, E., Strauss, G. and Wilpert, B. (eds) (1998) *Organizational Participation, Myth and Reality*, Oxford: Oxford University Press. (Contributors discuss the changing forms and character of organizational participation from a range of disciplinary perspectives. Strauss's contributions focus on collective bargaining, unions and participation.)
* Sayles, L. and Strauss, G. (1953) *The Local Union: Its Place in the Industrial Plant*, New York:

Harper & Brothers. (Strauss's classic work on leadership and participation in local unions.)

* Sayles, L. and Strauss, G. (1960) *Personnel: The Human Problems of Management*, New Jersey: Prentice-Hall. (Strauss's first comprehensive personnel management textbook, more than 700 pages.)

* Sayles, L. and Strauss, G. (1966) *Human Behavior in Organizations*, New Jersey: Prentice-Hall. (A textbook on organizational behaviour which integrates prescription, empirical research and critical analysis.)

* Sayles, L. and Strauss, G. (1977) *Managing Human Resources*, New Jersey: Prentice-Hall. (A textbook which draws on behavioural science research to explain the principles and processes of human resource management.)

* Spinrad, W. (1960) 'Correlates of trade union participation' *American Sociological Review*, 25 (2): 23–244. (An examination of union participation studies which identifies determinants of participation.)

* Strauss, G. (1977) 'Union Government in the US: Research Past and Future', *Industrial Relations*, 16 (1): 115–26. (Review article which evaluates knowledge in the field.)

* Strauss, G. (1989) 'Industrial relations as an academic field: What's wrong with it?', in J. Barbash and K. Barbash (eds) *Theories and Concepts in Comparative Industrial Relations*, University of South Carolina Press: 241–60. (Analyses the roots and development of the industrial relations field, developments in the 1980s and future research directions).

* Strauss, G. (1992) 'Present at the beginning: Some personal notes on OB's early days and later', *Laureates of Management Thought*, JAI Press: 145–90. (Strauss's reflections on his career and the development of organizational behaviour, including a list of Strauss's published works 1952–1992.)

* Strauss, G. (1998) 'Regional studies of comparative international industrial relations: symposium introduction', *Industrial Relations*, 37 (3): 273–81. (This review article compares industrial relations patterns in developing countries and the analytic methods of the contributors to the symposium.)

* Whitfield, K. and Strauss, G. (eds) (1998) *Researching the World of Work. Strategies and Methods in Studying Industrial Relations*, Ithaca: Cornell University Press. (This collection of papers explores trends in research strategy and method, and the practical and critical issues researchers face when studying industrial relations phenomena.)

Whitfield, K. and Strauss, G. (2000) 'Methods Matter: Changes in Industrial Relations Research and their Implications', British Journal Industrial Relations, 38: 1, 141–51. (A further recent contribution to understanding research methods in the field of Industrial Relations.)

* Whyte, W.F., with Dalton, M., Roy, D., Sayles, L., Collins, O., Miller, F., Strauss, G., Fuerstenberg, F. and Bavelas, A. (1955) *Money and Motivation: An Analysis of Incentives in Industry*, New York: Harper & Brothers. (A comprehensive study of the impact of monetary incentives in industry.)

See also: BARBASH, J.; COLLECTIVE BARGAINING; DUNLOP, J.T.; EMPLOYEE RELATIONS; HUMAN RELATIONS; HUMAN RESOURCE MANAGEMENT; INDUSTRIAL DEMOCRACY; INDUSTRIAL AND LABOUR RELATIONS; KOCHAN, T.; OCCUPATIONAL PSYCHOLOGY; ORGANIZATION BEHAVIOUR; ORGANIZATION BEHAVIOUR, HISTORY OF; PAYMENT SYSTEMS; PERSONNEL MANAGEMENT; SCHULER, R.; TRADE UNIONS

Stress

Overview

Early work on stress focused on explaining the nature of stress. It was originally perceived as an external force. More recently stress has been viewed as the reaction to pressure. The nature of stress will be explained and the physiological and psychological reactions will be described which can be used to identify increased levels of stress. Stress is becoming a global phenomenon affecting all countries, professions and all categories of worker. Stressors will be identified, both those created by individuals and organizational causes of stress. Studies have focused on particular categories of people including 1,100 executives and their experiences of stress. Strategies for stress management originally focused on individual approaches, concentrating on lifestyle and addressing work-related problems. With the threat of litigation, organizational initiatives are assuming growing importance. In the twenty-first century, interest will focus on helping organizations address stress issues to ensure employees are able to utilize their full potential.

1 Understanding stress

The term 'stress' is used in a variety of ways, often synonymously with pressure. Understanding of stress has developed from both medical and psychological research. Originally it was viewed from an engineering perspective and seen as an external force on the person, giving rise to strain and finally permanent damage. It is now widely viewed as the physiological and psychological reaction which occurs when individuals meet a threat or challenge and the individuals' perception, whether consciously or subconsciously, is that it is beyond their immediate capacity (see OCCUPATIONAL PSYCHOLOGY).

A recent report published by the Institute of Employment Studies (Rick *et al.* 1997) highlights the extent to which stress has become an umbrella term comprising three elements: stressors; strain – the symptom; and stress outcomes.

The physiological reaction is what is referred to as the fight/flight response. It equips the individual to face life-threatening situations by increasing their arousal level. This is a natural response and can be described as acute stress. When this occurs occasionally and the body quickly returns to a normal level of arousal, there are no detrimental effects. However, in the modern world, individuals are experiencing long-term, unacceptably high levels of arousal which give rise to chronic stress. This initially gives rise to tiredness, then exhaustion, and ultimately illness and long-term side effects. This chronic stress gives organizations most cause for concern and is the type most likely to lead to litigation for employers. Cases have been heard in a range of countries including the USA, Australia and Canada.

Most writers on the topic of stress usually make use of an extension of the Yerkes Dodson Law that demonstrates the relationship between performance/quality of working life and levels of pressure. Andrew Melhuish (1978) identifies a medical component as shown in Figure 1.

Figure 1 shows that low levels of pressure can be as unhealthy and stress-inducing as high levels of pressure. The relationship between pressure and stress levels is not linear. It also dispels the myth that the higher up one progresses in the organization, the more likely one is to experience excessive stress levels. People undertaking very routine work describe the stress experienced which results from boredom.

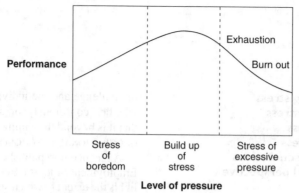

Figure 1 The relationship between stress and performance
Source: Adapted from Melhuish (1978)

At optimum levels of pressure the stress experienced is positive. People at this point on the performance curve describe feeling challenged, in control of the situation, achieving high levels of job performance and job satisfaction (see MOTIVATION AND SATISFACTION). Sports people concentrate on performing at these pressure levels to enable them to maximize their performance.

There is a fine line between optimum pressure and excessive pressure causing people to change their perceptions of the situation. At excessive levels of pressure people describe feeling out of control, unable to cope and overloaded. The point at which positive stress turns to distress is personal. It depends on the perceptions of people, personality characteristics and their perceived capacity to cope with the pressures of the situation. If people operate at excessive levels of pressure for lengthy periods, the excessive stress experienced can be extremely harmful to them. In a recent article (*Employee Health Bulletin* 11 October 1999), the Health and Safety Executive UK were cited as reporting stress as the second most commonly self-reported work-related illness next to musculo-skeletal disorders including back pain. They estimated a total of over five million working days lost a year in sickness absence.

Excessive stress is now viewed as a killer. A report in *Personnel Journal* (Solomon 1993) described an illness suffered in Japan, a nation known for its employees working very long hours. The fatal illness is known as *karoshi*. People die from high stress levels and the pressure of overtime work. In 1990 the Labour Ministry received 777 applications for compensation because of the illness (see JAPAN, MANAGEMENT IN). Not all symptoms of excessive stress are as serious, but it certainly impacts on quality of life and job performance as the next section will demonstrate.

2 Symptoms of stress

Care must be taken not to exaggerate the effects of excessive stress. While it is a killer, some illnesses known to be stress-related may develop for other reasons and excessive stress levels just exacerbate the problem. For example, the relationship between stress and heart disease remains controversial.

The symptoms of stress are best understood after having first explained the physiological reactions which take place when a person's stress level becomes raised either by a sense of danger, pressure at work or an irritation in daily life. The stressor sets off a complex chain of physiological and psychological reactions. This was described by Walter Cannon of Harvard as the 'fight or flight reaction'. The reaction was part of the survival mechanism of prehistoric man, needed to give extra energy to flee from life-threatening situations.

At the first sign of a threat, signals from the brain alert the body of the need for action. The adrenal glands produce adrenaline and noradrenaline and corticoids. These chemicals trigger activity in the short term, but if produced over long periods of time they can have negative effects.

Blood is diverted from the skin to the brain, increasing alertness, and to the muscles, fuelling them for action. In the short term digestion stops, the pulse becomes more rapid, blood pressure rises as a result of adrenaline and noradrenaline increasing the force and speed of contraction of the heart. The hormones also enlarge the airways so that more oxygen reaches the lungs. Glucose is released from the liver for energy and the cooling system is activated resulting in the person sweating.

This chain of reactions happens very quickly and if triggered to deal with a single emergency is not harmful. In today's climate this reaction is repeatedly triggered, which gives rise to long-term harmful effects. These include high blood pressure, the breakdown of the immune system, muscle tension resulting in headaches and backache, and constant perspiration resulting in skin allergies and eczema.

A range of symptoms are listed in Table 1. People tend to develop their own response patterns and when monitoring stress any changes in behaviour may be indicative of increased stress levels. Ashton (1993) identified a number of signs that can be used as stress indicators: reduced performance; increased absenteeism; excessive consumption of alcohol; irritability; rapid and inappropriate mood changes; indecisiveness; and an appearance of fatigue, nervousness and/or depression.

3 Causes of stress

The triggers of the stress reaction are many and varied depending on the person. Some writers, including Cooper et al. (1988), concentrate on identifying external sources of stress; others, including Arroba and James (1992), focus on self-imposed stressors. Another approach is to focus on life event changes, first developed by Holmes and Rahe (1967) in the 1960s and extended further by Cooper et al. (1988) (see ORGANIZATION DEVELOPMENT). This approach explores events in life which can be stress-inducing and

Table 1 Spotting the signs of stress

Physical reactions	Emotional reactions	Mental reactions	Behavioural reactions
Not all physical changes are caused by increasing pressure but many are:	A change in feelings often accompanies a change in pressure level:	A change in thought processes often accompanies a change in pressure:	There are many ways behaviour can be affected:
Indigestion/heartburn	Irritability	Inability to concentrate	Excessive drinking
Constipation/diarrhoea	Anxiety/panic	Difficulty establishing priorities	Excessive eating/loss of appetite
Tiredness	Anger	Indecisiveness	Craving for sweet food
Insomnia	Depression	Tunnel vision	Withdrawal from people/absence from work
Muscle tension/cramp and spasms	Guilt	Confused/illogical thinking	Clumsiness/accident prone. Changed driving behaviour
Palpitations	Feeling unable to cope	Procrastination	Irritability/hostile behaviour
Persistent headaches/ migraine		Forgetfulness	More speech/faster speech
Nervous twitches		Difficulty recalling information	Mood swings
Reduced resistance to illness			Loss of sense of humour

draws attention to the cumulative effects of several stressors which can result in chronic stress.

The Cooper model identifies six sources of work stress.

1 *The job itself.* This includes the working environment, hours worked including shift work, travel, workload and keeping up with new technology. This last factor was particularly experienced by Japanese executives (see INTERNAL CONTEXTS AND EXTERNAL ENVIRONMENTS).
2 *Role in the organization.* This covers role conflict, ambiguity of role, particularly lack of clarity, and responsibility for other people as part of the job role.
3 *Relationships at work.* One of the most stressful aspects of work is building and sustaining positive and supportive relationships with colleagues, bosses and subordinates (see ORGANIZATION BEHAVIOUR).
4 *Career development.* This includes job insecurity, redundancy, skill obsolescence, reaching one's career ceiling or being over-promoted (see CAREERS).
5 *Organization structure and climate.* This impacts on the extent to which individuals feel able to participate in decisions affecting them (see ORGANIZATION STRUCTURE).
6 *Home–work interface.* Increasingly, stresses at work escalate stress at home as partners experience difficulty providing the necessary support. There is also the challenge of dual career families. In the USA only 7 per cent of wives followed the conventional child-rearing role and family unit while in the UK 65 per cent of wives work. Studies have also suggested that husbands have greater difficulty than wives separating home and work when experiencing difficult relations with their children (see EQUAL EMPLOYMENT OPPORTUNITIES).

In the 1990s Cartwright and Cooper (1994) focused on three fundamental causes of stress: (1) change (resulting in uncertainty, job insecurity and changes in corporate culture which lead to significant changes in managerial style); (2) increased workload (as organizations strive to become leaner and increase their competitive position in Europe and internationally, fewer staff have more work to do); and (3) loss of control (as European and international networks become established, rules and regulations take away autonomy and control from organizations and individuals) (see HUMAN RESOURCE MANAGEMENT; HUMAN RESOURCE MANAGEMENT, INTERNATIONAL). The findings of Cartwright and Cooper (1997) were reinforced by Solomon (1999). She described a workplace riddled with tight deadlines, high expectations for productivity and fewer people available to do the job. In addition, managers have so much more work to do in less time with fewer people it in turn affects the way they communicate and deal with people. This results in people feeling isolated, unappreciated or having no say in the situation putting them under enormous pressure.

4 Studies on stress

The relationship between gender, work and stress

According to the *International Labour Organization Conditions of Work Digest* (1992), the relationship between gender, work and stress is complex and varied. A survey conducted in the USA reported women as being more affected by stress than men. Two reasons were cited: first, women are often earning less than men; and second, many companies lack policies covering family issues. Research conducted in Sweden concluded that women work longer hours than men. In Sweden 86 per cent of women work but spouses share duties equally at home (see EQUAL EMPLOYMENT OPPORTUNITIES).

Executive stress

Cooper *et al.* (1988) conducted a study of 1,100 senior to top-level executives in ten countries and discovered work pressure variations cross-culturally, particularly between developed and developing countries. US managers reported the stress of lack of power, incompetent bosses and a conflict of beliefs with the organization. Japanese managers cited the pressure of keeping up with changes in technology. German managers complained of work pressures and working with inadequately trained subordinates (see GERMANY, MANAGEMENT IN). In Brazil executives appeared to be under extreme pressure, with very high mental ill health and low job satisfaction (see BRAZIL, MANAGEMENT IN). Their stresses were work pressure, keeping up with new technology and inadequately trained personnel (see MANAGERIAL BEHAVIOUR).

IRS Survey June/July 1999

This survey covered 192 employers employing 741,002 staff. The survey explored:

1 trends in work-related stress
2 identifying stress
3 preventing stress
4 managing stress

Of the organizations surveyed, 99 per cent said that stress had moved up the management agenda largely as a result of an increased concern for employees' well-being and a growing problem of stress-related absence; 90 per cent reported a rise in sickness absence.

Stress was recorded as affecting the workplace in a number of ways, including absence due to sickness, morale, productivity, quality, customer care and lateness. A small proportion of companies also identified a rise in accidents at work.

Stress prevention in order to reduce the organizational sources of stress was tackled in a number of ways. Changes to jobs or working practices, and particularly changes which resulted in increased employee participation, were cited in approximately one-third of organizations. Stress policies were not widely used and only 36 organisations conducted stress audits.

Employees were given access to counselling in 91 per cent of organizations, while 74 per cent used a rehabilitation process for those returning to work from a stress related absence.

5 Managing personal stress

In today's world many are likely to need to manage personal stress. There is no one right way to manage it but different ways which will suit different people. Ashton (1993) describes stress management as one step in his twelve-week Executive Health Plan. Cranwell-Ward (1990) emphasizes the need for the right balance in life and the importance of physical, emotional and spiritual well-being. Cartwright and Cooper (1994) focus on how to respond to the fundamental causes of stress, particularly overload, relationship difficulties, the home–work interface and responding to unexpected events and changes in the organization (see DOWNSIZING). David Fontana (1989) and Arroba and James (1992) address personally induced stress. From the various approaches a number of core elements emerge.

1 Maintaining a healthy and balanced lifestyle – this acts for stress prevention as well as a cure. A balanced diet, adequate sleep, time for relaxation and taking regular physical exercise helps maintain stress at an acceptable level.
2 Participating in a programme of exercise – 3–4 sessions of 30 minutes per week. Exercise helps to reduce the sudden hormonal surges of the stress response and increases endorphins which reduce anxiety. It also helps to restore a normal sleep pattern.
3 Ensuring an adequate balance between home and work – avoidance of excessive overwork, taking work home and becoming involved in excessive business travel.
4 Keeping a positive outlook – the importance of turning negative stress into positive stress.
5 Self-management – the importance of prioritizing, being assertive and making the best use of time.
6 Effective problem solving – particularly when problems are causing stress.
7 Adopting realistic expectations for self and others – much stress is self-imposed resulting from excessive personal demands.
8 Ensuring adequate emotional support – both at home and networks at work to allow for release of emotions.
9 Managing the job effectively – ensuring pressure is kept at appropriate levels and if necessary seeking help from others.
10 Managing change appropriately – creating stability zones at times of change and facing up to change positively.

11 Stress monitoring – in terms of stress levels, signs of stress and triggers of stress.

12 Seeking outside help when necessary.

6 Organizational perspective

In recent years organizations have become much more aware of the need to help employees manage stress (see ORGANIZATION BEHAVIOUR). Help has taken a number of different forms, ranging from counselling help to cope with post-traumatic stress to stress prevention by creating a healthy environment, staff development and organizational development (see ORGANIZATION DEVELOPMENT).

Arroba and James (1992) suggest interventions at three levels to make organizations fitter to cope and perform well. At employee level, they emphasize the need to clarify expectations placed on staff, the importance of giving feedback on performance and developing the appropriate skill base to fulfil roles (see PERFORMANCE APPRAISAL). Teams can be developed to ensure effective teamwork and, at the organizational level, values, organization design and job design must be examined to ensure each is appropriate to achieve organizational objectives (see GROUPS AND TEAMS).

Rick *et al.*(1997) emphasized the need for much more focused interventions by organizations to deal with stress. Five key elements of good practice were identified in research:

1 assessment and diagnosis
2 solution generation
3 implementation
4 evaluation
5 on-going monitoring and feedback

Melanie Williams, in an article entitled 'Facing up to frontline stress' in *Managing Service Quality* (1993), explored the extent to which stress can be minimized in organizations. The Automobile Association, which deals with 4.8 million breakdowns a year, was given as an example of an organization which sometimes has to work under intense pressure and deal with very stressful situations and stressed customers. A number of measures are taken to ensure stress is kept to a minimum. Care is taken to recruit the right staff, train them adequately and empower them to make

their own decisions. A good team spirit is created and good use made of positive feedback.

As litigation by employees against employers increases in the USA for compensation for work-related stress illnesses there is likely to be a similar trend in the UK. Earnshaw and Cooper (1996) cite the successful personal injury action brought by a social worker, John Walker, against Northumberland County Council, England, UK. This is likely to focus attention more sharply on creating healthy organizations for employees. Williams (1994) outlines four elements of organizational health. He suggests a holistic approach to managing health of employees as the four elements – environmental factors, physical, mental and social health – all interact with one another and all have a bearing on stress.

Stephen Hoare, in an article entitled 'Life on the edge' (1998), emphasized the importance of organizations taking steps to help employees cope with the demands of a stressful job, for example, PPP, who offer support services to organizations, including counselling, stress audits and training services. In their view: 'Stress is fast becoming the single most important issue on the agenda for employers wishing to optimise efficiently and avoid litigation'.

Increasingly organizations are conducting stress audits as a way of identifying the nature and extent of the problem in a particular organization. Michael Reddy (1999) highlights the need to be very clear of the objectives of an audit. When conducting an audit it is important to tap into the unique causes of stress within an organization. Once root causes have been identified, focused constructive action can be followed up. According to Reddy, a stress audit should be viewed as a kind of employee opinion survey.

In a recent book, James and Arroba (1999) emphasize the importance of tackling organizational issues to ensure energy levels of employees are high enough to sustain a high level of performance. The starting point of their new model is developing a strategic approach for top performance. Revitalizing the organization depends on emotional focus with systematic thinking to develop a supportive culture which encourages higher peformance.

Stress is likely to remain a critical issue from an individual, team and organizational perspective (see OCCUPATIONAL PSYCHOLOGY). The focus for the twenty-first century is likely to be the healthy organization.

JANE CRANWELL-WARD
HENLEY MANAGEMENT COLLEGE

Further reading

(References cited in the text marked *)

* Arroba, T. and James, K. (1992) *Pressure at Work: A Survival Guide*, 2nd edn, Maidenhead: McGraw-Hill. (An excellent practical guide to help managers understand and keep pressure at a constructive level.)

* Ashton, D. (1993) *The 12 Week Executive Health Plan*, London: Kogan Page. (An excellent informative health plan to manage stress more effectively.)

* Cartwright, S. and Cooper, C. (1994) *No Hassle! Taking the Stress Out of Work*, London: Century. (A new approach to problems which generate stress at work and how to manage them.)

* Cartwright, S. and Cooper, C. (1997) *Managing Workplace Stress*, Thousand Oaks, London and Delhi: Sage. (A good overview of how to manage the major stresses of work.)

* Cooper, C., Cooper, R. and Eaker, L. (1988) *Living with Stress*, London: Penguin. (An excellent comprehensive summary of stress and how to manage it; particularly good at comparing different occupational and cultural groups.)

* Cranwell-Ward, J. (1990) *Thriving on Stress*, London: Routledge. (A workbook designed to help managers recognize and manage stress effectively.)

Cranwell-Ward, J. (1995) 'When the going gets tough', *People Management* 29 June, 1 (13): 22–5. (A review is made of some of the issues concerning stress in the workplace, drawing upon findings of a number of research studies and highlighting some of the costs involved. Four categories of stress are identified.)

* Earnshaw, T. and Cooper, C. (1996) *Stress and Employer Liability*, London: IPD. (A good overview related to stress and stress related issues for managers of employer liability.)

* Fontana, D. (1989) *Managing Stress*, London: Routledge and Kegan Paul. (A good overview on stress, the causes and how to manage them.)

* Hoare, S. (1998) 'Life on the edge', *CBI News* July/August: 33–6. (Emphasizes the importance of employers taking stress seriously. The actions being taken by companies to alleviate stress are summarized and there is a brief explanation of services such as employee assistance programmes and counselling.)

* Holmes T.H. and Rahe, R.H. (1967) 'The social readjustment rating scale', *Journal of Psychosomatic Research* 11: 213–8. (One of the first studies focusing on life event changes as a factor in stress.)

* International Labour Office (1992) *Preventing Stress at Work*, vol. 2, *International Labour Office Conditions of Work Digest*, Geneva, Switzerland: International Labour Office. (An excellent reference book summarizing current international research; good reading list.)

IRS Employment Review (1999) October, no. 689: 4–20. (The article outlines the findings of a survey of 126 UK employers investigating current policies and practices on work-related stress. Current trends are summarized and the processes of and approaches to identifying, preventing and managing stress are explored.)

* James, K. and Arroba, T. (1999) *Energising the Workplace: A Strategic Response To Stress*, Aldershot: Gower. (This book offers a new approach to the management of stress in organizations. Straightforward and practical, the book outlines a new model, which covers all the elements needed to manage organizational stress.)

* Melhuish, A. (1978) *Executive Health*, London: Business Books. (A good view of stress written by a medical practitioner.)

* Reddy, M. (1999) 'An introduction to stress audits', *IRS Employment Review* January (681): 5–6. (A review is made of stress audits and the factors involved in the stress audit process.)

* Rick, J., Hillage, J., Honey, S. and Perryman, S. (1997) *Stress: Big Issue, but What are the Problems*, Brighton: Institute of Employment Studies. (An informative report which gives an overview of stress, workplace stress interventions and well documented case studies of stress interventions.)

* Solomon, C.M. (1993) 'Working smarter: how H.R. can help', *Personnel Journal* June: 54–64. (Useful article on the human cost of overwork and how human resource professionals can help employees prioritize, make better decisions and lead balanced lives.)

* Solomon, C.M. (1999) 'Stressed to the Limit', *Workforce* September, 78 (9): 48, 50–4. (Stress is getting worse, the author contends: the need to recognize and deal with it is emphasized; actions which can be taken by human resources to deflect and defuse work stress are considered; the role of employee assistance programmes and organization culture is mentioned and

the importance of systems and policies is high-lighted.)

* Williams, M. (1993) 'Facing up to frontline stress', *Managing Service Quality* July: 11–14. (A useful article examining stress in organizations, exploring quality of management as a source of stress and describing a case study of an organization attempting to minimize stress in the workplace.)

* Williams, S. (1994) 'Ways of creating healthy organisations', in C. Cooper and S. Williams (eds), *Creating Healthy Work Organizations*, Chichester and New York: Wiley. (A useful collection of contributions focused on creating healthy organizations, with international examples. The chapter gives a useful overview of health from a holistic perspective, addressing the impact of the environment on physical, mental and social health.)

See also: BRAZIL, MANAGEMENT IN; CONTEXTS AND ENVIRONMENTS; DOWNSIZING; EQUAL EMPLOYMENT OPPORTUNITIES; GERMANY, MANAGEMENT IN; GROUPS AND TEAMS; HUMAN RESOURCE MANAGEMENT; HUMAN RESOURCE MANAGEMENT, INTERNATIONAL; JAPAN, MANAGEMENT IN; JOB DESIGN; MANAGERIAL BEHAVIOUR; MOTIVATION AND SATISFACTION; OCCUPATIONAL PSYCHOLOGY; ORGANIZATION BEHAVIOUR; ORGANIZATION CULTURE; ORGANIZATION DEVELOPMENT; ORGANIZATION STRUCTURE; ORGANIZATIONAL PERFORMANCE; ORGANIZATIONAL PSYCHOLOGY; PERFORMANCE APPRAISAL; PRODUCTIVITY; TOTAL QUALITY MANAGEMENT; WORK ETHIC; WORK AND LEISURE; WORK SYSTEMS

Strikes: see COLLECTIVE BARGAINING; INDUSTRIAL CONFLICT; TRADE UNIONS

Structure: see ORGANIZATION STRUCTURE; MULTINATIONAL CORPORATIONS, ORGANIZATION STRUCTURE IN

Subculture: see CULTURE

Sun Tzu

Overview

The emphasis in this article is on the ancient Chinese book *Sun Tzu Ping Fa* – often called *Sun Tzu's Art of War* in English – rather than on the life of Sun Tzu himself. This choice of emphasis is due partly to the fact that the authorship of the book is an unsettled question. The aphorisms contained in the book have influenced generations of Chinese, Japanese and other east Asian peoples.

Predating Carl von Clausewitz's *On War* by some twenty-two centuries, *Sun Tzu Ping Fa* is the oldest extant systematic military treatise in the world, yet some of its fundamental ideas have been described as ageless by the great twentieth-century military strategist Captain B.H. Liddell Hart. Overall, the book demonstrates the Chinese emphasis on the concrete and specific, awareness of complex multiplicity and interrelationships, the eschewal of the abstract and absolute, and esteem for both hierarchy and nature (Nakamura 1964). However, many of the principles expounded in the text are considered to apply outside purely military spheres, in particular in diplomacy, interpersonal relations and business strategy.

1 Introduction

Many of the principles expounded in *Sun Tzu Ping Fa* have, over the centuries, become part of the intellectual make-up of generations of Chinese, Japanese and other east Asian peoples, both soldiers and civilians (see ASIA PACIFIC, MANAGEMENT IN; BUSINESS STRATEGIES, EAST ASIAN). The book was probably introduced to Japan by the middle of the eighth century (Griffith 1963). Its influence could be seen, for example, in slogans written on the battle banners of Takeda Shingen (a famous general of the sixteenth century): 'Swift as the wind, Calmly majestic as the forest, Plundering like fire, Immovable as the mountains'. These words are identical to part of a paragraph in the seventh chapter of *Sun Tzu Ping Fa*, entitled 'Manoeuvre'. When discussing business or personal strategy with friends, east Asians will often refer to Sun Tzu's aphorisms. Chinese-language books on the application of Sun Tzu to business and management are among the best-selling titles in Hong Kong, Singapore, Taiwan and China, while Miyamoto Musashi's *The Book of Five Rings* (written around 1645 and itself influenced by Sun Tzu) has become recommended reading for MBA students at leading US business schools.

2 The question of authorship

'Sun' is a family name and 'Tzu' is an ancient title of respect for a learned or virtuous man; thus, 'Sun Tzu' means simply 'venerable Mr Sun', leaving the question of Sun Tzu's identity open. The primary meaning of 'ping' is soldier or weapons, and 'fa' means method. A literal translation of *Sun Tzu Ping Fa* would therefore be 'The Military Method of Venerable Mr Sun'. The use of the expression 'art of war' probably owes much to Machiavelli, whose *The Art of War* was published in 1520, and to the Prussian general Carl von Clausewitz, who favoured the notion of the 'art of war' over the 'science of war'.

The authorship of *Sun Tzu Ping Fa* has been a controversial question since at least the Sung Dynasty (AD 960–1126), when the *Seven Military Classics* were codified, and it remains unsettled to this day. According to the traditional view – based on the *Shih Chi* (Historical Records), which were completed shortly after 100 BC by the grand historian Szuma Chien – Sun Tzu was Sun Wu, whose book gained him an audience with King Ho-lü of Wu. Sun Wu had the two leading concubines decapitated to demonstrate the principles of military discipline and went on to an illustrious career as a general. According to this account, the thirteen chapters of *Sun Tzu Ping Fa* would have been composed around 500 BC during the Spring and Autumn period. However, if the book was indeed written by a single person, a number of significant anachronisms identified by Griffith (1963) suggest that it must have been written later, during the Warring States period, possibly between 400 and 320 BC. These anachronisms include the emergence of the professional general, the use of the crossbow and the deployment of armoured troops.

It is also possible that the text was written by different people at different times. Szuma Chien's chapter dealing with Sun Wu is entitled 'The biographies of Sun Tzu and Wu Chi' and covers the life stories of three people: Sun Wu, Sun Pin (who was a descendant of Sun Wu and who lived more than a hundred years later) and Wu Chi. All three were brilliant generals who wrote military treatises. Furthermore, the text that has come down to this day is referred to as *Sun Tzu Ping Fa as Commentated by the Eleven Authorities*; the commentaries, consisting of explanations, further elaborations and examples drawn from later periods, follow each sentence or paragraph and exceed the original text in length. The principal commentator was Ts'ao Ts'ao (AD 155–220), a famous prime minister and general during the period of the Three Kingdoms; it appears that he not only commented on the text, but edited it to reduce the number of redundancies (Griffith 1963). It is this text which has been preserved together with the commentaries, and the influence of the book derives from both the text and the commentaries.

3 Sun Tzu's main principles

Sun Tzu urged moderation and caution in relation to war:

> A sovereign should not start a war out of anger, nor should a general give battle out of rage. For while anger can revert to happiness and rage to delight, a nation that has been destroyed cannot be restored, nor can the dead be brought back to life.
>
> (*Sun Tzu Ping Fa*, Chapter 12)

Indeed, the aim of war is not necessarily the destruction of the enemy's forces, as it is in Clausewitz's system:

> In war, it is better to take a nation whole rather than broken, an army whole rather than broken. … For to win one hundred victories in one hundred battles is not the acme of skill. To subdue the enemy's forces without fighting is the summit of skill. The best approach is to attack the

other side's strategy; next best is to attack his alliances; next best is to attack his soldiers; the worst is to attack cities.

(Chapter 3)

Although preparations for war may take a long time, once war breaks out speed is of the essence:

What is precious in war is victory, not prolonged operations. ... Thus, while one hears of blundering swiftness in war, one never sees skilfulness that is prolonged. For there never has been a case of prolonged war from which the nation profits.

(Chapter 2)

Strategy, in the delimited sense of stratagems, ploys and deception, is an integral part of war. 'War is based on the method of deception. ... Therefore when strong feign weakness, when using something appear not to use it, when near appear far away, when far away appear near'. The principle of deception is intimately linked to that of surprise: 'Attack where and when he is unprepared; sally out where and when attack is not expected' (Chapter 1).

Sun Tzu's views on strategy lead to another key principle, that of flexibility or adaptability:

For the shape of an army is like that of water. The shape of water is to avoid heights and flow towards low places; the shape of the army is to avoid strength and to strike at weakness. Water flows in accordance with the ground; an army achieves victory in accordance with the enemy. Therefore the army has no constant shape just as water has no permanent form; it is an act of genius to achieve victory in accordance with changes in the enemy.

(Chapter 6)

These concepts of adaptability should not detract from the importance of the positional aspects of strategy:

In the old days, the skilful generals first made themselves invincible and then waited for the enemy to become vulnerable. Invincibility depends on oneself – the possibility of victory depends on the enemy. ... Therefore the skilful general stands on undefeatable ground and does

not miss an opportunity to defeat his enemy.

(Chapter 4)

Advantage on the battlefield does not depend on absolute numbers but on where, when and how one gives battle. To create a situation which assures victory is the ultimate responsibility of generalship:

Generally, the army that occupies the field of battle first and awaits the enemy is at ease; the side that arrives later to the battlefield and rushes into the fight is exhausted. Therefore the skilful warrior drives the other side and is not driven by him. ... If I can ascertain my enemy's shape while I have no shape (that is known to him), then I can concentrate my forces while he must divide his ... thus I can outnumber him by ten to one.

(Chapter 6)

This puts a premium on 'intelligence'. Sun Tzu is remarkably forthright in his views on the use of spies, arguing that generals have a duty to use them:

Armies confront each other for years to fight for victory on a single day. If, out of miserliness for ranks, emoluments and a hundred pieces of gold, one does not know the enemy's conditions, this is the ultimate in unkindness. Such a man is not fit to be a general, a support to his king, a master of victory. ... Advance knowledge cannot be gained from ghosts and spirits ... but must be obtained from people who know the enemy situation.

(Chapter 13)

According to Sun Tzu, one must also know the climate and, above all, the terrain. Much of chapters 8 ('The nine variations'), 9 ('Marches'), 10 ('Terrain') and 11 ('The nine types of ground') are devoted to discussions of ground and terrain.

4 Evaluation

To understand the tree, know the roots. The tap root of management strategy is war: its theory and practice. Indeed, the English word 'strategy' derives from the Greek words *stratos* (army) and *agein* (to lead), combined in the word *strategos* meaning generalship. Strategy has become an unconscious (and thus frozen) metaphor; a word which has become so familiar that it is treated as a literal term and our awareness of its metaphorical nature is lost (see STRATEGY, CONCEPT OF). The meanings of unconscious metaphors tend to be discontinuously shifted rather than continuously developed. The reading of Sun Tzu and other classics can provide a way to breathe life into ossified metaphors; they can remind us of the essentially metaphorical (and hence open) nature of many of the concepts which guide business thinking.

In approaching Sun Tzu's work and its relevance for contemporary management, it is useful and illuminating to contrast his work with that of Clausewitz. The two generals' philosophies have quite different emphases. Clausewitz stressed the logical ideal, the abstract and the absolute. The metaphor underpinning his work might be that of the machine, planned, built and then put into inexorable, predetermined motion. His writings reflect the modernist enlightenment philosophies of mechanism, cause and effect, and the clear separation of thought and action. In contrast, the *Sun Tzu Ping Fa* stresses the pragmatic, the contextual and the emergent. A key metaphor underpinning Sun Tzu's writing is that of water, and in this sense his work resonates with the wider Chinese philosophy of Taoism.

The contrasting approaches of Sun Tzu and Clausewitz are reflected in contemporary strategic management. The 'design school' of strategy (Andrews 1971; Mintzberg 1990) stresses rational conscious planning, explicitness and clarity, and the clear separation of formulation and implementation. Internal strengths and weaknesses, external opportunities and threats are assessed; a strategy (with its sub-components of goals and action plans) is formulated and then implemented. This approach echoes Clausewitz's philosophy and, indeed, the wider modernist axioms. In contrast, the more recent 'process school' of strategy – which is part antithesis, part extension of the design school – stresses process, learning, adaptability and contextuality (for example, Quinn *et al.* 1988). In this respect, the process school is closer in spirit to Sun Tzu.

However, attempts to pigeonhole Sun Tzu or Clausewitz are in many ways misleading and the much-invoked dichotomy between West and East may be regarded as ephemeral. For example, early Greek strategists such as Pericles have much in common with Sun Tzu, stressing the paradoxical nature of strategy and the need for the great strategist to combine nominally antithetical attributes. Moreover, Clausewitz regarded prescriptive systems as inadequate, stressing that theory cannot tell a person how to act but may help in developing judgement. The writings of both authors prefigured the shift in emphasis from 'planning' to 'thinking' that is occurring in strategic management today.

Three dangers are inherent in contemporary readings of ancient texts such as *Sun Tzu Ping Fa*. First, there is the danger of projection. Ancient texts can take on the role of a Rorschach inkblot, in which people find meanings that correspond to strongly held views or ideas of their own. It is perhaps not surprising, therefore, that Sun Tzu has been interpreted from a number of different perspectives and used to support disparate schools of strategic thought (for example, Chen 1994; Tung 1994; Wee *et al.* 1991).

Second, there is the issue of literalization. It is interesting to note that in the East business is closely equated with war, a notion summarized in the saying 'the marketplace is a battlefield'. The war metaphor is taken quite literally by many business people. Metaphors are more than simple analogies: they become ways of seeing and acting. Thus, one must ask: is war an appropriate metaphor for strategic management in contemporary society? Any answer must be equivocal. Possibly, as intimated above, one fundamental problem lies in the fact that we are not consciously aware of the metaphorical nature of the language often used to talk about business and strategy.

Finally, there is the question of transferability. It is not difficult to collect cases and stories about business and management, to arrange them under headings borrowed from Sun Tzu and to call this 'the application of Sun Tzu to modern management'. However, there are two problems with such an approach. First, there is the question of the transferability (or otherwise) of concepts and principles to a different sphere (from war to management), to a different era and to different nations and cultures (see CULTURE, CROSS-NATIONAL; ORGANIZATION CULTURE). Second, creative application requires the development of a new theoretical foundation on the basis of the old, just as Mao Tse-Tung articulated a theory of guerrilla warfare, which contains many concepts from Sun Tzu but which nevertheless offers new perspectives and insights appropriate to the conditions of time and place.

5 Conclusion

It is sometimes tempting to dismiss the writings of Sun Tzu as little more than 'common sense' aphorisms. However, the military strategist Captain B.H. Liddell Hart wrote: 'in that one short book was embodied almost as much about the fundamentals of strategy and tactics as I had covered in more than twenty books' (Griffith 1963). Yet, as suggested above, the paths to wisdom are not smooth. While simplistic codification or literalization of an ancient text may seem appealing, ultimately it is a sterile pursuit. It diminishes the past and impoverishes the present: the form of the original text is preserved but the essence lost. Essence cannot be reduced to mere theories or frameworks, but can only be approached with insight and inspiration. A careful study of texts such as *Sun Tzu Ping Fa* might pay dividends in providing the inspiration for a revision of contemporary strategic praxis.

YAO-SU HU

PIERRE BERTHON
HENLEY MANAGEMENT COLLEGE

Note

All translations in this entry are by the contributors.

Further reading

(References cited in the text marked *)

* Andrews, K.R. (1971) *The Concept of Corporate Strategy*, Homewood, IL: Irwin. (Regarded by many as the quintessential text on the design school of strategic management.)
* Chen, M. (1994) 'Sun Tzu's strategic thinking and contemporary business', *Business Horizons* (March–April): 42–8. (An attempt to transfer some of Sun Tzu's principles directly to contemporary business.)
* Griffith, S.B. (1963) *The Art of War*, Oxford: Oxford University Press. (A good translation, by a US Army general, of *Sun Tzu Ping Fa* and selected commentaries; also includes chapters on the text and its background, and on Sun Tzu's influence on Mao Tse-Tung and Japanese military thinking.)
  McNeilly, M. (1996) *Sun Tzu and the Art of Business: Six Strategic Principles for Managers*, Oxford: Oxford University Press. (Takes the principles of Sun Tzu and applies it for managers. Also has a website *http://www.cazmedia.com/suntzu/*)
* Mintzberg, H. (1990) 'The design school: reconsidering the basic premises of strategic management', *Strategic Management Journal* 11: 171–95. (An insightful exposition of the assumptions of the design school which triggered an ongoing debate in the literature.)
* Nakamura, H. (1964) *Ways of Thinking of Eastern Peoples*, Honolulu, HI: University of Hawaii Press. (A magnum opus that compares the ways of thinking of China, India and Japan.)
* Quinn, J.B., Mintzberg, H. and James, B. (1988) *The Strategy Process*, Englewood Cliffs, NJ: Prentice Hall. (A definitive collection of articles stressing the process school of strategic thinking.)
* Tung, R.L. (1994) 'Strategic management in east Asia', *Organizational Dynamics* 22(4): 55–65. (A description of four east Asian military classics: *Sun Tzu Ping Fa*, *The Book of Five Rings*, *The Three Kingdoms* and *The Thirty-six Stratagems*.)
* Wee, C.H., Lee, K.S. and Hidajat, B.W. (1991) *Sun Tzu: War and Management*, Singapore: Addison-Wesley. (A comprehensive discussion of Sun Tzu's ideas in terms of the traditional design-school model.)

See also: BUSINESS STRATEGIES, EAST ASIAN; CHINA, MANAGEMENT IN; COMPETITIVE STRATEGIES, DEVELOPMENT OF; MANAGEMENT EDUCATION IN ASIA PACIFIC; MILITARY MANAGEMENT; STRATEGY, IMPLEMENTATION OF

Supply chain management

1 What is a supply chain?

A supply chain is a set of suppliers and their suppliers, and customers and their customers, and the physical and information flows which link them together. The concept of a supply chain brings together insights and notions from a number of related sources – purchasing, physical distribution systems, logistics, industrial marketing, information systems and technology, and inventory management, to name a few. Negotiation, strategic alliances and customer relationship management are also often included under the supply chain umbrella. Most recently, the availability of communication through the Internet has added a new dimension to the management of the supply, bringing the prospect of increased efficiencies and improved customer service.

2 Evolution of supply chain management

Since the encompassing terms – supply chain and supply chain management – are often so broadly applied, it is helpful to trace the origins of the idea from its roots. The earliest reference to the flows of physical goods and information as a *system* is Forrester's seminal 1961 work *Industrial Dynamics* (see FORRESTER, J.W.). Forrester was first to visualize the system of industrial relationships and transactions, and to model them as examples of *information-feedback control theory*. Pushing the computer technology then available to its limits, he showed how '...organizational structure, amplification (in policies),

and time delays (in decisions and actions) interact to influence the success of the enterprise' (Forrester 1961: 13). Through *Industrial Dynamics* he offered a '... single framework for integrating the functional areas of management – marketing, production, accounting, research and development, and capital investment'.

Using insights from *servo-mechanism theory* which had evolved from his work during the Second World War at the Massachusetts Institute of Technology, Forrester (1961: 14–15) defined an 'information-feedback system' for an industrial organization:

An information-feedback system exists whenever the environment leads to a decision that results in action which affects the environment and thereby influences future decisions. This is a definition that encompasses every conscious and subconscious decision made by people. It also includes those mechanical decisions made by devices called servomechanisms.

Forrester showed how fragmented organizational structures and delays in processing and communicating information cause demand signals to become increasingly distorted (amplified) as they move upstream through the system (see ORGANIZATION STRUCTURE). This leads to misalignment of objectives, over-reaction, and instability for the system as a whole.

Although Forrester is rarely cited as its grandfather, supply chain management is in fact the first widespread application of ideas which he developed in 1961. Some of this delay in application can probably be explained by the fact that only recently has the computer technology existed to provide the information support which is required to operationalize his vision.

Proponents of *Time-Based Competition* explicitly recognize Forrester's 'pioneering work' (Stalk and Hout 1990), essentially replicating his efforts with modern computer technology, and focusing on the implications of time delays in information flows.

At the time Forrester's work was being published, the most closely related field was called *Physical Distribution Systems*:

A term employed in manufacturing and commerce to describe the broad range of activities concerned with efficient movement of finished products from the end of the production line to the consumer, and in some cases includes the movement of raw materials from the source of supply to the beginning of the production line ... Physical Distribution System activities include freight transportation, warehousing, material handling, protective packaging, inventory control, plant and warehouse selection, order processing, market forecasting and customer service.

(Bowersox *et al.* 1968)

This definition is extensive, but the focus is on the single firm and the 'efficient' outbound movement of finished goods to the customer, with consideration of inbound logistics 'in some cases'. While this describes a subset of a supply chain, it is less comprehensive, particularly in its lack of mention of associated information flows.

Ten years later, this field had evolved into *Business Logistics*:

Business logistics deals with all move-store activities that facilitate product flow from the point of material acquisition to the point of final consumption as well as the information flows that set the product in motion for the purpose of providing adequate levels of customer service at a reasonable cost ... Business Logistics is the study and management of goods and services flows and the associated information that sets these into motion.

(Ballou 1978)

This broader scope moves closer to Forrester's original ideas with the addition of the notions of 'goods and services flows' as well as information flows. But it remains focused on the individual enterprise, stopping short of involvement with suppliers and customers.

By the early 1990s, *Strategic Logistics Management* was clearly setting the stage for SCM. Lambert and Stock (1993) defined strategic logistics management as:

... the process of planning, implementing and controlling the efficient, cost-effective flow and storage of raw materials, in-process inventory, finished goods, and related information from the point-of-origin to point of consumption for the purpose of conforming to customer requirements.

Today the *supply chain* and *supply chain management* encompass all of these predecessors, adding explicit consideration of the *system* – Forrester's original idea. Developments in computer hardware and software, and recent burgeoning notions of the power of the Internet (see INTERNET), make possible more of the potential which has been noted earlier.

3 Systems effects

Conceptualizing the organizational, information, physical goods and flow characteristics of a firm's operations as a system leads to interesting and potentially valuable insights into behaviours, actions, decisions and their implications. If we understand that a real supply chain is a complex system, then we know something about it. For example, systems theory teaches us that it is better to suboptimize the whole system than to optimize subsystems individually and then try to put them together:

$$SUBOPT_{(system)} \to \to OPT_{(sub1)} + OPT_{(sub2)} + OPT_{(sub3)} .... + OPT_{(subN)}$$

This means that, while it is worthwhile to attempt to optimize one segment of a supply chain, the greatest benefit will come from analysis and management of the whole supply chain. This also alerts managers to the very likely existence of unintended effects emanating from an exercise focused on optimizing only one segment of a supply chain.

The best-known supply chain system phenomenon is the *bullwhip effect* – the amplification of variability as order information passes from one stage to another in a distribution system. The combination of time delays and inventory management decisions leads to increasingly severe swings as order information passes upstream from a retailer to a wholesaler to a distributor and finally to a manufacturer (Stalk and Hout 1990; Lee *et al.* 1997). (*The Beer Game* is the most widely known illustration of the bullwhip effect: this exercise is a mainstay of supply chain management courses and programmes [Hammond 1994; Sterman 1989]). As each link in the supply chain attempts to optimize its own position, decisions at each stage create an increasingly difficult situation for upstream suppliers.

4 Supply chains: design, analysis and management

Design of a supply chain should be an inextricable part of the product design and development process. In practice, however, a supply chain is more likely to be inherited by a manager than explicitly designed *de novo*. Whether designed from the ground up or inherited, the key management tasks are the same – establishing, maintaining and continuously improving physical and information flows to ensure flawless service to the customer. The analyses required to support this objective are substantial, and the techniques and methodologies have their roots in industrial marketing, logistics, inventory management and, more recently, information systems design.

In practice, analysis and management of a supply chain is likely to be spread throughout an organization, involving traditional departments – sales/marketing, purchasing/procurement, accounts payable/credit, warehousing/stockroom, production control and traffic/transport, to name a few. Engineering design, manufacturing/process engineering and quality assurance departments are typically involved as well, particularly for engineered products and/or components. The result is generally less than a *system*: it would be more accurately described as a supply *tangle* than a supply chain. When the supply chain extends beyond a single organization, ownership and control become central issues. As experience with Just-In-Time (JIT) systems demonstrates, it is no simple matter to establish and maintain lean supply lines (see JUST-IN-TIME PHILOSOPHY).

Supply-chain management makes a lot of sense conceptually. The difficulty is in implementation...In many cases the supply-chain management concept is a philosophical change in the way business should be done, but many organizations are still struggling to better manage processes with one supplier ... The term *supply chain* is obviously a misnomer. If we start off with a purchasing organization as a starting point and work down the supply side, it has a number of suppliers, each of which in turn has its own set of suppliers, and so on. The result is a supply network or a series of chains.

(Leenders and Fearon 1997)

Figures 1 and 2 are graphic representations of the differences between 'the supply chain' often depicted in books and articles and a real supply network. Figure 1 – 'A supply chain' – is the typical rendition with a focus on the flow of a set of goods through links in the chain. For example, this could be a representation of one stream through the supply network of a ball bearing manufacturer who ships to a great number of distributors and to some OEMs. The sequence (from the left) would be scrap steel conversion into steel rod at the first operation; conversion of steel rod into seamless tube at the second operation; and conversion of seamless tube into the races for ball bearings at the third operation. Obviously, this is only one chain within the supply network for the ball bearing product: other chains and networks would have to be shown to include the balls, spacers, packaging materials, etc.

Figure 2 is a simplified representation of a real supply chain: the focus is in the centre on a manufacturer of aircraft precision parts and components. Two of the suppliers are within the same company, as is one of the customers. Customers are suppliers, suppliers of suppliers are competitors, and customers are also suppliers. This network diagram shows graphic evidence of *system complexity* within a supply chain.

The managers who inherited this supply situation design the occasional new 'supply chain' when new parts and/or components are introduced, typically using many of the exist-

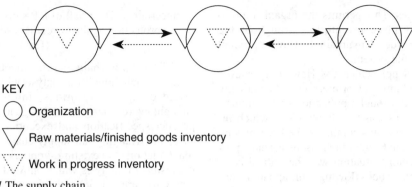

KEY

◯ Organization

▽ Raw materials/finished goods inventory

▽ Work in progress inventory

Figure 1 The supply chain

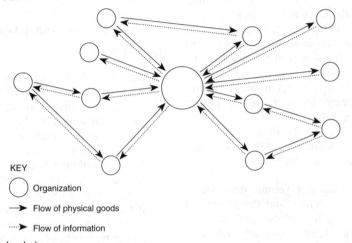

KEY

◯ Organization

→ Flow of physical goods

⋯► Flow of information

Figure 2 A supply chain

ing certified suppliers. Use of one of the internal suppliers is mandated.

Figure 1 shows inventory positions along the chain – the upside-down triangles. For simplicity these are not shown in Figure 2, but obviously that 'chain' abounds with physical stocks.

Physical flow and stoppage: inventory management

When the physical flow of goods is impeded, the result is inventory – arguably the most dangerous element in a supply chain. So the design objective is to keep physical goods moving as expeditiously as possible from one value-adder to the next. The simplest case of a supply chain is one in which the goods are physically under one roof, and are owned by one entity which can decide on each detail of the flow of goods from one operation to the

next. This never happens. Instead, a real supply chain is characterized by geographic distances, multiple and ever-changing ownership and complex inter-relationships among suppliers and customers, resulting in substantial issues of control.

Davis provides a description of Hewlett Packard's 'framework for addressing the uncertainty that plagues the performance of suppliers, the reliability of manufacturing and transportation processes, and the changing desires of customers' (Davis 1993: 35). The methodology takes a manufacturing organization as its focus and characterizes suppliers and customers by the uncertainty surrounding their supply and demand. It also characterizes manufacturing processes by the uncertainties of their supply on upstream activities. The modelling tool which results can then be used to examine the impact of these uncertainties, analyse them and assess the effects of changes in policies. This permits the organization to carefully place inventories throughout the chain in order to maintain the flow of product through the system.

The supply chain for Hewlett Packard's Deskjet family of printers was dramatically improved through application of the modelling tool, as was the supply chain which included shipments coming to the USA by ship from the Far East. In each instance, analysis of the inventory situation was the critical issue for keeping goods flowing. This apparent contradiction – stoppages (inventory) facilitating flow – is a hallmark of a complex system.

In each of the two Hewlett Packard situations, inventory *rationalization* — not just inventory reduction – was at the heart of the solution. This means the right stock level at the right place for the right reason. The net results were dramatic inventory savings as well as improved customer service. The analysis was possible because the data about uncertainty were available. Or, to be correct, the data were made available:

> … there are many performance measures, like supplier lateness and the associated variability, required to adequately model a supply chain. Ideally, this data would be collected routinely. After all, these are fundamental measures. However, we have yet to work with an organization that has the data readily available … While organizations typically imagine that they can collect the necessary data within just a few weeks, it invariably takes six months or longer.
>
> (Davis 1993)

The Hewlett Packard modeling exercise has led to results which they describe as 'downright unnerving':

> In HP factories and at the corporate level, we have exerted tremendous pressure on suppliers to improve their performance. Only a small percentage of the total stocks stems from late deliveries, etc. That is, if all deliveries arrived exactly when expected, HP's total inventory needs would drop just a few percentage points. … The same is true in manufacturing. HP processes are well-tuned … The chief culprit is demand

uncertainty. Over half of HP's inventories are protection against irregular orders.
>
> (Davis 1993: 44)

HP's supply chain improvements came about through thoughtful analysis with appropriate data. The solutions, interestingly enough, were changes to the generic/local product specification and execution in one case, and changing the supply chain through renegotiation with existing suppliers based on the results of analysis which showed the potential for dramatic inventory savings.

Information flows and delays

In 1961 Forrester wrote:

> Until recently we have been insufficiently aware of the effect of time delays, amplification, and structure on the dynamic behaviour of a system. We are coming to realize that the interactions between system components can be more important than the components themselves … Careful observation of the information network of an organization is essential to understanding its true character. Its dynamic behaviour cannot be represented without a proper treatment of the flows, levels, delays, and distortions that lie in the information channels that interweave the separate organizational channels.

A supply chain encompasses the information network which surrounds the physical flows of goods and services. Supply chain management therefore must include analyses of and decisions about the information flows within the system. For example, here is Taiichi Ohno's (see OHNO, T.) description of a unique characteristic of the Toyota Production Systems:

> In the Toyota production system, the method of setting up this daily schedule is important. During the last half of the previous month, each production line is informed of the daily production quantity for each product type. At Toyota this is called the daily level. On the other hand, the daily sequence schedule is sent only to one place – the final assembly line. This is a special characteristic of Toyota's information sys-

tem. In other companies, scheduling information is sent to every production process.

(Ohno 1988: 49)

The reason for this 'special characteristic' is that the actual daily sequence may in fact vary from that planned because Kanbans – linked to actual customer demand – will be used to sequence assembly. Production will be driven by the most recent information available. The low inventory positions within the Toyota production system are only possible with this close linkage with fresh information.

The Boston Consulting Group has provided details about the impact of decision delays on organizations. Stalk and Hout (1990: 76) report that:

> ... the amount of time required to execute a service or an order, manufacture and deliver a product is far less than the actual time the service or product spends in the value-delivery system. For example, a manufacturer of heavy vehicles takes 45 days to prepare an order for assembly, but only 16 hours to assemble each vehicle. The vehicle is actually receiving value for less than 1 percent of the time it spends in the system ... The 0.05 to 5 rule highlights the poor 'time productivity' of most organizations since most products and many services are actually receiving value for only 0.05 to 5 percent of the time they are in the value delivery systems of their companies.

They go on to provide details of what is happening during the non-productive time:

> During the 95 to 99.5 percent of the time a product or service is not receiving value while in the value-delivery system, the product or service is waiting. The waiting has three components, which are the amounts of time lost while waiting for:
>
> – completion of the batch a particular product or service is a part of as well as the completion of the batch *ahead* of the batch a particular product is a part of
>
> – physical and intellectual rework to be completed

> – management to get around to making and executing the decision to send the batch on to the next step of the value-adding process.

> Generally the 95 to 99.5 percent of the time lost divides almost equally among these three categories.

(Stalk and Hout 1990: 76–7)

The 'value-adding process' is essentially the supply chain. The numbers above are examples of the impact of information delays (where a decision is a piece of information) and demonstrate the potential benefits for excellence in supply chain management.

5 Supply chain management

Supply chain management is what the name implies – the management of a complex system with its complex of suppliers, customers, physical and information flows, and issues of geography, ownership and control. Given the nature of the supply chain, supply chain management is necessarily a strategic business (see STRATEGY, CONCEPT OF). Looking back to its precursors, supply chain management at the strategic level can – and should – encompass the fields and analyses which comprised physical distribution management and logistics.

A convenient and helpful context into which supply chain management can be placed is the classification scheme first introduced by Anthony (1965) – a taxonomy for managerial activity which is based on task and information requirements. As an accountant, Anthony was concerned about the quantities, characteristics and nature of information being provided to organizations as computer-based systems began to infiltrate business and industry. His 'framework' seems simple today but at the time of its introduction it was a profound insight – the three levels of managerial activity require different types of information from different sources: simply aggregating and summarizing historical accounting data, for example, does not provide sufficient information for managerial control. With its focus on management information, Anthony's taxonomy provides an appropriate outline for the managerial activities, analyses and decisions which permeate management of a supply chain.

Anthony's framework distinguishes between strategic planning, managerial control and operational control (emphasis added):

> *Strategic planning* is the process of deciding on objectives of the organization, on changes in these objectives, on the resources used to attain these objectives, and on the policies that are to govern the acquisition, use, and disposition of these resources … *Management control* is '…the process by which managers assure that resources are obtained and used effectively and efficiently in the accomplishment of the organization's activities … *Operational control* is … the process of assuring that specific tasks are carried out effectively and efficiently.
>
> (Anthony 1965)

Supply chain management assumes the existence of relationships between and among organizations, some of whom may be competitors. This can include high-level 'strategic alliances', 'strategic partnerships', collaborative arrangements among numbers of separate independent organizations and enterprises, etc. At this level, there can be little doubt that supply chain management is a strategic undertaking. If evidence is required, the United States Congress enacted legislation to distinguish appropriate supply chain collaboration from non-competitive behaviour which would be actionable under American antitrust legislation:

> The basic notion of supply chain management is grounded on the belief that efficiency can be improved by sharing information and by joint planning. The enactment of the Cooperative Research and Development Act of 1994, as amended in 1993, signaled a significant shift in the federal government's antitrust position to encourage firms to work cooperatively to foster increased competitiveness. Widespread realization that cooperation is both permissible and encouraged has stimulated interest in the formation of supply chain relationships … The supply chain perspective shifts the channel arrangement from a loosely linked group of independent businesses to a coordinated effort focused on efficiency improvement and increased competitiveness. In essence, overall orientation is shifted from inventory management by each individual participant to a pipeline perspective.
>
> (Bowersox and Closs 1996: 101)

Managerial control is required within supply chain management, so issues, activities, tasks and analyses which comprise logistics management are necessary – distribution channel management, customer service definition and provision, transportation management, warehousing and inventory management, purchasing and procurement, decision support, etc. The need for the analyses and decisions implied within each of these examples from logistics management does not disappear when supply chain management is invoked. The difference is that this is done within the context of strategic decisions and resource allocations, with constant awareness of both the power and peril of local optimization. At the operational control level, supply chain management moves towards day-to-day execution and control in the context of the managerial decisions which were in turn made in the context of strategic plans.

An interesting example of supply chain management which is not dependent on a computer-based solution is the *JIT II* system developed and successfully implemented by the Bose Corporation in Framingham, Massachusetts (Dixon and Porter 1994). Sole-source suppliers of non-core goods and services provide Bose with an *inplant* – a managerial-level person who works for the supplier but is resident at the Bose facility. The supplier is responsible for determining and fulfilling Bose' requirements. To accomplish this, *inplants* have access to Bose' manufacturing and assembly schedules: no Bose employee actually orders goods from the supplier. So, for example, the supplier of small plastic parts has his own computer with him at Bose and makes his own scheduling decisions based on what he sees in the Bose schedules.

JIT II means that Bose has no purchasers for small plastic parts, and the supplier has no sales personnel calling on Bose. The cost savings from this are real, but the primary benefit is superb delivery performance on the part of the supplier. There are now more than ten such suppliers within Bose, from printing to stamped metal parts to inbound/outbound freight. Improvement in the flow of information has provided the foundation for improvements in delivery performance, cost, quality and inventory positions for the partners.

The JIT II concept begins at the strategic level with a surprisingly simple and straightforward 'evergreen' contract (a rolling one-year agreement). Inplants and their Bose counterparts are the managerial controls who make decisions at the master schedule level. Operational control is spread between the Bose employees who make products and the suppliers' employees who supply goods and services.

Supply chain management encompasses the supply activities of the firm, from the highest to the lowest level in the organization, and it implies crossing organizational and enterprise boundaries. As such, it clearly is a systems view of the flow of information, materials and services – and the decisions which encourage or impede the flow – through organizations. In practice, the scope of a supply chain under management is likely to be more narrowly focused, most likely on a particular firm's immediate upstream (Tier 1) suppliers and immediate downstream customers.

6 Conclusion

Information systems and technology development now make possible dramatic improvements in information flows within and among organizations, at least in theory. The Internet, in particular, has been viewed as a revolutionary change in information capability. However, as recent events have shown, software and hardware alone do not guarantee smooth, effective and efficient information flows, nor do they necessarily generate decisions which result in optimal sub-systems, much less good sub-optimal systems.

What current technology does promise is the capability to improve an organization's productivity and competitiveness through information support. But this can only be real-ized through sound decision-making supported by old-fashioned analyses which can now be expanded to cover broader aspects of the organization's supply arrangements.

LINDA G. SPRAGUE
UNIVERSITY OF NEW HAMPSHIRE, USA, AND
CHINA EUROPE INTERNATIONAL BUSINESS
SCHOOL

VASSILIOS P. VALSAMAKIS
ROLLS-ROYCE PLC

Further reading

(References cited in the text marked *)

* Anthony, R.N. (1965) *Planning and Control Systems: A Framework for Analysis*, USA: Harvard University Graduate School of Business Administration.
* Ballou, R.H. (1978) *Basic Business Logistics*, USA, Prentice-Hall.
* Bowersox, D.J and Closs, D.J. (1996) *Logistical Management: The Integrated Supply Chain Process*, USA: McGraw-Hill. (Comprehensive description of logistics activities, application of logistics principles to gain competitive advantage and discussion on logistics integration.)
* Bowersox, D.J., Smykay, E.W. and LaLonde, B.J. (1968) *Physical Distribution Management: Logistics Problems of the Firm*, revised edn, New York: Macmillan Company.
* Davis, Tom (1993) 'Effective supply chain management', *Sloan Management Review* (Summer), 35–46.
* Dixon, L. and Porter A.M. (1994) *JIT II: A Revolution in Buying and Selling*, USA: Cahners Publications. (Origins and implementation of a unique collaborative arrangement in a supplier-customer relationship: 'in-plant' supplier personnel assume customer functions traditionally performed by customer personnel, thereby ensuring better, faster communication and lower costs.)
Ford, D. (ed.) (1997) *Understanding Business Markets: Interaction, Relationships and Networks*, London: The Dryden Press. (Focuses on understanding and analysing industrial markets: individual interactions between buyers and sellers are viewed in the context of a relationship in which both parties are active and can influence mutual behaviours.)
* Forrester, J.W. (1961) *Industrial Dynamics*, USA: MIT Press. (Pioneering work into the study of industrial systems which shows how organizational structure, policies, and time delays in de-

cisions and actions interact to influence stability and growth for the system as a whole.)

* Hammond, J.H. (1994) *The Beer Game*, USA: Harvard Business School (#9-694-104). (Current version of a popular exercise which demonstrates the impact of time lags and information gaps in a 4-level supply chain system.)

* Lambert, D.M and Stock, J.R. (1993) *Strategic Logistics Management*, Homewood, IL: Irwin. (Textbook on logistics covering customer service, transportation, warehousing, distribution channels, procurement, forecasting, and inventory management.)

* Lee, H.L., Padmanabhan, V. and Whang, S. (1997) 'The bullwhip effect in supply chains', *Sloan Management Review* (Spring) 93–102.

* Leenders, M.R. and Fearon, H.E. (1997) *Purchasing and Supply Management* 11th edn, Homewood, IL: Irwin. (Classic textbook on purchasing strategies, policies and procedures, including a chapter on supply-chain management and supplier relationships.)

* Ohno, T. (1988) *Toyota Production System: Beyond Large-Scale Production*, USA: Productivity Press. (English translation of the original Japanese edition *Toyota seisan hoshiki*, Japan: Diamond, Inc., 1978.)

Simchi-Levi, D., Kaminsky, P. and Simchi-Levi E. (1999) *Designing and Managing the Supply Chain: Concepts, Strategies and Cases*, USA: McGraw-Hill/Irwin. (Award-winning textbook with broad coverage of SCM issues; includes cases and problems.)

* Stalk, G., Jr and Hout, T.M. (1990) *Competing Against Time*, USA: The Free Press. (Focused on the importance of time as a competitive weapon: reviews strategies employed by time-based competitors to gain competitive advantage through lead-time compression and supply-chain integration.)

* Sterman, J.D. (1989) 'Modeling managerial behaviour: misperceptions of feedback in a dynamic decision making environment', *Management Science* 35 (3): 321–39.

See also: FORRESTER, J.W.; JUST-IN-TIME PHILOSOPHY; MANUFACTURING STRATEGY; OHNO, T.; ORGANIZATION BEHAVIOUR; ORGANIZATION STRUCTURE; TAYLOR, F.W.; TOTAL QUALITY MANAGEMENT

Sweden, management in

Overview

Swedish managers have for more than 100 years contributed to the international success of Swedish multinational organizations. However, they are often perceived by non-Swedes as puzzling on account of their 'soft' management style and their unclear communication style. The very employee-oriented Swedish management style is firmly rooted in Swedish culture and has evolved during the twentieth century in symbiosis with the political and industrial arena. Some of the most distinctive characteristics of management in Sweden include egalitarianism and empowering, cooperation and teamwork, conflict avoidance and consensus seeking, as well as rationality, fairness and pragmatism. The decentralized, flat Swedish organizations characterized by informal control are paralleled at the individual level by employees who prefer their independence and abhor supervision. The view of management presented in this article is in itself a strong reflection of the employee-oriented values prevalent in the Swedish culture.

1 Introduction

The Kingdom of Sweden has a 1000-year-old history as a sovereign state. Sweden has had a parliamentary democracy since 1917. The major parties represent political views ranging from conservative, liberal, Christian, environmental and socialist to communist. The Social Democratic Labour Party has been in power for most of the twentieth century. From the 1990s and into the twenty-first century, Sweden witnessed a stronger polarization between conservative and socialist supporters, while the in-between parties have been marginalized.

Sweden is the fifth largest country in Europe, but it is small in terms of population with 8,863,000 inhabitants. Sweden is ethnically and religiously very homogenous although this has been slowly changing during the last centuries. Currently roughly 89 per cent of the population are ethnic Swedes and about 86 per cent of the population belong to the Evangelical Lutheran State Church of Sweden. Philosophically, Sweden has been strongly influenced by Rousseau's egalitarian ideas and the idea of the 'noble savage', while Hobbesian thinking was strongly rejected, particularly during the twentieth century. Another important source of influence is Descartes, in particular his thoughts on rationality and 'I think, therefore I exist'.

Sweden is a capitalist market economy with a large public sector. In this way, private ownership co-exists with a strong welfare state. Sweden has a comparatively large percentage of women in the salaried workforce (about 80 per cent of the 20–64 age bracket). A majority of the employees in the public sector are women and about 50 per cent of the representatives in parliament are women. In the private sector women dominate in the insurance, banking and finance, retailing and restaurant industries. However, there is a striking gender imbalance across hierarchical levels (Höök 1995). Only 9 per cent at the executive level are women. In Sweden's 70 largest firms a mere 3 per cent of top management and 4 per cent of the board members are women. Consequently, management in Sweden is homogenous not only from a cultural, but also from a gender perspective. To be a manager was not seen as an occupation per se before the latter half of the twentieth century (Maccoby 1991). Consequently, management education and training was not pursued to any large extent. Managers were most often internally recruited engineers from a very small group of individuals with a similar educational, social and cultural background. The frequent choice of engineers as managers was not surprising given the engineering foundation and focus of the majority of Swedish companies. Slowly, together with a demand for market-oriented managers, this attitude has changed (Maccoby 1991), and managers are recruited from the business schools. Managers-to-be also participate in management development programmes both within and outside Sweden.

Sweden experienced late industrialization and early internationalization, which transformed in large parts of Sweden a poor agricultural society into a highly developed industrial society. In some areas, the flourishing protoindustry within woodwork, metalwork and textiles during the nineteenth century was not only a step towards industrialization but also a natural part of agricultural life (Magnusson 2000). Before 1870, the urban population was around 10 per cent. Less than a hundred years later, more than 80 per cent of the population were living in cities. The rich natural mining and forestry resources were important for the Swedish economy at an early stage, with some of the mills dating from the thirteenth century (Sölvell, Zander and Porter 1991). In the seventeenth and eighteenth centuries, the Bergslagen region in Sweden was the leading world supplier of iron. In the twentieth century, the pulp and paper production companies are leading international suppliers. The development of the mechanical and engineering industries was based on a number of significant Swedish inventions, or improvements of existing technology; for example, Alfa-Laval was established due to Gustaf de Laval's centrifugal separator and Nobel Industries started

with Alfred Nobel's invention of dynamite. Many of the companies were internationally active at an early stage. The small domestic market in Sweden made this a necessity. Companies such as AGA, Asea, SKF and Swedish Match had subsidiaries abroad, e.g. in South America and Asia, before the First World War. International trade and exchange has always been important in Sweden and the value of exports amount to 40 per cent of GDP. On a per capita basis, Sweden has more multinational corporations than any other country in the world (Maccoby 1991).

2 Decentralized organizations with centralized informal control

Swedish companies' undamaged production facilities together with their technological leadership in several industries were a powerful combination in the post-war era. It is often said that Swedish companies in those days did not employ any salespeople since they only needed order-takers. Consequently, premium prices could be charged for the high-quality sought-after products that were offered. Companies grew quickly, predominantly through green-field investments and established mother–daughter structures rather than working through international divisions operated from the home country (Hedlund and Åman 1984). Thus, the managing directors of the subsidiaries were pioneers, developing the local company and market. They took initiatives, enjoyed high autonomy and reported directly to the president of the parent company, subjected only to informal personalized control. The strong position of subsidiaries was one of the reasons that Swedish multinationals, as they grew and diversified, initially did not adopt global product division structures. Instead, many opted for a matrix structure where both subsidiary and product division managers are in charge. Another reason is that matrix organization functions reasonably well in a Swedish context, since authority is competence based and hierarchical lines are bypassed when necessary in Swedish corporations (see CULTURE, CROSS-NATIONAL).

Another feature of Swedish industry is that a few ownership groups dominate and constitute the main labour market for young ambitious managers. These include both financial and industrial corporations similar to those found in both Germany and Japan. The two largest spheres are controlled by the Wallenberg family and Svenska Handelsbanken, a major bank, and were established at the beginning of the twentieth century. Swedish industry consists of constellations of corporations characterized by cross-ownership, interlocking boards of directors, within-group manager transfers and access to capital (Collin 1993). These groups are the means of spreading risk through diversification within the group without losing control, since the interlocking boards of directors together with the transfer of managers facilitate both coordination and centralized control. Thus, Swedish corporations are characterized by decentralized organizational structures with centralized informal personalized control (including evaluation of performance and feedback), and a management style based on initiative and independence.

3 Constructive cooperation and collaborative coaching

Beginning in the 1930s, the Swedish political scene has been characterized by what is often referred to as the 'Swedish Model', a model that resulted in constructive cooperation between labour and capital. The governing Social Democrats, the unions and the employers have all placed importance on collective bargaining and industrial relations (85 per cent of the workforce are union members). For example, human resource issues have been handled at a societal level instead of company level since negotiations were carried out between groups rather than between individuals (Berglund and Lövstedt 1996) (see HUMAN RESOURCE MANAGEMENT IN EUROPE). Furthermore, the alliance between labour and capital strongly contributed to the social forces resulting in Sweden becoming a member of the European Union in 1995 (Bieler 2000). At the end of the twentieth century, Sweden faces a tougher economic climate, a more fragmented industry and a declining belief in the efficiency of collective bargaining as a system. A move towards more individualistic ideals permeates social as well as work-related issues concurrently, which may bring the curtain down on the Swedish Model (Berglund and Lövstedt 1996).

One of the important cultural elements underlying the Swedish Model was a belief in the superior efficiency and results of cooperation and collaboration compared to competition and confrontation. That good governance should be based on connecting subordinates' interest with superordinates' interests was expressed as a Swedish value as early as 1809 (Linnell and Löfgren 1995). Teamwork is strongly emphasized in the Swedish educational system as well as at all levels in organizational life. Self-managing teams, e.g. Volvo's production plant in Kalmar, received international attention in the 1970s. Twenty years later, several of the Swedish multinational companies declare that working in teams is a part of their corporate culture. Furthermore, Swedish employees consider that their managers should encourage cooperation and make the employees feel part of a team. In other words, the manager in Sweden should act as a coach (Zander 1997).

4 Avoiding conflict and achieving consensus

If cooperation is the preferred *modus operandi* in Swedish organizations, consensus is the preferred decision-taking vehicle. A consensus-based process ensures that when a decision is taken it is well aired, discussed from all parties' perspective and agreed upon by all parties involved. This facilitates not only a smooth and fast, but also a relatively tension-free implementation phase. Thus, influence is based on consultation and participation. Confrontation or aggressiveness is viewed as leading to conflict, which is perceived as negative since conflict should be avoided at all costs. There is also a rational aspect to conflict avoidance in that there is a strong belief that conflict is ineffective and will hamper any process rather than energize and inspire it (Jönsson 1996).

The consensus-oriented decision making is perceived as slow and cumbersome, and

Swedish managers are often seen as indecisive by employees in Swedish companies' foreign subsidiaries. However, the consensus process is an important mechanism for ensuring coordinated activities in decentralized Swedish corporations. A high level of conflict avoidance is prevalent in all parts of Swedish society, in particular within the family and in the workplace. The importance of agreeing is exceptional. A typical Swedish reaction when differing opinions are expressed is that 'there is no use in discussing this since we disagree'. It is difficult to express disagreement or negative opinions, as well as criticize others. If differing or negative opinions are expressed aggressively, they are often taken personally. One reason is that honesty is an important value in Sweden. If honesty can lead to hurt feelings or conflict, it is seen as better to remain silent. Thus, in the attempts to be careful and diplomatic, misunderstandings can occur. For example, it has been argued that Swedish managers are the only managers who can fire non-Swedish employees and leave them with the impression that they have received a promotion.

5 Egalitarian ideals and empowering realities

An overarching political goal in post-war Sweden has been to build a society labelled 'folkhemmet' (the home of the people). The power of the 'folkhemmet' concept lies in the fact that it can be seen as representing a shared base of cultural Swedish values (see DENMARK, MANAGEMENT IN; NORWAY, MANAGEMENT IN). One of the important values, egalitarianism, has influenced and shaped life in Sweden in general and Swedish management in particular. Taxes are used as an income redistribution tool and the income gap in Swedish society has been substantially reduced. Equality in the workplace in the form of employee influence and participation in decision making at all levels was legislated in Swedish law when it could no longer be handled by agreement by the labour market parties (Berglund and Lövstedt 1996). The egalitarian vision was also pursued in the area of communication by abolishing the extensive use of titles and the formal way of addressing

people. This further reduced the gap between different groups in society as well as in organizations. The gaps that do still exist are not easy to identify in Swedish culture where it is important to be modest and downplay one's achievements (Lawrence and Spybey 1997). Overt display of status, authority or wealth is abhorred. There is a social requirement not to stand out, not to believe in any way that one is special. This is expressed in an old Swedish saying: 'Any one person is as good as any other person'.

In parallel to the development of the employee participation legislation and the activities aimed at reducing status differentiation in Swedish society, Swedish companies transformed from hierarchical organizations to flat decentralized structures. In these organizations, decision-making responsibility is also delegated to employees at lower levels. In the 1990s, employees want their managers to empower them even further (Zander 1997). They want to be given responsibility, to participate not only in decision making but also in strategy discussions. In addition, they consider that their managers should appreciate not only their initiatives but also their advice.

6 Independent self-reliance and social caring dependence

The importance of independence and self-reliance is expressed not only in the desire for empowerment, but also in the limited appreciation of supervision (Zander 1997) (see EMPOWERMENT). In general, supervision is seen as an expression of the manager's distrust in the employees' ability and competence. The need for independence and self-reliance is part of the historical baggage of a people suffering hardships under power-hungry kings, as well as experiencing strong influence from the Protestant ethic. To be dependent on others is seen as something negative that should be avoided. It is viewed as important to rear responsible, independent individuals who make their own decisions and form their own lives at an early age (Sjögren 1993). Also, schoolchildren are encouraged to take initiatives, to question authority, and to develop their sense of responsibility. In Sweden, it is also important to be 'duktig'. This means both to be good at what you do, skilful and competent, and to be good-hearted as a person. To be 'duktig' often involves taking responsibility as well as taking the initiative to do something or to volunteer to do something that is needed. In the 1990s, it was intensively debated whether Swedish women had fallen into the 'goodness trap' ('duktighetsfällan') in their attempts to be the perfect wife and mother and at the same time succeed in their careers.

In Sweden, over the years, there have been elements of reliance on the state that are often expressed as 'being cared for from the cradle to the grave'. This 'caring' is expressed in a range of public services and welfare benefits as well as liberal employee benefit plans (e.g. a five-week minimum annual paid vacation and more than one year of paid paternal leave). On a positive note, people feel secure, supported and 'taken care of' by the state whenever it is necessary. The negative side is that it is also experienced as a 'Big Brother attitude' and the Swedish authorities are perceived as interfering in people's lives in a paternalistic manner. Thus, paradoxically, independence and self-reliance co-exist with dependence and reliance in Sweden. Independent self-reliance is valued in the family and at work, while dependence on social caring and security is a characteristic of Swedish society. Swedish management is characterized by employee independence and self-reliance as well by as their reluctance to be supervised.

7 The logic of order and the principle of fairness

Swedes are seen as good organizers, sometimes referred to as the Prussians of the North. This was presented as a typical Swedish characteristic at the beginning of the twentieth century (Linnell and Löfgren 1995). For example, Sweden is internationally renowned for its demographic statistics where citizens' births, marriages, deaths and movements from one parish to another have been registered since 1749. Rationality, reason, logic, facts, function and order have been valued in the Swedish context for a long time. This ensures excellence not only in organizing, but also in

engineering and science. In the eighteenth century Carl von Linné presented his binomial nomenclature categorization of about 6000 species, and Anders Celsius established the Celsius scale for the thermometer. In Sweden, it is also important not only to base work on reason and logic, but also to argue non-emotionally based on factual and rational arguments in order to convince and succeed. To Swedes this is not only to be rational, but also to be 'modern', which is seen as an important basis for future development (Daun 1992).

Law and order, fairness and universal application of laws and regulations are viewed as valuable cornerstones that permeate family life and education as well as Swedish society as a whole. Swedish society is heavily regulated in terms of rules, regulations and recommendations. There is a strong belief in the authorities, and that they will act in the people's best interest. Trust that the legal system will ensure justice is strong. The office of the 'Ombudsman' was established in 1809 with the responsibility of overseeing that laws are enforced and that justice and fairness are created. In Swedish organizations however, there are few rules and regulations, but these rules are intended to be followed and not to be broken. Experience, pragmatism, fairness and 'commonsense' rule in both Swedish companies and society at large. Thus, belief in rationality and facts together with a universal application of law is, according to Swedes, the basis of a modern country and a description of Swedish society. Consequently, Swedish management and the organization of work is based on the logic of order and the principle of fairness, but with a much lesser amount of formal rules and regulations. To communicate with facts and figures rather than colourful emotional arguments is a necessity given the Swedish belief in rationality and modernity.

8 Conversation is silver and communication is gold

Swedes in general are often experienced as 'reserved' or 'stiff' with a limited, if any, capacity for small talk (which in Swedish is translated into 'cold talk'). Silence and shyness are seen as something positive in the

Swedish culture. In the upbringing of children this is expressed by the compliment 'a nice quiet child'. According to an old Swedish saying, 'talking is silver and silence is gold'. A silent person is seen as someone who is a good listener, who thinks before speaking and when speaking reflects good judgement. It is also, according to Swedish values, impolite to interrupt someone. Verbal acrobats and strong debaters are viewed with the suspicion that the person is 'all talk and no action'.

Paradoxically, the silent Swedes who are unwilling to engage in personal talk outside work and in small talk when doing business prefer frequent communication with their managers and colleagues about both work and personal-oriented matters (Zander 1997). Communication within the organization is perceived as important for coordination and informal control, as well as for decision making and consensus seeking. Swedish managers are, however, often seen as indirect and unclear in their communication and they are often referred to by non-Swedes as 'managing by nods and winks' (Hedlund and Åman 1984) (see ORGANIZATION CULTURE). It is difficult for non-Swedes to capture the subtleties of the highly context-based communication. Since conflict is to be avoided in the Swedish context, there are very many ways of disagreeing or saying no without explicitly saying so. Swedes have in this respect been said to be the Japanese of the North (Daun 1986). Since Swedes draw a clear line between private and work life, there is usually very limited talk about non-business-related topics when doing business. Trust in business life is primarily created by fulfilling business commitments rather than establishing a relationship based on non-business-oriented discussions.

9 Conclusions

Swedish management style is often perceived by non-Swedes as 'soft' and difficult to understand. The *perceived softness* is primarily due to three reasons. First, that the Swedish management style is based on egalitarian ideals expressed in employee empowerment, in the form of delegation of responsibility and appreciation of individual initiative. Second, that supervision is not a part of the Swedish

manager's role. Swedish managers carry out only limited follow-up, and informal personalized control is exercised. Commonsense, the logic of order and the principles of fairness have to a large extent replaced formalized rules and regulations. However, when rules are applicable, they are universally applied. Third, it is believed that cooperation is a superior mode of working and that the manager should act as a coach and encourage the employees to work together and to feel part of a team.

The Swedish manager is also *perceived as difficult to understand* by non-Swedes. The first reason for this is the conflict-avoiding, consensus-achieving, context-dependent nature of the manager's communication. The second reason is the rational, fact-based, unemotional and unflavoured character of argumentation carried out by Swedish managers. The third reason is the Swedish manager's limited small talk outside the organization, while there is an abundance of general as well as personal communication inside the organization.

The major challenge for Swedish management in the twenty-first century is to understand the expectations of an increasingly multi-cultural workforce and to successfully manage the diversity of expectations to which this situation gives rise.

LENA ZANDER
INSTITUTE OF INTERNATIONAL BUSINESS
STOCKHOLM SCHOOL OF ECONOMICS

Further reading

(References cited in the text marked *)

Austin, P. B. (1968) *On Being Swedish*, London: Secker and Warburg. (Reflections on Swedish society, Swedish character and social norms in the 1960s.)

* Berglund, J. and Lövstedt, J. (1996) 'Sweden: the fate of Human Resource Management in a "folkish" society', in T. Clark (ed.) *European Human Resource Management*, Oxford: Blackwell. (Develops the idea that human resource management issues in Sweden have not been handled by companies, but by society.)

* Bieler, A. (2000) *Globalisation and Enlargement of the European Union: Austrian and Swedish Social Forces in the Struggle Over Membership*

(Warwick Studies in Globalisation), London: Routledge. (This book analyses why Austria and Sweden joined the EU at such a moment (1995) when in fact the EU's development towards a neo-liberal economic policy – embodied in the Internal Market and the convergence criteria of Economic and Monetary Union – endangered their traditional Keynesian economic policy making, and at a time when the steps towards a Common Foreign and Security Policy threatened their neutrality.)

Brewster, C., Lundmark, A. and Holden, L. (1993) *'A Different Tack' An Analysis of British and Swedish Management Styles*, Stockholm: Studentlitteratur; Chartwell Bratt Ltd. (Contrasts the experience of British managers in Sweden and Swedish managers in Britain, placing the focus on expatriation and management.)

* Collin, S.-O. (1993) 'The brotherhood of the Swedish sphere', *International Studies of Management and Organization*, Spring. (Argues that transaction-cost theory fails to explain financial groups in Sweden by using 'market' or 'hierarchy', instead proposes 'brotherhood'.)

Czarniawska-Joerges, B. (1993) 'Sweden: a modern project, post-modern implementation', in D. J. Hickson (ed.) *Management in Western Europe*, Berlin: Walter de Gruyter. (Discusses management of private organizations in terms of pragmatism and reorganization, and public organizations in terms of identity and modernity.)

* Daun, Å. (1992) 'Modern and modest. mentality and self-stereotypes among Swedes', in A. Sjögren, and L. Janson (eds) *Culture and Management – In the Field of Ethnology and Business Administration*, Stockholm: The Swedish Immigration Institute and Museum, and Institute of International Business. (Discusses Swedish mentality in terms of perceptions and self-stereotypes.)

* Daun, Å. (1986) 'The Japanese of the North – The Swedes of Asia?', *Ethnologia Scandinavica*: 5–15. (Compares Swedish and Japanese mentality from an ethnological perspective; several articles and books on Swedish mentality written by Daun and other ethnologists are in Swedish.)

Gannon, M.J. and Associates (1994) *Understanding Global Cultures: Metaphorical Journeys Through 17 Countries*, London: Sage Publications. (The Swedish summer house is used as a metaphor to describe Swedish culture.)

Hampden-Turner, C. and Trompenaars, A. (1993) *The Seven Cultures of Capitalism*, London: Currency Doubleday. (Analysing Swedish leadership, management, organization, human resource issues, product quality and company

development from a national cultural perspective.)

* Hedlund, G and Åman, P. (1984) *Managing Relationships with Foreign Subsidiaries – organization and control in Swedish MNCs*, Stockholm: Sveriges Mekanförbund. (Examines management of foreign subsidiaries in Swedish corporations by studying organization, goals, control and cross-cultural relationships.)

* Höök, P. (1995) 'Women at the top – a survey of Swedish industry', in A. Wahl (ed.) *Men's Perceptions of Women and Management*, Stockholm: Ministry of Health and Social Affairs. (Maps the presence of women executives, and perceptions and actions towards change versus preserving the current situation.)

* Jönsson, S. (ed.) (1996) *Perspectives of Scandinavian Management*, Kungälv: Gothenburg Research Institute and Gothenburg School of Economics and Commercial Law. (Scandinavian researchers compare management in four Nordic countries; the project has resulted in many books and articles published in Swedish.)

Laine-Sveiby, K. (1987) *Svenskhet som strategi*, Stockholm: Timbro. (An ethnological study where Swedish management is contrasted with Finnish management, and Swedishness is discussed as a strategic advantage.)

* Lawrence, P. and Spybey, L. (1997) 'Sweden: Management and Society', in D. Hickson (ed.) *Exploring Management Across the World: Selected Readings*, London: Penguin Books. (Explores the relationship between Swedish society and management mobility and motivation from a British perspective.)

* Linnell, B. and Löfgren, M. (eds) (1995) *Svenska krusbär: En historiebok om Sverige och Svenskarna*, Stockholm: Bonnier Alba. (Authors from different disciplines writing in Swedish about Sweden, the Swedes and Swedish mentality from 1434 to 1993.)

* Maccoby, M. (ed.) (1991) *Sweden at the Edge: Lessons for American and Swedish Managers*, Philadelphia: University of Pennsylvania Press. (Articles covering the transition of industry and public sector, organizational transformation in Swedish companies and Swedish activities in the United States.)

* Magnusson, L. (2000) *Economic History of Sweden*, London: Routledge. (This book represents the first recent attempt to provide a comprehensive treatment of Sweden's economic development since the middle of the eighteenth century. It traces the rapid industrialization, the political currents and the social ambitions that transformed Sweden from a backward agrarian economy into what is now regarded by many as a model welfare state.)

Phillips-Martinsson, J. (1981/1991) *Swedes As Others See Them – Facts, Myths or a Communication Complex?*, Lund: Studentlitteratur. (Discusses facts and myths about Sweden, Swedish communication and management style, and offers advice for doing business in Sweden.)

* Sjögren, A. (1993) *Här går gränsen: Om integritet och kulturella mönster i Sverige och Medelhavsområdet,* Stockholm: Arena. (Explores integrity and cultural patterns in Sweden and the Mediterranean region – summary in English.)

* Sölvell, Ö., Zander, I. and Porter, M. E. (1991) *Advantage Sweden*, Stockholm: Norstedts. (Explores the evolution of competitive firms, industries and clusters of industries in the Swedish economy.)

* Zander, L. (1997) *The Licence to Lead – An 18-Country Study of the Relationship between Employees' Preferences Regarding Interpersonal Leadership and National Culture*, Stockholm: Institute of International Business. (Published PhD dissertation examining employees' preferences for empowering, coaching, directing and communication from a national cultural perspective.)

See also: CULTURE, CROSS-NATIONAL; DENMARK, MANAGEMENT IN; EUROPE, MANAGEMENT IN; FINLAND, MANAGEMENT IN; HUMAN RESOURCE MANAGEMENT IN EUROPE; INDUSTRIAL RELATIONS IN EUROPE; MANAGEMENT OF TECHNOLOGY IN EUROPE; NORWAY, MANAGEMENT IN; PERSPECTIVES ON MANAGEMENT IN EUROPE; STRATEGY IN EUROPE

Switzerland, management in

Overview

Switzerland is the most prosperous country in Europe and is one of the best managed. It has many large multinational companies and, in spite of its small population, has an impact on international business disproportionate to its size. In spite of a lack of natural resources it has grown rapidly economically by seeking export markets for both manufactured products and services, value-added via quality, and by investing in people. Yet some see its very economic virtues as potential vices, given the structural problems in the economy, as we move into the new millennium.

1 Introduction

Switzerland lies at the heart of western Europe and has a commanding strategic position. It has been united as a confederation for over 700 years and has followed a policy of armed neutrality for centuries. It is multilingual and is basically divided into three major language zones, German, French and Italian, along with one minor zone, Romansch. It is landlocked, mountainous and has little arable land (around 10 per cent of its land mass). It was until recently poor, but the past century has seen the fast growth of its economy, and today it has strong chemical and manufacturing industries, banking and insurance sectors and tourism as sources of wealth. Although its agriculture is somewhat protected, industry and services no longer have any meaningful tariff barriers. Swiss managers have to look outwards to survive.

2 Economy

The Swiss economy is the envy of its neighbours and is often held up as a model. Based on a cautious macroeconomic policy, tight money is the order of the day. Its economy looks like a safe haven. Its gross national product (GNP) per capita is still the highest in Europe, estimated at over $40,000 in 2000. With a small but highly educated and trained population of just over seven million, it has a great deal of wealth to share around. Quality of life is high, with a life expectancy of around 78 years and an educational and healthcare structure of a particularly high standard. Unemployment was listed as just under 2.5 per cent in 2000.

The economy is prosperous and stable but has in recent years been affected by both the world recession and its structural weaknesses, which include a very high wage structure and a relatively over-valued currency. Swiss bankers are traditionally conservative and inflation has been low, just under 1.5 per cent in 2000. Reductions in public spending are aimed at having a balanced budget by the year 2001. Although Switzerland has stayed outside both the European Union (EU) and the European Economic Area, exports are heavily geared to the EU market (see EUROPEAN UNION; EUROPE, MANAGEMENT IN). Growth in 2000 was an estimated 3 per cent of its gross domestic product (GDP).

3 Competitive advantage and management

Porter (1990: 308ff) sees Switzerland's competitive advantage in terms of a remarkably wide range of advanced manufacturing and service industries given its small population base. It has provided almost full employment for its citizens and immigrants at the highest wages in Europe. There were many multinational corporations, including Nestlé, Novartis and Schindler in recent decades. They have in recent years formed many International Joint Ventures, in the People's Republic of China for example. Most firms are export-orientated, as in other small advanced countries like Denmark, Finland and The Netherlands. Switzerland is a perfect example of how a country with few natural resources and a small internal market can generate high living standards.

Swiss managers are, like the rest of the workforce, highly educated and trained. As in Germany, vocational preparation for work is well developed (Danthine and Lambelet 1987). There is a strong craft tradition flowing from older industries like watchmaking. The apprenticeship system is on Germanic lines, with on-the-job training for all young Swiss who do not go to university. In-house prorammes are available at all levels including management. Firms invest heavily in skills, and have sophisticated human resource management policies (see HUMAN RESOURCE MANAGEMENT). Army service for young males is compulsory, and until recently included renewed training each year. This helps foster a strong sense of social solidarity and discipline which spills over into work. Graduates are usually expected to become officers and have longer periods of military reserve duty, which may be inconvenient for firms. However, not being an officer may cause problems careerwise.

The work ethic is predictably strong and managers work very hard. They are linguistically deft and many speak at least two national languages plus English. Engineers are top-class and Swiss manufacturing quality is of an international standard. Bankers are also able to offer sophisticated financial services in most major languages. Tourism management is similarly of a high degree (see TOURISM MANAGEMENT).

Research on Swiss managers shows that their values tend to be aligned with their linguistic zones of influence. Hofstede (1980) notes that Swiss-German scores in his study shadow those of the Germans, while the French-speaking Swiss follow the French national score (see FRANCE, MANAGEMENT IN; GERMANY, MANAGEMENT IN). There is a wide culture gap, especially on power distance. The Swiss feature as part of the Germanic area because of the numerical strength of the Swiss-

Germans in the Hofstede sample (1980: 336–7): they represent 65 per cent of the population, alongside 18 per cent French, 10 per cent Italian and 1 per cent Romansch, plus 6 per cent others. The Swiss-French are more critical of social norms than the SwissGermans, and the latter more conformist. The young are less and less quiescent and youth culture is as strong as elsewhere in the large cities. The work ethic is less strong than previously for this age group.

Business values dominate Swiss society generally and managers have high status (Lawrence and Edwards 2000: 121–34). High-technology has long been a strength and many managers are top engineers from the Federal Polytechnics of Zurich and Lausanne. Management education has been sponsored by leading Swiss firms, like Nestlé. The International Institute for Management Development (IMD) at Lausanne is well-known and the University of Geneva's HEC offers an MBA. There is also a high-level graduate management school at the University of St Gallen, as well as programmes at many other major higher education or university centres (see BUSINESS SCHOOLS). The Swiss select their international executives from a broad field, including more from abroad as chief executives of their MNCs.

Swiss industry is generally peaceful, with few strikes since the social pacts of the 1930s. Labour relations are mostly non-confrontational and collaborative (although this varies by industry). This is in spite of strong union representation in manufacturing and public services. Until recently labour shortages were a drag on growth. 'Guest' workers came in and often stayed. Selective immigration was a compensating factor, but there is less tolerance for newcomers than in former years, as is the tendency in other European countries nearby.

Service employment has grown as elsewhere in Europe, especially in banking, insurance, management-support services, software creation, temporary work placement and tourism. Companies like Manpower and Interim are active in the large cities supplying firms with part-time employees. These sectors have very weak union representation, if any at all.

4 Conclusion

Switzerland has still not decided whether to join the EU. Swiss-French cantons favour the idea, but the Germanic areas are less keen, especially the less urbanized parts. Big business is, as elsewhere, much more enthusiastic about a larger market, although the existing trading arrangements give them a great deal of tariff-free access to European consumers. Swiss firms have survived the recession but the currency is free-floating; it is much in demand as a safe currency-hedge, but at the price of a high cost-structure for manufacturing and service industries like tourism. Structural problems, like those in Germany, may erode competitive advantage. Productivity growth has been slow (Porter 1990). Managers in Switzerland face many challenges in the coming decades.

MALCOLM WARNER
JUDGE INSTITUTE OF MANAGEMENT STUDIES
UNIVERSITY OF CAMBRIDGE

Further reading

(References cited in the text marked *)

Bernauer, T. (1999) 'Measuring and explaining Switzerland's public sector', *Swiss Political Science Review*, 5 (2): 1–20. (This recent article argues that Swiss society may be converging with that of western Europe.)

* Danthine, J.P. and Lambelet, J.C. (1987) 'The Swiss case', *Economic Policy* 5 (October): 149–79. (Describes the Swiss economy and the contribution of training.)

Financial Times (2000) 'Survey on Switzerland', *Financial Times*, 21 March 2000, pp. I–VI. (An updated account of business in Switzerland, with several sections dealing with the economy and business).

* Hofstede, G. (1980) *Culture's Consequences*, London: Sage Publications. (Well-known study of management values across the world, including Switzerland.)

Hofstede, G. (1991) *Cultures and Organizations: Software of the Mind*, London: McGraw-Hill. (Updated analysis of Hofstede's earlier cross-national research.)

Lawrence, P. (1978) 'Executive head-hunting', *New Society* 25 May: 416–17. (Analysis of cultural differences in recruitment styles between Switzerland and the UK.)

* Lawrence, P. and Edwards, V. (2000) *Management in Western Europe*, London: Macmillan Business. (A recent up-to-date text on management in Europe, including Switzerland.)

* Porter, M. (1990) *The Competitive Advantage of Nations*, London: Macmillan. (Porter deals with Swiss factor-advantages in chapter 7.)

Saner, R. and Yiu, L. (1993) 'Conflict-handling styles in Switzerland', *Die Unternehmung* 2 (1): 10–22. (Interesting article relevant to management–labour relations in Switzerland.)

de Saugy, J. and Chapuis, P. (1994) *Banking Secrecy and Tax Law in Switzerland*, Amsterdam: Kluwer. (Study of specific banking secrecy provisions in Swiss banking systems.)

Steinberg, J. (1996) *Why Switzerland?*, 2nd edn, Cambridge: Cambridge University Press. (An excellent broadbrush study of Swiss society.)

See also: BUSINESS SCHOOLS; CULTURE, CROSS-NATIONAL; EUROPEAN UNION; EUROPE, MANAGEMENT IN; FRANCE, MANAGEMENT IN; GERMANY, MANAGEMENT IN; ORGANIZATION CULTURE; TOURISM MANAGEMENT

System vulnerability and disaster recovery

1 **Technology and vulnerability**
2 **Disaster recovery plan**
3 **The Year 2000 (Y2K) problem**

Overview

Information systems, like any other operation, are not immune from disaster. The cost of lost business and subsequent recovery from such disaster could be monumental. More importantly, if no prior recovery programme is in place, system recovery may prove an insurmountable task, resulting in the complete breakdown of business operations. When talking about disaster and business recovery from such an upheaval, it is helpful to define the nature of the problem at the outset. A common-sense definition of a disaster is a large-scale disruption inflicted upon a system by some unforeseen event upsetting the continuity of a system. In the case of an information system, there is a dividing line between a security breach and a disaster, and it is important to recognize the difference. While a lack of security may contribute to a man-made catastrophe, the vast majority of security breaches do not cause disasters. Disaster recovery is then closely related to the security and availability of data. This involves policies, procedures and products which allow the timely resumption of the computer system of an enterprise, allowing business operations to continue following a large-scale disaster.

There are many reasons why computerized information systems are vulnerable and disaster prone. Some of the common threats stem from technical, organizational and environmental factors such as fire, electrical and telecommunications problems. The effects of a disaster in an automated system are generally severe and are more so when the system is based around an open network such as the Internet. Computer hardware, software, data files and other auxiliary equipment can be destroyed by fire, power failure and other natural disasters such as flood, tornado, earthquake and hurricane. Such disasters can not only disrupt the whole operation, but it also may take a long time to regain the continuity of service. Organizational operations are often so heavily dependent upon information systems that one such disaster can bring an entire business to a standstill. In the following sections we shall explore this problem and the protections needed to avoid serious consequences. In addition, the special situation of the so-called millennium bug or Year 2000 (Y2K) problem is considered.

1 Technology and vulnerability

As information systems become more dependent on distributed computing, they expose themselves to greater vulnerability. The business community is well aware of this changing environment and many businesses are trying to protect themselves from the effects of disaster.

In recent years, significant progress has been made in protecting data centres. New technologies have emerged and the importance of mainframe computers has diminished in day-to-day business operations. Along with change, information systems experience risks from other areas such as local area networks, multi-location distributed systems and, more recently, Internet applications. Unfortunately, many businesses have not been able to secure their data centres with these changes.

According to Comdisco's 1997 Vulnerability Index, a survey of 200 of the largest computer users in the USA, Canada and the UK, most corporations are at significant risk in the event of a disaster. The survey noted that only 12 per cent of companies have an effective disaster recovery programme in place for their enterprise computing system. The average enterprise vulnerability index for information systems was placed at 70, with 100 being the most vulnerable and 0 being the least vulnerable. The relative index was placed at 60 for local area networks and 43 for data centres. At the same time there is a continual shift in mission-critical applications to more decentralized environments, making organizations more vulnerable to disaster. The Comdisco survey also found that the proportion of companies using data centres declined from 70 per cent in 1987 to 61 per cent in 1997. Over half the companies surveyed are currently using multi-location distributed systems.

Business continuity planning remains an overwhelming task in this changing technological environment. Many systems professionals admit that ensuring safeguards at data centres continues to be a challenge. The task is even more daunting for multi-location systems. Despite the size of the challenge, the need will continue to grow and business continuity professionals must work to limit the risk and ensure recoverability at the enterprise level. While the budget is often limited, businesses must prioritize activities to improve return on business continuity investments. It is possible that companies with disaster recovery programmes are likely to experience as much disruption as those without a plan. However, it is a well-established fact that companies with recovery plans generally experience significantly shorter disruptions to their computer systems.

Organizations generally have a backup procedure to protect data but most distributed systems are far more lax. Enterprise data is generally stored on network servers and protected by backup procedures. But much data is often unidentifiable and stored all over the system, including on the hard drives of workstations. Too often companies have no recovery plan for such data and will not recover in the event a disaster strikes. New software tools are, however, emerging in the market to help companies to protect such databases.

Finally, vulnerability can be attributed to a lack of substantial resources that are needed to put a workable recovery plan in place. The problem is in part compounded by an inability to adequately measure the return on investment in recovery plans.

2 Disaster recovery planning

Organizations generally believe that they have an effective disaster recovery plan to take appropriate action to recover the system quickly to maintain the continuity of operations. The claim, however, often appears questionable because it is the testing of the recovery system and practice that makes any such plan workable in real emergencies. In most organizations the testing and practice of a recovery plan takes only a secondary role in the scheme of the operation. Perhaps the most active group of professionals in disaster recovery are consultants and vendors who offer and assist with recovery services.

There are two alternatives when considering disaster recovery planning: the first is the use of external service bureaus and the second a do-it-yourself or in-house approach. Regardless of how it is carried out, it is essential to have a programme in place. For a do-it-yourself plan, organizations need to have a replacement strategy in the event disaster strikes. A company may make a reciprocal backup agreement with another company with a similar hardware configuration with spare processing capacity. A company-owned off-site facility can offer an alternative processing capability. An external plan generally includes outside vendors with a secured recovery service. Both external and internal plans enjoy various advantages and suffer from various disadvantages; organizations therefore need to weigh the costs and benefits of different plans. Regardless of the approach taken, disasters cannot be eliminated and therefore organizations must prepare recovery measures.

To prepare for disaster an organization needs to have a well-thought-out programme in place. Such programmes are called *disaster recovery plans*. The plan details what is to be done and who should do it in the event of a disaster. Such plans must go beyond merely the recovery of information systems and comprise a broader framework for business continuity.

Experts have suggested a step-by-step approach in developing such a programme. A disaster recovery plan generally includes several steps such as:

1 Management commitment to the plan: top management commitment is essential since such a plan requires substantial resources.
2 Establish a planning committee: this is necessary to gain across-the-board cooperation and coordination of activities.
3 Perform risk assessment and risk analysis: this establishes which operations will be hurt by a disaster and the severity.
4 Prioritize recovery needs: essentially this will establish mission-critical applications. This involves identification and classification of the critical nature of applications into such categories as:
   - *Critical* (cannot be replaced with a manual system)
   - *Vital* (can be replaced with a manual system for a brief period of time)
   - *Sensitive* (can be replaced with a manual system at great cost.
   - *Non-critical* (may be interrupted for an extended period without significant additional costs).
5 Select a recovery plan: this emerges from the evaluation of possible alternative plans by considering such factors as risk, cost and training needs.
6 Select vendors: selected from several external vendors. Key criteria include vendor's ability to provide a more effective response to disaster than in-house-staff, past experience and support services.

Once the vendor is selected, the recovery plan needs to be fully developed and implemented. This is necessary to ensure that the role and responsibility of each business unit is informed and clearly understood. The plan needs to be tested; this may include utilizing mock disasters. In a mock disaster, the coordinator measures the time it takes to implement the plan and its effectiveness. Finally, continuous tests and evaluation must be carried out from time to time. Without such periodic tests the plan is easily forgotten and becomes only an archive collection. The most important thing to recognize in a disaster recovery plan is that it is an insurance policy and one hopes that disaster will never strike, but in the rare event that it does the plan must work. The plan, therefore, needs to be periodically tested to keep it viable. Complacency is the worst enemy and a guarantee of disaster.

Ultimately, the organization must establish links between the disaster recovery plan and its business recovery plan. While the disaster recovery plan focuses on getting centralized database computer systems running, a business recovery plan focuses on the client-server or distributed computing environment. This business recovery plan is a more comprehensive programme with a list of consistent actions that needs to be taken before and after a disaster. These actions are intended to minimize disruption and ensure orderly recovery, the availability of critical resources and the continuity of business operations.

3 The Year 2000 (Y2K) problem

Much was said in the media during the last years of the twentieth century about the so-called millennium bug media and many predicted it would be a doomsday event. Essentially, the Y2K problem could be classified as a potential man-made disaster and therefore it would be appropriate to discuss the issue in the context of disaster recovery. It is useful, however, to discuss the nature of the problem first before digging deeply into it.

In the early days of computing, data storage space was relatively expensive. To avoid the high cost of data storage, many business applications were written to use only the last two digits instead of all four digits in the year portion of the data field, and the first two digits of the year were always assumed to be 19. In addition, many older mainframe operating systems and library functions included with language compilers also used 6-byte or 8-byte strings such as MMDDYY or MM-DD-YY to identify dates, using only the last two digits for the year. Similar Y2K problems also existed for many desktop applications because the older personal computers also use the two-digit year field and therefore the year 2000 is read as 1900. As a result, these past actions created the monumental task of finding these occurrences and converting two-digit year representations to four digits so that dates ending with '00' or '01' could be read as '2000' and '2001' and not as '1900' or '1901'.

The problem thus seems very simple – too few digits in the year, only the last two digits are used to describe a year. To solve the problem, however, a new mini-industry emerged during the twilight years of the twentieth century. While many users were baffled about their needs and requirements, so-called 'Year 2000' software became highly prized in the information technology industry. For most businesses it was the scale of the problem that was proven to be overwhelming. Therefore, at the initial stage detailed source analysis was required. Date-related data names needed to be tracked on a program-by-program basis. Such analysis had to be capable of allowing the programmers to make the change towards Y2K compliance quickly and effectively. This was done by creating some sort of smart edit session where necessary changes were required. Having made the necessary source changes, the next step was to test these changes. An obvious requirement was to be able to run the program in order to receive a year 2000 date from the operating system. A date simulation package was used by most to achieve this goal and to test their performance. It soon became apparent that it was the testing of the software performance that takes time and many businesses were late in starting the process.

There was a growing expectation that despite all the efforts some systems would fail. Even if a business could guarantee its own internal system would work, it would be difficult for some to do so because businesses depend on so many external computer-based systems, such as those of the suppliers of raw materials and other basic resources such as power, water, communications and transportation. The threat from external disruption could be bigger than from the internal system, and was far less predictable. Thus, the Y2K problem was widely viewed as a business continuity threat. Businesses needed to develop sound plans to deal with this special, but potentially disastrous problem.

The Y2K problem was deemed particularly critical in the case of electronic data interchange (EDI) because of the external nature of its activities. This is because an enterprise cannot control when and how its business partners would resolve the problem.

Besides, there were no standard-based guidelines to follow. As a result, most businesses using EDI were deemed likely to be affected by the Y2K problem in one way or another.

By the years 1998–99, many Y2K problem-solving tools were made available for mainframe software. These can be separated into several categories such as:

- needs assessment
- impact analysis
- source code conversion
- date simulator
- date testing tools.

Needs assessment tools take the form of cost/benefit analysis to assess the extent to which the existing systems are vulnerable to Y2K problems and estimate the cost for keeping the system functioning properly. *Impact analysis* is a very time-consuming process of code conversion. It generally involves searching source codes for text strings that simulate date, or more specifically year, to find potential problem areas. The *source code conversion* generally entails expanding the date fields and date variables to accept date values with a four-digit year. Thus, the source codes are recompiled and data files are redesigned, converted and reformatted as needed. A *date simulator* is essentially used to generate dates beyond 1999 that are used in testing the performance after conversion of the system. *Testing* is by far the most expensive part of the conversion process. Almost one-half of the cost of fixing the Y2K problem was spent on testing efforts. Because of the high cost of making an error, the intensity of date testing was more acute than for normal business recovery programmes. Date simulation packages were widely used to test the performance of the conversion.

The Y2K problem seemed akin to a disaster and its effects could have been more devastating than a natural disaster, but it did not happen on a large scale. Its resolution was essential for smooth business continuity. Interdependency is perhaps the most critical factor and in the chain of computerized links, even a minor failure at one point could have caused havoc in the entire chain of operations. The

USA passed the 'Year 2000 Information and Readiness Disclosure Act', encouraging disclosure with respect to Y2K preparedness. Such readiness disclosure provided businesses with protection from liability arising from Y2K-related problems.

Most organizations were on alert on the night of transition from one millennium to the next, armed with expert personnel to tackle any potential disaster. The anxious moments arrived with many midnights as we passed through the world's time zones, and saw sighs of relief from many corners of our interdependent world. The long-awaited potential disaster did not strike. Certainly, there were many glitches but they were easily fixed. A year later, the transition from year 2000 to 2001 also occurred without any serious problem.

As was said earlier, Y2K was a man-made problem and was finally conquered by human ingenuity and hard work. The lesson we learned is that we can avert a potential disaster to our vulnerable systems and recover from a system failure, but we need to be prepared. Preparedness for disaster recovery is a continuous process and there is no room for laxity.

SUFI M. NAZEM
UNIVERSITY OF NEBRASKA AT OMAHA

Further reading

Butler, J. (1992) 'How to stay in business when disaster strikes', *Software* August. (Discussion on disaster prevention planning.)

Chapman, C. (1996) 'Before disaster strikes', *Internal Auditor* December. (A reading on security and disaster prevention.)

Hotle, M. and Conway, B. (1997) *Year 2000 Testing Crisis: An Overview*, Gartner Group. (A special industry report on the Y2K problem.)

Jones, C. (1997) 'Year 2000; what's the real cost?', *Datamation* March. (Discussion on issues related to the Y2K problem.)

Laux, D. (1998) 'New technology, new risk: business continuity not keeping pace in distributed systems', *Disaster Recovery Journal* Winter. (Contemporary reading on disaster recovery and business continuity.)

Song, K.W., Monaco, A.M. and Sellaro, C.L. (1994) 'Disaster recovery planning: suggestions to top management and information systems managers', *Journal of Systems Management* May: 28–33. (Comprehensive analysis and framework on disaster recovery planning.)

See also: CRISIS MANAGEMENT; ELECTRONIC DATA INTERCHANGE; FIRE-WALL SYSTEMS; SECURITY AND INFORMATION SYSTEMS

Systems

Overview

The word 'system' is always taken to refer to a set of elements joined together to make a complex whole. The word may be used to refer to an abstract whole (the principles constituting a system of justice, say,) or a physical whole (a railway engine); but in both cases the justification for using the word is the same: the whole is seen as having properties which make it 'more than the sum of its parts'. This is the everyday-language expression of the idea of so-called 'emergent properties', that is to say properties which have no meaning in terms of the parts which make up the whole. Thus, a heap consisting of the individual parts of a bicycle does not have vehicular potential. However, when the parts are linked together in a particular structure to make the bicycle as a whole, which does have the potential to get someone with the ability to ride from A to B, that is an emergent property of the bicycle as a whole.

The idea of emergent properties is the single most fundamental systems idea and to use this (and other) systems ideas in a conscious organized way is to do some 'systems thinking'. To use systems thinking to tackle some perceived problem is to take 'a systems approach' to it. Since the field of management deals with complex matters, and systems thinking has been developed to cope with complexity, it is not surprising to find systems thinking closely associated with the field. Indeed, many systems ideas and several versions of both systems thinking and a systems approach have all been developed in work on management problems.

This entry will briefly review the origin and nature of systems thinking and describe a number of varieties of it as they have been developed to tackle problems in the management field.

1 The origins of systems thinking

Around the turn of the century, when biologists were considering the fundamental nature of their science, a school of thought arose which argued that biology's object of concern was the living organism as a whole. It was suggested by these 'organismic' biologists that the science should develop by creating descriptions of the basic processes which characterize a living organism, processes of growth and decay and so on. They developed the concept of an organism as an 'open' entity which exchanges materials, energy and information with an environment to which it can adapt (a metaphor which has been much taken up in organization theory). Starting in the 1940s Ludwig von Bertalanffy (1968) argued that the ideas about organisms which he and his colleagues had developed could in fact be applied to wholes of any kind: to 'systems' in general. This initiated systems thinking in a formal sense and in 1954 the first institution in this new field was set up. This was the Society for General Systems Research (SGSR), committed to the development of a General System(s) Theory (GST) which could be applied within any field in which phenomena concerned with organized complexity were studied. The pioneers hoped that communications between different scientific fields would be helped by such theory.

These aspirations of the pioneers have not been fulfilled; rather, systems thinking has been developed within particular fields – although the outcomes continue to provide, in systems ideas, a language applicable within many different disciplines. This means that as a field, systems has the same status as mathematics: it is a meta-discipline, a language, which can be used to talk *about* the subject matter of other areas. Thus, for example, there are systems thinking geographers, sociologists and management scientists, and other geographers, sociologists and management scientists who do not use the systems language (see ORGANIZATION BEHAVIOUR, HISTORY OF).

2 The nature of systems thinking

Throughout the systems literature the core image upon which systems thinking is based is that of the adaptive whole. The concept is of some whole entity (which may be seen as a whole because it has emergent properties) existing in an environment which may change and so deliver shocks to it. The *adaptive* whole may then survive in the changing environment if it can adapt to the changes.

Ordinary everyday experience offers many examples of this process, which is what makes systems thinking intuitively attractive. Thus, when the temperature of our environment rises, our bodies open pores and produce sweat which evaporates and helps to cool us down; the Boy Scouts movement survives for a hundred years, but is not the same organization its founder created: it has adapted to a changing society; manufacturing companies using oil as a raw material had to change their policies and operations very rapidly when the price of oil increased fourfold between 1973 and 1974 and then doubled again in 1979, if they were to survive in their changed economic environment. All these happenings can be expressed in systems language. They represent the behaviour of entities which may be treated as adaptive wholes.

In order to describe something as an adaptive whole, four fundamental ideas are needed. First, the whole will be seen as a system (rather than simply as an aggregate) if an observer of it can identify some *emergent properties* of it as an entity. Second, the whole system may contain parts which are themselves smaller wholes (or 'sub-systems'). Thus, the human body can be regarded as a system but also within it sub-systems such as the respiratory system or the blood-circulation

system can be identified. This means that systems thinking postulates a *layered* or hierarchical structure in which systems, part of wider systems, may themselves contain sub-systems, which may contain sub-sub-systems, and so on. Finally, if a system is to survive in a changing environment it must have available to it processes of *communication* and processes of *control*. It must be able to sense the change in the environment and adopt a suitable response in the form of some so-called 'control action'. In our bodies many such actions are automatic, as when our core temperature is maintained within quite narrow limits. In designed systems, engineers have to create mechanisms which keep performance within chosen limits, Watt's governor controlling the speed of a steam engine being the paradigm example.

With the four concepts of emergent properties, a layered structure and processes of communication and control a very wide range of wholes may be described as systems capable (within limits) of surviving in a changing environment. Systems thinking applies these ideas to a wide range of observed features of the world, the purpose being, in general, either to understand the world better or to intervene to improve some part of it.

Three broad categories of work can be seen in which the idea of an adaptive whole has been developed and exploited. Biologists and, especially, ecologists study the wholes that nature creates, which are often referred to as 'natural systems', for example, frogs, forests, the biosphere of the planet. Engineers, on the other hand, create 'designed systems', systems planned to exhibit some desirable emergent properties and to survive under a range of environmental conditions. Note also that designed systems may be abstract rather than concrete, as in systems of philosophy or a set of connected principles (as in, say, a 'design philosophy').

It is the third broad area of systems thinking, however, which is of greatest interest to those studying the problems of management. For example, it was realized in the 1970s, in action research which tackled messy real-world problem situations, that a connected set of human activities, joined together to make a *purposeful* whole could, with the addition of a monitoring and control sub-system, be treated as a new kind of system (Checkland 1981). Models of such systems can be built and used to explore real-world purposeful action. This yields a wide-ranging approach to the problems within and between organizations, since the taking of purposeful action is a ubiquitous characteristic of human affairs at many different levels, from the short-term tactical to the long-term strategic and over many timescales.

These three broad categories of work are all similar in that they exhibit the key characteristic of systems thinking, namely the conscious use of systems concepts, especially that of the adaptive whole, to understand some phenomena in the world or to guide intervention aimed at improvement. In more technical language, systems ideas provide an epistemology within which what counts as knowledge for the systems thinker will be defined.

3 The evolution of the systems movement in the field of management

The systems movement has evolved steadily since the late 1940s when GST emerged. In the 1950s much of the work done was of a practical kind and represented the application to civilian situations of the lessons learned from the development of operations research (OR) during the second world war (see OPERATIONS RESEARCH).

The application of the lessons learned in wartime OR to post-war activity in industrial and other organizations led to a number of organized forms of inquiry and problem solving. Bell Telephone Laboratories, for example, formalized their approach to new-technology projects in 'systems engineering' (Hall 1962); the RAND Corporation developed 'systems analysis' (Optner 1973); and when the first mainframe computers became available the analysis needed to design and establish a computer system drew on the same set of ideas (see SYSTEMS ANALYSIS AND DESIGN).

This was the dominant systems thinking in management in the 1950s and 1960s. Its essence was to define very carefully a desirable objective or need, to examine possible alternative systems which might achieve the objective or meet the need, and to select among the alternatives, paying great attention to formulating the criteria upon which selection is based. This is what is now known as 'hard systems thinking', a *systematic* approach to achieving defined objectives.

It was in the 1970s and 1980s that a more *systemic* use of systems ideas was developed in a programme of action research aimed at finding better ways of tackling the kind of ill-structured problem situations in the real world in which objectives are multiple, ambiguous and conflicting (Checkland 1981). This produced what is now known as 'soft systems methodology' (SSM), a much-used complementary approach to that of systems engineering/systems analysis. Many practitioners around the world have contributed to this development of so-called 'soft' systems thinking.

SSM is a learning system, a system of inquiry. It makes use of models of purposeful human activity, each based on a particular, declared, world view (since purposeful activity seen as 'freedom fighting' by one observer may be interpreted as 'terrorism' by another). These models are used as devices to explore problematical situations. Comparing models with the perceived real world structures a debate about change, a debate which tries to find accommodations between conflicting interests which enable 'action to improve' to be taken.

The difference between 'hard' and 'soft' systems thinking lies in how systems thinking is used. In the 'hard' mode the world is assumed to contain systems; and they can be 'engineered' to work effectively. In the 'soft' mode the world is taken to be problematical, but it is assumed that the *process of inquiry* into it can be organized as a system. It is this shift of systemicity from the world to the process of inquiry into the world which marks the hard/soft distinction. In practical terms the 'hard' approaches are appropriate where objectives or needs are well-defined, the 'soft' approaches in 'messier' situations.

More recently, Ulrich's (1983) development of the work of Churchman (1971) has drawn attention to the need, where practical social planning is concerned, to open up the proposals of experts to examination by lay persons who will be affected by what the planners design. Ulrich's 'critical heuristics' stresses that every definition of a problem and every choice of a system to design and implement will contain normative assumptions which need to be teased out and subjected to critical scrutiny. The aim is to enable practical uses of systems thinking to be emancipatory both for those who are involved and those who are affected.

4 Varieties of systems thinking

It is not possible in a short article to cover all the many varieties of systems thinking. But it is possible to define a set of categories which at least enables us to make sense of any version of systems thinking which we may come across, whether in the literature of the past, in present practice or in potential future developments. The categories which make this possible are shown in Figure 1.

It is important to see Figure 1 not as a map of systems work but as a way of making sense of the wide range of examples of such work. Any actual use of systems ideas may draw on several categories; but it will be describable using these categories. It will be useful to give some examples of this.

Thus, area 1 in Figure 1 would include the development of cybernetics, which its pioneer

Wiener (1948) called 'the entire field of control and communication theory whether in the machine or in the animal' (see WIENER, N.). Many people have used cybernetics within area 2.1 and users of organizational cybernetics (Beer 1979) could do so in several ways, consciously using the cybernetic model either as an account of the real world (area 2.11) or as a device to explore complex reality (area 2.12) – or, indeed, both.

Similarly, a study in an organization, using SSM, part of area 2.12, might well reach the conclusion that, say, a system to control product quality to meet certain criteria ought to be set up. Designing and implementing such a system might then be done using the approach of hard systems engineering, area 2.11. As a final example, a RAND-style study (Optner 1973) using, say, cost-benefit analysis to help managers facing a major policy decision (area 2.13) would be enriched by placing the decision in question in a systems context such as could be provided by soft systems thinking.

The systems literature contains more than enough accounts of systems approaches in the management field. This article concentrates on methodologies which have been used extensively, have generated secondary literature and have been shown to be transferable from the pioneers to other groups of users. Several have been described above: systems engineering, RAND systems analysis, SSM, critical

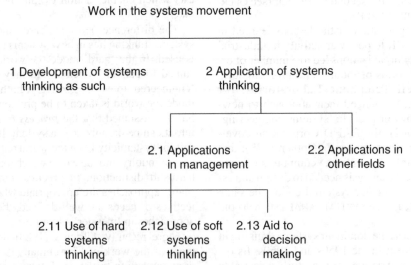

Figure 1 Categories which can make sense of the wide range of work within the systems movement

heuristics. This section will end with brief indications of six other approaches which have had a significant impact on management practice.

1 Studying inventory problems in manufacturing companies, Forrester (1961) developed a simple way of modelling material storage and flows governed by policy criteria. This 'industrial dynamics', as it was first called, was later generalized to 'system dynamics' (SD) and extended well outside the field of inventory problems. SD modelling was the basis of the world models which were in vogue in the 1970s (Meadows *et al.* 1972). The SD community flourishes but has remained rather isolated within the systems community, with its own journal and conferences.

2 When the technology of the UK coal-mining industry was changed radically in the 1950s, the change affected not only the technical aspects of winning coal from a harsh environment but the whole social structure of the industry (Trist *et al.* 1963). Studying this, the researchers from the Tavistock Institute proposed a 'socio-technical system' as an explanatory device. Based upon viewing an organization as an open system in interaction with its environment, the sociotechnical model makes technology, social system and environment interdependent: you cannot change one without changing all. This has been a very influential concept, a mainstream of thinking in organization theory of a functionalist kind, concerned to explain how the parts of an organization contribute to a coherent whole (see TRIST, E.L.).

3 After forty years of experience in the world of affairs, Sir Geoffrey Vickers sought in retirement to make sense of what he had experienced. He found systems thinking helpful and developed his theory of 'appreciative systems' as an account of the social process (1965). In an appreciative system we notice certain features of our world as significant, as a result of our previous experience. We discriminate and judge such features using standards of good/bad, interesting/uninteresting and so on, and we take action in terms of managing networks of relationships which are important to us.

However, the *source* of the standards is the previous history of the system itself, so that our social world continuously reconstructs itself out of its own past. Interest in Vickers' work is spreading as its relevance to modern management is perceived (see VICKERS, G.).

4 In his 'interactive planning' Ackoff (1974) argues for a systems approach to societal problems. His influential work is based on the idea that the real world is characterized not by 'problems' but by 'systems of problems' or 'messes' and requires a highly participative approach based on planning. He describes five interacting phases, planning for ends, means to those ends, resourcing achievement of ends, organizational arrangements necessary to achieve them and implementation and control – the latter being important since all outputs call for revision in the light of experience. The central idea is to start from an imagined ideal future for the system being planned for, one which ignores all constraints. The effort is then directed to getting as close to that ideal as possible (see ACKOFF, R.L.).

5 Though Wiener's original cybernetics (1948) focused on the nature of control systems, whether in machines or animals, the best-known work on organizational or management cybernetics, that of Beer (1979), extends that concept. Beer develops a sophisticated model, the viable systems model (VSM), having five interacting subsystems which, he argues, are necessary and sufficient for the survival of an autonomous whole in its environment. In terms of an organization, system one is a set of operational elements which make up an organizational entity; system two is an anti-oscillatory mechanism; system three the management unit responsible for system one, internally, now; system four is responsible for the external and future; system five for monitoring the three-four interaction. The sophistication of the model lies in its never-ending, recursive nature: systems two, three, four and five constitute the system one of another level. Many managers have made use of the VSM in understanding and ordering their organizations (see WIENER, N.).

6 Finally there is currently interest in the implications of a systems model created by Maturana and Varela (1980) to make sense of living systems. Their autopoietic (self-producing) model has elements whose action creates the system itself as a stable pattern of relations. They have reservations about applying the model to a social whole, such as an organization, but it is proving to be at least a rich metaphor for thinking about organizational phenomena.

5 The future of systems thinking

In everyday language we speak casually of 'the legal system', 'the education system', 'health care systems' as if these were systems unequivocally existing in the world. In fact, these features of our world reveal very imperfect versions of systemic properties as these have been defined in the field of systems. Everyday language uses 'system' to mean simply some complex whole. Systems thinking has supplied a variety of accounts of that complexity and has created an epistemology and a language which can be used to discuss many different phenomena – natural or designed, concrete or abstract. 'System', properly used, is the name of a concept which may or may not map the world as we experience it.

In the past, most work in the systems movement followed everyday language in assuming the world to consist of interacting systems. More recently emphasis has been on using the systems language to try to make sense of the world as we experience it, in particular modelling processes rather than entities.

Helped by the ease and density of instant communication, old boundaries dissolve and former taken-as-given hierarchies become irrelevant. Managers increasingly need to 'read' their world as if it were a text which can be interpreted in multiple ways. The crucial management skill remains that of making sense of the complexity faced. Process modelling based on systems thinking offers a powerful tool for managers in the future.

PETER CHECKLAND
LANCASTER UNIVERSITY

Further reading

(References cited in the text marked *)

* Ackoff, R.L. (1974) *Redesigning the Future*, New York: Wiley. (An accessible account of 'interactive planning' by its major pioneer.)

* Beer, S. (1979) *The Heart of Enterprise*, Chichester: Wiley. (The Viable System Model discussed in detail by its creator.)

Berlinski, D. (1976) *On Systems Analysis*, Cambridge, MA: MIT Press. (A polemical attack on some of the pretensions of GST and Systems Analysis.)

* Bertalanffy, L. von (1968) *General System Theory*, New York: Braziller. (Collected articles by a founding father of GST: the authentic flavour is conveyed.)

Boulding, K. (1956) 'General systems theory – the skeleton of science', *Management Science* 2 (3): 197–208. (The most famous systems paper? An intuitive classification of system types according to their complexity.)

* Checkland, P. (1981) *Systems Thinking, Systems Practice*, Chichester: Wiley. (Republished 1999 with the addition of a 30-year retrospective on SSM's development.)

Checkland, P. and Casar, A. (1986) 'Vickers' concept of an appreciative system: a systemic account', *Journal of Applied Systems Analysis* 13: 3–17. (Vickers' account of the social process presented in the form of a systemic model.)

Checkland, P. and Scholes, J. (1990) *Soft Systems Methodology in Action*, Chichester: Wiley. (Republished 1999 with the addition of a 30-year retrospective on SSM's development.)

Churchman, C.W. (1968) *The Systems Approach*, New York: Dell Publishing. (Enjoyable philosophical ruminations on what it means to use 'a systems approach'.)

* Churchman, C.W. (1971) *The Design of Inquiring Systems*, New York: Basic Books. (Deep examination of systems design through the ideas of Leibniz, Locke, Kant, Hegel, Singer.)

Espejo, R. and Harnden, R. (eds) (1989) *The Viable System Model*, Chichester: Wiley. (Articles discussing the interpretation and use of Beer's VSM.)

Flood, R. and Jackson, M.R. (1991) *Critical Systems Thinking: Directed Readings*, Chichester: Wiley. (Articles concerning the need to examine the normative implications of systems-based problem-solving methodologies.)

* Forrester, J.W. (1961) *Industrial Dynamics*, Cambridge, MA: Wright-Allen Press. (The book that established the field which became known as 'system dynamics'.)

* Hall, A.D. (1962) *A Methodology of Systems Engineering*, Princeton, NJ: Van Nostrand. (The classic account of 'hard' systems engineering, generalized from Bell Telephone's experience.)

Katz, D. and Kahn, R.L. (1966) *The Social Psychology of Organizations*, New York: Wiley. (Organizations treated as open systems with functional parts, interacting with an external environment.)

* Maturana, H. and Varela, F. (1980) *Autopoiesis and Cognition: The Realization of the Living*, Dortrecht: Reidel. (A seminal account of a self-producing system as an epistemological device for understanding living systems.)

* Meadows, D.H., Meadows, D.L., Randers, R. and Behrens, W. (1972) *The Limits to Growth*, New York: Universe Books. (System dynamics applied on a world scale; this was controversial but modish for a time.)

Miller, J.G. (1978) *Living Systems*, New York: McGraw-Hill. (A mammoth work describing living systems as containing nineteen necessary sub-systems; contrast this with the autopoietic model.)

Mingers, J. (1995) *Self-Producing Systems*, New York: Plenum Press. (An excellent discussion of autopoiesis and its implications in many fields.)

Miser, H.J. and Quade, E.S. (eds) (1985; 1988) *Handbook of Systems Analysis*, New York: North Holland. (A two-volume compendium on all aspects of (mainly 'hard') systems analysis in real-world problem solving.)

Open Systems Group (eds) (1984) *The Vickers Papers*, London: Harper & Row. (A valuable collection of Vickers's writing, tackling issues at world, societal, organizational and individual levels.)

* Optner, S.L. (ed.) (1973) *Systems Analysis*, Harmondsworth: Penguin. (Articles on RAND-style systems analysis, including Charles Hitch's 1955 account of RAND thinking.)

Rosenhead, J. (ed.) (1989) *Rational Analysis for a Problematic World: Problem Structuring Methods for Complexity, Uncertainty and Conflict*, Chichester: Wiley. (The book now seen as establishing 'soft OR', though that phrase is not used.)

Sage, A.P. (1992) *Systems Engineering*, New York: Wiley. (Usefully updates Hall's 1962 book, covering systems methodology and systems design and management.)

* Trist, E.L., Higgin, G.W., Murray, H. and Pollock, A.B. (1963) *Organizational Choice*, London: Tavistock Publications. (The emergence of the 'socio-technical system' concept.)

* Ulrich, W. (1983) *Critical Heuristics of Social Planning*, Bern: Haupt. (A conceptual framework aiming to reveal and reflect upon the normative implications of *inter alia* plans and designs.)

* Vickers, G. (1965) *The Art of Judgement*, London: Chapman and Hall. (Vickers' original account of the social process as 'an appreciative system', republished in 1984 by Harper & Row.)

* Wiener, N. (1948) *Cybernetics*, Cambridge, MA: MIT Press. (The classic account of communication and control in machines and living things.)

See also: ACKOFF, R.L.; ORGANIZATION BEHAVIOUR; ORGANIZATION BEHAVIOUR, HISTORY OF; SYSTEMS ANALYSIS AND DESIGN; TRIST, E.L.; VICKERS, G.; WIENER, N.

Systems analysis and design

Overview

Systems analysis and design is a systematic approach to the improvement of business through the help of computer-based information systems. The people who accomplish these tasks are known as systems analysts. The systems development life cycle approach to systems development took hold in the 1960s and it remained highly popular throughout the 1980s. In the last part of the 1990s much of the work of the systems analyst moved to developing Web sites for e-commerce applications on the World Wide Web. In addition, analysts designed applications of push and pull technologies that allowed users to either 'pull' information from the World Wide Web as is done with common search engines, or developed systems so that users could have information 'pushed' directly to their desktops. Two examples of this type of system are those of Web news services that push information to a user's desktop and information sent to decision makers via corporate intranets (see E-BUSINESS). CASE (computer-aided software engineering) tools have been adopted by many systems analysts. CASE tools automate many traditionally labour-intensive tasks, while also adding new capabilities to the systems analyst's work. Analysts also adopted a variety of microcomputer-based software including automated forms design and graphics packages to improve their productivity, increase their ability to communicate with design teams and users, and to minimize re-creation of standard reports and screens.

To analyse, design and document a system, a systems analyst might draw entity-relationship diagrams, create data flow diagrams, build a data dictionary and data repository, provide detail on process specifications and logic, and draw structure charts. In addition an analyst needs to design the output, input and user interface.

New, alternative approaches to the structured development methodology are also being tried. These methods include prototyping, project champions, ETHICS, Soft Systems Methodology, Multiview and using metaphorical analysis. Object-oriented systems analysis and design is becoming increasingly important.

1 Introduction

Systems analysis and design seeks to analyse in a systematic way the data input, data flow and information output of businesses in order to improve their functioning through the use of computer-based information systems. This work is performed by systems analysts who are professionally trained in universities or technical schools to develop or improve information systems with the purpose of helping organizations to reach their goals. Systems analysts require people-orientated, interpersonal skills as well as technical computer skills, since they often manage complex projects with large budgets, involving numerous resources and large numbers of people such as computer programmers and users of information systems. They may develop a wide variety of systems including transaction processing systems (TPS), management information systems (MIS), office automation systems (OAS), decision support systems (DSS), group decision support systems

(GDSS), executive information systems (EIS), expert systems, e-commerce Web sites and applications using push and pull technologies to facilitate users' work on the World Wide Web (Kendall and Kendall 1999). In addition, they design client/server systems, intranets and extranets, recommendation systems and applications for many other types of emerging information technologies (Kendall 1997, 1999). It is clear that analysts' future work will engage the realm of artificial intelligence (AI), as analysts work to design intelligent agents to understand their interests and pull desirable information from the Web (Kendall 1996) (see ARTIFICIAL INTELLIGENCE; MANAGEMENT INFORMATION SYSTEMS; DECISION SUPPORT SYSTEMS; EXECUTIVE INFORMATION SYSTEMS; KNOWLEDGE-BASED SYSTEMS; E-BUSINESS).

The approach to developing information systems that is most familiar, most widely taught and used in practice is the systems development life cycle (SDLC), wherein the analyst proceeds systematically through several predetermined phases in the life cycle of information systems. This can be divided into seven sequential phases: (1) identifying problems, opportunities and objectives; (2) determining information requirements; (3) analysing system needs; (4) designing the recommended system; (5) developing and documenting software; (6) testing and maintaining the system; and (7) implementing and evaluating the system. Many of these phases are interrelated and often are accomplished simultaneously. Users, also called end users, are consulted about the information required to complete their jobs and make decisions, especially throughout the early phases of the life cycle. Systems analysts are often members of a systems development team who are chosen for their competency and compatibility. As a matter of course they set goals for project productivity and motivate the team to achieve them (Kendall and Kendall 2001).

The SDLC took a powerful hold in the 1960s and remained a popular approach to systems development throughout the 1990s. Many proprietary and specialized structured methodologies were developed to accomplish the SDLC in a methodical and systematic way. STRADIS (Structured Analysis and Implementation of Information Systems) is a prime example of a structured methodology approach (Gane and Sarson 1979), while in the UK Structured Systems Analysis and Design Method (SSADM) is widely used in the Civil Service (Downs et al. 1988). Another approach to structured methodology was developed by Yourdon (1989).

Another popular structured methodology is Jackson Systems Development (JSD) (Jackson 1983). In this approach the information system itself is thought of as a large programme which is developed as if, in essence, it were a machine. This allows the system to be maintained. The approach omits the topic of user participation. Instead, JSD's strength as a methodology has been described as residing in its treatment of concurrency, timing and process scheduling. As a methodology, it is widely used and prized for its machine-like precision.

Slowly, systems analysts have begun using automated tools to accomplish their own work. The number and complexity of CASE (computer-aided (or -assisted) software engineering) tools has proliferated with the widespread availability of microcomputers from the mid-1980s onward. Systems analysts adopt CASE tools in order to increase their productivity in systems development, to improve communication among analysts and users and to integrate life-cycle activities. A synonym for CASE tools is the term 'analyst/ programmer workbench.' Some CASE tools include code generators to eliminate or reduce the amount of computer programming necessary to programme an information system. It is even possible to input existing program code in one computer language, modify it using a common structured tool, and output it as another computer language. This process is called re-engineering.

Early examples of CASE tools include commercially marketed products such as Visible Analyst (Visible Systems) and Information Engineering Facility (Texas Instruments). An early successful re-engineering tool, marketed by Siemens AG Ústerreich, is called XperCASE in the USA and EasyCASE throughout the rest of the world. All of these run on microcomputers, which makes them very flexible and accessible.

All of the structured methodologies and CASE tools use a series of tools which help the systems analyst design, document and maintain the information system. Although extremely useful, they do not replace the human, intellectual qualities of the systems analyst whose training, subjective professional judgement and expertise are valued for the creative approaches they bring to bear in solving complex organizational problems. The following sections describe some of the tools used in structured methodologies. Note that different tools are appropriate for different phases in the SDLC.

2 Entity-relationship diagrams

Systems analysts must determine what part of the organization can be considered part of the problem to be solved, and what is not part of the proposed system. This activity is called defining systems boundaries. One way a systems analyst can accomplish this is to use an entity-relationship model. It is critical for a systems analyst to understand early on the entities and relationships in the organizational system.

The elements that make up an organizational system can be referred to as entities. An entity may be a person, a place or a thing, such as a passenger on an airline, a destination or a plane. Alternatively, an entity may be an event, such as the end of the month, a sales period or a machine breakdown. A relationship is the association that describes the interaction between entities.

The standard notation for drawing an entity-relationship (or E-R) diagram uses only two symbols: a rectangle and a diamond. The rectangle is used to show the entity, while the diamond represents the relationship between that entity and another entity.

Figure 1 shows an entity-relationship diagram for passengers of an airline that has set up a frequent flyer award programme. The airline wishes to keep track of passengers, their accumulated miles and when they use their frequent flyer awards. In the centre is the airline passenger. Other entities are the flights, the frequent flyer club, frequent flyer miles accumulated, the upgrade to first class and the airline itself.

Several types of relationship exist between the entities. For example, an airline establishes only one frequent flyer club, so the relationship is shown as one-to-one (1: 1 on the diagram). The club, however, keeps track of many frequent flyer miles so the relationship is one to many (1: M). Many passengers can take many flights, so the relationship is called many-to-many (M: N).

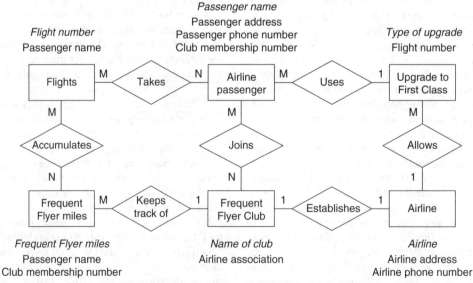

Figure 1 An entity-relationship diagram for an airline that established a frequent flyer club

Every entity can be described and has other data associated with it. For example the airline passenger entity contains data such as passenger name, address and phone number, and the club membership number. This information is used in designing a database to assist in organizing and tracking passenger data.

3 Data flow diagrams

Through the use of a structured analysis technique called data flow diagrams (DFD), the systems analyst is able to put together a graphical representation of data processes through the organization. The data flow approach emphasizes the logic of the data processes underlying the system. By using combinations of only four symbols, the systems analyst is able to create a pictorial depiction of processes that eventually can provide solid-system documentation for use in understanding, improving and maintaining the system. Figure 2 provides an example of such a diagram.

The double square is used to depict an external entity (a business, person or machine) that can send or receive data from the system. The external entity is also called a source or

destination of data. Each external entity is labelled with an appropriate name. Although it interacts with the system, it is considered external to the boundaries of the system.

The arrow shows movement of data from one point to another, with the head of the arrow pointing toward the data's destination. Data flows occurring simultaneously can be depicted using parallel arrows. Each arrow is labelled with an appropriate data flow name. Data flows depict data in motion in the organization.

A rectangle with rounded corners is used to show the occurrence of a transforming process. Processes always denote a change in or transformation of data; hence, the data flow leaving a process is always labelled differently than the one entering it.

The fourth basic symbol used in data flow diagrams represents a data store, and is depicted by an open-ended rectangle. This is drawn with two parallel lines, which are closed by a short line on the left side and open-ended on the right. These are drawn only wide enough to allow lettering between the parallel lines. In logical data flow diagrams the type of physical storage (for example, tape or diskette) is not specified. At this point the data

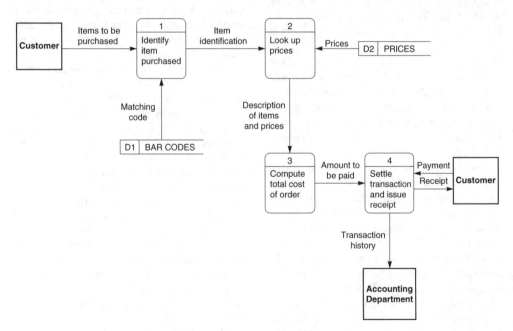

Figure 2 A data flow diagram of a customer transaction

store symbol is simply showing a depository for data that allows addition and retrieval of data. Data stores depict data at rest in the organization.

The data flow diagram seen in Figure 2 shows a customer purchasing an item, paying for it, and getting a receipt. It also shows the Accounting Department keeping track of the transaction. The Customer (in the upper left hand corner of the figure) initiates the transaction by bringing items to purchase. The items are identified by matching the bar code on the item to the codes in the data store called D1.

In this example, the data flow that comes from the data store is called 'matching code'. Data then flows from Process 1 to Process 2, 'Look up Prices'. Once again, the data is obtained from a data store, D2, and the new information flows to Process 3, and so on. After Process 4, the entity Customer appears again. A data flow called 'Payment' comes from the Customer and another called 'Receipt' flows to the Customer. At the same time the Accounting Department receives a data flow called 'Transaction History'.

The logical data flow diagram does not identify the physical features of the transaction. Only the logical data flows and processes are identified. Therefore, the reader of the data flow diagram does not know how payment is given by the customer (cash, cheque or credit card). The reader is also unaware of how the prices are stored (on paper or on a disk). Another type of data flow diagram, called a physical data flow diagram, is sometimes drawn later to clarify these issues, but the most common diagram is the logical data flow diagram seen here.

Data flow diagrams are usually drawn from the top down. The first diagram drawn is called a context diagram, and shows only the entities and one process, the system itself. Next the context diagram is 'exploded' to show more detail, as has been done for Figure 2. At this point, data stores are shown. The diagram can be exploded further to include child diagrams. For example, Process 3 can be exploded into steps showing that, in order it calculate the total cost of the order, items have to be categorized as taxable and non-taxable items.

4 The data dictionary and data repository

After data flow diagrams are created, the systems analyst uses them to begin compiling a data dictionary, which is a reference work containing data about data (meta-data) on all data processes, stores, flows, structures and elements within the system being studied. The data dictionary is a specialized instance of the kinds of dictionaries used as references in everyday life. The data repository is a larger collection of project information. The data dictionary is compiled by systems analysts to guide them through analysis and design. As a document it collects, coordinates and confirms what a specific data term means to different people in the organization.

Systems analysts identify and catalogue different terms that refer to the same data item. Most organizations face a proliferation of uncoordinated names (or aliases) for data items because a variety of computer programs and systems are developed over time by different systems analysts. Creating a data dictionary helps to avoid duplication of effort, allows better communication among organizational departments sharing a database and makes maintenance of computer programs more straightforward. The data dictionary also serves as a consistent, organization-wide standard for data elements.

Many CASE tools now feature automated data dictionaries and extensive data repositories which include re-usable program codes as well as data elements. These are valuable for their capacity to cross-reference data items, since necessary program changes can be made to all programs sharing a common element. This supplants changing programs on a haphazard basis or waiting until the program will not run because a change has not been implemented across programs sharing the updated item. Also, automated data dictionaries are important for large systems that produce several thousand data elements requiring cataloguing and cross-referencing. Additionally, data repositories can help reduce the amount of new computer program codes that must be written.

Many database management systems now come equipped with an automated data dictionary. These can be either elaborate or simple. Some computerized data dictionaries automatically catalogue data items when programming is done, others simply provide a template to prompt the person filling in the dictionary to do so in a uniform manner for every entry.

Understanding the process of compiling a data dictionary can aid the systems analyst in conceptualizing the system and how it works. The upcoming paragraphs allow the systems analyst to see the rationale behind what exists in automated data dictionaries.

One way to think about what should be in the data dictionary is to visualize how it should be used. As the basic reference work for finding the names and attributes of data items used throughout the organization's systems, it must be inclusive of all data items. Because it should be as inclusive as possible, it is never complete. It should be updated as changes are implemented, just as other documentation would be.

In order to be useful, data dictionary entries should contain specific categories of information, examples of which are listed below:

1 Name and aliases of the data item. (Different programs or departments may use their own names for common data items, so the data dictionary should include not only the data item's most common name but the synonym or alias for each element. All of these need to be recorded in the data dictionary to facilitate communication and cross-referencing between departments and their programs.)
2 Description of the data item in words.
3 Data elements related to the entry. (If an employee is the data item described then the data elements could be name, salary, social security number, phone extension and so on.)
4 Permissible range of the data item. (For example, the month can only be greater than or equal to one and less than or equal to twelve.)
5 Its allowable length in characters. (If the data element is a US Social Security Number the length of the data element should never exceed nine characters, or eleven characters if the two dashes are included in

the field. Length is always given in terms of the space taken up by the actual printed characters, not by the amount of computer storage required.)
6 Its proper encoding.
7 Any other pertinent editing information.

The data dictionary, when compiled correctly, is useful in serving as a standard source for systems development, modification, and maintenance.

The data repository also may contain specific elements:

1 Information about the data maintained by the system, including data flow, data stores, record structures and elements.
2 Procedural logic.
3 Screen and report design.
4 Data relationships, such as how one data structure is linked to another.
5 Project requirements and final system deliverables.
6 Project management information, such as delivery schedules, achievements, issues that need resolving and the project users.

New CASE tools prompt and assist the systems analyst in creating the data dictionary and the data repository at the same time as the information system is being analysed, thereby reducing the time necessary for documentation after the system is complete.

5 Process specifications and logic

Many of the early phases of the SDLC are devoted to information requirements analysis, during which time the analyst learns what decisions are made on the job by organizational members. Once the analyst identifies data flows and begins constructing a data dictionary, it is time to turn to decision analysis. The three methods for decision analysis discussed here are structured English, decision tables and decision trees.

A large part of a systems analyst's work will involve structured decisions; that is, decisions that can be automated if identified circumstances occur. A structured decision is repetitive, routine and has standard procedures to follow for its solution. An example of a structured decision is the approval of a credit card purchase by a credit card company. In order to classify a decision as structured, the analyst must define four variables in the decision being examined: conditions, condition alternatives, actions and action rules.

One way to describe structured decisions is to use the method referred to as structured English, where logic is expressed in sequential structures, decision structures, case structures or iterations. Structured English uses accepted keywords such as If, Then, Else, Do, Do While and Do Until to describe the logic used and is indented to indicate the hierarchical structure of the decision process.

Decision tables provide another familiar way to examine, describe and document decisions. Four quadrants (viewed clockwise from the upper left-hand corner) are used to: (1) describe the conditions; (2) identify possible decision alternatives (such as Yes or No); (3) indicate which actions should be performed; and (4) describe the actions. Decision tables are advantageous since the rules for developing the table itself, as well as the rules for eliminating redundancy, contradictions and impossible situations, are straightforward and manageable. The use of decision tables promotes completeness and accuracy in analysing structured decisions.

The third method for decision analysis is the decision tree, consisting of nodes (a square depicts actions and a circle depicts conditions) and branches. Decision trees are appropriate when actions must be accomplished in a certain sequence. There is no requirement that the tree be symmetrical, so only those conditions and actions that are critical to the decisions at hand are found on a particular branch.

Each of the decision analysis methods has its own advantages, and the systems analyst uses each according to the demands of the systems problem. Structured English is useful when many actions are repeated and when communicating with others is important. Decision tables provide complete analysis of complex situations while limiting the chance of impossible situations, redundancies or contradictions. Decision trees are appropriate when proper sequencing of conditions and actions is critical, and when each condition is not relevant to each action.

6 Structure charts

A top-down approach to systems development means that the systems analyst uses a general overview of the system and organization to gain a contextual perspective, and then each level is subsequently broken down into more detailed levels until the system is well understood and defined. Once the top-down design approach is taken, a modular approach is useful in programming. Using this the analyst breaks the programming into logical, manageable portions called modules. This kind of programming fits well with top-down design because it emphasizes the interfaces or relationships between modules rather than neglecting them until later in systems development. Ideally, each module should be functionally cohesive so that it is charged with accomplishing only one function in the program.

Modular programme design has three main advantages. First, modules are easier to write and debug (correct errors) because they are virtually self-contained. Tracing an error in a module is less complicated, since a problem in one module should not cause problems in others. A second advantage of modular design is that modules are easier to maintain. Modifications usually will be limited to a few modules, not spread over an entire programme. A third advantage of modular design is that modules are easier to grasp since they are self-contained sub-systems. This means that a reader can pick up a code listing of a module and understand its function.

The recommended tool for designing a modular, top-down system is called a structure chart. A structure chart is simply a diagram consisting of rectangular boxes (which represent the modules) and connecting lines.

Figure 3 shows four modules, labelled 000, 100, 200 and 300. The main module is labelled 000 and the subordinate modules are connected by lines. Off to the sides of the connecting lines, two types of short arrows are drawn. The arrows with the empty circles are called 'data couples'. In Figure 3, Raw Input and Sorted Part Numbers are both examples of data couples. The arrows with the filled-in circles are called 'control flags'. These arrows indicate that something is passed either down

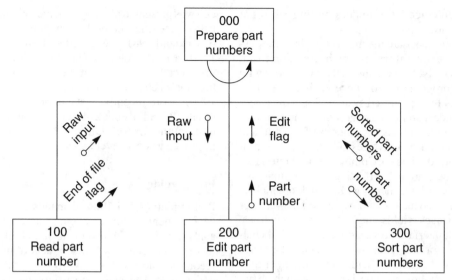

Figure 3 A structure chart that shows how to build program modules

to the lower module or back up to the upper one. In Figure 3, End of File Flag and Edit Flag serve this purpose.

Ideally, the more modularized, the easier it is to change the system. When these modules are actually programmed, it is important to pass the least number of data couples between modules.

Even more important, numerous control flags should be avoided. Control is designed to be from the top down, but on rare occasions it will be necessary to pass control upwards using control flags. Some examples of necessary control flags are messages that tell the higher module that the end-of-file was reached, a transaction was not valid or no such employee exists.

Another symbol used in structure charts is the loop. This symbol indicates that the procedures found in module 000 are to be repeated until finished. Still another symbol used in some structure charts is the small diamond. The diamond would appear on the bottom of one of the rectangles to signify that only one of the modules below the diamond will be performed.

7 Designing output, input and the user interface

Output is any useful information or data delivered by the information system or decision support system to the user. There are six main objectives in designing output of information systems: (1) to design output to serve the intended purpose; (2) to fit the user; (3) to deliver the right quantity of output; (4) to deliver it to the right place; (5) to provide output on time; and (6) to choose the right output method. Previously limited in scope to paper or screens, output now can take virtually any form including print, screen, audio, microforms and electronic output such as e-mail and faxes. The output of different technologies affects users in different ways. Output technologies also differ in their speed, cost, portability, flexibility, storage and retrieval possibilities. The systems analyst considers all of these factors when deciding on output methods from among such forms as print, on-screen, audio, microforms, electronic or a combination.

Proper flow of both forms and screens is important. Designers working within the Microsoft Windows environment can use windows, prompts, dialogue boxes and defaults on-screen to assure the effectiveness of the design. Icons and colour can also be used to enhance user understanding of input screens.

Interfaces are the means by which the system user interacts with the machine. Typically, the systems analyst will work with the programmer to conceptualize the interfaces for a proposed system. Some interfaces include: natural language, command language question-and-answer, menus, form-fill and graphic user interfaces (GUI, which is pronounced 'gooey'). Combinations of interfaces can be extremely effective. For example, using pull-down menus within GUI, or employing nested menus within question-and-answer interfaces yields interesting combinations. Each interface poses a different level of challenge for programmers, with natural language being the most difficult to programme. Systems analysts also design queries, which are designed to allow users to extract meaningful data from a database.

An important part of design includes the development of system or program feedback for the user. System feedback is necessary to let users know: if their input is being accepted; if input is or is not in the correct form; if processing is going on; if requests can or cannot be processed; and if more detailed information is available and how to get it.

8 Alternative systems development methodologies

Although structured methodologies and CASE tools were pervasive in the early 1980s, alternative methodologies and development approaches were also being introduced. In many cases they arose out of dissatisfaction with the SDLC and a firm commitment to increasing user participation in the systems development process. Prototyping was adapted and offered as a response to extended development times incurred in the SDLC. Project champions were offered as a participative approach for involving one key person to ensure systems success (Beath 1991). Another approach, ETHICS (Effective Technical and Human Implementation of Computer-based Systems) (Mumford and Weir 1979) was introduced as a sociotechnical methodology to combine social and technical solutions. Soft Systems Methodol-

ogy was presented as a way to depict organizational life that is both rich and chaotic (Checkland 1981) (see SYSTEMS). In the late 1980s a methodology called Multiview was introduced to make use of the many competing approaches (Avison and Wood-Harper 1990). More recently, metaphorical analysis (Kendall and Kendall 1993) was used to understand users' language in order to improve systems development.

Prototyping

Prototyping (Alavi 1984) demands the rapid development of some system features; high analyst and user involvement; the ability to incorporate changes quickly according to feedback; and a willingness to scrap what is undesirable. The analyst goes through several iterations of use and feedback, refining features until the user is satisfied with the system (Naumann and Jenkins 1982) (see INFORMATION AND KNOWLEDGE INDUSTRY). Prototyping is rife with uncertainty about user requirements, user behaviour and the feasibility of technical design solutions.

Project champions

The project champion is usually one user, chosen by the organization and the systems analyst, who is seen as pivotal in gaining the acceptance of a new technology (Beath 1991). Project champions are enthusiastic, knowledgeable about the technology, have influence with key user groups and basically stake their future careers on the success of the new technology by actively promoting its acceptance in the organization. The project champion possesses particular personality characteristics, leadership behaviour and career experience.

ETHICS

ETHICS examines the quality of work life, helping users design solutions to problems that not only fulfil technical objectives, but also give consideration to social interactions (Mumford 1983; Mumford and Weir 1979). The ETHICS method is of a participative nature, emphasizing user involvement. The sociotechnical approach upon which ETHICS is based improves the relationship between the groups and its work. The ETHICS method attempts to fulfil users' information needs in a social context, whether the solution is a manual procedure or the use of a computer. A work group needs to spend time together in order to recognize its true needs. With the ETHICS method there is a strong sense of group support for improving their life together, a personal commitment to values and an alternative orientation and concern for the group's overall lifestyle.

Soft Systems Methodology

Soft Systems Methodology (SSM) was created by Checkland (1981, 1989). It is concerned with helping the organization in learning; in prescribing general problem formulation approaches rather than tools and techniques. At its core is the 'root definition' that spells out verbally the critical aspects of the organization. It concerns itself with wholes rather than parts and denies the existence of organizational objectives, needs and performance objectives. Checkland believes that human activity systems possess goals that are not quantifiable, and describes organizations wrestling with these goals as the organizational conversation. There is not just one commonly-agreed upon goal, rather, there is an alternative orientation. SSM discusses the chaos (messiness) of the organizational situation in which users and analysts find themselves.

Multiview

The Multiview methodology (Avison and Wood-Harper 1990) discusses defining an information system as a social process. Multiview sees analysts as acting in a society, or social system, with the possibility of taking on several different societal roles; for example, either as a technical expert, a liberal teacher, an agent for social progress or a change catalyst. Multiview maintains an alternative-orientated perspective. The developers of Multiview characterize it as a flexible framework that does not force the analyst to choose among competing methodologies,

rather it provides a framework for how to use different tools, with adjustments being made according to the particular problem being faced.

Metaphorical analysis

Metaphors are ways of saying that something is something else, for example, an aggressive and acquisitive organization is a lean and hungry tiger. Using metaphorical analysis of users' own language in an organization can help with the analysis, improve the design, and provide a more successful implementation. At least nine user metaphors have been identified in organizations using this approach. They are the game, machine, journey, jungle, family, zoo, society, war and organism (Kendall and Kendall 1993).

9 Object-orientated systems analysis and design

Object-oriented analysis, design and programming have been developed as a response to the need for flexibility in computer-based information systems. The increasing popularity of object-oriented programming languages has resulted in a number of attempts at object-oriented systems analysis and design (Coad and Yourdon 1991; Booch 1991). Although these methods differ in their approach and notation, they share some basic concepts, including objects and classes, messages, encapsulation, inheritance and polymorphism. An object is a computer representation of some real world thing or event. Classes are groups of similar objects. Messages are the way objects communicate with each other. Since all of an object's internal data is buffered from other objects by its behaviour, objects are said to 'encapsulate' their data. Inheritance concept refers to the ability to create 'derived' classes based in part on old ('base') classes. Derived classes can inherit all or part of the structure and behaviour of base classes and extend these with new structures and behaviours. Polymorphism means that a base class may take the form of any of its derived classes when the circumstances demand it. Encapsulation, inheritance and polymorphism are intended to provide complex systems with mechanisms for fast, easy and reliable program maintenance and change.

JULIE E. KENDALL

KENNETH E. KENDALL
RUTGERS UNIVERSITY

Further reading

(References cited in the text marked *)

* Alavi, M. (1984) 'An assessment of the prototyping approach to information systems', *Communications of the ACM* 27 (6): 556–63. (A classic article on prototyping which demonstrates the risks associated with this approach.)
* Avison, D.E. and Wood-Harper, A.T. (1990) *Multiview: An Exploration in Information Systems Development*, Oxford: Blackwell. (Introduces an original, integrative approach to systems development called Multiview.)
* Beath, C.M. (1991) 'Supporting the information technology champion', *MIS Quarterly* 15 (3): 355–72. (Sets out an original vision of how the project champion initiates and supports changing information technology in organizations.)
* Booch, G. (1991) *Object Oriented Design with Applications*, Redwood City, CA: Benjamin/Cummings. (A new approach to systems design using an object-oriented paradigm.)
* Checkland, P.B. (1981) *Systems Thinking, Systems Practice*, Chichester: Wiley. (The original explication of soft systems methodology which is an alternative to traditional, structured development approaches.)
* Checkland, P.B. (1989) 'Soft systems methodology', *Human Systems Management* 8 (4): 271–89. (Revisits and enriches the author's original soft systems methodology after about a decade of use.)
* Coad, P. and Yourdon, E. (1991) *Object-Oriented Analysis*, 2nd edn, Englewood Cliffs, NJ: Yourdon. (An important book detailing a new approach to systems analysis.)
* Downs, E., Clare, P. and Coe, I. (1988) *Structured Systems Analysis and Design Method: Application and Context*, Hemel Hempstead: Prentice Hall. (Details the use of SSADM in the UK.)
* Gane, C. and Sarson, T. (1979) *Structured Systems Analysis and Design Tools and Techniques*, Englewood Cliffs, NJ: Prentice Hall. (Classic reference for structured approaches. Provides clear examples.)
* Jackson, M. (1983) *Systems Development*, Englewood Cliffs, NJ: Prentice Hall. (A presentation of the author's original, precision-like approach to systems development.)
* Kendall, K.E. (1996) 'Artificial intelligence and Götterdämerung: the evolutionary paradigm of the future', The *DATA BASE for Advances in Information Systems* 27 (4): 99–115. (Predicts the next 50 years of design work for systems analysts using the operas of Wagner's *Ring of the Nibelung* cycle as a methodology.)
* Kendall, K.E. (1997) 'The significance of information systems research on emerging technologies: seven information technologies that promise to improve managerial significance', *Decision Sciences* 28 (4): 775–92. (An original framework to classify and interpret emerging information technologies.)
* Kendall, K.E. (1999) *Emerging Information Technologies: Improving Decisions, Cooperation, and Infrastructure*, (edited) Thousand Oaks, CA: Sage Publications, Inc. (Comprehensive explanation and application of emerging information technologies whose applications are typically designed by analysts including recommendation systems, AI, virtual teams, ecommerce, push and pull technologies, and data warehousing.)
* Kendall, J.E. and Kendall, K.E. (1993) 'Metaphors and methodologies: living beyond the systems machine', *Management Information Systems Quarterly* 17 (2): 149–71. (An alternative approach that matches key metaphors of users such as war and family with those in well-known methodologies.)
* Kendall, J.E. and Kendall, K.E. (1999) 'Information delivery systems: an exploration of Web push and pull technologies', *Communications of AIS* 1 (14). (Names and classifies eight types of push and pull technologies designed by systems analysts for users of the World Wide Web.)
* Kendall, K.E. and Kendall, J.E. (2001) *Systems Analysis and Design*, 5th edn, Upper Saddle River, NJ: Prentice Hall. (A comprehensive text covering all aspects of modern systems analysis and design.)
* Mumford, E. (1983) *Designing Participatively – A Participative Approach to Computer Systems Design*, Manchester: Manchester Business School. (An elaboration of the author's earlier work on her original ETHICS methodology, with examples.)
* Mumford, E. and Weir, M. (1979) *Computer Systems in Work Design – the ETHICS Method*, London: Associated Business Press. (Introduction of an original sociotechnical approach to systems analysis and design.)

* Naumann, J.D. and Jenkins, A.M. (1982) 'Prototyping: the new paradigm for systems development', *Management Information Systems Quarterly* 6 (3): 29–44. (Classic article on prototyping that introduced the approach to information systems.)
* Yourdon, E. (1989) *Modern Structured Analysis*, Englewood Cliffs, NJ: Prentice Hall. (An elaboration of the author's well-accepted approach to structured systems development.)

See also: DECISION SUPPORT SYSTEMS; EXECUTIVE INFORMATION SYSTEMS; EXPERT SYSTEMS; INFORMATION AND KNOWLEDGE INDUSTRY; INFORMATION TECHNOLOGY; MANAGEMENT INFORMATION SYSTEMS; RE-ENGINEERING; SYSTEMS

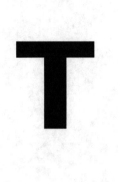

T

Taiwan, management in

1 The political environment
2 The business environment
3 State-run enterprises
4 Labour and human capital
5 Infrastructure
6 Conclusion

Overview

During the last four decades, Taiwan has undergone massive political and economic changes. From an agrarian society, when KMT, the nationalist party, moved to Taiwan in 1949, it emerged rapidly as an exporter of manufactured goods. At present, Taiwan is well on its way to become the world's leading exporter in a wide sector of high-technology products. These positive changes have taken place despite anything but a favourable political environment: initially a friend of the West and one of the bulwarks against mainland Chinese communism, Taiwan was also a recipient of US economic aid and a founding member of the United Nations (UN).

Since Taiwan's expulsion from the UN in 1971 and President Carter's resumption of diplomatic relations with the People's Republic of China in 1979, Taiwan's foreign relations never ceased to be overshadowed by its relationship with the People's Republic. No official diplomatic ties exist with any Organization for Economic Cooperation and Development country. Indeed, Taiwan has to celebrate every diplomatic trifle as a major breakthrough away from China's stranglehold.

The ninth biggest trading nation of the world has prospered on a trade diet that refutes the (World Bank) proponents of free trade. Taiwan's illiberal trade regime utilized customs and excise to generate income and to protect its own infant industry. Only on the eve of the WTO (World Trade Organization) negotiations in 1994–5 did the government commit itself to make far-reaching concessions to a more liberal trade regime, notably the politically sensitive areas of agriculture, cars and liberalizing markets formerly catered for by state monopolies, for example alcohol and designated sectors of telecommunications.

1 The political environment

Taiwan has correctly been described in the Western press as one of the most vibrant and open democracies in the region and the democratic transition that began in the last years of Chiang Ching-kuo's (Chiang Kai-shek's son and political heir) reign has now, in 1998 with the second round of legislative elections, been successfully completed. The Taiwan born president, Lee Teng-hui, was reaffirmed in office in the first ever direct election in 1996, and he represents for the Taiwan people the middle ground they would like to adapt in the tense and strained relations with China (see CHINA, MANAGEMENT IN).

The continuing diplomatic isolation and the politically sensitive relationship with China have had an important impact on Taiwan's economy. China views Taiwan as a renegade province and ultimately aims at re-unification. The KMT government itself, while officially committed to eventual peaceful reunification, now strives for equal 'temporary' recognition of both republics of China and re-entry into the United Nations (UN).

Trade with China via Hong Kong has greatly increased since the mid-1980s and was relatively unimportant before that, as Taiwan found an ideal market in the USA. In the past, Hong Kong therefore served as a gate to the outside world, not just as an entrepôt for trade, but also for people travelling between Taiwan and Europe, as Taiwan's isolation from international air traffic was virtually complete until the early 1980s. Even after China's resumption of sovereignty over Hong Kong in July 1997, Hong Kong continues to be of vital importance to Taiwan, as Taiwan still has no direct trade links with China. A couple of 'direct shipping links' were opened with much fanfare in 1996, but since the designated ports in China are insignificant and off the map for Taiwanese traders, actual trade volume remains negligible. However, the access to Hong Kong and its markets, as well as Taiwan's massive direct investment in China (estimated in 1997 to stand at an accumulated US$30bn according to Chinese official sources) will serve the Chinese government as a leverage to speed up unification negotiations with Taiwan.

However, Taiwan's increasing economic clout has induced all major trading partners to have a camouflaged diplomatic mission in the capital of Taiwan, disguised as 'trade missions'. The most important one to Taiwan is the American Chamber of Commerce. Economic links as well as the political weight given to improving diplomatic ties with the USA have heavily influenced Taiwan's foreign policy.

2 The business environment

In contrast to Hong Kong, Taiwan's legal framework is influenced by the German and Japanese legal systems, and is consequently based on codified law. While on an everyday basis, informal contracts are the means of conducting business, Taiwanese accept more and more the perceived need of a formal contract when dealing with foreign partners (Genzberger *et al.* 1994). Traditionally, Chinese society is not very litigious and more 'harmonious' means of dispute settlement prevail. Although legal claims brought before court are more frequent, arbitration as a means of solving disputes is more likely to create a mutually acceptable result. Observers have also voiced concern over the impartiality of the judges which might influence a fair trial. In addition, bringing a lawsuit against a Taiwanese business partner might irreparably damage the plaintiff's relationship not only with the defendant, but also with other prospective clients and partners in Taiwan.

One school of management thought postulates the pre-eminence of Confucian values in Chinese/Taiwanese management structures. Filial piety, frugality, industry and most importantly the paternalistic attitude of the employer towards his employee are seen to be the key elements. A survey by Liu *et al.* (1994) finds a more differentiated view, in that 49 per cent of managers interviewed put trustworthiness, quality control, cautiousness and innovation as key elements in their business philosophy (see BUSINESS CULTURES, ASIAN PACIFIC; HONG KONG, MANAGEMENT IN; SINGAPORE, MANAGEMENT IN).

Personal relationships, or *guanxi*, are the *sine qua non* of management practices in Taiwan. The business landscape varies widely in Taiwan, from world-leading multinationals to family sweatshops in the backyard (Chen 1994), yet all have to rely on a network of personal contacts to be able to succeed in their enterprises.

The fragmented economic landscape of Taiwan – 97 per cent of all enterprises belong to the small- and medium-sized category – is thus not as fragmented as it might appear at first glance. On nearly every level of enterprises, there exists a complicated network of sub-contracting, based on trust and long-term relationships (Shieh 1992: 93). For smaller firms, sub-contracting often means working for relatives; while for larger firms, the equivalent would be strangers introduced, however, by a common business friend or personal friends.

None the less, the sub-contracting system is not as pronounced or as stable as those for example found in Japan. The line between business and social relationships is blurred, yet economic rationale is said not to overtake obligations or feelings of friendship (Deglopper 1972).

Personal relationships taken to the extreme, one could argue, give rise to the existence of Mafiosi-like organizations in Taiwan. Trust, absolute loyalty and long-term commitment form the basis of the Taiwanese triads. Importantly, these triads are not a criminal institution *per se*, but rather the Taiwanese equivalent of an old boys' network – with slight alterations. Government officials, bankers and businessmen are often involved in Mafiosi affairs. Channelled through a tight network at all levels of society, the triads' influence on politics, mostly on a county level, and in economic decision making has long been a concern of the Taiwanese populace.

3 State-run enterprises

After the KMT resumed sovereignty over Taiwan in 1949, state-run firms were a vital tool for revitalizing the economy. The generation of savings, creation of investment and employment initially depended heavily on state enterprises (Wade 1990). During the late 1950s, the government decided to 'privatize' important industries by selling them to businessmen with appropriate political credentials and background.

In contrast to South Korea, the Taiwan equivalent of *chaebols* (business conglomerates) is not very prevalent (see CHAEBOLS). However, business groups do exist and they continue to determine important sectors of the Taiwanese economy. Although not in government hands, by the very nature of the regime these corporations have to accommodate themselves with the government. Some were even, as mentioned above, founded on a basis of 'friendship' and a feeling of obligation by the owner towards the ruling party. Firms such as Evergreen, Taiwan Plastics and Taiwan Steel are privately owned yet used, at times, as a governmental vehicle to achieve developmental or political goals. The KMT is very adept at using a carrot and stick policy to steer the direction of corporate investment. As land becomes increasingly dear in Taiwan, planning permission, especially in the Taipei area, is often politically motivated (Moore 1989). A good example of a private enterprise colluding/collaborating with the government is Evergreen. One of the biggest container companies in the world, Evergreen launched a new airline in 1992. The chairman of Evergreen is a notoriously good friend of President Lee Teng-hui. EVA Airways Corporation has now taken over the function of a 'flag carrier' and flies to countries where the official Taiwanese airline would never get landing permission because of Taiwan's peculiar political status.

Until 1991, the financial sector was firmly under governmental control (Chui 1992). The three commercial state-owned banks, the 'Big Three', dominated the commercial credit market for enterprises. They are specialized banks with a clearly defined developmental role and under a tight reign to implement government policy. In the wake of the government's drive to promote Taiwan as a regional operations centre – and to join the World trade organization – the government has initiated an ambitious privatization plan which also includes the 'Big Three'.

This signifies an important policy shift as state monopolies were a convenient source of income for the government. For example, the import of apples was monopolized in the past. Apples are an auspicious fruit of the Taiwanese and price elasticity was very low, one apple could cost up to US$3. Beer production is still firmly under government control, but even here, the government envisages privatization in the medium term, with the result of 'streamlining' the production redundancies. Other important state monopolies that are – or will be – privatized include the Telecommunications sector and Taiwan Petroleum. Even in the holy grail of agricultural protection, tariffs are planned to be lowered, once Taiwan has joined the World trade organization, and the import of rice will be regulated by quotas rather than completely banned.

4 Labour and human capital

Taiwan has a highly skilled workforce (see HUMAN RESOURCE MANAGEMENT IN ASIA PACIFIC). At any given year, some thirty thousand students study abroad, many of them on government grants. The proportion of US-educated PhDs at universities and research institutions is very high, at the most prestigious institutions well over 50 per cent. Expenditure on education is in the region of 7 per cent of gross national product (GNP).

The commitment of the government to providing education is mirrored by the commitment of students and parents alike (Lin 1983). Families are willing to make high financial sacrifices to send their children to preparatory schools, so-called 'cram schools', in order to obtain a university place. Pressure on high-school students is high, as only 30 per cent of students who sit the university entry exam pass the test.

Since the 1950s, Taiwan has actively controlled and promoted the creation of human capital. In the earlier years of the republic, emphasis (and entry control) was on vocational training to keep up with the demand of blue-collar workers. With the rapid changes in economic structure and economic growth, Taiwan faces the enormous task of improving its educational infrastructure. Realizing that this could not be done at the speed demanded, the government continues to implement scholarship schemes worth millions of US dollars to send students to the USA and Europe to complete their higher education.

Thus, Taiwan is in the paradoxical situation where a high output of skilled labour meant, on the one hand, a certain saturation in less booming sectors, while on the other hand an acute shortage is felt in relatively 'new' sectors of the economy, that is finance, information technology and 'modern' management. Consequently, the government has, albeit reluctantly, relaxed the limit on the number of expatriate experts working in Taiwan. However, strings are attached to this offer, as the government expects a high level of technology transfer (Myers 1986).

Taiwan also suffers from a lack of low wage and unskilled labour, a situation similar to those faced in Singapore and Hong Kong. With wage levels approaching those of countries in the Organization for Economic Cooperation and Development, dangerous and manual jobs, particularly in the construction sector, are occupied by workers from low-income neighbouring countries, especially the Philippines. In fact, the fishery sector employs mainland Chinese, circumventing the law that Chinese citizens cannot reside on Taiwan by offering them housing on ships off the Taiwanese coast, often in very poor conditions.

The shortage of both blue- and white-collar workers is said to have had an impact on the relatively peaceful labour relations. Dissatisfied workers, fired or leaving out of their own free will, have no difficulties in switching employers (Genzberger et al. 1994). Historically, labour unions are, unlike the militant unions in Korea, extremely weak, and labour activism has been consistently suppressed by the government and employers. Unions are comparatively passive and willing to compromise when it comes to protecting labour rights. Additionally, the present labour market gives little incentive for joining labour unions.

5 Infrastructure

Taiwan's society and infrastructure are much less 'internationalized', both in terms of catering for the needs of expatriate workers and tourist flows. This is partly due to government restrictions, but also to the homogeneous nature of Taiwanese inhabitants, who have as yet been very little exposed to an influx of foreigners on a scale comparable to Hong Kong. While academics often speak excellent English, the use of English is not very common in the Taiwanese business community, nor in the population at large.

The government aims at improving English literacy in the population: English-language media do exist but do not provide in-depth information of important political and economic events. The major (and more independent) newspapers specializing in finance and economics are published in Chinese only.

The transportation infrastructure in Taiwan is being modernized, and after many delays Taipei's elevated light railway-cum-underground system is partially operational. Cars and buses continue to be the main means of transport in the cities, but the introduction of bus lanes in Taipei has led to a noticeable improvement and cut down journey times. Other important infrastructural projects, such as the construction of a rail link from Taiwan's main international airport to Taipei, and a high speed rail link from the most northern tip down to the south, are still embroiled in allegations of corruption and bid rigging. However, this should not distract one from the fact that Taiwan boasts an extremely well-developed air transport system which is safe and reliable, and makes commuting across the island almost a pleasure.

6 Conclusion

Taiwan's stunning economic development was marked by a low volatility of growth rates and peaceful labour relations. Taiwan's main challenge in the 1990s, as perceived by the government, is both to regain international status and to upgrade its domestic technology. Plans were unveiled during 1994–5 to make Taiwan a regional hub in terms of finance, telecommunications, air and sea transportation. While the aim to overtake Hong Kong and Singapore is over-optimistic, Taiwan thereby confronts the perceived need of modernizing its economic infrastructure. The 1997 economic and financial turmoil that has hit its main competitors hard, namely Singapore and Hong Kong, has left Taiwan relatively unscathed. Despite some temporary restrictions on speculative capital flows following the financial crisis in east Asia, Taiwan's economy is open to foreigners and foreign influence, and its firms are increasingly on the cutting edge of information technology. Moreover, Taiwan's society is affluent and peaceful, and the negative impact of China's takeover of Hong Kong is much smaller than some observers feared.

JOHANNA BOESTEL
SCHOOL OF ORIENTAL AND AFRICAN STUDIES
UNIVERSITY OF LONDON

Further reading

(References cited in the text marked *)

Chan, S. and Clark, C. (1992) *Flexibility, Foresight and Fortuna in Taiwan's Development: Navigating between Scylla and Charybdis*, London: Routledge. (A case study of Taiwan's political economy and development.)

* Chen, J.-S. (1994) *Cooperation Network and Social Structure: A Socio-Economic Analysis of Taiwan's Small- and Medium-Sized Enterprises*, (in Chinese), Taipei: Lian Jing Press. (A thorough analysis of the peculiarities of small and medium-sized enterprises, the backbone of Taiwan's economy.)

Chow, P.C.Y. and Gill, B. (2000) *Weathering the Storm: Taiwan, Its Neighbors and the Asian Financial Crisis*, Washington, DC: Brookings Institution Press. (Entire section explaining how Taiwan's economy was able to weather the storm that was the Asian financial crisis.)

Chu, Y.P. and Wu, R. (1998) *Business, Markets and Government in Asia-Pacific*, London: Routledge. (Provides an up-to-date analysis of the ways in which governments in the Asia Pacific are coping with rapid industrial and economic change.)

* Chui, P.C.H. (1992) 'Money and financial markets: the domestic perspective', in G. Ranis (ed.), *Taiwan, from a Developing to a Mature Economy*, Boulder, CO: Westview Press. (A good overview of financial liberalization in Taiwan.)

Clancy, M. (ed.) (1998) *Business Guide to Taiwan*, MA: Butterworth Heinemann. (Part of the 'Business Guide to Asia' series, provides detailed information on setting up and running business ventures in Taiwan.)

* Deglopper, D.R. (1972) 'Doing business in Lugang', in W.W. Willmott (ed.), *Economic Organisation in Chinese Society*, Stanford, CA: Stanford University Press. (An anthropological study on Taiwanese business practices.)

* Genzberger, C.A. *et al.* (1994) *Taiwan Business*, San Rafael: World Trade Press. (A very useful guide to Taiwan, with broad coverage of important issues one needs to know when starting a business in Taiwan.)

Harwood, A., Litan, R.E. and Pomerleano, M. (1999) *Financial Markets and Development: The Crisis in Emerging Markets*, Washington, DC: Brookings Institution Press. (This volume brings together market economists, policymakers, development specialists and academics from developed and emerging market economies to examine the underlying causes of the Asian financial crisis and ways of preventing future crises in emerging markets.)

* Lin, C.-J. (1983) 'The Republic of China', in R.M. Thomas and T.N. Postlethwaite (eds), *Schooling in East Asia*, New York: Pergamon Press. (A broad overview of education and government investment in schooling in Taiwan.)

Lin, P.A. (1991) 'The social sources of capital investment in Taiwan's industrialisation', in E.K.Y. Chen (ed.), *Business Networks and Economic Development in East and South East Asia*, Hong Kong: Centre of Asian Studies, University of Hong Kong. (A description of the networking process in Taiwan.)

* Liu, P.C.K., Liu L.C. and Wu, H.-l. (1994) 'Emergence of new business organisation and management in Taiwan', *Industry of Free China* November: 33–62. (Analysis based on survey data of the changing managerial landscape in Taiwan.)

* Moore, J. (1989) 'Taipei's roaring real estate prices spark street protests', *Far Eastern Economic Review* 146 (42): 65. (A short observation on the growing lobbying pressure of the middle classes with regards to housing policies shortly before the elections.)

* Myers, R.H. (1986) 'Economic development of ROC on Taiwan, 1965–1981', in L.J. Lau (ed.), *Models of Development*, San Francisco, CA: Institute for Contemporary Studies. (A short comparative study of Taiwan's economic growth.)

Selya, R.M. (1995) *Taipei*, Chichester: Wiley. (A city guide of Taipei with a historical and political input.)

* Shieh, G.S. (1992) *'Boss' Island*, New York: Peter Lang Publishing. (An anthropological, in-depth analysis of the micro sub-contracting network in Taiwan.)

Smith, H. (2000) *Industry Policy in Taiwan and Korea in the 1980s*, Edward Elgar. (Smith re-ignites the contentious debate of the role of the state using East Asian economic development in general with particular emphasis on Taiwan and Korea. Includes comprehensive discussion of strategic industry policy with an application to East Asia; discussion of the impact of the 1997–8 financial crisis in Korea; and a critique of the structuralist/revisionist literature in the light of the financial crisis.)

Vines, S. (2000) *The Years of Living Dangerously: Asia – From Financial Crisis to the New Millennium*, London: Texere Publishing. (Hard-hitting book by foreign correspondent Stephen Vines argues that the 1997 collapse could be repeated because many of Asia's leading companies remain fundamentally weak and that the rapid recovery of the financial markets has engendered a false sense of security.)

* Wade, R. (1990) *Governing the Market: Economic Theory and the Role of Government in East Asian Industrialisation*, Princeton, NJ: Princeton University Press. (A thorough rejection of the World Bank paradigm that the east Asian tigers followed a free trade and financial regime.)

Woo, W.T., Sachs, J.D. and Schwab, K. (eds) (2000) *The Asian Financial Crisis*, MA: MIT Press. (The book makes clear that there is little particularly Asian about the Asian financial crisis and argues that the spread of the crisis reflects the rapid arrival of global capitalism in a world economy not used to the integration of the advanced and developing countries.)

See also: ASIA PACIFIC, MANAGEMENT IN; BUSINESS CULTURES, ASIAN PACIFIC; CHAEBOLS; CHINA, MANAGEMENT IN; HONG KONG, MANAGEMENT IN; HUMAN RESOURCE MANAGEMENT IN ASIA PACIFIC; JAPAN, MANAGEMENT IN; SINGAPORE, MANAGEMENT IN

Takeovers: see ACQUISITIONS AND DIVESTMENTS: MERGERS, ACQUISITIONS AND JOINT VENTURES

Tanzania, management in

1 Introduction
2 Analysis
3 Evaluation
4 Conclusion

Overview

This entry introduces the key issues affecting the process and practice of management in Tanzania. Despite an abundance of natural resources, Tanzania is one of the least developed countries in the world. Endemic poverty has had a strong impact on the prevalent type of management: a tendency towards *laissez-faire*. For nearly three decades, post-independence Tanzania pursued a socialist orientation, and put the bulk of the economy into state corporations. The pattern of management in such corporations – characteristically inefficient and corrupt – came to overshadow the entire framework of management in the country. Political and economic restructuring began towards the end of the 1980s, and the country is entering the new millennium with a new outlook as well as new management perspectives.

1 Introduction

A combination of many interrelated factors has influenced the pattern of management in Tanzania (see AFRICA, MANAGEMENT IN). Among these factors, three stand out clearly. The first is the very low level of social and economic development in the country. The second relates to the dominant role that the state has historically played in Tanzania in practically all public affairs. Third, the social and cultural features of what is essentially a rural traditional society have also influenced the practice of management. Section 2 of this entry examines how these and other aspects have influenced the country's management pattern.

Tanzania lies on the east coast of Africa, just below the equator. Covering some 945,234 square kilometres, it is by far the largest country in the region. Tanzania is larger than neighbouring Kenya and Uganda combined. Except for a narrow belt of 900 square kilometres along the coast, most of Tanzania lies above 200 metres in altitude, and much of the country is higher than 1000 metres above sea level.

Estimates put the country's population for 1999 at just over 32.9 million. Close to 85 per cent of the people live in rural areas – mostly as smallholder peasants. The population growth rate is just over 3 per cent – one of the highest in the world. Indeed, the urban areas register an annual growth rate of over 8 per cent. Like other countries in Africa, Tanzania's population is relatively young – people under 15 years of age constitute more than 40 per cent of the population.

Apart from its relatively large size, the country has abundant natural resources. There are considerable deposits of minerals: gold, diamonds, gemstones, gypsum, and tanzanite – a mineral found in Tanzania only. As for agriculture, practically every tropical crop grows in one or more of the country's three main ecological zones. There is wheat, coffee, tea, potatoes and pyrethrum in the highlands lying along the frontiers. The plateau area in the centre of the country produces maize, rice, sorghum, sisal, millet, cotton and tobacco. On the other hand, coconuts, cashew nuts and many types of spices abound on the coastal strip and on the Indian Ocean islands.

Despite this apparent endowment in natural resources, however, Tanzania is one of the poorest countries in the world. With an annual income per capita of just under US$200, the country ranks amongst the world's ten least developed countries. The mineral deposits are largely untapped, the agricultural sector is backward, and the country's infrastructure is very poor. While fairly vibrant, the industrial and commercial sectors are relatively small.

The economy, therefore, is quite shaky (Stewart *et al.* 1992). External debts – accumulated over decades – annually rob the country of the bulk of whatever surpluses the economy is able to generate. With a debt per capita value that is far above the country's per capital income, Tanzania is in the World Bank's category of *severely indebted low-income countries*. Throughout the 1980s and 1990s, the balance of payments deficit increased annually. In 1997 it constituted about 10 per cent of the country's gross domestic product.

Unlike the other countries in the region, Tanzania has had a chequered political career. The country has gone through a number of very different political regimes. The European scramble for African colonies in the nineteenth century had placed the bulk of what is now Tanzania under German rule. The defeat of Germany during the First World War shifted Tanganyika – as the mainland part was then called – into the British Empire as a United Nations trusteeship territory. Independence from Britain came at the end of 1961, and in 1964 Tanganyika united with the next door island of Zanzibar to form *The United Republic of Tanzania*. The first two and half decades of independence saw a one-party political system with a socialist orientation. Finally, the coming of multi-party politics towards the end of the 1980s coincided with the introduction of liberal policies on the economic front. The country has therefore gone through a series of very distinctive and radically different epochs that few other African countries have experienced.

Like other African countries, Tanzanian society is still in the process of formation. The landmass that Germany conquered and ruled from 1885 to 1918 consisted of more than 100 traditional societies. These were at different levels of development and had varied social structures and systems. The Germans used a variety of techniques – including very brutal 'pacification drives' – to amalgamate them into a single economic entity. The main role of the colony was to supply Germany with agricultural raw materials, particularly cotton, rubber and sisal. Using an approach that combined integration with 'divide-and-rule', the British later continued with this mission of turning the country into a true colonial appendage – not only economically, but also culturally.

The struggle for colonial independence had nationalism as its strongest expression. Its main voice was to transcend ethnic divisions, in addition to conquering foreign occupation. This appeal for nationalism was so successful that the anti-colonial movement became by far the strongest political movement in Eastern Africa. The post-independence regime pursued this same agenda of nationalism for well over two decades – vigorously championing 'nation-building' in all economic and social policies. Indeed, it is economic nationalism that drove even the socialist policies. Nationalization of the 'commanding heights of the economy' in 1967 was more of a nationalistic than a class ideology (Shivji 1985).

Having a common language, *Swahili*, the country has achieved a level of national consciousness that is unmatched in any other country in eastern and southern Africa. While ethnic cleavages do still erupt periodically, the spirit of nationhood has reached a fairly high level. The relative peace that has characterized Tanzanian society for all the years of independence is a reflection of this spirit.

2 Analysis

The social setting

The social conditions in Tanzania have a bearing on the process and pattern of managing the country's institutions. In this regard, the society's poverty is a critical factor. Tanzania is a very poor country, by any standards. Gross domestic product figures for 1997 were US$8.8 billion – a per capita domestic product of only about US$240 million. Close to 30 per cent of gross domestic product is not even part of the monetary sector: it represents the estimated value of household subsistence goods and services. Individual earnings for the vast majority of the people are therefore very low. Even in urban areas – where living conditions tend to be higher – people spend, on average, more than half of their incomes on food alone.

The physical and economic infrastructure is a major hindrance to organizational performance. In the countryside, practically every year sees areas experiencing a shortage of food while other areas have surpluses. It is not uncommon for villages to suffer a series of disasters emanating from floods in one season, and from drought the following season. Inadequate road and rail transport facilities are a major hindrance to productivity improvement in agriculture. Similarly, the poor calibre of financial services is an obstacle to the development of industry and commerce.

Government policy during the first 25 years of independence – from 1961 to 1986 – was socialist. The government created hundreds of state corporations to handle various sectors of the economy: banking, manufacturing, insurance, large scale farming, import and export trade, etc. Apart from wholesale and retail business, state enterprises dominated the bulk of economic activities in the country outside peasant agriculture. The 'parastatal' sector was therefore by far the largest sector in the modern economy. Its management style has had tremendous influence on the country's management pattern as a whole (Bol et al. 1997).

This socialist epoch contributed three important positive features to management in Tanzania. First, by putting emphasis on attaining self-reliance in technical expertise, it rapidly increased the number of skilled people in the country. For close to three decades, the government provided free or highly subsidized college education to all those who qualified – both within the country and outside. The number of training institutions for secondary school graduates increased tenfold in the first 20 years of independence. As a result, at the time of independence in 1961, Tanzania had less than a dozen graduates, by the mid 1980s some 4000 university graduates were joining the labour market annually. In addition, 10,000 more with diplomas in various fields –

engineering, nursing, agriculture, teaching, accounting, etc. – were leaving a myriad of colleges annually. For a small economy like that of Tanzania, these are not small numbers (see MANAGEMENT EDUCATION IN THE EMERGING COUNTRIES).

By 1990, Tanzania had more high level technical and professional skills than any other country in the region. Indeed, the number of qualified staff in such areas as engineering, finance, law, medicine, etc. was far higher than the country's economy and technology could justify or support. Low earnings and growing unemployment pushed a substantial portion of these graduates into the Southern Africa labour market where wages are higher. The best ones got jobs in Europe and North America or joined international organizations.

Second, the socialist policies of the time also enhanced access to basic education in the country (United Nations Development Programme [UNDP] 1995). Enrolment in primary school increased tremendously between 1961 and 1990. As a result of various educational efforts and reforms, during the 1980s Tanzania attained one of the highest primary school enrolment rates in sub-Saharan Africa: 96 per cent. In this way, the country created a *literate* labour force. In the context of Africa, this was a major achievement. It is therefore a characteristic of the labour market in the country that technical skills are generally available, and that unskilled labour is literate.

Third, improvements in basic education also brought about gender equality in education. In the mid 1980s, primary school enrolment achieved a 50:50 representation ratio between boys and girls (UNDP 1995). This success, however, was not repeated at secondary and higher levels of the education system. Social and cultural factors were a bigger obstacle to women attaining post-primary education – and therefore acquiring management positions – than they were for men. Even at the end of the 1990s, females constituted only about 20 per cent of university students, and about 5 per cent of technical college students.

It is therefore another characteristic of management in Tanzania that it is almost entirely male. Women have fewer opportunities than men to move into management positions.

While studies show that women do not suffer wage discrimination, women nevertheless do not have the same opportunities either at the point of entry or in terms of the rate of advancement. Even during the era of 'parastatal' bodies, women constituted a tiny proportion of management staff. In 1990, there were hardly any women holding top management positions in pubic enterprises. There was, for instance, only one female board chairperson compared to 449 males, no female managing directors, and only two female directors compared to 72 male ones. The situation in private enterprise was far worse. Things have improved somewhat since then, but not significantly.

Management education and training also benefited – albeit indirectly – from these early policies. A faculty of commerce and management opened its doors at the country's main university in the 1970s; when at least three other national institutions were beginning to give diploma level education in various aspects of management. Denied the autonomy to structure their own remuneration and incentive packages, state corporations often sent their managerial staff for training both locally and overseas as a way of rewarding them. In this way, management education and training received a notable boost.

The pattern of management

One of the glaring features of public life in Tanzania is obviously the low level of institutional capacity. It is not difficult to observe that institutions in the country generally have a very low capacity to discharge their functions. State institutions best illustrate this low level of management. Public agencies are unable to collect garbage from the streets, to carry out maintenance of the infrastructure, or even to collect revenues due to them. Similarly, public institutions that supposedly operate commercially to provide various utilities are grossly inefficient and ineffective. Within government, administrative systems and procedures are both cumbersome and outdated.

This scenario of weak management is of course not unique to Tanzania. Indeed, it is a common feature of Africa and other developing areas. There is no single factor that is the ultimate cause of this state of affairs. Rather, it is the product of a complex web of factors. Many authors (Jaeger and Kanungo 1990) have noted that institutions in developing countries operate under social, economic and political conditions that are, at once, both the *cause* and the *result* of poor performance (see HUMAN RESOURCE MANAGEMENT IN THE EMERGING COUNTRIES).

As elsewhere, the private sector operates quite differently. Wholesale and retail traders dominate this sector, but medium and small-scale industries are also sprouting. The sector faces stiff competition from imports, and therefore tries to carry itself in accordance with world standards. Multinational companies began moving aggressively into the economy in the 1990s, and these are making an impact on the style and pattern of management in the country.

3 Evaluation

There are a number of features that characterize the process of management in Tanzania. The process itself is dynamic, and the features are therefore in a state of constant evolution.

First, the work ethic is relatively weak. The low levels of living standards – coupled with very small rates of economic growth – have created a sense of *powerlessness* among people. Even managers easily exhibit a *laissez-faire* attitude to duties and responsibilities. Experience with the public sector strengthened this attitude. Indeed, the policy of public enterprises banished the sense of personal accountability, extolled corruption to high levels, and created an arena where staff in organizations – including managerial staff – openly engaged in looting their employing institutions.

This feature is of course changing. In practice at least, the country abandoned this socialist orientation from the mid-1980s. With guidance and insistence from the World Bank and the International Monetary Fund, the government embarked on economic restructuring (see INTERNATIONAL MONETARY FUND (IMF); WORLD BANK). It began selling enterprises, closing non-profitable ones, and liberalized trade and investment. Tanzania therefore entered a new epoch in the early 1990s. It is an epoch that is gradually changing the pattern of management– among many other things.

Second, the country inherited from the socialist epoch a cadre of managers that is lop-sided in its structure. The vast 'parastatal' sector that Tanzania built for over two decades consisted largely of monopolies. Its managers therefore tended to have a *production* rather than a *market* focus. They have had ample experience in overseeing the internal operational aspects of institutions, but lack the skills and experience of dealing with customer issues and problems. Tanzania is therefore left with a cadre of managers for a monopolistic environment.

For this reason, the multinational companies that – with economic liberalization – have rushed into the country have had no problems finding qualified engineers, lawyers, economists or scientists. They have, however, had difficulties finding people who can design marketing strategies. This feature is, of course, also changing fast. It will, however, take time before the lop-sided nature is fully corrected.

Third, the dominance of the state in organizational life during the socialist epoch meant that government mediated most institutional interactions in society (Shivji 1985). The state always mediated all transactions – arranging for credit, organizing distribution channels, importing and exporting, etc. The managers who therefore tended to excel in their respective organizations were those with competencies in dealing with government. Such managers had the influence to win political concessions, and the skills to manoeuvre through bureaucratic red tape. They have bequeathed a management orientation for taking short-cut measures to obtain short-term objectives. It is not a management orientation for formulating long-term strategies.

It is significant that even the private sector has tended to copy this approach to some extent. In the past, the most successful private businesses were those with connections to government officials. Thus, a tendency has grown whereby, rather than struggle to enhance its entrepreneurial capacities, the private sector also tends to look to government for solving the sector's problems.

Finally, management in Tanzania has had an inclination to be parochial in its outlook. The decades of state enterprises largely excluded foreign managers. The few who did work in the country came mainly at the behest of the state sector, and therefore had little influence over the style of management in the country. Indeed, theirs was largely a technical rather than a managerial role. As a result, Tanzanian managers have for a long time been able to shield themselves from the flow of ever-changing management ideas and practices that have been engulfing the rest of the world. For example, empowerment, total quality management, customer focus, re-engineering, etc. are generally untried management concepts in the country.

4 Conclusion

Tanzania left the twentieth century on a weak footing. The country, however, entered the new millennium with a great deal of expectations. A new political dispensation began in the early 1990s with the introduction of multi-party politics. It will take at least until the end of the first decade of the new millennium for the political system to stabilize fully. Investment in the key areas of the economy – mining, agriculture, and tourism – has now started to flow.

However, there are fundamental contradictions. For one, a de-emphasis on social services has already led to a downturn in education, health and welfare generally. The extent to which wealth generated through new investments is not siphoned out of the country is also, as yet, an open question.

Still, the prospects for a brighter future are better than at any other time. While the past bears heavily on the country's conscience, the opportunities are nevertheless irresistible. Above all, the structural reform of the civil service and the 'parastatal' sector is bringing a radically different management pattern to the country. This pattern will definitely have ramifications throughout society.

HENRY MAPOLU
REDMA – MANAGEMENT CONSULTANTS

Further reading

(References cited in the text marked *)

Austin, J.E. (1990) *Managing in Developing Countries* London: The Free Press. (A treatise on corporate management in the context of developing countries.)

* Bol, D., Luvanga, N. and Shitundu, J. (eds) (1997) *Economic Management in Tanzania*, Dar es Salaam: Tema Publishers. (Discusses the experience of different phases in the management of Tanzania's economy.)

Bryceson, D.F. (1993) *Liberalizing Tanzania's Food Trade*, Dar es Salaam: Mkuki na Nyota. (Case study on state policies on the management of the food industry in the country.)

Havnevik, K.J. (1993) *Tanzania: The Limits to Development from Above*, Dar es Salaam: Mkuki na Nyota. (Examines the interaction of policy makers, donors and experts on a major economic project in the country.)

* Jaeger, A.M. and Kanungo, R.N. (eds) (1990) *Management in Developing Countries*, London: Routledge. (Analysis of the various issues and features related to managing institutions in countries like Tanzania.)

Semboja, J. and Therkildsen, O. (eds) (1995) *Service Provision Under Stress in East Africa*, Dar es Salaam: Mkuki na Nyota. (Analysis of the role of the state and people's organizations in Kenya, Uganda and Tanzania.)

* Shivji, I. G. (ed.) (1985) *The State and the Working People in Tanzania*, Dakar: Codesria. (Contributions on the role of the state and different sectors and groups in Tanzania.)

* Stewart, F., Lall, S. and Wangwe, S. (eds) (1992) *Alternative Development Strategies in Sub-Saharan Africa*, London: The Macmillan Press. (Examines alternative policies for managing development in sub-Saharan Africa.)

* United Nations Development Programme (1995) *Human Development Report*, New York: United Nations Development Programme. (Contains very useful information on human development status in Tanzania.)

See also: AFRICA, MANAGEMENT IN; HUMAN RESOURCE MANAGEMENT IN THE EMERGING COUNTRIES; INDUSTRIAL RELATIONS IN THE EMERGING COUNTRIES; INTERNATIONAL MONETARY FUND; NIGERIA, MANAGEMENT IN; SOUTH AFRICA, MANAGEMENT IN; WORLD BANK

Tata, Jehangir Ratanji Dadabhoy (1904–93)

Personal background

- born 29 July 1904, Paris, of a French mother and an Indian (Parsi) father who belonged to a wealthy industrial family
- received his school education in Paris, Bombay, Yokohama and the UK but did not attend college
- became Bombay Flying Club's first pilot to obtain a flying licence in 1929
- participated in the Aga Khan Trophy in 1930, becoming the second Indian to fly UK–India or India–UK solo
- married Thelma Viccaji in 1930
- in 1932, his Karachi–Bombay flight for Tata Airlines inaugurated civil aviation in India
- in 1938, became chairman of Tata Sons, parent company of the Tata Group, the largest industrial group in India
- started the international airline Air India in 1948
- became the first national voice to call for the control of India's population in 1951 and started the Family Planning Foundation of India in 1970
- died 29 November 1993, in Geneva

Summary

Jehangir Ratanji Dadabhoy Tata (1904–93), better known as J.R.D., was the father of civil aviation in India and an industrialist. In 1938, he became chairman of the Tata Group of fourteen companies, comprising steel, electric power, textile, oils and soaps, and the famous Taj Mahal Hotel. When he stepped down in 1991 the Group had ninety-five companies – three of them among the ten largest in India.

From 1932 to 1978, J.R.D. remained active in the field of civil aviation. On the fiftieth anniversary of his inaugural flight launching India into civil aviation, at the age of 78, he repeated the performance in a vintage single-engine Leopard Moth.

1 Introduction

J.R.D. Tata's father, Ratanji Dadabhoy Tata, was an Indian industrialist related to Jamsetji N. Tata (1839–1904) who brought the industrial revolution to India through steel, hydro-electric power and the funding of its first university of science and technology. R.D. Tata was married to a French woman, Suzanne Brière. Their second child, Jehangir, was born in Paris. His school education was disrupted more than once as he spent a couple of years in Paris with his mother who then moved to India to be with her husband. In 1916, during the First World War, she suffered from tuberculosis and moved to Yokohama with her son, who was educated there.

After the war he returned to school in Paris. A place was reserved for him at Cambridge but prior to going there he was sent to a crammer to brush up on his English, his mother tongue being French. When he was ready to enter Cambridge the French authorities passed a conscription law and he joined a French cavalry regiment called 'Le Saphis' where, he complained, he was allowed to fire only five shots in one year! On completion of his conscription year his father summoned him to India. Eight months later his father died and J.R.D. had to step into his shoes as the director of Tata Sons (which prior to 1917 was called Tata & Sons). He was 22 years old.

2 Aviation

J.R.D. Tata's forty-six-year career in aviation began with the era of wood and fabric one-engined planes and ended with the jumbo jet. His love for aviation was born on the coast near Boulogne in France where his father had a summer cottage. Their neighbour was Blériot, the first aviator to fly across the English Channel. When Blériot's plane landed J.R.D. would help to push it into a makeshift hangar. When he was 15 years old he was given his first joy ride in France and it was then that he decided he would one day become a pilot. Ten years later, in 1929, he joined the Bombay Flying Club and graduated as its first pilot; he also received the first licence awarded by the Fédération Aeronautique International (FAI). In 1930 he competed for the Aga Khan Trophy of £500 to be awarded to the first person to fly solo from India to England or from England to India. Tata was flying from Karachi to London, while one of his main competitors, the pilot Aspy Engineer, was flying from London to Karachi. At Alexandria, J.R.D. found his competitor stranded for want of a spark plug and lent him an extra one. The competitor went on to beat J.R.D. by a couple of hours.

Soon after the contest, an English pilot called Nevill Vintcent proposed that J.R.D. start an airline to connect with the Imperial Airlines flight from London to Karachi, which carried mail from Europe. On 15 October 1932, J.R.D. carried the first mailbag from Karachi to Bombay. He nursed Tata Airlines with care and established standards which he kept up when Air India International was launched in partnership with the government. His dream of such partnerships continuing in other industrial ventures did not come to fruition.

After the war, the government continued to license more airlines than could be sustained by the market, in spite of repeated warnings from J.R.D. Finally, the airline industry was in such a crisis that the government nationalized the industry. J.R.D. was invited to be the chairman of all the domestic airlines as well as of Air India. He chose to remain the chairman of Air India alone, and guided the enterprise with zeal and skill, often giving half his working day to aviation and the rest to his industrial empire. It was his desire that Air India should be one of the best airlines in service, if not the largest in size. He became President of IATA (International Air Transport Association) in 1958 and made a significant contribution to its deliberations for two decades as a member of the executive committee. Sir William Hildred, IATA's Secretary General, wrote how 'the Committee has benefited at every meeting from your questing mind, your knowledge and experience and commonsense. ... I think without doubt there is no one geographically who could dream of replacing you' (Lala 1992a: 159). Air India won worldwide recognition under J.R.D.'s leadership but in 1978 he was relieved of the chairmanship:

Unpaid Air India Chief is Sacked by Desai

The air chief credited with making Air India one of the world's most successful airlines, basing its appeal on the beaming 'little Maharajah' emblem, has been fired by Mr Desai, the Prime Minister. His abrupt removal, apparently for political reasons, after 30 unpaid years at the helm of the national flag carrier, has left the business community in uproar and brought Mr Desai some of the worst publicity since he took office. Mr J.R.D. Tata, 73, is a legendary figure, known to legions of executives around the world and envied by most for his success ... with a fleet of only 14 aircraft, Air India last year flew more than 1 million passengers and made a profit of £11 million pounds. But despite this, and without warning, Mr Tata was replaced.

(*Daily Telegraph* 27 February 1978)

Even if Prime Minister Desai did not recognize J.R.D.'s contribution, others did. A number of awards followed, including one in the name of Tony Jannus – the entrepreneur who started the world's first airline in Tampa, Florida, in 1914 – and among whose recipients were the founders of Pan-Am and Eastern Airlines, and the inventor of the jet engine, Sir Frank Whittle. In 1988, J.R.D. was awarded the Daniel Guggenheim Medal, the first recipient of which was Orville Wright.

In 1984, evaluating J.R.D.'s contribution, Anthony Sampson in his book *Empires of the Sky* wrote:

The smooth working of Air India seemed almost opposite to the Indian tradition on the ground – not least at its home base, Bombay Airport, with its chaotic huts, shouting porters and primitive equipment, which was one of the least alluring gateways to the East. Tata, a domineering but far-sighted tycoon, could effectively insulate Air India from the domestic obligations to make jobs and dispense favours; he could impose strict discipline and employ highly-trained engineers, of whom India has a surplus; and Air India could make more intensive use of its jets than most major airlines. Tata continued as chairman until 1977, the most long-lasting of all the pioneer aviators.

(Sampson 1984)

3 Industry

When he entered industry in his early twenties, unqualified in any technical field, J.R.D. felt that his major contribution would be in the context of people management, employing the finest people and encouraging their talent (see MANAGERIAL BEHAVIOUR). He observed:

Every man has his own way of doing things. To get the best out of them is to let them exploit their own instincts and only intervene when you think they are going wrong. Therefore all my management contributions were on the human aspect through inducing, convincing and encouraging the human being. ... As I had no technical training, I always liked to consult the experts. ... When I have to make a decision I feel I must first make sure that the superior knowledge of my advisors confirms the soundness of my decision; secondly, that they would execute my decision not reluctantly but being convinced about it; thirdly, I see myself in Tatas as the leader of a team, who has to weigh the impact of any decision on other Tata companies, on the unity of the group. I think this policy has paid off.

(Lala 1992b: 225)

On the question of consensus, he commented that when he became chairman of the group at the age of 34, all of the other directors were older than him, so he became a 'consensus man'. Consensus, he said, is weak in some respects but strong in the long run. Revealing the secret of his teamwork, he said:

If I have any merit, it is getting on with individuals according to their ways and characteristics. At times it involves suppressing yourself. It is painful but necessary. ... To be a leader you have got to lead human beings with affection. ... Consensus never works 100 per cent but by and large I think I have succeeded.

(Lala 1992b: 225)

J.R.D. received his initial training in 1926 in Tata Steel which, prior to the Second World War was reputed to be the largest integrated steel plant in the British Empire. In 1943, he proposed in a note the need for a personnel management section, at a time when very few industries had such departments and it was left to the departmental heads to cope with their workers and staff (see HUMAN RESOURCE MANAGEMENT). In 1938, when elected chairman of the Tata Group, he decided that he would get the best professionals from outside to run the organization. Among the people he picked was Dr John Matthai, later Finance Minister of India. Another of his directors, Sir Ghulam Mohammed, became Finance Minister and later Governor General of Pakistan.

J.R.D.'s unique contribution lay in trying to maintain ethical values in business and industry when all around him they were declining (see BUSINESS ETHICS). Some critics argued that his value system inhibited the growth of the Tata Group at a time when latecomers were gaining ground. Even so, when he stepped down as chairman of Tata Sons, the parent company, there were ninety-five companies in the group, including India's largest automobile plant, TELCO, which J.R.D. himself had founded.

J.R.D. advocated liberal policies for business and a partnership between the government and private enterprise as he had earlier proposed for Air India. Instead, state control of the 'commanding heights of the economy' became the policy of the Indian Government. For thirty years, J.R.D. continued his struggle, hoping that his voice would have some influence on the socialist policies of successive governments. He lived to see the day, in 1991, when the Indian Government made a U-turn in its policies to encourage liberalization and privatization of the economy (see PRIVATIZA-TION AND REGULATION).

R. Venkataraman, who served as India's president from 1987–92, writes in his autobiography:

> J.R.D. Tata's contribution to the industrial development of India is unique. The Tata Group has expanded into every conceivable field of industrial activity and has set standards of enterprise, efficiency and integrity. J.R.D. Tata was the doyen among industrialists in India.
>
> I suggested to Prime Minister Narasimha Rao that we break the routine of honouring only politicians and confer *Bharat Ratna* (Jewel of India) on J.R.D. Tata. The Prime Minister readily agreed and for the first time an eminent industrialist was honoured with the highest award of *Bharat Ratna*.
>
> (Venkataraman 1994: 602)

J.R.D. was also a member of the Advisory Committee of the Chase Manhattan Bank which had one or two top industrialists from each country. He served there for twenty years and twice each year conferred with the top industrialists of the world (see INDIA, MANAGEMENT IN). For all his accomplishments he was a humble man. To the end he regretted his lack of a university education, but it was this deprivation that gave him the drive to excel in all he attempted. Profit was never the driving force of his life. It was the joy of achievement (see LEADERSHIP).

At the age of 86, when he stepped down as chairman of Tata Sons in favour of his distant cousin Ratan N. Tata, *The Economic Times* wrote:

> Under Mr Tata's leadership, the group has earned a special place in India's corporate life in two important ways. First, it has professionalised management to a degree that few other indigenous business houses have done, and done it to a point where professionals have emerged as corporate stars in their own right. Second, it has consistently stayed in tune with national priorities, and ventured into the fields which urgently require private investment. ... In J.R.D.'s own time, the group has diversified into automobiles, chemicals, exports and power.

> Throughout, the emphasis has been on building solid businesses, and not on seeking quick returns, capitalising on shortages, or manipulating government policy to personal advantage. This group culture should hold it in good stead in the future as well. ... Mr J.R.D. Tata has ensured that a shared business vision and strong ethical traditions provide the bonds of partnership in a clutch of companies which see a mutual strength in staying together.
>
> (*The Economic Times*, Bombay and New Delhi, 26 March 1991)

4 Social contribution

J.R.D. Tata was known not only for his contribution to aviation and industry but for his social consciousness, which resulted in his raising the issue of family planning with Prime Minister Nehru. The Prime Minister's first reaction was to dismiss J.R.D.'s views with the words 'population is India's strength' – that was in 1951. Undeterred, J.R.D. continued to argue in favour of population control. In 1970, he started the Family Planning Foundation. He studied the problem for forty years and did all that he could to promote the implementation of the idea of population control.

As an industrialist, J.R.D. was concerned not only about the welfare of his employees, but in 1970 had the Articles of Association of some of his companies amended to enable them to serve people living in the areas where their industries were based. Around Jamshedpur, for example, where some of the biggest Tata factories for steel and automobiles are located, approximately 300 villages benefit from social and economic measures implemented by J.R.D.'s companies.

J.R.D. was associated with a number of major philanthropic institutions. He founded the Tata Institute of Fundamental Research, which was set up as a result of his support for a budding young scientist, Dr Homi Bhabha. This institution of higher physics and mathematics became the cradle of India's atomic energy programme. His support made possible the founding of the National Centre for the Performing Arts at Bombay. In his later years, he established the National Institute of Advanced Studies in Bangalore.

A great advocate of exercise and good health, J.R.D. went skiing in the Alps each year until he was eighty-five years old. In 1991, he suffered from health problems and underwent four angioplasty procedures. He was fully active up until about three months before he died, aged 89, at a state hospital in Geneva on 29 November 1993.

R.M. LALA
SIR DORABJI TATA TRUST

Further reading

(References cited in the text marked *)

Harris, F.R. (1958) *J.N. Tata – A Chronicle of his Life*, Bombay: Blackie & Sons. (Interesting biography of J.N. Tata.)

Lala, R.M. (1984) *The Heartbeat of a Trust – Fifty Years of the Sir Dorabji Tata Trust*, New Delhi: Tata/McGraw-Hill. (The story the Sir Dorabji Tata Trust which founded many institutions of national importance.)

* Lala, R.M. (1992a) *Beyond the Last Blue Mountain – The Life of J.R.D. Tata (1904–1993)*, New Delhi: Penguin. (Detailed analysis of Tata's contribution to aviation and industry, and his philanthropy and social concerns.)

* Lala, R.M. (1992b) *The Creation of Wealth – The Tata Story*, Bombay: India Book House. (Covers the growth of the Tata organization and its effects on atomic energy, health, education, industrial relations and the performing arts.)

* Sampson, A. (1984) *Empires of the Sky*, London: Hodder & Stoughton. (Examines the politics, contests and cartels of world airlines.)

Tata, J.R.D. (1986) *Keynote*, edited by S.A. Sabavala and R.M. Lala, Bombay: Tata Press. (Excerpts from J.R.D.'s speeches and chairman's statements to shareholders.)

* Venkataraman, R. (1994) *My Presidential Years*, London: HarperCollins. (Autobiography of Venkataraman, India's President 1987–92.)

Further resources

Tata group website
http://www.tata.com

See also: HUMAN RESOURCE MANAGEMENT; HUMAN RESOURCE MANAGEMENT IN THE EMERGING COUNTRIES; INDIA, MANAGEMENT IN; LEADERSHIP; MANAGERIAL BEHAVIOUR; PRIVATIZATION AND REGULATION

Taxation, corporate

1 Introduction
2 Defining the tax base
3 Company investment policy
4 Company financial policy
5 International issues
6 Conclusion

Overview

Almost every country in the world levies some kind of tax on company profits. Yet companies are, in a sense, no more than the sum of their employees and shareholders, linked together with customers and suppliers by a web of contracts. Since most of these people will be paying tax themselves, the role of a separate tax on companies is not straightforward. The strongest justification for a separate corporate tax is as a withholding tax on investment income, in the absence of an adequate capital gains tax. Other possible arguments for a separate tax, based on the benefits of limited liability or on the value of public services to the company, are less persuasive.

The key features of any given corporate tax system are the base on which tax is levied, the rate, and the relationship with other parts of the tax system. The immediate effect of the corporate tax is to transfer funds from company to government. But the structure of the tax system can alter real decisions on how much, in what and in which country to invest. It can also alter financial decisions on how to fund investment, and on what proportion of profits to pay out as dividends, as companies try to minimize their tax liability. The actual impact on financial decisions will depend on the level of integration between corporate and personal taxes, and on the relative personal tax burdens on dividends, interest and capital gains. That said, tax is only one of many factors involved. Investment is driven mainly by the likely returns, and managers will always trade-off the benefits of a low-tax financial structure against the non-tax costs. Empirical studies indicate that non-tax factors dominate most important corporate decisions.

The growth of international capital and product markets puts new strains on domestic corporate tax systems: on the one hand, companies have more opportunity to arrange their affairs to reduce their overall tax burden but, on the other, they face new obstacles to seeking out the most profitable investments, as more than one government seeks to share in their profits. Fundamental questions are raised about whether corporate taxes are sustainable in a world capital market and how governments can best cooperate to raise revenue without limiting new investment opportunities.

1 Introduction

Why are companies taxed? A number of arguments have been given for imposing a special tax on companies. For example, the fact that companies gain benefits from incorporation, such as the advantage of limited liability, has been given as one reason for a corporate tax. However, companies pay for the benefits of limited liability through the costs of raising debt finance, and it is not obvious why they should be taxed for a contractual arrangement with their investors. Alternatively, the fact that companies benefit from the use of public goods and services provided by governments, such as transport services and a well-educated workforce, has been given as another reason for the tax. Here, however, the level of public goods available to the company, or used by the company, bears little relationship to the level of profits that a company makes, which is the basis for corporate taxes.

It has also been argued that companies should pay a tax on their income for equity reasons: individuals pay income tax so companies should also pay their 'fair share' of income tax. However, this argument ignores the fact that companies do not actually pay tax in an economic sense; people pay taxes. If

Table 1 Taxes on corporate income as a percentage of total taxation

Country	1970	1975	1980	1985	1990	1993
Canada	11.3	13.6	11.6	8.2	7.0	5.7
France	6.3	5.2	5.1	4.5	5.3	3.4
Germany	5.7	4.4	5.5	6.1	4.8	3.6
Italy	6.5	6.3	7.8	9.2	10.0	8.5
Japan	26.3	20.6	21.8	21.0	21.6	14.9
UK	9.1	6.7	8.3	12.5	10.8	7.2
USA	12.7	10.8	10.2	7.1	7.4	7.9
OECD average	8.7	7.5	7.4	7.8	7.6	6.9

Source: Revenue statistics of the OECD member countries (1994)

companies were not taxed, people would continue to pay tax on dividends (the income stream to shares), interest income (the return to bonds) and on capital gains (arising from retained profits which increase the value of their shares). The most convincing argument for a corporate tax is that it prevents people from allowing their income to build up inside a corporation free from tax. Since capital gains are usually taxed on disposal of the asset concerned, rather than as they accrue, or are not taxed at all, this could happen if corporate income were not taxed. So the corporate tax acts as a withholding tax on income invested in corporations.

How important are corporate taxes in raising revenue for governments? This is demonstrated in Table 1, which shows the proportion of total tax revenue raised by taxes on corporate income in the G7 countries and the average for the OECD (Organization for Economic Cooperation and Development) countries as a whole. Since 1970, the proportion of total tax revenue accounted for by taxes on corporate profits has fallen in six of the seven G7 nations, with only Italy increasing the proportion of revenue collected from the corporate sector. The fall in revenue has been particularly marked in Canada and the USA. Japan has relied more heavily on corporate taxes, while Germany and France have had historically low levels of company taxation, at least at the national level. Figures like these disguise the fact that some countries also levy taxes on corporate income at lower levels of government, which is true not only in low and medium tax countries, such as Germany and the USA, but also in some high tax countries such as Japan.

Where does the incidence of these corporate taxes fall? The question does not have a simple answer, for although corporate tax is a direct tax on companies, there may be opportunities for the owners of companies to pass on the burden of the tax to others. Part of the tax may be shifted onto consumers of the good or service being produced, through higher prices; part of the tax may fall on employees, through the payment of lower wages; and part may fall on the owners of other less mobile factors of production, such as land and natural resources. The extent to which the burden of the tax is shifted will depend upon many factors, such as the relative openness of the economy, the mobility of capital (whether portfolio or physical capital) and the characteristics of the market the firm operates in.

Consider the case of a small open economy with perfect capital mobility. If the domestic level of corporate tax is raised above the level of corporate taxes abroad, capital will shift out of the country into similar investments abroad, which now have a higher post-tax rate of return. This outflow of capital leads to a fall in wages in the domestic economy, since the fall in the ratio of capital to labour reduces labour productivity (assuming that labour cannot simply follow the capital out of the country too). It may also lead to a fall in the price of other resources, such as land and natural resources, as investment in the domestic economy declines. The flight of capital will stop when the rate of return before tax in the domestic economy rises enough to make the post-tax rate of return at home equal to the rate of return available after tax in the rest of the world. In the long run, for a small open economy facing perfect capital mobility, the entire burden of the increase in tax may be shifted onto less mobile factors of production.

In practice, it is unlikely that the full incidence of a change in tax will be shifted away from capital, for several reasons. Investment in physical capital is not perfectly mobile across borders, due to the adjustment costs involved in relocating a factory or office block, for example. In addition, some of the return to business investment can come from 'location-specific' rents, that is, benefits to the company which depend upon producing in a particular place, such as a high quality of local transport services or labour, or consumers with a special preference for their particular product. This rent will be lost if the company moves abroad, so at least part of the incidence of a corporate tax will fall on capital, even in an open economy. The effects of this tax on capital will depend upon the extent to which it distorts the behaviour of companies, both in their real decisions over investment levels and types of investment projects and in their financial decisions over sources of funding for that investment.

2 Defining the tax base

The level of taxes that companies pay depends upon the rate of corporate tax, the definition of the tax base and the relationship between the corporate tax and other parts of the tax system. The tax base specifies what exactly is going to be taxed, for example, the flow of income from employment in the case of personal income tax, the increase in the value of an asset for capital gains tax, or expenditure on particular goods for consumption taxes.

The starting point for the corporate tax base is usually the profits shown in company accounts. Normal costs which arise in the day-to-day running of a business, current expenditure for example, can be subtracted from income. These include costs such as raw materials and wages and salaries, and also include interest payments made on debt. Treatment of

the cost of capital expenditure, such as the purchase of plant, machinery and buildings, varies from country to country, but most allow the company to write off the cost of a capital investment over a few years, recognizing the fact that the asset's value depreciates. These capital allowances are given either according to standard accounting conventions or in ways set down in the tax rules themselves.

In addition to this, most countries allow a deduction for losses. When a business makes a trading loss, that loss may usually be carried forward and subtracted from taxable profits earned in future years. Some countries also allow companies to carry losses back to earlier years, often subject to certain time limits. The treatment of profits and losses is not symmetrical, however. When a company makes a profit, it is expected to pay tax on that profit soon after it has finalized the accounts for that year, but when a company makes a loss, it is not given an immediate refund of tax. Unless the real value of the tax losses can be carried forward, this creates a disincentive for companies to carry out high-risk investment.

Other differences do occur in the definition of the tax base between countries, which will influence the overall level of corporate tax paid by companies. For example, some countries give a deduction for increases in the value of inventories due to inflation, and although most countries include capital gains made from assets sold in the tax base, not all tax those gains at the full corporate tax rate.

One final issue to consider briefly in the definition of the tax base is the treatment of inflation. In a neutral corporate tax system, only the real return to capital employed would be subject to tax, hence only the real economic profits. Therefore, capital allowances would be indexed for inflation, and only capital gains over and above inflation would be taxed. Similarly, only real interest payments would be deducted from taxable profits, and not the nominal portion of the payment. Where the system does not account for inflation, distortions in the system arising from a non-neutral tax will be exacerbated by the presence of inflation. This reflects the fact that any flaws in the way that profits are measured in company accounts are likely to be reflected in the base of corporate tax, since the base is derived from these accounting measures.

3 Company investment policy

This section looks at the effect of corporate tax on the company's investment policy, using the concept of the 'cost of capital'. The economic definition of the cost of capital given here extends the definition of the cost of capital given in the finance literature. The essential difference is that here the cost of capital depends not only on the weighted cost of debt and equity used by the firm for financing investment, but also on the treatment of different types of investment by the tax system, through depreciation rules (see CAPITAL, COST OF).

The cost of capital and the level of investment

The cost of capital is the required rate of return that an investment project must earn in order to be carried out by the firm. The cost of capital depends upon two components: the cost of finance for the project and the fall in the value of assets employed in the project, or economic depreciation. The tax system may affect the cost of capital in several ways, through lowering the rate of return earned by the project, changing the cost of different forms of finance and changing the cost of different forms of investment.

The cost of finance is the rate of return which could be earned by investors by holding other financial assets at a similar level of risk. As a simple example, an investor can place £100 in a bank account for one year and receive the £100 back at the end of that year plus £5 in interest, which represents a rate of return of 5 per cent. If the manager of a company asks for the £100 instead to finance a small project that is no more or less risky than putting the money in the bank, the investor will only agree to give £100 to the company rather than the bank if the project will also earn a rate of return of at least 5 per cent. The total cost of finance faced by companies will depend upon this minimum rate of return required by investors, and the proportion of debt and equity used to finance investment. Let ρ denote the cost of finance.

Economic depreciation measures the cost of holding an asset for a period of time, and is itself made up of two components: the physical rate of wear and tear of an asset, minus any capital gain which might arise from holding the asset (or plus any capital loss, since this is a measure of the cost of holding the asset) (see FIXED ASSETS AND DEPRECIATION). For example, a piece of machinery purchased this year for £100 might have a working life of ten years, and in each year of use it wears down by the same amount, that is, it loses 10 per cent of its value each year. The rate of depreciation for this machine is 10 per cent. Let δ be the rate of depreciation. If the real cost of replacing the machine with a new one increases while it is being used, the asset earns a capital gain. This measures the advantage of buying the machine this year, if it will be more expensive to purchase the same machine next year, and so should be deducted form the cost of holding the asset. If g is the capital gain made during the year, then the rate of economic depreciation will be given by $\delta - g$.

For an investment project to be worth carrying out, it must be expected to earn a rate of return which is at least as high as the cost of capital. The cost of capital is the cost of finance plus the cost of economic depreciation, or $\rho + \delta - g$. If R is the expected gross rate of return on the project, then a project will only be viable if:

$$R \geq \rho + \delta - g$$

For example, a company has a possible investment project which can earn a gross rate of return of 7 per cent. The company managers calculate that the cost of capital on the project is 5 per cent, so they will go ahead with the project. Assume now that the government imposes a tax on corporate income, which leaves the investment earning an after-tax rate of return of less than 5 per cent. This means that the project is no longer worth carrying out, because it cannot earn a rate of return which at least covers the cost of the capital needed to finance the investment. The managers will now decide not to go ahead with the project.

This result implies that a tax system which only taxes the return to investment over and above the cost of capital will not affect managers' decisions of whether to invest. If the government only taxes the 2 per cent return the project earns over and above the 5 per cent cost of capital, that is, the pure profit, then the decision to go ahead with the investment will not change even though a tax has been imposed. In this case, the rate of return on a marginal investment – an investment which just earns the cost of capital but no more – will be the same before and after tax, and the tax system will be neutral with respect to the decision of whether to invest.

For managers to carry out an investment project, the current value of the future stream of income net of all costs from a project (its net present value) will have to be greater than zero. This depends, among other things, upon the cost of finance and the future value of capital allowances and tax rates (which is one of the reasons why companies, like individuals, prefer taxes to be relatively stable year after year, in order to calculate their future income and assess their investment decisions).

From this description of the cost of capital it is clear that the mechanics of the tax system will be very important. A tax system which gives a deduction for the cost of debt financing, in the form of interest payments, and no equivalent deduction for the costs of equity finance makes equity finance relatively more expensive than debt. This introduces a tax incentive for managers to finance investment using debt rather than equity, and the implications of this are discussed in the section on capital structure below. The existence of personal taxes on interest and dividend income, and the nature of the interaction between the corporate tax system and the personal tax system, will also affect the cost of finance by changing the return to debt and the return to equity for individual investors. The mechanism and implications of this are discussed in the section on dividend policy.

In addition, the actual operation of depreciation allowances in the tax code is unlikely to correspond exactly to the true rate of economic depreciation, and this will introduce tax incentives for and against investment in different types of asset. This is the final aspect of the interaction between tax systems and company investment to be discussed here.

Depreciation and investment decisions

The long-run cost of investment in physical capital includes the fall in its value over time, measured by its rate of depreciation. However, the true economic rate of depreciation will only be known once the asset has worn out or has been rendered obsolete by changes in technology. This is because an accurate measure of depreciation requires knowledge of the asset's life and its value on replacement. In practice, calculating accurate rates of depreciation for many different classes of asset is very complicated, and countries frequently apply two basic depreciation rules (straight line or declining balance) or variations of them, at fixed rates to broad groups of assets (such as plant and machinery, buildings, inventories).

The result is that the depreciation, or capital, allowances given in the tax system will be too high relative to true depreciation for assets with longer lives than the average chosen for their group, and depreciation allowances will be too low for assets with shorter lives. Although the tax system may be right 'on average', it will tend to favour long-lived investment projects, such as the building of a new factory, over short-lived projects, such as installing a new assembly line. In addition, where no allowance is given at all for the change in value of some types of investment, this will introduce a tax bias. However, it is possible that the costs of operating capital allowances for assets that are difficult to value may be more severe than the costs of having no capital allowance at all.

Countries may not actually want the tax system to be neutral over the types of decision the company makes. Governments may want to use the corporate tax system as a policy tool, in order to encourage some forms of investment and discourage others. For example, some countries offer an additional tax allowance in the first year of a new investment in the hope of increasing investment during a recession, or allow accelerated depreciation for investment in specific parts of the country to regenerate poorer regions, or give investment tax credits to particular industries or activities they wish to encourage, such as pollution control. As a result, the cost of capital will tend to vary deliberately according to the type of asset and the type of finance used. These different costs of capital can be estimated, over time and across countries, in order to measure the size of tax incentives towards different forms of investment and different forms of finance (King and Fullerton 1984). There is a large body of literature investigating the effects of taxes on company investment, and although most of the results agree that taxes do influence investment decisions, the size and permanence of these effects are in dispute (Chirinko 1986).

4 Company financial policy

We now turn to the effect of corporate tax on financial policy, and in particular the impact of tax on the level of debt finance and on the incentive to pay dividends. Seminal articles on corporate finance in the early 1960s argued that, in a simple world with perfect information, no taxes and no transactions costs, the value of the firm must depend, in the end, on the profits it can generate. It cannot depend on the way those profits are divided between shareholders and bondholders, nor on the overall level of dividends (Modigliani and Miller 1958; Miller and Modigliani 1961).

In the real world, directors and shareholders alike are concerned about the appropriate level of dividends, while financial analysts queue up to offer companies alternative ways to raise finance, all aimed at raising the share price. The force of the Modigliani–Miller view is that we have to look for explanations of behaviour in the real world in the factors they assume away, such as the existence of imperfect information, transactions costs or taxes.

There are no hard and fast rules here: the impact of corporate tax will often be buried in the detail of tax law and the company's profits, prospects and past history. The key tax question for a financial director or tax manager will always be:

Does a change in financial policy raise or lower the company's tax bill? If so, is this change offset by a higher/lower bill for someone else (who can pass the costs on to me) or a higher/lower bill for me later?

Corporate tax and dividend policy

The impact of tax on dividends will depend on the reasons why companies pay dividends in the first place. If dividend levels are mainly determined by simple managerial rules or on the level of profitable investment, then tax should have little or no effect on payout ratios. If dividends depend on capital market factors (such as the need to monitor managers, or to signal future profitability), then the tax system may alter payout ratios.

Survey evidence suggests that managers often follow simple rules relating payouts to long-run profit levels. If managers really stick to these rules, there is no reason why tax incentives should alter dividend payments. However, this view is very limited; it does not tell us how managers choose the right long-run payout ratio nor why ratios vary so much between companies.

A more sophisticated view is that dividends depend mainly on the company's investment opportunities. Most mature companies rely on retained earnings to finance the larger part of their investment. For some companies, dividends will be residual profits, paid out to shareholders because the company has exhausted its profitable investment opportunities. For these companies, dividends are the difference between profits and investment, and will be paid regardless of the taxes incurred (see DIVIDEND POLICY).

This argument cannot hold for all companies at all times. It would imply that companies would never pay dividends and raise new capital at the same time, and that dividends would be more volatile than profits or investment. In fact, companies pay dividends even when they also need to raise new equity, and dividends are generally smoother than either profits or investment.

Alternative views focus on capital market factors, and in particular the value of dividends in providing information to shareholders and extending market discipline to management. For example, 'monitoring' theories argue that individual shareholders do not always have the incentive or the ability to monitor company managers directly. Instead, they demand high dividend payments, reducing managers' discretionary control over profits and forcing them to the capital markets more often. When companies raise new capital, they have to justify investment plans and past performance to prospective new investors, and this also serves the interests of existing investors. 'Signalling' theories suggest that managers can use dividends to convey information to shareholders on the company's prospects. Managers often have better information on likely future profits than shareholders, but may find it difficult to communicate this information with any credibility. Only companies with high future profits will be able to sustain high dividend levels in the long-term. If there are penalties attached to cutting dividends, high current dividends should be a signal that managers genuinely expect good future profits.

On either of these views, managers will balance the tax cost of a particular level of dividends against non-tax costs and benefits. This view is borne out by empirical studies, which generally find that tax incentives do alter dividend levels, but the effect is small and swamped by other factors.

The tax incentive to follow a high- or low-dividend policy varies from country to country, but in each case the key factor is the degree of integration between corporate and personal tax systems. Under a 'classical' system, for example, the company and its shareholders are treated as completely separate. The company pays tax on its profits and the shareholder pays tax on dividends distributed from those profits, so that distributed profits are taxed twice. More complicated systems seek to reduce or eliminate this 'double taxation of dividends' by reducing either the corporate or the personal tax charge. Integration schemes fall into three basic categories: 'shareholder relief' systems, 'imputation' systems and 'split-rate' systems, discussed in more detail below.

Under a 'classical' system of corporation tax, the company pays tax on all of its profits, whether they are paid out to shareholders or not. So the corporate tax system itself has no effect on dividend policy. However, shareholders still have to pay income tax on the dividends they receive as well as capital gains tax when they sell shares that have risen in value. So a lower tax rate on capital gains, than on dividend income, should lead shareholders to press for lower dividends, other things being equal, even if the corporate tax system itself has no effect.

More formally, for every £1 the company pays as a dividend, the shareholders receive $£(1 - m)$, where m is the rate of personal income tax on dividend income. For every £1 retained within the firm to increase the share value, shareholders receive value of $£(1 - z)$, where z is the effective rate of tax on capital gains. The investor receives the same return on the investment, and so is indifferent between the decision to retain or distribute, only if the effective tax rate on capital gains is equal to the effective rate of tax on dividends, so that $£(1 - m) = £(1 - z)$.

This straightforward result only applies in the USA and in a few other countries that still operate 'classical' systems. Most countries have developed some form of integration between the tax paid by the company and that due from its shareholders. The impact of tax on dividend policy will depend on the exact form of this integration.

The simplest form of integration is 'shareholder relief', which involves lowering the personal tax charge on dividends. One could imagine a system which exempted both dividends and capital gains from income tax altogether. When the relief does not go as far as complete exemption, the incentive to pay dividends depends on the relative values of m and z, as it does under a classical system.

The key drawback to this type of system is that there is no guarantee that the company has actually paid tax on the profits, since the relief given to the shareholder does not relate to the level of corporate tax paid. Most countries instead use the more complex 'imputation' system. Under an imputation system, as under a classical system, companies are subject to corporate tax on their income. However, when this income is distributed to the shareholder, some credit is given for corporate taxes paid. Under a full imputation system all of the corporate tax paid is available to credit against the shareholder's income tax bill, while under a partial system only part of the tax is credited to the shareholder. The tax incentive to pay dividends will now also depend on the proportion of the company tax which is imputed to the shareholder.

As in the example above, the firm has £1 of post-corporate tax profits to distribute to the shareholder or to retain and use to reduce new share issues. On distribution, the shareholder receives £1 of dividend income plus a credit towards their income tax bill. This can be done by attaching a tax credit to the dividend related to the amount of corporate tax paid by the firm. If c is the rate of imputation, the individual receives £$1/(1 - c)$ in dividend income, which is then taxed at their marginal income tax rate. The shareholder's final income from the £1 of post-corporate tax profit is then £$(1 - m)/(1 - c)$ and tax has no effect on dividends only if $(1 - z) = (1 - m)/(1 - c)$.

The key difference compared to shareholder relief is that in the imputation system, the government can limit or claw the credit back if the company has not paid enough tax on its own account. This may be the case if, for example, the company pays dividends out of reserves, or has been able to take advantage of very generous investment allowances, or is paying dividends out of foreign profits. In the UK, France and Germany, for example, the corporate tax system is designed to levy a special tax charge where the company would not otherwise pay enough tax to match the credits paid to its shareholders. The effect of this kind of clawback is that different companies face different incentives, depending on the level and source of their profits, and on the allowances they can claim. (The taxation of foreign profits is discussed further in the section on international issues.)

Another approach again is a 'split-rate' system of different tax rates on distributed and retained profits. Suppose τ_R is the rate of corporate tax on retained profits and τ_D is the rate of tax on distributed profits. If the company distributes the profits, £1 of profits becomes £$(1 - \tau_D)$ after corporate tax, and the shareholder is taxed on that distribution at their personal tax rate, receiving £$(1 - \tau_D)(1 - m)$. If the company retains the profits, the shareholder receives £$(1 - \tau_R)(1 - z)$, after com-

pany and personal taxes. Tax will have no impact on dividend policy only if

$$(1 - \tau_R)(1 - z) = (1 - \tau_D)(1 - m).$$

We can summarize the various incentives to retain or distribute in a single number called a 'tax discrimination parameter', which measures the extent of an individual's preference for or against the payment of dividends. We define this parameter as the ratio of the two tax burdens under alternative decisions of the firm, so that:

$$\gamma = \frac{(1 - \tau_D)(1 - m)}{(1 - \tau_R)(1 - c)(1 - z)}$$

If there is only one corporate tax rate, , on both retained and distributed profits, this becomes $\gamma = (1 - m)/(1 - c)(1 - z)$, and in the case of a classical system, where $c = 0$, $= (1 - m)/(1 - z)$. If $\gamma > 1$, the tax system favours dividends; if $\gamma < 1$, it favours retentions.

It becomes immediately obvious that different shareholders may have very different preferences for dividends, depending on their tax rates. Under a imputation system, for example, the tax system favours dividends for a tax-exempt investor, but favours retention if the shareholder faces a high rate of tax on dividends and a low rate on capital gains. Table 2 gives some example values of for the G7 countries in 1994 as calculated by the author of this article. These values vary between different types of investor, between different countries for the same type of investor, and will vary over time for the same investor as tax rates change. The proportion of shares owned by different types of investors also varies widely between countries and over time, which will affect how much these preferences for or against dividends actually affect company behaviour.

Capital structure

Turning to capital structure, most corporate tax systems are taxes on equity profits only; they allow interest payments to be deducted from income in measuring the tax base. If there were no other taxes, and if debt and equity were perfect substitutes, then we would expect companies to fund all their investment through debt and pay no corporate tax all. We

Table 2 Tax incentives for and against dividends in 1994

Country	Shareholder's tax status		
	Exempt	Average rate	Top rate
Canada	1.25	0.75	0.85
France	1.50	0.82	0.72
Germany	2.05	1.25	0.96
Italy	1.92	1.34	0.75
Japan	1.00	0.75	0.75
UK	1.25	1.00	0.75
USA	1.00	0.90	0.88

Notes:

1. The table gives values of γ in 1994 for the G-7 countries. If $\gamma > 1$, the tax system favours dividends, if $\gamma < 1$ it favours retentions.

2. Exempt shareholders are those shareholders who do not pay tax on their dividend income or capital gains, such as individual pensioners, or non-taxpaying institutions such as pension funds. An 'average' taxpayer is someone being taxed at the marginal rate of an individual on average earnings. The top-rate taxpayer is someone being taxed at the highest marginal rate.

3. The figures for the UK assume an effective rate of capital gains tax of zero.

do not observe this in practice, in part because personal taxes on interest shift the balance back in favour of equity, and in part because tax is only one factor determining capital structure (see CAPITAL STRUCTURE).

The precise tax incentive to use debt finance depends on the rate of tax on equity returns relative to the rate of tax on interest receipts. If equity returns are heavily taxed, then companies must make higher returns in order to meet tax payments and still compete with the bond market. If corporate interest receipts are heavily taxed, then companies must pay higher interest rates in order to compete with other prospective borrowers.

Using the same notation as before, equity investors will require dividends and capital gains to at least match the market rate of interest. Ignoring the risk premium, and assuming equal personal tax rates on dividends and interest, this implies that:

$$d(1-m)/(1-c) + g(1-z) \geq i(1-m)$$

where d is the net dividend and g the capital gain. In the simple case where equity returns are paid entirely as dividends, the company must pay at least $i(1-c)$ for equity finance and $i(1-\tau)$ for debt finance. So there is a net tax incentive to use debt finance only if the imputation rate, c, is lower than the corporate tax rate, τ. The actual incentives will depend on how far companies retain and reinvest their profits, rewarding their shareholders with capital growth as well as dividend payments.

In an extension of these arguments, Miller (1977) suggests investors will sort themselves by tax rate, dampening the effect of interest deductibility. Those facing a low tax rate on interest relative to equity returns will buy bonds, while those facing higher tax rates on interest will invest in equity. Provided there are enough investors with appropriate tax rates, the company will be able to choose whichever level of debt it prefers.

Even this result is complicated by the provisions of tax codes in the real world. Companies can only benefit from interest deductibility if they make sufficient taxable profits before interest payments. If a company is 'tax-exhausted', that is, if it has no corporate tax liability, due to losses in current or previous years or due to high levels of depreciation allowances, the incentive to use debt finance is greatly reduced. So the net cost of debt finance will depend on the company's investment plans, and the level of allowances in the tax code, as well as its past history of losses.

This limit on interest-deductibility becomes even more important when we consider other factors influencing capital structure. In particular, using debt finance raises the possibility of bankruptcy, with all its attendant administration costs. Most tax systems do not allow interest-deductibility in loss-making years nor do they provide for refunds if the firm eventually fails. So the owners of a bankrupt company lose the benefit of tax reliefs in addition to their pre-tax losses.

As with dividends, views on the value of capital structure focus on the relationship between company and investors. In particular, debt finance may act as a signal of future profitability, and we also have to consider the monitoring costs incurred by lenders in minimizing their own risk and by the company in sticking to, for example, restrictive covenants designed to minimize lender-risk. The tax system interacts with these other costs, usually raising the benefits to be set against the costs relative to equity finance.

There is a large empirical literature on the effect of tax on capital structure in practice. Most of the studies find small but positive effects on overall debt levels, and rather stronger effects as companies become tax-exhausted. But, as with dividends, the key conclusion is that even quite large tax incentives have a limited effect on the main financial decisions for most companies. Clearly, other factors matter.

5 International issues

All of the above discussion of the tax system on the investment and financial decisions of the firm becomes even more pertinent when an international dimension is added. Even the question of who should receive revenue from the operations of an individual company does not have an obvious answer when that company operates in many different nations. For example, when a Japanese car company develops a new engine part in a laboratory in Germany, produces the car in a factory in the UK and sells the finished product in Belgium, it is not clear where the profits which are to be taxed have actually arisen. What is clear is that distributing such revenues 'fairly' between countries, without contributing to new distortions in resource allocation or imposing very high compliance costs on companies, is not an easy task.

Source-based and residence-based taxation

There are two basic principles for taxing profits earned in different parts of the world. Taxes can be levied on a *source* basis, where the country concerned taxes all income arising within its territory, regardless of the final destination of the profits. Hence, on a source basis, any profits earned in the UK by the UK-based subsidiary of a US firm would be taxed by the UK tax authorities, since the *origin* or source of the profits was the firm's activities in the UK. The alternative is to levy

taxes on a *residence* basis, that is, to tax all of the income earned by the residents of a particular country, regardless of where that income originated. So, on a residence basis, a shareholder in the USA would be taxed by the US authorities on their dividends from US firms and their dividends from Japanese or French firms, since the *destination* of the profits was the USA.

In fact, countries tend to tax profits both by the source and by the residence principle. A withholding tax on dividend income is often levied on dividends paid by a resident firm to its foreign shareholders (taxing by the source principle), at the same time as a corporate tax is imposed on income earned abroad and repatriated by a resident firm (taxing by the residence principle). In addition, personal income taxes can be levied on dividends arising from a foreign source. This can lead to the reintroduction of the double taxation of dividends at the international level, even if it has been reduced or eliminated at the national level.

The tax treatment of foreign source income is an important issue because, without international coordination, the operation of completely independent tax systems is likely to lead to higher tax burdens on some companies simply because they operate in more than one country, distorting their decisions over where, and how, to invest. There are two ways in which tax systems can influence the allocation of investment. If tax rates vary between countries, companies may find it cheaper to invest in a low tax country, even in cases when it costs more (before tax) to produce in that country. (When this occurs, this indicates an absence of 'capital export neutrality'.) Alternatively, if tax rates on two companies differ, one company may be able to sell its goods more cheaply than the other, even though it produces them at greater cost. (This is the absence of 'capital import neutrality'.)

Capital export neutrality (CEN) exists when there is no tax incentive for an individual to invest their capital at home or abroad, that is, the after-tax return on an investment is the same regardless of the location of the *investment*. For example, a German citizen will face CEN when the effective tax rate on the return from shares in a UK company is the same as the tax rate on the return from shares in a

French company. This can be achieved by taxing profits on a residence basis and giving full credit for foreign taxes paid.

Capital import neutrality (CIN) exists when both domestic and foreign suppliers of capital receive the same rate of return after tax on a given investment in a given national market, that is the after-tax return on an investment is the same regardless of the location of the *investor*. For example, this implies that an investment in a new project in Japan will give an after-tax rate of return of 5 per cent, regardless of whether the investor is Japanese or Spanish or Australian. This can be achieved by taxing income on a source basis, while exempting all foreign source income from domestic tax in the residence country of the investor and giving foreign investors the same tax status as domestic investors in the country that is the source of the profits.

Hence, CEN implies that countries should use the residence principle to tax profits, and give full credits for foreign taxes, while CIN implies that countries should use the source principle, and exempt income from foreign sources. The only way to achieve both CEN and CIN at the same time is for every country to operate exactly the same type of system, on exactly the same tax base, levying exactly the same rates. Not only would it require an unrealistic level of international coordination to achieve this result, it would also remove any possibility of countries following independent tax policy objectives. The realistic alternative to complete harmonization has been for countries to adopt bilateral tax treaties, introducing credit and exemption rules for the treatment of foreign source income.

Credit or exemption?

Under an exemption system, income from foreign sources is exempt from domestic tax. Corporate tax is only paid on foreign income in the country where the income is earned. Under a credit system, the company calculates its domestic tax liability on its income from all over the world, then subtracts any taxes on income that have been paid abroad. However, the size of tax credits is often limited to the minimum of the amount actually paid abroad or the amount which would have been due if the profits were all earned at home. Companies then find themselves paying tax on their foreign source income at whichever rate is higher, the foreign or the domestic tax rate.

Credit systems are operated in a number of ways, two of the most important being on a country-by-country basis, or on a worldwide basis. The former compares the tax paid abroad with the tax which would have been paid at home, for each country the firm operates in individually. This is less generous than a worldwide credit, which compares the total tax paid abroad with the tax which would have been paid on worldwide income if it had all been earned at home.

The limiting of credits introduces a bias against companies that operate in many different national markets. Individual countries do not give unlimited tax credits despite this bias, because they might find themselves refunding credits at the personal level to shareholders in domestic companies for corporate tax revenue which has been received by another country. Examples of the problems which arise from the limiting of credits are the existence of surplus or unrelieved 'advance corporation tax' (ACT) in the UK and excess foreign credits in the USA. ACT is a tax payment made by the firm when it pays a dividend, and surplus ACT occurs when a company cannot subtract all of its ACT payments from its total UK corporate tax bill or carry it back to set against earlier tax payments. This is because the deduction of ACT is limited to a proportion of the amount of UK taxable profits that companies earn. In the USA, companies can find themselves in an excess foreign credits position, when the maximum tax credit available on taxes paid abroad exceeds their US tax liability, but no refund of the extra foreign tax paid is given.

Exemption also creates problems, however. While a credit system ensures that the firm's total tax bill is defined by the domestic tax rules of its country of residence, an exemption system gives a tax bill which depends upon the rates applying in all of the countries that the firm operates in. Where a company and its wholly owned subsidiary operate in two different countries with very different corporate tax rates, the company's overall tax bill can be reduced by shifting profits from the high-tax country to the low-tax country. This can be done through manipulating transfer prices, in order to 'earn' profits in a lower tax area.

Transfer prices are the prices charged for goods and services between connected companies, for example, the price charged by the subsidiary of a car manufacturer for the engine parts it supplies. If the subsidiary is based in a high-tax country, it might understate the cost of the parts in order to ensure that more of the profits from the sale of the car are earned in the low-tax country that the parent company is based in. A principle of imposing 'arm's-length' prices on transactions between connected companies has been adopted by tax authorities in order to reduce this type of behaviour. The arm's-length principle requires that companies only charge a price similar to the one which would have been used if the two companies were not connected at all. However, this relies on the existence of an alternative price for the tax authorities to base an arm's-length price upon. Given the nature of multinational companies and their activities, there may not be a market between unconnected companies to act as a guide for these prices, nor even a close substitute for the product in a free market.

Difficulties in finding the appropriate arm's-length price to use has led to some movement, especially in the USA, away from using transaction-based methods and towards using profit-based methods, to achieve the arm's-length principle. Each approach has its own followers, but the general intention of tax authorities is to negotiate agreement over the 'fair' level of profits to be taxed in their own jurisdictions.

The main alternative to the arm's-length principle as a method for achieving a 'fair' distribution of tax revenues across countries is formula apportionment, also known as 'unitary taxation'. Under this system, countries would agree a formula for the division of income between themselves, based upon the proportion of sales, assets and employment occurring in each country that a company operates in. Such a system would allow different countries to impose different tax rates, since the division of tax revenue would not depend upon where countries formally declare their profits. The division of tax revenue would

depend, however, on the exact nature of the formula used, since the relative weights of different components of the formula will determine the size of each country's tax base (see TRANSFER PRICING). At the international level, this system has been considered for the members of the European Union (EU) and for the OECD member countries, but the level of international coordination necessary to agree the formula and the initial administrative costs of setting up such a system make it unlikely to be adopted, despite the potential long-term benefits.

Harmonization

The difficulties of moving towards a common, or harmonized, treatment of corporate tax have been discussed at the international level for many years. Why do countries want harmonization? The discussion above of the interaction between different countries' tax systems through credit and exemption systems highlights the difficulties of finding a tax treatment of foreign profits that neither penalizes companies for being successful in international markets nor allows them opportunities to avoid paying tax on those profits. The goal of harmonization might be to reduce, as far as possible, the distortions that are introduced into company behaviour by independent operation of very different tax regimes across the world.

An example of how the operation of very different regimes, either in the definition of the tax base or the rate tax charged, might alter company decisions can be seen in the existence of the 10 per cent rate of corporation tax levied on manufacturing firms in the Irish Republic. If a company compares the cost of locating its new plant in Ireland or Germany, and finds that before tax it is more cost-effective to locate in Germany, but that after tax the return is higher in Ireland, the company is likely to locate the new plant in Ireland (all other things being equal). Although Ireland is better off in terms of the level of investment within Ireland, Europe as a whole may be worse off, since the plant is producing goods at a higher cost than would otherwise have been the case. The lowering of a tax rate by one country may also inspire competitive tax cuts in other countries to protect their own stock of investment, with the result that the overall level of corporate taxes may be lower than any of the countries involved would prefer. This tax competition may lie behind the decline in revenue from corporate taxes shown in Table 1.

The countries of the EU have been attempting to reach agreement over the way to harmonize corporate taxes since the early 1960s. Proposals suggested by various EU committees have ranged from recommending the common adoption of a classical system, through the split-rate system and partial imputation, to giving no firm recommendation at all. Countries can agree that withholding taxes on the dividend income of foreign residents is discriminatory and should be brought to an end, but seem unable to agree on much more. Complete harmonization may be unlikely, but a reduction of the most obvious distortions may be achieved through less comprehensive arrangements.

6 Conclusion

The existence of a corporate tax raises a number of interesting issues for economists, accountants and policy makers alike. The most important aspect of a corporate tax is whether it significantly affects the decisions of companies over how much to invest, what to invest in, how to finance that investment and where to locate the investment. Tax incentives towards certain projects, debt levels and countries can be deliberate, but can also arise through the operation of tax systems that are not sufficiently well designed to minimize the level of distortions.

Although empirical studies suggest that non-tax factors continue to be far more important than tax factors in the decisions of company managers, the existence of these unintentional distortions reduces the overall level of investment, preventing companies from being able to carry out their best investment projects at the lowest cost, and hence resulting in a welfare loss for the international economy. The extent of these effects is hard to measure, but it is clear that they do exist.

The recent decline in the importance of corporate tax as a source of revenue for most of the countries in the OECD has led some commentators to believe that the future of corporate taxation is uncertain. However, the tax remains an important source of income for many countries. Despite the liberalization of exchange controls and other restrictions on international capital flows, which increase the openness of every economy and makes capital more sensitive to differences in national tax systems, the extra incentive this gives for tax competition has not led to a complete erosion of revenue from corporate taxes. While location-specific economic rents exist, and while the adjustment costs of relocating physical investment are significant, countries will continue to be able to raise revenue from corporate taxes.

LUCY CHENNELLS
INSTITUTE FOR FISCAL STUDIES, LONDON

Note

The author would like to acknowledge the contribution of Harold Freeman in the preparation of this article.

Further reading

(References cited in the text marked *)

Boadway, R. and Bruce, N. (1984) 'A general proposition on the design of a neutral business tax', *Journal of Public Economics* 24 (2): 231–9. (A theoretical model for the design of a neutral business tax.)

* Chirinko, R.S. (1986) 'Business investment and tax policy: a perspective on existing models and empirical results', *National Tax Journal* 39 (2): 137–55. (A critical review of the theoretical models for testing the effects of tax policy on investment and some discussion of results.)

Devereux, M.P. and Pearson, M. (1989) *Corporate Tax Harmonisation and Economic Efficiency*, IFS Report Series no. 35, London: Institute for Fiscal Studies. (A careful explanation of the harmonization arguments, plus some empirical results.)

Easterbrook (1984) 'Two agency cost explanations of dividends', *American Economic Review* 74 (4): 650–9. (Considers reasons for paying dividends based on monitoring costs and asymmetric information.)

Edwards, J. (1984) 'Does dividend policy matter?', *Fiscal Studies* 5 (1): 1–17. (Sets out the conflict between dividend policy in theory and in practice.)

Edwards, J., Kay, J. and Mayer, C. (1987) *The Economic Analysis of Accounting Profitability*, Oxford: Clarendon Press. (Explains the problems arising from using accounts data to measure profits.)

Harberger, A.C. (1962) 'The incidence of the corporation income tax', *Journal of Political Economy* 70 (3): 215–40. (The seminal article on the incidence of corporation tax, using a simple model.)

Jorgenson, D. and Yun, K.-Y. (1991) *Taxation and the Cost of Capital*, Oxford: Clarendon Press. (An accessible work explaining the cost of capital in detail, with reference to the US tax system.)

King, M.A. (1977) *Public Policy and the Corporation*, London: Chapman and Hall. (Thorough and readable study of the effects of personal and corporate taxes on companies.)

* King, M.A. and Fullerton, D. (eds) (1984) *The Taxation of Income from Capital*, Chicago, IL: Chicago University Press. (The first international comparative study of the taxation of capital income using a common methodology.)

Meade Report (1978) *The Structure and Reform of Direct Taxation*, London: Allen & Unwin. (A fundamental review of direct taxation, with a thorough assessment of 'good' tax structures, referring to the UK tax system.)

* Miller, M.H. (1977) 'Debt and taxes', *Journal of Finance* 32 (2): 261–75. (Sets out the argument that even with full interest deductibility in corporate tax, firm value is independent of capital structure.)

* Miller, M.H. and Modigliani, F. (1961) 'Dividend policy, growth and the valuation of shares', *Journal of Business* 34 (4): 411–33. (Sets out

the original dividend irrelevant hypothesis for dividend policy in a perfect capital market.)

Mintz, J. (1995) 'The corporation tax: a survey', *Fiscal Studies* 16 (4): 23–68. (A thorough and accessible survey of the issues with an extensive bibliography.)

* Modigliani, F. and Miller, M. (1958) 'The cost of capital, corporation finance and the theory of investment', *American Economic Review* 48 (3): 261–97. (Pioneering work on the theory of capital structure, showing that financial decisions are irrelevant in perfect capital markets.)

Nadeau, S. (1988) 'A model to measure effects of taxes on the real and financial decisions of the firm', *National Tax Journal* 41 (4): 67–81. (Empirical study using US data, 1934–80, finding large effects from dividend taxes.)

OECD (1991) *Taxing Profits in a Global Economy: Domestic and International Issues*, Paris: OECD. (The definitive international comparison of the corporate taxes of the OECD countries, using the King and Fullerton 1977 methodology.)

Ross, S. (1977) 'The determination of financial structure: the incentive signalling approach', *Bell Journal of Economics* 8 (1): 23–40. (Presents the signalling theory approach to the level of dividend payments.)

Stiglitz, J.E. (1973) 'Taxation, corporate financial policy and the cost of capital', *Journal of Public Economics* 2 (1): 1–34. (Sets out the deviations from neutral taxation of corporations, using the US system as an example.)

See also: ACCOUNTING; FINANCIAL ACCOUNTING; FIXED ASSETS AND DEPRECIATION; INFLATION ACCOUNTING

Taxation, international

Overview

Tax systems generally can be classified as either global or territorial; these differ most notably in the manner in which they treat resident entities. Countries with global systems tax the worldwide income of their resident entities. An overwhelming majority of nations have global tax systems, including Australia, Canada, Germany, Italy, Japan, the United Kingdom, and the United States. In contrast, a territorial system generally taxes resident entities only on profit arising from sources within the country's borders. Territorial systems include those in Costa Rica, France, Guatemala, Malaysia, Panama, Singapore, South Africa and Uruguay.

The definition of a resident entity varies among countries. For example, the United States considers any corporation incorporated in the United States to be a resident entity; where the corporation does business or conducts its management activities is irrelevant. As an objective definition of residence, incorporation situs provides a measure of certainty to both taxpayers and governments. Most other countries define resident entities solely on the basis of central management or on the combined basis of central management and incorporation situs. For example, Portugal defines a resident entity as one that has its head office there or is effectively managed from Portugal. A resident entity in Germany is one managed and controlled from within Germany or incorporated under German law. Countries generally operationalize the place of management in terms of the location of the head office, the place where board meetings occur or some similar criterion.

All tax systems, whether global or territorial, limit the taxation of non-resident entities. Generally, a non-resident entity that conducts business in a country through a fixed facility or dependent agent (hereafter permanent establishment, or PE) is taxable at the same tax rates applicable to resident entities, but only on income attributable to the PE. In contrast, the investment income of non-resident entities from sources within a country is subject to a withholding tax (such as 30 per cent) on the gross earnings (i.e. no deductions are allowed). Global and territorial systems typically do not tax non-resident entities on business profits in the absence of a PE. Also, investment income is usually exempt unless sourced within the country.

This entry identifies tax issues that many multinational companies face and suggests possible tax-minimization strategies (see MULTINATIONAL CORPORATIONS). To the extent possible, multinationals seek to avoid double taxation and take advantage of opportunities to exempt or defer income recognition. Often, these strategies are implemented through adopting appropriate transfer pricing and profit remittance practices. Multinationals also must be concerned about the tax liabilities of individuals who are transferred across national borders since corporate policy generally calls for employee reimbursement of any additional tax incurred.

1 Avoiding double taxation

Since the tax systems in any two countries differ (sometimes drastically), the multinational corporation (MNC) is often exposed to the possibility that more than one country will claim jurisdiction to tax the same income stream (see MULTINATIONAL CORPORATIONS). This double taxation can arise in three general ways. First, two countries may claim jurisdiction over the same entity under their internal definitions of residence. For example, country A may assert its right to tax an entity because it is incorporated in country A, while country B may claim jurisdiction over the entity because its head office is in country B. Second, under overlapping source of income rules, two countries may assert their separate rights to tax the profit from a single transaction. Third, one country may claim jurisdiction to tax the party earning the income (i.e. as a resident entity), while another country may claim jurisdiction over the specific transaction generating the income. This latter type of double taxation is the most common and the most difficult to eliminate.

Without some effective remedy, double taxation can greatly increase the cost of doing business abroad, and may curtail international business and investment activities. A primary objective of international tax policy and planning is to mitigate the impact of double taxation.

Unilateral methods

Countries can take unilateral measures to reduce instances of double taxation. Most nations with territorial systems depend primarily on the exemption method. Under their internal laws they simply exempt income arising beyond their borders. For example, France does not generally tax the profits of resident entities derived from a branch (or PE) in another country. In theory, a PE in another country subjects business profits attributable to the PE to foreign taxation; thus France decides not to tax the profits a second time. A major advantage of the territorial system is that investors are able to determine their after-tax returns from foreign activities simply by reference to the host country's laws. A disadvantage is that losses incurred abroad through foreign branch operations, which often characterize the start-up years, may not be currently deductible against domestic profits. Because this disadvantage can curtail foreign investment, France departs from pure territorial principles and allows foreign branch losses to be deducted if authorization is obtained from the French Ministry of Economics and Finance. If a resident entity obtains such permission it must include the branch's operating loss (or profit) in its own tax return.

Some global systems use the exemption method too (e.g. in the Netherlands), but most rely primarily on a foreign-tax credit mechanism to reduce double taxation. In brief, a country with a global tax system taxes the worldwide income of resident entities but allows a credit for any foreign income tax paid on the same income. For example, assume a US corporation has 600 of domestic income and 400 of income from a PE in Germany. Both the United States and Germany consider the 400 income to be under their respective jurisdictions. Thus both countries tax the income, but the United States allows taxes paid to Germany as a credit on the resident corporation's US tax return. As in this example, the home (rather than the host) country is the jurisdiction that generally provides tax credit relief.

In addition to a credit for direct taxes paid, many countries allow an indirect or deemed-paid credit for foreign income taxes that a foreign subsidiary pays. The purpose of an indirect credit is to achieve some parity between operating abroad through a foreign branch and a foreign subsidiary. Since a foreign branch is not a separate entity from its domestic company, the income tax the branch pays is allowed as a credit in the home country. In contrast, a foreign subsidiary is a separate legal entity from its parent company. Absent an indirect credit, the domestic company receives no double-taxation relief from foreign income taxes paid by its foreign subsidiary. Thus an indirect credit is allowed in order to achieve some measure of equity. A dividend triggers the indirect credit mechanism. Generally, the percentage of the foreign subsidiary's earnings and profits paid as a dividend to its parent is the percentage of the foreign subsidiary's foreign income-tax payments that is allowed as an indirect credit to the parent company.

Assume a company residing in country A has a wholly owned subsidiary in country B. After the first year the subsidiary accumulates before-tax profits of 140, out of which it pays 40 in foreign tax. Thus its earnings and profits are 100. Then the subsidiary pays a dividend of 70 to its parent company out of its net earnings. Under these facts, the parent company is entitled to an indirect credit of 28 in the home country (i.e. $70/100 \times 40$).

Calculation of the indirect credit often is very complex, especially when income is earned in one year and dividends from those earnings are paid several years later. For this reason, some countries only allow a foreign-tax credit for taxes an entity pays directly. None the less, an indirect credit might be permitted in these countries if granted through a treaty.

Most countries granting a foreign-tax credit limit the credit to the domestic tax paid on foreign income. In other words, no credit is generally allowed against the domestic tax paid on domestic income. As a rough rule of thumb, the effect of any limitation is that the worldwide effective tax rate (ETR) on a given income item is the greater of the ETRs in the two countries imposing their taxes (before considering any credit). Assume an entity's home country has a global tax system that uses a foreign-tax credit to relieve double taxation and limits the credit as noted above. The home country imposes a 30 per cent ETR. Income of the entity subject to a foreign ETR of 40 per cent pays an overall ETR of 40 per cent (i.e. the higher of the two ETRs). If, instead, the foreign ETR is assumed to be 25 per cent, the overall ETR is 30 per cent once the profits are remitted to the home country.

Most countries permit any foreign tax that cannot be credited because of this limit to be carried over to other taxable years. For example, the United States allows excess credits to be carried back to the two previous years and, if all the excess credits do not result in a refund, forward to the next five years. In contrast, Japan effectively allows a three-year carryback and a three-year carryforward, and Norway permits a ten-year carryforward.

Bilateral methods

Income-tax treaties provide bilateral means of mitigating the effects of double taxation. Some countries have extensive networks of treaties. For example, Canada, Denmark, Finland, Germany, Italy, the Netherlands, Norway and Sweden each have more than fifty income-tax treaties in force. The French and United Kingdom income-tax treaty networks are two of the most impressive in terms of sheer numbers, at approximately ninety each.

Treaties reduce double taxation through common rules that both countries agree to follow. For example, a given entity might be considered a resident under the internal laws of two or more nations (i.e. dual resident status). Perhaps the entity is a resident of one country because it is incorporated there, while it is considered a resident of the other country because management activities occur there. Treaties with most member nations of the Organization for Economic Cooperation and Development (OECD) usually dictate that the entity resides only in the country from which it is effectively managed. In the case of treaties with the United States, however, only the country where the entity is created can claim it as a resident. To a lesser degree, treaties may resolve double-tax problems in which two countries claim jurisdiction over the same transaction through common source of income rules.

Treaties often use the exemption method to prevent double taxation of certain types of income from occurring. The exemption method limits the ability of the host country to impose its tax on certain income streams. For example, income from transporting people or cargo between two treaty countries is generally taxable only in the home country. Also, treaties normally preclude the host country from taxing business profits unless the profits are attributable to a PE in the host country. In the absence of a PE, the treaty exempts the business earnings from host country tax. Thus, mere export sales between treaty countries generally result in no tax liability to the host country (see EXPORTING).

2 Exempting or deferring taxes

Establishing a subsidiary in a no-tax or low-tax foreign jurisdiction can often result in significant tax advantages. The advantages can range from the complete exemption of part or all of the subsidiary's profits to a long-term deferral of taxation in the home country until profits are remitted.

Tax holidays and tax sparing

Developing countries sometimes offer tax holidays to attract foreign investment (see ECONOMICS OF DEVELOPING COUNTRIES). Tax holidays exempt foreign investors who engage in specified activities from taxation over a specified period of time. In some cases the tax holiday is part of the country's domestic law and is available to all foreign investors. At other times tax holidays are separately negotiated ad hoc agreements with foreign investors.

Assume a developing country normally imposes a 25 per cent tax rate on business profits. However, it is willing to allow complete exemption from income taxation to foreign investors that establish manufacturing operations in a region with high unemployment. The tax holiday is guaranteed for ten years. A foreign investor from a global-system country decides to invest and earns 100 the first year. The global-system tax rate, payable to the home country, is a flat 40 per cent.

If the developing country had not granted the tax holiday the foreign investor would have paid a 25 foreign tax. The home-country tax would have been 40 less 25 foreign-tax credit, or 15. Thus the total tax on the 100 profit would have been 40 (i.e. 25 + 15). How did the tax holiday benefit this investor? Under the tax holiday the investor pays no tax to the developing country. However, the tax to the home country is 40; no foreign-tax credit is allowed in the home country since no foreign income tax was paid. Thus the tax holiday provides no net tax benefit to the foreign investor. Whether or not the tax holiday is granted, the result in each case is that the investor pays 40 in taxes. No incentive to invest in the developing country results. Even worse, the effect of the tax holiday is simply to shift tax revenues from the developing country to the developed country. In effect, the developed country, not the investor, is the beneficiary of the tax holiday.

To ensure that tax holidays accomplish their intended aim of attracting foreign capital, treaties between developed and developing countries often provide for a tax-sparing credit. Tax sparing allows the investor to claim a foreign-tax credit in the home country

as if no tax holiday existed. In the example above, the tax holiday would exempt the foreign investor from host country tax. In the home country the investor would pay a tax of 40 less 25 tax-sparing credit. In effect, the investor is assumed to pay tax to the developing country even though no tax is actually paid. Thus the tax-holiday incentive accomplishes its intended purpose. Although many developing countries routinely include tax-sparing clauses in their treaties, the United States does not as a matter of policy. This might explain why the United States has concluded fewer income-tax treaties with developing countries than have several of the European nations.

Subsidiaries in tax havens

Establishing controlled foreign subsidiaries in low-tax jurisdictions or tax havens can often lead to long-term tax deferrals in the home country. The longer the tax deferral, the greater the present-value benefits. Some tax havens, such as the Cayman Islands and Vanuatu, either impose no general income tax or impose relatively low taxes. Other tax havens impose low or no taxes on specified activities even though their general income tax rates are relatively high.

Assume the multinational establishes a controlled foreign corporation in a no-tax haven (see MULTINATIONAL CORPORATIONS). The foreign subsidiary carries on international business and becomes very profitable but is careful not to remit any of its profits to the parent company in the home country. Absent some anti-deferral legislation in the home country, the subsidiary can accumulate large amounts of earnings that neither the host nor the home country taxes. Assuming a 10 per cent cost of capital, every 100 of home country tax deferred for ten years costs only 39 in present-value terms.

Many developed countries have laws that curtail tax-haven activities such as the one described above. The United States' so-called Subpart F legislation, which is similar to anti-haven laws in several other countries, identifies certain types of transactions for which tax deferral is disallowed. For example, a controlled foreign subsidiary that purchases goods for resale from its US parent, engages in no manufacturing activities in the country where it is created and sells to customers outside the country of incorporation results in 'tainted' income. A good business reason for the subsidiary to be established where it is does not seem to exist. The presumption is that the foreign location was selected for tax haven activities or to obtain a long-term tax deferral. Income from these transactions is treated as a constructive dividend to the US parent company. The constructive dividend results in current taxation of the foreign profits and thus precludes a tax deferral.

As noted above, the US Subpart F approach is to identify certain transactions that suggest tax-haven activities. In contrast, the method that some countries use is to identify 'tax-haven subsidiaries' and end tax deferrals on all profits through such companies. Japan generally defines a tax-haven subsidiary as one that is subject to a foreign ETR of 25 per cent or less. Similar legislation in South Korea defines a tax-haven subsidiary as any company whose main or head office is located in a country that imposes an ETR not greater than 15 per cent. Other countries, such as Austria, currently have no anti-haven tax rules.

3 Pricing transactions between related entities

Unless they are prevented in some way, cross-border transactions between related or controlled entities provide almost unlimited opportunities to shift income from high-tax to low-tax jurisdictions through price manipulations. For example, assume that a manufacturer produces an item at a cost of 60 and sells it abroad for 100, resulting in a 40 profit per unit exported. The problem is that the country where the manufacturer resides imposes a 50 per cent tax rate on the profit. To reduce the tax bite a related sales company is established in a no-tax country. Thereafter the manufacturer sells each unit of its product to the newly created sales company for 66. The sales company performs nominal tasks, such as labelling, and resells the product to ultimate consumers at 100 each. Absent some restrictions on pricing, this arrangement reduces the tax on each unit sold from 20 (i.e. 40 profit taxed at 50 per cent) to 3 (i.e. 6 profit taxed at

50 per cent). The remaining 34 of profit on each unit sold is captured in the sales company's country, which imposes no tax. Though this example involves the sale of tangible goods, similar pricing schemes can be developed for the use of tangible assets (rents), sales or transfers of intangible assets (royalties), loans or advances of money (interest), and performance of administrative or oversight services (management fees).

To prevent such abuses most countries allow their tax authorities to reallocate or reapportion income, deductions, credits or other allowances among related or controlled entities if necessary clearly to reflect income or prevent tax evasion. In effect, these anti-abuse provisions require that affiliated or related entities price transactions among them at arm's length. In other words, entities are expected to determine the prices applicable to similar transactions between *unrelated* parties and to charge those prices on transactions with related entities. In some countries, such as Mexico and the United States, the taxpayer has the burden of proof in transfer pricing disputes. Other countries, such as Denmark, place the burden of proof squarely on the taxing authority. Also, very stiff penalties apply to transfer prices that are substantially out of line in some countries, such as the United States.

Arm's-length pricing is the standard under many tax systems. However, the operational definition of arm's-length pricing varies from one country to the next. As a result, countries do not always arrive at the same transfer price for a particular transaction. In some cases, more than 100 per cent of the profit from a transaction may be taxed. Assume that a company in country A sells goods costing 80 to an affiliate in country B for 90. The affiliate, in turn, sells the goods to a consumer residing in country B for 100. If country A accepts 90 as the correct transfer price between the related parties, the company in country A has a profit of 10. If country B adjusts the transfer price down to 85 the affiliate's subsequent sale in country B results in a profit of 15. Though the total profit on the sale is only 20 (i.e. 100 less 80), Countries A and B together are taxing profit of 25 (i.e. 10 plus 15). In this situation the two companies might request that the taxing authorities in the two countries try to arrive at a common transfer price. This procedure, known as invoking competent authorities, is a common method for resolving instances of double taxation and often is allowed through treaty.

To curb controversies proactively some countries, such as the United States, now permit advance pricing agreements. Taxpayers that wish to use these procedures can disclose their pricing methodology in advance of a dispute. The government examines the methodology and, if it is acceptable, reaches a contractual agreement with the taxpayer to the effect that such methodology will not be questioned. Such agreements can save both the taxpayer and the government countless hours and high litigation costs.

4 Remitting profits

Foreign subsidiaries can remit profits to the home country in several different ways. Earnings can be remitted through dividends. Alternatively, contractual arrangements may allow some earnings to be remitted as interest, royalties, rents or management fees. Deciding on the best remittance method or combination of methods requires careful analysis of at least two factors.

First, some remittances result in tax deductions, while others do not. Dividends are distributions of earnings and profits rather than expenses of doing business. Thus dividends are not deductible. In contrast, interest, rents and royalties are considered to be deductible business expenses in most countries, and thus might be the preferred method for remitting profits. Management fees are often also deductible if determined according to arm's-length standards.

Second, many host countries impose withholding taxes on remittances that vary depending on the remittance method. For example, Italy generally withholds a tax of 27 per cent on dividends and 12.5 per cent on interest paid to non-residents. Italy's withholding tax on royalties is normally 22.5 per cent. If the recipient resides in a treaty country, however, the applicable withholding rates are often lower. Italy withholds only 15 per cent on dividends, 10 per cent on interest and 10 per cent on royalties paid to New Zealand residents.

The thin capitalization rules in some countries restrict the amount of debt in a company's capital structure. Thus the amount of profits that can be remitted as interest *vis-à-vis* dividends may be limited. Many countries, for example Canada and Japan, have adopted the general rule that debt cannot be more than three times the amount of equity. Some countries with thin capitalization restrictions, such as Luxembourg and the United States, do not have an explicitly stated ratio of debt to equity. Other countries, such as Denmark, have no thin capitalization rules at present.

At times, profits can be remitted to the home country with a smaller withholding tax if a less direct route is taken. Assume a company in country A owns a subsidiary in country C. Dividends from country C to country A are subject to a 30 per cent withholding tax since there is no tax treaty in force between these countries. One possible solution is to interpose a holding company. That is, the company in country A owns an intermediate holding company in country B, which, in turn, owns the subsidiary in country C. If treaties exist between A and B and between B and C, the total withholding tax might be reduced. For example, the treaty between B and C might exempt dividends entirely, while the treaty between A and B might impose only a 10 per cent withholding tax. Using a holding company in this fashion to build a 'treaty bridge' between two countries without a treaty is called treaty shopping. Many income-tax treaties disallow or restrict treaty shopping. Also, international tax planners sometimes have differing opinions about whether a given instance of treaty shopping is ethical, especially when a significant non-tax business reason for the intermediate holding company is unclear (see INTERNATIONAL BUSINESS ETHICS).

5 Transferring employees

Ventures into the international market often involve the transfer of individuals across national borders (see HUMAN RESOURCE MANAGEMENT, INTERNATIONAL). Managers and technicians from the home country may be needed in the start-up phase of offshore manu-facturing. Individuals from the target com-pany may need training that can best be obtained in the country where the business has been conducted for several years already. For-eign sales operations usually require that some sales people be available on location to promote products or to take orders. A subsid-iary's board of directors may include one or more directors who reside in the country where the parent company is located. In each case the transferred employee or board mem-ber is potentially subject to double taxation, once in the host and once in the home country. Many multinationals reimburse employees for all or part of any double tax resulting from foreign transfers (see MULTINATIONAL COR-PORATIONS).

Treaty exemptions

Income-tax treaties normally contain a com-mercial traveller article that, when satisfied, eliminates host-country taxation of an employee's income. To qualify for exemption employees must generally limit their presence in the host country to 183 days during the year and receive their compensation from an entity that does not reside in the host country. Also, a PE in the host country usually cannot deduct the compensation without forfeiting the exemption. More lenient exemption rules generally apply to employees of ships or air-craft involved in international transportation.

Apprentices and trainees that are tempo-rarily present in a treaty country for full-time training are usually exempt from their com-pensation if two conditions are met. First, an entity or party outside the host country must pay the compensation. Second, the purpose of the payment must be for the individual's maintenance or training. Some treaties spec-ify that the exemption is limited to a specified time, such as one year from the date of trans-fer.

Some income-tax treaties explicitly ad-dress which countries can tax director fees. In those cases treaties allow the host country to tax any portion of such fees for services ren-dered in that country. Income from services rendered in a director's home country is gen-erally not taxable in the host country.

Totalization agreements

Tax planning for cross-border transfers of individuals often focuses on ways of mitigat-ing the impact of double income taxation. However, double social-security taxation is possible also. As with increased income-tax liabilities, multinationals often bear all or part of the cost of the double social-security taxes that transferred employees incur.

Totalization agreements exist between some nations that exempt transferred employ-ees from the host country's social-security taxes during temporary visits. In most agree-ments five years or less is considered tempo-rary. In the absence of a totalization agreement the host country can impose its social-security taxes on any individual who becomes a resi-dent. Double taxation results if the home country also continues to cover the individual during his or her term abroad. For example, the United States continues to impose so-cial-security tax on all US employees who work abroad for American employers.

Totalization agreements are not as wide-spread as income tax treaties. For example, Norway and the United States have less than twenty agreements in force.

6 Conclusion

Multinationals engaged in international busi-ness or investment activities are potentially subject to taxation in both their home and host countries (see MULTINATIONAL CORPORA-TIONS). The primary objective in international tax planning is to avoid double taxation as far as possible. The internal laws of some coun-tries reduce or eliminate double tax on certain types of income. Income-tax treaties and other international agreements are also helpful in reducing host-country taxation.

Once this primary objective is achieved multinationals can turn their attention to other goals. Tax holidays in some countries and the possibility of tax deferrals in tax havens can be the means of reducing a multinational's worldwide ETR. However, many developed countries have anti-haven domestic laws that curtail long-term tax deferrals. Transfer pric-ing and remittance policies can also be used to reduce worldwide income taxes in many cases.

Over the next several years international tax advisers expect to see an increased number of tax treaties signed and ratified. The treaty activity should be particularly heavy with the 'newly independent' nations of the former Soviet Union and countries in the Pacific rim and, perhaps, South America. To develop economically these countries must negotiate income-tax treaties so they can attract foreign capital. At the same time, the potential new markets in these areas are very attractive to developed countries. Thus both developing and developed countries are highly motivated to conclude new tax treaties that promote and encourage international commerce.

Transfer pricing laws in many countries have undergone considerable changes in the past few years. Controversies involving transfer pricing issues will continue to plague both taxpayers and taxing authorities. Also, disputes between governments on appropriate arm's-length standards are likely to erupt as each country seeks to ensure it obtains its fair share of tax revenues. An alternative to the arm's-length approach that has gained some momentum in recent years is the unitary or formulary apportionment method. This method uses a prespecified formula to apportion worldwide income among affiliated companies. If widely adopted, this formulary approach may replace the heavy dependence on arm's-length pricing some day, but probably not in the near future.

ERNEST R. LARKINS
GEORGIA STATE UNIVERSITY

Further reading

Arnold, Brian J. and McIntyre, Michael J. (1995) *International Tax Primer*, The Hague: Kluwer Law International. (Provides a terrific overview of international tax systems that is simple to read.)

Deloitte Touche Tohmatsu International (1999) *International Tax and Business Guide*, New York: Deloitte. (Multiple-volume set that summarizes foreign tax systems and other international tax topics.)

Diamond, Walter H. (1999) *Foreign Tax and Trade Briefs*, Albany, NY: Matthew Bender. (Looseleaf service that summarizes the tax systems of many countries and also provides trade information.)

Diamond, Walter H. and Diamond, Dorothy B. (1999) *Tax Havens of the World*, Albany, NY: Matthew Bender. (Nicely arranged loose-leaf service covering all major tax havens in a readable format.)

Doernberg, Richard L. (1997) *International Taxation in a Nut Shell*, 3rd edition, St Paul, MN: West Publishing. (Gives a lay introduction to the international aspects of the US tax system.)

Dogart, Caroline (1997) *Tax Havens and Their Uses*, London: Economist Intelligence Unit. (Gives an introduction to low-tax jurisdictions around the world and how to take advantage of them.)

Larkins, Ernest R. (1991) 'Multinationals and their quest for the good tax haven: taxes are but one, albeit an important, consideration', *International Lawyer* 25, summer: 471. (Examines tax and non-tax factors that cause various tax havens to be popular.)

Larkins, Ernest R., Oakly III, Elwood F. and Winkle, Gary M. (1999) 'Tax and accounting aspects of global expansion', *Tax Adviser* 30, June: 416. (Presents a broad overview of relevant issues companies face when first going global.)

Ogley, Adrian (1992) 'Tax systems and their interaction', *Tax Planning International Review*: 3. (Provides an easy-to-read conceptual overview of principles common to many tax systems.)

PriceWaterhouseCoopers (1999) *Corporate and Individual Taxes: Worldwide Summaries*, New York: John Wiley & Sons. (Presents tax-system summaries for more than 100 countries in a uniform way.)

Tretiak, Philip L. (1993) 'Tax planning for U.S. multinationals', *International Tax Journal* 19, winter: 67. (Focuses on fundamental tax planning ideas for US companies engaged in international business.)

See also: BUSINESS ETHICS; CAPITAL, COST OF; CAPITAL STRUCTURE; DIVIDEND POLICY; ECONOMICS OF DEVELOPING COUNTRIES; EXPORTING; INTERNATIONAL BUSINESS ETHICS; MULTINATIONAL CORPORATIONS; TRAINING; TRANSFER PRICING

Taylor, Frederick Winslow (1856–1915)

Personal background

- born 20 March 1856 in Philadelphia, Pennsylvania, into a middle-class Quaker family, but did not go to college
- trained as an apprentice and eventually studied at night school
- married Louise M. Spooner, 1884
- developed what he called the 'scientific' study of work
- formative influence on work-study and industrial engineering
- early death in Philadelphia on 21 March 1915 from pneumonia

Major works

Shop Management (1903)
The Principles of Scientific Management (1911)
Two Papers on Scientific Management (1919)

Summary

F.W. Taylor (1856–1915) was the initiator of scientific management and a major influence on the development of production management as a subject. He set out to systematize the study of workflow organization by breaking tasks into minute detail and devising ways to speed up their accomplishment. Taylor aimed at a 'mental revolution' in order to break down the barriers to good labour relations between workers and management. His ideas on efficiency were propagated by his disciples after his death through an international movement to promote such management techniques. While he was a controversial figure in his time, Taylor's contribution still continues to provoke lively debate in many management texts.

1 Introduction

Taylor is widely seen as the initiator of the scientific management movement, although his work has also been described as a synthesis of already existing notions. He has become one of, if not the, best known 'management gurus' of all time (see GURU CONCEPT). His contribution to the study of organizations has been described as original in that he set out to study jobs scientifically and to measure workflows in order to achieve higher productivity (see ORGANIZATION BEHAVIOUR; ORGANIZATION BEHAVIOUR, HISTORY OF). He believed that management normally tried to push workers to achieve output, without an objective yardstick to measure a proper day's work. He therefore tried to devise a science of work to resolve this problem. Taylor thought that he was transforming what had previously been a crude art form into a firm body of knowledge.

Taylor set out to analyse tasks into their smallest details, diagnose the abilities of workers and then fit the two together to achieve greater efficiency. Job techniques would be redesigned to make maximum use of operatives' skills. In proposing these notions, he combined an engineer's outlook with an obsession for control. The main concept in Taylor's work was the 'task-idea', based on the principle that management should specify what must be done in the minutest detail and how it could be done. If these instructions were followed, industry would become more productive and trouble-free. While many writers have positively recognized Taylor's contribution (Merkle 1980; Kelly 1982), others have negatively referred to it as 'the degradation of work' (Braverman 1974).

2 Biographical data

Taylor was born into a Quaker, middle-class family on 20 March 1856, just outside the city of Philadelphia. Having completed his apprenticeship during the Depression in the 1870s, he went on to perform labouring work at the Midvale Steel Company in Philadelphia. In order to get out of this low-level employment, he decided to study engineering at the Stevens Institute's evening classes, eventually receiving his Master's Degree in Mechanical Engineering in 1883. Once qualified, he began a set of time studies at Midvale Steel in the early 1880s, out of which grew what was later called the Taylor System of Scientific Management. He started with the analysis of machine speeds in metal cutting in order to achieve greater efficiency.

In 1895, he gave a paper to the American Society of Mechanical Engineers entitled 'A piece-rate system: a step toward partial solution of the labor problem'. It was not the first paper on incentives, but it contained the basis of the distinctly Taylorist system and was founded on twelve years' experience at Midvale Steel, by which time he was chief engineer. It combined technical and organizational expertise, synthesizing several currents of efficiency management at hand. Taylor aimed to subdivide tasks, time them and find a way to speed them up. To prevent fatigue, carefully timed rest periods were to be built into the system. He continued his work in a new post at Bethlehem Steel, where he was made their management consultant in 1898, until 1901 when he lost his job on the sale of the company (Kanigel 1997).

After *Shop Management* was published in 1903, he became a well-known writer and lecturer and was elected President of the American Society of Mechanical Engineers. By this time, he had acquired several disciples, including C.G. Barth, H. Emerson and F.B. Gilbreth (see GILBRETH, F.B.; GILBRETH, L.E.M.). An important implementation of his new methods of standardizing tools and tasks was later tried out between 1909 and 1912 at the Watertown Arsenal in Cambridge, Massachusetts (Aitken 1960). It led to the adoption of similar practices in arsenals all over the USA. In 1911, he published his *Principles of Scientific Management* and became an increasingly public and controversial figure giving talks to top industrialists among others. He was invited as a visiting lecturer to the newly formed Harvard Business School and taught there once a year from 1909 until his death.

After organized labour tried to block rationalization techniques in industry influenced by Taylor's ideas in 1910–11, Taylor was confronted with Congressional investigation (Nelson 1980). A special House Committee summoned him as a leading witness in 1912. While the Committee conceded that Taylorism offered advantages to industry, it still believed Taylorism gave employers too much power. Taylor was demoralized by this confrontation and it may have contributed to his early demise. In the years following his death in 1915, Taylor's followers were to improve their relations with organized labour by recognizing the role of the unions in negotiating the introduction of new working methods, but still Taylor had gained a reputation as 'the enemy of the working man' (Morgan 1997: 22) (see TRADE UNIONS).

3 Main contribution

Taylor saw 'slacking' by workers as the main source of inefficiency in industry. The labourer, he reasoned, would not exert himself; the manager would use guesswork. Both had to be guided towards rational behaviour. To this end, he invented what he called a 'science of shovelling' while working in the steel industry in the early 1880s. To illustrate his notion of a fair day's work, he trained a labourer called Schmidt to increase by four times his workload of loading mouldings called 'pigs': the latter gained a bonus of 50 per cent as a result of the rationalization of his job. Piecework rates were devised to boost motivation, with what Taylor liked to call 'first-class men' setting the pace (see PAYMENT SYSTEMS). He believed his system was more than a mere efficiency device: it involved a complete 'mental revolution' on the part of management as well as workers, and involved a coming together of capital and labour, a delusion according to most of his critics.

Taylor also tried to extend the division of labour (see SMITH, A.) to management, believing that there should be no fewer than eight kinds of functional foremen, dealing with work speed and repairs. He believed that 'a good organization with a poor plant will give better results than the best plant with poor organization' (Taylor 1903: 65). The planning department was to play a pivotal role in Taylor's schema, as it would work out the detailed work schedules for the employees to follow in order to increase output.

At the Congressional inquiry, Taylor argued that better production methods were not only in the interests of management but also of the workers. He believed that:

The new way is to teach and help your men as you would a brother; to try to teach him the best way and show him the easiest way to do his work. This is the new mental attitude of the management toward the men, and that is the reason I have taken so much of your time in describing this cheap work of shovelling. It may seem to you of very little consequence, but I want you to see, if I can, that this new mental attitude is the very essence of scientific management; that the mechanism is nothing if you have not got the right sentiment, the right attitude in the minds of the men, both on the management's side and on the workman's side. Because this helps to explain the fact that until this summer, there has never been a strike under scientific management.

(cited in Pugh 1991: 139)

Against the notion of the survival of the fittest which was prominent at the time, Taylor offered a strategy of collaboration. He argued that wasteful conflict was inefficient and therefore wrong (see INDUSTRIAL CONFLICT). It was this moral element in his thought that inspired his disciples and generated a crusade for scientific management according to his defenders (Merkle 1980).

4 Evaluation

F.W. Taylor promoted not only systematic time-and-motion study, production control methods and incentive pay, but a wider philosophy and methodology of work organization (Drucker 1999) (see WORK SYSTEMS). Scientific management would create an atmosphere of trust in industry based on a value-neutral approach, probably a dubious notion from the start. He always stressed the word scientific: he thought it would increase his credibility with managers and engineers and even ordinary workers who were sceptical about the impersonal forces of the market. Science, he thought, would create both high wages and high profits.

Taylorism has been criticized by many writers on organizational behaviour for its individualist assumptions that gave priority to distinctly individual motivation, rewards and controls in order to break the collective power of work groups (see MOTIVATION AND SATISFACTION; GROUPS AND TEAMS). Furthermore, time-and-motion study techniques and financial incentives were seen as part of management's definition of what were appropriate workloads and work methods in order to increase managerial control. Other critics of Taylor's theories have argued that his work did not deserve the term scientific and that Taylorism took too narrow a view of work:

Time-study; the confusion of human labour with the play of inanimate mechanisms; the ignorance of the physical and mental functioning of the organism and its own demands; the procedure adopted to stimulate and reward effort; the place of vocational guidance; the selection by output, and finally the empiricism of generalizations elevated to the status of 'laws' – everything proves that we have here a system created by a man who was doubtless a great technician but who could not see beyond the confines of his engineer's universe.

(Friedmann 1955: 64–5)

None the less, Taylor carried out several important field experiments at both the Midvale Steel works and Bethlehem Steel, and later as an industrial consultant at Watertown Arsenal, for example, passing on his findings to meetings of bodies such as the American Society of Mechanical Engineers, although not without criticism and even Congressional scrutiny. The later phase of Taylor's work was, however, more linked with what were to become mainstream developments. For example, there was a considerable continuity between late Taylorism and early industrial psychology (Kelly 1982) (see OCCUPATIONAL PSYCHOLOGY). During and after the First World War, industrial psychologists started to investigate the conditions for industrial cooperation. Union–management cooperation was encouraged as part of the war effort as were

joint consultation mechanisms (see INDUS-
TRIAL AND LABOUR RELATIONS). In spite of
proposing greater managerial control and
increased specialization of tasks, Taylor
emphasized many features of what later
became subsumed under the human relations
heading, including motivational factors, such
as promotional prospects, friendly supervisors, positive work rhythms and clear working
goals, which remain important concerns of
managerial practice (see HUMAN RELATIONS).

Taylorism evolved into an experimental
approach which was to persist in most capitalist economies long after its founder's death:
Japanese management was appreciably influenced by Taylorism in the inter-war years and
in much of its post-1945 development
(Warner 1994) (see JAPAN, MANAGEMENT IN;
UENO, Y.). Even in the Soviet Union, Taylorism
was encouraged as part of an ambitious
programme of social engineering as carried
out by the Russian efficiency expert Gastev in
the early 1920s. Taylor's name was openly
used along with studies of work physiology,
labour fatigue and selection methods. After
initial opposition to such ideas, Lenin observed that 'Socialism plus Taylorism would
equal Communism' because of businesslike
methods and one-man management. Soviet
and later Chinese industry continued to be influenced by scientific management as adapted
to their respective systems (Kaple 1994).

5 Conclusions

Taylor's four Principles of Scientific Management (1911) are: (1) to establish a science
of production; (2) to select and train workers
to achieve this; (3) to apply such a science to
operatives' tasks; and (4) to build cooperation
between the workers and management
to achieve common goals. Its impact on contemporary society and its so-called 'McDonaldization' (see Ritzer 1996) has been considerable. Taylorism was not a single innovation,
but a series of notions and practices elaborated
by the initiator and his collaborators. The
movement promoted an international crusade
for efficiency in the 1920s and 1930s with its
effect being felt long after. Taylor's epitaph in
Philadelphia reads: 'Father of Scientific Management' (Kakar 1970: 1). Drucker (1999: 81)

remarked that 'Taylor was the first to apply
knowledge to work.' Without his innovations
(and later those of Henry Ford), assembly-line
mass production as we know it today would
not have been possible (see FORD, H.). In anticipating the routinization of everyday life,
'History may judge that Taylor came before
his time' (Morgan 1997: 26).

MALCOLM WARNER
JUDGE INSTITUTE OF MANAGEMENT STUDIES,
UNIVERSITY OF CAMBRIDGE

Further reading

(References cited in the text marked *)

* Aitken, G.H. (1960) *Taylorism at the Watertown
  Arsenal: Scientific Management in Action,
  1908–1915*, Cambridge, MA: Harvard University Press. (A detailed monograph on a specific
  application of Taylor's work in arms manufacture, which is probably of interest mostly to
  specialists.)
* Braverman, H. (1974) *Labor and Monopoly Capital: The Degradation of Work in the Twentieth
  Century*, New York: Monthly Review Press. (A
  controversial work based on a critique of
  Taylorism from a Marxist perspective, which
  has played an important role in generating the
  de-skilling debate.)
  Copley, F.B. (1923) *Frederick W. Taylor: Father
  of Scientific Management*, 2 vols, New York:
  Harper & Co. (A definitive, extended biography
  of Taylor, published not long after his death,
  which is dated but contains useful detail.)
* Drucker, P.F. (1999) 'Knowledge worker productivity: the biggest challenge', *California Management Review* 41 (2): 79–94. (This
  prize-winning article reviews Taylor's contribution to the topic.)
* Friedmann, G. (1955) *Industrial Society: The
  Emergence of the Human Problems of Automation*, Glencoe, IL: The Free Press. (A
  well-known work on automation by a renowned
  French industrial sociologist who was a critic of
  Taylorism.)
* Kakar, S. (1970) *Frederick Taylor: A Study in Personality and Innovation*, Cambridge, MA: MIT
  Press. (A psychoanalytic biography of Taylor,
  which concisely examines the personal factors
  in his life that influenced his behaviour and the
  specific direction of his work.)
* Kanigel, R. (1997) *The One Best Way: Frederick
  Winslow Taylor and the Enigma of Efficiency*,
  New York: Viking. (A new insightful,
  up-to-date biography of Taylor and his work

which argues that his techniques owe more to 'guesswork' than to 'science'.)

* Kaple, D.A. (1994) *Dream of a Red Factory: The Legacy of High Stalinsim in China,* Oxford: Oxford University Press. (An account of Taylorist influence on both Soviet and Chinese communist industrial practice.)

* Kelly, J. (1982) *Scientific Management, Job Design and Work Performance,* London: Academic Press. (This book constitutes an excellent critique of Taylor's work, which is distinctive in that it sees the later development of his thought as overlapping with the human relations school.)

* Merkle, J.A. (1980) *Management and Ideology: The Legacy of the International Scientific Management Movement,* Berkeley and Los Angeles, CA: University of California Press. (The author has written an interesting monograph on Taylorism as a social movement with reference to its influence on the UK, France, Germany and the Soviet Union.)

* Morgan, G. (1997) *Images of Organization,* Thousand Oaks, CA: Sage (A provocative textbook which has attempted to re-write modern organizational theory.)

* Nelson, D. (1980) *Frederick Taylor and the Rise of Scientific Management,* Madison, WI: University of Wisconsin Press. (A more recent account of Taylor's life and work, placing it in the context of US economic history.)

Prujit, H.D. (1997) *Job Design and Technology: Taylorism-vs-Anti-Taylorism.* London: Routledge. (A timely account of anti-Taylorist innovations in European firms)

* Pugh, D.S. (ed.) (1991) *Organization Theory: Selected Readings,* Harmondsworth: Penguin. (This is a set of useful readings covering more of the field and including detail on Taylor's evidence to the Congressional investigation.)

* Ritzer, G. (1996) *The McDonaldization of Society,* Newbury Park, CA: Sage. (An imaginative attempt to link Taylorism and later phenomenon like McDonalds and Disney.)

Shingo, S. (1981) *The Toyota Production System,* Tokyo: Japanese Management Association. (Shingo describes the links between Taylorism and the Toyota system.)

* Taylor, F.W. (1903; 1919) *Shop Management,* New York: Harper Brothers. (Taylor's first major publication on work-study which made his reputation as a thinker and practitioner in the field.)

* Taylor, F.W. (1911) *The Principles of Scientific Management,* New York: W.W. Norton & Co. Inc. (Taylor's classic exposition of his views which has become internationally known as one of the classics of management theory.)

Taylor, F.W. (1919) *Two Papers on Scientific Management,* London: Routledge. (This book constitutes the late work of Taylor, which was published posthumously.)

Warner, M. (1994) 'Japanese culture, Western management: Taylorism and Human Resources in Japan', *Organization Studies* 15: 509–33. (This paper explicitly points to the role of Taylorism in the development of the Japanese employment system.)

Wrege, C.D. and Greenwood, E.G. (1991) *Frederick Taylor, the Father of Scientific Management: Myth and Reality,* Toronto, Ontario: Irwin Professional. (A definitive biography of Taylor.)

See also: BEDAUX, C.E.; COLLECTIVE BARGAINING; FOLLETT, M.P.; FORD, H.; GILBRETH, F.B.; GILBRETH, L.E.; GROUPS AND TEAMS; GURU CONCEPT; HUMAN RELATIONS; HUMAN RESOURCE MANAGEMENT; INCENTIVES; INDUSTRIAL AND LABOUR RELATIONS; INDUSTRIAL CONFLICT; JAPAN, MANAGEMENT IN; JOB DESIGN; JOB EVALUATION; LABOUR PROCESS; MAYO, G.E.; MOTIVATION AND SATISFACTION; OCCUPATIONAL PSYCHOLOGY; ORGANIZATION BEHAVIOUR; ORGANIZATION BEHAVIOUR, HISTORY OF; PAYMENT SYSTEMS; PRODUCTIVITY; RECRUITMENT AND SELECTION; SYSTEMS; TRADE UNIONS; WORK SYSTEMS

Teams: see GROUPS AND TEAMS

Technological development: see STRATEGY AND TECHNOLOGICAL DEVELOPMENT

Technology diffusion in Japan

Overview

Japan is widely regarded as the most successful of all nations in importing technology. It was the first non-Western nation to use Western industrial and military technologies to become a world power. Japanese firms are now well entrenched in positions of international leadership in high technology industries and, although it is now a leader in creating new technology, Japan continues to be the world's largest importer of technology.

Two factors account for much of this success. First, the Japanese population is unusually competent and motivated to use foreign technology. It is well-educated by world standards and has been so since before Japan was opened to world commerce in the nineteenth century. Throughout their modern history the Japanese have believed that the best way for Japan to protect its culture is through the effective use of foreign technology. Second, Japanese business firms, trade associations and the government have been particularly well structured to import, adapt and improve foreign technology.

1 Introduction

When the Japanese encountered Western civilization in the late sixteenth century they showed a remarkable ability to assimilate the high technology of the time, quickly developing the ability to produce their own guns and artillery, and even introducing refinements. Nevertheless, Japan soon cut off most contact with the West and for nearly a century books about the Occident were banned (Perrin 1979).

When their country was forcibly opened up to the outside world by a US fleet in the mid-nineteenth century, the Japanese were amazed to see such technological wonders as steam engines, telegraphy equipment and modern firearms. Despite the Japanese lack of familiarity with the latest Western military and industrial technologies, Japan had its strengths in science and technology. In the seventeenth century a Japanese mathematician had invented a form of calculus. In 1805 a Japanese doctor had been the first surgeon in the world to use general anaesthesia in removing a breast tumour, and smallpox vaccinations were introduced in 1807. Japanese engineering and public works were advanced by world standards. Literacy rates were relatively high: around 40 per cent of boys and 10 per cent of girls attended school. Although Japan had a substantial gap with the West in industrial and military technology, its strengths

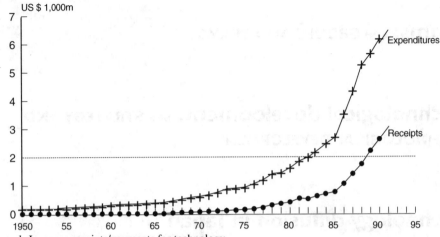

Figure 1 Japanese receipts/payments for technology

would help in closing that gap (Bartholomew 1989) (see FUKUZAWA, Y.; INNOVATION AND TECHNOLOGICAL CHANGE).

Japan's abrupt exposure to Western technologies in the mid-nineteenth century sparked concerns about national survival. Most other Asian countries had already been colonized by Westerners. The response in Japan was not an effort to protect Japanese values by blocking the introduction of Western technology, but rather a movement to combine Western technology with Japanese values to strengthen the nation so that it might maintain its independence. Both industrial and military development were heavily promoted. This sense of insecurity has never disappeared (Samuels 1994).

It seemed clear to the Japanese that quick progress would have to be based on importing and adapting technology rather than attempting to develop it independently. This notion guided Japanese government and corporate policies on technology not only during Japan's early industrialization, but until at least the 1970s. Foreign technical advisors were brought to Japan, and the government also invested heavily in sending Japanese scientists overseas for study. A widespread criticism in the years before the First World War was that so much was spent for this purpose that little money was left for domestic research (Bartholomew 1989).

Nevertheless, despite occasional nationalistic reactions to the reliance on foreign technology, there was a general tendency in Japan to look overseas for technology and to undervalue indigenous efforts. During the Second World War, the Japanese military was startled to find that the Japanese Yagi antenna was being used in captured US and British aircraft – the Japanese were not yet using this technology.

Japan's isolation in the 1930s and during the Second World War widened the gap between Japanese technology and that of the West. After the war, the country marshalled its limited resources to catch up by importing massive amounts of foreign technology. Between 1950 and 1997 nearly 90,000 agreements to import technology were signed by the Japanese. These agreements cost the Japanese nearly $100 billion (see Figure 1). In the late 1990s Japan was spending more on foreign technology imports than any other country. Some 3,000 new agreements were being signed by Japanese firms each year, about two-thirds of them with US firms (Japanese Science and Technology Agency).

2 Education

As part of its drive to industrialize in the late nineteenth century Japan established a new mass education system combined with a new system of higher education (see MANAGEMENT EDUCATION IN JAPAN). Emphasis was given to foreign languages and to technical and engineering education. While the system was very effective at training industrial workers and some engineers, most people did not have access to the universities. Under post-war reforms guided by US occupation authorities, however, the system of higher education lost this elitist orientation.

More than 90 per cent of the Japanese now complete secondary education, and more than thirty per cent of these go on to colleges and universities. Japan graduates a far higher per capita number of engineers than the US, Germany and other countries and also leads in the number of researchers as a percentage of the workforce (Japanese Science and Technology Agency).

Despite this success in building its technological human resources, critics point out that the Japanese educational system awards only about one half as many degrees in the physical sciences as Germany and one-quarter as many as the US. Furthermore, Japanese graduate programmes, even in engineering, are small by international standards. This could suggest that the Japanese education system is far more geared to training people capable of adapting and incrementally improving technology than to making scientific or technological breakthroughs.

Comparative studies of engineering education in Japan and the USA have found that course offerings are very similar. The major difference in curriculum is the attention paid to foreign language education in Japan. Japanese students are far better prepared than their US counterparts to undertake foreign language technical literature searches. Indeed, many Japanese firms send their technical and other employees to study at educational institutions in the USA and Europe.

3 Business

Employment practices common in large Japanese firms have important consequences for intra-firm, inter-firm and international flows of technology. These practices include the career-long employment system, the systematic rotation of engineers among functions and the strategic use of professional associations (see INDUSTRIAL RELATIONS IN JAPAN).

While career-long employment obviously inhibits the firm-to-firm diffusion of technol-ogy carried by job changing technologists in Japan, it may have made it easier for the Japanese to develop collaborative research arrangements. There is less concern about the loss of key employees to other firms. Career-long employment also makes it more rational for Japanese firms to send employees overseas for study because the firm has the rest of the employee's working life to capture the benefits of what they may have learned.

Career-long employment has also allowed Japanese firms to develop systematic job rotation as part of the training of engineers and as a mechanism to build intra-firm communication networks. Far greater numbers of Japanese than US engineers are sent to research and development divisions as part of their training, for example. Furthermore, career-long employment makes it possible for firms to develop systematic strategies for sending to professional meetings those who are best equipped to find key information and direct it to the appropriate people within the firm (Lynn et al. 1993).

On the negative side, career-long employment makes it harder for technology-based start-up firms to find the human resources they need. The system can also be wasteful, in that technical people may find it difficult to leave firms that can no longer use their expertise.

Some aspects of the Japanese enterprise system have developed in response to the pressing need for Japanese firms to introduce foreign technologies. The functions of technology transfer, product and process innovation, applied research and engineering, for example, were assigned to individual factories rather than to headquarters or staff sections, as would be typical in most other countries. During the period when Japan lagged far behind the West this practice offered the advantage that those with the best scientific and technical education, rather than more senior but less well-trained managers, were responsible for technology transfer. Managers closer to the production phase were also better able to enlist the aid of workers to adapt technologies to Japanese conditions. The well-known 'quality circles' and other small workplace problem solving groups are a contemporary manifestation of this close interaction between engineers and workers (Fruin 1992) (see ISHIKAWA, K.).

The Japanese enterprise system also developed a reliance on interdependent networks of firms. Firms belonging to groups, often known as *keiretsu*, specialize in the collection of certain types of technologies, sharing technologies they could not use with affiliates. The international networks of trading company offices monitor technological developments on behalf of group companies. Mitsubishi's trading company, for example, was instrumental in the late 1950s and early 1960s in importing most of the European and US technologies used by Mitsubishi Petrochemical in its new petrochemical complexes. Mitsui's trading company located technology and raised much of the capital needed in the formation of Mitsui Aluminium in 1968. More recently, as major Japanese firms have developed their own abilities to scan world technological developments, and as increasing numbers of technologies have become too complex for the technical generalists at the trading companies to monitor, this role of trading companies has diminished (Yoshihara 1982).

As the Japanese economy struggled through an extended recession in the 1990s, the nature of Japanese employment came under increasing pressure to change. It is not yet clear, however, how much change will actually take place.

4 Trade associations

Another type of organization that has helped Japanese firms keep abreast of foreign development in technology is the trade association. Partly because of a less restrictive antitrust regime in Japan, Japanese trade associations engage in a far broader range of activities than their counterparts in the USA.

Japanese trade associations routinely collect foreign technical journals, conference proceedings and patents. They abstract and index these documents, and provide translations to members. Often this information is offered online. Japanese trade associations organize study tours for their members and invite foreign experts to Japan. They maintain files of foreign product catalogues. Associations in the machinery industry have bought foreign made machine tools and placed them in laboratories for study by member firms.

Many of these functions are less important nowadays than they were in the past for larger firms (which now have their own international monitoring capabilities), but continue to be vital to smaller firms. Trade associations are also instrumental in the organization of collaborative research between firms in various industries (Lynn and McKeown 1988).

5 Government

After the Second World War and throughout the 1970s, the Japanese government used foreign exchange controls to exercise substantial control over technology imports. These controls helped Japanese firms get technology under very favourable terms. Government departments, most notably the Ministry of International Trade and Industry (MITI), withheld or threatened to withhold approval of agreements that were not judged to be favourable to the Japanese side (see BUSINESS STRATEGY, JAPANESE). When the controls were most fully in effect, during the 1950s, MITI intervened to force changes in about 40 per cent of the technology import agreements. The government also attempted to organize potential buyers of foreign technology to prevent them from bidding up prices. As a consequence, in the case of at least some technologies, royalty costs paid by the Japanese were a small fraction of those paid by firms in other countries. Earlier, when foreigners distrusted the ability of Japanese firms to make royalty and other payments, the government guaranteed the payments (Lynn 1982).

One factor motivating this extensive system of controls, particularly in the early 1950s, was that the purchase of foreign technologies was viewed by many Japanese government officials as potentially damaging. It could waste scarce foreign exchange. Worse, it could tempt companies to neglect the development of domestic technology. These concerns soon eased and preferential tax measures and tariff exemptions were introduced to encourage the import of technology during the late 1950s.

As Japan increasingly became a major part of the world trade community foreign pressures mounted for the dismantling of the controls. Japan joined the Organization for Economic Cooperation and Development (OECD) in 1964. Although the controls were increasingly liberalized, their basic framework remained in place until 1980. Today, the Japanese government no longer employs unusual measures to regulate technology imports.

Technology import controls were beneficial to Japan at a time when it was emerging from pre-war and Second World War isolation. Japan was recovering from wartime devastation, and the environment was one in which economic growth clearly depended on a relatively small number of technologies. As these factors ceased to apply, some of the problems with technology import controls became more evident. Japanese firms sometimes found, for example, that government intervention only made it harder for them to get advanced technologies from foreign firms that were in strong bargaining positions.

Aside from interventions in technology import agreements, the Japanese government has also played other roles to facilitate the efficient introduction of foreign technology. In 1957, the Science and Technology Agency established the Japan Information Center of Science and Technology. By the 1990s the Center was receiving more than 600,000 documents annually and providing online access to them. A number of other government agencies are also responsible for promoting the distribution of scientific and technological information in Japan.

In the late 1990s the Japanese government annually sent nearly 7,000 researchers from national research institutes and more than 13,000 researchers from academic institutions overseas, most often to the USA. The government was also sponsoring foreign researchers at Japanese laboratories.

6 Current issues

Since the 1970s it has been increasingly evident that Japan's emphasis on importing technology could not be sustained. First of all there was growing sensitivity in Japan to the widely held stereotypes of the Japanese as free riders on the world technology system, or of the Japanese as lacking in creative ability.

Second, there was concern that Japan could no longer prosper simply by borrowing technologies. Many Japanese researchers believed that the emphasis on borrowing technologies had resulted in an underfunding of original research. While Americans often fault themselves for a 'not-invented-here-syndrome' in which firms are irrationally unwilling to use technologies developed by others, the Japanese increasingly saw themselves as having the opposite problem, an irrational avoidance of the use of technologies developed in Japan. More generally, there was a growing sense that Japan should move to a stronger role of leadership in the world community, that it should make a stronger contribution to technology as in other domains.

A series of policies was adopted both at the governmental and corporate levels to bring more foreign researchers to Japan. Some of these have already been noted. In addition, a number of well-publicized international joint research projects were launched in the 1980s and 1990s. Other policies were directed at changing the education system away from its emphasis on rote learning.

Probably more because of the maturation of the Japanese technology system, however, than because of any of the government policies, Japan has become an increasingly important member of the world technology community. For some years Japanese nationals have led all foreigners in the number of US patents granted. Furthermore, citation evidence suggests that the Japanese patents are of high quality (Frame and Narin 1990). Japan's share of the number of papers published in the world's major scientific journals climbed from sixth in the world in the early 1970s to third (after the USA and UK) by the late 1980s. Japanese receipts for technology sold climbed from less than a quarter of a billion US dollars per year in the mid-1970s to more than $7 billion per year in the late 1990s (see Figure 1). This was still far less than the over $30 billion in annual receipts for the USA, but it was exceeded receipts for Germany, France or the UK (Japanese Science and Technology Agency). In a number of industries, such as steel, Japan has long had far more technology to sell than it needed to buy.

At the end of the twentieth century national technology systems were quickly merging, and Japan was a major part of this trend. Foreign firms were building research facilities in Japan to tap into the technological resources available there, while Japanese firms were building facilities throughout Europe and the USA. Strategic alliances between Japanese, European and German firms were jointly developing new technologies (Sakakibara and Westney 1992).

LEONARD H. LYNN
CASE WESTERN RESERVE UNIVERSITY

Further reading

(References cited in the text marked *)

* Bartholomew, J. (1989) *The Formation of Science in Japan: Building a Research Tradition*, New Haven, CT: Yale University Press. (Describes how science institutions developed in Japan, especially in the period 1868–1920.)

* Frame, J.D. and Narin, F. (1990) 'The United States, Japan and the changing technological balance', *Research Policy* 19 (5): 447–55. (An analysis of US and Japanese company patents issued in the USA.)

* Fruin, W.M. (1992) *The Japanese Enterprise System*, New York: Oxford University Press. (Argues that the distinctive 'Japanese enterprise system' evolved to facilitate import of foreign technology.)

*Japanese Science and Technology Agency (Annually) *Indicators of Science and Technology*, Tokyo: Ministry of Finance Printing Bureau. (Annual of science and technology data from various government ministries. Many of the tables have English headings.)

Goto, A. and Odagiri, H. (1997) (eds) *Innovation in Japan*, Oxford: Oxford Univwersity Press. (13 chapters by leading Japanese experts.)

* Lynn, L.H. (1982) *How Japan Innovates: A Comparison with the U.S. in the Case of Oxygen Steelmaking*, Boulder, CO: Westview Press. (Compares processes of technology import in North America and Japan.)

* Lynn, L.H. and McKeown, T. (1988) *Organizing Business: Trade Associations in America and Japan*, Washington, DC: American Enterprise Institute and University Press of America. (Shows how some Japanese trade associations monitor world technological developments.)

* Lynn, L.H., Piehler, H. and Kieler, M. (1993) 'Engineering careers, job rotation, and gatekeepers in Japan and the United States', *Journal of Engineering and Technology Management* 10 (1): 53–72. (Results of a survey of a large number of US and Japanese engineers regarding their careers.)

Morris-Suzuki, T. (1994) *The Technological Transformation of Japan: From the Seventeenth to the Twenty-first Century*, New York: Cambridge University Press. (An authoritative history, drawing extensively on both Japanese and English-language sources.)

Odagiri, H. and Goto, A. (1996) *Technology and Industrial Development in Japan*, Oxford: Oxford University Press. (Describes how various Japanese industries built technological capabilities.)

Partner, S. (1999) *Assembled in Japan: Electrical Goods and the Making of the Japanese Consumer*, Berkeley: University of Califronia Press. (Provides interesting information on the transfer and diffusion of electrical and electronics technology.)

* Perrin, N. (1979) *Giving up the Gun: Japan's Reversion to the Sword, 1543–1887*, Boston, MA: Godin. (How the Japanese quickly mastered and improved Western firearms, then ceased to use them as weapons.)

* Sakakibara, K. and Westney, D.E. (1992) 'Japan's management of global innovation: technology management crossing borders', in N. Rosenberg, R. Landau and D.E. Mowery (eds), *Technology and the Wealth of Nations*, Stanford, CA: Stanford University Press. (Discusses globalization strategies being pursued by Japanese research and development managers.)

* Samuels, R.J. (1994) *'Rich Nation Strong Army': National Security and the Technological Transformation of Japan*, Ithaca, NY: Cornell University Press. (Argues that a national sense of insecurity has motivated Japanese approaches to technology.)

* Yoshihara, K. (1982) *Sogo Shosha: The Vanguard of the Japanese Economy*, Oxford: Oxford University Press. (Describes the evolution of roles of general trading companies in the Japanese business system.)

See also: ASIA PACIFIC, MANAGEMENT IN; BUSINESS CULTURE, JAPANESE; BUSINESS HISTORY, JAPANESE; BUSINESS STRATEGY, JAPANESE; INDUSTRIAL RELATIONS IN JAPAN; KEIRETSU (ZAIBATSU); JAPAN, MANAGEMENT IN; TOYODA FAMILY

Technology and organizations

Overview

In the study of organizations, 'technology' is often defined as an operational tool, the design of which is dictated by the demands of efficiency within given market conditions. In the past technology has been treated as an independent or exogenous causal factor shaping organizational design. It is evidently the case that machines designed to transform materials, information or people (through means such as medicine or transport) can incorporate design principles that are not readily understood outside an engineering discipline and are therefore not easily challenged. However, organizational theorists have questioned the immutability of engineering design along a number of dimensions.

Taken more broadly, technology can be interpreted as all the means used by humans to control their environment, including bureaucracy or organization itself. Thus, like organizational structure, technological configurations can be regarded as modes of control or of means of reducing uncertainty in the exercise of managerial power. As such, they can provide more or less ability to monitor and meter their performance by central management. Communications and information technology (CIT) can be seen to be rapidly taking the place of bureaucratic modes of operational metering and monitoring within contemporary society.

As well as contributing to the value-adding functions of the organization, technology has always been incorporated into the service provided by many consumer products. Competitions or contests between rival corporations are now increasingly based on product innovation rather than price; hence the study of the management of innovation and of means of creating conditions conducive to creativity among organizational members has recently experienced an enormous revival. Nevertheless it remains true that the speed of technological innovation is presently accompanied by enormous social costs. Without adjustment in national and international infrastructures designed to cope with technological change, long-term effects on wider society may ultimately be described as destabilizing.

1 Defining technology

At its simplest, technology is defined as a tool. It is commonplace among historians to see the use of increasingly sophisticated tools as providing a convenient means to divide the evolution of society into epochs or periods of civilization. We even speak of pre-history as Stone, Iron or Bronze Ages. At this higher level of generality we can speak of all organized knowledge as the tool by which humans attempt to control their social and material environment. In other words, all modes of organizing people for the purposes of controlling or coordinating their activities can be considered a form of technology.

This ambiguity in definition is more than a semantic issue. It is difficult to escape the endogenous influences of technology within modern thinking and acting. However, it could be useful to consider these structuring technological influences in descending levels of abstract conceptualization. First, they are contained in *ideologies* of industrialization or modernization in which technological (or administrative) innovation is regarded as 'progress', and resistance from whatever source is labelled 'conservative' and viewed with approbation. It has underpinned the spirit of modern nationalism and perspectives on comparative national development for much of the last 150 years. Today it infuses almost all managerial and organizational literature.

Second, bodies of *disciplined knowledge* have emerged in which causal and systemic relations between material and/or social elements in specified situations are postulated and related to empirical observations (empirical positivism). Their origins can be traced to the European Renaissance, through what is often described as the Age of Reason or the eighteenth century Enlightenment. Observation, categorization and the related conceptual explanation can be seen as constituting more or less scientific knowledge in terms of its reproducibility and generalizability.

Third, there are *techniques* or procedures to be adopted in processing information relating to data on social or material operations. This knowledge may gain its explanatory and predictive value from scientific observation or from the accumulation of experience in the operations themselves (the so-called 'learning curve'). Techniques may be more or less codified in the form of texts and manuals or embodied in tacit routines. In the latter mode they often relate to the specific organizational system in which they arise and can be regarded as contributing to its unique competence (Nelson and Winter 1982).

Finally, these techniques can be incorporated in the mechanical, material or electronic *design and programming* of hardware and software, in other words in machines and capital equipment. This is the most articulated form of technology.

Technological innovation is often described as moving through these layers of abstraction from scientific discovery or invention to the design of new operational techniques, tools and consumer devices. In fact, it appears that the reverse is often the case. Improvements in design can result from user experience in operating with existing tools, and bottlenecks or 'reverse salients' in the development of new operational systems can shape the direction of research done in so-called 'pure' science. The influence exercised respectively by the customer-user or by the scientist or technologist is often described as providing either a pull or a push in bringing about innovation (Rothwell 1977).

A further definitional distinction to be made is that between product and process (or production) technology. At the level of the firm or sector it is evidently important to distinguish between the importation of technological resources and the exportation (to other firms, sectors or to final consumers) of the value added product. Studies of technology often reflect this dichotomy in their author's preoccupation, either with the installation and implementation of 'imported' process technology or with the invention and design of new products. Over the last two decades there has been a growing emphasis in the management literature on the relationship that each type of innovation has for the other, particularly in designer-user inter-firm transactions within the value chain (Womack *et al.* 1990).

2 The social construction of technology

The most prevalent critique of an autonomous and objective technological logic stems from its use as a device to control the actions of others. Contemporary studies highlight the social shaping of the range of options that usually exist in most critical decision making on technology. Choices often appear to be determined by implicit or explicit conspiracy on the part of one group to control the future actions of another. For example, Noble's (1985) account of the manner in which computer numerically controlled (CNC) machines were introduced in the GE and Lockheed Corporations emphasizes the importance that management and their US Government customers attached to removing control over the programming of their machines from the existing shop floor operatives.

Other studies emphasize the importance of the socio-emotive needs of actors reflected in their responses to technology rather than from any direct concern for its mechanical effectiveness. The early work of Rogers (1983) on the diffusion of new technology suggested the existence of layered networks through which new ideas were channelled, filtered and reconstructed in socially compatible terms by opinion leaders. More recently, Callon (1992) has demonstrated the manner in which technological knowledge is constantly reconstructed in interpersonal transactions as it traverses social networks.

Perhaps the most controversial and, at the same time, most influential exploration of innovation in knowledge creation is that put forward by Kuhn (1962), in his explanation of changes in scientific modelling and research. At any one time the scientific community is seen to give precedence to a dominant explanatory model or *conceptual paradigm* (see ORGANIZATION PARADIGMS). Its influence in shaping scientific work is not simply based on its efficacy in providing solutions to intellectual 'puzzles'. This is because the technical procedures prescribed by the model have acquired a normative significance within the moral order of a specialized group of scientists. Paradigmatic change is, therefore, a long drawn out process in which social, as well as intellectual, provision must be made for the retention of group solidarity within the profession. In recent years the Kuhnian concept of the paradigmatic interpretation of technological possibilities in both product and process applications has been applied to various managerial situations.

National culture has also been found to provide significantly different bases for the meaning given to technology and to technological innovation at all levels of organizational hierarchy. Qualitative micro studies of attitudes among operatives in the 1970s contributed a qualitative dimension to the broader societal comparisons of Maurice *et al.* (1982). In the latter work, the widely different organizational structures used in conjunction with similar plant and equipment by German and French employers are explained in terms of the institutional context of business, and most particularly in the occupational qualifying processes deployed in each country. Similar findings have emerged from Sorge *et al.*'s (1983) study of computerized manufacturing systems in Germany and the UK, and in a larger six-nation comparison of the utilization of information technology (IT) in retailing, banking and healthcare delivery (Child and Loveridge 1990) (see BUSINESS SYSTEMS; ORGANIZATION CULTURE).

3 Technology as social control

The most fundamental of the social constructionist critiques is possibly that of feminists. The history of the emergence of the concept of scientific 'objectivity' is seen to have provided a bridge to pre-industrial religious belief in at least one important respect. This was the discounting of personality characteristics perceived to be inextricably linked with the female gender. By alienating the intellect from emotive and affective sources of social action the 'mechanical' philosophers of the eighteenth century legitimated the continued closure of knowledge work to women. By the same token the historical contributions of women to the 'advance of science' have been effectively written out until recently. More insidiously, women have been socialized into an acceptance of an ancillary role within this 'advance' and as a consequence have lost status in each succeeding wave of innovation (Faulkner and Arnold 1985).

Beyond this powerful critique, organizational writers are often divided somewhat crudely into neo-Marxian or neo-Weberian, called after these German founding fathers of social science. Weber (1924) saw the pursuit of mechanical and bureaucratic efficiency as providing an essentially neutral arena in which groups could compete for market or status advantages (see WEBER, M.). In the neo-Marxian interpretation of history the process of standardization, routinization and specialization in the design of organizational tasks is seen as representing the steady and relentless expropriation of operational knowledge by owners of capital. Moreover, the relations of production present in the workplace, or labour process, are usually seen as the primary influence shaping the institutions of modern (civil) society (see LABOUR PROCESS). The history of the development of the principles and procedures embodied in production management and epitomized in the work of F.W. Taylor (for example, *The Principles of Scientific Management*, published in 1911) was used as the basis for the most influential of recent analyses in this genre, that of Braverman (1974) (see TAYLOR, F.W.; BRAVERMAN, H.).

Neo-Weberians vary in the importance attached to the pursuit of status advantage among interest groups. Those who elevate it to a central role in the creation of societal institutions, as for example in the formation of new occupations around particular modes of technology, are often conjoined with Marxian authors, under the label of 'conflict theorists'. Many other analysts see the managerial pursuit of control as being solely related to the survival of the organization and to the satisfaction of a diversity of stakeholders. Conflict is viewed as explicable and soluble within this more limited frame. Hence, much of the organizational literature on process innovation is concerned with overcoming resistance to technological change among existing operative staff (Wilkinson 1983) (see CONFLICT AND POLITICS).

These strategies usually involve the alignment of the localized task commitments of the operative with those compatible with the aims of strategic management (see STRATEGY, CONCEPT OF). They differ in the degree and type of involvement allowed to, or required of, recipients of management communications. They also vary in the extent to which organizational designers accept the design parameters embodied in pre-existing machines and their configuration in the workflow. Over much of the last century a debate has been carried on between behavioural scientists and those whom Taylor described as 'scientific managers' (see TAYLOR, F.W.). 'Behaviouralists', for the most part social psychologists, have argued that the rationalization and fragmentation of labour services recommended by Taylorist systems have led to the demoralization, and ultimately to the alienation, of labour. Perhaps the most radical among social science approaches to job design was that arising out of the so-called 'action research' conducted during the 1950s in the UK and India by the Tavistock Institute, and in the USA by the Institute of Social Research at Ann Arbor, Michigan. These researchers advocated the design of workflow and accompanying activities in a manner that 'optimized' its match with the sentient needs of operatives (see GROUPS AND TEAMS).

Contained within all levels of this debate there exists a tension between the managerial need for control over a stable ordering of activities and an accompanying need for entrepreneurial flexibility and creativity. A second strand in the job redesign argument advocates the devolution of responsibility as a means of encouraging 'bottom up' innovation rather than simply attempting the self-development of individual employees. The most important contemporary development in this approach to line management is to be found in the concept of total quality management (TQM) (see TOTAL QUALITY MANAGEMENT). Originating from the work of production engineers, it recognizes the impossibility of metering and monitoring even relatively simple line tasks as advocated in old-style scientific management. Instead, it advocates operator or group selfmonitoring of their own performance.

Unlike earlier human relations approaches, the TQM approach attempts an alignment of work group goals with those of the corporation, rather than shaping the latter around operative needs. Group membership is formally prescribed rather than spontaneously entered into and, through the operation of IT, group performance can often be more easily monitored centrally than under bureaucratically administered Taylorist systems (Pollert 1988). For all of these reasons some observers prefer to describe TQM as 'top-down' innovation.

4 Technology as information

In the 1950s the emergence of organizational behaviour as a management discipline was heavily shaped by prescriptive approaches to the control–commitment debate. Another school of researchers sought to describe influences acting on contemporary organizational structures before arriving at their design prescriptions. Among the most significant of the exogenous influences, or contingencies, to be investigated was seen to be the mode of operational technology employed by the organization. A small study of 100 British engineering firms in the mid-1950s provided one of the most important empirical bases for this approach. Woodward's findings (1958) suggested that organizational structure could be related fairly closely to the size of the batches produced and to the operational exigencies resulting (see WOODWARD, J.). Later, Bright

(1988) produced a detailed typology of operations technology based on a larger sample of US manufacturers. This emphasized the degree of integration between stages of materials process and provided a taxonomy not unlike that of Woodward, although not claiming the same causal importance in shaping the overall organizational configuration.

Woodward's typology gained, and retains, credibility both from its conceptual proximity to the axioms of batch engineering disciplines and from its rich case history description. During the 1950s and 1960s the findings of social anthropologists and industrial sociologists demonstrated differences in operator behaviours and commitments associated with the particular configurations of process technology.

Other writers interpreted operational processes at a higher level of abstraction, seeing organizational structures as attempts by managers to reduce their level of uncertainty or risk. This approach contained within it the possibility of moving away from the problems entailed in arriving at an agreed objective measure of technology. Instead, observers defined strategically important contingencies as those subjectively adjudged to be so by senior executives. In practice Perrow (1986) chose to see executive uncertainty as arising from: (1) variability in information flows including their scope and regularity (roughly equating with Woodward's linkage between batch size and variations in market demand); and (2) with the ability of the executive to comprehend and analyse the operational processes (that is, to embody operational knowledge in codified techniques or machines). Along these dimensions Perrow plotted the levels of discretion allowed to operatives in the different modes of organization arising from these higher order contingencies (Figure 1).

Stated in another way, executives were seen to attempt to guard against dependency upon others in the interpretation of information on strategically important operational matters. This more abstract definition of contingency surfaces in many more recent approaches to organizational analysis, most notably that of Williamson (1980). The latter author suggests that executive desire to absorb uncertainty is reflected in the type of contrac-

Figure 1 An informational typology of operational processes
Source: Adapted from Perrow (1986)

tual linkage established between suppliers of services, for example employees, and the organization's management (see Figure 2).

Previously, in the 1960s, a group of researchers at what is now the Aston Business School had attempted to measure the extent of commonality required in the administration of organizations (see ASTON GROUP). Taking technology as comprising both its material and knowledge components, but placing emphasis on integration between stages of the workflow, they concluded that as the size of the organization grew, the influence that the structure of shop floor operations had in shaping administrative structures diminished. Control passed to 'procedures dictated by standardization of the new specialists who devise the procedures' (Pugh *et al.* 1969: 124) (see ORGANIZATION STRUCTURE).

Although subject to methodological criticism, the Aston studies contributed *inter alia* to an understanding of two evident problems for Western management at that time. The first was that the coordination and control of

Figure 2 Internally segmented market
Source: Williamson (1980)

the segmented activities of large-scale organizations was itself a significant cause of cognitive complexity and uncertainty for strategic managers. The second was the association of formal bureaucratic control with grievance-related conflict and unionization among employees. The two-way nature of control within bureaucracies had been illustrated by the studies of shop floor employees described earlier. One carried out among auto components manufacturers in Ohio and Michigan in the 1950s (Sayles 1958) suggested that work groups reacted differently to attempts at control (see Figure 3).

5 Technology and innovation

The grievance-related behaviour described by Sayles and others might be seen as typical of post-Second World War industrial relations in Anglo-Saxon countries (see INDUSTRIAL AND LABOUR RELATIONS). Often it was triggered by attempts at 'top down' or imposed innovation. Groups defended their vested interest in prevailing bodies of technological knowledge or sought greater recognition in both status and market terms.

Equally, descriptions of the prevailing managerial model of 'bottom-up' technological innovation were rooted in pluralistic conflict. In most Anglo-American histories of innovation, whether brought about by the adoption of external inventions or through internal design, the process was, and is, presented as one full of conflict. Wilkinson (1983) and others suggest that junctures between the stages that mark the passage of implementation and use of innovation within routine operations can each become the locus of contestation. The propose-dispose dialogue that takes place represents a segmentation of interests within organizations.

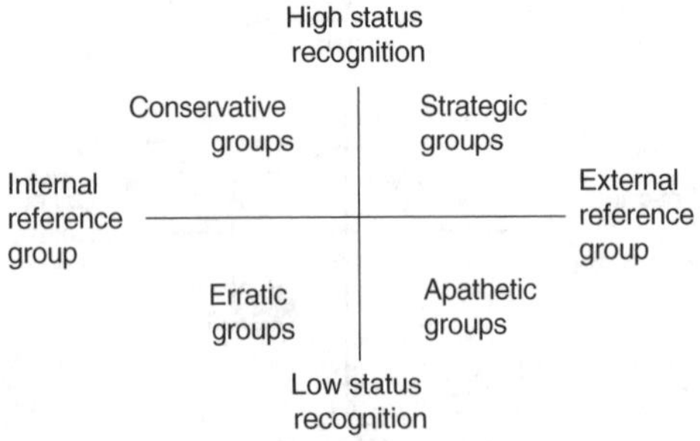

Almost all case histories make use of Schon's (1963) concept of the need for innovators to acquire a sponsor or product champion in the higher echelons, or 'clan'. Burgelman and Sayles (1988) go so far as to suggest that a system of sponsorship or patronage should be built into the formal structures of 'hi-tech' firms in a manner that enables innovation to diffuse across departmental, divisional or other functional, intellectual or cost/profit centre boundaries within the organization (see Figure 4). These latter have grown out of a need to establish predictable order but, by the same token, have become institutionalized barriers to the absorption of technological change.

In a much earlier study, Sayles and Chandler (1971) had suggested that the management of intellectually complex projects, such as that facing the moon landing planned by the National Aeronautics and Space Administration of the US Government (NASA), could be too complex to be controlled through a centralized bureaucracy. It was accomplished by delegating and devolving responsibility through market-based contracts, combined with continuous open dialogue around problem definition and design solutions. This market-led dialogue produced a culturally normative commitment to project goals while keeping boundaries fluid (see INNOVATION AND TECHNOLOGICAL CHANGE; ORGANIZATION CULTURE).

This network model of inter-organizational collaboration in the development and design of new technology has grown both in prescriptive, as well as descriptive, significance since the 1970s. The notion of conjoining the chain of linked production stages present within the organization in sequence with those outside its boundaries, in a vertical collaboration along the value-adding chain, is central to the concept of 'lean production' seen by Womack et al. (1990) to be the dominant new mode of organization in the automobile industry.

High status
recognition

Conservative groups	Strategic groups
Erratic groups	Apathetic groups

Internal reference group

External reference group

Low status
recognition

Figure 3 Patterns of grieving among shop-floor operatives
Source: Adapted from Sayles (1958)

Levels \ Key activities	CORE PROCESSES		OVERLYING PROCESSES	
	Definition	Impetus	Strategic context	Structural context
Corporate management	Monitoring	Authorizing	Rationalizing	Structuring
		Organizational championship ————		Selecting —
New ventures management	Coaching stewardship	Strategic building	Delineating	Negotiating
		Product championship		
Department leader/venture manager	Technical and need linking	Strategic forcing	Gatekeeping Idea generating Bootlegging	Questioning

Figure 4 The stepped process of bottom-up innovating
Source: Adapted from Burgelman and Sayles (1988)

The more unlikely condition of horizontal collaboration across competing organizations in the development of technology (as opposed to defensive cartels) has also become the widely accepted basis for joint ventures. A more Utopian concept is that of 'flexible specialization', in which small artisanal enterprises are seen to collaborate in the provision of an external, regionally based, infrastructure. This allows them to attain the economies of scale and scope necessary to compete on equal terms with large multinational corporations (MNCs). In spite of its aspirational nature, the notion of inter-firm collaboration on a regional, or 'industrial district', basis has received policy recognition by the European Commission and some states in the USA (see INTER-ORGANIZATIONAL RELATIONS; NETWORKS AND ORGANIZATIONS).

The influence of information technology

Underlying many accounts of these collaborative ventures is the importance of IT in enabling, and even creating, the means by which organizational boundaries have been pierced, and organizational hierarchies flattened (see INFORMATION TECHNOLOGY). Responsibility for carrying out the required tasks can be devolved to operational staff or to sub-contractors, who can be offered a measure of autonomy in their performance within parameters set or agreed centrally.

IT has effectively provided the means whereby many of the metering and coordinating activities of the bureaucracy can be automated, thus enabling the electronic monitoring of materials or people processing activities from the centre. The ultimate deployment of IT is seen to constitute a form of 'systemofacture' (Kaplinsky 1984) or total business system that fully integrates all of the functional activities of the organization and enables them to be related to centrally set series of strategic goals and related benchmarks (see INFORMATION AND KNOWLEDGE INDUSTRY).

Systems integration in this manner is likely to become increasingly technically practicable over the first decade of the twentieth-first century. For rationally deterministic theorists such as Perez (1985), the simple availability of a 'virtually unlimited' cheap supply of the new information technology will, as in previous historical epochs, result in the proliferation of a new managerial paradigm of organizational 'best practice'. This will entail the adoption of a much more flexible approach to the division of labour within the firm, both across tasks, and contractually, in the employment of 'spot' labour (see Figure 2).

A similar segmentalism can be seen to have evolved in the manner that corporations choose 'preferred' suppliers and users or distributors of their products, as described by Womack *et al.* (1990). In the USA, strategic theorists have adopted the term 'switchboard corporation' to describe the skeletal administration of managerial/service workers (clan) required to maintain short-term contracts with (loose teams of) professional and spot workers.

6 Post-Fordism, post-industrialism and post-modernism

Perez's description of the new 'techno-economic' paradigm currently utilized by managers is not entirely technologically driven. Emphasis is placed on a shift in consumer tastes that is seen to have taken place towards a greater individualization within social habits and, therefore, in diversity in consumption (1985: 449). She, like other writers, has been influenced by the description of the historical disjuncture seen to have occurred both in patterns of trade and in technology over the last quarter of the twentieth century. Over this period academic debate has increasingly focused on 'world view' or over-arching explanations of this change.

Of particular importance for neo-Marxian writers has been the analysis of the French *regulation* school (Aglietta 1975). The symptoms of bureaucratic sclerosis described earlier are seen to have been a by-product of the increased ability of the large firm to create a mass market for its standardized goods in the urbanized setting of industrialized countries. Since Henry Ford recognized and articulated the principles of this 'regime' in 1922, it has been described by these Marxian analysts as 'Fordist' (see FORD, H.). By the same token, changes in consumer tastes, accompanied by technological innovation, are seen to have led to the new organizational modes referred to as *post-Fordist*.

Throughout the 1960s the movement from manufacturing to service work was the subject of governmental concern in all industrialized societies. Daniel Bell (1973) was one of the early commentators on a so-called *post-industrial* society in which ultimate value in exchange would derive from knowledge inputs rather than from manual effort. His was a generally optimistic view on the outcomes, from the application of automation to manufacture, and the resultant deployment of labour in the provision of direct services. One such mode to have gained prominence in projections of the future is that of 'teleworking' or working from an IT link to the individual service provider's home. The merging of work with leisure is sometimes seen to be part of a 'professionalizing' of society.

At a still more abstract level the term post-industrialism has been extended to mean the relinquishment of the modernist basis of intellectual disciplines. Influenced by the work of French linguistic sociologists many recent management writers have gone further in predicting an abandonment of systems-rational modes of managing. Paradoxically, the onset of *post-modernism*, as this position is often described by its advocates, is seen as having been heralded and shaped by the algorithmic reasoning embodied in IT software (see DE-CONSTRUCTION ANALYSIS AND MANAGEMENT).

All three holistic views on the societal outcomes of technological innovation have framed much of the academic debate around the current crisis in Western manufacturing over the past decade. Others adopt a more contingently open view. Some industrial economists see the present disjuncture in organizational forms as merely the latest adjustment to business 'climacterics' coinciding with so-called long waves of technological development. Each of these waves has contributed to a movement over two centuries of industrialization, from the use of manual energy and primitive machines to the current development of IT. Shifts in generic technologies, such as new energy sources, can bring about convergent market developments which destroy sectoral boundaries. Freeman *et al.* (1982) and others see these movements as giving rise to new sources of sectoral or industry specialization. Thus IT is seen as having brought about an erosion and revision of these boundaries since 1970.

At sector level, the familiar life cycle metaphor is often used to describe the diffusion of a standardized 'best practice' across firms providing similar products. The four phases of the historical process of standardization of 'best practice' (shown in Figure 5) is that derived

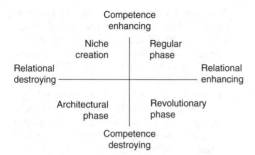

Figure 5 Phases in sectoral or corporate learning
Source: Adapted from Abernathy *et al.* (1983)

from the history of the automobile sector by Abernathy *et al.* (1983). Their separation of the social basis of trading relationships from the technological bases of operational competences, upon which the corporate reputation is based within the sector, provides important analytical scope for explanation of technological development along socially differentiated trajectories across different regional and organizational communities. Tushman and Anderson (1986) adopt a similar bifurcated approach to their analysis of the disruptive effects of innovation within the strategic context of the corporate portfolio.

In effect, these contingent analyses of technological innovation see emergent organizational forms as relating the continued success of corporate responses to the opportunities and threats present within phases in sector formation – and reformation. The analysis of Williamson quoted earlier sees these responses as being shaped by the overhead costs of corporate governance. Others emphasize the *scope* of the firm's diversified usage of its core technological capability. Yet others weigh the achievement of *synergy* across all such activities more heavily. These benefits are enhanced within the MNC by its ability to transfer technology across national boundaries by virtue of its internal jurisdiction over information flows (Teece 1987).

7 Balkanization or synergy in approaches to technology?

Given the permeation of technology into all areas of social activity, and the manner in which social aspirations shape technology, it is hardly surprising that Nelson and Winter

(1982) should speak of the 'Balkanization' of technology studies. Yet since the 1980s there has been a growing acknowledgement of the existence of differing theoretical perspectives within the academic community itself. This awareness has been brought home by the strategic position taken up by operational management in the design of new organizational forms. In addition, the former distinction between Marxian and Weberian approaches to innovation has also been blurred by the new significance attached to growing consumer influences by post-modernist theorists. However, there is a clear distinction between optimists and pessimists in the interpretation of present trends in technological development: this often coincides with a division between those interested in modelling successful technology management for prescriptive purposes and those more concerned with its wider social effects.

The movement in research has been towards the establishment of contextual configurations of institutional settings within which innovation takes place. This may be exemplified by the significance attached to occupational qualification structures in shaping changes in the workplace division of labour in the already quoted studies by Sorge *et al.* (1983). Such cross-national comparisons have been extended to the effectiveness of other societal institutions, such as the family and financial sources, in providing infrastructural contexts, or national innovation systems (Kogut 1993).

Success in national industrial policy can be seen to be related to the extent to which existing institutions channel the development of new knowledge streams in a productive or non-productive manner. For this to occur there has, of course, to be some agreement around a complementarity in purpose between strategic goals and institutional bases. It appears possible that this occurs within the more successful social orders of certain nations such as Germany and Japan (Altmann *et al.* 1992). The trusting or clan-like nature of inter-organizational and intra-organizational relationships within these national systems are not easily reproduced in the contexts of Western liberal societies.

As in other areas of organizational analysis, the effects of culture have come to be seen as critical in shaping more or less innovative stances towards the adoption or rejection of new process or product technologies. Unfortunately there is little detailed evidence in recent case research to provide strong anthropological foundations for claims in either direction. Many of the workplace changes described earlier as involving devolved modes of responsibility are regarded sceptically by some industrial sociologists, who describe the effects of exposure to recessionary market forces as being as coercive as those experienced under overt bureaucratic regulation. Furthermore, the emergence of new forms of strategic networking can result in a systemic rationalization whose effects lie outside of the influence of either local management or employee representatives (Altmann *et al.* 1992).

If, as some suggest, the modernization project is bringing about a convergence between the institutions and ideals of those nation-states, it is evidently not complete. Indeed, the differentiated nature of the institutions of industrializing countries appear to make them more or less effective vehicles for the implementation of new technology. It remains with the citizens of those countries to determine the ultimate costs and benefits of allowing regional institutions to be shaped by a technological contest between MNCs.

RAY LOVERIDGE
UNIVERSITY OF ASTON IN BIRMINGHAM

Further reading

(References cited in the text marked *)

* Abernathy, W.J., Clark, K.B. and Kantow, A.M. (1983) *Industrial Renaissance*, New York: Basic Books. (An attempt to diagnose the structural failure of US manufacturing by modelling the historical development of the automobile industry.)

* Aglietta, M. (1975) *A Theory of Capitalist Regulation*, trans. D. Sernbach, London: New Left Books, 1979. (A description of a general theory of modern capitalism in which the regulation of civil society through the creation of consumer markets is seen as complementing that of the prevailing mode of control over the labour process.)

* Altmann, N., Kohler, C. and Meil, P. (1992) *Technology and Work in German Industry*, London:

Routledge. (A collection of essays by members and associates of Institut Für Sozialwissenschaftliche Forschung, Munich on current debates around developments in German process technology and their impacts on skill formation and job structures.)

* Bell, D. (1973) *The Coming of Post-industrial Society*, New York: Basic Books. (One of the earliest prognostications on the effects of the decline of employment in the manufacturing sectors of Western economies. Still one of the most prescient, although heavily criticized at the time for neglect of analysis of social class implications.)

* Braverman, H. (1974) *Labor and Monopoly Capitalism*, New York: Monthly Review Press. (A study of Taylorian influences on workplace regulation. Led to a revival of Marxian analysis of workplace relations particularly among European sociologists.)

* Bright, J.R. (1988) *Automation and Management*, Cambridge, MA: Harvard Business School Press. (Bright continued the work of Woodward (1958). In her later work she responded to critics by moving away from the closely determinate significance attributed to process technology.)

* Burgelman, R.A. and Sayles, L.R. (1988) *Inside Corporate Innovation: Strategy, Structure and Managerial Skills*, New York: The Free Press. (The authors suggest an analysis of the design–innovation process based on product champions within a large US hi-tech firm.)

* Callon, M. (1992) 'The dynamics of techno-economic networks', in R. Coombs, P. Saviotti and V. Walsh (eds), *Technological Change and Company Strategies*, London: Academic Press. (An overview of the approach taken by French anthropologists to the social shaping of innovations through transactions along 'filiere' or networks.)

* Child, J. and Loveridge, R. (1990) *Information Technology in European Services*, Oxford: Blackwell. (Study of the use of IT in the European service industry.)

* Faulkner, W. and Arnold, E. (1985) *Smothered by Invention*, London: Pluto Publishing. (An example of the feminist reinterpretation of the male-dominated record of technological invention and the effects of its implementation on women's role in the process.)

* Freeman, C., Clark, J. and Soete, L. (1982) *Unemployment and Technical Innovation: A Study of Long Waves and Economic Development*, London: Frances Pinter. (An interesting re-interpretation of the work of Kontratiev (1925), Schumpeter (1934) and Mensch (1979)

on the historical existence of long waves of technological development.)

* Kaplinsky, R. (1984) *Automation: The Technology and Society*, London: Longman. (This might be considered as the most significant of a long series of government-inspired reports dating back to the 1950s which attempted to predict the effects of automation. Kaplinsky maps the stages of development through which machine control has moved and extrapolates to what is now familiarly known as total 'business systems'.)

* Kogut, B. (ed.) (1993) *Country Competitiveness*, New York: Oxford University Press. (An interesting collection of papers on how national institutions have encouraged or inhibited technological innovation with analytical contributions from the editor.)

* Kuhn, S.T. (1962) *The Structure of Scientific Revolutions*, Chicago, IL: University of Chicago Press. (Since the publication of this work the debate between so-called relativists and positivists among both natural and social scientists has gained in strength. Subsequently the debate has been extended to challenging the Kuhnian notion of the incommensurability of paradigms.)

* Maurice, M., Sellier, F. and Silvestre, J.-J. (1982) *Politique d'éducation et organisation industrielle en France et en Allemagne: essai d'analyse sociétal*, Paris: Presses Universitaires de France. (When this comparative study of workplace hierarchies within France and Germany was first published in the early 1970s, it provided a pioneering attempt at explanation of the labour process through wider societal institutions.)

* Nelson, R. and Winter, S. (1982) *An Evolutionary Theory of Economic Change*, Cambridge, MA: Harvard University Press. (Regarded by many industrial economists as providing a new bridge to organizational analysis; describes organizations as moving along path-dependent innovation trajectories. These represent incremental learning curves in the adaptation of knowledge 'routines'.)

* Noble, D. (1985) 'Social choice in machine design', in D. MacKenzie and J. Wajcman (eds), *The Social Shaping of Technology*, Milton Keynes: Open University Press. (A study of the political process of decision making leading to the introduction of CNC machines into the craft-dominated areas of aerospace manufacture.)

* Perez, C. (1985) 'Microelectronics, long waves and world structural change', *World Development* 15 (4): 441–63. (Part of a series of works from the Science Policy Research Unit at the University of Sussex. It offers one of the most explicit definitions of the new organizational paradigm emerging from scholarly debates in the 1980s.)

* Perrow, C. (1986) *Complex Organisations: A Critical Essay*, New York: McGraw-Hill. (Examines the degree of indeterminacy created by process technology, along with other elements in the managerial environment, as shaping organizational responses.)

* Pollert, A. (1988) 'Dismantling flexibility', *Capital and Class* 2 (3): 42–75. (Describes the devolved modes of organization as being exploitative, so long as TQM and other modes of diffusing responsibility are not complemented by decentralized authority. Suggests that terms such as 'flexibility' and 'empowerment' are often used to cover socially coercive modes of management better defined as neo-Fordist.)

* Pugh, D.S., Hickson, D.J. and Hinings, C.R. (1969) 'An empirical taxonomy of structures of work organization', *Administrative Science Quarterly* 14: 115–26. (This paper is one of a series published by the Aston School at the end of the 1960s and through the 1970s. The work of the School possibly represents the high point of structural positivism in the study of organizations.)

* Rogers, E.M. (1983) *Diffusion of Innovations*, 3rd edn, New York: The Free Press. (First published in 1970, this overview of research on technological diffusion relied heavily on the so-called two-stage model of communication popular in market research in the 1940s and 1950s. It remains, in this updated version, one of the most insightful social-psychological texts on the subject.)

Rose, M. (1988) *Industrial Behaviour*, 2nd edn, Harmondsworth: Penguin. (A comprehensive and insightful account of the development of behavioural science in Europe and North America with respect to developing management needs. This edition contains an extensive review of the comparative national systems approach.)

* Rothwell, R. (1977) 'The characteristics of successful innovations and technically progressive firms', *R&D Management* 7 (3): 258–91. (This paper has been a significant contributor to the development of the concept of product champion in case histories of product innovation within British companies.)

* Sayles, L.R. (1958) *Behaviour of Industrial Work Groups: Production and Control*, New York: Wiley. (One of a number of US and British participant observer studies of the workplace undertaken in the 1950s. Most illuminating in the discussion of the interaction between techno-

logical configurations and patterns of shop floor relationships.)

* Sayles, L.R. and Chandler, M. (1971) *Managing Large Systems: Organizations of the Future*, New York: Harper & Row. (An early case study of inter-organizational networking, focusing on the birth and development of NASA.)

* Schon, D. (1963) *Displacement of Concepts*, London: Tavistock. (Possibly the most quoted source of the concept of product champion, deriving from a staged series of British case studies carried out by SPRU and collectively known as the SAPPHO Project.)

* Sorge, A., Hartmann, G., Warner, M. and Nicholas, I. (1983) *Microelectronics and Manpower in Manufacturing, Applications of Computer Numerical Control in Great Britain and West Germany*, Aldershot: Gower. (Useful comparison of computerized manufacturing systems in Germany and the UK.)

* Teece, D.J. (1987) 'Profiting from technological innovation: implications for integration, collaboration, licensing and public policy', in D. Teece (ed.), *The Competitive Challenge*, Cambridge, MA: Ballinger. (One of the most original exponents of the concept of transaction costs in the analysis of the appropriation of technological knowledge and skills.)

* Tushman, M. and Anderson, P. (1986) 'Technological discontinuities and organizational environments', *Administrative Sciences Quarterly* 31 (2): 439–65. (The authors analyse the corporate responses to technological and market discontinuity in their environment.)

* Weber, M. (1924) *The Theory of Social and Economic Organization*, trans. T. Parsons, New York: Oxford University Press. (In this work Weber defines the organizational dimensions making up the ideal type of bureaucracy.)

* Wilkinson, B. (1983) *The Shopfloor Politics of New Technology*, London: Heinemann. (One of the earliest and best of the many workplace studies carried out in Europe during the 1980s, largely directed at discovering obstacles to the adoption of what was generically labelled 'new technology'.)

* Williamson, O.E. (1980) 'The economics of organization: the transaction cost approach', *American Journal of Sociology* 87 (November): 548–77. (This paper has inspired a range of studies using transactional cost approaches to technological knowledge as an appropriable asset.)

* Womack, J.P., Jones, D.T. and Roos, D. (1990) *The Machine that Changed the World*, London: Macmillan. (One of a series of reports on the automobile industry from this MIT-based team. Gained worldwide popularity from its case comparisons of production modes in the USA, Germany, Japan, France and the UK, coining the term 'lean production' to describe Western adaptations of Japanese organizational procedures.)

* Woodward, J. (1958) *Industrial Organization: Theory and Practice*, Oxford: Oxford University Press. (Woodward's original typology spanned eleven categories of process technology and took in a range of organizational variables such as span of control and the number of hierarchical levels.)

See also: COORDINATION AND CONTROL; DESIGN MANAGEMENT; INFORMATION TECHNOLOGY; INFORMATION TECHNOLOGY AND SOCIETY; INNOVATION AND TECHNOLOGICAL CHANGE; LABOUR PROCESS; ORGANIZING, PROCESS OF; SCHUMPETER, J.

Technology strategy, international

1 Technology and strategic function
2 Japan (Asia)
3 Germany (Europe)
4 The United States of America
   (North America)
5 Conclusions

Overview

Technological change as a response to outside environmental forces has in the past to a large degree determined the fate of individuals, organizations and nation states. Today more than ever before, the key to survival hinges on the ability to capitalize on the opportunities of technological change and implementation. The present is a very exciting time for both the understanding and the practice of management and technology; there is a growing awareness that the success of organizations is directly dependent on the effective management of technology in order to create competitive advantage.

The management of technology has as its goal the improvement of the products and the productive capability of an organization. There are a number of models of technology management, but none are considered to be universally applicable. There are different international perspectives on the management of technology; within the Triad (Europe, with Germany at the core, Asia, with Japan at the core and North America, with the USA at the core), there are different approaches to the value of management or technology activities. One important cause of these differences is differing emphases on technology in higher education within the various regions; for example, more than 25 per cent of all US university students take some type of business degree, while over 50 per cent of students in Japan and Germany take technical degrees. This fact alone may result in different approaches to the management of technology.

There are also different concepts of the role of technology within the organization. Technology is not the sole domain of the research and development personnel of an organization. Successful business use of technology requires strategic decisions concerning factors such as innovation, knowledge, time, value-added costs, strategic alliances as well as other functional areas such as marketing, production and finance.

Understanding the relative contributions of several different models of technology, and how these models relate to one another, can lead to a greater appreciation of the importance of the management of technology. This entry looks at three of these models and assesses their relative emphases and values.

1 Technology and strategic function

Value chain model

The research on which this entry is based chose two strands of theory in its approach to the international management of technology: the value chain and strategic alliance frameworks introduced by Porter (1985), and the concept of the Triad, first developed by Ohmae (1980) (see GLOBAL STRATEGIC ALLIANCES; OHMAE, K.). These two approaches allow the subject to be approached simultaneously from both an international and a strategic perspective.

The two key categories in the value chain model are the internal (value chain) organizational activities and their integration. According to Porter, each organization is a collection of nine generic and discrete activities which add to or detract from the organization's total value (see PORTER, M.E.). Porter goes on to divide these value chain activities into two broad groups which are called *primary activities* and *support activities*.

Primary activities are those involved in the physical creation of a product or service that can be sold in the international marketplace. Porter uses five typical organization functions in his model; to this can now be added a sixth, internationalization, based on European research. The six primary or 'functional' activities are:

1 inbound logistics;
2 production or operations;
3 outbound logistics;
4 marketing and sales;
5 service;
6 internationalization.

The four support or 'secondary' activities are:

1 infrastructure, which encompasses ownership and activities such as management, organizing, controlling, accounting, legal and strategic planning;
2 technological development, which encompasses innovation, product design and research and development activities;
3 human resource management, including the recruiting, training, organizing and development of personnel;
4 procurement, which is defined as obtaining the necessary organizational inputs.

In an international or transnational organization, strategy often involves making management decisions on how to spread the activities listed above among countries (see GLOBALIZATION; MULTINATIONAL CORPORATIONS). Coordination is also required so that activities in different countries are integrated with each other. In making these decisions, management faces an array of strategic options. Factors such as economies of scale, product/market life cycles, competitive advantages and disadvantages, joint venture policies and foreign direct investment policies are all important. Porter (1980, 1985) also suggests that an organization must make the key strategic decision of whether to emphasize price, focus or differentiation as a means of gaining competitive advantage in the world marketplace.

Against this background of Porter's very normative descriptive theory of strategic organizational behaviour, we applied the framework of a situational hypothesis in testing whether 'triad' organizations actually used the nine or ten activity value chain along with a goal involving margins (profit) or some type of modification of Porter's work. External coordination allows a firm to react to a dynamic world of shifting competitive advantages, and also gives the organization the flexibility of

responding to suppliers, buyers, competitors and new innovations. Porter's modified strategic alliance model is shown below. It is modified as follows.

1 The traditional state of the art, which is one of the five elements of competition according to Porter, is replaced by a value chain involving the firm in question.
2 The other elements of competition are included as value chains.
3 'New technology' is used to replace Porter's concept of 'substitutes'.
4 The addition of international (regional and global level) competition adds a third dimension to the model. The first dimension involves the value chain model of the firm which includes the nine or ten internal generic activities. The second dimension involves national competition with (local) suppliers, customers, competitors and new technology. The final dimension involves the above mentioned four competitive forces on an international/global scale. We will continue with the theoretical analysis of strategic alliances in the Triad section of this paper. The revised three dimensional model is shown in Figure 1.
5 Government is a difficult dimension to introduce into the model since it permeates at all levels and affects all actors. We have placed it at the top of the model on this assumption.
6 New technology is often used in the recent literature instead of substitutes.

The above modifications and changes are generally in line with the 'improvements' that have been made to Porter's work since 1985. It is beyond the scope of this entry to treat these in detail. Essentially, our cases from Asia, Europe and North America have pushed us in the situational (contingency theory or divergency theory are two of the most common terms used here) direction of explanation rather than the 'one best way' (convergency theory or universal explanation are the terms used).

The role of education

Education, particularly higher education at a university level, plays a major role in management performance and hence in organizational

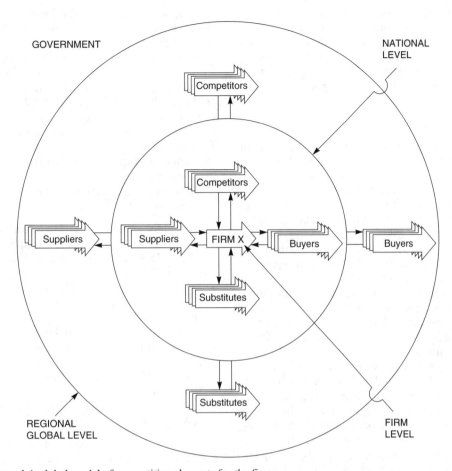

Figure 1 A global model of competitive elements for the firm

performance (see ORGANIZATION BEHAV-
IOUR). Thus the structure, purpose and content
of education have an influence on the management of technology and on business performance. Regional and cultural differences in
education emphasis can be seen to have an
important impact on technology strategy.

Education can be included in the model if
one uses the casual logic of education impacting on individual management behaviour,
which in turn impacts on organizational behaviour:

EDUCATION → INDIVIDUAL MANAGE-
MENT BEHAVIOUR → ORGANIZATION
PERFORMANCE

However, one may also reject the idea that
one universal model of the management of

technology exists, or can be developed. Presenting different international perspectives on
the management of technology improves our
understanding of the concepts and processes
involved. Technology is not the sole domain
of the research and development personnel of
an organization. Successful business use of
technology requires strategic decisions about
innovation, knowledge, time, value-added
costs and strategic alliances, as well as other
functional areas such as marketing, production and finance. Bridging the cultural gap
between different departments in an organization, as well as bridging the cultural gaps between different regions of the globe, are of
central interest here.

Since education is a complex and all-
encompassing theme, the focus here is restricted to higher education at the university

level. It is also assumed that education plays a major role in management performance and hence in organizational performance. Thus the structure, purpose and content of education have an influence on the management of technology and on business performance.

The Triad

The aim of the research was to develop an aggregate model of international behaviour for each of the three main regions of the Triad, Asia, Europe and North America (see ASIA PACIFIC, MANAGEMENT IN; EUROPE, MANAGEMENT IN; UNITED STATES OF AMERICA, MANAGEMENT IN THE). Within these regions the bias is towards Japan, Germany and the USA, since these are the major countries representing the three regions. The research was founded on a number of case studies (70 in Europe, 26 in the USA and 11 in Japan over the period 1990–98), mostly of large international firms. An earlier study of smaller European firms has also been conducted (Joynt 1991). The cases were completed by executives in Europe and the USA after taking part in masters programmes in management. The structured action research task they were given was to develop a value chain and key strategic alliance for their organization. Each executive was required to survey the organization decided upon (Joynt 1991); the cases averaged 15–20 pages for each organization. Japanese executives participated in the US sample.

2 Japan (Asia)

The Japanese concept of existence and thinking is built on harmony where everything in nature should be balanced (see JAPAN, MANAGEMENT IN). Business and work are an essential part of life and can be considered as an 'art of life' and not as an 'art of capitalism'. As such, behaviour in a firm is more of a vocation, a lifelong task and a fulfilment of life (Törnvall 1992).

At the same time, Western ideas have been a part of the Japanese culture for the past 400 years. In the past cultural influences from the West have widened individualism in the form of freedom, scepticism, private religion and organizational behaviour. The Japanese have always been interested in the West and have used techniques such as copying and scanning to absorb elements of Western culture. It is interesting to note that many Japanese management concepts such as quality and low-cost production have their origins in the West; the works of authors such as Drucker on organization structure, Deming on productivity and Thorsrud on group work have found a wide audience in Japan (see DEMING, W.E.; DRUCKER, P.F.).

Törnvall (1992), in a study of over 300 Japanese students, found that:

1 most of the students wanted to be teachers, civil servants or engineers and technicians (the profession which appeared lowest on the list of desired jobs was 'inventor');
2 schoolwork is believed to help develop the student into a harmonious person with perseverance and duty;
3 hard work is a Japanese tradition;
4 the Japanese attitude towards work comes from tradition and not from philosophies such as Confucianism, Shintoism or Buddhism;
5 a professional worker follows traditions and has long-term training.

The typical Porter value chain for a Japanese firm includes the activities of logistics and procurement, which upon further investigation can be seen to be part of the overall production activity. Human resource management is also not considered as a separate activity but is integrated with other management activity in all parts of the firm (see INDUSTRIAL RELATIONS IN ASIA PACIFIC). In conclusion, the Japanese firms studied tended to emphasize fewer generic activities than Porter's US-orientated model would suggest.

In generating a model involving key strategic alliances, the network relationships with suppliers were possibly the most important. This has always been a trademark for Japanese firms. The alliances also differed remarkably from their counterparts in Europe and the USA in that they were 'soft' long-term alliances, rather than 'hard' short-term alliances. As an example, just-in-time (JIT) alliances with suppliers often require a physical long-term plant location commitment by key suppliers in order to have the necessary time requirements (see JUST-IN-TIME PHILOSOPHY). Cutting lot sizes, reducing inventory holding points and eliminating work-in-progress inventories as well as quick reactions to new technology were all advantages gained by Japanese firms through using softer relationships with suppliers.

A 'soft' relationship often involves higher degrees of flexibility as well as an intention of understanding the total production process on the part of both the firm and the supplier. Flexible low prices and high quality are also an essential part of the soft relationship. Finally, the 'soft' relationship usually involves a time framework of years rather than the normal one-year contract with suppliers that is subject to bidding and renewal at the end of each year.

The network or benchmarking activities concerning competitors are part of a long tradition for Japanese firms as well (see BENCHMARKING). Initially called 'copying', the language has changed in recent years to 'scanning', since many Japanese organizations are on the threshold of new products. The Japanese accomplish the scanning of competitors through a variety of activities such as reading trade journals, attending exhibits and visiting competitors directly. These 'benchmarking' strategies are perhaps one of the most popular new trends by Western firms in their attempts to match good Japanese management practices.

The most interesting element in our analysis of Japanese firms has to do with the management of technology. The process can be called the management of 'incremental technology'. This incremental aspect is the key to the main difference between the Western and the Eastern approaches to innovation. In the West the new idea, the new product and invention are often key objectives in the technological process; in the East, the key objectives are rather to improve, make small changes and make incremental changes to an existing product (see JAPANIZATION; MANUFACTURING STRATEGY).

Car manufacture provides a good example. Japanese firms tend to locate their research and development (R&D) functions (technology) close to production, and closer to the customer. The function then becomes a 'broker'

arrangement where the customer's ideas are acted upon and implemented in an incremental fashion. One can argue that most of the changes to a car are made by customer reactions, and invention is no longer the key element in the technological process. True, a new electric motor or new materials may be invented in the future, but in terms of frequency, the small incremental change, often initiated by customer feedback, is more important in both the long and the short run. Indeed, Figure 2 might almost include the customer as part of the system of strategic alliances, except that in reality there is both an internal and an external process which can best be described rather than illustrated in a model.

In conclusion, Japanese management has a flexible attitude to the management of technological development, and it is not felt that there is any need to wait until the next new model before making small changes to the product. Relationships with customers do not necessarily involve marketing only, and a close scrutiny of customer feedback is carried out in order to make incremental changes to products.

3 Germany (Europe)

While the USA has 950,000 people employed in research, Europe is not far behind with some 580,000 and Japan has approximately 435,000. During the fifty years prior to 1990, Europeans won 86 Nobel Prizes, compared with 143 for US researchers and 5 for Japanese researchers. The twelve European Union (EU) countries spend 2 per cent of their combined GNP, while the USA and Japan spend around 2.9 per cent (*The Economist* 1993) on applied research.

In Germany there has long been a close relationship between management and engineering (see GERMANY, MANAGEMENT IN). Prior to the First World War, Germany had introduced a special degree in *Wirtschafts-Ingenieur* (economics and engineering) with classes in both disciplines. Until recently there has been no MBA degree offered in Germany, but a high degree of managers in any large firm have doctorates. Praxis is important, but as Locke (1985: 182) points out through the eyes of a personnel manager 'the

The typical Asian firm (Firm J) consists of a value chain with activities of production, technology, infrastructure and marketing. The strongest strategic alliances involve those with suppliers both at the national and international/global levels as well as competitors particularly at the international/global level.

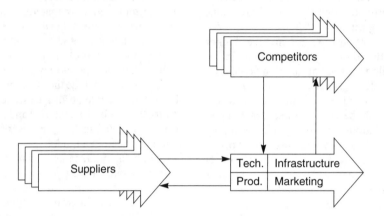

Figure 2 A scanning model for Japan

manager needs to know how decisions are made in the firm' and how planning processes are done, but the skill dimension is the province of the firm.

It is difficult to generalize from Germany to Europe for many reasons, yet it is also important to realize that the countries of Europe are converging as members in the EU. The EU goals which were set during the 1980s with the launch of programmes such as JET, Eureka, Esprit and Race include the following:

1 the development of home-grown expertise, especially in generic activities involving clean manufacturing techniques;
2 the achievement of economies of scale in R&D;
3 integration of firms in various countries;
4 to encourage equal ratios of spending for R&D in all countries.

Perhaps the most important trend in the EU has to do with the introduction of accepted standards across borders within Europe (see EUROPE, MANAGEMENT IN). This is eliminating a great deal of unnecessary product duplication. A manager from Belgium formerly required three different mobile telephones to communicate with company units in Belgium,

The Netherlands and Germany; a single standard means that only one telephone will be needed. At an even simpler level, standardization of electrical appliances means that in the future travellers will not have to buy an adapter in order to be able to use their shavers in the morning when travelling from country to country. At the company level, a welding firm will be able to manufacture to about twenty standards, as opposed to the thousands of different standards that exist in the USA and Japan. The economies of scale resulting from making twenty products instead of thousands of thousands will give European firms a considerable competitive edge within Europe (Figure 2).

Another impulse towards technological development involves the European Space Agency (ESA), which manages the Ariane space project. The agency has six major goals, which have both technological and political aspects:

1 the encouragement of space science as a new scientific discipline;
2 the use of space technology on earth through such means as cartography and weather prediction;
3 improving telecommunications;

4 developing applications from new technology in fields such as pharmacy, fluid dynamics and chemistry;

5 profit;

6 the political impact of a large European space project.

It is close to impossible to model the 'typical' European firm using a value chain with its associated external networks with strategic alliances. What is important is the concentration by firms on making the EU work at the economic, if not the political, level. The progress made on standards and economies of scale in the management of technology inspires most firms towards a better future. There is a danger, however, of a Europe which concentrates so hard on becoming unified that it forgets the outside world.

Education has played an important role in the development of the management of technology in Germany as well as in the creation of management culture in general (Locke 1985). Since the mid-nineteenth century, German universities have stressed the importance of scientific research. This research imperative in turn requires a specific approach to

the nature of knowledge, which is tested constantly through scientific investigative processes and deepened, changed and perfected. *Wissenschaft* implies that all fields of knowledge are subject to systematic, disciplined research and development; this applies not only to the natural sciences (*Naturwissenschaften*) but also art, history and the humanities (*Geistewissenschaften*).

Initially, students of engineering and business attended technical schools, but by 1890 students were allowed to acquire doctorates – the first engineering doctorates in the world – and the technical schools were placed on the same level as universities. The first higher business education schools (*Handelshochschulen*) were established around 1900, and by 1920 it was possible to acquire a full range of graduate degrees in business economics. Schmalenbach and Nicklisch were well known writers in this era. Locke (1985) quotes from a Vienna Congress on Commercial Education in 1910:

One could clearly see how the business schools in German speaking regions had begun to develop into teaching and re-

Our model for Europe is very general at this time as the EU is in its infancy. The model suggests a heavy concentration on the region of Europe, suggesting that international/global networks may be secondary firm strategies for the European firm at this time.

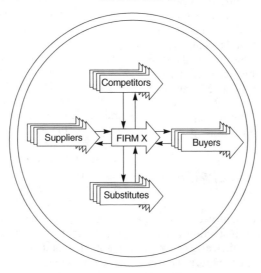

Figure 3 A regional model for Europe

search institutions and how the Latin countries with their very different academic goals, strived more and more to copy and to hold fast, to routine business practice.

(Locke 1985: 170)

German business schools reached full maturity before 1940; by 1958, in that year alone 24,000 students received economics degrees in West Germany, and 6,200 received doctorates. Firms were studied as an integrated, multi-faceted discipline in which the functional and institutional disciplines were for the most part submerged, with accounting overshadowing the others. Accounting sought to amalgamate the production and marketing function. The result was a flexible instrument of managerial control; accounting science could be applied to any kind of firm. However, following advances in the USA in areas such as marketing and finance, the university reforms in the 1960s produced changes in the curricula. Operations research and human resource management were introduced, along with elements from other disciplines such as law, sociology and psychology. Case studies were introduced and students were encouraged to undertake periods of work in firms.

In conclusion, the model for education – management behaviour – firm performance is very weak at this time; the technical aspects work with the model but other aspects may not, as the educational system has not concentrated on leaving these as a responsibility for firms. However, if we use the German model, one can see the impact that a technically oriented business education has had on the firm. It remains to be seen if this will eventually be the situation for all of Europe. Management culture in Germany, including the management of technology, has been strongly affected by the emphasis on science in education.

4 The United States of America (North America)

The most important value chain activity in the North American analysis is marketing, and the most important strategic alliance is between the firm and the customer (Figure 4) (see UNITED STATES OF AMERICA, MANAGEMENT IN; MARKETING). One language is spoken by the majority of the population in one of the largest regions in the world, so the above result is not surprising. However, the relationship between the customer and the firm can be taken to a further phase, the integration of the university or research centre that serves as an information gathering unit for all firms in the same customer branch. We found this to be true in about half of the US international firms studied.

While benchmarking has become a popular management technique in the USA, where firms look to competitors for 'best practices' behaviour, the integration of the university into the firm–customer relationship allows a neutral and objective third party the opportunity to collect information on new products, new markets, cost analysis, customer trends, market share trends and other valuable information (see BENCHMARKING). This research is often financed by the firm and its competitors working together, in other words by an entire manufacturing or industry segment.

One could argue that the present American model has its origins in the start-up firms of the past that were often formed by entrepreneurs from universities and funded by venture capital. However, in the recent past entrepreneurs without an academic background, such as Steven Jobs of Apple and Mitchell Kapor of Lotus, have not followed this mode (Kenney 1988). The tradition of relationships between universities and business that has served the USA well in the past, has worked less well in more recent years. The dean of the business school at Carnegie Mellon University complained that while US firms were not willing to finance research projects at his school, Japanese firms proved more than willing.

The university–firm relationship has a long tradition in the area of technology in the USA. However, there may now be a shift in the balance from an innovation/entrepreneurial start-up role for the university, to one of assistance in marketing and information gathering. If the new role of assisting in marketing is replacing the old role of assistance with technology, there is a possibility that Asian researchers may step into the old role; the Carnegie example suggests that this may already be happening.

Universities in the USA grant close to one million degrees each year. Over 25 per cent of those are in business, 10 per cent are in the so-

The American model suggests that the strongest value chain behaviour is marketing and the key strategic alliance is with the customer. Using the traditional university–firm linkage, one finds that many groups of firms are using the university to analyse the trends in the firm–customer relationship in detail.

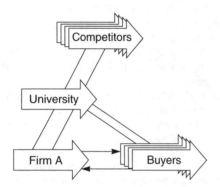

Figure 4 A marketing model for the USA

cial sciences, 9.5 per cent are in education, 9 per cent are in engineering and 6 per cent are in health. Further down the list is psychology, the study of the individual, with 4.5 per cent, which is high in comparison with other countries. The USA has ranked very low in testing youth on the basics of knowledge such as reading, writing and mathematics, and there is a great deal of concern about quality at the lower levels of education. The USA has, however, some of the best universities in the world. Many of these have a very high foreign student ratio at the graduate level, as it is difficult for many Americans to compete. The USA, with its large English-speaking population, is one of the largest markets in the world, and the business school curriculum reflects this. This is also reflected in firm behaviour.

5 Conclusions

In conclusion, it can be suggested that one should study the Japanese techniques for the upstream management of technology and production, analyse the Europeans concerning the advances made on standardization, and concentrate on the USA for the management of the marketing information function.

Competitive and comparative analysis is the name of the new game. While this entry has illustrated that the US model relies on a marketing emphasis, the key organization activities for the models of Europe and Japan suggest that upstream activities associated with the management of technology are more important. The models presented need more development and refinement, but the process of technology, the work done in any organization, emerges as a key competitive factor in this comparative analysis using the three largest trading nations (the Triad) as a focus. The issue is perhaps best summed up by Robert Reich, one of the leading writers and researchers in the area of technological strategy (see REICH, R.M.):

> Technology literacy is fundamental. The emerging global economy requires people at all levels who understand technology, design engineering and manufacturing engineering, energy, production and so on.
> (*Directors* 1991: 16)

PAT JOYNT
HENLEY MANAGEMENT COLLEGE, UK
BODO GRADUATE SCHOOL OF BUSINESS,
NORWAY

Further reading

(References cited in the text marked *)

Campbell, A. and Warner, M. (1992) *New Technology, Skills and Management: Human Resources in the Market Economy*, London: Routledge. (A look at the relationship between technology and training in modern management.)

* *Directors* (1991) 'A conversation with Bob Reich' (Fall): 16. (Interview with a leading US thinker on technology and strategy.)

Drucker, P. F. (1991) 'The new productivity challenge', *Harvard Business Review* (November–December): 69–79. (Work on the relationship between technology and performance by a leading management thinker.)

* *The Economist* (1993) 'Europe's technology policy', 9 January. (Short article on technology strategy in Europe.)

* Joynt, P. (1991) 'International dimensions of managing technology', *Journal of General Management* 16 (3): 73–84. (Longer look at different international aspects of technology management and strategy.)

Joynt, P. (1993) 'International strategy: a study of Norwegian firms', in P.J. Buckley and P. Ghauri (eds), *The Internationalization of the*

Firm: A Reader, London: Academic Press. (A look at Norwegian firms, which exhibit some distinctive national characteristics, in international operations.)

Joynt, P. and Warner, M. (eds) (1991) *Managing in Different Cultures*, Oslo: Universitetsförlaget. (Important and useful work on cross-cultural management.)

* Kenney, M. (1988) *Biotechnology: The University-Industrial Complex*, London: Yale University Press. (A study of the role of education in new technology, focusing in this case on biotechnology.)

Larsen, N.M. and Joynt, P. (1994) 'High-speed management and organizational communication: time as a competitive advantage in global markets', in D.P. Cushman and S.S. King (eds), *High Speed Management and Organizational Communication in the 1990s: A Reader*, Albany, NY: State University of New York Press. (A look at another aspect of technology management, that of the importance of time.)

* Locke, R. (1985) 'The relationship between educational and managerial cultures in Britain and West Germany', in P. Joynt and M. Warner (eds), *Managing Different Cultures*, Oslo: Universitetsförlaget. (Cross-cultural comparison between the UK and Germany.)

Lorange, P. and Roos, J. (1992) *Strategic Alliances: Formation, Implementation and Evolution*, Oxford: Blackwell. (Leading work on global strategic alliances.)

Moss Kanter, R.M. (1999) 'Managing the extended enterprise in a globally connected world', *Organizational Dynamics*, summer issue. (The Harvard Professor argues for key factors in managing the extended global enterprise. The management of technology is one of the most critical factors in this process.)

* Ohmae, K. (1980) *Triad Power: The Coming Shape of Global Competition*, New York: The Free Press. (Highly influential work which helped define the nature of global competition.)

* Porter, M. (1980) *Competitive Strategy: Techniques for Analyzing Industries and Competitors*, New York: The Free Press. (Textbook on the fundamentals of strategy.)

* Porter, M. (1985) *Competitive Advantage: Creating and Sustaining Superior Performance*, New York: The Free Press. (Another highly influential work by the leading US writer on strategy.)

* Törnvall, A. (1992) *Work in Japan: Proceedings from Workshop on Managing in Different Cultures*, Cergy-Pontoise: EIASM. (Useful cross-cultural comparison with Japan.)

Warner, M. (ed.) (1997) *Comparative Management*, London: Routledge. (The subject of comparative management has come a long way in the last years – an essential factor in the comparative framework is the management of technology.)

See also: ASIA PACIFIC, MANAGEMENT IN; BENCHMARKING; DEMING, W.E.; DRUCKER, P.F.; EUROPE, MANAGEMENT IN; INNOVATION AND CHANGE; INNOVATION MANAGEMENT; INNOVATION AND TECHNOLOGICAL CHANGE; JAPANIZATION; JUST-IN-TIME PHILOSOPHY; MANUFACTURING STRATEGY; MARKETING; OHMAE, K.; ORGANIZATION BEHAVIOUR; PORTER, M.E.; REICH, R.M.; TECHNOLOGY DIFFUSION IN JAPAN; TECHNOLOGY AND ORGANIZATIONS; UNITED STATES OF AMERICA, MANAGEMENT IN THE

Technology transfer: see EDUCATION AND BUSINESS PARTNERSHIPS; GLOBALIZATION; INFORMATION TECHNOLOGY IN DEVELOPING COUNTRIES; INNOVATION AND TECHNOLOGICAL CHANGE; INTERNATIONAL TRADE AND FOREIGN DIRECT INVESTMENT; MULTINATIONAL CORPORATIONS; SCHUMACHER, E.F; TECHNOLOGY DIFFUSION IN JAPAN; TECHNOLOGY AND ORGANIZATIONS; TECHNOLOGY STRATEGY, INTERNATIONAL

Telecommunications

Overview

We live in an era in which telecommunications has a great impact on our daily lives. Telecommunications technology has improved the way we communicate with, and understand, each other, and has altered the way we do business throughout the world. For the past two decades the structure of the telecommunications industry has been undergoing revolutionary changes worldwide. These changes have contributed to an accelerated growth in infrastructure development in all geographical regions of the world, albeit with varying degrees of success.

The rapid and dynamic changes that have taken place and those still to come pose a challenge to both users and providers. Technology has a great potential in assisting the effective use of telecommunications to enhance efficiency and to gain competitive advantages. New development of telecommunications systems includes, but is not limited to: digital wireless technology, the Internet, and applications of optical fibre.

1 Telecommunications infrastructures around the world

During the past two decades we have heard much about the 'information society' of the future, and in the present decade we hear a great deal of the 'global economy'. As we move into the new millennium we shall experience a new era in human civilization with the 'knowledge-intensive global economy'. The technology of digital telephony remains at the heart of such a global information society. Communication networks will facilitate such a transformation just as the technology of transportation brought the nations of the world and their people closer.

Business restructuring is a phenomenon well known to us and we are only just seeing the beginning of a change in the structure of our industrial society. There are many bottlenecks, and sometimes overlooked are the simple constraints that can cause serious problems for the full deployment of available technology. Some situations may affect the cost of service for the providers. For example, in the area of customer service, a lack of universal use of dualtone multi-frequency telephone sets, otherwise known as touch-tone telephones, is a handicap for automated voice-activated customer service. Universality of communications technology and its universal use is a necessary requirement in any society for full participation in the knowledge-intensive civilization of the future.

Unfortunately, the development of the communications infrastructure has been at best uneven in most countries and at worst virtually non-existent. Essentially, the nations of the world can be grouped into three different categories that can be identified depending upon their history, economy and culture. The first group of countries comprises such industrialized nations as the USA, Germany, the UK, France, Australia and Japan. While these countries provide leadership in development and deployment of modern communications technology on the domestic front, they also provide both capital and technology to facilitate infrastructure development in countries abroad. It is important, however, to note that 'universal access' to technology still remains a problem even within these developed countries. This is particularly true for those people with lower incomes and those rural residents who live in sparsely populated regions. While the USA has had a long-standing commitment to 'universal service', many other industrial nations have only just begun to address such an issue.

The second group of countries includes the former republics of the USSR and eastern European countries, such as Romania, Bulgaria and Albania. While these countries enjoy a high degree of literacy and considerable growth in technology, they suffer from an inherent socio-political bias against the free flow of information. Over the past half-century the leadership in these centrally planned nations has pursued an information policy that essentially barred the residents of these countries from open communication with the rest of the world. Naturally, there has been little desire on the part of the centrally controlled economic planners to provide open access to cross-border communication. The legacy of the past can be seen today in the Newly Independent States (NIS) of the former Soviet Union, where telecommunications for the most part is still in a state of disarray and where the slow speed of infrastructure development remains frustrating for both the citizens of these countries and outsiders alike. One can easily see that the past policy of these countries has not lent itself to the development of an effective communications infrastructure.

The third group of countries comprises those that are simply poor and have considerable difficulty in finding the money to upgrade their telecommunications infrastructures. A vast portion of the globe falls into this category, including such large countries as India, Egypt, Indonesia and Mexico, as well as numerous small nations such as Benin, Nepal, Vietnam, Gambia, Thailand, the Philippines and Tunisia, to name but a few. Today, however, this third group of countries forms several diverse sub-groups in terms of telecommunications development. The oil-producing countries in the Middle East as well as Venezuela and Brunei with their new-found wealth have had considerable success in acquiring technology from industrial countries to upgrade their telecommunications systems. Today, many people in these nations enjoy the benefits of modern communications technology. However, the vast majority of the population even in these relatively rich countries does not have access to telecommunications. The other sub-group of countries, such as Malaysia, the Philippines and Tunisia, are benefiting from liberal industrial policies that have attracted both foreign investment and technology. Telecommunications development in some large countries such as India has recently become a priority as they move ahead with a combination of indigenous technology together with some foreign collaboration.

To be successful in the information society of the new millennium, it is apparent that communications both at home and in business are a 'must' (see E-BUSINESS; INTERNET AND BUSINESS; NEW ECONOMY). While in the USA people argue about how to introduce 'fibre to home', the rest of the world still needs 'wire to home' or some form of wireless communication to the home. Some basic statistics may be surprising to many of us. One simple measure, such as the number of access lines or simply 'telephones per 100 population' usually used for the purpose of measuring penetration of communications technology, may be illuminating in discussing this issue. Such measures vary from over sixty in the Scandinavian and

Table 1 Telecommunications infrastructure in selected countries

Country	Access lines per 100 people	
	1985	*1995*
Brazil	5.3	8.1
China	0.3	2.3
Egypt	1.9	4.3
France	41.7	54.7
Hungary	6.9	17.0
India	0.4	1.1
Italy	30.5	42.9
Kazakstan	5.7	11.6
Kenya	0.6	0.9
Mexico	4.8	9.3
Poland	6.7	13.1
Russia	10.2	16.2
South Africa	6.8	9.5
Spain	24.3	37.1
Thailand	1.2	4.7
UK	37.4	48.9
USA	49.4	60.2
Venezuela	7.1	10.9

Source: World Statistics Pocketbook, United Nations, New York, 1997

North American countries, to over ten in the former Socialist bloc and South American countries, to barely over one in populous countries in Southeast Asia such as India and in much of the African continent. Although many countries have made significant progress in developing their telecommunications infrastructures, the world average still remains only a modest 16 access lines per 100 people, indicating much development is yet to come. Table 1 includes comparative statistics for a cross-section of the nations of the world. The information included is for the two years 1985 and 1995, enabling a comparison of recent development of infrastructures.

A positive sign, however, is the recognition of the need for change in the communication environment by all nations around the globe as well as by the major multinational telecommunications companies (see GLOBALIZATION). Over recent years, joint ventures and a variety of financial and trading agreements between the private and public sectors have taken place and such new ventures continue to unfold. Liberalization and privatization are two keywords we hear often around the world since the collapse of the centrally planned Soviet economy and its former satellite countries. While the telecommunications sector stands out in the race for privatization and liberalization on its way to supporting future market economies, this industry in most countries still has a long way to go. But, given the emotional, cultural and political ties of this industry to government, the telecommunications industry is setting the pace on its way towards a market economy. As a result, for the past two decades the worldwide telecommunications infrastructure has been undergoing revolutionary changes.

The technology of communication has been continually unfolding. Over the past two decades this momentum has clearly accelerated. The combination of changes in technology and subsequent market force has created a need for regulatory reform which is evidenced by the new telecommunications laws in many countries, for example the Telecommunications Act of 1996 in the USA. This landmark legislation effectively deregulated both wireline and wireless communications, potentially permitting all cable, local and long-distance companies to compete with each other in all forms of telecommunications services: voice, data and video.

The telecommunications industry in the USA generated over $210 billion in revenue during 1995, making this nation by far the largest single market in the world. Long-distance service remains the most vibrant market with a fast-growing revenue base. During 1995 long-distance revenue generated by the carriers amounted to over $81 billion. Cellular and radio telephone service has made a slow start in the USA but is now poised for accelerated growth potential from its current (1995) revenue base of $21 billion.

The European Union (EU) still endures the legacy of regulatory barriers and a restrictive ancient Post Telegraph and Telephone (PTT) culture and lacks a high-quality compatible cross-border data traffic network. While the European Commission and Council of Ministers of the member states have been playing a proactive role, the community as a whole has a long way to go towards a fully competitive telecommunications industry. In general, the EU pursues a more competitive service provision for the telecommunications market, although boundaries between competitive and non-competitive segments of the industry have been, and will continue to be, a controversial issue among the member countries. The 1987 Green Paper laid out the objectives of the future direction of the telecommunications industry. The key elements include an open and competitive policy for the telecommunications industry and services. Since then much of Europe has gradually created a competitive market, although some member countries such as the UK and Finland have moved faster than others.

The populous Asian and Pacific regions include a group of countries with diverse economic and political environments, which has resulted in their being at various stages in their telecommunications development (see ASIA PACIFIC, MANAGEMENT IN). Countries such as Japan, Singapore, Australia and New Zealand enjoy sophisticated networks, while others such as Indonesia, Thailand and the Philippines are battling with scarce resources to build the infrastructures necessary to provide basic telecommunications services. The lack of capital has been a chronic problem for most countries in this region, although some private foreign capital as well as grants and loans from international organizations, such as the World Bank and Asian Development Bank, have proven very beneficial. Some countries such as Malaysia and Thailand recognize the need for private capital, which has encouraged those countries as well as others to seriously consider opening up the telecommunications market to private investors, both domestic and foreign. This approach has proved very successful in Malaysia and to some extent in Thailand. The telecommunications market in economically developed countries such as Japan is open and highly competitive. Liberalization of the industry has encouraged new companies to enter the telecommunications market. The New Common Carriers (NCC) have rapidly become formidable competitors for the old monopoly provider, Nippon Tele-

graph and Telephone (NTT). Along with its expanding economy, China has made a serious commitment to improve her telecommunications infrastructure. Over the past ten years China has expanded her telecommunications infrastructure eight-fold from 0.3 access lines per 100 people in 1985 to over 2.4 in 1995.

2 Emerging technologies

New technologies in communication, needless to say, will play an important role in our future information society (see INFORMATION AND KNOWLEDGE INDUSTRY). These developments are evolutionary and can be viewed from two different perspectives, communication media and networking systems. The combined effect can be seen in emerging communication services.

Media can be divided into two categories, namely, wireline and wireless technologies. While wireline technologies provide much of the communication backbone among the industrialized nations, developing countries find greater opportunities in wireless systems requiring a lower capital investment. Wireline technology ranges from old twisted pair copper wires at the local level, to coaxial cable for higher-speed long-distance communications, to modern fibre optic cable providing wider bandwidth and greater reliability for long-distance transmission. Today, telecommunications companies as well as most cable companies have moved to utilize fibre cable for their long-haul transmission. Copper can be effective in local area networks (LAN), including those with wide bandwidth such as asynchronous transfer mode (ATM). Cable companies are utilizing coaxial cable for distribution at the local level while installing fibre for long-distance networks. In fact, copper and fibre often complement each other. Unlike copper, glass fibre transmits light waves which can travel afar without the amplification necessary for coaxial cable. Fibre's higher reliability, wider bandwidth and lower maintenance costs make it a highly attractive media.

The technology of optical fibre transmission is continually improving and new wave division multiplexing (WDM) technology promises both very wide bandwidth and higher speed. For example, it is now capable of transporting 20 Gbps through multiple frequencies of light. Companies such as Lucent and Ciena are capable of providing such service using the technology known as dense wave division multiplexing (DWDM). To meet the demand for transmitting a combination of voice, data and video, a global standard known as synchronous digital hierarchy (SDH) has been created. This synchronized optical network (SONET) is known as SDH-SONET in North America, and operates in multiples of OC1 (or 51.85 Mbps) and extends up to OC-192. For example, QWEST communications has recently activated its OC-192 network.

Despite the technological advantages of fibre, copper wire appears likely to stay with us for some time to come. As a result, new technologies such as asynchronous digital subscriber loop (ADSL) are being marketed by telephone companies as an alternative widerband and higher-speed service. Customer acceptance so far remains limited because of both cost and technical glitches.

Wireless technology

Growth in wireless technology has created new opportunities in telecommunications. While radical transformation in global communications can be credited to satellites, microwave and other fixed wireless transmission have made a significant contribution to the development of wireless communications. Most wireless communications rely upon some form of wireline technology to provide an efficient and diverse array of services. Rapid growth in the types and number of satellites, however, remains the driving force in wireless communications.

The traditional geosynchronous earth-orbit (GEO) satellites are launched at 22,250 miles above the earth's surface and remain stationary relative to a point on earth. Most of these do not provide global coverage, but a few of them providing extensive coverage require high-powered transmission. These satellites are expensive to build and launch. The latest technology has created two new classes of satellites that are launched at a lower altitude. These are known as medium-earth-orbit (MEO) and low-earth-orbit (LEO) satellites. The MEO satellites are placed around 1,500 to 6,500 miles above the earth's surface while the LEO satellites are placed at a lower altitude of only 550 miles from the earth's surface. Both of these types of satellite move relative to a point on the earth and consequently a number of them are required to provide global coverage. LEO satellites move more rapidly than do MEO satellites and require a larger number to form a constellation capable of providing global coverage. Both of these satellites are relatively inexpensive to build and launch compared to the geosynchronous satellites. These low-altitude satellites require low-powered transmitters and, unlike GEO satellites, experience only a negligible delay because of their proximity to the earth's surface. These low and medium altitude satellites are, in fact, the technology of choice today, and a number of constellations are currently being launched. Iridium system is already in operation and others such as Teledesic, Odyssey, Hughes Spaceway and ICO Global are on their way towards various stages of completion. Some of these new systems will provide specialized service such as the Internet but others will offer multiple services. Satellites have already facilitated new services such as direct TV to home and the Internet and other audio/video services will follow with the passage of time.

Wireless technology offers an inexpensive alternative for communication, particularly for the developing countries without extensive wireline networks. As a result, countries such as China and India are the potential beneficiaries of wireless communication technology. A combination of mobile cellular technology and low altitude satellites enables these countries to build communications infrastructures much faster than was previously possible and with a lower capital investment.

The Internet and the Web

The advancement of telecommunications technology has made the Internet a reality (see INTERNET AND BUSINESS). Today the Internet and the World Wide Web (or the Web) together represent an enormous possibility for global electronic communications and transactions. Essentially, the Internet consists of many different networks all attached through a common backbone network. The World Wide Web, on the other hand, is simply an address or facility where information can be stored. The Internet provides the connection to these facilities and special application programs known as Web browsers (e.g. Netscape) are used to review such information. The Web represents a new philosophy with respect to accessing and distributing information using the Internet. However, it is the diffusion of the Internet and the Web that is likely to change the world forever. The Internet has opened up exciting possibilities of communication between all constituents of human society, including business, consumers, educators, students and all other government and non-government agencies around the world. While Web usage is still in its infancy, its product development and deployment are moving at a very fast pace. There are two groups of new entrepreneurs involved in this process. The first group comprises Internet Service Providers (ISP) while the second group consists of those who essentially develop products and services that can be marketed over the Internet via the Web.

The number of Internet Service Providers has grown rapidly over the past several years, creating the most vibrant sector in the telecommunications industry in many countries. Some consolidation in this market is inevitable and appears to be taking place. A major case in point is the acquisition of CompuServe by America-On-Line (AOL) in 1997, making AOL a major player in this market. Included in the second group of businesses are those that provide search tools and information and services. Companies such as Microsoft and Netscape primarily provide platforms for posting various information and services. On the other hand, companies such as Yahoo, Amazon.com, Geocities, to name a few, are providing information and other services over the Internet using these platforms. There are, of course, numerous businesses and other organizations that now provide services over the Internet and advertise their products and services on the Web.

The Internet is the outcome of the old ARPA (Advanced Research Project Agency) project originally intended for military, government and academic researchers and scientists to share their ideas over a wide area network. The original Web was created by Timothy Bernes-Lee at CERN (French acronym for European Laboratory for Particle Physics) in Geneva. In 1989 a global web was proposed for hypertext documents that would allow physicists affiliated to CERN to work together from different locations. The Web is a multimedia system that can link computers around the world via a communications protocol called HyperText Transfer Protocol (HTTP) using a standard software authoring language called Hyper Text Markup Language (HTML). Today the Internet is the transportation system and the Web provides the application system; the pair represent a formidable part of the future in the telecommunications industry which will eventually transform our life, our work and civilization itself as we know it.

Technological changes in telecommunications are not new, but the Internet offers an exciting challenge to the old Public Switched Telephone Network (PSTN). Internet vendors are slowly but surely getting into voice telephony and thus invading the traditional turf of the old telephone companies. The existing communications protocol and limitations in available bandwidth have encouraged many new companies such as QWEST and Level-3 Communications to build and expand their networks based upon Internet Protocol (IP). The IP-based system offers an opportunity to transport data cheaply and efficiently and is almost certain to change the landscape of the telecommunications industry significantly.

3 Conclusion

Telecommunications, clearly, is the technology that will provide the lifeline of our civilization in the next century. With the increasing globalization of national economies and growing interdependence among the nations of the world, the need for communications cannot be over-emphasized. Rapidly evolving communications technologies certainly have the capacity to integrate the world. The challenge is to make telecommunications access available to every individual around the world, irrespective of their geographical and national boundaries. To this end, some progress has been made over recent years but we still have a long way to go to provide this technology to all people on our planet.

SUFI NAZEM

YONG SHI
UNIVERSITY OF NEBRASKA AT OMAHA

HEESEOK LEE
KOREA ADVANCED INSTITUTE OF SCIENCE
AND TECHNOLOGY

Further reading

Bates, R.J. and Gregory, D. (1998) *Voice and Data Communications Handbook*, New York: McGraw-Hill. (A comprehensive book of telecommunications technology.)

Datapro (1992) *Reports on International Telecommunications,* Defrum, NJ: Datapro. (A source of contemporary situations in telecommunications around the world.)

FCC (1992) *Statistics of the Communications Common Carriers,* Washington, DC: Federal Communications Commission. (An annual report which includes statistical data on US telecommunications.)

ITU (1992) *Telecommunications Indicators of the Former Soviet Union,* Geneva: International Telecommunications Union. (A special report on the status of telecommunications in the former Soviet Union.)

Minoli, D. (1997*) Internet and Internet Engineering*, New York: McGraw-Hill. (A comprehensive book on network technology.)

United Nations (1997) *Statistical Yearbook*, New York: United Nations. (A source book on national statistical data.)

See also: E-BUSINESS; E-COMMERCE AND BUSINESS; FIRE-WALL SYSTEMS; NEW ECONOMY; SECURITY AND INFORMATION SYSTEMS; SMART CARDS

Teleworking

Overview

The basic concept behind teleworking is that workers can work 'at a distance' from the office site, at their own times, by using advanced computing and telecommunications technologies then electronically transferring the results to the office or to another location. Teleworking constitutes an additional step taken by organizations in their search for increased flexibility in response to the rapidly changing business and human resources environment. The growing need for flexible work patterns may be regarded as stemming from social, economic and technological developments. As employers reorganize their businesses, focusing on optimizing productivity and reducing costs, they are also trying to respond to many of the challenges facing the modern employee – work and family obligations, career development and stressful lifestyles. The rapid and far-reaching advances of telecommunication devices during the last decade has afforded employers the option of employing salaried workers remotely from their office, in more supportive environments for performing tasks requiring long hours of uninterrupted concentration. The employment of remote workers without constant continuous presence at the workplace makes it possible to work from home or from distributed work centres. One form of telework, the home-based employment, was quite common historically, and a conventional form of work before the Industrial Revolution led to the currently dominant work pattern – working in offices according to a fixed time schedule. An attempt to quantify the overall losses or gains from teleworking to the individual worker, the employer and society would be problematic due to the multiplex concept.

1 Introduction

The idea of working from a distance, that is telecommuting, also known as teleworking, has in the last decade become a natural technology-enabled development (see INTERNET). Myriad terms have been coined to sum up the notion of that phenomenon: teleworking; telecommuting; flexiplace; distance work; remote work; off-site work; telecottage; electronic cottage; home work. Although these terms can be used interchangeably, each term actually implies a slightly different connotation of the concept. For instance, the term 'telecommuting' is a transportation-based expression, whereas 'teleworking' is an equipment-based one. Both expressions, however, refer to the same phenomenon: the use of computer and telecommunications equipment to do office work away from the central conventional office (Shamir 1993). It should be noted that while office work is performed at conventional dedicated central workplaces, remote work is performed outside such places and time-span. The relevant dimension behind this distinction is the amount of time or proportion of work activities that is performed outside the conventional office. That is, teleworkers are provided with a relative freedom in scheduling the time and location of work, guided by individual needs and the needs of the tasks.

Eventually, as the concept of managing home work gained credibility worldwide, it became acknowledged as 'the SO-HO business', which stands for 'Small Office – Home Office'. However, while considering that protean terminology, insinuating to the same notion, a profound disagreement is revealed over a conventional definition of what is meant by the various terms. In fact, there exists no clear-cut definition which would capture the varied multilateral notion of telework.

One possible basis for a definition lies in the transportation itself – the substitution of telecommunication for travel. However, that was found to be inadequate as the desire to save on commuting reflects only one of the several advantages of telework. Another definition which has gained some informal currency in common speech is one which perceives telework as a sub-category of home work. It is defined as 'a work which is carried out at home involving the use of information technology' (Huws *et al.* 1990).

Of relevance is a further distinction between *working at home* and *working from home*, since there are some workers who work partly at home and partly elsewhere. The first expression refers to people who actually work at home most of the time and the second to people who use the home mainly as a base for receiving messages and doing paperwork.

A further possible basis for a definition of telework lies in the technology itself, that is 'all activities which require electronic communication between the central office of an employer and an employee working at a distance'. In fact, that definition would yield a category so large as to be meaningless, as it would include all organizations with branch structures which have internal electronic communications systems.

An alternative basis for definition is that of the worker's contractual relationship to their employer. Such a definition would distinguish between three types of contractual arrangements: *substitute, complementary* and *independent*. The first type refers to salaried workers who are located at their own homes, which serve as a substitute for the workplace. The second type refers to full-time employees doing job-related work at home, especially in the evenings and weekends, as a complementary effort to work done in the workplace. The third type refers to self-employed workers, who operate a full-time home-based business.

As has been inferred, none of the prevalent definitions have been sufficiently universal or unambiguous to use as the basis of empirical investigation. However, teleworking can be characterized in terms which are technological, organizational, locational or contractual. It is not a mono-directional or mono-dimensional phenomenon, thus it can be defined by different parameters. A comprehensive definition which takes into account all of these factors together can provide the basis for the accurate formulation of telework at any particular point in time. Such a definition suggested by Huws *et al.* (1990) focuses on three variables: the location of work, the use of electronic equipment and the existence of a communications link to the employer or contractor. Thus, it can be defined as work, whose location is independent of the location of the employer or contractor and can be changed according to the wishes of the individual teleworker and/or the organization for which the employee is working. It is work which relies primarily, or to a large extent, on the use of electronic equipment, the results of which work are communicated remotely to the employer or contractor. The remote communications link need not be a direct telecommunications link but could include the use of mail or courier services.

2 Origins

Technological innovations combined with the continuing concern about the environment and the changing needs of modern society, as well as the changing conditions in the business arena, can be seen as potential contributors to the introduction of telework. The innovations in communication technologies taking place over the last decade opened up new challenges and possibilities to the global business community, which became known as a 'small village'. With the increasing availability of sophisticated computer and microchip technology and the communication services, telecommuting is becoming a viable option for many companies striving to survive (see INFORMATION TECHNOLOGY). The exodus from the office is made possible by the proliferation of relatively inexpensive computers, fax machines, electronic and voice mail systems, satellites, cellular telephones, conference calls, personal pagers and laptop or notebook computers. High-speed modems, ISDN (integrated services digital network) and other products and services are making network access from the home more effective. Workers are given the chance to work at home whenever they feel inspired and according to their biological clock, even in unconventional work hours.

In order to develop an understanding of the dynamics of telework it is essential to view it in the overall context of general office automation. Today, most offices have a number of systems for handling information, such as meetings, telephone, telex, mail, photocopies, fax, mainframe computers, individual personal computers and typewriters. The introduction of the computer and new storage media devices along with the application of communication technologies has led to organizations being able to cope with the vast quantities of information, which they need to process and manage in order to survive in the competitive business arena. While microelectronics has the raw power to process huge amounts of information, information gains its full value only when communicated. With the addition of electro-optic fibre, the technology of communicating with light, telecommuting could bring the office environment directly to a worker's home and increase the number of workers who 'commute' to work electronically.

A growing concern for the preservation of the physical environment on Earth, in addition to the massive competition over limited energy resources have also served as driving forces towards telework. The renewed interest in telework first arose during the oil crisis of the early 1970s, its impetus coming from the desire to minimize fuel consumption in order to save energy. In addition, a growing interest in national factors such as air pollution and transportation issues contributed to the importance of the telework concept. In the USA, the home office trend began to take off in 1990, when Congress passed amendments to the Clean Air Act mandating that companies with more than 100 employees reduce the number of workers commuting to work by car. National interest in telecommuting is growing, and several thousand US employers now have formal telecommuting programmes. In the San Francisco Bay area, for example, many employees stayed home and became telecommuters following the 1989 earthquake, although most have since returned to the workplace.

From the point of view of the company's management, teleworking represents a general trend of seeking new and more adaptive ways of coping with the changing demands of the workforce that have arisen as a result of social changes. In fact, telework meets the values, behaviours and family orientations of the post-Second World War baby boom generation, that is, those born between 1946 and 1964 (Hall and Richter 1990). The growing number of dual-career families, the accelerating concern about linking work, family and leisure time, the concern for autonomy, self-actualization and self-expression are all significantly impacting industry. Those changes in workers' aspirations are yet another reason for instituting more flexibility in organizations (see FLEXIBILITY). Furthermore, social developments and changes in labour relations – such as the need to improve the quality of life in the workplace, or the need to safeguard workers and their health, or the need to adapt to technological changes and shortage of entry-level workers – called for flexible work patterns in order to maintain complex organizational systems as fully operational. In most industrialized countries, the retention and recruitment of scarce skilled workers remains a strong motive for adopting the concept of telework. In some cases, companies can hold on to good workers who would otherwise leave the company due to family relocation by allowing them to work remotely, without any need to either change residence or make long journeys.

In many Western countries social and economic changes have created the need to provide employment opportunities for certain social groups that cannot be readily integrated into the generally prevailing work patterns: married women and mothers raising children who are joining the workforce in ever-growing numbers, youngsters, the disabled, working students, retirees and, in particular, workers who have been made redundant as a result of economic recession. Given the constant turbulence in today's business environment, the organizational systems themselves are also in need of flexible work arrangements. In this age of cutbacks in manpower, telework may be regarded as a flexible working arrangement aiming to improve competitiveness and to increase productivity from fewer workers. Many organizations are subject to 'seasonal' fluctuations and peaks of workloads. Working in the home makes it possible to increase the workload without having to add to the work area and to staff services. This allows for better utilization of human resources.

In addition, the currently dominant work pattern – working in an organizational environment according to fixed time schedules – is now found to be dysfunctional (see HUMAN RESOURCE MANAGEMENT). Instead, the issue of long and irregular working hours is becoming increasingly significant. With the globalization of the business environment, businesses no longer compete only with their nearest rivals, but internationally. Moreover, it is clear that a global community can only be in place if workforces on opposite sides of the globe consent to conduct their business outside the conventional nine-to-five timeframe.

The number of information-related activities in the workplaces of modern societies has increased immensely. The progress of information technologies coupled with technological feasibility is expected to bring an increase in the practice of teleworking. Controlled experiments conducted in the USA suggest that the most suitable sector to adopt telework seems to be the information sector – in which 85 per cent of employees can work remotely and 30 per cent can work from home. Activities, such as those of architects, designers, accountants, consultants, translators, computer programmers, clerical workers, typists and market researchers need not be conducted in central offices any more. Business and telecommuting visionaries embraced the concept of working at home not only for its solution to human problems, but also for the savings that they felt it would generate.

Research has revealed a degree of consensus – although largely unsubstantiated – that the benefits to employers considerably outweigh the losses. Efficiency is the main benefit for employers. For organizations, employees working at home means substantial saving in operating expenses such as transportation, travelling time, parking spaces, administrative expenses and better time utilization of computers and people. However, no such consensus exists in relation to teleworkers, where there is an ongoing debate on the subject (Huws *et al.* 1990).

One of the most frequently cited economic advantages of employing teleworkers is the saving on office overhead costs. Organizations like Rank Xerox and British Telecom have found that teleworking can reduce costs, such as on office space and overheads. This was given as a major justification for setting up the Rank Xerox networking scheme in the UK. Individual staff members were moved out of the company's Central London premises, so that it was possible to vacate a building formerly housing 42 staff, allowing continuing total overhead savings. Overheads costs are likely to be offset by savings resulting from lower rental costs and other advantages of being away from the city centre. The prevalence of electronic mail, faxes and other telecommuting equipment has made ex-urban management more plausible, prompting some firms to move their headquarters from big cities to smaller towns, where costs are lower. One plus factor of telework to employers is that much of the training cost can be transferred to the employee's free time. Even in the case of home-based telework, office overheads may not disappear altogether. Some costs may be transferred to the teleworker, who may be faced for instance, with higher fuel bills for heating and lighting a part of the home which would not otherwise be used during the day. There is also often a hidden cost involved in allocating space in the home for work use. Other costs to the homeworker may include extra maintenance and cleaning, and in some cases, additional insurance on the home and its contents. However, telework could save a lot of expense for entrepreneurs at a time when a newly-born business is not yet profitable. Research shows that half of all employees either have a job that lends itself to telecommuting or are interested in telecommuting. Thus, this factor, which is an advantage for the employer, may become a disadvantage – albeit a relatively unimportant one – for the worker.

In addition, there are so many variables with regard to equipment costs that it is impossible to make meaningful generalizations. The question of cost allocation arises. When work is carried out in a central office, the employer is the undisputed owner of the equipment and is expected to bear the cost. However, when workers are based at home, there is no such automatic assumption, and a number of different ownership and payment options exist. In some cases, companies make arrangements to hire their machines to teleworkers. In other cases, they provide loans so that individual teleworkers can purchase the equipment, or employers simply expect the teleworker to supply whatever equipment they may require in order to carry out the work effectively. In all these cases, costs are effectively allocated to the teleworker.

Obviously, telework involves a reduction in transportation costs, but it does not eliminate them. Most workers are expected to travel into the office once or twice a week, or else it is necessary for some work to be physically transported to and from the remote work site. In addition, some telework schemes may involve visits by safety officers or managers to the remote sites. Many new transportation costs involved in telework, such as delivery of work by messenger, or travel to meetings by teleworkers, their co-workers or managers, may now be claimed by the teleworker from the employer as business expenses.

One of the major expenses incurred in telework is, of course, the cost of communication, both between the teleworker and the employer and between the teleworker and any client of the employing organization, with whom the employee has dealings. Cost saving is dependent on a number of factors. One variable is the mode of communication used. While postal delivery, telephone communication and electronic mail may be comparatively cheap, full video-conferencing facilities are expensive. The level of these costs will therefore play a significant role in the decision making of either an organization or of an individual freelance.

3 Scope of the phenomenon

Various attempts were made to estimate and quantify the size of the teleworker population. A literature survey indicates that the potential of the telework concept is beginning to be recognized, although it has by no means yet become a reality. To the extent it is happening, telework is still a comparative rarity. It is occurring in a piecemeal way in all but the most highly organized offices in the industrialized countries. Although it seems somewhat difficult to support more accurately the size of the phenomenon, its growth trend is commonly accepted. The LINK Resources market research firm estimates that 32 million Americans engage in job-related work at home at least part of the time.

4 Implications

Teleworking is significantly impacting the structure of work, the office and the organization. In addition, it has implications for the individual and society as a whole.

Work structure

The type of work that lends itself best to telecommuting is characterized by routine information processing, heavy telephone or computer use, a project-specific orientation and a minimal need for complex support or work space. Teleworking is most suitable for people with a lot of autonomy in their work. The main criterion that determines whether a task is suitable for being performed at home is its level of interdependence, that is, the extent to which the task involves the work of other people, the amount of personal interchanges needed, the frequency with which feedback is required, matters of data security and confidentiality and the availability of the information needed to carry out the task.

Work at home is best suited to two types of tasks, from opposite ends of the work spectrum. At one end are the straightforward routine tasks, such as computer data entry or data transfer, that do not involve a high level of complexity or social interaction. At the other end are the tasks of data analysis and processing, programming and computation, which are complex, non-routine, and require individual creativity, rather than teamwork and interactive professional consultation (Richter and Meshulam 1993).

Work at home must be integrated with the other components of the system in such a way that it allows for the fulfilment of the organization's business needs. In case the organization decides to implement such an arrangement, management must consider a number of issues. First, unlike the conventional organizational structure, work at home relieves the organization of the need to establish a strict hierarchy. Second, the 'invisible' structure paves the way for large spans of control that are suitable for the management of both complex and simple tasks. If properly structured, work at home can lead to a reduction in the number of management level positions, thereby bringing real savings to the organization, and at the same time increasing the opportunities for personal growth and development of the employees. Third, the issue of the employee's maturity emerges as a crucial factor in deciding on the appropriate organizational structure.

The structure of organizations is moving towards a flatter, more decentralized organizational form. The move towards participative and team leadership practices is one of the reasons for today's downsized and de-layered organization. With the recent dramatic advances in telecommunications and computing, many companies are shifting facilities away from expensive centralized urban organizations to more loosely arranged organizations in less populated ex-urban areas. As companies decentralize and reform themselves around their information networks – connecting branch offices, telecommuting employees, and customers together with private networks, satellites, laptop computers and fax machines – the result is sometimes the end of entire layers of middle management. All manner of service-sector companies are becoming 'virtual employers' with no centralized home. For example, Journal Graphics, a vendor of transcripts of television shows, has Grant Street in Denver, Colorado, as its home address. However, the company's operations are conducted elsewhere, in employees' homes. Shows are taped on personal video recorders, transcripts are made there, and the material is directly uploaded to satellite channels, digital FM sideband networks, and on-line databanks for access by subscribers within hours of a show's original transmission.

In actuality, considerable work related to personnel management, planning and support can be done outside the organization; it may therefore be transferred to subcontractors or to employees working partly at home. Although it is not always the case, it frequently happens that the decision to decentralize workers via telework is accompanied by a change in their status to that of independent contract workers. When this takes place, there is a considerable saving to the employer in health insurance, sick pay, maternity pay and holiday pay, pension contributions and other welfare benefits. In this instance, what is a credit item for the employer becomes a debit for the teleworker and in the long run it is damaging to morale and staff loyalty.

Current practice reveals a number of different types of contractual relationships between teleworkers and their employers or clients. US case law suggests that the critical factor in deciding whether or not a worker is an employee is the degree of dependence on the supplier of work. Criteria used for assessing this can be summarized as: the degree of control over the work; opportunities for profit and loss; whether risk capital is supplied; the degree of permanence of the relationship and the amount of skill and initiative contributed by the worker. Even if there is a written agreement that a worker is a contractor, companies cannot unilaterally turn their employees into contract workers. By extension, employees cannot be compelled to give up any of their rights, including pensioned workers' compensation. In both lawsuits and additional private letter rulings, the rights of telecommuting workers have been slowly defined, as legislatures prepare to act. Some companies issue a policy guideline for telecommuters stating that telecommuting is a cooperative arrangement between the employer and employee, not a right.

In the UK, the situation is similar, and there is no simple rule of thumb which can be applied to determine whether a particular worker is an employee. In Germany, we find an additional legal status category affecting employees who work outside a conventional office environment: the home worker, covered by the Homework Law. People working as home workers as defined by this law are not classified as employees but as a category of people enjoying *employee-equivalent* status covered by special legal provisions. It is possible that a general lack of clarity about the legal status of teleworkers may have acted as a deterrent to the setting up of telework schemes in some cases.

Although that would lead to widespread workforce reductions the ultimate result is a decrease in companies' expenses, better utilization of workforce and increased productivity. By doing the work at home, equipment – mainly the central computer – can be utilized via telecommunications during the less busy hours. The organization suffers less from the traditional disciplinary problems, such as absenteeism and unpunctuality and may significantly reduce turnover rates and increase workers' satisfaction. At times of shortage of labour, the supply of workers can be increased by employing them in their homes, at a distance from the organization's premises.

Teleworking is not commensurate with organizational careers, with a central issue being the appropriate procedure for promotion. It is very difficult to manage invisible workers. Indeed, when a manager decides to promote a worker, he would undoubtedly give priority to the worker sitting in a room next to him, rather than to a teleworker. The promotion and advancement opportunities issues become problematic, as the careers of teleworkers may be severely hampered. There is a significant drawback of telework for those who intend to take managerial roles. One cannot take a managerial role when working alone. This is because career advancement in organizations requires visibility and involvement with many organizational activities beyond the performance of one's tasks. One not only has to conform to organizational norms, one must also demonstrate conformity to those that count. This often entails demonstrating punctuality at meetings, wearing the right clothes, speaking at the right time, and so forth. A lot of informal contacts and politics, taking place at the cafeteria or in the corridors, can lead to promotion of certain workers and not others. For regular workers, overtime work at home is a signal of career investment that is often rewarded by promotion. Paradoxically, this sign of career investment and commitment is unavailable to home workers, for whom overtime is not visibly separated from regular work.

Telework, as well as making work more independent of place, is also often associated with a reduced rigidity of working time, mainly on a short time-scale. In many telework schemes, especially home-based ones, supervision over the work is impossible or at least impracticable. Supervision of the teleworkers' performance and productivity thus relies mainly on the evaluation of output or work results. In many cases, this pattern of control is reinforced by contracts which stipulate that the teleworker is self-employed. In some cases, organizations try to increase supervision by telephone and hold regular meetings between teleworkers and project managers.

The blurring of home work boundaries resulting from transferring work to the residence is bound to affect the employee's sense of autonomy. Telework suits a mature individual who does not need direct supervision and is capable of working independently, one who is willing to trade personal benefits or power that arise from working in a social organization for freedom and flexibility. The main priority of such employees will be autonomy and control of their time.

Office sphere

The essence of teleworking for business is to allow people who would traditionally be part of a group working together in one place to work at their own time in a private space of their own, where they can better control the pace and pressures created by others. A growing number of workers find an intermediary solution near their residence, adopting flexible work arrangements. Telework can be categorized by the location in which it is performed. It may take the following equally valid organizational forms: satellite centres; neighbourhood work centres; and work at home. The principle motivation behind all of these alternatives is the saving of travel time and cost of commuting.

Telecommuting does not necessarily mean employees working at home. Satellite work centres are relatively independent units of a parent company which have been physically relocated and separated from the parent firm. The emphasis is on locating the separated units at a relatively convenient commuting distance for most of the workers. In the BC Tel Program for example, workers report for work at a specially established satellite office in a suburb rather than commuting to downtown Vancouver. Neighbourhood work centres are offices in which employees from several companies share space and equipment in a location close to their residences; these offices are equipped and financially supported by several different organizations.

Work at home, the most decentralized form of remote work, allows optimal choice of working hours. The incubator-like home environment reduces the distractions of an office and encourages the optimum use of time. It also allows for flexible hours, personal comfort and, because the commute is eliminated, a longer working day and the freedom to live anywhere, without considering how far is it from the office. Working at home eliminates geographical boundaries. The biggest challenges for those who work at home are maintaining a professional stance among clients and colleagues and ensuring that family and friends respect work schedules. In view of this factor, there is a need to moderate the interface between the family and work roles of home workers. There should be an apparent distinction marking the physical boundaries of the two spheres, in order to reduce mutual interference. That can be done by allocating a separate and isolated room, keeping the door closed while working, in addition to purchasing office furniture and equipment. One way to promote a professional image is to install a separate telephone line for the office and to buy an answering machine or sign up with an answering service for those times when no one is available to answer the phone. In addition, home workers' equipment should be compatible with office machines and telecommuting employees should report to the central office once or twice a week for meetings and messages.

Organizational strategies – management of workforce

To be effective, the organization needs to ensure that the effort of working remotely fits the business needs as dictated by the changing organizational environment. More specifically, remote work must be economically worthwhile, must enhance competitiveness, provide business opportunities, or address some major issues such as productivity and improvement in the utilization of resources. To achieve both effectiveness and efficiency in implementing telework, it is not sufficient to provide employees with appropriate rewards. Off-site work requires different characteristics on the part of the employee's managers, who must adapt their style to fit the different conditions. A major characteristic required of managers is flexibility and they will also be required to come up with non-conventional, innovative ideas for career development, involvement and communication with the employees. Many facets of conventional work environments are lost, or acquire a different meaning in the telework framework: power, status, position, grade, accepted informalities of structure, the staff/line structure. Additional options that the organization might consider for its teleworkers include a flexible career ladder, and a rotation programme that allows for job swapping at reasonable intervals.

Workers' compensation is just one aspect of the legal issues that could affect companies with employees who work at home. This complex subject takes into account variables such as employment status, sex, age, number of dependents, occupation and educational qualifications. Whatever the morality of the question, the fact remains that for a number of employers, substantial savings in salary are being made as a result of telework schemes. A central element in teleworking for management is for teleworkers to be monitored by results. Managers would have to change their performance evaluation methods by relying more on measured output, which might be the production of reports, and less on observed input. This effectively involves a greater degree of self-management by workers and might therefore be expected to lighten the workload of managers. Most companies already involved in telecommuting have measured substantial increases in productivity, and that constitutes a good measure of the attraction of this method of work for many employers. The financial advantages of this extra productivity accrue to teleworkers only when they are paid by results, at a rate which is genuinely comparable to that paid to equivalent on-site workers. Although figures on productivity gains vary from 20 per cent to 100 per cent it is widely supported that telecommuting will increase the organization's productivity.

In practice, managerial attitudes and organizational structure and culture do not form an absolute barrier to telework, but they do constitute a major restraint on its development. Many managers may resist the concept, fearing they will lose control of workers. Such a shift requires managers who have been accustomed to relying on direct supervision methods to learn to plan better the work activities of their subordinates and to define clear performance goals for them (or with them). Periodical site meetings with management and the working group are very important. These scheduled meetings will also serve to ensure that the basic values of the organizational culture, such as openness, trust and innovation are maintained and to assure that the teleworker is kept up to date with business developments. Clear rules are needed that define the responsibilities and obligations of the employee and the organization. Work schedules must be strictly adhered to, and objectives clearly specified. Finally, the organization must ensure that the appropriate screening procedures are available for identifying the right people for working at home. These will probably be employees who have been socialized in the organization and are mature enough to manage themselves. Young and inexperienced employees are probably not immediately well suited for this mode of employment.

The individual

It is not easy to assess the advantages and drawbacks of telework from a human point of view. Many depend on the individual personalities concerned, and others vary according to the type of work in question and the particular domestic situation of the worker concerned. Nevertheless, the telecommuting employee is likely to be a white collar professional, and in particular a knowledge worker, in a supervisory level position or above. Most telecommuters live in large metropolitan areas and may actually work at regional telecommuting centres closer to home or at home.

The benefits of teleworking for the employee are very likely to fall into the soft or intangible category. Besides avoiding commuting hassles and saving work-related expenses, teleworking allows a better control over time schedules, an opportunity to manage better family demands and schedule one's own work with fewer disturbances from colleagues during working time.

Indeed, telework fits very well into the profile of the baby boom cohort: a strong concern for basic values, a sense of freedom to act on values, strong sense of self-awareness, need for autonomy and questioning of authority, less concern for advancement, entrepreneurship and a total life perspective. Nowadays, workers are relatively well-educated, value-driven, independent and quality-orientated. The need for freedom and the impatience with formal hierarchical authority is probably the most salient feature of workers. Workers value achievement and autonomy but do not want to submit to authority nor exercise it. There appears to be less of a driving passion to move up the hierarchy. Perhaps related to this lower need for advancement is the worker's orientation towards high quality in the current job. The critical motivation for workers is the intrinsic reward which comes from crafting one's work and doing a high quality job in the service of a useful purpose. In contrast to earlier times, when people had to conform to the structure of the workplace, the structure of assignments can now be more responsive to people's needs. When weighing up the psychological advantages and disadvantages of remote work, the greatest human benefit is undoubtedly the flexibility telework offers, which makes it much easier to integrate work into domestic life.

Teleworkers enjoy a high degree of flexibility in work content. The autonomy and intrinsic challenges give employees freedom to generate their own solutions to work problems and to implement them in their own ways. Working at home may explain the growing trend among highly-skilled professionals of showing greater commitment to their profession than to their employing organization. The self-directed, authority-questioning worker of the baby boom generation behaves in ways that are congruent with basic values such as self-development and self-fulfilment. However, that may not be compatible with the goals of the employing organization and the interpersonal commitment which is commonly found in organizations. Professional workers or managers may become restless and start thinking about starting up their own business. That would be a financial loss for the employing organization, not to mention the loss of another source of ideas, innovation and energy.

The majority of teleworkers seem to find that the greatest advantage of telework is the ability to combine work demands and family obligations in a flexible manner. For instance, when childcare responsibilities are present, the ability to combine care of children or other dependents with work seems to be a great advantage. Women who choose to work at home do so partly because it allows them time for domestic labour, and in turn to spend more time on domestic tasks than office workers. Working at home also poses a problem of overlap or conflict between domestic life and work commitments. Although the worker may derive a greater measure of gratification from functioning, in practice, as an independent operator, the degree of autonomy actually enjoyed by the employee may be less than anticipated due to the demands made by family members, by virtue of the individual's mere presence at home. One of the problems encountered by home workers is the invisibility of work: assuming that home workers are not 'really working', friends and neighbours will not hesitate to call for a social chat, drop in for a visit or send their children over to play. Even spouses sometimes fail to regard home work as 'real work'.

The greatest problem for a large majority of teleworkers is undoubtedly social, as well as professional, isolation. Social isolation is generally considered to be the greatest disadvantage of home-based telework from the human point of view, and is the main reason given for opposing telework by those who do so. In the usual workplace, there exists transfer of information among colleagues on a regular basis, a sort of mutual fertilization.

However, when working alone there is no one to consult. Self-employed workers need professional contact in order to be constantly updated, as well as to gain exposure and market the business. Independent workers, running their own private business, should conduct self-marketing efforts in order to gain credibility in the business community. They should read a lot of professional material and take part in conferences as a compensation for the lack of conventional work meetings. For salaried workers, isolation can be minimized by the use of neighbourhood work centres, organizing regular social gatherings, providing good communication links between teleworkers and their colleagues and structuring jobs which partly require work in the office. Work at home limits the employee's opportunities for learning and for obtaining feedback from others. Under these conditions, feedback can be provided on task performance only, since behavioural performance cannot be evaluated.

Society

Telework affects the development of societal and economic issues, such as energy consumption, property, legal, taxation and labour relation's issues as well as education, community and family matters.

National factors contribute to the growth of teleworking. A study by the US Department of Transportation provided evidence that telecommuting has the potential to substantially reduce petrol consumption and lessen traffic congestion. It also leads to a considerable saving of resources, reduction of traffic peaks, more parking spaces, cut in energy demands, lower investments in roads, decrease of air pollution and useful exploitation of training plans by preventing an early retirement of workers.

Telecommunication technologies, which are already widespread and growing in popularity, become an alternative to railroads and highways. In Japan, remote work centres are constructed in order to overcome the overcrowding of the town centres. A trade-off between telecommunications and transportation would result in a net reduction in petrol consumption. However, it is not entirely obvious that this would be on a sufficiently large scale to justify major investment.

Besides, the rapidly expanding telecommuting market has already offered business opportunities for a broad range of enterprises. A need may arise for new office service industries such as stationery suppliers, fax or photocopying services, suppliers of migration paths as electronic mail providers, computing and telecommunication suppliers, vendors of telecommuting software, developers of videoconferencing and data compression systems, manufacturers of home-office electronic equipment and delivery services.

Another important issue is the decentralization of work into rural areas. The implication of population shifts from urban to rural areas would be far-reaching. Property assets are likely to decline in value in cities, and those who will benefit most from these trends include property owners in fringe suburbs and scenic rural areas. In addition, that shift would bring a regeneration of depressed regions, with high levels of unemployment, poverty and peripherality.

An additional issue that needs to be considered relates to labour relations. A definite constraint on the future spread of telework is the policy of trade unions towards the introduction of information technology. On the one hand, the unions will certainly support the extra freedom at work, the better utilization of the employee's time, and the provision of opportunities for mothers of young children to join the workforce. On the other hand, the unions may perceive work at home as a threat to their power and influence.

Telework has implications for education and training policies. Workers should be trained to use information technologies in order to gain the ability to search databases as well as send and receive electronic mail. Other skills should be taught such as: organizing one's time effectively, avoiding social and professional isolation, legal rights and obligations, in addition to the management of remote workers. Computers must be made more accessible to the elderly.

5 The future

The workplace of the future will differ from today's workplace. The rapid improvements in communications technology over the past decade have made the prospect of working at home not just desirable but practical as well. High-speed modems, ISDN and other products and services are making network access from the home more effective. Future advances in videophones, wireless networking and hand-held computers will make telecommuting even easier and more productive.

Economic factors, continuing concerns about the environment and employee needs are ensuring the growth of telecommuting. Even though the changes will be slower than often forecast, they will be more varied and more complex. Teleworkers do not only need technical skills and knowledge, but also psychological preparation. Facility managers will not only have to design plans for dealing with the now-vacant work spaces, but they will also need to develop strategies for assisting with home office design.

JUDITH RICHTER
TEL AVIV UNIVERSITY

Further reading

(References cited in the text marked *)

Bailyn, L. (1989) 'Toward the perfect workplace', *Communications of the ACM* 32 (4): 460–71. (This study presents the experience of home-based workers compared with their office-based counterparts in a UK computer firm.)

Bailyn, L. (1992) 'Changing the conditions of work: responding to increasing work force diversity and new family patterns', in T. Kochan and M. Useem (eds), *Transforming Organizations*, New York: Oxford University Press. (This paper sheds light over the personal as well as the organizational implementation of telework schemes.)

Bailyn, L. (1993) 'Patterned chaos in human resource management', *Sloan Management Review* 34 (2): 77–83. (This article suggests that organizations have to learn to respond with more flexibility to their employees.)

Daniels, K., Lamand, D.A. and Standen, P. (eds) (2000) *Making Telework: Perspectives from Human Resource Management and Work Psychology*, London: Thomson Learning. (Provides an integrated and comprehensive account of the human resource management of teleworkers.)

Gray, M., Hodson, N. and Gordon, G. (1994) *Teleworking Explained*, New York: Wiley. (The authors suggest a series of three training sessions: for teleworkers, their managers and a joint session for both of them.)

Hall, D.T. (1993) 'The role of workplace: flexibility in managing diversity', *Organizational Dynamics* 22 (1): 5–18. (This study, based on a survey of executives suggests that while telework provides an employee-friendly environment, it can also promote the organization's strategic objectives.)

Hall, D.T. and Richter, J. (1988) 'Balancing work life and home life: what can organizations do to help?', *Academy of Management Executive* 2 (3): 213–33. (An analysis of everyday boundary and transition issues in the relationship between work/home domains and the options organizations can consider to ease those transitions.)

* Hall, D.T. and Richter, J. (1990) 'Career gridlock: baby boomers hit the wall', *Academy of Management Executive* 5 (3): 7–22. (An illuminating article which examines the ways in which work organizations have been affected by baby boomers.)

* Huws, U., Korte, W.B. and Robinson, S. (1990) *Telework: Towards the Elusive Office*, New York: Wiley. (This useful book, based on major European studies, provides a broad spectrum examination into the concept of telework.)

Moktarian, P.L. and Salomon, I. (1994) 'Modeling the choice of telecommuting: setting the context', *Environment and Planning* 26 (5): 749–66. (A theoretical paper which introduces a conceptual model of the individual decision to telecommute.)

Ogozalek, V.Z. (1991) 'The social impacts of computing: computer technology and the graying of America', *Social Science Computer Review* 9 (4): 655–66. (A review of interdisciplinary literature which concludes that electronic technologies are making it more feasible for the elderly to work from home after retirement.)

Olson, M.H. (1988) 'Corporate culture and the home worker', in K.E. Christensen (ed.), *The New Era of Home-based Work*, Boulder, CO: Westview Press. (The author reports that supervisors' control was the main implicit criterion for organizational evaluation of the telecommuting pilot projects that she studied.)

Perin, C. (1990) 'The moral fabric of the office: Panopticon discourse and schedule flexibilities', in P.S. Tolbert and S.R. Barley (eds), *Research in the Sociology of Organizations*, Greenwich, CT: JAI Press Inc. (An account of several cases which indicate that the adoption of home work is problematic from both the organizational and the individual points of view.)

* Richter, J. and Meshulam, I. (1993) 'Telework at home: the home and the organization perspective', *Human Systems Management* 12 (3): 193–203. (An illuminating theoretical paper introduces the daily challenges faced both at home and in the organizational arenas by telework.)

* Shamir, B. (1993) 'Home: the perfect workplace', in S. Zedeck (ed.), *Work, Families and Organizations*, San Francisco, CA: Jossey Bass. (A theoretical survey and analysis of adjustment problems that emerge from telework, which points out some research implications from a self-concept perspective.)

See also: FAMILY–WORK ISSUES; HUMAN RESOURCE MANAGEMENT; INFORMATION AND KNOWLEDGE INDUSTRY; INTERNET; WORLD WIDE WEB

Term structure of interest rates

Overview

Financial securities that promise one or more fixed cash payments in the future are known as fixed interest securities. Examples include central government bills and bonds, local government (municipal) bonds, corporate bonds and mortgages. The rates of return offered on these various securities differ for a number of reasons, including the risk of default and the tax treatment of the promised payments. The term structure of interest rates describes the relationship between fixed interest securities that differ only in their time to maturity, that is, the length of time until the principal amount of the loan is repaid. The differences between interest rates for payments at different maturities reflect expectations about future interest rates and the preferences of investors.

Pure discount (zero coupon) bonds make a single cash payment at a fixed future date. The rates of return on pure discount bonds are the interest rates that make up the term structure. In many practical situations, the pure discount bond market does not cover the full maturity spectrum of all fixed interest securities, and sophisticated mathematical techniques are required to estimate the term structure. In addition, models have been developed to describe the behaviour of the term structure over time. Knowledge of the term structure is important for the accurate comparison of fixed interest securities, particularly newly issued securities against existing securities, and for understanding the future direction of general interest rate movements.

1 Interest rates

Most individuals would prefer to receive a certain cash sum now rather than wait until some future date. To induce saving, an appropriate rate of exchange has to be offered, a point first made by Fisher (1965). For example, an individual may be prepared to forgo spending £1 now, and invest this sum in exchange for receiving £1.10 next year. The rate of exchange between money now and money in the future is expressed as a percentage annual rate of interest, in this case, of 10 per cent.

The rate of exchange characteristic of interest rates permits cash payments and receipts that occur at different times to be compared consistently and exchanged through time. For example, suppose that we were offered the choice between receiving £1 today, or £1.10 next year. If the interest rate on a one-year investment is 10 per cent, then the two alternatives are equivalent. If we receive £1 today, we are able to invest the cash for one year at 10 per cent interest and receive in return £1.10 next year. So, receiving £1 today is worth the same as receiving £1.10 next year. However, if the interest rate were greater than 10 per cent, say 15 per cent, we would prefer to receive £1 now since this will be worth £1.15 next year. Similarly if the interest rate were less than 10 per cent we would prefer to receive £1.10 next year, since the £1 received today would be worth less than £1.10 next year.

So far, we have compared two cash alternatives at some future date, that is, we have compared the future values of the two alternatives. However, it is more usual to compare the present values of various cash alternatives. This is because the present business environment within which the alternatives are being compared has less uncertainty than any future business environment. In the previous example, the future cash sum of £1.10 has a present value of £1.00 if the interest rate is 10 per cent. We say that we have discounted back the future sum to its present value, and often refer to the interest rate as a discount rate. However, if the interest rate were less than 10 per cent, say 8 per cent, the present value of £1.10 would be (approximately) £1.02. In that case, receiving £1.10 next year is worth more (in today's terms) than receiving £1.00 now. However, the £1.10 cash payment occurs next year, which may not match our spending plans now. In that circumstance, we could borrow £1.02 today, on the promise to pay back £1.10 (£1.02 plus interest at 8 per cent) next year. Since we know that we are sure to receive that £1.10 payment next year, we know that we will be able to repay our loan.

More generally, if we denote the interest rate as i, the future cash sum as F, and the present value as P, the mathematical relationship between them can be written as:

$$P = \frac{F}{(1+i)} \qquad (1)$$

This formula can be extended to cover situations where cash is invested for more than one year, or where cash is to be received in more than one year's time. If we invest £1.00 for two years at an interest rate of 10 per cent, and reinvest the interest received at the end of the first year, the future balance of the investment at the end of the second year will be £1.00(1.10)(1.10) = £1.10(1.10) = £1.21. We have received interest totalling £0.21 on the investment of £1.00. The £0.21 is comprised of two £0.10 (10 per cent) interest payments on the initial sum invested, plus the amount of £0.01 which is one year's interest (at 10 per cent) on the £0.10 interest reinvested at the end of the first period. Thus, the future value of a sum invested for n years can be written as:

$$F = P(1+i)^n \qquad (2)$$

where the other terms are as previously defined. This compound interest formula can be rearranged to give the present value of a sum to be received in more than one year's time, that is:

$$P = \frac{F}{(1+i)^n} \qquad (3)$$

For example, the present value of £1.21 to be received in two year's time is £1.00, if the interest rate is 10 per cent.

In many circumstances, a particular investment may make or require more than one future cash payment. The formulae for the future and present value of a single cash payment can be extended to include cases of multiple cash payments. If we denote the series of cash payments as $C_1, C_2, \ldots C_n$, where C_j refers to the cash payment at the end of year j, then the future value of this series of cash payments is given by:

$$F = C_1(1+i)^{n-1} + C_2(1+i)^{n-2} + C_3(1+i)^{n-3} + \ldots + C_n \qquad (4)$$

and the present value of the series of cash payments is given by:

$$P = \frac{C_1}{(1+i)} + \frac{C_2}{(1+i)^2} + \frac{C_3}{(1+i)^3} + K + \frac{C_n}{(1+i)^n} \qquad (5)$$

In both equations (4) and (5), the interest rate that is being used to compound or discount each payment is the same regardless of the date at which the payment is made. This need not be the case and, in general, different rates will apply for different payment dates. However, each payment date will have a unique interest rate associated with it. The set of these unique interest rates is known as the term structure of interest rates.

2 The pricing of fixed interest securities

Pure discount bonds promise a single fixed cash sum at a fixed date in the future. Pure discount bonds are so called because they are sold at a price which is less than (at a discount to) the fixed future cash sum, and are free of further payments, tax liability, default risk or special provisions. Treasury bills issued by the government in a number of countries are an example of pure discount bonds. The price of a pure discount bond is determined by discounting the future cash sum at the interest rate that is appropriate for the payment date of the future cash sum. For example, a pure discount bond that will pay £100 in one year's time, will be priced at £90.91, if the interest rate for payments occurring in one year's time is 10 per cent. However, it is more usual to consider the interest rate as being determined by the price of the pure discount bond, rather than the price being determined by the interest rate, as follows:

$$R_1 = \frac{£100 - £90.91}{£90.91} = 0.1 \qquad (6)$$

where R_1 is the interest rate for cash payments occurring in one year's time. Similarly, the current prices of pure discount bonds of other maturities will have interest rates associated with those maturities. The set of these interest rates is the set of rates that makes up the term structure of interest rates. These interest rates are also known as spot interest rates, or spot rates. So, in the above example, the one-year spot rate is 10 per cent (see CAPITAL MARKETS, REGULATION OF).

To prevent arbitrage opportunities all securities which include a payment at the same date as this pure discount bond, must also command this same interest rate. An arbitrage opportunity is a trading opportunity which permits immediate, unlimited and risk-free cash payments. For example, if two one-year pure discount bonds, both promising £100 at maturity, had prices of £90.91 and £89.29, then this would imply two one-year spot interest rates, of 10 per cent and 12 per cent respectively. Rational investors would respond to this opportunity by selling the higher priced bonds and reinvesting in the lower priced bonds. This would not affect the future cash inflow, since either bond would pay the investors £100, but the switch would save them £1.62 now. The demand to effect this switch between the two bonds would be unlimited unless the bond prices adjusted so as to eliminate the arbitrage opportunity.

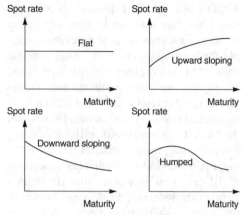

Figure 1 The different shapes of the term structure of interest rates

In the absence of arbitrage opportunities, the term structure of interest rates is uniquely defined. However, at any given moment in time, the interest rates associated with different future payment dates need not be the same. So, the one-year spot rate could be 10 per cent while the two-year spot rate could be 12 per cent. Figure 1 illustrates a number of possible shapes of the term structure.

The term structure of interest rates can be used to determine the prices of other fixed interest securities, since most fixed interest securities are composed of different combinations of pure discount bonds. This procedure can be illustrated by considering the case of default-free coupon paying bonds. Examples of these bonds include US Treasury bonds and UK gilt-edged stocks. A two-year 10 per cent annual coupon bond with a repayment at maturity of £1000 will make the following three cash payments. At maturity, in two year's time, it will pay the £1000 face value of the bond plus a coupon equal to 10 per cent of this value. In one year's time from now, the bond will also make a £100 coupon payment. The price of this bond is equal to the present value of these future cash payments, and can be calculated using equation (5).

$$P = \frac{£100}{(1.1)} + \frac{£100}{(1.12)^2} + \frac{£1000}{(1.12)^2}$$

$$= £90.91 + £79.72 + £797.20 \qquad (7)$$

$$= £967.83$$

This equation demonstrates the building block characteristic of pure discount bonds. This two-year bond gives the same cash payments as a combination of a one-year pure discount bond and eleven two-year pure discount bonds. To prevent arbitrage opportunities, the two-year bond must be priced consistently with the embedded pure discount bonds.

For pure discount bonds, the rate of return on the investment is uniquely defined. In contrast, the coupon bond has two rates of return in its pricing formula. An average rate of return on a coupon bond can be calculated by finding the interest rate that equates the price of the bond to the present value of the cash payments:

$$£967.80 = \frac{£100}{(1+y)} + \frac{£100}{(1+y)^2} + \frac{£1000}{(1+y)^2} \quad (8)$$

$$\Rightarrow y = 11.90\%$$

The interest rate y is known as the yield to maturity (or redemption yield) of the bond. For pure discount bonds, the yield to maturity is equal to the spot interest rate, and for this reason the term structure of interest rates is often referred to as the yield curve. Unlike the term structure of interest rates, there is a distinct yield curve for each coupon level, with the zero coupon yield curve being the term structure of interest rates curve.

3 Measuring the term structure of interest rates

The determination of the prices of coupon paying bonds, and other more complex fixed interest securities, requires reliable observations of the term structure of spot interest rates. Spot interest rates can be calculated from the prices of pure discount bonds. However, in practice, pure discount bonds tend to have short maturities, so that the pricing of

longer maturity coupon bonds is not possible. Thus, the identification of the term structure of interest rates is undertaken using coupon paying bonds. Consider the following example of the prices and cash payments of two coupon bonds, as shown in Table 1.

The prices, coupons and spot interest rates are related as:

$$£94.54 = £104.00 \left[\frac{1}{1+R_1} \right]$$

$$£96.78 = £10.00 \left[\frac{1}{1+R_1} \right] \qquad (9)$$

$$+ £110.00 \left[\frac{1}{1+R_2} \right]^2$$

which can be solved to give:

$$\left[\frac{1}{1+R_1} \right] = 0.9091 \Rightarrow R_1 = 10\%$$

$$\left[\frac{1}{1+R_2} \right]^2 = 0.7972 \Rightarrow R_2 = 12\% \qquad (10)$$

This method can be extended using additional bonds until the term structure has been identified along the whole of the maturity spectrum. This amounts to solving the following equation simultaneously for all the bonds in the market, to extract the interest rates that are discounting the cash flows to the current price of each of the bonds:

$$p = \frac{C}{(1+R_1)} + \frac{C}{(1+R_2)^2}$$

$$+ \frac{C}{(1+R_3)^3} + \ldots + \frac{C+F}{(1+R_n)^n} \qquad (11)$$

In this equation, p is the price of a bond, F is the face value which is paid in n period's time,

Table 1 Prices and cash payments of two coupon bonds

	Price	Cash flows	
	Now	End of year 1	End of year 2
Bond 1	£94.54	£104.00	–
Bond 2	£96.78	£10.00	£110.00

and C is the per period coupon payment. The term structure of interest rates is the set of interest rates $R_1, R_2, R_3, ... R_n$. The simultaneous solution of equation (11) for all bonds requires some matrix algebra, and will work provided that the number of bonds greatly exceeds the number of coupon payment dates. Techniques using the mathematics of approximation theory have been developed for cases where bonds do not have regular payment dates and so the number of payment dates exceeds the number of bonds. These methods also permit the identification of spot rates for dates at which no existing bond makes a payment. The approximation method has become the standard technique for term structure estimation (Schaefer 1981; Steeley 1991).

4 Explaining the term structure of interest rates

Theories of the term structure provide an economic rationale for the varying shapes of the term structure of interest rates that can be observed. These theories can be separated into those which seek to explain the current shape of the term structure, and those which seek to explain the movement of the term structure through time.

According to the expectations theory, the shape of the term structure is determined by expectations of future one period spot interest rates. If the term structure is upward sloping, then short maturity spot interest rates are expected to rise in the future. Conversely, a set of decreasing spot rates indicates that future short maturity spot rates are expected to fall.

This theory can be represented more precisely by considering the earlier example where the one-year spot rate was 10 per cent and the two-year spot rate was 12 per cent. The expectations theory says that in one year's time, the one-year spot rate is expected to be greater than its current value of 10 per cent. Consider an investor who wishes to invest £100 for two years. An investment at the two-year spot rate of 12 per cent would produce £100(1.12)(1.12) = £125.44 at the end of the two years. Suppose that the investor expects the one-year spot rate in one year's time to be 15 per cent, then by investing at the one-year rate of 10 per cent and rolling over

the proceeds into the expected one-year rate of 15 per cent, the investor would receive £100(1.10)(1.15) = £126.50. The rollover strategy would be preferred by this investor. If a future one-year spot rate of 15 per cent was expected by all investors, no investors would want to buy the two-year investment. Indeed, they would like to borrow at the two-year rate in order to invest in the rollover strategy, since they expect their proceeds (£126.50) to outweigh the repayment of their borrowing (£125.44). Market forces will adjust the two-year rate until it reflects aggregate market expectations of the future one-year rate.

The future one-year rate implied by a two-year rate of 12 per cent (and a one-year rate of 10 per cent) is 14.04 per cent. This rate is called a forward interest rate, and will be denoted f_2. The subscript refers to the maturity date of the forward rate. It is not necessary to indicate the start date of the forward rate since most practical applications use one-period forward rates. The forward rate is calculated by equating the proceeds from the two-year spot rate and the rollover strategy at the end of two years:

$$(1+R_1)(1+f_2) = (1+R_2)^2$$
$$(1.10)(1+f_2) = (1.12)^2 \qquad (12)$$
$$\Rightarrow f_2 = 14.04\%$$

In general, the one-year forward rate for the year ending n years from now can be calculated using the formula:

$$f_n = \frac{(1+R_n)^n}{(1+R_{n-1})^{n-1}} \qquad (13)$$

The expectations hypothesis says that the forward rate for the year ending n years from now is the market's expectation of the one-year spot rate in $n-1$ years from now. If one-year spot rates are expected to rise, forward rates will be greater then one-year spot rates. If forward rates are greater than one-year spot rates, then spot rates of longer maturities will be greater than those of shorter maturities, and an upward sloping term structure will be observed.

While the expectations hypothesis connects the shape of the term structure to interest rate expectations, it does not specify the source of the interest rate expectations. Market interest rates are nominal interest rates, and reflect the actual cash payments. In the presence of goods price inflation, the real value of interest payments is less than the nominal interest payments. Real and nominal interest rates are related by the formula:

$$(1+R) = (1+\pi)(1+r) \qquad (14)$$

where R is the nominal rate, r is the real rate, and π is the inflation rate. While nominal spot interest rates are observable, the inflation rate over the same time period is unobservable, and so nominal rates are comprised of expected real rates and expected inflation rates. If the real interest rate is expected to remain constant through time, but inflation is expected to increase steadily, the term structure of nominal spot rates would be expected to slope upwards. Similarly, downward sloping term structures would tend to be observed when inflation rates are expected to fall in the future.

As inflation tends to cycle alongside general economic expansions and contractions of the economy, the shape of the term structure might be expected to cycle from upward to downward sloping (see BUSINESS CYCLES). However, an examination of historical term structures suggests that there have been more occurrences of upward sloping term structures than this explanation would predict. The preponderance of upward sloping term structures has been explained by the liquidity preference theory. If the term structure were flat, then borrowing and lending for any maturity would carry the same annual interest rate. This means that long-term borrowers would incur the same interest charges as short-term borrowers, and short-term lenders would receive the same interest payment as long-term lenders. Given most individuals' predisposition to spending sooner rather than later, they are going to prefer to lend over the short term and borrow over the long term, rather than the reverse. If the term structure is flat they will willingly do this. The only way to induce lending over the longer term and discourage borrowing over the longer term is to offer a premium on the interest rate at longer maturities. This premium is called a liquidity premium because it compensates investors for the loss of short-term liquidity when they invest over longer time horizons.

The segmented markets theories maintain that investors have strong preferences for particular maturities of debt, because they have risks of distinct maturities that need to be hedged. For example, commercial banks and corporate investors may prefer to hedge their risk in short-term securities, while investment institutions and pension funds may prefer to hedge their longer-term liabilities in longer-term securities. The strong desire to match the maturities of assets and liabilities leads risk-averse investors to desire a premium to be induced to move from their preferred maturity habitats.

Further explanations of the shape of the term structure are provided by models of the changes in interest rates. These models assume that the term structure moves through time in response to changes in one or more underlying random variables, known as state variables. Empirical evidence, using the technique of principal components analysis, has indicated that there are three random variables influencing the behaviour of the term structure over time. However, the first variable appears to control around 90 per cent of the behaviour of the term structure over time, while the second and third variables control around 7 and 3 per cent respectively (Steeley 1992). In response to this observation, term structure models have used one or sometimes two underlying state variables. In the spirit of the expectations hypothesis, where the term structure is explained by uncertainty regarding future one-period spot rates, one of these random variables is assumed to be the shortest maturity interest rate. The key feature of these state variables is that by assuming a particular model of the changes in these random variables over time, and a model of investor risk preferences, the whole of the current term structure can be calibrated with reference to the current level of these random variables.

These models are framed within the mathematics of stochastic calculus, and are therefore concerned with limiting values of continuous functions of random variables. For example, in the single state variable models, the random variable is the interest rate on a security which matures at the end of the next infinitesimal interval of time. A useful introduction to these models can be found in Hull (1993). The behaviour of this interest rate over subsequent infinitesimal time intervals is assumed to be determined by a stochastic differential equation. While the models can be derived more precisely within this framework, practical implementation requires an approximately equivalent model for use with data observed at small, but measurable, intervals.

The specification of the short interest rate process that has been used in the state variable models is of the following kind:

$$\Delta R_t = \alpha\left(R^* - R_{t-1}\right) + u_t \tag{15}$$

where R_t is the value of the shortest maturity interest rate at time t and $\Delta R_t = R_t - R_{t-1}$. In this model, the interest rate is pulled elastically towards a long term 'target' or 'equilibrium' level, R^*. In macroeconomic contexts, this adjustment process is often referred to as a partial adjustment model. The constant coefficient α measures the speed of the mean reversion by the interest rate. The variable u_t is a random disturbance term which causes the interest rate to deviate from its current mean reverting path to a new path beginning at the new level of the interest rate. This random disturbance term is assumed to take the value of zero, on average. In the case where the variability of the disturbance is assumed to be constant, the stochastic differential equation equivalent to this model is known as the Ornstein–Uhlenbeck process or elastic

random walk. However, the assumption of constant variance means that the interest rate can become negative, which is unrealistic for a nominal interest rate. If the variability is assumed to be proportional to the level of the interest rate, this possibility is avoided. However, the introduction of a form of heteroscedasticity into the disturbance term means that sophisticated econometric techniques must be used to identify R^*, α and the constant of proportionality in the interest rate variability. However, once the parameters of the state variable models have been estimated and the model of risk preferences has been established, the whole of the term structure can be calibrated. The relative sizes of the estimated parameters determine whether the models will generate upward sloping, downward sloping or humped term structures.

Although both one and two factor state variable models can capture many term structure shapes, they are unable to capture all of the shapes that have been observed in historical term structures. An alternative approach to modelling the behaviour of the term structure over time involves measuring the current term structure and then determining the possible future paths of this term structure that do not permit any arbitrage opportunities. These models are known as arbitrage free rate models, and were developed initially in the form of a binomial tree. Figure 2 illustrates this structure. At any point in time, the term structure can move up or down, and will follow a particular path through the binomial tree over time. It has been shown that this model can also be represented as a single state variable model. The approximate discrete time equivalent of this model is:

$$\Delta R_t = f(t) + u_t \tag{16}$$

where $f(t)$ is chosen to ensure that the model exactly fits the current term structure, and that arbitrage opportunities are absent. Specifically, the deterministic function $f(t)$ depends upon the level and a constant variability of the current short interest rate, and time. The function $f(t)$ can also be extended to include the mean reversion found in historical interest rate series, and the whole model can be extended to permit more flexible volatility structures.

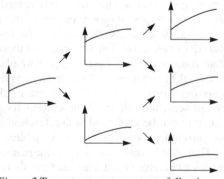

Figure 2 Term structure movements following a binomial tree

Table 2 Price and cash flows of two bonds

	8% coupon bond price = £100.00		4% coupon bond price = £97.20	
Marginal tax rate	After tax cash flow	After tax return	After tax cash flow	After tax return
0%	£108.00	8.0	£104.00	7.0
25%	£106.00	6.0	£103.00	6.0
40%	£104.80	4.8	£102.40	5.4

5 The effects of taxes on the term structure

In the presence of taxes on the cash flows of fixed interest investments, the before-tax and after-tax rates of return on the investment will be different (see CASH FLOW ACCOUNTING). This means that investors in different tax brackets will face different rates of return on the same fixed interest investment. As a result, the zero tax rate term structure of interest rates becomes one of a family of term structures that are defined with respect to each tax bracket. The calculation of after-tax term structures depends crucially on the tax rules that the investors are facing. In cases where coupon income is taxed at different rates to the capital change on the price of the bond, the term structure for a particular income tax bracket will depend on those bonds that are rationally held by investors in that income tax bracket. The example in Table 2 demonstrates this principle.

Table 2 shows the prices and cash flows of two bonds, each paying a single coupon at maturity in one year's time. The 8 per cent bond provides a cash flow of £108 to a tax exempt investor. Tax on the £8 coupon payment reduces these cash flows to £106 and £104.80 for investors in the 25 per cent and 40 per cent tax brackets. A smaller proportion of the cash flow on the 4 per cent bond is taxable. So, at the prices given, the 8 per cent bond gives a greater after tax return at tax rates below 25 per cent, and a lower rate of return at higher tax rates.

While the one-year spot rate is uniquely defined for the 25 per cent tax bracket, there are two spot rates (one associated with each bond) for all other tax rates. The correct spot rate is the one that is discounting those bonds that are

rationally held by investors in that tax bracket. In this case, no rational tax exempt investor would hold the 4 per cent bond, since it offers a lower rate of return than the 8 per cent bond. This means that the one-year spot rate for tax exempt investors is 8 per cent. Similarly, the spot rate for investors paying 40 per cent tax on coupon income is 5.4 per cent, since only the 4 per cent bond will be held by investors in that tax bracket. Clearly, the term structure for individuals in a particular tax bracket is determined by those bonds that they rationally hold.

If tax segmentation is not taken into account when the term structure is being estimated, the resulting estimates will be downwards biased. This is because the estimates will be an average of the correct term structure for that tax bracket and the lower rates available on bonds that are not rationally held by investors in that tax bracket. By averaging across the correct and the incorrect interest rates, the term structure that is unique to that tax bracket will not be identified.

In the presence of tax segmentation, the relationship between the price and cash flows of a bond, equation (11) will become:

$$p \geq \frac{C}{(1+R_1)} + \frac{C}{(1+R_2)^2} + \frac{C}{(1+R_3)^3} \\ + \ldots + \frac{C+F}{(1+R_n)^n} \tag{17}$$

where, now, C is the per period after-tax coupon payment, and the term structure of interest rates, R_1, R_2, R_3, $\ldots R_n$ is the correct term structure for that tax bracket. The equation holds as an equality only if the bond concerned is rationally held by investors in that tax bracket. Bonds that are not rationally held

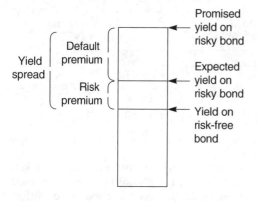

Figure 3 Default and risk premiums on bond yields

have a lower rate of return, and so higher price, than those that are rationally held. The inequality feature of this relationship has been exploited in a method to estimate term structures in the presence of tax segmentation. This method involves the technique of linear programming, which optimizes some objective function subject to inequality constraints. In the presence of tax segmentation, the matrix and approximation techniques that have been developed for term structure estimation in the absence of taxes, can be embedded within the linear programming framework (Hodges and Schaefer 1977; Schaefer 1980, 1981).

6 The effects of default risk on the term structure

Unlike government bonds, for corporate bonds there is a risk that the cash flows that are due to the holders of the bonds will not be made. In compensation for this risk, the expected yield to maturity on a corporate bond will be greater than that on a default-free bond with the same coupon rate and maturity date. The difference between these two yields is known as the bond's risk premium. The maximum yield to maturity on a corporate bond will be realized if the bond issuer does not default on any payments. This yield is called the promised yield to maturity. The difference between the promised yield to maturity and the expected yield to maturity is called the bond's default premium. The difference between the promised yield and the yield on

an otherwise equivalent default-free bond is called the yield spread. Figure 3 illustrates these terms.

The expected yield to maturity will depend on the likelihood of the promised payments being made. A number of econometric models have been developed to predict the likelihood that a bond issuer will default. Variables that have been used to predict the risk of default include corporate earnings variability, the length of time the firm has operated without defaulting on a payment, and various financial ratios calculated from the corporate balance sheet, such as leverage (or gearing) and asset turnover.

A number of agencies produce classifications of corporate bonds based upon their own assessment of the likelihood of default. The two most widely used services are operated by Standard and Poor's Corporation and Moody's Investors Service Inc. Bonds that are assigned to one of the top four categories are known as investment grade bonds, while bonds that are assigned to lower categories are known as speculative bonds. Very low rated bonds are often called junk bonds. The econometric models mentioned above have been used to attempt to reproduce the bond rating classifications given by Moody's and Standard and Poor's, with around 70–80 per cent accuracy. This is a useful exercise, for example, if a company wishes to borrow cash directly from a financial institution rather than by issuing securities. The model can be used to imply the classification attached to the borrowing, which in turn can be used to set the appropriate interest rate and assess the likelihood of repayment.

7 Conclusion

The variety of rates of return on fixed interest securities reflect many factors. These include the maturity of the investment, the likelihood of default and the tax treatment of the promised payments. The term structure of interest rates focuses on the most fundamental difference between fixed interest securities, that is, the relationship between the maturity of the investment and the interest rate offered.

This relationship is a complex one and sophisticated mathematical techniques may be required to measure and model the term structure. However, the pay-off to understanding the term structure is large. It provides information to investors and economic policy makers on interest rate expectations, liquidity and risk preferences, and statistically probable movements in interest rates.

JAMES M. STEELEY
BANK OF ENGLAND

Further reading

(References cited in the text marked *)

Alexander, G.J., Sharpe, W.F. and Bailey, J.V. (1993) *Fundamentals of Investments*, Englewood Cliffs, NJ: Prentice Hall. (Chapter 21 of this textbook provides an extensive discussion of the impact of default risk on interest rates.)

Cox, J.C., Ingersoll, J.E. and Ross, S.A. (1981) 'A re-examination of traditional hypotheses about the term structure of interest rates', *Journal of Finance* 36 (4): 769–99. (Provides a rigorous re-interpretation of the traditional theories of the term structure, using valuation techniques that were not available when the theories were first developed.)

Dobson, S., Sutch, R. and Vanderford, D. (1976) 'An evaluation of alternative empirical models of the term structure of interest rates', *Journal of Finance* 31 (4): 1035–66. (Considers the empirical evidence in support of the different traditional term structure theories.)

Fabozzi, F.J. (1989) *Bond Markets, Analysis and Strategies*, Englewood Cliffs, NJ: Prentice Hall. (Provides an overview of the market in fixed income securities, with particular reference to the US market.)

* Fisher, I. (1965) *The Theory of Interest: As Determined by Impatience to Spend Income and Opportunity to Invest It*, New York: Augustus M. Kelley Publishers. (This book, originally published in 1930, is the classic work on interest rates.)

* Hodges, S.D. and Schaefer, S.M. (1977) 'A model for bond portfolio improvement', *Journal of Financial and Quantitative Analysis* 12 (2): 243–60. (Provides the details of the linear programming framework for the pricing of bonds and the extraction of term structure estimates.)

* Hull, J. (1993) *Options, Futures and other Derivative Securities*, Englewood Cliffs, NJ: Prentice Hall. (Chapter 15 of this book contains an integrated presentation of the different models of the dynamic behaviour of the term structure, and their application to pricing bond options.)

Phillips, P. (1987) *Inside the New Gilt-Edged Market*, Cambridge: Woodhead-Faulkner. (The standard reference for participants in the UK fixed interest securities market.)

Schaefer, S.M. (1977) 'The problem with redemption yields', *Financial Analysts Journal* 33 (July–August): 59–67. (Explains the relationships between constant coupon yield curves and the term structure of interest rates.)

* Schaefer, S.M. (1980) 'Taxes and security market equilibrium', in W.F. Sharpe (ed.), *Financial Economics: Essays in Honor of Paul H. Cootner*, Englewood Cliffs, NJ: Prentice Hall. (Examines the impact of different tax rules on the pricing of financial securities.)

* Schaefer, S.M. (1981) 'Measuring a tax-specific term structure of interest rates in the market for British Government securities', *Economic Journal*, 91 (June): 415–38. (Shows how to estimate the term structure of interest rates where taxes are segmenting the bond market.)

* Steeley, J.M. (1991) 'Estimating the gilt-edged term structure: basis splines and confidence intervals', *Journal of Business Finance and Accounting* 18 (4): 513–29. (Shows how to estimate the term structure of interest rates using mathematical approximation theory and how to assess the accuracy of the estimates obtained.)

* Steeley, J.M. (1992) 'Some developments in measuring and modelling the term structure of interest rates', in S. Hodges (ed.), *Options: Recent Advances in Theory and Practice*, vol. 2, Manchester: Manchester University Press. (Presents evidence on the number of state variables influencing the term structure, and on the dynamic behaviour of interest rates.)

See also: CAPITAL, COST OF; CAPITAL MARKETS, REGULATION OF; INTEREST RATE RISK; TAXATION, CORPORATE

Testing

Overview

Testing refers to the manner by which organizations gather and use information to make staffing decisions (e.g. entry-level hiring, promotion). A test is any systematic procedure for measuring a sample of behaviour. These include, for example, standardized written paper-and-pencil tests designed to measure cognitive capabilities or personality traits, structured interviews that require the candidate to respond to particular questions, and work sample performance tests that call for the candidate to simulate important aspects of the job. Organizations use these tests to assess the various knowledge, skills and abilities (KSAs) needed to successfully perform the tasks of a job. These KSAs range from general cognitive capabilities and personality facets to more specific job knowledge and skills. Candidate scores on tests are indicators of whether individuals have the relevant competencies required to effectively perform a particular job. Thus, various staffing decisions can be made based on candidate test performance.

1 Introduction

Organizations tend to focus on areas such as strategy, structure, job design and people. As the new century begins, an emphasis has been placed on this last category, people, as a critical area of competitive advantage for organizations. Other types of competitive advantage are readily available (e.g. capital can be borrowed, technology can be copied). Only people with the skills and knowledge they possess are left to make the difference between organizational success and failure. Organizations must have the 'right' people with the 'right' stuff in order to effectively compete in today's business world. Assessment of personnel through testing provides the information needed to determine who are the 'right' people that have the 'right' stuff. Testing is used to measure if individuals have the skills and capabilities required for success in organizational positions.

The logic of testing is the following: (1) people have individual differences, (2) these individual differences matter in terms of performance, and (3) these individual differences can be measured. Tests are psychological instruments, techniques or procedures that measure these individual differences. Thus, testing revolves around the notion of prediction – the idea that scores on a test will predict performance on a job. In this employment context, tests are called 'predictors' while aspects of job performance are labelled 'criteria'. The testing model focuses on developing hypotheses regarding the relationship between predictors and criteria for particular jobs.

The testing model begins with determining which individual capabilities are required to be effective in a particular job position. A procedure called a job analysis is performed to obtain this information. The job analysis identifies the critical competencies (KSAs) required to effectively perform the tasks of the target job. The next step is to procure tests that measure these critical competencies. These tests can be built from scratch or may already exist for particular competencies. Finally, the tests are administered to job candidates. Candidate scores on these tests are then utilized to make staffing decisions (e.g. 'who to hire?', 'who to promote?') (see RECRUITMENT AND SELECTION).

The use of tests by work organizations has a long history that goes back to intelligence testing for armed forces recruits during the First World War. The Army General Classification Test was developed to select recruits for various military duties. This test was a paper-and-pencil written examination that focused on intellectual capabilities. The army also used other assessment devices such as situational tests to determine which persons were best suited for dangerous espionage jobs. These tests required recruits to perform 'hands-on' activities and focused on measuring their ability to perform under duress in difficult, trying conditions. However, in general, much of the early work on testing in personnel selection and placement focused on measuring intelligence using a written paper-and-pencil format. Building on the work of psychologists such as Alfred Binet and Lewis Terman who pioneered the concept of IQ (intelligence quotient) to examine children and educational issues, personnel psychologists adapted intelligence tests to predict job performance in work organizations.

Today, most organizations use some form of testing when making staffing decisions that include choosing persons to fill entry-level positions in an organization, determining who to promote to upper level managerial positions, and deciding which persons require various types of training. To accomplish these objectives, testing has greatly expanded beyond written paper-and-pencil intelligence tests to include numerous formats and a wide variety of tests that capture a vast array of aptitudes, abilities, interests and personality characteristics.

2 Evaluating tests

Before discussing the types of tests available to organizations, it is important to understand how to properly evaluate these tests. The three critical criteria used to evaluate tests are (1) validity, (2) adverse impact, and (3) utility.

Validity

Validity refers to the predictive capability of the test. It focuses on the accuracy of your predictorcriterion hypothesis. That is, do individual differences on the competencies measured by your test predict performance on the target job? One psychometric characteristic that validity rests upon is the notion of reliability. Reliability refers to the degree to which

the predictor produces dependable or consistent results. It is the extent to which the test minimizes sources of error (e.g. candidate fatigue or anxiousness) so that a 'true' picture of the applicant's ability is captured. In other words, scores on a test are theoretically composed of the 'true' score for the candidate and random error. To the extent that random error is reduced, test reliability is increased. There are multiple ways to estimate the reliability of a test. For example, 'testretest reliability' is administering the same test to the same candidate at two different times. If the test scores from the first and second test administration are close to equivalent, this indicates that the test is reliable.

Validity is the extent to which the test is accurate. In a selection context, validity is conceptualized in two ways. First, does the test measure accurately what it is supposed to measure? For example, does the test of extraversion in fact measure this attribute? Second, does the test accurately predict criteria? That is, does the test forecast aspects of job performance as hypothesized? For example, do scores on an extraversion test predict candidate performance in a sales job?

As noted above, reliability is a critical component of validity. However, while reliability is necessary for validity, it not sufficient for validity. If a test is not reliable, it cannot be valid. The logic is if the test does not capture a 'true' picture in a consistent manner, then it cannot validly predict criteria such as job performance. However, a test could be highly reliable, but have no validity. That is, the test could measure something in a consistent manner but not be predictive of any criteria.

Validity is a psychometric characteristic that is inferred from evidence that is gathered. Three strategies for gathering validity evidence are (1) construct validity, (2) criterion-related validity, and (3) content validity. Construct validity focuses on the extent to which the test accurately measures the competency it is supposed to. A common method of determining this is to see if the test correlates with other established tests of the same construct. Construct validity requires multiple research studies and an accumulation of evidence. Criterion-related validity involves directly examining if the test predicts performance on the job. Test scores are correlated with indicators of job performance to determine the strength of the relationship between the predictor and criterion. Criterion-related validity studies produce validity coefficients which range from -1.00 to $+1.00$. The stronger the correlation coefficient, positive or negative, the more evidence there is for the validity of the test. Content validity entails experts judging whether the test is related to critical aspects of job performance. Thus, rather than collecting data to evaluate the relationship between the predictor and criterion, experts make judgements regarding the strength of the predictorcriterion relationship.

These various strategies are used by organizations to determine the validity of a test. Validity is a critical facet of a test. It is a direct indicator of the usefulness of the scores produced by the test. If a test has high validity, this means that it accurately predicts performance on the target job. If the test has low validity, then it does not provide useful information on how persons will perform on the target job. It is important to realize that the validity of a test is a function of how it is used. While reliability is inherent in the test device itself, validity depends on what the test is used for. For example, a test of interpersonal skills may be valid in predicting job performance for a customer service representative but may not be valid in predicting job performance for a chemist.

Adverse impact

In addition to validity, adverse impact is another critical criteria of a test. Adverse impact focuses on whether tests discriminate based on demographic factors such as ethnicity, gender, religion, age, etc. The concern is that a test may be biased against such subgroups and therefore have a negative impact on test scores produced by group members. Different countries have different sets of regulations protecting against such bias. For example, the USA has a long history of executive orders and regulations that culminated in the passing of the 1964 Civil Rights Act which prohibited discrimination against individuals on the basis of gender, race, colour, national

origin and religion. In the decades that followed, the Civil Rights Act was updated (1991) and additional laws were passed to protect other groups (e.g. Age Discrimination in Employment Act of 1967; Americans with Disabilities Act of 1990). Similarly, European Union countries have legislation protecting against gender bias in staffing; however, not all of these countries consistently enforce such laws.

Legal issues regarding discrimination have had a powerful effect on the use of testing by organizations in the USA (see EQUAL EMPLOYMENT OPPORTUNITIES). The 1978 Uniform Guidelines on Employee Selection Procedures ('Uniform Guidelines') provide guidance to organizations on how to use tests in a legally defensible manner. The Uniform Guidelines were created by the Equal Employment Opportunity Coordinating Council (EEOC), the agency set up to enforce Equal Employment Opportunity legislation. These guidelines establish a set of standards for using testing procedures in a manner that complies with the legal acts and laws passed by Congress. In addition to the Uniform Guidelines, the American Psychological Association (APA) has produced documents designed to help maintain the appropriate use of tests. The Standards for Education and Psychological Tests issued in 1966 and updated most recently in 1985 as well as the Principles for the Validation and Use of Personnel Selection Procedures (produced by the Society for Industrial-Organizational Psychology, a division of APA) issued in 1975 and updated in 1987 provide additional information for organizations seeking to use tests.

While this information pertains to the USA, other countries have their own legal standards. The complexity of these laws varies. In the USA, the legal standards are complicated by the fact that state and local laws exist in addition to the federal Equal Employment Opportunity (EEO) legislation previously described. In addition, decisions in the courts continually interpret and reinterpret the EEO laws, forcing organizations to keep a vigilant eye on the changing standards for using testing in an appropriate manner. In comparison, other countries focus on different issues than the racial and gender-based discrimination cases that have dominated the US legal system. Some countries have focused on preferential treatment in hiring for legal citizens or veterans of armed forces. In general, many other countries provide stronger worker rights than those found in the USA, including rights with regard to selection and hiring. For example, Germany has specific legally fixed rules and regulations for many job-related features including hiring. Other countries such as France have placed restrictions, including due process, on the firing of employees.

Further complicating the situation is the growing number of multinational organizations that are under the jurisdiction of multiple countries. For example, which laws apply to a US-based organization that is using tests to hire workers for a factory they operate in Germany? This is a tough question that has not been answered. The laws of the various countries involved could be in direct conflict with one another, placing the organization in a difficult situation. The US Congress took an ethnocentric approach to this issue by stating in the 1991 Civil Rights Act that all Federal US EEO laws were meant to apply to multinationals. Obviously, other countries may not see the situation in the same way. As legal standards continue to shift and evolve, organizations must constantly monitor and adapt their use of tests in order to remain compliant with the laws of their host country, as well as the other countries within which they operate.

Utility

A final criteria used to evaluate tests is utility. Utility refers to the idea that the benefits of a procedure outweigh the costs of a procedure. With regard to testing, utility is the extent to which the organization gains dollars through increased performance of workers selected based on test scores. Therefore, test utility is the idea that the benefits of the information obtained from a test go beyond the actual expense of using the test. The expenses consist of both direct and indirect costs. Direct costs may include the price of the test device itself (e.g. price of test booklets, answer sheets, computer scoring programs, software packages). Indirect costs may include time spent developing or identifying tests, time

spent administering an exam, and time spent scoring a test and interpreting results. The benefits focus on the increase in productivity of workers hired using test scores compared to workers hired without using test scores.

Utility is a very practical criterion. Most organizations have budgetary constraints with regard to the amount spent on testing procedures. Utility analysis allows organizations to determine the financial gain associated with a testing system. Research shows that the economic value of gains from improved hiring methods are typically quite large (Schmidt and Hunter 1998). However, it is not always clear-cut how to estimate these gains. While the direct cost of a test instrument is relatively easy to calculate, it would be misleading to equate this cost with utility. For example, paper-and-pencil tests may be lower in direct cost compared to 'hands on' performance tests however their ability to predict job performance, and thus their benefit to the organization, may be low. It is important for personnel psychologists to consider all costs and benefits when conducting a utility analysis of their testing system.

Organizations must consider all of these critical criteria (validity, adverse impact and utility) when choosing a test procedure. This may be particularly difficult to accomplish because the criteria are not independent from one another. For example, a test with high validity and high utility may also have high adverse impact against minorities (e.g. written paper-and-pencil cognitive ability tests). On the other hand, a test with high validity and low adverse impact may have low utility because of the expense of the procedure (e.g. 'hands on' work sample performance tests). Organizations need to balance these various concerns depending on the given situation. For instance, with a low level entry position, an organization may not be as concerned with accurate prediction. Therefore, the organization may choose a less valid test that is inexpensive in order to control costs. However, for an upper level position, an organization may be more willing to invest money in the process in order to enhance validity because of the importance of choosing the right person for this critical job position. In summary, an organization will look to maximize all of these important criteria. However, because this is not typically possible, organizations need to carefully choose the proper testing procedure for each particular situation.

3 Testing techniques

A number of different testing techniques are used to measure target competencies or content areas. This provides organizations with a choice as to how to assess the critical competencies of a candidate. The primary techniques are the following: (1) written tests, (2) interviews, and (3) performance tests (see RECRUITMENT AND SELECTION). Written tests are referred to as 'paper-and-pencil' exams that require a written response by the candidate. This written response may be forced choice (e.g. multiple choice or true/false) or open-ended (e.g. essay). Obviously, forced choice written responses are easier to score because there is only one correct response. However, open-ended responses may provide a richer set of information to evaluate, even though it adds difficulty to the scoring process. Written tests have been designed to measure all types of competencies including cognitive skills, personality facets and specific job knowledge information.

The interview is the most common technique for testing a candidate for a job. During an interview, the interviewer asks questions that the test candidate answers. To enhance the validity of the interview, the test questions should be relevant to the competencies required for the target job. For example, asking a candidate for a sales job about their previous sales experience would be a job relevant question. Interviews vary in a number of ways, the most critical of which centres on the extent to which the interview is structured. A highly structured interview provides the questions that the interviewer will ask to the test candidate. It also establishes procedures for recording and subsequently evaluating the quality of the candidate's responses to the interview questions. The structured guide also ensures that all candidates are asked the same questions. This helps when comparing candidates on their suitability for the target job. Unstructured interviews do not provide guidance and the interviewer often ends up focusing on irrelevant information. Research shows that structured interviews are more valid than unstructured interviews.

Performance tests are a 'hands on' technique that requires the candidate to perform actual tasks. The test usually involves a replication of actual work situations that the candidate must handle. For instance, a performance test for a mechanic may have a candidate adjust the spark plugs on a car. A performance test for a secretary may involve word processing or typing a business letter. Performance tests require the candidate to simulate parts of the actual job. These types of performance tests are often called work sample exercises. Performance tests typically show a high degree of validity but are often expensive to create depending on what aspects of the job the test is replicating.

All of these different testing techniques can be used to gather information about particular competencies. However, the techniques go about collecting these data in a different manner. For example, to measure risk taking capabilities, a written test may present a series of multiple choice questions where the candidate has to choose which action he or she would be most likely to take in a given situation. These actions may vary in level of risk. The extent to which the candidate is a risk taker can be inferred from the number of times a high-risk answer is chosen. In an interview, the candidate can be asked questions about times he or she has engaged in high-risk behaviour and how comfortable he or she is in such situations. In a performance test, the candidate can be placed in a simulation where he or she has the opportunity to actually make high-risk decisions.

While often a competency could be measured using all of these different techniques, it should be noted that this is not always the case. Certain competencies are more suited to being measured using a particular technique. For example, oral communication skills are more easily measured using an interview or performance test rather than a written exam. On the other hand, written communication skills are more easily measured using a written exam or performance test rather than an interview. When choosing a testing technique, organizations should carefully consider the competency or content area being measured.

4 Testing content

Tests have been developed to measure a wide variety of competencies or content areas. A number of these are described below.

Cognitive ability

Tests of cognitive ability are designed to measure the intellectual capabilities of people. There are general tests of intelligence (e.g. general mental ability or 'g') and there are tests of specific mental and cognitive skills (e.g. spatial thinking, verbal ability and reasoning). A large amount of research has been conducted on the predictive power of both general and specific cognitive tests in work settings. Initially, it was hypothesized that general intelligence tests would be *too* general to be effective predictors of on-the-job performance. Researchers felt that designing specific cognitive tests tailored to particular types of jobs would lead to more success in selecting candidates. For example, a specific cognitive test of spatial thinking would be more predictive than a general cognitive test for jobs such as an architect or air traffic controller. While there has been some success with more specific cognitive tests, research has shown that general cognitive ability tests are extremely effective predictors of job performance.

In fact, many researchers view general intelligence tests as the single best predictor of future job performance. Research has shown that these tests of general cognitive ability are predictive across a wide range of jobs and occupations. However, it should be noted that general cognitive ability tests demonstrate stronger predictive power for jobs of higher complexity. Typically, general cognitive ability tests are relatively low in cost and easy to administer. Most general intelligence tests are standardized written paper-and-pencil exams, multiple choice in format, and therefore easily scored. These tests, such as the Wonderlic Personnel Test and the Weschsler Adult Intelligence Scale-Revised (WAIS-R), have been extensively studied in work organizations and are readily available for purchase. The main problem with general tests of mental ability is that they produce an adverse impact against minorities. Research shows that blacks tend to score significantly lower than whites on general intelligence tests. Therefore, some organizations are reluctant to use these tests because of the legal implications.

Recently, researchers have begun to re-examine the singular nature of intelligence as expressed by 'g'. Many researchers feel that despite the success of general intelligence tests, this unitary approach oversimplifies the complexity of the intelligence construct. It is felt that by expanding the conceptualization of intelligence, other cognitive competencies can be unearthed that may also predict job performance. For example, Robert Sternberg (1997) proposed the concept of practical intelligence, which focuses on how people perform in everyday work situations. It is analogous to the idea of being 'savvy', 'street smart', or 'world-wise'. Daniel Goleman (1998) and others have put forth the construct of emotional intelligence, which is the ability to use emotions effectively when making decisions. This ability is posited to be critical for effective leadership and management of others in work settings. Given that these concepts are relatively new in comparison to the over 100-year history of general intelligence testing, the creation of psychometrically sound tests has just begun. However, tests such as the Multifactor Emotional Intelligence Scale (MEIS) show promise in predicting job performance.

Mechanical aptitude

Mechanical aptitude tests focus on measuring the ability to identify, recognize and apply mechanical principles. The well-established Bennet Test of Mechanical Comprehension provides pictures reflecting various mechanical principles and asks the test candidate to answer practical questions about the pictures. The test is a standardized paper-and-pencil test with multiple choice responses. Mechanical ability tests such as the Bennet have demonstrated solid validity predicting performance in engineering and manufacturing jobs.

Sensory and motor skills

Tests have been developed to measure critical sensory and motor capabilities of candidates. For example, sensory tests have been created to measure visual acuity (e.g. eye chart) and hearing sensitivity (e.g. audiometer). Motor tests such as the O'Connor Finger Dexterity Test measures candidates' ability to manipulate small parts and objects. These types of tests focus on assessing fine or gross motor coordination. Sensory and motor ability tests show good validity for the narrow set of jobs that require those specific skills.

Personality characteristics

Personality focuses on how individuals interact with others and explains why people behave in a particular manner. While most people feel that personality plays a critical role in success at work, early research did not provide strong support for the predictive validity of such tests. However, much of this early research conducted prior to the mid-1980s used personality tests designed to measure dysfunctional personality characteristics. Researchers have had more success by shifting to tests that measure 'normal' personality. Currently, many personality tests focus on measuring five robust factors of personality known as the 'Big Five'. This includes extraversion, emotional stability, agreeableness, conscientiousness and openness to experience. The most consistently valid personality characteristic is conscientiousness. Conscientiousness characterizes someone who is dependable, hardworking and responsible, traits that are important for success in most job positions. Other personality characteristics are predictive but only for particular jobs. For example, extraversion is predictive of effective performance in sales and customer service job positions. Most personality tests used in work settings are in a paper-and-pencil-standardized format. Examples of 'Big Five' personality tests that have been successfully used by organizations include the Hogan Personality Inventory and the NEO-PI.

Integrity

Tests of integrity and honesty have seen a resurgence in use by organizations. While recent laws in the USA have greatly restricted the use of polygraph tests, written tests have been created that focus on predicting employee theft and other illegal activities. Overt integrity tests directly ask candidates about past illegal behaviours and their feelings regarding these actions. One concern with overt tests is that they may insult the test candidate, perhaps making it more difficult to hire them. Other integrity tests, labelled personality-oriented measures, contain questions that do not obviously refer to theft and illegal behaviours. These types of personality tests focus on predicting a wide variety of disruptive behaviours such as insubordination and absenteeism. Research provides strong support for the predictive power of integrity tests to forecast not only employee theft but also the broader domain of general disruptive behaviour at work. These latest findings enhance the usefulness of integrity tests in work organizations.

Job skills and knowledge

While the test content described thus far focuses on general human capabilities (e.g. intelligence, mechanical reasoning, personality traits), other ability tests have been developed that focus more directly on the competencies or KSAs required to perform the specific tasks of a specific job. The focus of a job knowledge or skill test depends completely on the target job. For example, a job knowledge test for a customer service position may contain questions about how to properly handle an irate customer. A job knowledge test for a paralegal may contain questions about where to locate particular information required to write a legal brief. A number of standardized job skills and knowledge tests exist. For example, the Minnesota Clerical Assessment Battery measures skills and knowledge necessary for clerical and secretary work. The test assesses abilities such as typing, proofreading and filing. Another example is the Judd Tests, which are designed to measure computer-based work skills in word processing, spreadsheet programs and database management.

Physical abilities

Physical ability tests focus on the physical capabilities of the test candidate. Many jobs have physical requirements that include characteristics such as strength, flexibility and stamina. Examples of such jobs include firefighters, police, construction workers and many other mechanical and labourer jobs. Tests of physical ability, when used to directly measure what is required in a given job, are extremely effective at predicting job performance and such outcomes as on-the-job injuries. One concern with such tests is potential discrimination against women, minorities and persons with disabilities. Organizations must pay close attention when using physical ability tests in order to comply with legal guidelines.

Biographical information

Tests that capture information on a candidate's general background are called biodata or biographical instruments. Biodata instruments are typically written multiple-choice tests that focus on a candidate's past experiences. The theory of biodata is that these past experiences and events shape our behaviours and attitudes. Because behaviours and attitudes are relatively consistent over the course of our lives, future behaviours and attitudes can be predicted based on these past experiences. Biodata instruments ask questions regarding a wide range of past experiences

including topics such as past academic achievements, participation in extracurricular activities and other events that occur throughout life. Biodata information has been shown to provide valid information in predicting future performance.

5 Using tests

The purpose of using tests is to successfully predict future performance of job candidates. Organizations have a number of issues to consider when choosing which tests they will use to evaluate job candidates. As noted previously, the primary goal of organizations is develop a testing process that balances the critical testing criteria. Table 1 presents the general research findings on various testing techniques and content areas with regard to these criteria. The table presents a general summary of the validity, adverse impact and utility of tests. The validity data, which include estimates of validity correlation coefficients, are based on the latest summary article by Schmidt and Hunter (1998). Also included in the table are reference checks and years of education. These are two commonly used predictors that do not provide much validity.

Organizations often use multiple tests, rather than a single test, to evaluate candidates. Because most jobs require a set of critical competencies, it makes sense to use multiple tests to measure these different competencies. For example, to perform effectively in a sales position, a person may need to be intelligent, influential, extraverted, conscientious and

Table 1 Validity, adverse impact and utility of tests

Predictor	Validity (r)	Adverse impact	Utility
Work sample test	High (0.54)	Low	Low
Cognitive ability test	High (0.51)	High	High
Interview (structured)	High (0.51)	Low	Medium
Job knowledge test	High (0.48)	High	High
Interview (unstructured)	Medium (0.38)	Low	Medium
Biodata	Medium (0.35)	Low	High
Conscientiousness	Medium (0.31)	Low	High
Reference checks	Low (0.26)	Medium	Low/Medium
Years of education	Low (0.10)	Medium	High

possess in-depth knowledge about the products to be sold. To measure this array of competencies, the organization may need a number of tests, rather than a single test. The combination of various tests is often called a multi-aptitude test battery. A few widely known batteries exist, such as the Armed Services Vocational Aptitude Test Battery (ASVAB) and the General Aptitude Test Battery (GATB). However, an organization could combine a set of cognitive and personality tests in order to form their own battery.

The use of multiple tests also allows an organization to enhance the critical criteria of the test process. For example, using the combination of a general cognitive ability test and a work sample performance test may result in a higher level of validity than the tests contribute individually. In addition, the use of multiple tests may mitigate negative aspects of an individual test. For example, combined use of the general cognitive ability test and work sample performance test may reduce the adverse impact produced alone by the general cognitive test.

When using multiple tests, decisions need to be made regarding how the data will be combined into a final score for a candidate. Tests that are combined may be weighted equally or unequally. The combining of tests can be done in different ways. A compensatory model combines the tests in a manner that allows the candidate to make up for a poor performance on one test with a good performance on another test. However, a multiple cut-off approach requires the candidate to attain a minimum level of performance on each test. In this model, the candidate cannot compensate. The multiple hurdle approach calls for a candidate to pass one test before being allowed to take another test.

Another important issue is whether to use pre-existing tests or to develop new tests. Organizations who develop their own tests can tailor these devices to their precise needs. However, test development requires a great deal of time and resources, which can have a negative impact on utility. To identify existing tests, organizations can use the *Mental Measurement Yearbook* (MMY) as a guide. The MMY is revised every four or five years. It provides detailed information about which tests are available to organizations, what type of validity they have shown in various situations, what they cost and how they can be obtained. This serves as a primary resource for identifying tests for organizations to use.

In comparing the use of testing procedures around the world, there is not a great deal of variance. However, Ann Marie Ryan and her colleagues (1999) found some interesting trends using a survey to take a global look at selection practices. They found that internationally, interviews and references were the most common selection techniques. Their survey also showed that in most foreign countries, personality measures were used more often than cognitive ability tests, which is opposite of what has been found in the USA. Another interesting finding was the use of graphology (handwriting analysis) in France, despite the lack of validity data for this device.

Despite the use of common testing practices around the globe, many test instruments must be adjusted in order to be used in a local country. A main issue that has emerged is translating an instrument into another language. While a test may be translated in terms of words, further review must be completed to determine whether the test items are suitable for the local country. There is also the issue of whether a translated measure is equivalent in terms of predictive validity. In addition, the items must be checked with regard to the legal constraints of the local country. Currently, the International Committee on Test Standards is working on guidelines for translating test instruments. These issues become more important as multinational organizations attempt to work globally across many countries.

6 Conclusion

Corporate success depends greatly on the KSAs of the people in the organization. As part of the personnel selection process, tests provide critical information on which people possess the important KSAs desired by the organization. By developing a testing system that has high validity, low adverse impact and reasonable utility, organizations ensure they are staffed with talented people who can perform their jobs effectively. Many future challenges exist for the field of personnel testing.

These include the development of tests that measure the skills required to work effectively across a wide range of cultures and countries, the creation of tests that validly measure new relevant content areas such as emotional and practical intelligence, and the building of testing techniques that leverage emerging technology to increase test utility (e.g. computer-based testing, the Internet).

HAROLD W. GOLDSTEIN
BARUCH COLLEGE
CITY UNIVERSITY OF NEW YORK

Further reading

(References cited in the text marked *)

* American Psychological Association (1985) *Standards for Educational and Psychological Testing*, 2nd edn, Washington, DC: American Psychological Association. (The standards outline a basis for evaluating the quality of testing practices as they affect the various parties involved.)

Anderson, N. and P. Herriot (eds) (1997) *International Handbook of Selection and Assessment*, New York: John Wiley & Sons. (A comprehensive handbook that covers a full spectrum of current international issues regarding personnel selection.)

Gatewood, R.D. and H.S. Field (2001) *Human Resource Selection*, 5th edn, Chicago: Dryden Press. (A comprehensive text book on personnel selection that reviews the development and design of various testing techniques.)

* Goleman, D. P. (1998) *Working with Emotional Intelligence*, New York: Bantam Books. (A book that highlights the impact of emotional intelligence as a significant predictor of performance at work.)

Hakel, M.D. (ed) (1998) *Beyond Multiple Choice: Evaluating Alternatives to Traditional Testing for Selection*, Mahway, NJ: Lawrence Erlbaum Associates. (Provides a full review of the options available for testing techniques beyond written multiple-choice paper-and-pencil test formats.)

Imparan, J.C. and B.S. Plake (eds) (1998) *The Thirteenth Mental Measurement Yearbook*, 13th edn, Highland Park, NJ: The Gryphon Press. (A comprehensive catalogue of existing tests for organizations to use for staffing purposes.)

Jeanneret, R. and R.F. Silzer (1998) *Individual Psychological Assessment: Predicting Behavior in Organizational Settings*, San Francisco: Jossey-Bass. (A book that covers cutting edge issues regarding individual assessment techniques and the challenges facing this field.)

London, M. and D.W. Bray (1980) 'Ethical issues in testing and evaluation for personnel decisions', *American Psychologist* 35: 890–901. (This article reviews the critical ethical issues that need to be considered when assessing persons in work organizations.)

* Ryan, A.M., L. McFarland, H. Baron and R. Page (1999) 'An international look at selection practices: Nation and culture as explanations for variability in practice', *Personnel Psychology* 52: 359–91. (This article reviews the findings of a survey conducted across fourteen countries on global trends in selection practices.)

* Schmidt, F.L. and J.E. Hunter (1998) 'The validity and utility of selection methods in personnel psychology: Practical and theoretical implications of 85 years of research findings', *Psychological Bulletin* 124 (2): 262–74. (Summarizes the 85 years of research on the validity and utility of various personnel selection testing procedures.)

Sessa, V.I., and J.J. Taylor (2000) *Executive Selection*, Greensboro, NC: Center for Creative Leadership. (An in-depth look at assessment procedures and processes used to staff managerial positions.)

* Society for Industrial and Organizational Psychology (1987) *Principles for the Validation and Use of Personnel Selection Procedures*, 3rd edn, College Park, MD: Society for Industrial and Organizational Psychology. (This document specifies principles of good practice in the choice, development, evaluation and use of personnel selection procedures.)

* Sternberg, R.J. (1997) 'The concept of intelligence and its role in lifelong learning and success', *American Psychologist* 52: 1030–57. (Expands the concept of intelligence to include other facets, such as practical and creative intelligence, that may predict performance at work.)

* Uniform guidelines on employee selection procedures (1978) *Federal Register* 43: 38290–315. (This document guides organizations on how to build tests that meet the legal requirements of US law.)

Westgaard, O. (1999) *Tests that Work: Designing and Delivering Fair and Practical Measurement Tools in the Workplace*, San Francisco, CA: Pfeiffer & Co. (Provides a systematic procedure for how to develop powerful, fundamentally sound tests to measure human performance.)

Wood, R., and T. Payne (1998) *Competency-Based Recruitment and Selection*, New York: John Wiley & Sons. (This book shows how competency-based testing fits into the overall selection system and describes various assessment procedures.)

See also: EQUAL EMPLOYMENT OPPORTUNITIES; HUMAN RESOURCE MANAGEMENT; HUMAN RESOURCE MANAGEMENT IN EUROPE; HUMAN RESOURCE MANAGEMENT IN NORTH AMERICA; HUMAN RESOURCE MANAGEMENT, INTERNATIONAL; PERSONNEL MANAGEMENT; RECRUITMENT AND SELECTION

Thailand, management in

Overview

At the start of the twentieth century, Thailand was an economy largely isolated from foreign influences and dependent almost entirely on agriculture. Industrialization began in the 1960s, accompanied by increasing urbanization. Following the Asian economic crisis of the 1990s, Thailand's recovery is under way at the start of the twenty-first century and economic growth has begun again, although perhaps more slowly than in earlier decades.

Thailand has a somewhat unique, hybrid management culture, which, evolving from the successful integration of Sino-Thai entrepreneurs, has proved to be largely resistant to Western management influences. Management culture is very much based on personality traits: Thai managers like to rely on informal and indirect forms of communication, showing a dislike for formal management meetings. They prefer to convey information obliquely, especially if they sense that that information will have unpleasant consequences. There is a tendency to rely on informal networks rather than the formal hierarchies and reporting channels of many foreign organizations, which can be a cause of confrontation for overseas firms operating subsidiaries in Thailand. However, a strategy of culturally sensitive negotiation may allow Thai managers to retain systems with which they feel more comfortable.

1 Introduction

During the 1980s and early to mid-1990s, the economy of Thailand exhibited very rapid rates of growth and the country began also to shift its economic focus from agriculture to industry. Although the Asian economic crisis, which began in Thailand in mid-1997 with the collapse of the currency (the baht) revealed that this growth was to some extent hollow, by 2000 recovery had begun and it seems likely that Thailand's economy will continue to grow, albeit perhaps more slowly and more cautiously than before.

The only country in Southeast Asia to escape foreign colonial domination, Thailand has to a large extent preserved its indigenous culture and society. Throughout the twentieth century, however, much of the Thai economy has been dominated by Chinese-born entrepreneurs and their descendants. This has been especially true since the Second World War, with the rise to prominence of the Chearavanont and Sophonpanich families. Unusually in Southeast Asia, however, these Sino-Thai entrepreneurs have for the most part integrated well into Thai society and have taken on aspects of Thai culture. The result has been to give Thailand a unique, hybrid management culture which blends aspects of indigenous Thai culture with other traits commonly found in overseas Chinese contexts. This culture has proved to be very strong and to a large extent resistant to the influence of Western management culture and practices.

2 History and economic background

Thailand began the twentieth century as an economy largely isolated from foreign influences and dependent almost entirely on agriculture. Ruled by a hereditary monarch from ancient times, the country had a strong and stable government. Unlike Malaysia and Indonesia, where Islam made many converts and became the dominant religion, Thailand remains strongly Buddhist; most Thais follows the Theravada school of Buddhism.

Uniquely among the countries of Southeast Asia, Thailand was never occupied by any colonial power, though French influence was strong from the 1880s to 1940 and imperial Japan treated Thailand as a client state from 1941 to 1945. During the Vietnam War the Thai government was closely aligned to US interests, particularly once the Pathet Lao and Khmer Rouge movements toppled the monarchies of neighbouring Laos and Cambodia. By and large, however, Thailand has preserved its independence, and as Andrews and Chompsuri noted, 'Beneath the surface ... the Thai kingdom has been able to retain its language, culture and tradition almost entirely intact' (Andrews and Chompusri 2001: 78).

From the 1960s, slowly at first and later with increasing pace, Thailand began to industrialize. In 1960 agriculture accounted for 82 per cent of employment in Thailand; by 1990 this had declined to 64 per cent (Hewison 1996). This rapid industrialization was accompanied by increasing urbanization, with Bangkok's population increasing to over 9 million by the middle of the 1990s, out of a population of about 60 million (see EAST ASIAN ECONOMIES).

Geographically, Thailand is divided into five zones, each of which has its own economic characteristics. The most important of these is Bangkok (Krung Thep), the capital and by far the largest city. Bangkok and its suburbs and satellite cities in the Chao Phraya river delta, such as Thon Buri and Nakhon Pathom, are the economic core of the country and are the sites of most of the recent growth; this area accounts for over half of national GDP. The centre of the country, the Chao Phraya valley, has shown some growth but remains largely agricultural; with 17 per cent of the population, it accounts for about 18 per cent of GDP. The mountainous north, centred around Thailand's second city Chiang Mai, depends on forestry, mining and tourism but is largely underdeveloped. The south, the northern half of the Malay peninsula, has a large tourism industry based around resorts such as Phuket and Ko Samui, but again most of the interior is undeveloped. The northeast, a large area consisting of the catchment basins of the Lam Chi and Mae Nam Mun rivers, is highly populous, agrarian and poor; with 35 per cent of the national population, it provides just 13 per cent of GDP. This area has provided many of the migrants which have swelled the urban industrial populations of Bangkok and its suburbs.

There are sharp differences between Bangkok and the rest of country. Average incomes are considerably higher in the capital, and the country's upper and middle classes are concentrated there. Education levels are higher, and the city is more cosmopolitan and receptive to outside influences. Much of rural Thailand remains highly conservative in its views and outlook. This unevenness of development played a not insignificant role in the events following July 1997.

3 The Asia crisis and recovery

From 1985 to 1996, Thailand exhibited the highest average economic growth rates in the world. Especially following liberalization of the financial markets in 1990–92, foreign investment capital poured into the country. Thai companies funded their rapid growth by borrowing in foreign currency, mainly dollars and yen, because this was cheaper than borrowing in baht. Adamson (2000) has noted how many of these foreign lenders, attracted by the prospect of high returns, lent with minimal security and little or no hedging. The Thai financial sector expanded rapidly, with more than 100 new banking and finance houses being established. The stock market increased in value by 2400 per cent between 1987 and 1995. Confidence in the Thai economy appeared boundless; there were predictions that by 2010 it would be the tenth largest in the world; in part this confidence was based on Thailand's apparently rapid conversion from an agrarian to a manufacturing economy; by 1996, 80 per cent of Thai exports were of manufactured goods (Adamson 2000).

However, the analysts had overlooked several key problems. First, this boom was almost entirely confined to Bangkok and the surrounding region, and the roots of growth were only shallowly laid. Second, the boom had been accompanied by a massive rise in debt; from 1992 to 1995 foreign debt doubled from $40 billion to $80 billion, most of this being corporate and private sector debt (Adamson

2000). Third, the Thai financial reforms at the beginning of the decade had been largely incomplete, and control and supervision mechanisms in the financial markets were wholly inadequate (see BANKING CRISES). Even as early as 1995, many Thai banks and corporations were houses of cards.

By 1996, wages in the Bangkok region had risen the point where many Thai exports were becoming uncompetitive in the face of cut-price competition, especially from China. Much of Thailand's export output goes to Japan, and another downturn in the Japanese economy that year also damaged the export effort. Late that year a large Thai bank became insolvent, and there were revelations of corrupt practices and false accounting. The baht, pegged at 25 to the US dollar, came under pressure, and the government began using its foreign exchange reserves to support the baht. In early 1997, even as some Western analysts were still boosting the Thai economy, the government sent 16 more banks into liquidation; by the middle of the year, more than 40 had followed, with total debts of around $40 billion. On 2 July 1997 the government finally gave in and allowed the baht to float – or sink. By the autumn of 1997 it had fallen to around 50 to the US dollar. The contagion spread, notably to Malaysia and Indonesia, but affecting to some degree every major economy in East Asia.

Adamson (2000) describes in detail some of the restructuring initiatives that have taken place since. One of the problems has been that the Thai economy, being quite 'new', lacks experience of crises of this sort and has been forced to import expertise from Europe and North America. Adamson, who has himself been a key figure in the reconstruction of the financial services sector, notes how not only the Thai borrowers but the foreign lenders were in a state of initial disarray, unable to agree on solutions. Those difficulties have now largely been sorted out, but Adamson points to continuing causes of underlying instability, notably lack of a tight regulatory regime and a more general lack of transparency. Laws now being enacted, in particular a new bankruptcy law, should deal with some of these problems, and the general view of Thailand now is one of cautious optimism.

4 Sino-Thai entrepreneurship

An important feature of Thailand's economy, as with every economy in the region, is the high degree of participation by overseas Chinese entrepreneurs (see ENTREPRENEURSHIP). There has been a long history of trade and intercourse between northern Thailand and southern China, and by the early twentieth century, Chinese traders made up a significant portion of the Thai middle class. Many of these early traders settled into Thai society and adopted Chinese names and customs, unlike countries such as Vietnam, Malaysia and Indonesia where Chinese immigrants were (and are) treated with reserve and even suspicion. Waves of immigration following the republican revolution of 1911, the ongoing civil war and Japanese invasion and the communist takeover in 1949 all swelled Thailand's Chinese population (see ASIA PACIFIC, MANAGEMENT IN). While the vast majority of these immigrants are small traders and manufacturers, several families have risen to prominence. In the 1950s the Sophanpanich family's Bank of Bangkok rose to become the largest bank in the country and, by the 1960s, the largest in Asia. Chin Sophanpanich, the head of the family, was at the centre of a business network of overseas Chinese leaders including Liem Sioe Liong in Indonesia and Robert Kwok in Malaysia, as well as domestic Sino-Thai business leaders such as the Chearavanont family.

It is the latter who today are the most visible manifestation of Sino-Thai entrepreneurship. The family fortunes began with Chin Ek-chor, an immigrant from Shantou province in China, who set up a small vegetable seed business, Chia Tai, in Bangkok in the 1920s. By the Second World War, this had grown into a sizeable import–export business, dominating the agricultural seed business and exporting agricultural produce to China. Consolidating within Thailand during the war, the business began to expand again in the 1950s. Chin's third son, Dhanin Chearavanont, became managing director in 1963 and began developing the business rapidly, in part using funds supplied by Sophanpanich's Bank of Bangkok. Chia Tai became Charoen Pokphand and diversified into wholesale agribusiness, contract farming and fish-farming, and became the largest business group in Thailand. In the 1980s the company moved downstream into food retailing and restaurants, notably acquiring the 711 retail store franchise for the country and opening over 1000 outlets in short order. There was further diversification into telecommunications, natural gas extraction and manufacturing of motorcycles, and Chearavanont had also led the group into major investments in property and retailing in the People's Republic of China, often in concert with other overseas Chinese tycoons. By the mid-1990s the CP Group, as it was now known, controlled over 250 subsidiaries in Thailand, Hong Kong and China and Chearavanont and his family were estimated to be worth around $5 billion (Hiscock 1997; Witzel 2001). The Asia crisis hit the CP Group hard but, concentrated around agribusiness rather than manufacturing, with a strong domestic core business and with limited borrowing, it came through the storm rather better than many Thai businesses and by 2000 was expanding once more.

5 Business culture

Thailand's business culture is in many ways typical of the region, and, especially in the Bangkok region, consists of a hybrid of indigenous Thai and overseas Chinese social values (see BUSINESS CULTURES, ASIAN PACIFIC). As the two sets of values are in many ways similar, there is little cultural clash between them; if anything, the effect of the indigenous Thai values is to strengthen or make more prominent those features of overseas Chinese business culture such as family orientation, emphasis on networks of relationships, informal structures and strong leadership.

Thai business culture strongly emphasizes the role of the leader. The nature of the leader's role can be compared to that of the father in Chinese family businesses, but also to the teacher in Buddhist communities. In Thai businesses, the leader/father/teacher is expected to provide guidance and make decisions. Decentralized decision making is not thought highly of in Thailand; it is the leader's responsibility to make decisions, that is why he or she has been chosen to lead. The leader is

also expected to be a guide, to assist and care for employees, and to help them with personal problems as well as problems at work. Above all, the leader is expected to be a motivator; studies of Thai employees show that the personality or character of the leader is a strong factor in motivation at work (Lawler *et al.* 1989) (see MOTIVATION AND SATISFACTION).

Although the leader is expected to be strong, in a typically Asian paradox, this strength should be exercised softly and without overt domination. Leaders should inspire loyalty rather than command obedience. They should speak softly to employees and never shout or threaten. The most admired trait in a leader is *baramee*, a Thai term implying both goodness and charisma or presence, with overtones of the Chinese trait of 'benevolence'. Justice and compassion are also highly valued traits. In general, the leader is expected to know and recognize his or her responsibilities to those who are led.

Personality traits also affect management culture. One of the most notable of these is a reliance on informal and indirect forms of communication. It has been noted that Thai managers dislike attending formal management meetings, and rarely participate actively in such meetings. They do not respond well to direct questions requiring direct answers, and prefer to convey information obliquely, especially if they sense that information will have unpleasant consequences. There is a very strong dislike of confrontation which permeates management and business activity at all levels. There is, finally, a tendency to rely on informal networks of staff and managers rather than formal hierarchies and reporting channels which, in the case of Thai subsidiaries of foreign firms, have often been imposed without much thought for Thai culture and circumstances.

Andrews and Chompusri (2001) report on one such case, where a British firm attempted to reorganize its Thai subsidiary so that its organization structure would match that of other subsidiaries. The attempt, which was at first couched as a set of orders from the London head office, met with strong levels of resistance within the subsidiary, and indeed there was a high degree of non-compliance. Eventually, head office agreed to discuss the problem with local managers and a solution was worked out, one which did lead to some degree of convergence with the structure of the international business and but which allowed the Thai managers to retain many of the systems with which they felt most comfortable. Andrews and Chompusri cite this as an example of the strength of Thai business culture and its ability to resist unfavourable adaptations to foreign cultures, and suggest that a strategy of 'cross-vergence' or rationalization but with concessions made to Thai business culture, should be followed by multinationals (see MULTINATIONAL CORPORATIONS) operating in Thailand:

> The corporate objective of imposing a 'blanket' program of organizational restructuring across its Southeast Asian units remains misguided and naive. Thai business norms appear to express qualitatively distinct ideas of what constitutes appropriate management practice. We therefore hold that an economy such as Thailand rests on institutional principles that provide an internal logic for competitive business activity. Accepted modes of managerial practice both shape and nourish locally embedded company–customer relations.
>
> (Andrews and Chompsuri 2001: 90)

6 Future prospects

At time of writing, the Thai economy is recovering from the Asia crisis and should exhibit relatively healthy rates of growth through the coming decade. Political and economic stability will need to be maintained, however, and the reform of the regulatory regime described by Adamson (2000) will need to be carried considerably further. Overseas investors will also need to act more responsibly and to assess risk and hedge their own operations in an appropriate manner.

Thailand's economic growth will also need to become more diversified, less dependant on exports and more deeply rooted. In particular, there is need to roll out economic growth and development from the capital to the regions, especially the centre and the poor northeast. During the 1990s, Thai economic and busi-

ness strategy was focused on moving out of Thailand into international markets. During the first decade of the twenty-first century, there is need for consolidation of growth inside Thailand. The example of CP Group, which despite its massive diversification stuck close to its core business in agriculture and food products, is a useful model here.

7 Conclusion

Although in many ways part of the greater Southeast Asian business sphere, Thailand possesses its own unique business and cultural attributes. Over the past two decades Thailand has exhibited rapid business growth and has produced some important and powerful entrepreneurs and large multinational corporations. That growth was temporarily stymied during the Asian crisis of 1997–9, which began partly as a result of structural problems in the Thai economy and partly as a result of a willingness by overseas investors to lend on an insecure basis. The unravelling of the crisis goes on, and Thailand is slowly reforming its economy; it is becoming a safer and better place to invest. The country's economy is heavily influenced by the Sino-Thai entrepreneurs who have built up many of its largest business corporations and banking houses, and can be considered a hybrid of domestic Thai culture and traits common to the overseas Chinese business community everywhere. A recognition of the importance and permanence of Thai business culture is essential for foreign companies and managers doing business there.

MORGEN WITZEL
LONDON BUSINESS SCHOOL

Further reading

(References cited in the text marked *)

* Adamson, S. (2000) 'Thailand's party and the hangover', *Corporate Finance Review* 4 (4): 5–11. (Account of the origins of the financial crisis in Thailand, by a corporate restructuring expert who has helped lead the recovery programme.)
* Andrews, T.G. and Chompusri, N. (2001) 'Lessons in "cross-vergence": restructuring the Thai subsidiary corporation', *Journal of International*

Business Studies 32 (1): 77–93. (Case study of interaction between a Western firm's headquarters and its Thai subsidiary, showing how the clash of cultures can have an effect even within a firm.)

Dixon, C. (1998) *The Thai Economy*, London: Routledge. (Description of the Thai economy, including the rapid growth of the mid-1990s before the crash.)

Godement, F. (1999) *The Downsizing of Asia*, London: Routledge. (General account of the Asian economic crisis.)

* Hewison, K. (1996) 'Emerging social forces in Thailand: new political and economic roles', in R. Robison and D.S.G. Goodman (eds), *The New Rich in Asia*, London: Routledge, 137–62. (Describes changes in modern Thai business culture and society, though written before the Asia crisis.)

* Hiscock, G. (1997) *Asia's Wealth Club*, London: Nicholas Brealey. (Short biographies of the wealthy business elites of Asia, including the Chearvananont and Sophonpanich families of Thailand.)

* Lawler, J.J, Siegenthai, S. and Atmiyannandana, V. (1989) 'Human resource management in Thailand: eroding traditions', *Asia-Pacific Business Review* 3: 170–96. (Reports on human resources management practices in Thailand, showing how these are in the process of evolution.)

* Witzel, M. (2001) 'Chearavanont, Dhanin', in M. Witzel (ed.), *Biographical Dictionary of Management*, Bristol: Thoemmes Press, forthcoming. (Brief biography of the entrepreneur who heads the CP Group.)

See also: ASIA PACIFIC, MANAGEMENT IN; ASIA-PACIFIC ECONOMIC COOPERATION (APEC); ASSOCIATION OF SOUTH-EAST ASIAN NATIONS (ASEAN); CHINA, MANAGEMENT IN ; GLOBALIZATION; MANAGEMENT EDUCATION IN ASIA PACIFIC; MULTINATIONAL CORPORATIONS; WORLD BANK

Theories of the firm: see COASE, R.; EVOLUTIONARY THEORIES OF THE FIRM; GROWTH OF THE FIRM AND NETWORKING; MANAGERIAL THEORIES OF THE FIRM; NEO-CLASSICAL ECONOMICS; WILLIAMSON, O.E.

Theory X and Theory Y: see GURU CONCEPT; HUMAN RELATIONS; LEADERSHIP; MCGREGOR, D.; ORGANIZATION BEHAVIOUR, HISTORY OF

Third-party intervention

1 Context
2 Historical evolution
3 Disputes over rights
4 Disputes of interest
5 Private and public interventions
6 The conciliation process
7 The mediation process
8 Arbitration processes
9 The conventions of arbitration
10 Conclusion

Overview

Any process of bargaining between parties with different interests in its outcomes creates some risk that they will not be able to agree and, accordingly, that they will break off the negotiation. Where the parties are able to select other bargaining partners with whom they can reach agreement, failure to agree presents no problem. Where, as in the case of bargaining between employers and workers, this option is either not open or open only at considerable cost to both parties, it is generally considered that some alternative course of action which avoids break-off or breakdown needs to be available to the parties.

In the context of collective bargaining, the mechanism takes one of three forms, which differ in the amount of discretion assigned to the third party:

- *Conciliation* is a method resolving differences by involving an impartial third party in the actual negotiating process with the object of assisting the parties to explore other methods of resolving their differences and to arrive at an agreement which accords with their values and interests. Of the three methods, this allows the parties' most discretion to decide the issue for themselves on their own terms.

- *Mediation* is a method of achieving the same result where an independent third party is either required by law or requested by the parties to make one or more recommendations on the way in which the difference might be resolved, leaving the parties some discretion to decide the form that any resolution should take.

- *Arbitration* is a method of resolving differences or disputes between two (or more) parties over the establishment, interpretation or application of the terms and conditions of a contract, by involving an independent third party who is either required by law or requested by the parties to make an award on the disputed issue(s) after considering the parties' evidence and arguments.

These mechanisms are often seen to provide an alternative method of resolving disputes to those found in the courts of law. Mediation and arbitration are, for example, being increasingly adopted either to settle disputes which do not lend themselves to resolution in terms of right and wrong – in which area the courts are well equipped – or to take advantage of their greater informality and lower cost (Mackie 1991). All three mechanisms offer distinct advantages where the disputes are concerned with the interests of the contending parties and where the constraining framework of law is at best replaced by a framework of convention developed largely by the parties themselves.

This entry identifies the main mechanisms that exist for avoiding or repairing breakdowns (which usually take the form of either strikes by the workers or lockouts by the employers) in the areas of labour and industrial relations. These are typically either:

1 judicial (involving the court system and the application of legal principles to determine who is right and who is wrong) (see EMPLOYMENT TRIBUNALS) or
2 quasi-judicial (involving processes of conciliation, mediation and arbitration and the application of principles derived mainly from customary values and conventions in an attempt to solve a problem in ongoing employment relationships).

I Context

Most industrial relations differences and disputes are resolved by the parties themselves in negotiations, but there is always a risk that they will not be able to reach agreement on the issues (see HUMAN RESOURCE MANAGEMENT; INDUSTRIAL AND LABOUR RELATIONS). Most countries that rely on collective bargaining as a way of reaching agreements rely on some form of third-party intervention to prevent or repair breakdowns in bargaining.

This mechanism may involve either the official court system or the quasi-judicial system identified with conciliation, mediation and arbitration. Resolution by reference to the courts is by far the most frequently used mode of resolving differences concerning questions of individual 'right', whether these are established by statutes or by contracts. Conciliators, mediators or arbitrators, who may have no connection at all with the judicial system, are more often used to resolve differences and disputes over collective 'interests' and rights. In most countries, conciliation is more frequently invoked in collective disputes than either mediation or arbitration, although these form important fall-back mechanisms for use in the event of failure in conciliation. In some countries, Japan and those of Eastern Europe, for example, arbitration is generally considered less appropriate than either of the other two mechanisms.

It is quite common to regard courts of law as ill-equipped to handle disputes over 'interests' (where one party is attempting to establish some new right in bargaining with a second party) and these are left for resolution in conciliation or arbitration in the event of failure to agree (see INDUSTRIAL CONFLICT). Collectivities or classes of people seeking to negotiate a new right into existence or to protect one already established are sometimes encouraged and sometimes legally required to make use of third-party assistance before embarking upon collective action which might disrupt commercial relations or result in possible social disorder.

Once rights have been established, individuals who consider that their rights have been infringed by another are at liberty to seek redress before a court. However, they sometimes have the option of going down the alternative route to arbitration; in the USA arbitration is widely used for this purpose and in Canada, Australia and New Zealand, it has been actually or virtually mandatory to follow this route.

The reasons for relying on alternative methods of collective dispute resolution are that both the principal parties and the wider society regard any breakdown in contractual relations as costly and without benefit or advantage to anyone, that resolution by means of court litigation is becoming increasingly time-consuming and costly, and that the courts may not be the best forums for resolving disputes which are not simply concerned with questions of right. The use of either mechanism to avoid breakdown may, therefore, be made mandatory or may be left to the decisions of the parties themselves. Practice in this respect varies from country to country, usually reflecting cultural attitudes towards the use of industrial action as a method of coercing the other party to agree to terms. Where their use is mandatory, the legality of industrial action is often made conditional upon their use and the processes of conciliation, mediation and arbitration then tend to be tied more closely into the judicial system.

Where, on the other hand, the parties are left to decide voluntarily whether they will make use of any of them, the legality of industrial action usually does not depend on their prior use (although it may be defined in other ways). In this context, conciliation, mediation and arbitration will often be undertaken by persons who have no necessary connection with the judicial system. The parties retain greater freedom to select the third party and to define the terms of reference.

2 Historical evolution

Although there is currently a limited movement towards using non-judicial methods of resolving differences in individual rights cases, such methods have in the past been associated with and largely dependent upon the growth of collective bargaining over workers' interests and rights. Whenever collective bargaining becomes established, the parties quickly recognize that a third party might be able to help them to reduce their differences and allow them to reach agreements without relying on strikes or lockouts to coerce the other party (see COLLECTIVE BARGAINING).

They may then voluntarily agree in advance of any breakdown in negotiations to the appointment of conciliators, mediators or arbitrators to assist them, should the need arise, what in Japan is referred to as 'leaving the dispute with someone' not connected with it. Governments may then recognize the virtue of

encouraging or mandating the parties to use these mechanisms to avoid open conflicts by enacting legislation which prescribes (as in some Eastern European countries) the use of a form of third-party intervention whenever a dispute threatens disruption; and/or creating a public service of conciliation, mediation and arbitration which the collective bargaining partners are free to use if they so wish (as in Britain or Japan).

Legislative prescription usually reflects a belief that disruption is normally more damaging to the worker than to the employer interest. The legislation then takes the form of giving each party to a difference or dispute the right unilaterally to refer the issue to a third party and disallowing any veto by the other party on this course of action. Many countries have adopted this approach in emergency conditions (Lockyer 1979) but others, such as Australia and New Zealand in the past (Hamani and Blanpain 1989) and the liberalizing economies of Eastern Europe more recently, see advantages in generally prescribing third-party intervention by law (OECD 1993), although arbitration may be involved only to a limited extent (Hamani and Blanpain 1989).

Where such legal prescription does not occur, these modes of dispute resolution remain part of the voluntary collective bargaining process. Even when the State organizes a public facility or agency for the purpose without prescribing its use, the parties are left to decide whether to write in any form of third-party intervention as final stages of their negotiating or disputes procedures (that is, the procedures they agree to follow in order to reach agreement). This clause may provide for unilateral reference to the third party, but more commonly *both* parties have to agree to refer an issue to a third party and (in the case of arbitration) to be bound by any award made.

Nevertheless, even where voluntary collective bargaining persisted (as for example in Britain in the 1960s and 1970s), legislation was extensively used to prescribe basic or minimum rights for individuals in employment. Resolving disputes about such rights was a task given to judicial tribunals in Britain and to ordinary courts elsewhere. As, subsequently, trade union power waned at workshop level and the judicial institutions assumed an ever-greater share of the work of resolving individual rights disputes, resolution became subject to considerable delay and to heavily increasing costs (see TRADE UNIONS).

3 Disputes over rights

Where the rights accorded to individuals by law are ones that reciprocate in another's duty, the courts are normally charged with the duty of hearing claims or complaints referred to them unilaterally by any aggrieved party for redress. Similarly, where they are established by contract a claim by one party that the other has breached its terms can also be pursued through the courts under contract law. Legislation usually then proscribes the use of any device which would deny a complainant access to the courts.

However, where workers' rights are established by collective agreement between trade unions and employers (individually or collectively), it is common to find that an alternative route to dispute resolution is followed. Commonly, such disputes are referred to as 'grievances', and sometimes, the parties to the collective agreement may be required by law (as in Canada, for example) to include a provision within the agreement for resolving grievances. In the USA, where the law rarely makes stipulation, it is still common for agreements to include such provisions.

In these countries, it is then common for the resolution of 'grievances' to be attempted through conciliation, mediation or arbitration, rather than through the ordinary or specialized labour courts. A complex set of arrangements have been made to ensure a supply of conciliators, mediators and arbitrators, as it were 'voluntarily', to facilitate such grievance resolution, but where collective agreements are recognized as contracts in law, such arrangements begin to look increasingly like distinct judicial systems with their own rules and procedures. In the USA, particularly, they also begin to match the tribunal and court systems in their high costs and long waiting times.

Elsewhere, the mounting costs of litigation before the labour courts and tribunals are leading to the greater use of alternative or supplementary methods of resolving disputes. Some countries, like Britain, have interposed in order to cut costs and workloads of the judicial bodies. Some countries are attempting to substitute mediation and arbitration as cheaper and quicker mechanisms for resolving disputes (Clark and Lewis 1992) (see EMPLOYMENT TRIBUNALS).

It is sometimes deemed expedient to use a form of arbitration, backed by judicial authority, to deal with rights accorded by law to collectivities, or with potentially controversial or complex industrial relations questions, usually on the ground that these require something less constrained than a judicial body. For example, when for a time British trade unions were by law accorded conditional recognition rights, the task of resolving claims and complaints on this score was allocated to the Central Arbitration Committee (CAC) whose function is both judicial and arbitral. In this case, the distinction between the alternative mechanisms becomes blurred.

In the simpler case, where a union seeks redress of complaints about the application of terms of a collective agreement, it usually prefers to use conciliation, mediation and arbitration rather than a court because it retains more 'control' over the criteria that will be relied on in making judgements. This is common practice in many countries, especially where, as in the USA, the collective agreements are legally enforceable contracts (see COLLECTIVE BARGAINING).

Where there is no legislative prescription of this kind, a reference to conciliation, mediation or arbitration normally depends on the prior agreement of both parties to refer a dispute in this way in the event of failure to agree. Unilateral references to arbitration are unusual, but may be provided for in collective agreements, although they usually occur where legislation gives one or other party this 'right'. In many cultures, however, unilateral references would be regarded as inhibiting the reaching of a preferred end-state of an agreement which the parties would accept as morally binding upon them (Bamber and Lansbury 1987).

4 Disputes of interest

It is common to deny the courts' competence to resolve disputes of interest, although it is increasingly difficult to identify with precision the dividing line between rights and interests issues (Weiss 1987). Many individual employers and some governments avoid referring interest claims to arbitration, although they may be less averse to proceeding to conciliation to facilitate a settlement. This reluctance stems from the belief that although it is proper to allow external adjudication of claims relating to established rights, it is either improper or inappropriate to allow a third party to establish them when the parties themselves cannot agree on their form.

It is, for example, widely considered that, if the law does not prescribe this course of action, it is not appropriate to place decisions about whether an employer should recognize a union as a bargaining agent for some of the workers, or about the levels of wages or the nature of other conditions, in the hands of a third party. In the circumstances, the issues are for the parties themselves to resolve in bargaining even if this risks the withdrawal of either party from the relationship as each seeks to compel agreement to its terms.

The number and types of issues referred to conciliation, mediation and arbitration are usually more limited than those involved in collective bargaining, for two main reasons:

1 The parties are often able to resolve some issues in negotiations and only those on which they fail to agree are referred for conciliation, mediation or arbitration. This is a consequence of the way in which bargaining over complex claims is conducted, although keeping all decisions open until the final package can be identified often helps to facilitate settlement

2 The parties, and particularly the employers, are less disposed (in the absences of mandatory legislation) to permit some claims to be determined by a third party over whom they cannot exercise a close control. This influences the types of third-party intervention that may be adopted in a country: it leads some to avoid arbitration entirely (as being less amenable to control) and others to accept only those 'awards' (usually in respect of 'rights') which are handed down by courts or tribunals.

Pendulum arbitration (in which the arbitrator is presented with a forced choice of the union's last claim or the employer's last offer) has been devised as a way of restricting the scope of the arbitrator and of retaining more control of the award in the hands of the parties (Burrows 1986). The arbitrator cannot then devise an award which accords with neither party's preferred position. It is not widely used (although it is more prevalent in North American countries than in others) because it does require the parties to be more precise in their bargaining behaviours.

5 Private and public intervention

The involvement of third parties in disputes resolution may occur in one of three main ways. They may be appointed privately under existing collective agreements to avoid open disputes with the aim of assuring the parties complete control of the intervention process. Alternatively, the parties may make voluntary use of any available public facility of this kind (that is, of the Labour Relations Commission in Japan or the Advisory Conciliation and Arbitration Service in Britain). In yet other cases, it may be mandatory upon the parties (or upon one of, them) to use some form of third-party intervention before they can take lawful industrial action.

Private arrangements are often the first form of third-party intervention to be adopted. They still occur under collective agreements made at local or sectoral levels, although, being private, information on their extent is not readily available. The parties appoint persons on whom they can agree should act as conciliators, mediators or arbitrators, either from within the industry or from outside it. The test applied is whether they are sufficiently knowledgeable about the issues involved and sufficiently independent and impartial to be trusted not to favour one party to the detriment of the other.

A public service of conciliation, mediation or arbitration need not be based on principles different from those applying in private arrangements. Tripartite control (by representatives of the State, the employers and the unions) may be adopted, as in the Japanese Labour Relations Commission, to give an indication of the intention to be impartial. In actual dispute conditions, steps are usually taken to ensure that the full consent of the parties is forthcoming before an intervention is made. Care is normally taken to ensure that the parties retain control over the processes involved – for example, in selecting the third party, or in supplying the information that the third party will rely on.

In most cases, it does not involve an injection of any greater third-party interest than occurs in the private arrangements (although the Australian award system did specifically provide for the State to address the Arbitration Court or Commission when issues of public interest were under consideration).

Where the State sets up a public service of conciliation, mediation and/or arbitration on which the parties must or can call as necessary, the conciliators may be drawn from the ranks of the agency's full-time staff and the mediators and arbitrators from a retained panel of 'outsiders' – as in the case of the British Advisory, Conciliation and Arbitration Service (ACAS). The problem faced by a State-provided facility is whether the parties will regard it as sufficiently distanced from the regulatory arms of government to convince them of its impartiality.

It is now common to find the people who are able and willing to act as third parties forming a distinct (if also small) cadre within the society. In some cases, as in Germany or the USA, they may form a professional body or institute from which the parties either must (in prescriptive systems) or may (in voluntary systems) select competent independents either to meet the legal requirements or to meet their particular need for assistance.

6 The conciliation process

The procedures followed in third-party intervention respond to the objective sought in each case, but also reflect the conventions which are designed to leave as much control with the parties as possible.

Collective conciliation is designed to help the parties to reach agreement on their own terms and in accord with their own values. In some systems (such as that adopted in Westphalia in Germany), the conciliator who may eventually be called upon to help may sit in on the negotiations from their inception, so that he or she is fully conversant with the arguments if called upon to act. In the more common system, the conciliator who is asked to help when an impasse has already been reached has to be briefed on the background and arguments before starting.

The conciliator will first acquaint him/herself with the background and nature of the difference(s) by discussing them with the parties separately, that is, using investigative methods. The conciliator may either visit the site where the negotiations normally take place (for example, the employer's premises) or more commonly bring the parties together in separate rooms on neutral premises. He or she needs to discover what the issues are, what value the parties place upon the various facets of the disputed issue, what they seek to achieve, and what ideas they have for resolving them. The conciliator can then use this information to modify the parties' perceptions of their problem and the possible solutions to it.

The outcome of this phase is usually a knowledge not only of the context, but an appreciation of what parts of the claim/offer are of particular significance to each party (or of what each expects to get out of the exercise). This enables the conciliator to act as an intelligent interpreter of their positions and problems in the interests of removing barriers to their agreement. He or she can explain to each party the nature of the other's objectives and difficulties, and, by developing a greater awareness of them, possibly bring the parties to a settlement.

Conciliators usually have to try to get the parties to modify their positions in order to narrow the outstanding differences between them, because the lack of awareness of the other's problems is not always the only barrier to agreement. Since disputed claims are often either composed of a number of separate elements or capable of being resolved in a number of different ways, the conciliator can explore whether the parties might find it easier to settle if the 'package' were composed differently. The conciliator's task of 'repackaging' complex claims and offers is facilitated if the parties have withheld agreement to parts of a complex package until all of them have been fully considered in relation to each other so that trade-offs can be explored.

In conciliation, the third party thus assumes the role of intelligent messenger who attempts to narrow the differences between the parties. If successful, the conciliator will invite them to reach their own agreement, although he or she may help them to formulate the terms to be used in it.

7 The mediation process

In its 'pure' form, mediation often appeals to the parties, and particularly the employer, because it is a proactive intervention which still avoids giving the third party an irretrievable power to resolve the issue in terms that might not be congenial to them.

The mediator has to be more proactive than the conciliator in suggesting (or recommending) one or more possible solutions until one is found that the parties can accept. The dividing line between the two processes is thin: although the conciliator does not formally have this proactive role, many of his or her suggestions are likely to be very similar to those of the mediator although they will not be presented as 'recommendations', nor are they as likely to be given in writing.

The mediator, in order to reach a position from which a recommendation can be made, may hear the parties together or separately, and may rely on either adversarial or investigative methods. Like the conciliator, he or she may suggest to the parties separately a succession of possible recommendations until one that is likely to be acceptable is found. Alternatively, he or she may simply hear the separate arguments and by dint of questioning them in the course of the hearing arrive at a conclusion as to which of a number of alternatives might be acceptable to the parties, and so recommends.

Mediation is more interventionist than conciliation, but does not involve imposition of a resolution of an issue. Both are essentially non-dictatorial and are often preferred to arbitration for this reason. They involve different ways of packaging the 'suggestions' made to the parties, but in both cases there is an aim of finding some solution to which the parties can agree. In Japanese culture, this aim is elevated to the level where the settlement is made to depend on the parties accepting their moral obligations and displaying goodwill towards the other party. In Western industrialized countries, a similar outcome is intended, although it is less often expressed in terms of morality.

Countries display different preferences for mediation and arbitration in dispute settlement. Mediation was in the past relatively little used in Britain, although its use is now increasing as an alternative to arbitration. By contrast, France tends to rely more upon mediation than arbitration (see FRANCE, MANAGEMENT IN). Practice thus tends to reflect cultural preferences for adversarial or investigatory methods of establishing the nature of reality.

Although the Japanese attempt to avoid using arbitration to impose a settlement on the parties, in other countries conciliation and mediation may be linked in series with arbitration (see JAPAN, MANAGEMENT IN). A conciliator may attempt to bring the parties together, and if this does not succeed, a mediator may be appointed to suggest a solution. But if this fails to produce a settlement, the mediator may proceed to arbitrate on the matter and make an award.

8 Arbitration processes

Arbitration is carried out either by a single arbitrator or by a board of arbitration, dependent on any requirements of law or the preferences of the parties. In cases which involve complex technical issues, arbitrators may be assisted by 'assessors' (or technical experts nominated by the parties) who are able to offer information or advice on them.

The single arbitrator is normally capable of reaching a decision in straightforward cases but the parties may feel more secure if the decision is in the hands of a, usually tripartite, board. This allows more minds to be brought to bear on the issues, and where the side-members are separately nominated by the parties themselves, these minds can be counted on to ensure that their distinct values will be brought to bear on the issues.

Before any hearing takes place, the parties normally agree the terms of reference which set the limits to the arbitrator's discretion in reaching an award. In framing them the parties may have assistance from conciliators who have previously been involved. They usually identify the parties, indicate what the difference between them is about (wages, dismissal, etc.) and indicate what issue the parties want the arbitrator to resolve (although because of their formality, they may not indicate the full extent of what the parties really want to see resolved). This may not be capable of presentation in formal terms and the arbitrator may uncover further complexities during the hearing.

The parties then produce written statements of argument or evidence for consideration by the arbitrator prior to the hearing. These usually include any detailed technical or statistical material about which it would be difficult to be eloquent, and the parties' definitions of the issue and their views of its provenance. These may be long or short documents, dependent upon either the kind of issue involved or the importance that the parties attach to it.

At the hearing, the parties expand on and amplify the information which they consider necessary to reaching a decision, and articulate the values which they, jointly or severally, consider relevant to the assessment that the arbitrator has to make (Lockyer 1979). The parties usually appear together in the hearing, so that they hear everything said to the arbitrator, but because it is the arbitrator who has to be persuaded, all arguments are addressed to him or her, not the other side.

The arbitrator is usually given a great deal of factual information (statistical data in the case of, for example, pay claims; the sequence of events leading to a disputed decision) intended to support the arguments and inform the arbitrator's mind. The parties explain why they have not been able to reach their own agreement. They also place the emphasis on the factors they consider to be important, and

indicate what each considers to be the fair or sensible solution.

The arbitrator is sometimes told much more than this, even if 'not in so many words'. There are occasions where what is said leads the arbitrator inexorably to a particular resolution which it appears that both parties recognize as the sensible one, even though their formal arguments may be at variance with it. This is the basis for regarding some references to arbitration as a process of finding a scapegoat to blame for a settlement.

On other occasions the parties may be very far apart, and no clues are given as to the settlement that *both* parties might find acceptable even if it is not their preferred one. Arbitrators must then reach a judgement as best they can. However, their task is made easier if there is a multifaceted claim and offer situation which allows them to offer some benefit, however small, to both sides. This allows arbitration to be branded as a process of splitting the difference.

However much or little 'help' the arbitrator gets from the parties, he or she must still reach the decision on the evidence and argument presented, and not import into the process other values to which the parties might not subscribe. This is fundamental to voluntary arbitration because it provides the only guarantee that the process remains voluntary – and, in particular, immune to influence by the State power. Where this principle is adhered to, the apparently interventionist process of arbitration remains consistent with a normatively controlled system of bipartite regulation.

9 The conventions of arbitration

The procedures followed in arbitration (and *mutatis mutandis* in other modes of third-party intervention not associated with the courts) are governed by conventions which allow the parties to retain control of the process and to avoid interference by the State with what is regarded as a private, voluntary process. Although particular parties may not wholeheartedly subscribe to these conventions in every instance, they may be regarded as a kind of 'common law' of third-party interventions:

1 Arbitration is embarked upon only with the consent of the parties to a dispute, and neither party can impose arbitration upon the other.

2 The parties will, in agreeing to put an issue to arbitration, also agree to accept the award of the arbitrator as binding (in honour or in law) upon them.

3 The parties may still continue negotiations on an issue after it has been referred to an arbitrator, but will suspend any industrial action which might have been with the aim of coercing the other party to settle.

4 The parties will, through their own chosen representatives, present the arbitrator(s) with whatever information is needed to enable a decision to be reached on the facts.

5 Arbitration will be carried out by one or more competent persons who are independent (both of the immediate parties and of the State) and impartial.

6 Arbitrators will reach their decisions exclusively on the basis of what is contained in the written and oral materials submitted by the parties and will respect the limits of decision indicated by the parties.

7 Arbitrators will reach their decisions on the basis of two main, broad criteria: what is likely on the evidence to resolve the immediate problem effectively; and what is likely to resolve the issue fairly or equitably (as these are defined by the values of the parties).

8 Arbitrator will serve the parties to the dispute and no other interest in reaching their decisions, and as a servant of the parties treat anything said by them as confidential.

It is not uncommon to find that, even when the State becomes more directly involved in these processes, its approach acknowledges these same conventions.

10 Conclusion

Third-party intervention, in whatever form, provides an alternative to overt industrial action as a way of compelling the other party in collective bargaining to agree the terms of a settlement, although it is not invariably used for the purpose. Its origins lie in convention-driven practices developed by the collective bargaining parties over time, but governments subsequently gave it some degree of statutory support in order to reduce the incidence of industrial action.

Although practically all industrialized nations have institutionalized arrangements for conciliation, different countries reveal preferences for mediation or arbitration, with more relying more heavily on mediation than arbitration. Some countries require a reference to one or more forms of intervention to be made before industrial action can acquire legality (particularly in respect of the public sector or 'essential services') while others leave the decision to the parties themselves. Some provide a public service of conciliation plus, where others leave the arrangements to be made by the parties on an *ad hoc* basis.

The success of the mechanism appears to depend on the parties retaining or being allowed what, within the particular culture, they consider to be adequate control over the processes involved. This, in itself, and for most countries, tends to make conciliation a more acceptable process of third-party intervention than the other two. A good deal of evidence suggests that compulsion is unlikely to produce more peaceful industrial relations, but that a mechanism of this kind which can facilitate settlements of differences can help to reduce the incidence of breakdown in formal industrial relationships.

GEORGE F. THOMASON
UNIVERSITY OF WALES, CARDIFF

Further reading

(References cited in the text marked *)

* Bamber, G.J. and Lansbury, R.D. (1987) *International and Comparative Industrial Relations*, London: Allen and Unwin. (A description of the main features of industrial relations systems in a number of countries, with brief descriptions of the modes of third-party intervention adopted in them.)

* Burrows, G. (1986) *No-Strike Agreements and Pendulum Arbitration*, London: Institute of Personnel Management. (A description of no-strike and pendulum arbitration clauses in collective agreements and an account and evaluation of the experience of their use and effects in North America.)

* Clark, J. and Lewis, R. (1992) 'Arbitration as an option for unfair dismissal claimants', *Personnel Management* June: 36–39. (Explores the feasibility of using arbitration as an alternative to industrial tribunals in resolving unfair dismissal claims.)

* Hanami, T. and Blanpain, R. (eds) (1989) *Industrial Conflict Resolution in Market Economies*, Deventer: Kluwer Law and Tax Publishers. (A review, in the form of contributed chapters (which include case studies), of the systems in use in Australia, the Federal Republic of Germany, Italy, Japan and the USA.)

* Lockyer, J. (1979) *Industrial Arbitration in Great Britain*, London: Institute of Personnel Management. (A description of the history and procedures of industrial relations arbitration in Britain compiled by a senior officer of the Advisory Conciliation and Arbitration Service (ACAS).)

* MacKie, K.J. (ed.) (1991) *A Handbook of Dispute Resolution*, London: Routledge. (A series of papers on the many varieties of difference or dispute, including those of industrial relations, commercial contracts, families and communities, that have attracted non-curial methods of resolution in various countries.)

Owen-Smith, E., Frick, B. and Griffith, T. (1989) *Third Party Involvement in Industrial Relations: A Comparative Study of West Germany and Britain*, Aldershot: Gower. (A review of the history and structure of third-party intervention in Britain and Germany, with a comparative and theoretical analysis, supported by eight case studies of particular interventions in the two countries.)

* Organization for European Cooperation and Development (1993) *Preventing and Resolving Industrial Conflict* (Final Report of a Seminar on Industrial Conflict Settlement in OECD Countries and in Central and Eastern European Economies in Transition), Paris: OECD. (A summary record of the issues raised and conclusions reached in discussions on disputes resolution in the Warsaw Seminar, supported by appended papers on the systems of dispute resolution in Poland, Hungary and the Czech and Slovak Republics.)

Rojot, J. (1989) 'The role of neutrals in the resolution of interest disputes in France', *Comparative Law Journal*, 10 (3), Spring: 324–38. (A description of the conciliation, mediation and arbitration provisions in law and practice in France, set against a background of the relevant aspects of the legal system and the practice of collective bargaining, and demonstrating the considerable reluctance of the collective bargaining parties to involve third parties in dispute settlement.)

* Weiss, M. (1987) *Labour Law and Industrial Relations in the Federal Republic of Germany*, Deventer: Kluwer. (A general description and discussion of the law and collective bargaining practice in the Federal Republic, which contains specific statements on the structure of the labour courts and their roles in the resolution of individual (pp. 96–103) and collective labour disputes (pp. 184–6).)

See also: COLLECTIVE BARGAINING; DISCIPLINE AND DISMISSALS; EMPLOYERS' ASSOCIATIONS; EMPLOYMENT TRIBUNALS; EQUAL EMPLOYMENT OPPORTUNITIES; HUMAN RESOURCE MANAGEMENT; HUMAN RESOURCE MANAGEMENT, INTERNATIONAL; HUMAN RESOURCE MANAGEMENT IN EUROPE; INDUSTRIAL CONFLICT; INDUSTRIAL AND LABOUR RELATIONS; INDUSTRIAL RELATIONS IN EUROPE; INDUSTRIAL RELATIONS IN JAPAN; INDUSTRIAL RELATIONS IN NORTH AMERICA

Thompson, James David (1920–73)

Personal background

- born 11 January 1920, Indianapolis, USA
- married Mary L. Mettenbrink, 1946
- earned doctorate at the University of North Carolina, 1953
- founded *Administrative Science Quarterly*, 1955
- specialized in the analysis of interdependence
- died September 1973 while at Vanderbilt University, Nashville, Tennessee

Major works

Comparative Studies in Administration (with P.B. Hammond, R.W. Hawkes, B.H. Junker and A. Tuden) (1959)
Organizations in Action (1967)
The Behavioral Sciences: An Interpretation (with D.R. Van Houten) (1970)

Summary

James David Thompson was a catalyst for the development of administrative science, specializing in the analysis of interdependence and its processes. He identified sources of interdependence and described their linkages with technology, power and authority, decision strategies and goal setting. Thompson presented typologies for interdependence and its dynamics which provide a strong conceptual base for further theory development and application.

1 Introduction

Thompson was instrumental in the development of the field of administrative science (see ORGANIZATION BEHAVIOUR). He served as a catalyst for the field and contributed to theory through identifying and analysing sources and dynamics of interdependence and its essential nature in organized systems. Although many young scholars in the organizational sciences are unaware of his efforts, his commitment for a science of administration has taken root and borne fruit.

An early advocate of the study of administrative processes, Thompson championed this cause in publications and active work throughout his career. In 1955, he founded *Administrative Science Quarterly*, the first journal devoted specifically to the systematic study of administration, and served as editor for two years and on the editorial board until his death in 1973.

A key aspect of Thompson's work, particularly later in his career, was the application of his ideas on organizational processes to other fields, including education, social welfare, public administration and health care. Toward this end, he led the Pittsburgh area Committee on Common Elements in Administration (1959–60) and wrote essays and articles illustrating common elements in administration across academic fields (Thompson 1961, 1962a). However, Thompson's most recognized contribution to the study of organization theory lies in his analysis of interdependence and its premises and effects.

2 Main contribution

Contributions to theory

A dominant theme throughout Thompson's work is the importance of interdependence as both a source and a consequence of uncertainty, the management of which he saw as an essential function of administration. 'Uncertainty appears as the fundamental problem for complex organizations, and coping with uncertainty, as the essence of the administrative process' (Thompson 1967: 159).

Sources of interdependence

Thompson identified sources of interdependence arising both externally to the organization as well as internally (see ORGANIZATION NETWORKS). Sources of external interdependence he cited include general uncertainty, 'lack of cause/effect understanding in the culture at large' (Thompson 1967: 159) and contingency, in which organizational action outcomes are determined in part by the actions of environmental elements. He described internal interdependence as stemming from relationships between component parts within organizations and between parts and the whole organization. His differentiation of internal interdependence was based on the nature of the existing relationships and consisted of three types: pooled interdependence, sequential interdependence and reciprocal interdependence.

In the first internal interdependence type, pooled interdependence, 'each part renders a discrete contribution to the whole and is supported by the whole' (Thompson 1967: 54). Sequential interdependence is a serial form in which there is direct interdependence and the order of the interdependencies can be specified. Finally, reciprocal interdependence describes a situation in which outputs of each part become inputs for the others, that is, each unit or part poses contingencies on the others. Thompson felt that identifying the type of uncertainty was much more important than measuring the amount. The three types of internal interdependence he identified have implications for the coordination of technology and other processes within organizations.

Technology/interdependence linkages

Thompson defined technology as sets of man–machine activities or techniques that together produce a desired outcome (see TECHNOLOGY AND ORGANIZATIONS). He identified three variations in technology and described their links to interdependence. First, mediating technology is a variation in which the primary purpose is to link clients or customers who seek to be interdependent, such as in a telephone company linking callers; thus, this technology is linked to pooled interdependence. Second, long-linked technology involves sequential interdependence in which

each act or event rests on the completion of the preceding one, such as in a mass production assembly line. Finally, intensive technology draws on a variety of techniques to change an object, and the selection, combination and ordering of techniques are determined by feedback from the object itself, such as in a hospital emergency room in which the state of the patient suggests which techniques and actions are required. In intensive technology, actions by each part create contingencies for other parts; thus, this technology is linked to reciprocal interdependence.

The technology/interdependency linkages Thompson described are important in the modern context of rapid change. Much more emphasis is being placed on interdependence in companies that are increasingly pursuing lateral and team-based approaches as well as integration forward toward the consumer (Gailbraith and Lawler 1993).

Power and authority/interdependence linkages

Thompson also extended his analysis of interdependence and uncertainty to power and authority relationships (Thompson 1956b). Technology and the task environment continuously present sources of uncertainty. He described power as resulting from increased interdependence which arises from a desire and capacity to reduce this uncertainty (see POWER). Individuals, units and organizations move in the direction of their dependency to pursue critical resources and create interdependencies to reduce uncertainty. The role of interdependence in defining power and authority and its relationship with the control of uncertainty have become increasingly prevalent in organization theory literature (Mackenzie 1986) (see ORGANIZATION BEHAVIOUR, HISTORY OF).

Task environment/interdependence linkages

Much of Thompson's discussion of interdependence focused on elements in the task environment, which he defined as 'parts of the environment which are relevant or potentially relevant to goal setting/attainment' (Thompson 1967: 27). He developed notions of buffering to absorb environmental fluctuations, smoothing or levelling to reduce fluctuations, and forecasting to adapt to anticipated fluctua-

Table 1 A typology of decision making

		Preferences about possible outcomes	
		Agreement	*Lack of agreement*
	Agreement	Decision by computation	Decision by bargaining/ compromise
Beliefs about cause/effect			
	Disagreement	Decision by majority judgement	Decision by inspiration

tions. His concepts of boundary and boundary-spanning roles which link organization members and non-members introduced key sources of organizational adaptation (Thompson 1962b). Many of his articles related task environment interdependencies to organization structure (see ORGANIZATION STRUCTURE). He described disaster situations in which communities created temporary 'synthetic organizations' through allocation and integration processes in response to critical contingencies (Thompson and Hawkes 1962).

Thompson defined his domain broadly, applying his ideas on task-environment interdependencies to society as well (Thompson 1974a, 1974b). He believed that the number and variety of boundary-spanning groups related directly to the heterogeneity and dynamism of the task environment (Thompson 1968) (see CONTEXTS AND ENVIRONMENTS). The relevance of his boundary concepts is reflected in the increasing number of networked organizations and alliances worldwide, which serve as a testimonial to his accurate predictions.

Decision strategies/interdependence linkages – a typology

Thompson pioneered several typologies which led to the development of many contingency models, often pointing out previously unseen relationships between variables. Most notable is one that defines decision issues based on two dichotomized variables: preferences about possible outcomes and beliefs about cause and effect (Thompson 1974a) (see DECISION MAKING). The two variables are analysed against the concepts of agreement or lack of agreement to yield a four-cell

typo-logy, as shown in Table 1. In the original presentation of the typology (Thompson *et al.* 1959), the latter concept was labelled as 'disagreement'; the later version reflects a move to a more general concept that includes, but is not limited to, cases of active disagreement. This revision demonstrates a concept refinement process that Thompson engaged in throughout his career.

The decision issues defined are linked to types of uncertainty and interdependence and appropriate strategies are suggested (see STRATEGIC CHOICE). Four strategies arise out of various combinations of agreement and lack of agreement on the two variables: computation, bargaining/compromise, judgement and inspiration. Thompson's focus on *how* decisions are made rather than *what* decisions are made is unique and differs from the usual approaches. In a later article, he further relates his typology to goal-setting strategies (Thompson 1964).

Goal-setting strategies/interdependence linkages

Thompson maintained a strong interest in goals in his work, and he saw goal setting as a necessary, recurring and dynamic aspect of organizational activity. He felt goals grew out of the interaction and interdependence within an organization (see ORGANIZATION NETWORKS) and between an organization and its environment. In 1958, he proposed his ideas in a well-known article with McEwen, which had been reprinted at least fifteen times by the mid-1990s. His proposed strategies for dealing with organizational environments include competition and cooperative strategies, with the latter further divided into bargaining, co-optation and coalition. His analysis placed goal setting in a more strategic form of reciprocal interdependence of the task environment and the organization.

Methodological contribution

Thompson's method of research often rested on creating innovative typologies and developing propositions stated in 'testable form' (Thompson 1960; Thompson 1967: 163). He felt administration was dynamic and that strategies for investigating organizations should focus on dynamics, not statics. Writing at a time when few researchers discussed process, Thompson referred often to patterned sequences of behaviour (Thompson 1967; Thompson *et al.* 1959), task environments (Thompson 1967, 1968) and the dynamics of organizations (Thompson *et al.* 1959).

A collaboratively written early article on the study of administration emphasized the importance of process – which the authors defined as 'how particular patterns bring about functional consequences' – and the need for process models (Thompson *et al.* 1959). The authors called for movement away from the reliance on 'spurious correlations' or associations and 'single-factor' analysis – statistical methods which dominated the field at the time. In fact, Thompson presented a process model for each of four transaction processes he analysed in an article on organizations and output transactions (Thompson 1962b). Given the dominant theme of his work – interdependence and its dynamics – his attraction to this approach is understandable. Leaders in the movement toward quality and organization redesign have pursued similar conceptual approaches (Deming 1982; Mackenzie 1986, 1991).

Although rarely an empiricist in practice, Thompson advocated the application of theory to experience and guided others in their pursuit of a science of administration that focused on simplified, testable models which considered unanticipated consequences and alternative means. He suggested that researchers seek out incidents which did not fit, as these were 'the only sure way of finding those points at which theory needs revision' (Thompson 1956a: 110).

Another aspect of Thompson's approach is his attempt to relate macro and micro structures and processes, seeing the field as a whole. He sought to define the field broadly, linking society, occupations, careers and families. This 'boundary-spanning' approach is currently being pursued under the label 'meso'.

3 Evaluation

Thompson was an early, effective and lifelong advocate of building a science of administration of complex organizations (see OCCUPATIONAL PSYCHOLOGY; ORGANIZATION BEHAVIOUR). He participated vigorously at the abstract, conceptual level but engaged less in the development of measurement, tools and the application of his concepts to the actual administration of organizations. He chose to lead by developing concepts for others to follow.

Citations of Thompson's work show 470 references in the period 1971 to 1975, 817 from 1981 to 1985, 698 from 1989 to 1993 and 768 from 1994 to 1998. Clearly, others are beginning to follow him down the conceptual paths he pioneered. It is his ideas about the nature and types of technology, the impact of uncertainty on decision making and the nature of interdependence that continue to influence scholars almost three decades after his death. Thompson foretold the collapse of the large bureaucracy and the rise of networked organizations (Thompson 1967, 1973) (see ORGANIZATION NETWORKS). These ideas are of central importance to organizations as they downsize, get re-engineered, implement increasingly sophisticated information management and movement systems, and adapt to regulation (Hammer and Champy 1993).

The globalizing effects of competition and the rapid transfer of technology are creating new interdependencies in the form of strategic alliances and networks (see GLOBALIZATION). The rapid pace of change makes Thompson's discussion of goal setting, task environments and the nature of power and authority timeless. He continues to be well worth reading because his work has proven seminal.

Thompson was not enamoured with statistical thinking and static reasoning. He always emphasized the dynamics of administrative processes. Increasingly, managers and scholars are becoming more aware of the limitations of statistical reasoning and static comparison and are focusing more on processes and values (Keeney 1992). It could very well be that the most significant legacy of Thompson's work is the need to understand and use the processes of administration. After all, the action in organization lies in its processes.

4 Conclusions

In his writing, Thompson demonstrated how the concept of interdependence transcended academic disciplines and provided a reference point for a more holistic analysis of the behavioural sciences (Thompson and Van Houten 1970). Being an essential feature of all organized systems, interdependence is an important topic for research. Thompson's ideas, articulated in his classic propositions and typologies, provide a strong conceptual base for the further development of theory. Beyond that, they stimulate useful questions, the pursuit of which will lead to the refinement of administrative science and progression of the field that Thompson sought so fervently.

KENNETH D. MACKENZIE
ELAINE C. HOLLENSBE
UNIVERSITY OF KANSAS

Further reading

(References cited in the text marked *)

* Deming, W.E. (1982) *Quality, Productivity, and Competitive Position*, Cambridge, MA: MIT Press. (A useful account linking processes to quality; provides a bibliography for advanced study.)
* Gailbraith, J.R. and Lawler, E.E. (1993) *Organizing for the Future*, San Francisco, CA: Jossey Bass. (A useful book on lateral and team-based approaches for managing complex organizations.)
* Hammer, M. and Champy J. (1993) *Reengineering the Corporation: A Manifesto for the Business Revolution*, New York: HarperCollins. (An account of business process re-engineering through the radical redesign of process, organization and culture.)
* Keeney, R.L. (1992) *Value-Focused Thinking: A Path to Creative Decision Making*, Cambridge, MA: Harvard University Press. (An illuminating book on decision making and the need for integrating values and ethics in processes.)
* Mackenzie, K.D. (1986) *Organizational Design*, Norwood, NJ: Ablex. (An account of organizational audit and design technology, virtual positions, interdependence, boundaries and task processes.)
* Mackenzie, K.D. (1991) *The Organizational Hologram: The Effective Management of Organization Change*, Boston, MA: Kluwer. (A theory of the organizational hologram, a means of enhancing organization productivity, adaptability and efficient adaptability.)
Mackenzie, K.D. (1997) 'Organizational work, part I: The theory', *Human Systems Management* 16 (1): 9–26; Mackenzie, K.D. (1997) 'Organizational work, part II: The distribution of work', *Human Systems Management* 16 (2): 99–115; Mackenzie, K.D. and Benoit, C.A. (1997) 'Organizational work, part III: Empirical results', *Human Systems Management* 16 (2): 117–137. (This trilogy of papers looks at how organizational processes have an implicate structure by types of process and by level of aggregation. They also detail how to describe and compare processes and then use archives to test eight hypotheses from the processes of actual companies.)
Mackenzie, K.D. (2000) 'Processes and their frameworks', *Management Science* 46 (1). (This paper details useful advances in the field since Thompson, looking at processes in general and describing their analytical properties, relates the process approach to the variance approach, and discusses some methodological issues in describing processes.)
Porter, M. (1990) *The Competitive Advantage of Nations*, New York: The Free Press. (A classic analysis of strategy and competition in an international environment.)
* Thompson, J.D. (1956a) 'On building an administrative science', *Administrative Science Quarterly* 1 (1): 102–11. (Thompson's arguments for developing a science of administration that focuses on simplified, testable models.)
* Thompson, J.D. (1956b) 'Authority and power in "identical" organizations', *American Journal of Sociology* 62: 290–301. (An analysis of relationships involving power and authority.)
* Thompson, J.D. (1960) 'Organizational management of conflict', *Administrative Science Quarterly* 4 (4): 389–409. (An analysis of conflict as a dynamic organizational phenomenon.)
* Thompson, J.D. (1961) 'Common elements in administration', in E.W. Reed (ed.), *Social Welfare Administration*, New York: Columbia

University Press. (An essay that illustrates common elements in administration across academic fields.)

* Thompson, J.D. (1962a) 'Common and uncommon elements in administration', in *The Social Welfare Forum: Official Proceedings of the National Conference on Social Welfare*, New York: Columbia University Press. (An examination of the elements of administration.)

* Thompson, J.D. (1962b) 'Organizations and output transactions', *American Journal of Sociology* 68: 309–24. (A description of process models for four transaction processes.)

* Thompson, J.D. (1964) 'Decision-making, the firm, and the market', in W.W. Cooper, H.J. Leavitt and M.W. Shelly II (eds), *New Perspectives in Organization Research*, New York: Wiley. (An article that relates Thompson's typology of how decisions are made to goal-setting strategies.)

* Thompson, J.D. (1967) *Organizations in Action*, New York: McGraw-Hill. (A major work which identifies sources of interdependence and emphasizes the role of uncertainty.)

* Thompson, J.D. (1968) 'Models of organization and administrative systems', in *The Social Sciences: Problems and Orientations*, The Hague: Mouton/Unesco. (An outline of Thompson's views on boundary concepts.)

* Thompson, J.D. (1973) 'Society's frontiers for organizing activities', *Public Administration Review* 33: 327–35. (An article that predicts the collapse of the large bureaucracy and the rise of networked organizations.)

* Thompson, J.D. (1974a) 'Technology, polity, and societal development', *Administrative Science Quarterly* 19 (1): 6–21. (Discussion of a typology that defines decision issues based on two dichotomized variables.)

* Thompson, J.D. (1974b) 'Social interdependence, the polity and public administration', *Administration and Society* 6 (1): 3–21. (The application of Thompson's ideas on task-environment interdependencies to society.)

* Thompson, J.D., Hammond, P.B., Hawkes, R.W., Junker, B.H. and Tuden, A. (eds) (1959) *Comparative Studies in Administration*, Pittsburgh, PA: University of Pittsburgh Press. (A landmark work presenting comparative essays on the dynamics of administration.)

* Thompson, J.D. and Hawkes, R.W. (1962) 'Disaster, community organization, and administrative process', in G.W. Baker and D.W. Chapman (eds), *Man and Society in Disaster*, New York: Basic Books. (An analysis of organization processes at work in disaster situations.)

* Thompson, J.D. and McEwen, W.J. (1958) 'Organizational goals and environment: goal-setting as an interaction process', *American Sociological Review* 23: 23–31. (A well-known article that proposes strategies for dealing with organizational environments.)

* Thompson, J.D. and Van Houten, D.R. (1970) *The Behavioral Sciences: An Interpretation*, Reading, MA: Addison-Wesley. (An analysis comparing and relating behavioural sciences on a macro level.)

See also: DECISION MAKING; ORGANIZATION BEHAVIOUR; ORGANIZATION NETWORKS; ORGANIZATION STRUCTURE; POWER; TECHNOLOGY AND ORGANIZATIONS

Time-based competition (TBC)

Overview

Speed is an increasingly important dimension of competition for firms in global markets. Firms compete on the speed with which they can respond to customer demands and bring new products and technologies to market. This competition in terms of response time is called *time-based competition*.

Faster response gives a firm a powerful, almost dominant, competitive advantage because, other things being equal, customers will invariably select the supplier who can respond most quickly to their demands: no one prefers to wait. For the faster firms, time is money; they tend to be more profitable, more productive, and have higher growth rates than their competitors.

The keys to developing time-based capabilities are rooted in the just-in-time (JIT) production system (or 'lean manufacturing'). However, to be successful at time-based competition, a firm must go beyond fast-cycle manufacturing and develop complete processes that are more responsive to customers. Today's time challenges are found *off* the factory floor – in customer service, in the supply chain, and in new product (or service) development. The fundamental skills learned in perfecting JIT production systems translate readily to these other processes.

The emergence of the Internet and the new information economy has magnified, rather than invalidated, time-based competition. As the time to transfer information diminishes, differences in speed of fulfilment become more significant factors in determining customer loyalty. In the new economy and the old, time-based firms that can develop processes that permit them to respond to customers faster than the competition will have the potential to dominate their markets.

1 Time as a critical dimension of competition

The term *time-based competition* was first introduced to the management lexicon in 1988 by George Stalk in his *Harvard Business Review* article 'Time: the next source of competitive advantage' (see PORTER, M.E.). Stalk explained how firms could achieve a position of dominance in their industry by using speed of response to customer demands (or time-based competition) as the linchpin of their strategy.

Although the term *time-based competition* is relatively new, the concept is not. Speed of response has always been a key performance measure – in war, as well as in business. Military commanders have long understood the strategic advantages of time: the Duke of Wellington noted that 'In military operations, timing is everything'. As early as the fourteenth century Dutch shipbuilders introduced fast-cycle production systems that were precursors of contemporary JIT production systems (see JUST-IN-TIME PHILOSOPHY).

As firms increasingly compete across great distances in global markets, speed can be an even more powerful competitive advantage. Moreover, as quality standards have risen to the point that they are 'order qualifiers' rather than 'order winners', customer expectations have tilted increasingly towards time as a differentiator among products and services. Firms across a variety of industries – from Toyota to Wal-Mart to Dell Computer – have used time-based competition to stake out positions of market leadership in their industries.

As Larry Carter of Cisco Systems put it, 'It's no longer about the big beating the small, it's about the fast beating the slow' (*The Economist* 1999).

There are two important reasons why the fast are beating the slow, and why speed has been so important to these firms' financial success. First, faster response wins customers, increases sales and market share. Second, firms that acquire speed by developing lean, responsive processes tend to see dramatic gains in productivity and quality as they reduce throughput times: production costs fall as time is compressed. As a competitive weapon, time is a double-edged sword: simultaneously increasing sales and lowering costs.

The competitive advantages of speed in the marketplace follow directly from an elementary principle of customer behaviour: given a choice of two equivalent products or services, customers will choose the one that can be delivered first. We prefer our packages to be delivered overnight, photographs developed in an hour, and mortgages approved without lengthy delays.

Speed is relative, and speed relative to the competition is what determines competitive advantage in a time-based world. However, the standard for response times, or *clockspeed* (Fine, 1998), varies by industry. In the custom furniture business, a leisurely industry in which response time is typically measured in months, response in weeks can be a powerful advantage. What qualifies as quick response in furniture would be snail-like in the personal computer (PC) business. With its ability to assemble-to-order and ship a custom PC in under four days (depending on delivery time), Dell Computer's *Dell Direct* process has revolutionized the PC business and made obsolete the traditional, but slow, manufacturer–distributor–retailer supply chain (Dell and Fredman 1999).

Not only is time relative, but the customer's *perception* of time is the critical metric. What matters is a firm's speed of response relative to the competition – *as measured by the customer*. To customers, a firm's internal processing speed is not relevant; they only care about the time required to complete the order cycle from 'need to satisfaction'. To be a time-based competitor, a firm must have a perceptible response time advantage to other firms in the same industry.

To the traditional operations manager, the statement that time-based competitors tend to have lower costs and higher quality sounds like a contradiction. Conventional wisdom maintains that 'haste makes waste': so, in pursuing speed, the time-based competitor must incur higher costs and/or lower quality because the low-cost producer is shielded by an unavoidable tradeoff, and the quicker competitor will be forced to charge higher prices. Unfortunately, there is more convention than wisdom in this. Several researchers have found that the time-driven efforts to reduce throughput time actually increase productivity and lower costs. (Schmenner 1988; Lieberman *et al.* 1990). As will be noted again below, the process of developing quicker response also leads to, if not forces, significant improvement in quality (see TOTAL QUALITY MANAGEMENT).

To see clearly the competitive advantage of speed, consider the dilemma of a manufacturer that is at a speed *dis*advantage. The traditional cost-based competitor with slower response time can only match the time-based competitor's offerings by carrying additional inventory to create the illusion of faster response. This drives up costs and diminishes the profitability of the slower firm; it also explains why time-based competitors in an industry tend to have higher growth rates and profitability. The traditional cost-based competitor has little defence against firms that can provide products with the most value for the lowest cost *with the fastest response time*.

2 Time is money: valuing faster response

Blackburn (1991) and Stalk and Hout (1990) suggest that the time-based competitor can charge higher prices, achieve higher market share and be more profitable than competitors. Other researchers (Li and Lee 1994) have used equilibrium models of market competition to *prove* that faster delivery does make a significant difference: given two competitors, the firm with faster delivery speed can charge higher prices and achieve greater market share.

In most industries, then, the price of a product or service is a decreasing function of the supplier's response time. Although this generic relationship exists, few managers have an appreciation for the marginal value of faster response in their own industry. Quantification of the time value of money allows managers to make informed decisions about efforts to further develop speed as a distinctive competence by making, for example, investment in better, faster information systems or improved logistics to move closer to customers.

Our empirical research (Blackburn *et al.* 1991, 1992) in three industries – book distribution, machine tools, and plastic injection mould manufacturing – found that, although the marginal value of time varies across industries, response time is generally undervalued, and the faster firms gain unexpectedly large returns at the expense of their slower competitors.

Plastic injection mould manufacturing is an illustrative example because in this industry many of the less profitable mould builders underestimate the value of faster response and have little appreciation for the strategic benefits of faster delivery to their customer, the moulder. The small, conventional mould builders tend to have similar lead-times of about 14 weeks to customers. They bid against one another for contracts and share a common belief that lead-time is 'not much of an issue in their industry'. However, a small set of faster, time-based mould builders existed, who used the latest technology, could deliver moulds up to nine weeks faster, and could command a price premium of up to 30 per cent. Each week of faster response was worth about a 3 per cent price premium to the faster mould builders. Their customers were high-tech manufacturers for whom development time of new plastic components was on the critical path for their new product introductions. As shown in Figure 1, primarily because their speed made a substantial price premium possible, these time-based mould builders tend to be 4 to 5 times as profitable as their slower counterparts who compete in the traditional way on price.

In other markets, such as make-to-stock manufacturing, price premiums cannot be charged for faster response, but there is a sizeable cost of delay. That is, product cost is an increasing function of response time. As cycle (or replenishment time) is reduced, the cost of (pipeline, safety stock, obsolescence) inventory is reduced. A failure to appreciate the real cost of delay has led some manufacturers to move offshore in search of lower labour cost and actually *in*crease their total cost because of a time trap. By moving offshore, a manufacturer adds more than a month to the replenishment time cycle, and this cost often far exceeds the labour cost differential. Undervaluing closeness to customers and the time value of money in search of cheaper labour can lead to misguided plant location decisions.

In industries with rapid, intense innovation, the cost of time delay may actually be greatest in new product development, where being late to market can carry severe penalties in terms of lost profitability. For example, a study of the automotive sector (Clark *et al.* 1987) indicated that, for the case of a $10,000 car, each delay in introducing a new car model into the market represents, conservatively, one million dollars in lost profits. The financial markets also extract severe delay penalties: a study of public announcements in the financial press of new product introduction delays found that the average market value of the firm decreased 5.25 per cent on the news (Hendricks and Singhal 1997).

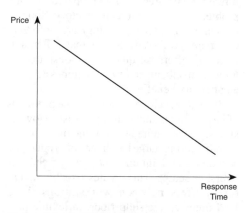

Figure 1 Profitability of faster response

3 Origins of time-based competition

The fundamental capabilities for developing faster response processes were first demonstrated in factory floor operations of manufacturing firms. Toyota, through its *Toyota Production System*, developed and refined the prototype process that is now better known as just-in-time (JIT) or 'lean manufacturing' (see JAPAN, MANAGEMENT IN; JUST-IN-TIME PHILOSOPHY; TOYODA FAMILY). By focusing on basic work processes, Toyota rethought the process and redefined the way discrete manufacturing is viewed. As they sharpened and simplified the process into a model of lean manufacturing, speed, productivity, quality and flexibility increased. Manufacturing cost was also sharply reduced. This example is important for time-based competitors not only for the dramatic reduction in cycle times produced on the factory floor, but because it provides a clear roadmap for successful time-compression of the firm's other activities – product development, order entry, supply chains and other business processes.

Misconceptions about JIT often blind us to its importance to time-based competition. For many firms, JIT is merely a programme to lower incoming inventory by requiring frequent shipments from suppliers. This accomplishes little more than shifting inventory further back into the chain onto the suppliers' balance sheet. Other firms view JIT as an inventory reduction device and, with this limited goal, are often unprepared for the problems that arise on the factory floor as mandates to reduce inventory are enforced. Compared to the advantages that JIT manufacturing offers for quicker response to customer demand, inventory reduction is actually an ancillary benefit.

JIT was developed to address the problems of large batch manufacturing – waste, slow response times, limited variety and high cost. In manufacturing, large batch runs of product are scheduled to minimize the cost of changeovers, or setups. This creates sizeable inventory buffers between workstations, long lead-times on the shop floor, inflexible production schedules, and barriers to increased product variety. Toyota recognized that the

basic problem to be solved (and a major cause of waste) was setup, or changeover, time and a concentrated effort to reduce changeover times and batch sizes is essential to effective JIT.

Figure 2 describes the key steps in a JIT implementation, beginning with setup, or changeover, time reduction. Although much has been written about each step of this process, the aim here is only to sketch the process and to draw out the essential elements that are keys to time compression. Many of the benefits ascribed to JIT come from attacking waste and isolating those essential activities that add value for the customer, then eliminating remaining non-value-adding activities, not in doing tasks faster. Another source of time delays and quality problems is large batch production. Therefore, a concentrated effort to reduce changeover times and batch sizes is an essential starting activity for JIT. Manufacturing cells based on grouping products into flow systems based on product families are another way to reduce setup times (or the need for setups). As setup times and batch sizes are reduced, opportunities for parallel, rather than sequential, processing arise. As cycle times and batch sizes are reduced, new, compact

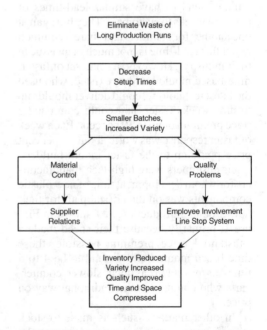

Figure 2 JIT process evolution

Table 1 Setup reduction process steps

1	Organize and charter the team
2	Create visual performance measures and track performance with time metrics
3	Develop a detailed map of the setup activity sequence
4	Label activities: non-value adding (waste), in-line and off-line
5	Eliminate non-value adding activities
6	Complete off-line activities prior to setup
7	Seek to move in-line activities off-line
8	Overlap activities
9	Smooth and simplify, before automating

layouts are designed to speed and simplify the work flow.

In JIT, reducing the waste of changeover time facilitates the production of smaller batch sizes, offers the possibility of more flexible and responsive production, and reduces the cost of variety. However, smaller batches tend to create material flow and communication problems on the factory floor. Smaller batches also expose quality problems, heretofore hidden by the excesses of large batch production, that now threaten to shut down the system. Therefore, the attack on the waste of large batch production stimulates a programme of continual process improvement that forces the organization to (1) solve critical quality problems; (2) redesign layouts for space compression and smoother flow; and (3) develop new methods of material flow control (such as Kanban). The net effect is lean production – a process that is much faster, more flexible, higher in quality, and operates at lower cost. Contrary to conventional wisdom, *this* is why faster response time reduces cost.

Of all the activities that encompass a JIT implementation, setup reduction is the key learning activity for an organization that seeks to become a time-based competitor. Setup reduction is time compression in microcosm. The activities (shown in Table 1) which are required to reduce a setup are identical to those required to eliminate time from any process.

The procedure for successful setup reduction provides an ideal template for compressing the time of any process. A team-based, metrics-driven approach to process improvement that begins with rigorous process mapping and value-added analysis is central to a setup reduction and to any other time-compression activity. A firm that 'cuts its teeth' on setup reduction gains more than the ability to achieve small batch production: it has developed a capability that can be propagated throughout the organization to accelerate processes of faster response.

4 Developing processes for quick response

Although the fundamental skills for developing quick response processes have been developed on the factory floor, the processes off the factory floor in the so-called 'white collar factories' offer some of the best opportunities for significant time compression (Blackburn, 1992). Speed in these processes is equally important to those of manufacturing because

Table 2 Comparison of conventional practices in manufacturing and administrative processes

Parameters	Conventional batch manufacturing	Conventional administrative processes
Batch sizes	Large batch production: transferred in large batches	Information processed and transferred in large batches
Layouts	Job shop	Functional by department
Process flow	Sequential activities	Sequential
Scheduling	Centralized scheduling	Centralized control
Employee involvement	Individual; low	Individual; low
Quality	High defect ratios; re-work	Re-work; re-checking and correcting information
Automation	Islands of automation; isolated robots or transfer devices	Isolated systems (e.g. stand-alone word processors)
Lead times	Long	Long

Table 3 Analysis of cycle times and value-added activity times in common administrative processes

Industry	Process	Average cycle time	Value-adding time	Percentage value-adding time
Life insurance	New policy application	72 hours	7 minutes	0.16
Consumer packaging	New graphic design	18 days	2 hours	0.14
Office equipment	Order entry	5 days	5 minutes	0.21
Footwear	Prototype development	25 weeks	2 days	1.60
Commercial bank	Consumer loan	24 hours	30 minutes	2.1
Hospital	Patient billing	10 days	3 hours	3.75
Motor vehicle equipment	Financial end-of-month closing	11 days	5 hours	5.60

customers care only about the total cycle time – time consumed anywhere in the 'value-delivery' chain is of equal value to customers. To be a time-based competitor, the lessons learned in lean manufacturing must be applied to all of the firm's critical processes.

Fortunately, white-collar processes can be attacked by the same methods used to reduce cycle times in traditional manufacturing because the processes are structured similarly. Table 2 presents a comparison of conventional manufacturing and administrative processes. The problems of large batch processing afflict both: white collar processes and conventional manufacturing processes tend to be slow for similar reasons.

The roadmap for time-compressing administrative processes follows the sequence of activities outlined in the previous section for a JIT implementation. The initial steps are selecting a critical process, chartering (and empowering) a team, and establishing key process performance metrics. Then the team's most important activity should be to prepare a detailed process map of the process and carry out a value-added analysis of all activities.

Isolating the value-adding (VA) activities in a process and seeking to eliminate the rest produces most of the time reduction in an administrative process. To understand why, we first introduce a definition of VA activities that restricts them to those absolutely essential for the process.

Definition of VA Activity: For a process activity to be classified as value adding, it must satisfy the following three criteria:

1 the customer must care about it (that is, be willing to pay for it);
2 the product or service must be transformed;
3 the activity must be done right the first time.

All other activities are classified as non-value-adding (NVA), or waste. Waste abounds in most administrative processes. As shown in Table 3, examples from some common processes make it clear that the fraction of total process cycle time spent on waste, or non-value-adding (NVA) activities when nothing of value is being done for the customer, frequently exceeds 95 per cent. The powerful message for process improvement teams is that by simply by removing the waste (and doing nothing to the value-adding activities), process improvements of up to 20 times are possible. A key progress metric for the improvement team is the ratio of VA time to total cycle time.

Time spent by the entire team preparing a map of the current process and debating the value of activities typically uncovers many opportunities for breakthroughs in process improvement. For example, eliminating waiting and queuing – which typically consume more than 50 per cent of the time in an administrative process – can produce significant reductions. The team will find that quality problems account for a large proportion of the NVA time, and this will spark lively debates among the improvement team about whether inspections are a VA activity or, at minimum, are necessary for the process. Further analysis

Table 4 Comparison of JIT practices in manufacturing and administrative processes

Process parameters	JIT manufacturing	JIT administrative processes
Batch sizes	Small batch production; transferred in small lots	Information processed and transferred in small batches
Layouts	Product layout	Grouped by process team
Process flow	Coordinated activities	Overlapping activities; concurrent information processing
Management	Localized control; high level of employee involvement	Local control; management by process team
Quality	Low defect rates	Less re-work; fewer information corrections
Automation	Integrated systems; automation follows process simplification	Automation of information flows; integrated, networked systems
Lead times	Short	Short

will reveal that when quality problems exist, entire sequences of activities become NVA because the process must go through a rework, or corrective, cycle. Therefore the time-compression process increases pressure to solve quality problems.

The next steps in the improvement process frequently produce smaller, incremental gains. A model for the conversion from a batch flow to a JIT model for administrative processes is shown in Table 4. Following the JIT model, the improvement team seeks to reduce batch sizes and move toward one-piece flows. Layouts are changed for space compression and to facilitate smoother flows. As NVA activities are removed, activities are grouped and assigned to a single staff member; handoffs are reduced. Opportunities for overlapping, or concurrent, activities are examined.

5 Time-based new product development

In many industries – notably consumer electronics, financial services, and others in which software is dominant – firms compete less in terms of manufacturing speed and more in the speed with which they can bring new products and services to market. As noted earlier, the cost of delay often reaches its highest values in new product development. Although there are concerns with being too fast to market with products that the market is not prepared to accept, a fast time-to-market process gives the

firm a choice of when to launch. With a slow process, the only option is to be a follower and try to play catch up.

Despite the strategic advantages of speed, the typical product development project is late to market and over budget. The research on worldwide product development practice that we carried out, as shown in Table 5, indicates that conventional product development processes share many of the features of conventional, large batch manufacturing, including long leadtimes (Blackburn, 1991). In short, firms tend to develop products in the same way that they make them.

The similarities between conventional practices in manufacturing and new-product development are surprisingly strong:

- *Batch sizes:* Long changeover times and large batch sizes pervade manufacturing, and large batches are the direct cause of long lead-times and excessive WIP inventories. Studies of new product design have shown that, as in manufacturing, information is commonly processed in large batches – tossed 'over the wall' from one developer to another. This reinforces a sequential, functional approach to development.

- *Layouts and process flow:* In conventional batch manufacturing, machines are grouped by function as in job shops. In new product development, the layout is analogous to the job shop: groups tend to be located in offices according to their function and the partitioned layout encourages

Table 5 Comparison of conventional practices in manufacturing and new product development

Parameters	Conventional batch manufacturing	Conventional new product development
Batch sizes	Large batch production; transferred in large batches	Information processed and transferred in large batches
Layouts	Job shop	Functional by department
Process flow	Sequential activities	Sequential
Scheduling	Centralized scheduling	Centralized control
Employee involvement	Low	Low
Supply relations	Little coordination with suppliers	Low involvement with suppliers in design of components
Quality	High defect ratios; re-work	Numerous engineering changes re-work
Automation	Islands of automation; isolated robots or transfer devices	Isolated systems (e.g. CAD systems with negligible integration)
Lead times	Long	Long

sequential performance of development activities. This further supports batch, 'over the wall' processing.

- *Supply relations:* Traditional supplier relationships in manufacturing tend to be arm's-length and adversarial. In development, suppliers are rarely involved; no attempt is made to take advantage of the supplier's technology or design expertise.
- *Quality:* Both conventional batch manufacturing and conventional product design are beset by quality problems for reasons due to large-batch processing. Quick detection of defects is necessary to determine the cause of the quality problems. Not getting it right means rework (or reworked designs) – a major cause of long lead times in development cycles.
- *Automation:* Automation in conventional manufacturing has been applied sporadically and inconsistently; 'islands of automation' are created to relieve a bottleneck or quality problem. In product design, similarly, automation has been applied to isolated segments of the process.

The net effect of these factors is that – in new product development as in large batch manufacturing – lead-times are long and non-competitive.

Just as there is a JIT model for manufacturing, there is a similar model for new product development which is shown in Table 6. In each case the key measure of performance is

the batch size: small-lot production, made possible by reduced changeover times, is the cornerstone of JIT. In product design, the analogue of the batch size is the amount of information to be processed or the scope of the problem to be solved. Faster-developer firms tend to bite off small chunks of the design problem at successive stages, reducing the information batch size. In an overlapping approach, information is released in incremental units – the batch size for information transfer from one design stage to the next is reduced to the smallest unit possible – a JIT approach to design.

As with JIT, overlapping among activities in product development and transfer of design information in smaller batches fosters similar layout changes. Instead of organizing by function or department, the project team is 'co-located', which fosters frequent, multi-channel communication among team members. Faster developers typically have suppliers heavily involved in the development process. The concept of a coordinated supply chain is applied to development.

In new product development, high quality means minimal rework or redesign. Reducing the batch size of information processing leads to earlier detection of design problems, shorter 'find and fix' cycles, and more rapid development. The proper role of automation in a JIT system can be summed up in the phrase 'First simplify, then automate'. In new product development the real power of design

Table 6 Comparison of JIT practices in manufacturing and new product development

Process parameters	JIT manufacturing	JIT new product development
Batch sizes	Small batch production; transferred in small lots	Information processed and transferred in small batches
Layouts	Product layout	Grouped by project team
Process flow	Coordinated activities	Overlapping activities; simultaneous engineering
Management	Localized control; high level of employee involvement	Localcontrol; management by project team
Supply relations	Close coordination with suppliers	High involvement with suppliers in design of components; technology and information exchange
Quality	Low defect rates	Few engineering changes
Automation	Integrated systems; automation follows process simplification	Automation of information flows; integrated CAD/CAE/CAM
Lead times	Short	Short

automation is realized when the firm already has in place a smoothly functioning design team with overlapping activities.

Just as the lean production model, built around small batch production, has helped time-based firms turn manufacturing speed into a distinctive competence, the lean development model, built around small batch production and transfer of information, has given those same firms the strategic capability to be first-to-market with new features and technology.

6 Time-based competition in the new economy

Fundamental changes in the structure of the economy raise questions about the validity of time-based strategies. The growth in the service sector is outpacing manufacturing, and manufacturing is now managed not as a stand-alone unit but as part of a service-oriented supply chain. The Internet and advances in information technology have fundamentally changed the nature of relationships with customers and suppliers. Of what value are time-based strategies in this new economy?

The rapid ascendance of the Internet and the information economy may have changed the nature of time-based competition, but it has magnified, rather than diminished it. An examination of the more successful competi-

tors in the new economy suggests that time is now even more important because the speed at which business is transacted and customer expectations for timely response have increased. In the new economy, there will be even greater pressure for time-based business process improvements.

To understand how a disruptive technology such as the Internet magnifies the importance of speed, consider the book distribution supply chain. Under the old system, the total time in the order-shipment cycle took ten days: four days to send and process the order and six days to fulfil – that is, pick, pack and ship to the customer. With the Internet, the order processing time can be shrunk essentially to zero. With no changes in fulfilment time, the competitive standard for response is now six days. A firm with a one-day fulfilment time advantage now has about a 20 per cent advantage over the competition, instead of a 10 per cent advantage in the old economy. The Internet does not eliminate the need for speed; it makes speed the *sine qua non* of performance. In the personal computer assembly and distribution chain, Dell Computer has leveraged quick fulfilment and their abilities to use the Internet to forge direct links with customers to become a dominant, time-based competitor (Dell and Fredman, 1999).

Time-based competition is a deceptively simple proposition. The power of a time-based strategy is that, by focusing on speed, the firm develops world-class quality and the process flexibility to deliver a wider variety of products and services without the burden of increased cost. Speed will continue to be a critical dimension of operations performance for the simple reason that it is important to customers. Time-based competition is a race that never ends.

JOSEPH D. BLACKBURN
OWEN GRADUATE SCHOOL OF MANAGEMENT
VANDERBILT UNIVERSITY

Further reading

(References cited in the text marked *)

* Blackburn, J.D. (ed.) (1991) *Time-Based Competition: The Next Battleground in Manufacturing*, Homewood, IL: BusinessOne Irwin. (An overview of time-based competition from basic principles to applications.)

* Blackburn, J.D., Lindsley, W. and Elrod, T. (1991) 'Time-based competition in the book distribution industry', *Journal of Operations Management* 10 (3): 344–62. (Describes an industry study of the monetary value of quicker response.)

* Blackburn, J.D., Elrod, T., Lindsley, W. and Zahorik, A. (1992) 'The strategic value of response time and product variety', Ch.13 in C.A. Voss (ed.), *Manufacturing Strategy: Process and Content*, London: Chapman & Hall. (Describes industry studies that quantify the value of speed and show how it is used for strategic advantage.)

* Blackburn, J.D. (1992) 'Time-based competition: white-collar activities', *Business Horizons* 35 (4): 96–101. (Explains how Just-in-Time principles can be applied to time compress non-manufacturing processes.)

* Clark, Kim. B., Chew, B. and Fujimoto, T. (1987) 'Product development in the world auto industry', *Brookings Papers on Economic Activity* 3: 729–71. (This paper documents the cost of time delays in product development, specifically in the automotive sector.)

* Dell, M.S. and Fredman, C. (1999) *Direct from Dell: Strategies that Revolutionized an Industry*, New York: Harper Business. (Describes the Dell Computer model that has made them the leading time-based competitor in the PC industry.)

* Fine, C.H. (1998) *Clockspeed: Winning Industry Control in the Age of Temporary Advantage*, Reading, MA: Perseus Books. (Describes the

variation in standards of time performance across industries.)

Gates, W.H., III (1999) *Business at the Speed of Thought: Using a Digital Nervous System*, New York: Warner Books. (This book by Microsoft's CEO gives his views on the importance of speed in the new economy.)

Handfield, R.B. (1995) *Re-engineering for time-based competition: benchmarks and best practices for production, R & D and purchasing*, Westport,CT: Quorum Books. (Provides benchmark data on cycle time performance for different processes in manufacturing.)

* Hendricks, K.B. and Singhal, V.R. (1997) 'Delays in new product introductions and the market value of the firm: The consequences of being late to the market', *Management Science* 43 (4): 422–36. (An investigation into the reaction of financial markets to announcements of delayed product introductions.)

* Li, L. and Lee, Y.S. (1994) 'Pricing and delivery-time performance in a competitive environment', *Management Science* 40 (5): 633–46. (A theoretical investigation of the relationships between response time and price.)

* Lieberman, M.B., Lau, L.J. and Williams, M.D. (1990) 'Firm level productivity and management influence', *Management Science* 36 (10): 1193–215. (An empirical investigation of the relationship between throughput time and productivity in the auto industry.)

* Stalk, G. Jr. (1988) 'Time—the next source of competitive advantage', *Harvard Business Review* July–August: 41–51. (The article that first introduces the term time-based competition and discusses its strategic implications.)

* Stalk, G. Jr. and Hout, T.M. (1990) *Competing against Time*, New York: The Free Press. (An excellent examination of the strategic advantages of time by the men who introduced the concept of time-based competition.)

* Schmenner, R.W. (1988) 'The merit of makings things fast', *Sloan Management Review* Fall: 11–17. (One of the first papers to examine the relationship between speed and productivity in global manufacturing.)

Shingo, S. (1985) *A Revolution in Manufacturing: The SMED System*, Cambridge, MA: Productivity, Inc. (The classic book on setup time reduction as a key to the Toyota Production System; setup reduction is a fundamental skill for time-based competition.)

Suri, R. (1998) *Quick Response Manufacturing: A Companywide Approach to Reducing Lead Times*, Portland: Productivity Press. (A how-to book that shows, with examples, how to reduce cycle times in manufacturing.)

See also: GLOBALIZATION; JAPAN, MANAGE-
MENT IN; JUST-IN-TIME PHILOSOPHY;
MANUFACTURING STRATEGY; NEW PROD-
UCT DEVELOPMENT; PORTER, M.E.; SUPPLY
CHAIN MANAGEMENT; TOTAL QUALITY
MANAGEMENT; TOYODA FAMILY

Time management

Overview

Time is perhaps the most valuable resource in any organization or personal endeavour. Even though time is an endless commodity, it is the one resource that is constantly depleted, cannot be reproduced, and once lost can never be recovered. Time management is the art and science of using time effectively. Some would argue that time itself is not manageable, that time simply *is* (Wright 1999). What *can* be managed is how we use time, and how we select the priorities, activities and tasks that use our time.

Time management is a key element of effective business management. Organizations and people who use time well are better equipped to face both the personal and professional challenges of the world. Time has become not only a tool for organizational study, but also a means to gain competitive advantage in the marketplace. Time-based management, cycle-time reduction and value-added time are key features of competitive strategy.

1 Time as an organizational and personal issue

Organizational issues of time management include the development of a corporate vision, goal setting, priority establishment, organization design, planning, scheduling, application of technology, systems, work processes and consistent follow-up. Organizational time management also focuses on time competition, 'just-in-time' methodologies and flexible work patterns (see FLEXIBILITY, PRODUCTIVITY).

Personal time management is at the root of effective management: as organizations become more reliant on effective minimal management, time becomes the factor that enables the critical work processes to be accomplished as required.

According to Covey, the essence of time management is characterized by a single phrase: 'organize and execute around priorities'. How best to do that is the focus of a number of different tools and approaches. Through its evolution time management has developed in three distinct phases. The first phase was characterized by the use of 'to do' lists and notes, in an effort to give some structure to the daily tasks that had to be accomplished. The next phase was characterized by the use of calendars and appointment books, the planning tools. Generation three, the time management concepts of the 1990s, concentrates on the importance of goal setting, priorities and defining work as having value based on how well it contributed to meeting the goals and priorities set. The fourth generation of time management is based on the recognition that the basic challenge of time management is not so much the management of time as it is the management of ourselves.

Just as each of us has at one time or another asked 'Where does the time go?' an unscheduled and uncontrolled organization can experience as much as 50 per cent 'lost time' in its daily operations as the result of seepage, poor planning and execution and lack of consistent follow-up. Missed schedules, overtime costs, excessive work-in-process time, all become built-in or buried in the overall cost of doing business. The work processes are weighted down with non-value-added activities or outmoded and costly methods of doing business.

In order for organizations to control their activities to use time effectively, they must first begin to value it as a resource and identify how it is being spent. Factors in organizations that cause time to be wasted or 'lost' include a myriad activities that do not add value to the customer, whether internal or external to the enterprise. Such factors include failures in management and control, ineffective scheduling, poor planning, misunderstanding or misalignment of corporate goals and priorities, methods and procedures that are outdated or could be replaced by technologies and different techniques, and processes and procedures that are simply not followed.

People in most organizations devote time to tasks that do not ultimately add value to the product or service that is offered to clients. Tasks can be categorized as: those that add value; those that are necessary but do not directly add value; and those tasks that are not necessary and do not add value. Experience indicates that less than 25 per cent of the time in most organizations is actually spent on work that adds value to the client. About 15 per cent of the time is spent on work that is necessary, but does not directly add value to the client. Of the remaining 60 per cent, typically 40 per cent of the time is spent in non-value-producing activity. The other 20 per cent is considered statutory time-off, holidays, vacation and sick leave.

In order to understand time management it is necessary to understand the kinds of tasks that may rob an organization of its ability to manage its resources effectively. By classifying work into basic categories of value-producing, necessary and non-value-producing, many of the typical organizational time traps are highlighted.

Some of the conditions that detract from value are:

Lack of a clear vision. Organizations that lack vision can spend time and other resources pursuing activities and events that do not actively support the achievement of their goals. Organizational visions that are not understood or clearly communicated also rob the organization of effectiveness. When people working for a company do not share in the corporate vision, they too begin to lose effectiveness. Wright (1999) identifies this as having 'purpose', without purpose, both people and the organizations that they form cannot be effective. Without purpose, goals lack coherence, order, direction and power.

Lack of goals and objectives. The organizational process is hindered and time wasted by people working on goals and objectives that do not meet the organization's requirements. Each set of organizational goals must be prioritized and managed effectively. By setting goals, you know where you are going. Without goals, it is easy to become distracted, and to devote precious time to extraneous activities that are not effectively supporting the desired outcome.

Mismatched capacities. Time is wasted when parts of the work process are not coordinated into a smooth flow. This results in excessive waiting time in parts of the operation, or bottlenecks in the flow.

Uneven work schedules, and resources not matched to the workload. Resources may be wasted in attempting to meet unrealistic deadlines. Most people routinely underestimate the amount of time to complete a given task. Dr Jan Yeager in her book, *Creative Time Management for the New Millennium* (1999), suggests that it is important to add at least 10 and often 20 per cent to estimated completion times in order for schedules to come out on time.

Lack of training or inadequate instruction, causing rework or errors. If follow-up is not timely, errors are not corrected when they are made, but are left to become more costly, as additional operations are added without adding real value.

Lack of meaningful work. People slow their pace when there is little work or work on things that do not add value.

Excess cycle time in the work process. As a product or service is fed through the work process, there are often built-in cushions, safety factors or gaps that actually waste time and provide no effective return. 'Just-in-time' manufacturing management and inventory management systems are designed to reduce not only the cost of excessive inventory but also the amount of time actually spent in the production cycle. The compression of cycle time is emerging as a clear competitive business advantage, and has led some organizations like Sun Microsystems and Wal-Mart into the practice of time-based management.

Lack of systems or methodology to relate work to time for purposes of scheduling. Unless the actual workload is known, and the rate at which the work can be completed, there is no meaningful way to schedule an operation or a task. Predictive methods can be used and evaluated for their effectiveness, but the base must be an accurate assessment of the time required to complete a given set of tasks.

Layout of work areas. The physical layout of the work area may cause more transport or travel time than necessary. Work-flow layout may be illogical in relation to parts, tools, machines and sequence of work. Personal workspace should be organized to eliminate unnecessary moves, steps or strains.

Pacing. People or groups pace their work according to the amount of time assigned to them, resulting in less output but an appearance of constant activity. When a person is assigned one task it will often be completed. When assigned two, one may be completed. When assigned seven or eight, most if not all will be completed.

Scrap, rework and errors. Time is spent producing work that does not conform to requirements if the latter were not been communicated or understood, or if the physical process cannot consistently maintain work at the required level.

Lack of specific assignment. The wrong work being done at the wrong time often results in lost time because the work sequence as a whole is not as productive as is desirable.

Work assignments are not equitable or demanding enough. Work expands to fill the time available. Workers each set their own pace. Often in these situations the worker has no real understanding of the desired or reasonable work pace. The result is inequities in the workplace, and a tendency generally to slow the pace rather than move more quickly.

Lack of alternative assignments. This occurs in situations where work of high priority may fluctuate and workers pace themselves according to the high priority work. There is no second or alternative assignment that will fill in the 'slack' periods when the higher priority work is not immediately available. Careful planning and assignment of alternative work will reduce work backlogs and increase productive effort.

Lack of discipline. Where discipline with regard to the time an employee should start work or take lunch and break times is very loose, this could cause a seepage of time,

sloppy work habits, and could lead to an undisciplined organization.

Assumption that individualization is desirable. When the work group is not trained in techniques that encourage maximum flexibility, the result is small groups of specialists who cannot be used for other jobs when required.

Failure to make use of inter-departmental flexibility. This is generally the result of a failure to establish communication channels and systems for shifting people from one area to another in order to be where the work is. Often managers will make work in their area in order not to move their workers out of it. This is often the result of poor predictive systems and lack of visibility in the scheduling of work activity.

Uncontrolled use of overtime. This occurs when overtime is not planned based on accomplishing the required work with a minimum of people at a desirable pace of work. Sometimes the need for overtime is assumed rather than 'real' in that it may be possible to shift priorities and accomplish the desired work at the regular rate. Typical also in the workplace is the problem of 'seeping overtime', where people just stay a 'few minutes more' to accomplish a job. A few minutes a day paid at premium rates are a costly time management issue, and one that is often overlooked.

Misuse of capacity and space. When the logistics of the scheduling process are not controlled, it is easy to waste valuable space with unnecessary stockpiling of inventories, or use capacity on items that are not required to meet customer needs.

Failure to get into the detail. Lost time often occurs when people work on projects that may not be consistent with the real needs of the company, because the assignments are made based on limited knowledge or poor communication of requirements.

Inadequate communication. When requirements are not clearly communicated between departments or work groups, time may be lost because the right work is not done at the right time. Lost time also occurs when too many or too few people are assigned to a task, or inappropriate skills are applied to resolving a problem.

Failure to recognize lost time. Recognition of lost time requires training, thought and objectivity. It is important to be able to step back from a situation and identify where events can be more effectively managed. Often it is difficult to see lost time as it happens, and techniques such as short-interval scheduling, batch-work processes, and just-in-time have been effectively employed to eliminate lost time systematically from the work environment.

Poor or inconsistent management. The management may not be motivated to eliminate the waste in an organization, or the organization may be placing its emphasis on the wrong indicators of performance. Even in organizations that value control as part of their culture, poor or inconsistent management will send signals that it is 'acceptable to do things that are counter-productive'.

Wrong emphasis in existing systems. An organization's systems may fail to keep pace with the changes in their business or changes in the work culture. Systems must be consistent with the work they are designed to control and the work process they are designed to support. Changes in the work process are often not reflected in management or operational control systems.

Duplication of effort. Often difficult to spot in larger or multifaceted organizations, duplication of effort may occur when one department or work group is producing work to support its needs, while another is doing essentially the same work for different purposes, and neither is aware of the other's effort. It often occurs with crosschecks of predominantly accurate information that are completed in the name of 'quality': the system or process might easily be changed to eliminate the need for crosschecks altogether.

Inflexibly or lack of innovative thought. This kind of thinking can perpetuate lost time and is counterproductive to time management. Questioning or ordering different priorities and encouraging original thinking may cost time in their inception, but save time in their execution; however, original drought may become imperiled by a static or archaic management thought process.

Poor standards, lack of revision or upgrading. Standards for performance are poor if, despite being based on historical data, time study or best practice, they are not updated for changes in process and procedure or evaluated in the light of how to make the processes most effective. When standards are set, they should be done from a perspective of constantly questioning the value of each step or task performed to determine if the methods can be improved.

2 Goals and objectives

In order to gain effective control over how an organization spends its time, goals and objectives must be created and used to support the corporate mission (see ORGANIZATION BEHAVIOUR). The mission of an organization is its general intent, usually in relation to how it views its position, describes its values and delivers its products or services. Goals are specific and measurable accomplishments to be achieved in a given timeframe within a given cost structure. Objectives are the tactics and techniques to be used in order to achieve the goals. They must be complementary to the goal and to the mission.

Effective time management begins with the establishment of effective goals and objectives. If there is no goal or recognized point of accomplishment, there is no need for time management. Events will control individual and organizational reactions rather than the reverse.

The establishment or selection of desirable goals and objectives is controlled by the corporate vision and value system, and by its desire to serve its customers, meet its market obligations, keep its commitment to its employees, suppliers, community and shareholders, and benefit by so doing (see BUSINESS AND SOCIETY).

Organizational objectives must be consistent with the corporation's goals. If the corporation desires to be the lowest-cost producer or provide the most responsive delivery, the organizational objectives must be developed to support that goal. There is no real difference between short- and long-term goals: each part of the organization should be orchestrated to meet the long-term goal and develop interim steps or 'short-term objectives' that are consistent with reaching the desired result. Decisions taken solely in the interest of the short term can rob the company of valuable resources in a way that saps the collective strength, and can force the company into a cycle of squandering the future for the sake of the present. It is one thing to set a goal and quite another to actually achieve it.

The relationship between goals and objectives depends upon the approach used to meet the goals. Whether it is most appropriate to develop several objectives to meet each goal, or one objective to meet one goal or several objectives to meet several overlapping goals depends upon how the needs of each are best satisfied.

Goal setting is only the first step in effective time management. It is also necessary to establish priorities for the accomplishment of the goals. There are three different types of goal: (1) essential – needed for the accomplishment of, or progress towards, the mission; (2) problem solving – leading to a more appropriate or desired condition; and (3) innovative – designed to make something that is good even better. To develop priorities, it is necessary to understand the kinds of goal to be set.

Essential goals identify necessary everyday activities that must be accomplished if the goal is to be met. A problem-solving goal identifies a current situation or opportunity that must be addressed in order for the goal to be met. These goals are vital to growth and development, but may not be essential to success. Innovative goals improve the conditions or set higher limits for achievement.

Goals identify the direction of the organization and the individual and represent the ultimate destination of our dreams, needs and desires. Goals, once set should not change; the objectives or tactics for reaching the goals may and should change as conditions change. Essential goals should not be passed over in favour of problem solving or innovative goals.

The most important steps in goal development are as follows:

1 Classify goals by type: essential, problem solving or innovative.
2 Prioritize the goals in terms of relative importance, time sequence and cost/benefit relationship.

3 Establish standards of performance: a timeframe for review of progress; a quantitative method for determining progress. Critical to this process is the selection of the appropriate measurement for effectiveness. Many companies consider their performance standards only in financial terms when they should consider them both in financial terms and in evaluative measures that are specific to describe desired performance.
4 Identify obstacles to goal achievement: develop contingency plans to overcome environmental, organizational and human or management obstacles.
5 Identify the personal motivations: define the benefit or value derived from achievement of the goals.

The establishment of objectives is based on the specific events that must take place in order to meet the goals. To develop the objectives it is necessary to determine what has to be done to meet the goal, what is the most appropriate resource to do it, how and when the objective should be carried out, and when it is considered completed (see STRATEGIC CHOICE). In addition to the key implementation and monitoring steps, it is also necessary to establish the relative points at which the objective is to be reviewed and revised. Effective organizations make timely decisions because they have timely information on which to base them. The development of incremental review points helps to establish a performance-based decision pattern that enables organizations to assess quickly how well they are performing at any moment in time, and to make the appropriate decisions to support continued success (see ORGANIZATIONAL PERFORMANCE).

3 Time as a competitive advantage

Effective time management is one of the factors affecting the ability of a company to deliver its promise to customers. Reduced cycle time, i.e. reduced time from idea to market and from order placement to delivery have long been desirable aspects of business. Now *they* are not only desirable, but are factors in the selection process (Hamel and Prahalad 1994).

Many traditional beliefs about the advantage of long production runs and the value of lot sizes are being challenged by studies showing that lean, fast and flexible work groups are consistently able to react more quickly to changing demand and get products produced more quickly, thus capitalizing on the fact that most customers are willing to pay for less elapsed time (see MANUFACTURING STRATEGY).

The sources of competitive advantage will continue to change, as companies find new ways of creating or increasing customer value. In the business of the 1990s, the basis for competitive advantage is a combination of quick response and increasing variety. While many companies jumped on the bandwagon of restructuring and re-engineering for the future, the companies that have the edge are those who are actively managing time and practising time compression (see RE-ENGINEERING). Time compression and restructuring are two different paths to the future. Restructuring is essentially a process of 'sorting down' procedures and processes, compressing activities around fewer people. Time management, on the other hand, is more of an integrating process. Time compression actually makes more connections and integrates more into the whole. Time compression is not wholly centred on reduction or restructuring, but on making connections that are faster and more responsive. Time-based companies themselves can often make what they had previously outsourced.

Restructuring and returning to 'basics' goes a long way towards developing the groundwork for time-based management. In order to keep and improve the results gained through restructuring, companies need to do move than reduce overheads and streamline operations and work processes. The future belongs to those who are able to innovate faster.

Since the early 1980s, the concept of getting and 'being close' to the customer has been popular. The means to define how well that happened was time. Time-based competitors were able to enhance their ability to respond to the needs of their customers. They were successful because they were able to carry out their vision, believing that time itself is the organization's main competition (Stalk and Hout 1990).

4 Personal time management

Businesses are concerned with the management of resources: physical, human, capital, information and time (see MANAGERIAL BEHAVIOUR). All those resources can be manipulated in different directions to cause different results – all, that is, except time. Time is not something that can be created or changed. Time is constant and must be used at the very moment it is there; once used, it cannot be replaced. In fact, we cannot manage time, we can only manage ourselves in relation to time.

Time management is not really about time, but about what we individually and collectively do with time. The first step in effective self-management is the establishment of goals and objectives. To make the most effective use of time, some consideration must be given to personal goals and objectives.

Like organizational goals, personal goals must be demanding as well as achievable. They must also be specific and measurable. Personal goals must also be written down and agreed by those who will achieve them. Personal goal setting also involves the establishment of priorities for accomplishing the tasks that are to be performed.

Establishing priorities involves the evaluation of each of the tasks that are to be performed, and assessment of how important they are relative to all the other tasks that must be performed. Priority setting is often confused with goal setting or the establishment of objectives. Priority setting is a process of deciding which objectives require immediate attention and which require attention at a relatively later date. Priority setting requires looking at objectives and ranking them in terms of their short-range urgency or long-term importance.

Some things must be done within time limits that cannot be manipulated; such things tend to become short-range objectives. As an example, if a financial transaction must be completed before the bank closes at three o'clock, that would have a higher relative short-range urgency than preparing a report that is not due until the following afternoon. The report, however, may appear to have a higher priority because management is demanding it. Other objectives, therefore, may have less urgency but significant importance. Careful planning and thought are required to discriminate between the two.

Priorities are used as a guide for daily endeavours. Once established, the priorities will determine when certain tasks are performed. Perhaps a bank transaction could be handled during the lunch break and still leave time for the rest of the daily workload. A list of objectives that must be completed on a given day should become part of the routine. The standard rule of thumb is to complete ten things per day. If only eight are completed, the day has been less than totally productive; if twelve are completed, then the plan may not be met consistently. A 'to do' list should be prepared each morning, listing all the tasks that are to be completed that day. As those tasks are completed, they should be checked off and the priorities for the remaining tasks reviewed. This method will help to establish order in the day and also serve as a reinforcement of accomplishments towards fulfilling the established goals.

When ordering priorities, it is also a good idea to place the most challenging objectives in such a position that they may be accomplished when the energy level is highest. This requires a study of work patterns and the energy peaks and valleys of the day to determine the most productive time. The day should be scheduled so as to accomplish the most pressing priorities first.

The last step in the effective management of objectives to make the best use of the time available is to stay on schedule. This is perhaps the most difficult task of all. Once a schedule is established, actually carrying it out and completing the tasks listed requires a great deal of concentration. If the day is effectively planned, then each hour is productive, and fewer of the distractions that were part of the routine are allowed to interfere. The organization will have a pattern of communication and a style of work that are evident to the observer. Are people comfortable with informal meetings, hallway chats? Is there a formal

structure that forces all meetings to be documented and arranged? How do people relate to their colleagues? Is communication open and free-flowing? Are interruptions a part of the daily routine? Personal time management must work around the organizational barriers that exist.

Priorities will constantly compete for attention. MacKenzie (1990) has outlined some of the time bandits related to personal time management as these:

(1) *Crisis management.* Effective management of events begins with careful planning and an understanding of priorities in relation to those events. When a crisis occurs, it is usually the result of some unforeseen circumstance that was not considered during the planning process. It is important to distinguish between a crisis, on the one hand, and a problem that can be avoided through planning and preventive measures, on the other. A carefully planned schedule can be disrupted by a 'crisis'. The organization should be examined to determine if it is 'crisis-prone'. Is there a value associated with stepping in to resolve a situation, a reward associated with crisis management? Perhaps the crisis is something that could actually be handled as a manageable problem, but is treated as a crisis so that a 'hero' can emerge. Before jumping in to manage a crisis, it is important to find out first if there is a crisis. What is the worst thing that could happen if nothing were done? Panic is contagious. Sometimes it is more important to wait, rather than to overreact and 'manage' a situation into crisis proportions (see CRISIS MANAGEMENT).

(2) *Telephone.* Both an effective business tool and a major source of interruption, the telephone breaks concentration and is a distraction from achieving objectives. But some control is possible. Most people will answer a ringing telephone, not because of the telephone itself but because of what the call represents. The telephone-answering response is deeply rooted in human nature. There are several reasons for this:

- The presumption of legitimacy – people tend to assume that every call is a legitimate demand for attention. We assume that every call that interrupts work is more important than the work already under way.

- Fear of offending – we answer telephone calls when we should not and talk longer than we should, because we fear causing others offence by cutting the calls short.
- Desire to be informed and included in what is happening – people pause momentarily without realizing it when a call is answered by an assistant; there is a strong urge to know what the call is about.
- Ego – the simple fact that someone would call us for information makes us feel important.
- Pleasure of socializing – some people cannot resist the engagement in social conversation, leaving the business part until after the 'visit'.
- A built-in excuse – sometimes the telephone is a welcome relief from a difficult or undesirable task.

Dealing with telephone interruptions is a question of managing priorities. It is a matter of developing a method for screening and returning calls that will work with the schedule rather than interrupt it. This is done by first identifying which calls must be handled, and then developing a routine for returning or referring those calls that can be handled differently. Some can be postponed, others referred to someone else for handling. On an organizational level it might be necessary to create a time during the day when no calls within the company will be made, a time for uninterrupted concentration.

Telephone routines should be actively developed in such a way that interruption can happen without guilt or without causing offence. Use can be made of voicemail or other aids to record calls when people are not personally available. E-mail should be used when possible, especially when someone is difficult to reach. The advantage of e-mail is that there is a written record and the message can be delivered intact.

(3) *Inadequate planning.* Planning the goals and priorities for the day is the most important part of time management. In order to carry out the plan effectively, it must be written down. A written daily plan is the tool for controlling how time is spent. Without it the day is often lost to 'crisis', telephone interruptions and false starts.

(4) *Attempting too much.* If there is a need to take on more than can be accomplished in a day, why is this? It is important to develop a sense of real capability and to identify which items can and should be delegated. Tasks should not be accepted or commitments made that are not realistically achievable or controllable within the personal span of direction or control.

(5) *Drop-in visitors.* As with telephone interruptions, it is necessary to control the amount of time and energy expended on people who drop in without warning. Techniques for screening visitors and identifying how best to handle the interruption need to be developed. Appointments should be set where possible so that time can be managed more effectively.

(6) *Ineffective delegation.* No one is required to do everything. We should do nothing that can be done by someone else! (As long as it is done by the person with the necessary skills or knowledge.)

(7) *Personal disorganization.* Time is wasted when routines are not established or priorities not set.

(8) *Lack of self-discipline.* It is important to learn the difference between dealing with the daily workload and letting the workload be in control.

(9) *Inability to say 'no'.* People sometimes feel they have to do everything that anyone asks of them. It is appropriate in many cases to defer to others in the organization who might have more time or could be trusted to accomplish the required tasks. If saying 'no' will cause discomfort, this should be compared with the discomfort of saying 'yes' and then failing to accomplish those tasks. A healthy self-evaluation and assessment of capabilities is a requirement for successful management of time and associated stress.

(10) *Procrastination.* The excuse that most procrastinators use is that they 'work best under pressure'. This is simply not true. No one works best under pressure. Even if someone has an outward appearance of calm, the internal stress factors still carry weight, and procrastination causes distress to the others in

the organization who are counting upon support (MacKenzie 1990).

5 Time in the instant age

Since the 1990s, the advances in technology, the reality of cyber-space, the Internet and e-business have changed the perception of time. Access to information that often took days in the past became instantaneous. Perhaps the greatest positive aspect of the technological age is the removal of time as a barrier to progress. Most workers in the 1990s acknowledge that the personal computer is the most timesaving technological advance of that decade. Most will also identify the portable cellular telephone as the singular most important time saver in communications.

Even with advances in technology, and an ever-increasing ability to 'speed-up' the pace of activity, time still must be actively managed. Just as with any new skill or knowledge set, the use of computers or technology requires time to learn, build confidence and effectively apply.

In addition, a few additional activities are required for using technology in the 'instant age' (Yeager 1999):

1 Budget time for learning new systems, software or hardware.
2 Develop ways to back-up work products, and filing systems to ensure easy retrieval.
3 Keep pace with the technology and how it can revolutionize the way you work.
4 Remain focused on your objective. Avoid distractions.
5 Increase your skill with the keyboard, or use voice recognition software.
6 Manage yourself.

Even the software developers who specialize in Time Management software rely on the tried and true principles of basic time management. As Winston (1999) points out, 'the process of getting organized is the same as it has always been. It is a mental process, a process of making decisions. 'Organizing is a conceptual process that stays constant regardless of the tools used for its execution.'

The use of electronic devices to help manage time requires the same sort of disciplined approach that is required for traditional pen and paper activity. Planning, organizing and goal setting are still required. Effective follow-up, whether prompted by a beeper or a file folder is still necessary.

6 Conclusion

In personal management and business management the same factors apply to the management of time. Goal setting, objective setting, priority setting and understanding of the critical factors that rob an organization of this resource are essential to effective time management. Actions that are designed to prevent lost time and to use time as a competitive advantage in getting goods and services to market more quickly are a large-scale application of personal and organizational time management. The key to effective time management is to manage ourselves.

It is critical that time be viewed as a finite resource, one of the most valuable. Even with the technological advances of the 1990s no one yet has been able to manufacture time. Time once used is gone, it cannot be stretched or recalled or reworked. While it is critical to set realistic goals and objectives, it is altogether essential that tasks once scheduled are periodically reviewed to ensure completion in a timely manner. In addition, priorities, and goals, must be set so as to make the most effective use of the time and resources available.

KATHIE S. SMITH

Further reading

(References cited in the text marked *)

* Covey, S.R. (1990) *The 7 Habits of Highly Effective People*, New York, Simon and Schuster. (A holistic, principle-centred approach to solving personal and professional problems.)

Goldratt, E. and Cox, J. (1993) *The Goal*, London: Gower. (A novel that describes an approach to management thinking that deals with the theory and management of constraints. A manufacturing manager fights to save his company and is required to use techniques that eliminate bottlenecks, reduce changeovers, and downtime.)

Hamel, G. and Prahalad, C.K. (1994) *Competing for the Future*, Boston, MA: Harvard Business School Press. (Consultants describe the future nature of competition based upon development of marketable competencies, control of organizational structures and management of resources.)

Hochheiser, R.M. (1992) *Time Management*, New York: Barron's Educational Series Inc. (A guide to personal time management.)

* MacKenzie, A. (1990) *The Time Trap*, New York: AMACOM. (A comprehensive guide to making time work for you.)

Panaia, G. and Smith, K. (1994) *Process Improvement for Task Forces*, Orlando, FL: Proudfoot (USA) Creative Services Division. (A workshop and guidelines for the management of work processes, through scheduling, time and resource management through the effective use of teams.)

Rouillard, L. (1993) *Goals and Goal Setting: Planning to Succeed*, Los Altos, CA: Crisp Publications Inc. (One of a series of sixty-minute guides to help define and communicate goals and objectives.)

* Stalk, G., Jr and Hour, T.M. (1990) *Competing Against Time. How Time Based Competition is Re-shaping Global Markets*, New York: The Free Press. (Turning time to market into a distinct advantage in the marketplace explores the reduction of cycle times, process times, market and business cycles.)

Williams, Paul B. (1996) *Getting a Project Done on Time*, New York: American Management Association. (The core skills required to manage time and deliver projects on schedule.)

Winston, S. (1994) *The Organized Executive*, New York: Warner Books. (A programme for productivity; new ways to manage time, paper, people and the electronic office.)

* Wright, Robert J. (1999) *Beyond Time Management – Business With Purpose*, Newton, MA: Butterworth-Heinemann. (Illustrates the practical application of principles and purpose to daily life and work.)

* Yeager, Jan (1999) *Creative Time Management for the New Millennium*, Stamford, CT: Hannacroix Creek Books, Inc. (An effective guide to managing personal time that provides knowledge and skills to help attain a competitive edge, and peace of mind.)

See also: COMPETITIVE STRATEGIES, DEVELOPMENT OF; MANAGERIAL BEHAVIOUR; ORGANIZATION BEHAVIOUR; PRODUCTIVITY; SMALL BUSINESS STRATEGY; STRATEGY, IMPLEMENTATION OF

Toffler, Alvin (1928–)

Personal background

- born 4 October 1928 in New York City
- graduated from New York University (1949)
- associate editor of *Fortune* magazine (1959–61)
- member of faculty at the New School for Social Research (1965–67)
- since the publication of his *Future Shock* in 1970, a world-renowned author and consultant
- developed the theme of The Third Wave, which offered a framework for understanding the global changes engulfing the world today

Major works

Future Shock (1970)
Third Wave (1980)
Power Shift (1990)

Summary

Since 1970, Alvin Toffler has co-authored with his wife Heidi Toffler some of the most influential books on the subject of change. His widely discussed trilogy of works – *Future Shock, Third Wave, Power Shift* – provide an unusually broad vision of the fundamental changes affecting societies throughout the world. Toffler has elaborated the concept of the Third Wave to illuminate what he considers to be three gigantic waves of change. *The First Wave* corresponds to the agricultural revolution which dominated human history for thousands of years. *The Second Wave* – industrial civilization – which began in the seventeenth century and which soon dominated the globe is now facing exhaustion according to Toffler. *The Third Wave*, which began with the birth of the post-war service economy and the information technology of the 1950s, now threatens the previous industrial civilization. The institutions, practices and values of industrialism face annihilation by the forces of the Third Wave. Toffler argues that it is the dynamic created by the clash between the second and third waves that helps explain most of the key developments that characterize contemporary societies.

1 Biographical data

Alvin Toffler was born just before the outbreak of the Great Depression. The experience of economic stagnation and of inequalities had a radicalizing impact on him and led him towards leftist activism during his days as a university student. Indeed, after graduating from University in 1949, he and his wife Heidi worked on a factory production line. Apparently, this interest in union activism was motivated not only by his left-wing leanings but also by an early interest in technology and its effect on everyday life. This venture into the factory floor was followed by a career in journalism. He became a Washington correspondent for a number of newspapers in the late 1950s and during the years 1959 to 1961 he went on to serve as the associate editor of *Fortune* magazine. During this intense phase of journalistic work the Tofflers wrote for a wide variety of publications – from *Fortune* to *Playboy* through to the *Annals of the American Academy of Science*. This period of journalistic work was succeeded by a move into academia. Toffler went on to serve on the staff of a number of universities during the years 1965 to 1970.

The elaboration of the Tofflers' insights into the relationship between technology and social and economic change occurred in the 1960s, when IBM asked them to write a study of the long-term social and organizational consequences of the computer. This study initiated a phase of intense study into the wider socio-economic impact of technological change. Some of the key ideas that were to characterize the Tofflers' work in the decades ahead were the product of this period. Many of the themes were first presented in an article published in 1965, entitled 'The future as a way of life'. The thesis of the article was that change was likely to accelerate and that the outcome of this process would be to fundamentally disorient people who were unprepared for the future. The Tofflers coined the concept 'future shock' to underline the sense of dread that societies which were stuck in the past would experience. Alvin Toffler's *Future Shock* went on to become an international best-seller and since that time he has never looked back. Toffler emerged as not only one of the most pre-eminent futurologists of our times; he also became one of the most successful popularizers of the notion of the information society. His contribution has been recognized internationally and he has won numerous awards for his writings in countries as varied as China, France, Italy and the United States.

2 Main contribution

Toffler's main contribution has been to illuminate the outcome of the process of technological change to an unusually wide readership (see TECHNOLOGY AND ORGANIZATIONS). Probably more than any one else he has also succeeded in sensitizing the business community to the profound implications of continuous change during the last three decades of the twentieth century. It was his educated intuition of the transformative impact of the knowledge industry that allowed him to pinpoint at a relatively early stage what would become some of the most significant trends of our era. By the mid-1960s, he had grasped the central role that information technology would play in the economic life of the future. From this insight he concluded that technological change would be qualitatively more rapid than in the past.

Toffler's concept of *Future Shock* expressed a vision of society that was more and more torn apart by the premature arrival of the future. His thesis, that the pace of change was

too fast for society to handle, reflected the mood of the 1960s. This was a time when less and less could be taken for granted. The institutions and value systems associated with industrial civilization had become subject to the irresistible force of change, argued Toffler. He believed that change was fuelled by the growth of knowledge. This massive explosion of knowledge had created an environment where the future would become virtually unrecognizable in the present. Transience had become a way of life – and this process was revolutionizing every aspect of life, from the economic to the realm of individual lifestyle. His advice to government and business was straightforward: be prepared for anything and certainly do not expect the future to be anything like the past. Today, this perspective has a strong influence on management theory, but back in the early 1970s, Toffler's vision of unchanging change was often dismissed as somewhat bizarre and eccentric.

In his book *The Third Wave*, Toffler sought to elaborate a more comprehensive framework for making sense of the changes that were working towards the creation of what he considered to be a new post-industrial civilization (see GLOBALIZATION). According to Toffler, The First Wave of change coincided with the agricultural revolution, which took off roughly ten millennia ago. But before this First Wave of change had exhausted itself, it was overtaken by the industrial revolution in Europe, which unleashed a Second Wave of planetary change. This Second Wave of change swiftly engulfed most of the world, although the agricultural and industrial modes of culture continued to coexist and compete with each other in large parts of the world. The Second Wave of change rapidly transformed life and revolutionized the institutions of the economy and of society. The consequences of the Second Wave of changes are still experienced throughout the world.

But even as societies continue to be influenced by the institutions and practices of the Second Wave, a new, even more significant process of change has begun to alter economic and social life. Toffler contends that industrialism, which peaked after the Second Wave, has been succeeded by a Third Wave of change which has transformed virtually every aspect of the human experience. The Third Wave, symbolized by the computer, commercial jet travel, the birth control pill and high-tech industry, has fundamentally altered the way we live and produce. For Toffler, the dynamic of this process is most strikingly expressed in the shift from manufacturing to the knowledge industry.

Toffler's study of the dynamic of the interaction between the Second and Third Waves of change has been taken up by academics, politicians and business managers to make sense of their circumstances. Toffler's analysis is clearly focused on the fundamentals of wealth creation. He noted that the Second Wave of changes led to the emergence of a factory-based system of wealth creation. Such a system depended on the principles of mass production, standardization, maximization and large bureaucratic business organizations. This industrial culture based on material factors of production has been severely undermined by changes brought about by the explosion of information technology. Toffler suggests that the Third Wave has fundamentally altered the very essence of wealth creation. Wealth today, according to Toffler's model, is based on instant communication and the dissemination of data, ideas and symbols.

Toffler has dismissed the idea of 'de-industrialization'. Instead, he argues that industry has been transformed by the knowledge revolution. In the Third Wave, the Tofflers coined the term 'de-massification' to describe trends that move economic life beyond mass production, mass distribution, mass media and mass homogeneity. The outcome of the process of *de-massification* is a shift from mass production towards increasing customization, from mass marketing towards niches and micro-marketing and from the monolithic hierarchical and control organization to a decentralized network.

Toffler's systematic study of the changing relations of power in his *Power Shift* provides intriguing insights into the role of knowledge in contemporary society. For Toffler, knowledge has become the essence of power. Both wealth and the means of physical violence depend on knowledge. His writings continually warn politicians and business managers about the danger of ignoring knowledge as a factor of production since economic success depends on a capacity to manipulate high-quality knowledge.

Toffler's theory of change has both a pessimistic and an optimistic side. His work provides a detailed account of both the destructive and the constructive side of the Third Wave (see FUTUROLOGY). He believes that most conflicts at both the global and the interpersonal level can be understood as a product of a clash between the forces steeped in the industrial civilization of the Second Wave and the forces which are the beneficiaries of the Third Wave. He argues that it is the shift in the foundation of power from violence and material wealth to knowledge that provides the impetus for these conflicts. Toffler projects a future where the scramble for the control of new knowledge resources becomes the foundation for the power struggles to come. There is also a democratic vision in this perspective. Since knowledge cannot be centralized or monopolized, a wide variety of interests have the potential to gain access to this new source of power.

Knowledge as the source of power is Toffler's key idea for making sense of the tensions that afflict economic and political life throughout the world today (see POWER). His work provides an important resource for making sense of the ways in which the knowledge industry has altered social and economic life.

3 Evaluation

Toffler's ability to integrate material and experience from a variety of subject areas is truly impressive. His key works have succeeded in synthesizing research from the fields of sociology, technology, science, cultural studies and psychology. The criticism made by academics that this feat is achieved at the expense of depth is undeniable. But despite all its shortcomings, Toffler has succeeded in putting forward the big picture and a framework for making sense of what otherwise appear as unconnected diverse processes.

Toffler's work also represents some of the finest examples of trend-spotting. He is at his best when he isolates developments before they have made an impact on the public imagination and draws our attention to their significance.

At the same time, Toffler's work suffers from the attempt to say too much too soon. His attempt to link together a variety of experiences – family breakdown, the rise of self-help groups, growth of new lifestyles, the rise of the paperless office, the home as the new place of work, the disintegration of the nation state – can only be sustained at the level of description. But just because these experiences occur at roughly the same time, there is no reason to suppose that they are all products of the same processes. It appears that virtually any new or not yet comprehensible process becomes integrated into the Third Wave precisely because it is new.

In a sense, Toffler's strength also constitutes his weakness. His focus on change tends towards an exaggeration of its effects. It is difficult to accept the view that everything from the family to the nation through to work has so fundamentally altered. Even in an age of information, most people still work with their hands instead of their brains. And even in the service sector, many of the jobs involve the kind of unskilled, repetitive tasks that characterize the labour of the past. And certainly when we compare the experience of the second half of the twentieth century with the transformative experience of the industrial revolution, the intensity of our own pace of change may not appear all that unusual (see INDUSTRIAL REVOLUTION).

As a popularizer of other people's work, Toffler invariably overstates his case and simplifies the issues at stake. His work is littered with extravagant phrases and simplistic sound-bites. But, unlike many academic works which deal with the issue of change, Toffler sticks his neck out and offers a stimulating argument.

4 Conclusion

In an important sense, Toffler personifies the temper of the late twentieth century. At a time when societies are prone to exaggerate the quality of change – terms like post-industrial, post-historical, post-geographical, post-

modern abound – Toffler provides a systematic statement of a future almost unconnected to the past. This disposition towards sensing change allows Toffler to help grasp some of the developments that will influence our future.

For the layperson, Toffler offers an exhilarating and even democratic vision, where the dominance of knowledge gives an ever-widening section of society access to power. For the world of business, Toffler provides the important insight of 'do not live off the past'. And though he falls short of giving us answers, Toffler continually stimulates his reader to think the unthinkable.

FRANK FUREDI
UNIVERSITY OF KENT IN CANTERBURY

Further reading

(References cited in the text marked *)

Badham, R. (1984) 'The sociology of industrial and post-industrial societies', *Current Sociology* 32: 1–36. (Reviews the contribution of Toffler and Daniel Bell to the establishment of the post-industrial perspective in sociology.)

Cohen, M.J. (1997) 'Risk society and ecological modernisation; alternative visions for post industrial nations', *Futures* 29: 105–119. (Examines how many of the trends outlined by Toffler are analysed by risk society theorists.)

Frankel, B. (1987) *The Post-Industrial Utopians*, Oxford: Polity Press. (A useful critique of Toffler's work, which offers a balanced account of the strength and weakness of Toffler.)

Gibson, R. (ed.) (1997) *Rethinking The Future*, London: Nicholas Brealey Publishing. (A collection of articles from leading business thinkers, which elaborate many of the insights found in Toffler's work.)

Kumar, K. (1995) *From Post-Industrial to Post-Modern Society*, Oxford: Blackwell. (This comprehensive survey of the post-industrial perspective helps situate Toffler within the wider sociological tradition.)

Marien, M. (1996) 'New communications technology – a survey of impacts and issues', *Telecommunications Policy* 20: 375–87. (An interesting biblioessay, which examines a wide range of literature on the impact of the new communications technologies on society.)

* Toffler, A. (1970) *Future Shock*, London: The Bodley Head Ltd. (Toffler's pioneering work which argues that the magnitude of change had

become so great that its effect was a future of trauma.)

* Toffler, A. (1980) *The Third Wave*, London: William Collins Sons & Co. (This is Toffler's most important analysis of social transformation.)
* Toffler, A. (1990) *Power Shift*, New York: Bantam Press. (This work is devoted to the exploration of the relationship between knowledge and power, particularly economic power.)
Webster, F. (1995) *Theories of The Information Society*, London: Routledge. (Webster's study of theories of The Information Society helps situate Toffler in the wider discussion of the subject.)

See also: FUTUROLOGY; GLOBALIZATION; INDUSTRIAL REVOLUTION; ORGANIZATION BEHAVIOUR; POWER; TECHNOLOGY AND ORGANIZATION

Total productive maintenance (TPM)

1 Introduction

Today, virtually all organizations make substantial use of equipment. Manufacturing firms make extensive use of a wide range of computer-controlled and manual machine tools, process equipment, robotics, handling equipment, assembly equipment and computer-based planning and control systems. The service sector is increasingly dependent on equipment: banks and insurance companies have broad ranges of computers and ATMs, airlines' revenues depend on sophisticated aircraft ready to fly, and medical services use computer-based equipment as well as computer information systems for all aspects of health and medical care delivery.

As every customer knows well, equipment is prone to failure: failure to operate at all, or failure to operate correctly. The impact of equipment failure can range from mildly annoyed customers to life-threatening (even disastrous) consequences.

The role of maintenance is to keep equipment operating correctly, thus contributing to the organization's effectiveness, efficiency and profitability. 'Downtime' describes the time when equipment is not available to do the task it is meant to; time spent on maintenance is therefore included in downtime. Recently organizations have been facing increased pressures to keep downtime to a minimum. In the service sector the pressures are for more reliable, effective, faster and cheaper services; in the manufacturing sector there are severe external pressures for shorter lead-times, on-time deliveries, greater product variety and lower costs, and internal pressures for greater equipment utilization and lower stock levels, all of which mean equipment must operate correctly when needed. As a result, organizations are placing heavier loads on their equipments, using these physical assets more intensively. At the same time, cost pressures throughout organizations demand the contradictory combination of low maintenance costs and zero breakdowns.

The management approach to maintenance has undergone significant change in the last two decades, changing from a low-level technical nuisance to a potentially important contributor to the organization's success. Total productive maintenance (TPM) is increasingly part of capacity management and planning efforts, and plays an important role in the improvement of productivity and service delivery.

2 What is TPM?

Traditionally the attitude of equipment users and operators alike towards maintenance staff has been 'I use, you fix'. Preventive maintenance was taught and encouraged, but in practice was generally implemented half-heartedly, if at all. The combination of budget pressure and maintenance departments' focus on repairing equipment already in trouble doomed most preventive maintenance programmes.

The term TPM was defined in 1971 by the Japan Institute of Plant Engineers (now the Japan Institute for Plant Maintenance). The word *total* in TPM means three things:

1 *Total effectiveness*: pursuit of economic efficiency or profitability
2 *Total PM*: maintenance prevention and activity to improve maintainability as well as preventive maintenance
3 *Total participation*: autonomous maintenance by operators and small group activities in every department and at every level' (Nakajima 1989).

It is not an accident that this has the familiar ring of Total Quality Management (see TOTAL QUALITY MANAGEMENT). TPM is an integral part of the Toyota Production System (Ohno 1988). With its focus on the elimination of waste and Just-In-Time manufacture, Toyota could not survive with maintenance by fire-fighting. Toyota was an active participant in the development of TPM through the Japan Institute for Maintenance Engineers, later called the Japan Institute of Plant Maintenance (JIPM) (see JUST-IN-TIME PHILOSOHY; OHNO, T.; TOYODA FAMILY).

In the late 1970s, the JIPM tracked the progress of its member plants as they moved through four stages of development towards TPM:

Stage 1   Breakdown maintenance: fix what's not working
Stage 2   Preventive maintenance: fix what's not working and follow a schedule of periodic service and overhaul
Stage 3   Productive maintenance: fix what's not working, follow a schedule of periodic service and overhaul and begin monitoring equipment to diagnose equipment during use
Stage 4   Total Productive Maintenance: all of the above, but within an overall context of strategic management of equipments to support the business (Nakajima 1989).

The JIPM published the first comprehensive explanation of TPM in 1982; this was available in English translation in 1989 (Nakajima 1989). *TPM Development Program: Implementing Total Productive Maintenance* remains the definitive work which lays out the fundamentals of TPM. Nakajima edited this work; at the time he was Vice Chairman of the JIPM. The other authors were consultants with the JIPM who worked with member companies, Toyota included, to develop and codify TPM (see JAPAN, MANAGEMENT IN).

Nakajima (1989) described the 'five goals' of TPM which had been developed through the work of the JIPM:

1   Maximize equipment effectiveness (improve overall efficiency).
2   Develop a system of productive maintenance for the life of the equipment.
3   Involve all departments that plan, design, use, or maintain equipment in implementing TPM (engineering and design, production, and maintenance).
4   Actively involve all employees – from top management to shop-floor workers.
5   Promote TPM through *motivation management*: autonomous small group activities.

In 1994, Willmott argued that there is a 'problem of definition … because the word "maintenance" has a much more comprehensive meaning in Japan than in the Western world …'. He offered an adaptation of TPM taking into account cultural and language differences between the Japanese developers and those attempting to implement TPM in English-speaking facilities. Here is Willmott's rendition of the 'five pillars for the application of TPM'.

1   Adopt improvement activities designed to increase overall equipment effectiveness (OEE) by attacking the six losses.
2   Improve existing planned and predictive maintenance systems.
3   Establish a level of self-maintenance and cleaning carried out by highly trained operators.
4   Increase the skills and motivation of operators and engineers by individual and group development.
5   Initiate maintenance prevention techniques including improved design and procurement'.

TPM is not as widely implemented as, for example, Total Quality Management (TQM). In general, TPM is simply not implemented; TQM is more likely to be tried so there are more reported implementation failures. The contrast shown above suggests that watered down TPM-like activities may be more widely implemented than is known, but TPM is not as widely known and implemented as other aspects of so-called Japanese production methods.

However, in 1993 Chen studied TPM practices at Japanese-owned factories in the USA – referred to as 'transplants'. These plants, all located in the Midwest United States, ranged from an automotive parts supplier to a machine tool builder; one was a high-volume auto assembly plant. They were owned by different Japanese companies. Chen (1994) found that:

There is remarkable similarity among the Japanese approaches to preventive maintenance and quality assurance. There is an overall philosophy of continual improvement, and a high value placed on the contribution of good preventive maintenance practices on the overall quality and productivity of the firm. These firms are characterized by managing the maintenance function aggressively and placing a great emphasis on training.

At least in the USA, it appears possible for TPM to be implemented relatively intact.

3 The 'six big losses'

A central notion of TPM is *equipment effectiveness* – a measure of the equipment's contribution to production value-added (Nakajima 1989):

Overall Equipment Effectiveness = availability × performance × quality

All three factors are affected by the quality of maintenance. TPM is intended to maximize OEE. A first step is understanding the six types of losses which affect OEE.

The six losses are:

- Breakdown
- Setup and adjustment
- Idling and minor stoppage
- Reduced speed
- Quality defect and rework, and
- Startup losses.

TPM aims to reduce to zero or at least minimize all of these losses.

Breakdown losses

There are two possible losses to a firm when equipment breaks down – the time lost (which is basically a loss of capacity), and the quantity lost through creation of defective product. Unexpected breakdowns are typically obvious and relatively easy to correct. However, chronic breakdowns may be symptoms of greater problems to come. It is very difficult to completely eliminate sporadic breakdowns. At the least, systematic examination of breakdowns can provide information leading to the design of procedures which will minimize downtime when a breakdown occurs.

Setup and adjustment losses

When equipment must be changed and/or adjusted when switching from making one product to working on another, time is lost and often product is lost as the equipment is adjusted. The usual target within manufacturing organizations is to reduce setup/adjustment times to less than ten minutes: Single Minute Exchange of Die (SMED), for example. Change from one product to the next is required to meet delivery, flexibility and inventory objectives; minimizing setup/adjustment times is the appropriate approach to managing time and/or product loss where setup/adjustment is required.

Idling and minor stoppage losses

Minor stoppages are not breakdowns but short-lived interference or interruption in operations caused by a machine jam, feeding and handling problems, temporary power interruption, etc. Idling is caused by such interruptions, or from the lack of parts and/or labour. Close monitoring and the elimination of defects must be undertaken to avoid such losses.

Reduced speed losses

Reduced speed losses occur when the actual operating speed is less than the equipment design speed. While there is a variety of explanations for this gap, it remains a waste of time which should be eliminated. Common explanations for reduced speed are that the equipment design speed is not known and/or the actual operating speed has not been systematically determined. An equally serious problem is machine wear which changes its capabilities.

Quality defects and rework

As with equipment breakdown, there are two losses – the product may be lost but time is also lost since the work must be repeated. And, as in the case of equipment breakdown, evaluation of the explanation for the quality defect must be the basis of prevention of future defects.

Startup losses

In process industries, the magnitude of startup losses is generally known and efforts are made to minimize them. Other industries – particularly those with infrequent new product startups – may not appreciate the full impact of 'running in' a process or product. Operators' skills as well as maintenance level of jigs, fixtures and dies can be important factors in the cause and ultimately correction of such losses.

4 Maintenance engineering

The field of maintenance management includes a wide variety of technical sub-fields that are best described as aspects of maintenance engineering. Some examples are: reliability engineering –often part of aircraft and aircraft spare parts design (Kececioglu 1995; Moubray (1997); early equipment management – usually applied to the installation of new equipment (Gotoh 1991); engineering maintenance management which includes cost estimating, scheduling and planning, and compensation (Niebel 1994); maintenance materials control (Duffuaa *et al.* 1999) and computer-based maintenance management systems, including continuous equipment monitoring (Levitt 1996); to name a few. These engineering specialities can be integrated into a TPM system since all can translate their results into the impact on the availability of the firm's productive assets.

From the point of view of general management, TPM is focused on the company's physical assets – equipment and machinery whether used by employees or customers – with the objective of ensuring that it performs when and as required. It is also aimed at ensuring that these assets are being properly utilized – in order words, that the company is getting its money's worth from its capital equipment investments.

From the point of view of maintenance personnel, particularly those in upper management levels, it is crucial that they recognize and understand the business implications of their work. (Kelly 1997a; 1997b) In addition to a positive impact on profitability, TPM offers the prospect of increased worker productivity and safety.

For a company making equipment and machinery to be used by others, TPM concepts can be applied during the design phase to improve customers' long-term satisfaction with the product. The Otis Elevator Company, for instance, offers an elevator with continuous electronic monitoring built in: maintenance teams are called in automatically, often before users recognize that there is a problem.

5 Implementation issues

In the past few years there have been a number of studies examining the impact of TPM on manufacturing, and the impact of newer manufacturing technologies on maintenance management. In 1997, Kelly *et al.* examined the 'Impact of maintenance policies on the performance of manufacturing cells'. They concluded that:

> … utilizing preventative maintenance procedures generally results in better average flowtime and % tardy performance while deteriorating the average tardiness performance in some cases. Furthermore, the results show that performing preventive maintenance and machine setups simultaneously improves average tardiness performance while maintaining the same average flowtime performance compared to the case where these activities are performed separately.

Two years later, Swanson (1999) reported that:

> For a manufacturing plant considering the implementation of AMT [Advanced Manufacturing Technology], it appears that managers need to go beyond considering changes in the direct workforce. Managers should be aware that additional capabilities will be required of maintenance. By planning for the additional capabilities required and changing the maintenance practices that are in use, maintenance may be better able to support the operation of the new equipment.

In a much broader investigation, McKone *et al.* (2001) found that:

> ... TPM ... has a strong positive impact on multiple dimensions of MP [Manufacturing Performance]. While TPM directly impacts MP, there is also a strong indirect relationship between TPM and MP through JIT [Just-In-Time]. Our results are important for two reasons: (1) Maintenance programs have long been used as a means to control manufacturing costs. Out results show that TPM does more than control costs, it can improve dimensions of cost, quality, and delivery. TPM can be a strong contributor to the strength of the organization and has the ability to improve MP. (2) World Class Manufacturing programs, such as JIT, TQM, and TPM, should not be evaluated in isolation. They are closely related and in combination can help foster better MP.

Taken together, these studies support the early claims for the value of TPM to the organization. They also point to the (not surprising) synergy between TPM and the Toyota production system which includes both TQM and JIT. Results in the USA for plants owned by Japanese firms are consistent with those from Japan. In other words, TPM does travel well.

6 Conclusion

The original '*TPM development program* brought together the five TPM development activities – autonomous maintenance, equip-ment improvements, maintenance planning, education and training, and early equipment management – emphasizing their integration and approach' (Gotoh 1991). As such, it includes substantial technical material which may be of only modest interest to general managers. However, the overall system offers substantial benefits to enterprises which value service, performance and improved profitability.

The typical view of TPM is in application within a manufacturing plant. However, there is actually more – and at least as complex – equipment in many service operations. The transportation industry – trucking, rail, air – is the most obvious, as are public utilities and the telephone and telecommunication industry. But the number of industries which are increasingly involved with complex equipment (particularly computer gear) has grown dramatically in the past decade to include grocery stores, restaurants, hospitals, financial and insurance organizations, and banks. While many of these new entrants into large-scale maintenance of complex and expensive equipment will outsource the maintenance, a TPM approach would probably benefit them as well, helping improve customer service levels.

ANDREW J. JOHNSTONE
CRANFIELD UNIVERSITY

LINDA G. SPRAGUE
UNIVERSITY OF NEW HAMPSHIRE, USA AND
CHINA EUROPE INTERNATIONAL BUSINESS
SCHOOL

Further reading

(References cited in the text marked *)

* Chen, F. (1994) 'Benchmarking: preventive maintenance practices at Japanese transplants', *International Journal Quality & Reliability Management* 11 (8): 19–26.
* Duffuaa, S.O., Raouf, A. and Campbell, J.D. (1999) *Planning and Control of Maintenance Systems*, New York: John Wiley & Sons. (Maintenance from an engineering perspective, describing the use of statistical and optimization techniques for planning maintenance systems.)
* Gotoh, F. (1991) *Equipment Planning for TPM: Maintenance Prevention Design*, USA:

Productivity Press Inc. (Translation of *Setsubi kaihatsu to sekkei*, Tokyo: Japan Institute of Plant Maintenance, 1988.) (Follow-on to the Nakajima book, providing substantial detail on one aspect – maintenance prevention design.)

* Kececioglu, D. (1995) *Maintainability, Availability, Operational Readiness Engineering*, vol. 1, Upper Saddle River, NJ: Prentice-Hall. (Introduction to maintainability engineering and prevention and corrective maintenance policies.)

* Kelly, A. (1997a) *Maintenance Strategy*, Oxford: Butterworth-Heinemann. (Focus on strategic issues including plant selection, life-cycle costs, development of maintenance schedule. Includes case studies.)

* Kelly, A. (1997b) *Maintenance Organization and Systems*, Oxford: Butterworth-Heinemann. (Focus on operational issues including workload and resources, planning and controlling maintenance activities, stores and documentation and computer-based systems.)

* Kelly, C.M., Mosier, C.T. and Mahmoodi, F. (1997) 'Impact of maintenance policies on the performance of manufacturing cells', *International Journal of Production Research* 35 (3): 767–87.

* Levitt, J. (1996) *Managing Factory Maintenance*, New York: Industrial Press, Inc. (The management of operations including budgeting, planning and implementing choosing appropriate maintenance approaches and developing supervisors.)

* McKone, K.E., Schroeder, R.G. and Cua, K.O. (2001) 'The impact of total productive maintenance practices on manufacturing performance', *Journal of Operations Management* 19: 39–58.

* Moubray, J. (1997) *Reliability-centred Maintenance,* 2nd edn, Oxford: Butterworth-Heinemann. (Extensive coverage of condition monitoring and functional analysis and failure modes.)

* Nakajima, S. (ed.) (1989) *TPM Development Program: Implementing Total Productive Maintenance*, Portland, OR: Productivity Press Inc. (Translation of *TPM tenkai*, trans by T. Masaji, Tokyo: Japan Institute for Plant Maintenance, 1982. (Original book introducing details of the TPM system.)

* Niebel, B.W. (1994) *Engineering Maintenance Management*, 2nd edn, New York: Marcel Dekker, Inc. (Basic maintenance operational issues, including estimating maintenance work and materials costs and work sampling maintenance workers with a view to improving their efficiency and effectiveness.)

* Ohno T. (1988) *Toyota Production System: Beyond Large-scale Production*, Portland, OR: Productivity Press. (Translation of *Toyota seisan hoshiki*, Tokyo: Diamond Inc., 1978.) (Introduction to the fundamentals of the Toyota Production System by its chief developer; provides clear evidence that TPM is critical in an organization using JIT systems.)

* Swanson, L. (1999) 'The impact of new production technologies on the maintenance function: an empirical study', *International Journal Production Research* 37: 849–69.

* Willmott, P. (1994) *Total Productive Maintenance: The Western Way*, Butterworth-Heinemann. (An introduction to the principles of TPM and how to apply them successfully; includes detailed case studies.)

See also: JAPAN, MANAGEMENT IN; JUST-IN-TIME PHILOSOPHY; MANUFACTURING STRATEGY; OHNO, T.; ORGANIZATION BEHAVIOUR; ORGANIZATION STRUCTURE; TAYLOR, F.W.; TOTAL QUALITY MANAGEMENT; TOYODA FAMILY

Total quality management (TQM)

Overview

Total Quality Management is a holistic approach to the management of the operations of an enterprise (commercial organization or public sector body) which recognizes that the quality of a delivered product or service is dependent on *all* the activities in the producing organization and its supply chains. In fact, the term 'Total Quality Management' is increasingly being replaced by the term 'Business Excellence' which is a more accurate description of the subject.

The concept is really the fusing together of two different philosophies of 'quality management' – the management system-based quality assurance approach (basically an Anglo Saxon-inspired concept) and the, often statistically-based, process analysis and control based-approach (typified by Japanese and Continental European traditions).

The overall concept is now frequently implemented via well-established models with the accompanying use of various tools and techniques for structured problem solving, process analysis, audit and assessment. The Malcolm Baldrige model from the USA and the European Foundation for Quality Management EFQM) are the leading models which have provided the genesis for others.

The danger for the future is that over concentration on the detailed implementation of one of the business excellence models, with its requirement for formal self-assessment and use of score cards, will obscure the aim – which is the efficient supply of quality products and services to meet customer expectations.

1 Development of the subject from original inspection-based quality control

Although we apply Total Quality Management to the delivery of both products and services, the subject developed from the need to measure and assure the quality of manufactured products.

Before the development of what we might call 'organized manufacture' – typified by the ideas of Frederick Taylor and others who separated out manufacturing tasks and produced the factory model – the primary quality control action was that of the craftsmen who inspected his own work and rectified or replaced it if it was, in his judgement, defective (see TAYLOR, F.W.). But even in those apparently simple and straightforward times there were 'outside' inspectors. We find Samuel Pepys, when he was controller of the Royal Navy in the 1670s, instigating audit inspections of timber supplies. In the Netherlands at about the same time there were established practices for independent audit inspections of cloth samples.

With the development of the factory organizations and the consequent division of labour there developed a separation between those who produced and those who inspected. This perhaps necessary tension (and sometimes conflict) persisted as normal industrial practice until almost the present day. There were some significant improvements in this inspection-based approach to quality control and assurance. As so often, a major war provided the spur to major change.

The rapidly increasing demand for wartime supplies during the Second World War put manufacturing industry in the affected nations under considerable pressure. The traditional inspection-based approach could not cope, so statistically-based sampling inspection was introduced. This provided a mathematical measure of the risks involved in sampling inspection (both the risk of accepting poor product and the risk of rejecting good product on the inspection of a sample). The original statistical ideas were developed in the 1920s by Shewhart and Taylor but were adapted to industrial inspection by a team at Columbia University (which, incidentally, included Milton Friedman). This statistically based sampling inspection approach (SQC – Statistical Quality Control) prevailed as the standard approach until the 1960s. Although valuable, it has obvious limitations.

Carried out correctly, SQC limits the risk of the customer receiving faulty product but it is inherently wasteful. Product is produced and then inspected, leading to waste if product is found to be inadequate. This is costly both in time and materials. It might be an acceptable philosophy for low added-value items (e.g. small components produced in a mass production system) but increasingly came to be seen as inadequate and costly for complex, high value-added items, especially those with a long design/production lead time and where a delay in supply caused significant consequential costs to the customer.

These concerns were particularly acute for purchasers of large, complex products (e.g. defence departments, public utilities, petrochemical companies) where the design and construction phase could last a number of years and where a quality deficiency in one major sub-system could have significant knock-on effects. Analysis of project data of the 1960s from the UK Central Electricity Generating Board (the UK electric power utility at that time) showed that the consequential costs of a quality-related delay in a major sub-system could be many times the value of the sub-system itself. This scenario will have been the same for other purchasers of complex, high value items.

The route to solving this situation was the adoption by the major purchasers of a 'quality assurance' model. They reasoned, with justification, that if their suppliers had well organized management systems which were designed to control and assure quality, then many quality problems could be avoided. This was a significant change in philosophy.

Instead of inspecting product *after* manufacture the quality emphasis was placed on the manufacturing processes to provide defect *prevention*. The reasoning was: if the processes are well under control, and can be demonstrated to be so, then it is highly likely that the product will be correct. This new philosophy could be implemented because the customers (being large organizations) could impose it on their suppliers. So developed the concept of formal quality assurance by adherence to defined procedural standards, checkable by system audit. This was the genesis of the well-known ISO 9000 series of international standards on quality management systems. Note that this approach was customer led and was designed to serve the customer's interests, *not* necessarily those of the manufacturers.

It is worth noting that this emphasis on quality assurance was very much a US/Western European initiative, as it reflected a situation of a relatively high growth economy coupled with significant defence expenditure as a result of the build up of NATO (the North Atlantic Treaty Organization). This led to a 'seller's market' such that quality assurance was seen as a sensible tool to protect purchasers' interests. By contrast, the Japanese economic strategy during this period was to build market share in manufactured products, so the emphasis was on developing more elaborate and discriminating quality control measures or tools for use by manufacturers to self-improve. As we shall see, Total Quality Management is, in effect, something of a fusion of these two strands of thought. Most of the quality tools we now take for granted were either developed or improved in Japanese industry (see JAPAN, MANAGEMENT IN).

The process-oriented preventive approach was developed and carried forward through the progressive development of various national and eventually international standards from the 1970s up through the late twentieth century. The standards (the ISO 9000 series) evolved from an engineering/manufacturing bias to a more business friendly state (the latest 2000 issue): also, these reflect the needs of the supplier (whether of goods or services). They are truly quality management standards which focus on the business processes.

These quality management standards do not attempt to define quality standards (i.e. product or service performance characteristics) as these are in practice specified in individual contracts between supplier and customer and cannot be 'standardized' except in the sense of minimum safety related characteristics. The widespread adoption of these ISO standards and the perceived necessity of demonstrating conformance to them has led to the development of a significant international business in the third party auditing of quality management systems and the granting of 'certification'. The 'ISO 9000' approach and the various industry specific derivatives (for automotive and aerospace) have without doubt contributed greatly to the performance of industry worldwide. This is particularly so for SMEs (small- to medium-sized enterprises) where the required externally applied discipline has been very valuable. The danger, as with all such sound initiatives, is that there can be over-concentration on the mechanics of the process of identifying and carefully documenting the quality system to satisfy external auditors, to the detriment of producing quality products.

The next stage of development, therefore, was the emergence of the concept of 'Total Quality Management' (TQM) as an all-embracing philosophy to cover *all* facets of an organization (they all contribute in some way to the quality of the output) and to avoid over-emphasis on process issues (although process management still forms the core of the concept, as it must) and, even more so, avoid the narrow and rather mechanistic approach so often experienced in ISO 9000 certification. This is not to say that the idea of TQM was suddenly invented in the 1970s. Indeed, many of the basic ideas had been propounded by Juran and Deming (the 14 points, the Plan-Do-Check-Act cycle, as examples) much earlier (see DEMING, W.E.; JURAN, J.M.). It was at about this time, though, that business began to seriously embrace the topic. TQM is designed as a framework to help provide strategic direction to an organization's quality activities. It is dependent on the use of well known quality tools and techniques, many of them statistically based and sharing a distinct lineage to the statistical ideas of 50+ years previously.

In the 1990s, the focus changed slightly to emphasize the fact that quality is an integral part of any organization. The term 'TQM' was increasingly being superceded by the concept of 'business excellence'. In fact, we might argue that TQM is only one of a number of concepts (management fashions almost) which seek to improve business performance. Concepts such as Just-in-Time, Business Process Engineering, Six Sigma, Lean Manufacturing, etc. are all addressing the same issue and have many elements in common with TQM. The point of difference is that TQM is a holistic approach which covers *all* aspects of an organization's activities.

2 Fundamental philosophy/concept

Customers buy products and services from commercial organizations. Public sector bodies supply services (healthcare, transport infrastructure, utilities, security, waste disposal) to citizens. In each case there is an expectation that the products and services so supplied are of the requisite 'quality'. What level of quality is required, or can be reasonably expected, is a matter for debate. In the commercial sector the debate is primarily driven by the realities of competition and the issues of cost effectiveness and value for money. In the public sector the debate is primarily driven by political realities (what quality of service will citizens expect and how much taxation will they accept to pay for it). This being so, the issue of quality management in a general sense is to do with the *mechanisms* by which we obtain or demonstrate the achievement of 'quality' rather than the *absolutes* of 'quality' (the performance standards). This is an important distinction which is not always understood, but it underlies the whole philosophy of TQM – and, indeed, that of the earlier ideas of quality assurance.

As its name implies, Total Quality Management (TQM) is concerned with the *total* operations of an organization. An organization exists to deliver products or services and all activities within that organization (including such seemingly peripheral activities as office cleaning and security) contribute in some way to the output. This fundamental concept is easy to understand, what is perhaps less straightforward is how the concept is applied. The concept is realized in two complementary ways:

- via a model of the management structure which highlights the key issues related to quality
- via the use of tools and techniques, often statistically based, to measure and monitor quality and to identify critical issues for improvement.

Understanding the development of these two complementary approaches is instructive and helpful in applying the concepts. The models arise from the 'management' approach to the subject, which has been strongly influenced by US and Western European thinking: it can perhaps be described as an Anglo Saxon approach (see UNITED STATES OF AMERICA, MANAGEMENT IN THE). The development and early use of the tools and techniques (apart from the original statistical quality control ideas of the 1940s) has been pioneered primarily by Japanese manufacturing industry. Japanese industry, with its consensus approach and strategic aim of building market share immediately after the Second World War, needed to put its quality effort into the details of improving processes and

product by continuous, incremental steps. By contrast, in the US and Western Europe, the primary challenge was seen as integrating and then focusing the managerial activities. Both approaches, of course, are needed but the relative importance of the two can depend on local situations and strategic commercial needs.

3 The quality models

There are a number of quality models – the best known and most widely used are the Malcolm Baldrige Award Model (USA), The Deming Prize Model (Japan) and the EFQM (European Foundation for Quality Management) Business Excellence Model. These three models are, in reality, very similar. Other national models which have been developed – usually to form the basis of and award (such as the Indian CII-EXIM model) – are based on one of these three.

The aim of the models is to identify, describe and, crucially, assign rankings to various attributes of an organization. The models were originally developed for the improvement of manufacturing industry but, over time, they have been updated and adapted to cover public and private sector commercial organizations.

The outline of the EFQM model is shown in Figure 1 as a typical example. The attributes are divided into 'enablers' – those attributes

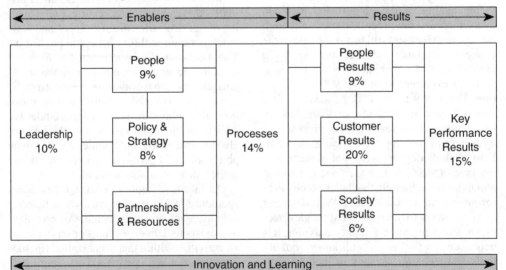

Figure 1 The EFQM 1999 model (© EFQM)

that are needed to enable quality to be delivered, and 'results' which are the quality outcomes. Processes are the core of the model. It should also be noted that 'results' includes, as it must, the impact on people (i.e. the organization's own employees) and on society at large as well as the customer. For the latter, this includes financial indicators (i.e. profit) for a private sector body, although it is not limited to financial metrics, and measurable (but non-financial) outcomes for public service organizations. It can be seen that the models take a holistic view of an organization. Addressing each of these attributes properly provides a searching analysis of an organization's overall quality management approach.

As indicated, the attributes are given weightings and organizations are encouraged to undertake a self-assessment and mark themselves against each. Guidance is provided on the type of evidence appropriate to a given mark; this can range from anecdotal through extensive longitudinal documented evidence. The idea is for organizations to benchmark themselves against their peers and/or, more constructively, to carry out regular self-assessments to monitor their improvement.

Rigorous and objective self-assessment requires that an assessment team have certain skills as well as knowledge of the model, so formalized training schemes are widely offered under the auspices of the model owners. This degree of formality in assessment is necessary because, in each case, the models form the basis of prestigious national or international quality awards. The danger, as with ISO 9000 certification, is that achieving a high score can be seen as the desirable aim, rather than delivery of quality to the customer in a cost effective manner. The existence of 'professional' assessors with the necessity of their concentrating on unambiguous documentary evidence can too easily lead to a 'tick in the box' approach to using the model, which could repeat, but at greater expense, the worst fears of the ISO 9000 third party certification regime.

4 Tools, techniques and implementation

TQM (or business excellence) models provide the management framework to link together in a structured way the various actual methods of measuring and monitoring quality, and provide structured analysis of quality problems. Prior self-assessment according to one of the models will indicate critical areas – either where quality actions are deficient or where quality actions are most critical to success. The two parts of TQM, the managerial model and the actual methods for quality improvement, can be seen to be necessary and complementary.

We can categorize tools in various ways but a strict categorization is not particularly helpful to the potential user. What *is* important is what the tools do and how easy they are to use. This section is a summary of the review of quality tools given by Barnes and Rogerson (1992).

Basic tools

These are often called the seven basic tools (as defined particularly by Ishikawa) and are:

- Flow charts
- Pareto diagrams
- Check sheets
- Cause and effect diagrams (Ishikawa or fishbone charts)
- Histograms
- Control charts
- Scatter diagrams

Although simple, the regular use of these tools brings a structure and discipline to problem solving. Being graphical, their message in any given case should be readily understood by anyone in the organization. A company can make a big leap forward in its performance using only these basic tools coupled with enquiring minds and cooperating personnel.

More elaborate analytical tools are grounded in statistics, and can include the tools of operational research. Such tools require specialist knowledge to be used properly, but they introduce more rigour and objectivity into the analysis and understanding of processes. Examples of these techniques are:

- Sampling methods
- Parameter estimation

- Hypothesis testing
- Basic experimental design

Advanced experimental design, multi-variate analysis and the tools of operational research form the most sophisticated set of tools. These are usually concerned optimization and, in most cases, will be used infrequently. Organizations other than those with their own in-house expertise in this area will normally need to call in outside advice.

There is a wide variety of other techniques frequently used to enhance quality performance. Examples include:

- Benchmarking
- Nominal group technique (a variation on brainstorming)
- Time charting and analysis
- Six sigma
- Five whys
- Cost of quality
- Quality function deployment (QFD)
- Failure mode and effect analysis (FMEA)
- Moments of truth

Some of these are so simple as to seem almost trivial and hardly worth mentioning. However, anything which can help get an organization moving on the road to total quality is to be fully utilized on the basis that the simple approach is often the most effective. On the other hand, some (Benchmarking, QFD and FMEA for example) require a time-consuming and rigorous approach to deliver useful results.

Benchmarking is the analysis of comparable processes in a different organization (not necessarily a competitor in the same field) to learn from them and adapt the best practices. If used properly, it is a 2-way process and works best when there is complete openness between the benchmarking partners and therefore is most successful when partners are not competitors, or are different branches of the same organization.

The *nominal group technique* is a variation on traditional brainstorming, there being an initial period for private contemplation of ideas, which are then made public in the usual round-robin way. The ideas are then ranked by each team member in private and a consensus

view is obtained without any one team member able to dominate proceedings (provided that the facilitator has remained in control).

Time charting and analysis uses flow charts to map activities showing where time is spent (and wasted) and where alternative methods might reduce it. The idea is to highlight improvement opportunities.

Six sigma focuses on extreme departures from a norm of some quality attribute. This first requires that some performance measure, however crude, be constructed for the activity. The people involved monitor their own performance through a time plot of the measure, taking note of any undesirable high or low values. In this way, a 'feel' for likely causes of adverse performance can be built up. If valid control limits based on statistical theory can be constructed, so much the better; if not, the plot can indicate step changes, trends and cycles in the activity provided that management assists in interpreting the plot and does not cast blame for which might be only part of the 'noise' in the performance measure.

The *Five whys* merely observe that if the reason for some activity is questioned, then a supplementary question is usually generated and after about five such iterations, an improvement opportunity will often be obvious or perhaps a further promising line of enquiry will be indicated. Such a simple approach can lead to the cause of a difficulty being traced rather than trying to make progress by treating symptoms.

The *cost of quality* is a big topic and very much has been written about it. It is an attractive proposition to evaluate the costs associated with defect prevention, with quality appraisal and quality failure costs so that these can be compared to the 'benefits' of a quality programme. This expresses quality in the language that all managers are familiar with – money. However, some external failure costs are, in Deming's words, 'unknown and unknowable'. What is important is to be able to monitor trends in costs related to quality issues and to know their location. It is the reported experience of organizations which have followed the total quality route that dramatic savings are not usually observable against specific improvement projects but rather there is a gradual increase in profitability over a time scale, often of several years.

Quality function deployment (QFD) is a technique used to relate customer needs to the technical features of a product or service. The idea is to rank customer needs and identify which are the most important technical characteristics that must be considered in catering to these needs. The assembly of a multi-disciplinary team to carry out such a design activity is frequently found to be one of its main strengths. It can then focus on inter-relationship of all departments involved and, by so doing, can lead to shorter product development times and a product which is easier to manufacture, works successfully the first time and satisfies the customer. All of these desirable features are likely to lead to overall reduced cost.

Failure mode and effect analysis (FMEA) is a structured approach to identifying ways in which a product or service could fail (the mode) and examining the likely consequences of such failures (the effect). Weightings, of necessity usually subjective, are given to the severity of any given failure, the chance of its occurring and the chance of it not being found before release into the marketplace. These scores are combined into one value, either by adding or multiplying them, and then ranked in order of size. The highest scores suggest which possible failure modes should be eliminated first.

Moments of truth refer to those times when a customer is in contact with any aspect of the organization. It is at such times that there is the potential for the customer to become dissatisfied and at worst, take their business away. Perhaps that is not the worst – they might sue for damages, and win! The trick here is to put oneself in the place of the customer and examine all likely contact points with one's organization and assess possibilities for something fouling up. An early example of this is the suggestion to senior managers that they telephone their organization from outside to see how their switchboard answers. This is important since the operator may be one of the lowest paid staff but is in a key position to influence customers. In an extreme case, a real potential customer might be lost forever without anyone every knowing – part of the 'unknown and unknowable' cost of quality (or lack of it).

5 Expected future developments

Trying to predict the future is always risky but we can certainly try to predict how and to what degree the known changes in business practice are likely to affect TQM and its implementation.

First, we are in an increasingly global economy, so 'comparative advantage' operates on a worldwide scale. Identification of the unique selling point will be more and more important and, for the developed world, this means a premium on innovation and new product development. Competition solely on the basis of labour costs is not feasible. Second, customers are increasingly demanding for both products and services, whether supplied by the public of private sector. Therefore 'the voice of the customer' must be understood and predicted with much greater accuracy. Third, there is growing concern about environmental issues, although whether these will override straightforward economic issues if there is a conflict, is debatable. However, providing goods and services in as environmentally friendly way as possible will be an aim. Fourth, developments in Information Technology (IT) –which are increasing at an ever accelerating rate – will seriously affect supply chain relationships, purchasing, resource management and allocation, customer relations, all of which have a 'quality' aspect.

The first three developments will certainly have the effect of strengthening the need for TQM (by whatever name we will call it) but will, at the same time, require a greater focus on two areas:

- New product development, including issues such as customer feedback and marketing, as well as the product and service innovation processes themselves;
- Environmental and sustainable issues, which will have to encompass the whole supply chain and include such topics as disposal/reclamation of product after use.

In meeting these new demands it may well be necessary to modify details of the established models, which may well provide the initiative for generating new quality tools –

particularly those for managing and monitoring the new product introduction process. There are models for new product introduction but they are, as yet, not integrated into the quality (or business excellence) models.

The effects of the developments in IT are less easy to predict, not least because IT developments themselves are very rapid and the difficulty of estimating which of the new information and data transmission media, for example, will be the dominant one. Nevertheless, the effects will be significant, not so much on the issues but on the speed, accuracy and detail of processes which can be generated and disseminated. To take one example: software now exists and is routinely used for 'data mining' in the retail industry to analyse customer buying patterns. This information can have a profound (and rapid) effect on issues such as procurement, JIT and the required flexibility of manufacturing and delivery processes.

Finally, we must recognize that management techniques such as TQM can be very fashionable in one period but then lose some of their appeal, usually because the business world expects them to deliver more than they reasonably can.

The Bain Survey published in May 2000 showed that usage of TQM is declining from its peak usage in the mid-1990s. The concepts, and particularly the tools, are still relevant but we might expect to see a decline in the use of the explicit models because they are perceived as too prescriptive.

JOHN H. ROGERSON
CRANFIELD UNIVERSITY

Further reading

(References cited in the text marked *)

* Barnes, J.A. and Rogerson, J.H. (1992) Tools and Techniques in TQM-Quality Methods Association conference, Coventry, October.

Deming, W. Edwards (1982) *Quality, Productivity and Competitive Position*, Cambridge, MA: MIT Press. (A classic statement of the views of one of the well known 'gurus'.)

* *The EFQM Execellence Model* (1999) Brussels: EFQM. (A description of a major TQM model and how it should be assessed.)

Feigenbaum A.V. (1991) *Total Quality Control*, revised 3rd edn, New York: McGraw-Hill. (This has been a standard work for many years. The third edition provides a good all-round view of the subject.)

Grant E.L. and Leavenworth R.S. (1988) *Statistical Quality Control*, New York: McGraw-Hill. (Another standard work, now in its sixth edition.)

Juran, J.M. (1988) *Juran on Planning for Quality*, New York: Free Press. (Another guru whose view of TQM differs slightly from that of Deming.)

Juran F.M and Gryna, F.M.(eds) (1988) *Quality Control Handbook*, 4th edn, New York: McGraw-Hill. (This is a comprehensive reference book which covers topics from quality policies and objectives, through quality economics, quality planning and organization, production, marketing, field performance, manpower to motivation. It also contains substantial descriptions of useful statistical methods and articles on quality assurance in many difference industries.)

Malcolm Baldrige National Quality Award (1999) *Award Criteria*, Washington, DC: National Institute of Standards and Technology. (A description of a major TQM model.)

Rooney E.M. and Rogerson, J.H. (1992) *Measuring Quality Related Costs*, London: Chartered Institute of Management Accountants. (A simple guide to measuring quality related costs.)

Taguchi, Genichi. (1986) *Introduction to Quality Engineering (Designing Quality into Products and Processes*, White Plains, NY: Unipub/ Klaus International Publications; Dearborn, MI: American Supplier Institute Inc. (Contains 175 pages of text and is a comprehensive account of Taguchi's philosophy. It covers off-line quality issues.)

Watson, Gregory H. (1993) *Strategic Benchmarking: How to Rate Your Company's Performance Against the World's Best*, New York: John Wiley. (A practical guide to the subject.)

See also: GLOBALIZATION; JAPAN, MANAGEMENT IN; JUST-IN-TIME PHILOSOPHY; ORGANIZATION BEHAVIOUR, HISTORY OF; TAYLOR, F.W.; UNITED STATES OF AMERICA, MANAGEMENT IN THE

Tourism management

Overview

Few industries have evolved as rapidly, broadly and prosperously as tourism in the relatively short span of recent decades. Despite its age-old origins, its phenomenal expansion followed the Second World War when, prompted by its envisioned economic prospects, both developed and developing countries rediscovered tourism and seriously committed themselves to, and heavily invested in, its development and promotion locally, nationally and internationally.

As this unprecedented worldwide popularity continued to spread at a steady rate, tourism quickly evolved into a vigorous industry, an internationally competitive business and a global trade, ranked just below the oil industry, then on a par with it, then above it and now as the largest industry in the world, according to the published data and estimates of the inter-governmental World Tourism Organization (WTO) and the industry-driven World Travel and Tourism Council (WTTC). Notwithstanding this already impressive and well-established magnitude, tourism is now believed to be in its infancy, about to soar to untold heights in this new century.

This recent burgeoning of global tourism has not been limited to its business and operational aspects only. Its pronounced economic towering has inspired the planting of its seeds on the fertile grounds of university campuses. Today, tourism occupies an impressive spread of academic footholds worldwide, with perhaps over a thousand institutions of higher education committed to offering training and education programmes in tourism and to developing knowledge in this new field of study. For some time now, university degrees in tourism have included the BSc, MSc and, beginning a few years ago, PhD.

What is so special or unique about tourism? What factors have brought about its global popularity and vast operation networks? What management principles and practices apply to the diverse tourism businesses, and what rethinking is in order? While these and other basic questions cannot be addressed in a short space, at least some attempts can be made here to provide an overview of tourism's present structure and nature, with some brief comments on its future prospects as an industry and an academic subject.

1 Definition of tourism

There are many different definitions of tourism. Some have been developed with reference to the traveller or tourist, some define tourism according to its operational components, some limit it to its economic dimensions, and still others view it as a sociocultural phenomenon. A definition which captures some of these elements, especially the business and research dimensions, suggests that tourism is a study of people away from their usual habitat, of the industry which responds to their needs, and of the impacts that both they and the industry have on the host and guest sociocultural, economic and physical environments (Jafari 1994).

In viewing this tripartite definition, the first aspect is the study of people (or tourists) away from their usual habitats. Tourists have regularly been studied by, for example, psychologists (what motivates them to travel), sociologists (functions of their touristic pursuits), economists (their expenditures on various goods and services), anthropologists (influences of the tourist culture on visited destinations) and many other academic as well as professional groups. Benefiting from these vast multidisciplinary perspectives, tourists and their touristic worlds and views are understood relatively well, with new research questions still being posed and addressed.

Second, as the definition suggests, tourism is also the study of the industry, composed of a vast network of businesses and operations committed to attracting, receiving, accommodating, managing and serving the tourists. The industry, obviously heterogeneous in nature, includes, partly or totally, such enterprises as hotel, restaurant, transportation, recreation, travel agency and several other tourism-orientated businesses. The definitional debate on the industry's parameters, on what falls inside and outside, will undoubtedly continue. However, what is commonly agreed upon by all is that no matter how the parameters are drawn, tourism still constitutes a mega industry with untold developmental potentials and consequences.

Third, as already noted, tourism is also the study of the impacts that both tourists and the industry have on the visited destinations (as well as tourists' home regions/countries). This last definitional component brings into focus that area of research where tourism's nature, structure and function are studied and continue to receive a magnifying attention. Significantly, this is where the tourism-generating markets (the demand or guest subsystem), the tourism-receiving destinations (the supply or host subsystem) and the intermediary touristic infrastructures (networks of telecommunications, computerized reservation systems or CRSs, and other facilitating forms and mobilizing forces) are combined for a broad and holistic view and a coherent treatment of the subject.

Various research observations, sharpened with analytic and synthetic tools, can begin to reveal generalities in tourism as an industry and as a phenomenon. Tourism's demand and supply subsystems can be distinguished and studied both separately and together, thus allowing analysis of tourism-generating structures: where potential tourists are located, which factors lead to their outbound travels, where the individuality of each market can be discerned, where different marketing and management techniques can be applied, etc. Such treatments cover both the theoretical and

practical domains in which tourism demand is formed (and why) and channelled (how and where) (see CONSUMER BEHAVIOUR). At the same research junction, a focus on the tourism-receiving structures sheds light on the operational fields: where most tourism-orientated enterprises are located, where tourism goods and services are produced, where actual touristic consumptions and practices take place, where tourists act out their fantasies, where their anticipated visits can be compared with the actual offerings of the destination, and more. These two analytically dissected tourism demand and supply subsystems are linked by the touristic networks, intermediary and channelling forms, and managerial tools and practices, among other things.

These tripartite tourist, industry and impact frames together bring into view not only tourism's hubs and spokes in action, but also constitute an ideal tourism model or system, of which the above definition is one example among many. It is within such a consolidated context that tourists by type and practice, the industry by size and operation, and their respective impacts by quality and quantity can be studied, assessed and understood. It is the examination of this holistic text which has already led to the formation of knowledge and its application to tourism planning and development at local, national and international levels. It is here that the management principles and practices applicable to this unique service industry are rendered meaningful (Jafari 1994), and it is from this whole that the main components of the tourism industry are selected for comments on the following pages.

2 The tourism industry

According to the World Tourism Organization (WTO) and the World Travel and Tourism Council (WTTC), tourism is the largest worldwide industry, with a total output of US$3.78 trillion in 1997. Of this, over 90 per cent is domestic (people travelling within their countries of residence) and less than 10 per cent is international. However, it is often international tourism, because of the foreign exchange it generates, which receives pronounced attention and serious competition between and among countries and regions of the world. In 1998, it involved 635 million international travellers, who spent close to US$440 billion (Waters 1999).

The sheer economic magnitude of tourism (domestic and international together) and its employment record of 127 million jobs are both impressive. However, its growth rate is also among the fastest. Between 1950 and 1998, for example, international tourist arrivals (about which more reliable data are available) increased by 2,512 per cent and receipts by 20,923 per cent. By 2010, according to WTO estimates, 1,047 million tourists will travel internationally.

Although tourism is ubiquitous and world-wide, its arrivals and receipts are unevenly shared among countries and regions, with only a handful having lead positions. For example, in 1998, the top five tourist destinations of France, Spain, the USA, Italy and the UK hosted 35.4 per cent of the total international arrivals and enjoyed 41.3 per cent of the total receipts. In the same year, the USA, Germany, Japan, the UK and Italy were the top tourism spenders, with 39.8 per cent of total expenditures. Since practically all countries and regions are eager to increase their share of international arrivals and receipts, according to the World Tourism Organization, this is where major competition among them lies. For a focus on the tourism industry, its operation and management can be considered at four levels: scope, ownership, industry sector and managerial function, as shown in Table 1. These levels will now be examined individually.

3 Scope

Those who are concerned with the *macro* effects of this industry have analysed its consequences on the economy, ecology and sociocultural milieu of the host community. Economists have developed mathematical models to estimate the direct and indirect impacts of income injected by tourists into the local, regional, national or international economies. Furthermore, they have analysed tourism's contributions to the national balance of payments, employment generation and foreign currency earnings. Ecologists, geographers and regional planners, among others, have studied environmental effects of tourism on air, water and noise pollution, soil and beach erosion, destruction of natural habitat and loss of flora and fauna (see ENVIRONMENTAL MANAGEMENT). Regional planners have formulated development models for physical planning and design of tourism which would minimize some of the negative impacts and protect the quality of life of the local community. Sociologists and anthropologists, as examples of other concerned groups, have examined the real and perceived consequences of host–guest sociocultural interactions. Additionally, these aspects have been studied with respect to arts, cultural expressions, values and norms, community organization, intra-familial relations and social stratification resulting from the host–guest interface and influenced by the tourism operational practices and managerial policies.

Researchers and scholars interested in the *micro* aspects of tourism have studied tourism businesses (such as hotels, restaurants, theme parks, transportation, etc.) and/or tourist/

Table 1 Classification of tourism management

Scope	Ownership	Industry sectors	Management functions
• Macro	• Public	• Lodging	• Marketing
• Macro	• Private	• Food service	• Financial management
		• Transportation	• Legal aspects
		• Travel agents and tour operators	• Management information systems
		• Conventions and meetings	• Human resources management
		• Theme parks and attractions	

consumer behaviour. While management specialists have analysed organizational processes and decision making in tourism enterprises, marketing experts and psychologists have formulated models that explain tourist behaviour and motivation.

4 Ownership

The provision of goods and services to travellers is normally done by both the public and private tourism enterprises. Except for some centrally planned economies where the state owns and operates them (such as hotels, restaurants and travel agencies), *public* tourism organizations are chiefly committed to the marketing and promotion of tourism in their regions. Other functions conducted by most public organizations include representation of tourism abroad, facilitation of travellers upon their arrival, and research and trend analysis. Some national organizations are also involved in tourism education and training, conservation of tourism-related resources (such as natural resources and cultural heritages), and regulation of the industry (such as hotel classification, licensing of *travel* agents and tour operators).

Public tourism organizations can be found at the national, regional and local levels. At the national level, they are normally referred to as National Tourism Organizations (or administrations), and are in most cases governmental bodies (for example, the former US Travel and Tourism Administration or the British Tourist Authority). At the regional and local levels, they can be either a governmental body, such as the former Florida Division of Tourism and the English Tourist Board, or a non-profit membership organization, such as the New York City Convention and Visitors Bureau. At all levels, these organizations are concerned first and foremost with the promotion and marketing of their respective destinations. They are funded through public sources, chiefly budget allocations, general taxes and/or tourist taxes, membership dues (such as Convention and Visitors Bureau dues), or from a combination of taxes and dues. Most national and regional governments intervene to a certain extent in the operation of tourism enterprises through legislation, regulations or financial aid and incentives (subsidies, reduced interest rate loans, land grants, credit guarantees, special exchange rates for tourists, etc.).

Private enterprises make up the bulk of the tourism industry and specialize in the provision of commercial services to travellers. They range from large multinational corporations which own thousands of properties throughout the world (such as hotel and fast-food chains) to small family-owned restaurants and inns. Horizontally or vertically integrated multinational companies such as Hilton, SAS and American Express are the visible giant forces (see MULTINATIONAL CORPORATIONS), but the tourism sector is still densely populated and energized by local resources, capital and manpower worldwide. The industry sectors, described below, offer additional insights into the subject.

5 Sectors

Tourism is composed of several distinct sectors, some of which have grown into industries in their own right.

Lodging

The world accommodation or lodging sector is of significant magnitude. In 1997, it consisted of more than 14.9 million rooms worldwide. Europe had more than 5.8 million rooms, followed by the Americas with 4.9 million and the East Asia/Pacific region with 3.3 million. The USA alone had more than 3.9 million rooms. (World Tourism Organization as quoted by Waters, 1999.) Chain hotels and resorts, such as Holiday Inns and Club Med, occupy special accommodation niches, nationally and internationally. Networks of single country/region hotel chains are also rapidly expanding. As in the past, the bulk of hotel rooms are still in the hands of individual operators.

The field of lodging management is concerned with the operation of hotel (resort, inn or motel) establishments, including managing customer demand, ensuring customer service, improving employee performance, increasing productivity, protecting assets and achieving satisfactory levels of return on investment.

The hotel operation is normally divided into several functions which are organized into departments, divisions or units. The front office function sells rooms, checks guests in and out, provides information on hotel services, prepares room status reports, maintains guest accounts, creates guest history files, etc. The food and beverage function operates the hotel's restaurants, coffee shops, bars and lounges, and serves meals and drinks to hotel guests, as well as to outsiders. The guest services function is responsible for the provision of entertainment, relaxation and miscellaneous services. The maintenance and engineering function oversees the physical operation of the property. The security function protects guests from crimes against their persons and property and safeguards the hotel property itself. The reservation function is responsible for receiving enquiries, checking availability and processing all reservation and booking matters. The human resources management function is responsible for all personnel matters, including recruitment, selection, orientation, performance evaluation, promotion, and training and development. The accounting function provides a framework for the accumulation of all financial data which enables management to understand its financial position and evaluate its operation (Powers 1988).

Food service

Unlike lodging, the field of food service operations is not necessarily restricted to serving people away from home. The majority of these establishments serve most of their meals and drinks to local residents. Despite this, the relative contribution of tourism to food service operations is very significant. In the USA, it is estimated that 32 per cent of all food service sales are made to tourists. This amounted to US$108 billion in 1998 (Waters 1999).

The food service sector can be divided by type and ownership. It is common to classify food service operations into independent restaurants, hotel and bar restaurants, and institutional food service. The latter can further be subdivided into business and industry, schools and universities, healthcare, correc-

tional and vending. As to ownership, food service operations can be either independent or franchise. While currently the bulk of the operations throughout the world are still independent (that is, sole proprietors), the situation in most developed countries is changing rapidly and it is expected that by 2010, the majority of food service units will be franchises (such as McDonald's, KFC, Pizza Hut). Franchises already exist in fast-food restaurants, full service restaurants, family-style restaurants, coffee shops, ice-cream parlours, baked goods and doughnut shops.

The management of food service operations, whether independent or franchise, includes the service delivery system (storage, preparation, cooking, etc.), production planning (menu, recipes and recipe standardization, ingredient control, production forecasting, production scheduling), consumer food preference (formation of preference, factors affecting it), menu planning (influencing factors, menu design and display), physical design (layout planning, equipment selection), nutrition (ingredients, nutrient values), purchasing (specifications, order sizes, suppliers, ordering procedures), quality assurance (raw material, inspection, handling and storage, equipment, sanitation, preparation, service, consumer satisfaction), cost control (menu control, cost accounting control, food cost control, food storage and inventory control, labour cost control, food service management information systems), and marketing (markets, positioning, marketing campaigns) (Spears 1991).

Transportation

Like food service, commercial passenger transportation services are not all part of the tourism industry. Only those that transport tourists to, from and within destinations are considered to be in tourism. Commercial transportation services can be divided into land, sea and air.

Land transportation

Land transportation services consist of rail, motorcoach (buses), car rentals, taxis and limousines. The relative magnitude of each of these components and their importance to the tourism industry vary from country to country. While the railway is widely used by tourists and residents alike throughout Europe and many parts of Asia, it is not popular in North America and Australasia. The same is more or less true for the motorcoach industry. In North America, buses are mostly used by tourists for short sightseeing trips (that is, city tours) and not for intercity travel or multiple day tours, as they are used throughout Europe and many other parts of the world. In the USA, trains and buses are neither luxurious nor do they offer the comfort and facilities that their European or Asian counterparts do. Other reasons for the underuse and lack of popularity of trams and buses in North America are a serious neglect and lack of developmental funds in the railway system and a negative public attitude towards travel by these transportation means. Car rentals are by far the fastest-growing commercial land transportation mode in North America, Europe and Asia. The bigger car rental companies, such as Hertz, Avis, National and Budget, have services in virtually every major airport and every destination throughout the world. Limousines are used mostly by business tourists for travel to and from airports, while taxi services are used by tourists as a mode of intra-city travel.

Sea transportation

Sea transportation services are dominated by the cruise sector which is currently experiencing a phenomenal growth. In 1997, 5.1 million North American cruiseline passengers (81 per cent of the world market share) took deepwater cruises and generated US$14.5 billion of revenues (out of the worldwide total of US$18.0 billion). Some 205 cruise ships operate in deep waters worldwide. Major cruiselines operate in the Caribbean, Mediterranean, Pacific, northern Europe and Alaska. Most modern ships are actually floating luxury hotels or resorts which provide a vast range of amenities and services. These vessels can accommodate anywhere from 100 to over 3,000 passengers. Owing to recent expansion and consolidation, three major cruise lines now carry half of the world's cruise passengers. The cruise lines, Carnival Corp., Royal Caribbean Cruises Ltd and Princess Cruises, are expected to increase their capacity by 58.2

per cent over the next five years (Waters 1999).

Air transportation

The airlines can be singled out as the transportation mode which has totally revolutionized the tourism industry and made travel to long-haul destinations accessible, inexpensive and comfortable. This worldwide system is composed of 715 airlines, which own about 18,000 aircraft worth some US8.4 billion. In 1997, the world airlines carried 1.45 billion passengers and flew 2,571 billion passenger/kilometres. North America is the biggest market; in 1997, 39.7 per cent of world passenger/kilometres were flown in this region. As the top five scheduled airlines, Delta, United, American, US Airways and Northwest dominated the combined domestic and international markets, with a 26 per cent market share of passengers flown in 1997 (Waters 1999) (see AIRLINE MANAGEMENT).

A typical airline organization consists of flight operations, engineering and maintenance, and marketing and services. Staff functions consist of finance and property, information services, personnel, corporate communications, economic planning, legal and medical. The function of flight operations is the nucleus of airlines and is concerned with flying, air traffic, safety, flight procedures, training and crew scheduling. Engineering and maintenance oversee all base (overhaul) and line maintenance activities for aircraft and aircraft equipment. Marketing and services perform the functions of advertising, sales and sales planning, food service, and services (ground services such as reservation and ticketing, and on-board services such as flight attendants and entertainment). The most crucial managerial issues in airlines relate to forecasting, pricing, costs, scheduling, fleet planning, labour relations and marketing (Richardson 1990).

Travel agency and tour operation

A travel agency is a business that sells a variety of tourism products, individually or packaged. Travel agents, as intermediaries, sell the goods and services produced by airlines, hotels, cruise lines, car rentals, and the like. In performing their tasks, they supply information and advise clients on destinations, itineraries and facilities, issue tickets on any mode of transportation, sell insurance policies for persons and luggage, make hotel reservations, arrange for excursions and visits to various tourist attractions, and provide/assist with a range of miscellaneous services such as visas, money orders, theatre and museum tickets, etc. Their revenue is generated from predetermined commissions paid by most of these suppliers, and not from their clientele. In 1997, there were 79,743 licensed agents, accredited by the International Air Transport Association (IATA), to sell tickets on international airlines. Of this total, over half were located in the USA and sold a record US$73 billion in travel. While many tourism suppliers are highly dependent on travel agents for the marketing and sale of their products, the industry is under increasing pressure from airlines and the Internet to produce more efficiently. In 1995 the airlines imposed a US$50 cap on commissions paid for US domestic roundtrip tickets. This has forced many travel agencies to consolidate operations and concentrate on the higher priced international fares. For example, in 1997, 57 per cent of all domestic airline tickets were sold by travel agents in the US, down from 80 per cent in 1994. However, travel agents still sold 80 per cent of all international airline tickets which was down only slightly from 1994 when they sold 85 per cent, and they continue to book 95 per cent of all cruise line passengers. But the future of this business has been challenged, with the popularity of e-tickets and their direct purchase over the Internet. Most travel agencies are small and employ fewer than ten individuals. Their main management functions include marketing and sales, delivery of services, human resources management (including training, wage and salary administration), and general administration such as accounting, budgeting and office automation (Lehman 1988; Waters 1998).

Tour operators or tour wholesalers are companies that combine various tourism products (a consolidating function) and sell the resulting packages directly or through retail outlets and travel agents to the public. Tour operators can be either independent, airline dependent (working exclusively with one airline), or travel agents who package tours themselves. Although the exact number of tour operators throughout the world is unknown, experts estimate this number at around 10,000. In the USA alone, in 1997 there were more than 2,000 tour operators. According to the US Tour Operators Association (USTOA), 1997 was a banner year and 1998 was expected to be even better. In 1995, tour operators' products accounted for 17 per cent of all domestic and international bookings made by travel agents in the USA, generating US$17.2 billion in revenue. The most important managerial aspects of the tour operation business include selection of destinations, planning, preparing and marketing vacation tours (Poynter 1993; Waters 1998).

Convention and meeting business

This sector is concerned with generating, attracting and accommodating travel for the purpose of attending meetings, conventions, congresses, trade shows and expositions. These gatherings, which vary in size from a few dozen participants to tens of thousands, can be regional, national and/or international in scope. Every year, millions of worldwide meetings, attended by hundreds of millions of participants, generate billions of dollars. In the USA these meetings are attended by more than 1 million people and generate over US$40 billion of direct and indirect expenditures per year, the bulk of which is spent in the tourism industry. Most meetings are held in popular destinations such as London, Brussels, Geneva, Paris and Vienna in Europe, Chicago, Montreal, Orlando, San Francisco and Vancouver in North America, and Bangkok and Singapore in Asia (Falk and Pizam 1991).

The actors in this sector are meeting planners and convention managers, associations, trade shows, hotels, convention and visitors bureaux, exhibitors, exhibit designers, transportation services, exposition service contractors, destination management companies and food service operations. For example, meeting planners are responsible for planning and organizing professional meetings, and their functions include site and hotel selection, hiring a destination management company, programme planning, arranging for audio-visual equipment, booking in-city transportation, contracting food functions and special events, hiring security services, promoting the meetings and conducting advance and on-site registration (Chon and Feiertag 1990).

Theme parks and attractions

Theme parks and attractions are the newest member of the tourism industry. They represent particular built locations where, usually for a single admission fee, visitors are offered a mix of recreation and entertainment. Today, most such attractions are centred around a unified theme or motif such as history, culture, geography, fantasy and future. Although the majority of large theme parks are in the USA, other countries such as France, the Netherlands, Korea and Japan have also developed parks of significant size and tourist attendance.

Of the forty North American parks that annually attract visitors in millions, over 50 per cent of the attendance is in the parks owned by the Walt Disney Corporation (Disney World, Florida and Disney Land, California), Anheuser Busch (Sea Worlds in Florida and California, Busch Gardens in Tampa), Universal Studios (Florida and California) and Knott's Berry Farm (California). Outside North America, the largest parks are Euro Disney in Paris, Lotte World in Seoul, Tivoli Gardens in Copenhagen, Lisberg in Gothenburg, Sweden and De Efteling in Tilburg, The Netherlands. Although published data on the management and operation of theme parks and attractions is almost non-existent, the few publications that address this subject indicate that the most important issues relate to human resources management, consumer behaviour, forecasting, new product development, and maintenance and engineering (Milman 1993; Walsh-Heron and Stevens 1990).

6 Management functions

Managerial functions in the field of tourism are somewhat similar to those of other industries, with some adapted to reflect better the needs and unique situation of this service industry.

Marketing

In principle, the discipline of marketing as applied to tourism enterprises is unlike the marketing of manufactured goods, but it is very similar to the marketing of services (see SERVICES, MARKETING OF). Tourism practitioners and academics are concerned with several marketing issues that have a direct bearing on the financial success of their organizations. They include market segmentation, selection of target markets, branding and branding strategies, pricing, market positioning, effectiveness of the promotional mix, market feasibility, tourist motivation and decision-making process, and tourist behaviour and satisfaction (Lewis et al. 1995).

Financial management

Financial managers in tourism enterprises, similar to those working in other industries, make financial decisions by interpreting and analysing financial data (see FINANCIAL MANAGEMENT, INTERNATIONAL). They are directly involved in raising capital funds, are responsible for asset management and allocate funds through the preparation of capital and operations budgets. They are also directly involved in budget preparation by establishing financial objectives, forecasting revenues, estimating expenses, determining net income and establishing budgetary controls (Kwansa 1993).

Those who are involved in managerial accounting are responsible for recording, summarizing and interpreting financial data. In most of the hospitality industry (that is, hotels, restaurants and food service institutions), recording and summarizing are accomplished through the use of uniform systems of accounts. These systems offer a formal structure within which financial data is accumulated and organized for the reporting of financial position and operation results. Some of the common tools applied by managerial accountants in tourism/hospitality enterprises include ratio analysis, cost–volume–profit analysis, actual to planned cost analysis, food and beverage cost analysis, payroll cost analysis, and the like (Coltman 1994).

Legal aspects

Tourism enterprises are affected by the legal system in which they operate. Legal systems regulate supplier–consumer relations (which are governed by contracts, tort and regulatory law), commercial relations, competitive marketing relations and international relations (see LAW, CONTRACT). In most countries, tourism operators have legal obligations to their guests. For example, in the USA and most European countries, innkeepers' legal obligations include receiving and accommodating guests, providing safe accommodation, protecting guests from harm, serving safe food and ensuring guest privacy.

A large portion of the most common legal problems in the tourism industry occur in the airlines. They include failure to honour ticket reservations (overbooking), travel delays, changes and cancellations, delayed, damaged or lost luggage and physical injury or death. These plague the airlines on a regular basis and result in countless litigations. To reduce the incidence of these and other problems, tourism enterprises train their employees in the legal issues affecting their business, and have elevated their legal staff to a high organizational position (Cournoyer *et al.* 1993). The recent formation of the International Forum of Travel and Tourism Advocates (IFTTA) signals both the importance and magnitude of this management issue, nationally and internationally.

Management information systems

Most tourism enterprises throughout the world own and operate management information systems (MIS) (see MANAGEMENT INFORMATION SYSTEMS) or property management systems (PMS). These systems are composed of computer hardware and specialized software used to operate tourism properties efficiently. Information systems are used for a multitude of tasks such as reservation, guest registration, accounting, purchasing and inventory control, scheduling, manpower planning and energy management.

Because of the rapid escalation in the use of sophisticated computers and complex software, many tourism enterprises devote a significant amount of their resources to training their personnel in the use of such systems. While the function of MIS was practically non-existent in most tourism enterprises ten or fifteen years ago, today all airlines, all hotel and restaurant chains, most individual operations and all tour operators have organizational units solely devoted to this function (Kasavana 1992).

Human resources management

The management of human resources in tourism is similar to other service industries. It incorporates the functions of recruitment and selection of employees, orientation, motivation, communication, leadership, training and development, salary and benefits, performance evaluation, promotion, health and safety, discipline, termination, collective bargaining and other related concerns (see HUMAN RESOURCE MANAGEMENT). During recent years, many advances in these and other human resources areas have occurred and new management strategies adapted to tourism enterprises and their diverse operations are being designed (Woods 1997).

7 The future

As already noted, tourism is now a well-established global mega-industry (the largest in the world), with a very promising future, especially as both disposable income and time – two essential ingredients or forces mobilizing tourism – continue to grow, and as new technology allows people to visit places near and far faster, more frequently and more comfortably.

In the years ahead, tourism will be a better-integrated industry, as it is presently fragmented and disunited on many fronts. Its present low (frivolous) image, in the eyes of some governments and publics, will be enhanced and the recognition that it deserves will follow. The many thousands of trade associations, whether representing tourism as a whole (such as the World Travel and Tourism Council) or its sectors (such as the International Hotel and Restaurant Association), will adapt their management and marketing efforts for an emerging/repositioned industry. Government recognition and support for tourism as a major economic force and development alternative, as studies show, will multiply. Both the government and the industry itself will begin to recognize further that tourism is not all benefits, but many costs are associated with its development and management. In particular, its environmental and sociocultural consequences will receive penetrating attention. Planning and development of tourism will be based more on techniques backed by research and enriched with the wisdom gained from past developmental successes and failures. Controlled tourism development, with special emphasis on sustainable forms, will demand the attention of public and private sectors.

With the increase in the status of the tourism industry, professionalism among its managers will increase. Managerial salaries and working conditions will improve and a specialized university education in tourism management will be required for many entry positions; 'hands-on' experience and 'promotion from within only' will no longer be the norm. Like managers in other service industries, tourism managers will use sophisticated quantitative and qualitative managerial techniques in order to facilitate decision making in uncertain situations.

Tourism as an academic field will also witness striking changes and new popularity. Study of tourism will continue to borrow theories and research techniques from other fields, as it already has amassed a platform of knowledge to its credit. This advancement will allow tourism to 'export' knowledge to the very fields and disciplines from which it has so generously been borrowing for the past decades.

In short, based on published reports and available data, as the new century unfolds, a much brighter and broader horizon awaits tourism – as an industry, as a profession and as an academic field of investigation.

JAFAR JAFARI
UNIVERSITY OF WISCONSIN-STOUT

ABRAHAM PIZAM
UNIVERSITY OF CENTRAL FLORIDA

Further reading

(References cited in the text marked *)

* Chon, K.S. and Feiertag, H. (1990) 'The essence of meeting management', *The Cornell Hotel and Restaurant Administration Quarterly* 31 (2): 95–7. (A short review of the subject of meeting and convention management.)

* Coltman, M.M. (1994) *Hospitality Management Accounting*, 5th edn, New York: Van Nostrand Reinhold. (A primary text on management accounting for the hospitality industry.)

* Cournoyer, N.G., Marshall, A.G. and Morris, K.L. (1993) *Hotel, Restaurant, and Travel Law. A Preventive Approach*, 4th edn, Albany, NY: Delmar. (An advanced text on the US legal environment in the hospitality and tourism industry.)

* Falk, T.F and Pizam, A. (1991) 'The United States meeting market', *International Journal of Hospitality Management* 10 (2): 111–18. (A review of the size and magnitude of the convention industry in the USA.)

* Jafari, J. (1994) 'Structure of tourism: three integrated models', in S. Witt and L. Mountinho (eds), *Tourism Marketing and Management Handbook*, 2nd edn, New York: Prentice Hall. (A discussion of models which allow tourism to be viewed as a field of study and as an industry.)

Jones, P. and Pizam, A. (eds) (1993) *The International Hospitality Industry: Organizational and Operational Issues*, New York: Wiley. (An advanced text/reader on operations management in the hospitality industry worldwide.)

* Kasavana, M. (1992) *Managing Computers in the Hospitality Industry*, 2nd edn, East Lansing, MI: Educational Institute of the American Hotel and Motel Association. (A primary textbook on hospitality information systems.)

* Kwansa, F.A. (1993) 'Financial management', in M. Khan, M. Olsen and T. Var (eds), *VNR's Encyclopedia of Hospitality and Tourism*, New York: Van Nostrand Reinhold. (A short article describing the nature of financial management in hospitality enterprises.)

* Lehman, A.D. (1988) *Travel Agency Policies and Procedures Manual*, Albany, NY: Delmar. (A combination textbook and practitioner's manual on the subject of travel agency operations.)

* Lewis, R., Chambers, R.E. and Chacko, H.F. (1995) *Marketing Leadership in Hospitality*, 2nd edn, New York: Van Nostrand Reinhold. (An advanced text on marketing in the hospitality and tourism industry.)

* Milman, A. (1993) 'Theme parks and attractions', in M. Khan, M. Olsen and T. Var (eds), *VNR's*

Encyclopedia of Hospitality and Tourism, New York: Van Nostrand Reinhold. (A review article on the nature and magnitude of the theme parks and attractions industry worldwide.)

Nebel, E.C. (1991) *Managing Hotels Effectively*, New York: Van Nostrand Reinhold. (An advanced text on hotel management with special emphasis on the USA.)

* Powers, T. (1988) *Introduction to Management in the Hospitality Industry*, 3rd edn, New York: Wiley. (A primary text on hospitality management in the USA.)

* Poynter, J.M. (1993) *Tour Design, Marketing and Management*, Englewood Cliffs, NJ: Regents/Prentice Hall. (A combination textbook and practitioner's manual on the subject of tour operations.)

* Richardson, J.D. (1990) *Essentials of Aviation Management*, 4th edn, Dubuque, IA: Kendall/Hunt. (A primary text on the US airline industry.)

* Spears, M. (199 I) *Foodservice Organizations*, 2nd edn, New York: Macmillan. (A primary text on food service management.)

* Walsh-Heron, J. and Stevens, T. (1990) *The Management of Visitor Attractions and Events*, Englewood Cliffs, NJ: Prentice Hall. (A primary text on the management of attractions and events.)

* Waters, S.R. (1998) *Travel Industry Worm Yearbook. The Big Picture 1997–98*, vol. 41, New York: Child & Waters. (An annual publication summarizing and evaluating the performance of the travel and tourism industry worldwide.)

* Waters, S.R. (1999) *Travel Industry Worm Yearbook. The Big Picture 1998–99*, vol. 42, New York: Child & Waters. (An annual publication summarizing and evaluating the performance of the travel and tourism industry worldwide.)

Weirich, M.L. (1992) *Meetings and Convention Management*, Albany, NY: Delmar. (A primary text on meetings and convention management.)

* Woods, R.H. (1997) *Managing Hospitality Resources*, 2nd edn, East Lansing, MI: Educational Institute of the American Hotel and Motel Association. (A primary text on human resources management practices in the US hospitality industry.)

* World Tourism Organization (1994a) *Yearbook of Tourism Statistics*, 46th edn, vol. 1, Madrid: WTO. (A compendium of annual tourism statistics.)

* World Tourism Organization (1994b) *Global Tourism Forecasts to the Year 2000 and Beyond*, vol. 3, Madrid: WTO. (A compendium of forecast tourism statistics for the years 2000 and 2010.)

See also: CULTURE, CROSS-NATIONAL; DIRECT MARKETING; EMERGING COUNTRIES, MANAGEMENT IN THE; EXECUTIVE TRAINING; GLOBALIZATION; MARKETING

Toyoda family

Summary

There is no one 'great person' who bears the name Toyota in the same way as Henry Ford. The Toyota Motor Company, which in 1982 became Toyota Motor Corporation (TMC), was founded by the Toyoda family. The company took on the name Toyota after staging a contest to select a new name in 1936. TMC has become the most powerful Japanese car manufacturer and one of the world's largest manufacturers of motor vehicles, third in size after General Motors (GM) (see GENERAL MOTORS CORPORATION) and Ford. The success of TMC has been associated with its production system, which has given TMC the reputation of being highly efficient and of producing high-quality cars and trucks. Much of TMC's success can be attributed to the achievements of the Toyoda family.

Personal background

See Figure 1 for details of the Toyoda family tree.

Major works

Toyota – Fifty Years in Motion: An Autobiography by the Chairman, Eiji Toyoda (1987)
Toyota, a History of the First Fifty Years (1988)

1 Introduction

Toyota Motor Company was established in the summer of 1937 and in 1956 it became the largest car producer in Japan. In 1959 Nissan surpassed Toyota, but in 1965 Toyota once again became the largest car maker in Japan and was still dominant in 1995. Since the mid-1980s, prompted by the rise in the value of the yen and by periodic tendencies towards protectionism in its export markets, the Toyota Motor Corporation (TMC) has made major investments in overseas manufacturing plants, most notably in the USA, Canada, the UK and Australia, but also in other countries.

In 1974, when most of the world's car companies were making losses, Toyota continued to make a modest profit. Competing manufacturers began making visits to Toyota to discover the key to that company's success. What they discovered was the Toyota production system, which Toyota had continued to develop over forty years.

2 Biographical data

Sakichi Toyoda (1867–1930)

The founding father of the Toyota Group, Sakichi was born in Yamaguchi on 14 February 1867, the son of Ikichi Toyoda. As the first born, Sakichi was the *kacho*, or head of the household, and it was his duty to carry forward the obligations of his father and his trade as a carpenter. However, Sakichi was not as committed to carpentry as he was to contributing to society, so in 1885 he decided instead to become an inventor. Over the next forty-five years Sakichi worked on improving weaving looms. In 1906 he became a partner in Toyoda Loom Works, from which he resigned in 1910. He later started his own business, Toyoda Spinning and Weaving Company. In 1924, with the aid of his son Kiichiro, he developed a fully automatic loom, and in 1927 Sakichi formed another company, Toyoda Automatic Loom Works. In 1929 he sold the patent rights of the automatic loom to the British firm Platt Brothers & Co. Ltd for 1 million yen. He was awarded Japan's highest civilian honour by the Emperor in 1927, and died on 30 October 1930.

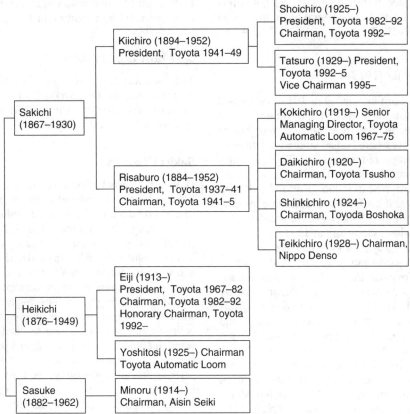

Figure 1 The Toyoda family: members in director positions with Toyota
Source: Adapted from Kamiya (1976: 100–1) and Cusumano (1985: 184) and personal

When the people of the Nagoya region laid Sakichi to rest, they honoured him as a man who made his dreams reality, who had embraced the challenges and opportunities of the Meiji Restoration, and who had helped lead his country into the modern world.

(Togo and Wartman 1993: 39)

Kiichiro Toyoda (1894–1952)

The founder of Toyota Motor Company, Kiichiro, was born in Yamaguchi in 1894, the eldest son of Sakichi Toyoda. He graduated in 1920 from Tokyo University as a mechanical engineer and joined his father's company, Toyoda Spinning and Weaving Company, in that same year. In 1930, at the bequest of his father, Kiichiro began work to produce cars. He began by sectioning off an area of the Toyoda Automatic Loom Works in which to disassemble and study a small engine. In

December 1930 the directors of Toyoda Automatic Loom agreed to fund an automotive department, and in August 1934 Kiichiro and his staff completed their first prototype engine, type A. The first truck prototype was completed in August 1935.

The cost of the automotive department was a great burden on the Loom company and Kiichiro reasoned that the only way to become established in the market was to expand. With the board's approval, the acquisition of credit and the sales of shares, Toyota Motor Company was formally established in the summer of 1937. Kiichiro was executive vice-president and in 1941 he became president of the company. But by 1950 the company was in turmoil as the entire workforce went on strike, protesting against a proposed reduction in employees. In an attempt to smooth labour relations, Kiichiro resigned from the company. He was due to return as president in 1952 to manage and advance the production of cars, but unfortunately he died of a cerebral haemorrhage on 27 March 1952.

Eiji Toyoda (1913–)

Eiji was born in Nagoya in 1913, the second eldest son of Heikichi Toyoda, Sakichi Toyoda's brother. He graduated from Tokyo University, where he had studied mechanical engineering, and joined the Toyoda Automatic Loom Works in 1936 at the newly established car research lab. Eiji lodged with Kiichiro and his family and became an integral part of their household. He transferred to Toyota Motor Company in 1937.

In 1950 Toyota and Ford were beginning talks of a joint venture; part of the deal was to accept Toyota trainees at Ford's facilities, and Eiji Toyoda was the first person sent by Toyota. In 1951 he redesigned Toyota's plants to incorporate more advanced methods and machines. Eiji became president in 1967 and in 1982 chairman of the new Toyota Motor Corporation (TMC). In this same year Eiji began talks with General Motors (GM) about an important joint venture, New United Motor Manufacturing Incorporated (NUMMI), which would produce a Corolla-type car (a Toyota model) at a recently closed GM plant in Fremont, California. The project was widely hailed as a success, and demonstrated that the Toyota production system could be adapted to a Western context.

Dr Shoichiro Toyoda (1925–)

Shoichiro, the eldest son of Kiichiro, was born in 1925. He graduated from Nagoya University in 1949 with a degree in engineering and joined Toyota Motor Company in 1952. In 1955 he earned a doctorate in engineering at Tohoku University, with a thesis on fuel-injection systems. He assumed the presidency of TMC Sales Co. Ltd in 1981. After its merger with Toyota Motor Company the following year, he became president of the new Toyota Motor Corporation, and in 1992 chairman of the board. He presided over Toyota's becoming a global corporation. In May 1994 he became chairman of Keidanren (Japan Federation of Economic Organizations), the most powerful organization in Japan.

3 Main contributions

TMC's success reflects the foresight and determination of the Toyoda family. Each of the above members contributed to the development of the Toyota philosophy.

Sakichi Toyoda

Having no formal educational qualifications, Sakichi learnt by trial and error; he believed that he could learn all that he needed to know by working on machines with his hands. Sakichi also recognized that industry in Japan had to advance in small steps and to fill particular markets not met by Western companies. He came to recognize the importance of constantly improving machines regardless of what the competition was doing. Sakichi believed that no process ever reached a point where it could not be improved; this policy of *kaizen* (continuous improvement) became part of his basic philosophy (see JAPAN, MANAGEMENT IN).

Despite much opposition, Sakichi was sure that cars would be a worthwhile product of the future. When he sold the patent rights to Toyoda's automatic loom, he told his son, Kiichiro Toyoda, that he was giving him a million yen, but there was one condition: Kiichiro had to use the money for research on car production. Kiichiro agreed.

Kiichiro Toyoda

Kiichiro took on Sakichi's business style and formally established Toyota Motor Company. However, his contribution to the Toyota story did not stop there. Kiichiro realized that in order to compete with such powerful Western companies as Ford and GM, Toyota needed to invest in research and development. Hence, in 1936, he established a research lab in Tokyo. Japan differed from the USA in its lack of space and other resources. The US manufacturers could afford to stockpile parts and could build big warehouses. Kiichiro wanted to develop a Japanese production system that provided higher-quality, more cost-effective products that reflected the country's lack of space and resources, as well as the flexibility and versatility of its people. Consequently he bought specialized machines and his plan was to modify them into multi-purpose machines.

In the past the process of building cars had been 'learning by doing'. This had generated waste, which the Japanese could not afford. Kiichiro envisaged a system in which no component would be produced unless it was needed, hence eliminating the need for stock piles and waste. Therefore, in his factory, he hung a sign that read 'Just in time'. He told the workers that no component for a car should be produced before it was needed; in other words, components should be made just in time (JIT) (Togo and Wartman 1993: 79) (see JUST-IN-TIME PHILOSOPHY). The practices of *kaizen* and JIT became an important part of the philosophy. However, the philosophy was not developed fully until Taiichi Ohno joined the team (see OHNO, T.).

Eiji Toyoda

In February 1951 Eiji Toyoda developed a five-year modernization plan. This plan involved the modernization of equipment and the transformation of production methods. Like Kiichiro and Sakichi before him, Eiji recognized that Toyota would have to utilize conveyor systems; workers would have to search for continuous improvement and waste had to be minimized. Eiji employed Taiichi Ohno to implement these changes.

Ohno had begun his career with the Toyoda family in 1933 and was familiar with their philosophies. He introduced *kanban* cards (which keep track of stock), taught workers to understand *kaizen*, fully implemented the JIT system, rationalized the machinery and assembly lines, and introduced multi-skilling. Eiji was supportive of Ohno's work, and within two years Eiji and Ohno had devised a radical new principle of factory operation. Whenever a problem developed in assembly, the production line was to be shut down, thus providing an incentive for a speedy and effective remedy.

By the 1960s the JIT system had been instituted throughout the company and Toyota Motor Company began asking its suppliers to adopt the same system. It took Eiji Toyoda and Ohno more than twenty years to implement this set of ideas fully (including JIT) within the Toyota Motor Company supply chain.

Eiji also set another precedent. He decided that the future of the company depended on how well it built cars, even more than on how well it designed them. He proclaimed that production was the most important thing that happened at Toyota. The mission of designers and engineers was to enable the production staff to do their best. Accordingly, the status of assembly-line workers was elevated.

Shoichiro Toyoda

A novel production system had improved Toyota's efficiency and had enabled the company to put cars on the market at competitive prices. The quality, however, was still inadequate. Shoichiro Toyoda, then managing director of corporate planning, came to realize that the company was practising *kaizen* at too late a stage. Having to mend cars after they came on the market was damaging Toyota's reputation. In search of a means to improve quality, Shoichiro came across the work of Deming (see DEMING, W.E.). Toyota had instituted some aspects of Deming's approach in the early 1950s. Shoichiro realized that for Toyota Motor Company to improve, two aspects of its quality process needed to change: first, it had to become more systematic; and, second, it had to be extended to every department. Therefore, Shoichiro implemented a quality programme throughout the company and in 1965 Toyota Motor Company won the coveted Deming Prize for quality.

Toyota Motor Company

Following the first 'oil crisis', by 1974 the international car industry was in a state of flux. Toyota was one of the few car manufacturers in the world that was consistently profitable. Competing manufacturers wanted to know how Toyota could be profitable in a bad market. Toyota was able to achieve extremely high levels of quality (few defects) and productivity in manufacturing (output per worker that was as much as two or three times higher than in US or European plants in the late 1980s). Toyota was also able to achieve high levels of flexibility, producing relatively small batches of different models with little or no loss of productivity or quality. Accordingly, this Japanese style of manufacturing and product development has come to be studied and emulated around the world. By the mid-1990s the best US-owned car manufacturing plants appeared to have achieved relative parity with all but the most efficient Japanese plants.

Many believed that Toyota's most critical factor for success was its production system and underlying philosophies, sometimes known as 'Toyodaism'. The Toyota production system includes:

- JIT production
- minimal in-process inventories and efficient use of resources
- geographic concentration of assembly and parts production
- good communications
- elimination of waste
- manual demand-'pull' with *kanban* cards
- production levelling
- rapid set-up
- machinery and line rationalization
- work standardization
- foolproof automation devices
- multi-skilled workers
- high levels of subcontracting
- selective use of automation
- continuous incremental process improvement (*kaizen*)
- teamwork

Since the publication of *The Machine that Changed the World* (Womack *et al.* 1990), Toyota's production system has also become known as 'lean production'. Lean production has been put forward as a model of 'best practice which can be successfully implemented even in cultures very different from Japan, not merely in the car industry but in other industries too.

4 Evaluation

The success of Toyota's production system has helped to transform Japan into the second capital of the automotive world and has also led to improved productivity and efficiency in Western manufacturing. For example, following a change to lean production at the GM–Toyota joint venture plant (NUMMI), performance in terms of quality, productivity and other indicators improved dramatically from one of the worst in the USA to one of the best. A typical body-stamping die-change time was reduced from twelve hours to fifteen minutes. Lean production involves significant differences from and advantages over Fordist and neo-Fordist mass-production factory regimes, as illustrated in Table 1, and the key components of lean production can contribute to a major improvement in competitiveness (Shadur and Bamber 1994).

Nevertheless, as manufacturers around the world have tried to copy TMC's methods, there have inevitably been criticisms. Compared to Fordism, lean-production systems place greater demands on managers and supervisory staff since they are responsible for managing a broader range of issues in their unit, such as human resource management, safety, absenteeism and continuous improvement. There are also more demands on them to maintain extensive information systems for each work unit and optimize performance on each item they measure.

Critics argue that the pace of work in such Japanese production plants is frantic (for example, Kamata 1982; Williams *et al.* 1992). The JIT system creates pressures for operators to maintain production at a pre-set rate, and the demands of smaller batches and shorter set-up times can lead to pressure on them to work harder. But advocates of Toyodaism hold that it requires people to work smarter, not necessarily harder. Others have argued that lean production uses labour as a buffer for a fragile production system and that the workers have little real control over their job design. Such criticisms have led some authors to describe lean production as 'management by stress' (Parker and Slaughter 1988).

From the perspective typical of Toyota, however, such criticisms are merely seen to be

Table 1 Critical differences between Fordism, neo-Fordism and lean production

	Fordism	Neo-Fordism	Lean production
Innovation	Wholly technocratic	Mostly technocratic	Technocratic/ continuous improvement
Quality control	Inspected in	Part inspected and built in	Built in
Operations management	Bulk supply	Bulk supply/JIT incipient	JIT
Throughput efficiency	Operational	Operational	Process
Approach to HR	Individual/plant	Individual/some teams	Teams
Authority structure	Highly vertical	Vertical	Vertical/some decentralization
Information to workers	Minimal	Some provided	Extensive
Role of workers	Appendages of machines	Important part of production	Crucial part of production
Role of supervisory staff	Directive	Controlling/ organizing	Facilitating/organizing/ training
Company's role for union	Non-recognition	Adversarial	More cooperative

Source: Shadur and Bamber (1994)

a reminder that the lean notion itself should be subjected to continuous improvement. While US, European and other car makers continue to study and, at least in part, try to emulate Toyota's manufacturing and engineering practices, it has become apparent to many Japanese managers, policy-makers and industry observers that the notion of 'continuous improvement' – continually pushing for gains in manufacturing and engineering efficiency – can precipitate new problems and has some practical limits. *Kaizen* continues at TMC, as Toyota and other Japanese car makers are exploring ways to modify their approaches.

5 Conclusion

The Toyota Motor Corporation (TMC) had its beginnings in 1929, when Sakichi Toyoda gave his son Kiichiro Toyoda a grant to produce cars. Since its establishment TMC has grown to be the world's third-largest car manufacturer, with plants in many countries. Toyodaism has been emulated around the world and has been widely advocated as a paragon of best practice. Most of the other Japanese car companies had lost their independence by 2000 as they had formed various alliances with American or European companies. However, TMC and its production system continued to attract much international acclaim. In spite of the rise in the value of the yen and economic recessions, Toyota has remained competitive, as it continues to improve its production and 'humanware' systems, including the working environment, health and safety.

KELLIE CAUGHT
QUEENSLAND UNIVERSITY OF TECHNOLOGY

GREG J. BAMBER
GRIFFITH UNIVERSITY

Note

C. Kurokawa and N. Horii of TMC helpfully supplied information that assisted greatly in compiling this entry. The author acknowledges with thanks that K. Caught co-authored this entry in the first edition of the IEBM.

Further reading

(References cited in the text marked *)

Berggren, C. (1992) *Alternatives to Lean Production: Work Organisation in the Swedish Auto Industry*, Ithaca, NY: Cornell University Press. (Also published in London by Macmillan under the title *The Volvo Experience: Alternatives to Lean Production in the Swedish Auto Industry*; challenges the superiority of Toyodaism, arguing for a more human-centred approach, contrasting and comparing the Swedish and Japanese styles.)

Clark, K.B. and Fujimoro, T. (1991) *Product Development Performance: Strategy, Organization and Performance in the World Auto Industry*, Boston, MA: Harvard Business School Press. (Shows that Toyota and other Japanese companies develop products more quickly and efficiently than Western manufacturers.)

* Cusumano, M.A. (1985) *The Japanese Automobile Industry: Technology and Management at Nissan and Toyota*, Cambridge, MA: Harvard University Press. (Provides an account of the developments of Nissan and Toyota, contrasts their different systems and highlights ways in which Japanese manufacturing diverged from US and European practices.)

* Kamata, S. (1982) *Japan in the Passing Lane*, New York: Pantheon. (A radical journalist's critique of working life in a Toyota plant in Japan, based on participant observation.)

* Kamiya, S. (1976) *My Life with Toyota*, Nagoya: Toyota Motor Sales. (A personal history of Shotoro Kamiya, his life with Toyota and the Japanese automobile industry.)

Kimoto, S. (1991) *Quest for the Dawn*, Milwaukee, WI: Dougherty. (An insight into the origins of Toyota Motor Company, based on translations of diaries, memos and other documents written by Sakichi and Kiichiro Toyoda and their contemporaries.)

Krafcik, J.F. (1988) 'Triumph of the lean production system', *Sloan Management Review* 30 (1): 41–52. (An account of the superiority of the Toyota production system, which manufactures a wide range of models but maintains high degrees of quality and productivity, as revealed by research of the International Motor Vehicle Program (IMVP), Massachusetts Institute of Technology.)

MacDuffie, J.P. and Frits, K.P. (1995) 'The international assembly plant study: update on round two findings', IMVP Research Briefing Meeting, Toronto, 5 June (mimeo, Wharton School, University of Pennsylvania and International Motor Vehicle Program (IMVP), Massachusetts Institute of Technology). (A comparison of the findings of IMVP's surveys conducted in 1989 and 1993 which show general improvements in plant performance, but Japanese plants in Japan appeared to be the most productive in both surveys.)

Monden, Y. (1983) *The Toyota Production System*, Atlanta, GA: Industrial Engineering and Management Press. (An explanation of Toyodaism dating from before it was popularized by the IMVP's publications.)

* Parker, M. and Slaughter, J. (1988) 'Management by stress', *Technology Review* 91 (7): 37–44. (A critique of Toyodaism by two radical critics based in Detroit with the Labor Education and Research Project.)

* Shadur, M.A. and Bamber, G.J. (1994) 'Toward lean management? International transferability of Japanese management strategies to Australia', *The International Executive* 36 (3): 343–64. (Reports a study of an attempt to transplant Toyodaism to Australia.)

Shimada, H. (1989) *The Economics of Humanware* (in Japanese), Tokyo: Diamond. (Introduces the notion of 'humanware' as one of the secrets of success of successful Japanese investments in US car manufacturing.)

* Togo, Y. and Wartman, W. (1993) *Against All Odds: The Story of the Toyota Motor Corporation and the Family That Created It*, New York: St Martin's Press. (An account of the Toyoda family and the development of the Toyota Motor Corporation from 1867 to 1990.)

* Toyoda, E. (1987) *Toyota – Fifty Years in Motion: An Autobiography by the Chairman, Eiji Toyoda*, New York: Kodansha International. (An account of the life of Eiji Toyoda, from his birth to the chairmanship of Toyota.)

* Toyota Motor Corporation (1988) *Toyota, a History of the First Fifty Years*, Japan: Toyota Motor Corporation. (An official synopsis of Toyota Motor Corporation's fifty-year history, spanning 1937–87, with reference to Toyota's beginnings and the development of its management style.)

Toyota Motor Corporation (1995) *You 'Ain't Seen Nuthin' Yet!*, Japan: Toyota Motor Company. (Toyota Annual Report 1995: a review of operations, finances, board of directors and share information for the 1994–5 financial year.)

* Williams, K., Haslam, C., Williams, J. and Cutler, T., with Adcrost, A. and Sukhdev, J. (1992) 'Against lean production', *Economy and Society* 21 (3): 321–54. (A critique of the lean-production system.)

* Womack, J.P., Jones, D.T. and Roos, D. (1990) *The Machine that Changed the World*, New York: Rawson/Macmillan. (Examines the differences between mass production and lean production in the automotive industry in Japan, North America and Western Europe; reports the results and implications of the International Motor Vehicle Program (IMVP) study.)

See also: DEMING, W.E.; FORD, H.; INDUSTRIAL RELATIONS IN ASIA PACIFIC; JAPAN, MANAGEMENT IN; JAPANIZATION; JUST-IN-TIME PHILOSOPHY; MANAGEMENT IN JAPAN; OHNO, T.; PRODUCTIVITY; SLOAN, A.P.; TOTAL QUALITY MANAGEMENT

TQM: see **TOTAL QUALITY MANAGEMENT**

Trade: see **COUNTERTRADE; INTERNATIONAL TRADE AND FOREIGN DIRECT INVESTMENT; NORTH AMERICAN FREE-TRADE AGREEMENT**

Trade, international: see **INTERNATIONAL TRADE AND FOREIGN DIRECT INVESTMENT**

Trade unions

Overview

Trade unions are associations established for the purpose of maintaining or improving the conditions of the working lives of wage earners. Although some contemporary unions may trace their origins to the medieval guilds, trade unions as we know them today are primarily the result of the industrial revolution and the large wage earning class which it created. Unions exist in almost every contemporary nation-state where they are typically considered to be a principal representative of the interests of employees.

Historical Background

The first modern trade unions began to appear in Great Britain in the eighteenth century, when medieval institutions collapsed leaving the wage earner without protection from the vagaries of the market for labour. The first unions were formed by craftsmen and drew upon craft guild traditions (Slomp 1990; Adams 1995). Most of the early unions were confined to specific cities, although contact with organizations in other towns led quickly to informal arrangements to aid itinerant workers. The policies and objectives of the early unions were eclectic. They provided a forum whereby workers in the same trade could socialize with like-minded individuals and they helped members in time of need. Many of the early unions assumed the functions of friendly societies and as such provided financial assistance to sick or unemployed members. One early service was the provision of insurance in order that a deceased 'brother' or 'sister' would be able to have a proper burial.

In difficult times it was natural that these organizations would petition employers to uphold or improve terms and conditions of employment. During the nineteenth century, some of the early worker associations petitioned the government to uphold protective regulations. In situations where they were strong the early craft unionists often would agree among themselves not to work for less than a basic 'trade rate' and to work only for employers who respected union rules.

The early unions were fragile. They proliferated in prosperous times and disappeared during recessions and depressions. Employers were generally opposed to the unions because they challenged long established authority relations, attempted to impose work rules considered to be confining and pushed for higher wages. The state was also wary of unions because they were considered to interfere with efficient market operations and because they posed the threat of becoming a base for the making of working class political demands. After the French Revolution of 1789 European states generally attempted to discourage the formation of working class organizations. In most countries unions were banned for at least some period of time (Adams 1993).

1 Ideology

Despite the opposition of both employers and the state, the 'labour movement' slowly grew in size and strength throughout the first half of the nineteenth century. Isolated local unions consolidated into national unions and by the second half of the nineteenth century unions in many countries had formed national federations of unions (see WEBB, B. AND WEBB, S.). The most pressing concerns of the early unions were survival and the solution of specific problems as they arose. From about the mid-nineteenth century, however, labour leaders began to think more consciously about ideology and long term objectives. Although a wide variety of ideological perspectives competed for the allegiance of the working class organizations four types emerged as dominant: Revolutionary, Reform, Christian and Business (Larson and Nissen 1987) (see INDUSTRIAL AND LABOUR RELATIONS).

The revolutionary perspective and Marxism

The revolutionary perspective was put forth most vigorously by Karl Marx, who argued that the industrial revolution had ushered in an era of 'capitalism' in which two major social classes clashed (see MARX, K.H.). Capitalists, the owners of the means of production, were pulled by the desire for profits and pushed by competition to 'exploit' workers by making those dependent on the sale of their labour work long hours for low pay. According to Marx, these systemic forces were so strong that efforts by individuals, unions or companies to stand against them would be futile. The working class could improve its conditions only by revolting against capitalism and establishing socialism – a system in which the means of production were owned in common and rational decisions could be made about the distribution of goods, services and purchasing power.

The Marxist prescription for improving the working lives of wage earners called for the formation of both unions and labour political parties. The unions would have the responsibility for organizing the working class and educating workers about the nature of the capitalist system as well as defending and improving working conditions within the capitalist system. The party would have the function of developing working class strategy for bringing about the transition from capitalism to socialism. According to Marx, the party should be accorded primacy within the labour movement.

The appeal of Marxism

The Marxist analysis and prescription had great appeal to labour leaders in the second half of the nineteenth century. At that time working people had few rights and labour leaders within civil society were considered only slightly more legitimate than criminals. As noted above, in most European countries as well as the United States, trade unions were outlawed for some time. In France the 'Loi le Chapelier' forbade all associations intermediary between the individual and the state. In Britain the Combinations Acts of 1799-1800 branded all associations of working people as 'conspiracies' in constraint of trade and thus illegal (Hepple 1986). The same doctrine became law in the United States as a result of a court case in 1806. By the mid-nineteenth century these laws were being revised, but the stigma of unionism as a less than proper activity continued on for many decades. Marxist philosophy glorified the working class and labour leadership. It insisted that the working class was a force of history that would inevitably lead to the destruction of the capitalist system and the establishment of a more just and perfect society. Thus Marxist philosophy elevated labour activism from contemptible to laudable.

Revolutionary syndicalism
The ideology of revolution attracted a wide following among trade unionists in the second half of the nineteenth century. It became the dominant philosophy of labour on continental Europe, either in its Marxist form or in its variant of revolutionary syndicalism (van der Linden 1990). The syndicalists shared the Marxist analysis of the nature of capitalist society but were very distrustful of political parties and of government bureaucracies and thus called for direct worker action to bring about the revolution through the general strike. Whereas Marxists would initially replace the capitalist state with a strong socialist state, the syndicalists called for the destruction of the state to be replaced with voluntary arrangements between worker-controlled production organizations. Syndicalism became the dominant labour movement philosophy in France, where the revolution of 1789 and several additional revolutions in the name of the common people had failed to bring about significant change in the conditions of the working class.

'Productionist unionism'
When the revolution actually occurred in Russia in 1917, the new rulers had to consider the proper role of unions in socialist as opposed to capitalist society. It was decided that the unions would be given the tasks of managing social programmes, negotiating the implementation of the central plan and statutory labour standards in specific enterprises, representing worker grievances to management and, most unlike unions under capitalism, assisting in the mobilization of workers to achieve high productivity. This type of unionism became known as 'productionist' as opposed to the union focus on consumption in capitalist countries (Grancelli 1988). When

communism spread from the Russian core to the USSR and later to Eastern Europe, Asia and some African nations this trade union model was generally adopted in those countries as well. Within the communist world neither free collective bargaining, nor the right to strike, nor union independence of the party and the state was seen as appropriate.

The reform philosophy

In Western Europe, the ideology of revolution began to be challenged in the late nineteenth century. Reformers agreed with the Marxist proposition that society needed to be changed so that the conditions of work and life were made more comfortable for the many. They argued, however, that change could be brought about through reform rather than through revolution. By this time labour/socialist parties had been established in many countries; regulations protecting the safety of workers in mines and factories had been introduced and the right to vote was being extended to a larger part of the adult population. These developments encouraged the reformers to believe that capitalist society could be gradually changed through the extension of democratic institutions. Particularly active in developing the philosophy of reform socialism was Eduard Bernstein in Germany and British Fabian Society in Britain (Landauer 1959).

This philosophy had considerable appeal among trade union leaders whose rank and file members were more interested in their daily conditions of work than they were in macro sociopolitical change. It also won increasingly large numbers of adherents from labour/socialist party leaders after those parties began to win political power. By the 1920s reform socialism had become the dominant philosophy of European unions (Adams 1995).

Christian unionism
A third labour philosophy that began to appear in the latter part of the nineteenth century was Christian unionism. Marxist ideology held that the capitalist state was supported by many institutions, including Christianity. Christian doctrine held that even though the lot of the

working person might be difficult on earth, if workers led sin free lives they could expect a better existence in heaven. Marx argued that this doctrine helped to perpetuate capitalism by diverting workers attention from their mundane problems to their potential reward in heaven. They were led to focus on 'pie in the sky' rather than the achievement of change on earth. Thus Christianity acted as a bulwark to capitalism and was an enemy to working class aspirations.

Christian unionism and the Church

As swelling numbers of workers were recruited to organizations that officially embraced Marxist ideology, the Christian churches became increasingly alarmed. Church leaders in many European towns encouraged Christian workers to form their own unions. In 1891 Pope Leo XIII issued the encyclical Rerum Novarum in which the formation of Christian unions was encouraged (Fogarty 1957). During the first two decades of the twentieth century Christian unionism spread significantly across not only Europe but also notably South America. It also became a significant force in the Canadian province of Quebec.

Initially the Christian unions were dominated by the church, which discouraged conflict and cajoled Christian workers and employers to conciliate their differences. The church held that workers had a duty to do a fair days work and that employers had a responsibility to treat their employees fairly and with dignity. Church leaders offered their services as mediators and conciliators when disputes occurred. From about the 1930s the influence of church leaders on these unions began to decline along with the general decline of religious influence on civil society. In the decades following the Second World War most Christian union movements became entirely independent of the church hierarchy although they continued, in many countries, to be guided by Christian principles. In some countries, of which France is a good example, there was a transition away from Christianity to an entirely independent stance. Never as important globally as socialist unionism, Christian unionism has declined in strength in recent decades.

Business unionism, pure and simple

The fourth important labour philosophy is that of business or pure and simple unionism. This philosophy holds that the purpose of unions is to win the best conditions of employment for their members within liberal democratic society. It also insists that it is improper for unions to become involved in partisan politics. Union members have many different political interests and thus should be free to join and support the political party of their choice. The proper interest of the union in politics is to ensure that the state permits the labour movement the freedom to negotiate effectively with employers over conditions of work and that it adopt legislation in the interests of union members. Generally, business unionism does not affirm the Marxist analysis of modern society as being split into two antagonistic classes. Instead it tends to accept the theory of the pluralist state as an arena of myriad interest groups none of which is strong enough to dominate. Unlike Marxism, this philosophy does not hold that the labour movement has any long term mission. Its sole purpose is continually to improve the conditions of its members (Perlman 1928).

The appeal of business unionism

Business unionism became the dominant philosophy in the United States by the end of the nineteenth century and it continues to hold that position today. Because some variant of socialism is dominant in the labour movements of most other modern nations, the US situation is regarded as extraordinary and 'American labour exceptionalism' has been a major topic of scholarly inquiry. The philosophy has also been of importance in many other countries where it has competed with socialist and Christian unionism. Whereas the labour movements of Northern Europe moved to reform socialism from the doctrine of revolution, the British and Canadian labour movements moved to reform socialism from the opposite end of the ideological spectrum. During the nineteenth and early part of the twentieth century they had been more business-like and only slowly moved towards a more political strategy.

Business unionism has had considerable appeal to unions of white collar employees. In many countries, white collar workers during the nineteenth and into the twentieth century had privileges not enjoyed by blue-collar workers and thus found revolution and reform less appealing. White collar unionism first appeared as an important force during the First World War. In many countries white collar unions have seen fit to remain independent of the mainstream movement, generally because of differences over ideology.

2 The international trade union movement

Although autonomous power within labour movements resides primarily at the level of the nation-state, trade unions have established important international organizations.

International trade secretariats

In the 1880s and 1890s, International Trade Secretariats began to be formed. These were organizations composed of national unions in particular crafts or industries. Among the first to come into existence were those for boot and shoe workers, miners, printers, metal workers and clothing and textile workers. By the second decade of the twentieth century, there were nearly 30 such organizations but the number has declined over the years primarily as the result of mergers. Most recently (1 January 2000), four of the ITS's catering primarily to white collar workers combined into Union Network International, which claims to represent over 15 million workers worldwide. Today there are fewer than fifteen separate international secretariats (Windmuller and Pursey 1998 and *http://www.icftu.org*).

The ITS's carry out research and disseminate information on subjects such as terms and conditions of employment. They also act as vehicles for coordinating the efforts of their members with respect to strikes and boycotts. Most provide assistance to unions in less developed countries.

International trade secretariats and other international organizations

The ITSs also lobby international organizations such as the International Labour Organization and the United Nations on their member's behalf. In recent decades a principal concern has been the activities of multina-

tional corporations. In response to the growth of those organizations, several international trade secretariats have set up committees to exchange information and coordinate the activities of trade unionists working for the same company in different countries. For several companies international councils have been established which confer with the management about a range of issues of mutual concern. Pressure exerted by international labour organizations has resulted in organizations such as the Organization for Economic Cooperation and Development, the International Labour Organization and the European Economic Community developing acceptable standards of behaviour for multinational companies in their dealings with employees and their representatives (see INTERNATIONAL LABOUR ORGANIZATION [ILO]).

The ITS's have also begun to work closely with non-governmental organizations concerned with environmental and human rights issues in order to promote a 'social dimension' to international trade. The object is to require of nations, as a condition for participation in international trade agreements, effective respect for a set of core labour rights that have been widely affirmed to be fundamental human rights. The core includes freedom of association, the right to bargain collectively and effective protection against forced labour, exploitative forms of child labour and discrimination in employment. Trade unions, along with their civil society allies, have also begun to insist that these standards be adhered to by multinational corporations and in response, corporations have increasingly been adopting codes of conduct committing the organization to respect human and labour rights and the environment.

Central trade union federations

A second type of international trade union organization is composed of central labour federations. Conferences of such organizations (in some cases in conjunction with political parties) were held from the late nineteenth century. From these meetings emerged a secretariat which, from 1913, was known as the International Federation of Trade Unions. Ideological splits within the labour movements of particular countries were eventually reflected in the international arena. After the

Second World War three major international union federations of worldwide scope came into existence: The International Confederation of Free Trade Unions attempted to group all social democratic and business union federations; the World Federation of Trade Unions brought together all of the union organizations in countries under communism as well as those federations in other parts of the world who affirmed communist ideology and the International Federation of Christian Trade Unions. In 1968 this latter organization changed its name to World Confederation of Labour, to reflect the more independent and secular programme that its member federations had adopted by that time.

The International Confederation of Free Trade Unions

The most representative of the three global internationals is the ICFTU. It includes union federations from all of the most developed countries but also has many affiliates in Asia, Africa and Latin America. It claims to represent 125 million workers grouped into 215 national trade union centres in 145 countries. Since the collapse of communism in 1989 many of the new union federations in central and eastern Europe have also affiliated. The ICFTU represents general labour interests to international organizations, assists labour movements in the less developed world and carries out research and educational work.

The World Confederation of Labour (WCL)

Since it moved away from its Christian identity, the WCL has had a difficult time defining its unique reason for being. Several of its important affiliates have abandoned it for the ICFTU. Its major supporters today come from Belgium, the Netherlands and Latin America. Its programme of action is similar to that of the ICFTU. It claims to represent 26 million trade unionists from 113 countries (*http://www.cmt-wcl.org*).

The World Federation of Trade Unions and other federations

Since the collapse of communism many of the previous constituents of the WFTU have disbanded or completely changed their programmes. The previous singular government-supported union federation that existed in most communist nations has been superseded in most East and Central European nations by several federations with philosophies ranging from business-like to various versions of democratic socialism. Although many individuals active in the unions under Soviet communism continue to be active in the post-communist era, totalitarian communism as a working philosophy has all but disappeared in Eastern and central Europe. Many of the new federations have joined the ICFTU. Nevertheless the WFTU continues to exist and at its most recent international congress attracted participants from over 80 countries.

In addition to the ITS's and the international union confederations, there are also regional groupings of trade union federations, some of which are independent and some of which are sub-units of the international confederations. Among the most important of the independent regional organizations is the European Trade Union Confederation (ETUC), which brings together national trade union federations affiliated with the ICFTU and the WCL and some with no international affiliation. Its primary function is to represent labour interests within Europe. ETUC is the voice of labour within the European Union and is labour's representative in the so-called 'social dialogue', a multinational bargaining process established by EU rules. Roughly similar organizations exist in Africa, Asia, the Middle East, the South Pacific and the Caribbean.

Finally, there are trade union organizations whose function is to represent labour's interests within particular international organizations. The Trade Union Advisory Committee (TUAC), for example, is labour's representative within the Organization for Economic Cooperation and Development (*http://www.tuac.org*).

3 Union objectives and methods

With the recent changes noted above there are today two dominant independent union types in the global arena: social democratic (or reform socialist) and business. Business unions take as their major object the representation of the interests of their own members, while social democratic unions have the wider aspiration of representing the interests of all working people whether or not they are members of a trade union. Typically social democratic unions are closely associated with a labour or socialist party and political strategies for improving the conditions of the working class are coordinated with the party. Union leaders often hold party office simultaneously and in many countries unionists also hold political office (von Beyme 1980). In countries where such unions and parties are strong, social and welfare legislation tends to be more highly elaborated than in nations where these organizations are weak. Pure and simple unions by definition are not officially associated with any one political party, although they may support specific candidates and may support particular parties in specific circumstances. A major activity of both sorts of unions today is the influencing of legislation of particular interest to their constituents. In addition, in many nations, in order to avoid economic disruption and price instability, unions have been invited to cooperate with employer organizations and the state in the formation of overall socioeconomic policy (Trebilcock 1994). This phenomenon has become known as 'neo-corporatism' or 'tripartism'.

Collective bargaining

A major activity of both business and social democratic unions today is collective bargaining with employers over terms and conditions of employment (see collective bargaining). In all of the industrialized, market economy countries collective bargaining is a dominant contemporary method of trade unions (Windmuller *et al.* 1987; Adams 1995). In Western Europe, due to the prevalence of multi-employer bargaining and the extension of agreements to non-associated employers, collective bargaining is the predominant method for the establishment of wage levels, hours of work and other general conditions of employment. Collective bargaining is also a primary activity of unions in North America; however, because unions represent only a minority of the labour force and because of decentralized bargaining and the absence of agreement extension, most North American employees have their basic conditions of work established unilaterally by employers. Collective bargaining is also in evidence throughout

most of the developing world. However, because of union weakness basic conditions of employment are frequently established unilaterally by employers or specified by the state.

The right to strike

The primary basis of union power is the right to strike. The strike or the strike-threat plays a critical role in collective bargaining in most countries. Unions generally insist on the general acceptance of the right to strike and according to the interpretation of the International Labour Organization that right is implicitly a part of freedom of association. In a few countries (Italy, France) the right to strike has been embedded in the national constitution. Because it is disruptive of economic activity and the stable delivery of critical services, some countries have outlawed the strike for certain employees such as police and firefighters. In some cases nations have attempted to convince unions to accept arbitration in lieu of the right to strike. The most extensive experiment with arbitration as a substitute for the right to strike was undertaken in Australia and New Zealand. In both of those countries it was a national institution for most of the twentieth century, but the availability of arbitration and the forbidding of strikes did not actually result in the absence of strike activity in either country.

Administering social and economic policies

In addition to co-determining socioeconomic policy and terms and conditions of employment, unions in many nations serve on agencies established to administer social and economic policies. For example, trade unionists serve on agencies designed to administer labour market policy, training, health and safety, pensions, workers' compensation for industrial accidents and human rights. In some countries (Sweden, Belgium) unions have been given primary responsibility for administering the unemployment insurance system. Unions also provide assistance to individuals who believe that their rights under collective agreements or social legislation have been violated. In some countries (United States, Canada) unions have been instrumental in the development of 'grievance procedures' ending in binding arbitration for the settlement of collective agreement disputes. In other nations (Germany, France) unions are active in representing their constituents before tribunals such as labour courts.

4 Structure and government

Within any country unions today are typically organized at three levels: local, industry or occupation and national (Bean 1994, Bamber and Lansbury 1998).

Local level organization

At the local level there are three major types of organizational format. In many countries industrial (e.g. the chemical industry) or occupational (e.g. nurses) unions are organized locally on a geographic basis. All members within a given city or district belong to the local union. Some unions prefer, however, to organize on a plant basis. This type of union groups all employees who work in a particular plant or location in the same union and it is common among industrial unions in North America. A third local form is the enterprise union which differs from the plant union type in that all members of a single company (e.g. Toyota) belong to a single union. Enterprise unionism was pioneered in Japan and has been spreading to other countries in recent decades.

Industrial or craft unions

Local unions are typically grouped in national unions. Initially there were two major types of national union: the industrial union and the craft union. However, over the years, as a result of amalgamations and mergers, these two types have become increasingly intertwined. As a result a common form of union today is referred to simply as the general union.

Craft unions were the first unions to endure as going concerns but when unskilled and semi-skilled workers began to organize *en masse* at the beginning of the twentieth century industrial unions began to be more prevalent. Socialist movements generally prefer the industrial union form because it is more consistent with their egalitarian principles. By the mid-twentieth century industrial unionism dominated throughout the world, but craft unionism continued to be important in a few countries, notably Britain and others strongly influenced by British traditions such as the United States, Canada and the Australasian countries. In continental Europe craft unionism continued to be important only in Denmark.

National-level organization

At the national level one finds union federations divided by ideology (e.g. Social democratic vs. Christian or formerly Christian vs. business). One also finds divisions based on occupational identity. In several countries (France, Sweden, Germany) there are separate central organizations for white collar workers.

Union governance

In Europe trade unions were major elements in the struggle for democracy and everywhere unions are formally organized on democratic principles. At each level union officers are elected. Before entering negotiations unions typically survey members to ensure that their concerns are represented and usually before official strikes take place union members must vote in favour of such action. In many nations tentative collective agreements must be approved by union members before they go into effect.

Often there is tension within union organizations between the democratic imperative and the need for leaders to possess the authority to take quick and decisive action. The latter consideration has led many North European unions to give their negotiators the right to enter into collective agreements on their own initiative without the need to subject the tentative agreement to a member vote.

Most union organizations schedule frequent local union meetings but they are usually poorly attended and thus draw criticism from democracy adherents. To quell such criticisms some union movements go so far as to fine members who do not attend such meetings.

5 Contemporary issues and challenges

The 1960s and 1970s was a period of rapid economic growth, generally low unemployment and price instability. In that milieu union membership generally grew, strike activity was high and union economic and political influence was considerable. Wages, benefits and social programmes expanded considerably. In many countries governments offered unions political concessions in return for their pledge to moderate wage demands and forego strikes. That period came to an end as a result of the deep recession of the early 1980s. Subsequent to the recession, unemployment in many European countries reached levels unknown since the worldwide depression of the 1930s. Economic growth in South America and Africa came to a halt and real wages fell. In Asia, however, Japan and the newly industrializing economies of Hong Kong, South Korea, Taiwan and Singapore continued to expand and prosper, providing enhanced worldwide competition (see ASIA PACIFIC, MANAGEMENT IN). With the exception of newly industrializing Asia these developments undermined union strength. Membership generally decreased and unions were unable to organize effective strike activity (Adams 1991).

During this period, employers in many nations seized the initiative in labour relations and successfully demanded economic concessions, freedom from union- and government-imposed constraints and more flexibility. They also took the initiative to reorganize production in order to take better advantage of employee skill and creativity. These developments led to more bargaining at the level of the enterprise. Many states ceased to involve unions in socioeconomic decision-making. However, in several countries where tripartite consultation had become firmly embedded (e.g. Germany, Japan, Austria) it continued in effect.

Independent trade unions appeared in all of the ex-communist countries and, during the 1990s, institutions similar to those common in the West were constructed.

By the turn of the third millennium, perhaps the dominant issue of concern to unions around the world is the phenomenon of globalization. Due to the rapid advance of technology and especially communications and transportation technology, multinational corporations have begun to source production globally. The development of a global market for capital as well the removal of trade barriers has increased the power of management in labour negotiations because of its credible threat to migrate unless it is able to achieve acceptable terms. To counter this development trade unions have increasingly been making alliances with human rights and environmental organizations, with the goal of establishing effective international labour and environmental standards and decision-making processes. Should this trend continue, and that appears likely, the multinational arena is likely to attract a good deal of labour union attention in the twenty-first century.

6 Conclusion

Although the contemporary era has been a difficult one for the trade unions, they continue to be a salient feature of most nations of the world. They are generally considered to be a fundamental pillar of democracy and as long as political democracy continues to be a dominant force in the world trade unions will continue to play a significant role in society.

ROY J. ADAMS
MCMASTER UNIVERSITY

Further reading

(References cited in the text marked *)

* Adams, Roy (1993) 'Regulating Unions and Collective Bargaining: A Global, Historical Analysis of Determinants and Consequences', Comparative Labor Law Journal 14 (3): 272–301. (A global review of government policy towards unions and collective bargaining over the past two centuries.)
* Adams, Roy (ed.) (1991) *Comparative Industrial Relations, Contemporary Research and Theory*, London: Harper Collins. (A review of industrial relations developments from the 1960s in industrialized, developing and communist countries.)
* Adams, Roy (1995) *Industrial Relations Under Liberal Democracy, North America in Comparative Perspective*, Columbia: University of

South Carolina Press. (A systematic comparison of the development and current practice of industrial relations in Europe, North America and Japan.)

* Bamber, G. and Lansbury, R. (eds) (1998) *International and Comparative Employment Relations*, London: Sage. (Chapters on industrial relations in the major industrialized market countries.)

* Bean, R. (1994) *Comparative Industrial Relations*, 2nd edn, London: Croom Helm. (Chapters on comparative industrial relations issues in both developed and developing countries.)

* Fogarty, M. (1957) *Christian Democracy in Western Europe, 1820–1953*, London: Routledge and Kegan Paul. (The most comprehensive treatment of the development of Christian trade unionism.)

* Grancelli, B. (1988) *Soviet Management and Labor Relations*, Boston: Allen and Unwin. (Discussion of the practice of industrial relations under communism.)

Heery, E. and Solomon, J. (eds) (1999) *The Insecure Workforce*, London: Routledge. (Up-to-date account of labour market and HRM pressures on trade unions.)

Hepple, B. (ed.) (1986) *The Making of Labour Law in Europe: A Comparative Study of Nine Countries Up to 1945*, London: Mansell. (The most comprehensive treatment of the subject.)

* Landauer, C. (1959) *European Socialism*, Berkeley: University of California Press. (Most comprehensive treatment of the subject.)

* Larson, S. and Nissen, B. (eds) (1987) *Theories of the Labor Movement*, Detroit, MI: Wayne State University Press. (Multiple perspectives on the nature and purpose of trade unions. Excerpts from basic sources.)

Ng, S.H. and Warner, M. (1998) *China's Trade Unions and Management*, London: Macmillan. (Analyses trade unions and management in China, Hong Kong, Singapore and Taiwan.)

* Perlman, S. (1928) *A Theory of The Labor Movement*, New York: The Macmillan Company. (The most widely referenced statement of the nature of business unionism. Also an apologetic from American exceptionalism.)

* Slomp, H. (1990) *Labor Relations in Europe*, New York: Greenwood Press. (The history of labour relations in Europe.)

* Trebilcock, Anne *et al.* (1994) *Towards Social Dialogue: Tripartite Cooperation in National Economic and Social Policy-Making*, Geneva: International Labour Organization. (A review of efforts by labour, management and the state to reach consensus on national issues.)

* van der Linden, M. (1990) *Revolutionary Syndicalism: an International Perspective*, Brookfield, VT: Gower.

* von Beyme, K. (1980) *Challenge to Power, Trade Unions and Industrial Relations in Capitalist Countries*, London: Sage. (An international comparison by a prominent German political scientist.)

Webb, S. and Webb, B. (1894) *History of Trade Unionism*, New York: Longmans, Green and Co. (The first major study of trade unions.)

* Windmuller, J.P. and Pursey S.K. (1998) 'The International Trade Union Movement', in R. Blanpain and C. Engels (eds) *Comparative Labour Law and Industrial Relations in Industrialised Market Economies*, 6th and revised edition, Deventer, Netherlands: Kluwer. (Development and contemporary status of the concept.)

* Windmuller, J.P. *et al.* (1987) *Collective Bargaining in Industrialised Market Economies: A Reappraisal*, Geneva: International Labour Office. (Comparative overview and review of bargaining in several countries.)

See also: COLLECTIVE BARGAINING; EMPLOYEE RELATIONS, MANAGEMENT OF; EMPLOYERS' ASSOCIATIONS; EMPLOYMENT AND UNEMPLOYMENT, ECONOMICS OF; FLEXIBILITY; HUMAN RESOURCE MANAGEMENT; INDUSTRIAL CONFLICT; INDUSTRIAL DEMOCRACY; INDUSTRIAL AND LABOUR RELATIONS; MARX, K.H.; THIRD PARTY INTERVENTION; TRAINING, ECONOMICS OF; WEBB, B. AND WEBB, S.

Tradeoffs management

Overview

Technological change essentially rewrites the notion and management of tradeoffs that underpin established business in all sectors. Global customers do not want tradeoffs between price, quality, speed, customization, reliability, etc. – they want it *all*. Global producers are thus forced to adjust and *eliminate the tradeoffs*. The elimination of tradeoffs has become a part of the global management paradigm (GMP) and the mantra of the e-business and commerce.

At the very least, new, adjusted patterns of tradeoffs are emerging, while old-fashioned 'business as usual' in the management of tradeoffs is fading. For example, customization vs. price tradeoff is all but eliminated through the advances of digital business and mass customization. Common bundling of products and services implies significant implied tradeoffs and cross-subsidies. Not all customers want 'the mix' but specific, item-by-item, individual customer-focused bundling. Another tradeoff: offer a wider range of products to the same customers, or exploit the value-added reserves through seeking a larger share of each customer's purchases? Digital business changes it all: disintermediation, vertical disintegration, direct customizing – industry value chains have to be redefined.

1 Introduction

A new, somewhat discomforting, possibly radical and certainly challenging idea has started making the rounds in better business management literature: *'Are tradeoffs really necessary?'*

The answer is no: *tradeoffs are not necessary*. Pursuing and achieving lower cost, higher quality (and improved flexibility), all at the same time, is not only possible but clearly desirable and – within a New Economy – also necessary.

Tradeoffs can be postulated among different, conflicting objectives or criteria. Conventional wisdom recommends dealing with such conflicts via 'tough choices' and a 'careful analysis' of the tradeoffs. Yet, many Japanese factories have achieved lower cost, higher quality, faster product introductions and greater flexibility, all at the same time: Lean manufacturing has apparently eliminated the tradeoffs among productivity, investment and variety.

Quality and low cost and customization and low cost were long assumed to be tradeoffs, but companies are forced to overcome the traditional tradeoffs (see JAPAN, MANAGEMENT IN; JUST-IN-TIME PHILOSOPHY).

There is a *basic asymmetry* between the producer's and the customer's view of tradeoffs. The producer wants to produce either low-cost *or* high-quality *or* high-speed-delivery products. The customer wants to purchase both low-cost *and* high-quality *and* high-speed-delivery products – all at the same time. These two traditionally opposing vantage points are being reconciled and matched with the help of information technology and systems (IT/S) (see INFORMATION TECHNOLOGY; SYSTEMS).

Turning to more professional literature, in *The Need to Make Tradeoffs*, the authors concluded:

> Recently, tradeoffs have been called into question as operations are being designed which have better quality, lower cost and faster delivery than the competitors. These operations have moved to a new level of performance rather than making tradeoffs on an existing level. Because of these new insights, the exact nature of tradeoffs is no longer clearly understood.
>
> (Anderson *et al.* 1988)

How can traditional tradeoffs be 'eliminated' or 'overcome'? Are not tradeoffs generic to multiple-criteria conflicts? Can we have it both ways? Can one decrease cost and increase quality at the same time – and continue doing so? The answer is yes; tradeoffs are properties of badly designed systems and thus can be eliminated by designing better, preferably optimal, systems. The tradeoffs-free (TOF) management and design of resources is the key. Enterprise Resource Planning (ERP) systems have to include the notion of the optimal *portfolio of corporate resources*.

2 Multiple objectives and tradeoffs

Consider the following quote:

There are no conflicting objectives per se. No human objectives are in conflict by definition, that is, inherently conflicting. Everything depends on the given situation, the historical state of affairs, the reigning paradigm, or the lack of imagination.

We often hear that one cannot minimize unemployment and inflation at the same time. We are used to the notion that maximizing quality precludes minimizing costs, that safety conflicts with profits, Arabs with Jews, and industry with the environment. Although these generalizations may be true, they are only conditionally true. Usually inadequate means or technol-

ogy, insufficient exploration of new alternatives, lack of innovation – not the objectives or criteria themselves – are the causes of apparent conflict.

(Zeleny 1982)

Tradeoffs among multiple objectives (there can be no tradeoffs when only a single objective is considered) are *not* properties of the objectives themselves, but of the set of alternatives or options they are engaged to measure.

For example, tradeoffs between cost and quality have little if anything to do with criteria of cost and quality themselves: rather, they are implied by the limits and constraints on the characteristics of available alternatives they measure. Measuring sticks are neutral and any apparent relations (like tradeoffs) are only induced by the objects measured.

3 Tradeoffs graphics

Suppose that objectives f_1 = profit and f_2 = quality. Both of these objectives are to be maximized with respect to given resource constraints (feasible options).

In Figure 1, the polyhedron of system-feasible options is a well-defined System I. Maximizing functions f_1 and f_2 separately leads to two different optimal solutions and levels of criteria performance (designated as *max*). If System I remains fixed, observe that the maximal, separately attainable levels of both objectives lead to an *infeasible* 'ideal' option. The tradeoffs between quality and

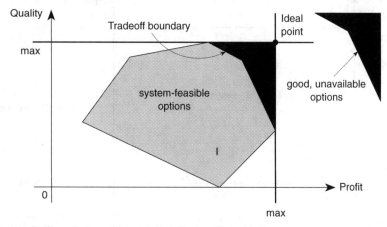

Figure 1 System I: given design with natural quality–profit tradeoff

profits are explicit and must be dealt with (selecting from the heavy boundary, i.e. non-dominated solutions, of System I.

In Figure 1, the system I is poorly designed because there exists a set of good, currently unavailable options which would make the 'ideal' point feasible and thus would allow the maxima of f_1 and f_2 (Profits and Quality) to be attained both at the same time.

Any manager's lifetime of work in System I will unfailingly yield the following wisdom: There is always a tradeoff between profits (or costs) and quality, one cannot have it both ways, one has to pay for quality. As more and more managers derive (from their own experience) the same wisdom, textbook writers and instructors accept the wisdom as conventional, embed it in their own educational efforts and teach it to multitudes who had no such prior experience.

In other words, reshaping the feasible set (reconfiguring resource constraints) in order to include the 'missing' alternatives would lead to a superior system design with higher levels of criteria performance.

Such desirable 'reshaping' of the feasible set is represented in Figure 2, where System II of system-feasible options is sketched. Given System II, both objectives are maximized at the same point (or option): System II is superior in design to System I.

There is one system configuration, given some cost or effort constraint, that yields the best possible performance. Such a system (like System II in Figure 2) will be superior with respect to both profit and quality and no tradeoffs between them are possible. Tradeoffs have been eliminated through optimal system design.

In Figure 2, a system with no quality–profit tradeoffs is presented. Observe that the maximal separately attainable levels of both criteria now form a feasible ideal option. Consequently, the tradeoffs between quality and profit have ceased to exist (the heavy tradeoff boundary of System I has disappeared in System II).

Any manager's lifetime of work in System II will unfailingly yield the following wisdom: There is no tradeoff between profits (or costs) and quality, one cannot have one without the other, quality pays for itself. As more and more managers derive (from their own experience) the same wisdom, textbook writers and instructors accept the wisdom as conventional, embed it in their own educational efforts and teach it to multitudes who had no such prior experience.

4 Numerical tradeoffs

Let us consider a simple production problem involving two different products, say suits and dresses, in quantities x and y, each of them consuming five different resources (nylon through golden thread) according to technologically determined requirements (technological coefficients). Unit market prices of

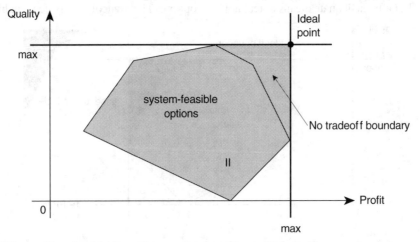

Figure 2 System II: optimal design with no apparent quality–profit tradeoffs

Table 1 Original data for production example

Unit price	Resource		Technological coefficients Number of units	
$	x = 1, y = 1	Raw material	Resource requirements	Resource portfolio
30	Nylon	4	0	20
40	Velvet	2	6	24
9.5	Silver thread	12	4	60
20	Silk	0	3	10.5
10	Golden thread	4	4	26

resources are also given, as are the levels (no. of units) of resources currently available (portfolio of resources). The data are summarized in Table 1.

In the above example, observe that producing one unit of each product x and y (x = 1 and y = 1) requires 4 units of nylon (4×1 + 0×1), 8 units of velvet (2×1 + 6×1), etc. Total number of available units of each material (given resource portfolio) is given in the last column of Table 1.

Current market prices of resources (first column) allow us to calculate the costs of the given resource portfolio:

$$(30×20) + (40×24) + (9.5×60)$$
$$+ (20×10.5) + (10×26) = \$2600$$

The same prices can be used to compute unit costs of producing one unit of each of the two products:

$$x = 1: (30×4) + (40×2) + (9.5×12) + (20×0)$$
$$+ (10×4) = \$354$$

$$y = 1: (30×0) + (40×6) + (9.5 × 4) + (20×3)$$
$$+ (10×4) = \$378$$

In other words, it costs $354 to produce one suit and $378 to produce one dress. Suppose that we can sell all we produce at current market prices of $754/unit of x and $678/unit of y.

Expected profit margins (price – cost) are:

$$x: 754 – 354 = \$400/unit$$

$$y: 678 – 378 = \$300/unit$$

As profit maximizers, we are interested in maximizing the total value of function $f_1 = 400x + 300y$.

As a second criterion, let us consider some quality index: say 6 points per x and 8 points

per y (scale from 0 to 10), so that we can maximize the total quality index or function $f_2 = 6x + 8y$.

We are now in a position to analyse the above outlined production system with respect to profits and quality. Maximizing levels of x and y (best product mix) can be easily calculated by techniques of mathematical programming (here we need only the results).

1 Function f_1 is maximized at x = 4.25 and y = 2.25, thus achieving maximum of (400×4.25) + (300×2.25) = $2375 in profits.
2 Function f_2 is maximized at x = 3.75 and y = 2.75, achieving maximum of (6×3.75) + (8×2.75) = 44.5 in total quality index.

This situation corresponds to the situation in Figure 1. The two maximizing points are the endpoints of the tradeoff boundary. One can trade off quality for profits by moving from x = 3.75, y = 2.75 to x = 4.25, y = 2.25 and back again, trading profits for quality. Because we can produce only one product mix at a time, we can choose either to maximize profits (x = 4.25, y = 2.25) or to maximize quality (x = 3.75, y = 2.75), but not both. The choice is difficult because of the tradeoffs between profits and quality. Their importance is difficult to evaluate.

Let us heed our productivity consultant's advice and purchase a portfolio of resources different from that in Table 1, other things being equal. We keep this new production system comparable and compatible in all respects, except the last column of Table 1. The new portfolio of resources in Table 2 has been proposed by the consultant.

Table 2 New data for production example

Unit price	Resource	Technological coefficients No of units		
$	x = 1, y = 1	Raw material	Resource requirements	Resource portfolio
30	Nylon	4	0	16.12
40	Velvet	2	6	23.30
9.5	Silver thread	12	4	58.52
20	Silk	0	3	7.62
10	Golden thread	4	4	26.28

We are now in a position to analyse the newly proposed production system under the same conditions.

1. Function f_1 is now maximized at x = 4.03 and y = 2.54, a maximum of (400×4.03) + (300×2.54) = $2375 in profits.
2. Function f_2 is maximized at x = 4.03 and y = 2.54, achieving a maximum of (6×4.03) + (8×2.54) = 44.5 in total quality index.

Both previously achieved maximum values of f_1 and f_2 have been matched. More importantly, *both* maximum profits ($2375) and maximum quality index (44.5) are achieved through a single product mix: x = 4.03 and y = 2.54. This particular product mix, or ideal point in Figures 1 and 2, was infeasible in the previous system. By allowing its feasibility now, we have eliminated all and any tradeoffs between the criteria of profits and quality.

The previous tradeoffs-based system (Table 1) was operated at the cost of $2600. The newly designed tradeoffs-free system (Table 2) is realizable at the following cost:

(30×16.12) + (40×23.3) + (9.5×58.52) + (20×7.62) + (10×26.28) = $2386.74

The superior performance of the newly designed system comes at $213.26 cheaper than the sub-optimal performance of the original system.

5 Optimal portfolio of resources

The above example demonstrates that the chosen portfolio of resources is crucial for assessing the maximum achievable levels of profits, costs, quality, flexibility, etc., at which the corresponding production system can be operated, other things being equal.

In our example, should any company choose to operate *any other* resource portfolio (at cost $2600) than that of Table 2, other things being equal, then its performance with respect to f_1 and f_2 would be necessarily inferior. Simple rearrangement of resource levels (comparing Table 1 with Table 2) 'reshapes' the management system (of feasible opportunities) from Figure 1 to Figure 2 and provides superior performance at the same or even lower costs.

The explanation is simple. Productive resources should not be engaged individually and separately because they do not contribute one by one according to their marginal productivities. Productive resources perform best as a whole system: they should be determined and engaged jointly as a portfolio and in an optimal fashion.

Consequently, any company running anything other than an optimal portfolio of resources cannot outperform a company running the optimal portfolio, *ceteris paribus*. A company based on Figure 1 has, under these conditions, no chance of successfully competing with the company based on Figure 2. Regardless of its product-mix positioning along its tradeoff boundary, the tradeoffs-free company is bound *always* to do better.

We have identified the portfolio of resources to be the key to a system's potential performance and maximum productivity. The issues of technology, education, skills, work intensity, innovation, flexibility, quality, etc. are all very important in business. But they could only come to their full fruition if applied to an optimally designed, tradeoffs-free system.

Profit maximization. Free market systems are rooted in the assumption of profit maximization by individuals and their corporations.

This time-honoured premise is usually not specified or elaborated further, as if there were only a single form of profit maximization.

Yet, rational economic agents can maximize profits in *at least two* fundamentally different – often mutually exclusive – ways:

1 Manage (operate) a *given* system so that a profit function is maximized.
2 *Design* a system so that its management (operation) would result in maximal profits.

These two forms of profit maximization are not the same.

In the first case, one is doing one's managerial best and squeezing maximum profits from a *given* system. This is known as profit maximization.

In the second case, one designs (re-engineers) a profit-maximizing system: doing one's best managing leads to maximum profits. This is, undoubtedly, also profit maximization.

The two modes are mutually exclusive because one cannot follow the second course without first dismantling the first one. It is not sufficient to (continually) improve the given system: because there is *only one* optimally designed system, all *other* systems must be sub-optimal by definition.

One mode of profit maximization leads to consistently lower profits than the other, other things being equal. This could not have been intended by Adam Smith.

Because the second case is, *ceteris paribus*, always superior to the first, we are facing two strategically different concepts of profit maximization. It *does* matter – in business, economics and management – which particular mode of profit maximization the individuals, corporations or cultures mostly adhere to: free markets are committed to rewarding those who consistently adhere to *the second* mode of operation.

6 Conclusion

The race is on to transform production and management systems from tradeoffs-based to tradeoffs-free. This race moves well beyond the assorted world-class, TQM, lean production or mass customization labels. Corporate portfolios of resources will have to be optimized *before* all other relevant efforts could become effective. The ERP systems should become the right enablers in this effort.

There are two fundamental dimensions to management: *what* is your system and *how* do you operate it? One can operate a bad system well or a good system quite badly. The main competitive challenge, yet to be recognized and achieved, is to *operate good systems very well*. Global managers may operate well, often performing virtual miracles with inadequate and outdated systems. But running optimally designed, high-performance, tradeoffs-free systems would put back joy, pride and self-confidence into the business and management endeavours of the IT/S era.

MILAN ZELENY
FORDHAM UNIVERSITY AT LINCOLN CENTRE

Further reading

(References cited in the text marked *)

* Anderson, J.C. *et al.* (1988) 'Operations strategy: a literature review', *Journal of Operations Management* 8 (2), April: 137.
Hayes, R.H. and Pisano, G.P. (1994) 'Beyond world-class: the new manufacturing strategy', *Harvard Business Review* January–February: 77. (Argument for tradeoffs-free strategy in manufacturing, opening the way for mass customization.)
Lee, E.S. (2001) 'Optimal-design models', in *International Encyclopedia of Business & Management*, 2nd edn, London: Thomson Learning. (A good coverage of De novo programming methodology, including the optimum-path ratio and fuzzy aspects of goal setting in resource allocation.)
Li, R.-J. and Lee, E.S. (1990) 'Fuzzy approaches to multicriteria De novo programs', *Journal of Mathematical Analysis and Applications* 153 (1): 97–111. (Fuzzy sets extensions of De novo programming for calculating optimal portfolios of corporate resources.)

Li, R.-J. and Lee, E.S. (1990) 'Multicriteria De novo programming with fuzzy parameters', *Computers and Mathematics with Applications* 19 (5): 13–20. (Fuzzy sets extensions of De novo programming for calculating optimal portfolios of corporate resources.)

Li, R.-J. and Lee, E.S. (1993) 'De novo programming with fuzzy coefficients and multiple fuzzy goals', *Journal of Mathematical Analysis and Applications* 172 (1): 212–20. (Fuzzy sets extensions of De novo programming for calculating optimal portfolios of corporate resources.)

Pine II, B.J. (1993) 'Mass customizing products and services', *Planning Review* July–August: 6–15. (Another of the 'Planning Review' articles that brings forth a new concept and extends mass customization from manufacturing to services.)

* Zeleny, M. (1982) *Multiple Criteria Decision Making*, New York: McGraw-Hill. (A textbook on decision making with multiple criteria, containing many topics on tradeoffs, tradeoff analysis, management and elimination, as well as the first formulation of De novo programming for resource optimization.)

Zeleny, M. (1986) 'Optimal system design with multiple criteria: De novo programming approach', *Engineering Costs and Production Economics* 10: 89–94. (Optimal portfolio of corporate resources can be computed via the De novo programming methodology. Some practical examples are included.)

Zeleny, M. (2001) 'Optimality and optimization', in *International Encyclopedia of Business & Management*, 2nd edn, London: Thomson Learning. (An extensive treatment of optimality concepts in all their forms, including optimal and tradeoffs-free designs.)

See also: DECISION MAKING, MULTIPLE CRITERIA; ENTERPRISE RESOURCE PLANNING; INFORMATION TECHNOLOGY; JAPAN, MANAGEMENT IN; JUST-IN-TIME PHILOSOPHY; MANUFACTURING STRATEGY; OPTIMAL-DESIGN MODELS; OPTIMALITY AND OPTIMIZATION; PROJECT MANAGEMENT; SYSTEMS

Training

1 Training needs analysis
2 Training design and delivery
3 Training evaluation

Overview

Training is any systematic process used by organizations to develop employees' knowledge, skills, behaviours or attitudes in order to contribute to the achievement of organizational goals. It is also referred to as human resource development. Training is used to improve the performance of employees in their present positions; to prepare workers for positions to which they are likely to be promoted in the future; and to respond to changes in the workplace, such as new technology and systems, internationalization, global competitiveness and the need for greater service orientation. In addition, training is provided by governments and organizations to improve the future employability of the hard-core unemployed, under-employed minority groups and workers whose present skills are becoming obsolete. Training is directed toward employees at all levels of the organization, from workers on the shop floor through to executives, and covers applications from specific technical skills to complex social and cognitive skills.

Most organizations dedicate substantial resources to training and see it as an integral function of achieving their goals. In the USA alone training expenditures have been estimated to be as high as $100 billion per year and training professionals have estimated that organizations' commitment to training is likely to grow.

Despite its pervasiveness in industry, however, training must be viewed as only one of several human resource interventions used to improve the match between the knowledge, skills, behaviours or attitudes possessed by employees and those required in particular jobs. Alternatives to training include changing the way in which personnel are selected; changing job requirements through job redesign or technological change; and changing the way in which performance is managed (for example, introducing goal setting, feedback or reward systems). All of these alternatives can be used in place of, or in conjunction with, training initiatives.

The development of training programmes involves three phases: (1) training needs analysis; (2) training design and delivery; and (3) training evaluation. In the first phase, specific training needs which address organizational objectives are identified. Within the training design and delivery phase, training objectives are set, specific training content is identified and principles that will maximize learning and transfer of skills are applied. In training evaluation, criteria are established and a method of evaluation is developed: (1) to ensure that training has met its objectives; and (2) to make necessary changes to improve the programme's effectiveness.

1 Training needs analysis

In order for training to contribute to the achievement of an organization's goals, training needs must be identified through an analysis which links training to relevant organizational outcomes – a process referred to as training needs analysis. In the first major book written on organizational training, McGehee and Thayer (1961) presented a three-part system for training needs analysis which, despite slight changes in terminology, is still the most prevalent model presented in textbooks today. Their approach involves three analyses: (1) organization analysis; (2) task analysis (sometimes referred to as operations analysis or job analysis); and (3) person analysis (originally referred to as man analysis, sometimes called individual analysis). The purposes and commonly used procedures for each of these three analyses are summarized in Table 1.

Table 1 The McGehee and Thayer approach to identifying training needs

Analysis	Purpose	Examples of specific needs analysis techniques
Organization analysis	To determine where in the organization training is needed.	Identify knowledge and skill requirements from organizational goals, objectives, business plans
		Compare efficiency and quality indices against expectations
		Conduct personnel and succession plans, including personnel audits which identify knowledge/ skill-base of present employees
		Assess organizational climate for training
Task analysis	To detemine what training content should be	For individual jobs, identify performance outcomes/standards, tasks required to achieve them and knowledge, skills, behaviours and attitudes necessary for successful task completion
Person analysis	To determine who should receive training and what training they need	Using performance appraisals, identify knowledge/ skill, causes of performance discrepancies
		Collect and analyse critical incidents
		Conduct training needs analysis serveys

Organization analysis

An organization analysis (see ORGANIZATION BEHAVIOUR) is conducted to determine exactly where in the organization training is needed. Organizational goals, objectives and business plans are reviewed to identify knowledge and skill requirements of the organization. For example, an Australian beef export firm which wishes to increase sales in Asia may determine that its product quality and uniformity must first be improved and that training in quality improvement processes will be necessary to achieve its goal.

In addition to reviewing goals, efficiency indices (for example, production figures, scrap rates and quality data) are compared with targets to identify performance discrepancies which might be addressed by training. Personnel (workforce) and succession plans are conducted to determine future staffing requirements and the replacement of people who vacate positions due to promotion, retirement or leaving the organization. These plans typically include a *personnel audit*, in which the knowledge and skills of employees are compared with future requirements to identify training needs.

Goldstein (1993) has suggested that, as part of an organization analysis, the climate for training should also be assessed. Conflict between the goals of a training programme and those of a particular group in the organization (for example, management, union), or between behaviours taught in training and those supported by trainees' supervisors, indicates that trainees are unlikely to apply newly learned skills to the job, and thus that the organization is not ready for the training.

Task analysis

While organization analysis is conducted at the level of the entire organization or within divisions, task analysis is conducted at the level of a specific job. Through task analysis the specific content of the training is identified. Similar to job analysis used for personnel selection (see JOB EVALUATION), task analysis involves the identification of performance outcomes and standards for a job, the tasks which must be completed for an individual to achieve those outcomes, and finally the knowledge, skills, behaviours and attitudes required for successful task completion.

Comprehensive overviews of alternative approaches to training task analysis have been provided by DuBois *et al.* (1997/8) and Zemke and Kramlinger (1982).

Person analysis

A person analysis is used to determine who in the organization needs training and what training each person needs. Performance appraisals can be used for person analysis by identifying areas of discrepancy between individuals' expected and actual performance and by determining whether such discrepancies are due to a lack of knowledge or skills, thus indicating training needs. Based on what the employee and supervisor determine to be the employee's training needs, through performance appraisals and a discussion of the employee's career goals, a *learning contract* (also known as a learning agenda) can be developed between employee and supervisor.

A person analysis can also be conducted using critical incidents, in which supervisors record actual occurrences of particularly effective or ineffective job behaviour. Unlike performance appraisals, in which training needs are identified on an individual basis, critical incidents are grouped across all individuals in a particular job to identify training needs at a group level.

Alternatively, surveys can be used for person analysis. Employees or their supervisors are asked to indicate training needs, usually by checking or rating each of a list of knowledge and skill areas. Such surveys have been expanded in two ways for the identification of managers' training needs: (1) subordinate and peer ratings are often used to supplement self-and supervisor ratings; and (2) two rating scales for each knowledge/skill area are frequently used, one indicating the optimal level of proficiency for the job and one the actual proficiency of the individual. Training needs are indicated where a significant gap exists between these two actual and optimal performance levels.

Training needs analysis surveys are popular because they are relatively easy to administer and analyse and because they provide quantitative information, but they suffer from a fundamental weakness: they do not necessarily link training to organizational goals. Responses to needs analysis surveys may reflect respondents' own (unstated) personal objectives more than those of their organization. Evidence of this limitation is found in studies which have compared, and found significant differences between, self-rated and supervisor-rated training needs. Further research is needed to determine whether these differences reflect different objectives for identifying training needs or simply different views of what training is needed to meet the same objectives.

Demographic analysis

Some writers have extended the three analyses (organization, task and person) to include a fourth, demographic analysis, because studies comparing self-reported training needs of various levels of management, of different ethnic groups and of male and female employees have often indicated statistically significant (albeit small) differences. They suggest that training practitioners should look for differences in training needs identified by various groups of employees (see WOMEN AND WORK).

Equal employment opportunities and training

Related to the concern for differences in the training needs of various demographic groups of employees, training personnel should ensure that women and minority groups have equal access to training and equal probabilities of successfully completing training (see EQUAL EMPLOYMENT OPPORTUNITIES). For example, if a minority group does not receive the same access to training necessary for promotion as its majority group counterpart, the training can be viewed as failing to provide equal employment opportunities. Similarly, if minority group members have a lesser chance of succeeding in training required for promotion, the training can be considered to have an adverse impact on that group.

Performance analysis

While McGehee and Thayer's (1961) organization–task–person analysis model is the most
widely recognized approach to training needs
analysis in textbooks, an alternative approach
referred to as performance analysis has
become popular among practitioners. The
basic process of performance analysis is presented in Figure 1. Gaps between expected
and actual job performance are identified, as
in performance appraisals for person analysis.
Unlike performance appraisals, however, performance analysis looks for factors in the
work environment (for example, rewards or
punishments) which sustain poor performance, instead of assuming that the gap is
caused by a deficiency in employee skills,
knowledge or attitudes.

Performance analysts have criticized the
traditional training needs analysis approach

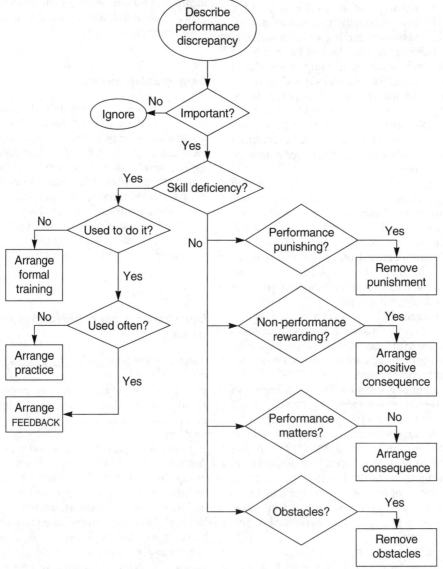

Figure 1 The performance analysis approach to identifying training needs
Source: Mager and Pipe (1984)

for failing to link training to organizational outcomes by relying too heavily on needs analysis surveys and for overlooking the role of (often subtle) rewards and punishments in the work environment when assessing the causes of performance discrepancies (Gilbert 1978; Mager and Pipe 1984). This latter criticism is much the same as some writers' suggestion for greater cooperation between training and organization development (see ORGANIZATION DEVELOPMENT), which focuses more broadly on long-range planned organizational change.

The extent to which organizations actually use these training needs analysis techniques is surprisingly low. In one study, organizations in four out of five European countries reported that they identified training needs most frequently through employee and line manager requests (Holden 1990) (see HUMAN RESOURCE MANAGEMENT IN EUROPE). Similarly, only 27 per cent of 611 companies surveyed in a study of organizations in the USA indicated that they had practices or procedures for determining training needs (Saari et al. 1988). In a sample of large organizations in New Zealand, most reported using no formal training needs analysis procedures (O'Driscoll and Taylor 1992). Some training practitioners may be unfamiliar with these procedures or see little value in applying them. McGehee and Thayer (1961) suggested that practitioners rarely apply a systematic needs analysis procedure because of the pressure to get training started quickly. Further research is needed to understand and resolve the practice–theory gap in training needs analysis.

2 Training design and delivery

In order to design an appropriate training programme to meet identified needs, training objectives must be established, for they guide the development of training content, training method and evaluation criteria. Training objectives can state what trainees will know after training; what they will do on the job, referred to as *behavioural objectives*; or what end results will be achieved for the organization through training. For example, a safety training programme may have the knowledge-related objective that 'each trainee will be able to accurately describe the correct procedure for lifting heavy items off the floor'; a behavioural objective that 'observed violations of safety procedures should occur no more than one time per year per employee'; and a results objective that 'lost-time accidents at the plant are reduced by 30 per cent'. Knowledge, behavioural and results objectives each can be stated in terms of either desired performance levels (as in the first two examples above) or performance changes (as in the last example).

Of the three types of training objectives, behavioural objectives have received the most attention because virtually all organizational training efforts are expected to affect outcomes relevant to the organization through changed employee behaviour. Guidelines for the development of behavioural objectives can be found in Mager and Pipe (1984) and Goldstein (1993).

Once training objectives have been developed, specific training content is established. General tasks to be learned are broken down into smaller, component tasks, which are sequenced so that each component builds upon those that have been presented earlier. Principles of learning are applied to the development of the training process in order to maximize skill retention and transfer of training to the workplace. These principles have been developed largely from behavioural, social learning, educational and cognitive psychologies. Learning principles most commonly employed in training include:

1 operant conditioning (in which desired behaviours are intentionally reinforced during and after training);
2 modelling (in which desired behaviours are modelled through videos, as well as by trainers and trainees' supervisors);
3 knowledge of results (in which trainees are given frequent and accurate performance feedback);
4 distributed practice (in which sessions are spaced rather than massed together);
5 identical elements (in which the similarity between what learners face in training and job situations is maximized).

Goldstein (1993) has provided a comprehensive review of these and other learning principles which have been applied to training.

Various training methods have been developed which combine principles of learning and available technology for particular applications. Training is usually thought of in terms of programmes conducted in classroom settings, but also includes on-the-job learning activities such as job rotation, apprenticeships and vestibule training. Many training programmes in organizations employ multiple methods. For example, while most training programmes have a lecture component, few would use lecture alone. Further details on training methods can be found in Craig (1987) and Nadler and Nadler (1990). Commonly used training methods are described below.

Job rotation

Employees at virtually all levels of an organization may be rotated through a series of jobs to expand their knowledge and skills. Job rotation allows the organization greater flexibility because employees' responsibilities can be shifted easily with changing human resource needs. In the interest of flexibility some organizations have adopted pay-for-knowledge schemes (sometimes referred to as competency-based pay), in which a portion of workers' pay is influenced by the knowledge and skills they have acquired through voluntary job rotation and formal training experiences. Job rotation can also be used to prepare workers for promotion and to provide a more enriching work experience for employees. Job rotation may not be appropriate when workers are paid on a piece-rate system and would be less productive in jobs other than their primary one (see WORK SYSTEMS).

Apprenticeships

In the trade field apprenticeships are a common means of providing training to new employees. The apprentice serves as an assistant to a more senior worker, often for a fixed period of time, receiving one-to-one, on-the-job modelling, instruction and feedback. This method is usually cost-effective because the organization receives the benefit of the apprentice's work, usually at a relatively low rate of pay. Apprenticeships are only appro-priate when there are enough skilled individuals to work on a one-to-one basis with new employees. A further limitation is that, because apprenticeship periods are usually fixed, they do not take into account individual differences in pre-apprenticeship skill levels and learning rates.

Vestibule training

New employees who are to work on production lines that require a particular speed or skill level may be trained on a simulated production line which often operates at a slower rate. Using this technique organizations avoid having to slow down regular production lines or risk product damage or poor quality due to the introduction of unskilled workers.

Lecture

The lecture method consists of a trainer presenting information to trainees, and is one of the least expensive forms of training because it incurs little development costs and can be used with large training classes. Despite criticism that it lacks the opportunity for practice and feedback, evaluations of training using the lecture method have shown that it can have at least a moderate level of effectiveness.

Conference

The conference method uses structured discussion between trainer and trainees in relatively small groups. While the lecture method involves one-way communication, the conference approach provides for two-way discussion and so can be used to test participants' understanding and to invite reactions to what is presented. Because it entails a high degree of participant involvement, the conference method is particularly effective for enhancing trainee commitment or attitude change.

Video

Video can be used in training to stimulate interest in the training topic, to present information, to model the use of skills and to provide trainees with accurate feedback about their use of newly learned skills. Videos can be used to present course information to employees at remote sites, which can be a cost-effective alternative to bringing trainer and trainees physically together. In behaviour modelling training video is used to present trainees with a positive role model of the skills they are learning, shown in realistic settings to enhance credibility. Trainees are often videotaped as they practise complex interpersonal skills, such as in simulated selling situations, and immediate playback provides them with feedback.

Video use in training evolved from the use of slides and films, and is growing increasingly sophisticated and powerful through computer and laser disk technologies. These developments allow trainees to interact with video material, which can stimulate interest and provide very controlled feedback. For example, management trainees may be shown a simulated discussion concerning a job performance problem and asked how they would respond. Based on their response, realistic replies by the video-simulated employee would be shown.

The primary disadvantage of using video to present training material is cost, of both the initial development and of making later modifications. Videotaping of trainees for the purpose of feedback is not as costly but requires considerably more training time. Despite these disadvantages the use of video in training is likely to continue to grow.

Computer-assisted instruction

Computerized training permits the presentation of information in a logical sequence, testing trainees' understanding, providing feedback and tailoring lessons to the knowledge/skill level of individual trainees through an assessment of their responses (called *branching*). Computer-assisted instruction (CAI) developed from programmed instruction, which followed the same basic approach of presenting information and testing understanding in a logical sequence, but using either workbooks or teaching machines. Programmes designed to teach a wide variety of knowledge and skills have been developed using CAI, from tutorial programmes that accompany PC software to complex interpersonal and problem-solving skills.

Despite initial enthusiasm about CAI as an innovative training method, research comparing its effectiveness to more traditional training approaches has found little difference. Furthermore, rapidly changing computer hardware has made it difficult to develop CAI programmes that will not be soon outdated. For example, large investments were made in PLATO, a mainframe-based CAI environment, during the early 1970s, but the unexpectedly high processing power and memory of PCs that followed have rendered PLATO obsolete. As PC hardware grows increasingly standardized, the development of CAI training programmes becomes more cost-effective.

Simulation

Simulations are carefully developed exercises, modelled on realistic situations, in which trainees participate and receive feedback. Simulations are particularly useful for jobs in which the risk and costs of mistakes are high (for example, pilot training) or in which direct observation and feedback are typically absent (for example, managerial decision making). With the aid of computer technology, machine simulators (such as flight simulators) can be created to be amazingly realistic. Simulations are frequently used in management training and include assessment centre exercises such as in-tray (or in-basket) exercises, business games and case studies. Management training simulations allow participants to collect information and make decisions as if they were in a real situation and to receive feedback on their behaviour based on careful observation by other participants and training staff.

A particularly popular simulation for managers has been outdoor training, which includes a series of exercises in a wilderness setting that, according to its proponents, simulate job-related group and individual problem-solving situations. For example, a group of trainees might be instructed to scale a high wall without the use of any equipment. After each exercise the trainer links behaviour on the task with trainees' work environment, facilitating feedback to individuals under the assumption that their behaviour on the exercise is similar to how they address challenges at work. The fidelity of outdoor training exercises is not as high as more job-related simulations mentioned earlier, and so the effectiveness of such training may depend on the trainer's ability to show links between the outdoor exercise and job behaviour.

Role play

Role playing is used in teaching interpersonal skills such as managerial and sales interactions. Trainees adopt relevant roles (for example, manager and staff member; salesperson and customer) and play out a particular kind of discussion (for example, taking disciplinary action; making a sale). Background information on the nature of the roles is provided for the role players but the interaction is generally unscripted.

A particularly effective role-playing approach is behaviour modelling training, developed from social learning theory. Participants are first shown a model of someone using a set of clearly defined skills appropriately (typically an actor on video) and then asked to role play; they then receive feedback on a similar interaction using those same skills.

Burke and Day (1986) have conducted a major review of training research which compared the effectiveness of various training approaches. They found that all methods which they included in their review yielded at least moderately positive effects. Which particular training technique is used seems of less importance than the determination of training content, despite the fact that much of the past training research has focused on comparing new training methods with traditional approaches. Future research could focus less on the effectiveness of alternative training methods and more on developing generalized training content for common jobs and tasks.

While earlier training design research focused on the application of learning principles and comparing training methods, later research has focused on techniques which can be added to training to increase transfer of skills to the job. For example, having trainees set goals concerning how they will apply newly learned skills to their jobs, identify po-

tential causes of reverting to pre-training behaviours and to brainstorm solutions have all been shown to increase training transfer if added at the end of training sessions.

Transfer of training is not only a function of how training is designed but is also related to characteristics of trainees and their work environment. For example, researchers have demonstrated that trainees' self-efficacy (their beliefs about their skills and likelihood of success) influences training transfer. In the work environment factors which affect training transfer include the opportunity to apply newly learned skills and the degree to which trainees' supervisors support the use of trained skills.

While organizations can do little to change trainees' individual characteristics to increase training transfer, their work environments can be positively influenced, such as through the provision of supervisory support workshops to accompany training. Given the concern that a substantial proportion of training does not get transferred to the workplace (Baldwin and Ford 1988), research into ways that training transfer can be maximized is likely to continue to be important.

3 Training evaluation

In addition to ensuring that training has met its objectives, training evaluation provides critical information for several organizational decisions. Training programmes are often piloted and evaluated to determine whether they should be continued throughout the organization and, if so, to identify changes that could be made to improve them. Favourable training evaluations within an organization can document that training dollars have been well spent, which enhances the future credibility of training initiatives. An evaluation of training effectiveness in one organization can be useful to other organizations in deciding whether to implement a particular programme.

Like all other human resource interventions in organizations, training can only be evaluated in relation to criteria, which should be based on training objectives established at the beginning of the training design and delivery phase. Kirkpatrick (1983) developed a set of four criteria for training evaluation, including trainees' *reactions, learning, behaviour* and *results*. (Note the parallel between the last three training evaluation criteria and the three types of learning objectives discussed earlier.) These four criteria are often referred to as levels of training evaluation. Trainee reactions represent Level I evaluation, while results reflect Level IV.

Reactions are trainees' impressions, usually sought at the conclusion of training sessions through a brief questionnaire. Most reaction questionnaires include both open-ended questions such as 'What could be done to improve the training?' and questions with anchored response scales such as 'Overall, how effective did you find the training? 1 – quite ineffective, 3 – somewhat effective, 5 – very effective'.

Learning is typically measured with paper-and-pencil tests which are administered both before and after training. For example, managers of a multinational firm who attend training to prepare them for working in another country could be tested for their knowledge of facts concerning that country. Such tests must contain a representative sample of the training content.

Behaviour refers to change in employees' on-the-job behaviour after training and is usually rated by trainees themselves and those working closest to trainees, such as managers, co-workers or subordinates. Ratings are often made on behavioural observation scales (BOS). For example, subordinates of supervisors attending training might be asked to complete a BOS concerning the extent to which their supervisors engage in each of a list of effective managerial behaviours, such as asking for their help in solving problems. When ratings are made by trainees' supervisors either BOS or existing performance appraisal rating forms may be used.

Results refers to changes in organizationally relevant outcomes of trainee behaviour such as increased production rates of supervisors' work groups after supervisors have attended training. Ultimately the purpose of training is to contribute to the achievement of organizational goals, and the most meaningful level of training evaluation is results. Unfortunately changes in organizational results due to

training are difficult to isolate from those caused by factors outside trainees' control. For example, salespeople who attend training may improve their sales strategies, which should increase their organization's volume of sales, but increased cost-cutting by competitors may reduce the organization's sales over the period surrounding training.

Training professionals have become increasingly concerned with measuring and demonstrating the financial benefits of training initiatives to the organization. The findings of behaviour- or results-level training evaluations can often be interpreted in terms of the training programme's financial utility, and a variety of approaches are available to do so (see Swanson 1998).

There are also special difficulties in measuring behavioural change due to training. Those rating trainees' behaviours usually know whether training has been attended and their expectations of the effect of training can bias ratings. In addition, it is difficult to determine if differences in self-rated behaviour before and after training are due to genuine changes in behaviour rather than trainees interpreting the rating scale differently after attending training.

These difficulties in evaluating training at the behavioural and results levels may account in part for why practitioners continue to rely most heavily on reaction-level training evaluations (Holden 1990; Saari *et al.* 1988). Another explanation for the infrequent use of behavioural and results evaluations is that much of training in organizations is provided as an end in itself, rather than to change specific on-the-job behaviours and results, and so evaluation at more than the level of trainees' reactions is considered unnecessary.

Training validity

In order to establish the validity of a training programme, namely, whether a training programme has achieved its stated objectives, evaluation criteria must be measured through an *evaluation design* which permits unambiguous interpretation of results. Consider, for example, an evaluation of technical training provided to new employees, using a comparison of pre- and post-training ratings of on-the-job behaviour for a single group of trainees. Higher post-training ratings could be a result either of the training or of increased job experience, leaving interpretation ambiguous. Controls in the evaluation design are required to eliminate potential threats to the validity of the conclusions.

A common control used in training evaluations is the use of a control group, which does not receive the training and serves as a comparison. If individuals are assigned to training and control groups randomly, which is called an *experimental design*, group differences in post-training performance can be attributed to training with some degree of certainty. Unfortunately, random assignment of individuals to training and control groups is not often practical in work situations because existing work groups frequently must be trained together. Designs that use intact work groups as training and control groups are referred to as *quasi-experimental designs*. Results of the quasi-experimental design cannot be interpreted as clearly as those from true experiments, mainly because we are uncertain about pre-existing differences between the groups, but they are still considered superior to evaluations with no control group at all.

In cases where control groups are difficult to establish, a *time series design* may be an effective alternative. Criterion measures are taken repeatedly for a period of time before training and again after training. The repeated measures before training act as a control, and so a single individual, group or even organization can be studied without a control group. Time series designs are most appropriate when the criterion can easily be measured repeatedly over time, such as when existing records, called archival data, can be used.

Training evaluation studies are subject to many potential threats. A study of these potential threats and suggested evaluation designs to address them have been developed and are reviewed in Goldstein (1993). One of the most ubiquitous threats in training evaluation is referred to as the Hawthorne Effect, named after an assembly plant in which individuals' productivity increased for short periods after virtually all of a series of experimental changes to working conditions, some of which would logically be expected to have either no or even detrimental effects. In the Hawthorne study these increases were attributed to employees' knowing that they were part of an experiment. In training evaluations the Hawthorne Effect could account for positive reactions immediately after training; favourable self-reports of learning, behaviour change and results; or even temporary increases in actual job performance.

Even a true experimental design does not control for the Hawthorne Effect because those trained may respond favourably to the fact that they are part of a training group being studied while the control group does not. One suggested way of addressing the Hawthorne Effect is to provide the control group with bogus training, often called *placebo training*. For example, the control group might only view a video, read a book or have a discussion on the training topic. Because both the training and control groups are expected to be influenced by the Hawthorne Effect in this design, differences in post-training performance between groups can be unambiguously attributed to the effect of training. Placebo training is often not practical. Another solution is to take post-training measures some time after training has been completed, when a potential Hawthorne Effect might be expected to have worn off.

Training validity has been extended beyond the traditional four criteria since Kirkpatrick first introduced them in the 1960s. Training *content validity* has been presented as a means of reflecting the match between training content and job content, much as the content validity of a test reflects the match between test and job content. People familiar with the job (frequently supervisors) specify all elements of the job and of the training programme and a comparison of the two reflects the degree of the training programme's content validity. However, content validity cannot serve as a replacement for criterion-related validity because the extent to which training criteria are achieved is influenced by multiple factors, including the training methods used and characteristics of trainees and their work environments.

Goldstein (1993) has also extended the way in which training validity is viewed by proposing four levels of validity relevant to training programmes:

1   training validity (whether trainees achieve performance criteria established within the training programme);
2   transfer validity (whether trainees apply newly learned skills to the job);
3   intra-organizational validity (whether the training is also effective with subsequent training groups within the organization);
4   inter-organizational validity (whether the training is also effective when conducted within other organizations).

Few published studies of training effectiveness have extended beyond the first two of these four levels (Burke and Day 1986).

The traditional approach to experimental training evaluation compares trained individuals' performance on a criterion with either their pre-training performance or the performance of an untrained control group. Inferential statistics are used to determine whether differences between trained group and control group scores (or between post-training and pre-training scores) are greater than would be expected by chance alone at a particular significance level (for example, 0.05). Three criticisms of this traditional approach have been raised.

The first criticism is that the typical training evaluation lacks sufficient statistical power to detect statistically significant differences when, indeed, the training has had a true effect. Statistical power is a function of many variables, but in training evaluation the primary cause is small sample sizes. The second criticism, also related to the inferential statistics used in the traditional training evaluation design, is that statistical tests of significance tell us only whether training has had an effect, but not the size of that effect. We know from the cumulation of training evaluation studies that training is generally effective across a variety of methods and applications, and so the question of whether training has had an effect is less informative than what the size of the effect has been.

Determining the size of the effect indicates training's practical significance and can help organizations estimate the utility of training, which is its value to the organization in monetary terms. Training utility estimates can be used to compare the anticipated value of a training programme to other training programmes; non-training human resource interventions (for example, improving employment selection procedures); and investments in other areas of the organization (for example, marketing programmes, equipment upgrades, research and development).

The third criticism of the traditional approach to training evaluation concerns a frequent mismatch between how training objectives are stated and training is evaluated. Objectives of training are often stated in terms of trainees attaining a particular level of performance (for example, 'observed violations of safety procedures should occur no more than one time per year per employee'), but training is usually evaluated using a *change model* (for example, 'Significantly fewer violations of safety procedures were observed among employees who attended safety training than among those of a comparable control group'). When training objectives refer to obtaining a particular performance level after training, the method of evaluation must focus on whether that level has been achieved. Together, these three criticisms suggest that training evaluation practices and future research should focus on the practical, rather than just statistical, significance of training effects and should link more closely training evaluation with training objectives.

In conclusion, training has become an increasingly important function within business and industry, due largely to technological advances, workers' need for greater involvement in decision making and organizations' interest in developing workforces which reflect their particular values and cultures. Systematic approaches to determining training needs, developing programmes to meet those needs and evaluating training effectiveness are required to ensure that training meets its objectives.

PAUL TAYLOR
UNIVERSITY OF WAIKATO

Further reading

(References cited in the text marked *)

* Baldwin, T.T. and Ford, J.K. (1988) 'Transfer of training: a review and directions for future research', *Personnel Psychology* 41 (1): 63–105. (An extensive review and integration of theory and research on transfer of training, including an exhaustive bibliography.)

Blanchard, N. and Thacker, J. (1999). *Effective Training: Systems, Strategies and Practices*, Englewood Cliffs, NJ: Prentice Hall. (An easy-to-read, introductory text on training.)

* Burke, M.J. and Day, R.R. (1986) 'A cumulative study of the effectiveness of managerial training', *Journal of Applied Psychology* 71 (2): 232–45. (A quantitative review of various managerial training content and methods.)

* Craig, R.L. (ed.) (1987) *Training and Development Handbook*, 3rd edn, New York: McGraw-Hill. (A comprehensive training text for practitioners.)

* DuBois, D.A., Shalin, V.L., Levi, K.R. and Borman, W.C. (1997/8). 'A cognitively-oriented approach to task analysis', *Training Research Journal* 3: 103–42. (A comprehensive review of recent developments in training task analysis, particularly those that have developed from cognitive psychology.)

* Gilbert, T.F. (1978) *Human Competence: Engineering Worthy Performance*, New York: McGraw-Hill. (Provides a detailed description of the performance analysis approach to training needs analysis.)

* Goldstein, I.L. (1993) *Training in Organizations*, 3rd edn, Monterey, CA: Brooks/Cole. (A comprehensive overview of training useful to both academics and practitioners, including an extensive bibliography.)

* Holden, L. (1990) 'European trends in training and development', *International Journal of Human Resource Management* 2 (2): 113–31. (Reports on a major survey of training practices in five European countries.)

Human Resource Development Quarterly. (A schorlarly journal published by the American Society for Training and Development, which reports new theory and research in training.)

* Kirkpatrick, D.L. (1983) 'Four steps to measuring training effectiveness', *Personnel Administrator* 28 (11): 19–25. (Presents the commonly referred to four levels/types of training criteria.)

* Mager, R.F. and Pipe, P. (1984) *Analyzing Performance Problems*, 2nd edn, Belmont, CA: Lake. (Provides an easy-to-read guide for writing behavioural training objectives and for using performance analysis to identify training needs, primarily for practitioners.)

* McGehee, W. and Thayer, P.W. (1961) *Training in Business and Industry*, New York: Wiley. (The first major text on training, which provided seminal ideas about training needs analysis.)

* Nadler, L. and Nadler, Z. (eds) (1990) *The Handbook of Human Resource Development*, 2nd edn, New York: Wiley. (A compilation of training topics for the practitioner which includes chapters on some specialized and practical topics not found elsewhere.)

* O'Driscoll, M.P. and Taylor, P.J. (1992) 'Congruence between theory and practice in management training needs analysis', *International Journal of Human Resource Management* 3 (3): 593–603. (Reports on a survey of training executives concerning how training decisions have actually been made.)

Phillips, J. (1994) *In Action: Measuring Return on Investment*, Alexandria, VA: American Society for Training and Development. (Useful resource for developing results-based training evaluation strategies.)

Prior, J. (ed.) (1994) *Gower Handbook of Training and Development*, Aldershot: Gower. (Practitioner-orientated handbook covering a wide field of training topics.)

* Saari, L.M., Johnson, T.R., McLaughlin, S.D. and Zimmerle, D.M. (1988) 'A survey of management training and education practices in U.S. companies', *Personnel Psychology* 41 (4): 731–43. (Presents findings from a large survey of training practices in US companies.)

* Swanson, R.A. (1998). 'Demonstrating the financial benefit of human resource development: Status and update on the theory and practice', *Human Resource Development Quarterly* 9 (3): 285–96. (A recent overview of approaches to demonstrating the financial value of training, including a comprehensive bibliography.)

Training & Develoment Journal. (A magazine published by the American Society for Training and Development, which reports new developments in training of interest to training practitioners.)

Training Research Journal. (A bi-annual, scholarly journal reporting new research in the field of training.)

Wexley, K.N. and Latham, G.P. (1999). *Developing and Training Human Resources in Organizations*, 3rd edn, New York: Harper Collins. (A leading training textbook for both academics and practitioners, with an extensive bibliography.)

* Zemke, R. and Kramlinger, T. (1982). *Figuring Things Out: A Trainer's Guide to Needs and Task Analysis*, Reading, MA: Addison-Wesley.

(A thorough overview of alternative approaches to training needs analysis, aimed at training practitioners.)

See also: EMPLOYEE DEVELOPMENT; EQUAL EMPLOYMENT OPPORTUNITIES; HUMAN RESOURCE MANAGEMENT; HUMAN RESOURCE MANAGEMENT, INTERNA- TIONAL; HUMAN RESOURCE MANAGEMENT IN EUROPE; INDUSTRIAL RELATIONS IN JAPAN; JOB DESIGN; OCCUPATIONAL PSY- CHOLOGY; ORGANIZATION BEHAVIOUR; ORGANIZATIONAL PERFORMANCE; PRO- DUCTIVITY; TRAINING, ECONOMICS OF; WOMEN AND WORK; WORK SYSTEMS

Training, economics of

1 Definition and importance
2 Nature of evidence
3 Human capital theory
4 Institutional factors

Overview

The economics of work-based training comprises two overlapping approaches: human capital theory and institutional analysis. Human capital theory focuses on the economic incentives to employers and trainees to develop skills, resulting in a broadly optimistic view of training outcomes in an unregulated market. Its elaboration to allow for recruitment costs, informational failure and wage rigidity leads to a more institutionally oriented and less optimistic account. Further institutional influences, neglected by human capital theory, include managerial strategy, industrial relations, labour market structure, collective organization, system-wide interdependences and historical path dependence.

1 Definition and importance

The term 'training' denotes the learning of work-related skills and knowledge (see TRAINING). The scope of the definition is, however, variable. Economists include all forms of work-related learning, ranging from vocational education to learning by doing. Managers typically include only structured learning under instruction. This survey focuses on *on-the-job training*, that is, work-based learning, covering apprenticeship and learning by doing but excluding full-time vocational education.

Economic interest in training reflects several attributes. Vocational learning, of which it is part, contributes strongly to the economic performance of companies, regions and countries (Prais 1995; Huselid 1995). For individuals, increased skill is associated with higher pay and lower unemployment (Blundell *et al.* 1996). Training is central to theories of inter-

nal labour markets, efficiency wages and labour market segmentation. Finally, as market failure is endemic to training, public intervention may improve outcomes. Indeed, training is widely favoured as the policy response to unemployment (Grubb and Ryan 1999: ch. 4).

2 Nature of evidence

Empirical work on training is beset by measurement problems. In addition to varying definitions, the jointness of training with production impedes the measurement of its incidence and effects. Surveys of employer outlays on training produce unreliable estimates (see PERFORMANCE APPRAISAL). Case studies offer better estimates but they are costly and rare (Jones 1986; Ryan 1991). Age-earnings profiles yield indirect estimates of training expenditures, but restrictive assumptions limit the validity of the results (Polachek and Siebert 1993). The empirical literature is accordingly dominated by qualitative, partial indicators – e.g. for workers, trainee status; for employers, share of employees with trainee status. The reliability of such indicators is limited (Barron *et al.* 1997).

3 Human capital theory

The economics of training has been dominated by human capital theory, in which training is treated as an investment. A near-term sacrifice of income is accepted in return for a subsequent gain in income (see HUMAN CAPITAL; HUMAN RESOURCE MANAGEMENT). Agents are rational egotists, undertaking all investments for which discounted net benefits are positive. Markets are assumed competitive: pay adjusts to clear markets for trained, trainee and untrained labour alike (Becker 1975).

Training provision and finance (in the absence of public intervention) can be analysed in a two-period model, in which the first period comprises work-based training and the second, work without additional learning. In Figure 1, Q represents individual output (net marginal value product) for trained, unskilled and trainee workers (subscripted s, u and t, respectively). Assuming identical abilities, no unemployment, full information, and no learning in unskilled work, the total costs and benefits of training are then areas *abcd* and *cefg*, representing respectively the initial loss and the subsequent gain in output when an employee receives training instead of doing unskilled work. If discounted net benefits are positive, the training is economically viable.

The division of costs and benefits between employer and trainee is mediated by payroll costs (W, henceforth 'pay') for the three employee categories. When skills are *general*, that is as valuable to many other employers as to the employer that provided the training, the pay profile tracks the output one and trainees bear all of the costs – i.e. forgone earnings amounting to *abcd*. Any employer which subsidizes general training (for example, by paying W_1 to trainees, incurring costs of *abih*) has to pay its trained workers less than they produce (for example, W_2) in order to earn a return on its investment. Other employers who do not pay for training can then lure away its trained workers by paying them their full

value (Q_s). As the employer must therefore meet the market price for skilled labour, it refuses to invest in general training. That need not be a problem: trainees will be willing to bear the entire cost themselves, as the external market ensures high pay once they become skilled, thereby providing the return on their investment. Training for costly general skills therefore involves a prolonged period of low pay – even explicit training fees – for trainees, but employers meet trainee demand in full as it costs them nothing to do so.

The problem is that trainees may not be able to finance the investment. As human capital is embodied in people, legal and motivational factors prevent potential trainees from using it as collateral to secure a training loan. Trainees who lack other assets cannot finance training. Training volumes are accordingly low, and skilled pay high, relative to optimal levels.

An apprenticeship contract may remove the financial problem. The trainee contracts to receive low pay, the employer to teach a skill, and each party to avoid separation, for a fixed duration, which must exceed that required to learn the skill. If the trainee's net product rises during the course of the contract from less than to more than his or her pay, the employer

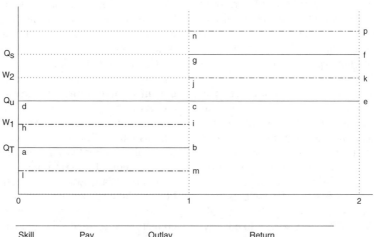

Skill	Pay	Outlay		Return	
		trainee	employer	trainee	employer
general	abgf	abcd	0	cefg	0
specific	hijk	hicd	abih	cejk	jkfg

Figure 1 Pay, outputs and investments in training
Note: Investments and returns have not been discounted to present values

then invests in training during the first phase and reaps a return during the second one. By relieving the financial strain on the trainee without laying the employer open to the 'poaching' of skilled workers before its investment has been recouped, an apprenticeship contract can make both parties better off than can one-period contracts.

The contemporary (as opposed to historical) relevance of the apprenticeship contract as a solution to trainee financial problems is undermined by the first of two anomalies in the financing of general training in practice. The first is that employers often invest significant sums in any general training that they provide (including apprenticeship contracts taken as a whole) and may even pay trainees enough to live on without having to borrow. Examples include manual and technical skills, both certified and uncertified, traded in external labour markets (Ryan 1984; Acemoglu and Pischke 1999). Secondly, at the other extreme, some employers exploit trainees by offering them little training as well as low pay, benefiting more from their output during training than from their skills when trained (see LABOUR MARKETS). 'Contracts of apprenticeship, in which the main advantage accrues to the employer, leaving very little to the apprentice who has been "trained" are only too familiar' (Hicks 1969: 140). The exploitation of trainees is commonly encountered in both traditional, unregulated apprenticeship and public 'training' programmes for the unemployed (Ryan 1994).

The two anomalies are exemplified by pay profiles *dcgf* and *lmjk*, respectively. As neither anomaly could constitute an equilibrium in competitive markets, the assumption of perfect competition must be abandoned. Two approaches to the task are promising: oligopsony power and wage rigidity.

Oligopsony (i.e. few buyers) power is present whenever an employer's labour supply would not disappear totally were it to cut pay. When it concerns skilled workers, oligopsony power allows an employer to pay them less than their marginal product while retaining enough of them to earn a return on its investment in training. It can be generated by imperfect information, concerning e.g. the training that a skilled worker has received or the ability

of trainees, as well as by heterogeneous training content (Acemoglu and Pischke 1999). Employers then provide and finance costly training that is useful to other employers (anomaly one) as long as the alternative – increased recruitment of skilled workers – is more expensive. Hiring costs for skilled labour do indeed influence apprentice numbers in the UK (Stevens 1994). Oligopsony power can also account for the second anomaly, when it is trainees who are on the receiving end. Trainees who lack information about the content of training programmes or whose outside alternatives are depressed by unemployment or labour market segmentation may accept training programmes that offer little scope for learning despite low pay.

Wage rigidity takes the form of a compressed wage structure: i.e. differences in pay (between the three categories of labour in Figure 1) that are smaller than those in marginal products. It becomes possible when the pay profile in Figure 1 is set by law, collective agreement or job evaluation rather than by market clearing. When such rules specify a trainee wage greater than trainee productivity, employers must finance whatever training they provide – and consequently tend to reduce their provision of general training (Stevens 1996). Evidence of such effects has been found for statutory minimum wages and collective agreements (Hashimoto 1982; Ryan 1984).

Theories that invoke wage rigidity should explain it. One factor has been trade union pursuit of high trainee pay. Several motives are possible. Unions may respond to the interests of trainee members seeking higher pay. Unions may seek to curb trainee exploitation (anomaly number two) by raising the price of trainee labour. Better training would have the same effect but, given asymmetric information and in the absence of the external regulation of training quality, the enforceability of collective agreements is greater when they cover trainee pay rather than training quality (Ryan 1994).

At the other extreme, skills may be *specific*, that is, of value only to the employer that provided the training. As a mutually beneficial asset is then destroyed should employer and trained worker separate, each party requires protection against separations initiated by the other. An efficient contract therefore allocates to each party a significant share of both costs and benefits, reassuring each that the other will lose significantly by ending the relationship – as under pay profiles such as *hijk* in Figure 1 (Becker 1975). The difficulty is that both parties may seek opportunistically after training to 'hold up' the other by bargaining for a higher share of the joint benefit. Not only is such bargaining costly in itself; the prospect of it impedes agreement to undertake the training in the first place. The efficient contract therefore covers both periods and specifies skilled pay in advance.

The optimal separation rate for trained workers will not, however, usually be zero: given uncertainty about future conditions, specific training may not work out for one or both parties. Various contractual provisions, concerning duration, wage growth and restrictions on separation rights, prove optimal according to the *ex ante* productivity and job satisfaction of trained workers. For example, employers must bear more of the costs when: (1) higher pay for trained workers raises layoffs by more than it reduces quits; and (2) when less is known *ex ante* about the productivity and job satisfaction of trained workers in the training firm than elsewhere (Hashimoto and Yu 1980).

Specific training provides an explanation for the existence of both long-term employment and a positive association between length of service and pay. The difficulty of measuring specific skills makes the theory hard to test, but empirical difficulties have surfaced nevertheless (see EMPLOYMENT AND UNEMPLOYMENT, ECONOMICS OF). The prediction that senior employees are paid less than their productivity conflicts with evidence that Japanese employers often pay 'window watching' senior employees more than their value (*np* and *gf* respectively). The existence of mandatory retirement rules intensifies the problem: why would employers oblige senior employees to retire were their productivity to exceed their pay? These anomalies can be explained by interpreting long-term employment and seniority pay as vehicles for the motivation of employees, via deferred compensation and tournament promotions, rather

than for the financing of specific training (Hutchens 1989). Indeed, as employers finance most or all of the costs of the in-service training that they provide, the human capital theory of the finance of specific training lacks empirical support.

Human capital theory sheds only limited light on international differences in training and training-related pay structures. In Sweden and France, initial vocational learning occurs largely in formal schooling; in the UK, USA and Germany, largely in association with work. Only the latter category lies within scope here, but differences are marked there too. German training relies primarily on two- to four-year apprenticeships undertaken early in working life; training often begins in the USA only after several years of work experience and increases in frequency over the first half of the work-life. German apprentices receive allowances well below earnings in the occupation for which they are training; US trainees are normally paid at the rate for the job for which they are being trained. More generally, the relative pay of young trainees varies considerably from country to country (Marsden and Ryan 1991b).

Such differences can hardly be understood primarily in terms of the worker preferences and technology to which human capital theory looks. US youth may indeed be less willing to invest in its future than German youth, and German production methods may require more general skills than US ones, but such differences are expected to cause only second-order differences in national outcomes – and may themselves be by-products of national training systems. An explicitly institutional approach is needed in order to understand the heterogeneity of national training systems.

4 Institutional factors

Human capital theory, as part of the 'new institutional economics', interprets such institutions as long-term employment, seniority rights and apprenticeship as the result of rational choices under imperfect information and skill specificity (see INSTITUTIONAL ECONOMICS). The contribution of the new institutionalism is, however, limited by its attachment to methodological individualism and its predilection for unique, efficient outcomes. A truly institutional account of training patterns and outcomes must also consider managerial strategy, industrial relations, labour market structure, non-market coordination, systemic interdependencies and path dependence.

A role for managerial strategy is visible in differences in the training efforts of employers who compete in the same product market. For instance, automobile producers who opt for flexible production offer more training to their employees than do those who prefer mass production. The benefits for productivity and profits of their increased training provision prove greater in the presence of lean production, teamwork and other human resource management practices (see HUMAN RESOURCE MANAGEMENT). Moreover, Japanese and European automobile employers train more extensively than do their US counterparts, even when production strategy is held constant (MacDuffie 1995).

Second, training is often intertwined with industrial relations. Craft regulation of training in the post-war British national newspaper industry provided an extreme case (Stuart 1994). More generally, the pay structures that determine incentives to demand and supply training (above) reflect the goals of the unions and employers that negotiate them. The training implications of wage structure are often ignored. Thus British, Swedish and Italian pay negotiators appear to have neglected the implications for training of egalitarian pay policies; their German counterparts, by contrast, to have avoided compressing trainee pay differentials, in order to protect apprenticeship (Marsden and Ryan 1991a).

Labour market structure also affects training. Occupational markets encourage skilled workers to move between employers, relying on certified skills rather than any particular employer for employment security. Occupational structures tend to rely on low trainee pay, formalized by apprenticeship contracts, to encourage employers to offer training. Internal labour markets are organized around particular workplaces and employers. Job vacancies are filled by internal mobility; skills are learned along career promotion ladders. The dichotomy between occupational and internal markets corresponds partly to that between general and specific skills but, as similar products and technologies are sometimes associated with differences across countries in labour market structure, the latter must be important in its own right. Internal structures predominate in many Japanese, French, Italian and US labour markets; occupational ones in German, Swiss and, historically, UK ones. The decay of occupational markets has posed serious skill problems in the post-war UK (Doeringer and Piore 1971).

Fourth, general training (particularly apprenticeship) requires a degree of coordination between the interested parties that purely contractual relations cannot provide. The simpler aspect is employer–employer cooperation. The employer who considers financing general training acts as a player in a Prisoners' Dilemma game, in which all employers will jointly do best if all train (the cooperative solution), all will do worst if none train, but any one employer will do best of all if it (alone) avoids training and 'poaches' trained workers (Chapman 1993). Cooperative solutions are possible in a repeated game if discount rates are low and players who violate them can be punished effectively. The latter option usually requires an employers' association possessing the authority to deter free riding. The weakness of employers' associations in the UK and the USA accounts partly for those countries' poor performance, in terms of apprenticeship training at least (Soskice 1990).

Tripartite cooperation between employers, unions and government is also required if training is to transcend specific skills and attain the wider occupational and educational goals to which apprenticeship caters. Neocorporatist structures to regulate training are influential in Germany and neighbouring countries, weak in most English-speaking ones (Streeck et al. 1987; Ryan 2000).

A fifth aspect is interdependence among national institutions relevant to training, creating the possibility of multiple equilibria. The UK and USA have been depicted as stuck in 'low skill equilibria' as a result of mutually reinforcing influences, including weak employer associations, Fordist managerial strategies (mass production using deskilled production techniques), managerial short-termism (imposed by takeover threats and penalising investment in intangibles like training), arm's-length, insecure relationships between suppliers and producers, low social respect for skill, and political short-termism, driven by partisan advantage rather than consensual institutional development. Japan and Germany enjoy high skill equilibria as a result of the interlocking across the same dimensions of favourable attributes within each one (Finegold and Soskice 1988).

These national systems constitute equilibria in that, firstly, agents act rationally within their wider institutional context and, secondly, changes in only one component, for example increases in public training subsidies, often fail, given systemic inertia. The efficiency claims of competitive equilibria are absent. Such holistic interpretations tend, however, to slight intra-national variation. For example, some UK employers have maintained high skill strategies, notwithstanding an unfavourable institutional context (Gospel and Druker, 1998).

Finally there is path dependence: the content of a national training system reflects a unique, cumulative historical path, in which random effects and positive feedback produce enduring international differences – in contrast to the universalism of human capital theory (David 1986). Path dependence helps account for the persistent heterogeneity of national training systems within an increasingly integrated global economy. A low skill equilibrium represents, however, only one of several historical possibilities, and opportunities to change radically a national training system do arise episodically. At such times, its redirection may be informed by economic theory and comparative evidence.

PAUL RYAN
UNIVERSITY OF CAMBRIDGE

Further reading

(References cited in the text marked *)

* Acemoglu, D. and Pischke, J.-S. (1999) 'Beyond Becker: training in imperfect labour markets', *Economic Journal* 109: F112–42. (Oligopsony power in skilled labour markets and its implications for work-based training.)

* Barron, J.M., Berger, M.C. and Black, D.A. (1997) *On-the-Job Training*, Kalamazoo: W.E.Upjohn Institute. (The measurement, incidence and effects of employer provided training in the US.)
* Becker, G.S. (1975) *Human Capital*, 2nd edn, Chicago, IL: University of Chicago Press. (The original, lucid account of human capital theory, using job training as the exemplar.)
* Blundell, R., Dearden, L. and Meghir C. (1996) *The Determinants and Effects of Work-Related Training in Britain*, London: Institute for Fiscal Studies. (Training incidence and effects in a UK population cohort.)
* Chapman, P. (1993) *The Economics of Training*, Hemel Hempstead: Harvester Wheatsheaf. (A textbook that discusses human capital and institutional approaches to training.)
* David, P.A. (1986) 'Understanding the economics of QWERTY: the necessity of history', in W.N. Parker (ed.), *Economic History and the Modern Economist*, Oxford: Blackwell. (Path-dependent economic outcomes illustrated from the history of the standard keyboard layout.)
* Doeringer, P.B. and Piore, M.J. (1971) *Internal Labour Markets and Manpower Analysis*, Lexington, MA: D.C. Heath & Co. (A classic eclectic account of internal and occupational labour markets.)
* Finegold, D. and Soskice, D. (1988) 'The failure of training in Britain: analysis and prescription', *Oxford Review of Economic Policy* 4 (3): 21–53. (British training interpreted as a multidimensional low skill equilibrium.)
* Gospel, H. and Druker, J. (1998) 'The survival of national bargaining in the electrical contracting industry: a deviant case?', *British Journal of Industrial Relations* 36 (2), 5–20. (How an industry-wide organization of pay bargaining and apprentice training has functioned in an institutionally unfavourable environment.)
* Grubb, W.N. and Ryan, P. (1999) *The Roles of Evaluation for Vocational Education and Training*, Geneva: International Labour Office and Kogan Page. (Methods and findings in the evaluation of training.)
* Hashimoto, M. (1982) 'Minimum wage effects on training on the job', *American Economic Review* 72 (5): 1070–87. (Presents theory and evidence of adverse effects of minimum wages on youth training.)
* Hashimoto, M. and Yu, B. (1980) 'Specific capital, employment contracts and wage rigidity', *Bell Journal of Economics* 11 (2): 536–49. (Contractual options for specific training.)
* Hicks, J.R. (1969) *A Theory of Economic History*, Oxford: Oxford University Press.

* Huselid, M.A. (1995) 'The impact of human resource management practices on turnover, productivity and corporate financial performance', *Academy of Management Journal*, 38 (3), 635–72. (Evidence that greater training provision by employers is associated with higher productivity and profits.)

* Hutchens, R.M. (1989) 'Seniority, wages and productivity: a turbulent decade', *Journal of Economic Perspectives* 3 (4): 49–64. (An accessible account of debates over the role of training in seniority-pay relationships.)

* Jones, I.S. (1986) 'Apprentice training costs in British manufacturing establishments: some new evidence', *British Journal of Industrial Relations* 24 (3): 333–62. (Case studies of employer investments in engineering apprentices' skills in Britain.)

* MacDuffie, J.P. (1995) 'Human resource bundles and manufacturing performance: organisational logic and flexible production systems in the world auto industry', *Industrial and Labour Relations Review*, 48 (2), 197–221. (The association between training and productivity across plants in the world automobile industry.)

* Marsden, D.W. and Ryan, P. (1991a) 'Initial training, labour market structure and public policy: intermediate skills in British and German industry', in P. Ryan (ed.), *International Comparisons of Vocational Education and Training for Intermediate Skills*, Brighton: Falmer. (An account of divergent post-war training paths in the UK and Germany drawing on human capital, institutional and path dependence themes.)

* Marsden, D.W. and Ryan, P. (1991b) 'The structuring of youth pay and employment in six European economies', in P. Ryan, P. Garonna and R.C. Edwards (eds), *The Problem of Youth: The Regulation of Youth Employment and Training in Advanced Economies*, London: Macmillan. (Institutional background to trainee pay in the EU.)

* Polachek, S.W. and Siebert, W.S. (1993) *The Economics of Earnings*, Cambridge: CUP. (Textbook exposition of the human capital theory of life-cycle investments in skill.)

* Prais, S.J. (ed.) (1995) *Productivity, Education and Training*, Cambridge: CUP. (Sector-level investigations of links between vocational skill and productivity in matched sectors in the UK and other European countries.)

* Ryan, P. (1984) 'Job training, employment practices and the large enterprise: the case of costly transferable skills', in P. Osterman (ed.), *Internal Labour Markets*, Cambridge, MA: Massachusetts Institute of Technology. (Wider implications of a case study of shipyard welder training.)

* Ryan, P. (1991) 'How much do employers spend on training? An evaluation of the "Training in Britain" estimates', *Human Resource Management Journal* 1 (4): 55–76. (Difficulties of costing training, with estimates for the UK.)

* Ryan, P. (1994) 'Training quality and trainee exploitation', in R. Layard, K. Mayhew and G. Owen (eds), *Britain's Training Deficit*, Aldershot: Avebury. (The determinants of trainee exploitation and trade union responses.)

* Ryan, P. (2000) 'The institutional requirements of apprenticeship: evidence from smaller EU countries', *International Journal of Training and Development*, 4 (1): 42–65. (The extent to which national apprenticeship systems depend on collective action and public regulation.)

* Soskice, D. (1990) 'Reinterpreting corporatism and explaining unemployment', in R. Brunetta and C. dell'Arringa (eds), *Labour Relations and Economic Performance*, London: Macmillan. (Employer associations and public policy options.)

* Stevens, M. (1994) 'An investment model for the supply of training by employers', *Economic Journal* 104: 556–71. (Costs of recruitment and borrowing as influences on the volume of apprenticeship training in the UK.)

* Stevens, M. (1996) 'Transferable training and poaching externalities', in A. Booth and D. Snower (eds), *Acquiring Skills*, Cambridge: CUP. (The supply of training for 'transferable' skills is proved sub-optimal in the absence of collective action or public intervention.)

* Streeck, W., Hilbert, J., Kevalaer, K.-H. van, Maier, F. and Weber, H. (1987) *The Role of the Social Partners in Vocational Training and Further Training in the FRG*, Berlin: European Centre for Vocational Education and Training (CEDEFOP). (An account of the multi-layered, tripartite regulation of German apprenticeship.)

* Stuart, M. (1994) 'Training in the printing industry: an investigation into the recruitment, training and retraining agreement', *Human Resource Management Journal* 4 (2), 62–78. (The decline of craft union regulation of training in a traditional stronghold.)

See also: HUMAN RESOURCE DEVELOPMENT; HUMAN RESOURCE FLOWS; INDUSTRIAL AND LABOUR RELATIONS; MANAGEMENT DEVELOPMENT

Training, executive: see EXECUTIVE TRAINING

Transaction cost economics

Overview

The aim of this entry is to discuss the new avenues opened up to economic enquiry by the consideration of transaction costs. The origins of transaction cost economics (TCE) can be traced back to a classic article on the theory of the firm by Ronald Coase. In it, Coase tried to explain the existence of multiple person hierarchies (firms) in terms of market failures, which he claimed were due to the high costs of exchanging (transacting) in markets. Coase later extended his analysis to attribute the existence of Law and the State to market transaction costs.

After a long gestation period, Coase's ideas have been taken up, elaborated, extended and criticized by numerous economists. The emergent new perspective has found applications not only in explanations of economic phenomena, such as the market, the firm, the transnational corporation and the state, but also in sociology, economic history, development, organization studies and strategic management. It would appear that TCE has the potential to transform not only economics and social science, but also, perhaps, to provide the elements of a unified social sciences research programme. It comes as no surprise therefore that the originator of TCE, Ronald Coase, was awarded the 1991 Nobel Prize for economics. Moreover, the 1993 Prize went to a disciple of TCE, Douglass North. In his work, he has attempted to explain economic history by pursuing a brand of TCE theorizing that goes beyond conventional economic thinking. TCE is also currently finding applications in macroeconomics and is rapidly influencing both government policy on competition and industry, and the competitive and corporate strategies of firms.

Despite its widespread influence, TCE has been the focus of widespread criticism from various vantage points, such as economics, sociology and management studies, and a number of alternative perspectives have been proposed. This entry is intended to offer a bird's-eye view of these developments. Section 1 looks at the origin and development of the Coasean tradition and pays particular attention to the TCE explanation of the nature, and boundaries of the firm. Section 2 discusses some critiques and alternatives, while section 3 outlines the policy implications of TCE, anticipates future developments. Section 4 provides an assessment.

1 The Coasean tradition

Coase's main concern in the 1937 article was to explain the existence of firms (see COASE, R.). His starting point was that resource allocation in market economies is ordinarily regarded by theorists as taking place through the price mechanism. Yet he observed that economists often also employ the assumption that such allocation depends on the entrepreneur. These two assumptions, however, are incompatible. In Coase's view, the distinguishing mark of the firm is the supersession of the price mechanism. The question then arises as to how such alternative institutional forms of resource allocation come about.

Coase's answer is that the operation of the market is costly and that by forming an organization and allowing an entrepreneur to direct the resources (firm or hierarchy) certain 'marketing costs' are saved. 'Marketing costs' are the costs of using the price mechanism. Examples given by Coase include the cost of discovering the relevant prices and the cost of negotiating and concluding separate contracts for each transaction. Contracting costs in particular, he observed, are not eliminated but are greatly reduced if the entrepreneur (seen as one of the 'factors of production' within the firm) does not have to make a series of contracts with the other parties with whom he or she is cooperating (the other factors of production), but substitutes them for one contract; under the terms of this contract, the other factors agree to obey the directions of the entrepreneur within certain limits: 'It is the fact of direction which is the essence of the legal concept of "employer and employee"' (Coase 1937: 409).

Coase's argument was that, given the assumption that the market pre-exists or is a natural starting point, the very existence of firms implies that firms reduce costs associated with the price mechanism. This revolutionary insight was potentially damaging to the neo-classical tradition as it provided a reason why planning (including, perhaps, central planning) might be preferable to the market.

Although some insights resembling Coase's were developed in the 1960s and early 1970s, particularly by writers on the theory of the transnational corporation, it was not until Oliver Williamson's *Markets and Hierarchies* (1975) that an attempt to develop Coase's work into a full-blown research programme in economics was made (see COASE, R.; INSTITUTIONAL ECONOMICS; WILLIAMSON, O.E.).

Williamson on markets and hierarchies

Williamson's starting point was the same as Coase's, namely the assumption that 'in the beginning, there were markets' (Williamson 1975: 20). Given this, the core methodological elements of the perspective that Williamson outlined in *Markets and Hierarchies* are:

1 the transaction is the basic unit of analysis;
2 human agents are subject to bounded rationality and are characterized by self-interest and guile (opportunism);
3 the critical dimensions for describing transactions are frequency, uncertainty and

transaction-specific investments, or asset specificity;
4 the attempt to keep transaction costs to a minimum is the principal factor that explains viable modes of contracting and should be the main concern of organizational design;
5 the assessment of transaction costs differences is a useful exercise in comparing institutions.

According to Williamson, a transaction occurs when a good or service is transferred across a technologically separable interface. Transaction costs are the costs of running the economic system, (Arrow 1970). Williamson thinks of these in contractual terms. Coase (1960) and North (1981) list search and information costs, measurement costs, bargaining and negotiation costs, and policing and enforcement costs as examples of transaction costs (see also Eggertsson 1990).

Williamson's concept of human agency has two important elements. First, there is 'bounded rationality', which refers to behaviour that is intended to be rational but is so only to a limited extent. Limits to rationality arise from limited knowledge, foresight, skill and time. Second, there is self-interest with guile; agents can be selective in information disclosure, can distort information or can try to deliberately mislead. Self-interest with guile is called 'opportunism' (also 'moral hazard' or 'agency'). The importance of these two behavioural assumptions, Williamson claims, is profound: given bounded rationality, all complex contracts are unavoidably incomplete and given opportunism, contracts unsupported by credible commitments cannot be regarded as promises. It follows that transactions should be organized so as to minimize these problems.

'Transaction-specific investments' (asset specificity) refers to the extent to which assets can be redeployed to alternative uses and to different users without loss of productive value. Forms of asset specificity include site specificity, human asset specificity, physical asset specificity and dedicated assets. Of the three critical dimensions for describing transactions, asset specificity is claimed to be more important and distinctive than uncertainty and frequency.

The co-existence of asset specificity, bounded rationality and opportunism creates a situation where market transaction costs can be so high that it is advantageous to supersede the market and organize resource allocation within a firm. This is due to a 'fundamental transformation'; from a potentially large numbers condition pre-contract, to a small numbers bilateral dependence, once a contract has been made. In the context of specific assets, opportunistic behaviour may lead to excessive market transaction costs, which render integration, seen as the internalization of the market, preferable. The 'internalization' of the market by the firm is due to the latter's ability to reduce transaction costs arising from the co-existence of all three factors. If any one of the three factors does not exist, markets can still allocate resources economically compared to firms. If rationality were not bounded, all potential problems could be settled from the outset and the problems of opportunism and asset specificity could be solved within the market. If there were no opportunism, the 'principle of stewardship' (whereby transactors can be relied upon to keep promises) could be used instead of a hierarchy of the sort found in a firm. Finally, if there were no asset specificity (and therefore no sunk costs), contestable markets – markets characterized by perfectly easy entry and costless exit – would exist.

Williamson considers the co-existence of all three factors as pervasive, implying the possibility of market supersession by hierarchies. The advantage of internal organization is that it facilitates adaptive, sequential decision making in circumstances where complex, contingent claim contracts are not feasible and sequential spot markets are hazardous. Problems from bounded rationality are thus reduced. Internal organization also attenuates opportunism, both because of the ability of authority to stop prolonged disputes and because members of a hierarchy are likely to feel that they are part of a whole. Convergent expectations are more likely to appear, which reduces uncertainty. Bargaining costs arising from asset specificity can similarly be reduced through the use of authority.

While hierarchical organization looks desirable for the reasons given above, William-

son points out that there are problems. These arise because the 'high-powered' incentives of markets can be blunted or lost by hierarchies. A related problem is the possibility of high transaction costs within firms or 'management costs' (Demsetz 1988). Thus there is a trade-off between high-powered incentives and bilateral adaptability. The combination of management costs and the loss of high-powered incentives can help to explain the boundaries between firms and the market (given the assumption of pre-existing markets). As Coase claimed, 'At the margin, the costs of organizing within the firm will be equal either to the costs of organizing in another firm or to the costs involved in leaving the transaction to be "organized" by the price mechanism' (1937: 404). The idea of leaving the transaction to be organized by the price mechanism is crucial here, as it implies that in the absence of internalization, markets (continue to) exist.

Transaction cost economics on the nature, integration and internal organisation of firms

Transaction cost economics (TCE) has been used by Williamson, to explain a number of important issues: the employment relation (between employer and employee), vertical integration, the evolution of multidivisional structures within firms, the conglomerate and transnational corporations (Williamson 1981) (see MULTINATIONAL CORPORATIONS). Of these, the employment relation was Coase's almost exclusive concern and it is arguably the most important (Malcolmson 1984; Kay 1992). This is because it seems that only the employment relation has the potential to explain the emergence of hierarchies from pre-existing markets. All the other issues listed above presuppose the existence of firms (Pitelis 1991) (see ORGANIZATION STRUCTURE). This idea is examined briefly below.

Vertical integration
Williamson explains vertical integration (VI; the extension of a firm's activities 'upstream', for example to raw materials, or 'downstream', for example to distribution) within his perspective on organizational failures. His

approach is directly derived from Coase's observation that firms will tend to expand (integrate) up to the point at which it is equally costly not to. It follows that VI occurs for the same reason that makes firms come into existence. In Williamson's case, VI is due to post-contract hold-up problems in the context of asset specificity and opportunism, leading to high transaction costs.

With or without specific assets and/or opportunism, the TCE of VI is both powerful and widely regarded today as a most convincing explanation of VI (see, for example, Caves 1996 and Marris 1999). Empirical studies of vertical integration do provide evidence in favour of TCE-type factors (see Caves 1996) (although the interpretation of the econometric results can sometimes be doubtful).

Nevertheless, while arguments about opportunistic suppliers, specific assets and *ex post* bilateral dependencies may be legitimate explanatory factors of firms' decisions, the fact is that integration involves the internalization of more market transactions by an existing hierarchy; no explanation of new hierarchies from markets is offered.

Multidivisional (M-form) firms

Alfred Chandler (1962) analysed the emergence of firms with a multidivisional structure (M-form firms), which started to replace unitary firms (U-form firms) in the USA soon after the Second World War. The structure of the U-form firm involved a central office, which was responsible for both long-term strategic decisions and day-to-day operational decisions, and a number of divisions, such as production, marketing, finance, personnel, etc. The M-form firm, on the other hand, consists of a general office, which is responsible for strategic decisions alone, and a number of operating divisions, each one organized in the way the U-form firm was. The operational decisions are left with the divisional managers in this structure. Chandler's idea was that the adoption of the M-form was a response to firms' needs for diversification. By the early part of the twentieth century, a number of firms were already vertically integrated and realized that their know-how could be profitably applied in new product lines (Chandler 1977). The U-form created difficulties when

the need arose to administer activities in different markets. The M-form was a way forward, as a firm would only have to add another division in a new product market to achieve its diversification plans. In this sense, Chandler's thesis was that strategy caused structure.

Williamson tells a different story. He claims that U-form firms were becoming so large that 'bounds on rationality were reached as the U-form structure labored under a communication overload, while the pursuit of subgoals by functional parts ... was partly a manifestation of opportunism' (Williamson 1981: 1555). This was because central offices were taking both strategic and operational decisions. The M-form firm, by creating 'semi-autonomous operating divisions (mainly profit centers) organized along product, brand or geographical lines' (*ibid.*: 1555), the operating affairs of which were managed separately, was able to reduce managerial opportunism, ease the confusion between strategic and operating goals and, importantly, re-establish the profit motive by reuniting ownership and control. In Williamson's view, the adoption of the M-form was due to its inherent control advantages, which reduced transaction costs. In this sense, it was size that led to the M-form firm: structure caused strategy.

In addition to these TC-related efficiencies, the M-form has also served to reduce transactions costs related to the external capital market. The M-form operates as an internal capital market, thus solving TC-related external capital market failures.

The debate on the M-form is big and ongoing. In this author's view (Pitelis 1991), moreover, there is little reason to see the two views as conflicting. Both Chandler-type and Williamson-type factors could be operative.

Worth noting, finally, are the problems of the M-form. Fransman (1994) observes that failure of the M-form to attenuate opportunism has led large firms, such as ATT and IBM, to introduce a more segmented form, the S-form, which allows much more authority to the various divisions than the M-form.

However, the merits of the two explanations of the M-form structure or of a synthesis is another case of the organizational form of an existing hierarchy.

Conglomerates and transnationals

In the case of the conglomerate firm, Williamson's argument is in terms of internalizing the external capital market because of failures in that market (Williamson 1975, 1981). Internalization increases the availability of information and the ability to control auditing, and facilitates performance assessment of the M-form-type divisionalized profit centres. Economies in transaction costs can be made by internalizing the production of separate goods. This is due to the possibility that firms will be better able to exploit the quasi-rents from the ownership of specialized resources, either physical capital or human know-how. In both cases, conglomeration, as compared to leasing or selling in the open market, can help reduce market transaction costs arising from opportunism, the problem of which is particularly acute in the case of organizational know-how because of its tacit and tangible nature. There is evidence in support of this analysis (Caves 1996); it is clear, however, that what is being explained is the behaviour of existing hierarchies. There is an explanation of why some market transactions are superseded, but not why hierarchies arise from markets (see CORPORATE CONTROL).

Williamson's treatment of the transnational corporation (TNC) is not extensive (see Williamson 1981). In essence, the TNC is once again attributed to hold-up problems due to asset specificity. There is a large debate on the role of transaction costs in the theory of the TNC, recently summarized in Pitelis and Sugden (2000). Williamson's version is one of at least three. Buckley and Casson's (1976) TC-based internalization theory of the TNC focused on appropriability problems of intangible assets, usually with a knowledge component, which are hard to sell in open markets due to the public good aspects of knowledge. Teece's (1986) assessment of the TC theory of the TNC suggests that TCE can help discriminate between transaction costs that need to be internalised or not. Hennart (2000) suggests that TNCs internalized inefficient labour markets abroad, given TNCs' superior ability to control foreign labour. Caves (1996) has a TC theory which, however, has elements of the resource-based theory (see below). He finds empirical support for this theory.

Criticisms of the TC explanation to the TNC involve its alleged failure to consider failures in the final product markets (see Hallwood 1994). It is also observed that in the case of the TNC both specific and non-specific assets are internalized (Kay 1992). Finally, it is argued that TNCs are not the result of market failure at all, but rather that firms are better than markets and other firms in transferring tacit knowledge (Kogut and Zander 1993). For our purposes, suffice it to note that the TNC too cannot explain why firms; TNCs, are already existing firms.

The employment relation

It seems that only the employment relation might have a legitimate claim to explain how new hierarchies arise from markets. Coase was aware of this and in his 1937 paper it is the employment relation that receives near exclusive attention (although more recently (Coase 1991) he has expressed regret for this and claimed that the firm involves more than the employment relation). In the Coasean tradition, it is 'failures' of pre-existing markets for labour which explain the emergence of hierarchies (the firm). TC explanations of vertical integration, M-form firms, conglomerates and transnational corporations simply explain the further internalization of markets by existing hierarchies. This raises the question of why labour markets 'fail' and what the exact nature of such failure is. It is useful to examine this in a historical context.

The capitalist firm, as embodied in the factory system, was the way of organizing work that succeeded the 'putting-out' system (see INDUSTRIAL REVOLUTION). In the putting-out system, a merchant-manufacturer 'put out' raw materials to dispersed cottage labourers to be worked up into finished or semi-finished products. In most cases, the labourers used their own equipment, such as looms or forges. Material was moved from home to home in batches under the direction of the merchant-manufacturer. In the factory system, on the other hand, labourers 'accepted' working under the employers' authority and doing as they were told, provided that the employer's behaviour fell within certain limits of acceptability. This agreement – the employment contract – replaced the market-type relationship that existed under the putting-out system.

What were the critical factors that led to the replacement of a market-type putting-out system by a factory system? In Williamson's story, the general reasons relate to TC economizing. Workers can possess 'idiosyncratic' job-related skills, which increase their bargaining power with employers. This and worker opportunism gave rise to the TC difficulties of such market-type employment relationships as the putting-out system: for example, protracted haggling. The long-term employment contract of the sort associated with Coasean firms can ameliorate, albeit not fully solve, the problem of asymmetric information between employers and employees. The employer can provide incentives to the employee to increase cooperation; for example, in the internal labour market the wage rate attaches to the job, not the worker (see LA-BOUR MARKETS). This can reduce individual bargaining and thus opportunism. Employees accept voluntarily the reduction in their freedom, but retain the right to cancel the authority relationship by leaving the employer. Although shirking by employees is not prevented, 'consummate' (as opposed to 'perfunctory') cooperation is encouraged. Employers' opportunism is reduced for reasons of reputation, a point going back to Coase (1937). Cheating firms become known quicker than cheating workers. This and the existence of unions (see TRADE UNIONS), which monitor the firm's commitments, make cheating by firms less likely. Overall, according to this story, it is idiosyncratic transactions (ones that arise from a labourer having a particular skill) and opportunism which necessitate the emergence of the long-term employment relation.

There is substantial evidence to support the claim that the workers' ability to behave opportunistically under the putting-out system was high (Landes 1966). Accordingly, from the merchant manufacturers' point of view at least, there were good reasons why the market-based putting-out system should be replaced by the firm-like authority relation (similar considerations would apply in the case of 'purer' market-type employment contracts, for example of the spot contracting type). By making the ability to work (labour power) rather than a certain amount of product the subject of the contract, employers could increase their ability to control quality and monitor workers. The impetus for the factory system, according to North, was 'monitoring of the production process by a supervisor' (North 1981: 169). Williamson notes that this monitoring had obvious productivity advantages, such as the appropriation of the benefits of innovation and the checking of embezzlement and similar deceits.

There can be little doubt from the above that, from the merchant manufacturer's point of view, superseding the putting-out system by a more hierarchical organization had obvious advantages in terms of efficiency. This appears to be in line with Williamson's claim that such changes are driven by efficiency. However, this 'Williamsonian synthesis' is not uncontroversial.

2 Critiques, and alternatives

Markets first

As already suggested, the starting point of the Coase–Williamson framework is the idea that the market is the natural and/or original means of resource allocation and that non-market institutions need to be explained. However, there are problems with this idea. That markets predate firms is questionable, both conceptually and empirically: conceptually, because (single person) firms may be required for the production of exchanged products and thus for the market; and empirically, because, historically at least, it is not obvious that price-making markets predated (at least some) hierarchies, such as the state (North 1981) or the family. Williamson claims that the pre-existence of markets is a methodological assumption and one can get the same results by starting from hierarchies. This, however, is far from obvious. Starting from firms implies that markets are the making of firms too; at the very least, this questions the assumption of substitutability between markets and hierarchies.

Efficiency through economizing, strategizing, and power

The assumption that firms are the result of efficiency through 'economizing' (in transaction costs), and that this results in increasing efficiency, is questionable. First, it is possible that hierarchies result from, and in, efficiency of a non-TC economizing type (see below). In addition, one may question the process through which an efficient institution (the firm) comes to replace an inefficient one (the market). It is common among TC theorists to employ evolutionary arguments in order to explain the replacement process. North, for example, suggests that 'competition in the face of ubiquitous scarcity dictates that the more efficient institutions ... will survive and the inefficient ones perish' (1981: 7). While this possibility cannot be excluded, it is also possible that competition can lead to monopoly (Marx 1867); market inefficiencies need not necessarily lead to efficient firms. In addition, by way of counter-argument, one could suggest that many institutions tend to contain a self-sustaining pattern of actions; once a pattern is established, it may be maintained despite being socially sub-optimal (see, for example, Foss 1993).

A second line of criticism concerning the efficiency argument relates to the nature of efficiency and its beneficiaries, including the concept of Pareto efficiency. As suggested above, the move from putting-out to the factory system incorporated productivity gains through, in particular, the reduction of employee opportunism. But why should labourers have accepted the loss of their opportunity to be opportunist? It seems odd that independent craftsmen and women should have been willing to sacrifice their independence and obey employers' orders. It is plausible to expect that they would have been against such a change. If so, the firm was not efficient in the Pareto sense. Someone (the merchant) became better off, while someone else (the labourer) became worse off. A counter to this argument would be that from a purely pecuniary point of view both labourers and merchants might have become better off. Although this is a realistic possibility, the question arises as to whether the focus on pe-

cuniary cost-benefits should not be extended to incorporate psychic cost-benefits. If it should be, the preference of putting-out labourers for independence (which Coase himself acknowledges) would appear to invalidate the claim that firms are Pareto-efficient in comparison to markets.

A related criticism is that the TC scenario ignores or downplays the role of power considerations. Such considerations can refer both to market power and to power in its more general sense, that of the ability of an agent to impose his or her will on others through coercion or even charisma. Regarding market power, it was noted above that competition can lead to monopoly, which is one of the major aspects of structural market failure according to conventional welfare economists. The ability of firms to give rise to, rather than solve, market failure has been extensively remarked. Particularly damaging, however, is the observation that market power and TC considerations may be inseparable, as it is often the case that firms attain monopoly power by reducing market transaction costs.

Williamson's response to the issue of power is two-fold. First, he re-interprets evidence on market or overall power in terms of efficiency. He then goes on to say that even if power considerations have merit, power issues have not been operationalized and are less operationalizable. This criticism, however, may be inaccurate (Pitelis 1998) and could well submit too much to the power argument (see Demsetz 1995).

Problems with methodology

Another problem with the TC approach concerns its ability to offer refutable hypotheses that differ from other perspectives. Methodologically, this is done by varying governance structures while holding the transaction constant. This, however, may be illegitimate, as changes in governance structures normally imply changes in the nature of the transaction costs involved; in other words 'a 'better' transaction may be a different transaction' (Dow 1987: 18).

The reliance of the TC perspective on methodological individualism – the reduction of institutions (see INSTITUTIONAL ECONOM-

ICS) or other social phenomena to individual action alone could be questioned too. An alternative would be to explain individual behaviour in terms of institutions, or to at least recognize some sort of interaction between the two; the unit would then be not the individual but the social individual.

Another methodological problem is that the TC perspective is effectively a comparative static approach. A most important issue is how firms behave over time; arguably, the real issue is the 'innovative firm' (see Lazonick 1991). TCE assumes technology and innovation as constant. This is a most important problem. Arguably, the most important issue in economics is wealth creation through productivity enhancements through innovations. This is the agenda of Schumpeter (1942), Penrose (1959), Nelson and Winter (1982) and a host of important contributors in the field (see, for example, Lazonick 1991; Langlois 1992). Many such contributions acknowledge the importance of transaction costs, but see these as a dynamic, real time, historically informed phenomenon, usually blended with resource-knowledge-based and production costs-benefits (see Pitelis 1991).

Transaction costs' static nature also precludes it taking seriously into account the issue of knowledge as distinct from information (Fransman 1994), and the issue of knowledge creation (Penrose 1959) as opposed to its asymmetric distribution.

Other criticisms

Other criticisms of the TC perspective include its disregard of the macroeconomic structure as a potential factor in explaining the existence of various institutional functions (Pitelis 1991). Others have observed that the distinction between markets and firms is not as clear cut as the TC framework implies, so that firm-type behaviour in markets and interpenetrations of markets and hierarchies can often be found. Cowling and Sugden (1998) have suggested that if one focuses on control rather than ownership, certain market-type relations, for example between TNCs and their sub-contractors, can be seen as intra-firm, rather than market, transactions.

Other critiques refer to TCE's comparative neglect of institutional devices between markets and hierarchies, such as networks, strategic alliances, clans and other forms of relational contracting.

In his seminal 1972 contribution Richardson (1972) pointed to the extensive cooperation between firms, suggested that cooperation stands between market and hierarchy, and explained markets, hierarchies and cooperation in terms of the similarity and complementarity of activities, building on the work of Penrose (1959).

Concerning the particulars of Williamson's contribution, his emphasis and focus on bounded rationality, opportunism and asset specificity has been questioned by no less than Coase (1993) himself and Demsetz (1995). Coase (1993) has gone as far as to question the importance of anything that involves the term 'rationality' and questioned the importance of asset specificity. On 'opportunism', there is an ongoing debate (see Williamson 1993). This involves specific criticisms, for example, Williamson's exclusive focus on opportunistic suppliers or workers, but not employers. In contrast, Dow (1987) believes that authority is itself an inducement to opportunistic behaviour. Kay (1997) observed that in the case of the TNC both specific and non-specific assets are involved. He has also questioned whether transactions should always be viewed in contractual terms.

Concerning the links between Williamson's triad, and building on Coase (1993), it is not obvious how one can be (boundedly) 'rational' and opportunistic at the same time. Opportunism may well involve behaving in an apparently irrational way to achieve one's own long-term purpose, given recognition of rivalrous behaviour by others, if only one's self-interest is revealed. While such actions aim to be eventually rational, they are apparently irrational. How can one define rationality in this context, except by trying to define the other parties' 'real' interests? This, however, is clearly far too dangerous to be proposed by anyone. In its absence, rationality plus opportunism may not go together. Lastly, is bounded rationality also procedural as suggested by Simon (1991)? How does it link to collective rationality?

Demsetz (1995) has claimed that the Coase–Williamson treatment of uncertainty is too cavalier, and indeed Coase's critique of Knight's (1921) risk distribution theory of the firm inadequate. For Demsetz, one can generalize Knight's risk distribution theory of the division of tasks between employers (risk undertakers) and employees (who choose security for a stable wage) in terms of overall uncertainty reductions – one could say, transforming fundamental uncertainty (where probabilities cannot be assigned to events) with risk (where probabilities can be assigned). More generally, it could be suggested that TCE deals with risk, but not with fundamental uncertainty.

The ability of TCE to determine the boundaries of the firm has also been forcefully criticized by Marris (1999). Echoing earlier contributions by Penrose (1959; who noted that there are no obvious reasons why average administrative costs should increase as firms expand), Marris suggests that there is no reason to expect that average management costs increase over time, and that there is not necessarily an optimal point, where a declining average TC curve meets a rising administrative costs one.

Indeed the list of potential critiques is limitless, which, however, should not obscure the important contribution of both TCE and Williamson (see below).

The criticisms outlined above are indicative of the strong interest that TCE has aroused. Alternative perspectives have been proposed (although not necessarily as a direct response to TC ideas). Most notable among them are the pure neo-classical approach of Alchian and Demsetz (1972), the resource-based perspective and the radical perspective of Marglin (1974).

A neo-classical alternative

The starting point for Alchian and Demsetz's neo-classical approach is that there is no difference between the firm and the market, and that the firm is essentially a market: 'the firm can be considered as a privately owned market; if so, we could consider the firm and the ordinary market as competing types of markets' (Alchian and Demsetz 1972: 138). In a now famous quote, Alchian and Demsetz reject the idea that the firm has the power to settle issues by any authority superior to that available in ordinary markets: 'Telling an employee to type this letter rather than to file that document is like my telling a grocer to sell me this brand of tuna rather than that brand of bread' (*ibid.*: 120). Overall, the firm is a nexus of contracts and involves continuous renegotiation of the contracts between employers and employees in terms acceptable to both parties. Thus, there is a perfectly symmetrical relationship. The right to quit implies that firing can be bi-directional. The employer fires the employee and similarly the employee fires the employer by leaving.

Alchian and Demsetz suggest that the employer 'is the centralized contractual agent in a team production process – not some superior authoritarian directive or disciplinary power' (*ibid.*: 120). Team production, however, involves problems of metering performance, of rewarding good performance and punishing bad performance. To achieve this, a monitor is required to minimize shirking. To make sure that the monitor is monitoring him or herself, he or she should have the right to claim the residual profit. Thus, the employer is regarded as the coordinator or orchestrator of a private market (the firm). The right to claim residual profit ensures efficient production (compared to the ordinary market). Competition among potential coordinators, moreover, ensures that team members are not exploited.

The Alchian and Demsetz challenge has been criticized for pushing the ubiquitous presence of markets too far even by insiders of the TC tradition. More recently, both authors have independently accepted the existence and importance of direction in firms. Despite shortcomings, the Alchian and Demsetz scenario is valuable in that it re-emphasizes the well-known point that, from the point of view of exchange and in the purely legal sense, there is no essential difference between employers and employees, a point going back to Marx (1867). It is recognized that this equality may be constrained through the actions of one or the other party within the process of exchange (Putterman 1986), but not that agents can be unequal to start with, in their different roles in the production process, as employers and employees.

Important in Alchian and Demsetz moreover is the focus on the role of agency, ownership and teamwork. As observed below, the focus on teamwork (suitably re-interpreted) actually renders Alchian and Demsetz precursors of the resource-based perspective! In addition, the focus on shirking, monitoring, ownership and the role of a residual claimant has informed the huge literature on agency (see Jensen and Meckling 1976), property rights (see Barzel 1989) and the incomplete contracts theory of Grossman and Hart (1986) and Hart (1988) (see Foss 1993 and Holmstrom and Roberts 1998 for critical assessments and comparisons of these perspectives).

The resource/knowledge-based perspective

This perspective can be traced of the work of Adam Smith, Karl Marx and Joseph Schumpeter, among others, but arguably owes its recent motherhood to Edith Penrose's (1959) classic, *The Theory of the Growth of the Firm*. In brief, Penrose's view is that firms, seen as bundles of human and non-human resources under administrative coordination providing services, are better than markets in creating new knowledge, through teamwork and learning (learning by doing, learning by working with others, learning to learn, etc). New knowledge implies increased productivity and, *ceteris paribus*, excess resources, for use by profit-seeking entrepreneurs at zero marginal cost. This leads to endogenous growth and (through) endogenous innovations. Resources, knowledge and innovations thus generated also determine, up to a point, the direction of expansion. There is no limit to firms' size, but only to the rate of growth. This is mostly the result of management. Experienced management to plan and implement expansion is always required, but not available in the market. Therefore the availability and quality of management constrains at any point in time the rate of growth. Differential resources, thus services, knowledge, innovations and capabilities, and attempts to remove constraints to growth can help explain firm

strategies; firms are better at doing some things than markets.

It is beyond the scope of this subsection to discuss these issues further. Suffice it to note that the resource-based theory is currently the main contender to TCE (for example, see Foss 1993 1997).

Worth noting are the following. First, contributions to TCE already mentioned, notably Caves (1996) and Teece (1986), invoke resource/knowledge-based arguments. Second, Demsetz (1995), building on Demsetz (1988), re-interprets the Alchian and Demsetz contribution in terms of intra-firm differential productivity benefits of teamwork. This brings him very close to the resource-based camp. Third, Williamson (1999) sees merit and promise in the resource-based view, but questions its record so far and its ability regarding operationalization.

It would appear that the future should involve elements of both TCE and resource/knowledge-based theorizing.

A radical perspective

Another alternative to the TC perspective is Marglin's account of the rise of the factory. In Marglin's 'What do bosses do?' (1974), the main claim was that, in contrast to neo-classical perspectives, the rise of the factory from the putting-out system had little or nothing to do with the technical superiority of large-scale machinery. The key to the success of the factory, as well as its aspiration, was the substitution of capitalists' for workers' control of the production process: 'discipline and supervision could and did reduce costs without being technologically superior' (Marglin 1974: 46). Marglin suggested that the reason for the factory system was the desire of capitalists to increase their control over labour. Given that workers had greater autonomy under the putting-out system, it cannot be presumed that they preferred the factory system. The factory system arose for reasons of control-distribution rather than efficiency. Marglin provided historical evidence to support his views. His perspective has been applied to a number of areas, including explanations for the M-form organization and the TNC (Pitelis 1991 provides a survey).

Williamson's response to Marglin's challenge is cautious and rather surprising. He accepts that there is merit in all explanations, including ones relating to power. He then re-interprets Marglin's analysis in a way consistent with his own views and suggests that Marglin's evidence is in line with the efficiency hypothesis (or a combined efficiency-power hypothesis). He goes on to suggest, however, that the main problem with power ideas is that they are even harder to operationalize than TC ideas.

Markets as hierarchies, agency and self-interest

Additional problems with TCE relate to the fact that the perspective downplays the production side (see, for example, Pitelis 1991; Demsetz 1995). Focus on the production side is important, as in capitalist economies the very existence of employers and employees (or principals and agents) implies an inequality whereby the one accepts the other's authority. Even if one agrees with the TCE view that this is a contractual process, the inequality still implies that every employment relationship is a hierarchical one, including the putting-out system. This would suggest that, seen from the point of view of capitalist production, markets too involve hierarchy. Accordingly, what Williamson and Marglin debate is not markets versus hierarchies but rather market versus non-market hierarchies. To take this point further, in hierarchically organized capitalist societies, where the production process is controlled by a minority of the stakeholders, hierarchy is inherent and what we observe is only the evolution of hierarchical forms (for example, from putting-out to the factory system). The evolution itself is due to the principals' (employers') aim of furthering their interests, by reducing worker opportunism (according to Williamson) or by increasing labour exploitation (according to Marglin) – which amount to the same thing anyway.

These observations have two other important implications for the TCE scenario. First, they expose the need for a discussion of agency: who drives the process of change? Coase and Williamson do not address this issue and it is implicit in their accounts that both principals and agents are behind the contractual process of change in their pursuit of mutual interest. However, this is conceptually suspect and historically uninformed. Conceptually, as Coase himself has observed, it is not obvious that someone will voluntarily relinquish autonomy to someone else, even given the possibility of material gain. For Coase, one's usual preference would seem to be for being one's own master (Coase 1937). This raises the possibility of imposition by one group over another, which is not only conceptually plausible, but is also supported by historical experience (see, for example, Heilbroner 1991). It is by basing his account on extensive historical analysis that North has taken the principals (in the outline of the decline of putting-out given above, these are the merchant manufacturers or emerging capitalist class) and their pursuit of their own interests to be the driving force behind institutional change.

The second important implication flowing from the idea that the driving force behind the evolution of hierarchies is the self-interest of principals is this: once we attribute to a particular actor (the principal in this case) the attribute of being the main orchestrator of institutional change, it follows that we cannot legitimately separate the actor's objectives and the reasons for the change, as it is the former that instigates the latter. Put this in the framework of the firm and it follows that one cannot first explain the existence of the firm (for example in terms of transaction costs) and then discuss its objectives. Existence and objectives are inseparable, as it is the principal's objectives that lead to the firm's existence. It follows that the objective of the analysis becomes the examination of the factors that motivate actors. It is this that will answer the question as to the objectives of firms.

It has been claimed elsewhere (Pitelis 1991, 1998) that conceptually and historically we can explain institutional change, including the emergence and evolution of the capitalist firm, in terms of principals' attempts to further their interests by seeking maximum benefits. This involves conflict with agents (labour) and rivalry with other principals (firms). In this framework, an important consideration faced by principals is the removal of constraints to growth, which is the means of achieving maximum long-term profits under conditions of uncertainty. Such constraints are found in the product market, labour market and capital market; they can also be managerial or technological. A number of important institutional changes can be explained within this framework, including the emergence of the capitalist state.

A theory of the state

Building on work by Coase (1960), Pitelis (1991) argues that it is possible to generalize the neo-classical perspective on the state (which is based on instances of market failures, like public goods, externalities and monopoly) in terms of TC reductions. In this framework, the state internalizes the private sector (market and firms) up to the point where additional transactions can be carried out equally inexpensively by the private sector. It follows that the observed institutional mix is optimal, that is, it reduces transaction costs. This, though, can be criticized for ignoring issues of agency (principals) and thus of predation and also the issue of production costs. Applying the framework referred to above, the state has also been explained in terms of principals' efforts to enhance their systemically determined interests. Transaction costs also feature in Douglass North's work (1981). In his 'neo-classical' theory of the state North assumes a ruler who tries to maximize rents and then, subject to this happening, to reduce transaction costs. Rulers face competition by rivals, which induces them to grant privileges to powerful groups, which generates the conditions for 'capture' of the state by special interests. This explains the emergence and persistence of inefficient property rights in economic history. North goes on to observe the need to include ideology in the analysis, thus moving his perspective well away from conventional and TC-type theorizing despite his own reference to 'neo-classical'. There is insufficient space to discuss North's contribution here. Worth noting in passing are the similarities between his perspective and alternative views, including the neo-liberal focus on self-interest seeking by state functionaries and state capture, as well as alternative views that focus on self-interest-seeking principals, capture and the ideology of legitimacy. North himself points to such similarities, which goes to show how exciting economics is now becoming. This, in part at least, is due to the TC perspective.

3 Policy implications and the future

The remarkable contribution of TC theorizing is not so much what some of its proponents believe it to have been, namely the explanation of the firm and the law, as the observation that economists' previous concern with minimizing costs of production assumed as constant the costs of exchange. Once it is recognized that exchange is not costless, a legion of possible new avenues for research appear. For example, potentially beneficial trades may not take place because of excessive transaction costs. Countries may fail to develop because their structure of property rights does not facilitate exchange and thus trade and growth. Institutions other than the firm and the state can be explained by similar theorizing. Macroeconomic (market and government) failures may be explained in terms of transaction costs (Pitelis 1991). The list is endless. Indeed, the TC perspective provides the possibility of an interdisciplinary economics and even a unified social science, although one should not disregard its considerable problems.

The TC perspective has substantial implications for both public strategy on industrial competition and for the competitive and corporate strategies of firms (see Williamson 1975; Teece 1986). The policy implication of conventional industrial economics and organization has traditionally been that oligopoly and monopoly are forms of market failure; government intervention is required to curb monopoly power and increase competition, for example through strong antitrust policies. TC analysis raises doubts about this prescription. If large firms result from TC-reducing conduct, efficiency will be the result and this has to be considered by public authorities.

The TC approach is also relevant to the competitive and corporate strategies of firms. It provides firms with an account of the conditions under which they should make or buy, integrate or dis-integrate, use U- or M-form organization, license or undertake foreign direct investment. It suggests what combination of market and hierarchy (for example, networks, strategic alliances, sub-contracting, etc.) might be appropriate. This is a most exciting potential development in strategic management. The revolutionary possibilities of the TC perspective are far from exhausted.

4 Assessment

In the view of this author, TCE has been one of the two major contributions to economics this century (the other being the resource- or knowledge-based perspective). Since the mid-1970s, it has changed the way we view virtually everything in economics: markets, firms, networks, history, economic development, the whole lot. The credit is due to Ronald Coase. Coase himself acknowledges that modern TC economics owes as much to Oliver Williamson. Despite Coase's own suspicion, and extensive critiques of the concepts of asset specificity, opportunism and (bounded) rationality, and despite extensive criticisms by others, Williamson's contribution to TCE and to economics more generally is hard to overestimate. Many fundamental ideas have emerged as criticisms of TCE. Valuable syntheses have emerged and are emerging. With all limitations and criticisms, it is very hard now to imagine E without TC.

CHRISTOS PITELIS
JUDGE INSTITUTE OF MANAGEMENT STUDIES
AND QUEENS' COLLEGE, UNIVERSITY OF
CAMBRIDGE

Further reading

(References cited in the text marked *)

* Alchian, A. and Demsetz, H. (1972) 'Production, information costs and economic organization', *American Economic Review* 62 (5). (The classic statement of the view that firms are internal markets, characterized by team work and requiring monitoring of shirking, including self-monitoring of the monitor through him or her being a residual claimant.)

* Arrow, K. (1970) 'The organization of economic activity: issues pertinent to the choice of market versus non-market allocation', in R.H. Haveman and J. Margolis (eds), *Public Expenditure and Policy Analysis*, Chicago, IL: Markham. (A TC-based explanation of the organization of economic activity that also deals with the government, and which precedes Williamson's 1975 book.)

* Barzel, Y. (1989) *Economic Analysis of Property Rights*, Cambridge: Cambridge University Press. (A property rights-based approach to economic analysis, which, among others, extends Alchian and Demsetz's analysis.)

* Buckley, P.J. and Casson, M.C. (1976) *The Future of Multinational Enterprise*, London: Macmillan. (A TC-based explanation of 'internalization' of markets by TNCs, which focuses on appropriability problems of intangible assets, which appeared almost simultaneously with Williamson's 1975 book.)

* Caves, R.E. (1996) *Multinational Enterprise and Economic Analysis*, 2nd edn, Cambridge: Cambridge University Press. (Updated classic by Caves. Among others, he proposes a TCE-based theory of the TNC, and discusses evidence in its favour. His version of TCE blends well with resource-based arguments.)

* Chandler, A.D. (1962) *Strategy and Structure: Chapters in the History of American Industrial Enterprise*, Cambridge, MA: MIT Press. (The evolution of the multidivisional structure, or M-form, in major US industrial corporations from the 1920s through the 1950s.)

* Chandler, A.D. (1977) *The Visible Hand: The Managerial Revolution in American Business*, Cambridge, MA: Harvard University Press. (The rise of the vertically integrated US managerial enterprise as the foundation for the further evolution of the multidivisional structure.)

* Coase, R.H. (1937) 'The nature of the firm', *Economica* 4 (16): 386–405. (The classic statement of the firm internalizing the market due to excessive market transaction costs.)

* Coase, R.H. (1960) 'The problem of social cost', *Journal of Law and Economics* 3: 1–44. (Coase's application of his 1937 thesis to the case of law, and the first statement of what was later termed 'Coase's theorem'.)

* Coase, R.H. (1991) 'The nature of the firm: meaning' and 'The nature of the firm: influence', in O.E. Williamson and S.G. Winter (eds) *The Nature of the Firm: Origins, Evolution and Development*, Oxford: Oxford University Press.

(Coase's reflections on the history and influence of his 1937 article.)

* Coase, R.H. (1993) 'Coase on Posner on Coase', *Journal of Institutional and Theoretical Economics* 149 (1): 90–8. (Among others, why the master dislikes bounded rationality and even that he regards 'the concept of "rational utility maximization" as meaningless'.)

* Cowling, K. and Sugden, R. (1998) 'The essence of the modern corporation: markets, strategic decision-making and the theory of the firm', *The Manchester School* 66 (1) January: 59–86. (Critical assessment of TC-based arguments on the firm that focuses on the role of strategic decision making and questions distinctions between markets and firms.)

* Demsetz, H. (1988) 'The theory of the firm revisited', in *Ownership, Control and the Firm: The Organization of Economic Activity*, vol. 1, Oxford: Blackwell. (A strong general critique of the TC perspective and extensions.)

* Demsetz, H. (1995) *The Economics of the Business Firm: Seven Critical Commentaries*, Cambridge: Cambridge University Press. (Vintage Demsetz. Excellent critical comments and developments on the state of the art of the theory of the firm. An absolute must.)

* Dow, G.K. (1987) 'The function of authority in transaction cost economics', *Journal of Economic Behavior and Organization* 8: 13–38. (A powerful critique of the TCE approach's neglect of the possible hazards of authority.)

* Eggertson, T. (1990) *Economic Behaviour and Institutions*, Cambridge: Cambridge University Press. (Excellent survey of developments in TCE, with a detailed account of new perspectives.)

* Foss, N.J. (1993) 'Theories of the firm: contractual and competence perspectives', *Journal of Evolutionary Economics* 3 (2): 127–44. (One of the best critical assessments of TCE and the resource-/knowledge-based perspective.)

* Foss, N.J. (ed.) (1997) *Resources, Firms and Strategies*, Oxford Management Readers, Oxford: Oxford University Press. (Very useful reader on the resource-based perspective.)

* Fransman, M. (1994) 'Information, knowledge, vision and theories of the firm', *Industrial and Corporate Change* 3 (3): 713–57. (Critique of treatment of knowledge in neo-classical and TC theorizing, and examination of alternative treatments, such as the Penrosean, resource-based one.)

* Grossman, S. and Hart, O. (1986) 'The costs and benefits of ownership: a theory of lateral and vertical integration', *Journal of Political Economy* 94: 691–719. (Important treatment of the role of ownership on integration, in an incomplete (nexus of) contracts framework.)

* Hallwood, C.P. (1994) 'An observation on the transaction cost theory of the (multinational) firm', *Journal of Institutional and Theoretical Economics* 150 (2): 351–61. (Critique of the of TCE approach to TNCs, in terms of its alleged failure to deal with imperfections in final markets.)

* Hart, O. (1988) 'Incomplete contracts and the theory of the firm', *Journal of Law, Economics and Organisation* 4 (1): 119–40. (Incomplete contracts-based approach to the firm that does not presuppose markets.)

* Heilbroner, R. (1991) *The Worldly Philosophers*, 6th edn, London: Penguin Books. (Classic treatment of the worldly philosophers with, among others, refreshing insight on real markets in history.)

* Hennart, J.-F. (2000) 'Transaction costs theory and the multinational enterprise', in C. Pitelis and R. Sugden (eds), *The Nature of the Transnational Firm*, 2nd edn, London: Routledge. (An employment contract-based theory of the TNC that builds on Coase, with elements of differential capabilities.)

* Holmstrom, B. and Roberts, J. (1998) 'The boundaries of the firm revisited', *Journal of Economic Perspectives* 12 (4) Fall: 73–94. (Critical observations and comparison of TC and incomplete contracts perspectives.)

Holmstrom, B. and Tirole, J. (1989) 'The theory of the firm', in R. Schmalensee and R.D. Willig (eds) *Handbook of Industrial Organisation*, vol. 3, Amsterdam: North-Holland. (Extensive critical survey of transaction costs and other theories of the firm.)

* Jensen, M.C. and Meckling, W. (1976) 'Theory of the firm: managerial behaviour, agency costs and ownership structure', *Journal of Financial Economics* 3: 304–60. (Classic treatment of agency, building on, and extending, Alchian and Demsetz.)

* Kay, N. (1992) 'Markets, false hierarchies and the evolution of the modern corporation', *Journal of Economic Behavior and Organization* 17: 315–33. (Criticisms of Williamson's reliance on asset specificity and of the new institutionalists' reliance on evolutionary process arguments, with particular emphasis on the U-form versus M-form debate.)

* Kay, N.M. (1997) *Pattern in Corporate Evolution*, Oxford: Oxford University Press. (Linkages-based theory of corporate evolution, with resource/knowledge-based focus and new insights.)

* Knight, F. (1921) *Risk, Uncertainty and Profit*, New York: Houghton Mills. (Knight's 1921 classic, on, among others, why firms exist, as well as his famous distinction between risk and uncertainty.)

* Kogut, B. and Zander, U. (1993) 'Knowledge of the firm and the evolutionary theory of the multinational corporation', *Journal of International Business Studies*, 4th quarter: 625–45. (Tacit knowledge-based theory of differential abilities by TNCs, critical to TCE and closely linked (albeit not referring) to Penrose's approach.)

* Landes, D.S. (ed.) (1966) *The Rise of Capitalism*, New York: Macmillan. (A very important source of historical insights on the rise of capitalism.)

* Langlois, N.R. (1992) 'Transaction costs economics in real time', *Industrial and Corporate Change* 1 (1): 99–127. (Critical assessment and extension of TC analysis, focusing on dynamic transaction costs, in real time.)

* Lazonick, W. (1991) *Business Organization and the Myth of the Market Economy*, Cambridge: Cambridge University Press. (Discussion of the 'innovative firm' and important critique of TC-based arguments.)

* Malcolmson, J. (1984) 'Efficient labour organisation: incentives, power and the transaction costs approach', in F. Stephen (ed.), *Firm Organizations and Labour*, London: Macmillan. (An expression of the powerful view that TC economizing could lead to increased market power.)

* Marglin, S. (1974) 'What do bosses do? The origins and functions of hierarchy in capitalist production', *Review of Radical Political Economics* 6: 60–112. (The classic statement of the view that the factory system served the interest of the capitalist by increasing control over labour.)

* Marris, R. (1999) 'Edith Penrose and economics', *Contributions to Political Economy* 18: 47–66. (Marris suggests that TCE fails to determine the size of the firm, while Penrose fails to determine the rate of growth. He suggests a way out.)

* Marx, K. (1867) *Capital*, vol. 1, London: Lawrence & Wishart, 1954. (Among others, distinguishes between firms and markets and presents the view that competition and monopoly are not polar opposites and that the one can lead to the other.)

* Nelson, R.R. and Winter, S.G. (1982) *An Evolutionary Theory of Economic Change*, Cambridge, MA: Harvard University Press. (Classic analysis of organizations in terms of evolutionary metaphors, including the introduction of the concept of 'routines'.)

* North, D.C. (1981) *Structure and Change in Economic History*, London and New York: W.W. Norton & Co. Inc. (North's classic application of his version of TCE to economic history.)

* Penrose, E.T. (1959) *The Theory of the Growth of the Firm*, Oxford: Oxford University Press; 3rd edn, 1995. (Penrose's classic resource/knowledge-based theory of the firm's endogenous growth, innovations, limits to growth, firms' evolution, monopoly and competition, and much more.)

* Pitelis, C.N. (1991) *Market and Non-market Hierarchies*, Oxford: Blackwell. (A critique and extension of the Coasean perspective to the theory of the state and macroeconomics.)

Pitelis, C.N. (ed.) (1993) *Transaction Costs, Markets and Hierarchies*, Oxford: Blackwell. (A useful set of critical readings on the TC perspective.)

* Pitelis, C.N. (1998) 'Transaction cost economics and the historical evolution of the capitalist firm', *Journal of Economic Issues* XXXII (December): 999–1017. (Critique of TCE in terms of, among others, history-based considerations and links with resource-based perspectives.)

* Pitelis, C.N. and Sugden, R. (eds) (2000) *The Nature of the Transnational Firm*, 2nd edn, London: Routledge. (Useful set of readings on the theory of the TNC, with critical assessment and extensions of TC-based theories.)

* Putterman, L. (1986) *The Economic Nature of the Firm: A Reader*, Cambridge: Cambridge University Press. (A very useful selection of readings, including many classic pieces.)

* Richardson, G. (1972) 'The organisation of industry', *Economic Journal* 82: 883–96. (All-time classic on why and when market, hierarchy and, importantly, cooperation.)

* Schumpeter, J. (1942) *Capitalism, Socialism and Democracy*, London: Unwin Hyman; 5th edn, 1987. (Another all-time classic; competition is a dynamic process of creative destruction through innovations that lead to ephemeral monopoly; and much more.)

Shelanski, H.A. and Klein, P.G. (1995) 'Empirical research in transaction cost economics: a review and assessment', *Journal of Law, Economics and Organisation* 11 (2) October: 335–61. (Extensive coverage of evidence on transaction costs, in support of the perspective.)

* Simon, H.A. (1991) 'Organizations and markets', *Journal of Economic Perspectives* 5 (2) Spring: 25–44. (On the prevalence and importance of organizations *vis-à-vis* markets, with a critical assessment of TCE.)

* Teece, D.J. (1986) 'Transaction costs economics and the multinational enterprise: an assessment', *Journal of Economic Behavior and Organization* 7: 21–45. (TC-based explanation of the TNC with some resource-based insights.)

* Williamson, O.E. (1975) *Markets and Hierarchies*, New York: The Free Press. (The original attempt to re-introduce the Coasean perspective, by one of its major proponents.)

* Williamson, O.E. (1981) 'The modern corporation: origins, evolution, attributes', *Journal of Economic Literature* 19 (4): 1537–68. (A very useful summary of Williamson's main ideas by himself.)

Williamson, O.E. (1986) *Economic Organisation: Firms, Markets and Policy Control*, Hemel Hempstead: Harvester Wheatsheaf. (A very useful selection of essays by Williamson on the topics mentioned in the title.)

* Williamson, O. E. (1993) 'Opportunism and its critics', *Managerial and Decision Economics* 14: 97–107. (Why opportunism matters for the (TC-based) theory of the firm, and critique to critics.)

* Williamson, O.E. (1999) 'strategy research: governance and competence perspectives', *Strategic Management Journal* 20: 1087–108. (Critical assessment of competence-based theory from a TC-based perspective; comparison and points for future developments.)

See also: BUSINESS ECONOMICS; CHANDLER, A.; COASE, R.; CORPORATE CONTROL; DYNAMIC CAPABILITIES; GROWTH OF THE FIRM AND NETWORKING; INDUSTRIAL REVOLUTION; INSTITUTIONAL ECONOMICS; LABOUR MARKETS; MANAGERIAL THEORIES OF THE FIRM; MARSHALL, A.; MULTINATIONAL CORPORATIONS; NEO-CLASSICAL ECONOMICS; ORGANIZATION STRUCTURE; TRADE UNIONS; WILLIAMSON, O.E.

Transfer pricing

Overview

Many intra-firm transactions are non-market transactions and therefore lack a market determined price. A transfer price is the price assigned to such non-market intra-firm transfers. Transfer prices are especially important for multinational corporations since a parent company typically has subsidiaries or branches in other countries and transfers are often made between the component parts of the multinational.

As the world has become more internationally dependent, these transactions and the associated transfer prices have come under increased scrutiny. The fear often expressed by governments is that a multinational corporation may manipulate transfer prices in order to transfer profits from one country to another and thereby affect various government policies. Most notably, transfer prices can affect the tax revenues of both the home and host country.

After a brief description of international tax systems that is necessary to understand transfer pricing incentives, transfer price manipulation is discussed with respect to three broad areas: the taxation of outbound investment, the taxation of inbound investment, and non-tax factors. The empirical evidence relating to the extent of transfer price manipulation for these three broad areas is summarized. The inter-relationship between transfer pricing and tax competition is then discussed.

A general international consensus is that the appropriate transfer price is the 'arm's length' price. This is the price that would be charged by two unrelated parties. However, it is often difficult to find such a comparable transaction. Practical solutions to this problem are offered at the end of the article.

1 Introduction

Modern corporations are often organized as a set of separate entities (see MULTINATIONAL CORPORATIONS). A typical organization might involve a parent corporation and a set of subsidiaries. The parent is typically the major stockholder in its subsidiaries, often controlling 100 per cent of a subsidiary's stock. Various transactions may occur between the parent and its subsidiaries. For instance, a subsidiary may provide an input that is used in the parent's production process or the parent may provide a trademark or technical advice to a subsidiary. The price attached to these intra-firm transactions is referred to as the transfer price.

While transfer pricing occurs (implicitly or explicitly) with any intra-firm transfer, the feature that has made transfer pricing so important and controversial is its use in a multinational corporation. The transactions between a multinational corporation's parent and its foreign subsidiaries cross international boundaries and this raises a host of important issues. For instance, suppose that the parent is located in a high-tax country while the subsidiary is located in a low-tax country. Assuming that the multinational is trying to minimize its total tax payments, the multinational will try to price transfers so that most of its profits appear in the low-tax country. For example, if the subsidiary is providing the parent with an input, there is an incentive to charge a very high price for the input. Since this will result in high revenue in the low-tax country and high costs in the high-tax country, the effect will be to transfer profits from the high-tax to the low-tax country. The multinational's taxes will be lower and its after-tax profits higher than would otherwise be the case. This example illustrates the central role that transfer pricing plays both for governments and for multinational firms.

2 Theoretical context

International tax systems

The primary reason that governments have been interested in the transfer pricing practices of multinationals has been in relation to taxes. To understand the role that transfer pricing plays in minimizing worldwide taxes, one must have at least a rudimentary understanding of the taxation of multinational corporations (see GLOBALIZATION). All countries claim the right to tax income generated within their borders. Since the income of a multinational is generated in more than one country, there is the further question of whether income generated outside of the home country's borders is considered taxable. In principle, two systems have been developed: the territorial (source) system of taxation and the worldwide (residence) system. The former exempts income earned outside of a country's borders while the latter taxes it. Since the worldwide system taxes income earned abroad twice (once by the foreign country and again by the home country), a credit is usually given for taxes paid to foreign countries. To avoid giving refunds for high foreign taxes, the credit is limited to tax that would have been paid had the income been earned in the home country.

While countries generally do not adhere strictly to one system or the other, it is useful to list the system used by some major countries, since this will influence the transfer pricing incentives. Foreign source dividend income is treated on a worldwide basis by the USA, the UK, Turkey, Spain, Portugal, Norway, New Zealand, Japan, Italy, Ireland, Iceland and Greece. These countries use one of two methods to determine credit for foreign taxes. One method treats income in each foreign country separately in determining the credit. The second method determines the credit on a worldwide basis; that is, tax paid to all foreign countries is added together and credit is given as long as the weighted average is less than the home country tax. Of the countries listed, the USA, Japan, and Iceland provide credit on a worldwide basis; the others use a per country limit in determining the foreign tax credit. Other countries of the OECD treat foreign source dividend income on a territorial basis; that is, it is exempted from home country tax. Foreign source interest income is generally treated on a residence basis.

Transfer pricing and the taxation of outbound investment

Transfer pricing can be used to reduce taxes for either the territorial or the worldwide tax system. The simplest cases can be illustrated for a multinational that has foreign profits generated in a single foreign country as well as profits generated at home. Abuses under the territorial system are perhaps the most obvious: taxes can be reduced by transferring profits out of the high-tax country and into the low-tax country.

A purported advantage of the worldwide system is that this incentive disappears for a multinational that invests in a single foreign country with a tax rate lower than the home country. In this case, income derived from the foreign investment will be taxed at the home country tax rate and the incentive to shift income is eliminated. This is called capital-export neutrality.

However, several complications of the tax systems of countries that purport to use the worldwide system of taxation make it so that multinationals can use transfer pricing to reduce taxes. First, consider a multinational that invests in a single high-tax country. (In the tax jargon, such a firm would be in 'excess credits'.) Some of the foreign tax will not be credited since the credit for foreign taxes is limited; hence, taxes can again be reduced by using transfer prices to shift profits to the home country. Second, since multinationals typically have investments in a variety of foreign countries, the way in which the credit is computed is important. As mentioned above, the USA, Japan and Iceland aggregate income over all foreign countries in determining the limit. Hence, for these countries, a multinational with a large proportion of income coming from investments in high-tax countries and a small proportion of income coming from investments in low-tax foreign countries will not obtain full credit for foreign taxes paid. This firm would then have an incentive to use transfer prices to shift income from high-tax to low-tax foreign countries and thereby obtain credit for all foreign taxes paid. Third, the USA defers home country tax on income earned by multinationals in foreign countries until that income is repatriated. This is called 'deferral' and effectively converts a worldwide tax system into a territorial system. Although Subpart F provisions in the USA have limited deferral, the transfer pricing problems associated with territorial tax systems become relevant when a worldwide system incorporates deferral.

Transfer pricing and the taxation of inbound investment

Transfer pricing incentives as discussed thus far have centred on home country corporations that invest abroad (i.e. outbound investment). However transfer pricing may also be used by foreign corporations operating in the home country (i.e. inbound investment) to transfer profits out and so avoid home country taxes. This second issue has become important, especially in the USA, because the aggregate rate of return for foreign-controlled companies in the USA is observed to be much lower than the rate of return of domestically controlled companies. A concern expressed by the US Congress is that foreign-controlled US corporations are not paying US tax; the suggested culprit is transfer pricing.

There are, however, several reasons other than transfer pricing that might explain low rates of return of foreign-controlled companies operating in a home country. First, foreign companies may at first experience a lower than average rate of return because of the revaluation of the value of existing assets for tax purposes for new acquisitions or because of the start-up costs of a new business. Second, a low average rate of return in any one year may not be indicative of a long-run trend. That is, although foreign companies may have difficulty in adjusting to the nuances of a foreign market at first, one would expect this to change over time as the firms mature. Moreover, unexpected changes in exchange rates

can have a large effect on profits. An unexpected fall in the dollar, for instance, would increase the cost of components imported into the USA and therefore temporarily decrease the profits of a foreign-controlled company in the USA. This effect also would be expected to diminish over time.

Non-tax factors

The tax related effects of transfer pricing are important and have received a great deal of attention. However, several non-tax factors deserve mention as well. The most important non-tax factors include a parent company's perceived need to exert control over the operations of its subsidiaries, money laundering, and diversification of political and foreign exchange risks. Consider first the need of a multinational to exert central control over the firm's operations. Much of the accounting literature emphasizes the need for central control in order to maximize profits for the entire firm. The idea is that an intra-firm transfer by definition entails some monopoly or monopsony power. In such an environment, an uncontrolled transfer price will be set to maximize the profit of a division of a corporation, but this will hurt the overall profit of the corporation.

A second non-tax factor involves political and foreign exchange risk. To the extent that such risks vary over time and can be predicted, transfer pricing can be used to transfer profits out of politically unstable regions or out of currencies that are expected to fall in value relative to the home currency. Finally, profits from illegal activities can be transferred in a covert way by inflating the profits of a legitimate business transaction.

3 Empirical evidence

The evidence on the extent of transfer pricing suggests that transfer pricing is quantitatively important. Outbound investment by US multinationals has been investigated by Harris *et al.* (1993), who use Compustat data to investigate whether taxes paid to the USA are influenced by the location of the multinational's profits overseas. Since the USA taxes multinationals based on a worldwide system and computes the foreign tax credit by aggregating on a worldwide basis, the multinational can get credit for income tax paid in a country with a tax rate higher than the US rate. Further, judicious use of transfer pricing can shift income from a high-tax to a low-tax location so as to avoid hitting the limit. Harris *et al.* find that a multinational that has a subsidiary in a low(high)-tax country has a lower (higher) than average ratio of US tax to US assets. This is consistent with the use of transfer pricing to minimize worldwide taxes, although they find that the aggregate effect on US tax revenues is moderate.

Hines and Rice (1994) investigate transfer pricing of outbound investment by concentrating on the use of 'tax havens' (a set of very low-tax foreign countries) by US multinationals. They find that reported profit rates are sensitive to local tax rates, although they note that this may not be bad for US revenue. A US multinational whose foreign source income comes primarily from a high-tax country will not be subject to additional US tax. If, however, the multinational is able to shift income so that its foreign source income appears to come primarily from a low-tax country, the US will gain tax revenue equal to the difference between taxes paid and what would be paid in the USA.

Inbound investment in the USA is investigated by Grubert *et al.* (1993). They use data from the tax returns of US corporations to investigate the difference in taxes paid by foreign-controlled as opposed to US-controlled corporations. The aggregate data suggest a much lower ratio of taxable income to assets for foreign-controlled corporations. However, the authors find that the revaluation of assets after merger or acquisition, exchange rate changes, and a maturation effect account for about half of the difference. The remaining difference could be due to transfer pricing, and the authors present some evidence that indicates that foreign-controlled companies tend to be more concentrated and persist longer at zero taxable income. This indicates that transfer pricing is used to some extent to reduce taxes, although less than might at first be feared.

Pak and Zdanowicz (1994) compare the implied prices of products from international transactions using data from the US Commerce Department. The data set is very disaggregated in terms of individual transactions and the implied prices offer some striking examples of prices that deviate from the norm. The implied prices are probably best interpreted as resulting from all forms of illegal pricing activity, including money laundering.

4 Tax competition and transfer pricing

Transfer pricing presents a problem for tax authorities when the taxes paid by a corporation differ according to the country from which it derives revenue. It is the difference in taxes that gives rise to incentives to shift income from a high-tax to a low-tax country. Why do taxes differ between countries and what impact do these differences have on transfer pricing incentives?

Certainly there are many reasons for taxes to differ between countries. One country may simply prefer to provide more public services and hence will need to collect more in taxes. A country may also use its tax system to stimulate investment by, for instance, lowering corporate tax rates. This topic has generated much debate of late. The OECD is compiling a list of countries that engage in 'harmful' tax competition (Weiner and Ault 1998). Ireland has for many years created much controversy in the EU with its low 10 per cent tax rate for certain manufacturing firms that invest in Ireland. Although Ireland has agreed to repeal this special tax break, it is being replaced by a low 12.5 per cent corporate tax rate.

A long literature that studies fiscal structure in a federation addresses many of the conceptual issues since it inherently involves the taxation of resources that are mobile (Goodspeed 1998). Part of this literature discusses tax competition, which is usually thought to occur when the tax system of one government affects the tax system of a second government, usually through an effect on the second government's tax revenues. This literature shows that tax competition can be efficient or inefficient, depending on whether taxes paid reflect the benefits of public services received.

There is little empirical work that attempts to assess the impact of tax competition, possibly because of empirical difficulties. (For an exception, see Goodspeed 2000.) For instance, although there are many aspects to the controversy involving Ireland and other EU countries, one difficulty in assessing the various arguments is that many governmental policies are at work simultaneously. For instance, although the EU complains about a low Irish tax rate, they also attempt to stimulate investment in Ireland through the EU grant system. In addition, any investment incentive created by a low Irish tax rate would be offset if the parent multinational were from a worldwide taxation country and that country taxed the residual. Yet many Irish tax treaties with EU countries contain tax sparing agreements which exempt the difference between the standard and tax holiday rates. Exemption countries also implicitly allow the incentive to stand since they exempt foreign source income from tax. In either case, the possible avenue for transfer pricing abuse is created, though it is not clear whether the fault lies with Ireland or with the other countries that implicitly allow tax differences through their own tax system.

In addition, the interconnection of transfer pricing and tax competition are rarely discussed. One exception is the work of Elitzur and Mintz (1996), who study a model of a multinational that is present in two countries. They find that a country that raises its tax rate will lower revenues in each country as the multinational lowers production in both countries. The model does not consider capital flows between countries, however.

5 Practical solutions to the transfer pricing problem

Transfer pricing may theoretically be used to evade taxes. Some rules must therefore be set by governments to control tax evasion. A generally accepted international standard is 'arm's length pricing'. The basic notion is that a transaction between a parent and its subsidiary should be priced as if it had occurred between two unrelated parties in a competitive market. Transfer prices that correspond to this are not always easy to calculate, however, since there may not exist comparable transactions by unrelated parties. Indeed, many

legitimate reasons for transfer pricing such as royalties from a brand name result because of the inherent existence of monopoly power that generates economic rents. The correct transfer price in this case would not be that of a competitive market. Still, governments must provide some guidance as to what is acceptable.

Specific international standards for transfer pricing rules that try to approximate arm's length transfer prices have recently been proposed by the OECD (1995). Specific rules that are acceptable to a country's taxing authority generally vary from country to country. While directly comparable transactions by unrelated parties are often preferred, no comparable transactions between unrelated parties are observable for many transactions that involve transfer prices. The rules therefore try to set some bounds on transfer prices. Generally, an attempt is made to approximate unrelated party transactions by reference to some industry average such as a rate of return on assets or a margin on sales. The methodology used to determine the proper transfer price has become increasingly sophisticated. Frisch (1989) and Witte and Chipty (1990) suggest the use of the capital asset pricing model to determine a proper return for a project. Horst (1993) suggests using regression analysis to determine an appropriate rate of return.

Some new issues emerged in the 1990s. Two of these are the taxation of global trading of financial instruments and certain cost-sharing agreements known as 'buy-ins'.

Many of the issues involved in the taxation of global trading of financial instruments have been discussed by the OECD (1998) and Alworth (1998). Technological change and the use of derivatives have resulted in financial firms organizing their activities on a global 24-hour basis. Questions arise as to the source country for income and expenses related to these activities. The OECD suggests that these activities can be dealt with using current arm's length rules or other currently used methods such as a profit split, or perhaps sourcing based on bonuses paid to employees. Alworth (1998) is less sanguine, and suggests that it would be desirable for large businesses to be taxed on accrual of gains and losses, although the record keeping necessary for this approach makes it difficult for individual taxpayers. In any case, exchange of information is likely to prove to be important in enforcing residence tax systems in this area as in others in the information age.

A technical issue that emerged in the 1990s involves 'buy-ins'. A buy-in is a payment for pre-existing intangible assets. New technology-related companies have used buy-ins to allocate the development costs of an intangible asset in a joint development project involving a parent and a subsidiary (usually located in a low-tax country). Costs are normally allocated according to anticipated benefits of the project, but it is the fact that anticipated benefits are unknown that creates the controversy. Morgan (1999) argues that the arm's length price for the buy-in can be approximated by the subsidiary's cost of capital, while corporations argue that the buy-in payment should be much lower, effectively increasing the amount of income in the low-tax subsidiary.

6 Conclusion

Intra-firm transactions are common in large corporations. The price attached to such non-market transactions is called the transfer price. Transfer prices are particularly important for a multinational corporation since such a firm's transactions typically cross international borders. As the world has become increasingly interdependent, such transactions have become more commonplace, and have come under a great deal of scrutiny. Of primary concern to governments has been the tax consequences of transfer prices. A multinational corporation may be able to use transfer prices to transfer revenue to low-tax subsidiaries and costs to high-tax subsidiaries and thereby transfer profits from high- to low-tax countries. The empirical evidence indicates that multinationals are able to successfully reduce their worldwide taxes to some extent. To control these possible abuses, a generally accepted international practice is to use the arm's length method, which attempts to price a transaction as if it had occurred between two unrelated parties.

TIMOTHY J. GOODSPEED
HUNTER COLLEGE

Further reading

(References cited in the text marked *)

* Alworth, Julian S. (1998) 'Taxation and integrated financial markets: the challenges of derivatives and other financial innovations', *International Tax and Public Finance* 5: 507–34. (Contains a detailed discussion of the consequences of taxing various types of financial instruments.)

Dunning, John H. (1993) *Multinational Enterprises and the Global Economy*, New York: Addison-Wesley. (Chapter 18 provides a comprehensive and non-technical review of (especially non-tax) factors affecting a firm's transfer pricing decision.)

* Elitzur, Ramy and Jack Mintz (1996) 'Transfer pricing rules and corporate tax competition', *Journal of Public Economics* 60 (3): 401–22. (Develops a model that illustrates certain sorts of interactions between transfer pricing and tax competition.)

* Frisch, Daniel J. (1989) 'The BALRM approach to transfer pricing', *National Tax Journal* 261–71. (A discussion of how BALRM (the basic arm's length return method) can be interpreted in terms of the capital asset pricing model, a foundation of modern finance.)

Giovannini, Alberto, R. Glenn Hubbard and Joel Slemrod. (eds) (1993) *Studies in International Taxation*, Chicago: University of Chicago Press. (Provides several empirical studies on the effect of transfer pricing including the chapters by Harris, Morck, Slemrod, and Yeung and Grubert, Goodspeed, and Swenson mentioned in the text.)

* Goodspeed, Timothy J. (1998) 'Tax competition, benefit taxes, and fiscal federalism', *National Tax Journal* 60 (3): 579–86. (Discusses the issues involved in tax competition from the perspective of the fiscal federalism literature and the difficulties in empirically estimating the effect of tax competition.)

* Goodspeed, Timothy J. (2000) 'Tax structure in a federation', *Journal of Public Economics* 75 (3): 493–506. (An empirical examination of tax competition in a federation.)

* Grubert, Harry, Timothy J. Goodspeed and Deborah Swenson. (1993) 'Explaining the low taxable income of foreign-controlled companies in the United States', in Alberto Giovannini, R. Glenn Hubbard and Joel Slemrod (eds) *Studies in International Taxation*, University of Chicago Press, ch. 7: 237–70. (Empirical study of inbound transfer pricing for the USA; explains about half of the difference in returns between US and foreign

controlled companies by reasons other than transfer pricing.)

Grubert, Harry and John Mutti (1991) 'Taxes, tariffs, and transfer pricing in multinational corporate decision making', *Review of Economics and Statistics* 68: 285–93. (An empirical study of transfer pricing on outbound transactions that finds support for the tax minimizing hypothesis.)

* Harris, David, Randall Morck, Joel Slemrod and Bernard Yeung (1993) 'Income shifting in U.S. multinational corporations', in Alberto Giovannini, R. Glenn Hubbard and Joel Slemrod (eds) *Studies in International Taxation*, University of Chicago Press, ch. 8: 277–302. (Empirical study of transfer pricing for outbound investment that finds support for tax minimizing behaviour, although the magnitude is not large.)

* Hines, James R., Jr. and Eric M. Rice (1994) 'Fiscal paradise: foreign tax havens and American business', *Quarterly Journal of Economics* 149–82. (An empirical study of transfer pricing activities of US multinationals in very low-tax countries (tax havens).)

* Horst, Thomas (1993) 'The comparable profits method', *Tax Notes International* 14 June: 1443–58. (A discussion of the rules suggested by the Internal Revenue Service of the USA for dealing with transfer pricing and some practical problems with those rules.)

Lowell, C.H., M. Burge and P.L. Briger (1994) *US International Transfer Pricing*, Boston, MA: Warren, Gorham and Lamont. (A complete guide for the practitioner, including regulations, methodology, penalties, treaties and rules for several foreign countries.)

* Morgan, R. William (1999) 'Buy-in payments and market valuations', *Tax Management Transfer Pricing Report* 8 (10): 449–54. (Discussion of the issues and controversy surrounding buy-in payments.)

OECD (1991) *Taxing Profits in a Global Economy*, Paris: OECD. (A large study that calculates effective tax rates for the OECD countries; of interest here is the description of the international tax systems of member countries.)

* OECD (1995) *Transfer Pricing Guidelines for Multinational Enterprises and Tax Administrations*, Paris: OECD. (Guidelines that confirm the commitment of the OECD to arm's length pricing.)

* OECD (1998) *The Taxation of Global Trading of Financial Instruments*, Paris: OECD. (Description and discussion of the issues raised by global trading of financial instruments.)

* Pak, Simon and John Zdanowicz (1994) 'A statistical analysis of the U.S. merchandise trade data base and its uses in transfer pricing compliance and enforcement', *in Tax Management Transfer Pricing Report*, 11 May: 50–7. (Empirical tabulations using reported data of actual transactions that show some large discrepancies between certain products and their normal price.)

Rugman, A.M. and L. Eden (eds) (1985) *Multinationals and Transfer Pricing*, London: Croom Helm. (A discussion of many of the non-tax issues in transfer pricing.)

* Weiner, Joann M. and Hugh J. Ault (1998) 'The OECD's report on harmful tax competition', *National Tax Journal* 60 (3): 601–8. (A discussion of the OECD's report on harmful tax competition.)

* Witte, Ann and Tasneem Chipty (1990) 'Some thoughts on transfer pricing', *Tax Notes* 26 November: 1009–24. (Develops some issues in transfer pricing, including use of the capital asset pricing model employed in finance.)

See also: ECONOMIC INTEGRATION, INTERNATIONAL; GLOBALIZATION; GROWTH OF THE FIRM AND NETWORKING; INTERNATIONAL MONETARY FUND; MULTINATIONAL CORPORATIONS; WORLD BANK; WORLD TRADE ORGANIZATION

Transnational corporations: see MULTINATIONAL CORPORATIONS

Treasury management: see CREDIT MANAGEMENT; INTEREST RATE RISK; FOREIGN EXCHANGE RISK, MANAGEMENT OF

Trist, Eric Lansdown (1909–93)

1 Introduction
2 Main contribution
3 Evaluation
4 Conclusion

Personal background

- born 11 September 1909, Dover, England, into a maritime family
- educated at Dover County Boys' School and Pembroke College, Cambridge; took a First in English and in the Moral Sciences Tripos (1928–33)
- married Virginia Traylor (1900–60) in New York, 1935, while a Commonwealth Scholar at Yale University (1934–5); married Beulah Joyce Varney in London, 1959
- developed the sociotechnical approach to work design, the 'search conference', and the concepts of the turbulent environment and the social ecology of organizations
- died in Carmel, California, 4 June 1993

Major works

Exploration in Group Relations (with C. Sofer) (1959)
Organisational Choice: Capabilities of Groups at the Coal Face under Changing Technologies: The Loss, Rediscovery and Transformation of the Work Tradition
(with G.W. Higgin, H. Murray and A.B. Pollock) (1963)
'The causal texture of organisational environments' (with F.E. Emery) (1965)
Towards a Social Ecology: Contextual Appreciations of the Future and the Present (with F.E. Emery) (1973)

Summary

Trist based his work as a management scholar on social science research. During the Second World War he designed War Office Selection Board procedures for officer selection and established Civil Resettlement Units for returning prisoners of war. He founded and later directed the Tavistock Institute of Human Relations, and studied work organization in British coal mines using a sociotechnical approach to work design, an alternative to traditional management. With his Australian colleague Fred E. Emery, Trist devised the 'search conference', a management tool for long-range planning; together they also presented a theory of organizational settings, among which was the 'turbulent' environment. In the USA and Canada, Trist developed his study of social ecology.

1 Introduction

Eric Trist's father was a master mariner and his mother was a Scot with a deep interest in education. Trist was educated in Dover at St Martin's School and the Dover County Boys' School. He won a scholarship to Cambridge, where I.A. Richards introduced him to humanistic psychology and Trist learned the social psychology of Kurt Lewin (see LEWIN, K.). A brilliant student, Trist graduated with a distinction, and in 1934–5 he studied at Yale under Edward Sapir (1864–1939) on a fellowship with the Commonwealth Fund. On returning to the UK, he and his wife researched the impact of structural unemployment in Dundee, Scotland, and for a year afterwards he headed the St Andrews University Department of Psychology.

In the Second World War, Trist worked at the Maudsley Psychiatric Hospital, studying the psychological effects of head injuries and the anxieties of those who suffered in the London blitz. He joined the army group of psychiatrists from the Tavistock Clinic and helped devise the experimental War Office Selection Boards, which selected officers for the army. Later, Trist contributed to the Civil Resettlement Unit scheme for prisoners of war. This involved the establishment of therapeutic communities with a radically different organization from the army. His experience in these army projects taught Trist that he could create social systems quite unlike those he had worked in before (Trist and Murray 1990).

With funds from the Rockefeller Foundation, Trist and his associates from the army established the Tavistock Institute of Human Relations in 1946 (see HUMAN RELATIONS). Trist went into psychoanalytic training so that he could work in groups and organizations with the detachment that clinicians normally have with patients. His aim was to use social psychological knowledge to resolve the problems in industry that faced the British government after the war. The Tavistock Institute secured government funds for one industrial project at the Glacier Metal Company, another to train young people in industrial fieldwork and a third to study groups of miners; this last would later bring Trist to the attention of organization theorists (Trist and Murray 1990). Trist also helped establish the journal *Human Relations*, because there was no British journal that would publish interdisciplinary social science. In 1951, Foundation funding ceased, so Institute members went directly to industry for support. Most of their work at this time centred on selection of executives (for which the experience with War Office Selection Boards was invaluable), studies in organizational change and consumer research.

In 1960–1, while Trist was a Fellow at the Center for Advanced Studies in the Behavioral Sciences in Palo Alto, he co-wrote *Organisational Choice* (Trist *et al.* 1963). He was later invited to lead experiential groups at Bethal. In 1965, Trist, with Fred Emery (1925–97), made a breakthrough in socio-organizational ecology in the famous paper 'The causal texture of organisational environments'. Trist joined the University of California at Los Angeles in 1966 as a professor of organizational behaviour and social ecology, and in 1969 he joined the faculty of the Wharton School at the University of Pennsylvania.

In Pennsylvania, Trist undertook a study of coal mines and the community of Rushton, and later did similar research in northwestern New York State – the Jamestown project (Trist and Murray 1993). Both were innovative programmes in industrial cooperation. In 1971, Emery joined Trist at Wharton, where the two drew their work together in *Towards a Social Ecology: Contextual Appreciations of the Future and the Present* (1973).

After supervising much postgraduate research, Trist retired from the Wharton School in 1978 and joined the Faculty of Environmental Studies at York University, Ontario, to teach organizational behaviour and social ecology. He consulted for Labor Canada, for projects concerned with the quality of working life and for community studies, and also introduced search conferences in Alberta. Trist's last efforts were directed to the publication of the three-volume *Tavistock Anthology* (Trist and Murray 1990, 1993; Trist, Emery and Murray 1997).

2 Main contribution

Trist's first contribution was as a psychologist on War Office Selection Boards. With the Directorate of Army Psychiatry, Trist studied morale among officer cadet training units, designed a psychological technique for selecting candidates and later advised on ensuing problems. His second contribution was to help establish Civil Resettlement Units for returning prisoners of war and others distressed by the return to civilian life. For this he developed the concepts of 'social reconnection' and 'de-socialization', and showed that therapeutic communities could be developed within the military authority structure. In both contributions, Trist used Wilfred Bion's ideas on group processes and followed Kurt Lewin's action research principles (Trist and Murray 1990).

Trist's next contributions were to British industry. These centred on the Glacier Metal project with Elliott Jaques, which showed how psychoanalytic ideas may be used to clarify conflicts at work, and on the coal projects with Ken Bamforth, which illustrated the productive value of semi-autonomous work groups (Trist *et al.* 1963) (see OCCUPATIONAL PSYCHOLOGY; ORGANIZATION BEHAVIOUR).

Trist wrote on many subjects in management: the role of the absent leader, accidents as a means of withdrawal, diagnostic performance tests, communication issues, social structure and psychological stress, human relations training, systems theory, organizational democracy, quality of working life, action research methodology, and the weaknesses of scientific management. His most notable idea was the sociotechnical approach to organizations (Trist and Murray 1993) (see JOB DESIGN).

The sociotechnical approach developed between 1946 and 1963 out of Trist's research and ideas from Emery. It was a practical alternative to the view of industrial organization that for generations had fused bureaucratic administration, technological imperatives, autocratic management and economic rationalism. The sociotechnical approach had the following features:

1 work was no longer to be considered as a list of discrete jobs, but as a system of activities that had a unity of its own;
2 the work group, not the job holder, was the central concern;
3 external regulation by supervisors was not appropriate – instead, internal regulation was more effective;
4 when work systems needed changes, the functions performed were to be regarded as

redundant, not the people who performed the functions – consequently people would acquire many skills rather than just one;
5 work roles were no longer prescribed, but became alterable at the discretion of the job holder;
6 people complemented machines at work, rather than being mere extensions of them;
7 rather than standardizing operations, increasing their variety was the appropriate way to meet changing influences from outside the organization.

Redesigning work to these specifications was enormously productive, and was augmented by a closer, more rational commitment by employees to the organization's goals.

In 1960, Trist and Emery devised the search conference. Using concepts from the applied social psychology and clinical skills acquired with small groups, Trist and Emery introduced a new use of group psychology that has become accepted worldwide (Trist and Murray 1993).

In 1965, again with Emery, Trist published one of the most widely quoted papers in the social science of industrial management, 'The causal texture of organisational environments'. Until then it had been commonly thought that organizations functioned and were maintained largely by internal authorities. The impact of the environment – beyond mere market forces – was rarely considered, until their paper showed that organizations operate in four types of societal context. The most interesting of these was the 'turbulent environment', which now has a secure place in management theory (see ANSOFF, H.I.).

Trist's work thereafter centred on the quality of working life, the social ecology of organizations and the design of alternatives to the inward-looking and autocratic procedures of traditional management. His international experience as a researcher and consultant showed that modern industry operated in a turbulent environment. The steady-state and equilibrium theories were no longer useful for managing such turbulence because when organizations responded in accordance with these theories, they increased confrontational and defensive working relations; employees tended to feel infantilized and humiliated, and, like outsiders in their own workplaces, withdrew effort and commitment to workplace goals. Today's technocratic bureaucracies fail to work at high levels of complexity; because they curtail the participation of individuals and the use of innovative practices, and limit the quality of work experience, they fall perilously short of the productivity levels of self-regulating organizations. Failure to see this, Trist argued, would lead to a global industrial catastrophe from which recovery via conventional, entrenched, defensive, bureaucratic methods would be slow, impoverished and unproductive.

To overcome the problem, Trist recommended principles of co-designing organizations by working through the changes that turbulent environments bring about. The first step, he thought, was to understand the seriousness of the problem, to recognize the danger of a global industrial catastrophe. At the same time, it was important to realize that such a nightmarish scenario could not be managed by blaming others and treating them like hostile competitors, because that would perpetuate the conditions that promote irreversible disaster.

The solution was to consider the ordinary good life; it is this, with its ups and downs, that has to be valued, rather than the single-minded, popular and pathological pursuit of nothing but one goal (such as 'excellence'). Out of this, various productive imperatives emerge:

1 Variation in human capacity should be used to help tune into the turbulent environment, see new material as it appears and value ambiguous information. This leads to the idea that different procedures must be developed to match the changing effects of a turbulent environment.

2 The emotional upheaval and pain of seeing old securities and identities lose ground has to be accepted and tolerated. This is a great problem in entrenched industrial bureaucracies, and as yet there is no clear way to manage the pain except through findings from social science research.

3 People must recognize that a great cultural shift in organizational design will not happen by itself or be caused by outside forces such as the 'market'. People must accomplish it together, consciously and deliberately, with plans that have many evolving purposes, not just one.

4 These plans should be orientated towards ideas and purposes, and have a self-reviewing function attached to them.

5 Work has to be done openly, with organizations that have an overarching sense of community; the conventional form of control through autocratic bureaucracy must be rejected. Guidelines from social science research should be used to cope with the anxieties that will necessarily emerge with the move to open work systems.

6 A network of leaders and supporters is needed to turn negative identities and anxieties into positive images. This is another unknown for which social science offers appropriate methods and theory.

7 Finally, outsiders and consultants who are suited to tuning into turbulent environments and redesigning organizations as internal resources should be brought in, along with co-contributors, co-learners and action-research learners.

3 Evaluation

Trist's work was based on professional social research into changing organizations and not on the popular techniques and schemes that regularly dominate management fashions. As a result it is not possible yet to evaluate scientifically the impact of his efforts. Nevertheless, the academic recognition accorded to Trist in his later years indicates that his work has had a significant impact on professional management thought. On retirement, he was made Emeritus Professor of Organisational Behavior and Ecology at the Wharton School; Warren Bennis, one of the USA's most renowned organization theorists, described him as one of the few heroes of organizational psychology; in 1979, the International Academy of Management made Trist a Fellow for his outstanding contribution to the science and practice of management; in 1983, York University conferred the degree Doctor of Laws, *Honoris Causa*, on him; and in 1989, he was noted as the most outstanding organization development consultant of the year by the Organization Development Institute and the

International Registry of Organizational Development Institutes.

While institutions honoured Trist generally, individual social scientists and co-workers valued him as a teacher, colleague, collaborator, guide and mentor: he could get people excited about their own ideas and make them feel clever in his presence; he motivated them to learn more; he encouraged them to think on their own, to be intellectually honest, and to see wisdom not in books or theories, but in honest reflection on their own lives, and on the connection between their own mental chaos and the turbulent world they were in. He was known by many for his relentless drive to create a better future.

Trist's work had four features that gave him his distinguished position in the field of organization and management. First, his ideas and concepts were thought-provoking, clear and unambiguous; among them he particularly advocated self-direction at work, sociotechnical systems theory, open systems planning, ecology of work, and change processes. Second, he was always a collaborator; his power lay in cooperation with others and in demonstrating that social science had real human consequences. Third, Trist helped found a transnational network of colleagues, an alternative kind of global organization that openly spread ideas about human organization based on partnership and on new organization design principles that could replace autocratic bureaucracy. Finally, these elements were mediated by his personal qualities: quiet, impish humour, playfulness (especially with ideas), an acceptance of others, generosity of spirit and the courage to act quietly and simply in any situation.

4 Conclusion

Trist was one of the few prominent British social researchers in industry after the Second World War. He advanced the theory of sociotechnical systems, practised what he learned from research and offered his work to overcome problems in modern management. He advocated the principle that social scientists had to earn the right to be consulted on management problems and strengthened the use of psychoanalysis and field theory in organization research. His intellectual and personal debts were to Ivor Richards for literary skills, Kurt Lewin for social psychology, Wilfred Bion for clinical insights into group dynamics and Fred Emery for systematic conceptualization of his work.

RICHARD TRAHAIR
LA TROBE UNIVERSITY

Further reading

(References cited in the text marked *)

Clark, A.W. (1976) *Experimenting with Organisational Life: The Action Research Approach*, New York: Plenum. (Reports several studies of action research in introducing and practising organizational change under the guidance of social scientists.)

Emery, F.E. and Thorsrud, E. (1976) *Democracy at Work*, Leiden: Martinus Nijhoff Publishers. (An account of field experiments in industrial democracy in Norway.)

Ketchum, L.D. and Trist, E.L. (1992) *All Teams Are Not Created Equal – How Employee Empowerment Really Works*, Newbury Park, CA: Sage Publications. (A study of work groups and how they function.)

Trist, E.L. (1993) 'Guilty of enthusiasm', in A.G. Bedeian (ed.), *Management Laureates: A Collection of Autobiographical Essays*, vol. 3, Greenwich, CT: JAI Press Inc. (This biographical entry includes the most comprehensive published list of Trist's publications.)

* Trist, E.L. and Emery, F.E. (1965) 'The causal texture of organisational environments', *Human Relations* 13 (1): 21–32. (A seminal theory of four types of environment – placid randomized, placid clustered, dynamic clustered and turbulent – that affect an organization's change process.)

* Trist, E.L. and Emery, F.E. (1973) *Towards a Social Ecology: Contextual Appreciations of the Future and the Present*, New York: Plenum. (Two substantial intellectual discussions of the concepts and methodology needed for an organization to reduce the complexity of and adapt to the vagaries of post-industrialism.)

* Trist, E.L., Emery, F.E. and Murray, H. (eds) (1997) *The Social Engagement of Social Science: A Tavistock Anthology*, vol. 3: *The Socio-Ecological Perspective*, Philadelphia PA: University of Pennsylvania Press. (Concerns the coevolution of systems and their broad environments which shape sociotechnical organizations, and the institutional

and cultural worlds that confront the individual.)

* Trist, E.L., Higgin, G.W., Murray, H. and Pollock, A.B. (1963) *Organisational Choice: Capabilities of Groups at the Coal Face Under Changing Technologies: The Loss, Rediscovery and Transformation of the Work Tradition*, London: Tavistock Publications. (Reports on the first Tavistock coal-mining studies, which showed the value of cohesive primary groups committed to holistically organized tasks, and the power of responsible autonomy in work groups.)

* Trist, E.L. and Murray, H. (eds) (1990) *The Social Engagement of Social Science: A Tavistock Anthology*, vol. 1: *The Social-Psychological Perspective*, Philadelphia, PA: University of Pennsylvania Press. (Uses the object-relations approach of psychoanalysis for the study of groups and organizations.)

* Trist, E.L. and Murray, H. (eds) (1993) *The Social Engagement of Social Science: A Tavistock Anthology*, vol. 2: *The Social-Technical Perspective*, Philadelphia, PA: University of Pennsylvania Press. (Offers an alternative to conventional management techniques and suggests using action research to change organizations.)

Trist, E.L. and Sofer, C. (1959) *Exploration in Group Relations*, Leicester: Leicester University Press. (Reports on the concepts and techniques discovered during the early development of group relations training at Leicester University by Tavistock workers.)

See also: HUMAN RELATIONS; INDUSTRIAL DEMOCRACY; JOB DESIGN; OCCUPATIONAL PSYCHOLOGY; ORGANIZATION BEHAVIOUR; ORGANIZATION BEHAVIOUR, HISTORY OF; ORGANIZATION DEVELOPMENT; ORGANIZATION TYPES; ORGANIZATIONAL POPULATIONS; WORK SYSTEMS

Trust

Overview

The increasing interest in trust in the economics and business literature is part of a more general resurgence of interest in the social and institutional determinants of economic activity and performance. A basic theme in this literature is that trust plays an important role in promoting and sustaining economic exchange in situations characterized by some form of uncertainty. Arrow (1972), for example, has argued that trust is an element of any transaction conducted over time, such as when goods or services are provided in exchange for future payment. Within organizational research, it has been argued that trust lowers transactions costs and promotes risky investments in transaction-specific assets (Lorenz 1988; Nooteboom 1993). Fukuyama (1995) has identified trust as a key factor in national economic performance, and a growing empirical literature drawing on survey-based measures of trust has sought to confirm this hypothesis (Knack and Keefer 1997; La Porta *et al.* 1997).

Both individuals and institutions may be the object of one's trust. Trust is commonly defined as a belief concerning the likely behaviour of an individual, organization or institution that matters for the trustor's decision making. For example, one may have to decide whether to place a sum of money in a financial institution which runs the risk of going bankrupt. Or, you may have to decide whether to buy a used car which could turn out to be a lemon. Both of these situations are characterized by the fact that the trustee's behaviour matters for the actions of the trustor and that the trustor's actions have to be made prior to or independently of the possibility of monitoring the behaviour of the trustee (Gambetta 1988; Luhmann 1988).

As the above references to trust directed to either individuals or to society's institutions suggest, one finds multiple notions of trust in the literature. Corresponding to these different ideas about what trust amounts to, one finds different approaches to analysing the sources of trust. Different notions of trust in turn pose different problems of measurement in order to make trust an operational concept. These various issues are taken up in the sections below.

1 Notions of trust

One of the most common distinctions made in the literature is that between 'personal trust' and 'system trust' (see ORGANIZATIONAL TRUST). This distinction is associated with the work of Luhmann (1979) and has been developed by Giddens (1990) in his work on modernity. The distinction concerns the object of trust rather than its sources, with personal trust referring to trust in a particular individual or group of individuals, while system trust designates trust in societal systems such as the legal system or the banking system. Personal trust entails a belief in the trustworthiness of an individual or group of individuals, while system trust implies no such belief. That is to say, one's trust in the banking system or the legal system transcends interpersonal experience or face-to-face relations. It does not necessarily imply that one trusts the individuals who constitute these systems. This raises the question of the foundations for such beliefs, a point returned to below.

In the organizational literature, there is a tendency to conflate inter-organizational trust with interpersonal trust (see ORGANIZATION BEHAVIOUR; ORGANIZATION NETWORKS). The quality of the relationship between a subcontractor and a client or between two firms engaged in a technological alliance is often discussed in the same terms as the quality of a relationship between an individual buyer and seller on the market. One can attempt to provide a micro-foundation for this form of trust by drawing on Livet and Reynaud's (1998) notion of 'organizational trust', which they define as a form of trust that depends on the members of a group involved in some collective endeavour holding the 'reasonable' belief that each is implicitly committed to it. Extended to inter-firm relations, this would imply, as Sako (1998) has suggested, that inter-organizational trust depends on multiple channels of communication being established between the two organizations at various functional levels. For extremely large organizations operating over large geographical spaces, however, it seems implausible that this condition could be respected. This suggests, much as Sydow (1998) has argued, that the notion of impersonal or system trust may provide a better starting point for understanding the forms of trust that link organizations.

A key issue raised in the literature on modernity is whether in technologically advanced societies there is a tendency for system trust to replace personal trust. This idea is often associated with Giddens (1990), who argues that impersonal forms of trust emerge in the presence of abstract systems where relations are 'disembedded' or lifted out from their local contexts and restructured across indefinite spans of time and space. It is also possible to read Luhmann's (1979) discussion of how system trust underwrites the development of personal trust as supporting this view concerning the evolution of trust in modern society.

The literature offers a number of useful distinctions concerning the properties of personal forms of trust (see Lazaric and Lorenz (1998) for a more complete review). One basic property is the distinction between 'intentions trust' and 'competence trust' (Sako 1992). The former refers to an individual's beliefs concerning the possible opportunism of another and more generally to questions of honesty and to whether explicit or implicit commitments will be respected. The latter form refers to trust in another person's ability to undertake a task or to fulfil a commitment, irrespective of that person's intentions. Intentions trust can be taken to signify that the trustor has formed a belief concerning the trustee's interests and the degree to which

their relationship is marked by incentives alignment problems, while competence trust does not imply that any such judgement has been made.

Another key distinction is that between 'generalized trust' and 'person-specific trust'. The former notion of trust, developed especially in the literature on social capital, refers to the trust one holds for people in general about whom one has no specific knowledge. The latter form refers to the trust one may hold for an identified individual about whom one has knowledge, based either on one's past experience in dealing with that individual or on information provided by some trusted third party. An issue raised in the social capital literature is whether strong forms of inter-personal trust act to prevent the development of the more diffuse and impersonal forms of trust that support economic exchange in advanced economies. For example, Fukuyama (1995) in his book on trust and economic performance argues that strong family or group-based ties restrict the development of trust beyond the confines of the family or the group. Yamagishi (1988) and Yamagishi *et al.* (1998) draw on this distinction to account for the counterintuitive experimental finding that Japanese society, though characterized by the prevalence of strong social ties, produces less general trust than US society, where social and interpersonal ties are weaker.

2 Sources of trust

In accounting for trust or its absence, the literature focuses primarily on the question of personal forms of trust. One of the most common distinctions made is between trust based on values or norms and trust based on a calculation of one's self-interest. As regards norm-based trust, it is important to point out that the argument is not that norms directly produce trust, understood as a belief. Rather, norms are thought to produce trustworthiness understood as certain types of behaviour, such as behaving honestly in one's commercial dealings. The trust one may hold for another is then seen to be dependent on what one knows about that person's norms and values. Thus, it is quite possible for a trustworthy individual to distrust and to decide not to enter into a transaction with another because of what is known about his or her norms or values. Similarly, it is quite possible for an untrustworthy individual to trust and to seek to enter into relations of exchange with those who are thought to be trustworthy. On this account the amount of trust, and hence cooperative exchange, displayed by a community will depend on how widely diffused are norms prescribing trustworthy forms of behaviour.

The calculative view of trust, on the other hand, would argue that the trust one holds for another is based on what is known about the other person's interests, and in particular upon the evidence one has than the other person has an interest in behaving in a trustworthy manner. Pushed to an extreme, this argument reduces trust to rational choice in the form of maximizing one's expected utility. A popular tool used in developing this optimizing approach to trust is the theory of repeated games. Thus Kreps (1990), in his treatment of reputation effects, argues that trustworthy behaviour will be displayed in settings where the present discounted value of the future gains from acting in a way designed to maintain one's good reputation are greater than the one time gains achieved from reneging on one's commitments and thus losing one's good reputation. (Other authors adopting a rational choice approach to trust include: Axelrod 1984; Coleman 1990; Dasgupta 1988; Hardin 1998.)

The strongest methodological critique to this way of analysing trust has come from Williamson (1993), who argues that if trust simply amounts to calculation then it adds nothing important to the traditional analysis of decision making under risk (see WILLIAMSON, O.E.). Correspondingly, he argues that trust should be reserved for relations based on strong personal ties, such as ties of friendship, which on his account are of limited relevance to economic analysis. Regardless of what one thinks of Williamson's position on the importance of personal ties, there is clearly something valid in his critique. It is difficult to see, for example, that the notion of trust adds anything essential to Kreps' (1990) discussion of reputation effects in the context of the infinitely or finitely repeated prisoner's dilemma.

Arguably the strongest rebuttal to Williamson's stance is to argue that the notion of trust can usefully contribute to economic analysis in so far as one takes bounded rationality seriously and does not simply reduce it to subjective expected utility optimization in the face of risk, as Williamson (1993) implicitly does in arguing that individuals are farsighted and are able to anticipate changes in the environment. Bounded rationality, in the sense of truly unanticipated contingencies and limits on the possibility of calculating one's interests, creates a role for trust in an explanation for sustained cooperation in which a concern for one's self-interest is not absent (Lorenz 1993, 1999; Nooteboom 1993; Sabel 1992). Trust, on this account is a tentative judgement based on past experience and previous interactions, and it remains open to revision, based on what one discovers about another in an ongoing relationship.

Another set of distinctions that are often drawn upon in analysing the sources of trust are those proposed by Zucker (1986) between process-based, characteristic-based and institution-based trust. These distinctions focus on the mechanisms that produce trust rather than on the question of the rationality of trust. Process-based trust refers to trust derived from the knowledge one gains about another individual, either through repeated interactions or through information provided by trusted third parties. Characteristic-based trust refers to trust based on ascribed characteristics of an individual which cannot be produced at will, such as one's family ties, ethnicity or religious affiliation. Institution-based trust refers to the way formal institutions, such as systems of law, can promote trust between individuals independently of any personal knowledge based on direct interaction or otherwise.

Zucker's (1986) notion of institution-based trust, while focusing on the mechanisms which produce trust in interpersonal dealings, implicitly raises the question of system trust, or the trust one has in societal institutions, such as the legal system. For example, one's belief that an individual will live up to his or her contractual commitments may be shaped in part by how much confidence one has in the courts and the legal system. Moreover, in a manner that is complementary to Giddens (1990), Zucker (1986) argues that characteristic-based trust is in scarce supply in modern societies, which are characterized by an increasing reliance on institution-based trust, given that dealings go beyond the boundaries of the group or family connections.

3 Measuring trust

Most empirical efforts to measure trust concern 'generalized trust' or the trust an individual may hold for another about whom he or she has no knowledge based on past interactions or reputation. Within the economics discipline, much of the interest in this form of trust has been fuelled by the debate on social capital and by the possibility of drawing on survey-based indicators of trust which can be entered into macroeconomic growth regressions in much the same manner as measures of human capital (see HUMAN CAPITAL); key contributions include: La Porta *et al.* 1997; Knack and Keefer 1997; Zak and Knack 1998. A second type of empirical research is based on laboratory experiments, where small groups of subjects are confronted with decision making in the context of social dilemmas which pose the issue of trust; see, for example, Berg *et al.* 1995; Glaeser *et al.* 1999; Robin and Ruffieux 1999; Yamagishi 1988.

Survey work

The two principal survey sources drawn on in the social capital literature in order to measure trust are the World Values Survey (WVS) for cross-national comparisons and the General Social Survey (GSS) for studies focusing on the USA. The WVS, which provides information on 29 market economies, is meant to be a random sample of between 500 and 3000 persons in each country, while the GSS has been administered 20 times in the USA since 1972 to a sample of between 1000 and 2000 persons (see Inglehart (1994) for a discussion of likely biases in the WVS sample frame). The question in the WVS and the GSS that is used to measure trust is: 'Generally speaking, would you say that most people can be trusted, or that you can't be too careful in dealing with people?' The standard trust indicator in empirical research is the percentage of the respondents replying that 'most people can be trusted'.

Based on this measure, there are significant variations in the level of measured trust across the countries surveyed in the WVS, ranging from a high of about 60 per cent in Norway to a low of about 7 per cent in Brazil. Amongst OECD countries, France, with a score of about 25 per cent, ranks lowest on the trust scale (Knack and Keefer 1997: 1285). The GSS survey indicates considerable variation across states in the USA, with high values of trust being concentrated in the north/northwest and the lowest values being found in the southeast (Alesina and Ferrara 2000: 33).

In addition to measuring the level of generalized trust, this literature seeks to assess its determinants, its consequences for economic performance and its relation to measures of confidence in societal institutions, such as the educational system or the legal system. There is not sufficient space here to systematically review this literature and only certain key results will be highlighted.

A number of studies find a positive and significant relationship between generalized trust and growth in per capita income using a Barro (1991) type specification controlling for education and the price of investment goods. (See, however, the study by Helliwell (1996) which shows that trust is significantly negatively related to productivity growth in a sample of 17 OECD countries.) Knack and Keefer (1997: 1260) find that the impact of trust on growth in per capita income is higher in poorer countries, which they interpret as supporting the view that trust is more essential for economic growth in countries where contract enforcement mechanisms are poorly developed and where access to formal sources of credit is limited. They also present regression results showing a positive and significant relation between trust and levels of output per worker and levels of physical and human capital per worker. They find no significant relation between trust and investment's share of GDP.

Knack and Keefer's (1997) results also show that there is a positive relationship between trust and a synthetic measure of confidence in society's institutions. The latter measure is based on responses in the WVS to how much confidence respondents have in their country's legal system, education system, police and civil service. If we take this synthetic measure as an indicator of respondents' levels of 'system trust', then the results suggest a positive link between the two types of trust.

As regards the determinants of generalized trust, the literature drawing on the GSS for the United States has been largely concerned with the relation between respondents' individual characteristics and trust, while the internationally comparative research has focused as well on the relationship between trust and certain structural characteristics of the nation under consideration. A key finding based on the GSS surveys is that measured trust is declining for later age cohorts. This supports Putnam's (1995) contention that social capital is declining in the USA. Other 'stylized facts' from this research are that generalized trust increases with income and education and is lower among racial minorities (Glaeser *et al.* 1999). Alesina and La Ferrara (2000) also report that women trust less in the USA. Studies based on the WVS show no significant relation between the age cohort and trust for most countries, while showing a more pervasive positive relationship between trust and schooling and between trust and income (Knack and Keefer 1997).

In terms of structural determinants, one of the key concerns of this literature is to explore the relation between generalized trust and measures of economic and religious polarization. Two of the more robust results are that trust is negatively correlated with a country's gini coefficient and that trust is lower in countries with a 'dominant hierarchical religion' as measured by the percentage of the population that is Catholic, Orthodox Christian or Moslem (La Porta *et al.* 1997). In a cross-state comparison of the USA, Alesina and La Ferrara (2000) similarly find a negative relation between trust and the gini coefficient. They find that the effect of religious affiliation on trust is insignificant and conclude 'that it is not the religious beliefs per se but the organized forms of religion in different parts of the world that may influence different social behavior.'

Experimental work

The most common design used in experimental research on trust is the 'investment game' associated with the work of Berg *et al.* (1995). The basic idea in this game is to divide subjects between two populations, senders and recipients. Each sender is allocated a sum of money and is asked to send some portion of it to an anonymous recipient. The experimenter then doubles or perhaps triples the amount sent and the recipient is asked to return some portion of the increased amount back to the anonymous sender. Sending money is interpreted as a show of trust on the part of the sender, while returning money is interpreted as an exhibition of trustworthiness or reciprocity on the part of the recipient.

One of the issues addressed in the experimental literature is whether observed behaviour conforms to the behaviour predicted by rational choice theory. Berg *et al.* (1995), in an experiment using a group of University of Minnesota undergraduates as subjects, reject the unique Nash equilibrium prediction for this game of sending zero money, since the large majority of their subjects send some. The authors conclude that trust is an economic primitive which should be included as part of the rational choice paradigm.

By relaxing the anonymity condition between sender and recipient, Glaeser *et al.* (1999) use a similar experimental design on a population of Harvard University undergraduates in order to assess how variations in social connections and certain ascribed characteristics influence trusting behaviour. Their results are partially asymmetric as regards trust and trustworthiness. The amount of trust (i.e. the amount of money sent) rises significantly with the amount of time the two individuals have known each other, while the effects of matching people with different nationalities or race, though negative, are not statistically significant. As regards trustworthiness, not only are the effects of the length of time the two subjects have known each other significant, but both racial and national effects are also sizeable and significant. Overall the authors conclude that racial or national heterogeneity may decrease trust in social groups. This result is consistent with a finding based on the GSS surveys that regions in the USA marked by greater racial heterogeneity are characterized by lower levels of generalized trust. This would appear to be contrary to the argument of Zucker (1986) that characteristic-based trust is of limited importance in modern societies.

4 Conclusions

Research over the past decade has considerably improved our understanding of trust and its relation to economic exchange and performance. Despite this, the literature remains marked by problems of conceptual clarity, while efforts to empirically measure trust are open to a number of criticisms. On the conceptual level, perhaps the most serious problem is the divide that exists between those, such as Zucker (1986) or Knack (2000), who argue that any factor serving to reduce uncertainty in economic exchange can be considered to be a source of trust, and those, such as Berg *et al.* (1995), who would argue that trust is what remains after eliminating the role of such factors as reputation in repeated interactions, contractual pre-commitments and possible threats of punishment in sustaining cooperation. Where the former would see trust at work, the latter would see behaviour motivated either by farsighted calculation or by the exercise of power.

In terms of accounting for trust, the sources of 'system trust', or the trust that individuals may place in such institutions as the public service or the legal system, remain poorly understood. While in the case of personal trust one may plausibly argue that one places one's trust in another because of what one knows about the other's interests or values, it should be obvious that this explanation cannot hold for complex systems, such as the legal system, or even for large and possibly geographically dispersed organizations. Societal institutions or large organizations are not unitary entities with well-defined interests or values, and their size and complexity preclude that any individual might have a clear understanding of the routines and operating procedures which determine their behaviour. One the other hand, as Hardin (1998) has argued, few would be satisfied with an account of trust in institu-

tions that simply reduces it to a prediction of future behaviour based on induction from past behaviour. Gaining a better understanding of the nature and sources of system trust remains one of the key challenges facing those committed to the trust research agenda.

Survey-based empirical work, while making plausible the claim that trust is positively correlated to economic performance, has made little progress in identifying the mechanisms that underlie this relation. Moreover, this research is marred by the use of ambiguous indicators of trust. In the case of the WVS and GSS surveys, for example, it is not at all clear whether in responding positively to the question, 'would you say that most people can be trusted?' respondents are referring to most people they regularly transact with or to a wider population. Experimental work, by controlling what subjects know about each other, arguably provides superior measures of trust and trustworthiness. For the moment, however, this work has been confined to analysing the behaviour of a few unrepresentative populations of university students in controlled laboratory settings and its relevance to the everyday behaviour of people in general must remain in doubt.

In conclusion, while much progress has been made in analysing the determinants and consequences of trust, there is a need for greater conceptual clarity. In particular, there is a need for clarity on whether the use of legal sanctions or the exercise of power is compatible with a trusting relationship. Resolving such ambiguities is a necessary condition for defining appropriate measures for empirical research on trust. It is only through addressing such outstanding problems that the notion of trust will come to be generally recognized as having an important role to play in the analysis of economic exchange and business activity.

EDWARD LORENZ
CENTRE D'ETUDES DE L'EMPLOI,
NOISY-LE-GRAND, FRANCE

Further reading

(References cited in the text marked *)

* Alesina A. and E. La Ferrara (2000) 'The determinants of trust', NBER Working Paper No. 7621.

(This text shows how individual and community characteristics influence how much people trust using data drawn from US localities.)

* Arrow, K. (1972) 'Gifts and exchange' *Philosophy and Public Affairs* 1: 343–62. (In this paper Arrow introduces the notion of trust into his analysis of uncertainty.)

* Axelrod, R. (1984) *The Evolution of Cooperation*, New York: Basic Books. (A path-breaking attempt to use basic game theoretic concepts to explain the success and failure of cooperation.)

* Barro, R. (1991) 'Economic growth in a cross section of countries', *Quarterly Journal of Economics*, 106: 407–44. (Presents Barro's standard growth specification controlling for education and the price of investment goods.)

* Berg, J., J. Dickhaut and K. McCabe (1995) 'Trust, reciprocity, and social history', *Games and Economic Behavior* 10: 122–42. (The authors develop an experiment to study trust and reciprocity in an investment setting.)

* Coleman, J. (1990) *Foundations of Social Theory*, Cambridge MA: Harvard University Press. (Coleman is one of the major proponents of the rational choice approach to trust.)

* Dasgupta, P. (1988) 'Trust as a commodity', in D. Gambetta (ed.) *Trust: Making and Breaking Cooperative Relations*, Oxford: Basil Blackwell, 49–72. (Applies game theoretic concepts to the analysis of trust in economic exchange.)

* Fukuyama, F. (1995) *Trust: The Social Virtues and the Creation of Prosperity*, New York: Free Press. (This study links trust and networks to differences in national economic performance.)

* Gambetta, D. (1988) 'Can we trust trust?' in D. Gambetta (ed.) *Trust: Making and Breaking Cooperative Relations*, Oxford: Basil Blackwell, 213–38. (A multi-disciplinary volume which has done much to put trust on the research agenda in the social sciences.)

* Giddens, A. (1990) *The Consequences of Modernity*, Cambridge: Polity Press. (Links trust in systems to the 'disembedding' of social relations from local contexts in modern society.)

* Glaeser, E., D. Laibson, J. Sceinkman and C. Soutter (1999) 'What is social capital? the determinants of trust and trustworthiness', NBER Working Paper No. 7216. (Presents two experiments analysing trust and social capital using a sample of Harvard undergraduates.)

* Hardin, R. (1998) 'Trust in government', in V. Braithwaite and M. Levi (ed.) *Trust and Governance*, New York: Russel Sage Foundation, 927. (Considers the limits of a rational choice framework for explaining trust in societal institutions.)

* Helliwell, J. (1996) 'Economic growth and social capital in Asia', NBER Working Paper No. 5470. (This study purports to show that trust is negatively related to productivity growth in a sample of OECD countries.)

* Inglehart, R. (1994) *Codebook for World Values Surveys*, Ann Arbor, MI: Institute for Social Research. (Describes the likely biases in the World Value Survey sample frame.)

* Knack, S. (2000) 'Trust, associational life and economic performance', The World Bank, April. (Presents empirical evidence on trust and economic performance using a 25-nation OECD sample.)

* Knack, S. and P. Keefer (1997) 'Does social capital have and economic payoff? A cross-country investigation', *Quarterly Journal of Economics* 112: 1251–88. (Shows that trust and civic norms are stronger in nations with higher and more equal income and with better-educated and ethnically homogeneous populations.)

* Kreps, D. (1990) 'Corporate culture and economic theory', in J. Alt and K. Shepsle (eds) *Perspectives on Positive Political Economy*, New York: Cambridge University Press, 90–144. (Draws on the theory of repeated games to analyse the role of trust in organizations.)

* La Porta, R., F. Lopez-de-Salanes, A. Shleifer, and R. Vishny (1997) 'Trust in large organisations' *American Economic Review Papers and Proceedings* 87: 333–8. (Tests the proposition that trust promotes cooperation, especially in large organizations, using data from the World Value Survey.)

* Lazaric, N. and E. Lorenz (1998) 'The learning dynamics of trust, reputation and confidence', in N. Lazaric and E. Lorenz (eds) *Trust and Economic Learning*, Cheltenham: Edward Elgar Press, 1–22. (Provides a critical overview of recent work on trust and economic cooperation.)

* Livet, P. and B. Reynaud (1998) 'Organisational trust, learning and implicit commitments', in Lazaric, N. and E. Lorenz (eds) *Trust and Economic Learning*, Cheltenham: Edward Elgar Press, 266–84. (Provides a general definition of organizational trust based on the notion of 'reasonable' implicit commitments.)

* Lorenz, E. (1988) 'Neither friends nor strangers: informal networks of subcontracting in French industry', in D. Gambetta (ed.) *Trust: Making and Breaking Cooperative Relations*, Oxford: Basil Blackwell, 194–210. (Draws on case study material to analyse the role of trust in inter-firm relations.)

* Lorenz, E. (1993) 'Flexible production systems and the social construction of trust', *Politics and Society* 21 (3): 307–24. (Contrasts various ap-

proaches to explaining trust in economic relations.)

* Lorenz, E. (1999) 'Trust, contract and economic cooperation', *The Cambridge Journal of Economics* 3: 301–15. (Links trust to uncertainty and presents a critique of the treatment of uncertainty in the incomplete contracts literature.)

* Luhmann, N. (1979) *Trust and Power*, Chichester: John Wiley. (This path-breaking work develops Luhmann's classic distinction between personal and system trust.)

* Luhmann, N. (1988) 'Familiarity, confidence, trust: problems and alternatives', in D. Gambetta (ed.) *Trust: Making and Breaking Cooperative Relations*, Oxford: Basil Blackwell, 94–107. (Distinguishes the concepts of familiarity, confidence and trust.)

* Nooteboom, B. (1993) 'Networks and transactions: do they connect?' in J. Groenewegen (ed.) *Dynamics of the Firm*, Aldershot: Edward Elgar Press, 9–26. (Argues that trust lowers transaction costs and promotes risky investments.)

* Putnam, R. (1995) 'Tuning in, tuning out: the strange disappearance of social capital in America', *PS: Political Science and Politics* 28 (4): 664–83. (Presents Putnam's view that social capital is declining in the USA.)

* Robin, S. and B. Ruffieux (1999) 'L'Economiste au Fond du Puits: L'Expérimentation de la Confiance', in C. Thuderoz, V. Mangematin and D. Harrison (eds) *La Confiance: Approches Economiques et Sociologiques*, Paris: Gaëtan Morin Editeur. (Presents the results of an experiment based on the investment game developed by Berg *et al.* (1995).)

* Sabel, C. (1992) 'Studied trust: building new forms of cooperation in a volatile economy', in F. Pyke and W. Sengenberger (eds) *Industrial Districts and Local Economic Regeneration*, Geneva: IILS, 215–50. (Argues for a link between social amnesia and trust in communities.)

* Sako, M. (1992) *Prices, Quality and Trust: Inter-firm Relations in Britain and Japan*, Cambridge: Cambridge University Press. (Compares the role of trust in inter-firm relations in Japan and the UK.)

* Sako, M. (1998) 'The information requirements of trust in supplier relations: evidence from Japan,

Europe and the United States', in N. Lazaric and E. Lorenz (eds) *Trust and Economic Learning*, Cheltenham: Edward Elgar Press, 23–47. (Provides empirical evidence on the nature of trust in the US, UK and Japanese auto parts industries.)

* Sydow, J. (1998) 'Understanding the constitution of interorganizational trust', in C. Lane and R. Bachmann (eds) *Trust Within and Between Organizations*, Oxford: Oxford University Press, 31–63. (Examines the role of system trust in inter-firm relations.)

* Williamson, O.E. (1993) 'Calculativeness, Trust and economic organization', *Journal of Law and Economics* 36: 453–86. (Argues against the use of the concept of trust in economic analysis.)

* Yamagishi, T. (1988) 'The provision of a sanctioning system in the United States and Japan', *Social Psychology Quarterly* 51: 265–71. (Presents the results of a cross-societal experiment comparing cooperative tendencies in social dilemmas.)

* Yamagishi, T., K. Cook and M. Watabe (1998) 'Uncertainty, Trust and commitment formation in the United States and Japan', *American Journal of Sociology* 1: 165–94. (Develops the distinction between social commitment and trust based on experiments performed in the USA and Japan.)

* Zak, P. and S. Knack (1998) 'Trust and growth', IRIS Center Working Paper No. 219. (Presents empirical evidence showing that trust is positively associated with investment rates and growth in per capita income.)

* Zucker, L. (1986) 'Production of trust: institutional sources of economic structure, 1840–1920', *Research in Organizational Behavior* 8, 53–111. (Develops Zucker's classic distinctions between process-based, characteristic-based and institution-based trust.)

See also: EMPLOYMENT RELATIONS; EVOLUTIONARY THEORIES OF THE FIRM; GROWTH OF THE FIRM AND NETWORKS; INDUSTRIAL AND LABOUR RELATIONS; ORGANIZATIONAL TRUST

Tung, Rosalie L. (1948–)

1 Introduction
2 Main contribution
3 Evaluation

Personal background

- born in Shanghai, China, 2 December 1948
- raised and educated in Hong Kong, emigrated to Canada after finishing high school
- received BA in 1972 from York University, MBA in 1974 and PhD in 1977 from the University of British Columbia
- served on the faculties of the University of Oregon (1977–80), Wharton School at the University of Pennsylvania (1981–6) and the University of Wisconsin-Milwaukee (1986–90) before joining Simon Fraser University in 1991
- holder of Wisconsin Distinguished Professor (July 1988–December 1990) at the University of Wisconsin-Milwaukee and The Ming & Stella Wong Professor of International Business (January 1991–present) at Simon Fraser University
- has served as a visiting professor at Harvard University, UCLA, University of Manchester (Institute of Science and Technology), Copenhagen Business School, Shanghai Jiaotong University (China) and the Chinese University of Hong Kong
- elected as Vice President-elect of the Academy of Management in 2000, a professional association of over 10,000 professors of management and practitioners. She will become President of the Academy of Management in 2004.

Major works

Management Practices in China (1980)
U.S.–China Trade Negotiations (1982)
Business Negotiations with the Japanese (1984)
Key to Japan's Economic Strength (1984)
Strategic Management in the United States and Japan (1986)
The New Expatriates (1988)
International Encyclopedia of Business and Management (subject editor for International Management) (1996) (2nd edition; 2001)
IEBM Handbook of International Business (1999)

Summary

Rosalie L. Tung is a pioneer and recognized authority in international management, a research area within the larger field of international business studies. Born in China, raised in Hong Kong and educated at Canadian universities, Tung has made effective use of her cross-cultural background to integrate management thoughts and practices from the East and West. She is most widely recognized for her work in international human resource management and international comparative management studies. More recently, Tung has extended her research to investigate intranational diversity and Chinese business networks both in and outside of China (see ASIA PACIFIC, MANAGEMENT IN).

1 Introduction

Rosalie L. Tung was the first female scholar in business administration to be elected as a fellow of the Royal Society of Canada (established in 1882 under a charter of Queen Victoria of England), the first Asian-born management scholar to hold an endowed chair/professorship in a major university in both the USA and Canada, and the recipient of the Leonore Rowe Williams Award from the University of Pennsylvania. She was selected as one of the best 75 graduates from the University of British Columbia in that university's 75th anniversary celebration. According to the 1994 issue of *Journal of International Business Studies*, Tung was ranked among the world's top five most cited researchers in the field during 1989–93. In 1991, she was named by the same journal as the world's ninth most prolific author in the field. She is listed in many *Who's Who* and related honorific citations, including: *Who's Who in America*, *Who's Who in the World*, *Who's Who in Finance and Industry*, W*ho's Who in Canadian Business*, *Who's Who of Canadian Women*, and *The Directory of Distinguished Americans*, among others. More recently, Tung received the 1997 Outstanding Academic Contribution to Global Markets Research from the American Society for Competitiveness, was elected as a Fellow of the Academy of Management (a professional association of over 10,000 professors in management) and a Fellow of the International Academy of Intercultural Research. She was recipient of the 1998 Vancouver Woman of Distinction Award in Management, Professions and the Trades. Tung has also served on the United Nations' Task Force on Human Resource Management. In 2000 she was elected as the Vice President-elect of the Academy of Management where she will serve a five-year term culminating in the presidency of that professional association. She is the first non-Caucasian, first academic in international business, and first faculty from a non-US university to be elected to that position.

2 Main contribution

Tung's research has made original contributions to the theory and practice of cross-cultural understanding and communication within the context of economic collaborations between entities from different nations. There are two areas where her contributions are most widely recognized. First, in the area of international human resource management, her pioneering research on expatriate effectiveness has led to the development of a theoretical framework for the selection and training of personnel for international assignments (see HUMAN RESOURCE MANAGEMENT, INTERNATIONAL). This framework was tested using data collected from samples of American, European, Japanese and Australian multinational firms. Results support the theoretical

framework and identify key factors that affect the success and failure of international assignments. These factors include: due consideration of the family situation, possession of good human relations skills in a cross-cultural setting, appropriate criteria for selection and training of personnel in different categories of international assignments, and use of effective repatriation programmes. Based on this research, Tung formulated a contingency paradigm for the selection and training of managers for international assignments. The recent explosion of research interests in international human resource management is largely a result of Tung's seminal work in this area. In 1997, with the assistance of Arthur Andersen Inc., she completed a major study of attitudes and experiences of American expatriates in 54 countries around the world (see EXPATRIATE MANAGERS; MIGRANT MANAGERS). The study was based on a 14-page questionnaire survey of 409 expatriates in 49 multinationals. It investigated expatriates' motivations for undertaking international assignments, their mode of acculturation abroad, the mechanisms that they found most useful in coping with living and working in a foreign country, and their concerns about repatriation.

Second, in the area of international comparative management, Tung has conducted original and insightful research into the mindsets of East Asians as they affect management thoughts and practices (see BUSINESS STRATEGIES, EAST ASIAN). Until the early 1980s, much of the international comparative management literature was written by scholars who came from mono-cultural backgrounds. Mono-cultural researchers often lack the insight and perspective possessed by their bi-cultural colleagues in interpreting research findings and developing knowledge which can advance theory and research in new ways. Drawing upon her unique cultural background and upbringing, Tung has conducted path-breaking research on cross-cultural business negotiations between Americans and East Asians (Chinese, Japanese and Koreans). This work has significantly advanced our theoretical and practical understanding of how people with different cultural mind-sets can influence the way they communicate, process information, interact, compete and collaborate. For example, following the Yin/Yang principle, East Asians are more adept at handling contradictions and appear to have a special ability to comprehend the interdependent relationships of situations, something not readily perceptible from a Western perspective. Given the increased involvement of firms in international strategic alliances and network organizations, these skills are becoming more important to meeting the managerial challenges of the twenty-first century.

3 Evaluation

As an Asian-born management scholar trained in the North American research traditions, Tung has distinguished herself as one who can effectively integrate management thoughts and practices from the East and West. This ability, coupled with her genuine concern for interpersonal effectiveness, have provided Tung with both the intellectual and motivational foundation for her pioneering research on cross-cultural understanding and communication. From the very beginning, she has been careful not to let the established theories and concepts from the West restrict her thinking and inquiry. In the best tradition of an empirical researcher, she collected systematic and reliable data from cross-national samples of managers and companies and let the data speak for themselves. The many contributions that Tung has made to the international management literature are the result of this investigative approach.

While Tung's work has been widely cited by colleagues in the international management field, it has also been criticized by some for lacking in methodological sophistication. These criticisms usually come from colleagues in the traditional organizational behaviour and human resource management areas who have a domestic research focus. Tung's supporters would argue that these traditional research areas are at a more advanced stage of paradigm development than international management. Thus, one should not use the same criteria to judge research work in a less developed area. Additionally, most of Tung's early work was done when international management was transitioning from case- to survey-based research, a stage where descriptive exploratory studies are most commonly conducted.

In recent years, Tung has extended her research in two major ways. First, she has applied her earlier research on cross-national interactions to theory development in the management of intra-national diversity, a challenge faced by the USA, Canada and other countries. Intra-national diversity refers to the increasing multi-ethnic composition of the domestic workforce. Tung's research found that there are many similarities in the dynamics and processes associated with managing international and intra-national diversity, such as mode of acculturation and communication patterns.

Second, she has initiated new studies that investigate business networks in the Chinese society (both in and outside of China) and how these may affect foreign investors' performance in the People's Republic of China. Given her outstanding prior research records, we can expect more and greater scholarly contributions from Tung in the coming years.

JOSEPH L. C. CHENG
UNIVERSITY OF ILLINOIS AT
URBANA-CHAMPAIGN

Further reading

(References cited in the text marked *)

Caligiuri, P.M. and Tung, R.L. (1999) 'A comparison of male and female expatriates' success', *International Journal of Human Resource Management,* 10 (5): 763–82. (Empirical study of male and female expatriate performance in international assignments around the world.)

Paik, Y.S. and Tung, R.L. (1999) 'Negotiating with East Asians: how to attain win-win outcomes', *Management International Review* 39 (2): 103–22. (Empirical study examining the similarities and differences in negotiating styles between Japanese, Chinese and Koreans.)

Tung, R.L. (1981) 'Selection and training of personnel for overseas assignments', *Columbia Journal of World Business* (Spring): 68–78. (Presents a contingency framework of selection and training of expatriates for international assignments; provides empirical data from US multinationals to support the framework.)

Tung, R.L. (1982) 'U.S.–China trade negotiations: practices, procedures and outcomes', *Journal of International Business Studies* (Fall): 25–37.

(Presents results from an empirical study of business negotiations between US and Chinese firms; examines the major issues under negotiation and identifies success factors in collaborating with the Chinese.)

Tung, R.L. (1987) 'Expatriate assignments: enhancing success and minimizing failure', *Academy of Management Executive* 1 (2): 117–25. (Compares and contrasts the expatriation process in US, West European and Japanese multinationals; examines the reasons for the varying rates of expatriate failure among these firms.)

Tung, R.L. (1993) 'Managing cross-national and intra-national diversity', *Human Resource Management Journal* 23 (4): 461–77. (Examines the similarities and differences in the dynamics and processes associated with managing international and intra-national diversity; offers suggestions on how to manage such diversity.)

Tung, R.L. (1994) 'Human resource issues and technology transfer', *International Journal of Human Resource Management* 5 (4): 804–21. (Presents a theoretical framework highlighting the significant role that human resources play in the transfer of technology from one country to another.)

Tung, R.L. (1994) 'Strategic management thought in East Asia', *Organizational Dynamics* 22 (1): 55–65. (Drawing upon the four ancient Chinese and Japanese works, this article presents the principles that guide strategic management thought in China, Japan, and Korea.)

Tung, R.L. (1998) 'A contingency framework of selection and training of expatriates revisited', *Human Resource Management Review* 8 (1): 23–7. (Assessment and update of Tung's 1981 contingency paradigm of selection and training for international assignments.)

Tung, R.L. (1998) 'American expatriates abroad: from neophytes to cosmopolitans', *Journal of World Business* 33 (2): 125–44. (Study of the attitudes and experiences of 409 American expatriates toward international assignments around the world.)

Tung, R.L. (1999) 'Expatriates and their families abroad', in W.A. Oechsler and J. Engelhard (eds), *International Management: Effects of Global Challenges on Competition, Corporate Strategies and Labour Markets*, Wiesbaden, Germany: Gabler Verlag, pp. 468–77. (Empirical study of the role families play in affecting expatriate performance abroad.)

Yeung, I.Y.M. and Tung, R.L. (1996) 'Achieving business success in Confucian societies: the impact of guanxi connections', *Organizational Dynamics* 24 (3): 54–65. (The study operationalizes the 'guanxi' construct and examines its relationship to firms' financial performance.)

See also: ADLER, N.; ASIA PACIFIC, MANAGEMENT IN; BUSINESS STRATEGIES, EAST ASIAN; CHINA, MANAGEMENT IN; CULTURE, CROSS-NATIONAL; DIVERSITY; EQUAL EMPLOYMENT OPPORTUNITIES; EXPATRIATE MANAGERS; GLOBALIZATION; HOFSTEDE, G.; HUMAN RESOURCE MANAGEMENT, INTERNATIONAL; JAPAN, MANAGEMENT IN; LUTHANS, F.; MIGRANT MANAGERS; MULTINATIONAL CORPORATIONS; ORGANIZATION BEHAVIOUR; ORGANIZATION BEHAVIOUR, HISTORY OF; ORGANIZATION CULTURE; SUN TZU

Turner, Ted (1938–)

Personal background

- born 19 November 1938 in Cincinnati, Ohio
- attended Brown University, but was expelled
- worked for his father's billboard business as general manager of Turner Advertising in the early 1960s and became president and chief executive officer (CEO) after his death
- in 1970, purchased an independent UHF television channel in Atlanta and renamed it WTBS
- founded the Turner Broadcasting System (TBS) in 1979
- in 1980, created the Cable News Network (CNN) and two years later added CNN Radio and Headline News
- in 1985, co-founded the Better World Society to promote world peace
- in 1985, purchased the MGM/UA Entertainment Co.
- in 1986, sold United Artists (UA) and the non-library portion of MGM and created the Turner Entertainment Company to oversee the libraries
- acquired the Hanna-Barbera animation studio in 1992
- in 1993, TBS purchased New Line Cinema and Castle Rock Entertainment
- merger with Time Warner in 1996
- after the AOL Time Warner merger in 2000, Turner lost control of the cable programming assets (e.g. CNN, HBO, TBS)
- in 2001, created Turner Ventures International which pursues purchasing a stake in Russia's NTV television

1 Introduction

Robert Edward Turner III was born on 19 November 1938 in Cincinnati, Ohio. His family moved to Savannah, Georgia, when he was nine years old. His father was so busy and preoccupied with his work that Turner was largely raised by a family employee by the name of Jimmy Brown. According to Turner, 'my friendship with Jimmy Brown [an African American] has made me a great believer in equal rights and equality for all people' (Booker 1994). It was Brown who taught Turner to hunt, fish and sail.

Turner attended Brown University. While at Brown he was vice-president of the Debating Union and commodore of the Yacht Club. Unfortunately he was expelled from Brown University for violating visitation rules when he was caught with a woman in his room (Farhi 1996). When his father committed suicide, Turner was 24 years old and inherited his father's financially troubled billboard business. 'Against the advice of financial consultants, Turner canceled the sale of the business and then proceeded to restore it to success.' Seven years later he expanded the business into broadcasting with the purchase of an Atlanta TV station (renamed WTBS) (*Contemporary Theatre, Film and Television* 1988; *Celebrity Biographies* 1998).

He has been married three times and has five children. Robert Edward IV and Laura Lee are from his first marriage to Judy Nye. Rhett, Beauregard and Sarah Jean are from his marriage with Jane Smith, whom he wed in 1964. Turner and Jane Smith divorced after twenty years of marriage. In 1991 he married the actress Jane Fonda at Avalon, his plantation in Capps, Florida (*Contemporary Theatre, Film and Television* 1988; *Celebrity Biographies* 1998). After nine years of marriage, Turner and Fonda divorced in 2000 (Rouse 2000).

Turner was named Yachtsman of the Year four times, won the cherished America's Cup in 1977 and received the Fastnet Trophy for yachting in 1979. *Sales and Marketing* magazine named him Outstanding Entrepreneur of the Year in 1979. Turner received the President's Award from the National Cable TV Association in 1979. He was named International Communicator of the Year by sales and marketing executives in 1981. Ted was named *Time* magazine's Man of the Year in 1991, and inducted into the TV Hall of Fame in 1992 by the Academy of Television Arts and Sciences. The *Sporting News* named Ted Turner the 1993 Most Powerful Person in Sports. In 1995, he received the David Susskind Lifetime Achievement Award in Television (Elliott 1993; *Contemporary Theatre, Film and Television* 1988; *Celebrity Biographies* 1998).

He serves on several boards, including Better World Society (chairman), Atlanta Chapter of the National Association for the Advancement of Colored People (NAACP) and Martin Luther King Center for Nonviolent Change. His outspoken and aggressive style contributed to Turner being called the 'Mouth of the South' and 'Captain Outrageous'. On several occasions he has acted in movies, e.g. *Southern Voices, American Dream, Gettysburg* (*Contemporary Theatre, Film and Television* 1988; *Celebrity Biographies* 1998).

2 Main contribution

In the early 1960s, Turner worked for his father's billboard business as general manager of Turner Advertising. After his father's death, he became president and CEO of the company. In 1970 he entered broadcasting when he purchased an independent UHF television channel in Atlanta and renamed it WTBS. Since 1976 WTBS has been widely distributed by cable systems. He owned the Atlanta Braves baseball team (acquired in 1976) and Atlanta Hawks basketball team (acquired in 1977), and televised their games on WTBS. He founded the Turner Broadcasting System (TBS) in 1979. In 1980, Turner created the Cable News Network (CNN), the first 24-hour news network. Two years later he expanded his news coverage by adding CNN Radio and Headline News (*Contemporary Theatre, Film and Television* 1988; *Celebrity Biographies* 1998). In 1986 he cre-

ated the CNN Center in Atlanta after purchasing the Omni International site.

In 1985 Turner purchased the MGM/UA Entertainment Co. for $1.5 billion. After purchasing MGM Turner was financially overextended and sold shares in TBS, reducing his ownership in the firm to 51 per cent. Turner agreed to allow the cable owners who had invested in his firm to approve all purchases over $2 million (Fabrikant 1989). In 1986 he sold UA and the non-library portion of MGM as he was primarily interested in the MGM film and TV libraries. He created the Turner Entertainment Company to oversee these libraries. Turner has been criticized for the colourization of classic black and white movies acquired from MGM. In 1987 he created a new cable network called Turner Network Television (TNT). He acquired the Hanna-Barbera animation studio in 1992, and the following year TBS purchased New Line Cinema and Castle Rock Entertainment. By 1994 Turner had six cable networks: CNN, TBS, TNT, Headline News, Cartoon Network and Turner Classic Movies (Hall 1994; *Contemporary Theatre, Film and Television* 1988; *Celebrity Biographies* 1998). Turner's merger with Time Warner in 1996 created the world's largest media and entertainment company (*Chicago Tribune* 1996). After the 1996 merger with Time Warner, Turner became a vice-chairman responsible for the cable programming assets, e.g. HBO, CNN, TBS (Reuters Financial Service 1996; *PR Newswire* 1996).

In 2000 America On-Line (AOL) merged with Time Warner ($143 billion deal) and Ted Turner was the largest shareholder after the merger with 4 per cent (Furman 2000). Under the terms of the AOL Time Warner merger, 'Turner was stripped of his day-to-day operating role in a management reorganization …' (Hofmeister 2000). Several new stories reported that Turner was furious about the AOL deal and being stripped of his authority over CNN and other components of the Tuner media empire (e.g., Furman 2000; Hofmeister 2000). Turner remains a vice-chairman of AOL Time Warner and publicly he has not spoken negatively about the merger. In fact he told journalists that he is 'happy as a clam' (Grantham 2000). 'Asked what life would be like without CNN, he said: "There was a time when there was no CNN and Turner was doing OK, so I guess I could live without it again'" (Rouse 2000).

Since the AOL Time Warner merger, Turner has led a group of investors interested in purchasing 25 per cent of Russia's NTV television and other Media Most holdings for $300 million (Higgins 2001). 'Mr. Turner has set up a new company, Turner Ventures International, to handle his Russian media project, which is separate from his role as vice chairman of AOL Time Warner Inc.' (Higgins 2001).

3 Evaluation

Turner is known for accomplishing in business what most have considered impossible. For example, 'He took an unknown, unheralded station that in nine years grew to 33 million viewers' (Cuff 1985). Turner attempted but failed to purchase the CBS (1985) and NBC (1993–4) television networks (Farhi 1996). This, however, did not necessarily reduce the impact he has had on the television industry.

It has been said that '[h]e is pushing television ... to its farthest frontiers' (*Contemporary Theatre, Film and Television* 1988). He was a leader in foreseeing consumer demand for news and creating the first global 24-hour news network. CNN has been available to viewers around the world since 1989 (Hall 1994). Turner has been credited with revolutionizing the broadcast industry by making it possible actually to see news in the making (Booker 1994). In 1991 'his Cable News Network presented the Gulf War, the Hill-Thomas hearings, the end of the Soviet Union, and the William K. Smith trial, all those great events, while they were happening' (Vecsey 1992).

Turner has made some enemies over the years. Perhaps most well known are his outspoken conflicts with his competitor Rupert Murdoch of News Corporation Ltd. When Murdoch announced that Fox News would be challenging CNN, Turner called Murdoch 'the schlockmeister' and 'promised that CNN would "squash [Murdoch's new venture] like a bug"' (Farhi 1996).

After being frustrated by the absence of Soviet athletes during the 1984 Los Angeles Olympic Games, Turner organized and co-sponsored the 1986 Goodwill Games in Moscow (*Celebrity Biographies* 1998). He has been outspoken against gratuitous violence on TV and in films, and has tried to present family-style content on his entertainment networks (Hall 1994). In 1985 Turner co-founded the Better World Society, an organization which promotes world peace. He continues to be active in the peace, environmental and population control movements (Green 1986; Farhi 1996). In a 1994 interview Turner stated: 'I'm planning right now to give half of what I have away. ... There are so many problems in the world that need addressing' (Hall 1994). Ted Turner has lived up to his promise and in 1997 pledged to donate a historic $1 billion to the United Nations (UN) to support the UN economic, environmental, social and humanitarian causes. 'Complementing the Turner pledge was the Turner promise – to encourage other leaders from the world of business and philanthropy to follow his lead in supporting UN causes' (*PR Newswire* 1997).

The *Forbes'* listing of the wealthiest Americans ranked Ted Turner at number 25 with $9.1 billion (*www.forbes.com* 2000). Turner owns 1.7 million acres of land in nine states, making him America's largest private non-corporate landowner (International Paper owns 7.3 million acres). 'They are places where rare and endangered species of wildlife, native grasses and even the lowly rattlesnake, coyote and prairie dog merit equal protection. It is a largely unfenced landscape with bison [24,000] and without cattle, as it was before White settlers arrived' (O'Driscoll 2000).

As a tribute to Ted, Time Warner Chairman Gerald Levin insisted that the new stadium for the Atlanta Braves be named 'Turner Field' (Hofmeister 2000). Among his personal accomplishments is his battle with manic depression, which he has fought and overcome (*People* 1995). Turner does not have plans ever to retire, but has shifted more of his efforts towards philanthropy. He has said: 'I try to relax. But I end up doing a lot of work wherever I am, out in Montana or wherever' (Hall 1994).

STEPHEN J. HAVLOVIC

UNIVERSITY OF WISCONSIN – WHITEWATER

Further reading

(References cited in the text marked *)

* Booker, S. (1994) 'TV's Ted Turner reveals black man served as his "second" father', *Jet* 18 April: 33. (Takes a look at Jimmy Brown and his impact on Turner.)
* *Celebrity Biographies* (1998) 'Turner, Ted'. (Gives personal and professional biographical information.)
* *Chicago Tribune* (1996) 'Time Warner, Turner shareholders approve $7.5 billion merger', *Chicago Tribune*, News, 10 October: 1. (Announces merger.)
* *Contemporary Theatre, Film and Television* (1988) 'Ted Turner', vol. 5. (Gives personal and professional biographical information.)
* Cuff, D.F. (1985) 'The formidable Ted Turner', *New York Times*, Section D, 5 April: 1. (Takes a look at Turner's aggressive approach to business.)
* Elliott, Stuart (1993) 'Ted Turner earns top sports honor', *New York Times*, Section D, 27 December: 7. (Announces award.)
* Fabrikant, Geraldine (1989) 'Some promising signs for Turner's empire', *New York Times*, Section D, 23 January: 1. (Reviews how Turner refinanced his business empire.)
* Farhi, P. (1996) 'Mogul wrestling: in the war between Murdoch and Turner, similarity breeds contempt', *Washington Post*, Style, 18 November: C1. (Discusses and analyses the animosity between Turner and Murdoch.)
* Furman, P. (2000) 'Turner shows his ire', *Daily News*, Business Section, 27 May: 43. (The article discusses Ted Turner's reaction to AOL's purchase of Time Warner.)
  Goldberg, R. and Goldberg, G.J. (1995) *Citizen Turner: The Wild Rise of an American Tycoon*, Harcourt Brace & Co. (A biography of Ted Turner.)
* Grantham, R. (2000) 'CNN Turns 20', *The Atlanta Journal and Constitution*, 2 June: 7E. (The article examines Ted Turner's life after the AOL merger with Time Warner.)
* Green, M. (1986) 'Ted Turner stages his own Olympics – and tries to rescue the planet', *People* 14 July: 62. (Takes a look at the Goodwill Games in Moscow and his personal life.)
* Hall, J. (1994) 'We're listening Ted', *Los Angeles Times*, Calendar Section, 3 April: 9. (An exclusive interview with Ted Turner where he discusses his professional and personal lives.)
* Higgins, A. (2001) 'Western investors advance on stake in Russia's NTV', *The Wall Street Journal* 16 February: A9. (Article reviews Turner's attempt to purchase a stake in NTV and Media Most.)
* Hofmeister, S. (2000) 'He's angry over diminished AOL Time Warner Role. Some expect Fireworks', *Los Angeles Times* 26 May: A1. (Article reviews the AOL purchase of Time Warner and impact on Ted Turner.)
* O'Driscoll, P. (2000) 'Turner builds ultimate preserve', *The Arizona Republic*, 18 July: A2. (A review of Turner's private land holdings and his environmental restoration projects.)
* *People* (1995) 'Ted Turner', *People*, 25 December: 87. (Turner was selected as one of the twenty-five most intriguing people of 1995.)
* *PR Newswire* (1996) 'Time Warner creates operating structure and management team for Cable Networks Group', *PR Newswire*, 17 September. (News release.)
* *PR Newswire* (1997) 'Ted Turner names Tim Wirth to oversee gift in support of UN causes', *PR Newswire*, 19 November. (News release.)
* Reuters Financial Service (1996) 'Time Warner N, Turner A team together', *Reuters Financial Service* 17 September. (News release.)
* Rouse, L. (2000) 'Turner steps aside at CNN', *The Guardian*, 1 June: Guardian City Pages 28. (The article discusses the 20th anniversary of CNN and Turner losing control of CNN after the AOL Time Warner merger.)
  Time Warner Corp. (1997) *1996 Annual Report*.
* Vecsey, George (1992) 'Sports of the Times', *New York Times*, Section B, 10 January: 11. (Profiles *Time* magazine's Man of the Year.)
* www.forbes.com (2000) 'List of wealthiest Americans'. (Annual listing of Americans with the most personal wealth.)

Further resources

AOL Time Warner website
http://www.timewarner.com or
http://www.aoltimewarner.com

See also: GLOBALIZATION; MULTINATIONAL CORPORATIONS

U

Ueno, Yôichi (1883–1957)

Personal background

- born Shiba, Tokyo, 28 October 1883, into a middle-class family; his father died when he was twelve years old
- gained a BA degree in psychology at the Tokyo Imperial University, 1908
- married Teruko Miimi, 1910; following her death in 1922, he married Shige Koehi
- promoted industrial efficiency movement, based on F.W. Taylor's notion of scientific management, in pre-war Japan
- established a school for industrial efficiency in 1942
- died at home of heart failure, 15 October 1957, aged 73

Major works

Shinrigaku tsûgi (Introduction to Psychology) (1914)

Hito oyobi jigyô nôritsu no shinri (Psychology of Efficiency of People and Business) (1919)

Jigyô tôseiron (Control of Enterprise) (1928)

Sangyô nôritsu-ron (Industrial Management) (1929)

Nôritsu gairon (An Introduction to Management) (1938)

Nôritsu handobukku (Management Handbook) (1939–41)

Nôritsu-gaku genron (Principles of Management) (1948)

Summary

Trained as a psychologist, Yôichi Ueno (1883–1957) was a pioneer in many fields in pre-war Japan. He is best remembered as the promoter in Japan of the notion of production efficiency based on the theory of scientific management devised by F.W. Taylor and developed by Taylor's followers. Ueno firmly believed in Taylor's idea that efficient work organization, informed by 'mental revolution', would reduce conflict and thereby lead to better relations between workers and management. Through consultancy, writing, lecturing and teaching, Ueno worked tirelessly to introduce the practice of industrial efficiency into the Japanese workplace. The philosophy of efficiency he developed was deeply influenced by the spiritual discipline of Zen Buddhist thought and could be extended to apply to life itself. Through pioneers like Ueno, Taylorism influenced Japanese management before the Second World War and provided the basis for further development in post-war Japan.

1 Introduction

Yôichi Ueno's professional life can be divided into four major phases. After his graduation in 1908 and until 1919, he worked to establish himself as a psychologist. Towards the end of this phase he became interested in industrial efficiency, introducing the works of F.W. Taylor and others to Japan (see TAYLOR, F.W.). From 1919 to 1925, he practised as an industrial efficiency consultant and visited the USA, where he contacted Taylor's followers. During the period 1925–42, he established the Japanese chapter of the Taylor Society of America, participated in international activities and published Taylor's works. Later, when the official economic and industrial organizations became dominated by the military, Ueno concentrated on private consultancy work. During the final period of his life, he devoted himself to the development of his own school of industrial efficiency while continuing his writing and consultancy work.

2 Biographical data and main contributions

Ueno's family originated in Nagasaki, where his grandfather, Shunnojô Ueno (1791–1852), had been a scientist and industrialist. Shunnojô introduced the first camera into Japan and is today regarded as Japan's 'father of photography' (Misawa 1967). Ueno's father, a skilful photographic technician, left Nagasaki for Tokyo to establish himself as a professional photographer. However, this venture did not succeed and he changed jobs several times. He died in the year Ueno completed the eight years of his elementary education. The family returned to Nagasaki to live under the protection of Ueno's uncle, Hikoma, himself a successful photographer.

Ueno went to a missionary school where all the textbooks, except those used for Japanese and Chinese language studies, were in English. This early exposure to English was to serve him well. At the age of seventeen, he returned to Tokyo with a strong desire to study at Tokyo Imperial University, which was then the foremost educational establishment in Japan. Working as a live-in English language assistant to an eminent educationist, he also taught English in the evening to finance his admission to the university as an auditing student in 1903. Continuing to work throughout his years at university, he first acquired full student status and, finally, in 1908 gained a degree in psychology.

Psychology and industrial efficiency

The experience Ueno gained in his first job as an editor at Dôbunkan, a major publisher, was important for his subsequent activities. While he was with Dôbunkan, he began lecturing, writing, editing and publishing in psychology-based disciplines. Psychology was established as an academic subject in Japan by Ueno's teacher, Yûjirô Motora, a professor at the Tokyo Imperial University. Between 1909 and 1921, Motora and his graduates gave monthly public lectures to popularize psychology. The lectures, edited by Ueno and published by Dôbunkan, proved to be popular. The success of the venture led to the launch of a monthly psychological journal, *Shinri kenkyû* (The Study of Psychology) in 1912, with Ueno as its chief editor. In 1926, it amalgamated with another journal to become *Shinri-gaku kenkyû* (Journal of Psychological Studies), the journal of the Japan Psychological Society.

Ueno's comprehensive psychology textbook, published in 1914 for student teachers, became both the best seller among his early publications and a long-selling book. The first revision in 1926 incorporated new psychological developments, including Sigmund Freud's psychoanalytic theory (see FREUD, S.), and by 1942 it had run to sixty-five editions. This success established Ueno's reputation as a psychologist and brought him financial independence (Saito 1983).

Turning his attention to the study of industrial efficiency, Ueno found the practical application of psychology to industry fascinating. At university he had read a journal from the USA in which Gilbreth, one of Taylor's followers, demonstrated the use of photography in the motion study (see GILBRETH, F.B.; GILBRETH, L.E.M.). Ueno wrote to ask Gilbreth for further explanation and thus made contact with a leading exponent of scientific management. In 1912, he was asked to contribute to a special edition of the journal *Jisugyôkai* (Business World), centred on scientific management. In writing this article, he studied the work of H. Münsterberg to establish a connection between psychology and scientific management and came to see Gilbreth's work in this light. To *Shinri-gaku kenkyû*, he contributed papers describing the accomplishments of Taylor, Gilbreth and Thompson and translated the work of Münsterberg. In 1919, using the material Gilbreth had sent, Ueno wrote and published his book *Hito oyobi jigyô nôritsu no shinri* (Psychology of Efficiency of People and Business). This achievement marked the end of the period when his study of industrial efficiency largely involved introducing the works of western scholars.

Industrial consultancy

From 1916, Ueno taught the psychology of advertising at Waseda University. In 1919, while working in this capacity, he came into contact with the director of marketing at the Kobayashi Company, the maker of Lion Brand tooth powder. The company wanted to improve its existing packing process, giving Ueno the opportunity to work on the practical application of theories of industrial efficiency to production. Using the time-and-motion technique, he introduced a change in the flow of work and a team-based work group and achieved a 20 per cent increase in output, a saving of 30 per cent in space, a reduction of waste and a decrease in the working hours. His success at Kobayashi established him as the first industrial consultant in Japan. The success of other assignments such as those at Nakayama Taiyôdô, a cosmetic firm, and Fukusuke Tabi Company, the maker of Japanese-style socks, helped to popularize the practical application of scientific management and brought Ueno a stream of speaking engagements and consultancy contracts.

In 1921, Ueno became the head of the *Sangyô Nôritsu Kenkyûsho* (Efficiency Research Institute), an arm of *Kyôchôkai*, a body established in 1919 to promote cooperation and adjustment between capital and labour through improvements in production efficiency. Ueno's achievements in industrial efficiency convinced the members of *Kyôchôkai* that there was a scientific basis to the notion of cooperation between capital and labour (see INDUSTRIAL RELATIONS IN ASIA PACIFIC).

Before starting work at the institute, Ueno was sent to the USA and Europe on a ten-month fact-finding tour. The tour turned out to be immensely significant for the subsequent development of his career. Helped by Gilbreth, he visited many universities, businesses, governmental offices and private associations, mainly in the USA. He met many people, including F.W. Taylor's widow, the known followers of Taylor and many other exponents of scientific management. At the spring conference of the Taylor Society held in Philadelphia, Ueno gave an impressive speech to an audience of 500 people (Misawa 1967). The contacts he made with the members of the Taylor Society led to many lasting friendships. In Europe, he visited London, Paris, Munich and Berlin. He wrote *Nôritsu gakusha no tabinikki* (The Travel Diary of the Efficiency Management Scholar), describing his visits.

In the first part of the 1920s, Japan was ready to embrace the idea of industrial efficiency and Ueno was extremely busy running the institute, working as a consultant and writing (see JAPAN, MANAGEMENT IN). One of the institute's major achievements was its programme for training efficiency experts. Four courses held in 1923 qualified 450 people as efficiency supervisors, who became the backbone of the efficiency movement in subsequent decades (Misawa 1967). However, the institute was closed in March 1925, due mainly to lack of funds.

Keen to continue the institute's work, Ueno took it over as his personal consultancy business, with the same aims and staff, under the name of *Nihon Sangyô Nôritsu Kenkyûsho* (Japan Institute of Industrial Efficiency). His activity extended to Manchuria, China, when it came under Japanese control. The institute's office moved, in 1933, to Ueno's home. In 1927, *Nihon Nôritsu Rengôkai* (National Management Association of Japan), was formed as an amalgam of six existing regional efficiency institutes, with Ueno as one of its committee members and later as its director-general. He also edited the association's house journal, *Sangyô Nôritsu*. (In pre-war Japan, the tenn *nôritsu*, or 'efficiency', which was employed by Harrington Emerson, was more commonly used in Japanese industrial circles than the term *keikei*, or 'management'.)

Furthering the aims of scientific management

In 1925, Ueno established the Japan chapter of the Taylor Society, the first outside the USA. In the following five years, many leading US experts in scientific management came to Japan, and most of them were at the World Engineering Congress held in Tokyo in the autumn of 1929.

In the spring of 1929, Ueno attended the fourth *Comité International de l'Organisation Scientifique* (CIOS) congress in Paris, both as director-general of the National Management Association of Japan and as a representative of the Japan Branch of the

Taylor Society. One item of interest at the congress was an historical map submitted by Ueno which showed the development of scientific management (*L'histoire graphique de l'organisation scientifique du travail, 1856–1929*). This map charted the four stages of the movement's development, the names of its major proponents, their publications and their contacts (Saito 1986).

A year later, the Taylor Society of America invited Ueno to lead a party of sixteen Japanese industrialists on a very successful tour of US factories. His next project was the publication of a three-volume comprehensive collection of works by Taylor and on Taylor. Only two volumes were published, however. The third volume, a projected biography of Taylor, was abandoned for financial reasons.

In 1934, Ueno extended his work to include the promotion of efficiency in the distribution/retail sector. Keen to introduce the idea of efficiency into people's lives, both at home and at school, he joined *Kanamoji-kai* (Phonetic Scripts Society), a society aimed at popularizing a simplified version of written Japanese which uses fewer Chinese script symbols. Aware of the implications for clerical and personal efficiency, Ueno also introduced the practice of writing Japanese from left to right.

In 1935, having received a grant from *Nihon Gakujutsu Shinkôai* (the Japan Society for the Promotion of Learning), Ueno and the staff of the efficiency institute began the task of compiling a management handbook. Ueno wanted to produce a book on scientific management, framed within the Japanese concept, for the Japanese. The whole work was published in three volumes between 1939 and 1941.

Although Ueno enjoyed passing his knowledge and experience in management on to students, he remained largely outside mainstream management education at a higher education level in pre-war Japan, which was heavily influenced by the German tradition based on management economies (see MANAGEMENT EDUCATION IN JAPAN). He taught at Waseda and Nihon Universities as a part-time lecturer, although from 1943 to 1945 he was professor in charge of the departments of Economics and Management at St Paul's University, Tokyo (now more commonly known as Rikkyô University). Of greater significance was his time at the Yokohama Polytechnical School (today's Kanagawa University), where he became the director of a newly inaugurated department of industrial management in 1939, after some years spent teaching the history of scientific management. The satisfaction Ueno got from contact with students there was an important factor in his decision to establish his own school of efficiency, *Nihon Nôritsu Gakkô*, in 1942.

Ueno's school of industrial efficiency

Ueno first discussed the idea of establishing a school of industrial efficiency in his book *Nôritsu gairon* (An Introduction to Management), published in 1938. In this text, he outlined the basic principles of efficiency as applied to the entire way people live and learn: 'The principle of efficiency is not just the method and technique but it is a philosophy and the way, and beyond learning one must act to disseminate the philosophy' (Saito 1983: 104).

In addition to being a writer and consultant, Ueno became directly involved in establishing his own teaching organization. The first stage of this development was the establishment of *Nôritsu dôjô* (the Efficiency Training Centre). This was underpinned by Ueno's emerging philosophy of efficiency', which rested on the five elements of: the right food, the right posture, learning without prejudice, the right belief and the right use of language. Followers of Ueno's efficiency activities in the Kyoto/Osaka region started several study circles called *Ochibo-kai* (the Society of Fallen Ears of Rice). The movement spread to Tokyo and Hakata in 1941. Based on this experience, Ueno opened a school in 1942, but it had to be closed the following year because of the Second World War.

In 1947, the Allied Occupation Force invited Ueno to serve on the *ad hoc* personnel committee for the creation of *Jinjiin* (the National Personnel Agency) and the civil service personnel structure. His post was equivalent to that of a cabinet minister, an unusual appointment for a person not connected with the government. During his four years in this post, he introduced the 'Jinjiin Supervisory Training' (JST), a training programme for clerical supervisors. It was the 'first training programme made by the Japanese and for the Japanese' (Saito 1983: 124).

In 1948, Ueno published *Nôritsu-gaku genron* (Principles of Management), an original work on his philosophy which brings together the results of his life's work in management. In this book, the notion of three 'mu', namely muda (waste), muri (inappropriateness) and mura (unevenness) – the avoidance of which is central to efficiency – is presented as an integral part of his philosophy.

While working for the occupation force, Ueno was elected chairman of the All-Japan Federation of Management Associations, which replaced the war-time association. He also played an important role in establishing the Japan Association of Management Consultants, which gave official recognition to management consultants' professional status in 1951.

Ueno's school, when it reopened in 1947, became a vocational school catering for the needs of adults through evening classes. In 1950, it obtained two-year junior college status, offering production and clerical efficiency programmes. In 1953, it introduced correspondence courses in four subjects, becoming Japan's only higher education institution providing working adults with part-time management education. After completing his tenure as a bureaucrat, Ueno devoted his remaining years to the development of the college *Sangyô Nôritsu Tanki Daigaku* (the Industrial Efficiency Junior College).

Ueno published over 100 books, particularly in the area of scientific management. Another area of publishing that was important to him as a communicator was his editorship of a succession of journals and the numerous articles he contributed to those publications. Starting with *Shinri kenkyû* (The Study of Psychology), he went on to become involved in the publication of *Nôritsu Kenkyû* (Efficiency Review) by the Japan Efficiency Study Group from 1923 to 1927, followed by *Sangyô Nôritsu* (Industrial Efficiency), published by the National Management Association from 1927 onwards. These journals had a more public character than his previous work.

In 1935, Ueno began publishing his own house journal, *Ochibo* (The Fallen Ears of Rice), which was renamed *Nôritsudô* (The Way of Efficiency) in 1942 and ran until his death. Through these journals, he communicated his experiences in consultancy work, introduced works of efficiency scholars from the USA and elsewhere and propounded his own philosophical views and educational ideas for the furtherance of scientific management.

Ueno's enthusiasm for the promotion of industrial efficiency never waned. He represented Japan at the tenth CIOS congress in Sao Paulo, Brazil, in 1954. A year later, he travelled to India and Thailand as adviser on flood prevention and other matters for the Economic Commission for Asia and the Far East. Towards the end of his life, he worked on a book about creativity, which was published a month after his death. The evening before his death from heart failure, Ueno was teaching at his college.

3 Evaluation

Although he was not the first person to introduce Taylor's theories of scientific management to Japan (Greenwood and Ross 1982), within his own country, Ueno was probably the person who best understood what Taylorism truly stood for. Certainly, he worked steadfastly and passionately throughout his life to promote scientific management, which was encapsulated in the notion and practice of industrial efficiency. While mainstream Japanese management academics were concerned essentially with the textual interpretation of the German school of management economics (see GERMANY, MANAGEMENT IN) represented by Nicklisch (Saito 1986), Ueno played a leading role in spreading the American concept of 'efficiency' by applying it at a practical level.

Perhaps, because it was in the pioneering stage, Ueno's work, although highly successful, began with small companies and did not involve large and heavy engineering concerns. Large companies tended to introduce 'Taylorist' practices through the mediation of their own trained industrial engineers, often in piecemeal fashion, with the result that their understanding of the principles of scientific management was often incomplete. Large companies were also suspicious of consultants such as Ueno, outsiders who offered their 'advisory' services for a pecuniary return, as it was customary for such 'non-concrete' expertise to be offered free of charge in Japan in the 1920s and 1930s (Saito 1983). Nevertheless, Ueno contributed enormously to raising the business community's concern for efficiency, by organizing the fragmented regional societies for the promotion of efficiency into a national-level organization.

A considerable part of Ueno's contribution to Japanese management was in the area of international exchange. Through the establishment of the Japan branch of the Taylor Society of the USA, he was able to organize an industrial mission to the USA and invite prominent disciples of Taylor (who were also Ueno's personal friends) to Japan to give talks to Japanese businessmen. Ueno was an active participant in international conferences on scientific management, raising the profile of Japanese management internationally.

Ueno's influence on efficiency activities at a national level waned from the early 1930s, when Japan was dominated increasingly by the military. This loss of influence was occasioned probably by his close association with the USA as well as by his lack of political adroitness (Saito 1983). However, the fertility of Ueno's mind was such that he continued to extend the notion of efficiency beyond the manufacturing sector, to advertising, retailing, the service industry and clerical work, promoting it through his writing and consultancy. There is no doubt that his work prepared Japanese businesses for the promotion of productivity in the early 1950s.

Ueno's death in 1957 occurred just as enthusiasm for new management techniques gripped Japanese managers (Okazaki-Ward 1993). Industry was in the process of large-scale capital investment into new technology imported mainly from the USA (see TOYODA FAMILY). A flood of new American management ideas and techniques was to enter Japan, to be seized upon by managers and management academics (see DEMING, W.E.; JURAN, J.M.). Many American management experts were invited to Japan to give lectures, and hundreds of industrial missions were sent to the USA. It is hard to ignore the role played by the tradition of the Taylorist management practices, established in pre-war Japan by people like Ueno, in providing a receptive climate for new American management ideas after the Second World War. However, because Ueno's work was concerned with the practical aspects of industrial management, his pioneering contribution to management in Japan is not properly appreciated by the academic community (Saito 1983).

Ueno never was a mere mouthpiece for Taylor's theory, nor was he a simple follower of the practitioners of scientific management in the USA. He stood equal to them in stature, and continued to evolve the practice of scientific management by incorporating the Japanese approach, not only to work but to the way of living, to create a unique synthesis. Once, he debated the possibility of such an approach to management being exported back to the USA (Saito 1983), presaging the worldwide interest which the so-called Japanese-style of management created in the 1980s.

4 Conclusion

As an early advocate and interpreter of American scientific management, Ueno worked tirelessly for its adoption into Japanese industrial culture. It was in recognition of this fact that he was given the title 'the Father of Industrial Efficiency' in Japan and also called 'Benefactor to the Efficiency Movement'. Also he was posthumously decorated.

His work is carried on by his son, Itchirô Ueno, through the Sannô Institute of Business Administration, a unique educational organization which brings together the two-year college, the university and postgraduate study in management, plus a research arm to serve a wider business community. The uniqueness of the organization that Yôichi Ueno bequeathed to posterity was that it was based on the concept of continuous adult education in business, the notion that managers needed ongoing training to manage efficiently. Today, Sannô University's postgraduate school in business administration is at the forefront of the new wave of MBA education in Japan for working adults, which began towards the end of 1989 and gathered momentum during the 1990s (L.I. Okazaki-Ward, 2001). It offers a fully accredited MBA programme through a course requiring college attendance in the evenings and at the weekend, and also a distance-learning course in conjunction with Globis in Japan and the Leicester University's Business School in the UK.

L.I. OKAZAKI-WARE
CRANFIELD SCHOOL OF MANAGEMENT

Further reading

(References cited in the text marked *)

Araki, T. (1955) *Nôritsu lchidaiki – Keieikomon 30nen* (Record of a Life in the Efficiency Profession – Thirty Years as a Management Consultant), Tokyo: Nihon Keici Nôritsu Kenkyûsho. (An account written by one of Ueno's junior colleagues.)

* Greenwood, R.G. and Ross, R.H. (1982) 'Early American influence on Japanese management philosophy: the scientific management movement in Japan', in S.M. Lee and G. Schwendiman (eds), *Management by Japanese Systems*, New York: Praeger. (Describes the early scientific management movement in Japan, in which Ueno figured prominently.)

* Misawa, H. (ed.) (1967) *Ueno Yôichi-den* (Yôichi Ueno, a Biography), Tokyo: Sangyô Nôritsu Junior College Press. (A short biography/autobiography of Ueno, the first half of which is written by him.)

Nihon Nôritsu Kyôkai (ed.) (1982) *Nihon Nôritsu Kyôkai Konsarutingu 40 nen-shi* (The Forty-Year History of Consulting Activities at the Japan Management Association), Tokyo: JMA. (A collection of writings about the JMA's consultancy work, covering the period *c.* 1940 to *c.* 1980.)

* Okazaki-Ward, L.I. (1993) *Management Education and Training in Japan*, London: Graham and Trotman. (A comprehensive study of how managers are developed in Japan today, with some historical overview.)

* Okazaki-Ward, L.I. (2001) 'MBA management education for the New Millennium in Japan', *Journal of Management Development* 20. (The paper will be included in an early publication of Vol. 20 in 2001.)

Okuda, K. (1985) *Hito to keiei – Nihon keiei kanri-shi kenkyû* (Men and Management – Research into the History of the Development of Scientific Management in Japan), Tokyo: Manejimento-sha. (A detailed history of the

development of scientific management in Japan before the Second World War.)

* Saito, T. (1983) *Ueno Yôichi – Hito to gyôseki* (Yôichi Ueno – The Man and his Achievements), Tokyo: Sangyô Nôritsu University Press. (A work published to commemorate the centenary of Ueno's birth; includes full biographical details.)

* Saito, T. (1986) *Ueno Yôichi to keieigaku no paionia* (Yôichi Ueno and the Pioneers of Management), Tokyo: Sangô Nôritsu University Press. (A collection of documents and correspondence relating to Ueno and his colleagues in the scientific management movement, interspersed with the author's comments.)

* Taylor, F.W. (1911) *The Principles of Scientific Management,* New York: W.W. Norton & Co. Inc. (Taylor's exposition of his views which is widely regarded as a classic of management theory.)

Ueno, Y. (1914) *Shinrigaku tsûgi* (Introduction to Psychology), Tokyo: Dainihon Tokyo. (Comprehensive textbook written for students of teacher training. First to apply psychology to education.)

* Ueno, Y. (1919) *Hito oyobi jigyô nôritsu no shinri* (Psychology of Efficiency of People and Business), Tokyo: Dôbunkan. (The first half covers the effect of an individual's personal characteristics upon efficiency, while the second deals with topics such as scientific management.)

Ueno, Y. (1928) *Jigyô tôseiron* (Control of Enterprise), Tokyo: Dôbunkan. (Ueno advocates the practical application to Japanese business of the concept of planning and control which lies at the root of scientific management.)

Ueno, Y. (1929) *Sangyô nôritsu-ron* (Industrial Management), Tokyo: Chikura Shobô. (Comprehensive work on the theory and practice of management which incorporates practical wisdom distilled from Ueno's consultancy work.)

* Ueno, Y. (1938) *Nôritsu gairon* (An Introduction to Management), Tokyo: Dôbunkan. (Argues that the principle of efficiency must extend to all areas of human life, not simply factories and other organizations. Advocates the need to view efficiency as a philosophical principle which offers guiding precepts for behaviour.)

Ueno, Y. (1939–41) *Nôritsu handobukku* (Management Handbook), Tokyo: Dôbunkan. (Three-volume text designed to fulfil the need for a comprehensive handbook on scientific management written in Japanese, for the Japanese, based on the actual situation in Japan.)

* Ueno, Y. (1948) *Nôritsu-gaku genron* (Principles of Management), Tokyo: Nihon Nôritsu Gakkô. (Summarizing Ueno's life works on efficiency,

this comes in two parts: the first dealing with the theory of management and the second with the history of industrial development and that of scientific management.)

Urwick, L.F. (1984) 'Yôichi Ueno', in L.F. Urwick and W.B. Wolf (eds), *The Golden Book of Management*, New York: American Management Association. (A collection of short biographies of 106 major international figures in management; Ueno is one of seven Japanese pioneers in management included in the collection.)

See also: ASIA PACIFIC, MANAGEMENT IN; ECONOMY OF JAPAN; FUKUZAWA, Y.; HUMAN RELATIONS; JAPAN, MANAGEMENT IN; JAPANIZATION; JUST-IN-TIME PHILOSOPHY; MANAGEMENT EDUCATION IN ASIA PACIFIC; ORGANIZATION BEHAVIOUR; ORGANIZATION BEHAVIOUR, HISTORY OF; TAYLOR, F.W.; TOTAL QUALITY MANAGEMENT

Uganda, management in

Overview

To the visiting foreigner, Uganda is a beautiful and scenic country with polite and friendly people. To the local business executive, entrepreneur or public service manager, however, it is a difficult country to manage. This entry discusses the factors which, over the years, have shaped the leadership, organization and management of the country's political economy. It concludes with a cautiously optimistic note about the future of the country and its management.

1 Introduction

Located at the northern shores of Lake Victoria and the source of the Nile, Uganda is an equatorial country endowed with natural beauties and resources. But it is also small, landlocked, underdeveloped, highly differentiated, and characterized by contrast, contradiction and conflict. The forces which have shaped the country's business development, leadership and management style and content include:

1 its history: pre-colonial, colonial, and post-colonial;
2 the country's variegated cultural and ethnic groupings including religious and sectarian differentiation;
3 a predominantly agricultural and resource based economy with a small but promising industrial sector;
4 socioeconomic status differentials, including sex roles. Computer information technology and globalization have not as yet had a direct significant impact on the country's development, work processes, or management thought and practice.

2 Analysis

History and management

Modern Uganda is glued together from previously independent or semi-independent traditional kingdoms and chieftaincies each with its own unique governance institutions, work organizations, languages, cultural values, religious beliefs and practices. Before colonial times, administrative systems were small in size, homogenous in membership and therefore easy to manage, used local technology and indigenous knowledge systems, and co-existed in relative harmony with the natural environment. Each had a formal hierarchy with the chief or king at the apex. Authority was due to conquest, heredity or special relationships with the supernatural. Even today, leaders attempt to emulate these traditional forms of authority which were also reinforced by the colonial administrators through a system of indirect rule. Consequently, symbolism and status are important in influencing leadership behaviour and managerial style (Kiggundu 1991).

Kinship and shared cultural values helped to cement relationships across administrative hierarchies. It also helped to foster a common understanding and thereby control any excessive abuse of power with indirect but socially effective checks and balances. The weakening of the traditional social controls and sanctions has contributed to current problems of governance and economic mismanagement. In addition, organizations which cut across traditional homogenous lines are prone to conflict, and are more difficult to manage.

The current stock of leaders and managers draw their experience and inspiration from the traditional leaders and colonial administrators. Most managers in the private sector have served their time in government or the military. Accordingly, leadership and management philosophy values, styles and practices are similar across sectors. Leadership is characterized by a formal hierarchy, and by auto-cratic, authoritarian and paternalistic behaviour with highly centralized decision making. Delegated participative management is rare. Symbolism, especially that drawn from traditional or even colonial images, is important. Power distance is high and senior managers often take on the role of father figure towards their employees. Lower level employees are given little or no autonomy in their work; middle and junior managers exercise close supervision. Trust across hierarchical levels is low. Those in leadership roles behave like the old traditional chiefs (Blunt and Jones 1992; see LEADERSHIP).

Differentiation without integration

Uganda and its formation as a modern state is a complex juxtaposition of ethnicity and religion with a more recent spicing of African nationalism, Islamic fundamentalism, and post-Cold War ideology. There are about 55 tribes in Uganda with a population of just over 21 million people (1996) and a total surface area of 241,139 square kilometres (about the size of Britain) of which about 20 per cent is covered with water and swamps. Religion is important in Uganda and there is competition among the Christian churches and with the Muslim community. According to the 1995 figures, 60 per cent of the population belongs to various Christian denominations of which the Catholic church (7.8 million) and the Anglican church are the most dominant. Muslims make up only 5 per cent of the population although they are much more dominant especially in politics, trade and commerce.

The historical and socio-cultural characteristics, reinforced by colonial and post independence administrations have resulted in a highly differentiated society. Besides ethnicity, language and religion, society is differentiated by race, education, income, wealth (e.g. land, cows), opportunity, the rural–urban divide, gender, age, family connections, heredity and political affiliations. This differentiation makes management and public administration difficult, and causes a certain disconnectedness especially between traditional institutions and modern organizations (Dia 1996).

Societal differentiation manifests itself in many different ways relevant for public administration and business management. For example, it explains why a relatively small country has over 20 political parties and an equal number of small commercial banks each servicing a small segment of the population. It also explains why so many small universities are mushrooming in spite of a generalized lack of resources for post-secondary education. It also explains the existence of wide disparities in education, income, wealth and opportunity among the various segments of society. It explains some of the tensions and conflict which characterize independent Uganda (Rupesinghe 1989).

Societal differentiation and its manifestations transcend to the level of individual institutions and business organizations. At the organizational level, it complicates leadership, management and supervision. For example, national institutions such as the civil service, the military and the central bank devote a lot of resources trying to reconcile different and often conflicting regional, tribal or religious differences. This may explain why, as of 1998, the Uganda Railways, left with only a 50 mile operating line from Kampala to Jinja, still employs over 2000 workers. It may also explain why top management of the corporation, after being found wanting, was reprimanded by being sent home on six months paid leave.

Leaders and top executives try to cope with organizational differentiation by taking on many societal extra-organizational roles. For example, a senior banking executive is president of a local youth organization, heads a religious or tribal group, chairs the board of governors of a local university, sits on the fund-raising committee for a local high school and advises political leaders. This means that these executives are spread too thinly and hardly have time to concentrate on the strategic aspects of the business or to keep up to date with industry trends. Ugandan managers tend to be more operational and tactical than strategic or long-term in their business decisions (Kiggundu 1989, 1996). This may explain at least in part the excessive dependence on outside consultants, especially in the public sector.

Differentiation contributes to organizational small size because it prevents the development of joint ventures, large scale partnerships, horizontal or vertical business integration. Indeed many organizations in Uganda suffer from being small in size, not only because of market limitations but also due to societal differentiation. This deprives management of economies of scale and results in highly cost inefficient operations. Entrepreneurs in Uganda complain of a lack of economies of scale, but are reluctant to take practical steps to merge operations because they are afraid of losing management control. Trust is low and information on corporate performance is not shared. As one CEO told me, 'we do not provide operational or performance data. If you are successful, they are jealous; if you fail, they laugh at you.'

The problem is not that differentiation in Uganda's organizations is too high. Indeed, organizations in other countries – especially in Africa – operate under similar differentiated environments (see AFRICA, MANAGEMENT IN). Rather, the problem is that no corresponding effective integrating mechanisms are in place. Integrating mechanisms such as shared corporate vision and how to achieve shared goals, effective horizontal linkages within and across organizations, mutual trust and a code of business ethics and employee empowerment have been difficult to institutionalize. This is the challenge for management in Uganda in the twenty-first century.

War and disease

The Ugandan population, including political, business and institutional leaders and managers has been traumatized by war and disease. By the year 2000, those who were born in the mid 1960s when the first incidents of domestic conflict started will be in their mid 30s. Those who were in their teens when Amin's 'state of blood' started in the early 1970s will be in their 40s. Those who were young adults when Obote and Muwanga's reign of terror started in the early 1980s will be in their 50s. Those who got their experiences, work values and ethics from the colonial era are retiring (Kasozi 1994).

The present generation of leaders and managers is made up of men and women who have grown up under reckless, highly stressful and traumatic conditions. There is no adult in the country who has not lost a close relative, friend, co-worker or business associate either due to conflict or disease. HIV/AIDS has been particularly devastating not only to the individuals and their families, but also to the social and economic fabric of society as a whole. It is estimated that by the mid-1990s, about 15 per cent of the adult population was infected with the human immunodeficiency virus (HIV), the causative agent for AIDS (Armstrong 1995).

Besides reducing the already limited stock of available management, entrepreneurial, professional and intellectual capital, or inexpensive unskilled rural labour, war and disease have created a generation of traumatized employees and their managers. Trauma manifests itself in many ways including fear, anger, learned helplessness, mistrust, depression, perceptual distortion, a sense of personal persecution and a variety of psychosomatic disorders. The full extent of the effects of these manifestations on the leaders and business managers in the country has never been studied. However, as a minimum, the managers' ability to analyse business decisions, take appropriate business risks, maintain healthy social and interpersonal relations, and sustain strategic thinking must be negatively affected. A lot of energy is spent camouflaging these feelings, especially when dealing with foreigners. Managers who have no faith in the future do not think strategically and tend to be corrupt. There is very limited respect for the sanctity of ordinary life. Investment decisions are made to protect capital from the consequences of war and disease rather than to maximize long-term profitability. Hoarding of capital, stock, information and other business assets is part of doing business. Yet, Ugandans are very resilient. In spite of almost 40 years of war and disease, they are busy rebuilding a society and economy which, if successful, will be the envy of all their neighbours (see BOTSWANA, MANAGEMENT IN).

Economic management

Agriculture is by far the most important sector of the economy accounting for 46 per cent of GDP (gross domestic product), 90 per cent of exports and 80 per cent of the total labour force. It is predominantly organized by small holdings with little or no application of modern technology or management. The development of the whole economy is heavily influenced by the performance of the agricultural sector which in turn is influenced by climatic conditions, internal security, rural infrastructure, availability of local cheap labour and global pricing. The few agricultural estates for tea, sugar and coffee are owned by foreign firms with their own global management systems largely independent of local management practices (Europa Yearbook 1998).

There is a small industrial sector based on agriculture/food processing, textiles, logging, mining and quarrying, which accounts for about 5 per cent of GDP. The industrial sector was developed from the colonial period through independence on the basis of import substitution rather than global integration and contained a dominant and pervasive public enterprise sector. Like the agricultural sector, the industrial sector contains many very small firms. Over 80 per cent of the firms employ 35 people or less, and 50 per cent employ 10 people or less. These firms are too small and too undercapitalized to take advantage of modern technology or management. The larger firms are either foreign owned, or currently undergoing privatization.

Most of the manufacturing sector produces the usual 'necessities' of life in poor developing countries: processed food, beer, soft drinks, soap, cigarettes, cement, electricity, paper, etc. These products tend to be politically sensitive and the firms seek protection or concessions against foreign competition. They therefore have little incentive to adopt modern management techniques since competition is muted. Most industries are located in the Kampula-Jinja-Tororo axis while the north and western regions (outside Mbarara) have very few industries. This uneven regional distribution accentuates problems of differentiation across the country (United Nations Industrial Development Organisation (UNIDO) 1992).

The sector has been adversely affected by several factors including the leftist policies of the 1960s, the expulsion of the Asians (1972), the break up of the East African Community, the security problems of the 1980s and associated brain drain, and the frequent looting during successive civil conflicts. During the 1990s the government has been preoccupied with the rehabilitation, development and privatization of the public enterprise sector. By the early 1990s the entire industrial sector was performing at only 30 per cent of capacity, and manufacturing accounted for about 7.7 per cent of GDP in 1995/96. Government policy aims at creating an enabling environment for private sector development including attracting private foreign direct and domestic investment. During the period 1992–95 government identified over 1600 new investment projects in various sectors of the economy. Experience elsewhere shows that public sector administrators rarely make good private sector managers.

The new class of African entrepreneurs and managers are developing their own approach to business development and management. Rather than concentrating on the growth of a single firm in a single sector, the tendency is to develop many small firms in many different sectors. This is particularly the case with entrepreneurial family owned firms. For example, one entrepreneur who started out in the financial services sector, over a period of 10 years, has developed an 'octopus' business structure that includes real estate, hotel and recreation, food processing, export, trading and post-secondary education (Jorgensen *et al.* 1986).

The management implications and challenges of the octopus approach to business are obvious. First, individual firms are likely to remain small and therefore unable to enjoy economies of scale. Small firms do not use modern management or technology, especially if market conditions are competitive. Second, the few available management capacities are spread too thinly across different and unrelated businesses. This makes industrial specialization difficult and the octopus entrepreneur runs the risk of running out of good managers across sectors. Third, integration within the same or similar sectors is difficult as investments in individual firms are considered not in the context of their respective sectors, but as part of a sprawling octopus with social and political implications for the entrepreneur rather than purely business considerations. These implications suggest that adoption of modern management and technology by these octopus entrepreneurs is likely to be slow.

One of the issues confronting the new African entrepreneurs is corporate governance (see CORPORATE GOVERNANCE). Most of the nouveaux riches do not yet understand the structuring, role and responsibilities of the corporate board of directors and the separation of responsibilities with the executive senior managers. Some board members are known to get involved in the day-to-day running of the business, thus interfering with managements' prerogative to manage. At the same time, executive managers are reluctant to provide board members with corporate sensitive information for fear it will be sold to the highest bidder. This problem is particularly serious in the early stages of privatization where overlapping directorships and changing minority interests are common.

The commercial banking system is in need of significant change. In 1994, more than half of the banks made losses with a large negative core capital. Aggregate non-performing assets were in excess of 50 per cent of total loans. Banks generally lacked financial discipline and administrative efficiency thus causing high intermediation costs. Even the Central Bank's financial position and institutional capacity are in doubt. The government has responded by privatizing its own Uganda Commercial Bank – forcing the closure of the worst of the non-performing banks – and strengthened the supervisory capacity of the central bank. Still the majority of the small entrepreneurs have no access to open market credit.

Privatization of public enterprises is expected to attract modern management and technology as the new owners seek better returns from their investments. However, this will only happen if privatization is accompanied by increased competition in the local economy and if there is a clear distinction between the new owners and those in government and their political or military masters. Crony capitalism impedes advances in business and management development. Available evidence suggests that the difference between management before and after privatization is rather blurred. Uganda has been ranked the twelfth most corrupt country in the world.

The Asian factor in Uganda's management

No discussion of management in Uganda is complete without examining the role of the Asian community. This is a small but important group of entrepreneurs originally from the Indian subcontinent who settled in Uganda, brought capital, enterprise and expertise and dominated the country's commerce and industry both in urban centres and rural areas. Although governments before and after independence attempted to limit the role of the Asians, they remained dominant until their expulsion in 1972. In the mid-1990s, they were invited back to repossess their businesses and some have accepted the challenge and restarted their business operations or opened new ones.

In spite of their dominant role, especially in small and medium-sized enterprises, the Asian entrepreneurs have never been instrumental in introducing modern management thought and practice. Instead, their employment practices, management styles and business philosophy are traditional and paternalistic. They have tended to exploit their superior economic status but are not interested in transferring their business acumen to the indigenous entrepreneurs. They have tended to crowd out the Africans, especially in the more profitable lines of business. True business partnerships based on a level playing field between the two groups are rare. Until this happens, coexistence will be difficult, and mutual mistrust will continue.

Unions and associations

Uganda does not have a strong independent trade union movement. The small size of the agricultural and industrial firms, the problems of societal differentiation, lack of union support from overseas and restrictive government legislation have all contributed to a weak labour movement. This gives managers a relatively free hand in shaping employee relations at their place of work.

There are several active employer associations in the country. For example, the Uganda Manufacturers Association, originally formed in 1972 and reactivated in 1989 has more than 200 medium and large-scale member companies in both the private and public sector. Together with the Federation of Uganda Employers, the Uganda Chamber of Commerce, Uganda Management Institute and the recently established Private Sector Foundation, these organizations play an active role in promoting industrial development and assisting local organizations to improve management thought and practice (see HUMAN RESOURCE MANAGEMENT IN THE EMERGING COUNTRIES; INDUSTRIAL AND LABOUR RELATIONS IN THE EMERGING COUNTRIES).

Women in management

Uganda is a basically male dominated society and this dominance pervades life in work organizations. Although the country has a long tradition of female education through Christian missionary schools, few women are active in business management and entrepreneurship, except in the social sector (e.g. education, health, welfare, non-government organizations). Status differentials also prevent the advancement of women, as existing women's organizations tend to concentrate on their narrow interests rather than reaching out to the grassroots including the poor and uneducated women. Ironically, AIDS, which cuts across social status, has had the effect of bringing Ugandan women together as they cope with the challenges of widowhood, single parenting and the vulnerability of their own health. The Aids Support Organization (TASO) is a case in point.

Although there are a few high profile women who have been successful in politics and public administration, the overall role of women in society leaves much to be desired. More women are needed, especially in the

higher levels of business, corporate management and entrepreneurship.

3 Conclusion

For a country that has been described as the 'pearl of Africa' and a 'state of blood', predicting the future is indeed a risky business. During the late 1990s, the country enjoyed positive international press and material support from the World Bank and Western donors. However, very little of the aid has trickled down to the poor. On the basis of monetary and economic macro-performance, these supporters predict favourable conditions for business and management development. This is particularly likely to be the case if the country's industrial strategy is linked to the agro-business sector taking advantage of a favourable climate, fertile soils, cheap unskilled labour, and a good track record of managing relatively small and simple value adding enterprises.

The real test will be the extent to which the country attracts substantial private foreign direct investment and maintains an environment within which local business can grow and eventually compete in the global economy. Critics point out that a combination of internal tensions, crony capitalism, mismanagement and poor utilization of resources and regional military adventurism may give rise to the development of 'Aminic' conditions leading to yet another reign of terror and destruction. History teaches us to be cautiously optimistic.

MOSES N. KIGGUNDU
SCHOOL OF BUSINESS
CARLETON UNIVERSITY

Further reading

(References cited in the text marked *)

* Armstrong, J. (1995) *Uganda's AIDS Crisis: Its Implications for Development*, Washington, DC: World Bank Discussion Papers, No. 298. (This field study shows that AIDS in Uganda will have a far-reaching impact on the social and economic fabric of the country's society and that it poses a serious threat to development including the rural areas where HIV is spreading rapidly.)

* Blunt, P. and Jones, M.L. (1992) *Managing Organizations in Africa*, New York: Walter de Gruyter. (Discusses the challenges and prospects for developing and managing effective organizations in Africa with illustrations from Uganda.)

* Dia, M. (1996) *Africa's Management in the 1990's and Beyond: Reconciling Indigenous and Transplanted Institutions*, Washington, DC: The World Bank. (Presents research evidence to support the view that problems of economic management in Africa are due to a structural disconnection between formal institutions transplanted from outside and indigenous institutions born of traditional African culture.)

* Europa Yearbook (1997) 'Uganda', *Africa South of the Sahara*, 26th edn, London: Europa Publications Limited. (Provides the statistics used in this section of the paper.)

* Jorgensen, J.J., Hafsi, T. and Kiggundu, M.N. (1986) 'Towards a market imperfections theory of organizational structure in developing countries', *Journal of Management Studies* 23 (4): 417–42. (Develops the concept of the octopus as a structural response to market imperfections in the development of small entrepreneurial organizations. Provides illustrations particularly relevant to the newly emerging indigenous small business organizations in Uganda.)

* Kasozi, A.B.K. (1994.) *The Social Origins of Violence in Uganda 1964–1985*, Montreal: McGill-Queen's University Press. (Spirited discussion of the causes of violence from the time of independence in 1962 to 1985 by a Ugandan social historian.)

* Kiggundu, M.N. (1989) *Managing Organizations in Developing Countries: An Operational and Strategic Approach*, West Hartford, CT: Kumarian Press. (Provides a framework with illustrations from Uganda for the analysis of strategic and operational aspects of organizations in developing countries.)

* Kiggundu, M.N. (1991) 'The challenge of management development in Sub-Saharan Africa', *Journal of Management Development* 10 (6): 32–47. (Discusses the effects of history on management development in Africa with examples from Uganda.)

* Kiggundu, M.N. (1996) 'Integrating strategic management tasks into implementing agencies: from firefighting to prevention', *World Development* 24 (9): 1417–30. (Provides a rationale and suggested approach for integrating strategic management and operational administration in organizations in Uganda.)

Mutibwa, P. (1992) *Uganda Since Independence: A Story of Unfulfilled Hopes*, London: Hurst and Co. (Discusses the unfortunate recent history of Uganda, pointing out the disappointment of many unfulfilled hopes and expectations.)

Ofcansky, T.P. (1996) *Uganda: Tarnished Pearl of Africa*, Boulder, CO: Westview Press. (Provides a pessimistic general overview of the country's recent history and political economy, and identifies the factors that help to explain the challenges of postcolonial development: poverty, disease, crime, instability, violence and refugee migrations.)

* Rupesinghe, K. (ed.) (1989) *Conflict Resolution in Uganda*, Oslo: International Peace Research Institute. (Discusses the causes of conflict in Uganda. For more recent historical accounts, see Wrigley 1996; Ofcansky 1996; Mutibwa 1992; and Twaddle 1993.)

Twaddle, M. (1993) *Kakungulu and the Creation of Uganda*, London: James Currey. (Describes the genesis of modern Uganda as a colonial state, and the roots of internal conflicts among ethnic groups in the country.)

* UNIDO (United Nations Industrial Development Organization) (1992) *Uganda: Industrial Revitalization and Reorientation*, Industrial Development Review Series, Geneva. (Discusses the structure and historical evolution of Uganda's industrial sector with a special emphasis on government initiatives since 1986.)

Wrigley, C.(1996) *Kingship and State: The Buganda Dynasty*, Cambridge: Cambridge University Press. (Wide-ranging and original study of one of Africa's most famous kingdoms.)

See also: AFRICA, MANAGEMENT IN; HUMAN RESOURCE MANAGEMENT IN THE EMERGING COUNTRIES; INDUSTRIAL RELATIONS IN THE EMERGING COUNTRIES; LEADERSHIP; NIGERIA, MANAGEMENT IN; SOUTH AFRICA, MANAGEMENT IN; WORLD BANK

Ukraine, management in

1 Introduction
2 Ukrainian management in transition
3 Management education and training
4 Conclusion

Overview

Prior to the collapse of the Soviet Union in 1991, management in the Ukraine involved operating (with all the practical day-to-day difficulties involved) within a framework of coordination from centralized sectoral ministries at the level of the republic or (more often) the level of the USSR government. The system of management remains hierarchical and clan-based, except that absolute power now typically resides in the hands of one director and associates rather than with a party machine or ministry. This in itself would not be a problem, were the mechanisms of accountability and competition more firmly in place; after initial liberalization the pace of reform slowed, leading to an environment in which state functionaries made it difficult for managers (whether foreign or Ukrainian) to carry out business effectively.

1 Introduction

Since the break-up of the Soviet Union in December 1991, Ukraine has gone through dramatic economic restructuring (see RUSSIA, MANAGEMENT IN). Many of the basic institutions of a market economy were quickly introduced. Prices at the wholesale and retail level were liberalized. At first policy-makers lost all control over prices and exchange rates, and inflation reached an annual rate of 10,000 per cent during the worst period shortly after independence. The exchange rate of the first national currency, *karbovanets*, fell from ten per US dollar to 180,000 per dollar over the years after its introduction. In the past few years, however, the government has made remarkable progress with macroeconomic stabilization, achieving an inflation rate

around 40 per cent in 1996 and less than half that in 1997. Meanwhile a new currency, the *hryvnia* (HRN), was introduced in 1996 and has remained stable within a currency corridor of 1.7–1.9 to the dollar for almost all of 1996–97. Ukraine's heavy trade exposure to Russia has already forced one effective devaluation of *hryvnia* as a result of the financial crisis in Russia. The currency was squashed down towards the bottom end of its new HRN2.50–3.50:$1 trading band, valued at below HRN4:$1 on the streets.

Viewed from every angle, Ukraine's economy has performed poorly in recent years, with real gross domestic product (GDP) having fallen by 62 per cent since independence; 10 per cent in 1996; 7.5 per cent in 1997. Ukraine's industrial output declined by 57.9 per cent between 1990 and 1997. Recently Ukraine's macroeconomic performance has been mixed, with strong progress having been made to curb inflation, but with instability still persisting in terms of high budgetary and inter-enterprise arrears.

Economic policy

In addition to the problems associated with moving from a planned to a market economy, Ukraine has to build a whole hierarchy of state institutions almost from scratch. This has complicated and confused economic policy-making. During Leonid Kravchuk's presidency economic policy was hostage to a political stalemate between left and right. Fiscal and monetary policies were very loose, with the budget deficit rising to 27.1 per cent of GDP in 1992 and 14 per cent in 1994. As a result, in late 1993 the economy spiralled into hyperinflation, with the new national currency, the *karbovanets*, losing half its value every month. Not surprisingly, Mr Kravchuk lost the presidential election in 1994 to Leonid Kuchma, who campaigned on a platform of economic reform as well as rapprochement with Russia. In November 1994 the new presi-

Basic data

Land area	The Republic of Ukraine (formerly the Ukrainian Soviet Socialist Republic, a constituent part of the USSR) is situated in eastern Europe. It is bordered by Poland and Slovakia to the west; by Hungary, Romania and Moldova to the southwest; Belarus in the north; Russian Federation in the east. To the south lie the Black Sea and the Sea of Azov. Ukraine covers an area of 603,700 sq km (233,090 sq miles), of which 58 per cent is cultivated.
Population and main towns	The total population at 1 January 1998 was 50.48 million. The largest cities are the capital Kiev (Kyiv, 2.635 million), Kharkiv (1.576 million), Dnipropetrovsk (1.162 million), Odessa (1.160 million), Donetsk (1.102 million), Lviv (808,000). The capital of the autonomous region of Crimea is Simferopol (352,000), although its largest city is Sebastopol (370,000). Almost 73 per cent of the population are ethnic Ukrainians, 22 per cent are Russian and 5 per cent other minorities. About 68 per cent of the population is urban.
Language	Ukrainian, a member of the East Slavonic group, is the official language; but Russian is as widely spoken in central and eastern Ukraine, where it dominates in urban areas.
Currency	The *hryvnia* replaced the *karbovanets* on 2 September 1996, at the rate of HRN1:Krb100,000. Average exchange rate in 1997: HRN1.86:US$1; on 12 October 1998: HRN2.50–3.50:US$1.
Legal system	A new constitution was approved by the *Verhovna Rada* (parliament) on 28 June 1996.
Major officials	President: Leonid Kuchma, elected with 52 per cent of the popular vote in June 1994. Prime Minister: Valery Pustovoitenko, appointed in July 1997. First Deputy Prime Minister: Anatoly Holubchenko. Deputy Prime Minister of Economic Reform: Serhiy Tyhypko. Finance Minister: Ihor Mityukov. Economic Minister: Vasyl Rohoviy. Foreign Economic Relations and Trade Minister: Serhiy Osyka. Foreign Affairs Minister: Borys Tarasyuk. Chairman of National Bank: Viktor Yushchenko. Head of the State Property Fund: Oleksandr Bondar.
National legislature	*Verhovna Rada* or Supreme Council, a unicameral assembly of 450 deputies.
Main political factions in parliament	As of 20 July 1998: Communist Party of Ukraine (120 seats); People's Democratic Party (87 seats); *Hromada* (45 seats); Socialists and Peasant Party bloc (33 seats); United Social Democratic Party (25 seats); Green Party (24 seats); Progressive Socialist Party (14 seats); other parties and independents (46 seats); unfilled seats (9 seats).

dent signed a stand-by arrangement with the IMF, under which Ukraine undertook to limit the budget deficit to 7.3 per cent of GDP in 1995. Almost immediately a range of price subsidies and trade restrictions were abolished, and the president promised to accelerate privatization (see PRIVATIZATION AND REGULATION). Despite stalling tactics by the left-wing opposition in parliament, the stabilization programme has been a success. In 1995 the consolidated budget deficit was 7.9 per cent of GDP, in 1996 4.6 per cent of GDP, and

in 1997 7.1 per cent of GDP. In addition, the proportion of the deficit financed by credits from the National Bank of Ukraine has fallen from 100 per cent in 1993 to zero in 1997. Year-end consumer price inflation dropped from 39.7 per cent in 1996 to 10.1 per cent in 1997. In early 1998 the band within which the currency was allowed to fluctuate was widened to HRN1.8:US$1–HRN2.25:US$1 to take account of volatility in the aftermath of an international crisis of confidence in emerging markets from late 1997.

Privatization

Though Mr Kuchma's stabilization programme has been a success, his ambitious privatization programme has not. Most small retail and high street businesses have been handed over to worker cooperatives, privatization of larger firms has proceeded extremely slowly, with controlling shares in many so-called privatized enterprises staying in government hands. Privatization revenue has been correspondingly small: by December 1997 revenue totalled only HRN165 million, or one-third of that year's budget target.

In addition to worker and management buy-outs (the most popular method of privatization in Ukraine) the State Property Fund (SPF) has held, with the help of the International Finance Corporation, a series of voucher auctions similar to those pioneered by the Czech Republic (see CZECH AND SLOVAK REPUBICS, MANAGEMENT IN THE). Though the public was initially sceptical about the scheme, because the government was slow in putting up attractive firms for sale, by January 1998 over 90 per cent of Ukrainian citizens had picked up their vouchers and half of them had exchanged them for shares. Some 28,000 state owned enterprises have been privatized since 1992, 16,265 of these in 1995 when the privatization process began in earnest. For the most part corporatization (the formation of joint stock corporations, whether open or closed) and privatization have not led to the expected productivity or efficiency gains. In December 1997 the head of the SPC, Volodymyr Lanovy, announced that in 1998, the government would try to sell more companies for cash, and hold international tenders for stakes in Ukraine's four electricity generators. The Prime Minister, Valery Pustovoitenko, has also announced the privatization of the national telecommunication monopoly, Ukrtelecom, in 1998, but this unlikely to happen before early 1999 at the earliest.

In November 1998, the head of the privatization fund gave a gloomy assessment of his chances of getting his plans for future sell-offs past parliament. Deputies have already called for privatization to be halted completely, and any planned sales may have to be forced through by presidential decree. The privatization fund is not performing well: it expects to achieve less than half its target of HRN1.04 billion ($303 million) in revenue this year. At this rate, even next year's target of HRN800 million is out of reach. In September 1998 Ukraine's government admitted that events in Russia would make it extremely difficult to sell some of the state firms being offered for privatization this year – particularly the oil-refining sector, which is reliant on the Russian market. As such, it now expects only to earn HRN500 million (US$200) from sell-offs this year, compared with a budget forecast of over HRN1 billion.

2 Ukrainian management in transition

Management in Ukraine reflects the fundamental changes occurring in the economy as a whole, changes wrought by national independence, the collapse of the traditional state economy and the implementation of market reforms. Leaving aside the substantive problems (loss of markets, finance, suppliers) the main trend has been decentralization, whether or not accompanied by formal changes in ownership status. Managers at enterprise level have de facto inherited powers of discretion and decision making that were previously the preserve of administrators or party officials at the level of the Ukraine (or the then USSR) as a whole. A generation of managers whose tasks were previously conceived in technical or routine administrative terms have been obliged to confront major strategic issues of enterprise survival in difficult conditions with few instruments at their disposal.

Ukraine, like a number of transitional countries, is characterized by chronic nonpayment, shortages of liquidity or investment capital, barter, lack of all but extremely short-term incentives, lack of effective regulation or accountability and meddling by (often self-interested) state and regional bureaucrats. This is an environment as conducive to sharp practice as to entrepreneurial innovation, perhaps significantly more so given the degree to which the official and business worlds appear intertwined. Semilegal means of survival (or enrichment) are widespread, to the extent that the shadow economy is estimated to account for 40–60 per cent of the economy as a whole. Typically the bosses of state (or former state) enterprises afflicted by crisis will have a parallel existence as owners of unofficial or semi-official small firms, the success of which usually has little to do with competitive advantage (see CHINA, MANAGEMENT IN; RUSSIA, MANAGEMENT IN).

Ukraine management relies heavily on personal networks, whether family-related or of the 'production' type – the hierarchical clan type networks that characterized Soviet economic management organizations. This orientation towards personal, as opposed to formal/institutional links sits easily with the economy's reliance on barter, variously estimated as accounting for 50–75 per cent of Ukraine's economy.

This in turn reinforces the overall lack of transparency in business and management. In part this reflects the Soviet legacy. In the past enterprise managers did not know their customers and suppliers as most if not all contacts with these were mediated through central agencies which had every incentive to minimize the flow of information. In many cases a similar situation pertains in post-Soviet circumstances, albeit with shadowy intermediary firms taking the place of the defunct ministries and agencies. 'Commercial secrecy' has replaced national security as a means of legitimizing the monopoly of information and coordination involved. The lack of information inhibits the development of genuine competition, the absence of which removes the incentive to improve efficiency or develop new products.

Structural reorganization

Decentralization has not only occurred between the state and enterprises, but is occurring also within the enterprises themselves, where the managers of subdivisions are increasingly extricating themselves from the control of the parent organization. This trend is true both for the core businesses involved as well as peripheral or service functions. These departments or businesses have been registering themselves as independent legal persons, and are increasingly establishing themselves

as joint stock companies (whether of an 'open' or 'closed' type) with a view to uniting at a later stage as a holding company. This process of disaggregation may be seen to have its roots in the Soviet-era system of *khozraschyot*, an extreme form of cost-centre management which (notwithstanding the centralized nature of the management system overall) had provided a degree of autonomy to departments and functions particularly in high technology industry, during the late 1970s and 1980s (the same period saw widespread adoption of cell production and project management approaches, although these came too late to save industry from the accumulated problem of very low productivity).

Decentralization was accompanied by the abolition and merger of the sectoral ministries that ran industry in Soviet times. In the most significant instance, nine such ministries were merged in 1992 to form the Ministry of Machine-Building and Conversion of the Military-Industrial Production of Ukraine, within which each sector (e.g. aviation, heavy engineering, etc.) is represented by a Principal Directorate. The years 1992–98 saw a succession of no less than six ministers, which testifies to the organizational problems involved in running this state conglomerate and developing any kind of effective overall policy, leading to the view that the ministry should be decentralized.

3 Management education and training

Management education for young managers occurs largely through higher education institutions, most notably the Kiev National Economics University. The University provides undergraduate and masters level courses in finance, management economics, accounting and audit, banking, insurance operations management and marketing. The University had a record of innovation in the late Soviet period when, as the Kiev Institute of National Economy, it had in the early 1980s become the first Soviet institute to provide courses in Western style management economics and labour economics (see MANAGEMENT EDUCATION IN CENTRAL AND EASTERN EUROPE).

Taras Shevchenko University (Kiev) and Kharkov University have also developed centres of management education, as have a number of the state-licensed regional training centres which provide training in both public administration and commercial management.

In addition there are an estimated 200 commercial higher education institutes providing vocational training for accountants, financial managers, bankers, traders and production/operations managers. However, the explosion in management education that occurred in the early 1990s has been followed by a period of retrenchment since the enterprises which used to pay for their staff to be trained in such institutes can no longer afford to do so. Economic stagnation has in any case removed much of the stimulus for enterprises and firms to invest in staff training, although this is partly offset by the heightened desire of individuals to acquire new skills and qualifications in business and management. Banking provides an exception in that high demand from the sector has led to the development of a strong network of training centres which train managers and staff of commercial banks and the central bank of Ukraine. Banking has also been the sector where large numbers of staff have received training abroad, notably in the USA, the UK, Germany and Canada.

Although training of new managers is more than catered for by the university sector and continuing education by the commercial institutes, there is arguably a vacuum regarding senior management training, The Higher Party Schools which had previously trained the top managers of the Soviet *nomenklatura* have, as elsewhere, been reincarnated as centres for civil service and public administration training. Similar centres for senior managers in private industry appear not to exist, except in part through the training programmes of the Employment Fund. The emphasis in management education thus seems to be on business school qualifications for younger managers – although this may itself reflect international trends.

The system of management training has thus undergone similar changes as has management in Ukraine generally – a shift from a highly centralized system to a market-based one strongly differentiated and decentralized by sector and by region. Economic stagnation has none the less seriously inhibited the ability of the decentralization drive to deliver tangible benefits except for a fortunate few.

4 Conclusion

Ukraine is in the process of developing a more flexible, decentralized approach to management, but it is still at an early stage in this process, and much management practice, certainly in the more traditional sectors, is inevitably conditioned by the past. Much needs to be done to accelerate change in this area, if the style of management is not to become a major constraint on the country's successful emergence from the current economic crisis. The continuing expansion of Western-style business education, particularly at graduate level provides grounds for some optimism none the less.

ELENA DENEZHKINA
UNIVERSITY OF BIRMINGHAM

Further reading

(References cited in the text marked *)

The Economist Intelligence Unit (EIU) (1998–99) *Country profile: Ukraine*. (Provides detailed economic data (by sector) along with detailed analyses of political and socioeconomic background. An ideal starting point for a country overview.)

The Economist Intelligence Unit (EIU) (1998) *Country report: Ukraine*, 3rd quarter. (The quarterly reports provide detailed updates on the themes covered by the country profile, but with more detail and with cumulative comparisons of trends.)

The Economist Intelligence Unit (EIU) *Business Eastern Europe. A Weekly Report: Business, Finance and Investment.* (Journalistic bulletin with useful quotes, expert opinions and case examples, very useful for comparison between transitional countries.)

Europa Publications (1997) *Eastern Europe and the Commonwealth of Independent States. Regional Surveys of the World: A Political and Economic Survey* 3rd edn, London: Europa Publications Limited, 789–817. (Very useful in terms of an integrated analysis, drawing on business, socioeconomic and political data to provide a broad and thorough picture of the position in each of the countries concerned.)

Eurasia Economic Outlook. WEFA Group. Ukraine. (Useful for recent news, forecast highlights, as well as statistical data.)

Jolly, A. and Kettaneh, N. (eds) (1998) *Doing Business in Ukraine,* London: CBI/Kogan Page. (Very helpful compilation of practical summaries of the business context, market potential, business opportunities in Ukraine, and how to go about building an organization to operate in the Ukrainian market. The only criticism would be that the problems encountered are so well described that this tends to belie the editors' optimistic conclusions.)

Konings, J. and Walsh, P. (1998) 'Disorganization in the transitional process: firm-level evidence from Ukraine', *Transitional Economics* Discussion Paper Series, No.1928, July, Centre for Economic Policy Research, London. (Useful analysis of the productivity effects of privatization, including survey data from Ukrainian enterprise directors.)

PlanEcon Report, Development in the Economies of Eastern Europe and the Former USSR, Ukrainian Economic Monitor (1111 14th Street, NW-Suite 801, Washington, DC 20005-5603). (Provides useful financial comparisons between transitional countries, analyses of trends and patterns of economic cause and effect between different countries including how the Asian financial crisis has affected Ukraine and other transitional countries).

Ukrainian Economic Trends, Monthly update, Tacis, 1998. (Brings together socioeconomic and public finance indicators.)

Ukrainian Ministry of Statistics *Monthly Statistical Bulletin.* (Monthly bulletin of the National Bank of Ukraine, Monthly and Quarterly Ukraine – statistical database.)

See also: ACCOUNTING IN CENTRAL AND EASTERN EUROPE; CHINA, MANAGEMENT IN; CZECH AND SLOVAK REPUBLIC, MANAGEMENT IN THE; GLOBALIZATION; INTERNATIONAL MONETARY FUND; MANAGEMENT EDUCATION IN CENTRAL AND EASTERN EUROPE; RUSSIA, MANAGEMENT IN; WORLD BANK

Uncertainty: see DECISION MAKING; INTERNAL CONTEXTS AND EXTERNAL ENVIRONMENTS; FUTUROLOGY; KNIGHT, F.H.; LAWRENCE, P.R. AND LORSCH, J.W.

Unemployment, economics of: see EMPLOYMENT AND UNEMPLOYMENT, ECONOMICS OF

Unions: see TRADE UNIONS

United Kingdom, management in the

1 Historical context
2 Social position, social origins and education
3 Careers
4 Managerial work
5 Professionalism and training
6 Industrial relations and employee participation
7 Public and private sectors
8 Future prospects

Overview

Changes in the economic and occupational orders of the modern-day UK have led to increasing proportions of workers in managerial and professional positions. Although it is difficult to define precisely the nature of the managerial role, definitions of managers taken from occupational censuses suggest that they comprise more than two million of the workforce. This is certainly the case if the two broad categories incorporating managers in central and local government and in large-scale commercial and industrial enterprises are included with those engaged in smaller establishments. There have been a wide range of studies in the UK covering different aspects of the managerial role and, as a consequence, there is an increasingly clear picture of the dominant characteristics of managerial attitudes and behaviour. Indeed, much is now known about patterns of share ownership among managers in the UK, industrial relations experience, job satisfaction and motivation, and views on the role of government and the enterprise culture. Moreover, specific aspects of managerial behaviour with respect to issues such as careers, training and education have increasingly been targeted as areas of particular focus.

Here, the intention is to delineate various aspects of the managerial role and of related managerial experiences in the UK. The entry begins with an analysis of the historical context, in which early debates on the separation of ownership from control and the concomitant emergence of a 'separate' and 'specialist' management function are assessed. This is followed by accounts of the social position, social origins and education of managers, together with issues of managerial careers with special reference to gender. Following this, details of the range and types of managerial work and related aspects of job satisfaction are then discussed. Issues of professionalism and training are then assessed, after which managerial attitudes towards industrial relations and employee participation are evaluated. There is then a review of public and private sector similarities and differences in the nature of managerial roles and behaviour. Discussion then focuses upon future prospects and identifies five key issues for special consideration: the corporate state and the enterprise culture; professionalism and management development; ownership, control and competing interests; the employment relationship; and the increasing internationalism of management. The special importance of British managers in shaping the future of the country's organizations and society is forcefully stressed as an overall conclusion.

1 Historical context

The rise of managers as an occupational group in the UK during the nineteenth and twentieth centuries is usually attributed to the growth in size and complexity of industry (facilitated by the emergence of the joint stock company), coupled with the expanding administrative activities of the state. Typically, this overall development has been analysed in terms of the separation of ownership from control at the top of the business enterprise: managers are understood to occupy the controlling positions, but have little or no involvement in the ownership of enterprises (which has passed increasingly to institutional shareholders) (see BIG BUSINESS AND CORPORATE CONTROL).

However, early theories about the relationship between ownership and control can be classified into two contrasting perspectives. The first argues that a separation of ownership from control has taken place at the top of the modern corporation and that, accompanying this development, a new type of manager who is essentially non-propertied, technically proficient and professional has replaced the old-style entrepreneur or owner-manager. The second asserts that this change has been overstated and that, even where it has occurred, management still tends to pursue policies in which the interests of business

ownership are to the fore. Essentially, the so-called 'managerialists' argued that a separation of ownership from control has taken place; these include such writers as Berle (1960), Burnham (1941) and Galbraith (1967). Berle contended that as companies grew in size the proportion of voting stock held by the largest individual shareholders declined, and thus there was a progressive movement from owner to management control in the enterprise. Moreover, Berle argued that this process would gradually bring about changes in business behaviour and ideology since whereas the old-style owner-manager pursued policies which maximized shareholder interests, the 'new' managers would ensure that the interests of all stakeholders in the enterprise would be accommodated – employees, consumers and the public at large as well as the owners. Burnham and Galbraith diagnosed similar trends to Berle but put forward somewhat different interpretations. Burnham considered that managers would ultimately pursue their own vested self-interests and that, particularly in the public sector, they would use their indispensable positions in the decision-making processes of organizations to ensure the dominance of managerial rather than ownership priorities. Galbraith on the other hand viewed power as shifting from ownership to a more broadly based *technostructure* consisting not only of managers but also of professionals, specialists and other key personnel within the enterprise.

The second perspective argues from an opposite view to claim that, for a number of reasons, ownership or large shareholder interests continue to be the dominant force in modern corporations despite the emergence of a specialist management function (Nichols 1969). First, devices such as non-voting shares and the difficulties in organizing large numbers of small shareholders means that the larger shareholders can effectively exercise corporate control, even with a minority of total shares. Second, even though top managers may hold a relatively small percentage of the total shareholdings issued, on an individual basis they are often sufficient to encourage managers to pursue policies which favour corporate ownership. Third, similarities in background, attitudes and values between owners and senior managers ensure that both groups subscribe to the primacy of large shareholder interests. Finally, and perhaps most important of all, external market pressures ensure that in the long run managers must pursue profit-orientated policies to the advantage of owners rather than others among the enterprise's stakeholders. This arises not least because of the risk of predatorial takeover by competitor companies if different policies are pursued (Nichols 1969).

In the UK the most influential early empirical work on these issues was conducted by P. Sargent Florence. In an early study, *The Logic of British and American Industry* (1953), he concluded that the managerial revolution had not proceeded as far as had previously been supposed. However, evolutionary trends along lines consistent with the arguments of the 'managerialist' thinkers were identified in a later work, *The Ownership, Control and Success of Large Companies* (1961). First, he found an inverse relationship between size of company (in assets) and the percentage of ordinary shares owned by the board. The percentages of director shareholding by size of company were, for smaller companies, 2.9 per cent; medium size, 2.1 per cent; and very large companies, 1.5 per cent. Second, for the same size ranges, the proportion of directors among the twenty largest shareholders was 30 per cent, 21 per cent and 16 per cent, respectively. Third, Sargent Florence found that the median percentage of directors' ordinary holdings in the very large companies had fallen from 2.8 per cent in the year 1936 to only 1.5 per cent in 1951 (see Nichols 1969 for a review of these data). However, as his critics have argued, the amount of wealth owned by directors and senior managers may still be considerable, and for the reason stated above, it is unlikely that they will pursue policies in any way detrimental to ownership interests. On the contrary, in the UK the propensity towards 'short-termism', associated with the renowned tendency to reward ownership interests particularly favourably, has been viewed as explaining in part the relatively poor long-term investment performance of British companies.

During the 1980s, in the UK there have been major changes in patterns of ownership. However, and as a consequence, the issue of ownership–control has become increasingly prominent in discussions on the role of the manager. For much of the twentieth century the growing scale and complexity of industry, coupled with public ownership of the means of production and distribution, appeared to have occasioned a significant degree of formal separation of ownership from control at the top of the business enterprise. Managers had come to occupy positions of control and, outside family firms, any participation in ownership was seen to be largely irrelevant for the managerial role. However, from the 1980s onwards, phenomena as diverse as the upsurge of entrepreneurialism, restructuring and privatization, profit-sharing and share ownership schemes and management buyouts have reflected a radical change. Indeed, the prospects of a substantial change in patterns of ownership (with capital being widely, if very unequally, distributed among modern working populations) have become more likely than at any stage since the rise of industry itself. The origins of these changes are complex but five are particularly worthy of mention:

1 Dislocations in political economies of the post-1970s brought about by 'oil shocks', turbulent currency movements, inflation, high unemployment and worldwide economic recessions.

2 A transformation in ascendant ideologies and values in which entrepreneurship and new forms of ownership have been sought as counterpoints to the traditional capitalist firm, the managerially dominated corporation and the impersonal state bureaucracy.

3 Legislative changes (reflecting these ascendant values) that have given a fiscal stimulus to profit sharing and share ownership and to similar departures, some of which have applied directly to managers; for example, executive share option schemes.

4 New technologies that have placed a heavy premium on the retention and the redeployment of core workforces (including managerial personnel) who require expensive retraining.

5 Large-scale organizational transformations brought about by increasing international competition and the processes of globalization.

Moreover, these developments appear to have impacted substantially on managers; an inference which is certainly reasonable on the basis of Institute of Management studies of managers in the UK, 1980 and 1990 (see Mansfield *et al.* 1981 and Mansfield and Poole 1991 for a comparison of data from the two studies). Taking direct shareholdings by managers first of all, in the 1980 study, unless attention is restricted to private sector board members, the evidence by and large supports the thesis that a separation of ownership from control has taken place in the modern business enterprise. However, it is clear that for managers in the 1980s the incentives to hold shares have had an appreciable effect on behaviour in this regard and, in consequence, this earlier conclusion now requires reappraisal.

In 1980 78.1 per cent of manager respondents did not own shares in the companies in which they were employed, leaving a balance of approximately one-fifth who had a direct financial stake in their enterprises. By 1990, although only a minority of managers overall owned shares in their companies, the pattern had altered considerably (64.2 per cent of respondents reported that they did not own shares in their employing organizations, leaving a balance of 35.8 per cent as owner-managers). However, if one concentrates on managers in publicly quoted firms, the majority (52.5 per cent) are now owner-managers. Moreover, although there are no direct data to compare with the situation in 1980, the 1990 findings are that most managers own shares (indeed, 64.4 per cent of managers possess shares in companies other than their own). Hence, it is clear that the bulk of British managers are now shareholders.

Of course, it is also important to know which of the various 'stakeholder' interests are endorsed by modern managers. In the Institute of Management surveys, the following groups' interests were identified: owners and shareholders; managers; other employee groups; consumers; suppliers; and the public at large. And there has, over time, been an increase in the percentage of managers who consider that owners' or shareholders' interests should be promoted by their organizations (81.8 per cent in 1990; 77.5 per cent in 1980). If anything, therefore, there is a greater degree of commitment to ownership interests

in the 1990s than in 1980, a situation which is not surprising given the increased number of managers who are currently owners of shares in their companies. But what is of particular interest is the apparently paradoxical commitment to consumer interests. In 1980, these were a significant concern for managers. Indeed, at that time 73.3 per cent considered that consumer interests should be promoted by their firms. By 1990 the relevant figure had risen to 84 per cent. Consumers rather than owners now have what the classical economists referred to as 'sovereignty'. In other words, according to managers, they comprise the most important single interest group among the various stakeholders in the modern corporation. The dominance of markets and market issues (alongside ownership) for managers are thus worth stressing, together with the growing significance of organization cultures – with their emphasis upon 'close to the customer' values – for management behaviour.

2 Social position, social origins and education

The position of managers in the system of social stratification in the UK has also been an issue of debate. According to one view, the main dimensions of stratification may be understood in terms of the ownership of the means of production, the purchase of the labour power of others and the sale of one's own labour power. On these assumptions, managers do not own the means of production (except in a limited way) or formally employ labour, but they are distinctive in that they control and supervise labour power (see Wright and Perrone 1977). Moreover, for Goldthorpe (1980), managers are a principal example of 'third parties' within modern capitalist societies brought about by the growth of joint stock companies and the increasing size of 'industrial plant and commercial enterprise'. More specifically, in most occupational structures, managers are broadly classified in either Class I or Class II categories. Incumbents of Class I have relatively high incomes, a wide range of discretion and considerable autonomy of freedom from the control of others and encompass 'all higher grade professionals, self employed or salaried; higher grade administrators and officials in central and local government and in public and private enterprises (including company directors); managers in large industrial establishments; and large proprietors'. Incumbents of the Class II category are typically seen to carry 'staff' status and conditions of employment but are subject to control from above (despite some degree of discretion and authority). Encompassed in this category are 'lower grade professionals and higher grade technicians; lower grade administrators and officials; managers in small businesses and industrial establishments and in the services; and supervisors of non-manual employees' (Goldthorpe 1980: 39–40).

Similar occupational categories have been used to assess changes in patterns of recruitment into management over time. Indeed, the Registrar General's Occupational Classification has five categories running from professional and administrative to unskilled manual and the early studies in the UK revealed a strong propensity for managers to be recruited from Category III families; that is, clerical and skilled manual occupations. Thus, in a study by Clements (1958), 55 per cent of managers were found to have fathers whose social origins were of this kind while in a study by Clark (1966) the percentage was 43.6. Indeed, in an investigation by Leggatt (1970) the relevant percentage figure was found to be as high as 62 per cent. Later studies using the Institute of Management (then British Institute of Management) as a sampling frame revealed a slightly different pattern, with the largest groupings being drawn from either Category II (which includes middle managers) or Category III (Mansfield and Poole 1991). In the 1980 study, the relevant percentages were 32.2 per cent and 28.4 per cent and, in the 1990 study, 29.4 per cent and 29.5 per cent respectively for these two categories. It is of course difficult to make comparisons over time, given the different samples involved, but there does seem to be evidence that managers have been increasingly recruited from a broader spectrum of occupational backgrounds than in the past. This reflects in part the changing employment structure of British society, but it may also be a result of managerial positions having gained in terms of pay and prestige

compared with other occupations during the post-war era.

In terms of educational qualifications it is, of course, frequently claimed that British managers are relatively poorly qualified compared to their counterparts in other countries. Unlike many other occupational groups there are no specific academic or professional qualifications required to become a manager, although specific jobs or particular employers may impose their own requirements. Under these circumstances it is to be expected that a wide range of educational experience will be found among them. However, given the relatively prestigious and highly paid status of managers, it is also the case that they are relatively well-educated compared to the norm of British society. From the surveys carried out for the Institute of Management, the majority of British managers have been educated at grammar or technical schools with a sizeable (but declining) percentage drawn from the independent sector. The overwhelming majority of managers have also undertaken some form of full-time or part-time further or higher education, including more than 30 per cent who have attended university. In addition, the 1990 survey shows that nearly 30 per cent of the sample have been educated at polytechnics (the 'new' universities) while only a very small proportion attended Oxford or Cambridge. Overall, it is clear that managers in the UK are significantly better educated than the population as a whole, but equally it is evident that they are not as well-educated as members of the learned professions where almost 100 per cent are graduates. It also has to be recognized that the percentage of graduates in any particular age group has risen steadily in British society over a lengthy period and this will explain in part any apparent improvements in the educational accomplishments of British managers (see EUROPE, MANAGEMENT IN).

3 Careers

Career progression is another important aspect of the experiences of managers in the UK (see CAREERS). Nicholson and West (1988) have characterized managerial careers in terms of a transition cycle comprising four stages: (1) preparation; (2) encounter; (3) adjustment; and (4) stabilization. Career development programmes are typical for managers in large bureaucratically-administered enterprises, particularly those in the public sector. They involve a planned progression up career ladders to help managers acquire the necessary experience for future jobs. Thus, job changes are driven by much more than simply the personal needs and desires of managers, although this is in part because the coupled forces of organizational hierarchy and human ageing cause a continuous process of managerial succession. However, the introduction of new technology, the redesign of jobs, intra-organizational transfers and the recruitment or shedding of personnel can all create uncertainties about career changes as well as less predictable career paths.

Over time there has almost certainly been an increase in inter-firm mobility among British managers, even though this may be contrary to many human resource management philosophies which view long-term commitment to the firm as essential. On human resource management assumptions, all employees (including managers) are viewed as assets and hence commitment to the organization is carefully nurtured (see HUMAN RESOURCE MANAGEMENT). It is for this reason that distinctive career ladders for the personal development of managers are designed. In the context of the UK in the 1990s, however, there is far more employment insecurity, changes of career, organizational restructuring and de-layering, all of which creates unpredictable job moves (Arnold 1997). Of particular interest is that, in an early study by Clements (1958), 34 per cent of managers were found to have been employed in a single firm, whereas Mansfield and Poole (1991) found this to be the case for only 11.6 per cent. Nevertheless, the dominant type of job change continues to be *in-spiralling* (movement within a single firm), although men with low domestic responsibilities and women with dependent children have the highest rate of movement between employers (Nicholson and West 1988).

Gender is a significant factor in British management, with few women reaching senior organizational positions. Indeed, although roughly 42 per cent of employees in the UK are female, only 7 per cent of senior managers are women. Successful women in management include so-called 'late starters', professionals, 'go-getters', entrepreneurs and the 'unconventional' (White *et al.* 1992). Moreover, other aspects of successful careers for women are the importance of an early challenge, a wealth of experience, prospects for movement, mentoring and the handling of power and politics. None the less, the overwhelming pattern is for women still to experience considerable gender problems associated with identity, social position and prescribed roles which substantially inhibit their career progress (Scase and Goffee 1990).

4 Managerial work

As a result of the increased complexity of organizations and industry, British managers, like managers in other countries, are engaged in a wide variety of disparate functions. The most common category is that of general management; but other areas include sales and marketing; finance and accounting; personnel, training and industrial relations; production; research and development; engineering and maintenance; strategic management; and information technology management. Arguably, in the UK there is a stronger emphasis on financial management than in other nations such as Germany, where production management is accorded a greater priority (see GERMANY, MANAGEMENT IN).

The modal category for managerial salaries in the early 1990s was between £20,000 and £30,000 per annum. Managerial salaries appear to have increased over the years and are substantially above those of other occupational groups in British society. This is particularly the case for those in senior managerial positions. On the other hand, employment is less secure because of uncertain economic conditions, mergers and acquisitions, and corporate de-layering (involving a substantial loss of those in middle-management positions). There are also more managers in the UK in commerce and service industries than in manufacturing; and a substantial number of British managers now work for overseas rather than British-owned companies.

British managers appear to work long hours. In the Institute of Management study (Mansfield and Poole 1991), 40.6 per cent claimed to work for more than fifty hours per week. Indeed, given that in an earlier study by Stewart (1976) an average working week of forty-two hours was recorded, it appears that managers in the UK are working increasingly hard. As far as job satisfaction is concerned, the job characteristics identified by Maslow (1954) have been used to study this. Managers have been asked to assess the characteristics of their work in terms of the extent to which it provides scope for various material and psychological rewards. These include: opportunities for independent thought and action; security; scope for feelings of self-esteem; pay; opportunities for personal growth and development; the opportunity to develop close friendships; and promotion opportunities. Accordingly, it is possible to assess the extent to which managers consider such characteristics *are* present in their jobs or *should* be present, and the importance which they attach to any given characteristic. Essentially, managers in the UK rank opportunities for independent thought and action, scope for feelings of self-esteem, pay and security relatively highly in terms of the characteristics which they deem to be present in their jobs. Overwhelmingly, too, they rate opportunities for independent thought and action as the most important characteristic to them in their work and strongly emphasize that this should be present in their jobs (Mansfield and Poole 1991). Given the difficult economic conditions and the continuous changes with which they have to cope, British managers appear to be more satisfied with their work than might have been expected. The areas of greatest concern appear to be possibilities for promotion, opportunities for personal growth and development, pay, security and scope for feelings of self-esteem.

5 Professionalism and training

The development of professionalism has been an important aspect of the general changes in the manager's role over the years. Indeed, the growth of bodies such as the Institute of Management may be viewed as a part of the pro-

cess of evolution in which a concern over professional standards and conduct of behaviour has increased. However, for managers the issue of professionalism has always been somewhat ambiguous. This is because the classic model of professionalism emphasizes the role and function of the professional body as a means of control over membership of the body. But managers are likely to have, primarily, an organizational-based identity and to be in control over specialists (including various professionals) who carry out the work process. From the Institute of Management study conducted in 1990, it is clear that the majority of British managers consider themselves to be professionals (62.7 per cent). Even though the characteristics of the sample may bias the responses towards professionalism to some extent, it is notable that 89.1 per cent claimed that the Institute of Management should promote and enforce standards of training for managers; 69.8 per cent endorsed the provision of courses and/or material or issues of importance to members and 75.4 per cent supported the enforcement of professional standards in management. Moreover, one of the main characteristics of professionalism is the establishment of professional norms (usually enshrined in a 'code of ethics'). In this respect, it is interesting that 76.9 per cent of the 1990 sample of managers endorsed this as an aim of the Institute of Management.

In the 1980s and 1990s in the UK a great deal of interest has focused upon the quality of management education and the related concerns over training and development (see MANAGEMENT DEVELOPMENT; EXECUTIVE TRAINING). Various studies have indicated that managers in the UK still receive less training than their contemporaries in competitor nations and also that delivery is less systematic (Handy *et al.* 1987; Constable and McCormick 1987). Against this background, in 1987 the Council for Management Education and Development (CMED) launched the Management Charter Initiative in 1987. A proposal in this initiative was to establish a coherent set of management qualifications and to set up a Chartered Institute of Managers. However, this has been the subject of considerable controversy among employers, training providers and professional institutes and associations. Even so, it is clear that British managers strongly endorse developments in training and management education and view these as important aids to management performance. A study by Warr conducted in 1991 found that 82 per cent of managers undertook some training in work time in that year (the median number of training days being five) (Warr 1993). Moreover, a formal management training policy was found to exist in 68 per cent of organizations in the sample.

In the 1990 Institute of Management survey, 87.8 per cent of managers 'agreed' or 'strongly agreed' with the statement that management development and training were important in helping them to do their job well and 86.3 per cent endorsed the statement that training is important in aiding them to develop as managers. In addition, 73.6 per cent of managers had heard of the Management Charter Initiative and the overwhelming majority supported its essential aims. In short, despite a concern over trends in training and management development in the UK, there does seem to be considerable support for major improvements in these respects (see Poole and Jenkins 1996; Storey *et al.* 1997). Indeed, the expenditure of a typical British company on management development would typically be far more than for technical and manual grades of employee.

6 Industrial relations and employee participation

Managing of the employment relationship is a major feature of the manager's role in the UK. Broadly speaking, it is possible to classify the overall approaches of UK managers into *pluralist* and *unitarist* approaches. Pluralism recognizes a coalition of diverse individual and group interests in the firm and is broadly associated with the recognition of trade unionism. Unitarism focuses on a unified authority structure in the firm and emphasizes common policies and objectives within an overall organizational identity (see INDUSTRIAL RELATIONS IN EUROPE). In the 1970s it was assumed that pluralism and so-called constitutional management (in which pay and conditions of work are regulated by collective bargaining and conducted through the medium of recog-

nized trade unions) would become increasingly ascendant. But these predictions were to be largely falsified by the events of the 1980s and 1990s. As a result of changes in labour and product markets, governments fostering market-orientated strategies and the introduction of labour legislation which circumscribed the role of trade unions, managements increasingly found themselves in a position to choose between diverse sets of industrial policies and objectives. Thus, in the UK the following developments have occurred:

1 the re-emergence of 'macho' or authoritarian styles of management in industries with highly competitive product markets and subject to substantial rationalization;
2 an increasing interest in 'paternal' industrial relations styles as a consequence of the enormous success of Japanese companies in world markets and direct Japanese investment in the UK;
3 a growing concern for employee involvement and direct forms of employee participation in expanding industries where skilled and educated workers remain scarce and where technological change is particularly rapid;
4 a decline in constitutional management outside the public sector and manufacturing industry occasioned by (a) the reduction of 'corporatist' economic management by the state and (b) the appreciable weakening of trade unions, reflected in a significant loss of union membership;
5 the growth of hybrid styles of industrial relations management (such as consultative–paternal) which incorporates elements of more than one industrial relations style.

These and other changes have reflected movements in the political, economic and legal environment that have impacted upon the competitive strategies that managers pursue and, in turn, on their industrial relations attitudes and behaviour. Market conditions and the firms' financial performance are reflected in the extent to which corporate-level managers involve themselves in industrial relations. Firms with unfavourable demand conditions are likely to seek greater control over pay settlements by increased intervention, whereas 'organizational slack' and local autonomy are more likely to occur where competition in the product market is relatively weak. The growth in company size is also reflected in division-alized structures, with financial decentra-lization (in terms of profit accountability) spreading down to enterprise level or below.

Changes in the wider environment and in competitive strategies tend to reinforce mana-gerial commitments to a free-enterprise sys-tem and to unitarism rather than pluralism in industrial relations. And of course, power and influence in industrial relations has shifted substantially, to the detriment of organized la-bour. Union membership fell by over three million in the 1980s from the peak of 1979 and remained strongest in job grades and employ-ment sectors that were in decline (manufactur-ing and the public sector). The 1980s also witnessed a decline in shop steward power and the rise of the so-called 'new realism', with labour movement solidarity giving way to an enterprise consciousness among certain trade unions (MacInnes 1987).

The manager's experiences of industrial relations has thus changed in major respects in the UK and is reflected in attitudes to trade unionism, personal commitments to collec-tive representation, experience of collective bargaining, and employee participation and involvement (see HUMAN RESOURCES MANAGEMENT IN EUROPE; INDUSTRIAL RELA-TIONS IN EUROPE).

Insofar as attitudes towards trade unions are concerned, on the basis of the Institute of Management surveys, it is clear that there is now less hostility to trade unions than was once the case. In 1980 82.1 per cent of manag-ers considered that unions in the UK had too much power, a figure which fell to 31.7 per cent in 1990. In 1980 just over half of manag-ers (52.9 per cent) considered that trade unions were more powerful than manage-ment; a figure which fell to 14.1 per cent in 1990. And although at both times the majority of respondents agreed with the statement that trade unions were not acting in the country's economic interests, those strongly agreeing with the view declined from 40.4 per cent to 11.4 per cent between 1980 and 1990 (Mans-field and Poole 1991). On the other hand, the willingness of managers to recognize trade

unions for collective bargaining purposes has declined. In terms of personal commitments to collective representation, managers appear to be increasingly individualistic in approach. Again on the basis of the Institute of Manage-ment surveys, whereas in 1980 only 32.8 per cent of managers felt that no kind of collective representation was relevant to them, this fig-ure rose to 43.2 per cent in 1990. Moreover, union affiliation has also featured promi-nently in the analysis of the managerial role. Broadly speaking, union membership in-creased dramatically in the 1970s (and not just in the UK). However, following the decline of the corporatist state and the increasing auton-omy of managers and enterprises experienced in the 1980s and 1990s, the extent of manage-rial collectivism has declined.

Theoretical interpretations of managerial unionism (and other modes of managerial collectivism) include: (1) the systematic list-ing of co-terminous factors; (2) the industrial relations focus on recognition policies; (3) sociological analyses based on the study of adaptations in market, work and status situa-tions; (4) 'radical analysis' by industrial rela-tions specialists and sociologists focusing on the labour process; and (5) social action mod-els emphasizing managers' orientations and perceptions. Thus, the issues which have been seen as encouraging managerial unionism in-clude economic pressures, fear of exclusion from national-level consultations/negotia-tions and fears over job security. Conversely, fear of loss of promotion, of losing the trust of employers and senior managers, and the inap-propriateness of trade unionism for managers' needs (for example, opposing philosophies and policies) have been seen as discouraging membership. However, the most potent forces appear to be presence and recognition of a trade union at the manager's level, commit-ment to collective rather than industrial repre-sentation of interests by the managers them-selves and employment in the public rather than the private sector (see Poole *et al.* 1983).

In any event, union membership among managers has declined in the 1980s and into the 1990s. On the basis of the Institute of Man-agement studies, it is apparent that three-quarters of managers (75.4 per cent) now have no collective representation of their interests.

Moreover, less than 20 per cent of managers in the early 1990s were trade union members compared with nearly a quarter at the beginning of the 1980s (Mansfield and Poole 1991). The period since 1980 has also witnessed a major shift in employer approaches towards regulating the employment relationship via collectivism and collective bargaining. Where collective regulation still exists, bargaining structures have become increasingly decentralized to the level of the firm. From the Institute of Management surveys it would appear that there has been a decline in managers experiencing formal collective bargaining (20 per cent in 1980; 17.4 per cent in 1990). Informal meetings with union representatives appear to have declined appreciably: 48.5 per cent of managers in 1980 were engaged in these types of practice, compared with only 31.3 per cent in 1990. But managers' handling of individual grievances brought by union representatives has declined far less sharply (42.2 per cent in 1980, 38.2 per cent in 1990). Indeed, it is clear that the formal aspects of industrial relations have changed less than the informal procedures. The decline in trade union power appears to have enabled managers in the UK increasingly to deal with individual employees rather than having to discuss issues first of all with a trade union representative.

Turning to employee involvement and employee participation, there have been many interesting developments in the UK since the 1980s. For a period, in the 1970s, the Bullock proposals on Industrial Democracy appeared to herald a major change to the board levels of the UK, with trade union representation appearing at this level. However, these proposals are no longer on the political agenda and although a series of European initiatives on company law, disclosure of information and, more latterly, the Social Charter became increasingly important, the focus of attention has been on employee involvement and on profit-sharing and employee shareholding schemes. Managers in a large number of firms have introduced various types of direct employee involvement (such as two-way communications and quality circles) while eschewing board-level practices. Above all, managers in the UK have encouraged the growth of profit-sharing and employee shareholding schemes. Indeed, a wide range of schemes may be identified in the UK, with over half of workplaces employing more than twenty-five employees having at least one such scheme. The most prevalent are those with profit-related payments and bonuses, but Inland Revenue approved profit-sharing schemes, 'save-as-you-earn' schemes and executive share option schemes are also common developments. Between 1979 and 1992 in the UK, 1015 general profit-sharing schemes were approved by the Inland Revenue under the auspices of the 1978 Finance Act. Between 1980 and 1992, 1058 share option schemes under the provisions of the Finance Act of 1980 were approved. Finally, no less than 5089 discretionary share option schemes under the provisions of the 1984 Finance Act received the Inland Revenue seal of approval by 1992.

7 Public and private sectors

The emergence of joint stock companies in the private sector and the rise of governmental activities (furthering the growth of large-scale public enterprises) have been the main forces underpinning a sizeable increase in the number of British managers over the years. However, it is also the case that the experiences of managers in these two sectors are different, even though recent developments may be indicative of a greater degree of convergence than was once evident. Essentially, public sector managers have been more constrained – in comparison with their private sector colleagues (in terms of autonomy and freedom to develop new products and services) – to act on the basis of a market logic and to take strategic decisions without reference to overall governmental policy (see CORPORATISM). Differences in respect of industrial relations are particularly noteworthy. First of all, attitudes towards trade unionism tend to be less hostile in the public sector and union density is higher. Managers in the public sector are also more likely themselves to want some collective representation of their own interests and, indeed, about half of British public sector managers belong to trade unions (Mansfield and Poole 1991). Collective bargaining is typically more centralized in the public sector.

Although direct experience of collective bargaining does not differ greatly between public and private sectors, managers in the public sector are far more likely to deal with individual grievances brought by union representatives (in the 1990 Institute of Management survey, the respective percentages were 61.4 and 32.2).

Reflecting differences in managerial autonomy, managers in the private sector are typically more satisfied than those in the public sector, with opportunities for promotion, personal growth and development, self-esteem and independent thought and action. However, as a result of major changes in the public sector (including privatization, contracting out of services and a far greater market logic being developed), corresponding adaptations in the manager's role are occurring. For instance, in the health sector there is more organized and ever-increasing 'purchaser power'. Indeed, the emphasis on the purchase/contractor has developed alongside the spawning of measures and indicators of relative performance (for example, league tables for schools). The upshot has been increasing pressure on public sector managers to adapt to a rapidly changing environment which is radically different from that previously encountered in traditional, bureaucratically-administered organizations (see Boyne *et al.* 1999).

8 Future prospects

The political and economic framework of the UK has changed substantially since the 1980s. Government intervention has been largely displaced by a belief in the virtues of the market economy. Entrepreneurism and the enterprise culture have become ascendant themes, while privatization programmes have reduced the state sector. Prices and incomes policies have been formally abandoned and replaced by practices such as profit sharing and profit-related pay. Trade unions have been substantially weakened by the exigencies of the early 1980s recession, the rise of the service sector and adverse legislation. Industrial democracy is no longer on the political agenda, replaced by developments such as worker involvement through employee

shareholding and by shop-floor level developments in quality circles and similar ventures. All of these far-reaching changes have impacted appreciably on the role of the manager.

Whether or not these developments will continue is debatable, but five ascendant themes for the future of British management merit attention at this juncture: (1) the corporatist state and the enterprise culture; (2) professionalism and management development; (3) ownership, control and competing interests; (4) the employment relationship; and (5) internationalization.

The corporate state and the enterprise culture

In the UK over the past decade there has been a major attempt to 'roll back' the powers of the State and to replace the neo-corporatism of the 1970s with the market economy. However, British managers have never been very corporatist in outlook (see CORPORATISM). They have tended to support strong state intervention in the sphere of industrial relations and there is some support for the control of foreign enterprises in the UK. However, they are against the statutory control of prices, wages and salaries; and few wish to see extensive import controls on the subsidization of exports. There is also strong opposition to the increasing powers of government ministers and to the principle of state monopolies (see Mansfield and Poole 1991). Indeed, rather than corporatism, they are far more likely to support an enterprise culture, reducing the regulatory powers of government, encouraging share ownership, reducing monopolies and encouraging competition. Looking to the future, it can be anticipated that there will be a continued underpinning of the enterprise culture by British managers even though certain types of state intervention in specific areas of interest to managers may well be encouraged.

Professionalism and management development

Arguably no issue is likely to affect the role of managers more in the future than the concern over professionalism and management development (see MANAGEMENT DEVELOPMENT).

The view expressed by, among others, Handy *et al.* (1987) and Constable and McCormick (1987) has been that British managers are less well trained than their competitors and that their experiences in this area are, by and large, less systematic. The Management Charter Initiative has been particularly symptomatic of the concern over management development more generally. However, the professional commitments of British managers appear to remain strong and are likely to increase in the future. Strong support for management development as an important company responsibility, for corporate support for management development, for the encouragement of continuous self-development, and for all members of the organization to obtain recognized qualifications is likely to continue (see Mansfield and Poole 1991). The attention devoted to these issues in the media and in management circles may have had a dramatic effect on managers' attitudes to their own training and development and to that of their colleagues. Managers themselves appear to be willing to invest more of their own time and resources in their attempts to obtain competence. This is encouraging for the prospects of an increasingly professional, well-educated and well-trained management emerging in the twenty-first century, even though the advance may not be sufficient to close the gap entirely with competitor nations (Woodall and Winstanley 1998).

Ownership, control and competing interests

One of the main developments in the UK in recent years has been the popular notion of a property-owning democracy in which the role of the state in economic management is reduced. This is in sharp contrast to the corporatist economic and political policies of the 1960s and 1970s, which relied heavily on state intervention and a substantial public sector. Moreover, economic restructuring and the privatization of state assets have encouraged managers and employees to take equity stakes in their firms and to endorse the ideals of a 'free' market economy in which the role of the consumer is paramount. Partly as a result, there has been a substantial increase in the

number of managers who own stocks and shares, and particularly in those who own shares in the companies in which they work. Indeed, as we have seen, if one excludes managers in the public sector and in voluntary organizations, the majority of managers who are eligible to do so now appear to have a stake in the ownership of the firms in which they are employed. The development of executive share ownership schemes, in particular, was an important part of this process in the 1980s. Accordingly, the formal separation of ownership from control at the top of business concerns has been substantially reduced over the last decade, a trend which may well continue.

With respect to managers' perceptions of whose interests should be most predominant within their own employing organizations, these are fairly comprehensive. However, in line with changes in ownership, it is scarcely surprising that owners' and shareholders' interests are a dominant concern. None the less, as has also been seen, in recognition of the importance of markets and the interests of customers, consumers have often replaced owners and shareholders as the single most important group whose interests managers should most actively pursue (Mansfield and Poole 1991). The focus on the market economy is thus clearly evident and, given the increasing measure of multi-party support for this proposition, there is every reason to suppose that such concerns will continue to predominate in the future.

The employment relationship

The reform of industrial reform and the curtailment of trade union activities have also affected managers in the UK. Above all, Thatcher era policies have adversely affected trade unions in a number of ways:

> Legislation limited the way unions could act and they were no longer consulted by government nor their agreement or cooperation on economic policy sought. The harshness of the new economic regime slashed revenues in manufacturing leading to a collapse of profits, record bankruptcies and a fall of about one-third in employment in established firms. This produced a very hostile climate for unions in the workplace.

In the public sector, unions also faced job losses and a hostile government and usually a new hostile management ... Finally unemployment, which rose by more than two million, weakened unions directly by reducing their membership and income and indirectly by threatening their workplace bargaining power. The unions suffered a series of severe defeats: particularly that of the miners, barely ten years after they could claim to have brought down a Conservative government. The unions were powerless to resist the government's challenge, much of which was popular with their own members.

(MacInnes 1987: 3)

Managers at enterprise level have been the principal beneficiaries of these changes. It is then, scarcely surprising there has been a decline in the direct experience of managers of formal collective bargaining and a substantial reduction in informal meetings with union representatives. The vast majority of managers now view themselves more powerful than trade unions. However, in part as a result, managers are now far less likely than at the beginning of the 1980s to consider that trade unions are not acting in the country's economic interests. None the less, greater protection for labour interests appear likely to stem from the 'Fairness at Work' White Paper of 1998.

Notwithstanding public and private sector differences, managers are now also far less likely to wish for collective representation of their own interests through managerial unions. Indeed, the percentage of managers belonging to trade unions has undoubtedly fallen. But does this involve a long-term change in patterns of employment relationships or merely a reaction to alterations in the wider environment? There can be no certain answer, but unless there are dramatic changes in the political environment of the 1990s, it would appear to be most unlikely that there will be any appreciable endorsement of collectivism by British managers in the medium term. It is also likely that, in the employment relationship, human resource management policies on the one hand and the non-union firm on the other will feature increasingly prominently (Poole and Jenkins 1998) (see HUMAN RESOURCE MANAGEMENT; INDUSTRIAL AND LABOUR RELATIONS).

The role of middle managers

Another concern in recent years has been the consequences of de-layering and downsizing for the role of middle managers, Flatter organizational structures and reduced levels in hierarchies in the firm have impacted considerably on the opportunities for middle managers. Those who remain work longer hours and with much wider roles than was previously the case. Some empowerment of middle managers has occurred but, in many instances, the impact on lifestyles has been considerable (Thomas and Dunkerley 1999). These trends are likely to continue as firms become increasingly cost conscious and 'knowledge workers' are able to take greater responsibility for their own work structuring and scheduling. This will have important implications, too, for managerial careers (Worrall and Cooper 1998).

Internationalization

Along with other countries, the increasing globalization of business has impacted substantially upon managers in the United Kingdom (see GLOBALIZATION). This has been accelerated by substantial investment into the UK by Japanese, US and German companies. The majority of large firms in the UK are multinational in any case and this brings in its wake problems of formulating adequate human resource policies and the tendency to create substantial numbers of expatriate managers. The early classification of staffing policies in the multinational firm distinguished between ethnocentric, polycentric and geocentric types. Moreover, the tendency towards ethnocentricism is greater than is sometimes supposed, although firms may adapt different staffing policies over time and the patterns in reality are complex. In any event, it is likely that global tendencies will increasingly affect the dominant modes of operation of British companies and, hence, the behaviour of managers themselves. British managers in the future are likely not only to be increasingly aware of overseas developments but to have substantial 'foreign' experiences, either from their own overseas assignments or from the impact domestically of the policies of particular multinational enterprises.

Finally, the conclusion must be that the attitudes and behaviours of managers are likely to become increasingly ascendant in shaping the future condition of British organizations and wider society. Accompanying the relative decline in influence of the state and trade unions, managers have become progressively more dominant in the UK and, for better or worse, it is the strategic choices made by them that are likely to fashion powerfully the destinies of the majority of the British people. What is even more certain, structural changes in the economy are creating greater demands for those with administrative and managerial skills.

MICHAEL POOLE
CARDIFF BUSINESS SCHOOL

RICHARD SCASE
UNIVERSITY OF KENT AT CANTERBURY

Further reading

(References cited in the text marked *)

* Arnold, J. (1997) *Managing Careers into the 21st Century*, London: Paul Chapman. (Details changes in careers and the implications for management.)
* Berle, A.A. (1960) *Power Without Property*, New York: Harper & Brace. (Classic argument for the separation of ownership from control, with managers occupying the controlling positions in the modern enterprise.)
* Boyne, G., Jenkins, G. and Poole, M. (1999) 'Human resource management in the public and private sectors: an empirical comparison', *Public Administration* 77 (2): 407–20. (Shows that there remain some differences between the public and private sectors in respect of human resource management practices.)
* Burnham, J. (1941) *The Managerial Revolution*, New York: Day. (Argues, like Berle, for a separation of ownership from control but focuses particularly on the rise of management in the public sector.)
* Clark, D.G. (1966) *The Industrial Manager: His Background and Career Pattern*, London: Business Publications. (One of the early studies of managers in the UK which is essentially empirical in compass.)
* Clements, R.V. (1958) *Managers: A Study of their Careers in Industry*, London: Allen & Unwin.

(Another very early study of managers in the UK which is essentially an empirical contribution.)
* Constable, J. and McCormick, R. (1987) *The Making of British Managers*, London: British Institute of Management and Confederation of British Industry. (Along with Handy *et al.* (1987), a key report on the low levels of training and education of British managers and one of the spurs to subsequent reforms.)
* Galbraith, J.K. (1967) *The New Industrial State*, Boston, MA: Houghton Mifflin. (Argues for the growth of a technostructure (rather broader in compass than management per se) as the key controlling force in modern industry.)
* Goldthorpe, J.H. (1980) *Social Mobility and Class Structure in Britain*, Oxford: Oxford University Press. (A key text locating managers in terms of their position in the social stratification system of British society.)
* Handy, C., Gow, I., Gordon, C., Randlesome, C. and Maloney, M. (1987) *The Making of Managers*, London: National Economic Development Office. (A key report tracing the need for greater training provision for managers in the UK.)
Heery, E. and Salmon, J. (eds) (2000) *The Insecure Workforce*, London: Routledge. (Deals with insecurity at work, including managerial policies and practices that affect job security.)
* Leggatt, T. (1970) 'Managers in industry: their background and education', *Sociological Review* 26 (4): 807–25. (Examines the social origins and educational experiences of British managers based on a large size of sample.)
Legge, K. (1995) *Human Resource Management: Rhetorics and Realities*, London: Macmillan. (A valuable, critical text on human resource management in the UK.)
* MacInnes, J. (1987) *Thatcherism at Work*, Milton Keynes: Open University Press. (Deals with the effects of the Thatcher years and the consequences for management power in the workplace.)
* Mansfield, R. and Poole M. (1991) *British Management in the Thatcher Years*, London: Institute of Management. (This is a longitudinal analysis of managers' attitudes and reported behaviour based on a comparison of fellows and members of the Institute of Management in 1980 and 1990.)
* Mansfield, R., Poole, M., Blyton, P. and Frost, P.E. (1981) *The British Manager in Profile*, London: British Institute of Management. (A national, formative study of managerial attitudes and behaviour in the UK.)
* Maslow, A.H. (1954) *Motivation and Personality*, New York: Harper & Row. (A classic study on

motivation which has been applied to managers in several countries.)

* Nichols, T. (1969) *Ownership, Control and Ideology*, London: Allen & Unwin. (An excellent review of the ownership–control debate which is highly critical in approach and compass.)

* Nicholson, N. and West, M. (1988) *Managerial Job Change: Men and Women in Transition*, Cambridge: Cambridge University Press. (A valuable, theoretically informed, empirical analysis of managerial careers focusing on socio-psychological concepts and ideas.)

* Poole, M. and Jenkins, G. (1996) *Back to the Line?*, London: Institute of Management. (Presents the results of a survey of managers' attitudes to human resource management issues, including material on training and development.)

* Poole, M. and Jenkins, G. (1998) 'Human resource management and the theory of rewards: evidence from a national survey', *British Journal of Industrial Relations* 36 (2): 227–47. (This study, based on fellows and members of the Institute of Management, analyses managerial commitments to human resource policies on rewards based on performance criteria.)

* Poole, M., Mansfield, R., Frost, P. and Blyton, P. (1983) 'Why managers join unions: evidence from Britain', *Industrial Relations* 22 (3): 426–44. (Seeks to examine the factors affecting the propensity of managers in the UK to join unions based on systematic data analysis.)

* Sargent Florence, P. (1953) *The Logic of British and American Industry: A Realistic Analysis of Economic Structure and Government*, London: Routledge & Kegan Paul. (An early empirical study suggesting that the notion of separation of ownership from control was not wholly supported by the evidence.)

* Sargent Florence, P. (1961) *The Ownership, Control and Success of Large Companies*, London: Sweet & Maxwell. (Argues that an evolutionary trend along the lines predicted by the 'managerialist' thinkers has been occurring.)

* Scase, R. and Goffee, R. (1990) 'Women in management: towards a research agenda', *International Journal of Human Resource Management* 1 (1): 107–25. (Isolates various studies of women managers and identifies ten major areas in a research agenda for the future.)

Sisson, K. and Storey, J. (2000) *The Realities of Human Resource Management*, Buckingham: Open University Press. (A good and readable analysis of recent developments in human resource management with a UK focus.)

* Stewart, R. (1976) *Contrasts in Management*, Macmillan. (A valuable contribution on the nature of managerial work in the UK based on careful empirical observations.)

* Storey, J., Edwards, P. and Sisson, K. (1997) *Managers in the Making*, London: Sage. (A comparative analysis of managers in Britain and Japan focusing on careers and development.)

Tayeb, M. (2000) *The Management of International Enterprises*, Basingstoke: Macmillan. (Points out the importance of internationalism for modern management and management systems.)

* Thomas, R. and Dunkerley, D. (1999) 'Careering downwards? Middle managers' experiences in downsized organizations', *British Journal of Management* 10 (2): 157–69. (A sensitive, qualitative account of middle managers in Britain in an era of de-layering and downsizing.)

* Warr, P. (1993) *Training for Managers*, London: Institute of Management. (A detailed empirical study of training provision and attitudes to training among British managers based on an Institute of Management sample.)

* White, B., Cox, C. and Cooper, G. (1992) *Women's Career Development: A Study of High Flyers*, Oxford: Blackwell. (Examines the factors accounting for the career development of women and some of the obstacles to this (not least in management).)

Winterton, J. and Winterton, R. (1999) *Developing Managerial Confidence*, London: Routledge. (Aims to provide a comprehensive analysis of modern management development.)

* Woodall, J. and Winstanley, D. (1998) *Management Development: Strategy and Practice*, Oxford: Blackwell. (This is an authoritative study of the increasingly important area of management development.)

* Worrall, L. and Cooper, C.L. (1998) *The Quality of Working Life*, London: Institute of Management. (A survey of managers' changing experiences at work based on a survey of Institute of Management fellows and members.)

* Wright, E.O. and Perrone, L. (1977) 'Marxist class categories and income inequalities', *American Sociological Review* 42: 32–55. (Seeks to develop sophisticated analytical categories of relevance for understanding the position of managers in the social stratification system of society.)

See also: BUSINESS CULTURES, EUROPEAN; BUSINESS SCHOOLS; CORPORATISM; EUROPE, MANAGEMENT IN; GERMANY, MANAGEMENT IN; HUMAN RESOURCE MANAGEMENT IN EUROPE; INDUSTRIAL RELATIONS IN EUROPE; MANAGEMENT EDUCATION IN EUROPE; UNITED STATES OF AMERICA, MANAGEMENT IN THE

United States of America, management in the

Overview

In the aftermath of the Second World War, management in the USA was the kind of management held in the greatest respect; in many ways it set the standard of excellence for the entire world. US-based multinational corporations dominated the international marketplace in a number of industries, from copiers and computers to industrial equipment and transportation vehicles. By the 1970s, however, this dominance had begun to fade, and during the 1980s it became clear to US managers that dramatic changes were needed. These were duly implemented, and included the use of advanced information technology, total quality management and the re-engineering of processes. US managers also recognized the need to develop learning organizations in order to stay ahead. In order to maintain their status, to be world-class organizations, management needed to change, not simply react.

In the 1990s and now into the new millenium, management in the USA did dramatically change, and the results have been very impressive. Whereas in the previous decades US managers crossed the Pacific to learn about Japanese management, now the Japanese and others from around the world are trying to learn about US management (see JAPAN, MANAGEMENT IN). Going into the twenty-first century, the US economy has had sustained robust economic growth and high productivity. Much of the credit for this boom is being given to US management (see Hitt 2000; Hodgetts *et al.* 1999)

Before looking at the recent developments in US management, this article will outline the traditional, time-tested approach. This discussion of classic organization design and management processes will serve as a foundation and point of departure for the examination of information technology, total quality management and re-engineering, and creative human resources management before analysing the future of management in the USA.

1 Classic management style

Traditionally, management in the USA has been characterized by identifiable organization design and management processes. Organization design primarily relates to the characteristics of bureaucracy and the concepts of departmentation, span of control and decentralization, while the management process involves the functions of decision making, communication and control (see ORGANIZATION BEHAVIOUR).

Organization design

The classic organization design used by US enterprises has its roots in bureaucracy, the ideal characteristics of which were established by the German sociologist Max Weber (see WEBER, M.). Weber believed organizations should be structured as follows:

1 a clear-cut division of labour;
2 a hierarchy of positions, with each lower one being controlled and supervised by the one immediately above;
3 a consistent system of abstract rules and standards to help ensure uniformity in the performance of duties and the coordination of tasks;
4 a spirit of formal impersonality in which duties are carried out;
5 employment based on technical qualifications and protected from arbitrary dismissal.

These Weberian bureaucratic characteristics have traditionally formed the structural basis of most large US organizations. They are coupled with the concepts of departmentation, span of control and delegation/decentralization.

Departmentation is the process of combining jobs into groups on the basis of common characteristics. The most popular arrangement is functional departmentalization, in which work activities are grouped on the basis of the job being carried out. An example is manufacturing firms, which have traditionally been departmentalized into three major functional departments: production, marketing and finance. Another common arrangement is product departmentalization, which groups together the activities associated with a particular product line. Firms in the motor industry have long used this type of arrangement by creating divisions that focus on a specific product, such as the Buick or Chevrolet divisions of General Motors (see FORD, H.; SLOAN, A.P.). A third common arrangement is customer departmentalization, which is designed to meet the needs of specific customer groups. For example, retail stores will have major departments for men's clothing, for women's clothing and for children's wear.

Span of control is the number of subordinates a manager directly supervises. Different factors influence this span, including the amount of time that must be spent with each subordinate, the competence and experience of subordinates and the ability of these subordinates to work on their own. While some enterprises tried to keep the span of control within a specified range, most organizations began to recognize contingency variables, such as the difficulty of the task and the personal characteristics of the manager.

Delegation is the process a manager uses in distributing work to subordinates. *Decentralization* relates to the number and importance of decisions made lower down the management hierarchy. Both delegation and decentralization represent transitionary concepts in relation to the development of organization design. For example, delegation has now evolved into empowerment, while decentralization is at the forefront of today's new network and virtual organization designs.

Management processes

Alongside the classic organization design characteristics described above, management

in the USA has also depended upon a process consisting primarily of decision making, communication and control.

Decision making is the process of choosing from among alternatives. This management function involves making rational choices by analysing situations, determining alternative courses of action, weighing the benefits and drawbacks associated with each and choosing the one that offers the best solution. Mathematical modelling and computer analysis are employed in managerial decision making, particularly in those areas where data quantification is given high priority. Examples include economic forecasting, comparison of alternative investments, decision-tree analysis, linear programming techniques and economic value analysis.

Decision making also relies heavily on non-quantitative or subjective analysis (see DECISION MAKING). For example, when making decisions that require creativity or innovation, quantitative modelling and analysis may be replaced by brainstorming, synectics or other creative problem-solving techniques. Some organizations have accomplished this by testing their employees to identify those that are heavily right-brain (creative, spontaneous, intuitive) and those that are left-brain (logical, sequential, rational), and creating heterogeneous teams that can draw on the analytical strengths of both types of thinkers. This approach has been widely used in advertising, design and new product development.

Communication as a management function involves the process of conveying meanings in order to spread information throughout the organization. Typical examples include: downward communication in the form of memos and reports; upward communication in the form of suggestion programmes and open-door policies that provide feedback on problem areas; and horizontal communication in the form of interdepartmental meetings and reports used to coordinate activities.

In addition to formal communication channels, there is widespread use of informal communication, represented by the so-called grapevine. While there are a variety of ways in which information can be informally passed on, the most common route is through a selective process in which some people are deliberately included on the grapevine and others excluded.

Different media are used to convey information. One of the most common is written communication, such as memos, reports, letters and organizational handbooks. Another is oral communication: face-to-face verbal orders, telephone discussions, speeches and group meetings. A third is non-verbal communication, as exemplified in the use of kinesics, proxemics and paralanguage. Kinesics deals with the use of body language, including facial expressions, gestures and posture. Proxemics deals with the way people use physical space to convey information, such as how close one person stands to another when carrying on a conversation. Paralanguage is how things are said, including the person's rate of speech, voice tension, inflection, pacing and volume level.

Today, of course, almost all communication in US organizations is done electronically – for example e-mail, Internet, intranets and extranets. This not only allows organizations to be paperless, but also has implications for organization design, management processes and human relationships.

Control is the process of evaluating performance according to plans and objectives and taking any action deemed necessary. This management function is closely related to decision making and helps to create a closed loop between the two functions, thus ensuring continual systems feedback. As a result, all three functions in the management process – decision making, communication and control – are in a constant state of adjustment and readjustment.

Managerial control in US firms has become quantitative through the use of accounting and information syystems that provide financial and numerical feedback to decision makers (see ACCOUNTING IN NORTH AMERICA). In addition, non-quantitative information may be used for control. For example, many managers rely on anecdotal feedback from their customers regarding the quality of service and how it can be improved. In recent years there has been some rethinking and changes made in control measures. For example, while firms have traditionally determined their cost of capital and used it as a factor in evaluating performance, there has been a

growing trend towards including equity capital in this calculation, thus requiring subsidiary managers to generate a profit that pays for the cost of borrowed funds as well as providing a return on invested capital. As in communication, the computer and information technology are playing an increasing role in the control process, for example electronic data interchange (EDI). Some of these developments are covered below.

2 Recent developments

The organization design and management processes described above have played a major role in US management over the years (see ORGANIZATION BEHAVIOUR). However, beginning in the 1980s things began to change dramatically. US organizations were challenged as never before, resulting in some significant alterations to the classic management approach and some entirely new ways of thinking and acting. Some of the most significant developments which affected US management starting in the 1980s included downsizing, the use of advanced information technology (IT) and now in the 2000s e-commerce.

Downsizing

By the mid-1980s, US organizations were finding themselves facing growing competitive pressure from abroad. To reduce costs and increase efficiency and productivity, a growing number of firms began to downsize (see DOWNSIZING). They did so by not filling the positions of those who left or retired and by eliminating jobs, first those of operating workers, then middle managers and staff personnel. In many cases high-tech equipment and computers/expert systems replaced people. The result of this downsizing (some firms began calling it 'rightsizing' to soften the blow to employees) was to flatten the organization structure and increase productivity and competitiveness in global markets (see Parker 1999).

Unfortunately, this downsizing also restructured employment and left many without jobs. Those remaining in organizations had greater responsibility and more demanding job requirements. They have become known as knowledge workers. One way that management tried to meet this new challenge was to increase the amount of training given to personnel. A second method was to cross-train personnel so they could be assigned to the growth needs of the organization and the employees themselves. A third way was by creating self-managed work teams to replace the individualism that previously dominated the work environment. Thus, as the Japanese did so successfully, US workers began to work in groups, using their cross-training combined with the new high-tech equipment and processes to dramatically increase productivity and, especially, quality. Once again they became leaders in certain industries.

These lean structures also increased the ability of companies to adapt to external conditions. For example, as the quality of goods and services started to improve, companies with bloated bureaucracies and inflexible management processes were forced either to change or to go under. Firms with flat structures found it easier to modify work processes, introduce change and incorporate quality management techniques into their operations. They also found that the flat, interfunctional structures increased their ability to respond to customer needs.

Unfortunately, there has also turned out to be a downside to this downsizing. There has been a negative impact on employee commitment and performance. The important human side of US organizations in the 1980s was slighted in the rush to beomce 'lean and mean'. These implications will be noted after the discussion of total quality.

Information technology

Along with the recent transformation in organization structure came the use of IT. Both in the form of computers and related transmission, retrieval and storage components, and in the form of telecommunications involving computers interacting with both telephone and television technology, IT greatly changed management in the USA. Many organizations began at first complementing and then replacing their large computer systems with microcomputers, most of which became networks. Management decision making, communica-

tion and control also began incorporating other forms of IT, including fax machines, electronic organizers and cellular telephones. Many organizations were thus able to expand the horizons of their electronic office. More personnel could leave the boundaries of the traditional organization and be assigned customer-contact responsibilities, and the firm was able to communicate with them no matter where they were physically located. For example, some firms now have knowledge workers pass work off at the end of the day to other time zones around the world to in essence obtain a 48-hour day to help in the necessary speed needed in today's competition. IT also facilitated the creation of flat organization structures and played a vital role in total quality management (TQM).

IT boosted productivity in a number of ways, one of which was by reducing the time needed to send and retrieve information. For example, by using electronic mail (e-mail), many managers were able to drastically reduce the number of inter-office memos and increase the speed with which written messages were sent and replies received. An accompanying benefit with e-mail was that everyone could communicate directly with everyone else. Thus, there was less need for the cumbersome chain of command and bureaucracy.

A second productivity-related benefit was the time savings in obtaining information. For example, Connecticut Mutual Life Insurance customer representatives now sit at IBM personal computers, where they are able to call up the necessary forms and correspondence needed to answer customer questions. As a result, the average time taken to respond to enquiries has declined from five days to two hours, 20 per cent fewer people are needed for handling customer questions and productivity has risen dramatically.

A third way in which efficiency was increased was through the use of electronic data interchange (EDI; see ELECTRONIC DATA INTERCHANGE). This process allows customers, companies and suppliers to exchange information directly, computer to computer. Where customers used to place orders by filling out paper forms, a company computer can now receive an order from a customer's computer and instruct the warehouse to fill the order while also checking inventory on hand to see if more needs to be ordered from suppliers. Almost all US firms use some form of EDI.

Still another way in which computer technology has affected productivity is through the use of computer monitoring. This process is used to collect, examine and feed back information about work results. The monitoring should not be used to keep a close check on employees nor for punitive purposes, its purpose being to improve performance and help develop employees. The most effective computer monitoring systems are designed on the basis of three objectives: (1) determining the type of information that will be most useful to the employees; (2) designing a system that gathers these data and allows for useful comparisons between, and within, specific tasks; and (3) ensuring that non-relevant information is not entered into the system. A number of US firms use computer monitoring. At Hughes Aircraft Company, for example, the process has been used to facilitate integrated production and quality control strategies and to help increase productivity.

Finally, managers in the USA are now using software that allows computers to emulate management decision making. This approach is a combination of those discussed above, but its applications are more varied. For example, many US banks have now developed expert systems which involve computer programs that allow the machine to perform a variety of functions. One such expert (or smart) system scans credit card usage for the purpose of identifying those cards that may have been stolen but not yet reported. Typical computer programs look for sudden and obvious changes in spending patterns, such as a person suddenly buying expensive clothing or jewellery or making large cash withdrawals.

To take such systems one step further, neural networks are now being developed. These are more sophisticated software packages. Applied to the credit card example, neural networks can scan transactions and more accurately spot credit fraud. This is possible because of their ability to identify those transaction patterns most likely to indicate complex fraud. For example, at the Mellon Bank's Visa and MasterCard operations in Wilmington, Delaware, neural networks keep track of 1.2 million accounts and are able to identify as many as 1,000 potential defrauders a day. Other examples of the application of neural networks include optical character recognition, stock trading, property appraisal and the evaluation of machine performance.

E-commerce

In the new millennium US firms are engaging in e-commerce. This involves more than just building a website and doing a few transactions on the Internet. For example Bill Gates, in his book *Business@the Speed of Thought* states: 'I'm trying to show that it's not just the transaction, it's the customer service, it's the collaboration at a distance, it's the decision about what skills you need inside your company vs. what things you can go out now on the web to take advantage of'. Although e-commerce does involve firms marketing and selling their products directly to the consumer through their web pages, such as Internet retailers (e-tailors) Amazon.com or multichannel established retailers such as Wal-Mart, or innovative firms such as Priceline.com, by far most e-commerce is business-to-business or intra-business on the Internet. For example, Cisco Systems has become a virtual organization by connecting through the Internet its various functions with other business partners. This business-to-business e-commerce is expected to grow to well over a trillion dollars in the next few years (see E-COMMERCE). US firms have found that e-commerce not only has an impact on revenue but also can greatly reduce costs and adjust quickly to changing customer needs.

3 From total quality to learning organizations

Traditionally, US management concentrated on quantity – how much could be produced at the lowest cost. However, starting in the 1990s it became clear that in order to compete in world markets, quality must assume greater importance. At first the emphasis on quality was a direct reflection of successful Japanese management practices and procedures. Some of the techniques, such as quality circles, were copied directly, but when this did not work, US management began to develop their own approach. Quality management involved both the development of an overall philosophy and perspective of total quality as well as the application of specific techniques such as empowerment and benchmarking best practices.

Philosophy and perspective of total quality

The philosophy of quality management in the USA is grounded in ten core values (see TOTAL QUALITY MANAGEMENT). These values are reflected in the overall approach taken. They serve as the basis for planning, implementing and controlling total quality efforts.

1 *Customer-driven focus.* All methods, processes and procedures are designed to meet both internal and external customer expectations.
2 *Leadership.* Management understands what total quality entails and fully supports the organization's efforts to achieve it.
3 *Full participation.* Everyone in the organization is provided with TQM training and is actively involved in implementing these ideas.
4 *Reward system.* A reward system is developed to motivate personnel and ensure continual support for the overall effort.
5 *Reduced cycle time.* Great effort is made to reduce the amount of time needed to deliver output by continually analysing work procedures and workflows and eliminating or streamlining the process.
6 *Prevention not detection.* The focus of all quality efforts is on preventing mistakes and errors from occurring, rather than detecting and correcting them later on; the guideline is, 'do it right the first time'.
7 *Management by fact.* Feedback on TQM efforts are databased and often quantitative, with minimum attention given to anecdotal references, intuition and gut feeling.
8 *Long-range outlook.* There is continual monitoring of the external environment in order to answer the question: What level of quality or service will have to be provided to our customers over the next twelve to

thirty-six months and how can this goal be attained?
9 *Partnership development.* A cooperative network system is created between organizations and their customers and vendors, thus developing a process for helping improve quality and keep costs down.
10 *Social responsibility.* Corporate citizenship and responsibility are fostered through the sharing of quality-related information with other organizations that can profit from these ideas, and by working to reduce negative impacts on the community by eliminating product waste generation and product defects or recalls.

Empowerment

Empowerment is the delegation of authority to employees in order for them to take control and make decisions (see EMPOWERMENT). The objective of empowerment is to encourage employees to become more personally involved in their jobs and to use their authority to get things done and deliver quality to (meet the expectations of) internal and external customers. Empowerment is becoming increasingly recognized and used by management in the USA. For example, at the Ritz-Carlton hotel chain, the only hotel firm to win the national quality award the Baldrige and the only firm to win it twice, employees are authorized to spend up to $2,000 to handle problems, such as mailing a suit to a customer who checked out and left it in his room, sending a pot of herbal tea and aspirin to a guest who has just checked in and has a cold, or renting a television monitor and video cassette recorder because all of the hotel's units are in use and a client needs this equipment for a meeting scheduled to start immediately. At AT&T Universal Card Services, employees are allowed to authorize whatever expenditures are necessary to reduce cost and improve customer service, such as sending out a replacement card by overnight delivery to a customer whose card has been lost and who needs a new one as soon as possible.

Empowerment is typically tied to training. Empowered employees are trained so they are aware of how to do their jobs correctly and can then take action that will help deliver quality service to customers. At Motorola, for example, employees are trained in both hard (technical, engineering) and soft (interpersonal relations, customer service) skills. As a result, each Motorola employee learns how to handle their own quality and productivity, create production schedules and job assignments, manage material supplies, set up equipment and conduct routine maintenance, provide input to both product and process design, design the workplace, develop and manage budgets, generate input for hiring decisions, provide information for peer-performance reviews and train new employees.

Empowerment is also closely tied to work improvement systems. For example, at Zytec the empowerment plan includes an element known as the implemented improvement system (IIS), a Japanese-style suggestion system that places major emphasis on employee involvement with the goal of generating new ideas for increased productivity (see JAPAN, MANAGEMENT IN). There are three stages to IIS:

1 the organization encourages employees to examine their jobs and work areas, think of ways of improving them and make small developments;
2 employees are educated and developed so that they are better equipped to analyse problems, devise ideal solutions and undertake more ambitious improvements;
3 the organization encourages employees to pursue major improvements to achieve significant financial benefits.

At the heart of this system is the concept of continuous improvement. Continuous or constant improvement focuses on never being satisfied with the status quo, always striving to improve quality to customers. Innovation, characterized by improvements in the creation and delivery of quality goods or services, plays a key role. Most firms stress constant improvement as reflected by on-going, small, incremental gains. In contrast to the dramatic gains that can result from highly innovative approaches, constant improvement provides more long-term gains because of its on-going nature. In addition, constant improvement places the emphasis on people, both employees and customers, not just technology, and

promotes group effort (in contrast to individualism).

Today, many US managers recognize that continuous improvement is necessary but not sufficient. Now discontinuous leaps in improvement are necessary to compete in the hypercompetitive global economy.

Benchmarking and best practices

Another dimension of total quality is benchmarking and best practices, a process of comparing current performance and practices with those judged to be the very best (see BENCHMARKING). There are two ways in which this can be used to manage quality: (1) by studying the best processes and practices used internally and seeing how these can be employed by the group conducting the best practices effort; and (2) by studying best practices for the purpose of picking up new ideas which can be copied or modified for use. In the case of IBM Rochester, which designed and built the successful AS/400 minicomputer, the group benchmarked both in-house and outside firms. In-house, the group learned how other IBM divisions successfully handled defect prevention, hardware process documentation and resource manufacturing capability. Outside, they learned about quality improvement techniques from Motorola, about resource manufacturing planning capability from 3M, about the effective use of service representatives from Hewlett Packard, about improved secretarial performance planning from Honeywell and about just-in-time (JIT) inventory from Japanese firms.

Learning organizations

Although the total quality approach has dramatically changed US management in the 1990s, it is now recognized that this is just the starting point for managing successfully in the twenty-first century. In particular, US management is attempting to move towards becoming learning organizations. These new paradigm organizations incorporate total quality but go beyond it (Luthans *et al.* 1994). For example, while total quality depends on single-loop and adaptive learning, learning organizations move towards double-loop and generative learning. Similarly, while the total quality approach continually adapts strategies to resolve problems and meet challenges, learning organizations anticipate change and analyse the causes of problems, thus preventing their recurrence.

Learning organizations have a number of common characteristics and values (see OR-GANIZATION LEARNING). One is an intense desire to learn how to prevent problems. This is commonly done by carefully analysing mistakes and failures to determine how their recurrence can be prevented. A second is a strong commitment to the generation and transfer of new knowledge and technology. This commitment typically encompasses information gathering and training programmes for personnel. A third characteristic is that of continuously scanning the external environment, learning of new developments and incorporating this information into all relevant aspects of the operation. A fourth feature is the use of shared vision and systems thinking to evoke a personal commitment from all participants. Systems thinking is also used to understand the inter-relationships between causes and effects and thus avoid the use of short-term solutions that lead to long-term problems.

Other characteristics of learning organizations can be seen in the contrast between the traditional resource-based enterprises and emerging knowledge-based organizations (see Senge 1993). Such differences include: the way in which shared vision is created; the formulation and implementation of ideas; the nature of organizational thinking; conflict resolution; and the role of leadership.

In traditional resource-based enterprises, vision was created by top management. In the new, knowledge-based learning organization, vision can emerge from anywhere, although top management remains responsible for the existence of such a vision and for promoting it through organizational processes (see KNOWLEDGE MANAGEMENT). In the same way, in a resource-based enterprise formulation occurs at the upper levels and implementation is at the lower levels. In the knowledge-based learning organization, both formulation and implementation are carried out at all levels. It is in such situations that total quality

techniques, such as empowerment, apply to learning organizations: empowered employees at any level can formulate the ideas and then implement them to get the job done right the first time and meet customer expectations at any cost.

The nature of organizational thinking differs between the two types of organizations in that employees in resource-based organizations understand their specialized jobs and what is expected of them. However, little attention is paid to how these jobs inter-relate with others. The flow of authority and the focus of attention tends to be in a vertical, downward hierarchy. In contrast, in learning organizations employees are taught to understand how their jobs and actions influence those of others in the enterprise, and vice versa. An example is provided by Hanover Insurance, a medium-sized property and liability insurer. This firm steadily increased local control of regional operations, promoting a greater sense of ownership among personnel. The company also developed a claims management learning laboratory to help local managers better understand how individual decisions interact. As a result of this learning, Hanover managers discovered that some well-accepted practices used in the industry were contributing to problems, such as escalating costs and premiums. By rethinking the ways in which settlement costs were handled, the company was able to reduce payouts.

Conflict resolution is also handled in different ways. In the traditional approach, disputes tend to be mediated politically. Learning organizations approach conflict management differently, operating under the premise that, frequently, conflicts cannot be solved through the sheer use of power or hierarchical influence. Effective solutions often require input from an array of organizational personnel throughout the enterprise. Collaborative learning and the integration of diverse viewpoints are encouraged. For example, the product development departments of learning organizations may create competing teams that develop different approaches to the same project. These teams will then debate the advantages and disadvantages of the approaches. Under the guidance of team leaders, the groups eventually develop a common agreement as to the best approach.

The role of leadership is still another critical difference between traditional and learning organizations (see LEADERSHIP). In the resource-based organization, the leader sets the direction. In the learning organization, leaders are responsible for the processes of building a shared vision. One of the most commonly cited examples of this contrast is the way in which leaders motivate their people. In resource-based enterprises, rewards and recognition as well as punishment are used, while in learning organizations the personnel are empowered and inspired towards full commitment. While the resource-based organization relies on external tools and techniques designed to control local actions, learning enterprises work at creating an internally motivated workforce that is willing to use its increased authority and training to get things done.

Since learning organizations are future-oriented, they also make use of techniques such as scenario analysis. This involves the formulation of future plans based on responses to possible situations that could develop in the future. While future environmental conditions are not totally predictable, the use of scenario analysis helps learning organizations predict likely developments and develop plans for addressing these conditions. This allows managers to stay ahead, not merely to adapt and react to changing environments.

4 The future: world-class organizations

The most recent development in US management with significant implications for the future is the move beyond learning organizations to become what could be called world-class organizations (see Parker 1999) (see GLOBALIZATION). These enterprises are recognized as global leaders in their respective industries; they dominate their markets. World-class organizations are additive in the sense of incorporating both total quality and learning organizations, but they extend beyond this. In particular, US managers of world-class organizations realize that change is not only desirable but necessary to compete successfully in an anywhere-anytime-anyplace twenty-first century environment. Today, US managers of world-class organizations continually monitor their environment and assess new technological developments not as threats but as opportunities (see GLOBALIZATION; MULTINATIONAL CORPORATIONS). They realize that their present stakeholders (customers, owners, employees, suppliers and communitites) and their current state of technology can be limiting or inhibiting to their future action (see Hodgetts *et al.* 1999). As the famous US manager Jack Welch said as his company GE was coming off another record year in 1999, 'We have to reinvent ourselves!', and as Rosabeth Kanter (1999) declares, 'the best way to predict the future is to create it'. There are several support pillars that can be used to characterize world-class organizations: (1) customer focus; (2) continuous improvement; (3) flexibility; (4) creative programmes for managing human resources; (5) an egalitarian climate; and (6) technological support (see Luthans *et al.* 1994). Once again, these are quite similar to what has been discussed under both total quality and learning organizations. Although the pillars use the same familiar terms, such as customer focus and continuous improvement, they are more comprehensive. Much of the following summary of the pillars, including the examples, has been suggested by Sang M. Lee and is drawn from Luthans *et al.* (1994).

Perhaps the most important pillar of the world-class organization is its *customer focus*. The organization puts the customer at the centre of its strategy, and all systems and personnel are organized to serve the customer. One way in which this is done is by flattening the structure and reducing the distance between the customer and the organizational personnel most directly serving customers. This type of structure can better gather information about customers' current and future needs. Organizations not only meet customer needs but also create new demand for their goods and services. For example, Pitney-Bowes, long known for its innovativeness in the postage meter/franking machine business, has continually developed creative products that have made it indispensable to the US Postal Service, as well as to a wide array of domestic and international customers, by expanding its focus from the postal business to the entire mailing business for its customers. The firm thus created both new product and service demand.

A second pillar is the need for *continuous improvement*, as reflected by the way world-class organizations learn to be faster and more effective than competitors. Large enterprises partly accomplish this by sharing information on a worldwide basis. For example, IBM research scientists are in constant on-line contact with each other. Research and development personnel in Europe and Asia know what their colleagues in US laboratories are doing, and vice versa. This practice is used by all major functional groups, thus ensuring global learning throughout the enterprise. Another approach is the use of process engineering to create virtual offices at home or at customer premises. Most US managers now have laptop computers and cellular phones. This allows them to set up virtual offices everywhere and, in the process, reduce employee working space and allow personnel to spend more time with customers. Emerging IT tools such as Dell's Premier Pages (small web pages linked to large customers' intranets, that let approved employees configure their PCs on-line, pay for them and track the delivery status) not only cut costs and improve quality (ordering errors), but also led to improved selling and customer service from freed-up Dell representatives.

The third pillar of world-class organizations is *flexibility*, the use of flexible arrangements that allow enterprises to respond quickly, decisively and correctly to changes in the environment. These enterprises become what is called a virtual corporation, which is a firm that acts just like a corporation but is organized through a network of partners and alliances (Davidow and Malone 1992). For example, while the virtual corporation produces goods and services and continually generates new offerings for the marketplace, many of these activities are often performed through an outside sourcing arrangement or the formation of temporary alliances with other companies. For example, Corning Inc. uses twenty-three strategic alliances to compete in a variety of high-tech markets. In this way, world-class companies are able to reduce costs and share risks with other firms.

Another example of flexibility is the way in which world-class organizations use JIT inventory systems and multiskilled personnel. For example, Kawasaki Manufacturing USA, in Lincoln, Nebraska, produces several models of motorcycles, all-terrain vehicles and jet skis. Relying heavily on its ability to switch production from one product to another, the company is able to achieve rapid set-up time, low cost and high-quality output. Some of the characteristics of this flexibility pillar include: the use of modular or matrix organizations; the use of multifunctional teams; the simultaneous processing of ideas; multiskilled workers; empowered teams; cross-training and job rotation of workers; and innovative approaches to cycle-time reduction.

Creative human resource management programmes represent the fourth pillar. Most US managers today recognize what has become known as high-performance work practices or HPWPs. Although there is not a single agreed-upon definition of HPWPs, a recent comprehensive review of the definitions and research literature concluded that the best definition is: 'an organization system that continually aligns its strategy, goals, objectives and internal operations with the demands of its external environment to maximize organizational performance' (Kirkman *et al.* 1999). The HPWPs can be operationalized as specific techniques such as multisource or 360 degree feedback, pay for performance, self-managed work teams and employee involvement/participation (Luthans *et al.* 2000).

Creative human resource management techniques have considerable research support linking them to organizational performance (Faris and Varma 1998) (see HUMAN RESOURCE MANAGEMENT). Yet in actual practice, only the world-class organizations fully utilize them. Pfeffer (1998) notes that only about half US organizations and their managers believe in the strong relationship between creative human resources techniques and bottom-line success. Of the half that do believe, only about half of them implement HPWPs, and then only half of the remaining one-fourth stick with these creative human resource management techniques long enough to reap the benefits of retention of the best people, productivity improvement and increased profit and growth. Pfeffer (1998) has documented that these one-eighth firms ($\frac{1}{2} \times \frac{1}{2} \times \frac{1}{2}$) are world-class organizations such as Southwest Airlnes, GE, Gallup, Norwest Bank and Microsoft.

Another pillar is the existence of an *egalitarian climate* in which the organization and its participants value and respect one another (see ORGANIZATION CULTURE). This philosophy also extends to those whom the organization serves: customers, owners, suppliers and the community. At Wal-Mart, for example, all employees are called associates, and store managers have weekly meetings during which they hold open discussions with the associates for the purpose of reviewing operations and freely discussing new ideas for improving customer service. Some of the most important features of this pillar are: open communication between all parties; a friendly environment; a mentoring, coaching, 'buddy' system; active employee involvement and participation in all phases of operations; and sponsored community, health and family programmes.

The final pillar supporting world-class organizations is technological support. Many of the creative, innovative or productive approaches of these organizations are made possible because of advances in technologies, such as computer-aided design, computer-aided manufacturing, telecommunications, expert systems, distributed database systems, intra-, inter- and extra-organizational information systems, multimedia systems and executive information systems. This technological support helps the enterprise use speed, information knowledge and differentiation to gain competitive advantages. An example is provided by American Express's company AmeriTax, which provides electronic tax filing by creating an electronic linkage between the IRS and tax preparation firms. Through this inter-organizational information system, AmeriTax offers a tax-return preparation service to its customers, while also developing a conduit for a larger set of financial products and services. The key elements of the technological support pillar include: technology–human interface; modern information/telecommunication systems; distributed information/database systems; shared ownership of information knowledge and intelli-

gence; decentralization of decision making to the lowest level possible; and continuous technical education and training.

5 Conclusion

US management has a strong foundation in classic organization design and management processes, but has undergone dramatic change of late. To some extent Japanese management techniques and competitive battles stimulated US managers to abandon the classical approach about 15 years ago, but, as has been discussed here, some changes are unique to the USA. In particular, there has been, and will probably continue to be, a great deal of focus on adjusting to the external technical and global environment. Customer service, quality management, reduced time to market, continuous improvement, outsourcing of goods and services, and creative human resource management programmes are all key factors in US management efforts to attain and maintain world-class levels of goods and services.

Not all US organizations have achieved world-class levels, but, even to survive, they know they need to continually improve to fend off competitors and maintain local markets. The concepts of total quality, learning and world-class organizations are increasingly being adopted by US managers in order to sustain and strengthen their position in the domestic economy, and now the reality of the global economy.

FRED LUTHANS
UNIVERSITY OF NEBRASKA

RICHARD M. HODGETTS
FLORIDA INTERNATIONAL UNIVERSITY

Further reading

(References cited in the text marked *)

Bowen, D.E. and Lawler, E.E., III (1992) 'The empowerment of service workers: what, why, how, and when', *Sloan Management Review* 33 (3): 31–9. (A detailed description of the use of empowerment in the service industry.)

* Davidow, W.H. and Malone, M.S. (1992) *The Virtual Corporation*, New York: HarperCollins. (A detailed description of the characteristics

and operations of this emerging type of corporation.)

Dixon, N.M. (1992) 'Organizational learning: a review of the literature with implications for HRD professionals', *Human Resource Development Quarterly* 3 (1): 29–49. (A review of the special implications that each of the five areas of organizational learning has for HRD professionals.)

* Faris, G. and Varma, A. (1998) 'High performance work systems: what we know and what we need to know', *Human Resource Planning* 21 (2): 50–5. (A comprehensive research summary of the impact of HPWPs on financial and operational performance.)

Fulmer, R.M. and Gibbs, P. (1998) 'The second generation learning organizations: new tools for sustaining competitive advantage', *Organizational Dynamics* 21 (1): 7–20. (This article and the rest of this whole special issue in Organizational Dynamics is the latest information and real-world examples of learning organizations.)

Glanz, E.F. and Dailey, L.K. (1993) 'Benchmarking', *Human Resource Management* 32 (1/2): 9–20. (This article provides specific examples of how benchmarking has been used by Digital Equipment and United Technologies.)

Hammer, M. and Champy, J. (1993) *Reengineering the Corporation*, New York: Harper Business. (A detailed description of how the re-engineering process works and of firms that have successfully used this approach.)

* Hitt, M.A. (2000) 'The new frontier: transformation of management for the new millenium', *Organizational Dynamics* 28 (3): 7–17. (An up-to-date description and analysis of the impact of the twenty-first century environment on effective management.)

* Hodgetts, R.M., Luthans, F. and Slocum, J.W. Jr (1999) 'Strategy and HRM initiatives for the '00s environment: redefining roles and boundaries linking competencies and resources', *Organizational* Dynamics 28 (2): 7–21. (After describing the twenty-first century environment, the article turns to new thinking strategy and innovative human resource management approaches.)

Howard, R. and Haas, R.D. (eds) (1993) *Learning Imperative: Managing People for Continuous Innovation*, Boston, MA: Harvard Business School Press. (A compilation of *Harvard Business Review* articles which describe organizational innovation in worldwide companies.)

* Kanter, R.M. (1999) 'Change is everyone's job: managing the extended enterprise in a globally connected world', *Organizational Dynamics* 28 (1): 7–23. (Richly describes the trends in global connectivity and the future of organizations.)

* Kirkman, B.L., Lowe, K.B. and Young, P.D. (1999) *High Performance Work Organizations*, Greensboro, NC: Center for Creative Leadership. (An innovative bibliography and summary of all HPWP articles published up to 1999.)

* Luthans, F., Hodgetts, R.M. and Lee, S.M. (1994) 'New paradigm organizations: from total quality to learning to world-class', *Organizational Dynamics* 22 (3): 5–19. (A description of the characteristics of organizations as they move towards world-class status.)

* Luthans, F., Luthans, K.W., Hodgetts, R.M. and Luthans, B.C. (2000) 'Can HPWPs (high performance work practices) help in the former Soviet Union? A cross-cultural fit analysis', *Business Horizons* (September/October): in press. (This article defines and reviews the research on HPWPs and then analyses the cultural fit of their use in former Soviet Union organizations.)

McGill, M.E., Slocum, J.W. Jr and Lei, D. (1992) 'Management practices in learning organizations', *Organizational Dynamics* 21 (1): 5–17. (A comparison of the characteristics of adaptive and generative learning organizations.)

* Parker, B. (1999) *Globalization and Business Practice*, Thousand Oaks, CA and London: Sage. (An up-to-date text on North American dominated MNCs.)

* Pfeffer, J. (1998) *The Human Equation*, Boston, MA: Harvard Business School Press. (A very readable professional book that makes a strong documented case for the very positive impact that human resources managed effectively has on the performance of organizations.)

Rodgers, C.S. (1993) 'The flexible workplace: what have we learned?', *Human Resource Management* 31 (3): 183–9. (A research study of white-collar and service-sector jobs which reports the demand by employees for more flexibility.)

Schonberger, R.J. (1992) 'Is strategy strategic? Impact of total quality management on strategy', *Academy of Management Executive* 6 (3): 80–7. (This article focuses on common strategic planning objectives: continuous improvement, responsiveness, flexibility and waste and cost elimination.)

* Senge, P.M. (1993) 'Transforming the practice of management', *Human Resource Development Quarterly* 4 (1): 5–32. (A detailed contrast of resource-based and knowledge-based organizations.)

Tully, S. (1993) 'The modular corporation', *Fortune* 127 (3): 106–15. (A detailed discussion of how major firms are using outsourcing and other modular organization concepts.)

Warner, M. (ed.) (1997) *Comparative Management*, 4 vols, London: Routledge. (The first volume of this collection of readings is devoted to North American management.)

See also: ACCOUNTING IN NORTH AMERICA; ADLER, N.; BANKING IN THE UNITED STATES OF AMERICA; BENCHMARKING; BUSINESS CULTURES, NORTH AMERICAN; BUSINESS PROCESS REENGINEERING; COMMERCE; CULTURE, CROSS-NATIONAL; DECISION MAKING; DOWNSIZING; DRUCKER, P.F.; ELECTRONIC DATA INTERCHANGE; EMPOWERMENT; FORD, H.; GATES, B.; GLOBALIZATION; HAMMER, M.; HUMAN RESOURCE MANAGEMENT; INDUSTRIAL RELATIONS IN NORTH AMERICA; JAPAN, MANAGEMENT IN; KANTER, R.M.; KNOWLEDGE MANAGEMENT; LEADERSHIP; MANAGEMENT EDUCATION IN NORTH AMERICA; MULTINATIONAL CORPORATIONS; ORGANIZATION BEHAVIOUR; ORGANIZATION CULTURE; ORGANIZATION LEARNING; SLOAN, A.P.; TOTAL QUALITY MANAGEMENT; WEBER, M.

Urwick, Lyndall Fownes (1891–1983)

Personal background

- born 3 March 1891 in Malvern, Worcestershire
- educated at Repton College, University of Oxford (New College) with History Exhibition; graduated BA (Oxon) in 1912, subsequently MA
- officer cadet service at Repton and Oxford
- 1912–14 worked in the family company; elected to partnership *in absentia* in 1916
- commissioned as Second Lieutenant in 1914 and served in British Army from August 1914 until December 1918; promoted to Captain; awarded Military Cross; selected for Divisional Staff appointment, 1916; promoted to Major, 1917, and appointed Officer of the Order of the British Empire (OBE)
- Fownes Brothers & Company, Worcester, 1919–21
- Rowntree & Company, York, 1922–6
- The Management Research Groups, 1926–8
- Director of the International Management Institute, Geneva, 1928–33
- founder, managing partner, and director of Urwick Orr & Partners, Consulting Specialists in Organisation and Management, 1934 onwards
- retired in 1965 and moved to Australia, where he died on 5 December 1983

Major works

Organising a Sales Office (assisted by E. Aston, F.H. Cordukes and C.H. Tucker) (1928)

The Meaning of Rationalisation (1929)
Management of Tomorrow (1933)
Committees in Organisation (1937)
Dynamic Administration (1941)
The Elements of Administration (1944)
The Making of Scientific Management (with E.F.L. Brech) (1946–8)
Patterns of Organisation (1946)
Morale (1947)
The Load on Top Management (1954)
The Golden Book of Management (1956)
Leadership in the Twentieth Century (1957a)
Is Management a Profession? (1958)
Sixteen Questions about the Selection and Training of Managers (1958)

Summary

Lyndall Urwick became interested in management during his early involvement with Army command and administration in the officer cadet service of the Territorial Army, and sought to apply positive lessons learned there into the industrial setting of the family manufacturing company. That approach was strengthened by experiences gained in his wartime Army service (1914–18), and he was manifestly successful in man-management during 1919–21. A wartime incident had brought to his attention the writings of F.W. Taylor, whose thinking he found closely concurrent with his own, and he set out to be a 'disciple' of the Taylor principles and doctrines. Through the ensuing four decades Urwick was unwavering in his promotion of sound managerial principles reflected into effective practice, with an accompanying urge towards management advancement. This was purveyed both in the sequence of employment roles and in an unstinting programme of voluntary service through the UK's institutional 'management movement' and the higher educational channels. He published a number of books as well as a plethora of papers, addresses and articles, the majority preserved in published reproductions.

1 Introduction

No other individual from the UK's industrial and commercial sectors, nor from the academic milieu, has made so extensive and varied a contribution as did Lyndall Urwick to the advancement of management in practice, as a subject or in specific education. While his three early books (Urwick *et al.* 1928; Urwick 1929, 1933) made a significant presentation of his pioneering thinking and recommended practice (see below), by far the majority of his contributions were made through innumerable addresses and lectures given by invitation to the membership of managerial societies and educational conferences. His first such address came about in April 1921 when, in consequence of a recommendation from his own employees in the family-owned Fownes Brothers & Company, he was invited to address the Rowntree Lecture Conference in Oxford on the subject of 'Management as a science'. The content was an Urwick interpretation of the thinking and principles of F.W. Taylor, adapted to better understanding by a British audience (see TAYLOR, F.W.).

The impact of Urwick's lecture was such that Seebohm Rowntree invited him to join the Rowntree company, in York, to assist in determining and implementing a programme of managerial improvement in the sales and administrative offices. This Urwick accepted, effective from January 1922, taking on the role of 'organization and methods' investigator. He met with considerable success due to his capacity for gaining cooperation from the working people whose activities and methods were being changed by improvement. The Rowntree directors allowed the story of his efforts, *Organising a Sales Office* to be published in 1928. This book was an early contribution to the ways and means of successfully carrying through the betterment of organization and methods, including the innovation of setting timing norms for repetitive tasks, with full employee cooperation.

2 Management research groups

Urwick's involvement with Rowntree had an additional and more significant consequence when Seebohm Rowntree sought to use Urwick's talents to initiate experiments in the UK with a concept he had seen at work in the USA: manufacturers' research associations. These were informal groupings of non-competing companies for the purpose of strictly confidential interchange of experience and ideas at director and senior manager level, in matters of policy, marketing programmes, development, financial control and the like. Urwick's initial role was to visit top managers in a cross-section of larger manufacturing companies to ascertain and assess reactions to the concept and to the proposal to inaugurate an experimental development.

By mid-1926, Urwick had gained sufficient positive response to justify the Rowntree family's Social Research Trust putting up preliminary funding for a small London office, with Urwick himself working full-time to launch the experiment. Four groups were established early in 1927 with eight to ten participating companies in each, structured by size grades in order to sustain good comparability: the grades were large (over 2,000 personnel employed), medium (500–2,000) and small (under 500). Within the year the number of groups had doubled, with increasing numbers of participating companies, and the 'management research group' (MRG) nomenclature was adopted in preference over the US title.

Urwick's dedicated and enthusiastic promotional efforts brought a gradually expanding participation in all three groups, despite the traditional British conservative attitudes with regard to disclosure of information. The fundamental principle of strict confidentiality of proceedings was rigorously maintained, the only occasional public references being brief notes that the MRG had been formed and that interested company directors were invited to contact the secretariat at the London address. A governing council had been formed, with Seebohm Rowntree as Chairman, as a coordinating focus for policy and development, but each group had its own committee for the planning and conduct of programmes of activities including exchange visits. By the end of 1928 the network was firmly established and still expanding. The very nature of the objectives ensured that the more progressive companies and firms were those that joined, thus developing a strong background influence for managerial progress. This was to become significant during the 1930s and 1940s, especially in 'Group No. 1' whose membership included nearly 30 of the country's largest manufacturing concerns.

Whereas the idea for forming the MRGs came from Seebohm Rowntree, it was Urwick's two years of executive application that propelled the movement into permanent progress and success, with an in-built strength and momentum which meant that it continued onwards even after Urwick's own departure. In September 1928, he was appointed Director of the International Management Institute in Geneva. A successor secretary was appointed to the London office, and Urwick himself was co-opted onto the MRG Council. He was already undertaking a task ongoing from that setting, arising from the World Economic Conference in May 1927, where he had attended as a member of the British delegation. A major subject had been 'rationalization' in the sense of managerial and productivity improvement. For their reporting on the conference, the delegation decided that fuller explanation would be useful on the home scene and invited Urwick to undertake this. The outcome was *The Meaning of Rationalisation*, which was published in 1929. The content was a structured presentation of principles and practice for systematic managerial application.

Continuing involvement within the MRG, even though only part-time and from a distance, afforded Urwick further opportunities for contributing to managerial advancement in the UK. Three opportunities were particularly significant. First, arising from the Geneva Conference, the MRG Council had by 1929–30 reached the conclusion that the UK needed a public central institution in the managerial context, and invited Urwick to draft ideas and proposals, a task he gladly undertook. His memorandum submitted in mid-1930 was entitled 'The British Institute of Management' (Brech, forthcoming), and set down in full the rationale, a proposed constitution and suggested lines of action. This was circulated among the participating companies, but regrettably no further action ensued.

The second opportunity lay in bringing the UK overtly onto the international scene by securing an invitation to host a forthcoming session of the triennial International Management Congress. Urwick was hoping to secure the session for 1932, with the MRG Council as the focus, especially if the proposed institute had been initiated in the preceding year. In default of this, the only alternative host body had to be the Federation of British Industries, which needed more time for preparation. The invitation was accepted for the London venue for the Congress of 1935; this was successfully carried through, although British participation was both limited and unenthusiastic.

The third contribution again stemmed from the Geneva Conference, in that the success of the *The Meaning of Rationalisation* prompted its publishers to invite Urwick to compile a collected presentation of the many addresses and lectures that he had been delivering at home and abroad. In accepting this invitation, Urwick chose to adopt the form of a consolidated treatise rather than a collection of reproductions. The result was *Management of Tomorrow* (1933). While the content covered the broad spectrum of management principles and practice, the presentation was philosophical in mode rather than aiming to be a textbook of action and technique. It had a remarkably perceptive and forward-looking content, portraying aspects of managerial thinking and development, and it set the foundations for the wide-ranging 'Urwick mentality' that was to become a predominating influence for the ensuing 20 years and more.

3 Professional consultant service

The closing of the International Management Institute in Geneva in December 1933 due to the prevailing financial crises brought Urwick back to the UK to start a new phase of his career. He was already a well-known name in the managerial context. His earlier successful re-organization service with the Rowntree Company suggested the initiation of a 'consultancy' practice, provided he could find a partner with comparable and even fuller experience in manufacturing managerial advancement. Fortuitous circumstances brought him this in the person of John L. Orr, who had a decade of experience with an industrial engineering background. Both had the goal of founding a well-rounded consultancy service covering, in due course, all aspects of managerial practice, and they shared both common and complementary characteristics.

The new jointly-owned company, Urwick Orr & Partners Limited, commenced business in September 1934, getting off to a good start with very commendable progress in the ensuing years, despite the relative novelty of a management consultancy service in the UK industrial and commercial scene. Within five years, 30 consultants were being employed by the company. All had substantial managerial experience and were given additional in-depth training by the two partners. The company described its service as 'consulting specialists in organization and management', indicative of the wide scope intended. Within those first five years specific teams had been developed for providing services in clerical methods and administration, in the effective process of delegation, in sales management and marketing, in the improvement of manufacturing productivity and in financial planning and control.

In all these services, a significant objective was the effective implementation of changes recommended for improvement of method and performance, involving preliminary and continuing consultation with the personnel concerned together with appropriate retraining for the changed and improved methods. One of the company's principles was the request for preliminary consultation with trades union representatives as and when pertinent. A second principle was to ensure that the supervisory personnel concerned in the assignments were competently trained in the improved organization and methods, as well as assisted to enhance their standards of man management in gaining cooperation.

4 Public institutional contributions

The company grew steadily in terms of service, size and reputation, becoming a nationally renowned institution. The personal standing which Urwick had attained, even by 1934–5, was a contributing factor. John Orr was a highly competent and successful industrial engineer and manufacturing management consultant, but he was a somewhat private person and not at ease in public display. He only rarely appeared in institutional programmes. Both partners were agreed that public contributions from the company, in the managerial institutional and educational context, formed an important obligation, as well as serving to foster promotion and reputation. This was to be primarily Urwick's sphere of activity in voluntary service towards the UK's emerging 'management movement', and he fulfilled the role comprehensively and generously. He had the personal advantage of language skills and fluency and an attractive personality, as well as the competence to advance progressive lines of thought and practice cogently and persuasively.

During the latter half of the 1930s Urwick was repeatedly invited by managerial societies and other institutions to address their meetings and conferences, and very frequently his contributions were subsequently reproduced in their journals or separately printed as booklets. Additionally, there were occasional articles (sometimes series) written for commercial magazines. The subject matter through all those contributions was customarily indicated or suggested by the institution concerned, but where the choice lay with himself, Urwick had the broad spectrum of *Management of Tomorrow* from which to select, knowing that his presentation would always be forward-looking. Among those many aspects and topics, two which held his particular personal interest were 'organization and delegation' and 'leadership in man management'. By any standards of assessment, Urwick's output during the 1930s, contributing to the advancement of managerial practice and of education for management, can only be described as immense.

Fortuitous circumstances gave rise to two special contributions in the latter years of the decade. The first stemmed from the International Management Congress of 1938, held in Washington, DC. The aftermath of the 1935 London Congress had revealed a growing level of institutional activity in the UK, but this was only loosely coordinated. In January 1937 there was formed a new national framework for those institutions, the British Management Council. This included some 30 organizations, though still only in loose coordination.

An immediate task was to compose and brief the British delegation for the 1938 Congress, with a major item in that briefing being an overview of the background to the emerging 'management movement' and the current state of development attained. Urwick was invited to compile the background report and he used volunteer research assistance to pull together a comprehensive review. In 1937 he presented an interim report to an Oxford Management Conference, one of a series of conferences which provided a forum for the presentation of knowledge and know-how in management practice. The full document of July 1938, at over 80 pages *octavo*, was a remarkable historical *tour de force* under the title *The Development of Scientific Management in Great Britain*. Reproduced subsequently in *The British Management Review*, it represented an immensely valuable pioneering contribution to knowledge in the UK.

The second item of 1938 stemmed from that compilation, as it led Urwick to recommend the British Management Council to seek Leverhulme Research Trust funding for the inauguration of a specific project investigating the contemporary provision and development of facilities for the pursuit of management studies within the UK educational system. The project was initiated late in 1938 with the service of a full-time research officer, E.F.L. Brech being the first such officer selected and appointed.

5 Education for management

During the Second World War, Urwick was on full-time service with government departments involved in developing and applying operational improvements in organization and methods, though he remained in office as chairman of Urwick Orr, in occasional attendance, while J.L. Orr took over the full general management role. Urwick did however continue with a restricted programme of voluntary institutional contributions, notably within the Institute of Industrial Administration (IIA) which was enjoying a marked revival of activities and membership growth.

One important non-institutional achievement early in the war period was to publish a collection of papers and addresses given over several years by Mary Parker Follett (see FOLLET, M.P.), an objective that Urwick had long had in his sights, despite the complexity arising from the necessity of having a US co-partner (H.C. Metcalfe). The volume was published in the UK in 1941 as *Dynamic Administration*. Within the IIA Urwick was an elected member of council, and in November 1944 he was appointed Chairman of the Institute's Education Committee, with a mandate to revise ('modernize') the professional diploma syllabus. Since 1928 this framework had been the UK's only structured system for promoting studies of 'the body of knowledge in management', a matter of long-standing special interest for Urwick himself. This committee setting afforded him opportunity for consultative contact with the higher educational authorities, enabling him to encourage national thinking towards a comprehensive approach in the advancement of management studies.

Urwick's standing and reputation among managerial societies and with the educational authorities ensured that his views were heard with respect. Within the new government (after the general election in July 1945) the Minister and Department of Education responded positively to his recommendation for a national review and acted promptly. In September 1945, the Minister invited all interested parties to an informal conference; representatives of 18 institutions were in attendance, including the two senior educational authorities. Among those attending were some institutions that had already established programmes of management studies and some with schemes prepared and awaiting inauguration. The conference found consensus for the national review, recommending the Minister to appoint a committee and unanimously indicating preference for Urwick to serve as chairman. This recommendation was accepted and immediately implemented, with the committee formed and initiating deliberations in October 1945.

The leadership and outcome of the Departmental Committee on Education for Management could well be regarded as Urwick's biggest single contribution to the nation's advancement of management, especially because of the consensus that he achieved in the pattern of recommendations. The Committee's terms of reference were simple, as was the membership composition. There were six persons from the industrial and commercial milieu, selected to serve in personal capacity rather than as representatives, but with adequate familiarity with the existing situation in management studies. Two further members represented educational interests and there was a departmental secretary. The Committee worked expeditiously, enabling a report of review and recommendations to be completed by August 1946 and circulated as a draft for consultation among the eighteen institutions. In the following December the Minister reconvened the representatives to a conference whereat the draft report was unanimously approved and the Minister indicated intention for immediate implementation. The report was published by HMSO early in 1947 (Ministry of Education 1947).

The significance of the Urwick Committee's contribution lay in two features. First, there was now a national policy favouring, advocating, supporting and providing facilities for management studies and examinations covering all aspects and all regions of the country. Second, an integrated pattern of syllabuses had been promulgated, providing for cover of those subjects that were common among different functions and sections of the managerial process, together with appropriate attention to naturally arising differentiations. There was no doubt that Urwick's knowledge and leadership skill had secured unanimity in that pattern, attained through a simple formula of a two-tiered syllabus with an intermediate level and a final level. The former was common to all the managerial societies operating educational programmes, and it was structured into three 'parts' for which outline content was laid down in the report, respectively designated 'introductory subjects', 'background subjects' and 'the tools of management'. With regard to the Engineering Institutions and the Institute of Cost and Works Accountants, the committee recommended that their councils should align their incidental requirements in 'management' subjects to the structure and content of the common 'intermediate' syllabus; this was accepted.

The 'final' syllabus catered for specific managerial institutional requirements, to be determined and prescribed by the councils of the institutions concerned, but with one strong recommendation for serious inclusion of 'management principles' and a broad review of 'management practice' in all the specialist programmes. Within this pattern for a 'final' level, the Committee laid down a syllabus for 'general management' appropriate for the IIA and for the newly-founded British Institute of Management as and when that body was ready to embark on programmes of studies. The new pattern was initiated in the scholastic year 1948–9, requiring some three to four years for effective implementation. By then a new era had opened for the UK's industrial and commercial sectors, offering for the first time structured programmes of managerial studies and examinations. The credit for this belongs primarily to Urwick.

Contemporary circumstances, however, necessitated continuing active responsibility and involvement in that inauguration process during the ensuing few years. The new phenomenon in the UK's industrial and commercial sectors of widening interest in the reality of 'education for management' had encouraged a number of technical and commercial colleges in the major conurbations to initiate programmes of evening courses, even while the consultative procedures for the Committee's report were in progress (1946–7), when the Ministry of Education had no focus of coordination for policy and programme in implementing the recommendations. The natural focus should have been the newly-created (January 1947) British Institute of Management, but that body's slow progress in establishment during the first couple of years rendered it incapable of taking up a role of that kind. The Ministry's only alternative was to invite the Council of the IIA to undertake the advisory and coordination responsibility for an interim period: acceptance of the invitation put Urwick, as Chairman of their Education Committee, actively into the lead role until the end of the decade.

It was fortunate for the national development of managerial education that the Urwick Orr Company were willing to concede their Chairman the time, opportunity and support facilities for competent fulfilment of that public duty. Urwick allied it with his continuing institutional contributions to managerial advancement through addresses to the membership meetings of several societies, as well as to specific educational conferences where the further implications of the new national policy were being reviewed. For Urwick himself this became the satisfying achievement of a personal objective, in so far as he had been advocating and promoting the serious pursuit of structured managerial studies since his first public address in April 1921. It was a fitting climax that 30 years later he was invited to lead a selective team within the Anglo-American Productivity Council's programme to review and bring back ideas and pointers for further British development from a review of the widely established US policies, programmes and facilities for management education.

6 'Management movement' contributions

The ensuing 15 years provided ample demonstration of Urwick's continuing contributions to the advancement of management thinking, practice and policies through addresses, lectures, articles and within the programmes of managerial societies, including the new national institute. He was recurrently invited to address their meetings and conferences, taking as subject matter the wide span of management principles and practice, oriented to the specific institutional slant involved. He had, of course, his own preferential topics, two of which were 'organization and delegation' and 'leadership'. Both had roots in the presentation of his thinking in his 1933 book, and the former topic came forward again as an early post-war item in the Manchester Lecture and Monograph on *Patterns of Organisation* (1946), as well as in two or three London lectures in the following years.

Leadership of a US seminar in 1951–2 provided an opportunity for consolidating Urwick's thinking and presentation in the form of *Notes for Guidance on the Theory of Organisation*, reproduced as a booklet by the American Management Association. His second personal topic (leadership) was introduced in public contributions both incidental

and specific, focusing on the high values that he had first placed on man management in the armed services, a feature that had underlain his thinking and attitudes since his first experience of it during his 1914–18 war service (see MILITARY MANAGEMENT). An invited lecture series in London in November–December 1955 provided the opportune occasion for consolidation of his approach, and the presentation was preserved for permanent reference by reproduction in book form as *Leadership in the Twentieth Century* (1957a).

It was fortunate for the nation's progress in managerial advancement that the institutional councils as well as the commercial magazine companies readily sought and/or provided reproduction of his addresses; their extent and scope during the 1950–65 period was demonstrated by a printed bibliography of some 20 pages compiled by the Urwick Orr Company in that latter year. Among the items there were, at times, topics specifically written by Urwick for publication in the company's name, for example: *Is Management a Profession?* (1958a), *The Life and Work of Frederick Winslow Taylor* (1957b) and *Sixteen Questions About the Selection and Training of Managers* (1958b). An unusual commercial publication in 1956 arose from the invitation of the CIOS International Committee to Urwick personally to research and compile biographical and professional activity notes on 70 'pioneers' (international in scope, but already deceased) contributing to the progressive evolution of managerial thinking and practice. This was published as *The Golden Book of Management* (1956).

Increasingly from the mid-1950s, Urwick's institutional activities were becoming international in scale. He was regularly invited to address assemblies and conferences by national institutes and management education centres in a number of countries, and on many occasions these were published in translation in the local language. Some consequential curtailment of contributions at home was unavoidable, though there was no detriment to his established reputation or to the esteem with which he was held. His contributions abroad earned acknowledgements and awards, starting in 1951 when the CIOS International Gold Medal was awarded to him. He was the first Briton to be elected to Fellow of the International Academy of Management, founded in 1958, and in the following year was awarded the Gantt Memorial Gold Medal. He was by then enjoying a nationwide reputation and acclaim in the USA comparable with that already attained at home.

E.F.L. BRECH
THE OPEN UNIVERSITY BUSINESS SCHOOL

Further reading

(References cited in the text marked *)

* Brech, E.F.L. (forthcoming) 'The concept and gestation of a central institute of management in Britain 1902–76'. (Includes appended reproduction of the Urwick memorandum of 1930 for the Council of the Management Research Groups proposing a 'British Institute of Management'.)
* Metcalf, H.C. and Urwick, L.F. (eds) (1941) *Dynamic Administration: The Collected Papers of Mary Parker Follett*, London: Management Publications Trust. (A collection of the addresses and papers given in the UK and the USA by Mary Parker Follett during 1921–32.)
* Ministry of Education (1947) *Education for Management:Report of the Departmental Committee*, London: HMSO. (The Committee was chaired by Urwick.)
* Urwick, L.F. (1929) *The Meaning of Rationalisation*, London: Nisbet & Co. (A review of the purposes and accomplishment of industrial and commercial company reorganization as discussed at the World Economic Conference in Geneva, May 1927.)
* Urwick, L.F. (1933) *Management of Tomorrow*, London: Nisbet & Co. (A consolidated exposition of the author's thinking on the principles and practice of management in the contemporary setting. Remarkably progressive.)
Urwick, L.F. (1937) 'Committees in organisation', *British Management Review* 2 (3). (A descriptive and critical review of the role that committees and formalized meetings can play in the conduct and coordination of managerial activity within a company.)
Urwick, L.F. (1938) 'The development of scientific management in Great Britain', *British Management Review* 3 (4).
Urwick, L.F. (1944) *The Elements of Administration*, London: Pitman & Sons. (A structured analytical study of the principles and processes underlying and supporting the exercise of managerial and administrative responsibility.)
* Urwick, L.F. (1946) *Patterns of Organization*. (Published as 'Monograph on Higher Management' by the University of Manchester. An exposition and review of the processes of delegation of managerial and supervisory responsibility within the organization structures of major industrial and commercial concerns.)
Urwick, L.F. (1947) 'Morale', published as 'Monograph on Higher Education', University of Manchester. (An exposition of the factors and features involved in maintaining good levels of morale and cooperation among managerial and supervisory colleagues within a company, as well as between those cadres and the employed personnel.)
* Urwick, L.F. (ed.) (1956) *The Golden Book of Management*, London: Newman Neame Limited. (Compiled for the International Committee on Scientific Management, comprising biographies and reviews of 70 contributors to the advancement of managerial principles and practice in several countries.)
* Urwick, L.F. (1957a) *Leadership in the Twentieth Century*, London: Pitman & Sons. (A compilation and review of contemporary observations on the nature and exercise of the leadership role, supplemented by the author's own thinking in that context.)
* Urwick, L.F. (1957b) 'The Life and Work of Frederick Winslow Taylor', address to the XIIth International Management Congress, London: Urwick Orr & Partners.
* Urwick, L.F. (1958a) *Is Management a Profession?*, London: Urwick Orr & Partners.
* Urwick, L.F. (1958b) *Sixteen Questions about the Selection and Training of Managers*, London: Urwick Orr & Partners. (Together with *The Load on Top Management: Can it be Reduced?* (1954), these monographs discuss topics of contemporary interest in industrial and commercial circles.)
* Urwick, L.F., assisted by E. Aston, F.H. Cordukes, and C.H. Tucker (1928) *Organising a Sales Office*, London: Victor Gollancz. (Portraying the conduct and outcome of a major departmental reorganization within the Rowntree Company's Chocolate and Cocoa works.)
* Urwick, L.F. and Brech, E.F.L. (1946–8) *The Making of Scientific Management*, 3 vols: Management Publications Trust. (The first volume contains summary biographies and reviews of 13 'pioneers' in management thinking, principles and practice; the second records various aspects of pioneering development in management practice, literature and education within Britain's industrial and commercial sectors; the third is a summary presentation of the 'Haw-

thorne investigations' by the Western Electric Company 1925–33.)

See also: EMPLOYEE DEVELOPMENT; EXECUTIVE TRAINING; MANAGEMENT DEVELOPMENT; MANAGEMENT RESEARCH, MANAGEMENT OF; ROWNTREE, J.; TRAINING

US Federal Reserve System

Overview

The Federal Reserve System, known as 'the Fed', is the most powerful financial institution in the United States. The Fed is an independent government entity that serves as the country's central bank. The system is comprised of a Board of Governors, located in Washington, DC, and 12 regional reserve banks. This article is organized as follows: Section 1 discusses the origins and functions of the Federal Reserve System, Section 2 explains the structure of the Federal Reserve, Sections 3 and 4 discuss the various roles of the Federal Reserve and the final section concludes.

1 Origins and functions of the Federal Reserve System

Congress established the Federal Reserve in 1913 as a response to several banking crises that occurred in the nineteenth century and particularly in response to the 'crash' of 1907 (see BANKING CRISES). Prior to the establishment of the Federal Reserve, opposition to central banking was high. Much of the opposition was rooted in a severe distrust of a centralized bank that controlled the financial system. Controversy between southern states and financial centres fuelled the opposition. The establishment of a 'decentralized' central bank was a clever structure that alleviated the concerns of centralizing power in one entity. The establishment of regional federal reserve banks allows different areas of the county to contribute to monetary policy decisions (Mishkin and Eakins 2000).

The original roles of the Fed are the same as they are today. These include:

1 conducting the nation's monetary policy;
2 providing a sound financial system;
3 providing financial services to the US government, consumers and financial institutions;
4 supervising and regulating banking institutions and protecting the rights of consumers (Board of Governors website, 2001).

The Federal Reserve System's main functions are the establishment and maintenance of monetary policies and providing a sound financial system. In very simple terms, monetary policy affects the rate at which the money supply grows. Rapid growth can result in inflation, and not enough growth can result in recession. The Federal Reserve wants to maintain high employment, stable prices and reasonable growth in the money supply such that the economy will grow. Section 3 reviews specifics about this critical role of the Fed. The other functions of the Fed include its role as the bank for the US government. Acting as the bank for the US government, the Federal Reserve receives tax payments as deposits. Recall that the Fed was created, in part, to ensure a smoothly functioning cheque clearing process. Federal Reserve banks collect and clear cheques for depository institutions and provide currency for financial institutions. Finally, acting as a supervisor and regulator, the Fed monitors bank solvency and ensures that banks are complying with bank regulations.

2 Structure of the Federal Reserve

The Federal Reserve is comprised of a seven-member Board of Governors and 12 regional Federal Reserve banks.

Board of Governors and the Federal Open Market Committee

Independent from Congress and the President, the Board of Governors is responsible for setting the nation's monetary policy (see BANKING IN THE UNITED STATES OF AMERICA). The Board of Governors is responsible for setting reserve requirements and approving discount rates. Appointed by the President of the United States and approved by the Senate, members serve staggered 14-year terms. One of the Board members' main responsibilities is their role on the Federal Open Market Committee (FOMC) These seven board members serve with the President of the New York Federal Reserve Bank and four other Presidents of regional banks on the FOMC. The FOMC meets eight times a year to direct open market operations, the Federal Reserve's main monetary policy tool (Federal Reserve System: Purposes and Functions 2001; Madura 2001).

Regional banks

There are 12 regional Federal Reserve banks that are headed by a President who is selected by a nine-member board of directors. The regional banks are the operating units of the Federal Reserve for different geographic areas of the country. The banks are located in the following cities:

- Atlanta, Georgia
- Boston, Massachusetts
- Cleveland, Ohio
- Chicago, Illinois
- Kansas City, Missouri
- New York, New York
- Dallas, Texas
- Minneapolis, Minnesota
- Richmond, Virginia
- Philadelphia, Pennsylvania
- St. Louis, Missouri
- San Francisco, California

These banks propose discount rates and assist in the supervision of bank holding companies and state chartered banks in their District that are members of the Federal Reserve System. They also assist in cheque clearing and the processing of electronic fund transfers (Federal Reserve System: Purposes and Functions 2001).

3 Monetary policy: tools and implementation

According to the Federal Reserve, its responsibility is to

> promote effectively the goals of maximum employment, stable prices and moderate long-term interest rates.
> (The Federal Reserve System: Purposes and Functions 2001: ch. 2, p. 1)

One of the ways the Federal Reserve meets this responsibility is through the implementation of monetary policy. Monetary policy affects the volume of money and interest rates. In turn, the volume of money and the level of interest rates affect employment, output and the general level of prices.

Before we turn to a discussion of the monetary tools and implementation, a few definitions are in order. The term 'money supply' is defined in several ways. The most narrow definition of the nation's money supply is M1. M1 includes all cash, chequeable deposits and traveller's cheques. M2, a broader definition, includes M1 plus savings and small time deposits, such as certificates of deposits under $100,000. M3 includes M2 plus large time deposits.

Now that we have defined the term 'money supply', we examine the Federal Reserve's balance sheet. An examination of the Fed's balance sheet is critical to the understanding of how the Fed can affect the money supply. Since the Federal Reserve is a bank, its balance sheet resembles those of other banks. Assets primarily consist of government securities and loans to member banks, while liabilities include currency in circulation and reserve deposits of financial institutions. Changes to these two liabilities, often called the monetary base, affect the nation's money supply. The Federal Reserve can affect the monetary base, and therefore, the nation's money supply through its monetary tools.

The Federal Reserve has three 'tools' with which it can affect the supply of money and therefore, conduct its monetary policy. They include establishing the reserve requirement, conducting open market operations, and setting the discount rate.

Establishing the reserve requirement

The Federal Reserve establishes the reserve requirement, the percentage of deposits that financial institutions must hold either as reserves at the Federal Reserve or as cash in the vault. Changes in reserve requirements are rare, and as such would be a major change in policy. In general, increases in reserve requirements are indicative of a restrictive monetary policy, and decreases in the requirements indicate an expansionary monetary policy. Suppose the reserve requirement is 10 per cent and one bank, Bank A, comprises the entire banking system. For every dollar that Bank A receives in deposits (liability), it must hold 10 cents on reserve (asset). The remaining 90 cents can be invested. In reality, deploying those assets is a complex process, but for simplicity's sake, assume that Bank A can invest all non-reserve assets in income generating loans. Examine the following balance sheet for Bank A under the assumption that $1000 of deposits are received and the reserve requirement is 10 per cent.

Bank A: Balance sheet –10 per cent reserve requirement

Assets		Liabilities	
Reserves	$ 100	Deposits	$1,000
Loans	900		
Total	$ 1,000	Total	$1,000

Now consider if the reserve requirement increases to 15 per cent. Clearly, lending is restricted. Bank A's balance sheet would appear as follows:

Bank A: Balance sheet –15 per cent reserve requirement

Assets		Liabilities	
Reserves	$ 150	Deposits	$1,000
Loans	850		
Total	$ 1,000	Total	$1,000

If however, the reserve requirement is only 5 per cent, lending is increased, and the economy has expanded.

Bank A: Balance sheet –5 per cent reserve requirement

Assets		Liabilities	
Reserves	$ 50	Deposits	$1,000
Loans	950		
Total	$ 1,000	Total	$1,000

Conducting open market operations

Open market operations is the most powerful and important tool the Fed has. Open market operations refers to the practice whereby the Federal Reserve buys and sells government securities. The rationale behind such purchases and sales is to control the amount of reserves in the banking system and the level of reserves ultimately affects the Federal Funds rate. The Federal Reserve can actually either target a certain quantity of reserves, thus allowing changes in reserves to affect the federal funds rate. Or, it can target the federal funds rate by adjusting the level of reserves. Over the years, the Federal Reserve has used combinations of these approaches. From the 1990s onward, the Fed has primarily targeted the federal funds rate (Mishkin and Eakins 2000).

Open market operations refers to the sale and purchase of government securities. When the Fed purchases government securities, the level of reserves increases. The Fed pays for those government securities by writing a cheque on itself. When the Fed sells government securities, the level of reserves fall. Acting on behalf of the Fed, the Trading Desk of the Federal Reserve Bank of New York (one of the 12 regional banks) conducts open market operations. The Trading Desk buys and sells government securities with designated 'primary dealers' (banks and securities broker-dealers). These dealers act as the counterparty to the purchase (sale) by the Fed of government securities. When the Fed buys government securities from a dealer, it 'pays' for those securities by crediting the reserve account of that dealer's clearing bank. Such actions increase reserves in the banking system. When the Fed sells government securities, the bank account of the dealer is debited, which drains reserves from the banking system (Federal Reserve System: Purposes and Functions 2001). The following examples exhibit how the purchase (sale) by the Federal Reserve creates (depletes) reserves. The Federal Reserve, one commercial bank, Bank A, and one primary dealer, Investment Bank Z comprise a simple economy. In the first example, the Fed purchases US Treasury bonds from Bank Z, the primary dealer, while in the second example, the Fed sells US Treasury bonds. Simple T-accounts will demonstrate changes in balance sheets for each entity in the economy. For simplicity, assume the bond transaction is $1 million.

Example 1: Purchase of US Treasury bonds

1 The Fed buys $1 million of bonds from Investment Bank Z.
2 The Fed pays for those securities by 'writing' a cheque on itself and crediting Z's clearing bank, Bank A.
3 The credit to Z's bank account simultaneously increases reserves at Bank A which are a liability of the Fed.

Example 2: Sale of US Treasury bonds by the Fed

1 The Fed sells $1 million of bonds to Investment Bank Z.
2 Z pays for those securities which results in a debit to its deposit account at Bank A.
3 The debit to Z's bank account simultaneously decreases reserves at Bank A which are a liability of the Fed.

Example 1

Federal Reserve

Assets	Liabilities
(1) + $1 million of US Treasury bonds	(3) + $1 million reserves

Investment Bank Z

Assets	Liabilities
(1) – $1 million of US Treasury bonds	
(2) + $1 million in deposits at Bank A	

Bank A

Assets	Liabilities
(3) + $1 million of reserves	(2) + $1 million Z's account

Example 2

Federal Reserve

Assets	Liabilities
(1) – $1 million of US Treasury bonds	(3) – $1 million reserves

Investment Bank Z

Assets	Liabilities
(1) + $1 million of US Treasury bonds	
(2) – $1 million in deposits at Bank A	

Bank A

Assets	Liabilities
(3) – $1 million of reserves	(2) – $1 million Z's account

These examples demonstrate how powerful open market operations are. In an instant, banking reserves can increase or decrease. When bank reserves increase (decrease), the federal funds rate, the rate at which banks lend reserves to other banks, decreases (increases). This can be explained in a simple supply and demand framework. As the supply of funds increases (reserves increase), the cost of those funds (fed funds rate) decreases. Conversely, as the supply of funds decrease (reserves decrease), the cost of those funds increases.

The Federal Reserve carefully monitors the fed funds rate. Approximately every six to eight weeks, the Federal Open Market Committee meets and sets monetary policy directives. These directives include a target for the federal funds rate. In fact, when the public press announces that the Fed 'changed the fed funds rate', the announcement is actually referring to a change in the *target* for the fed funds rate as the Fed cannot directly change the fed funds rate. The previous example about the effect of open market operations on the federal funds rate is a wonderful segue into how the Federal Reserve actually meets its target for the federal funds rate. Suppose the Federal Reserve announced an increase in the fed funds target from 5 per cent to 5.25 per cent. In order to accomplish an increase, the Fed would want to restrict reserves and would therefore sell government securities through open market operations. If the target were lowered, the Fed would buy government securities which would result in an increase in reserves.

Permanent and temporary changes in reserves
Most often, open market operations are conducted to temporarily change the level of reserves. The Trading Desk at the New York Federal Reserve therefore engages in what is called 'a repurchase agreement', or a 'Repo'. A buyer of a repo agrees to purchase a security and simultaneously the seller agrees to repurchase them within a specified period of time. A repo would initially increase the level of reserves. When a repo matures, the reserves that were initially added when the securities were purchased are then depleted. If the Fed desires to temporarily decrease the level of reserves, it would engage in a 'reverse repurchase agreement' or 'reverse'. Occasionally, the Trading Desk conducts outright purchases or sales of securities. This occurs if the Fed desires to permanently alter the level of reserves (Federal Reserve System: Purposes and Functions 2001).

Announcement effect of changes in the target of federal funds
When the Federal Open Market Committee announces its directive on federal funds, the financial press and financial markets usually react. Indeed, when the FOMC announces that the federal funds rate target has been lowered, equity markets usually respond favourably. The reasoning behind such a reaction can be explained both logically and mathematically. First, when the FOMC announces a lower federal funds rate, *ceteris paribus*, financial market participants interpret such news as lower interest rates in general. Theoretically, the expectation by market participants is that long-term interest rates will be lower. If the rate that banks charge each other on reserves is lower, market participants will expect that this lower short-term rate will result in lower long-term rates. Lower long-term interest rates allow companies to borrow more easily and more cheaply. All else being equal, this is 'good news' for companies and therefore, stock (equity) prices will rise. Mathematically, the rise in equity prices as a result of lower expected interest rates is also apparent. In a simple valuation model, a security's price is obtained as:

$$P_0 = CF_1/(1+k)^1 + CF_2/(1+k)^2$$
$$+ \dots CF_\alpha/(1+k)^\alpha$$

Where P_0 is a security's current price, CF_1 is the cash flow provided in period 1, CF_2 is the cash flow provided in period 2, etc., and k is a marginal investor's required return. Clearly, to the extent that a firm's cash flows are affected by interest rates, $CF_1 - CF_\alpha$ will increase as interest rates fall. Additionally, if the federal fund rate falls, other rates will fall, and thus, any investor's required return, k will be lower. P_0 will therefore be higher as a result.

Setting the discount rate

When the Federal Reserve lends money to its member banks, the rate that it charges is called the discount rate. A bank borrows from the Fed in order to meet its reserve requirement. The Fed offers three types of credit at its discount window. These include adjustment credit, for short-term liquidity needs, seasonal credit, for banks in agricultural areas that have seasonal patterns, and extended credit, which is given to banks experiencing severe liquidity problems (Federal Reserve System: Purposes and Functions 2001). The role of the discount window has changed considerable since the inception of the Federal Reserve. In its early days, lending at the discount window was the primary monetary policy tool. If the demand for reserves is very high (or the supply is extremely low), a bank can borrow reserves at the discount window. Typically, banks will try to secure reserves by borrowing them from other banks (at the federal funds rate). As stated before, when the Federal Reserve was created, one of its roles was to serve as the 'lender of last resort' in order to prevent financial panics. The role of the Fed as a 'lender of last resort' has potential moral hazard problems. Theoretically, a bank could take on great risk if it 'believes' that it can always borrow at the discount window when it is in financial trouble. The Fed, therefore, must be careful in its role as lender of last resort.

Adjusting the discount rate upward or downward has monetary policy implications. If the Fed lowers the discount rate, more discounts loans will be made, thus increasing reserves. If the Fed increases the discount rate, reserves are lowered. While it is clear that increases (decreases) in the discount rate will lower (raise) the level of reserves, it is hard to predict how much reserves will change. As such, the Fed has mostly relied on open market operations as their effect on reserves is much clearer.

In general, the actions of the Fed can be categorized as 'expansionary' or 'restrictive'. Expansionary actions include decreases in the reserve requirement, decreases in the federal funds target (purchases in open market operations), and decreases in the discount rate. All of these actions, in the short term, increase bank reserves and therefore increase the supply of money. Restrictive policies include increases in the reserve requirement, increases in the federal funds target (sales in open market operations), and increases in the discount rate. These actions reduce reserves in the short run.

Implementation issues

The Federal Reserve has a daunting task. As noted before, the Federal Reserve is charged with the maintaining of maximum employment, stable prices and moderate long-term interest rates. What is difficult about the accomplishment of these goals is the fact that many of them conflict with one another. While one of the goals of the Federal Reserve is to moderate long-term interest rates, its monetary tools mostly affect short-term rates. Excessive use of short-term 'tools' can undermine long-term goals. Suppose that the Federal Reserve continually lowered the target on the federal funds rate, thus increasing reserves. As we have already seen, this increases the money supply. In the short run, holding all other factors constant, such actions would lead to lower interest rates. However, if the money supply continued to increase, inflation would result which would ultimately be reflected in higher interest rates. In fact, the Fed has wavered between setting money supply targets and short-term interest rate targets. Depending on the decade, the Fed has favoured one or the other because it realized that to target both is an impossible goal (Federal Reserve System: Purposes and Functions 2001; Mishkin and Eakins 2000).

As a result, the Federal Reserve establishes short-term and intermediate targets in order to meet its long-term goals. As mentioned before, an example of a target is the establishment of a federal funds target. Through the use of targets, the Fed can ascertain if its directives are effective in attaining the long-term goals and simply change the targets if necessary.

4　Other roles of the Federal Reserve System

Services provided by the Federal Reserve System

Another role of the Federal Reserve System includes the services it provides to banks and the US government. One major service the

Fed provides to banks is cheque clearing. Since most banks hold reserves at one of the 12 regional Federal Reserve banks, the cheque clearing process functions smoothly. Very simply, when a cheque is written on Bank X, for example, the Federal Reserve deducts the amount of the cheque from Bank X's reserve account at the Fed. If the cheque is deposited into Bank Y, the Federal Reserve credits Y's reserve account. The transfer of funds between institutions is as simple as making changes to their reserve accounts at the Federal Reserve.

In addition to performing services for banks, the Federal Reserve acts as an agent for the US government. In this role, the Federal Reserve serves as the depository for the US Treasury. As such, cheques drawn on the Treasury department are cleared through the Federal Reserve. Tax and loan accounts serve as a receptacle for taxes paid by individuals and businesses. In addition to these services, the Fed manages the auction process of Treasury securities.

Supervision and regulation

Finally, the Federal Reserve also supervises and regulates the banking systems. The Fed's supervisory functions were initially established in order to prevent bank failures. Bank supervision is a complicated topic, and many agencies provide supervision of financial institutions. The Federal Reserve shares supervisory and regulatory roles with the Office of the Comptroller of the Currency (OCC), the Federal Deposit Insurance Corporation (FDIC), and the Office of Thrift Supervision. The Fed supervises and regulates all bank holding companies and state-chartered banks that are members of the Federal Reserve System. In its supervisory role, the Fed monitors and inspects banks to ensure they are complying with banking laws and regulations. For example, the Fed conducts on-site examinations of banks to determine if the bank is solvent. Examinations may include analysing a bank's capital adequacy, sensitivity to interest rate risk, and other financial factors. If a bank is found out of compliance with regulations and/or is deemed to be unsound, the Fed will take corrective action to rectify such deficiencies (Federal Reserve System: Purposes and Functions 2001).

The Fed also serves as a bank regulator. Since 1913, the powers of the Fed to establish regulations about a variety of banking activities have expanded. These regulations' names are simply letters of the alphabet. For example, Regulation Q set maximum interest rates that banks could pay on savings deposits. In 1986, Regulation Q was abolished. Regulation Z, known as 'The Truth in Lending Act' prescribes methods for computing interest charges as well as requiring that banks fully disclose credit terms. These are just some of the banking regulations that the Fed controls.

5 Conclusion

Established in 1913, The Federal Reserve is the central bank of the United States. Its main functions (roles) are to establish and implement monetary policy, provide a sound financial system, provide services to banks and the government and regulate and supervise the banking system. The implementation of monetary policy and the provision of a sound financial system are the most important roles of the Fed. As discussed, meeting such goals is complex and difficult. Through a variety of policy tools, the Federal Reserve is able to establish and maintain a sound financial system.

JACQUELINE G. FAUGHT
COLLEGE OF BUSINESS ADMINISTRATION
UNIVERSITY OF RHODE ISLAND

Further reading

(References cited in the text marked *)

* The Federal Reserve Board of Governors website, *http://www.federalreserve.gov/*. (Accessed 30 January 2001.)

The Federal Reserve Bank of Atlanta website, *http://www.frbatlanta.org/* (Accessed 30 January 2001.)

The Federal Reserve Bank of New York website, *http://www.ny.frb.org/* (Accessed 30 January 2001.)

The Federal Reserve Bank of San Francisco website, *http://www.frbsf.org/* (Accessed 30 January 2001.)

* The Federal Reserve System: Purposes and Functions (2001) *http://www.federalreserve.gov/pf/pf.htm*. (A publication of The Board of Governors of The Federal Reserve System, accessed 30 January 2001.)

Kidwell, D.S., Peterson, R.L. and Blackwell, D.W. (2000) *Financial Institutions, Markets, and Money*, Fort Worth: Dryden Press/Harcourt College Publishers. (A textbook on financial markets and institutions.)

* Madura, J. (2001) *Financial Markets and Institutions*, Cincinnati: South-Western College Publishing. (A textbook on financial markets and institutions.)

* Mishkin, F.S. and Eakins, S.G. (2000) *Financial Markets and Institutions*, Reading: Addison-Wesley. (A textbook on financial markets and institutions.)

Saunders, A. and Cornett, M.M. (2001) *Financial Markets and Institutions*, New York: McGraw-Hill/Irwin. (A textbook on financial markets and institutions.)

Scott, W.L. (1999) *Markets and Institutions*, Cincinnati: South-Western College Publishing. (A textbook on financial markets and institutions.)

See also: BANK OF ENGLAND IN CENTRAL BANKING THEORY; BANK OF JAPAN; BANKING; BANKING CRISES; BANKING IN THE UNITED STATES OF AMERICA; BANKING IN WESTERN EUROPE; BANKING, ISLAMIC; BANKING REGULATION; BANKING SYSTEMS; INTERNATIONAL BANKING

Value-added systems

Overview

In a market setting, a business undertakes many operations to provide products (goods or services) to its customers. Each of these operations receives an input (raw material, labour, throughput) and transforms it into an output. An operation is effective if it creates an output having more value than its input. The *value added* by each operation justifies its *raison d'être* in the business. An operation is efficient when its output is created at low cost. Traditionally, in the analysis of a business strategy, one takes the view that the advantage of a firm results from many operations that it performs in designing, producing, marketing, delivering and supporting its product. These operations take place in an interrelated environment including suppliers, competitors, distributors and consumers. Each operation of the system should add a value in the process of transforming its input to an output. Consequently, one should maximize the performance and minimize the cost of each of these operations so that the value of the good or service will exceed the cost of input. At the end, the agent (i.e. supplier, firm or distributor) will earn a margin when customers accept and pay for that value.

However, in the past two decades, it has been found that the optimization of individual operations in the production system does not necessarily create an overall advantage for the firm in the market. An efficient part of a production system does not necessary contribute effectively to the value of the final product and create a competitive advantage for the company. The reason is that the value added through individual operations is not always fully accepted and paid for by consumers. In fact, the operation-centring view is ineffective to meet consumer needs in a fast-paced changing market. Therefore the contemporary view is to look at the firm and its operations as a whole from a process-centring perspective. From this viewpoint, one needs to identify and implement an effective process for the company, which is a complete set of effective operations and efficient activities creating value for a customer.

1 Introduction

To be able to survive and enjoy sustained growth, a business entity should focus on its competitive advantage to satisfy customers' demand (see MARKETING). The strategy taken should result in relative cost position and/or product differentiation for the business. Cost position advantage results from low-cost material supply, effective production and efficient distribution. Product differentiation results from distinct aspects of the output, such as high-quality material, superior product design, and effective response to consumer needs. To analyse the competitive advantage, Porter (1985) proposed a framework in which the operations of a business are disaggregated into strategically relevant activities in a *value chain*. By studying the value chain of a business, one can understand cost behaviours, and the existing or potential sources of differentiation. Then the business may gain competitive advantage by performing these strategic activities at lower cost and/ or better than its competitors do.

In Porter's framework, the value chain of a business is a part of a larger stream of operations, called a *value system*, performed by its business partners and competitors. In this value system, suppliers have value chains that create and deliver the input to be used in a business. Then the products (goods or services) of the business pass through the value chains of distributors to the buyer. Distributors perform additional services relating to the product. At last, the final product becomes part of the buyer's value chain determining the buyer's needs. In each part of the value system, the agents create and add extra value as the product flows through the system to the final consumers.

Consequently, gaining and sustaining competitive advantage depends on understanding not only the value chain of a business but also how it takes part in the overall value system (see PORTER, M.E.). Then one considers appropriate strategies to add value to the value chain such that the final products will create a profit margin for the business and meet consumers' needs.

In production management, the traditional *operation-centring* view is to maximize individual activity/operation-related performance, sometimes at the expense of whole system. However, we find that consumers have not always accepted and paid for the product and service created by the firm. In addition, businesses have not been able to meet customers' demand in a timely manner. We have realized that an integrated approach to conducting business could avoid this problem. This view takes a *process-centring* approach proposed by Hammer (1996), in which we start from an overall perspective to define what a business can perform best to satisfy a consumer need. Then we design appropriate processes, namely a complete set of coordinated operations to create value to be accepted and paid for by customers.

2 Operation-centring value systems

The value chain model is an attempt to identify where actions should be taken to improve the company's performance. Competitive opportunity exists at every cell of a matrix defined by support and primary activities. Corporate strategists can use this matrix of value activities to determine in which cells current systems are located, and therefore in which cells gaps exist, or by successively considering the potential opportunity for each cell.

In addition, a firm's value chain is a part of a value system that is composed of the company's value chain and those of its suppliers,

its distributors and its customers. By focusing on the linkages in the value system, a company can add value not only to itself but also to those in the value system.

Value chain

The ultimate goal of any business is to provide value to its customers and earn a profit margin from its products (goods or services). A business will be profitable if the value that it creates or adds is greater than the cost to produce its product. In Porter's framework, each business has nine distinct value activities that are linked in a value chain. There are five *primary activities* to create, market and deliver a product to buyers, and then service and support it:

- *Inbound logistics* consists of receiving, storing and distributing materials that are inputs to the product. These activities comprise material handling, warehousing, inventory control, vehicle scheduling, and returns to suppliers.
- *Operations activities* transform inputs into outputs (goods or services), such as machining, packaging, assembly, equipment maintenance, testing, and facility operations.
- *Outbound logistics* facilitates the distribution of a finished product to buyers, such as finished goods warehousing, material handling, delivery operation, order processing, and scheduling.
- *Marketing and sales activities* facilitate the sale of products or services, such as advertising, promotion, sales force, distributing channel selection, channel relations, and pricing.
- *Service activities* provide repair and maintenance functions to enhance or maintain the value of the product, such as installation, repair, training, part supply, and production adjustment.

Each of these operations adds an extra value as a product or service is created. Depending on the industry in which the business operates, some operations may be vital to its competitive advantage. For instance, inbound and outbound logistics are the most critical operations to a distributor. But production is the most important operation for a manufacturer. However, all these operations exist to some degree in any business and play some role in its competitive advantage.

These primary activities are made possible by the four *support activities*. Each category of support activities could be divided into a number of distinct value activities that are specific to a given industry.

- *Firm infrastructure* includes organizational activities and functions that support the value chain. The infrastructure of a business consists of general management, planning, finance, accounting, legal, government affairs, and quality management. Unlike other support activities, infrastructure supports the entire value chain instead of individual activities.
- *Human resources management* relates to recruiting, hiring, training, and providing employee compensation and benefits. Human resource management affects competitive advantage of the business through the cost of hiring, training, and its role in the assignment of skills to tasks and the motivation of employees.
- *Technology development* activities improve a product or service with related know-how, procedures, and technology embodied in equipment specific to the operations of the business. Technology development takes form in basic research, product design, media research, process equipment design, and servicing procedures. Some technology development is related to the product and supports the entire chain, while others are associated with particular primary and support activities.
- *Procurement* refers to the function of purchasing inputs to be used in the value chain of a business, such as necessary materials, supplies, machinery, and building for the primary activities. The dispersion of procurement functions throughout a business may obscure the magnitude of total purchases, such that many purchases receive less scrutiny than others do. In many cases, the cost of procurement activities may have a large impact on the overall cost and differentiation of a business.

Depending on their goals and objectives, the value chains of businesses operating in an industry differ. The value chain of a specific business may differ in competitive scope from that of its competitors, representing a potential source of competitive advantage. How each operation/activity is performed, combined with its economics, will determine whether a firm is high or low cost relative to competitors. The performance of each value operation/activity will also determine its contribution to the product differentiation and the satisfaction of the buyer's needs.

Although businesses in the same industry may have similar chains, differences among the value chains of competitors are the main source of competitive advantage. The value chain of a specific business may vary for different items in its product line, different buyers, geographic areas or distribution channels.

In competitive terms, value is defined as the amount that buyers are willing to pay for the goods or services that a business provides. For a business, value is measured by total revenue derived from the price and the units of product sold. A business is profitable if the value, which it commands, exceeds the costs involved in creating the goods or services. In the value chain, value activities are the physically and technologically distinct operations that a business performs to create a product valuable to its buyers. Margin is the difference between total value and the collective cost of performing these operations.

Although value activities are the building blocks of competitive advantage, the value chain is a system of interdependent, linked operations. Linkages are relationships between how one value activity is performed and the cost or performance of another. Competitive advantage may derive from linkages among operations as well as from the individual operations themselves. Linkages can lead to competitive advantage through *optimization* and *coordination*. Linkages often reflect tradeoffs among operations to achieve the same overall performance, so that the business must optimize the linkages between activities to achieve competitive advantage. Linkage may also raise issues on the coordination of operations so that the business can reduce cost and/or enhance differentiation. The cost advantage or product differentiation of a business is not solely the result of reducing cost or improving performance in each value operation individually, but it should be considered in the value chain and value system as a whole (see COSTING).

Linkages can take many forms. Obviously, there are linkages between support and primary activities. The more subtle ones are those between primary activities themselves. The most difficult to recognize are those linkages involving activities in different categories or different types.

Linkages among value activities and operations arise from the following causes: (1) the same business function can be performed in many alternative ways by linking different activities; (2) the cost or performance of direct activities could be improved by further effort in indirect activities; (3) activities performed inside the company may reduce the cost to service a product in the field; (4) quality assurance inside the company can be performed in many alternative ways. Exploiting linkages usually requires information on the cross-functional activities of the business that allows optimization or coordination to take place.

Competitive scope can create advantage to the business as it has influence on the configuration and economic of the value chain. There are four dimensions that affect the competitive scope of a value chain:

- *Segment scope* is to serve different products or buyers' needs segments. Depending on how many market segments or products the business intends to serve or produce, the interrelationship of activities in its value chain will define a narrow or large scope.
- *Vertical integration* aims at the division of activities between a business and its suppliers, distribution channels and buyers. A business can purchase semi-products from suppliers instead of fabricating them. Similarly, it may let its distribution channels perform the delivery, marketing and service functions. Or it can let consumers perform some activities on the final goods, such as with 'do-it-yourself' products.
- *Geographic scope* may allow a business to reduce cost and/or enhance differentiation by sharing and/or coordinating operations to serve different geographic areas. The coordination may lead to division of operations such that a branch in one geographic area does not have its own complete value chain but just carries some value activities of the corporate chain.
- *Industry scope* involves interrelationships among the value chains of business units in related industries. The interrelationships may exist in any primary (e.g. shared sales forces) as well as support (e.g. joint research and development) activities.

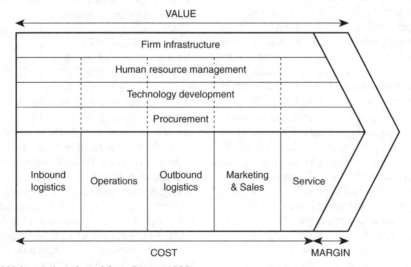

Figure 1 Value chain (adapted from Porter, 1985)

Value systems

A business can exploit the benefits of broader scope internally or it may form coalitions with other firms in the form of joint ventures, licences, and supply agreements. Coalition involves coordinating or sharing value chains with partners to broaden the effective scope of the company's chain. Competing in related industries with coordinated value chains can lead to competitive advantage through interrelationships in value systems.

Linkages also exist between the value chain of a business and those of suppliers and distribution channels. *Suppliers* provide input in the form of raw materials, semi-products and/or services that a business uses in its value chain. Suppliers' value chains also influence the business at other contact points (generally referred to as an extended value chain). For instance, suppliers can reduce the inventory, inspection and handling cost of a business. As such, these linkages can significantly affect the cost and differentiation of a business. It is possible to benefit both the business and its suppliers by influencing the configuration of suppliers' value chains to jointly optimize the performance of operations, or by improving coordination between the value chains of the business and its suppliers.

Distribution channels have value chains through which the product of a business flows to final buyers. Channels perform activities such as sales, advertising and display that may substitute for or complement some of the company's activities. There are multiple contact points between a company's value chain and channels' value chains in operations related to sales force, order entry, and outbound logistics. The channel mark-up over a firm's selling price may represent a large proportion of the price to final buyers. Therefore, coordination and joint optimization with channels can lower cost or enhance differentiation.

Buyers also have value chains, in which a firm's product represents a purchased input. Buyers could be industrial, commercial, institutional or individual. Individual buyers in households purchase many products for a wide range of activities. The value created in a buyer's chain is the buyer's perception of the utility of the purchased product or service. It is difficult to construct a value chain that encompasses everything a household and its members do. But one can always construct a representative chain for households for analysis purposes.

A company's differentiation stems from how its value chain relates to its buyer's chain. It is a function of how a company's product is consumed in a particular buyer activity and all other contact points between a company's value chain and the buyer's chain. Value is created when a business creates competitive advantage for its buyers, either by reducing the buyers' cost or increasing buyers' performance and/or satisfying their needs.

3 Process-centring value systems

The traditional view decomposes business processes into specialized tasks and operations and then focuses on improving the performance of these. Most current business entities are task-centred enterprises. However, in the changing environment of contemporary business, the competitive advantage is to design effective processes to respond quickly to what the market actually demands. The persistent problem that companies are

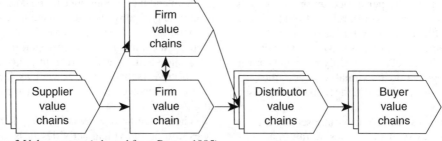

Figure 2 Value system (adapted from Porter, 1985)

faced with in gaining and maintaining their competitive advantage could not be addressed by means of task improvement. In our global economy, processes are inhibitors and determinants of business success, and only process-centred companies will be able to deal with them.

The current difficulties that are afflicting most current organizations are not task-related problems but process-related problems. The reason that one cannot deliver results in a timely manner to meet consumer demand is not that individual activities are performed slowly and/or inefficiently. It is because some existing ineffective activities, regardless of how efficiently they are performed, are unnecessary to achieve the desired result.

In addition, a business is inflexible in response to consumer needs not because it is locked into a fixed way of operating but because it lacks understanding of how individual activities combine to create a final result. High costs may result not from individual activities that are expensive but from the costly coordination of these individual activities so that the final product can be delivered to customers. Therefore, the problem lies not in the performance of individual tasks and activities – the units of work – but in the processes – how the units fit together as a whole. Process-centring means that everybody in the business should recognize and focus on their processes to see if all the activities together could produce the results for the customer that they are supposed to do.

In process-centring value systems, a *process* is a complete set of activities that together create value for a customer. The difference between activities (tasks, operations) and process is the difference between parts and a whole. A task is a unit of work, a business activity normally performed by one person. In contrast, a process is a related group of tasks that ultimately create a result of final value to a customer. None of these tasks by itself creates value for the customer. Only when they are all put together do individual work activities create value in the form of the final goods and services.

Business entities are composed of *business processes* such as purchasing raw materials, manufacturing products, taking orders, and distributing products to buyers (see BUSINESS PROCESS REENGINEERING). Each of these processes will create value and add it to the products as they go through the value chain and value system. A process is comprised of many work activities. However, not all activities in a process are beneficial to the firm. One can differentiate the value-creating activities in three broad categories:

- A *customer-value-added activity* is a task that a customer is willing to pay for, such as turning raw materials into goods.
- A *business-value-added activity* is a task that is essential to managing a business organization.
- A *non-value-added activity* is a task that customers will not pay for and that does not result in an increased value to the business.

To be profitable, a business has to design/redesign its processes in order to:

- Maximize customer-value-added operations so that its products will gain the acceptance of consumers in terms of providing utilities and satisfying their needs.
- Minimize the cost by maximizing the efficiency of business-value-added operations.
- Eliminate non-value-added activities by maximizing the effectiveness of business operations.

Companies moving to process-centring management do not have to create or invent their processes. The processes have always existed to produce the company's output, but in a fragmented, invisible, unnamed and unmanaged form. A process-centring strategy is to recognize and identify these processes, and ensure that everyone in the company is aware of them and their importance to the company. Then the company should manage processes in a permanent manner, strive for ongoing improvement and measure how well the processes are being performed from a customer perspective (satisfaction) as well as from a company perspective (financial cost and asset utilization).

The key point of *process thinking* is that it sees not the individual activities in isolation but the entire collection of activities that contribute to a desired outcome. In process-centring management, everyone should not be concerned exclusively with his or her own limited responsibility and how well it is met. This is liable to result in working at cross-purposes, misunderstandings and optimization of the part at the expense of the whole. A process perspective requires that everyone involved be directed toward a common goal so that no conflicting objectives will impair the common effort. To *re-engineer* current processes, unnecessary operations are eliminated, tasks are combined and reorganized, and information is shared among people involved in a process so that improvements in speed, accuracy, flexibility, quality, service and cost are realized.

Traditionally, when formulating strategy one first concentrates on identifying potentially attractive markets and business and then looks at whether it is feasible to enter them. In contrast, with a process-centred approach one starts by considering the possibilities of what a company might be able to do well, and then looking to see which are worthy of implementation. From a process perspective, an organization considers the following strategies (Hammer 1996):

- *Intensification*: improving processes to serve current customers better. The goal is to re-engineer the current processes, eliminating ineffective operations.
- *Extension*: using efficient existing processes to enter new markets to gain competitive advantage.
- *Augmentation*: expanding processes to provide additional services to current customers.
- *Conversion*: taking a process that the company performs well and performing it as a service to other companies.
- *Innovation*: applying existing processes that one performs well to create and deliver different goods or services.
- *Diversification*: creating new processes to deliver new goods or services.

4 Value-added systems and competitive advantage

The value-added concept suggests that one must examine each component of a process in terms of the value that component adds to the final product. If an activity, an operation or a linkage adds no value, eliminating it may improve overall productivity. Value is added through the processes by which raw materials are changed into semi-finished and then finished parts, and through assembly into a marketable product that is packed and shipped to a customer or distribution centre. What may not be recognized is that many activities/operations may add considerable cost to a product but no value at all. For instance, manually counting and handling inventory, or sorting out defects, rather than having a defect-free procedure, are typical ineffective operations that add cost but not value. The way to achieve excellence is to involve everyone in the value chain (employees of the firm) and value system (business partners) in detecting and eliminating operations that do not add value.

Consequently, the selection of appropriate business process can be based on a value-added analysis. This analysis focuses on how the works are combined in processes that clearly add to the worth of the product in terms of meeting the customer's expectations and needs. The customer will reluctantly pay more than the perceived value of the goods or service, regardless of how much it cost to produce. This is called the *non-cost principle* as it emphasizes that value instead of cost will determine the margin earned from a good or service. From this perspective, quality, reliability, appearance, service and specific features make up the customer's perception of value. For value to be added, some transformation activities, some material conversion in production, must take place effectively and efficiently in business processes. Value-added processes or activities must be emphasized in any analysis of performance and opportunities for improvement to achieve a competitive edge.

In manufacturing (supply chain) management, a decision made in one stage of operation, i.e. value activity, will influence operational performance in other stages (see SUPPLY CHAIN MANAGEMENT). Linking together the supply chain stages in an effective process will be an important success for firms engaging in the supply, manufacture and distribution of products globally.

One way to describe the desired result of value-added manufacturing is the maximization of the contributions of everyone involved in the system as a whole, as contrasted to the minimization of the direct labour content of the product. The effort includes each of the following:

- Eliminate activities and related costs that add no value.
- Reduce lead times in transportation, internal flows, supplier response, communications, and customer need schedules.
- Identify way to bring products to the market more quickly and with less debugging.
- Improve product manufacturability by working with manufacturing engineering and the tool and die shop.
- Achieve fitness for use and strive for quality throughout the system.

When work activities add considerable cost to a product but add no value at all, they are considered as waste. American Production and Inventory Control Society (APICS) addresses four major categories of waste:

- Inventory takes up space and ties up capital.
- Poor quality consumes material, time, capacity and energy without any usable output.
- Lead time makes the schedule rigid and requires an investment in replanning capability to make the inevitable adjustments.
- Material movement reflects the distance a part travels in being processed and then assembled, the space and equipment and people involved in carrying out the movement, and the energy absorbed.

A value-added system can become a driver for motivating creative, inspired employees to put organizations on a sustained learning and improvement curve. It offers a focus for the overall productivity effort. As such, one may avoid over-specification as well as escape the 'departmental' syndrome. In process-centring management, everyone in the business value chain and value system is involved in re-engineering to define effective business processes. From a process perspective, everybody participates in the detection and elimination of ineffective operations that do not add value to the final product that the business intends to provide.

Since a value-added system is composed of numerous technical operations and processes, technological changes will definitely influence the performance of the system. In gaining competitive advantage, information technology (IT), as an *enabler* of business process re-engineering, is an important support that can be used to perform operations effectively and efficiently. Modern managers should use the value-added systems concept to determine where and how IT can add value to the firm. They should identify activities in the business processes, determine the cost and value of each activity, and analyse how and where IT can add value (see INFORMATION TECHNOLOGY AND MARKETING). The advances in hardware and software technology have increased manufacturing flexibility, transportation speed and information availability, along with increased management complexity. In general, IT can provide value-added and competitive advantage in the following ways:

- IT improves or innovates the use of knowledge in the operations of the value chain and value system.
- IT improves products or services by increasing quality, reducing costs, or adding desirable features.
- IT provides timely and reliable information to enhance the decision-making process.
- IT improves communication between internal as well as external business entities to increase efficiency in production and distribution.

Specifically, the developments in manufacturing, such as cellular manufacturing and automated material handling, have increased throughput rates and the responsiveness of firms. Developments in telecommunications and other technologies such as Electronic Data Interchange (EDI) and global positioning systems provide businesses with access to operational real-time information. In addition, the development of software technology for Enterprise Resource Planning (ERP) helps organizations to manage their manufacturing processes efficiently. Finally, electronic commerce (e-commerce) has the ability to transform the way firms perform activities and process all along the value-added system. With an e-commerce-enabled value system, organizations can conduct their business on the Internet in a faster, leaner, and more flexible way and consequently have opportunities to add more value to, and earn larger margin from, their final products.

DAT-DAO NGUYEN
CALIFORNIA STATE UNIVERSITY
NORTHRIDGE

DENNIS S. KIRA
CONCORDIA UNIVERSITY
CANADA

Further reading

(References cited in the text marked *)

Bell, R. and Burham, J. (1991) *Managing Productivity and Change*, Cincinnati, OH: South-Western Publishing. (Besides treatments on managing productivity and change, this book discusses how to create value added in manufacturing.)

Davenport, T.W. (1992) *Process Innovation: Reengineering Work Through Information Technology*, Boston: Harvard Business School Publishing. (This book discusses the role of information technology in business process innovation and business strategy implementation.)

Hammer, M. (1990) 'Reengineering work: don't automate, obliterate', *Harvard Business Review* July–August: 104–12. (The classic article on why and how an enterprise should undertake a radical change of its business processes.)

* Hammer, M. (1996) *Beyond Reengineering: How the Process-Centered Organization is Changing Our Work and Our Lives*, New York: Harper Business. (The book proposes that what we do in re-engineering is not necessarily making a radical change, but taking a process view in making strategies.)

Hammer, M. and Champy, J. (1993) *Reengineering the Corporation*, New York: Harper Business. (This book examines the radical redesign of a company's processes, organization and culture to achieve a quantum leap in performance.)

Harmon, R.L. (1996) *Reinventing the Business*, New York: The Free Press. (This book discusses how enterprises should implement contemporary and future technology in their business processes to make significant improvements in productivity, customer service and quality, and to gain a competitive advantage.)

Kay, J. (1993) *Foundations of Corporate Success: How Business Strategies Add Value*, Oxford: Oxford University Press. (This book examines the strategic importance of business relationships and the architecture of the supply chain system.)

* Porter, M.E. (1985) *Competitive Advantage*, New York: The Free Press. (The classic treatment of the value chain, the value system and how a firm formulates its strategies to gain competitive advantage.)

See also: COSTING; JUST-IN-TIME PHILOSOPHY; MARKETING; ORGANIZATION BEHAVIOUR; PORTER, M.E.; STRATEGY, CONCEPT OF; SUPPLY CHAIN MANAGEMENT

Veblen, Thorstein B. (1857–1929)

Overview

This entry discusses the work of the American institutional economist Thorstein Veblen (1857–1929). It is argued that he provides some of the most fundamental and radical criticisms of neoclassical economics. Veblen's analytical approach to both technology and institutions is discussed here, as well as his explicit application of the evolutionary analogy from Darwinian biology to economics and social science. Finally, mention is made of Veblen's concept of cumulative causation and its relevance to an understanding of the possible trajectories of capitalist development.

1 Biographical details

Thorstein Veblen was born in 1857. He was the fourth son and sixth child of Norwegian immigrants who settled in eastern Minnesota in the United States. Educated at Carleton College, Johns Hopkins University, Yale University and Cornell University, he took various university posts at Chicago, Stanford, Missouri and New York. As a student at John Hopkins University he came in contact with the brilliant philosopher and founder of pragmatism Charles Sanders Peirce. At Yale University he came under the influence of William Graham Sumner, the Social Darwinist. He read widely in biology, psychology and philosophy, as well as the social sciences. As well as Peirce and Sumner, the works of Charles Darwin, William James, Karl Marx,

William McDougall and Herbert Spencer made an enduring mark.

Veblen's most important works date from the 1890s. In 1898 he published his classic article 'Why is economics not an evolutionary science?' in the *Quarterly Journal of Economics*. The following year saw the appearance of his first book *The Theory of the Leisure Class*. Although this is an original and sophisticated theoretical work, its satiric prose and mockery of the wasteful and idle practices of the rich turned it into a bestseller. Other academic articles followed in the *Quarterly Journal of Economics*, the *Journal of Political Economy* and elsewhere, the most important of which have been collected together in *The Place of Science in Modern Civilization and Other Essays* (1919a). Together these articles provide a devastating critique of neoclassical economics and the basis of a new approach to economics on 'evolutionary' lines. Neoclassical economics originated in the 1870s with the work of William Stanley Jevons, Alfred Marshal, Léon Walras and others, and is still the dominant school of thought in that subject. Veblen's critique was one of the first and most fundamental of this emergent paradigm.

In 1904 *The Theory of Business Enterprise* was published, followed by *The Instinct of Workmanship* in 1914, *Imperial Germany and the Industrial Revolution* in 1915, *An Inquiry Into the Nature of Peace and Terms of its Perpetuation* in 1917, *The Higher Learning in America* 1918, *The Vested Interests and the Common Man* in 1919, *The Engineers and the Price System* in 1921 and *Absentee Ownership and Business Enterprise in Recent Times* in 1923. Regrettably, the later works do not deliver the tacit promise of further theoretical development that is found in Veblen's writings from 1892 to 1915. He died in California in 1929.

Veblen was a radical and innovative thinker. He is remembered today as the founder of the school of 'institutional economics' which prospered in the United States between the First and Second World Wars. His writings sometimes bristle with biting and satiric phrases, critical of the institutions and practices of modern capitalism. Nevertheless, Veblen and his followers did not construct an integrated system of economic theory to follow that of Karl Marx, Alfred Marshall or Léon Walras (see MARSHALL, A.; MARX, K.). After the 1930s, the 'old' institutional economics lost ground to the rising generation of formal and mathematically inclined economists, led by Kenneth Arrow, Paul Samuelson, and others (see ARROW, K.; SAMUELSON, P.). By 1950 the institutional school was confined to a small minority of adherents. However, in recent years there has been a revival of the 'old' institutional economics in both Europe and America, and there is a renewed interest in Veblen's works. A large number of themes arise in Veblen's writings and a comprehensive review is not possible. Instead, a few topics of particular relevance for business and management are selected.

2 Veblen's critique of rational economic man

Veblen (1919a: 73) argues that neoclassical economics has a 'faulty conception of human nature' wrongly conceiving of the individual 'in hedonistic terms; that is to say, in terms of a passive and substantially inert and immutably given human nature'. Veblen's critique is directed at neoclassical economics and all theories in which the individual is taken as a given 'globule of desire', to use his satiric phrase. In *The Theory of the Leisure Class* and elsewhere, he argues that consumption is a 'conspicuous' and social rather than an individual process. Consumption is regarded as much more than the mechanical satisfaction of fixed individual needs; it is a cultural and communicative act by which humans signal status and social position, and thereby create further and future desires for others. Accordingly, tastes are malleable and the idea of unalloyed 'consumer sovereignty' is a myth. Indeed, Veblen's bestselling book is not only a major criticism of neoclassical economics but one of the founding texts in the modern science of marketing (see CONSUMER BEHAVIOUR; MARKETING).

In one of his early essays, Veblen (1919a: 73) lambasts the neoclassical view of the economic agent as 'a lightning calculator of pleasures and pains'. He describes the economic man of the textbooks as having 'neither antecedent nor consequent'. Neoclassical economics gives no account of how human wants were formed and developed and instead portrays human agents as utility-maximizing machines. Veblen proposes an alternative theory of human agency, in which 'instincts' such as 'workmanship', 'emulation', 'predatoriness' and 'idle curiosity' play a major role. The emphasis on habitual and 'instinctive' behaviour replaces the utilitarian pleasure–pain principle.

Veblen's conception of the human agent is strongly influenced by the pragmatist philosophy of Peirce and James. Following them, he rejects the Cartesian notion of the supremely rational and calculating agent, instead seeing agents as propelled in the main by habits and routinized behaviours. Instead of the continuously calculating, marginally adjusting agent of neoclassical theory there is an emphasis on inertia and habit.

Veblen argues that habits give the point of view from which facts and events are apprehended and reduced to a body of knowledge. When they are shared and reinforced within a society or group, individual habits assume the form of socio-economic institutions. Institutions create and reinforce habits of action and thought: 'The situation of today shapes the institutions of tomorrow through a selective, coercive process, by acting upon men's habitual view of things, and so altering or fortifying a point of view or a mental attitude handed down from the past' (Veblen 1899: 190–1).

In contrast, in neoclassical economics the self-contained, rational individual has autonomous preferences, seemingly formed apart from the social and natural world. He or she is seemingly capable of optimizing behaviour when faced with a complex problem with enormous numbers of interdependent variables. Instead, Veblen sees the individual's conduct as being influenced by culture and institutions and guided by habit. There is a radical break from the atomistic, individualistic and utilitarian assumptions associated with neoclassical economics.

3 Technology and institutions

One of Veblen's most important arguments against 'economic man' and other core assumptions of neoclassical theory is that they are inadequate for the theoretical purpose at hand. Veblen's intention is to analyse the 'evolutionary' processes of change and transformation in a modern economy. Neoclassical theory is defective in this respect because it indicated 'the conditions of survival to which any innovation is subject, supposing the innovation to have taken place, not the conditions of variational growth' (Veblen 1919a: 176–7). But Veblen sees it as important to consider why such innovations take place, and not to confine ourselves to a theory that dwells over equilibrium conditions with given technological possibilities. The question for Veblen was not how things stabilize themselves in a 'static state', but how they endlessly grow and change.

Accordingly, along with the assumption of fixed preference functions, Veblen also criticizes the widespread assumption of a fixed set of technological possibilities in economic theory. One of his concerns is to examine the conditions for human creativity. With ironic phrases such as 'idle curiosity' he rejects the view that business interests and the potential for technological advance are always positively correlated.

Although Veblen does not see a conflict with technology as universal, he argues that technological change can often challenge established institutions and vested interests. In *The Theory of Business Enterprise* and elsewhere Veblen distinguishes between industry (making goods) and business (making money). This critical dichotomy parallels the earlier suggestion in *The Theory of the Leisure Class* that there is a distinction between serviceable consumption to satisfy human need and conspicuous consumption for status and display. Accordingly, Veblen is strongly critical of apologetic tendencies in social science which regard existing institutions as necessarily efficient or optimal. He rebuts the assumption that institutions must necessarily serve functional needs of society. Instead, he describes particularly regressive or disservicable institutions as 'archaic', 'ceremonial' or even 'imbecile'.

4 Foundations of evolutionary economics

Veblen sees the evolutionary metaphor as crucial to the understanding of the processes of technological development in a capitalist economy (see EVOLUTIONARY THEORIES OF THE FIRM). He is the first economist to apply the Darwinian evolutionary analogy from biology to economics. He argues that economics should become an 'evolutionary' and 'post-Darwinian' science. There is a current revival in 'evolutionary' approaches in economics but the Veblenian precedent for this type of approach is not always acknowledged.

Biological evolution is based on three essential features. First, there must be sustained variation among the members of a species or population. Variations may be blind, random or purposive in character, but without them, as Darwin insisted, natural selection cannot operate. Second, there must be some principle of heredity or continuity through which offspring have to resemble their parents more than they resemble other members of their species. In other words, there has to be some mechanism through which individual characteristics are passed on through the generations. Third, natural selection itself operates either because better-adapted organisms leave increased numbers of offspring, or because the variations or gene combinations that are preserved are those bestowing advantage in struggling to survive. This is the principle of the struggle for existence.

The same three principles can be found in Veblen's work. For instance, habits and institutions are regarded as relatively durable and the analogue of heritable traits. Veblen (1899: 190–1) writes: 'men's present habits of thought tend to persist indefinitely, except as circumstances enforce a change. These institutions which have so been handed down, these habits of thought, points of view, mental attitudes and aptitudes, or what not, are therefore themselves a conservative factor. This is the factor of social inertia, psychological inertia, conservatism'. Likewise, Veblen (1914: 86–9) recognizes the role of creativity and novelty with his concept of 'idle curiosity'. Veblen's recognition of the open-endedness of the evolutionary process is evidenced in his conception of 'change, realized to be self-continuing or self-propagating and to have no final term' (Veblen 1919a: 37). Finally, without drawing Panglossian or laissez-faire conclusions, Veblen (1899: 188) subscribes to a notion of evolutionary selection in the socio-economic sphere: 'The life of man in society, just as the life of other species, is a struggle for existence, and therefore it is a process of selective adaptation. The evolution of social structure has been a process of natural selection of institutions.'

In this respect Veblen is a more suited mentor for evolutionary economics than Joseph Schumpeter (see SCHUMPETER, J.), who eschews all natural and physical metaphors and states in his *History of Economic Analysis* (1954: 789) that in economics 'no appeal to biology would be of the slightest use'. Schumpeter's frequent use of the word 'evolution' should not mislead us into believing that his work was a precedent for the employment of a biological analogy. He does not define the term in biological terms and we do not find in his work the use of the three principles of evolutionary change (heritable traits, generation of variety, and selection) as outlined above. Richard Nelson and Sidney Winter describe their seminal work *An Evolutionary Theory of Economic Change* (1982) as 'Schumpeterian', yet they make explicit use of a metaphor from evolutionary biology. In this respect there are strong resemblances with some of Veblen's ideas. Accordingly, their work is better described as 'Veblenian', although they make no reference in that work to the earlier economist.

5 Cumulative causation: against teleology

During his lifetime, half-understood biological analogies were being widely applied to the social sciences, in attempts to justify all sorts of ideological positions from socialism to capitalist competition. Veblen is a clear exception and his understanding of biology is much more sophisticated. Contrary to many of his contemporaries, Veblen saw that the idea of Darwinian evolution meant that the future was unknown, unpredictable and indeterminate. In this respect he treated Darwin not only as a critic of apologetic defenders of capitalism but also as a rebuttal of Marx's teleological suggestions that history was leading inevitably to a single and communist future.

Veblen's answer to both the Marxian suggestion of the inevitability of communism and his rebuff to the neoclassical concept of equilibrium is his theory of cumulative causation. He sees both the circumstances and temperament of individuals as part of the cumulative processes of change: 'The economic life history of the individual is a cumulative process of adaptation of means to ends that cumulatively change as the process goes on, both the agent and his environment being at any point the outcome of the last process' (Veblen 1919a: 74–5). Directly or indirectly influenced by Veblen, the notion of cumulative causation has been developed by a number of economists, notably Nicholas Kaldor and the Nobel Laureate Gunnar Myrdal. The idea relates to the modern notion that technologies and economic systems can get 'locked in' – and sometimes as a result of initial accidents – to relatively constrained paths of development. Hence there is 'path dependence' rather than convergence to a given equilibrium or track of development. History matters.

Veblen's concept of cumulative causation is an antidote to both neoclassical and Marxian economic theory. Contrary to the equilibrium analysis of neoclassical economics, Veblen sees the economic system not as a 'self-balancing mechanism' but as a 'cumulatively unfolding process'. As Myrdal and Kaldor argue at length, the processes of cumulative causation suggest that regional and national development is generally divergent rather than convergent. This contradicts the typical emphasis within neoclassical economic theory on processes of compensating feedback and mutual adjustment via the price mechanism leading to greater uniformity and convergence.

Contrary to much Marxist and neoclassical thinking, Veblen argued that multiple futures were possible. Equilibrating forces do not always pull the economy back onto a single track. This exposes a severe weakness in Marx's conception of history. Although Veblen has socialist leanings, he argues against the idea of finality or consummation in economic development. Variety and cumulative causation mean that history has 'no final term' (Veblen 1919a: 37). In Marxism the final term is communism or the classless society, but Veblen rejects the teleological concept of a final goal. This means a rejection of the ideas of the 'inevitability' of socialism and of a 'natural' or end-point in capitalist evolution. There is no natural path, or law, governing economic development. Accordingly, Veblen accepts the possibility of varieties of capitalism and different paths of capitalist development.

This standpoint is particularly relevant for recent debates about convergence versus divergence within global capitalism. Veblen's emphasis on the importance of institutions and culture, along with his notion of divergent and cumulative causation, suggests that multiple futures and multiple varieties of capitalism are possible. Despite the lack of an integrated and systematic theory in his writings, his analytical outlook makes him one of the most relevant economists and social theorists today.

GEOFFREY M. HODGSON
THE BUSINESS SCHOOL
UNIVERSITY OF HERTFORDSHIRE

Further reading

(References cited in the text marked *)

Dorfman, J. (1934) *Thorstein Veblen and His America*, New York: Viking Press. (The classic intellectual bibliography of Veblen.)

Hodgson, G.M. (1988) *Economics and Institutions: A Manifesto for a Modern Institutional Economics*, Cambridge and Philadelphia: Polity Press and University of Pennsylvania Press. (A critique of neoclassical economics from a perspective inspired by Veblen and other 'old' institutional economists. There is an extensive bibliography.)

Hodgson, G.M. (1993) *Economics and Evolution: Bringing Life Back Into Economics*, Cambridge, UK and Ann Arbor, MI: Polity Press and University of Michigan Press. (An extensive discussion and analysis of various approaches to evolutionary economics where the work of Veblen is prominent.)

Hodgson, G.M. (ed.) (1998) *The Foundations of Evolutionary Economics: 1890–1973*, 2 vols, International Library of Critical Writings in Economics, Cheltenham: Edward Elgar. (A collection of important essays on evolutionary economics by various authors, including several commentaries on the work of Veblen.)

* Nelson, R.R. and Winter, S.G. (1982) *An Evolutionary Theory of Economic Change*, Cambridge, MA: Harvard University Press. (A now-seminal application of the evolutionary analogy to the theory of the firm. Although the influence is unacknowledged, aspects of this work are highly redolent of Veblenian institutionalism.)

Rutherford, M.C. (1994) *Institutions in Economics: The Old and the New Institutionalism*, Cambridge: Cambridge University Press. (An erudite and thoughtful account of institutional thought with extensive attention to Veblen.)

Samuels, W.J. (ed.) (1988) *Institutional Economics*, 3 vols, Aldershot: Edward Elgar. (A useful anthology of essays on Veblen and other 'old' institutionalists.)

* Schumpeter, J.A. (1954) *History of Economic Analysis*, New York: Oxford University Press.

Seckler, D. (1975) *Thorstein Veblen and the Institutionalists: A Study in the Social Philosophy of Economics*, London: Macmillan. (Contains a sympathetic critique of Veblen. Sometimes misguided in its assessment, but contains extensive quotations and makes a number of useful points.)

Tilman, R. (1992) *Thorstein Veblen and His Critics, 1891–1963: Conservative, Liberal, and Radical*, Princeton: Princeton University Press. (A detailed and very interesting perspective on Veblen through the eyes of his critics.)

Tilman, R. (1996) *The Intellectual Legacy of Thorstein Veblen: Unresolved Issues*, Westport, CT: Greenwood Press. (An excellent overview of controversies surrounding Veblen's thinking.)

* Veblen, T.B. (1898) 'Why is economics not an evolutionay science?', *Quarterly Journal of Economics*, 12.

* Veblen, T.B. (1899) *The Theory of the Leisure Class: An Economic Study of Institutions*, New York: Macmillan. (Veblen's classic and highly influential analysis of the consumer behaviour of the rich. With this work the 'old' institutional school was founded.)

* Veblen, T.B. (1904) *The Theory of Business Enterprise*, New York: Charles Scribners, reprinted 1975 by Augustus Kelley. (A major and

influential work on modern capitalist enterprise.)

* Veblen, T.B. (1914) *The Instinct of Workmanship, and the State of the Industrial Arts*, New York: Augustus Kelley, reprinted 1990 with a new introduction by M.G. Murphey and a 1964 introductory note by J. Dorfman, New Brunswick: Transaction Books. (Regarded by Veblen as his most important book.)

* Veblen, T.B. (1915) *Imperial Germany and the Industrial Revolution*, New York: Macmillan, reprinted 1964 by Augustus Kelley. (A strikingly prescient and incisive work.)

* Veblen, T.B. (1917) *An Inquiry into the Nature of Peace and the Terms of its Perpetuation*, New York: Huebsch. (An attempt to lay bare the causes of war.)

* Veblen, T. B. (1918) *The Higher Learning in America: A Memorandum on the Conduct of Universities by Business Men*, New York: Huebsch. (A critique of business influence on universities.)

* Veblen, T.B. (1919a) *The Place of Science in Modern Civilization and Other Essays*, New York: Huebsch, reprinted 1990 with a new introduction by W. J. Samuels, New Brunswick: Transaction Books. (The most important collection of Veblen's essays. Veblen is often at his best in his essays and polemics and for this reason this work is invaluable both for the economic and the social theorist.)

* Veblen, T.B. (1919b) *The Vested Interests and the Common Man*, New York: Huebsch.

* Veblen, T.B. (1921) *The Engineers and the Price System*, New York: Harcourt Brace and World. (A work in which Veblen idiosyncratically sees the engineer as the agent of socialist revolution.)

* Veblen, T.B. (1923) *Absentee Ownership And Business Enterprise in Recent Times*, New York: Huebsch. (An early critique of the separation of ownership from both responsibility and control.)

See also: ARROW, K.; CONSUMER BEHAVIOUR; EVOLUTIONARY THEORIES OF THE FIRM; INSTITUTIONAL ECONOMICS; MARKETING; MARSHALL, A.; MARX, K.H.; SAMUELSON, P.; SCHUMPETER, J.; TECHNOLOGY AND ORGANIZATIONS

Venezuela, management in

Overview

Venezuela is a country that possesses an excellent geographical position, as a door to many other countries in South America, and as a connecting point between South America and the Caribbean, and Europe. It also possesses unique mineral resources (tremendous oil reserves and iron ore, among others). However, these privileges have brought the country less progress than these resources would indicate. Many political problems have plagued Venezuela during the last 100 years. Although the oldest Latin American democracy, Venezuela has been governed by politicians who have put their personal interests or the interest of a particular group ahead of the needs of the country as a whole. Thus Venezuela has not developed the appropriate infrastructure to take full advantage of its geographical position and its natural resources. Of course, there is always an exception to this situation. The oil industry has developed into a modern corporation capable of competing with the large global companies in this industry. The privatization movement of the 1990s is still too recent to evaluate.

In terms of the development of managerial philosophy, the country has been influenced for most of this century by the models developed in northern Europe and the USA, and more recently by Japanese practices. It is possible to speculate that significant cultural differences (e.g. northern Europe and the USA are low cultural context countries, while Venezuela is a high context country [Ferraro 1998]) have made it more difficult for Venezuela to adapt management ways of thinking from other regions. Although highly significant in the study of cross-cultural management, this dichotomy is not the focus of discussion here. However, the discussion of the evolution of the country would justify some of the differences in development between Venezuela and other countries. Still Venezuelan business schools and management practitioners make every effort to learn the latest managerial practices of the industrial world.

1 Introduction

Venezuela had a rather modest beginning, where there were no 'mighty Amerindian empires, no storehouses of golden objects, and no fabulous cities' (Lombardi 1982: 59). Lombardi (1982) also indicates that the Spanish explorers and conquerors only found various 'hunting and gathering tribes, some Indians engaged in low-intensity, sedentary agriculture, and many hostile tribes unwilling to cede control over their territories to the invading Spaniard' (Lombardi 1982: 59). From the 1500s until the early 1700s, Venezuela developed very slowly, to become a significant supplier of pearls, cocoa, fruits and other agricultural and farm products. In the eighteenth century, the commercial activity between the colony and Spain was more or less under the control of the *Compañia Guipuzcoana*, which was a Spanish monopoly. This organization could probably be considered as the first organized business concern of considerable size operating in the country. The style of management was basically an exploitative one, with a very direct line of command (see SPAIN, MANAGEMENT IN).

2 The practice of management

During this period, there were a number of family-owned businesses that started to develop as a result of the importance that Venezuela gained in areas such as stock raising, cocoa, fruits and other agricultural products, and a few mining operations. There were also a few small shops. Businesses dealing with agriculture and stock raising were generally characterized by being owned by an individual or a family with considerable amounts of land. This led to the development of the big haciendas. These haciendas are also known as *latifundios* (Lambert 1971). The style of management in these businesses was generally patriarchal, and with many exploitative actions against the peasant labourers. However, Lambert (1971) indicates that there was a relationship of personal dependence between the agricultural workers and the hacienda owners. He also indicates that this relationship could have been the result of the slave–master relationship that existed between them, before these workers were freed as a result of the abolition of forced labour.

The situation remained practically unchanged for almost 200 years. Moron (1970) indicates that this was the case until the late 1870s, when the first attempts to exploit and process oil on a commercial basis were made by the *Compañia Minera Petrolia del Tachira* (Mining Company Petrolia of Tachira, in the southwest of Venezuela). This company refined fifteen barrels of oil a day and later increased production to sixty barrels a day, but the company had failed by 1912. These were not the largest concerns. It was around 1916, when the rich oil reserves were confirmed, that the larger companies started to operate in the country, which marked the beginning of the Venezuelan oil industry. Venezuela became a point of interest to many large corporations of the time. The British/Dutch company Royal Dutch Shell was one of the pioneers in entering the country's recently born oil business. Then a subsidiary of Standard Oil of the USA entered the country, before the passing of antitrust laws which forced its break up. However, other companies followed.

The initial contribution of these companies to the development of managerial skills among locals was minimal if it occurred at all. These companies generally functioned in isolation from other areas of Venezuelan economic life. They made very limited local purchases of supplies and materials and paid very low local taxes. Their managerial expertise did not spread to the locals until the 1950s,

when Venezuelans are allowed to occupy middle-level managerial positions. It would take some fifteen more years for Venezuelan managers to reach higher levels of management in these international companies. The managerial style of these foreign companies was basically founded on the traditional classical theories of management from the early 1900s.

During the same period, a number of Venezuelan companies developed in other industries such as Electricidad de Caracas and Electricidad de Valencia (electricity); Telares de Maracay and Telares Los Andes (textiles); Cerveceria Caracas and Cerveceria Polar (breweries); Manufacturas de Papel (a paper manufacturer); Ron Santa Teresa (a rum manufacturer); and Ingenios el Palmar, Ingenio Venezuela, Ingenio el Tocuyo, and Ingenio Yaritagua (sugar cane growers and sugar processing plants); and the Grupo Mendoza (hardware stores, cement plants and others), to name a few. These Venezuelan companies developed their own managerial models among others, with very little influence from the foreign companies operating in the country. The Venezuelan companies' management style was extremely paternalistic, with family owners and their members controlling most of the important positions.

In summary, for many decades the style of management used by Venezuelan businesses was mostly dominated by two schools, basically determined by the origin and type of ownership of the companies. Foreign companies were characterized by a classical, bureaucratic management style. The local companies were characterized by their paternalistic style of management.

During the late 1940s and early 1950s, as a result of the Venezuelan dictator M. Perez Jimenez's *Nuevo Ideal Nacional* (a plan called 'the new national ideal', which was aimed at the modernization of the country), the Venezuelan government developed and managed large companies in non-petroleum industries. The country moved from an almost dormant position in these developing industries to the management of large industrial complexes. The government entered the iron ore industry, the petrochemical industry, aluminium, steel, large seaports, electric power generation and administration and the airline industry, among others. It is important to note that the investments to develop these industrial complexes were financed with increasing oil revenues. The predominant management style was, for the most part, the typical official bureaucracy, with a degree of favouritism (both political and personal) playing an important role in the selection of managers and directors. These managers did not really develop high skill levels, however, because they were managing with excess resources from oil revenues.

Venezuela has been too dependent on oil revenues for its subsistence. So, one of the official objectives of many industrialization and modernization programmes in the last three decades has been to promote the exportation of other products and services. These programmes have produced moderate results, but have also fomented the development of many other industries and have led to the creation of a small number of industrial zones in the country. The windfall of oil revenues in the 1970s led the government to increase its direct participation in the industrial and productive process. This effort included the nationalization of the oil industry, the steel industry, increased participation in aluminium, and others. On the whole, this movement produced very questionable results, due in great part to poor management. Some of these companies failed completely, and others were the main targets for privatization in the 1990s (see PRIVATIZATION AND REGULATION).

3 Academic side of Venezuelan management

The development in the country of what we know today as structured, formal academic programmes in business management had its origins in many different schools and at different levels of professionalism. The Venezuela of the 1940s saw the development of the first formal modern college degree programme in economics at the major state supported university in the country. In reality, during that time most private business sector managers were economists, as were most of the administrators in the public sector. From these

programmes in economics emerged the first schools of business administration and accounting, in recognition of the need for professionals with more specific education in the area of business management. The economic degree was not fulfilling the need for managers in the private sector. The country saw its first fully developed business school early in the 1950s. During the latter part of the 1960s and until early in the 1970s, there was a dramatic increase in the number of students enrolled in business programmes and in the number of universities offering academic programmes in business. Today most universities offer degrees in business administration, with two major degrees: a general business administration degree and an accounting degree. Graduates from these programmes are generally well accepted by the business community.

Not all the academic programmes were offered at college level. Up to the mid 1970s, the Venezuelan educational system offered high school level programmes in office skills. These programmes were delivered through schools that specialized only in this field, and most of the students specialized in the field of office management and related areas. There were also private courses aimed at the development of middle-level and entry-level professionals in the accounting and auditing fields. These were delivered in the form of a sequence of courses, which in most cases had very little government oversight. These accounting academies (*academias de contabilidad*), as they were known, issued an unofficial certificate as proof of the training received by participants. Generally, these professionals were highly qualified and accepted by the business community, although they were limited to the area of accounting.

The opening of the school of business mentioned above contributed to the death of the accounting academies. The programmes implemented by these schools provided progressive training in accounting to their students, very similar to those offered by the academy of accounting. These college courses in accounting were taken sequentially, beginning from the very first year in the programme. Additionally, government offices started to accept business students for the positions equivalent to those occupied by the graduates from the academies. The private business sector immediately followed suit, and started to employ business students in accounting positions as well. Most schools of business first opened and functioned for many years, exclusively, as evening programmes. This allowed their students to be employed in many different entry-level positions in accounting, office management, supervision, human resources, etc.

The area of human resources and personnel administration really started under the influence of the oil companies, which first initiated internal training of executives in these areas. There were no college level HRM programmes at any of the universities until 1964, when the University of Carabobo, in the state of Valencia, and the Andres Bello Catholic University of Caracas opened academic undergraduate programmes in this field. Coupled with this, the Venezuelan government created the Public Administration Commission (*Comision de Administracion Publica*), in early 1960s, which was charged with the overseeing of many administrative issues and procedures. This commission also gave birth to the Central Personnel Office and the National School of Public Administration. Initially this school offered programmes for the development of middle-level public employees in the areas of personnel and budget and planning. Later it diversified into other areas such as purchasing, organization, and other areas of interest to the public sector. Since the 1970s, public administration became a recognized field of study at many universities, and the School of Public Administration itself became recognized as an institution of higher education.

In the late 1960s, the country experienced graduate management education for the first time. The Institute of Graduate Studies in Administration (*Instituto de Estudios Superiores de Administracion* – IESA) was created to offer graduate programmes in management. They offered master degree programmes in management and executive development programmes. This institute is very well-known today, not only in the country but also abroad, because it is very actively involved in many international academic groups and in a num-

ber of professional associations. It has a number of academic agreements with many well-known universities in the USA and Europe. This private graduate management school is characterized by the high academic credentials of its faculty. Faculty members possess terminal degrees in business from a number of very well-known schools in the world, and they are also involved in research and other intellectual endeavours.

At around the same time, some of the major private and public universities of the country also developed their own graduate level programmes in business administration and management. These programmes also offer both full master degrees in a variety of majors, and a large number of executive development programmes. Most of these graduate college courses follow the American model of graduate management education. Also today there are at least two doctoral programmes in the developmental stage or fully functional. The country today enjoys many degree programmes in a variety of major fields. There are standard MBA programmes, and courses in management, advertising and marketing, human resources, labour relations, finance, etc (see MANAGEMENT EDUCATION IN LATIN AMERICA).

4 Contemporary management

Since the late 1970s, there have been a number of factors contributing to the subsequent development of the management field in Venezuela. One factor is that the country enjoyed a huge windfall in oil revenue, and a considerable amount of this extra income was used to finance more than 60,000 Venezuelans who went to universities in the USA and Europe from the 1970s to the 1990s to study in a large variety of fields. Many of them have returned to Venezuela after completing their MBA degrees and degrees in other areas of business. A second factor is that there has been an increase in the number of American investors in Venezuela, who have brought with them some approaches to management to be implemented in the companies receiving their investments, or in newly created concerns. Among these, there have been banks, insurance companies, financial companies and other financial institutions who try to influence how companies should be managed.

A third factor is the increase in the number of agreements between some major Venezuelan universities and some American and European universities. These agreements were initially in the areas of agriculture and other farming activities, petroleum and veterinarian medicine, among others. Business and management were not included in these agreements until the latter part of the decade of the 1980s. A fourth factor is the activity of institutions such as the International Monetary Fund (IMF) and the World Bank that, through the conditions attached to their financial interventions, have forced countries to pay more attention to how companies and other institutions should be managed (see INTERNATIONAL MONETARY FUND; WORLD BANK). These political and economic factors have a strong influence on the education and development of managers and other business professionals.

A fifth major factor is the globalization of the business world, which combined with the privatization process, has brought into the country many international businesses from different parts of the world (see GLOBALIZATION). There have been companies from Mexico, Argentina, Spain, Germany, England, the USA, Korea, Japan and others. Although the bulk of foreign companies in Venezuela are probably from the USA, most of them share common modern approaches to management. It is not to be unexpected that they bring with them a combination of the most contemporary ideas in management, which they implement in their businesses in Venezuela. These companies have adopted practices such as total quality management and continuous quality improvement, employee empowerment, reengineering, open information systems, improved customer service, cycle-time reduction, organizational learning, improved strategic planning processes, collaborating strategies, and visionary leadership, to name but some of them.

All of these factors are coming together to transform the business landscape in the world, and Venezuela is no exception. Many domestic Venezuelan companies are now struggling to accept, to understand and to cope with the set of rules in this new global business order.

These companies find themselves forced to learn new ways of doing business, and to forget (or unlearn) their old ways. But it is not an easy move to abandon culturally set paternalistic and traditional styles of management, and to function in an environment without the accustomed protectionist government. Some of these managers are now learning what it takes to become competitive and to stay in the global business game.

5 Issues for the future

The opening of markets everywhere has created a situation where a product manufactured in almost any country can be sold in almost any other country, and has changed the rules of the business game. Some are still resisting this transformation. Some of the excuses offered to explain the resistance is that this is an Americanization of the business community, that jobs will be lost, or even that the country's sovereignty is in danger. But some progressive businesses are moving ahead with the changes. They are making great efforts to retool their managers to get them ready to face the new challenges. These managers have now developed an increased understanding that the movement is not necessarily an Americanization of business, but a global phenomenon, in which businesses from other countries are also involved. They are learning that they can no longer function under the protectionist form of government, and that their traditional and paternalistic management practices are fast becoming obsolete. They are really understanding that the only protectionism available to business today is their own competitiveness and productivity.

It is important to recognize that not all the changes are due to the globalization of business, but that some are due to internal pressures in the country. One example of this is the recent transformation of the banking industry and other financial institutions in Venezuela, mostly as the direct effect of very serious corruption and the abuse of trust by many bankers – who are now exile in other countries in order to escape justice. Regardless of what causes it, the transformation of business is a reality that managers must deal with and must do so while still trying to run successful businesses.

In conclusion, Venezuelan organizations and their managers are in the midst of this major transition. Even the casual observer may notice that there are some managers and their companies that have been oblivious to the globalization of business, and continue with their efforts to continue in the way they have always done. There are others who could not transform in any way, and have already fallen victim to the more competitive concerns. Still others are enjoying the fruits of the transformation, or the opportunities that come with the challenges of a new global business order.

However, there are still major concerns about the formation and development of the managers who would be the ones responsible for leading the transition of their companies into this new business world. One of those concerns relates to the quality of the academic programmes offered by universities all over the country. It seems that too many educators and practitioners worry that these programmes have not kept up with the new developments in the business world, and the graduates from these schools do not emerge ready to meet the skills demanded by businesses today. Similar concerns exist about the executive development programmes offered by many schools in the country. There remains some degree of political instability in the country, in the sense that there can be no assurance that the programmes instituted by one government will be maintained or continued by the next. This does not give the business community the predictability or stability necessary to do business in the country.

HÉCTOR LUCENA
UNIVERSITY OF CARABOBO

R. IVAN BLANCO
CENTRAL CONNECTICUT STATE UNIVERSITY

Further reading

(References cited in the text marked *)

Enright, M., Frances, A. and Scott Saavedra, E. (eds) (1995) *Venezuela: The Challenge of Competitiveness*, New York: Palgrave. (Based on a comprehensive two-year study, this text represents a first-of-its-kind analysis of the competitiveness of the economy and industries of a developing nation. The authors also provide valuable recommendations on actions that firms and government can take to improve the nation's overall economic performance.)

* Ferraro, F.P. (1998) *International Dimensions of International Business* 3rd edn, Upper Saddle River, NJ: Prentice Hall. (This books offers a good discussion of the high/low cultural context dichotomy.)

Harris, P.R. and Moran, R.T. (1991) *Managing Cultural Differences* 3rd edn, Houston, TX: Gulf Publishing Company. (Offers a general discussion of managing across cultures, and briefings about doing business in different regions of the world, including Latin America.)

* Lambert, J. (1971) *Latin America: Social Structure and Political Institutions*, Berkeley, CA: University of California Press. (This book offers a very comprehensive discussion of the social, political and economic development of the Latin American countries.)

Leal, I. (1981) *Historia de la UCV*, Caracas, Venezuela: Universidad Central de Venezuela Press. (This books discusses the history of the Universidad Central de Venezuela, from 1721 to 1981.)

* Lombardi, J.V. (1982) *Venezuela: The Search for Order, the Dream of Progress*, New York: Oxford University Press. (Lombardi presents a thorough discussion of Venezuelan history.)

* Moron, G. (1970) *Historia de Venezuela* (Venezuelan History) 5th edn, Caracas, Venezuela: Italgrafica, S.R.L. (This is a Venezuelan history text that was a requirement for many courses taught in that country.)

Further resources

For more information on the contemporary issues and challenges faced by Venezuelan business organizations and schools, there are some periodical publications that offer discussions by local experts and Spanish translations of *Business Week* and *Fortune Magazine* feature articles. Some of these publications are: *Gerente, Inversiones* and *Numero*.

See also: ARGENTINA, MANAGEMENT IN; BRAZIL, MANAGEMENT IN; CHILE, MANAGEMENT IN; GLOBALIZATION; HUMAN RESOURCE MANAGEMENT IN LATIN AMERICA; INDUSTRIAL RELATIONS IN LATIN AMERICA; INTERNATIONAL MONETARY FUND; LATIN AMERICA, MANAGEMENT IN; MEXICO, MANAGEMENT IN; NORTH AMERICAN FREE TRADE AGREEMENT; STRATEGY IN LATIN AMERICA; WORLD BANK

Venture capital

Overview

The impact of venture capital on Western industrial economies in recent years has been immense, and continues to grow. It has backed new industrial enterprises that could not have taken shape in any other way. Venture capital has also facilitated large-scale restructuring through the division of large industrial organizations into smaller, more focused units. And thousands of venture capital investments have enabled small businesses to grow faster. There is no universally accepted definition of venture capital and there are some international variations in terminology. In the USA, 'venture capital' generally means financing start-up and early stage businesses. In the UK it has a broader meaning, covering most types of investment in private companies, including management buy-outs. 'Private equity' is the term increasingly used internationally to describe the full range of activity in this field of investment.

In this article, I am using both 'venture capital' and 'private equity' to mean the full range of investments from seed capital to management buy-outs (see below). The common denominator is that they are all investments in private companies – companies without stock market listings and therefore without the facility to 'trade' in stock. Partly because of this, they are generally higher risk investments. The level of risk varies widely and a key element of the venture capitalist's role is to assess the risk and to negotiate an investment which could yield a commensurate return. The essential core of venture capital is equity – a shareholding in the company which provides the investor with the potential for substantial capital growth. The equity finance provided is usually geared up with debt or other financial instruments (see below). The degree of in-volvement in each business varies widely but increasingly it is likely that the venture capitalist will play a significant role in the determination of both business strategy and the timing of realizing returns from the business.

Who provides venture capital? It is an area of finance which requires a range of skills and attributes, in particular the ability to judge markets, technologies and people. Venture capital is mainly provided by specialist venture capital or private equity companies whose funding is supplied by pension funds, insurance companies and other fund managers. One of the developments of the last few years has been an increasing involvement from corporate investors (e.g. Intel), wealthy private investors (particularly in the USA) and some professional partnerships. This article is written from the perspective of 3i, Europe's leading venture capital company, which has over 50 years experience in this field. (The name 3i stems from 'investors in industry'.) 3i was established in the UK in 1945 to fill a perceived gap in British capital markets – for businesses too small or too young to raise money from the stock markets. Today 3i operates from six countries in Europe, as well as in the USA and Asia. Venture capital is an international activity, although the vast majority of investors concentrate their investments in one country or region. In the 1990s we have seen several major US investors set up offices in Europe and vice versa. It seems likely that we will see more development of international firms, including global venture capital firms within the next few years.

As we enter the new millennium, venture capital is far better understood than it was ten years ago. The 1990s saw a dramatic growth in both the supply of venture capital finance and the demand for venture capital products. If anything, supply grew faster than demand resulting in increasing competition and innovation with new developments such as institutional buy-outs (see below).

I Venture capital products

Venture capital can be used in various ways for varying situations. Some may prefer to describe venture capital as a 'service' rather than the provision of a 'product'. However, for the purposes of this review, I will describe the principal 'products' of venture capital.

One of the current trends is towards specialization among venture capitalists. It has generally been the case that firms have specialized in certain sizes of transaction (e.g. small, medium or large), but increasingly investors are offering specialist skills and knowledge by the type of investment product (e.g. management buy-outs) or by industry (e.g. food, bio-tech).

Seed capital

The provision of seed capital is one of the most specialized niche areas. It is also probably the highest risk type of venture capital. Seed capital can be defined as finance required to explore the potential for a new business. This is usually before a company has been formed, before the full management team has been recruited, and before the business plan has been written. It is usually required for new technology applications, not for established industries. Seed capital is becoming familiar to universities and research establishments who recognize the potential value of their intellectual property and consequently the possibilities of raising commercial venture capital to supplement public sector funding and the grants for their requirements. 3i, for instance, has a joint venture with Scottish Enterprise, a public sector body, to provide seed capital for Scottish Universities. The Medical Ventures Fund is another joint-venture fund set up to look for commercial opportunities from the Medical Research Council in Britain, in which 3i has participated.

Seed capital is usually provided in relatively small amounts and in several 'rounds' as the research projects develop. Those projects that do become successful commercial ventures should offer very high returns to the venture capital investors to compensate for the high risk taken at a very early stage. The pay-back is unlikely to be fast.

Start-ups and emerging businesses

More conventional venture capital is the backing of start-up businesses, which probably provides the clearest illustration of the function of venture capital. Start-up businesses, by their nature, constitute a risky form of investment. However, if the enterprise prospers, the rewards for the original investors can be very large indeed, once the business has proved its success and reached an appropriate size for the investors to sell their investment. The rewards consist of the dividends payable on the investor's shares, plus the capital gains achieved if the business is sold or floated on the stock market (see SMALL BUSINESS FINANCE).

As with seed capital, a new business may require only a small amount of capital to get started. However, much larger sums are usually called for as the enterprise reaches the next stages of emergence as a business – to fund development, production and so on. As further rounds of finance are called for, probably with profits still not being earned, it is usual for venture capitalists to make additional investments in the young company.

Different providers of capital have different criteria for selecting young companies. Some investors are specialists in specific sectors, where they have built up experience in judging the chances of a venture prospering. All investors would agree, however, that a basic criterion is the character and level of experience of the founders of new businesses. Investors look for a good standard of managerial expertise. They will examine the track records of the business's founders, and take up references. They also hope to find entrepreneurial qualities – the extra characteristics that can bring outstanding business success. It is sometimes said that venture capitalists are risk averse in backing start-up ventures. 'There are plenty of good ideas but venture capitalists are reluctant to back them' is a frequently heard view. On the other hand, venture capitalists will often say they can't find sufficient quality investment opportunities. The missing 'third leg' to this situation is often quality management.

The venture capitalist wishes to be convinced not just that the basic business proposition is sound, but that there is a suitable

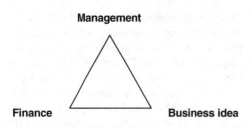

Figure 1

management team with the necessary commercial skills to make a success of the plan. The three basic ingredients for successful start-up are: the business idea; suitable finance; and a quality management team.

Investors usually expect the founders of a company to be willing to invest an appropriate amount of their own money, although they recognize that a young entrepreneur cannot be expected to have large personal resources. Venture capitalists look for commitment. By subscribing for shares the founders have a strong incentive to make the business succeed, because of the potential capital gains involved.

Appropriate technical knowledge is obviously vital in some start-ups, but potential investors will always look carefully at the founders' general management skill, and will be looking for a management team that incorporates a high level of financial management skill, either directly or through professional advisors, preferably both. Some successful start-ups have been launched by a team of managers who worked together in an established company and decided to use their skills to found a new business. This arrangement can provide reassurance for investors because it represents important management experience.

The explosion of high technology and e-commerce start-ups is a key feature of current markets (see E-COMMERCE). There are major transitions taking place in some industries caused by technological advances creating high-growth market opportunities. These provide potentially rich picking for venture

capital companies able to spot these opportunities, to take the risks and to move quickly. Many fortunes have indeed been made in recent years. In these circumstances, technological and market assessments are likely to be key, rather than managerial or financial experience, but venture capitalists need to assess all the risks! These situations help to explain why many venture capitalists are getting increasingly involved in the businesses in which they invest. Young, inexperienced management teams very often welcome the support, and particularly the personal introductions, which an experienced venture capitalist can provide. Apart from the technology itself, a key determinant of success for the venture capital investor is usually the timing of the 'exit' – through stock market flotation or the sale of the whole business.

Management buy-outs

In recent years, very large amounts of venture capital have been invested in management buy-outs (MBOs). Buy-outs have an advantage from the investors' points of view in that their money is going into an established business, not into a new situation, as in a start-up. In the USA these transactions are usually called 'leveraged buy-outs' (LBOs).

An MBO takes place when ownership of a company passes into the hands of new shareholders, who include the management team and their venture capital backers. Many MBOs arise because a large group wishes to divest itself of a subsidiary, and a buy-out is seen as a better option than selling to another company. The motive of the vendor company may be to realize capital, or to focus on what it regards as its core business by disposing of subsidiaries that do not fit into that core. Other MBOs take place when an independent business, such as a family business, is to be sold because the owners wish to retire. Companies that are the subject of an MBO vary in their degree of profitability. Some may have been very successful. Others may be under-performing – perhaps because the managers were unable to reach their full potential as part of a larger group. Whichever, when a venture capital company backs an MBO, the aim will be that the business's profitability will increase under the new ownership arrangements and thus prove to be a good investment. Investors recognize that a key to ensuring an enhanced performance is the financial incentive for the management team, arising from their new role as owner-managers. Like their backers, the managers should stand to make significant capital gains if the MBO succeeds.

The ownership structure of a company after a buyout can take a variety of forms according to the circumstances. In the case of a small MBO, it is often possible for the managers to acquire the majority of the equity, even though they may be able to raise only a small proportion of the full purchase price out of their own resources. However, their personal funds may enable them to subscribe enough capital to acquire, say, 65 per cent of the equity. The venture capital backer subscribes for the remaining 35 per cent, and also provides other forms of capital to meet the total capital requirement. There is a range of instruments, (described below) that can provide the remainder of the funds needed. In a larger MBO, it is unrealistic for the managers to have a majority of the equity, but they will probably acquire a significant minority.

Institutional buy-outs

An institutional buy-out (IBO) is a variation on the theme of an MBO. IBOs are another manifestation of the increasing competition in the venture capital world and the need for innovation and risk-taking. Whereas an MBO typically involves the venture capital investor responding to the opportunity to back a management team's plans to acquire a business, an IBO is usually the initiative of the venture capital company itself. The venture capitalists negotiate directly with the vendor of the business rather than through the management team and their advisors. The venture capital company will then secure a management team to run the business which may be the incumbent managers, may be outsiders, or it may decide to merge the business with another already in its portfolio of investments.

The advantages to the venture capital company of an IBO are its lead role and control of all the purchase terms and management contracts. The key disadvantage, and main risk, is the uncertainty created by not involving the incumbent senior management team who are best placed to know the value and prospects of the business.

Management buy-ins

A management buy-in (MBI) is another variant of the MBO and achieves the same purpose of changing the ownership of a company. However, in an MBI, an experienced manager or entrepreneur from outside the business comes in to play the leading role. He or she may bring his or her own team to run the new company, or may involve members of the existing team.

The basis of the financial structure of an MBI is the same as for an MBO. The ownership pattern is designed to provide both managers and investors with the prospect of substantial rewards if the new company prospers. As with MBOs, the initiative may have originally come from the vendor company, from the managers or from institutional investors, and once again intermediaries may play a role.

From an investor's point of view, MBIs, like IBOs, tend to carry a higher risk than MBOs. In the latter, the managers already know the company, and understand – or ought to understand – both the problems and the potential for growth. A buy-in, on the other hand, may have appeared to be an excellent opportunity, but the manager moving in can find 'skeletons in the cupboard'. Some MBIs (and also some MBOs) may represent a 'turn-round' situation, where the business requires radical change. In these cases the investors will require special qualities in the management teams they back. Experienced venture capitalists make it their business to get to know individuals who are able to bring about change successfully.

Growth capital, development capital

MBOs, IBOs and MBIs are uses of venture capital that result in the restructuring of a company's ownership and management structure. Arguably, however, the most important use of private equity in funding unquoted companies is simply to enable them to grow substantially under the same management. Most business growth tends to be financed by debt, but there are situations where the extent of the proposed growth, or the risks involved, means that the banks are unwilling to provide finance on the required scale. An injection of equity capital is the key. This strengthens the business and can make it much easier to approach lenders to supply the remainder of the cash needed. This type of venture capital is usually known as 'growth capital' or 'development capital'.

In planning substantial growth, a company that is quoted on the stock market can turn to the market for further equity, and sometimes an unquoted company with ambitious growth plans may decide that this is the time to float on the stock market. However, various funding instruments, described in more detail below, are available from venture capitalist investors, which provide alternatives to flotation or to total reliance on debt.

It is important for the shareholders of a business to find an investor whose ambitions are in line with their own. The 'exit' question, once again, is important. The shareholders may have their eye on an eventual flotation, or trade sale of the business, and bringing in a venture capital investor as a minority shareholder can be an effective first step. It is vital, however, that all interested parties are clear about their exit strategy. It may be that the management wish to continue as an independent company, and there would have to be a meeting of minds on this at the outset. Also, before investing growth capital in a business, venture capitalists will consider the quality of management, as in the case of MBOs and MBIs. Often they can help by suggesting names of individuals, who could be brought in to strengthen the management team if it has any gaps. Growth capital provided in this way has enabled many small and medium-sized businesses to grow larger and stronger, for instance, by investment in a new plant, by moving into new markets, by developing new products, or through the acquisition of other businesses.

Share purchases

Another venture capital 'product' is the share purchase (see FINANCIAL ACCOUNTING). This simply means that a venture capital investor acquires shares from an existing shareholder in a private company. It is an arrangement that can resolve various situations as if the company were quoted – where the shareholder could dispose of the shares on the stock market.

A common situation is where a shareholder wishes to retire and the other shareholders do not wish, or cannot afford, to acquire the shares. The fact that the shares pass into the hands of an independent organization may be more acceptable than if they were acquired by another individual or company.

Share purchases can also be used to enable shareholders to realize a part of their holdings for cash. This can be useful, for instance, in the case of entrepreneurial business that have grown from small beginnings to become successful companies. The owners decide that it is time for some of the value of the business to be realized, but they do not want to sell the whole company or to float it. A share purchase by a venture capital investor is a convenient means of selling a proportion of the shares.

2 Venture capital instruments

Every venture capital transaction is individually structured to meet the particular circumstances. The capital structure must reflect the risks involved and the need to provide appropriate incentives to all those involved. Much will also depend on the nature of the business. For instance, if it is a cash-generative business it is easier to use instruments that depend on the regular payment of interest. In most cases the emphasis will be on capital growth. Investors are probably looking for their return in a mix of dividend payments, interest payments and capital gains, with an emphasis on the last of these three. The basic elements in any venture capital package include the following.

Equity capital

The sharing of the ownership of a business is normally the key negotiation between shareholders, venture capitalists or otherwise. In many situations, particularly early-stage, technology companies, it is the means by which the venture capital investor will seek to achieve all their return on the investment. This may be at the time of flotation (or in the market subsequently) or, more usually, when the business is sold.

Equity capital, apart from providing permanent funds for the business, is often the key to raising other forms of finance. The equity provided by a venture capital company usually takes the form of a separate class of ordinary shares with specific rights to dividends, which are written into the agreement.

Dividends may be 'fixed' or 'participating'. A fixed dividend is normally expressed as a percentage of the amount divested. A participating dividend is expressed as an agreed percentage of pre-tax profits. Sometimes, the arrangement is that the larger of these two amounts is payable. The agreement will normally contain a definition of what is meant by profits, including stipulations to ensure that profits are not unfairly distributed in the form of extra emoluments to directors (see DIVIDEND POLICY).

Preference shares

These are shares that help to strengthen the capital base of the company, but do not participate in capital growth. They are commonly redeemable at a fixed price over an agreed period, say five to ten years, and have a right to a fixed dividend. Occasionally the agreement may be that some or all of the preference shares are convertible into ordinary shares in specific circumstances, for example flotation, to provide a further attraction to the investor in taking on the risk involved. Preference shares are therefore part of the shareholders' funds in a business but, unlike equity capital, do not form part of the permanent capital.

Loan capital

Loans can also form part of a venture capital package. They will generally be medium or long-term loans secured on the fixed assets and/or current assets of the business, normally with prior security being given to the company's bankers. Term loans may be matched to the life of a particular project. The period of each loan, the interest rates and schedules of repayment, would be negotiated along with the other details of the financial package.

Interest rates may be fixed or variable. Fixed rates can be particularly useful in situations where it is important to budget cash flow accurately. They are obviously also desirable if it is predictable that interest rates will rise over the period involved. Variable rates may be preferable if rates are currently high but expected to fall. There are various devices, such as 'caps' (maximum rates) and 'collars' (a range of interest rates to limit exposure and manage costs in highly geared businesses).

Mezzanine finance

Mezzanine, as the name implies, can be seen as lying somewhere between equity capital and loan capital. It combines an unsecured loan with some of the risk and reward elements of equity. It is used, usually in very large buy-outs and buy-ins, where the sums required to be raised cannot be fully met by equity and bank lending.

A mezzanine loan carries interest, usually at a variable rate three to four points above the base rate, and the interest rate composure is often limited by 'cap' or 'swap' (exchanging a fixed rate for a variable rate or vice versa) arrangements. The equity element in mezzanine usually consists of 'warrants' that allow the lender to subscribe for ordinary shares, normally when the business is sold or floated.

3 Conclusion

Venture capital can play a significant role in creating a dynamic and entrepreneurial business environment. It is a well-established part of the financial industry in the USA, the UK, and increasingly in continental Europe and elsewhere. Through the provision of risk capital alongside debt from banks and other sources, venture capital allows entrepreneurial managers with limited financial resources to start, to grow and to acquire businesses. It is the managerial skills and enterprise of the executive management, together with the financial resources and experience of the venture capital backers, which can combine to make a successful business venture and to create wealth for all the shareholders.

CHARLES RICHARDSON
DIRECTOR OF CORPORATE AFFAIRS, 3i,
LONDON

Further reading

Coopey, R. and Clarke, D. (1995) *3i: Fifty Years Investing in Industry,* Oxford: Oxford University Press. (Traces the history of 3i, Europe's leading venture capital company, and presents an inside view of the workings of this institution.)

The Guide to Venture Capital in Asia, Hong Kong, Asian Venture Capital Journal. Published annually. (Details providers of venture capital in Asia/Pacific region.)

Hay, M. and Peeters, J. (1999) *Venture Capital Handbook: Strategies for Successful Private Equity Investment,* London: Pitman. (Advises on the strategies and tools required to operate successfully in the venture capital market. Each section is illustrated with real-life case studies.)

O'Brien, V. (ed) (1995) *Buy-Outs*, London: Euromoney Publications. (A guide to all the processes involved in a successful MBO. It features practical advice from the experts on larger MBOs, buy-ins, structuring the transaction and life after the buy-out. Leading practitioners have contributed to this book which is not only a guide to undertaking a buy-out, but also to how to approach the new beginning by balancing the demands of backers, suppliers, customers and employees.)

Pratt's Guide to Venture Capital Sources, New York, Venture Economics. Published annually. (Details providers of venture capital in the USA.)

Robbie, K and Wright, Mike. (1996) *Management Buy-ins*, Manchester: Manchester University Press. (Presents the theory, development and characteristics of management buy-ins (MBIs). The authors draw from the Centre for Management Buy-out Research to trace the development of MBIs to compare and contrast the two main buy-out forms. The results of an extensive questionnaire survey of buy-ins are analysed and case study results compared. The book also draws on surveys of the appraisal processes and return criteria of venture capital firms and their attitudes to second-time entrepreneurs as well as the interviews with second-time and serial entrepreneurs.)

Venture Capital Report Directory 2000: Private Equity and Venture Capital in the UK and Europe, London: Pearson Educational. Published annually. (Details providers of private equity and venture capital in UK and Europe.)

See also: ACCOUNTING; BANKING; BANKING IN THE UNITED STATES OF AMERICA; E-COMMERCE; ENTREPRENEURSHIP; FINANCIAL ACCOUNTING; INNOVATION AND CHANGE; SMALL BUSINESS FINANCE

Vickers, Sir Geoffrey (1894–1982)

1 Biographical data
2 Main contribution
3 Conclusions

Personal background

- born 13 October 1894 in Nottingham, England
- served in First World War; awarded the Victoria Cross for exceptional gallantry
- graduated in Classics from Oxford University (1921)
- qualified as solicitor 1923; joined legal practice Slaughter & May (1926)
- in Second World War, became Deputy Director-General of the Ministry of Economic Warfare in charge of economic intelligence, for which work he was knighted in 1946
- returned to legal practice (1945)
- joined the National Coal Board as Legal Adviser (1947)
- became Director of manpower, training, education, health and welfare at the National Coal Board (1948)
- set up the Research Committee of the Mental Health Research Fund and was its chairman from 1951 to 1967
- was member of the London Passenger Transport Board (1941–46), the Council of the Law Society (1944–48) and the Medical Research Council (1952–60); also appointed to the Royal Commission on the Press (1947–49) and the Committee of Enquiry into the Cost of the National Health Service (1956)
- left the National Coal Board (1955)
- spent rest of his life mainly lecturing and writing on effective societal governance
- died 16 March 1982 at Goring-on-Thames, England

Major works

The Art of Judgment (1965)

Towards a Sociology of Management (1967)
Value Systems and Social Process (1968)
Freedom in a Rocking Boat: Changing Values in an Unstable Society (1970)
Human Systems are Different (1983)

Summary

Sir Geoffrey Vickers was the doer/ thinker par excellence. His careers embraced the Army, the legal profession, public administration, public health, the world of business and the field of mental health research. To each, he brought formidable intellectual power, undivided attention and profound understanding of human behaviour. Then, when just over 60, he retired from the world of action to reflect on, and write about, what his experience had taught him and his views for effective organizational governance.

Vickers' contribution to systemic thinking, which flows into better management decision making, was his concept of the 'appreciative system', the element of *judgement*, unique to human systems, which enters into the decision-making process. His basic tenet was that every human decision has an appreciative content rooted in one's culture which influences that decision. The meaning we give an action in fact determines how we assess it. This meaning is affected by our history which informs our culture, both sources of moral and political standards. Systemic thinking is based on the *interdependence* of the parts making the whole. Interdependence liberates as well as constrains. The notion of the autonomous individual is unrealistic, 'man-in-society' being the indivisible reality; and dangerous, our Western culture of individual independence blinding us to our responsibilities to others.

We should accept our factual interdependence and understand the contribution of history and culture to the decision-making process. In so doing, we evolve the more inclusive approach that leads to the more comprehensive and wiser decision and thus to more effective management and governance.

I Biographical data

Born on 13 October 1894, Geoffrey Vickers was brought up in a Victorian England at the height of its powers, in an environment of freedom and order, all of which gave him a strong sense of identity and stability. He had a very happy childhood. His father, a man of wide interests and large enthusiasms, instilled in him a love of nature, of learning and language. At 12, he was sent to Oundle, a typical English public school which conditioned him in many ways but could not change his inner sense of classlessness.

When Britain entered the war against Germany in August 1914, Vickers enlisted immediately. He showed exceptional gallantry in battle for which he was awarded the Victoria Cross and later the Croix de Guerre.

After the War, Vickers returned to Oxford and in 1921 took a degree in Classics. In 1923, he qualified as a solicitor. In 1926, by then an accomplished lawyer, he became a partner in the London legal practice of Slaughter & May. He specialized in international commercial law and was involved, in the 1930s, in the re-scheduling of the German debt. A highly successful lawyer, he enjoyed 'the comfortable, even pampered life of the self-employed professional who need not talk to anyone not willing to pay for the privilege', as he later described it.

The events in Munich in 1938 made him politically conscious. He started 'The Association for Service and Reconstruction' through which he got to know many eminent academics, in the physical and social sciences, who influenced his burgeoning ideas on society and politics.

In the Second World War Vickers re-enlisted immediately. Promoted colonel, he was seconded to the Ministry of Economic Warfare, as Deputy Director-General in charge of economic intelligence, for which work he was knighted in 1946.

At the end of the war, Vickers returned to his legal practice. In 1947, he was invited to join the National Coal Board (NCB) as Legal Adviser. He enthusiastically accepted the challenge, despite the loss of status and income involved. In 1948, he became directly involved in management, when appointed director for manpower, education, training, health and welfare, responsible for some 750,000 men – quite an undertaking, given the entrenched adversarial relations between the miners and their managers. His transition from being an international corporate lawyer to working in a nationalized industry was not easy. He reflected later that he felt more at home with the trade unionists than with his fellow directors, but he learnt a great deal at the NCB about motivation, industrial relations and the problems of operating a nationalized industry.

During his time there, his wife's ill health brought him into contact with psychiatrists which led him to study psychology, for him a new field of knowledge. He founded in 1951 the Research Committee of the Mental Health Research Fund, with scientists from various disciplines, which he chaired and kept going until 1967. It was the cognitive psychology he learnt here that enriched his systems thinking concepts and provided the foundation of the appreciative system he made his own in later years.

His other public appointments – to the London Transport Passenger Board, the Law Council, the Medical Research Council, the Royal Commission on the Press, the Committee of Enquiry into the Cost of the National Health Service – give an inkling of how much in demand he was and how much knowledge came his way as a result.

Important for Vickers, in the late 1940s, was discovering systems ideas, through the work of Norbert Wiener, Ludwig von Bertalanffy and Ross Ashby (see VON BERTALANFFY, L.; WIENER, N.). Systemic thinking somehow liberated him, confirmed his own insights. It gave him a way of looking at a situation within the wider picture into which he could better fit its components and also see it in the context of its connections – of great help to him, as a manager, in his efforts to change the conflictual relationship dividing miners and managers into a cooperative one of joint effort and endeavour.

Systems ideas also gave him a new language with which to better understand and explain his diverse experiences – intellectually very exhilarating and inducing in him the urge to learn more about the discipline. In 1955, just over 60 years of age, Vickers decided to retire from the business arena, 'to contribute to what I believed to be a revolution in human thinking which had been reaching and exciting me for the previous ten years', as he reminisced to Bayard Catron in his letter of 19 January 1981.

The Director of the School of Social Work at the University of Toronto in Canada immediately snapped him up for three terms. This gave Vickers the academic time and space to work through, and formalize, his ideas. His address in 1956 to the School on 'Values and Decision-Making', showing how both individual and societal values shape the goals we set up, already presaged the comprehensiveness of his thought that joined aesthetic and ethical norms with calculable analyses – integration of tangible and intangible factors, the fundamental of all his later writings (see DECISION MAKING; ORGANIZATION BEHAVIOUR, HISTORY OF).

Systems thinking was the linchpin that fixed his ideas into a coherent framework, the tool of understanding that set him on a most exciting and productive intellectual voyage. Between 1955 and 1982, he wrote nine books and published 87 papers. His books – *inter alia The Art of Judgment* (1965), *Freedom in a Rocking Boat: Changing Values in an Unstable Society* (1970), *Human Systems are Different* (1983) – show the constancy of his interests and concerns. The diverse range of his papers can be gleaned from the publications in which they appeared – *Acta Psychologica*, the European Journal for Psychology, *The Lancet*, the British medical journal, *Futures*, the futurology publication, *Organizational Dynamics*, *Human Relations* and *Policy Sciences* – to name but a few.

Vickers was much in demand in universities in the United States and made many friends there. In planning a Festschrift, their spokesman wrote to him in January 1981 'we want to acknowledge more than the power of your intellect. The character of the man, his warm and gentle humanity, his indomitable curiosity, and zest for life – these have touched us. . . . Having known you as a person

as well as author, we understand ourselves and our culture better.' No other words could have touched Vickers more.

In the UK, Vickers had been ignored, in the 1960s, by an academic community hidebound in its separate specialisms. But, in the 1970s, the growth of Systems Departments in the newer universities brought him admirers and followers. The Systems Groups of the University of Lancaster and of the Open University held him in high esteem. The latter invited Vickers as a regular speaker to its annual Summer School, commissioned a book which became *Human Systems are Different*, and edited, in 1984, in tribute, *The Vickers Papers*, a collection of his articles.

Vickers' wife had died in 1972. Unable to cope any longer on his own, he moved in 1977 to a residential home for the elderly. There, he spent his last years: serene and busy years during which he continued to write, receive visitors from home and overseas and, as always, carry on his extensive correspondence with friends, old and new.

2 Main contribution

Vickers was among the first, in the management field, to adopt and apply the concept of systems theory (see SYSTEMS). He used systemic thinking to analyse situations, in their complex richness, in their internal and external relations, to better understand their workings, their reciprocal interactions and underlying commonalities.

The other systemic protagonists eschewed this inclusive approach. To acquire academic respectability, they followed the quantitative methods of the physical sciences, excluding all elements that were not measurable and treating all systems – natural, man-made and human – as identical.

Vickers fought long and hard against their reductionism. For him, human systems had the extra element of judgement. Each human system is a network of relations which reflects its historical past and culture. It develops its own ways of looking at the world, its own values and standards. This is its appreciative framework which substantially influences its decision making. It is unique to the human system which cannot therefore be subsumed with the others.

In the *Art of Judgment* (1965) Vickers showed that a judgement consists of three reciprocally interactive strands:

- a 'reality' judgement – (deciding what is) covering the whole range of factors from direct cause-and-effect facts to tacit beliefs;
- a 'value' assessment – (what might, or could or should be) taking into account self-interest, moral constraints, individual and collective set goals; and
- the instrumental means – (how do we get there?) of getting from 'what is' to 'what could or should be', within the available resources.

What facts we select out of all those in a situation, the meaning we give them, the means we use to reduce the mismatch between existing and desired situations – all this flows from our appreciative system. It is not to be disregarded because, partly tacit, it cannot be easily measured. We are culture-bound creatures. To ignore the effect of culture in the decision-making process is to disregard one of its essential components and thus arrive at the truncated and perforce inadequate solution. It is essential to understand how our belief systems affect our decisions, the better to make them for long-term effective performance.

In addition to culture, Vickers emphasized the fact of our interdependence. The basic unit of society is the interdependent 'man-in-society', not the independent, autonomous individual conceived by Western culture since the Enlightenment. Interdependence highlighted the double-sided coin of rights and responsibilities. To be a member of a healthy community involved fulfilling responsibilities as well as demanding rights.

Vickers always saw everything in terms of processes and reciprocal interactions. In *Value Systems and Social Process* (1968), Vickers was concerned about the effect of rapid technological advance on our social systems. In *Freedom in a Rocking Boat* (1970), it was the threat to stable relations between human society and its ecological milieu that worried him. Underlying our multicultural di-

versity, we had to build a basic cultural consensus, to be able to agree on common action both in our social groupings and in relation to our environment – a difficult task but an urgent necessity.

3 Conclusions

Vickers' ideas were grounded in practical experience acquired through an unusually wide range of activities and backed by studies in both the physical and social sciences. Integrating theory and practice, his teaching has a breadth and depth of vision which startle by a foresight, which is in many instances, prophetic. In 1957, when the prevailing wisdom was that a health service was a self-limiting one, with little to do once the demands of health were fully met, Vickers was already warning of the effects of technology on expectations and of the conflict to arise between an ever-increasing demand and the inability to meet it – a situation all the more intractable today, for having been ignored for so long.

Vickers' appreciative system concept was very much ahead of the times in the mid-1960s. Today, we recognize to some extent the incidence of culture in the decision-making process; here and there, 'soft' systems methodologies are complementing the 'hard' ones in place. But the full significance of the concept has yet to be realized. It is of primordial relevance to managers who, working in the multinational company or the global organization, must understand the value systems of those in their teams to better communicate with them. Failure to do so invariably leads to the weak, ineffective solution and therefore to unsatisfactory results.

Vickers' insistence on the need for some shared or compatible cultural values is similarly of basic importance to managers. Through reciprocal interchange, multiculturalism enriches its constituent cultures but these have to be underpinned by a basic commonality of norms to provide consensus and the will for joint action. It is of the essence of leadership, whilst respecting and indeed welcoming diversity, to bring to the fore those values which join us in our common humanity, to build the team spirit for effective and satisfying performance.

Yet another strand of Vickers' philosophy, that of interdependence, directly applies to managers. Steeped in the Western culture of individual independence, especially prevalent in the appreciative systems of those in authority, interdependence is felt as weakness. The command/obedience syndrome still lingers in the managerial consciousness. Managers need to absorb and act upon the irreducible fact of their interdependence with their followers. Leadership is not always with the manager; it is sometimes with the follower, the expert in that particular situation who knows what to do. The need between managers and their followers is reciprocal. It is that interdependence between *all* the members of the group which regulates their relationships, builds mutual knowledge and understanding and creates the initiative and enterprise that takes the group forward.

Vickers' teaching is not of course of value to managers only. It is of universal application and increasingly relevant in our fast-changing and pluralistic world. Understanding our diversity, developing a common culture to underlie it, recognizing our interdependence with each other as well as with our environment: these are the directions Vickers gives us to evolve the scientific art of human governance.

PAULINE GRAHAM
LONDON

Further reading

(References cited in the text marked *)

Blunden, M. (ed.) (1994) 'Rethinking public policy-making, questioning assumptions, challenging beliefs', *American Behavioral Scientist* 38, September–October. (Essays in honour of Sir Geoffrey Vickers on his centenary.)

Open Systems Group (eds) (1984) *The Vickers Papers*, London: Harper & Row. (A wide selection of his articles, in four parts, with an essay on 'Geoffrey Vickers – an intellectual journey' by Margaret Blunden and a bibliography of his books and articles.)

* Vickers, G. (1965) *The Art of Judgment*, London: Chapman & Hall. (His seminal book, where he sets out his concept of the 'appreciative system'.)

* Vickers. G. (1967) *Towards a Sociology of Management*, New York: Basic Books. (On the basis that business is a social activity and management a form of social control.)

* Vickers, G. (1968) *Value Systems and Social Process*, New York: Basic Books. (His 1954–66 articles on the impact of technological change on social systems.)

* Vickers, G. (1970) *Freedom in a Rocking Boat: Changing Values in an Unstable Society*, New York: Basic Books. (Reflects his concern on the relations between human systems and their ecological milieu.)

Vickers, G. (1973) *Making Institutions Work*, New York: John Wiley. (To this end, we have to reduce our expectations from, and demands on, them.)

* Vickers, G. (1983) *Human Systems are Different*, London: Harper & Row. (A review why human systems are different from natural and man-made systems.)

Vickers, G. (1995) *The Art of Judgment*, Centenary Edition, Thousand Oaks, CA: Sage Publications, Inc. (With Foreword by G.B. Adams, B.L.Catron and Scott D.N. Cook; and 'The life of Sir Geoffrey Vickers' by Margaret Blunden.)

Vickers, J. (ed.) (1991) *Rethinking the Future: The Correspondence between Geoffrey Vickers and Adolph Lowe*, New Brunswick, NJ: Transaction. (The lifelong correspondence between Vickers and his friend, Adolph Lowe.)

See also: DECISION MAKING; GENERAL MANAGEMENT; ORGANIZATION BEHAVIOUR; ORGANIZATION BEHAVIOUR, HISTORY OF; ORGANIZATION CULTURE; SYSTEMS; VON BERTALANFFY, L.; WIENER; N.

Vietnam, management in

Overview

Management in Vietnam must be seen against the background of the country's history as a French colony, the war of independence and US intervention, as well as the context of an underdeveloped socialist economy. The former command economy modelled on Soviet lines has now been mitigated by economic reform and an 'Open Door' policy, similar to but on a much smaller scale than its Chinese neighbour. The level of wealth per capita is one of the lowest in Asia Pacific, although a more hospitable climate for foreign capital has made the country a destination for inward investment in the early and mid-1990s. More recently, however, Vietnam has been affected by the wider financial crisis in Asia, and by consequent declining investment flows and unemployment.

1 Introduction

Vietnam as a nation was largely a creation of the French colonial authorities in the late nineteenth century. The old kingdoms of Tonkin, Annam and Cochin were welded together under a single administration. Even today, substantial cultural differences exist between these three areas, and there are a number of other ethnic minorities as well, including a Chinese community which numbers about 3 per cent of the population. The principal religion is Buddhism, but there are minority religious groups including Christians and the twentieth-century indigenous faith of Cao Dai. Plurality and diversity, therefore, are part of the Vietnamese cultural heritage.

French colonialism created the infrastructure of economic development in Vietnam. It provided capital for the development of plantations, mines, light manufacturing and services. The French bosses ruled their workforces with an iron hand, and exploitation was rampant. The result was the rise of a revolutionary labour movement, which by the 1920s was being strongly influenced by Marxist-Leninism.

During the Second World War Vietnam was occupied by the Japanese, and the revolutionary leaders fought a low-key guerrilla war against the occupiers until the end of the war. After the Japanese surrender the guerrillas turned their attention to the French, who were seeking to re-establish their colonial authority. Now under the leadership of the charismatic Ho Chi Minh, who combined Vietnamese nationalism with MarxistLeninism, the rebels declared independence in September 1945, announcing the foundation of the Democratic Republic of Vietnam. Nine years of struggle against the French ended with military victory at Dien Bien Phu in 1954. The country was partitioned into two states, the north headed by Ho and the south headed by a succession of military and civilian leaders propped up by the USA.

During the late 1950s, with some Soviet aid, North Vietnam was able to undertake some improvements to its economy, developing its manufacturing industries and infrastructure. South Vietnam, similarly aided by the USA, also experienced prosperity. By the middle of the 1960s, however, the conflict between the two states had increased in scale and US military support for the South was increasing. The ensuing war saw widespread devastation of much of both North and South, and as many as a million Vietnamese were killed. Even the end of the war, with the American evacuation and the unification of Vietnam in 1975, did not bring peace; Vietnamese troops entered Cambodia to help overthrow the Khmer Rouge, and then fought a bloody border war with China. It was not until the middle of the 1980s that Vietnam was able to take its economy off a war footing.

Economic planning throughout this period had been fragmentary. The first five-year plan (1961–5) had seen some successes, but most of these had been wiped out in the war. The second and third five-year plans (1976–80, 1981–5) attempted to do too much too soon, setting ambitious targets which could not be met and, in some cases, worsening economic problems. Production stagnated and hyperinflation set in.

2 Economy and management since reunification

In 1986 the government of Vietnam, observing the increasing success of economic reforms in nearby China (see CHINA, MANAGEMENT IN), instituted its own reform policy with the aim of attracting foreign investment. The Sixth National Congress of the Vietnamese Communist Party announced the policy of *doi moi*, which broadly speaking means 'renovation' or 'rebirth', but has increasingly come to mean the wholesale regeneration of Vietnam's economy and management (Robinson 1995: 12). Further liberalization policies were announced by the Seventh National Congress in 1991. The 1987 Foreign Investment Law allowed foreign companies to invest in Vietnamese enterprises, and a succession of further legislation laid down a rudimentary framework for private enterprise. *Doi moi* initially proved to be highly successful. In the late 1980s and early 1990s, Vietnam came to be seen by Western investors as a rising star, even a potential recruit to the ranks of the tiger economies. Like its neighbour China, it has become a node for growth, although it lacks China's huge natural resources and labour surplus.

The population of Vietnam is nearing 80 million people. The greater majority still live in rural communities, although during the 1990s there has been a steady stream of migrants to the urban areas of the Red River and Mekong deltas. Gross national product (GNP) is growing rapidly; in 1994 the figure stood at $83.5 billion, and GNP increased by around 7–9 per cent annually from then until 1998.

The most rapid growth has been in industrial sectors, which have more than doubled their output since 1990, and in services; by 1995 manufacturing and services had overtaken agriculture as the highest-value sectors in the economy, though agriculture still accounts for the highest share of employment. In 1997, the last year before the Asian crisis began to bite, agricultural output grew by 4.8 per cent, while industrial output grew by 13 per cent. Inflation fell steadily over the same period, from over 60 per cent in 1990 to under 15 per cent by the end of the decade.

Vietnam's population is increasingly rapidly, and is expected to double before it finally stabilizes in the middle of the twenty-first century. The workforce is large, mostly young, mostly well-educated (literacy rates in Vietnam are over 90 per cent except in some border and tribal areas) and costs of living are low; average monthly wages range from US$30–$150. These wages are insufficient for most families to survive, and many people work two or more jobs. At the same time, one of the consequences of *doi moi*, compounded by the Asian crisis, has been an increase in unemployment and underemployment. The official national rate of unemployment is around 9 per cent, with the highest rates found in the north around Hanoi, but it is possible that the real rate is higher still. Since the mid-1980s, many state firms have dismissed or laid off workers; it is estimated that state manufacturing industries have downsized 30–40 per cent of their employees in this fashion (Greenfield 1997: 126). There is also a severe problem of underemployment, especially in rural regions, which is having two consequences: first, it is partly responsible for large-scale migration to the cities (which in turn is affecting unemployment) and second, it is creating increasing tension within the countryside itself, where relative poverty is actually increasing in some areas.

Until 1998, Vietnam's exports had been growing at a rate of about 20 per cent annually. Economic reform was responsible for most of this growth, as industries became more efficient. Throughout the 1980s Vietnam had had to import foodstuffs, but as early as 1990 it had become a rice-exporter, and is now one of the leading rice-exporters in the world. There is still a negative balance of trade, but the gap is narrowing, down to just over $2 billion by 1997. Although export earnings are comparatively small ($11 billion in 1997), they have made a significant contribution to the Vietnamese economy. This success is particularly notable given that trade with Vietnam's previous major trading partner, the Soviet Union and its satellites, effectively collapsed in 1991 and the value of exports to the rouble zone plunged sharply.

At the same time, foreign direct investment in Vietnam increased very rapidly in the 1990s as elsewhere in Asia. Especially after the lifting of US economic sanctions in 1995, Vietnam came to be seen as an ideal site for foreign investment, a future star performer. Most investment took the form of joint ventures, often with Vietnamese state companies. Primary sectors for investment were manufacturing and infrastructure. Asian countries provided the bulk of investment, but US, Canadian and Australian firms were also prominent. The Western multinationals tended to focus on the more capital-intensive and technologically sophisticated sectors, while Asian firms tended to enter the more labour-intensive manufacturing sectors. Most of the recent labour problems in Vietnam are centred on the latter firms, as many have moved their factories there to take advantage of the even lower wages that prevail in other parts of Asia where they have already been operating. Authoritarian industrial relations are the order of the day, as these overseas entrepreneurs and managers seek obedient and acquiescent operatives.

3 The Asia crisis and recovery

The Asia crisis of 1997–8 affected Vietnam badly; inward investment dried up, and some Western investors pulled out. Like the rest of the region, Vietnam has begun to recover, but that recovery has been patchy and uneven. Dapice (2000) comments that while some regions are surging ahead with imports growing rapidly, others remain stagnant. Dapice (2000) and Torode (1998) are just two observers who believe that Vietnam needs to liberalize its government and economy still further in order to achieve full recovery but, at the

time of writing, there are few such signs that such liberalization is imminent. Indeed Vietnam, like China, faces problems of unemployment and rural poverty which could be exacerbated if the economy begins to boom again, and at present, the signs are that the government plans to concentrate on rural issues and reform of the agricultural sector. This may deter Western investors still further. However, if Vietnam can manage to show signs of a general economic recovery, inward investment should begin to pick up regardless of political climate.

4 Issues in management

Management in Vietnam remains very much in a state of transition, a state that has to some extent been placed in suspension by the Asian crisis (see above). Vietnam's considerable advantages, in terms of natural resources, a literate and intelligent but low-paid workforce, and a diverse culture with the potential for a very high standard of living, remain. The future envisioned for Vietnam in the early 1990s was of a high-technology centre not unlike Taiwan or Singapore, but vastly larger.

There remain, however, considerable barriers to the reaching of such a goal. First and foremost of these remain the structural problems inherited from previous years. Vietnamese government and management suffered for years under the dual constraints of Soviet-style command and control ideologies (like China, Vietnam has been left with a large and inefficient state sector), and the pressures of fighting a war for survival against powerful enemies such as the USA and China. The present government has recognized the need to scrap the former; the legacy of the latter is proving harder to dispose of. Even modernizers in Vietnam evince an (understandable) distrust of the West and maintain that capitalism should not be allowed to flourish unfettered. Put another way, after almost a century of domination by foreign powers, the Vietnamese are reluctant to surrender control of their own destiny once more.

The opposite side of this particular coin, however, is that foreign investors are finding the investment climate in Vietnam increasingly less to their taste. According to Lamb

(1998), no US company has so far made a profit in Vietnam. The currency, the *dong*, is not convertible and is not likely to be in the near future. Problems of restrictive bureaucracy, corruption and an inability to repatriate profits are turning investors off. This has further repercussions, as Vietnam is still only part way through the process of modernizing its economy and urgently needs technology and investment for its agriculture, manufacturing and infrastructure sectors, and also to develop potentially lucrative new sectors such as tourism. That investment can only come from overseas.

Modernization is further hampered by poor provision and quality of training at almost every level. Although as noted, the Vietnamese are generally well-educated and literacy is high, specialist technical and managerial training is almost non-existent. There is an urgent need to improve technical and managerial skills. One of the few organizations involved in this field is the Asian Institute of Technology (AIT) in Bangkok, which has established regional centres in Hanoi and Ho Chi Minh City. In a consortium with the Swiss Agency for Development and Reconstruction and the Vietnam Ministry of Education and Training (MOET), AIT has launched the SAV programme, aimed at providing better administrative and managerial skills in Vietnam. A 14-month graduate programme, along with a number of shorter specialist programmes, is on offer. The Vietnam Management Initiative (VMI), backed by McKinsey, represents a pool of Vietnamese MBA graduates offering consulting services, and the efforts of groups such as this should do more to raise the profile of management education in the country.

The shortage of trained staff has a further consequence in the form of job-hopping. Qualified staff remain on fairly low wages, but they have come to expect large bonuses. If they fail to get these from their present employer, they are nearly always able to secure bonuses from other employers eager to recruit them. There is also a great deal of poaching, particularly of Vietnamese who are also graduates and are fluent in a foreign language. Wages in general, as noted, remain low, but there are tight regulations concerning labour contracts, and foreign investors also have to pay benefits and taxes on behalf of employees; it has been estimated that paying a Vietnamese worker a salary of $4,000 incurs the payment of a further $16,000 to the government.

Trade unions are official arms of the reunified state, as in China; they are organized on both industrial and geographical lines. There are 53 recognized trade unions, organized along geographical and sectoral lines. About three million workers belong to the unions, who form part of the Vietnam Federation of Trade Unions. Most state plants are formally heavily unionized, but only one in seven employees of non-state firms are organized. There have been around 150 strikes in Vietnam since 1989, over half of which have been at state companies. Initially strikes tended to be most likely at joint ventures, but recently Vietnamese state and private firms have increasingly been the targets.

One group within the country that could play an important role is the Chinese community. Before unification, the Chinese community of Ho Chi Minh City (then Saigon) provided much of the capital and entrepreneurship in the largely successful South Vietnamese economy. After 1975, tensions and open warfare between Vietnam and China led to many Chinese fleeing overseas or being expelled. Many have now returned, however, and they continue to form an important part of the small capitalist class in Ho Chi Minh City. The experience of other countries in southeast Asia suggests that Chinese entrepreneurship could make a difference in Vietnam, though whether government and people would be prepared to let so visible a minority in their midst take important economic roles is at present an open question.

5 Conclusion

A country with tremendous natural competitive advantages, Vietnam has endured a century of occupation and warfare, and only since the mid-1980s has it been able to focus on its economic needs. *Doi moi*, the policy of opening up to the West, was initially highly successful and attracted huge foreign capital inflows; Vietnamese businesses began to modernize, exports increased, and both GNP and personal prosperity began to rise. The Asian crisis, coupled with the obvious limits to economic liberalization, have, at the time of writing, arrested this development. However, with the Asian situation improving, it is possible that Vietnam will once again become a magnet for foreign investors, especially elsewhere in Asia. A pluralist, diverse society with a tradition of enterprise and education, Vietnam should still be capable of becoming one of the Asian economic stars of the twenty-first century.

MALCOLM WARNER
JUDGE INSTITUTE OF MANAGEMENT STUDIES

MORGEN WITZEL
LONDON BUSINESS SCHOOL

Further reading

(References cited in the text marked *)

* Dapice, D. (2000) 'Point of no return', *Vietnam Business Journey* February, *http://www.viam. com/02-2000/noreturn.htm.* (Highly critical article which casts doubt on Vietnam's ability to recover under its present government.)

Entous, A. (2000) 'Vietnam signs trade deal with America', *Independent* 14 July: 15. (Note on the further opening up of trade relations between Vietnam and the USA, which will have important consequences.)

Fahey, S. (1997) 'Vietnam and the "Third Way": The nature of socio-economic transition', *Journal of Economic and Social Geography* 88(5), 469–80. (A useful scholarly article on Vietnam's economic reform programme.)

Godement, F. (1999) *The Downsizing of Asia*, London: Routledge. (A wider account of the Asian economic crisis revealing its impact on the region.)

* Greenfield, G. (1997) 'Fragmented visions of Asia's next tiger: Vietnam in the twentieth century', in M.T. Bergerer and D.A. Borer (eds), *The Rise of East Asia: Critical Visions of the Pacific Century*, London: Routledge, 124–47. (A critical chapter on Vietnam's potential role as the next tiger economy as an 'elite vision'.)

Griffin, K. (ed.) (1998) *Economic Reform in Vietnam*, New York: St Martin's Press. (Good, sober overview of *doi moi*, its successes and failures, and future prospects.)

Hiebert, M. and Sitzer, J. (1996) *Chasing the Tigers: A Portrait of the New Vietnam*, Tokyo: Kodansha International. (Upbeat account of economic reform in Japan, highly optimistic about Vietnam's long-term future.)

* Lamb, D. (1998) 'Vietnam's open door now exit for investors', *Los Angeles Times*, 25 December. (Journalist's view of the exodus of foreign capital which took place in the immediate aftermath of the Asian crisis.)

Murray, G. (1997) *Vietnam: Dawn of a New Market*, New York: St Martin's Press. (Good overview aimed at the businessman and potential investor; like many of its kind, requires updating in light of the Asian crisis.)

Norlund, I. (1993) 'The creation of a labour market in Vietnam: legal framework and practices', in C.A. Thayer and D.G. Marr (eds), *Vietnam and the Rule of Law*, Canberra: ANU, 173–89. (A specialist account of Vietnam's emerging labour relations and labour law.)

Ralston, D.A., Thang, N.V. and Napier, N.K. (2000) 'A comparative study of the work values of North and South Vietnamese managers', *Journal of International Business Studies* 30(4): 655–72. (Excellent work wich highlights regional differences within Vietnamese business culture.)

* Robinson, J.W. (1995) *Doing Business in Vietnam*, Rocklin, CA: Prima Publishing. (A step-by-step guide to doing business in Vietnam.)

* Torode, G. (1998) 'Vietnam feels sharp pain of modernization', *South China Morning Post*, 31 December. (Newspaper article discussing Vietnam's economic growing pains.)

See also: ACCOUNTING IN THE EMERGING COUNTRIES; ASIA PACIFIC, MANAGEMENT IN; BUSINESS CULTURES, ASIAN PACIFIC; BUSINESS CULTURES, THE EMERGING COUNTRIES; CHINA, MANAGEMENT IN; CONFLICT AND POLITICS; CUBA, MANAGEMENT IN; CULTURE, CROSS-NATIONAL; INDUSTRIAL RELATIONS IN ASIA PACIFIC; INDUSTRIAL RELATIONS IN THE EMERGING COUNTRIES; MANAGEMENT EDUCATION IN ASIA PACIFIC; MANAGEMENT EDUCATION IN THE EMERGING COUNTRIES; RUSSIA, MANAGEMENT IN

Virtual organizing

Overview

The widespread use of computers combined with access to the Internet has created a new communications medium described alternatively as 'cyberspace', 'online' or 'virtual world'. This new medium essentially eliminates time and physical location as constraints on sending and receiving information. So long as a person is connected to a computer network, online activities can be pursued 7 days a week, 24 hours a day regardless of geographic location. This enhanced ability to exchange information introduced by the virtual world makes a range of new organizing options available that directly affect how people live and work.

1 What is 'virtual'?

A conventional way of obtaining information is to arrange for a face-to-face meeting with a person who has it. At an appointed time and place, we meet and gain access to the information. As an alternative to obtaining information in a face-to-face meeting, many people rely on sources accessed by computer. When people source and obtain information in this fashion, they are said to have engaged the virtual world.

By comparing alternative methods for finding a definition of the word 'virtual', one can readily understand how a virtual approach differs from a more traditional method (see VIRTUAL REALITY IN BUSINESS). Obtaining a definition of 'virtual' from a direct source such as a dictionary is an example of a conven-

tional method. The virtual method, in contrast, uses a computer connected to the Internet that is further connected to a website such as *www.dictionary.com*. At this site, 'virtual' is inserted as the word of interest, the 'go' command is pressed, and the computer responds.

This virtual search identified several sources on the Internet with entries defining the term 'virtual'. The American Heritage Dictionary defines the term 'virtual' to mean 'existing in essence though not in actual fact', 'existing in the mind', and 'created by means of a computer or computer network'. Webster's Revised Unabridged Dictionary indicates that 'virtual', means 'having invisible efficacy'. The Jargon File website and the Free On-Line Dictionary of Computing each define 'virtual' as the opposite of 'real' and 'physical'.

While these entries offer definitions of 'virtual', they do not quite define the term as it is used in the phrase, 'virtual organizing'. On the other hand, the search process does illustrate how interconnected computers usually respond to a query by offering several possibilities. As a user, one must then decide which of the possibilities is relevant. In the present context, to say something is 'virtual' is to indicate that people do things by employing computers rather than by using conventional methods. 'Virtual organizing' is a process that relies on interconnected computers to initiate, monitor or otherwise carry out information-related tasks such as requesting information, sharing ideas or coordinating activities. A 'virtual organization' refers to a group with an identifiable presence whose members use interconnected computers to communicate with one another or to carry out information-related tasks (Jackson and van der Wielen 1998) (see ORGANIZATION BEHAVIOUR).

People may employ virtual instead of conventional methods because of their convenience, efficiency or the increased range of alternatives that they often provide. The vir-

Alternative time–space worlds

	Real	Virtual
Working alone	A person looks up a word in a dictionary	A person searches many online sources
Interacting with others	A group gets information and exchanges ideas with one another	Unlimited numbers of people do many things with many others

Figure 1 Alternatives and participation possibilities expand as people organize virtually

tual world also enables people at geographically dispersed locations to directly interact with others who they may never meet in person. The left-hand side of Figure 1 presents examples of people who undertake information-related tasks by employing conventional methods. It highlights how conventional methods implicitly limit the number of participants and the number of alternatives explored. The examples on the right-hand side of Figure 1 highlight how, by entering the virtual world, the number of participants and the possibilities that may be explored are potentially limitless. In general, a virtual approach provides opportunities to increase participation and increase the number of alternatives considered.

2 The online medium/virtual world

In the virtual world, it is an interconnected computer network that enables the transfer of information (see INFORMATION TECHNOLOGY). As any computer on the network can both send and receive information, the virtual world is an interactive medium where the scale and pace of information exchange and the number of online relationships are essentially unlimited. Within a network, targeted computers receive communiqués almost immediately after they are sent. If desired, these communications can be stored in the computer's memory and retrieved for viewing at a later time. By enabling instantaneous and asynchronous communication, the virtual world minimizes time as a barrier to communication.

While the content of virtual communication was initially limited to text, advances in technology have enabled the inclusion of graphics and, to an increasing extent, voice and video. This combination of technologies makes it possible to deliver very large amounts of precise information. As a result, the volume of available information becomes a potential issue. Most people do not feel overwhelmed, however, because they can actively control the amount of information they send and receive. They can restrict themselves to exchanging e-mail with close associates, for example. They can connect to the Internet, enter websites they select, and participate in only those interactive discussions that are of interest to them. Senders and receivers are also able to maintain independent records of their interaction. While the volume of information that is available on the Internet is huge, people who use the technology can remain in control (see INFORMATION AND KNOWLEDGE INDUSTRY).

Much of the information available online comes from anonymous sources. The anonymity inherent in the virtual world makes online interaction different from face-to-face interaction in significant ways. In face-to-face communication, for example, a person's title, position or perceived power can inhibit participation, distort meaning or otherwise interfere with effective communication. In the virtual world this type of information is not included, and thus cannot affect communication. A further consequence is that people often say they have greater freedom to express themselves (Sproull and Kiesler 1991).

Many people accept the speed and convenience of the virtual world and take full advantage of its benefits even though they may know little about where the information they receive comes from or the purpose for which it was sent. To see how this can lead to problems, imagine receiving an e-mail message from a friend with the title: 'ILOVEYOU'. The literal meaning is clear. In May 2000, however, an e-mail labelled in this way was in actuality a computer virus that had originated in the Philippines. Until the destructive nature of the virus was identified and publicized, people didn't know the 'ILOVEYOU' e-mail was not the nice greeting from a friend that it appeared to be. Many people opened their e-mail because they expected the content to coincide with their understanding of the phrase 'ILOVEYOU'. Press reports estimate that within hours of its launch, the virus travelled around the world several times. While it is impossible to accurately assess the cost, the news media estimated that the virus affected millions of computers worldwide and that the damage totalled billions of dollars.

3 Forming virtual organizations

The virtual world has millions of websites designed to serve different interests. People can connect to a particular website and focus their attention on those aspects that are of interest to them (Figallo 1998). Even if a person frequently connects to the same Internet site but never interacts with other frequent visitors to that site, it is assumed that at some level, they share a common interest. Depending upon the frequency of their visits, this group of individuals can, in effect, constitute a virtual organization.

A virtual organization depends on interconnected computers and a shared interest or purpose. The use of a website is an option but not a requirement. An extended family or a project team, for example, can still be identified as a virtual organization if their members rely on frequent e-mail exchanges to pursue their mutual interests. Nevertheless, many virtual organizations have their own website in order to identify themselves more clearly, and to facilitate communication through an established Internet address. As access to a website is generally not restricted, membership in an associated virtual organization is typically open to anyone who wants to participate.

Visitors who regularly connect to the *Financial Times* website, for example, are in-

dividuals who have many different interests. Nevertheless, as they are all repeat visitors to this website, it can be assumed they at least share an interest in the news as it is reported and presented by the Financial Times. Even if none of the visitors directly interact with one another, their repeated connections to the Financial Times website itself are sufficient to identify them as members of the Financial Times' online virtual organization. In order to encourage new members, the boundaries to virtual organizations are largely left open. While many sites include a short registration process, most often there are no other barriers to entry.

The primary purpose of a website is to attract an identifiable audience of repeat visitors to a central address. Currently, there seem to be three broad strategies in use. Regardless of the specific strategy employed, a website's effectiveness is typically measured by the number of visitors that connect to the site, the duration of each visit, the number of transactions completed and other quantitative measures of activity (e.g. see Kotha 2000).

The following section identifies each of the three basic strategies and explains how each supports different types of virtual communication and facilitates the development of different types of virtual organizations.

4 Website strategies for virtual organizing

Focused channel strategies

Some websites focus on the interaction that takes place between the site and each individual visitor. These sites generally restrict interaction so visitors cannot communicate directly with each other. Information made available to visitors explains the purpose of the site and lists the transactions that can be completed. If it is a commercial enterprise, the site is also likely to include information about the sponsor's products or services and how to obtain them.

Businesses, public and non-profit organizations all sponsor websites that use focused channel strategies (see E-BUSINESS; E-COMMERCE). Generally, the intention is to provide a virtual mechanism as an addition to or a replacement for face-to-face communication. A commercial bank, for instance, may employ staff to assist customers to complete a range of transactions and also support a website that may enable many of the same transactions. Business to consumer (B2C) sites also use focused channel strategies. One can buy books online instead of at a conventional bookstore, or buy airline tickets online rather than in person from a travel agent. Further, government agencies and non-profit organizations use focused channel strategies. In most cases, individual visitors can ask questions, request documents, or complete similar transactions. Business-to-business (B2B) sites also use focused channel strategies.

As the number of visits to a site and the number of transactions that take place on a site increase, significant benefits can accrue to sponsors and visitors alike. As the number of transactions increases, for example, due to economies of scale, the incremental cost to the sponsor of each additional transaction is reduced. As sponsors monitor and discover the behaviour patterns of site visitors, they are frequently able to identify ways in which they can increase the range and quality of the services that they offer. As the number of options offered on a site expands, transactions often become more efficient and convenient. Interaction of this type between sponsors and site visitors ultimately leads to an increasingly sophisticated virtual organization.

When compared to conventional approaches, however, virtual approaches can still seem relatively strange and people may hesitate to use them. To overcome a visitor's hesitancy, website sponsors often use language and symbols to evoke parallels with conventional methods and real world experience. Internet sites may describe themselves, for example, as stores or shops and list their different departments. They may suggest to customers that they can place the items they wish to purchase in a shopping cart by clicking on an appropriate icon. At the end of a visit, they may ask them to click on an icon that will take them to a checkout counter or cashier. By using language that evokes conventional experience, site sponsors try to make virtual contexts seem familiar. If visitors accept the

analogy, their confidence increases and they may use websites more frequently.

Wide channel strategies

Websites that employ wide channel strategies focus on providing visitors with the opportunity and the means to communicate directly with the site and also with anyone else who visits the site. The aim is for visitors to exchange views on topics of mutual interest and in so doing, attract an ever-increasing number of repeat visitors.

The success of a website that pursues a wide channel strategy depends on the sponsor's ability to identify a specific focus or a range of interests that are common to the visitors that it wants to attract. A sponsor then structures its website to encourage these people to participate. The hope is that visitors will find the interaction that takes place to be so meaningful that they repeatedly use the website as the vehicle to continue their interaction with one another. The ultimate goal is for visitors to be transformed into participants who interact and continually make contributions to onsite discussions.

Effective wide channel strategies build on visitor curiosity and desire to interact with other like-minded people. There are many ways to identify people with common interests who may be motivated to interact with like-minded others. One way is to identify an organization whose specific theme simultaneously distinguishes it from other groups and at the same time links its members to each other based on shared interests or common goals. Examples of such groups include female engineers, young democrats, college professors, opera lovers and new fathers. Groups of this type usually include individuals who want to interact with other people who share their interests but who may not be able to do so in person because of scheduling conflicts or their geographical location.

Middle and high school students in the USA provide a daily illustration of how the desire for interaction with like-minded people may well be a universal phenomenon. Specifically, millions of these students continue their school social life at home after school hours by using the Internet and instant messaging technology. In similar ways, members of professional groups, unions, sports clubs and school districts can use the Internet to increase their interaction with one another and strengthen their shared identity.

An example of a site with a successful wide channel strategy is *www.linux.org*. For over a decade, this site has enabled an open-source contribution process in which volunteers from around the world discuss coding issues pertaining to computer operating systems and contribute 'copyleft' (rather than copyright) code to the site. Contributors identify themselves and receive recognition on the site for their contributions. The site archives all the exchanges between contributors for future reference (Raymond 1999). Relying on this contributory process, visitors to the site developed the Linux operating system.

Wide channel strategies that successfully identify the shared interests of visitors are in an ideal position to offer direct instruction, online counselling and mentoring as additional services. The website, *www.about.com*, for example, supports individual and group learning activities on a variety of different subjects and disciplines. Experts in each specialized field manage the sections of the website dedicated to their particular subject. Another well-known website, *www.ivillage.com*, uses wide channel strategies to develop discussion groups that focus on topics of importance to women.

Online auctions, multi-player games and similar sites utilize variations of basic wide channel strategies. Rather than allowing visitors to interact directly and freely with one another, sponsors of these sites provide structure and regulate how visitors can interact. Within these constraints, participants are free to pursue their own interests. The website, *www.ebay.com*, is illustrative. This site establishes rules of conduct to be used during its actions. So long as participants abide by these rules, they can then pursue their personal goals as they participate in the competitive bidding process. Other variations include multi-participant games in which each player adopts the role of an identified character and manages the character's behaviour while an interactive scenario unfolds on their computer screen (Turkle 1997).

Many sites are freewheeling and offer no rules concerning website activity. As a result, content can originate from anyone at anytime. Issues arise because visitors often have dramatically different expectations concerning appropriate site contributions and behaviour. This makes it difficult to control the direction that a discussion may take. Some sites emphasize openness and a tolerance for controversy. Other sites want their identified focus or particular style of communication to be maintained. For some websites that employ wide channel strategies, it seems to be a continuing managerial issue as to whether it is appropriate to monitor site content, regulate communications, or to try to enforce a particular style of interaction.

As site visitors have opportunities to repeatedly interact and exchange views with others, they may start to bond together emotionally. A website that supports these types of discussion may become the focal point of an evolving virtual community. The site's discussion history will influence its identity and contribute to the continuing development of its associated virtual community. If visitors continue to contribute to the site and their contributions maintain the interest of other visitors, the virtual community associated with the website will continue to strengthen. In such situations, frequent participants are often likely to want to exercise some control over the site. It is often left to a core group of participants who enjoy site prestige to unobtrusively guide and direct discussion.

A site that employs a wide channel strategy enables participants with many different perspectives to interact with one another. While no doubt this prompts some interesting discussions, it can also lead to sharp divisions among visitors concerning the subject matter and how it is discussed. In fact, vigorous, unrestricted discussion may lead to the fragmentation of a site. In such cases, visitors who share a particular interest but who no longer like the specific approach that is being taken on an existing website may withdraw, or they may break away and establish a new site to explore the same or similar issues in a way that they like.

Omnibus strategies

Internet portals

The third strategy can be referred to as an omnibus or portal strategy. This draws upon and combines key elements of the focused and wide channel strategies, and employs them on the same Internet site. These sites enable each visitor to engage in a variety of different interactions or complete a variety of transactions without leaving the site. At one level within the site, for example, a visitor can initiate a search for and obtain a local weather report. Then without leaving the site, they can switch to another level and send or receive e-mail. At still a third level within the site, they can enter a chat room and engage in a discussion and perhaps even initiate a new personal relationship.

By definition, portal sites are typically large in their scope. Their strategy is to seek new and repeat visitors by supporting many different types of activity including direct links to other sites. As survival of many portal sites often depends on their ability to generate advertising revenue, statistics showing the number of visitors and how they use site features are very important. Reflecting this priority, many portal sites use games, contests and other inducements to attract new visitors.

Intranet sites

Of particular interest are the portal sites that support virtual work. Business organizations often build Intranets to dispense company specific information and otherwise support the work of their employees. Such sites generally organize and transmit information about local and organization-wide issues and enable workers to initiate requests for information. Management may anticipate that a restricted portal site may enable workers to coordinate their work with the work of other employees at different job sites, or conduct information searches that will enable them to improve work procedures. They may anticipate that the site will enable workers to obtain information they need to work more effectively with clients, and even enable them to participate in individualized training programmes that can be delivered to their desktops (see HUMAN RESOURCE MANAGEMENT; TRAINING).

Some aspects of a company Intranet portal site can function very well. They can, for example, efficiently broadcast the same information to all employees. While general company information often helps employees become more fully aware of the broad issues that an organization faces, employees in different geographical locations may need additional information that is responsive to local conditions or needs. For these employees, the issue is often how to get the information that they want. Accordingly, the website's ability to assist workers to obtain individualized information or interact with others regardless of location is a major benefit.

By working in proximity to each other and by moving about corporate facilities, employees obtain information about their organization. They develop a first hand view of organizational activity and a sense of the workplace atmosphere. Information of this type is generally not available to employees who work virtually. The information management provides is usually not a good substitute because employees expect such information to be determined primarily by management's view of business needs and not by a desire to provide employees with the information they want. In such cases, people want to conduct their own surveillance and obtain information that is reflective of their own personal concerns rather than overall business issues that are defined by management (March and Feldman 1981).

5 Verifone: virtual organizing in action

When Hatim Tyabji became chief executive of Verifone in 1986, it was a small and financially struggling firm. In the turnaround that followed, Tyabji redesigned Verifone to be a worldwide virtual organization that developed new technology utilizing teams of employees located in different geographic regions. Verifone became consistently profitable and had growth rates averaging around 25 per cent per year. By 1996, its sales figures reached $400 million. By 1998, Verifone had over 3000 employees operating from more than 50 different locations. Despite competition from firms like GTE and IBM, Verifone achieved a 60 per cent market share in many markets.

Verifone's business mission was to create technology to support the automation of credit card authorization services worldwide. To achieve this, Tyabji divided Verifone into cross-functional teams, each with members located in different time zones so that work could proceed unabated 24 hours a day. The teams relied on e-mail and the firm's Intranet to coordinate their efforts. While each team's goals were determined by the firm's overall financial goals, team members determined how their team's goals would be achieved.

Tyabji directed employees to establish very close relations with customers and to respond quickly to their needs. Each day, teams posted the progress they had made and the problems they had encountered on the corporate Intranet so all employees would know or could learn what was taking place. As teams solved problems, they immediately shared this information with co-workers inside and outside their team. Verifone's speedy response to emerging issues astounded customers and competitors alike.

Tyabji reported that while the rapid exchange of information via e-mail over the firm's Intranet led to very high productivity, it also generated a great deal of tension and misunderstanding between people who worked on the same project team but at different locations. Frequently, matters got so intense that team members could only clarify information and otherwise resolve differences by holding face-to-face meetings. Tyabji estimates that at any particular time, a third of Verifone's employees were travelling to and participating in offline meetings where they discussed and resolved conflict and tension. They also became more aware of the constraints that they shared that were imposed on them by business circumstances and local conditions. Through such efforts, they were able to reestablish a sense of group identity and otherwise assist each other to focus 'on the same page'. The understanding and trust that team members developed through these face-to-face meetings helped them deal with frustrations that periodically arose as deadlines approached (see ORGANIZATIONAL INFORMATION AND KNOWLEDGE).

The communication and coordination issues that Verifone encountered may be inevitable consequences of the fast pace and increased number of information exchanges made possible by working virtually. People in different locations often employ different methods to attain the same goal and different criteria to evaluate their performance. As teams attempt to work together in order to meet deadlines, they may also apply different criteria when assessing work to be performed. As one location demands output, for example, another may insist on a focus on missing inputs; while one emphasizes quality another may emphasize speed; while some people strive to make direct contributions to task accomplishment, others may question their ultimate purpose.

Managers vary greatly in the extent to which they recognize that highly motivated team members who are in different locations are likely to develop different priorities and that these cross motivations can inadvertently sabotage performance. If these issues are left unattended, they will destroy any potential that virtual organizing arrangements have to facilitate cooperation among workers and increase productivity. Research in virtual organizing contexts is only just beginning (De Sanctis and Monge 1999). The sorts of conflicts that are likely to arise have been documented in other fields (e.g. Garud and Ahlstrom 1997) along with the types of personal and organizational flexibility that virtual work processes seem to require (e.g. Dunbar *et al.* 1996).

6 Recurring issues for the virtual world

Virtual organizations build on the communication options that are available in the virtual world and it, in turn, depends on the integrity of underlying computer networks. The ILOVEYOU virus demonstrates, however, that it is relatively easy to launch a program that disrupts computer networks. Such sabotage is difficult to stop and legal penalties can be imposed only after an attack takes place. Rather than rely on legal infrastructure to protect Internet activities, most people and organizations currently seem to prefer depending on mutual goodwill. For the foreseeable future, then, the virtual world is vulnerable to unexpected attacks of the ILOVEYOU kind.

In addition, a current priority for individuals and organizations alike is the ability to protect personal privacy and guarantee the security of data, document and money transfer. As there are continuing efforts by criminal elements to sabotage or bypass existing security systems, there are also ongoing efforts to improve encryption and countermeasure technologies in support of sites that intend to guarantee the security of information transfer.

The utility of each of the three virtual organizing strategies depends on the integrity of computer networks and on the ability to guarantee the security of specific types of transactions. For the moment, however, the problems inherent in maintaining network integrity and security do not have permanent solutions and in this sense, virtual organizations are vulnerable to attack. In addition to being frequently discussed in the media, these are matters of continuing governmental and private sector concern because when security or networks are compromised, the virtual world is threatened.

7 Conclusion

The virtual world has enabled us to send and obtain information anywhere and at any time. There seem to be at least three different virtual organizing strategies that build on these new capacities.

First, focused channel strategies enable an alternative to face-to-face communication. For a variety of transactions, focused channel strategies offer increased speed. They also provide sponsors with improved efficiency and users with enhanced services.

Second, wide channel strategies emphasize interaction between visitors and are used to foster mutual understanding and support among like-minded people. Such sites are in a unique position to offer counselling, mentoring, teaching and other instructional services. Virtual communities frequently develop around successful sites.

Third, omnibus strategies seek to exploit the different advantages associated with both focused and wide channel strategies. Perhaps, the most interesting aspects of this strategy are the various ways they can be used to support virtual work. The Verifone case demonstrates how the use of virtual work arrangements can create a highly successful organization. The case also reminds us that when organizations rely mainly on virtual communication, as performance pressures increase, tensions and major misunderstandings between workers often increase as well. There is little doubt that organizations can greatly increase their productivity by incorporating virtual work processes. Nevertheless, relationships between people are likely to determine just how far the work arrangements made possible by virtual technologies will go.

ROGER L.M. DUNBAR
STERN SCHOOL OF BUSINESS

JEROLD TOMAS
TOMACO CONSULTANTS

Further reading

(References cited in the text marked *)

Carmel, E. (1999) *Global Software Teams: Collaborating across borders and time zones*, Upper Saddle River: Prentice Hall. (A consultant suggests 'best practices' for managing cross-border software development teams.)

Daniels, K., P. Standen and D. Lamond. (eds) (2000) *Managing Telework: Perspectives from human resource management and work psychology*, London: Thomson. (Discusses issues that telework management must deal with.)

* De Sanctis, G. and P. Monge (1999) 'Communication processes for virtual organizations', *Organization Science* 10 (6): 693–703. (The article introduces this Special Issue that summarizes up-to-date research on communication in virtual organizations and then provides several examples.)

Dunbar, R.L.M. and R. Garud (2001) 'Culture in-the-making in telework settings', in C. Cooper, S. Cartwright and C. Early (eds) *Handbook of Organizational Culture and Climate*, London: Wiley. (Identifies the cultural issues that emerge as firms attempt to institute virtual work arrangements.)

* Dunbar, R.L.M., R. Garud and S. Raghuram (1996) 'Deframing in strategic analyses', *Journal of Management Inquiry* 5 (1): 23–34. (To work virtually, people often have to change their as-

sumptions about how to do things. This article describes the process people go through in changing their assumptions.)

* Figallo, C. (1998) *Hosting Web Communities: Building relationships, increasing customer loyalty and maintaining a competitive edge*, New York: Wiley. (Describes several web communities and builds a typology for distinguishing them.)

* Garud, R. and D. Ahlstrom (1997) 'Technology assessment: a socio-cognitive perspective', *Journal of Engineering and Technology Management* 14: 25–48. (Shows how different perspectives on technology assessment can quickly develop.)

* Jackson, P.J. and J.M. van der Wielen (eds) (1998) *Teleworking: International perspectives. From telecommuting to the virtual organization*, London: Routledge. (Provides an edited international overview of developments in virtual organizing.)

* Kotha, S. (2000) *http://www.netesteem.com/* (A website that presents website statistics and examines the implications for website reputation. The site includes specific case studies of prominent firms.)

Levinson, P. (1999) *Digital McLuhan*, London: Routledge. (Explains how Marshall McLuhan's ideas and insights on media relate to the Internet.)

* March, J.G. and M.S. Feldman (1981) 'Information in organizations as signal and symbol', *Administrative Science Quarterly* 26 (2): 171–86. (Summarizes different functions that information availability in organizations can serve.)

* Raymond, E.C. (1999) *The Cathedral and the Bazaar*, *http://www.tuxedo.org/~esr/writings/cathedral-bazaar/cathedral-bazaar.html* (Eric Raymond uses his website to publish insightful articles on virtual organizing and software developments. He is a leading thinker in the field and many hackers, firms, consultants, practitioners and academics cite his ideas.)

* Sproull, L. and S. Kiesler (1991) *Connections: New ways of working in the networked organization*, Cambridge, MA: The MIT Press. (A classic that summarizes the issues raised by virtual organizing and presents relevant research.)

* Turkle, S. (1997) *Life on the Screen: Identity in the age of the Internet*, New York: Touchstone. (Discusses how the virtual world confronts and changes identities.)

See also: E-BUSINESS; E-COMMERCE; GROUPS AND TEAMS; HUMAN RESOURCE MANAGEMENT; INTERNET AND BUSINESS; ORGANIZATION BEHAVIOUR; ORGANIZATIONAL INFORMATION AND KNOWLEDGE; TRAINING

von Bertalanffy, Ludwig (1901–72)

Personal background

- born 1901 near Vienna, Austria
- Ph.D. from the University of Vienna (1926)
- Dozent and then Professor at the University of Vienna (1934–48)
- Professorships at the University of Ottawa, Canada; University of Southern California, USA; University of Alberta at Edmonton, Canada (1948–69)
- Professor at the State University of New York at Buffalo, USA (1969–72)
- first on the European continent to develop open systems theory in biology as a working hypothesis for research and a prime mover of general system theory, both considerably influencing the theory and practice of business and management

Major works in English

Modern Theories of Development (1933)
Problems of Life (1952)
General Systems (founding editor and co-editor) (1956–1972)
Robots, Men and Minds (1967)
Organismic Psychology and Systems Theory (1968)
General System Theory (1968)

Summary

Ludwig von Bertalanffy was a biologist whose organismic conception of biology known as *open systems theory* came to pervade many disciplines, including business and management, the impact being vastly 'more than the sum of its parts'. He was the first person on the European continent to develop open systems theory in biology as a working hypothesis for research. It is central to his publications from mid-1920s. Open systems theory profoundly influenced the way organizations are conceived and consequently managed. It helped shape management and organization theory in the 1950s and 1960s. It pervades management practice in the 1990s. Von Bertalanffy was also a prime mover of *general system theory* that emerged in his work in the late 1930s. In particular, his associated idea of the unity of science is still discussed today. From the 1950s until his death von Bertalanffy applied open systems theory and general system theory to a wide range of social sciences, the result became known as his *systems view of people*. He is one of those rare people who had a wide influence on the way Westerners conceive their relationship to each other (at work and elsewhere) and the world in which they find themselves.

1 Biographical data

Ludwig von Bertalanffy was born near Vienna in Austria. He was awarded a Ph.D. from the University of Vienna in 1926, was appointed Dozent in 1934 and then became a Professor, remaining in post until 1948. Subsequently, von Bertalanffy pursued his career in North America, initially as Professor and Director of Biological Research at the University of Ottawa in Canada, then Director of Biological Research at Mount Sinai Hospital and Visiting Professor at the University of Southern California in the USA, then Professor of Theoretical Biology (later University Professor) and member of the Centre for Advanced Study in Theoretical Psychology at the University of Alberta at Edmonton in Canada, finally (in 1969) moving as Faculty Professor to the State University of New York at Buffalo in the USA.

Von Bertalanffy's career was distinguished. He was Fellow of the Rockefeller Foundation (1937–8), Fellow of the Centre for Advanced Study in Behavioral Sciences at

Stanford in California (1954–5), Alfred P. Sloan Visiting Professor at the Menninger Foundation (1958–9), Honorary Fellow of the American Psychiatric Association, Member of the Deutsche Akademie der Naturforscher, Fellow of the International Academy of Cytology and Fellow of the American Association for the Advancement of Science.

Von Bertalanffy published extensively in English and German and his books were translated into many languages (see Further reading). A full list of major works is documented in *General Systems* (1972), XVII: 221–8.

Von Bertalanffy's scholarly contribution to science can usefully be broken down into three interrelated categories: biology and open systems theory (from the mid-1920s), general system theory and the unity of science (from the late 1930s), and application of these theories to, for example, symbolism, psychology and education (from the mid-1950s). These categories reflect progression in his research. Concepts from each category influenced theory and practice in business and management to different degrees; the impact of open systems theory is profound, of general system theory is explosive; whilst work on symbolism, psychology and education bear on those subject areas. Each category is presented below in an allocated space commensurate with its importance to business and management.

2 Open systems theory

A breakthrough in Western thought is credited in part to von Bertalanffy's organismic biology. Until the late nineteenth century, science was founded on concepts of physics. Physics advocated reductionism. Reductionism seeks of any system of interest analysis of fundamental parts. Analysis involves identification of fundamental parts and the behaviour of and forces acting upon each one. Coupled to reductionism is the Second Law of Thermodynamics which states that systems move from ordered to disordered states, known as entropy. Physics thus sees only closed, isolated systems moving ever closer to disorder. Phenomena defying explanation of this sort were dismissed as metaphysical, transcending

the boundaries of science and not worthy of scientific study.

In the late nineteenth century researchers encountered limitations to reductionism. A counter position in biology took on a coherent form by mid-1920s. Several scientists began to think this way. Paul Weiss, Walter B. Cannon (credited with homeostasis) and in particular Ludwig von Bertalanffy came to the fore. Von Bertalanffy demonstrated that concepts of physics were helpless in appreciating dynamics of organisms. Existence of an organism cannot be understood in terms of the behaviour of some fundamental parts. A whole organism is more than the sum of its parts, it exhibits synergy. Furthermore, much of an organism's existence is characterized by increasing or maintaining order, which is negentropic. Biology therefore required new concepts to explain phenomena such as synergy and negentropy.

In this regard, von Bertalanffy developed a theory of open systems in biology, or organismic biology. Open systems theory employs functional and relational criteria rather than reductionist analysis of fundamental parts. Organisms exist in relation to an environment and their functions and structure are maintained by a continuous flow of energy and information between organism and environment. An organism is a complex system comprising many interrelated parts resulting in a whole with integrity. Key concepts here include *self-organization* by way of progressive differentiation, *equifinality* as the independence of final state from initial conditions, and *teleology* as the dependence of behaviour of the organism on some future purpose 'known in advance'. Open systems theory and related ideas from biology swept across and challenged the basis of other disciplines such as business and management, as evidenced below.

Closed system thinking assumes that the behaviour of organizations is based on fundamental principles and laws just like physics. Closed organizations are like Newton's closed mechanical universe; their managers are governors and engineers. Operations are routine, repetitive and perform predetermined tasks. There is a strict hierarchy of control, exact obedience by standardized parts and much emphasis is placed on their efficiency.

Closed system, or machine, thinking resonates with and reinforces ideas of classical management theory. Classical management theory is a 'machine view' for organizations borrowed from physics. The machine view characterizes theories of bureaucracy (Weber), scientific management (Taylor) and administrative management theory (Fayol) (see FAYOL, H.; TAYLOR, F.W.; WEBER, M.).

Open systems theory and other biological conceptions like homeostasis portray concepts of physics as helpless in appreciating dynamics of organizations as well as organisms. Rather, open systems theory observes organizations as complex systems made up of parts most usefully studied as a whole. An organization is open to its environment. Action is taken to hold an organization in the steady-state. The primary aim is to ensure survival, by transforming inputs and by adapting to changes when they occur. Since parts comprise people, management are concerned about the nature of people at work. Parts, or subsystems, have lists of needs that must be met. Individual motivation requires attention; for example, jobs can be enriched leading to greater satisfaction and productivity. The whole organizational structure may facilitate participation and leadership can encourage democracy and autonomy (see LEADERSHIP).

Open systems theory and other biological conceptions echo and reinforce ideas of organizational systems theory and human relations theory (1950s–60s) (see ORGANIZATIONAL BEHAVIOUR, HISTORY OF; ORGANIZING, PROCESS OF). These theories are to an extent the open systems view of organizations and their management borrowed from the biology of von Bertalanffy. The open systems view helps characterize systems theories of Parsons, Selznick, Katz and Kahn, Barnard; and human relations theories of Roethlisberger and Dickson, Herzberg, and McGregor.

Open systems theory has attracted criticism. It suggests structure and function in bounded organizations and that they are physical entities just like organisms. This encourages people to seek and to identify systems in the world. Writers such as Churchman, Vickers and Checkland, in various ways, stated that human systems are different. Human systems, they argued, are better understood in terms of the systems of meaning (ideas, concepts, values, etc.) people ascribe to the world. To appreciate human systems therefore requires learning and understanding about systems of meaning and the conflict that arises between them. Organizational boundaries diminish in importance or at least are redefined in this way. Ideas such as open systems theory then are useful insofar as they stimulate learning and understanding as one possible model for analysis. This is precisely Morgan's approach, employing an open systems metaphor as one possible image of organizations.

The impact of von Bertalanffy's open systems theory on the theory of business and management is profound. It helped shape management and organization theory in the 1950s and 1960s and pervades management practice today. Planning and decision making is often couched in terms of differentiation, environment, functions, growth, interrelatedness and teleology (dependence of the behaviour of an organization on some future events planned in advance). Open systems theory also turned out to be the forerunner of general system theory.

3 General system theory

Von Bertalanffy generalized the open systems concept for other fields, which led him to the idea of general system theory and a new vision of the unity of science. General system theory aims to formulate and derive principles applicable to systems in general and was given its first oral presentation at the Seminar of Charles Morns in Chicago in 1937. Von Bertalanffy developed general system theory throughout the 1940s and into the 1950s.

In 1954 he and three other distinguished scholars with similar ideas spent time together as Fellows of the Centre for Advanced Study in the Behavioral Sciences in Palo Alto, California. Von Bertalanffy along with Kenneth Boulding (economist), Ralph Gerard (physiologist) and Anatol Rapoport (mathematical biologist) became founding fathers of the systems movement. Kenneth Boulding recollects that the systems movement began in conversations of four Fellows around a luncheon table.

Von Bertalanffy was a prime mover in organizing the systems movement. He was central in establishing the Society for the Advancement of General Systems Theory which was initiated as a group of the American Association for the Advancement of Science at its Berkeley meeting in 1954. The society launched a yearbook and an annual conference in 1956 (both are still going today). The society was founded with the following aims:

- to investigate the isomorphy of concepts, laws and models from various fields, and to help in useful transfers from one field to another
- to encourage the development of adequate theoretical models in fields which lack them
- to minimize the duplication of theoretical effort in different fields
- to promote the unity of science through improving communication among specialists.

Von Bertalanffy's main worry was increasing specialization leading to a breakdown in science as an integrated realm. He saw specialists encapsulated in their own private universe, finding it difficult to get messages from one cocoon to another and he wanted to prevent closed, isolated research. He foresaw a system of laws and generalized theories to unify all sciences.

Robert Rosen (1979) described von Bertalanffy's general system idea with forceful simplicity. If two systems, S and S′, which are physically different but nevertheless behave similarly, there is a sense in which we can learn about S through S′. Learning, von Bertalanffy insisted, is through isomorphy or homology, not vague analogy.

Alexander Bogdanov (1873–1928; see further reading), a Russian thinker, developed 'tektology' which is likened to general system theory and was published in Russian 1912–28 but suppressed by Soviet authorities. In the 1980s tektology became available in English.

4 Systems view of people

Consolidated in the book *A Systems View of Man* (edited by La Violette, 1981), von Bertalanffy's reasoning on symbolism, psychology and education, illustrate applications of his systems theories. Besides certain biological differences, von Bertalanffy states, what distinguishes human beings from other creatures is the creation of symbols. Symbols are freely created, representative of some content and transmitted by tradition. They are conscious representations such as thought and values. Von Bertalanffy's systems thinking sees systems of symbols, or symbolic universes. Through this conception he suggests that language, science, art and other cultural forms, achieve existence transcending the personalities and lifetimes of their creators.

In the domain of psychology, von Bertalanffy wrote of people as intrinsically active psychophysical organisms that possess autonomous behaviour. This challenged the reactive, mechanistic stimulus–response model. He emphasized many organismic principles from open systems theory.

In the domain of education, von Bertalanffy saw a stifling of creativity in North American practices that taught within confines of disciplines. He recommended an interdisciplinary approach. Interdisciplinarity is a big topic in the 1990s, particularly in tertiary education.

5 Conclusion

In 1957 the Society for the Advancement of General Systems Theory changed its name to the Society for General Systems Research. Under this umbrella organization, systems thinking burgeoned into many offshoots including complexity theory, cybernetics, information theory, systems approaches to problem solving, systems engineering and systems philosophy. Offshoots then sprouted more offshoots; many national systems societies formed.

In 1980 the International Federation for Systems Research was incorporated, fittingly in Austria. The aim was to stimulate all activities associated with the scientific study of systems and to coordinate such activities at an international level. It launched the journal *Systems Research* (now incorporating *Behavioural Science*). The independent *International Journal of General Systems* was launched in 1974. In response to this growing plurality and competition, in 1988 the Society for General Systems Research changed its name to the International Society for the Systems Sciences. In 1988, the international journal *Systems Practice* (renamed *Systemic Practice and Action Research* in 1998) in which many new possibilities for systems thinking have emerged, was launched. Systems thinking has become diverse yet remains vibrant.

Ludwig von Bertalanffy was thus at the start of this remarkable movement, which began in 1954 at Palo Alto, California, in the conversation of four Fellows around a luncheon table. Central to these conversations was von Bertalanffy's open systems theory and general system theory. As seen, the outcome was vastly 'more than the sum of its parts'. Von Bertalanffy is one of those rare people who influenced widely the way Western people conceive their relationship to each other (at work and elsewhere) and the world in which they find themselves.

ROBERT L. FLOOD
UNIVERSITY OF HULL

Further reading

(References cited in the text marked *)

Ashby, R. (1958) 'General system theory as a new discipline', *General Systems*, 3: 1–6. (Classic paper on general system theory.)

Bogdanov, A. (1996) *Bogdanov's Tektology*, Hull University: Centre for Systems Studies Press (translated by V.N. Sadovsky and V.V. Kelle, edited by P. Dudley). (The first full English Language translation of the Tektology.)

Boulding, K.E. (1956) 'General system theory: the skeleton of science', *Management Science*, 2: 197–208. (Classic paper on general system theory.)

Boulding, K.E. (1972) 'Economics and general systems'. In Laszlo, E. (ed.) *The Relevance of General System Theory*, New York: Braziller. (Reflections on the establishment of general system theory plus its relevance to economics.)

Gray, W. and Rizzo, N. (eds) (1972) *Unity Through Diversity: A Festschrift in Honour of Ludwig von Bertalanffy*, (2 volumes) London and New York: Gordon Breach. (A celebration of von Bertalanffy's research.)

Klir, G. (1991) *Facets of Systems Science*, New York: Plenum. (Background and history of general system theory with contributions from many key researchers.)

* La Violette, P.A. (ed.) (1981) *A Systems View of Man*, Boulding, CA: Westview. (Collection of von Bertalanffy's papers on symbolism, psychology and education.)

Laszlo, E. (1972) *Introduction to Systems Philosophy*, New York: Gordon and Breach. (Systems philosophy from a general system theory viewpoint, including a notable foreword from von Bertalanffy.)

Rapoport, A. (1986) *General System Theory*, Tunbridge Wells: Abacus. (Recent general system theory from an old master.)

* Rosen, R. (1979). 'Old trends and new trends in General Systems Research', *International Journal of General Systems*, 5: 173–81. (Insightful reflections on general system theory with ideas for its development still relevant today.)

von Bertalanffy, L. (1933) *Modern Theories of Development*, Oxford: Oxford University Press (translated from German by J.H. Woodger). (1962) Harper: New York. German original (1928) *Kritische Theorie der Formbildung*, Berlin: Gugrüder Borntraeger. Spanish translation (1934) *Teoria del Desarrollo Biologico*, Buenos Aires: Universidad de La Plata (in two volumes, translated by M. Biraben). (First conceptions of organismic biology and open system theory.)

von Bertalanffy, L. (1950) 'The theory of open systems in physics and biology', *Science*, 11: 23–9. (Classic paper on organismic biology and open system theory.)

von Bertalanffy, L. (1953) *Problems of Life: An Evaluation of Modern Biological Thought*, New York: Wiley, London: Watts. (1961) Harper: New York. German (1949) *Das Biologische Weltbild*, Bern: A Francke AG. Japanese translation (1954) Tokyo: Misuzu Shobo. French translation (1960) *Les Problèmes de la Vie*, Paris: Gallimard (translated by M. Deutsch). Spanish translation (1963) *Concepción Biológica del Cosmos*, Santiago: Ediciones de la Universidad de Chile (translated by F. Cordon). Dutch translation (1965) *Een Biologische Wereldbeeld. Het Verschijnsel Leven in Natuur en Wetenschap*, Utrecht: Holland, Bijleveld. (Includes a survey of his research on organismic biology and open system theory.)

von Bertalanffy, L. (1956) 'General System Theory', *General Systems* 1: 1–10. (Classic paper on general system theory.)

von Bertalanffy, L. (1967) *Robots, Men and Minds: Psychology in the Modern World,* New York: Braziller. German enlarged edition (1970) *aber vom Menschen wissen wir nichts* Düsseldorf: Econ Verlag. Japanese translation (1972) Tokyo: Misuzu Shobo (translated by K. Nagano). Italian translation (1971) *Teoria Generale dei Sistemi* Milano: Istituto Librario Internazionale (translated by L. Occhetto Baruffi). Spanish translation (1971) *Robots, Hombres y Mentes,* Madrid: Guadarrama (translated by F. Calleja). Czech translation (1972) *Clovek-robot a mysleni,* Prague: Svoboda (translated by J. Kamaryt). (Organismic biology and open system theory applied to psychology, plus detailed references to temporal sequence of development of organismic biology and open systems theory.)

von Bertalanffy, L. (1968) *Organismic Psychology and Systems Theory,* Worcester, Mass: Clark University Press. (Organismic biology and open systems theory applied to psychology.)

von Bertalanffy, L. (1968) *General System Theory: Foundations, Development, Applications,* New York: Braziller. Enlarged edition (1971) London: Penguin, (1972) New York: Braziller. Japanese translation (1971) Tokyo: Misuzu Shobo (translated by K. Nagano). Italian translation (1972) *Il Sistema Uomo: La Psicologia nel Mondo Moderno,* Milano: Istituto Librario Internazionale (translated by E. Bellone). Spanish translation (1972) Madrid: Guadarrama. French translation (1972) Paris: Dunod. Swedish translation (1972) Stockholm: Wahlström and Widstrand. German translation (1973) Braunschweig: Vieweg. (A consolidated account of general system theory.)

See also: ACKOFF, R.L.; BEER, S.; BOUDLING, K.; BUSINESS ECONOMICS; CHECKLAND, P.; CHURCHMAN, C.W.; CYBERNETICS; DECISION MAKING; FAYOL, H.; MANAGEMENT SCIENCE; MORGAN, G.; NEO-CLASSICAL ECONOMICS; ORGANIZATION BEHAVIOUR; ORGANIZATION BEHAVIOUR, HISTORY OF; OPERATIONS RESEARCH; SYSTEMS; VICKERS, G.; WEBER, M.; WIENER, N.

Vroom, V.H.: see LEADERSHIP; MOTIVATION AND
SATISFACTION

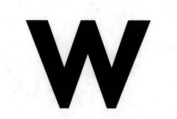

Wage bargaining, process of: see COLLECTIVE BARGAINING

Watson, Thomas (1874–1956)

Personal background

- born 17 February 1874 to a Methodist family of Scottish descent in rural New York State, USA
- early career as a travelling salesman paved the way for a meteoric rise through the ranks of National Cash Register (NCR), 1895–1913
- married 29-year-old Jeannette Kittredge in 1913
- hired as General Manager of the Computing Tabulating Recording company (CTR) in May 1914. CTR subsequently changed its name to International Business Machines (IBM), in 1924
- served 41 years as Chief Executive of CTR/IBM, releasing control to his eldest son, Thomas Junior, in 1956, six weeks before his death
- died 19 June 1956

Summary

Thomas J. Watson (1874–1956) was the progenitor of International Business Machines (IBM), formerly the world's most admired and profitable company. He was a persuasive salesman and, by all accounts, a charismatic leader, an autocratic man with a remarkable capacity for paternalistic benevolence. Towards the end of the twentieth century, Watson was credited with operationalizing a code of management practice and a corporate culture which together represented a powerful model of best practice for those grappling with the key problems of business and administration. As IBM's fortunes changed through the 1990s, such claims became increasingly controversial, provoking intense debate among management theorists and consultants.

1 Introduction

Watson has left an indelible mark on the folklore and legend of the computer industry. He is frequently portrayed as a shrewd and skilful businessman who carries significant personal responsibility for its early development, its structure and indeed for some of its less appealing features via the corporate power and influence of International Business Machines (IBM). Historically, IBM has been the target of criticism for its pricing methods, for monopolizing key markets and restricting trade in its favour. Anti-trust officials with the US Justice Department have been particularly vigorous in pursuing the company with charges of pre-empting competitive processes, thereby stifling the innovative potential of smaller, entrepreneurial companies and limiting consumer choice in the market-place. Lengthy legal battles were fought over anti-trust suits filed in 1932, 1952 and 1969, the latter culminating in a dramatic withdrawal by the Reagan Administration in January 1982.

Watson himself joined the Computing, Tabulating ad Recording company (CTR) with a convinction under US legislation, having been prosecuted with other National Cash Register (NCR) officials for earlier violations of the 1890 Sherman Anti-Trust Act. His penalty, a $5,000 fine and one-year jail sentence, was eventually quashed in March 1915 as the judgment was set aside on appeal. However, the experience undoubtedly left its mark, prompting the development of the clear and favourable corporate image that IBM projects to the outside world.

With lawsuits regularly fixing IBM in the public gaze, Watson, his successors and their officials guarded information on how the company actually operates. Commentators have frequently expressed surprise that the internal workings of such a large and successful company should remain so remarkably opaque. This has lent a certain mystique to Watson's public persona, producing different evaluations of his status and his contribution to IBM's achievements and failures.

One popular interpretation employs the 'great man' theory of history, presenting Watson as a visionary who worked his way out of a farmyard to become 'an industrial giant', perhaps the most enlightened businessmen of his time (Sobel 1981). A related view concentrates on his managerial skills, his flair for motivating employees and success in crafting an organization with a clear sense of direction and a culture that has tended to be purposeful rather than reactive. Watson was apparently conscious of the need to monitor competitors' attempts at dictating market conditions and to minimize the dangers for IBM by responding proactively to ongoing events. For his critics, this amounted to a monopolists' charter, a philosophy of control that nurtured discriminatory practices, producing a company that ruthlessly crushed its rivals (DeLamarter 1988). For all the anti-trust interest in IBM, Watson had little truck with such a view. His self-image was not of a lawbreaker but rather of an individual who had lived the American dream. Hard work and dedication had delivered success, along with sound marketing and superior management of his production staff and sales force. Circumstances were also propitious, since IBM's growth coincided with epochs that were receptive to information processing and computing equipment. Another view of Watson's success suggests that he happened to be in the right place at the right time. More recent IBM executives have not been so fortunate, facing crises of morale, performance and profitability. Difficulties in the

early 1990s notwithstanding, there is still a broad consensus that useful lessons can be gleaned from an understanding of Watsonian management at IBM. The debate centres on whether it constitutes an exemplar model, or a cautionary tale of unchecked corporate power.

2 Biographical data

Watson cut his business teeth as a teenager, selling pianos and sewing machines from the back of a wagon. After a few difficult years travelling the countryside, he took a job selling cash registers for NCR. Success came quickly, drawing the attention of Eugene Patterson, head of the company, who had installed Watson as his second-in-command by 1911. At NCR Watson established many of the convictions that later found expression in IBM's corporate culture. In fact he borrowed many of his concepts directly from Patterson, his own distinctive contribution relating to the missionary zeal with which they were refined and pursued. The armoury of sales techniques and paternalistic human resource strategies that later became synonymous with IBM have their roots in the quota systems, commission structures, company clubs and evangelistic pep talks that Patterson had pioneered as a way of motivating his sales force. Watson's antipathy for anti-trust legislation was also conditioned by his experience at NCR, his first brush with the authorities resulting from the aggressive sales tactics that Patterson favoured. Despite his admiration for Patterson, Watson was forced out of the company because his superior feared a challenge to his ultimate authority. With the anti-trust conviction of 1913 still hanging over him, his next step would be to CTR, the company that eventually became IBM.

Although Watson is often identified as the founder of IBM, its genealogy can actually be traced back to the inventor, Herman Hollerith. In 1896 Hollerith formally capitalized the Tabulating Machine Company, a business he had established by supplying US census agencies with 'statistical pianos' based on the Jacquard loom. With financial restrictions hindering its development, the company was subsequently absorbed into CTR, a conglomerate put together by Charles Flint, the so-called 'Trust King', who appointed Watson General Manager in 1914. While Hollerith had given the corporation innovative products, Watson's contribution centred on marketing, distribution and organizational arrangements. Due to the efforts of an increasingly professional sales force and highly motivated production staff, the company prospered through the early decades of the century, its change of name on 14 February 1924 signalling Watson's confidence about the prospects for trade outside the USA. By the end of the Second World War, IBM was an international icon, leading its industry with an annual revenue in excess of $140 million in 1948.

The post-war IBM was shaped under the leadership of three men, Thomas Watson, Sr and his two sons, Thomas, Jr and Arthur (known as Dick). In 1949, at the age of 75, Watson, Sr presided over its separation into a domestic US company and a subsidiary labelled IBM World Trade. The latter was controlled by Dick, while the parent company increasingly came under the direction of Thomas, Jr, who led the company fully into the computer age. Thomas, Jr was appointed Chief Executive Officer in May 1956, shortly before his father died of a heart attack (on 19 June 1956). Over the next fifteen years, IBM's gross income increased from $335 million to more than $7 billion, a rate of growth that prompted the August 1987 edition of *Fortune* magazine to proclaim Thomas Watson, Jr the greatest capitalist in history. Thomas, Jr retired in 1971 after a heart attack. In 1979 he was appointed US ambassador to Moscow by President Carter. He died in 1994.

3 Main contribution

IBM's success has been widely attributed to almost sixty years of continuous Watson management. Company brochures and business commentaries often project the image of an entrepreneurial family promoting a strong culture of managerial excellence through adherence to core values and behaviour patterns that were set out by Watson, Sr. The backbone of IBM's character is identified as the social creed that emerged from his sense of morality and his ethical fortitude. Three cen-

tral principles are usually linked to this: respect for individual employees, a commitment to customer service and the pursuit of excellence in all spheres of operation. These found expression in personnel programmes promoting full employment and open communications, and also in pronouncements and slogans that set the tone for the company, at least through its first forty years. Legends such as 'Think' and 'The best supervision is self supervision', together with company anthems and personnel practices, ostensibly fostered a feeling of community, even family obligation, among employees. The consistent fairness of the culture was considered to be functional in creating corporate loyalty and identification. The message for other companies was reaffirmed by Thomas, Jr in 1963. In a book entitled *A Business and its Beliefs: The Ideas that Helped Build IBM*, he argued that there was simply no substitute for good human relations and for the high morale they bring.

More recently, through the 1970s and 1980s, prominent management theorists and consultants have taken the Watson lesson to heart, extolling the virtues of IBM's enlightened corporate culture. Peters and Waterman provide the most notable example, their 1982 book *In Search of Excellence* proclaiming IBM to be the epitome of excellence, the greatest corporation in the world. These authors attribute IBM's prosperity directly to its internal management systems and relationships, rather than to merger and monopoly activity, or even technical innovation. On this reading, autonomy and entrepreneurship within the company combined to create customer loyalty that made IBM invulnerable to competitors. Such a view has found enormous favour with company insiders. F. 'Buck' Rodgers, an ex-marketing executive who describes himself as 'a born-and-bred, dyed-in-the-wool IBMer' gives it a glowing commendation: 'Every now and then – about as often as Halley's Comet streaks across the sky – a book like *In Search of Excellence* comes along and gets right to the heart of things' (Rodgers and Shook 1986: 3). He maintains that 'To understand IBM's success and its unshakable optimism, one needs some insights into its marketing systems and philosophy, and its unique relationship with employees and customers' (1986: 4).

Others take a less complimentary stance, criticizing Peters and Waterman for accepting an IBM public relations spiel. For Richard DeLamarter, one of the US anti-trust officials on the 1969–82 investigation, Peters and Waterman operate at the level of superficial images:

> According to the authors, IBM has benefited from a strong central philosophy that was originally laid down by its charismatic leaders, the Watsons. They present a simple, appealing model for IBM's success – excellence in management. But this view is dead wrong. IBM's success comes from the power of monopoly.
>
> (DeLamarter 1988: xvii)

According to DeLamarter, few lessons can be learned from IBM on management, the work ethic or technological innovation. Under the Watsons, its growth was based on a strategy of holding a near monopoly market share in which customer interests were regularly and systematically sacrificed. This position is heavily endorsed by Rex Malik. In his 1975 publication, *And Tomorrow the World?: Inside IBM*, he wrote:

> This book is about control. It is about a sham: an American company which masquerades as a multinational and has dozens of foreign subsidiaries, each with a board packed full of local worthies and executive flunkies, but which in reality is a company, in all meaningful senses of the word, consolidated, and in which power is about as widely distributed as is power in the Kremlin.
>
> (Malik 1975)

Ex-IBM employees have also flagged the dangers of monopoly power at IBM, relating these to concerns about inferior products and weak management. Gene Amdahl, a leading technologist with the company in the 1960s, reported in 1975 that IBM was sidelining engineering talent, employing two-thirds of the Western world's computing engineers without producing leading edge technology. Similar pragmatic concerns about the limitations of IBM's logic of management have recently prompted business periodicals to caution against the emulation mentality encouraged by Peters and Waterman. *Business Age* magazine is among the most prominent, noting in a March 1993 editorial that:

> *In Search of Excellence* provided many executives of companies that are now defunct with a false sense of security. It wasn't all wrong, but it just wasn't all right. There is a lot of responsibility on the shoulders of management gurus, especially those who write books and take people's money for it.
>
> (*Business Age* March 1993: 22–5)

4 Evaluation

So much has changed about IBM in recent years that efforts to attribute its record solely to superior management *or* monopoly power seem ill-informed and, ultimately, futile. Such absolutism deflects attention from contextual factors and contingencies, and downgrades the significance of reflective social action in formulating responses to environmental opportunities and constraints. In February 1993, when IBM announced a record corporate loss of $5.3 billion, it was clear that the information technology market had changed and that the company had failed to react. Regardless of whether the Watsons' management was essentially enlightened or monopolistic, the company was out of touch.

Ironically, given the mooted flexibility of IBM's culture, there was a broad consensus that bureaucratic priorities had taken hold. The dynamic organization had frozen. Perceptible rigidities enabled critics to hoist the company with its own petard. In their own analysis of the situation, senior IBM executives identified the core characteristics of the Watsons' management as a root cause of poor performance. Responding to early signs of a downturn in January 1988, then chairman John Akers announced a major reorganization, including changes to the open access policy that enabled employees to take their grievances progressively higher up the corporate ladder until they found an acceptable solution. By 1992, he was devolving decision making to the point where research and production centres could take responsibility for their own commercial well-being, changing employment and marketing policies if that was considered appropriate. Lou Gerstner, who assumed the mantle of chief executive in March 1993, was even more disdainful of the traditional culture, replacing Watson's three basic beliefs with eight objectives that would facilitate change. Respect for the individual came bottom of the list, confirming the new priorities to employees who had already lost the promise of lifetime employment when redundancies were instituted in early 1993.

Under Gertsner's influence, IBM has since been reinventing itself as less of a manufacturing operation and more of a provider of integrated computing services. Breadth of technology coverage and expertise have been crucial to this strategy, encouraging Gerstner to keep the company together, and to reverse Akers' earlier plans to fracture it into autonomous units that would compete in distinctive market segments. While some resonance can be found with Watson's image of a corporate family, insiders have reported that this has sparked a more forceful challenge to the founders legacy.

Enthusiasts detect a liberating effect through the destruction of a stifling, insular and bureaucratic culture via partnership deals and sourcing agreements that open IBM to collaborative ventures with telecommunications and software companies, and even to components manufacturing for competitors in personal computer and other product markets (Garr 1999). Others, especially in manufacturing, highlight job worries, redundancy figures – which Derber (1998: 68) puts at 200,000 employees over the ten years to 1995 – and the dramatic contraction of the human resource function as evidence for the final renunciation of Watsons 'social contract' with an appreciative staff. Meanwhile, the business media has commended Gerstner for engineering the corporate turnaround of the decade, and for delivering strengthening profits since 1994 (Kirkpatrick 1999).

Contrary to the views of Peters and Waterman, it would be easy to conclude from all of this that an over-indulgence in Watsonian management can be damaging to corporate health. Certainly, commentators on IBM's decline in the early 1990s argued that its demise

was inevitable given its inability or refusal to escape from Watson's legacy. Bill Gates of Microsoft famously predicted that the company would be extinct by 2002. Paul Carroll, author of *Big Blues* (1994) argued that IBM would never again hold sway over the computer industry. Gerstner has stolen some thunder from the obituary writers by launching his own assault on the Watson principles, enabling IBM to regain something of its corporate prominence in the process. Although some commentators are still cautious about its regeneration, others see a more threatening future of industry dominance by a company now purged of its social conscience and liberated from the expensive obligations of the Watson era:

> IBM, while often viewed as a dinosaur, remains the 800-pound gorilla of most sectors of the computer industry. ... A huge player in hardware, software and services, IBM is moving from manufacturing mainframes towards monopolizing cyberspace.
> (Derber 1998: 68)

5 Conclusion

Thomas J. Watson asserted that in order to respond to environmental contingencies, an organization must be willing to change everything about itself except its basic beliefs. Recent IBM executives have displayed a more fickle attachment to the principles that Watson espoused, and which were endorsed in the 1980s as determinants of business excellence. Although the Watson influence has undoubtedly waned within the company, many insiders bemoan the passing of the paternalistic 'social contract' which secured employment and contributed to employee commitment and productivity.

With Gerstner's reforms, many IBM workers have joined the ranks of what Robert Reich, former United States labour secretary, called the new anxious class. Their worries about cost-cutting and terms and conditions of employment may prove highly significant as the company aims for solid growth from its partnership and integrated solutions and services strategy. Reports have already highlighted staffing problems in the transition to new assignments as the company confronts a backlog of service orders and the need to strengthen consultancy and other expanding operations. In this context, the axemanship involved in changing the traditional paternalism may create motivational difficulties which restrict the sense of entrepreneurship and process-ownership which Gerstner is trying to foster. Perhaps there is a danger of throwing something valuable out with the bureaucratic bathwater, in which case the management of Watson's legacy will be the subject of continuing debate.

MARTIN BEIRNE
UNIVERSITY OF GLASGOW

Further reading

(References in the text marked *)

Black, E. (2001) *IBM and the Holocaust*, New York and London: Little, Brown. (New book contains allegations that Watson was, like Ford, and admirer of Hitler, and that IBM's activities in wartime Germany aided the Holocaust.)

* *Business Age* (1993) 'IBM: the death of the corporation', (March) 22–5. (Editorial which highlights the dangers of an emulation mentality in corporate management.)

* Carroll, P. (1994) *Big Blues: The Unmaking of IBM*, London: Weidenfeld & Nicolson. (An incisive review of IBM's predicaments and responses.)

Cortada, J. (1993) *Before the Computer: IBM, NCR, Burroughs, and Remington Rand and the Industry They Created, 1865–1956*, Princeton, NJ: Princeton University Press. (Provides historical detail on the rise of IBM.)

* DeLamarter, R. (1988) *Big Blue: IBM's Use and Abuse of Power*, London: Pan Books. (A landmark text by an anti-trust investigator who articulates a penetrating critique of IBM's business practices.)

* Derber, C. (1998) *Corporation Nation*, St.Martin's Press: New York. (A critical and sophisticated analysis which connects IBM to broader debates on corporate power and democratic accountability.)

Evans, H.S. (1941) *Fellowship Songs of the International Business Machines Corporation*, New York: IBM. (Provides a taste of the corporate community spirit at IBM, which was fostered in part through company anthems, slogans and innovative personnel practices.)

Foy, N. (1974) *The IBM World*, London: Eyre Methuen. (Offers an informative, if now rather dated, insight into IBM's internal work systems.)

* Garr, D. (1999) *IBM Redux: Lou Gerstner and the Business Turnaround of the Decade*, New York: Harper Business. (A flattering account of Gertsner's influence by an admirer and enthusiast for the recent changes at IBM.)

* Kirkpatrick, D. (1999) 'IBM: from big blue dinosaur to e-business animal', *Fortune* 26 April, 116–24. (An accessible commentary by a respected journalist with *Time* magazine.)

* Malik, R. (1975) *And Tomorrow the World?: Inside IBM*, London: Millington. (A useful counterweight to IBM in-house and officially endorsed publications.)

* Peters, T. and Waterman, R. (1982) *In Search of Excellence: Lessons from America's Best Run Companies*, New York: Harper & Row. (Initially influential with practitioners, this book illustrates the folly of de-contextualized, prescriptive advice in modern management consulting.)

* Rodgers, F. 'Buck' and Shook, R. (1986) *The IBM Way: Insights into the World's Most Successful Marketing Organization*, New York: Harper & Row. (A glowing endorsement of the 'IBM way' by a company insider.)

Rodgers, W. (1969) *Think: A Biography of the Watsons and IBM*, New York: Stein & Day. (An early account of the Watsons' influence at IBM.)

* Sobel, R. (1981) *IBM: Colossus in Transition*, New York: Times Books. (An interesting view of the pressures bearing on IBM as it entered the 1980s.)

* Watson, T., Jr (1963) *A Business and its Beliefs: The Ideas that Helped Build IBM*, New York: McGraw-Hill. (A straightforward commendation of Watsonian management through two generations.)

Watson, T., Jr (1990) *Father, Son and Co: My Life at IBM and Beyond*, New York: Bantam Books. (Thomas Watson, Jr offers some candid reflections on his family ties with IBM.)

See also: GURU CONCEPT; ORGANIZATION CULTURE; PETERS, T.J.

Webb, Beatrice (1858–1943) and Webb, Sidney (1859–1947)

1 **Biographical data**
2 **Main contribution**
3 **Evaluation**

Personal background

Beatrice Webb

- nee Potter, born 1858
- born into a rich railway owning family
- influenced by Spencer and Booth
- investigated Co-operative Movement
- private income allowed independence
- established 'our partnership'
- Poor Law Royal Commission member
- died in 1943

Sidney Webb

- born 1859
- son of radical London acccountant
- educated in Switzerland and Germany
- initially Colonial Office civil servant
- University of London LL B
- Poor Law Royal Commission member
- MP and Cabinet Minister
- created Baron Passfield
- died in 1947

Jointly helped found the following:

The Fabian Society
The Labour Party
The London Local Government
The London School of Economics
The *New Statesman* weekly magazine
The British Welfare State

Major works (joint)

The History of Trade Unionism (1894)
Industrial Democracy (1897)
Methods of Social Study (1932)

Soviet Communism: A New Civilisation? (1935)

Overview

The Webbs made an outstanding contribution to British society and to its study. As social reformers, they helped transform Britain in their lifetime, shaping many important institutions and the way their contemporaries thought about them. As democratic (and non-Marxist) socialist intellectuals, they helped launch the Fabian Society 'think-tank', the British Labour Party, London local government and the London School of Economics (LSE) amongst other political and social innovations, as well as laying the foundations for the modern post-Second World War Welfare State. They also helped set up an influential political weekly, the *New Statesman*, which was essential reading for socialist intellectuals for decades to come and is still in print. A major part of their activities as social scientists – they were also prolific writers on their own society – related to the study of industrial relations, public administration, social reform and so on. As good 'Fabians' they believed in building a new society, combining 'social justice' with 'efficiency'.

Sidney Webb was born in 1859, the son of a Radical London accountant, was educated in Germany and Switzerland and eventually became a civil-servant. He had been awarded a place at Trinity College, Cambridge to read Law but his duties prevented him from taking it up. He studied in his own time to take a LL B degree of the University of London. Webb was said to have a photographic memory for detail. He was fascinated by how institutions worked and the detailed rules and regulations to which they conformed. Plunging himself into politics, he became a founder of the Fabian Society, together with the playwright Bernard Shaw and other intellectuals of his day, becoming a 'seed-bed' for new ideas of

socialist thinking for the soon-to-emerge Labour Party. On marrying Beatrice, he embarked on a joint destiny, the details of which
are examined more fully below.

Beatrice Webb (nee Potter) was born in 1858
and was the daughter of a railway magnate.
Unlike most other members of her class and
gender, she decided to try to understand how
ordinary people lived outside her narrow social circle, became a social investigator and
wrote an important book on the new Cooperative Movement which had emerged in
Victorian Britain. She met Sidney Webb, a
most unusual match for a 'society-lady' but
was fascinated by his formidable mental capacities. Their marriage is described by her as
'our partnership'. After they formed this, their
lives became a seamless web and their
achievements are *grosso modo* hard to separate.

2 Main contribution

The Webbs made a huge impact on their country – and indeed beyond – in the period bridging the Victorian era and post-1945 British
society. They were what many would see as
archetypal socialist intellectuals who tried to
fuse thought and action, translating theory
into policy, as we shall elaborate in greater
detail below. They were probably generally
better-known in the post-war period than they
are today, except perhaps in the labour movement in Britain, in the world of the social sciences and for those studying industrial
relations (see INDUSTRIAL AND LABOUR RELA-
TIONS).

Their achievements were unusual in that they
were an effective working married couple engaged in joint literary, political and research
endeavours, like few others (see the
GILBRETH, F.B.; GILBRETH, L.E.M.) a 'partnership' as Beatrice called it, in most of their activities, although both also led distinguished
careers in separate capacities. Immensely prolific, it is said that they wrote over five million
words in their lifetime together as scholars
and researchers. In a new work Harrison
(1999) argues that Sidney made a greater input to their joint writings than formerly imagined.

Their contributions may be divided into
two main categories, namely *organizational*
and *intellectual,* but it should be noted that
they were private scholars who did not hold
academic posts. They were both life-long students, but their efforts were certainly not confined to study. They believed passionately in
putting ideas to practical uses. Promoting the
cult of the 'expert', they thought 'knowledge'
could be used as an instrument for social
change, paralleling the Pragmatist approach
of the American philosopher John Dewey, a
contemporary on this latter point. In this context the Webbs may be perceived as truly 'intellectuals in politics'.

They set up a university institution devoted
to the social sciences and the training of experts: the London School of Economics in
1895. Today, the LSE is ranked as one of the
top British academic institutions second only
to Cambridge and Oxford for its research excellence, although much smaller in resources
and student numbers. Sidney wanted to model
it on the élite French *Institut d'Etudes Politi-
ques*, set up in 1871, now popularly known as
'Sciences Po', which he mistook for what we
would today call a 'business school'. It is said
that Sidney thought the LSE would train
'managers' for the new society.

Ceaseless in their endeavours and energies,
(they had no children) they plunged into the
arena of political and social reform. Sidney
soon helped to create the modern system of
education and local government in London in
the LCC at the turn of the century. It emphasized technical education and the 'scholar-
ship-ladder', possibly anticipating later
national educational reforms after the 1944
Butler Report, which became the standard for
many decades in the post-Second World War
era.

As members of the 1908 Royal Commission on the Poor Law, they laid the foundations of the post-1945 British welfare state.
They proposed the notion of the 'national
minimum' standard of living in the key *Minority Report* of the Commission which they
signed in 1909. John Maynard Keynes once
said he had found the roots of his counter-
cyclical economic policies in the Webbs' proposals on that point made in that document,

long before the slumps of the inter-war years (see Warner, 1979) (see KEYNES, J.M.).

They had earlier founded a 'think-tank' to generate 'ideas' for the emerging labour movement, the Fabian Society, based on the 'inevitability of gradualness', which in time became one the building-blocks of the British Labour Party, which they believed would implement their ideas and policies. The Webbs may be said to have invented the notion of the 'think tank', as a vehicle for intellectuals to apply field-research to the solution of practical economic, political and social problems, in its contemporary meaning.

Sidney wrote the programme *Labour and the New Social Order* in 1918. He then became MP for Seaham 1922–8 and was a Cabinet Minister in the two first Labour Governments in 1924 and 1929. He was made a member of the House of Lords in 1929. They were never mere 'ivory-tower' intellectuals but placed themselves at the heart of politics. Beatrice's social connections were very useful in this domain, but Sidney had also built a solid base in the Labour Movement. Once Labour fell from political grace in the early 1930s, the Webbs lost their mainstream role. They were too closely identified with the fiasco of Ramsay MacDonald's government and its inability to cope with the economically and socially disastrous back-wash of the Wall Street Crash of 1929.

They unfortunately became infatuated, as did many socialist intellectuals of the inter-war period, with Stalinist Russia, which they hailed as a 'new civilisation', albeit with a question mark, in a book published in 1935. They saw the 'rule of the expert' and 'administrative efficiency' as *de rigueur* in the Soviet system; Lenin's fascination with Taylor's scientific management notions (see TAYLOR, F.W.) may provide a counterpoint here to the Webbs' predilection for such virtues. They particularly admired the state-run trade unions in Russia, characterized as they were as 'transmission-belts' of top-down 'progressive' strategies. This work unfortunately marred a solid record of scholarly achievement. At times, more visibly in their later years, they lacked balanced judgement and deeply liberal inclinations.

Apart from this, their major intellectual contributions were indeed formidable for their times and may be divided into three key domains respectively *vis-à-vis* (1) the analysis of poverty; (2) the systematic use of social research methods; (3) history and functions of local government; and (4) the study of trade unionism and collective bargaining.

Industrial relations

The Webbs' main contribution to the study of industrial relations and collective bargaining (see COLLECTIVE BARGAINING; INDUSTRIAL AND LABOUR RELATIONS; TRADE UNIONS) is set out in two major works: *The History of Trade Unionism* (1894) and *Industrial Democracy* (1897), both running into many editions. Both are substantial works of scholarship, with detailed footnotes and references. In this area of industrial relations, this kind of fine-focus description and analysis was highly novel. They are regarded as seminal works in the field, even today. The first is a major, indepth descriptive as well as analytical history of British trade unions. The second is a profoundly institutional analysis of the wider labour movement, with the propagation of a highly original theory of union structure and function. Both books are the result of many years of in-depth empirical and historical research, hardly trumped by later experts in the field. Their theories have been criticized by many subsequent writers in the field of industrial and labour relations but are nonetheless still regarded as classics in the profession. We may sum up their contributions as follows:

- Although the Webbs were not the first to write about trade unions as such, their contribution incorporated perhaps the earliest fully conceptual approach to the subject. The economic implications of unions were highlighted by the Webbs in their pioneering *History of Trade Unionism* which was published in 1894 (see Poole 1981). It was a long, detailed work, of almost 800 pages based on painstaking archival research but clearly written and is still accessible to a wider readership.

- They actually defined trade unions 'as a continuous association of wage-earners for the purpose of maintaining or improving the conditions of their working lives' (p.1 in the 1920 edition). In the first edition of 1894, they had used the phrase 'of their employment'. The term 'continuous' is critical here, as they saw the establishment of 'structure' as vital to ensure the achievement of 'function'.

- Their approach has been described by commentators on their work as 'structural', since they mainly focused on the change in economic relations which has set employee against employer in terms of their interests and function (Poole 1981: 16). The rise of unions had been impeded by the possibilities of getting on as an independent craftsman. They placed great emphasis on the change in economic relationships rather than technology or factory size. The rise of the factory had certainly reduced the independence of workers and made them wage-earners, but 'combinations' of working men had in fact arisen before the emergence of the factory system. The defensive reaction of ordinary workers had its roots in the ground of pre-industrial Britain (see INDUSTRIAL REVOLUTION). Unions have their origins much further back than most popular writers on workplace conflict believe (Fox 1985: 67).

- The origins of trade unionism, they believed, came from the craft trades, where independent associations could resist the will of the employers. These interest groups had either been protected by legal or customary regulation in areas like apprenticeships or by other forms of limitations on numbers of entrants into the trade (see INTEREST GROUPS). As Fox (1985) points out: 'Early unionism was predominantly a response not by those at the bottom of the industrial pile, but by those who were a significant distance from the bottom and who hoped to preserve their relative advantage' (Fox 1985: 63).

- The Webbs stressed (1) the salience of justice and social order which were embodied in the rule-making process; (2) the distinction between union structure and function; (3) the device of the 'common rule'; (4) the strong democratic thrust of unionism; (5) and that collective bargaining would be superseded by legal enactment (Poole 1981: 56).

- They firmly believed that 'in the absence of any Common Rule, the conditions of employment are left to "free competition", this always means in practice, that they are arrived at by Individual Bargaining between contracting parties of very unequal economic strength'. (Webb and Webb 1897: 560-1). Poole (1981: 56) finds much of their analysis has parallels with the work of the French sociologist Durkheim (see DURKHEIM, E.) especially their emphasis on the aforementioned 'common rule'. Later writers have criticized their structural approach and placed greater emphasis on 'objective' factors such as business cycles and union density, as well as 'subjective' ones such as the objectives or purposes of unions.

- Nassau Senior, a nineteenth century British economist, noted that wages issues could not be discussed apart from institutional analysis. The Webbs took this a stage further and their work solidly complements Alfred Marshall's work on the institutional setting of economic life (see MARSHALL, A.). Their immediate mentor was another economist of the period, W.S Jevons (and certainly not Karl Marx). They approved of 'national efficiency' and the 'economy of high wages'; the latter had considerably impressed Sidney when he visited the US, back in 1888. They had no taste for abstract economics, however, preferring to anchor their work in historical and institutional contexts.

3 Evaluation

Buried in Westminster Abbey, the Webbs were major figures in the reform of British society as it was transformed from a *laissez faire* Victorian society to a mid-twentieth-century welfare state. They played a major role in creating many new institutions in Britain, in education, local government, social science research and welfare. They also helped 'organized labour' become a political force, the Labour Party, and achieve its rise to power and eventually form a Government for the first time in 1924, as well as integrating it into the social and political Establishment of their time. Equally, they helped their contemporaries understand the role of trade unions and management in modern industrial society more clearly. They were what many would see as archetypal 'socialist intellectuals' who tried to fuse thought and action, translating theory into policy. They were among the major founding fathers (and mothers) of social science in their country. They were in addition important prophets of 'managerialism', promoting the 'rule of the expert' and 'administrative efficiency', in the name of a 'fairer society', above all other considerations.

MALCOLM WARNER
JUDGE INSTITUTE OF MANAGEMENT STUDIES
UNIVERSITY OF CAMBRIDGE

Further reading

(References cited in the text marked *)

Clegg, H. A. (1979) *The Changing System of Industrial Relations in Britain,* Oxford: Blackwell (A relatively recent general theory of trade unionism of considerable interest *vis-à-vis* the Webbs' original work.)

* Fox, A., (1985) *History and Heritage: The Social Origins of the British Industrial Relations System,* London: George Allen and Unwin. (A masterly, extended account of the wider historical and social roots of British Industrial Relations.)

* Harrison, R. (1999) *The Life and Times of Sidney and Beatrice Webb, 1895–1905; The Formative Years,* London: Macmillan. (A critical new biography which sets out to overturn previous 'myths' about their respective roles in the 'partnership'.)

* Poole, M (1981) *Theories of Trade Unionism,* London: Routledge Kegan and Paul. (A very clear and crisp analysis of industrial relations theory, especially as related to trade unions, with a close analysis of the Webbs' contribution to the field.)

McKenzie, N. and J. (1977) *The First Fabians,* London: Weidenfeld and Nicholson. (A highly readable account of the Webbs' life and works in the context of the rise of the Fabian Society.)

Webb, B. (1926) *My Apprenticeship,* London: Longmans Green. (First volume of Beatrice's fascinating historical source-document: her diaries.)

Webb, B. (1948) *Our Partnership,* London: Longmans Green. (Second volume of the diaries.)

* Webb, S. and B. (1894; 1920) *The History of Trade Unionism,* London: Longmans. (A seminal work on the history of trade unions in Britain, which has now become a classic work in the field.)

* Webb, S. and B. (1897) *Industrial Democracy,* London: Longmans. (A path-breaking institutional analysis of the British labour movement, exemplifying the Webbs' theories of collective bargaining.)

* Webb, S. and B. (1932) *Methods of Social Study,* New York: Kelley. (Classic account of social research methods and their approach to conducting empirical research.)

* Webb, S. and B.(1935) *Soviet Communism: A New Civilisation?* London: Longmans Green. (An uncritical appreciation of Stalin's 'new civilisation' based on an overly sympathetic reaction to the Soviet system.)

See also: COLLECTIVE BARGAINING; CLEGG, H.; DURKHEIM, E; DUNLOP, J.H; EMPLOYERS ASSOCIATIONS; EMPLOYMENT AND UNEMPLOYMENT, ECONOMICS OF; GILBRETH F.B.; GILBRETH L.E.M.; INDUSTRIAL AND LABOUR RELATIONS; INDUSTRIAL DEMOCRACY; LABOUR MARKETS; KEYNES, J.M.; MARSHALL, A.; OWEN, R.; ROWNTREE, J.; TRADE UNIONS

Weber, Max (1864–1920)

Personal background

- born into a middle-class family in Erfurt, Germany, 21 April 1864
- took his Ph.D. and began his teaching career at the University of Berlin
- moved on to a position as Professor of Economics at the University of Heidelberg
- experienced a nervous breakdown in 1897 and was unable to do any serious work for several years
- began to re-emerge in 1904, coincident with a trip to the USA
- published his best-known work, *The Protestant Ethic and the Spirit of Capitalism*, in 1904–5
- most of his major works published in the next decade and a half, or posthumously
- died on 14 June 1920 while in the midst of his most important work, *Economy and Society*

Major works

The Protestant Ethic and the Spirit of Capitalism (1904–5)
Economy and Society (1921)
General Economic History (1927)

Summary

Max Weber (1864–1920) was a major social theorist whose ideas are of great relevance to business and management. Embedded in Weber's world historical studies is a general theory of the rationalization of society. Time has been kind to Weber's theory; society today is even more rationalized than it was in his day. His theoretical ideas are of particular relevance to the understanding of, among other things, modern formal organizations, the capitalist market, the professions and economies as a whole. Not only do Weber's ideas continue to be relevant today, but neo-Weberians are developing new ideas that have even greater applicability to modern society.

1 Introduction

After Karl Marx (see MARX, K.H.), Weber is the most important German social theorist. In fact, Weber had to grapple with, and distance himself from, Marxian theory. Weber, like Marx, had much to say about capitalism. However, to Weber capitalism was merely part of a much broader problem – modern rational society. Thus while Marx focused on alienation within the economic system, Weber saw alienation as a far larger problem occurring in many other social institutions. While Marx condemned the exploitation of the capitalist system, Weber was concerned with the increasing oppressiveness of the rationalized society. Marx was an optimist who felt that the problems of alienation and exploitation could be solved with the overthrow of the capitalist economy, but Weber was a pessimist who believed that the future held only increasing rationalization, especially if capitalism were overthrown. Weber was no revolutionary, but rather a careful and insightful analyst of modern society.

2 Biographical data

Max Weber was born into a middle-class family in which his parents had very different outlooks on life. His worldly father was a classic bureaucrat who ultimately rose to a position of some political importance in Germany; in contrast, Weber's mother was devoutly religious and even ascetic in her outlook. In a later biography, Weber's wife Marianne (Weber 1975) comments that Weber's parents confronted him with a difficult choice as a child, a choice that he agonized over for much of his life and one which had a profound effect on both his personal life and his scholarly work (Mitzman 1969).

Weber earned a doctorate from the University of Berlin in 1892 in his father's field (law) and began teaching at that university. However, his interests were already shifting towards his lifelong concerns – economics, history and sociology. His early work in these areas led to a position as Professor of Economics at the University of Heidelberg in 1896.

Not long after his appointment at Heidelberg, Weber had a violent argument with his father, who died shortly thereafter. Within a short period of time Weber suffered a nervous breakdown from which he was never to recover fully. However, by 1904–5 he had recuperated sufficiently to publish one of his best-known works, *The Protestant Ethic and the Spirit of Capitalism* (Weber 1904–5; Lehmann and Roth 1993). The subject-matter of this work, as reflected in the title, exhibited a concern for both his mother's religiosity (she was a Calvinist, the key Protestant sect in the rise of capitalism) and his father's worldly interests. It also demonstrated the ascendancy of his mother's orientation over his father's; an ascendancy that was to be manifest in a series of works focusing on the sociology of religion (Weber 1916, 1916–17, 1921), especially the impact of the major religions of the world on economic conduct.

In the last decade and a half of his life, Weber was able to publish his most important works. At the time of his death he was working on his most important book, *Economy and Society* (Weber 1921) which, although incomplete, was published posthumously, as was the also significant *General Economic History* (Weber 1927).

During his lifetime, Weber had a profound impact on scholars such as Georg Simmel, Robert Michels and Georg Lukács. His influence remains strong to this day with the continuing, and perhaps even accelerating, production of a wide array of neo-Weberian scholarship (Collins 1985).

3 Main contribution

In the area of business and management, Weber has been best known for his work on bureaucracy (see ORGANIZATION STRUCTURE). However, that work is but a small part of his broader theory of the rationalization of Western society and many elements of that theory beyond his paradigm of a bureaucracy are relevant to scholars working in the area of business and management.

At the broadest level, the question that informs Weber's work is, why did the Occident develop a unique form of rationalization and why did the rest of the world fail to develop such a rational system? The paradigm case of the West's distinctive rationality is bureaucracy, but it is only one aspect, albeit a central one (along with capitalism), of a broad-based process of rationalization.

The rationalization concept in Weber's work is notoriously obscure, but the best definition of at least one key type – formal rationalization – is the process by which actors' choices of means to ends are increasingly constrained, if not determined, by universally applied rules, laws and regulations. The bureaucracy, a key domain of such rules, laws and regulations, is one of the defining products of this process of rationalization, but there are others such as the capitalistic market, systems of rational–legal authority, the factory and the assembly line. All have in common the fact that they are formally rational structures that constrain the individuals within them to act in a rational manner by pursuing ends through the choice of the most direct and efficient means. Furthermore, Weber saw more and more sectors of society coming under the domination of formal rationalization. Eventually, he envisioned a society in which people would be enslaved in an 'iron cage of rationality' made up of a near seamless web of these formally rational structures.

These structures, as well as the process of formal rationalization in general, can be seen as being defined by several dimensions (Eisen 1978). First, formally rational structures emphasize calculability, or those things that can be counted or quantified. The focus on quantity tends to lead to a de-emphasis on quality. Second, there is a focus on efficiency, or finding the best means available to an end. Third, there is great emphasis on predictability, or being sure that things operate in the same way from one time or place to another. Fourth, there is an emphasis on the control over, and ultimately replacement of, humans by non-human technologies. Finally, and reflective of Weber's profound ambivalence about the rationalization process, is the tendency of formally rational systems to have irrational consequences, in other words, the irrationality of rationality.

Rationality has many irrationalities, but the foremost among them is dehumanization. Modern formally rational systems tend, in Weber's view, to be inhuman places in which to function and this goes for the bureaucrat, the factory worker and the assembly-line worker, as well as the participant in the capitalist market. For Weber, there is a basic conflict between these formally rational structures devoid of values and individuals imbued with his notion of 'personality,' that is, those defined and dominated by such values (Brubaker 1984: 63).

The modern analyst of business and management is left with several concerns derived from Weber's work (see ORGANIZATION BEHAVIOUR; ORGANIZATION BEHAVIOUR, HISTORY OF). At the most general level is the continuing relevance of Weber's general theory of increasing formal rationalization to the modern business world. The business world in particular, as well as society as a whole, would seem to be even more rationalized today than it was in Weber's day. Thus, the process remains relevant and, in fact, we need to be attuned to its spreading influence throughout the business world and the larger society.

Beyond the broad theory are more specific aspects of Weber's work, the most important of which for our purposes is the process of bureaucratization and the resulting bureaucratic structure. As one aspect of the rationalization process, the process of bureaucratization persists and bureaucratic structures continue to survive and even spread throughout the West, as well as the rest of the world. At the same time, Weber's 'ideal type' of a bureaucracy continues to be useful as a heuristic device for analysing organizational structures. The goal is to see how well these structures measure up to the elements of the ideal-typical bureaucracy. The ideal-typical bureaucracy remains a useful methodological tool even in this era of radically new, debureaucratized organiza-

tional forms. The ideal type is of utility in determining how far these new bureaucratic forms have strayed from the form as it was first described by Weber.

While the bureaucracy continues to be important, one may question whether it still is the 'paradigm case' of the rationalization process. It could be argued, for example, that the fast-food restaurant is today a better paradigm for the rationalization process than the bureaucracy (Ritzer 1993).

The bureaucracy is the organizational form characteristic of one of Weber's three types of authority – rational–legal authority which rests on the legality of enacted rules (see ORGANIZATION STRUCTURE; ORGANIZATION TYPES). There is also traditional authority which is based on the sanctity of immemorial traditions. Finally, charismatic authority rests on the belief of followers that a leader has extraordinary qualities. These authority types remain relevant to thinking about those who lead businesses and other types of organizations. Since the three types of authority are ideal types, any given leader may have their authority legitimized on the basis of some combination of all three types.

With the rout of communism throughout most of the world, Weber's thoughts on the capitalistic marketplace take on renewed importance. The capitalist market was both a key site of the rationalization process and a formally rational structure defined by all of the key elements outlined above. Further, it was crucial to the dissemination of the principles of formal rationality to many other sectors of society.

Weber envisioned a mortal struggle taking place in the modern world between formal rationality and a second type of rationality, substantive rationality. While in formal rationality choices of means to ends are determined by rules, laws and regulations, in substantive rationality those choices are guided by larger human values. The Protestant ethic is an example of substantive rationality, while the capitalist system, which was an 'unanticipated consequence' of that ethic, is, as we have seen, an example of formal rationality. That they are in conflict is reflected in the fact that capitalism became a system that was inhospitable not only to Protestantism, but to all religion. To put it another way, capitalism, and more generally all formally rational systems, reflect the increasing 'disenchantment of the world'.

In the modern world, one of the places in which this conflict is being played out is in the struggle between formally rational systems like bureaucracies and the substantively rational professions like medicine and law. The classic professions are being threatened by both formally rational bureaucracies like those associated with the government or private enterprise as well as by increases in formal rationality within the professions. As a result, the professions as we have known them are embattled and in the process of losing much of their power, prestige and distinguishing characteristics. In other words, they are undergoing a process of deprofessionalization. This is nowhere clearer than in the most powerful profession of all, the American medical profession (Ritzer and Walczak 1988).

We have mentioned two of the types of rationality employed by Weber (formal and substantive), but it should be pointed out that there are two others: practical (the day-to-day rationality whereby people accept given realities and attempt to deal with them as best they can) and theoretical (the effort to master reality cognitively through increasingly abstract concepts). It could be argued that the USA achieved much of its economic success by creating and refining a wide range of formally rational systems, for example, assembly lines, time-and-motion systems, organizational principles such as General Motors' divisional system (see SLOAN, A.P., JR), and innumerable others. It also could be argued that its more recent failures are traceable to relying too long and too exclusively on such formally rational systems. In contrast, it could be argued that the Japanese have succeeded by using formally rational systems often developed in the USA (as well as developing their own such as the just-in-time system) (see JUST-IN-TIME PHILOSOPHY) and supplementing them with substantive rationality (importance of the success of the collectivity), theoretical rationality (strong reliance on research and development, as well as engineering) and practical rationality (for example, quality circles) (see TOTAL QUALITY MANAGEMENT). In other words, the Japanese have created a 'hyperrational' system and this gives them an enormous advantage over American industry that continues to rely heavily on only one form of rationality (Ritzer and LeMoyne 1991).

4 Conclusions

Weber's most lasting contribution has been his theory of rationalization. That theory posits four types of rationality (formal, substantive, theoretical and practical) and argues that formal rationality was a distinctive product of the Occident and one that has come to dominate it. This theory has proved useful in analysing such traditional issues as the bureaucracy, the professions and the capitalist market, as well as a series of recent developments such as the rise of the fast-food restaurant, deprofessionalization and the recent ascendancy of Japanese industry and the parallel decline of American industry. Thus, Weber's ideas continue to be relevant to an understanding of a variety of recent developments in the business world and in the world economy. Theorists continue to clarify and amplify his ideas and researchers continue to apply Weber's ideas to a wide range of social settings.

GEORGE RITZER
UNIVERSITY OF MARYLAND
AT COLLEGE PARK

Further reading

(References cited in the text marked *)

Bendix, R. (1960) *Max Weber: An Intellectual Portrait*, Garden City, NY: Anchor Books. (Now classic overview of the life and work of Max Weber.)

* Brubaker, R. (1984) *The Limits of Rationality: An Essay on the Social and Moral Thought of Max Weber*, London: Routledge. (The best single source on Weber's thoughts about rationality.)

* Collins, R. (1985) *Weberian Sociological Theory*, Cambridge: Cambridge University Press. (Excellent example of neo-Weberian theory.)

* Eisen, A. (1978) 'The meanings and confusions of Weberian "rationality"', *British Journal of Sociology* 29: 57–70. (Useful discussion of the various dimensions of formal rationality.)

Kalberg, S. (1980) 'Max Weber's types of rationality: cornerstones for the analysis of rationalization processes in history', *American Journal of Sociology* 85: 1145–79. (Excellent discussion of Weber's rationalization theory and the source for the four types of rationality employed in this biographical sketch.)

Lassman, P. (ed.) (1994) *Weber: Political Writings*, Cambridge: Cambridge University Press. (Essays dealing with another one of Weber's concerns – politics.)

* Lehmann, H. and Roth, G. (eds) (1993) *Weber's Protestant Ethic: Origins, Evidence and Contexts*, Cambridge: Cambridge University Press. (Collection of contemporary essays dealing with various aspects of Weber's classic work.)

* Mitzman, A. (1969) *The Iron Cage: An Historical Interpretation of Max Weber*, New York: Grosset & Dunlap. (A controversial psychobiography of Weber which focuses on his often unsuccessful effort to work out the conflict between his mother and his father in his work and elsewhere.)

Parsons, T. (1937) *The Structure of Social Action*, New York: McGraw-Hill. (The work that introduced, many would say in a distorted manner, Weber's theory (and others) to an American audience and laid the basis for Parsonsian theory and structural functionalism.)

* Ritzer, G. (1993) *The McDonaldization of Society*, Thousand Oaks, CA: Pine Forge Press. (The thesis of this book is that the fast-food restaurant is now a better paradigm of the rationalization process than the bureaucracy and that, if anything, that process is even more powerful today than it was in Weber's day.)

* Ritzer, G. and LeMoyne, T. (1991) 'Hyperrationality: an extension of Weberian and neo-Weberian theory', in G. Ritzer (ed.), *Metatheorizing in Sociology*, Lexington, MA: Lexington Books. (Creates the concept of hyperrationality to describe the co-existence of Weber's four types of rationality and uses that concept to explain Japan's economic successes and the recent failures of the USA.)

* Ritzer, G. and Walczak, D. (1988) 'Rationalization and the deprofessionalization of physicians', *Social Forces* 67: 1–22. (Argues that the medical profession is being swamped by formal rationalization and that this is leading to the deprofessionalization of medicine.)

Schluchter, W. (1981) *The Rise of Western Rationalism: Max Weber's Developmental History*, Berkeley, CA: University of California Press. (Important study of Weber's developmental history of rationalization.)

Sica, A. (1988) *Weber, Irrationality, and Social Order*, Berkeley, CA: University of California Press. (Unlike most other studies of Weber which focus on his work on rationality, this one deals with the issue of irrationality.)

Turner, S. (2000) *The Cambridge Companion to Weber*, Cambridge: Cambridge University Press. (A key work bringing together leading scholars on Weber and his work.)

* Weber, Marianne (1975) *Max Weber: A Biography*, trans. and ed. H. Zohn, New York: Wiley. (The definitive biography of Max Weber, by his wife.)

* Weber, M. ([1904–5] 1958) *The Protestant Ethic and the Spirit of Capitalism*, New York: Scribner's. (One of the classic works in sociology detailing the relationship between the ethos of Protestantism, especially Calvinism, and the rise of a spirit of capitalism in the West, a spirit that was ultimately connected to the development of capitalism and, more generally, formal rationality.)

* Weber, M. ([1916] 1964) *The Religion of China: Confucianism and Taoism*, New York: Macmillan. (Part of Weber's sociology of religion in which he discusses the barriers to the rise of capitalism and formal rationality within the major religions of China.)

* Weber, M. ([1916–17] 1958) *The Religion of India: The Sociology of Hinduism and Buddhism*, Glencoe, IL: Free Press. (Companion to *The Religion of China*. Here Weber shows how Hinduism and Buddhism served to impede the development of capitalism and formal rationality.)

* Weber, M. ([1921] 1963) *The Sociology of Religion*, Boston, MA: Beacon Press. (The most general statement of Weber's ideas on the sociology of religion.)

* Weber, M. ([1921] 1968) *Economy and Society*, Totowa, NJ: Bedminster Press. (Three volumes comprising the single best source for a sense of Weber's overall project and his general theoretical perspective.)

* Weber, M. ([1927] 1981) *General Economic History*, New Brunswick, NJ: Transaction Books. (Demonstrates that Weber saw the Protestant ethic as only one of many factors in the rise of Western capitalism and rationality.)

See also: CROZIER, M.; JAPAN, MANAGEMENT IN; MARX, K.H.; MICHELS, R.; OCCUPATIONAL PSYCHOLOGY; ORGANIZATION STRUCTURE; POWER; TOTAL QUALITY MANAGEMENT; UNITED STATES OF AMERICA, MANAGEMENT IN THE

Weick, Karl E. (1936–)

Personal background

- born 31 October 1936 at Warsaw, Indiana, USA
- graduated from the Ohio State University, Columbus, Ohio (1962, PhD in Psychology)
- Assistant Professor of Psychology at Purdue University, Lafayette, Indiana (1962–5)
- Professor of Psychology at the University of Minnesota, Minneapolis, Minnesota (1965–72)
- Professor of Psychology and Organizational Behavior, Cornell University, Ithaca, New York, (1972–84)
- Harkins and Co. Centennial Chair in Business Administration, University of Texas (1984–8)
- Rensis Likert Collegiate Professor of Organizational Behavior and Professor of Psychology, the University of Michigan, 1988 onwards
- editor, *Administrative Science Quarterly* (1977–85)
- re-directed the focus of organization theory from structures to processes, from organizational behavior to sensemaking

Major works

Social Psychology of Organizing (1969, revised edition 1979)
Sensemaking in Organizations (1995)
Making Sense of the Organization (2000)

Overview

Karl E. Weick's work has had a central role in shaping the discipline of organization theory in the 1980s and 1990s. He launched a new style in organizational theorizing by combining a sophisticated use of systems theory with insights from the world of music and literature, which steadily acquired a growing circle of followers. Some of his concepts are widely used throughout organization theory, e.g. organizing, loosely coupled systems, enactment of environment and sensemaking. He is keenly interested in the concerns of organizational practice and combines an interest in concrete organizational events with an imaginative theorizing.

1 The Social Psychology of Organizing

The origins of organization theory can be placed as late as the early 1960s. Previous to this, there was business and public administration, industrial psychology and sociology, and other subdisciplines which dealt with somewhat similar issues within their disciplinary frames (Waldo 1961) (see ORGANIZATION BEHAVIOUR, HISTORY OF). An encounter with systems theory led to a need to establish an object with boundaries able to interact with its environment. Thus 'organization' became viewed not as a state of affairs but as an entity (see SYSTEMS).

Among those works which attempted to make a massive loan from systems theory there was one which was especially prominent: Daniel Katz and Robert L. Kahn's *The Social Psychology of Organizations* (1966). Weick's book – *The Social Psychology of Organizing* – published in 1969 but best known in its revised edition from 1979, clearly announced its intention to continue but also advance beyond their perspective. The reason for it was that the concept of open systems became the mainstay of organizational analysis, but remained underdeveloped (Weick and

Sandelands 1990: 337). Weick undertook its development whilst simultaneously transcending it by the adoption of concepts related to autopoietic, i.e. self-regulating and self-reproducing systems (Maruyama 1974, Luhmann 1990). It is this later innovation that permitted him to extend biological metaphors to those coming from literature, poetry and the arts. Furthermore, it is Weick's understanding of how metaphors work which made him use biological concepts in organization theory so successfully (see ORGANIZATION BEHAVIOUR; ORGANIZING, PROCESS OF).

He argued that the focus of organization theory must be set in the process of *organizing*, that is assembling 'ongoing interdependent actions into sensible sequences i.e. generate sensible outcomes' (Weick 1979: 3). The result of organizing is *interlocked* cycles which can be represented as *causal loops* rather than a linear chain of causes and effects.

Organizing runs through stages reminiscent of biological evolution and is triggered by a change in environment that is followed by an *enactment*: organizational actors bracket out a certain segment of their environment for active treatment. This stage corresponds to variation. The subsequent treatment consists of *selection*, i.e. attempts to reduce the ambiguity of the ongoing events by applying accessible cognitive schemes to them, which makes it possible to (temporarily) assemble them together; this is then followed by *retention*, i.e. storing of the successful results of such sensemaking that enlarges and renews the repertoire of cognitive schemes, but, paradoxically, also limits the possibility of noticing subsequent changes in the environment.

Organizing is thus an ongoing encounter with ambiguity, ambivalence and equivocality being part of a larger attempt to make sense of life and the world. It is this assumption that sets Weick's theorizing organizations apart from the rest of the field that evolved around the notion of 'uncertainty', which is a negative state which must be eradicated for organizing to take place. He cherishes ambiguity and gives it a central place in evolutionary processes. While organizing is an effort to deal with ambiguity, it never completely succeeds. Furthermore, the ordering it involves does not consist of imposing the rules of rationality on a disorderly world, but is a far more complex and inherently ambiguous process of sensemaking.

Social Psychology of Organizing is exceptionally rich in metaphors, anecdotes, and pictures with everything from high and popular culture, jazz, business, politics and sports. The anecdote that is best remembered concerns three baseball umpires who represent the three most common variations of the theory of knowledge. Asked how they call balls and strikes, the objectivist says 'I calls them as they is'; the subjectivist says 'I calls them as I sees them', while the constructivist says 'They ain't nothin' till I calls them'. This last stance, together with the set of concepts introduced in this early work, was to characterize Weick's work in the years to come.

2 Loosely coupled systems

Like its outcomes, organizing itself does not develop along a linear sequence. Different stages are *loosely coupled* to one another in everyday organizational life. This loose coupling provides organizations with the flexibility and slack necessary for survival.

The idea of loosely coupled systems comes from Robert B. Glassman (1973) and was borrowed for organizational purposes by several organization scholars such as March and Olsen (1976) who used it in their notion of the garbage-can decision model. Weick originally applied the idea for understanding the erratic organizing typical of educational institutions (1976) and later for grasping the occurrence of disasters in high reliability organizations which tend toward tight coupling (Weick 1990). As the attention of organization researchers turned away from hierarchies and toward networks, the idea was then adopted by many researchers studying different organizational contexts. Its attraction lies in admitting the existence of both rationality and indeterminacy in the same system. There is a tendency, however, to mistake loosely coupled systems as the opposite of tightly coupled systems, rather than a combination of tightly coupled and decoupled systems: 'If there is responsiveness without distinctiveness, the system is tightly coupled. If there is distinctiveness without responsiveness, the system is decoupled. If there is both distinctiveness and responsiveness, the system is loosely coupled' (Orton and Weick 1990: 205). While the greatest promise of his notions is their ability to grasp complexity, the obvious danger awaiting his followers is the one of simplifying these notions and thus forfeiting their power.

3 Organizational cognition and learning

When represented, causal loops resemble maps, thus the concept of *cause maps* that is present in his first major work and is later developed (Bougon *et al.* 1977, Daft and Weick 1984). He refused the concept of 'cognitive schemata' that was already in use in psychology in favour of 'cause maps' because it allowed him to tackle the paradoxical observation that 'a map is often a territory', which builds a bridge to the notion of enacted environments. But 'maps' were more in tune with the second umpire and his subjectivist stance 'I calls them as I sees them'. People may act according to their cause maps but if sensemaking is an ongoing process then how long is a given map valid? Does it survive the longish process of depicting it? Above all, does it capture complexity or does it trade it off for complication? Inscribing cause maps in research may well aid the reification and 'confusing the map with the territory' which he considers dangerous for managerial practice.

His later work on organizational learning (Weick 1991, Weick and Westley 1996) refutes the structuralist strain of cognitive psychology in favour of espousing the paradoxicality of organizational cognition processes. Weick and Westley claim that 'organizational learning' is an oxymoron, as 'To learn is to disorganize and increase variety. To organize is to forget and reduce variety' (Weick and Westley 1996: 440). In order to grasp this paradox it is necessary to abandon the notion of organizational cognition as an aggregate of individual cognitive processes and focus the collective and embedded character of learning in organizations. Conceptualizing organizations as self-designing systems helps to reconcile the two opposing processes of learning and organizing in a pic-

ture of organizational change based on 'muddling through' (Lindblom 1959; in Weick's terms, 'small wins') rather than on stimulus–response or planned change models.

4 Enactment and crisis management

Another concept which turned out to be seminal in organization theory was that of enactment which is both the process of making ideas, structures, and visions real by acting upon them and the outcome of this process, 'an enacted environment' (Weick 1988). It reverses the idea of implementation – which is the putting of a plan into operation – by showing that people are able to act as if their ideas were already implemented. It exchanges the idea of environment as given for the one as constructed. This is not to be confused with wishful thinking as at best enactment is only partially successful, but the concept allows one a better understanding of the dynamics of collective undertakings.

The notion has been widely used as it blends well with the increasing constructivist strand in organization theory. Weick used it most spectacularly in studies on high reliability (or high risk) organizations. While crises are the everyday happening of all organizations, they become especially acute and visible in this kind of organization. The theory of crisis management, developed through the analysis of accidents, catastrophes and disasters (Turner 1978, Perrow 1984, Shrivastava 1987) conceptualized it in terms of reactions to the situation already existing (see CRISIS MANAGEMENT). The perspective of enactment erases the division between crisis prevention and crisis management, revealing how enactment can produce a crisis-prone environment, but also how the understanding of it may help to avoid crises and to reduce danger (Weick 1988, 1990). One way of doing this in practice is by producing and exchanging stories, especially of the kind which he calls 'near-miss narratives', i.e. when an accident is prevented and there is therefore no one to blame but a lesson to be learnt. This is but one example of sensemaking – the core of all organizing.

5 Sensemaking in Organizations

Organizational sensemaking in this work is compared with interpretation, i.e. Sense-giving and sense-taking. In the latter cases, a frame of meaning is already in place, and it is enough to connect a new cue to an existing frame. Where there is no frame or at least no obvious connection presents itself, one has to be created – and this is sensemaking. This distinction was not present in Weick's first book, where organizing equalled sensemaking, which seemed at the time to encompass all three processes.

Seven properties of organizational sensemaking were explored: 'identity, retrospect, enactment, social contact, ongoing events, cues, and plausibility' (Weick 1995: 3). Most of these were known from his earlier writings, but here they are all brought together. After discussing plausibility – which in organizational practice is much more important than accuracy, the fetish of perception studies – Weick concludes:

> If accuracy is nice but not necessary in sensemaking, than what is necessary? The answer is, something that preserves plausibility and coherence, something that is reasonable and memorable, something that embodies past experience and expectations, something which resonates with other people, something that can be constructed retrospectively but also can be used prospectively, something that captures both feeling and thought, something that allows for embellishment to fit current oddities, something that is fun to contrast. In short, what is necessary in sensemaking is a good story.
>
> (Weick 1995: 60–1)

This, in his opinion, is what is most needed 'in an equivocal, postmodern world, infused with the politics of interpretation and conflicting interests' (Weick 1995: 61). Such a postulate is consistent with another, also known from his earlier work: that of requisite variety, which suggests that complex objects must be met by complex models. Although stories simplify the world and are therefore useful as guides for action, they simplify it less than the

kind of formal models which we learned to revere as true science.

Scientists may not always make sense, but practitioners constantly try to. Even though sensemaking is an ongoing activity, it is not always equally intensive. After all, there are routines, stereotypes, 'received ideas' and inherited truths. The activity of sensemaking increases with ruptures and discontinuities, shocks and interruptions.

What does sensemaking consist of? A frame, which is relatively large and lasting (Goffman 1974), a cue, and a connection. The frames can be usefully conceived as inherited vocabularies of society, organization, work, individual life projects and tradition.

Sensemaking can be driven by beliefs or by actions. Beliefs shape what people see, and give form to the actions they take. Disparity of beliefs in any social context leads to argument which is one form of sensemaking. Beliefs can also be projected onto the future thus forming expectations. In discussing this last point, Weick retrieves Merton's notion of the 'self-fulfilling prophecy' (Merton 1948) as a 'fundamental act of sensemaking' (Weick 1995: 148).

Action-driven sensemaking, in organizational practice irrevocably connected with the belief-driven kind, generally assumes two forms which are creating commitment and manipulating the world. Weick observes that organized anarchies are the ones which excel at creating commitment as in them there is a continuous need for sensemaking, unrelieved by routines, standard operating procedures or organizational memories.

The book as a whole fulfils two functions. It summarizes two decades of organization theory inspired by his work and it sets the platform for the works to come.

6 Modelling the discipline

Karl Weick has played a central role in shaping the discipline of organization theory in the 1980s and 1990s. This role is highly unusual in that he was never a part of the so called mainstream, and yet his influence was not exerted from the margins of the discipline. He is neither a school builder nor the critical deviant but more a constructive deviant, in the sense that his deviation from standard concerns and perspectives at any given time gives shape to the concerns and perspectives to come. For this reason, many other organization theoreticians tried to assess and understand his influence upon the field.

Weick himself was of the opinion that 'theorists often write trivial theories because their process of theory construction is hemmed in by methodological strictures that favour validation rather than usefulness' (Weick 1989: 516). Favouring usefulness, he suggests that theory making is an organizing process, a sensemaking process which consists of 'disciplined imagination'. A desired result brings out 'a plausible theory, and a theory is judged to be more plausible and of higher quality if it is interesting rather than obvious, irrelevant or absurd, obvious in novel ways, a source of unexpected connections, high in narrative rationality, aesthetically pleasing, or correspondent with presumed realities' (Weick 1989: 517).

His critics agree and use his work as the best example for just this kind of theory. John Van Maanen (1995) argues that, instead of following methodological strictures, he has developed a unique style, which fulfils both the requirement of a high narrative rationality and an aesthetical satisfaction. Van Maanen calls this style 'allegoric breaching'. Allegory consists of conveying an abstract message through the narration of a concrete set of events, while breaching concerns conventional textual practices of the field. This style favours an essay form, ambiguity of reasoning, dialectic reconstruction, and a rhetorical strategy of presence (Van Maanen 1995). Much as these traits break against the recommended style of academic writing, the success of Weick's style speaks most eloquently for itself.

His influence on both form and context of theorizing organizations is profound. He turned the attention of organization students from structures to processes, from the relevance of academia to the relevance of the field, from mystification to imaginative interpretation. His exceptionally sophisticated use of biological metaphors permitted their combination with cultural metaphors in a seamless way. Although his importance for theory building is paramount, were managers to read only one book in organization theory in their lives, *Social Psychology of Organizing* is a serious candidate.

BARBARA CZARNIAWSKA
GÖTEBORG UNIVERSITY

Further reading

(References cited in text marked *)

* Bougon, Michel, Weick, Karl E. and Binkhorst, Din (1977) 'Cognition in organization: An analysis of the Utrecht Jazz Orchestra', *Administrative Science Quarterly* 22: 606–31. (Cybernetic analysis of cause maps held by the orchestra members.)
* Daft, Robert L. and Weick, Karl E. (1984) 'Toward a model of organizations as interpretation systems', *Academy of Management Review*, 9 (2): 284–95. (A conceptual treatise on cognitive organization theory.)
* Glassman, Robert B. (1973) 'Persistence and loose coupling in living systems', *Behavioral Science*, 18: 83–98. (Adapts cybernetic terms and systems theory to behavioral and social sciences.)
* Goffman, Erving (1974) *Frame Analysis: An Essay on the Organization of Experience*, Boston: Northern University Press. (The most complete treatment of Goffman's theory of everyday's life.)
* Katz, Daniel and Kahn, Robert L. (1966) *The Social Psychology of Organizations*, New York: Wiley. (A classic in the field; several editions exist.)
* Lindblom, Charles E. (1959) 'The "science" of muddling through', *Public Administration Review*, 19: 79–88. (An anti-reformist, incrementalist view of organizational change.)
* Luhmann, Niklas (1990) *Essays on Self-reference*, New York: Columbia University Press. (Explains the concept of self-perpetuating systems in the context of communication.)
* March, James G. and Olsen, Johan P. (1976) *Ambiguity and Choice in Organizations*, Bergen: Universitetsforlag. (A collection of studies using the garbage-can model of decision making.)
* Maruyama, M. (1974) 'Paradigms and communication', *Technological Forecasting and Social Change*, 6: 3–32. (Explains the notion of communication systems in cybernetics.)
* Merton, Robert K. (1948) 'The self-fulfilling prophecy', *Antioch Review*, 8: 193–210 (A classic article showing how collective beliefs can turn into reality.)

* Orton, J. Douglas and Weick, Karl E. (1990) 'Loosely coupled systems: A reconceptualization', *Academy of Management Review*, 15 (2): 203–23. (A review of the works using the loosely coupled systems concepts after 14 years of its introduction.)

* Perrow, Charles (1984) *Normal Accidents*, New York: Basic. (Taking the Three Mile Island accident as a starting point, it suggests that accidents are normal rather than exceptional events in complex systems.)

* Shrivastava, Paul (1987) *Bhopal: Anatomy of a Crisis*, Cambridge, MA: Ballinger. (An attempt to formulate a theory of crisis origins and of crisis management.)

* Turner, Barry A. (1978) *Man-made Disasters*, (2nd edn. 1997), Oxford: Butterworth/Heinemann. (The first book looking for systemic and organizational causes of disasters.)

* Van Maanen, John (1995) 'Style as theory', *Organization Science*, 6 (1): 133–43. (A passionate defence of variety and creativity in organization theory against attempts to solidify and standardize it.)

* Waldo, Dwight (1961) 'Organization theory: An elephantine problem', *Public Administration Review*, 21: 210–25. (A review article signalling the new era in organization theory.)

* Weick, Karl E. (1976) 'Educational organizations as loosely coupled systems', *Administrative Science Quarterly*, 21: 1–19. (Introduces the concept of the loosely coupled system to organization studies.)

* Weick, Karl E. (1979) *The Social Psychology of Organizing*, 2nd edn, New York: Addison-Wesley. (A classic, first published in 1969, for those interested in the concept of organizing.)

* Weick, Karl E. (1988) 'Enacted sensemaking in crisis situations,' *Journal of Management Studies*, 25 (4): 305–17. (Argues that crisis management can be active instead of reactive.)

* Weick, Karl E. (1989) 'Theory construction as disciplined imagination', *Academy of Management Review*, 14 (4): 516–31. (Presents a reflective view on the process of theory construction in organization studies.)

* Weick, Karl E. (1990) 'The vulnerable system: An analysis of the Tenerife air disaster', *Journal of Management*, 16 (3): 571–93. (The collision of two planes in Tenerife in 1977 is analysed as a prototype of system vulnerability to crisis.)

* Weick, Karl E. (1991) 'The nontraditional quality of organizational learning', *Organization Science*, 2 (1): 116–24. (Criticizes the traditional definition of learning borrowed from psychology.)

* Weick, Karl E. (1995) *Sensemaking in Organizations*, Thousands Oaks, CA: Sage.

* Weick, Karl E. (2000) *Making Sense of the Organization*, Boston: Blackwell. (A collection of papers edited by the author.)

* Weick, Karl E. and Sandelands, Lloyd E. (1990) 'Social behavior in organizational studies', *Journal for the Theory of Social Behaviour*, 20 (4): 323–46. (Summarizes main problems and achievements of organization research in the context of social science.)

* Weick, Karl E. and Westley, Frances (1996) 'Organizational learning: Affirming an oxymoron', in *Handbook of Organization Studies*, Sage: London, 440–58. (Redefines the concept of organizational learning setting it in the context of culture and language.)

See also: DECISION MAKING; LINDBLOM, C.E.; MARCH, J.G. AND CYERT, R.M.; MORGAN, G.; OCCUPATIONAL PSYCHOLOGY; ORGANIZATION BEHAVIOUR; ORGANIZATION BEHAVIOUR, HISTORY OF; ORGANIZATION PARADIGMS; ORGANIZATIONAL LEARNING; ORGANIZING, PROCESS OF

Welch, Jack (1935–)

1 Introduction
2 Main contribution
3 Evaluation

Personal background

- born 19 November 1935 in Peabody, Massachusetts
- received his BS in chemical engineering from the University of Massachusetts in 1957
- earned an MS (1958) and a PhD (1960) in chemical engineering from the University of Illinois
- engineer at the General Electric Company (GE) from 1960 to 1968
- General Manager of the Worldwide Plastics Division from 1968 to 1971
- promoted to Vice-President in 1972
- from 1973 to 1977 served as Vice-President and Chief Executive of the Components and Materials Group
- served as Senior Vice-President of the Consumer Goods and Services Division from 1977 to 1979
- promoted to Vice-Chairman and Executive Officer in 1979
- appointed Chairman and Chief Executive Officer (CEO) of General Electric in 1981

1 Introduction

John Francis Welch, Jr was born on 19 November 1935 in Peabody, Massachusetts. John, Jr (aka Jack) was the only child of John Francis, Sr and Grace Andrews Welch. His father was a railroad conductor on the Boston & Maine Railroad and spent a lot of time away from home. Welch was largely raised by his mother who was said to have been both demanding and supportive of her son. She told him '... that his serious stammer was not a speech impediment, but the result of a hyperactive brain working too fast for his mouth' (Rosen 1993).

Welch grew up in a tough working-class neighbourhood where fights were common (Smart 1992). He was an aggressive and determined athlete who played neighbourhood sports (e.g. baseball, basketball) in an abandoned quarry named 'The Pit' (Harris 1986). 'Friends say Welch was an accomplished, if not natural, athlete who always pushed himself to the limit' (Harris 1986). College classmates remember his intense competitive spirit and how much he hated to lose, 'even in touch football' (Harris 1986). Welch received his BS in chemical engineering from the University of Massachusetts in 1957. He continued his studies at the University of Illinois where he earned an MS (1958) and PhD (1960) in chemical engineering.

After finishing his graduate education, Welch joined the General Electric Company (GE) where he worked as an engineer from 1960 to 1968. During 1968–71 he was the General Manager of the Worldwide Plastics Division. In 1972 he was promoted to Vice President, and from 1973 to 1977 Welch served as Vice President and Chief Executive of the Components and Materials group. He served as Senior Vice-President of the Consumer Goods and Services Division from 1977 to 1979. In 1979 Welch was promoted to Vice-Chairman and Executive Officer, and in 1981 he made history when he became the youngest person (age 45) to be selected Chairman and CEO of General Electric (Rosen 1993).

From 1959 to 1987 Welch was married to Carolyn Osburn. In April 1989 Welch married Jane Beasley. He has four children (Katherine, John, Anne and Mark) from his first marriage (Rosen 1993; Harris 1986).

In 1995, at age 59, Welch underwent elective triple bypass heart surgery to relieve arterial blockages. Following the surgery he ran GE from his home and a month later he was back on the job (Smart 1995). Welch recently postponed his scheduled retirement in April 2001 (Hill 2000c), and he now plans to work through the end of 2001 to oversee the completion of the Honeywell acquisition (Murray *et al.* 2000).

2 Main contribution

'Within three years of his appointment as General Manager of GE's worldwide plastics division, Welch turned the fledgling division into a $400 million-a-year powerhouse. Promotions followed rapid-fire...' (Rosen 1993). Welch was nicknamed 'Neutron Jack' in the 1980s after his massive downsizing and restructuring had led to more than a 25 per cent reduction in employment at GE (Rosen 1993). 'Welch has trimmed GE's work force from 400,000 in 1981 to 220,000 today [circa 1994], has nearly doubled revenue from $26 billion a year and has transformed GE into truly a global corporation' (Swoboda 1994) (see MULTINATIONAL CORPORATIONS). By January 2000, GE's employment had increased with its business expansions to 340,000 (*The Financial Times 500* 2000).

During Welch's tenure as Chairman and CEO, GE has bought and sold companies/divisions to bolster overall corporate performance. After taking over the top job at GE in 1981, Welch stated that any operating unit which was not ranked number 1 or 2 in terms of world market share would be sold (Swoboda 1994). He divided the company's divisions into 'winners' and 'losers' and gave those on the loser list one year to turn their operations into winners, i.e. number 1 or 2 globally (Rosen 1993). In 1988, Welch even sold GE's Consumer Electronics group to Thomson SA of France after he became convinced that the group would not be able to meet his high profitability standards (Stein 1989). History supports Welch's prediction as Thomson's consumer electronics operations posted sizable operating losses in the 1990s, including a 1991 write-off of $365 million (Levine 1991; PR Newswire 1997).

During the 1990s, Welch has attempted to create what he refers to as a 'boundaryless company'. According to Welch, 'A boundaryless company ... will remove the barriers among engineering, manufacturing, marketing, sales and customer service; it will recognize no distinctions between "domestic" and

"foreign" operations .... [It] will ignore or erase group labels such as "management", "salaried" or "hourly", which get in the way of people working together' (Swoboda 1994). He has implemented a strategy of worker participation and empowerment in the 1990s. 'The cornerstone of Welch's New Age management is the Work-Out, an intense [2–3 day] forum in which rank and file GE employees and managers brainstorm about ways to make production more efficient in factories and other facilities' (Rosen 1993).

As part of his long-range strategy, Welch has led GE into new markets such as television (NBC and MSNBC) and established a new corporate intranet to significantly improve the utilization of information within GE (Smart 1996). In 1996, GE used the intranet and Internet to match GE buyers with outside sellers for $1 billion of goods purchased electronically. 'The payoff ... is that GE can select from a broader base of suppliers as well as cut its purchasing costs' (Smart 1996).

Under Welch's leadership GE has aggressively pursued 'e-business', with each GE unit required to form a team to reinvent itself in terms of opportunities and challenges posed by the Internet (see E-BUSINESS). This initiative is known as 'dyb.com' or 'destroy your business.com' after Welch's proclamation that if you don't change your business some 'dot.com' will destroy it (*The Economist* 1999b: 25). In 1999, Welch made 'e-business' the top priority for GE (Hill 2000b).

Sticking to his vision, Welch is in the process of further restructuring GE in order to ensure the company's ability to compete after his retirement (Bernstein *et al.* 1997). Most notable was Welch's influence in arranging the surprise acquisition of Honeywell in October, 2000 for $44 billion (Edgecliff-Johnson and Bowe 2000). As in the past, '"Plants and product lines may be closed or sold, wages cut, and work transferred to non-union plants and subcontractors both here and abroad"' (Bernstein *et al.* 1997).

3 Evaluation

'... Welch's intense intellect and hard-charging style have earned him a reputation as one of the country's toughest managers, as well as one of its emerging gurus of business management' (Lueck 1985). Welch is known for continually cutting costs and improving productivity throughout GE. There are also some signs that he is more sensitive than generally perceived. He resents the nickname 'Neutron Jack' and has stated that 'It was really painful for me and for the people [whose jobs were eliminated]...' (Swoboda 1994). He believes that job security is only provided by being able to compete effectively in a global marketplace. Welch loathes inefficient bureaucracies and continually strives to eliminate layers of management which he sees as impeding efficient decision making. At GE Welch has reduced the management hierarchy from nine levels to as few as four, and eventually to one in some divisions. (Byrne 1989; Ashkenas *et al.* 1995). He says that 'The role of a successful corporate leader ... is to create "shock" and then lead the company to recovery' (Swoboda 1994).

While Welch is often criticized for his harsh management style, he is frequently cited for his strategic leadership abilities. Many now believe that GE under the leadership of Jack Welch has been a trend-setting multinational corporation (MNC). '... Welch has been a pioneer of fundamental structural change in the American workplace' (Swoboda 1994). His influence has been further enlarged by his ability to mentor and nurture GE managers and executives who have gone on to lead other prominent organizations. For example, Welch has contributed to the development of CEOs such as Larry Bossidy of Allied Signal, Glen Hiner of Owens Corning, Jon Trani of Stanley Works, and Norm Blake of USF&G (Martin 1997; Reingold and Byrne 1997). Welch has also been invited to share his management philosophy with corporate executives at firms such as IBM (Hammonds 1994).

Despite all of his successes, Welch is not immune to mistakes and failures. For example, '... GE did not pursue research into magnetic levitation technology for railroads ... even as it boosted its investment in the manufacturing of conventional locomotives, whose revival Welch had optimistically and incorrectly predicted' (Rosen 1993). Shortly after GE purchased the brokerage firm of Kidder Peabody in 1986, Welch was embarrassed by a government bond scandal within the brokerage (Carroll *et al.* 1994). Internal fraud with GE's military accounts in the 1980s were also difficult for Welch to accept (Rosen 1993; Lueck 1985).

These problems have not hindered Welch from positioning GE to continue to produce 25 per cent or greater annual returns on equity (Bernstein *et al.* 1997). 'Thanks to his continual revolution since becoming boss in 1981, GE's revenues have quadrupled and its share price has risen thirtyfold' (*The Economist* 1999c: 17). GE was listed by *Fortune* magazine as one of America's 10 most admired companies (Stewart 1998), and *Forbes* magazine (20 April 1998) named GE the most powerful corporation in the United States. As of April 2000, GE was the most valuable company in the world, worth $534 billion in market capitalization (Peston 2000: 3). Welch credits the success to '...the company's continuing emphasis on globalization, growth in services, Six Sigma quality [the quality control method used by GE since 1995] and e-business' (Hill 2000a).

STEPHEN J. HAVLOVIC
UNIVERSITY OF WISCONSIN – WHITEWATER

Further reading

* Ashkenas, R., Ulrich, D., Jick, T. and Kerr, S. (1995) *The Boundaryless Organization*, San Francisco: Jossey-Bass. (Case studies of industry leaders such as GE, SmithKline Beecham and Morgan Bank on how they seek to attain the objective of boundarylessness. Provides useful guidelines to help organizations move toward that goal.)
* Bernstein, A., Jackson, S. and Byrne, J. (1997) 'Jack cracks the whip again', *Business Week*, 15 December: 34. (A review of Jack Welch's recent restructuring activities at GE.)
* Byrne, J.A. (1989) 'Is your company too big?', *Business Week*, 27 March: 84. (An examination of organization size and firm performance.)
* Carroll, M. *et al.* (1994) 'GE draws a line in the sand at Kidder', *Institutional Investor*, July: 13. (A review of the difficulties that Jack Welch and GE have experienced since the firm acquired Kidder Peabody.)
* Edgecliffe-Johnson, A. and Bowe, C. (2000) 'GE agrees $44bn for Honeywell', *Financial Times*, 23 October: 1. (Announcement of GE's acquisition of Honeywell.)

* Hammonds, K.H. (1994) 'Empty chairs in IBM's boardroom', *Business Week*, 7 March: 54. (New release.)

* Harris, M.A. (1986) 'He hated losing — even in touch football', *Business Week*, 30 June: 65. (An overview of the childhood through early career years of Jack Welch.)

* Hill, A. (2000a) 'GE powers towards record result', *Financial Times*, 21 January: 16. (News release.)

* Hill, A. (2000b) 'GE head rues slow start on Net', *Financial Times*, 27 April: 21. (News release.)

* Hill, A. (2000c) 'GE lays ground for orderly succession to Welch', *Financial Times*, 6 June: 19. (News release.)

* Levine, J.B. (1991) 'The heat on Alain Gomez', *Business Week*, 11 March: 66–7. (Shows the pressures to perform under the leadership of Jack Welch.)

* Lueck, T.J. (1985) 'Why Jack Welch is changing GE', *The New York Times*, 5 May 5: Section 3, 1. (An overview of organizational change at GE at the start of the Jack Welch era.)

* Murray, M., Cole, J., Deogun, N. and Pasztor, A. (2000) 'Staying On: On eve of retirement Jack Welch decides to stick around a bit', *The Wall Street Journal*, 23 October: A1, A32. (Announcement of Welch's decision to delay his retirement to oversee the integration of Honeywell with GE's operations.)

* Martin, J. (1997) 'Another GE veteran rides to the rescue', *Fortune*, 29 December: 282. (A review of John Blystone who follows the trend of former GE managers who become successful CEOs after leaving GE.)

* Peston, R. (2000) 'Rising and Midnight Suns Shine Brightly', *FT 500*, 4 May: 3. (A review of recent stock market volatility and the impact on the *Financial Times*' listing of the top global companies.)

* PR Newswire (1997) 'Thomson & Units Ratings Affirmed,' 3 June. (News Release.)

* Reingold, J. and Byrne, J.A. (1997) 'The Top 20 Heads to Hunt', *Business Week*, 11 August: 69. (Article looks at the most desired executives for executive search firms. GE leads the list with 5 of the top 20 and the authors predict a mass exodus from GE once Jack Welch's successor is named.)

Reuters (1998) 'GE is No. 1 on Forbes Super 100 List', *Business News*. (News release.)

* Rosen, I. (1993) 'Jack Welch', *Newsmakers 1993*, Issue 4. (Provides personal and professional biographical information.)

* Slater, R.I. (1993) *The New GE: How Jack Welch Revived an American Institution*, Homewood, IL: Business One Irwin. (Interviews with Jack Welch are used to interpret and explain organizational change and performance at GE.)

* Smart, T. (1992) 'How Jack Welch brought GE to life', *Business Week*, 26 October: 13. (A book review of The New GE: How Jack Welch Revived and American Institution by Robert Slater.)

* Smart, T. (1995) 'Who could replace Jack Welch?', *Business Week*, 29 May: 32. (The article discusses Jack Welch's medical problems and possible replacements for Welch as CEO.)

* Smart, T. (1996) 'Jack Welch's cyber-czar', *Business Week*, 5 August: 82. (A review of GE's information technology initiatives.)

* Stein, C. (1989) 'Ex-GE executive hired to run Wang', *The Boston Globe*, 24 August: Economy Section, p. 1. (Announcement of the hiring of former GE executive Richard W. Miller as President of Wang Laboratories.)

* Stewart, T.A. (1998) 'America's most admired companies', *Fortune*, 2 March: 70–82. (A listing and review of the top rated US firms.)

* Swoboda, F. (1994) 'Up against the walls', *The Washington Post*, 27 February: H1. (An analysis of Jack Welch's leadership and strategic change initiatives at GE.)

* *The Economist* (1999a) 'Dyb.com', 18 September: 25. (A look at Jack Welch's e-commerce initiative known as 'Destroy your Business'.)

* *The Economist* (1999b) 'The house that Jack built', 18 September: 23–6. (A review of the legacy of Jack Welch at GE.)

* *The Economist* (1999c) 'The revolutionary spirit', 18 September: 17–19. (An overview of the ability of GE to change and to reinvent itself.)

* *The Financial Times 500* (2000) 'The US 500', 4 May: 37. (The *Financial Times*' listing of the top 500 US firms by market capitalization.)

Tichy, N.M. and Sherman, S. (1993) *Control Your Destiny or Someone Else Will: How Jack Welch is Making General Electric the World's Most Competitive Corporation*, New York: Doubleday. (The authors provide an 'inside' view of Jack Welch's leadership style and accomplishments at GE.)

See also: DOWNSIZING; GLOBALIZATION; LEADERSHIP; MULTINATIONAL CORPORATIONS; STRATEGY, CONCEPT OF; STRATEGY, IMPLEMENTATION OF

Whistleblowing

Overview

Ethical conflict in organizations has increased as the complexity of working practices has increased. Most employees will experience situations in which they could blow the whistle, or see others doing so. A working definition of whistleblowing is the unauthorized disclosure of information that an employee reasonably believes evidences the contravention of any law, rule or regulation, code of practice, or professional statement, or that involves mismanagement, corruption, abuse of authority, or danger to public or worker health and safety.

A comparison of US and UK law shows that whistleblowing uniquely receives protection in the entire economy of the UK (public, private and not-for-profit sectors), but only public sector whistleblowers or those in contractual relations with the public sector in the USA are protected for. Most whistleblowers suffer harm, however justified their cause. Research on whistleblowing shows that the average whistleblower could be regarded as a model employee. A suitable code of practice can assist in harnessing the energies of whistleblowers.

1 Case histories

An element of organizational disagreement is not only normal, but may also be regarded as healthy (see ORGANIZATION BEHAVIOUR). Generally there is speedy resolution, and the organization then gets on with its day-to-day business. Sometimes this is not the case and there is an ethical trigger point that is set off within the employee, which means that the matter is perpetuated to an end that generally leaves one or both parties aggrieved (Vinten 1999a). One such ethical trigger was found in the case of Stanley Adams, who in 1973 blew the whistle on the trading practices of his company, Hoffman La Roche, which contravened European law. Another occurred when Vivian Ambrose wrote to Tony Benn MP on 14 July 1990 about the widespread corruption, nepotism and incompetence that he observed at the Bank of Credit and Commerce International (see BUSINESS ETHICS).

Concerns have been expressed over a number of years about the way employers disregard the health and safety of their workers, and face minimal fines when death occurs. It is possible to write a common report that would readily apply to every type of disaster: in each case, the findings of previous reports are concealed or not actioned, there is lack of independence or effectiveness of inspectorates, there is failure to adopt a participative management style, and finally there is the 'not required back' stamp for employees who complain of health and safety abuses. Increasingly there are anonymous telephone hot lines and safety ombudsmen so that those who know, and will suffer the consequences, have a sure means of communication that will be guaranteed an impact. In the social services, the North Wales Child Abuse Tribunal, chaired by Sir Ronald Waterhouse, found abuse at 40 homes, (mostly in seven) since 1974. TheTribunal report of February 2000 recommends that local authorities implement whistleblowing procedures.

There are many examples of employees suffering these consequences. In the UK, an oil rig welder and whistleblower, Vaughan Mitchell, reported safety violations by his drilling company on a North Sea oil rig, and was dismissed. Guardian Royal Exchange dismissed Charles Robertson, their Chief Tax Accountant, for writing abusive letters to his seniors. However, an Industrial Tribunal in November 1987 found that this was not the true reason; the company was obstructing Mr Robertson in his professional duty to report the company's true tax position to the tax authorities. Two cases involve the UK National Health Service. Dr Helen Zeitlin and Charge Nurse Graham Pink both believe that they were dismissed because they drew attention to inadequacies of resourcing for patients, particularly for elderly patients. Some staff consider their duties under their professional code take priority over those under their employment contract, and conflict is inevitable (Vinten 1992).

2 Research on whistleblowing

The limited research on this subject generally ignores the costs and the perspective of the organization and concentrates on the whistleblower. An exception is Vinten (1994). In a survey of eighty-seven whistleblowers in the USA, from both the civil service and private industry, all but one experienced retaliation, with those employed longer experiencing more. Harassment came from peers as well as superiors, and most of those in private industry and half of those in the civil service lost their jobs. Of the total, 17 per cent lost their homes, 8 per cent filed for bankruptcy, 15 per cent got divorced and 10 per cent attempted suicide.

A similar result emerged from a six-year-long US study of sixty-four whistleblowers. To qualify for inclusion in the study, each ethical resister (those who take a stand on matters of ethical principle) needed to have persuasive evidence to corroborate observations, and those appearing to be engaged in a personal vendetta or making a deal to exonerate themselves when charged with improper conduct were excluded. Most were in their thirties or forties, and were conservative people devoted to their work and organizations. They had built their careers by conforming to the requirements of bureaucratic life. Most had been successful until they were asked to violate their own standards of workplace behaviour (see OCCUPATIONAL PSYCHOLOGY). Whistleblowing was accompanied by economic and emotional deprivation, and led to career disruption and personal abuse (Glazer and Glazer 1989). In another US survey, a questionnaire was completed by 161 whistleblowers, 80 per cent being government employees. Severe retaliation and overwhelming personal and professional hardship were re-

ported by many in this group, which was found to be in many ways exceptional and tending to exhibit a distinctive approach to moral issues and decision making. Committed to certain values, the group was capable of acting on this sense of obligation despite the strong organizational and situational pressures to the contrary (see BUSINESS ETHICS).

The few UK studies come to similar conclusions. One study focused on the health service (Hunt 1995) and another more specifically on nurses working in psychiatric hospitals (Beardshaw 1981). It is instructive that the Commission of the Speaker of the House of Commons in *Encouraging Citizenship* provides a definition of citizenship which includes whistleblowing:

> The challenge to our society in the late twentieth century is to create conditions where all who wish can become actively involved, can understand and participate, can influence, persuade, campaign and whistleblow, and in the making of decisions can work together for the mutual good.
>
> (Stonefrost 1990: 1)

This was certainly the nearest one came in the UK to any official recognition of the value of whistleblowing within the context of citizenship and, indeed, the attribution of almost a constitutional role for the activity.

3 The legal position?

The USA's employee-at-will doctrine is that an employee hired for an indeterminate period of time may be discharged at any time for any reason or no reason at all. The idea was that there was a symmetry between the right of a person to sell labour upon such terms as is deemed proper, and the right of the purchasers of labour to proscribe the conditions of such labour, including termination-at-will. This was the position in Britain until the passage of the 1971 Industrial Relations Act, which gave every employee the right not to be unfairly dismissed by an employer (Vinten 1994).

Increasingly, in the USA, the courts have been prepared to allow a defence based on noteworthy public interest (see ENVIRONMENTAL MANAGEMENT; ENVIRONMENTAL REPORTING). This will depend upon the importance of the relevant public policy, where and in what context it was announced, how it fares when weighed against the employer's and society's broader interests, and whether the violation was so offensive as to justify carving an exception to the all-pervasive employer-at-will doctrine. Public sector employees in the USA enjoy considerable protection under the so-called whistle-blower protection acts, with compensation of up to $500,000, and an independent protection agency, the Office of the Special Counsel.

Under common law there is an implied duty not to misuse confidential information belonging to the employer, and this duty may continue to operate after the termination of the employment. There are, however, practical difficulties in dealing with ex-employees, and where matters of confidentiality are likely to be significant, the best course of action is to extract from the employee an express restraint clause. Not only is this more certain and effective, but, if valid, it may also stop the former employee from entering employment in which there is a high probability that the information may be used. The one exception to the duty not to misuse confidential information occurs where disclosure is in the public interest. This may apply where the employer is committing a criminal offence, but it goes beyond this to include situations where the public has a serious and legitimate interest in the revelation. The law will often weigh up the benefit of public disclosure.

The UK Public Interest Disclosure Act 1998

Following media coverage of disasters where whistleblowing might have saved life, a charity promoting the benefits of raising employee concerns at work, Public Concern at Work (PCAW) joined with the Campaign for Freedom of Information and Tony Wright MP, to draft the Whistleblowers Protection Bill, introduced under the ten-minute rule by Wright in early 1995. The Bill failed to proceed, lacking the employer-friendly factors of later versions and a conducive political climate. A revised version, The Public Interest Disclosure Bill, was introduced by Don Touhig MP at the end of 1995. The Bill entered the committee stage in the Commons,

but was talked out by the government in 1996. There was strong all-party support, with a lively five hour debate and individual cases presented to argue for legislation.

In December 1997, a new version of the Public Interest Disclosure Bill gained its second reading without debate. It was supported by all political parties, and by the Confederation of British Industry, the Institute of Directors, and the Trades Union Congress. The Bill progressed through the House in record time, and was the subject of an enactment order in early 1999. Although the Act encouraged and offered maximum protection to those who reported first internally, it recognized that this might be impossible, for example, where a cover-up might be predicted, or wherelives could be put at risk through the need to adhere to lengthy procedures. Media disclosure was approved in these most serious of cases. Tests for reasonableness and good faith were applied to the employee, as in the previous version of the Bill. Two conditions apply. The first is to fit the definition of a qualifying disclosure, the second relates to how the whistle-blower should pursue the matter. A qualifying disclosure involves reasonable belief of:

1 A criminal act;
2 The failure to comply with a legal obligation, including a breach of contractual obligation, the breach of statutory duty, or maladministration, where it may also be shown that administrative law has also been breached;
3 A miscarriage of justice;
4 Danger to health and safety;
5 Damage to the environment;
6 The concealment of information relating to any of these.

Whistleblowers need to be able to show that they:

1 Acted in good faith;
2 Reasonably believed that allegations are substantially true;
3 Have not acted for personal gain;
4 Had made a disclosure through existing procedures unless it may be shown that there was a reasonable belief that a cover-up would ensue or that the wrongdoing was so serious that immediate and appropriate action was necessary.

The question remains as to how much protection the common law really offers to the whistleblower, outside the UK Public Interest Disclosure Act. What is most likely to happen is that the whistleblower will be dismissed and may then have recourse to an employment tribunal. The odds here tend to be against the complainant, but success is less likely to result in reinstatement, and even where it does, the employer can ignore the order and simply pay damages, assuming that the complainant has the energy to take another legal action.

An award of damages is the more likely successful outcome, but this will rarely be any more than a token payment in view of the financial loss that most whistleblowers experience. Employers need to consider the large amount of staff time and costs needed to fight such cases, as well as the possibility that the organization may be shown in an unfavourable light. Legislation has been enacted in the UK, the USA, Canada, Australia and New Zealand, and all but the UK (which protects all valid whistleblowing) only encompass the public sector.

4 A code of practice?

There is much value in companies setting up a code of practice to deal with whistleblowing situations (Vinten 1999b). This can take the sting out of an occasion that will otherwise result in a lose/lose situation. Whistleblowing is, in itself, neither valid nor invalid, right nor wrong, but depends on the context, which is often one of high moral ambiguity with disputes as to the true nature of the situation and differing perceptions. Although a rugged individualism may suggest the civil liberty of an employee to blow the whistle at will, this has to be balanced against the smooth and relatively unencumbered running of an organization. The still, small voice of conscience, the Kantian categorical moral imperative, cannot be the ultimate arbiter, every employee may have a slightly different voice and acting on this voice could lead to organizational chaos.

The employee should in the first place avoid taking up employment that would lead to moral conflict. It also needs to be recognized that not all whistleblowers are correct in what they allege, and it may be problematic to establish the facts. Whistleblowing may sometimes be a subterfuge to disguise an employee's incompetence or illegal activity, or it may be a spurious counterclaim to disciplinary action taken against the employee. It may not be unsafe or unlawful activities that are in question, but the social policies of the management that the employee happens to consider to be unwise. There has to be an element of leadership and direction in any organization, and employees need to achieve a sense of proportion in how much protest and for how long is reasonable (see LEADERSHIP). Equally the employer needs to show fairness, patience and openness in dealing with such an inevitable, if hopefully uncommon, aspect of organizational life.

A code of practice would include:

1 Bringing the matter to the attention of one's superior, except where the superior is involved, in which case the next level up will apply. Failing a satisfactory outcome, go to the next managerial level up.
2 A right of confidential access to the managing director and/or chairperson.
3 A final court of appeal within the organization to a committee of non-executive directors.
4 Providing guidance on ethical dilemmas that may arise and ways of coping.
5 A clear statement by the company of the standards of ethical conduct it intends to follow.
6 The *ad hoc* appointment of an independent ombudsman to whom employees can appeal, perhaps with the agreement on both sides that the decision of this person will be final.
7 A recognition of the value of employees being ethically alert and therefore an intention not to discriminate against employees who blow the whistle.

5 Conclusion

Although there will still be cases in which any policy will be unsuccessful, by internalizing whistleblowing within an organization it should be possible to contain it, and even to harness it for the good of the company. Only the unethical organization will hesitate to take such action. Certainly it can be seen as wasteful to take action against the sort of employee who could be one of the organization's most valuable assets. Beyond this there is an increase in legal protection in several countries, plus gathering public and political support. Countries which abuse human rights may of course have little sympathy with the whistleblower.

GERALD VINTEN
SOUTHAMPTON BUSINESS SCHOOL

Further reading

(References cited in the text marked *)

* Beardshaw, V. (1981) *Conscientious Objectors at Work. Mental Health Nurses – A Case Study*, London: Social Audit. (Provides case study material and ways forward in a close-knit sector in which staff have sometimes conspired against the interests of patients, and resists those staff who voice dissent at such abuse.)
* Glazer, M.P. and Glazer, P.M. (1989) *The Whistleblowers: Exposing Corruption in Government and Industry*, New York: Basic Books. (Useful perspective and case studies.)
* Hunt, G. (1995) *Whistleblowing in the Health Service*, London: Edward Arnold. (Sector-based treatment.)
Miceli, M.P. and Near, J.P. (1992) *Blowing the Whistle*, New York: Lexington Books. (A US research-based text.)
Martin, B. (1999) *The Whistleblower's Handbook. How to be an Effective Resister*, Charlbury, Oxfordshire: Joon Carpenter. (How to assess options, prepare for action, use official channels, build support and survive the experience.)
* Stonefrost, M. (1990) *Encouraging Citizenship*, London: HMSO. (Places discussion in context of good citizenship.)
* Vinten, G. (1992) *Whistleblowing Auditors: A Contradiction in Terms?* London: Chartered Institute of Certified Accountants. (A comparison of the ethical standpoints and whistleblowing outcomes of internal and external auditors.)
* Vinten, G. (1994) *Whistleblowing: Subversion or Corporate Citizenship?* London: Paul Chapman. (A comprehensive treatment of whistleblowing in the USA, UK and the rest of Europe, from personal, professional, organizational, managerial and legal perspectives.)
* Vinten, G. (1999a) Whistleblowing – Hong Kong Style, *Public Administration and Policy*; A Hong Kong and Asia Pacific Journal. (Closely analyses a civil servant pharmacist whistleblower in Hong Kong who claimed support in Confucian ethics.)
* Vinten, G. (1999b) 'A Whistleblowing Code for Educational Institutions', *International Journal of Educational Management* 13.3: 150–7. (Examines cases of whistleblowing within academia, the dictates of the Nolan Committee, the new legal protections, and an approach towards formulating codes of practice.)
Winfield, M. (1990) *Minding Your Own Business: Self-Regulation and Whistleblowing in British Companies*, London: Social Audit. (A short survey of fifty-three British companies.)

See also: BUSINESS ETHICS; BUSINESS AND SOCIETY; ENVIRONMENTAL MANAGEMENT; HUMAN RESOURCE MANAGEMENT; INDUSTRIAL AND LABOUR RELATIONS; LEADERSHIP; OCCUPATIONAL PSYCHOLOGY; ORGANIZATION BEHAVIOUR; SOCIAL AND ENVIRONMENTAL REPORTING

Whitney, Eli (1765–1825)

Personal background

- born December 8, 1765, in Westborough, Massachusetts, son of a prosperous farmer
- showed early aptitude for the mechanical arts; at age 14 installed a forge in his father's workshop; during the American Revolution established a successful business manufacturing nails and knife blades
- set out to obtain an education at age 19; graduated from Yale College in 1792 (age 27)
- came under the influence of Catherine Greene at Mulberry Grove, Georgia, after a failed attempt to establish a career as a private tutor; with Greene's encouragement and inspiration invented the first successful cotton gin (1792)
- filed patent application on the cotton gin June 20, 1793; awarded March 14, 1794
- easily copied, pirated versions of Whitney's cotton gin were already in widespread use by the time he was able to complete tooling and manufacture his first production models
- despite the cotton gin's success, the lack of sales for Whitney led him to seek a government contract for the manufacture of muskets in 1798
- in 1801, Whitney put on a demonstration of the interchangeability of parts in ten muskets for government officials, including President Jefferson, in Washington, DC; this demonstration earned Whitney the sobriquet 'Artist of his Country' as well as faithful government support for his efforts to develop manufacturing techniques producing interchangeable parts
- the manufacturing techniques developed at Whitney's arsenal and in government arsenals over the next generation furnished the basis for the American System of manufacturing – division of labour and use of special purpose machine tools
- married Henrietta Edwards, 1817; four children
- died January 8, 1825, New Haven, Connecticut

Summary

Eli Whitney (1765–1825) was the inventor of the cotton gin as well as the first American manufacturer to attempt volume production of a relatively complex product using interchangeable parts. As inventor of the cotton gin he contributed significantly to launching an economic revitalization of plantation agriculture and plantation slavery in the American South. In his efforts to produce muskets based on interchangeable parts he pioneered the systematic use of special purpose machine tools and division of labour intended specifically to de-skill a manufacturing process. Whitney also clearly understood the potential for economies of scale achieved through the application of power driven machinery to produce large volumes of goods. In developing manufacturing techniques for volume production of firearms, he achieved considerable financial success. At the same time, he also established himself in the eyes of his contemporaries as the 'Artist of his Country'.

1 Introduction

Eli Whitney's cotton gin proved itself the technological *sine qua non* for Southern agriculture and the American cotton textile industry of the early nineteenth century. Although Whitney and his business partners saw little financial return on the development of the cotton gin, Whitney was widely recognized and celebrated for the invention. Following Whitney's successful demonstration of interchangeability of the parts for ten muskets before President Adams and President-Elect Jefferson in 1801, his contemporaries lionized him as a mechanical genius and the creator of an entirely new manufacturing system. Subsequent generations rather uncritically accepted a simplified and mythologized version of his accomplishments as inventor and as Father of the 'American System' of manufacturing (see UNITED STATES OF AMERICA, MANAGEMENT IN THE; MANUFACTURING PROCESSES). Scholarship in the twentieth century challenged numerous points both in the story of his invention of the cotton gin and in the standard account of Whitney as the 'inventor' of interchangeable parts.

2 Biographical data

From an early age Whitney showed strong mechanical aptitude. At age 14 he persuaded his father to instal a forge in the workshop on the family farm in Westborough, Massachusetts. With imports from Britain cut off by the American Revolution, Whitney entered business manufacturing nails and knife blades. While the hostilities lasted, he operated a successful venture. The end of hostilities, however, soon led to the reintroduction of British trade goods in American markets. Whitney tried manufacturing hatpins and walking sticks, but soon understood that his small establishment could not compete with the large volume of British trade goods that flooded into American markets at the end of the hostilities.

In 1783, at age eighteen, Whitney formed the plan to attend college. At this point he had achieved only a rudimentary education, but that apparent handicap did not deter him. He set about preparing himself to gain his own education by teaching school in neighbouring towns for the next six years. With a salary of $7 per month, he financed his own summer attendance at Leicester Academy, where he studied mathematics as well as Latin and Greek. In 1789, at the age of 24, he passed the entrance exam for Yale College.

Graduating from college in 1792 at age 27, Whitney was penniless. Almost by default, and because the offer came through his connections at Yale, he accepted a position as a private tutor on a South Carolina plantation.

He travelled to Savannah in the company of Phineas Miller, a Yale alumnus, and Catherine Greene, the widow of General Nathanael Greene, hero of the American Revolution. Miller and Greene would play a very important part in Whitney's life: Miller, Catherine Greene's plantation manager, would become his partner in the cotton gin venture. Catherine Greene soon adopted Whitney as a protégé, and she was to play in important part in the actual invention of the cotton gin.

When the promised tutoring position in South Carolina failed to materialize, Whitney accepted an invitation to take up residence at Mulberry Grove, the plantation owned by Catherine Greene. 'Green seed' cotton grew almost like a weed in the upland regions of the American South, but the difficulty of cleaning the seeds from the cotton by hand left the material worthless to the textile industry. There was a widely acknowledged need for a machine to separate the seeds from the short-staple cotton.

As the local notables gathered and discussed the cotton problem in Catherine Greene's drawing room, she urged Eli Whitney to invent a new machine. With her encouragement and support, Whitney had a crude working model within a week. It took several months of additional effort to build the full-sized prototype. A demonstration before a select few guests in early 1793 caused a sensation. On the strength of what they had seen (or heard), local planters ordered wholesale conversion of their cropland to the 'green-seed' cotton. Whitney was soon in partnership with Phineas Miller who would furnish the working capital and handled the local business arrangements while Whitney produced machines.

Whitney was to return to New Haven to produce machines. On his way there, Whitney stopped in Philadelphia to file a patent application. Once in New Haven, he set about establishing a works to manufacture gins, but had to overcome a number of problems, including a shortage of skilled labour and a lack of machine tools. He was not able to set out again for Savannah (with just six machines) until May 1794 – after nearly a year away. Upon arrival in Savannah, he discovered that, rather than selling machines, Miller had established a marketing scheme that called for their partnership to operate gins. They would clean the cotton for planters on a model derived from the traditional operation of grist mills, returning one pound of cleaned cotton for every five pounds of seed bearing bolls brought to their gin.

Such a scheme never had a realistic chance of working effectively. Miller and Whitney had significantly underestimated the volume of cotton planters could produce. They lacked the capacity to handle the 1794 crop. Moreover, their machine was so simple in its construction that pirated versions were already in operation even before Whitney arrived back in Georgia with his first six machines. Finally, the planters considered the pricing scheme onerous and unfair, with some justification. Had Miller and Whitney been able to get their price, they would have held title to one-third of the cotton crop produced in the American South.

Whitney and Miller found courts reluctant to enforce their patent. They pursued legal remedies together until Miller's death in 1803. Although the partnership did eventually get legal recognition in 1807 and some compensation for the illegal use of their invention, Whitney always claimed that he took less money out of the cotton gin venture than what it had cost to pursue the legal battle. As late as 1812 he was seeking a special act of Congress to extend the patent monopoly on the gin.

By 1798 Whitney possessed a complete manufacturing works outside New Haven. The lack of success in enforcing the patent on the cotton gin, however, meant that the works were nearly idle and he faced bankruptcy. At that point, events took a turn that allowed Whitney to change course in his life.

In 1798, the threat of war with France jolted the American Congress into voting a dramatic increase in defence spending. At a stroke, Congress allocated $800,000 for the procurement of arms from private firms as a supplement to the output of the new federal armouries. The intent was to stimulate the development of a domestic arms industry in the United States. Despite enjoying a reputation for high quality hunting rifles, the United States remained almost entirely dependent on European imports for military arms. The establishment of the national armouries at Springfield, Massachusetts (1795), and Harpers Ferry (1797) had not created the manufacturing capacity that would be necessary to meet even the needs of the military in case of a national emergency. The $800,000 appropriation was made with the knowledge that sufficient manufacturing capacity did not exist. It was intended to stimulate investment by private contractors.

In the government's desire to encourage the development of private manufacturers, Whitney saw a market opportunity. Even before final Congressional authorization for the funding, he was lobbying for support in seeking a contract to produce muskets using a new manufacturing process that would involve the use of machines powered by water and the production of uniform parts. Whitney had no experience as an armourer, but believed his idea for manufacturing musket parts as uniformly as if produced from a 'copperplate' would allow him to produce 10,000 stand of arms in two years. His proposal proved hopelessly optimistic, but within the plan lay the seeds of his contribution to the development of what became known in the nineteenth century as the 'American System of Manufacturing' – volume production based on interchangeable parts.

With the endorsement of Oliver Wolcott, Secretary of the Treasury (and a Yale alumnus), Whitney secured a contract to produce 10,000 muskets in 28 months. The contract, for $134,000, was awarded in June 1798, calling for the delivery of the first 4,000 muskets by September 1799. Delivery of the balance was due by September 1800. The government even allowed Whitney a cash advance of $5,000. Whitney had no experience as an armourer; nor was it widely believed he could deliver on time. Still, the threat of war, a lack of qualified arms competitors, and the backing of influential supporters meant that Whitney got the work.

He came nowhere near completing the contract on time. In 1799, when the first lot was due, he had barely begun outfitting his armoury with machines. He did not deliver the first 500 muskets until September 1801. The final delivery was not made until January

1809 – more than eight years late. During this time, Whitney not only managed to obtain one extension after another but enjoyed the vocal support of such influential backers as Oliver Wolcott and Thomas Jefferson. It was also during this period that the first of the Whitney legends about interchangeability and enlightened factory management had their birth. Even before the completion of the contract for the first 10,000 muskets, his armoury had become stop for travellers interested in new manufacturing practices and enlightened factory management (Smith 1981).

Despite difficulties, Whitney was developing the methods that would mark the emergence of American manufacturing as a distinct and powerful economic force (Livesay 1979). One measure of his personal success can be seen in comparing his initial contracting capabilities with his performance on later contracts. The 1798 contract for 10,000 muskets to be delivered in 28 months actually required 10 years and 6 months for completion. Most of the muskets in that order were actually produced during the final two years. In contrast, during the War of 1812, Whitney took a contract to supply 15,000 muskets and completed the order in somewhat less than two years (Olmsted 1972).

3 Evaluation

The young American republic of the early nineteenth century was hungry for home-grown heroes and a distinctive American identity. Eli Whitney's ingenuity, his pluck, the boldness of his ambitions, and the scope of his vision seemed to provide just the right mix needed to satisfy this national hunger. As early as 1795, Yale awarded him with an honorary Master of Arts in recognition of his invention of the cotton gin. Even as he struggled to put together the machines and the system needed to manufacture the first muskets, diarists and essayists lionized him and trumpeted his accomplishments as inventor, manufacturer, enlightened manager, and social visionary. By the early 1820s he was the richest man in prosperous New Haven and his factory village was widely acclaimed as a model of all that was good and virtuous in the young American republic. Whitney had, in fact,

already become an American folk hero. Along with his contemporaries Oliver Evans, Robert Fulton, and Francis Cabot Lowell he quickly entered the schoolbook lore of nineteenth century America as an exemplar of all that was best and most creative in the dynamic economic growth produced by industrialization.

Much of the early praise for Whitney was produced and accepted before the full meaning of his work could be understood. Not surprisingly, much of the fulsome praise as 'inventor' of interchangeablithy failed to stand the tests of critical scrutiny. Indeed, at the level of specifics, virtually every major claim about Whitney's accomplishments came under attack (more or less successfully) in the late twentieth century. Most significantly, the famous 1801 demonstration of interchangeability was unquestionably 'rigged', and Catherine Greene is now widely accepted as at least a co-author in the invention of the cotton gin. Claims about extraordinarily ingenious machine tools at Mill Rock have been discounted; and even the long accepted claim for Whitney as the inventor of the milling machine (1818) has been discredited (Smith 1981). Curiously, however, even these seemingly devastating revelations have done little to dim Whitney's historical reputation. Instead, the revisions shifted the grounds for evaluating his accomplishments.

Recognizing Catherine Greene's role in the story of the cotton gin is important. She certainly played a part. She directed Whitney to the problem, and she suggested the simplified approach (a brush) for pulling the cotton off the cleaning rollers. Beyond the issue of authorship, however, the important issue is that the invention truly revolutionized agriculture in the American South. This appears most forcefully in the figures on American cotton production immediately before and after the invention. In 1792 cotton exports from the United States totalled just 138,328 pounds. In 1794, the year the cotton gin first came into use, exports totalled 1,601,000 pounds. By the following year the United States was able to export 6,276,000 pounds of cotton. By 1800, American farmers produced 35,000,000 pounds and exported 17,790,000 pounds of cotton. Such figures speak not only of the revitalization of Southern Agriculture but also the development of the American cotton textile industry. Of course, such figures also speak to the revitalization of slavery in the plantation agriculture of the American South. The cotton gin helped set into motion economic forces that led to the American Civil War.

The fact that the 'interchangeable' parts used for the famous 1801 demonstration were specially selected and matched just for that occasion has been established beyond any doubt (Woodbury 1960). Whether there was any intentional 'fraud' involved, however, is far from clear. Whitney was demonstrating prototypes. He was still fully nine months away from delivering the first batch of 500 muskets. Moreover, even though those muskets (and all the muskets Whitney ever delivered) lacked true 'interchangeability', his work was not rejected or criticized by the government on these grounds.

His contemporaries, at least those involved in weapons production, certainly understood that Whitney had produced special prototypes for the 1801 demonstration. With the 1798 contract he was at the centre of a government effort to stimulate the development of a domestic arms industry. His contract for 10,000 muskets was just 1 of 27 contracts awarded for over 40,000 stand of arms. His contract price of $13.40 was just what the government expected to pay. It was a price that exactly matched the production cost of weapons produced at the Springfield Armoury, and it was above the market price the Army had been paying for European imports (Purvis 1995). His projected rate of production, which was 360 per month, while greater than what the national armouries had produced to date, actually proved to be less than what the Springfield Armoury provided across the time of Whitney's contract, which was about 390 units each month (Purvis 1995).

Whitney was at the centre of a movement among armourers to produce weapons using interchangeable parts. He was neither the first to conceive the idea, nor would he become first to accomplish the goal. He was, however, an articulate spokesman for the idea. He was also the first entrepreneur to base his business on the idea. Government officials such as John Adams, Oliver Wolcott, and Thomas Jeffer-

son expressed confidence in Whitney's ability to make progress toward the ideal of interchangeability. What he brought specifically to the implementation was the concept using numerous specialized machines, each doing a specific task. More specifically, he wanted machines – not craftsmen – to provide the precision of the parts. His concept was the use of special purpose tools and division of labour. Moreover, he clearly worked to de-skill the labour involved in manufacturing the parts of his muskets (Livesay 1979). His significance lies in his role as a champion and sponsor of interchangeability who was willing to commit to implementation. In that sense, the title of 'Artist of His Country' has genuine meaning. He conceived and worked toward a vision.

Despite the mythology, Whitney's Mill Rock plant contained no highly specialized or extraordinary machinery. Parts were filed to fit just as they were in the handicraft industries. Whitney's difference was in using unskilled labourers who filed parts against patterns. It was in the use of patterns, jigs, and fixtures that Whitney pioneered the volume production methods of the nineteenth century. He openly shared his techniques, gave visitors tours and advocated for the system. In 1815 he was at the centre of the movement to establish a long-range strategy for standardizing the manufacture of muskets in the national armouries. Effectively, the strategy was to extend the use of patterns, jigs, and gauges. Whitney's patterns and jigs did not produce true interchangeability, but implementation of this strategy in the national armouries led eventually (in the 1840s) to that end. In his role as visionary and champion for the manufacturing process, Whitney deserves recognition as 'Father of the American System'.

On the issues of Whitney's supposedly enlightened management practices, the revisionist social history of the late twentieth century ran squarely across the grain of the nineteenth-century mythologies. Mill Rock had continuing labour problems. Recruiting and maintaining a reliable and labour force proved beyond Whitney's capability. Despite public adulation for his enlightened factory management, his workers disliked his paternalistic practices, the low wages, and the tight enforcement of factory rules. In matters such as these, it is impossible to deny the validity of the specific claims about Whitney's practices and his failures. At the same time, however, it is important to place Whitney's labour practices into context against the standards of the broader world of the early nineteenth century. In that framework, he appears less enlightened than some, more progressive than most. He clearly cared for his workers and sought to improve their living conditions. Moreover, he made significant efforts to furnish continued employment during slack periods, and to provide adequate housing and communal facilities for his workers and their families. Like all factory managers of the early nineteenth century, he faced a workforce unfamiliar with factory work (see INDUSTRIAL REVOLUTION).

4 Conclusion

Eli Whitney played a significant role as a technologist, inventor, and entrepreneur in two areas of important economic developments associated with the early industrial revolution in America. First, the cotton gin clearly enabled an agricultural revitalization in the American South. Insofar as that agricultural revolution depended on slave labour his invention contributed to the circumstances that brought about the American Civil War. Of equal significance, his commitment to the manufacture of muskets using uniform parts provided a pioneering pathway leading to the American System of Manufacturing – high volume production based interchangeable parts. Although Whitney's boosters in the nineteenth and early twentieth century exaggerated his accomplishments, he certainly deserves to be known as the Father of the American System. Under his direction, his armourers never achieved full interchangeability, nor manufacturing at standards that would later come to be known as 'high armoury practice'. Nevertheless, Whitney did more than simply conceive the idea and make a first try at interchangeability. During the first quarter of the nineteenth century he was actively engaged in the developments that led to high armoury practice. He worked with, trained, and supported those figures such Simeon North, Roswell Lee, and John H. Hall who laid the foundation for high armoury practice and the fully developed American System.

DAVID S. LUX
BRYANT COLLEGE, SMITHFIELD,
RHODE ISLAND

Further reading

(References cited in the text marked *)

Green, C.M. (1956) *Eli Whitney and the Birth of American Technology*, Boston: Little, Brown and Company. (Still considered one of the standard biographies. A great deal of important scholarship has appeared since this work was published.)

* Livesay, H.C. (1979) *American Made: Men Who Shaped the American Economy*, Boston: Little, Brown and Company. (The chapter on Whitney offers an excellent account of the difficulties encountered with both the cotton gin and interchangeability. Places Whitney in the context of the history of American manufacturing.)

Mirsky, J. and Nevins, A. (1952) *The World of Eli Whitney*, New York: Macmillan. (A standard biography. Still useful, but now dated.)

* Olmsted, D. (1972) *Memoir of Eli Whitney, Esq.*, New York: Arno Press. (Olmsted's work was based on both documentary sources and personal knowledge of the inventor. The work first appeared as a magazine article in the 1832 issue of the *American Journal of Science*.)

* Purvis, T.L. (1995) *Revolutionary America 1763 to 1800*, New York: Facts on File. (A well-organized compilation of social and economic data for late eighteenth-century America. Very useful for putting Whitney and his achievements into context.)

Schur, J.B. (1999) 'The constitution community lesson plan: Eli Whitney's patent for the cotton gin'. Available [Online]: *http://www.nara.gov/ education/cc/whitney.html* [January 20, 2001]. (A social science lesson plan based on primary sources. Provides an excellent overview of the issues of larger social and cultural significance that followed from the invention of the cotton gin and the development of the American System of Manufacturing.)

* Smith, M.R. (1981) 'Eli Whitney and the American system of manufacturing', in C.W. Pursell Jr, *Technology in America: A History of Individuals and Ideas,* Cambridge, MA: The MIT Press. (Thorough consideration of Whitney's role in the early arms industry and the development of armoury practice. Discounts many tra-

ditional claims, but celebrates Whitney's accomplishments as organizer and promoter.)

Whitney, E. (1794) 'Eli Whitney's cotton gin patent drawing'. Available [Online]: *http://www. nara.gov/nara/searchnail.html* Document: NWDNC-241-PATENTRES-72X [January 20, 2001]. (The drawing is simple. Shows just how easy pirating the invention would be even for a local craftsman.)

* Whitney, E. (1812) 'Petition of Eli Whitney requesting the renewal of his patent on the cotton gin'. Available [Online]: *http://www.nara.gov/ nara/searchnail.html* Document: NWL-233-PETITION-12AF112-1 [January 20, 2001]. (Whitney based his petition primary on the value of the Southern cotton crop to the American economy. The petition provides an interesting glimpse into how Whitney saw his rights.)

* Woodbury, R.S. (1960) 'The legend of Eli Whitney and interchangeable parts', *Technology and Culture.* (Woodbury provided the evidence to show that Whitney's 1801 demonstration of interchangeable parts was based on specially prepared and marked pieces.)

Further resources

The Eli Whitney Museum
http://www.eliwhitney.org

See also: FORDISM; INDUSTRIAL REVOLUTION; MANUFACTURING PROCESSES; MANUFACTURING STRATEGY; OPERATIONS MANAGEMENT; TAYLOR, F.W.; UNITED STATES OF AMERICA, MANAGEMENT IN THE

Wholesaling

Overview

Wholesaling is a business function which can be best described as playing an intermediary role between the manufacturer and the retailer. As a consequence, wholesalers do not have a high level of visibility in the eyes of the final consumer. However, they do provide a broad range of services which are indispensable to both retailers and manufacturers, and which ultimately lead to a more effective system of distribution for products. The functions provided for the manufacturer include market coverage, selling, stockholding, order processing, market research and customer support, while benefits to retailers include availability, assortment, the breaking of bulk supplies into smaller units, credit, service and advice. In line with changes in the role of manufacturers and retailers in most countries, the wholesale function has also undergone some shifts in emphasis, affecting both the importance of wholesalers and the roles they play.

1 Wholesaling defined

There is some confusion as to what precisely constitutes a wholesaling organization. The primary cause of this confusion is the bewildering variety of terms which are applied to business establishments which perform some or all of the business activities which one normally associates with wholesaling.

One of the best definitions is that provided by the US Bureau of the Census (1982), which neatly captures the essence of wholesaling. In this definition, wholesaling is 'concerned with the activities of those persons or establishments which sell to retailers and other merchants, and/or to industrial, institutional and commercial users, but who do not sell in significant amounts to ultimate consumers'.

Thus, the wholesaler forms the bridge between the manufacturer/supplier and the retailer.

Categories of wholesaler

Rosenbloom (1989) has identified a number of business activities which wholesalers perform for both the manufacturer/supplier and the retailer. The extent of the range of services provided, however, depends on the category of wholesaler. The most common category is the merchant wholesaler; typically, this type of operation will provide a complete range of services including the assumption of risk (as it is the wholesaler who purchases inventory from manufacturers), the provision of storage and transportation, the maintenance of a sales force to service retail or industrial accounts, the provision of financing through the extension of credit and the dissemination of market information to both manufacturers and retailers. Bowersox and Cooper (1992) estimate that merchant wholesalers accounted for over 80 per cent of all wholesale firms in the USA in 1987.

The cash-and-carry wholesaler, by contrast, typically does not provide customer credit or delivery. Also known as merchandise agents, these are wholesalers who perform selected marketing functions while buying or selling for other firms. They take responsibility for negotiation, but do not take title to the merchandise which they handle. Other categories of wholesaler include:

1 Mail-order wholesalers, who typically provide a broad range of services but do not include personal selling. Instead, customers place their orders by phone or mail, having made their selections from a previously provided catalogue.
2 Drop shippers, who sell bulky commodity items such as timber and building materials. They arrange direct shipment from the manufacturer to retailer, thereby avoiding the need to take physical possession of the

order. However they do typically take ownership of the order (and the consequent risk that goes with it).

3 Symbol groups, which are to be found in the grocery wholesale sector. These have emerged as a response to the needs of small retail chains when competing with large multiple retailers. Groups such as Spar, Londis and Mace in the UK, for example, provide own brand/label products across a range of merchandise such as grocery, hosiery, tobacco and alcohol to small retail outlets. They have also extended this concept to restaurants and catering establishments including pubs and clubs.

2 Wholesaling in context

A crucial issue for manufacturers is the extent to which they wish to use wholesalers as part of their overall business strategy. In the context of channel management, it is often stated that it is possible to eliminate the middlemen but not the functions that they perform. Thus, a manufacturer has to consider whether it would be more profitable for the firm to perform some or all of the business functions which are normally performed by the wholesaler (see CHANNEL MANAGEMENT).

At a pragmatic level, wholesalers have a continuing presence in, and an intimacy with, local markets which a national supplier cannot possibly hope to attain. In addition, wholesalers make possible local availability of stock and, perhaps more significantly, handle small orders which many national suppliers would find too costly to service themselves. Similarly, the wholesaling function can play an important role in helping small, independent retailers to deliver a more professional and efficient service to the ultimate consumer. This is most commonly exhibited in the level of expertise that wholesalers can provide in areas such as store layout and design, cooperative advertising, price concessions on featured items and point-of-sale material.

However, Stern and El-Ansary observe that many of the descriptions of what a wholesaler can do for the manufacturer and/or retailer are based on an optimistic picture of the capabilities of individual wholesalers. In particular, they note that 'wholesaling firms are,

in general, much more preoccupied with logistics, credit and collection functions than they are with marketing strategy' (1988: 120). This focus has led in many cases to wholesalers failing to appreciate the realities and demands of the marketplace. By contrast, many of the large multiple retailers have taken advantage of large volume purchasing, warehousing and delivery operations, and have made the necessary capital investment in infrastructure (such as in information technology, for example) to allow them to run these operations profitably. Stern and El-Ansary argue that this has weakened the role of the wholesalers and has quickly 'relegated them to meeting the needs of smaller retailers' (1988: 120) (see RETAILING).

This in turn has led to the growth of the voluntary (wholesaler-sponsored) groups such as Spar and Londis, referred to earlier. Similarly, a number of retailer-sponsored groups have also emerged in various retail sectors. This type of operation is characterized by a number of small retailers who band together to form their own wholesale organization, from which they then agree to buy. A range of services is also supplied to retailers, including store design and layout, financing and advertising. A good example of this type of group is Ace Hardware in the USA.

In contrast to the consumer goods sector, industrial wholesaling has managed to retain its importance over the years. Many manufacturers realize the important role that distributors perform in establishing, cementing and improving relationships with the client base (see BUSINESS-TO-BUSINESS MARKETING). This role has taken on even greater significance with the decline in importance of individual brand names (as products become commodities) and the increasing ability of many distributors to add value to the product by providing specialist services. In many cases, wholesalers have become more than capable of justifying their role and importance in the channel. This is significant because there is an alternative option which many suppliers need to consider: like retailers, they could opt to integrate forward in the channel and take on wholesaling responsibilities themselves, possibly benefiting from cost savings in the process. However, the ability of industrial distributors to provide increasing levels of expertise, allied to the increased technical competence and product knowledge which they have acquired, has allowed them to carve out a core competence which suppliers find hard to rival.

Managerial considerations when using wholesalers

One of the key managerial issues which must be addressed is the potential loss of control which can occur when a manufacturer or supplier increasingly has to rely on intermediaries such as wholesalers. This is brought into sharper focus when it is recognized that the wholesaler is an independent entity which exists to maximize profitability for itself, and not the manufacturer. If the aims and objectives of both parties are incompatible, then clearly a situation arises where conflict emerges. This is best exemplified where the wholesaler perceives its role as one of selling an existing range of products to an existing customer base, and where the manufacturer expects the wholesaler to strive for new accounts and to be active in promoting its products. This is particularly germane to the case of industrial markets. Clearly in this case the onus is on the manufacturer to become more proactive in the level of commitment and support which it provides to the wholesaler. In particular, wholesalers need to be given assistance in the areas of pricing, promotion and product development related activities. This issue is particularly significant when dealing with industrial products, which have higher levels of product complexity and sophistication; the problem is less common in consumer markets (see BUSINESS-TO-BUSINESS MARKETING).

3 Future developments in wholesaling

In general terms, the twentieth century has witnessed a decline in the importance of wholesaling. As noted above, industrial wholesalers and distributors have managed to retain their importance in the channel, but consumer goods wholesalers have lost impor-

tance and relative power. These trends seem likely to continue.

Increasing levels of retailer and manufacturer concentration have made direct contact between them economically practical, reducing the need for a middleman. This trend has been reinforced considerably by the advent of more efficient management of information flows between the retailer and supplier. In particular, the adoption of electronic data interchange (EDI) and computer-to-computer systems has created the prospect of more accurate forecasting of product requirements and a reduction in order volume, as better knowledge of the processing cycle is allied to quicker delivery (see ELECTRONIC DATA INTERCHANGE). When these developments are added to recent advances in the management of the logistics function, it becomes apparent that the role of the wholesaler as a middleman between the large manufacturer and large retailer has been severely diminished (see LOGISTICS AND PHYSICAL DISTRIBUTION).

However, there is still a role for wholesalers, particularly in bridging the gap between the small independent retailers and national suppliers. Further, the undoubted decline in the fast-moving consumer goods (FMCG) sector should be set against the fact that other sectors still rely on wholesalers to a large extent. Davies (1993) cites the example of the fresh produce sector, where over two thousand wholesalers account for about 60 per cent of fruit, vegetables and flowers. Clearly there are many sectors where the wholesaler continues to have a role to play.

Another interesting development is the emergence of 'warehouse clubs'. These have been described as large-scale, members-only establishments that combine the features of both cash-and-carry wholesalers and discount retailers. Operating out of basic, even spartan premises, these establishments offer a diverse range of products, including car tyres, soft drinks, office supplies and home furnishings. The warehouse club concept blurs the demarcation line between what constitutes a retail operation as opposed to a wholesale operation. A court case at the end of 1993 (considering a planning application) classified them as wholesalers; however, single consumers can join such clubs on payment of a fee. This raises the possibility that traditional cash-and-carry wholesalers may come under threat from such operations.

In summary, the role of the traditional consumer goods wholesale function has declined – severely, in some sectors – in the last twenty years. However, it still provides a valuable service to the small independent retailer. By contrast, industrial wholesalers have survived and in some cases prospered, mainly due to the nature of the product and the inherent opportunity to add value to the basic service provision and thus create a niche based on specialization.

SEAN ENNIS
UNIVERSITY OF STRATHCLYDE

Further reading

(References cited in the text marked *)

* Bowersox, D.J. and Cooper, M.B. (1992) *Strategic Marketing Channel Management*, New York: McGraw-Hill. (This is a general work on channel management, and is useful for examining wholesalers in the context of the overall channel structure.)

Business Statistics Office (1989) *Business Monitor: Wholesaling*, Newport: Business Statistics Office. (A report with useful information for those who wish to capture a more detailed perspective of wholesaling in the UK.)

* Davies, G. (1993) *Trade Strategy Marketing*, London: Chapman. (An excellent review of the changing role of wholesaling.)

KeyNote (1991) *Cash and Carry Outlets*, 9th edn, Hampton: KeyNote Publications. (This is an industry report that provides a detailed review of the cash-and-carry sector in the UK.)

Michman, R.D. (1990) 'Managing structural change in marketing channels', *Journal of Consumer Marketing* 7 (4). (A salient article which addresses the issue of how certain functions are being performed by other channel participants.)

* Rosenbloom, B. (1989) 'The wholesaler's role in performing marketing functions', in L. Pellegrini and S.K. Reddy (eds), *Retail and Marketing Channels*, New York: Routledge. (This chapter is a concise examination of the functions performed by the wholesaler.)

* Stern, L.W. and El-Ansary, A.I. (1988) *Marketing Channels*, 3rd edn, New York: Prentice Hall. (A standard text on channel management with a detailed chapter on the wholesaler.)

* US Bureau of the Census (1982) *Census of Wholesale Trade*, Geographic Area Series WC82–A–52, Washington, DC: US Bureau of the Census. (Useful for a statistical analysis of the structure of wholesaling in the US; however, caution must be exercised, given the age of the statistics.)

See also: BUSINESS-TO-BUSINESS MARKETING; CHANNEL MANAGEMENT; EXPORTING; LOGISTICS AND PHYSICAL DISTRIBUTION; RELATIONSHIP MARKETING

Wiener, Norbert (1894–1964)

Personal background

- born 26 November 1894, Columbia, Missouri, USA
- at the age of 10, wrote his first paper entitled 'The theory of ignorance'
- studied mathematics and philosophy at Harvard University
- at 19 he received a doctorate in philosophy from Harvard University
- married to Margaret Engelmann, 1926
- pioneer of the new science of cybernetics
- spent most of his academic life at the Massachusetts Institute of Technology (USA) as professor of mathematics
- was author of over 200 papers in mathematical and scientific journals and eleven books
- received five prizes and medals – including the National Medal of Science from the US president – and three honorary doctorates
- died of a heart attack in Stockholm on 18 March 1964 at the age of 70

Major works

Cybernetics: or Control and Communication in the Animal and the Machine (1948)
The Human Use of Human Beings: Cybernetics and Society (1950)
Ex-prodigy (1952)
I am a Mathematician (1956)
God and Golem, Inc. (1964)
Invention: The Care and Feeding of Ideas (1993)

Summary

Norbert Wiener (1894–1964) was the father of cybernetics, an interdisciplinary new science that was born after the Second World War. Cybernetics created connections between wartime science and post-war social science by developing a non-causalistic and ecological view of systems, both physical and biological. In his books about cybernetics Wiener showed the existence of invariants in the communication and control mechanisms that are observed in both animals and machines. Cybernetic principles have provided, on the one hand, basic principles for the design of many sorts of machines such as radar, communication networks, computers and artificial limbs, and on the other hand, fundamental insights to the study of animal characteristics like learning, memory and intelligence. Cybernetic ideas have also been widely developed and used in the managerial sciences and in a much broader sociological context.

1 Introduction

Norbert Wiener was a mathematical prodigy who at the age of 19 obtained his doctorate in philosophy at Harvard University. He spent most of his academic life at the Massachusetts Institute of Technology (MIT) as professor of mathematics where he wrote over 200 papers in mathematical and scientific journals, and eleven books. Since his early scientific works in the development of a mathematical theory of Brownian motion and a mathematical interpretation of quantum mechanics, two of the more important research topics in theoretical physics at that time (1920s), Wiener appeared as an unusual mathematician because of the integration of the content of his mathematical work with his personal philosophy. For Wiener, mathematical theories were special instances in which general philosophical ideas are made concrete. His philosophical approach pointed to a unified view of the world, including human beings, where everything is connected to everything else, but in which the most general principles have an element of vagueness (Heims 1980: 140, 156).

Such a holistic (or ecological) view of nature was well ahead of its time for an early twentieth-century scientist.

2 Main contribution

During the Second World War, the US Office of Scientific Research and Development gave priority to the solution of the long-range problem of atomic bomb construction and the more immediate problem of finding a way to attack German bomb-carrying aircraft. While the work on the atomic bomb was centred at Los Alamos, the problem of tracking and shooting down aircraft was concentrated at MIT where Wiener was in charge of developing the necessary mathematical foundations for solving it. Working with a young engineer, Julian Bigelow, Wiener developed a mathematical theory of great generality for predicting the future as best one can on the basis of incomplete information from the past. This theory helped revolutionize the whole field of communication engineering and formed the basis of modern statistical communication theory (Heims 1980: 184). At that time (1940s) the theory immediately led to great improvement in radar observations of aircraft and was successfully applied in the design of noise filters for radios, telephones and many other devices of common use (Wiener 1993). This work was carried out independently around the same time that Claude Shannon was developing his 'mathematical theory of communication' (Shannon and Weaver 1949) (see SHANNON, C.).

One particularly interesting feature of the anti-aircraft problem was the cycle involving feedback: information from a radar screen was used to calculate the adjustments needed on gun controls to improve accuracy on the target, then the effectiveness of this adjustment was observed and communicated again via radar, and this new information used again to readjust the aim of the gun and so on. If the calculations are automated this is a self-steering device; if not, the whole system including the participating persons is a self-steering device. It was Wiener's crucial insight that a similar feedback mechanism is involved in all voluntary activity, for example, in the act of picking up a pencil from a table. Here information perceived mainly through observation continually guides the movements of the muscles in our arm and hand until this particular task has been successfully achieved. Wiener discussed these ideas with the Mexican physiologist Arturo Rosenblueth, who suggested that some common disorders of the nervous system, generically known as ataxia, could possibly be explained in terms of failures of this feedback mechanism. If you offer a cigarette to a person suffering from ataxia, they will swing their hand past it in trying to pick it up. This will be followed by an equally futile swing in the opposite direction, and then by a third swing back, until the motion becomes nothing more than a vain and violent oscillation.

The idea that some parallels between engineering devices and living organisms could be found through mathematical formulations received extraordinary support from many scientists of quite diverse backgrounds (see SYSTEMS). On 8 March 1946, in a hotel in New York, 21 scientists met to talk about these ideas. That was the first of a series of conferences sponsored by the Macy Foundation – a philanthropic medical foundation – out of which the principles of a new science were formulated: cybernetics. The group of scientists who met regularly during those years (from 1946 to 1953) is known as the 'cybernetics group' (Heims 1991), and included names such as the great mathematician John von Neumann, the neuropsychiatrist Warren McCulloch, the social scientist Gregory Bateson and the anthropologist Margaret Mead, along with Arturo Rosenblueth and Wiener himself.

In his classic book, *Cybernetics: or Control and Communication in the Animal and the Machine* (1948), Wiener named and presented the foundations of cybernetics (see CYBERNETICS), one of the youngest scientific disciplines of the twentieth century. Etymologically the name selected by Wiener came from the Greek κυβερνητης or steersman. In choosing this term he wished to acknowledge that the first significant paper on feedback mechanisms was an article on governors written by Clerk Maxwell in 1868, and that 'governor' is derived from a Latin corruption of *gubernatur*. Plato had used this term to describe the science of the steering of ships, while in the nineteenth century the French scientist Ampère had also borrowed the term as a name for the science of government.

By showing the fact that some underlying unity did indeed exist between communication and control mechanisms in different sciences, cybernetics made irrelevant the old philosophical controversy between vitalism and mechanicism, which had claimed that biological and physical systems were naturally distinct. In fact, cybernetics, in accordance with Wiener's philosophical standpoint, permitted a much broader classification of systems, reflecting its interdisciplinary nature (Wiener 1993: 84). A useful criterion for this classification is that of complexity. According to this category the main concern of cybernetics is the study of exceedingly complex (that is, so complex that they cannot be described in a precise and detailed fashion) and probabilistic (as opposed to deterministic) systems (Beer 1959: 18). Typical examples of these systems are the economy, the brain and the company.

To study the control and communication mechanisms of these sorts of systems Wiener and his colleagues developed a deep understanding of concepts like feedback, homeostasis and the 'black box'. Although the feedback mechanism has already been mentioned, it is interesting to look at its main characteristics in more detail. Each feedback loop involves some input information, such as the measurement of temperature, and some output, such as the heating of the room; moreover – and this is the crucial feature – the input information is affected by the output, for example, the output of the heater will determine the subsequent temperature reading, which in turn will determine whether the heater will be turned on or off. In this way it is continuously showing the difference between a desired situation and the existing one. If the control mechanism reduces this difference it is called a negative feedback (as in the case of the thermostat); if it increases the difference it is called a positive feedback (as in the case of power-assisted brakes which detect small manual movements made and enlarge them until the force applied is capable of stopping the moving car).

In his *Cybernetics* book (1948), Wiener showed that feedback mechanisms are found in many systems of a totally different nature, from machines to economics and from sociology to biology (see ORGANIZATIONAL BEHAVIOUR, HISTORY OF). A special group of feedback loops which appears to be essential for the continuation of life is found in what is known as homeostasis. The classic biological example is the homeostasis of blood temperature in which the body temperature varies very little although the body passes from refrigerator to furnace-room. A homeostat is thus a control device for holding some variables between desired limits. The well-known Watt's governor of a steam engine, which serves to regulate its velocity under varying conditions of load, is a typical homeostat. What is important to understand here is that the movement of the controlled variable away from its desired value (the speed is too high or too slow in the steam engine) itself operates the regulatory feedback (the valves are closed or opened respectively in Watt's governor). In other words, for as long as the mechanism does not break, the feedback controller cannot fail. The corollary of this statement is extraordinary because it implies that the feedback controller not only is guaranteed to operate against a given kind of disturbance, but against all kind of disturbances (Beer 1959: 29). This special characteristic of control systems is commonly known as ultrastability (Ashby 1956).

By now it should be clear that 'control' in cybernetics does not refer to its naive interpretation as a crude process of coercion, but instead refers to self-regulation.

Another important concept in cybernetics that has permeated many other sciences is that of the black box. Cybernetics, as stated above, is mainly concerned with the study of control and communication mechanisms of exceedingly complex and probabilistic systems. To study control cyberneticians use the concepts of feedback and homeostasis; to deal with the probabilistic characteristics of systems they use the statistical theory of information; and to deal with extreme complexity they use black boxes. By representing a system as a black box cyberneticians are tacitly accepting their cognitive limitations in understanding the huge range of possible states which an exceedingly complex system can be in at any moment in time. However, they recognize some inputs that can be manipulated and some outputs that can be observed. If the outputs are continuously compared with some desirable values some responses could be determined to affect the inputs of the black box in order to maintain the system 'under control'.

By modelling a system as a black box four sets of variables are identified: a set 'S' of possible states in which the system can be, according to some purpose defining the nature of the study; a set 'P' of perturbations that affect the current state of the system; a set 'R' of responses to these perturbations; and a set 'T', or target set, determining the accepted states (according to some established criteria) of the system. The system is said to be 'under control' if at any time its states are elements of the target set T. An extremely important cybernetic principle is obtained from this modelling: indeed, for the system to be under control it is necessary that a response should exist for any perturbation affecting the system in such a way that after applying this response to the system its subsequent state is in the target set. This principle was established by the British cybernetician Ross Ashby and is known as the 'law of requisite variety', commonly phrased as 'only variety absorbs variety' (Ashby 1956).

Wiener's experiences with machines began very early in his scientific career (Wiener 1993). In the 1920s, long before computers existed, he devised a method for evaluating a general class of integrals by passing a beam of light through some screens and measuring the intensity of the resulting beam. This invention was in fact an analog computer that was known as the Wiener integraph. About 20 years later, in 1940, he wrote a memorandum for the government in which he proposed five points to be followed in the design of computer development: it should be digital, rather than analog; it should use binary numbers; it should be electronic; its logical structure should follow the principles of a Turing machine; and it should use magnetic tapes for data storage. Although this memorandum was ignored for many years the same ideas developed independently by other scientists gave rise to the modern high-speed digital computers (see INFORMATION TECHNOLOGY).

3 Applications

Much of the early research associated with cybernetics involved the design and development of machines. The electronic tortoises built by the British neurologist Grey Walter were intended to demonstrate that by putting together a few simple mechanisms, with the correct system of feedback, extremely complex behaviour patterns could be produced of almost the same type as those seen in living systems. By the same time another British cybernetician, Gordon Pask, had developed a teaching machine initiating a process that years later gave rise to the development and publication of his *Conversation Theory* (1975). Pask's machine itself displayed the information that had to be learned, received the trainee's response and used this response as a feedback to proceed with the teaching process. In this way his machine was able to teach, by continuously adapting itself to the trainee's personal abilities to learn. Similarly, Wiener himself dedicated much of his time during the 1950s and early 1960s to the design of a device to replace an amputated limb, including its tactile sensibility. His work with a team of orthopaedic surgeons, neurologists and engineers (although unsuccessful at that time) paved the way for the subsequent development of the effective prosthetic known as the Boston Arm.

This initial work on machines had the dual intention of demonstrating the practical applicability of cybernetic ideas and, at the same time, being used as a tool for studying complex systems like the human nervous system as well as understanding animal characteristics like learning, memory and intelligence. As an example of the latter Wiener – in a second edition of his book on cybernetics (Wiener [1948] 1961) – explained in some detail how to build a machine to play chess at an acceptable level. Now almost any personal computer can easily beat most non-professional chess players. Unfortunately, and perhaps because of the initial impact caused by these practical applications of cybernetic ideas, the whole scientific discipline has come to be associated with hardware, particularly with computers, despite its principles still being used in other disciplines.

In the area of management sciences perhaps the most important development of Wiener's original ideas has come from Stafford Beer (see BEER, S.) who, by modelling a company as a set of interconnected homeostats and using Ashby's law of requisite variety, developed the viable system model (VSM) (Beer 1979, 1981, 1985). The VSM – an important achievement of the branch of cybernetics known as management cybernetics – has proved to be a useful tool for the diagnosis and even design of complex organizations, ranging from small companies to multinationals and from local government to the economy of a whole country (Espejo and Harnden 1989). In the same field, recent issues such as planning through creative decision processes (Beer 1994) and organizational learning (Senge 1992; Espejo *et al.* 1996) have been studied using cybernetic principles like feedback mechanisms.

By the end of the 1970s some social scientists were trying to extend and enrich cybernetics by merging it with sociology in what they called 'socio-cybernetics'. However, some paradoxes were found which seemed very hard to solve (Geyer and Zouwen 1986). It was work in the field of the biology of cognition (see for example, Maturana and Varela 1987; Foerster 1984) that established the platform for the development of social cybernetics. This theory, known as 'second-order cybernetics' (Foerster 1979), is a non-objectivistic approach to scientific enquiry that emphasizes the role of the observer in social systems.

In this way, second-order cybernetics, by stressing the autonomy of individuals and studying the continuous processes by which they construct their shared reality, points to a new paradigm in social research which could lead to – recalling the title of one of Wiener's books – a more 'human use of human beings' (Wiener 1950).

RAUL ESPEJO
UNIVERSITY OF LINCOLNSHIRE AND
HUMBERSIDE

ALFONSO REYES
UNIVERSIDAD DE LOS ANDES

Further reading

(References cited in the text marked *)

* Ashby, R. (1956) *An Introduction to Cybernetics*, London: Chapman & Hall. (Explains the concepts of cybernetics, including the law of requisite variety, and contains exercises.)
* Beer, S. (1959) *Cybernetics and Management*, London: The English University Press. (The author explains cybernetics and shows how it can be used to study management problems.)
* Beer, S. (1979) *The Heart of Enterprise*, Chichester: Wiley. (Describes the development of a logical model for studying systems such as any enterprise.)
* Beer, S. (1981) *Brain of the Firm*, 2nd edn, Chichester: Wiley. (The original development of the viable system model (VSM), it starts from insights derived from the human nervous system.)
* Beer, S. (1985) *Diagnosing the System for Organizations*, Chichester: Wiley. (A manual of how to apply the VSM; full of explanatory graphics and methodological tips.)
* Beer, S. (1994) *Beyond Dispute: the Invention of Team Syntegrity*, Chichester: Wiley. (Provides managers with a planning method that captures the native genius of the organization in a non-hierarchical way.)
* Espejo, R. and Harnden, R. (eds) (1989) *The Viable System Model: Interpretations and Applications of Stafford Beer's VSM*, Chichester: Wiley. (Contains a balanced, reflective and critical assessment of the VSM. Some practical applications are discussed.)
* Espejo, R., Schumman, W., Schwaninger, M. and Bilello, U. (1996) *Organizational Transformation and Learning: A Cybernetic Approach to Management*, Chichester, Wiley. (An application of cybernetics principles to facilitate understanding of organizational learning processes.)
* Foerster, H. von (1979) 'Cybernetics of cybernetics', in K. Krippendorff (ed.), *Communication and Control in Society*, New York: Gordon and Breach. (Considers the importance of self-referential systems, such as social systems, and shows the necessity of a second-order cybernetics to study them.)
* Foerster, H. von (1984) *Observing Systems*, Seaside, CA: Intersystems Publications. (A collection of papers moving towards constructivism; that is, seeing reality as invented rather than discovered.)
* Geyer, F. and Zowen, J. van der (eds) (1986) *Sociocybernetics Paradoxes: Observation, Control and Evolution of Self-Steering Systems*, Lon-

don: Sage Publications. (A series of articles exploring the possibilities and limitations of socio-cybernetics in the study of social problems.)

* Heims, S. (1980) *John von Neumann and Norbert Wiener: From Mathematics to the Technologies of Life and Death*, Cambridge, MA: MIT Press. (A double biography of two brilliant and innovative scientists, critically analysing their differences in personality and philosophy and their contributions to modern science.)

* Heims, S. (1991) *The Cybernetics Group*, Cambridge, MA: MIT Press. (The story of a remarkable group who met regularly between 1946 and 1953 to explore how to use cybernetics, information theory and computer theory as a basis for interdisciplinary alliances.)

* Maturana, H. and Varela, F. (1987) *The Tree of Knowledge: The Biological Roots of Human Understanding*, Boston, MA: Shambhala. (Presents an understanding of cognition not as reflecting an objective reality, but as a continuous bringing-forth of a world through our co-existence with others.)

* Pask, G. (1975) *Conversation, Cognition and Learning: A Cybernetic Theory and Methodology*, Amsterdam: Elsevier. (Describes a theory of person-to-person or person-to-machine conversations and cognitive processes.)

* Senge, P.M. (1992) *The Fifth Discipline. The Art and Practice of the Learning Organization*, London: Century Business.

* Shannon, C. and Weaver, W. (1949) *The Mathematical Theory of Communication*, Urbana, IL: University of Illinois Press. (Contains a simple explanation of the theory of communication and develops a rigorous mathematical account of concepts like 'information', 'noise', 'coding' and 'communication'.)

* Wiener, N. (1948; 2nd edn 1961) *Cybernetics: or Control and Communication in the Animal and the Machine*, New York: Wiley. (A relatively short and easy book explaining cybernetics, contains examples and some mathematical sections. In the second edition Wiener adds chapters showing the relevance of cybernetics to learning, artificial intelligence, adaption and language.)

* Wiener, N. (1950) *The Human Use of Human Beings: Cybernetics and Society*, English edn, London: Eyre and Spottiswoode (1954). (Describes cybernetics for the layperson, showing Wiener's ethical considerations in relation to science and the application of cybernetics.)

Wiener, N. (1952) *Ex-prodigy*, paperback edn, Cambridge, MA: MIT Press, 1964. (The first volume of Wiener's autobiography, it concentrates on his years as a child prodigy and his relationship with his father.)

Wiener, N. (1956) *I am a Mathematician*, paperback edn, Cambridge, MA: MIT Press, 1964. (The second volume of Wiener's autobiography, it covers his mature personal and scientific career and intellectual development.)

Wiener, N. (1964) *God and Golem, Inc.*, Cambridge, MA: MIT Press. (The sequel to *The Human Use of Human Beings*, outlining how cybernetics impinges on society, ethics and religion.)

* Wiener, N. (1993) *Invention: The Care and Feeding of Ideas*, Cambridge, MA: MIT Press. (A historical account of discovery and invention showing the importance of the intellectual, technical, social and scientific climate for the development of original ideas.)

See also: ACKOFF, R.L.; ARTIFICIAL INTELLIGENCE; BEER, S.; CYBERNETICS; INFORMATION TECHNOLOGY; ORGANIZATION BEHAVIOUR, HISTORY OF; SHANNON, C.; SYSTEMS; SYSTEMS ANALYSIS AND DESIGN; VICKERS, G.; VON BERTALANFFY, L.

Williamson, Oliver E. (1932–)

Personal background

- born 27 September 1932
- Professor of Economics at University of Pennsylvania, 1965–83
- Professor of Economics at Yale University, 1983–8
- applied and developed the transaction cost analysis of Coase
- Professor of Business, Economics and Law at University of California at Berkeley

Major works

Markets and Hierarchies: Analysis and Anti-Trust Implications: A Study in the Economics of Internal Organization (1975)
The Economic Institutions of Capitalism: Firms, Markets, Relational Contracting (1985)

Summary

This article discusses the work of the American new institutional economist Oliver Williamson. The key inspirations for Williamson have been the works of two Nobel Laureates, Ronald Coase and Herbert Simon. The article discusses how Williamson developed the earlier, transaction cost analysis of Coase to provide explanations of firm behaviour and structure. The relationships with the behavioural economics of Simon and Williamson's theory of organizational efficiency are both briefly evaluated.

1 Biographical data

Oliver Williamson (born 1932) is former Professor of Economics at Pennsylvania and Yale University and is currently Professor of Business, Economics and Law at the University of California at Berkeley. Williamson came to prominence in an article published in the *American Economic Review* in 1963 that argued that managers maximize their own utility, rather than, for example, profits or sales. However, it is for his application and development of the transaction cost analysis of Nobel Laureate Ronald Coase (born 1910) that he is most well-known (see COASE, R.). Williamson's first book in this genre was his *Markets and Hierarchies*, published in 1975. During the subsequent 25 years, Williamson has developed and extended this approach in a large number of books and articles, most notably his *Economic Institutions of Capitalism*, published in 1985 and his *Mechanisms of Governance*, published in 1996. His work is widely cited and has been inspirational for a large number of theoretical and applied researchers. His 1975 and 1985 books ranked as two of the three most highly cited books in economics in the Social Science Citations Index in 1990. His influence has not been confined to economics and it has extended significantly to both legal and business studies.

2 Williamson and transaction costs

A key work in the general development of the mainstream economic thinking about institutions was Williamson's *Markets and Hierarchies*, published in 1975. Williamson was the first to coin the phrase 'new institutionalism' and he used it to describe his approach (see INSTITUTIONAL ECONOMICS). With this phrase he simultaneously underlined his focus on the inner structures and workings of the firm and his distance from the 'old' institutionalism of Veblen, Mitchell and Commons (see VEBLEN, T.B.). In the next few years this term achieved a wide currency and the study of institutions has become commonplace for economists.

The main inspiration for Williamson was a much earlier and classic paper by Ronald Coase (1937). In this article Coase characterized the firm as an organization that supersedes the price mechanism and allocates resources by command rather than through price. As Coase (1937: 388) himself put it: 'Outside the firm, price movements direct production, which is co-ordinated through a series of exchange transactions on the market. Within a firm, these market transactions are eliminated and in place of the complicated market structure with exchange transactions is substituted the entrepreneur-co-ordinator, who directs production'. Coase explained this phenomenon by arguing that the firm arises because of the relatively greater 'cost of using the price mechanism' (1937: 390).

Following on from Coase, Williamson developed his central thesis that economic institutions such as the firm 'have the main purpose and effect of economizing on transaction costs' (Williamson 1985: 1). The approach of both Coase and Williamson can be characterized as contractarian, because institutions are seen as emerging from contracts between individuals. For example, firms with employment contracts emerge when the transaction costs of alternative market arrangements – such as using self-employed contractors – are too high.

However, the Coase–Williamson argument contrasts with other contractarian approaches that explain all firm and market phenomena solely in terms of contracts. Williamson recognizes a key polarity between 'markets' and 'hierarchies' and sees the latter as emerging because of specific, asset and information based efficiency considerations. However, a key difference between Coase and Williamson is that Williamson extends the transaction cost analysis from general comparisons of the firm and market to a comparison of different types of organization within the firm.

Much of Williamson's work is concerned with spelling out the implications of this approach. For example, he argues that if two firms trade with each other and rely on assets that are highly specific to that relationship and cannot readily or cheaply be traded elsewhere – an example is a steel mill relying on a local supply of iron ore – then the transaction costs of an enduring relationship are likely to be high and the firms are likely to have an incentive to vertically integrate in order to reduce those costs. Much of the empirical work on transaction costs looks at this issue of 'asset specificity'.

As another important example, Williamson compares two forms of hierarchical organization, the unitary ('U-form') and multidivisional ('M-form') structures. He argues that the M-form is often a more efficient way of administering particular types of transactions. It is argued that the M-form allows incentives to be aligned more closely to corporate goals and promotes the use of operational rather than functional criteria of managerial evaluation. On this basis it is claimed that the spread of the multidivisional firm in modern capitalism is explained.

A consequence of this widening of the scope of transaction cost analysis is that the cost of monitoring and enforcing all transactions, including employment contracts, are considered under the label of 'transaction costs'. This contrasts with Coase, who focused on 'marketing costs' and 'the cost of using the price mechanism'. Williamson's wider meaning of the term 'transaction cost' includes the internal cost of managing the workforce within the firm. The acknowledged danger in this approach is that the term 'transaction cost' becomes a 'catch-all phrase' including every possible cost under its head. Questions are then raised concerning the potential falsifiability of the theory.

3 Williamson and behaviouralism

In its close attention to non-market forms of organization, Williamson departs from much of mainstream economics. Furthermore, Herbert Simon and the behaviouralist school influenced Williamson; Simon is well known as a critic of mainstream assumptions of rationality (see SIMON, H.A.). However, on closer inspection it is evident that Williamson's break from neo-classical theory is partial and incomplete, and much of the core apparatus of neo-classical economics is retained. In fact, Williamson's claimed departure from orthodoxy sits uneasily alongside his repeated invocation that agents are marked by 'opportunism' (i.e. 'self-interest seeking with guile'). As conventionally presented, self-interested behaviour is a typical feature of 'economic man'.

Simon (1957) argued that complete or global rational calculation is ruled out, hence rationality is 'bounded'. Agents do not maximize but attempt to attain acceptable minima instead. It is important to note that this 'satisficing' behaviour does not simply arise because of inadequate information, but also because it would be too difficult to perform the calculations even if the relevant information were available. Contrary to a prevailing neo-classical interpretation of Simon's work, the recognition of bounded rationality refers primarily to the matter of computational capacity and not to additional 'costs'. Hence 'satisficing' does not amount to cost-minimizing behaviour. Clearly, the latter is just the dual of the standard assumption of maximization; if 'satisficing' were essentially a matter of minimizing costs then it would amount to maximizing behaviour of the neo-classical type.

Williamson (1989: 161) simply replicates this view when he accepts the term 'bounded rationality' rather than 'satisficing' because he regards the latter as 'a contentious and separate issue'. Clearly, Williamson adopts the neo-classical, cost-minimizing interpretation of Simon and not the one that clearly prevails in Simon's own work. In Williamson's work 'economizing on transaction costs' is part of global, cost-minimizing behaviour, and this is in fact inconsistent with Simon's idea of bounded rationality. The cost calculus remains supreme in his theory and there is no essential break with the neo-classical assumption of maximization.

4 Institutions and efficiency

According to Williamson, organizations with lower transaction costs are more likely to survive in a competitive world. In several passages Williamson (1975, 1985) asserts that because hierarchical firms exist, then they must be relatively efficient and more suited to survival. Thus, in his theoretical attempt to compare the efficiency of different types of firm structure, Williamson (1980: 35) concludes that 'it is no accident that hierarchy is ubiquitous within all organizations of any size. ... In short, inveighing against hierarchy is rhetoric; both the logic of efficiency and the historical evidence disclose that non-hierarchical modes are mainly of ephemeral duration'.

However, this argument has been widely criticized, particularly for the neglect of path dependency. It also contrasts with the recent work of other 'new institutionalists' such as Douglass North, where path dependence is recognized. The explanation of emergence and survival in evolution is not the same thing as an explanation of efficiency, even if the latter may enhance the chances of survival in the future. Strictly, in order to explain the existence of a structure it is neither necessary nor sufficient to show that it is efficient. Inefficient structures do happen to exist and survive, and many possible efficient structures will never actually emerge or be selected.

Essentially, Williamson's transaction cost argument involves comparative statics (see TRANSACTION COST ECONOMICS). Typically, the incidence of transaction costs in equilibrium is compared in two or more governance structures, and the structure with the lowest costs is deemed to be more efficient. In fact Williamson (1985: 1434) admits that a shift from considerations of static to those of dynamic efficiency is not encompassed by his theory: 'the study of economic organisation in a regime of rapid innovation poses much more difficult issues than those addressed here ... Much more study of the relations between organisation and innovation is needed'. It is questionable whether the comparative statics approach can do justice to important dynamic developments such as technological change. Particularly on this point, 'evolutionary' (Richard Nelson and Sidney Winter) and 'competence-based' (Edith Penrose) theorists of the firm claim they have overcome the limitations of comparative statics.

Transaction cost analyses reduce the interaction between individuals to the calculus of costs. Individuals act as utility-maximizing automata on the basis of given preferences. Social institutions bear upon individuals simply via the costs they impose. Consistent with the retention of the basic neo-classical model of optimizing behaviour, Williamson assumes that individual preferences are unchanged by the economic environment and the institutions in which individuals are located.

Importantly, the assumption of given individuals and preferences is antagonistic to the notion that institutions transform individual preferences, purposes, conceptions and beliefs. Clearly there is an important contrast here with the 'old' institutionalism of Veblen, Commons, Mitchell, Galbraith and others. The contractarian emphasis in the new institutionalism means that non-contractual relations such as trust and loyalty are neglected. Just as seriously, the conception of the given individual cannot readily incorporate notions such as learning and personal development.

Williamson assumes that individual preferences are unchanged by the economic environment and the institutions in which individuals are located. However, it can be argued that an important difference between the market and the firm is that actors tend to behave in a different manner with differing goals. According to this alternative perspective, a key to understanding the nature of the firm is its ability to mould human preferences and actions so that a higher degree of loyalty and trust is engendered.

5 Conclusion

Whatever its limitations, Williamson's work is one of the most important developments in the analysis of economic institutions. It has been of enormous benefit in bringing questions of internal and intra-firm organization to the fore. Indeed, despite criticism, the Coase–Williamson argument for the existence of firms remains persuasive for many economists. Furthermore, recent work has gone a long way to bring empirical richness to the transaction cost story. Finally, transaction cost analyses have inspired key developments in corporate and competition policy.

GEOFFREY HODGSON
UNIVERSITY OF HERTFORDSHIRE

Further reading

(References cited in the text marked *)

* Coase, Ronald H. (1937) 'The nature of the firm', *Economica*, 4, November: 386–405. Reprinted in Williamson, Oliver E. and Winter, Sidney G. (eds) (1991) *The Nature of the Firm: Origins, Evolution, and Development*, Oxford and New York: Oxford University Press. (The classic article that established the transaction cost approach to the theory of the firm – later developed by Williamson.)

Pitelis, Christos (ed.) (1993) *Transaction Costs, Markets and Hierarchies*, Oxford: Basil Blackwell. (A set of critical essays on the transaction costs approach.)

* Simon, Herbert A. (1957) *Models of Man: Social and Rational. Mathematical Essays on Rational Human Behavior in a Social Setting*, New York: Wiley. (An early statement of the behaviouralism that inspired Williamson.)

* Williamson, Oliver E. (1975) *Markets and Hierarchies: Analysis and Anti-Trust Implications: A Study in the Economics of Internal Organization*, New York: Free Press. (Williamson's first major statement of the transaction costs approach.)

* Williamson, Oliver E. (1980) 'The organization of work: a comparative institutional assessment', *Journal of Economic Behavior and Organization*, 1 (1): 5–38. Reprinted and revised in Williamson (1985, chs. 9–10). (An notable attempt by Williamson to develop a theory of comparative organizational efficiency.)

* Williamson, Oliver E. (1985) *The Economic Institutions of Capitalism: Firms, Markets, Relational Contracting*, London: Macmillan. (A milestone development of Williamson's approach.)

* Williamson, Oliver E. (1989) 'Transaction cost economics', in Richard Schmalensee and Robert D. Willig (eds) *Handbook of Industrial Organization*, vol. 1, Amsterdam: North Holland, pp. 135–82. (A concise statement of Williamson's approach and analysis.)

Williamson, Oliver E. (1996) *The Mechanisms of Governance*, Oxford and New York: Oxford University Press. (The third volume in Williamson's trilogy on the firm.)

See also: COASE, R.; DECISION MAKING; GALBRAITH, J.K.; GROWTH OF THE FIRM AND NETWORKING; INSTITUTIONAL ECONOMICS; MANAGERIAL THEORIES OF THE FIRM;

MARCH, J.G. AND CYERT, R.M.; MARSHALL, A.H.; NEO-CLASSICAL ECONOMICS; ORGANIZATION STRUCTURE; SIMON, H.A.; TRANSACTION COST ECONOMICS; VEBLEN, T.B.

Womack, James Potter, (1948–) and Jones, Daniel Theodore (1948–)

Personal background

Daniel Jones

- born in Sussex, England, 12 June 1948
- graduated in Economics from the University of Sussex, UK (1970)
- Voluntary service overseas on Lake Chad (1971–2)
- MSc in Economics, University of Manchester, UK (1973)
- Research Fellow, National Institute of Economic and Social Research, London (1973–7)
- Senior Research Fellow, University of Sussex (1977–89)
- Professor of Management, Cardiff Business School, UK (1989 onwards)
- developed and disseminated the idea of lean production

James Womack

- born in Little Rock, Arkansas, USA, 27 July 1948
- graduated in Political Science, University of Chicago (1970)
- time out travelling round the world, mainly in North West India (1971)
- read Transport Policy at the Kennedy School, Harvard (1973–5)
- Research fellow, MIT (1975–80)
- Principal Research Scientist, MIT (1980 onwards)
- received Ph.D. on comparative industrial policy in the auto industry in the US, Germany, France and Japan (MIT, 1983)
- developed and disseminated the idea of lean production

Major works

The Future of the Automobile (with Altshuler, A., Anderson, M. and Roos, D.) (1984)
The Machine that Changed the World (with Roos, D.) (1990)
Lean Thinking (1996)

Summary

James P. Womack and Daniel T. Jones are best known for their role in developing and disseminating the concept of 'lean production'. This concept evolved from two large scale studies on the international automotive industry in which Jones and Womack played leading roles. The best known of these was the 1985–90 International Motor Vehicle Programme (IMVP). This programme involved over 55 researchers world-wide, and demonstrated a substantial performance gap between Japanese and non-Japanese vehicle assemblers in terms of both productivity and quality. These performance differences were ascribed to a distinct set of organizing principles, found in their purest form in the Japanese automotive industry, termed 'lean production' principles. Womack and Jones argue that these principles apply not only to manufacturing operations, but to product development, distribution and retailing, and the organization of the supply chain.

Lean production quickly caught the imagination of academics and practitioners alike. The results of the IMVP sent shock waves around the automotive industry, prompting many companies to embark on programmes of manufacturing reform based on lean principles. These principles were eagerly adopted as the new best practice orthodoxy in operations management, though challenged by some, primarily from a critical social science perspective. During the 1990s the term lean production was gradually replaced by terms such as 'lean thinking' or the 'lean enterprise', as the principles were increasingly applied to contexts outside their original home in automotive manufacturing.

1 Biographical data

Pre 1980

Daniel Jones was born in Sussex, England in 1948. He graduated in Economics from the University of Sussex in 1970 and then embarked on voluntary service overseas for two years, running a Fisheries Extension project on Lake Chad. He undertook an M.Sc. in Economics at the University of Manchester, where he developed an interest in industrial performance. In 1973 Jones became a research fellow at the National Institute of Economic and Social Research in London, where he worked on two main projects. The first project investigated the innovation process in energy-related industries in the UK, Sweden and Germany. The second examined industrial performance and industrial structure in Germany, the UK and the USA, using both Industrial Census Data and detailed industrial case studies. Jones describes this work as a 'painstakingly rigorous piece of narrow, traditional industrial economics'. It was later written up in *Productivity and Industrial Structure* (Prais *et al.* 1981).

In 1977 Jones returned to the University of Sussex, where he was to stay for 12 years, first at the Sussex European Research Centre, and later at the Science Policy Research Unit. Due in part to his previous experience with collaborative projects, and in part to his ability to speak German, Jones' activity in international research ventures continued. Between 1977 and 1981 he was a principal researcher on a project into European Industrial Policy and the evolution of large firms, involving detailed studies of automotive, machine tool and chemicals industries in Europe.

In 1979 Dan Roos of MIT contacted Jones and invited him to participate in the International Automobile Programme, a project later written up in *The Future of the Automobile*.

The project was initially funded by the German Marshall Fund in the USA as a study into environmental and social issues facing the automotive industry with many other governments and foundations later offering additional support. It was in the early stages of this project, in 1979, that Jones and Womack first met, and in Jones' words, 'hit it off from very early on'.

James Womack was born in 1948. He read political science at the University of Chicago, which exposed him to a wide variety of writers, including Marx and Weber. Having completed his degree he took some time out to travel around the world, spending some time in India in the process. On his return to the USA, Womack studied transport policy at the Kennedy School at Harvard, but perceived the field to be dominated by microeconomics, which led him to focus more on issues of network analysis and system optimization. In 1975 he took a research position in transport policy at MIT. At this time, urban transportation was a major issue, and the Nixon administration had a policy objective of promoting underground transportation systems in major cities in the USA. Womack analysed the policy alternatives to motor-vehicle dominant transport systems, largely from a political science perspective.

As the 1970s wore on, environmental and social concerns about motor vehicles grew. Womack's brother worked as a lawyer for the Federal Government's National Highway Traffic Safety Administration based in Washington. This meant that Womack was always close to someone involved in debates about improving vehicle safety and energy efficiency. In addition, by 1979 Womack had concluded that underground transportation systems would have little impact on transportation patterns in the USA. It therefore seemed appropriate to concentrate on the dominant technology, namely the automobile. This drew him to the International Automobile Programme, coordinated out of MIT by Alan Altshuler and Daniel Roos. (Womack had worked with Altshuler in the late 1970s, contributing to Altshuler's *The Urban Transportation System*, published in 1979.) It was during the International Automobile

Programme that the Womack/Jones partnership began.

1980 onwards

As with many large scale collaborative projects, the International Automobile Program was characterized by a variety of perspectives on the part of the collaborators, and inevitably, conflict was a consequence of this. As project developed, the key issues to Womack and Jones (who had formed a good working relationship), was not the environmental impact of the automobiles but the competitive gap opening up between the Japanese and Western car industries.

Both Womack and Jones describe how the early stages of this project were formative experiences for them. Womack describes how a visit to one of the Big Three's Auto Assembly plants in the USA was 'a defining moment' for him. At the end of the factory were two gates; one marked 'major repairs', the other marked 'minor repairs'. All cars went through one gate or the other, and there were as many people employed in rework and repair as were building the vehicles in the first place. Jones describes how he and Womack were amazed at the superiority of what they saw during visits to auto plants in Japan in 1982. This theme of the relative performance of the Japanese and Western car industries became a major element of the project.

At a conference called to launch *The Future of the Automobile* in 1984 a senior industry executive encouraged Jones and Womack to prove definitively the performance gap between Japan and the West. Jay Chai, the head of the Japanese trading company C Itoh (America) and his wife and leading auto industry analyst Maryann Keller helped mobilize Japanese and US auto industry support for the endeavour. First Japanese and then US firms joined in and the IMVP was born, with the first European players coming on board a year later. Daniel Roos was the overall Director of the IMVP, Womack the Research Director and Jones the European Director.

The IMVP was completed in 1990, although there has been an IMVP II, in which Womack and Jones chose not to participate, feeling that they neither wanted to manage another huge project nor needed the MIT brand name. In 1989 Jones joined Cardiff Business School, initially as Professor of Motor Industry Management. Since then his interests have moved away from the motor industry to the application of lean principles in many different settings. In 1993 he founded the Lean Enterprise Research Centre (LERC) in Cardiff, which he has directed since then. By 2000 the LERC employed 20 staff (see further reasources for the website address). Since 1991 Jones has been involved in variety of research programmes in different industries, including benchmarking in the autocomponents industry, supply chain development, automotive distribution and raw materials production and distribution.

Womack largely withdrew from academic life following the publication of *The Machine that Changed the World*, though he continues to have an affiliation with MIT. Having talked about lean principles and process improvement he felt it appropriate to try to put the words into action and so invested in a small, up-market bicycle manufacturing business, in which lean principles were successfully applied to cost reduction. Both Womack and Jones have been in great demand as speakers and consultants following the publication of *The Machine that Changed the World*, and spent a considerable amount of their time advising companies on the implementation of lean principles. In addition to their consulting work, they spent a considerable amount of time researching approximately 50 organizations for *Lean Thinking*, which was published in 1996.

In 1997, when interviewed for an earlier version of this entry, Womack commented that 'The overt objective of the writing is to change the behaviour of the reader… we don't easily fit into the academic world … we're like two management priests or monks. We're catalysts, rather than analysts'. Their subsequent activities have demonstrated this. Although Jones has kept a foot in the academic camp with the *Lean Enterprise Research Centre* at Cardiff University, UK. However, between 1997 and 1998 Womack and Jones established independent 'Lean Enterprise Institutes' in the US and Europe respectively. In 2000, the mission of these Institutes was described as follows: 'Our global mission is to be the leading educators for society in maximizing value and minimizing waste. To accomplish this goal we develop and advance lean principles, tools, and techniques designed to enable positive change'.

The institutes have organized conferences and seminars since 1997. In 1999 there were three 'lean summit' conferences, held in the US, France and Brazil and attended by over 1,300 people. The activities of the institutes are centred on hands-on improvement projects with a particular emphasis on value stream mapping. There are comprehensive web sites which provide information on the institutes (see further reading at the end of this chapter) and a variety of workbooks and toolkits are available. The LEI (US) web site also provides a forum for an online community to share lean ideas, and in 2000 this community comprised approximately 1,500 members. The majority of these members were from manufacturing companies, especially aerospace and automotive companies.

2 The Future of the Automobile

The Future of the Automobile (Altshuler, Anderson, Jones, Roos and Womack) was published in 1984, and summarized the findings of the 1980–4 International Automobile Programme. The initial focus of the project was on the future of the automobile in the light of increasing concerns about its environmental impact, but as the project developed the competitive imbalance between the world's major auto produced assumed increasing significance. The number of collaborators involved was huge (131 researchers) under the overall direction of Altshuler and Roos, and the style and content of the book reflects the varied perspectives of those who contributed to it. The book sold over 40,000 copies in three languages.

The Future of the Automobile covers a wide range of issues: the development of the automotive industry, safety and energy issues, the relative performance of different carmaking regions and international trade issues. Inevitably, the result is a rather chaotic piece. Womack comments: 'I don't look back on [the book] with any satisfaction'.

However, Womack and Jones' fascination with the production practices of the Japanese producers, in particular the manufacturing accuracy which these practices are able to deliver, clearly comes across in the book. The scene was set for a more thorough investigation of this issue, and this culminated in the 1985–90 International Motor Vehicle Programme, and the subsequent publication of *The Machine that Changed the World* in 1990.

3 The Machine that Changed the World

This book has sold hundreds of thousands of copies, been translated into 11 languages, and has attracted extremes of praise and criticism. The book, voted business book of the year in 1990 by the *Financial Times*, is a synthesis of the findings of the 1985–90 International Motor Vehicle Programme.

Although IMVP covered all aspects of designing and producing automobiles, it was the study of the manufacturing performance of approximately 80 auto assembly plants across the world that took centre stage for most readers and reviewers. This study revealed a substantial superiority – approaching 2:1 – between assembly plants in Japan and their non-Japanese counterparts on measures of productivity and quality. In addition to the assembly plant study, IMVP covered new product development, relations with suppliers and retailing and distribution. The book has a strong story line, in which the traditional mass production methods of Henry Ford are portrayed as being swept away by the rise of 'lean production' methods – a new form of production organization, found in its purest form in Toyota in Japan. The book also deals with processes of automotive design and development, manufacturing, supplier relationships and distribution.

Lean production principles include: integrated single piece production flow, with small batches made just-in-time; an emphasis on defect prevention rather than rectification; production which is pulled by consumption, not pushed to suit machine loading; team based work organization, with flexible, multiskilled operators; active involvement in problem-solving activities by all personnel, eliminating waste, interruptions and variability; and close integration of the whole supply chain from raw materials to retailing and distribution, back up by close buyer–supplier relationships based on trust and collaboration rather than competition.

The Machine that Changed the World proved to be a powerful cocktail of ideas for a number of reasons. Mass and lean production are set in a chronology, the latter addressing many of the acknowledged weaknesses of the former. The size of the performance gap between the Japanese producers and the rest of the world had a tremendous shock value, demonstrating to many western manufacturers that change was imperative. Lean production systems not only promised an answer to their manufacturing performance problems, but also a more interesting and challenging work experience to those working within such systems due to opportunities for problem-solving. Importantly, Womack, Jones and Roos argued that the successful implementation of lean production methods was not dependent on the Japanese cultural context, pointing to the Japanese auto transplant factories in North America, whose performance levels were not too far behind those of their Japanese parents.

> We believe that the fundamental ideas of lean production are universal – applicable anywhere by anyone – and that many non-Japanese companies have already learned this.
>
> (Womack, Jones and Roos, 1990: 9)

> We think it is in everyone's interest to introduce lean production everywhere, as soon as possible.
>
> (Womack, Jones and Roos, 1990: 256)

The sales of *The Machine that Changed the World* are a testament to the appeal of the book. However, there have been critical responses as well, the most ardent of which are represented by a group of radical economists in the UK, who published a whole book as a rejoinder to lean production (Williams *et al.* 1994). They object to *The Machine that Changed the World* on both ideological and empirical grounds, accusing it of an 'unconscious managerialism' and claiming that the

firm as the unit of analysis is over-emphasized, to the neglect of economic and structural conditions. In addition, these critics allege that the IMVP method of plant productivity comparison is flawed, and that the 2:1 productivity superiority of the Japanese is not supported by secondary data. Furthermore, they claim that the exceptional performance of Toyota in Japan rests on a unique interplay between its production system and the market conditions and therefore cannot be ascribed to a universally applicable set of principles. Commentators writing from a labour process perspective have also challenged the claim that lean production methods lead to a superior work experience, arguing that the lean production methods lead to more intense work, and by implication, a more exploitative employment relationship.

4 Lean Thinking

Lean Thinking represented a significant shift in style from the earlier work of Womack and Jones. It was the first book that they had produced that was not part of a large project involving many collaborators and it did not address major issues of *public* policy, such as environmental impact or relative competitiveness. Although *The Machine that Changed the World* had been written for a practitioner audience, the book blended the authority of large scale comparative empirical evidence with a strong story about the evolution of different approaches to production and development, supply and distribution. In contrast, *Lean Thinking* was not concerned with international comparisons of productive performance, but was aimed at chief executives struggling with the implementation of lean principles. Perhaps it is this absence of a strong public story that explains the relatively muted response to the book by the media, though its appeal to practitioners may be seen from its sales over 100,000 in the year following publication – a faster rate of sales than *The Machine that Changed the World*. The book has been translated into at least eight languages.

Lean Thinking identifies five key lean principles:

- The precise specification of value from the end customer's perspective, in terms of product capabilities, price and availability.
- The identification of the entire value stream for a product or product family, and the elimination of wasteful steps within this.
- The facilitation of flow between the value-creating steps which remain, eliminating waiting, downtime and scrap within and between steps.
- Control of flow by customer 'pull', not production 'push', providing only what the customer wants at the time it is wanted.
- The continuous pursuit of perfection – continuous effort to reduce effort, time, space and errors.

These principles are illustrated throughout the book with case studies of various organizations, including a bicycle manufacturer, Pratt and Whitney jet engines, and Porsche. The potential benefits which typically accrue from the application of these lean principles are substantial – a doubling of labour productivity, a reduction in inventory and throughput times by 90 per cent and a halving of defect rates. These benefits may be expected during the first realignment towards lean principles; continuous improvement effort should result in a doubling of performance levels within two or three years (Womack and Jones 1996). In the light of these claims, it is not surprising that *Lean Thinking* has sold so well.

5 Conclusions

In their work to date, and particularly with *The Machine That Changed the World*, Womack and Jones and their collaborators have achieved something which is unusual amongst management writers. They have succeeded in leveraging the efforts of large international research teams, and (initially with the help of Dan Roos) have been very successful in raising substantial commercial sponsorship for these efforts. Their material has proved stimulating to both practitioners and to academics from many disciplines. Labour process academics have been intrigued by the implications of lean production principles for labour;

operations management academics have eagerly, if uncritically, adopted lean principles as a best practice orthodoxy. Across the world managers have attempted to implement lean principles, sometimes supported, sometimes resisted, by labour unions. Lean production principles have excited evangelism on the part of their supporters, and challenges on the part of their critics, who argue that issues of market constraints and economic structures are given too little attention. Whatever view one favours, there is no doubt that Womack and Jones have stimulated extensive and fruitful debate about the way humans organize for productive activity. In the course of their partnership, the emphasis has shifted from that of academic analysis to the active promotion of change, as the three books reviewed here demonstrate.

NICK OLIVER
UNIVERSITY OF CAMBRIDGE

Further reading

(References cited in the text marked *)

* Altshuler, A. with Womack, J.P. and Pucher, J.R. (1979) *The Urban Transportation System: Politics and Policy Innovation*, Cambridge, MA: MIT Press. (Described by Jones as part of Womack's apprenticeship in writing books.)
* Altshuler, A, Anderson, M., Jones, D., Roos, D. and Womack, J. (1984) *The Future of the Automobile*, London: George Allen and Unwin, and Boston: MIT Press. (Initially concerned with the social and environmental challenges facing the automobile, but contains some early observations on the superiority of the Japanese automakers.)
Cusumano, M. (1994) 'The Limits of Lean', *Sloan Management Review*, Summer, 27–32. (Discussion of the factors that may limit the application of lean production principles.)
Cusumano, M. and Nobeoku, T. (1998) *Thinking Beyond Lean*, Simon and Schuster: New York. (Analysis of the product development practices of the major car makers. Argues that a crucial source of competitive advantage lies not just in the factory but in an ability to leverage learning across different products and platforms during the development process.)
Fucini, J.J. and Fucini, S. (1990) *Working for the Japanese*, New York, Free Press. (Critical account of life inside Mazda's Flatrock assembly plant in the USA.)

Kochan, T.A., Lansbury, R.D. and MacDuffie, J.P. (eds) (1997) *After Lean Production: Evolving Employment Practices in the World Auto Industry,* Ithaca: Cornell University Press. (A useful collection of readings examining the take up of lean production principles in different countries. Challenges the 'universal applicability' argument by concluding that local context is important in shaping how lean principles are implemented.)

Liker, J.K. (ed.) (1998) *Becoming Lean: Inside Stories of US Manufacturers*: Portland, Productivity Press. (Up beat set of accounts from US manufacturers who claim to have successfully implemented lean concepts.)

Lillrank, P. (1995) 'The transfer of management innovations from Japan'*, Organization Studies* 16 (6): 971–89. (Describes the process by which ideas from one context are transferred to other environments.)

Ohno, T. (1988) *Just-in-Time for Today and Tomorrow*, Productivity Press: Cambridge, MA. (Description of the Toyota Production System by its chief architect.)

* Prais, S.J. *et al.* (1981) *Productivity and Industrial Structure*, Cambridge: Cambridge University Press. (Described by Jones as his apprenticeship in writing books.)

Wickens, P. (1993) 'Lean production and beyond: the system, its critics and the future', *Human Resource Management Journal* 3 (4): 75–90. (Observations on the lean production system by the ex Personnel Director of Nissan UK.)

* Williams, K., Haslam, C. Johal, S. and Williams, J. (1994) *Cars: Analysis, History, Cases*, Providence: Berghahn Books. (Argues the case for structural, rather than managerial explanations of company performance.)

* Womack, J.P., Jones D.T. and Roos, D. (1990) *The Machine that Changed the World: The Triumph of Lean Production*, New York: Rawson Macmillan. (The seminal work, containing dramatic performance comparisons tied together by a strong story line.)

Womack, J.P. and Jones, D.T. (1994) 'From Lean Production to the Lean Enterprise', *Harvard Business Review* March/April. (Argues for the need to think about whole value chains rather than individual enterprises.)

* Womack, J.P. and Jones, D.T. (1996) 'Beyond Toyota: How to Root Out Waste and Pursue Perfection', *Harvard Business Review* September/October. (Nice summary of the main points in *Lean Thinking*, with a case example.)

* Womack, J.P. and Jones, D.T. (1996) *Lean Thinking*, New York: Simon and Schuster. (The how-to-do-it version of lean production, with case examples.)

Further resources

* *http://www.lean.org.* (The web site of Womack's Lean Enterprise Institute in the US. Provides information about lean seminars and conferences, publications and other resources, and a discussion forum for those interested in sharing lean ideas.)

http://www.cf.ac.uk/UWCC/cards/lerc/. (The web site of Jones' Lean Enterprise Research Centre at Cardiff University). Contains information on LERC members, publications and useful links.)

* *http://www.leaneuro.co.uk/.* (The web site of the Lean Enterprise Institute [Europe]. Similar to the LEI (US) web site in content, though smaller and less interactive.)

See also: BUSINESS ECONOMICS; BUSINESS HISTORY; GLOBALIZATION; HAMMER, M.; INTERNATIONAL MARKETING; JAPANIZATION; JUST-IN-TIME PHILOSOPHY; MANUFACTURING MANAGEMENT; OHNO, T.; ORGANIZATION BEHAVIOUR; ORGANIZATION BEHAVIOUR, HISTORY OF; RE-ENGINEERING; SHINGO, S.; STRATEGY, CONCEPT OF; SUPPLY-CHAIN; TAYLOR, F.W.; WORK SYSTEMS

Women and work: see GENDER AND ACCOUNTING; GENDER AND ORGANIZATIONS; GENDER DIVERSITY IN ORGANIZATION

Woodward, Joan (1916–71)

1 Early work
2 Discovering the relationship between technology and organization
3 Woodward's work as part of contingency theory
4 Limitations of the contingency approach
5 Control systems in conjunction with technology
6 Legacy

Personal background

- born 19 June 1916
- 1936, BA (Hons), Class 1, Philosophy, Politics and Economics, University of Oxford
- 1938, MA Medieval Philosophy, University of Durham
- 1939, Diploma in Social and Public Administration, University of Oxford
- 1939–46, Industrial War Service, Lancashire textiles, Buckinghamshire electronics, Royal Ordnance Factory, Bridgwater
- 1946–8, Administrative class of Civil Service, Ministry of Supply
- 1948–53, University of Liverpool, Lecturer and Senior Research Fellow
- 1951, married Leslie Thompson Blakeman, who became Director of Labour Relations for The Ford Motor Company and a member of the Commission on Industrial Relations
- 1953–7, Director, Department of Scientific and Industrial Research Human Relations Research Unit, South East Essex Technical College

- 1957–62, University of Oxford, Lecturer and Special Tutor in Industrial Sociology
- 1962–71, Imperial College of Science and Technology: 1962–5 Senior Lecturer in Industrial Sociology; 1965–9 Reader in Industrial Sociology; 1969 Professor of Industrial Sociology
- 1960s, member of the Mallibar Committee on Government Industrial Establishments
- 1968–70, member of the Prices and Incomes Board
- died of cancer, 18 May 1971

Major works

Social Aspects of a Town Development Plan (with other members of the Department of Social Science, University of Liverpool) (1951)
Employment Relations in a Group of Hospitals (1951)
The Dockworker (with other members of the Department of Social Science, University of Liverpool) (1954)
Labour, Management and the Community (1956)
Management and Technology (1958)
The Saleswoman: A Study of Attitudes and Behaviour in Retail Distribution (1960)
Industrial Organisation: Theory and Practice (1965)
Experiment in Industrial Democracy: A Study of the John Lewis Partnership (with A. Flanders and R. Pomerantz) (1968)
Industrial Organisation: Behaviour and Control (1970)
Behaviour in Organizations (1970)

Summary

Joan Woodward was born on 19 June 1916. She gained a first-class degree in Philosophy, Politics and Economics at Oxford in 1936, in 1938 an MA in Medieval History from the University of Durham, and in 1939 a Diploma in Social and Public Administration from the University of Oxford. Her war service was spent in personnel and planning in industry, where she developed an abiding interest in seeking ways to improve the management process. This was confirmed in 1946 with a move to the Civil Service and a posting to the Ministry of Supply. In 1948 she was appointed to a lectureship in Industrial Sociology at the University of Liverpool. Posts at South East Essex Technical College and Oxford University followed. In 1962 she was appointed to a senior lectureship in Imperial College, London, where, in an institution famous for its science and engineering, her ground-breaking work in bringing together technological and social analysis was recognized in 1969 by her appointment to the founding Chair in Industrial Sociology. Her commitment to finding practical solutions coupled with her keen analytical mind resulted in appointments as consultant to large companies, such as Tube Investments, Pilkington and the John Lewis Partnership, as well as to government departments and quasi-governmental organizations, such as the General Post Office, the Department of Employment and Productivity and the Prices and Incomes Board.

As a woman, Woodward was a rarity in her academic discipline and in Imperial College, where she was only the second woman to become a professor in its entire history. Her legacy to organizational analysis through surveys, case studies and practical experience is impressive for its breadth and depth. She led a generation of industrial sociologists in the pursuit of knowledge, in a field in which it was as important to be practically relevant as it was to be theoretically interesting and rigorous. Her name became synonymous in Britain with the recognition of a crucially important relationship between social and technical systems. Groundwork in this area had been undertaken at The Tavistock Institute of Human Relations, and contemporary scholars in the UK and USA were making similar observations, but it is her name which, in the UK, is most frequently associated with the discovery of relationships between production technology, organization structure and behaviour.

I Early work

At the University of Liverpool, working with Professor Simey, Woodward tackled issues of social and organizational change with studies of employment relations in hospitals, social aspects of urban planning and industrial relations and management practices in the docks. Her monographs *The Dockworker* (1954) and *The Saleswoman* (1960) showed her to be a consummate field worker, able sensitively to establish different points of view, to locate them in a social and economic context and in particular to explore the human dimensions of technological and economic change.

As director of the Department of Scientific and Industrial Research's Human Relations Research Unit at South East Essex Technical College, she began her work on management organization. Formal management education was in its infancy, and it was current practice to advocate 'one best way to manage'. There were, however, two competing views on what constituted the 'best way'. On the basis of the principles of scientific management, managers were urged to design formal structures with clear lines of authority, restricted spans of control and standardized working practices (see TAYLOR, F.W.). However, others espoused the human relations tradition associated with the work of Mayo and emphasized supportive supervision and group-based working (see HUMAN RELATIONS; MAYO, G.E.). Through her experience in textiles, retail, the docks and engineering, Woodward had witnessed a wide variety of management practices, which were not obviously related to degrees of commercial success. While formal hierarchies predominated, informal patterns of influence could also be found. Sometimes production line management was dominant, but at other times technical or administrative specialists determined key points of strategy and operations. The contrast between the variety she observed and the emphasis on 'one best way' intrigued her. She embarked on a comprehensive study of all the firms employing more than a hundred people in her immediate locality of southeast Essex; 91 per cent agreed to cooperate, resulting in a study of 100 firms.

2 Discovering the relationship between technology and organization

The aim of the South East Essex study was to establish how and why industrial organizations varied in structure, and whether particular structures were associated with commercial success. General trends that emerged from the survey were to be explained in greater depth through case studies. Having looked in vain for an explanation of success in terms of any one particular set of organizational and managerial relationships, Woodward and her team discovered that systematic patterns could be discerned in the data when firms were grouped according to the complexity of their technology, which was also found to be related to the degree to which production processes were in themselves controllable and predictable, and the degree of uncertainty with which workers and their supervisors had to work. Taking a scale of technical complexity from unit prototype, craft or customized production, through the production of small, and then large, batches of products, on to the mass production of standardized goods and finally to continuous process production of liquids or gases, the research revealed two sets of relationships which, within each of the technologically based production groups, were strongly associated with commercial success. First, a set of linear relationships between technical complexity and a firm's organizational arrangements were established. For example, the number of direct workers to indirect workers decreased from unit to process, whereas the number of levels of management increased, and the ratio of managers to other staff decreased. However, not all relations were linear; curvilinear relationships were revealed between aspects of the social structure and technology. For example, the number of employees controlled by first-line supervisors was largest in mass production and lowest in both unit and process production. The

classic 'one best way' principles of scientific management were found to be associated with success in the mass and large batch production of standardized goods, whereas the human relations emphasis on supportive supervision and enhanced discretion was better suited to unit and process production.

The survey findings were initially published in a Department of Scientific and Industrial Research pamphlet entitled *Management and Technology* (1958). They had a profound effect on practitioners, for whom they made immediate intuitive sense, and to whom they offered something more than generalized prescription. In the more detailed publication *Industrial Organisation: Theory and Practice* (1965), Woodward described the case studies as well as the survey and developed the idea that effective management depends on analysis of 'situational demands' and consideration about how they can best be met through creating appropriate organizational structures and developing appropriate managerial behaviour. For example, short lines of command within functions and strong interpersonal communication between functions were found to be most appropriate to unit production, but inappropriate to large batch and mass production, where, Woodward concluded, functions were best kept fairly distant and independent. She found that although there was considerable variation in structure within technological groups, where a firm's structure conformed to the median for that technological group, it was more likely to be successful than if it deviated from it (see ORGANIZATION STRUCTURE).

3 Woodward's work as part of contingency theory

The findings supported work being undertaken coincidentally in the UK by Burns (1958), with his distinction between management systems which were organic and informal, and those which were mechanistic and formal. Meanwhile in the USA, Lawrence and Lorsch (1967), Perrow (1967), Thompson (1967), and Hage and Aiken (1969) were reaching compatible conclusions from their empirical work (see LAWRENCE, P.R. AND LORSCH, J.W.; THOMPSON, J.D.). Whereas

Woodward had concentrated on the effects of technology, some of her contemporaries were equally concerned with the effects of the market, and the Aston School had demonstrated the importance of size (Pugh and Hickson 1976; Pugh and Hinings 1976) (see ASTON GROUP).

These scholars in the UK and the USA are credited with the development of contingency theory, with its basic tenet that a firm's industrial performance is influenced considerably by the extent to which structure and managerial behaviour 'fit' with the degrees of complexity and uncertainty which are displayed in contingent factors such as technology, market position, product diversity and size. The more uncertain and complex the context (as created by age, size, technologies, product, capital and labour markets), the more organic and flexible the structure needs to be and the more need there is for information to flow vertically between levels and horizontally between functions (see CONTEXTS AND ENVIRONMENTS). In contrast, the more certain and less complex the context, the more structures can be mechanistic, with greater emphasis on hierarchy and standard rules and procedures. Woodward and her contemporaries were important in prompting further academic work (for example, the Harvard Organization and Environment Research Programme; see also Van de Ven and Joyce 1981; Mintzberg 1979). They also influenced generations of managers to see contingency theory as a useful guide for making decisions about the design of organization structures.

4 Limitations of the contingency approach

Notwithstanding its enormous impact, there are, however, a number of practical and theoretical limitations to contingency theory and they can be discerned in Woodward's work (Donaldson 1976; Wood 1979; Dawson 1992). Problems with the approach surround the hypothesized link between contingencies – including technology – and structures. First, different contingencies, such as technological complexity, product market characteristics and organizational size, may demand different and conflicting organizational responses. Which contingency is to dominate? Certainly

not always technology. Second, the nature of the contingencies evidenced in the technology or market will change over time, at different rates and in different directions. Third (and here Woodward readily acknowledged the limitation of any magic solution to organizational effectiveness), any 'fit' between contingencies and structures is the result of choices made by people within constraints which reflect decisions and actions taken at a previous time. Such choices reflect values and attitudes, not least about managerial effectiveness within the wider organizational context. Furthermore, at a general level, it is well established that many factors other than organization structure and managerial behaviour influence performance, for example, interest rates, commodity prices, international political change and so on. These points were first articulated by Child (1972).

Woodward's early death meant that she was unable to engage in debate about these issues. However, there is enough in her work to suggest that she did not favour an overly deterministic view of organizations. In her later work she was concerned to refine the concept of technology and so became interested in the exercise and limits of managerial choice, especially concerning the development of managerial control systems. She did not see organizations as static determined systems; she found scope for variability in organization design, particularly in the middle areas of batch production, and she attributed this to the exercise of choice.

5 Control systems in conjunction with technology

Working with colleagues at Imperial College, Woodward developed a typology of control systems based on two dimensions. First, the degree of personal direct control (for example, through the hierarchy) as opposed to impersonal control (for example, through technological or administrative systems). Second, the degree to which control systems were integrated, so that different standards and rules were presented in a common framework, or fragmented, with discrete sets of standards and rules applied by different departments to regulate and control performance. Re-analysis of the South East Essex data suggested that a consideration of control systems explained some of the curvilinear relationships. Unit and process production firms were found to operate to good effect with integrated control systems; in the former, the integration was through personal control, and in the latter through technologically integrated systems. In contrast, large batch and mass production firms operated with fragmented systems. This work is discussed in Woodward's edited collection *Industrial Organisation: Behaviour and Control* (1970).

Woodward suggested that types of technology and control systems determined and responded to the uncertainties and complexities in any organization. Both technologies and control systems were the creation of managers; relationships which existed were not somehow mechanistically created without human endeavour and were therefore influenced by different human interests. Furthermore, she readily acknowledged that control systems, although formally concerned with securing greater efficiency, also reflected and created differences of power and interest. However, she would only go so far in this analysis. She assumed that ultimately all parties engaged in one organization shared a common interest in working for the good of the organization. She wanted to help managers to identify things which they could, if possible, alter to increase effectiveness. She saw different interests arising from different locations in the product cycle of development, production and distribution, but she regarded the acceptance of overall goals and objectives as non-problematic. She was interested in challenging the ways in which management operated in order to increase their effectiveness but she was not interested in a critical reappraisal of the management function. Many, however, were far more prepared to take a more critical stance and subsequently several schools of radical or critical organization theory have become established (for example, Benson 1977; Reed and Hughes 1992) which stand in sharp contrast to Woodward's managerial approach.

6 Legacy

Woodward's immediate legacy was to stimulate work in the Industrial Sociology Unit which she had formed in Imperial College and which continued after her death under the leadership of Dorothy Wedderburn (Davies *et al.* 1973). Empirical studies were conducted of hospitals (Davies and Francis 1976), prison industrial workshops (Dawson 1975) and engineering companies, and a theoretical model of organizations as technically constrained bargaining and influence systems was developed (Abell 1975).

Woodward's work was ground-breaking and exciting. It showed managers that they should make informed choices on organizational design and gave them a framework for doing so. For scholars, she, together with Burns, established the basis for the empirical study of organizational effectiveness within the UK, and the importance of the relationship between technology, structure and performance. Her work stimulated intellectual debate and practical action. As such, she achieved her aim of wanting to bridge the gap between practising managers and academics; she fully expected further study and practice to lead to reappraisal of her work. Interestingly, in the years which have elapsed since her death no academic or manager considering organization theory or design has said that technology is unimportant. Some have emphasized the importance of other factors, some have stressed technology as a creature of human endeavour and therefore open to change, and others have challenged apolitical approaches to organizational development. The most significant reconceptualization of technology has come from those (De Sanctis and Poole 1994; Orlikowski 1992) who have sought to recognize technology as an external objective force and an outcome of strategic choice and social action arguing from a structuration view (Giddens 1979) that technology may be both a cause and a consequence of structure (Barley 1986; Weick 1990). Despite these caveats and additional perspectives, most managers recognize, when developing programmes of change, that they have still to have an eye on the human requirements generated by the technologies employed as well as designing technological solutions which fit the human context.

With increasing sophistication and penetration into all aspects of business and organization, technology as a constraint on action and as an opportunity for competitive advantage is of dual importance. When Woodward was conducting her research, technology was most obvious as a means of industrial production. It was based on mechanics and fairly simple electronics. With major developments in materials, electronics, telecommunications, genetics and the whole field of biomedical sciences, the relevance and use of technology in organizations has expanded beyond industrial production to lie at the heart of administration, distribution, decision making and communication and critically now at the heart of private and public service enterprises. The speed and capacity underlying sophisticated analytical techniques have revolutionized managerial activity. As both the creature and creator of management systems, technology is now of ubiquitous importance and is a major factor when decisions are made about future structures and strategies in the new global environment. Woodward was the first person in the UK to draw attention to its practical and theoretical importance in management.

SANDRA DAWSON
JUDGE INSTITUTE OF MANAGEMENT STUDIES,
UNIVERSITY OF CAMBRIDGE

JONATHAN FORD
JUDGE INSTITUTE OF MANAGEMENT STUDIES,
UNIVERSITY OF CAMBRIDGE

Further reading

(References cited in the text marked *)

* Abell, P. (1975) *Organizations as Bargaining and Influence Systems*, London: Heinemann. (A collection of papers showing work which continued at Imperial College after Woodward's death, with greater emphasis on power and control.)

* Barley, S. (1986) 'Techonlogy as an occasion for structuring: evidence from observation of CT scanners and the social order of radiology departments', *Administrative Science Quarterly* 31: 78–108. (Useful outline of structuration perspective in a practical setting.)

*Benson, J.K. (ed.) (1977) *Organizational Analysis: Critique and Innovation*, Beverly Hills, CA: Sage Publications. (A radical approach, challenging the positivist view and stressing the importance of action, power and process.)

* Burns, T. (1958) *Management in the Electronics Industry – A Study of Eight English Companies*, Edinburgh: Social Science Research Centre, University of Edinburgh. (Subsequently elaborated and published as Burns, T. and Stalker, G. (1961) *The Management of Innovation*, London: Tavistock Publications.)

* Child, J. (1972) 'Organisational structure, environment and performance: the role of strategic choice', *Sociology* 6: 1–22. (The first article in the UK which challenged the static nature of contingency theory.)

* Davies, C., Dawson, S. and Francis, F.A.S. (1973) 'Technology and other variables', in M. Warner (ed.), *The Sociology of the Workplace*, London: Allen & Unwin. (A development of Woodward's work.)

* Davies, C., and Francis, F.A.S. (1976) 'Perceptions of structure in NHS hospitals', in M. Stacey (ed.), *The Sociology of the NHS*, Sociological Review Monograph 22, Keele: Keele University. (A development of Woodward's work.)

* Dawson, S. (1975) 'Power and influence in prison industries', in P. Abell (ed.), *Organizations as Bargaining and Influence Systems*, London: Heinemann. (A development of Woodward's work.)

* Dawson, S. (1992) *Analysing Organisations*, 2nd edn, London: Macmillan. (Chapters 3–5 give an overview of the development of contingency theory from Woodward and others, and a discussion of its limitations and contribution to practice and theory.)

* De Sanctis, G. and Poole, M.S. (1994) 'Capturing the complexity in advanced technology use: adaptive structuration theory', *Organization Science* 5: 121–47. (Useful outline of structuration theory as an explanatory frame for understanding the use and application of advanced technology.)

* Donaldson, L. (1976) 'Woodward, technology, organisational structure and performance – a critique of the universal generalisation', *Journal of Management Studies* (October): 255–74. (Gives a critique of Woodward's work but concludes in broad support.)

* Giddens, A. (1979) *Central Problems in Social Theory: Action, Structure and Contradiction in Social Analysis*, Berkeley, CA: University of California Press. (Original exposition of structuration perspective by Giddens as an integrative theory for social science.)

* Hage, J. and Aiken, M. (1969) 'Routine technology, social structure and organizational goals', *Administrative Science Quarterly* 14: 366–76. (A study which resulted in conclusions similar to those of Woodward.)

* Lawrence, P.R. and Lorsch, J.W. (1967) *Organisation and Environment*, Boston, MA: Harvard Business School Press. (Placing greater emphasis on the environment, these authors developed a similar analysis to that of Woodward.)

*Mintzberg, H. (1979) *The Structuring of Organisations*, Englewood Cliffs, NJ: Prentice-Hall. (A sophisticated development of contingency theory, developing five ideal structural models which are appropriate to five different technological and environmental scenarios.)

* Orlikowski, W. (1992) 'The duality of technology: rethinking the concept of technology in organizations', *Organization Science* 3: 398–426. (Valuable discussion locating technology as derived from objective and subjective processes.)

* Perrow, C. (1967) 'A framework for the comparative analysis of organisations', *American Sociological Review* 32: 194–208. (A similar emphasis on technology is found in this approach by a US author.)

* Pugh, D.S. and Hickson, D.J. (1976) *Organizational Structure in its Context*, The Aston Programme, vol. 1, Farnborough: Saxon House. (UK study which stressed size rather than technology as a determinant of structure.)

* Pugh, D.S. and Hinings, C.R. (1976) *Organizational Structure: Extensions and Replication*, The Aston Programme, vol. 2, Farnborough: Saxon House. (Companion volume to *Organizational Structure in its Context* (1976).)

* Reed, M. and Hughes, M. (eds) (1992) *Rethinking Organization: New Directions in Organization Theory and Analysis*, London: Sage Publications. (A series of papers challenging a positivist contingency paradigm.)

* Thompson, J.D. (1967) *Organizations in Action*, New York: McGraw-Hill. (A US scholar who was working at the same time as Woodward and producing compatible results.)

* Ven, A.H. Van de and Joyce, W.F. (eds) (1981) *Perspectives on Organisation Design and Behaviour*, New York: Wiley. (A development of contingency theory.)

*Weick, K.E. (1990) 'Technology as equivoque: sense-making in new technologies', in P.S. Goodman and L. Sproull (eds), *Technology and Organisations*, San Francisco, CA: Jossey-Bass. (Important theoretical work linking technology and structure.)

* Wood, S. (1979) 'A reappraisal of the contingency approach to organisation', *Journal of Management Studies* 16 (3): 334–54. (Argues that if contingency theory is anything more than a statement that there is no one best way of organizing, it implies a technocratic systems approach and does not give adequate emphasis to the political realities of organizations and change.)

Woodward, J. (1951) *Employment Relations in a Group of Hospitals*, London: The Institute of Hospital Administrators.

Woodward, J. (1956) *Labour, Management and the Community*, London: Pitman.

* Woodward, J. (1958) *Management and Technology*, London: HMSO. (The initial findings of the South East Essex study.)

*Woodward, J. (1960) *The Saleswoman: A Study of Attitudes and Behaviour in Retail Distribution*, London: Pitman. (A fine example of field work.)

* Woodward, J. (1965; 2nd edn 1980; 3rd edn 1994) *Industrial Organisation: Theory and Practice*, Oxford: Oxford University Press. (Woodward's classic work containing the results of the South East Essex study.)

*Woodward, J. (1970; 2nd edn 1982) *Industrial Organisation: Behaviour and Control*, Oxford: Oxford University Press. (A book of papers with contributions from her colleagues at Imperial college, developing her work on technology and control.)

Woodward, J. (1970) *Behaviour in Organizations*, London: Imperial College of Science and Technology. (Woodward's inaugural lecture as Professor of Industrial Sociology.)

Woodward, J. *et al.* (1951) *Social Aspects of a Town Development Plan*, Liverpool: Liverpool University Press. (A study of the County Borough of Dudley, written in association with other members of Liverpool University's Department of Social Science.)

Woodward, J. *et al.* (1954) *The Dockworker*, Liverpool: Liverpool University Press. (An excellent piece of field work, written in association with other members of Liverpool University's Department of Social Science.)

Woodward, J., Flanders, A. and Pomerantz, R. (1968) *Experiment in Industrial Democracy: A Study of the John Lewis Partnership*, London: Faber & Faber.

See also: HUMAN RELATIONS; MANAGERIAL BEHAVIOUR; MAYO, G.E.; OCCUPATIONAL PSYCHOLOGY; ORGANIZATION BEHAVIOUR; ORGANIZATION BEHAVIOUR, HISTORY OF; ORGANIZATION DEVELOPMENT; ORGANIZATION STRUCTURE; STRATEGY AND TECHNOLOGICAL DEVELOPMENT; TAYLOR, F.W.; TECHNOLOGY AND ORGANIZATIONS

Work ethic

Overview

The work ethic is an important concept, since working is an essential activity in every economy. A considerable amount of cross-national research evidence is available and some findings have practical policy relevance. The original historically derived concept of a 'Protestant work ethic' is no longer appropriate, since particularly high work ethic (centrality of work) scores exist in Japan, Israel and Slovenia. However, almost everywhere one or more of four values are thought to characterize working; it can be seen as a burden, a constraint, a responsibility, or a social contribution. Another useful distinction shows that people distinguish between work as an obligation or an entitlement. The USA, for instance, has very low entitlement expectations while several European countries have high scores on entitlement and Japan is in a middle position.

It should also be noticed that the term 'work' in the work ethic concept should include many important but usually unpaid activities, like rearing children, looking after a household, and doing voluntary jobs for local as well as international societies and charities.

The most policy-relevant practical findings from the available literature suggest that work ethic values everywhere are high with people who have interesting, varied jobs which enjoy a fair amount of autonomy or self-regulation. This would suggest that investment in education and job design are appropriate policies for strengthening the work ethic.

1   Some introductory thoughts

Those of us who study work are unsurprisingly convinced of its importance while ... (for) those who merely do it, it may have less cosmic significance.

(Albert Cherns)

In everyday usage, the term 'work ethic' is almost indistinguishable from work satisfaction or simply attitudes to work. Do people value work or not, or are they in various degrees indifferent to it? Since most adults are expected to work and most do so in order to make a living, the work ethic in this popular use of the term is, on average, positive for most people. Nevertheless, there are bound to be variations in this average and in the distribution around the average for different groups of people.

Social scientists tend to define the term with greater precision and want to compare and contrast the emphasis people tend to give to working with their valuation or preference for other activities in their lives, most obviously leisure, but also religion, community, the family, hobbies and so on. In such an approach, human activities are seen to offer choices. Working may still be very central, but at the margin, people will have other preferences and the margin may be different for a variety of reasons that are interesting to explore. Another approach is to differentiate attitudes that regard work as an obligation – something we owe society – or an entitlement – something society owes us.

Probably the most influential writing on the work ethic comes from the sociologist Max Weber (1930) (see WEBER, M.). In trying to explain why people pursue wealth and material gain for its own sake, not because of necessity, Weber found the answer partly in Puritan asceticism and the concept of 'calling'. Puritans sought to achieve salvation through economic activity. Weber believed the introduction of capitalism as a mass phenomenon was facilitated by factors like urbanization, the development of cooperatives and guilds, the development of a legal system, bureaucratic nation-state, and the development of a moral system, which he called 'the

Protestant Work Ethic', the core notion of the Protestant work ethic being the idea of calling and Puritan asceticism. The notion of calling requires individuals to fulfil their duty in this world and interpret occupational success as a sign of being elected, and the notion of Puritan asceticism adds the positive evaluation of hard, continuous, bodily or mental labour, and a negative view of idleness, luxury, and time wasting. The term Protestant work ethic is still used to describe a positive attitude to hard work, possibly unconsciously as a way of indicating an expectation of social approval. As we shall see, modern research casts doubt on the Protestant connection in the twentieth century, though it appears to have had such an influence in the past.

Another related concept that has become very popular among managers and organization psychologists is work commitment or attachment to work (see OCCUPATIONAL PSYCHOLOGY; ORGANIZATION BEHAVIOUR). The assumption here, as well as with the work ethic, is that people who demonstrate high values on these characteristics are somehow more effective or productive and consequently more valuable as employees and managers. Such a causal relationship is more often assumed than tested. Causality, as we shall see, is more likely to run in the other direction. People having high levels of education and skill and occupying jobs with a fair measure of autonomy are likely to hold high work ethic values. People with lower skills, education and control over their work tend to espouse low work ethic values (MOW 1987: 261–3).

2 Research evidence

Research has discovered a relationship between the work ethic and social policy values, such as lack of sympathy for the unemployed, who are regarded as lazy and therefore responsible for their own predicament (Furnham 1987). People who hold these values believe that economic, social and other outside environmental conditions should not be considered to be causal agents or excuses for social deprivation, poverty and related misfortunes. There is clearly an association between these private beliefs and political values, but the rapid and substantial rise in unemployment in the last decades of the twentieth century in parallel with unprecedented changes in technology and several severe economic depressions has made these views less plausible.

Extensive tests to measure the work ethic have been developed and have shown association with achievement, motivation, ambition, and other personality factors and attitudes like economic, political, and social conservatism, and self-control and self-reliance. (Technically known as 'internal locus of control', self-control is a measure which shows that a person perceives him/herself as having control over one's own behaviour rather than being influenced by external environmental factors.)

For all those who are not unemployed or retired, work takes up a major slice of the week; this is true even when work is unpaid, as for large numbers of women. Work is, therefore, closely associated with self-identity and feelings of self-worth. This is why involuntary retirement and unemployment create many individual problems, tensions and stress. Stress can also be a consequence of excessive work. Stress-related illness seems to have increased in the run up to the twenty-first century and has received a lot of attention from social scientists. It is sometimes attributed to inappropriate forms of leadership (Fiedler *et al.* 1992) (see LEADERSHIP; STRESS). Work stress can also be self-induced and, among managers in some organizations, long hours and homework have become a cultural prescriptive that cannot easily be rejected. The workaholic's singular dedication tends to exclude the variety of human experience we associate with civilization; it narrows or excludes social intercourse, including family relations, and has been likened by some to a form of psychopathology.

In the last decade of the twentieth century, as a result of combination of technological development and economic conditions, part-time work has grown rapidly, particularly in Europe, and women have taken up a larger share of the labour market (see LABOUR MARKETS). These labour market developments, if sustained, will have an effect on the work ethic.

While intellectual enquiries into the work ethic are usually considered to be within the field of the behavioural social sciences, economics has recently claimed a stake. Buckley and Casson (1994) have argued that the main threat to the position of economics as an explanation of economic behaviour 'comes from accumulating evidence that cultural factors are key determinants of economic performance'. They argue that culture (see CULTURE) can be considered to be a major component of human capital. The argument is that people in two different countries may have identical skills, but one country's workers may be more productive 'because the moral content of the local culture makes them better motivated' (Buckley and Casson 1994: 1040). The 'moral content of the local culture' seems very similar to our description of the work ethic but the validity of the argument that local cultural differences or the work ethic can be considered as 'key determinants of economic performance' has not been established.

A fair amount of cross-national research on the work ethic has been carried out.

3 International perspectives

In the past decade the Meaning Of Working Study and its offspring (MOW 1987; Ruiz-Quintanilla 1991) have collected evidence on how cultural, societal and individual factors shape the work ethic. Intensive personal interviews were conducted with respondents representing all segments (occupational, educational, age-groups) of societies in Europe, the USA and Asia. In some countries additional data were collected for societal groups of special interest, like socialization agents (teachers). In other countries the study was replicated eight years later to estimate changes on the group level. Three-year longitudinal studies were undertaken with youngsters entering the labour market and additional evidence was collected in complementary case studies. All in all, more than 30,000 respondents from Belgium, Bulgaria, the Czech Republic, China, England, France, Germany (both former Federal Republic as well as Democratic Republic), Hungary, Israel, Italy, Japan, the Netherlands, Poland, Portugal, Slovenia, the Slovak Republic, Spain and the USA were involved in one or other study. To summarize such a large amount of data we will confine ourselves to major cross-cultural similarities and differences, and their sources.

Employment and working is characterized by one of four values: work can be seen as a burden, a constraint, a responsibility (give and take) or a social contribution (see EMPLOYMENT AND UNEMPLOYMENT, ECONOMICS OF). This is true whether we talk to a professional athlete or an unskilled factory worker, in Beijing or Antwerp, or to a person starting their working career or entering retirement. For about 95 per cent of the respondents in any given society, one of these work values clearly dominates their understanding and, thus, their evaluation of work. Comparing the dominant view across countries we learn that the work as responsibility view dominates in Japan, two-thirds of the respondents endorsing it, while the same portion of the Slovak and Czech Republics sees work as a social contribution. Seeing work as a burden or constraint became more prominent in the USA between 1982 and 1989 (Ruiz-Quintanilla and England 1993).

We have seen that work can be perceived as an obligation (something one owes society) or as an entitlement (something society owes to a person). Differences between countries on these values are important considerations to help us understand contractual relations between employees and the organization (Rousseau 1995). While there is high agreement between Western and Asian societies in what contributes to entitlement (for example, responsibility to receive retraining or participation in decision making) and what belongs to the obligation side of the equation (for example, to give value and quality, etc.), this black-and-white picture becomes blurred in the former communist states and Israel. In the latter, respondents have a hard time distinguishing between rights and duties of work. This can be understood as a consequence of a mixture between an individualistic and more collectivistic approach in the dominant ideology. Being able to distinguish between rights and duties assumes that people tend to distinguish between themselves as 'private' person and citizen, and their role in the world of work, between employees and employers, or between the partners of a contract. Comparing the entitlement/obligation results for Belgium, Germany, the USA, and Japan (Ruiz-Quintanilla and England 1993) we can summarize that the two European labour forces have the highest entitlement expectations; the Japanese follow and the Americans have the lowest entitlement expectation. The reverse is true for the obligation scores. In addition, these results proved to be fairly stable over a period of six to nine years. Obviously, the respective labour forces start from different expectation points about what society or the organization owes individuals in terms of interesting and meaningful work, work as a right versus a duty, and whether the organization or the employees themselves should plan or provide for their own future. We can assume that this result derives from a different understanding of 'what is fair and what isn't' in these countries. Finally, in all countries the obligation orientation becomes more dominant and the entitlement expectations weaker with age and with higher educational and occupational level.

In the seven-country MOW study the measure of work centrality was highest in Japan and lowest for the UK. The US sample came somewhere in the middle. Israel and Slovenia had high work centrality, and Germany and the Netherlands had low scores. In the same countries the research took samples of different occupational groups. The findings show that jobs requiring high skills and relatively low centralized control (that is to say a higher measure of independence) had high work centrality (chemical engineers, self-employed and teachers).

Adding other research data, it seems that people who have high work ethic values have skilled and moderately autonomous jobs, are older rather than younger and come from countries like Japan, China, the Slovak Republic, Slovenia and Israel that have only recently moved away from agriculture and towards industrialization. The work ethic is lower but emphasis on hobbies, sport, recreation and social activity is higher in countries like the UK, Germany and the Netherlands, which had their industrial revolutions some two and a half centuries ago.

The Strathclyde Centre for the Study of Public Policy (1994) has carried out survey work in ten central and eastern European countries and included a question on what people would do if by luck they unexpectedly came into a lot of money. One theoretical alternative was: 'To try to get a better job'. The answers varied from 4 per cent in Slovenia to 16 per cent in Croatia. An alternative that attracted many was: 'Start business, buy farm'. In every country the answer was 20 per cent or above, 57 per cent in Romania, 41 per cent in Croatia and 40 per cent in Bulgaria. There were also substantial variations in those who wanted to take the money and stop working: 4 per cent in Slovakia and Romania, but 19 per cent in Bulgaria and 21 per cent in Belorussia.

To be really useful this type of data would have to be followed up with analysis of the degree of realism or fantasy these answers imply. For instance, the question about a realistic opportunity of starting a business or buying a farm; are the 57 per cent of Romanians who answered that question indulging in a daydream or are they genuinely motivated to become entrepreneurs? This type of survey work needs to be followed up. In general, country differences are interesting but are difficult to explain and have little policy relevance.

4 Work ethic and policy

There can be little doubt that at the moment and for the vast majority of people, work occupies an important place in life and takes up a considerable amount of the available time between the end of education and retirement. There is now a trend in western as well as eastern countries for education to take up more time and for retirement to come earlier, while at the same time life expectancy is increasing. The consequence of these developments suggests that in future over the life span from birth to death, work as traditionally conceived will become less important or at least will take up less of the available time (Heller 1991).

Nevertheless, the work ethic usefully underpins the economic system. The goods and services, including food production, which we need for survival as well as for higher standards of living, require human activity. That part of activity for which people receive pay is called work. In this sense the term 'work' in the phrase work ethic is slightly misleading because men and women undertake many different activities that are important for our standard of living that require considerable effort – the equivalent of hard work – and are capable of being characterized as being rational, frugal, achievement-orientated and deserving. Child rearing and housewifery are probably the best modern examples, but one can also include studying, amateur sports and unpaid work for voluntary organizations like the Red Cross and Amnesty International.

We will stay with the term 'work ethic' but mentally include the important range of unpaid activities that sustain the social fabric of our society. The importance of the work ethic is its provision of a motivational dynamism that gets things done. It is this characteristic that Max Weber identified when he attributed the rise of modern capitalism in part to the Protestant ethic. Today, as we have seen, this ethic thrives in several parts of the world which espouse different religions. In the older western industrialized countries the centrality of working retains an important position but is complemented by other salient life interests, like the family and recreational activity.

What implications do these findings have for policy at organizational and national levels? Accepting that, other things being equal, a high work ethic has practical utility, what can be done to increase it in companies or countries where it is considered to be exceptionally low? It is not sensible to increase the age level in an organization because we know that older people have a higher work ethic, nor can one advance or retard industrialization by a century or so. We know from other social science research that exhortation alone is not very effective in changing attitudes or behaviour, though parental and school influences can be important. It seems that findings which relate the work ethic to the nature and designs of jobs offer useful policy recommendations but need to be tested further. Several studies have shown that high work ethic values are related to educational achievement, senior level jobs and work which allows self-expression, a measure of autonomy and self-regulation (Penn *et al.* 1994; Lundberg and Peterson 1994; MOW 1987).

These factors are interconnected but an underlying dimension is the nature of skill. Rose (1991), using the results of a large-scale survey on social change and economic life in the UK, comes to the conclusion that the nature of a person's job and the level of skill largely determine the strength of the work ethic. From the data Rose concludes that work involvement and the work ethic can be strengthened by improving education and skill training (see CAREERS; TRAINING, ECONOMICS OF). Similar improved work ethic effects would result from redesigning jobs to have higher and more varied skill content.

Here, then, are several practical and feasible policy options at the level of a country (educational improvement) and at the level of organization (work design changes) which seem capable of having a positive effect on the work ethic.

FRANK HELLER
TAVISTOCK INSTITUTE, LONDON

S. ANTONIO RUIZ-QUINTANILLA
CORNELL UNIVERSITY

Further reading

(References cited in the text marked *)

* Buckley, P. and Casson, M. (1994) 'Economics as an imperialist social science', *Human Relations* 45 (9): 1035–52. (Argues that economics has a methodology capable of also analysing the social and political environment and that economists should pay more attention to people's values.)
* Fiedler, F., Potter, E., III and McGuire, M. (1992) 'Stress and effective leadership decisions', in F. Heller (ed.), *Decision-making and Leadership*, Cambridge: Cambridge University Press. (Gives empirical evidence in support of a theoretical model which analyses the effect of stress on the under-utilization of human competence.)
* Furnham, A. (1987) 'Work related beliefs and human values', *Personality and Individual Differences* 8: 627–37. (The study examines the relationship between work beliefs and general human values.)
  Furnham, A. (1990) *The Protestant Work Ethic: The Psychology of Work-related Beliefs and Behaviour*, London: Routledge. (A comprehensive discussion of the Protestant work ethic and related concepts including measures and methodological issues.)
  Grossein, JP. (1999) 'Can the Protestant ethic and the spirit of capitalism be read in French?' *Ar-*

chives *Europeennes de Sociologie* 40 (1): 125–47. (A careful analysis of the French translation of the Protestant ethic and the spirit of capitalism reveals an accumulation of errors that seriously alter Weber's concepts and analysis.)

* Heller, F.A. (1991) 'Reassessing the work ethic: a new look at work and other activities', *European Work and Organization Psychologist* 1: 147–60. (Argues that while nearly everybody has to work in order to sustain life, in future nonwork activities will become more important over a total life span as work will start later in life and end earlier.)

* Lundberg, C.D. and Peterson, M.F. (1994) 'The meaning of working in US and Japanese local governments at three hierarchical levels', *Human Relations* 47 (12): 1459–87. (Presents the results of a research project on the work ethic based on community organizations in the USA and Japan.)

* MOW (1987) *The Meaning Of Working: An Eight Country Comparative Study*, London: Academic Press. (An empirical study comparing work related values and attitudes across eight nations and a diversity of occupational groups.)

* Penn, R., Rose, M. and Rubery, J. (1994) *Skill and Occupational Change*, Oxford: Oxford University Press. (A chapter on the changing British work ethic based on a large-scale survey comes to the important conclusion that the strength of the work ethic reflects skill levels.)

* Rose, M. (1991) 'The work ethic: women, skill and the ancient curse', presidential paper to section N (sociology), British Association for the Advancement of Science. (Based on a large-scale survey, it argues that women's commitment to work differs little from men's but their employment opportunities are inferior.)

* Rousseau, D.M. (1995) *Promise in Action: Contracts in Organizations*, Newbury Park, CA: Sage Publications. (A behavioural theory of contracts and the fundamental role they play in organizations with special emphasis on how changing contracts impact on the employer–employee relationship.)

* Ruiz-Quintanilla, S.A. (ed.) (1991) *Work Centrality and Related Work Meanings*, Hove: Law-

rence Erlbaum. (A collection of articles discussing work ethic assessments across nations and time.)

Ruiz-Quintanilla, S.A. and Claes, R. (2000) 'MOW research programs', in Jerome Katz (ed.) *Databases for the Study of Entrepreneurship*, Vol. 4, Amsterdam: JAI/Elsevier Inc. (Summarizes the MOW research studies replication studies, and recent empirical work exploring attitudes towards work and the market economy in central and eastern Europe.)

* Ruiz-Quintanilla, S.A. and England, G.W. (1993) *Balanced and Imbalanced Societal Norms about Working*, CAHRS working paper no. 93–120, Ithaca, NY: Cornell University Press. (The empirical work compares two normative orientations: work as an obligation and work as an entitlement among representative samples from the US, German, Belgium and Japanese labour forces.)

Ruiz-Quintanilla, S.A. and England, G.W. (1996) 'How working is defined: structure and stability', *Journal of Organizational Behavior* 17: 515–40. (A cross-national study supporting the belief that one dominant dimension ranging from individual cost to social contribution underlies the way in which people define working.)

* Strathclyde Centre for the Study of Public Policy (1994) 'Between State and Market', Glasgow: University of Strathclyde. (Professor Richard Rose has carried out a series of attitude surveys in central and eastern Europe; attitudes to work are included.)

* Weber, M. (1930) *The Protestant Ethic and the Spirit of Capitalism*, London: Allen & Unwin. (Classic study of the apparent relationship of Protestantism with the rise and development of capitalism.)

See also: HUMAN RESOURCE MANAGEMENT; HUMAN RESOURCE MANAGEMENT, INTERNATIONAL; MOTIVATION AND SATISFACTION; ORGANIZATION BEHAVIOUR; ORGANIZATION BEHAVIOUR, HISTORY OF; WORK AND LEISURE

Work groups: see GROUPS AND TEAMS

Work and leisure

Overview

Human work and leisure are being radically redefined. The key words are empowerment, self-reliance, autonomy and self-service, replacing the more traditional notions of division of labour, specialization, manual work and the physically remote workplace of the mass production, mass assembly and mass consumption era. Most human activities – work, labour, jobs, leisure, recreation and the overall ways and quality of life – have changed and are going to change even more so in the future.

1 Definitions

Human action can be loosely differentiated into work (creation) and leisure (recreation) activities (see MOTIVATION AND SATISFACTION). This is not an exhaustive distinction – there could also be non-voluntary human activities that are neither work nor leisure (breathing, eating, sleeping), or either work or leisure depending on the person (sex, escort or companionship for money), or even mixtures of work and leisure (hobbies such as gardening and do-it-yourself).

The key to any useful differentiation of this kind must be the *purpose*, the why, the motivation of the activities being carried out. If the purpose is a direct or indirect economic exchange – for money, goods, time or any other reciprocity of economic value – then humans engage in work. If the purpose of such activities is not directly economic or exchange motivated, then we can speak of leisure. That is

why somebody doing 'absolutely nothing' in exchange for money would be working, while somebody sweating in the garden for their own pleasure and satisfaction would be at leisure – and even having a 'good time'. Professional sports are work, amateur sports are a mixture of leisure and work, and recreational sports activities are leisure.

Also, domestic, household and at-home work or chores, as well as all forms of do-it-yourself and self-service, represent bona fide work because their purpose is substituting for an exchange or economic alternative, like having such in-house work performed by paid (external, for exchange) help or professionals. The purpose of a given activity provides the key. Yet, some governments still consider taking care of one's own children as leisure and taking care of someone else's children as highly taxable work – with the obvious societal impacts. The sheer exertion of neuromuscular energy does not necessarily amount to work if it is not economically motivated and cannot or would not be exchanged. An individual going out to plant some tulips, for relaxation and enjoyment, is at leisure. An individual going out to plant the same tulips in order to avoid the high costs of landscaping services, is working.

Leisure activities must be voluntary, non-contractual and unforced, seeking recreation rather than economic gain or exchange of value. Forced unemployment or serving a jail term are not leisure as they have no alternative. Forced labour is work only if remunerated, at least partially. Work and leisure are not mutually exclusive and exhaustive categories.

'Work' can be defined as economically purposeful activity requiring substantial human coordination of task and action. 'Job' designates the kind of work that is performed contractually, that is, explicitly for remuneration and in the employ of others. 'Labour' (often used as a synonym for hard work or toil) can more properly be related to performing simplified work-components or tasks without engaging in their substantial coordination towards given purposes. Work often involves labour but not vice versa. Work involves coordination of tasks while labour relates only to their performance. Building a fish pond is work, digging a hole is labour (see MASLOW, A.H.; HERZBERG, F.). 'Leisure' and activities of leisure are motivated by non-economic and non-exchange purposes, like relaxation, pleasure, joy, recreation, satisfaction and so on.

2 Division and re-integration of labour

If we divide the work into its components we break it into labour. Historically, since the time of Adam Smith (see SMITH, A.), we refer to such a division as the 'division of labour' (although division of work would be more appropriate). Any work-task can be broken down into a large number of sub-tasks and operations. Such task disaggregation allows parallel processing and may translate directly into increased productivity. This kind of 'division of task' is directly related to the number of parts constituting the product. Some products consist of thousands of parts, including all sorts of accessible or less accessible screws, nuts, washers, bolts, caps and pins.

In order to realize the parallel processing of thousands of specialized tasks, different tasks have to be performed or controlled by different workers: labour itself has to be appropriately divided. Only in this sense can we talk about the division of labour. Division of task may or may not be accompanied by the division of labour. Together with the division of labour, we are also disaggregating, dividing and dispersing the knowledge necessary for the coordination of work. When one person makes a chair, from cutting the proper wood to selling the product at the market, such a person commands a full contingent of the chair-making knowledge. As the task and labour become divided, each person can claim only a part of the overall knowledge. The knowledge itself has become divided and the phenomenon of the 'division of knowledge' must be considered.

Modern concepts of 're-engineering' are helping to redefine work through reunifying the previously broken down tasks into coherent work processes (see RE-ENGINEERING). The traditional industrial paradigm – the division of labour, economies of scale, hierarchical control and so on – represented the old ways of doing business. 'The division of labour around which companies have been organized since Adam Smith first articulated that principle – simply don't work anymore', insist Hammer and Champy (1994: 17). Modern re-engineering of work processes is based on the following efforts:

1 Re-integrating the task: combining smaller process sub-tasks and sub-activities into larger, integrated units and packages; reducing the number of parts, components, segments and constituents in products and processes.
2 Re-integrating the labour: allowing workers to perform and coordinate larger rather than smaller portions of the process; encouraging multi-functionality, job rotation, despecialization and integrated process design; letting people work in autonomous teams and coordinate an integrated process rather than labour individually on narrowly defined and linearly conceived tasks of assembly lines.
3 Re-integrating the knowledge: workers must know (that is, be able to coordinate successfully) larger and larger portions of the process and product, not smaller and smaller portions. Knowledge is the ability to coordinate one's actions purposefully. If one is specialized, atomized, reduced to a machine appendage – one cannot coordinate action (work), but only perform single and simple commands (labour).

As Hammer and Champy explain:

Today's airlines, steel mills, accounting firms, and computer chip makers have all been built around Smith's central idea – the division or specialization of labor and the consequent fragmentation of work. The

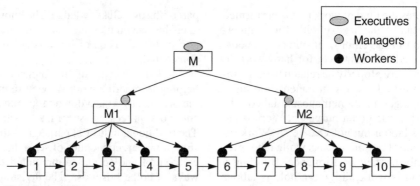

Figure 1 Division of labour

larger the organization, the more specialized is the worker and the more separate steps into which the work is fragmented. This rule applies not only to manufacturing jobs. Insurance companies, for instance, typically assign separate clerks to process each line of a standardized form. Then they pass the form to another clerk, who processes the next line. These workers never complete a job; they just perform piecemeal tasks.

(Hammer and Champy 1994: 12)

It appears that Smith's and Marx's concepts of the 'division of labour' have been overcome in the 1990s (see SMITH, A.; MARX, K.H.).

In Figure 1, observe how the division of labour leads to the emergence of coordinating agents (M1, M2 and M), organized properly in a coordinative hierarchy, because of the individually limited span of control. Although the productivity increases, the complexity and the cost of coordination are increasing even faster. Division of labour is limited by its own requisite transaction cost and complexity of coordination, not simply by the extent of the market.

Every subsequent doubling of the number of specialized sub-tasks (and labourers), as in Figure 1, leads – under the conditions of a finite span of control (how many people a manager can effectively manage) – to more than a doubling of the requisite number of coordinators (managers). Coordinative hierarchy is therefore bound to grow in size, complexity and costs (see ORGANIZATION BEHAVIOUR; ORGANIZATION STRUCTURE).

Through the re-integration of task, labour and knowledge, labour is again becoming work, meaning is replacing alienation, professionalism and skill are replacing expertism and specialization. Basic coordinative mechanisms of the traditional administrative management of labour-performing operators are being replaced by the self-coordinative systems of mutual adjustment and consensual reciprocity of teams of empowered skilled workers.

In Figure 2 we present these three re-integrations schematically. Compared to Figure 1, if each worker now performs two instead of just one task (with the aid of the requisite high technology), task productivity

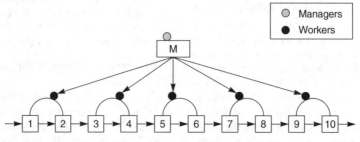

Figure 2 Re-integration of labour

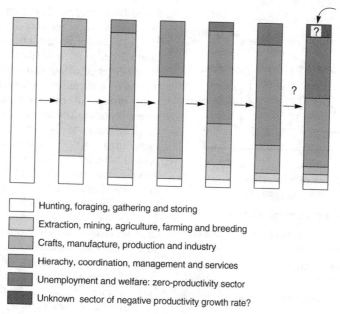

Hunting, foraging, gathering and storing

Extraction, mining, agriculture, farming and breeding

Crafts, manufacture, production and industry

Hierachy, coordination, management and services

Unemployment and welfare: zero-productivity sector

Unknown sector of negative productivity growth rate?

Figure 3 Sectoral evolution and differentiation (in a rapidly maturing economy)

would be maintained, the number of workers cut in half, the number of managers cut by two-thirds and the whole process made simpler, more streamlined, cheaper, more flexible and of higher quality.

3 Sectors of work and employment

Re-integration of work is accompanied by very strong co-trends towards self-service and do-it-yourself modes of work activities. Mature economies, especially in the USA, are characterized by a large percentage of people working in the service sector. In the 1980s, services in the USA added 21 million jobs and employed almost four out of five workers. Some 70 per cent of the total US workforce is in the services. However, the service sector is no different from any other economic sector, for example agriculture or manufacturing, that went into irreversible loss of employment decades ago. The accelerating productivity growth rates in those sectors have caused a steady decline in their job-generating capacity. The service sector is simply following the pattern: increasing automation, increasing productivity, global competitive pressures,

high relative costs and overgrown hierarchies are annihilating its own employment opportunities.

In Figure 3 we display the general sectoral dynamics that all economies, slowly or rapidly, sooner or later, are bound to follow. Due to its productivity growth rate, each sector has to emerge, grow, persist, stagnate, decline and dissipate in terms of its employment-generating capacity.

The high-productivity growth sectors are emerging and dissipating first, the low-productivity growth sectors (like services) are completing their cycle only now. Different productivity growth rates in different sectors are accompanied by essentially uniform growth rates in wages and salaries across all sectors. This simple empirical fact implies that the costs and prices grow relatively faster in low-productivity sectors and relatively slower in high-productivity sectors (see PRODUCTIVITY).

In other words, in mature economies, the prices of food and manufactured goods are getting relatively cheaper and the prices of services are getting relatively more expensive. In slow-developing or laggard economies of the Third World this may still be the

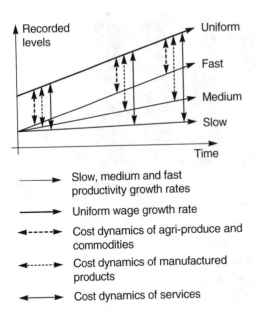

Slow, medium and fast
productivity growth rates

Uniform wage growth rate

Cost dynamics of agri-produce and
commodities

Cost dynamics of manufactured
products

Cost dynamics of services

Figure 4 Price gap: differential productivity
growth rates, combined with the uniform wage
growth in the whole economy, cause the prices to
grow faster in the 'lagging' sectors

other way around: food and manufactured
goods are most expensive while services remain relatively cheap. That is, in developed
countries, chicken, bread, computers and cars
are getting cheaper, while insurance, healthcare and education costs are skyrocketing
without adequate quality, productivity or
availability improvements. In Figure 4 we
represent this phenomenon.

4 Towards self-service

The fundamental systemic disharmony of Figure 4, that is, between differential productivity
growth rates and the uniform wage/salary
growth rates across sectors, points to a self-
organizing, spontaneous mode of resolving
the tension.

Rational economic agents will exhibit and
support the tendency towards substituting relatively cheap capital-intensive manufactured
goods for relatively dear labour-intensive services. Consumers will tend to use goods instead of services wherever economical and
possible, while the producers will tend to re-

spond by supplying them with goods instead
of services wherever economical and possible. As a collective result of this individually
rational decision making, one shall observe
the emergence of automated teller machines
instead of bank tellers, self-service petrol stations instead of full-serve stations (except
where prohibited by law), self-driving instead
of chauffeurs, do-it-yourself pregnancy kits
rather than hospital test services, self-handled
optical scanners rather than cashier-handled
services and personal computers instead of
centralized mainframes. In other words, self-
service and do-it-yourself activities are replacing the traditional, other-person-deliv-
ered services at an increasingly accelerating
rate. Mature economies are entering the era of
self-service and do-it-yourself societies.

Self-service activities are characterized by
high efficiency: they can be delivered when,
where and at whatever quality the user desires,
at lower costs and in a shorter time period.
They require user-friendly requisite products
with easy-to-use, reliable instructions and
support, sufficient time and the high costs of
alternative services. All these conditions are
present in mature economies. The self-service
society is characterized here by increasing autonomy of workers and consumers, growth of
work-at-home, telecommuting, self-employment, community self-help, home office, part-
time and seasonal work, early retirement, barter and exchanges, networking, flexible work
hours, self-management, decline in supervisory and administrative 'services', decentralized self-reliance and so on.

5 New work and leisure

There is no conspicuous increase in leisure
and leisure-related activities perceived in the
modern economy: the traditional leisure activities are themselves becoming overpriced services and thus being substituted by self-
service. There is a tendency for job-holders to
work even longer hours, although the overall
amount of time worked per person is declining. The time spent for self-service and do-it-
yourself activity is one of the few expanding
categories of economic activities, and it is
sketched in Figure 5.

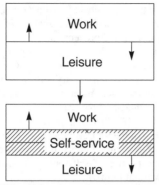

Figure 5 Transition from the sharp separation of work and leisure to a self-service 'grey' region of working

Households are again becoming primary investment/production units, producers and consumers are merging into 'prosumers'. One of the fastest-growing sectors in developed industrial economies, especially in the USA, is 'work at home'. Work at home relates to self-employment, part-time self-employment, work after regular office hours, work instead of regular office hours, self-service and do-it-yourself, typically relying on a home office, telecommuting, neighbourhood networks, virtual office, personal computers, modem, fax, multiple and cellular telephone lines and similar technologies. Work at home is the most potent job-generating sector, moving the self-reliant population towards more productive and efficient self-service activities, reducing the pressures on energy, ecology, human stress, traffic congestion and the cost-intensive physical commuting inherited from factories from the turn of the century. Clearly, individual or corporate telecommuting presents a powerful alternative to the traditional emphasis on 'railroads, highways and bridges'.

Modern production is primarily based on the processing of information, not on the hauling of goods, humans and machinery over large distances. One can more effectively 'haul the information', to produce goods and provide services locally. Information and knowledge travel effortlessly through electronic superhighways, through telecommunications networks and the World Wide Web. Citizens and employees working at home are now in control of their time, can take care of their own children, can invest in home technologies; they do not have to pay excessively for petrol, insurance and childcare and waste most of their precious off-work hours on commuting to work. Temporary, freelance, contingent and interim workers are increasingly forced into or voluntarily choose new modes of economic action. They support and accompany empowerment, autonomy, self-reliance and professionalization – main attributes of the future work and jobs. Knowledge, enhanced by education and training, is taking over as the main form of capital. Self-employed people (in the USA) earn about 40 per cent more hourly than those employed by others. Hired operators, labourers and farmhands are rapidly declining in their importance as well as pay.

The most qualified workforce – in terms of education, computer literacy and worker motivation – is found in Singapore, Denmark, Germany, Japan and the USA. However, over 96 per cent of Japanese students attend high school, Hong Kong's per capita spending is $810, and Korea moved from $33 in 1975 to $450 per student by 1989. Such numbers underline that educational spending is rapidly becoming the main arena of global competition: in search of the knowledge capital, human and social (see ASIA PACIFIC, MANAGEMENT IN).

In spite of the continued governmental obstacles and barriers, there were already about 40 million Americans working at home in 1992. This is to be compared with only some 25 million in 1988. From these 40 million home workers, there are 12.1 million self-employed, 11.7 million part-time self-employed, 8.6 million working at home after regular office hours, and 6.6 million working at home instead of regular office hours. High technologies – e-mail, computer teleconferencing, real-time teleconferencing and video teleconferencing – are all helping to create the electronic networks necessary for self-help and work-at-home business styles (see INFORMATION REVOLUTION; INFORMATION TECHNOLOGY). However, the distributed and asynchronous communication systems are the key: they allow global interaction to take place at different places and at different times – creating time/space collaborative systems of unprecedented productivity. The physically 'going-to-work-with-a-lunch-box' type of interaction is becoming rapidly outmoded: unless there is an actual physical transformation taking place *in situ*, all the necessary information processing is becoming location-independent.

The US economy appears to serve as an experimental laboratory for many new forms of work and leisure, from work at home and telecommuting to self-employment and virtual offices. Spending on home improvement products by individuals was about $25 billion in 1980, but has reached about $95 billion in 1995, and the trend is accelerating rather rapidly.

MILAN ZELENY
FORDHAM UNIVERSITY AT LINCOLN CENTER

Further reading

(References cited in the text marked *)

Champy, J. (1995) *Re-engineering Management*, New York: HarperCollins. (The follow-up book to *Re-engineering the Corporation*, calling for the re-engineering of management.)

* Hammer, M. and Champy, J. (1994) *Re-engineering the Corporation*, New York: Harper Collins. (One of the first and simplest introductions to re-engineering of a business process.)

Heery, E. and Salmon, J. (eds) (1999) *The Insecure Workforce*, London: Routledge. (A discussion of the flexible labour market.)

Kochen, M. and Zeleny, M. (1981) 'Self-service aspects of health maintenance: assessment of current trends', *Human Systems Management* 2 (4): 259–67. (Self-service aspects of modern medical care and prevention.)

Schor, J.B. (1992) *The Overworked American: The Unexpected Decline of Leisure*, Cambridge, MA: Harvard University Press. (Extensive study of the dilemma of less work and less leisure for modern Americans.)

Zeleny, M. (1979) 'The self-service society: a new scenario of the future', *Planning Review*, 7 (3): 3–7, 37–8. (One of the earliest arguments predicting the rise of self-service, do-it-yourself and work-at-home.)

Zeleny, M. (1980) 'Towards a self-service society', *Human Systems Management* 1 (1): 77. (Simple exposition of basic principles of self-service.)

Zeleny, M. (1989) 'Knowledge as a new form of capital, part 1: division and reintegration of knowledge; part 2: knowledge-based management systems', *Human Systems Management* 8 (1–2): 45–58, 129–43. (Extensive discussion of the demise of the division of labour and the rise of integrated knowledge.)

Zeleny, M., Cornet, R. and Stoner, J.A.F. (1990) 'Moving from the age of specialization to the era of integration', *Human Systems Management* 9 (3): 153–71. (Management and business viewpoint of the decline in the division of labour and the rise in re-integration of labour.)

See also: BRAVERMAN, H.; INFORMATION TECHNOLOGY; INTERNET AND BUSINESS; LABOUR PROCESS; PRODUCTIVITY; RE-ENGINEERING; SMITH, A.; TAYLOR, F.W.; WORK ETHIC

Work and organization systems

Overview

Around the world, the issues associated with changing work organization and work systems are important for practitioners and scholars in several fields, including human resources, industrial relations and organization design, and for those concerned with the broader issues of management, public policy and political economy. How has work organization developed since the nineteenth century? After outlining the historical context and offering a definition, the entry discusses a series of approaches to work organization: craft, bureaucracy, Taylorism/Fordism, sociotechnical, neo-human relations, labour process, lean management, empowerment, service areas and the influence of unions.

The development of work organization is influenced by many factors including technology; national, industry and enterprise culture; product and labour markets; and government and union regulation. However, there also appears to be scope for 'strategic choice'. This entry examines competing views of determinism versus choice and argues that some choice was exercised even in the most mechanistic work organizations. Nevertheless, the role of choice should not be exaggerated.

1 Historical context

As early as 2000 BC in ancient Mesopotamia there were records of the organization and management of work. Work plays a central role in the lives of most of us. People derive several meanings from work. Through work, we seek to justify our own existence, to develop a feeling of participation in a design which is grander than our personal lives.

Through work, we join a community of individuals with common experiences, skills or goals. Through work, we derive feelings of competence and achievement, making contributions which enable us to believe in our own worth.

People's understanding of and relationship to work has changed throughout history and varies across cultures. For example, in the days of ancient Greece, work was deemed the plight of those to whom Plato referred as 'the meaner sort of people'. The role that such privileged philosophers occupied was seen as separate from and above work. More recent conceptions of work placed a divine importance on the need for and importance of work. The Protestant work ethic, puritanism and Calvinism extol the virtues of work as a means to greater divine salvation. Others argue that work is in essence a social process, and culture is the ultimate determinant of what meaning and value people assign to work (see WORK ETHIC).

2 What is work organization?

People combine their skills and knowledge in an effort to produce and distribute goods and services. It becomes necessary to combine the various inputs in the work process: labour and capital (including raw materials and energy) in the context of the available technologies, such as equipment and buildings, then produce an output of goods or services. Work organization is the manner in which these variables are arranged.

Work organization determines the way that employees undertake their specific tasks. This usually involves the formation of a hierarchy which shapes the relationships between members of an enterprise, an arrangement for the division of labour and a set of explicit or implied work rules. Through these arrangements, certain individuals may be subordinate to, and controlled by, others.

3 Different ideal types of work organization

Different models of work organization can be compared by examining in each such factors as hierarchy, authority structure, units of responsibility (individual versus group), formalization of work rules, structure of job design and flexibility or division of labour. Actual policies and practices can be better understood by comparing them with an 'ideal type' – an exaggerated abstraction that simplified types of organization. This does not imply a moral value of an 'ideal prescription' for the management and organization of work. In practice, no exact replica will be found of the ideal type, but examples will usually display variations of the key characteristics.

There are at least three reasons why work organization changes over time and across cultures. First, work organizations are influenced by their context, such as product and labour market demand, geography, demographics and culture. In view of the economic and social distinctiveness of Japan, managers there have developed different forms of work organization from those in Western countries (see JAPAN, MANAGEMENT IN).

Second, work organization is influenced by technology (see TECHNOLOGY AND ORGANIZATIONS). For example, in the first half of the twentieth century, industrial engineers used assembly lines to change work organization fundamentally. More recently, others have used microelectronics to revolutionize processes and products. Such technological change may precipitate significant alterations to work organization. The notion of technological determinism is that technology tends to determine a particular pattern of management and work organization. However, although technology may be an important influence, it is by no means the sole determinant (Bamber and Lansbury 1988).

Third, there is scope for key decision makers to exercise a strategic choice about work organization, although they are constrained and possibly partially determined by the above-mentioned variables, including national and corporate cultures as well as technology, labour markets and payment systems (see STRATEGIC CHOICE). Work organization is also constrained by employers' and unions' policies, styles and organizational structures (including centralization or decentralization), the extent to which decision making is participative and the way in which innovations are introduced and maintained.

Craft production

Images of craftwork before industrialization have often been idealized. Craftworkers' jobs were broadly defined. Such work came to be seen as satisfying, because it provided workers with feelings of identity and control over their labour processes. Before the Industrial Revolution work organization could be characterized by a relative lack of a division of labour, an absence of an explicit means of worker control and little formalization of job design. Craft production or cottage industry often involved an extended family. Only a few individuals were involved in production, usually working as a team. These self-employed people might have owned some means of production and sold what they made at a market. Production was set at the pace dictated by the head of the family business and was strongly influenced by demand and by the supply of materials. Loyalty was to a family or an individual rather than to a larger enterprise. While workers had access to intensive collective knowledge of their craft or occupation, most of this knowledge was not systematically organized or recorded. One example of such work organization was the family farm. Although there were general methods for core activities such as ploughing a field or fitting parts of machinery, there was a degree of variation in these activities. Family members, owners and employees decided the specifics of how and by whom these tasks would be carried out.

Workshops had a decentralized control system: most owners had only a nominal control of a semi-autonomous workforce. Work was loosely organized around the traditional apprentice–master system. This gave a degree of structure to the relationships of those involved. In some cases such arrangements were regulated by guilds, the forerunners of craft unions. Different products might be designed and built in the same workshop and, depending upon their complexity, by the same people. These enterprises predominantly employed skilled craftworkers that combined their skills to build products, mainly by hand. There was a limited division of labour which was based upon different crafts including fitters, turners, welders and painters. For example, in the earliest production of coaches, parts were hand cut and produced by skilled contractors. These parts would probably be assembled into a coach elsewhere, by other craftworkers. There was little standardization and parts would vary. Those assembling the product would have to manipulate the parts further, filing and cutting them as necessary. Many products were built to the specific needs of customers. There was, therefore, considerable scope for choice in, for example, the design of work, the development of authority structures and the relationship between people and technology. After industrialization, work organization was fragmented, as illustrated by Adam Smith's famous analysis of pin making in *The Wealth of Nations* (see SMITH, A.). He argued that increasing the division of labour (by process) led to higher labour productivity. As the nineteenth century drew to a close, managers began to use more complex arrangements for the division and control of labour to supplement craft-based approaches. Craft production was not completely eliminated, but survived to varying extents, especially in agriculture and to service niche markets. However, a bureaucratic approach based on mass production became more typical.

Bureaucratic work organization

In the twentieth century more systematic forms of work organization began to be introduced to facilitate increases in efficiency, standardization and quality. Weber made an important contribution to the understanding of such work organization (see WEBER, M.). He diagnosed a fundamental process of rationalization that characterized the modernization of industry. This process was considered inevitable due to the increasing role that technology and structured enterprises were having in the lives of working people. The former decentralized and loosely structured craft-

work organization was being replaced with more centralized organizations characterized by formal rules, regulations, hierarchy and formal structures. Weber saw such a progression in organization as the office equivalent to the change from non-mechanized to mechanized forms of factory production.

Weber's conception of a bureaucratic enterprise built on the work of Adam Smith, Babbage and others who analysed the division of labour and the importance of a systematic system of management. Weber provided several characteristics of the ideal bureaucratic form of work organization:

1 fixed, clearly understood and demarcated, division of tasks;
2 hierarchical means of authority governed by clear rules and regulations;
3 focus on impersonality (that is, power and authority which emanates from the position, not the person, and maintains control over other positions);
4 separation of management and ownership of the enterprise;
5 clear method of hiring and promotion based on merit.

Weber argued that bureaucratic work organization was more efficient than the relatively haphazard work organization found in most family enterprises or small firms. Weber was writing against a background of class consciousness and work organization in Europe. His notion of *impersonality* and *rationality* in the management of the enterprise was conceived in opposition to the overemphasis on *personal interests* in small family-run businesses and many state-operated enterprises (for example, the military), at the expense of the needs of clients and employees.

Taylorism and Fordism

Several others attempted to develop more prescriptive methods by which bureaucratic organization could be implemented most effectively. Both Frederick Winslow Taylor and Henry Ford had a profound impact (see FORD, H.; TAYLOR, F.W.). They were concerned with raising labour productivity. Taylor argued that tradition be replaced by management based on scientific study, hence his term 'scientific management'. The need for a systematic approach to management had already been identified by others, however Taylor was possibly the most influential in conceptualizing these approaches.

Taylor was working against a background of rapid industrialization. The USA, for example, was changing from craft production to a factory system. There was no existing blueprint for the scale of labour organization that was then occurring. Scientific management partially filled this gap. While working as a steel-company engineer, Taylor attempted to find the solution to the problem of employee 'soldiering' (employees not working to their potential). He developed four principles designed to deal with the problem of soldiering and, in general, of organizing labour effectively (Taylor 1911):

1 scientific study should be used to develop the best way for doing a task;
2 workers should be scientifically selected and trained;
3 management should cooperate with employees to make sure workers use the scientific principles;
4 work and responsibility should be clearly divided, with management responsible for planning and deciding upon work issues and workers executing the work.

Taylor recommended that time-and-motion studies be used to gauge and plan the amount of work that an employee should do. The employee was then given strict instructions on this method, as well as a monetary incentive to undertake these tasks. The method was exemplified with his dealings with a pig-iron handler, Schmidt. Taylor wanted to increase the amount of pig iron loaded from 12.5 tonnes per day to 47.5. He gave strict instructions to Schmidt to obey a manager (presumably one versed in the science of loading heavy objects). In return, Schmidt was paid as a 'high-priced man' (he received US$1.85 instead of US$1.15 a day). The following is an excerpt from their discussion:

Well, if you [Schmidt] are a high-priced man, you will do exactly as this man tells you tomorrow, from morning till night. When he tells you to pick up pig and walk, you pick it up and you walk, and when he tells you to sit down and rest, you sit down. You do that right straight through the day. And what's more, no back talk.

(Taylor 1911: 39)

Such work was analysed and the best procedure for doing each task was determined. These tasks would then be assigned to those who were specially trained in doing them. A high degree of control was needed to make this work successfully. The methods by which jobs are designed have subsequently changed, but job design as a method of productivity improvement has since become a central strategy in the management of work organization (see JOB DESIGN).

Scientific management also emphasized areas other than job design: the formalization of authority and responsibility, standardization of means for control, development of task specialization and separation of responsibility and authority. These strategies are still used to varying degrees in contemporary work organization.

Henry Ford refined and built upon the work of Taylor. The opening of his mechanized assembly line in the USA in 1913 revolutionized manufacturing and heralded the age of mass production. Mass production is typified by long production runs of a standard product and the use of a moving assembly line. However, it is important not simply to equate Ford's techniques strictly with the assembly-line form of mass production which prevailed in some industries for much of the twentieth century. Ford also developed innovative techniques in factory layout, stock handling and labour usage before the adoption of the assembly line. His innovations exemplify the potential for choice in even the most mechanistic work organization: according to Williams *et al.* (1992: 525) 63 per cent of the 1910–16 labour hours reduction and 70 per cent of the material cost reduction was achieved without benefit of assembly lines. Ford adopted innovative techniques which were subsequently forgotten, and it was not until later the term 'Fordism' became synonymous with mass production.

Taylorism and Fordism provoked a great deal of controversy among managers, workers and others. Critics argued that such mechanistic approaches de-skilled and de-humanized working people. This was apparent in increased rates of turnover, for example, which on Ford's first assembly line was approximately 380 per cent per year. Ford also had to double wages to US$5 per day before he could maintain a relatively stable workforce. However, these methods appeared to induce tremendous productivity gains. These gains, coupled with the large amount of power that employers wielded in their own establishments, meant that Taylorism and Fordism had a major impact upon work organization, especially in larger manufacturing enterprises in the USA, Europe, the former USSR and elsewhere. Fragmented forms of work organization were institutionalized by job regulation (custom and practice, collective bargaining, arbitration or professional codes). Industrial engineers, job evaluation specialists and labour negotiators further defined jobs and demarcations.

The advent of bureaucratization, Taylorism and Fordism was partially induced by industrialization. However, different countries and enterprises adopted varying bureaucratic methods. Bureaucracy was a means by which management could extend a greater degree of control over the means of production. While it took a degree of control of the individual elements of work organization away from skilled workers, perhaps managers and owners could then exercise a greater degree of choice in the direction and control of the enterprise and the pattern of work organization. Clawson (1980: 57) argues that moves to such fragmented forms of work organization came before a technological revolution and were not determined by it. According to Thompson and McHugh, the 'minute division of work was not necessarily more efficient; rather, it provided a role for the capitalist to play in organizing production and to take a greater portion of the rewards' (1990: 49).

Taylorism, while providing standards for individual work tasks, was applied in varying ways and influenced by different reactions from managers, employees and unions. Taylorism was not a precondition of industrialization, but was a chosen method of control.

'Human relations' was an alternative approach.

Human relations

In partial reaction to the drawbacks of Taylorism and Fordism, the human relations school advocated that management should focus on the role of employees and work groups (see HUMAN RELATIONS). People could not or would not always follow instructions exactly and there were other problems with regard to working conditions and the importance of job satisfaction which Taylorism and Fordism neglected. Led by Elton Mayo (see MAYO, G.E.), the human relations school was inspired by reports of experiments at Western Electric's Hawthorne Plant which began in 1924. These experiments found that employee motivation increased with attention from higher-status people (see HAWTHORNE EXPERIMENTS).

The human relations school argued that informal social processes could have a large impact on issues such as productivity, morale and the effectiveness of work organization. Therefore, when constructing a work organization, social issues could be as important as technical requirements, though management's potential choice of organization systems is not necessarily increased. The methodology and conclusions of the Hawthorne experiments have been widely criticized. However, human relations theory has had a major effect on subsequent approaches to work organization, with managers paying more attention to interacting with employees. Under Taylorism, work organization was seen as primarily a technical (engineering) problem and hence it advocated a 'one best way' approach, as determined largely by technology. The human relations school contradicted this argument. Two advocates, Roethlisberger and Dickson (1939), when describing their experiments, invoked the notion of a social system. Given the dominance of 'structural functionalism' in sociology in the subsequent period, it is unsurprising that other studies of work used a similar paradigm.

Sociotechnical systems

Another approach to work organization is derived from research and consulting by the Tavistock Institute of Human Relations, which ranged from British coal mines to Indian textile mills. Its adherents saw a sociotechnical system as consisting of two elements: (1) *technical factors* such as mechanical equipment, technical processes and the physical environment; (2) *social factors* such as the relationships amongst workpeople and their individual and collective attitudes to the system and to each other. The idea of a work organization as a system includes a series of assumptions:

> that it comprises a set of interdependent 'parts' such that a change in one part will affect some or all of the others, but that the whole system is more than just an aggregation of these parts; that there is some relatively clear continuity about this set of interdependent parts so that it can be considered the same enterprise despite the changes which may take place; and that it has a relatively clear *boundary* which separates it from a wider 'environment'. In addition, most conceptions of enterprises as systems assume that there is an overarching set of values and/or goals which secures the *integration* of the system; and, in open system models, that the maintenance of the system (and the achievement of its goals) are secured by exchanges between the system and its environment.
>
> (Brown 1992: 42–3; emphasis added)

The Tavistock analysts' insights included the notion of work being arranged around people. Compared with scientific management (which underlined the technical aspect of work) and human relations (which emphasized the social aspects), a sociotechnical understanding recognizes the importance of both of these vital aspects of work organization.

Tavistock researchers criticized the formal methods used to introduce new technology and to organize tasks. They argued that employees could not be treated as separate individuals isolated from their work groups. The sociotechnical school emphasized the need to find a proper fit between the social and technical systems. They argued that when this did not occur, low productivity, poor morale and high turnover of staff often resulted (Trist *et al.* 1963).

The organization of work by sociotechnical precepts includes two main characteristics. First are semi-autonomous work groups; work groups should have a degree of freedom in regulating the manner of their work. Although details of this approach were published in the 1950s, relatively few managers in the English-speaking world seem to take its message fully into account when embarking on technological and organizational change. The message has had more impact in Scandinavia. For instance, at Volvo's Uddevalla plant, production employees were given control over the pace of work and the division of tasks (Berggren 1992: 146–83). However, the concept of employee self-regulation may apply beyond the work-group level. Joint labour–management consultative committees are also recommended as appropriate for making decisions about the organization of work.

Second is the adoption of ergonomically sound methods of production and the de-emphasis of assembly lines in favour of 'cellular production'. Semi-autonomous teams of workers are given responsibility for a whole task or a whole unit of production.

How can 'social' objectives be incorporated into the design of a technical system of work organization? Such questions apply in general to the design of work organizations and the use of new technologies. Graversen (1989), for instance, draws on the sociotechnical approach in a Danish study of the phases of the design of work organization in a new brewery. He identifies four different patterns:

1 technical systems are designed without regard to social systems;
2 objectives for, and the design of, social systems are separated from the design of technical systems;
3 objectives for, and the design of, social systems are introduced after the design of technical systems;
4 technical and social objectives and solutions are integrated in the design process.

Heller (1989) draws on French and British examples to argue that engineering solutions ('the technological fix') are often designed to maximize technological effectiveness, on the assumption that people, being adaptable, will make all the necessary adjustments to work with any technologies. He shows that such one-sided solutions can fail completely and advocates the sociotechnical approach as appropriate for analysing the range of choices available when designing technologies.

The notion of choice, as conceptualized by the Tavistock school, has been criticized. The Tavistock researchers argued that the social, technical and economic variables must be mediated. However this may indicate a decrease in choice. According to Rose, if the consideration of social requirements is a 'necessary precondition of more productive arrangements ... [then] the socio-technical concept may be seen as a device for helping production engineers to discover better "best ways"' (1975: 216). This is a concept shared with Taylorism.

The 'technological imperative' tends to ignore the requirements of people and thereby usually fails to realize its full potential. The sociotechnical approach implies an integrated solution rather than a compromise. Both the technical–economic system and the social system may operate at sub-optimum levels, but overall efficiency may be maximized by allowing the social as well as the technical factors to operate in coordinated harmony.

A labour process perspective

Braverman (1974) inspired a revival of interest in the Marxist notion of the labour process. This is the management function which converts people's potential for work into productive work effort under conditions which permit capital accumulation (see LABOUR PROCESS). This perspective can highlight the influence of technology on work organization. Braverman's major criticism of the earlier scientific management approach is not of the technological imperative as such, but the underlying drive for capital accumulation and control.

Since the mid-1970s there has been much debate about work organization and management from a labour process perspective. Such research has made an important contribution by directing attention to managerial strategies and the importance of skills. Braverman and some of his followers, however, tend to regard new technology as inevitably causing de-skilling and the degradation of work. They appear to assume that most managers invariably follow a technological imperative, use scientific management principles and give the utmost priority to maximizing the control of labour.

In spite of the de-skilling argument, technological change can be associated with re-skilling and a demand for new skills. Depending on the choice of work organization, flexible automation may provide operators with opportunities to use a wider range of skills than traditional machine tools (Child 1984). New technologies may provide possibilities for technicians to use mechanical and electronic engineering skills, and for operators to programme and maintain their machines and to supervise themselves. By arguing that perceived skill is often associated with the use of new technology, however, Braverman's work has highlighted how elusive the whole notion of 'skill' can be in analysing work organization.

It may be true that the principal reason for introducing new technology during the early stages of assembly-line manufacturing was to reduce direct labour costs through economies of scale and standardization of production. In the more advanced stages, however, the main objective for introducing technological change in manufacturing is to achieve greater quality and flexibility in the production process, through the use of innovations such as computer-aided design/computer-aided manufacturing (CAD/CAM) and robotics. Although most managements aim to achieve consistent profitability and thereby retain the goal of minimizing labour costs, increasing emphasis is being given to customizing products and achieving fast responses in terms of changes in specification, delivery times and so on.

When deciding about new technologies, most employers are primarily concerned with achieving greater control over production processes, improved product quality and cost reduction. Labour processes and work organization are invariably of secondary importance and are often considered only in the implementation stage, rather than initially when making high-level corporate decisions about technological innovation.

Braverman has been criticized for underestimating the potential for worker resistance, union action and even of worker control of aspects of labour regulation, and his adherents for concentrating too narrowly on the point of production and exaggerating the pervasiveness, coherence and conspiratorial nature of management. In reality, business strategy specialists tend to focus on finance, marketing, research, production and corporate structures, while neglecting work organization and the labour process.

Zuboff (1988) highlights two stark options in the introduction of information technology (IT). IT may be used to *automate* work, robbing people of whatever skill and gratification they may have had and increasing management's impersonality. Alternatively, IT can be used to *informate*, empowering people with knowledge about production and distribution processes, which in turn may provide new opportunities for individual workers and their employing enterprises.

Zuboff asked people 'to draw pictures that represented their "felt sense" of their job experience before and after conversion to the new computer system' (1988: 141ff.). One set of pictures and captions drawn by clerks and their supervisors shows 'both the sense of the isolation of the individual office worker and a new sense of distance between the clerical function and those who supervise it' (1988: 151). IT had been used to automate rather than to informate the clerks' jobs; that is, to push them away from acting with other people to acting on office machines. Paradoxically, this may allow some informating of supervisors' jobs so that they can become more closely integrated into management.

Taylorist styles of work organization appear to be inimical to the adoption of an information approach. Hierarchical control is not suitable for the new informating regime. Zuboff's analysis shows how an 'information process can provide the impetus for new models of organization and management' (1988: 223).

A neo-human relations approach

Several of Peters and Waterman's (1982) prescriptions are consistent with elements of the earlier human relations school (see PETERS, T.J.). Peters and Waterman do not formulate a new behavioural model, but include a series of common-sense prescriptions, based on their observation of the USA's most successful companies. They recommend, for example, that 'employees should be trusted':

> Treat people as adults. Treat them as partners; treat them with dignity; treat them with respect. Treat *them* – not capital spending and automation – as the primary source of productivity gains. These are the fundamental lessons from the excellent companies' research. In other words, if you want productivity and the financial success that goes with it, you must treat your workers as your most important asset.
>
> (Peters and Waterman 1982: 238; original emphasis)

Although their book has been a best-seller internationally and has inspired similar studies elsewhere, outside the USA many scholars regard the remedies of Peters and Waterman as inapplicable, on the grounds that they are too prescriptive and too ethnocentrically American. Even in the USA, work organization issues for such renowned 'excellent' companies as McDonald's and Walt Disney Productions in the private service sector are very different from those that might confront practitioners in the public sector, mining or manufacturing. Within manufacturing, work organization issues differ greatly, for example, depending on the technologies, methods of production and type of business strategy. Even in the private service sector, work organization strategies may vary depending, for example, on whether the business policy is to concentrate on specialist market niches with emphasis on high quality (and high pay) as the basis for a competitive advantage, or to concentrate on mass markets with an emphasis on the quantity of low-cost output (and low pay), which gives a fundamentally different competitive advantage.

Lean management

Particularly since the 1973 oil shock, the ability of Japanese enterprises simultaneously to produce high-quality and relatively low-cost goods gave these firms a competitive advantage over most of their Western counterparts. The work organization systems of these Japanese enterprises are an aspect of their success.

In breaking the assumed nexus between high quality and low productivity, Japanese enterprises overthrew much of the accepted 'wisdom' about the modern organization of work. They altered the prevailing way in which work systems are judged. Traditional mass producers emphasized output *quantity* as a key measure of success. Other criteria, such as *quality*, were considered subordinate and even incompatible with this focus. A certain proportion of defective output was seen as acceptable; it could either be rectified later or scrapped.

To survive in the face of Japanese and international competition, many non-Japanese enterprises saw a need to increase the efficiency of their work systems and the quality of their outputs. In North America, Europe and elsewhere many managers and academics sought to apply the 'secrets' of Japanese success. Furthermore, many of their enterprises tried to emulate Japanese work systems or to develop forms of work organization which could build a similar competitive advantage.

Deming, Juran and others who advocated the approach to quality observed in large Japanese manufacturing enterprises found Western business leaders were an enthusiastic audience (see DEMING, W.E.). They developed strategies for improving quality and productivity, the adoption of which changed work organization.

Deming stresses the importance of training, especially in statistical tools of process control. Operational employees are the main target of this training. They are given greater control over production processes and are expected to supervise the quality and efficiency of their own work. This decreases the need for direct supervision. In return for such *empowerment* the enterprise can expect an increase in quality and productivity.

The concept of the 'internal customer' is crucial. All employees in the enterprise are seen as customers of those who supply them with parts, information, services and so on. Ideally this concept extends to all levels of an enterprise and can change the relationships that develop in work organizations. For example, a finance officer would provide budgetary advice to other departments of an enterprise. This advice is expected to equal or surpass the service that an external finance consultant could provide, and is judged on this basis.

In the early 1980s, in response to Japanese competition, the Ford Motor Company embarked on an 'After Japan' (AJ) strategy. This was an attempt to change from Fordist mass production to Japanese-style management practices. Ford aimed to change its workforce from being relatively unskilled and untrained to more highly skilled and trained. Ford's leaders saw these changes as a way of building higher quality cars more productively. This was a means to an end: winning a more satisfactory return on its investment.

In the 1980s the Massachusetts Institute of Technology's (MIT) International Motor Vehicle Program (IMVP) undertook a major study into the sources of the competitive success of Japanese car manufacturers. The IMVP researchers argued that most of this success could be traced to the type of work system; they contended that just as mass production (Taylorism and Fordism) replaced craft production, lean production 'will become the standard global production system' (Womack *et al.* 1990: 278).

The IMVP coined the idea of 'lean' because lean production uses 'less of everything compared with mass production – half the human effort in the factory, half the manufacturing space, half the investment in tools, . . . [and] far less than half the needed inventory on site' (Womack *et al.* 1990: 13).

Lean production is primarily concerned with achieving a competitive advantage by operating at the highest levels of efficiency possible. This is accomplished by the continuous reduction of everything used in the production process and specifically every process not involved in adding value to the product. The notion of *kaizen* (continuous or incremental improvement) is a key to lean production.

This drive for continuous improvement has de-emphasized the role of technical experts as the sole source of innovation in work systems. Operational employees are closest to the point of production, and hence much of the *kaizen* effort is focused upon their efforts. MlT's Commission on Industrial Productivity argued that a focus on *kaizen* can be more effective than the older notion of aiming to achieve large technological breakthroughs (Dertouzos *et al.* 1989: 74). *Kaizen* is promoted in training and suggestion schemes. Frequent rewards are given for suggestions. These rewards tend to encourage all suggestions, no matter how small (Shadur and Bamber 1994).

The *andon* system is an aspect of lean production whereby operators are given responsibility for stopping the production line to remedy problems at their source. The *andon* system played an integral part in improving the quality and efficiency of Japanese car manufacturers. However, it is not easy to adopt such methods in older Western assembly plants with entrenched customs and practices.

Another important aspect of lean production is just-in-time (JIT) (see JUST-IN-TIME PHILOSOPHY). Units of production are delivered by suppliers (internal and external) 'just in time' to meet the demands of the next stage of production. Such a process helps to cut costs by removing inventory, the resulting storage space and the workers required to handle inventory. There is a growing interest in these approaches in most industries including the service sector. For this reason we prefer the term lean *management*, rather than lean *production*.

Lean management is also supported by an array of human resource management strategies such as teamworking, multi-skilling and cross-functional training. With regard to teamworking, teams normally consist of five to fifteen members. In large Japanese enterprises teams tend to be compulsory, whereas in non-Japanese enterprises they are frequently voluntary. In either case, teams are expected to work towards the solution of specific problems and make general quality improvements (see GROUPS AND TEAMS; TEAMS IN MANUFACTURING).

Non-Japanese enterprises that also arrange their employees into teams (like Federal Express, General Electric, Hewlett Packard, Honeywell and Rank Xerox) do so as a means of improving performance. There are several advantages of operating in teams rather than individually. When dealing with tasks, the combination of individuals' knowledge and experience found in a team will produce quicker and higher quality results than individuals. Teams may also foster creativity and innovation.

To operate successfully, teams may depend upon an increase in the inputs to the work system, such as cross-functional training. Team members can be trained in the functions of all members of the team. Members can therefore cover the jobs of absent colleagues. However, where the team concept is implementedthere may be considerable peer pressure to minimize absenteeism. Also, cross-trained team members can be readily shifted to respond to changing production requirements. Teams are often given a greater degree of autonomy than individual employees. Consistent with the notion of built-in quality, teams are responsible for their own quality.

Japanese firms pioneered the use of cross-functional teams in the design and manufacture of cars. Japanese cars are designed more quickly and are often more manufacturable than comparable US ones (Womack *et al.* 1990: 97). Lean-managed enterprises can respond more quickly and effectively to changing consumer preferences. Similarly, multi-function teams are being used effectively in many leading-edge companies to deal quickly with current or potential problems.

The sociotechnical school of thought was one inspiration for the later advocates of teams and self-managing work groups. However most sociotechnical analysts are critical of such later developments of the team concept. For it would appear that, in Japan and other countries, teams are being adopted in a subordinate role to the technological infrastructure. Sociotechnical researchers tend to be critical of Japanese-style work organization. Instead, Berggren (1992) recommends the sociotechnical forms of work organization pioneered by Swedish enterprises.

Supporters of the sociotechnical style of work organization claim that the changes to work systems associated with lean management enhance the quality of employees' working lives. However, detractors hold that, from an employees' point of view, these methods may lead to a degradation of human dignity. After a study of several US and Japanese firms, Klein (1989) is also critical of JIT, arguing that a reduction in inventory often leads to an increased work pace and worker dissatisfaction. Such critics suggest that these systems do not augment the skills of employees – instead, for most workers, they imply de-skilling.

Lean management aims to eliminate as many 'buffers' as possible. Hence the work system is operating as close to its failure point as possible. Some critics argue that this system places undue stress on employees and represents a return to Taylorism. Other critics cite the pace of work as a key drawback. For example, at Toyota in Japan, supervisors reportedly run to the workstations to assist employees to keep up with the line or alleviate problems. Attempts at continuous improvement create increasing demands on employees and managers (see TOYODA FAMILY).

At the enterprise level two more strategies are influencing work organization: empowerment and the decentralization of authority. These strategies can be encapsulated within the broader models of quality improvement and lean production mentioned above. However, they also merit further discussion.

Empowerment

Empowerment is defined by Vogt and Murrel as a process by which employees achieve individual and cooperative goals by working in teams (1990: 8–10) (see EMPOWERMENT). While this emphasizes the *team* focus of empowerment programmes, empowerment is also reported as an *individual* process whereby employees can become increasingly involved in the maintenance and improvement of their enterprise. By working in self-managing teams, employees can take more direct control over their own jobs. Empowerment, then, resembles the major tenets of the sociotechnical school.

Empowerment may increase the effectiveness of a work system, for an empowered workforce should be able to initiate and make changes and adjustments in a work system more quickly than if each process were controlled strictly by management. Thus, an enterprise with such a workforce could be more responsive to their various customers' needs. Operational employees are the closest to the point of production and often have most knowledge about it, and many of these employees are excellent 'troubleshooters'.

To assist the strategy of empowerment, enterprises are trying to decentralize and devolve authority. There are several other reasons for this: first, a holistic approach to quality improvement requires a large degree of communication up, down and across organizational structures (see ORGANIZATION STRUCTURE). This is easier in enterprises with 'flatter' hierarchies. Second, there have been attempts to remove as many non-value-adding costs and employees as possible. Middle managers and supervisors are being either removed or given greater autonomy. Third, tall hierarchical organizations tend to be less responsive to market conditions than flat organizations. Many levels of authority may actually create work and can lead to an insular focus. Feedback from employees who deal with customers tends to be slower to reach upper management. Moreover, it is more difficult to change an enterprise with a long chain of command. MIT's Commission on Industrial Productivity found '[in] virtually all successful firms ... [Investigated] ... the trend is toward greater functional integration and fewer layers of hierarchy, both of which promote greater speed in product development and greater responsiveness to changing markets' (Dertouzos *et al.* 1989: 122).

Work and organization systems

It is not easy to find the most appropriate balance between centralized control (to adjust work organization in the face of a rapidly changing environment) and decentralization (to give organizational units sufficient autonomy to focus on their areas of business). Lawrence and Lorsch (1967) identified this issue in their concepts of differentiation and integration. To cope with complexity in their environment, it may be appropriate for organizations to develop specialized units (differentiation). On the other hand, differentiation carries with it forces that tend to divide the organization and move these parts in different directions – therefore integration devices are required.

It may be possible to derive benefits from differentiation while maintaining integration. Many Japanese enterprises, and more recently Western firms (to an extent learning from the Japanese), have attempted to increase the degree of employee participation within their enterprises. Employee participation is not a singular concept but has been used to describe a variety of processes. Wagner (1994: 312) defines participation as 'a process in which influence is shared among individuals who are otherwise hierarchical unequals', Employee involvement (EI) programmes try to harness the potential of workforce participation. While there are many different EI programmes, most involve some form of *group* involvement. (An exception to this generalization may be the notion of employee surveys, though these may also have group dimension, for example, if their results are discussed in focus groups.) Effectively implemented, EI programmes may assist organizations to be flexible and responsive to changing market demands (taking advantage of differentiation), while maintaining integration within the workforce.

Integration encompasses the standardization of organizational units and implies a standardization of processes and control mechanisms most clearly observed in traditional bureaucracies. Yet integration can take forms other than the standardization of structures and processes. Much recent literature has reported the competitive benefits that can stem from having an integrated and involved workforce; yet traditional bureaucracies may be less amenable to EI programmes. Enterprises that have serious EI programmes may facilitate integration through the 'culture' of the organization, and not through traditional bureaucratic control mechanisms. Reinforced with standardised support mechanisms, such as training and performance assessment, integration and control can be stronger in enter-

prises that have EI programmes than in traditional bureaucracies. Other involvement strategies, such as cross-functional teams, can be employed to increase communication and interaction between different organizational sub-units, further facilitating integration.

The use of EI is by no means the only way to increase flexibility and differentiation. In an effort to benefit from participation, many enterprises have adopted *empowerment* schemes or other individualized approaches to work organization. In comparison with EI, empowerment may focus on teams or individuals; participation processes tend to be less formal and are less likely to encompass formal group involvement programmes. These individualistic approaches to work organization are usually accompanied by individual, performance-based contracts and individual, rather than, collective bargaining. Flexibility can be increased because work organization, hours and pay can be adjusted relatively quickly to meet changes in the environment. Productivity may increase as employees' pay is related to performance. Most union officials have been opposed to these approaches to work organization. They argue that such methods may give managers excessive power at the expense of the other employees.

High performance work systems

The high performance work system (HPWS) is a concept used increasingly to describe high-commitment or high-involvement models of work organization. High performance systems represent a significant departure from Taylorist work methods based on an acute division of labour, close supervision, and minimal work involvement. HPWS, in contrast, involves lean management and quality management practices in combination with human resource management practices that foster employee empowerment and involvement. Some claim that this type of work system can outperform Taylorist work systems, especially in the provision of high-quality goods and services (Wood 1999b).

A key component of HPWS is the focus on creating a work environment or culture that recognises and supports customer expectations and needs. HPWS employs new flexible technologies and flatter organizational structures to improve internal communication and responsiveness to customer and market demands. The use of quality circles creates opportunities for continuous improvement in the design and operation of work methods. Quality circles also enable workers to become more directly involved at work. Employee participation is further enhanced with the use of semi-autonomous work groups. To support the more active engagement of employees at work, there is a heightened need for training and staff development (Farias and Varma 1998).

Research indicates that firms employing HPWS do experience improved organizational performance in terms of financial success, productivity and decreased employee turnover. Higher levels of performance tend to occur where organizations adopt a 'bundle' of integrated human resources practices rather than individual practices. Performance is also improved if there is a close 'fit' between business strategy, productions systems and human resources strategies (Farias and Varma 1998; MacDuffie 1995).

Work organization in service areas

Services generate approximately 70 per cent of gross domestic product in the most highly developed countries. The importance of this sector is increasing since the distinction between manufacturing and service enterprises is blurring, and many manufacturing enterprises attempt to increase the level and quality of, for example, their customer service, distribution and finance operations. White-collar support staff, comprising approximately one-third of the employment in the US service sector, also are a large component of the total workforce of manufacturing enterprises. Despite the apparent importance of services, the general productivity of services appears to lag behind manufacturing.

The increasing importance of services and the need to improve the efficiency of this sector has implications for contemporary work organization. Work organization that was designed for the manufacturing sector may be inappropriate for the service sector. Traditionally, commentators recommended a Tayloristic production-line approach to services. Some argue that McDonald's is the archetype of this strategy, with its set procedures for greeting customers, taking and assembling orders. This kind of organization system results in a standardized, highly efficient operation in which customers know exactly what they will receive. This production-line approach to services has been criticised, however, on the grounds that customers are beginning to demand a more customized service.

In parallel, many employers are seeking to change the work organization among their managerial cadres too. The production-line approach may not be applicable to knowledge-based services that encompass a range of managers, executives and professionals such as doctors and lawyers. Nor may it be applicable to white-collar support functions that are highly complex and difficult to standardize. For example, while there have been attempts at extending the features of lean management to staff areas, lean management has so far had less influence on white-collar staff than on operational employees. Many Japanese enterprises that have pioneered lean production on the shop floor are overstaffed and less well organized in the white-collar areas. The adoption of quality management strategies in US service enterprises has also had only sporadic success. The adoption of these strategies, which were initially developed in a manufacturing setting, relied on standardization. It is difficult to transpose such strategies to the management of services despite the rapid introduction of advanced telecommunications and information technologies. These technologies have increased the mechanization of services, especially in the white-collar support areas, but there has not been a correlated increase in the efficiency of services.

There have been calls for the adoption of a work system for services which shares many of the underlying philosophies of lean production yet is more flexible and stresses empowerment over the standardization of tasks. However, such strategies as flatter management hierarchies are probably more suitable in enterprises with highly skilled and polyvalent operational workers who may seek greater autonomy than their less skilled and univalent counterparts. Perhaps such 'unskilled' workers can effectively be managed by Theory X approaches of 'direct control', but typically the highly skilled are more appropriately managed by a Theory Y-type strategy (see HUMAN RELATIONS). Transformations have been taking place in the management hierarchies of enterprises. Some are aiming to be less bureaucratic and to share information horizontally as well as vertically. As Burns and Stalker (1961) found, such flexible (organic) organizational structures are more appropriate than bureaucratic (mechanistic) ones in enterprises which face turbulent environments.

The influence of unions

As unionism grew in the nineteenth and early twentieth centuries, it reflected the contemporary forms of work organization. Consequently a pattern of occupationally structured unionism is evident to varying extents in many countries including the UK, Ireland, Canada, the USA, Australia and New Zealand. (Independent forms of occupationally based unionism were virtually destroyed in Germany and Japan in the 1930s.) As unions tend to be defensive, they may appear to be suspicious about attempts to change work organization. Many employers are opposed to unions participating in decisions about work organization. When unions are not consulted in advance but are merely confronted with a *fait accompli* about new work systems, it is not surprising if their initial response is negative.

There is some evidence that conflict about work organization changes is less likely if the changes are also associated with technological change. None the less, where there have been industrial disputes about technological change, the conflicts have often involved the introduction of new technology that may impinge on the work organization of traditional occupations which are threatened with extinction, or at least a transformation, such as railway firemen, miners, dockers and printers. For example, working with hot metal was the basis of the newspaper printers' old craft. The craftworkers and their unions feared the prospect of extinction by the introduction of computerized typesetting, with direct keying by journalists. Several newer occupations have also been involved in disputes about technological change, including computer staff, TV and telecommunications technicians, air traffic controllers and chemical workers.

Despite the media's focus on such industrial conflicts, complete resistance by unions to changing work organization associated with new technology is relatively rare. In recent years there have been many such changes, most of which have been introduced peacefully. Most innovations are not accompanied by industrial disputes (and are, therefore, less newsworthy). Only 7 per cent of a large British sample of managers of manufacturing establishments using new technologies reported opposition from the shop floor or unions as a major difficulty (Northcott *et al.* 1985: 37).

Unions have long sought to exert some control over work organization through various means, including collective bargaining and government action (see TRADE UNIONS; COLLECTIVE BARGAINING). Increasingly, some unions have been seeking to shape the introduction of organizational and technological change, which they realize can have a significant impact over the quality of their members' working lives. Why have certain national union movements had much more influence than others? As one observer puts it:

> The unions which have been most effective in securing positive outcomes for their members seem to have been those which have adopted a strategic response involving generally positive attitudes towards technological and organizational change and a willingness and ability to engage in consultation and collaboration with management at the workplace level.
>
> (OECD 1992: 252)

Union responses are not the only variable, however – the role of the State is also important. The role of governments tends not to be that of direct intervention, rather of helping to establish a climate, while perhaps providing minimum standards. Governments can also play a powerful leadership role by fostering appropriate education and training, disseminating information about 'best practice' exemplars and providing advice and assistance to managers, employees and unions.

4 Conclusions

As the above discussion of different approaches to work organization was approximately in a chronological order, one might infer that, within a century, conventional wisdom about work organization has almost turned full circle, from autonomous craftwork with flat hierarchies, through bureaucracy, Taylorism/ Fordism and tall hierarchical bureaucracies, to semi-autonomous work groups and flatter hierarchies again. Decision makers' views of 'best practice' work organization vary according to their particular circumstances, but dominant coalitions in many enterprises are aiming to reorientate work, away from individuals to teams, with more emphasis on decentralization. They are seeking more input from employees, for instance, by participating in making and implementing decisions.

There is, however, a fundamental difference between nineteenth-century autonomous craftwork and late twentieth-century semi-autonomous work groups. Typically, the latter are allowed to have only a degree of 'relative autonomy' about some details of how they work and they usually remain employees (or sub-contractors) of a large enterprise that has sophisticated control mechanisms. The late twentieth-century emphasis on total quality management (and, as the Japanese put it more bluntly, total quality *control*) has often induced a rigorous and systematic approach to management that resembles Taylorism.

Is there an international convergence of 'best practice' work organization? There were parallel moves in most industrialized market economies in the 1990s in an attempt to introduce forms of lean management. None the less, there are also differences of approach between countries. To begin to characterize these differences, Anglo-Saxon approaches tend to be seen all too often as trying a one-off 'quick fix' that is not integrated with enough appropriate training and other elements of corporate strategy. By contrast, Japanese approaches are integrated with complementary elements in the political economy, and foster a mind-set that sees training as an investment rather than a cost. Scandinavian approaches build on a legacy of industrial democracy, with pervasive union and employee influences, so that Volvo's form of teamworking is quite different from Toyota's approach.

Anglo-Saxon countries can be characterized as having an adversarial industrial relations context. By contrast, Japan and another group of countries can be characterized as currently having a more consensual approach, for instance, Scandinavia, Germany and Austria (where there was little pre-capitalist industry, as they were primarily agrarian societies and the industrial workforce was recruited rapidly from peasants). Other things being equal, employers in these latter countries have tended to be more innovative in terms of work systems and have introduced more integrated approaches than most of those in the Anglo-Saxon countries.

Although there are many exceptions – some enterprises in Anglo-Saxon countries have been innovative in terms of work organization and have a consensual rather than an adversarial approach – there are many similarities between different countries. Hence such generalizations can be sustained more easily for particular industries, occupations, or organizations.

In most of the countries characterized as consensual, there have been substantial public policy initiatives emphasizing novel forms of work organization. Such initiatives have been complemented by a high priority devoted to education and training. There is less likelihood of fully flexible work organization being successfully implemented and maintained in countries with an adversarial context than in some of the continental European countries, where there have been more constructive moves away from Taylorism, with a backcloth of public policies that aim to improve the working environment. The broader context is crucial. Reformers, unions and their members are better able to exert a constructive influence in countries, industries and enterprises that have a relatively harmonious tradition and a long-term approach to training, career development and investment, rather than a tradition of conflictual industrial relations and short-termism.

There are numerous examples of convergence in work organization. Management styles in Japan are changing to incorporate a greater degree of variation in management practice. In the USA, UK, Australia and New Zealand, Japanese enterprises are having remarkable success at transplanting lean management systems which are almost as successful in terms of productivity and quality as those in Japan. Similarly, US enterprises such as Ford, Motorola and Hewlett Packard are adopting forms of work organization which resemble those in Japan, but also incorporate insights from the sociotechnical and other schools. Scandinavian enterprises are having difficulty maintaining their distinctive approach to work organization. The closing of Volvo's Uddevella plant, as well as General Motors' takeover of Saab may signal the end of the Swedish car industry's divergence from others. However, these examples draw upon the experience of large enterprises. There may be less convergence among small to medium-size enterprises, especially those which service niche markets.

International and comparative research reinforces the view that there are no universally applicable prescriptions for 'best practice' work organization. A contingency approach is likely to yield more useful insights into work organization. Accordingly, the most effective managers draw selectively on research and experience, analyse their own national and corporate cultures and constraints, diagnose the opportunities and problems which they face, then devise the policies and practices which are most appropriate in their precise circumstances. This is a contingency approach to designing work organization, which is more demanding than buying 'off-the-shelf' prescriptions. For most managers, however, a contingency approach is more likely to be successful in the longer term. An important aspect is that those who are involved in conducting their own investigations and devising their own solutions tend to feel a sense of ownership and are then committed to their success.

While most contemporary enterprises use more advanced technology than their predecessors, they also have more informed choices about its introduction, management and change. Arguably, technologies can provide a competitive advantage, but only if they are well integrated with work organization, drawing insights from several of the above-mentioned schools of thought. These findings are consistent with our analysis of different approaches to work organization. Each approach is constrained by various technological and environmental factors, however, these are not the sole determinants of work organization. While proponents of various approaches to work organizations, such as Taylorism and lean production, argue that these represent 'one best way', there is considerable diversity in the practical application of these forms of work organization, and the associated choices of key decision makers. Several different styles of work organization can exist at any one time in any given industry. For example, aspects of each 'ideal-type' work organization discussed above can be found in the car industry.

Innovation in work systems has been influenced by technological change, as well as by such factors as greater expectations on the part of consumers for high-quality and low-cost products; shortening of product life cycles; overcapacity in some markets (for example, cars); privatization; growing international trade; de-regulation, and the growth of regional trade blocs (for example, the European Union and North American Free Trade Agreement); increasing competition and the growth of small and medium-sized enterprises. Policy-makers may have a degree of choice in the way in which work organization is designed. Nevertheless, as shown by this discussion of the development of work organization, choice does not occur in a vacuum, but is strongly influenced by contextual factors.

GREG J. BAMBER
GRIFFITH UNIVERSITY

CAMERON ALLAN
GRIFFITH UNIVERSITY

DAVID E. SIMMONS
FORUM CORPORATION, INC.

Acknowledgement

We acknowledge the kind help of Ken Lovell and Mary Moloney

Further reading

(References cited in the text marked *)

Ackroyd, S. and Procter, S. (1998) 'British manufacturing organization and workplace industrial relations: some attributes of the new flexible firm', *British Journal of Industrial Relations* 36 (2): 163–83. (Describes the 'new flexible firm' that has come to dominate large manufacturing plants in the UK.)

* Bamber, G.J. and Lansbury, R.D. (1988) 'Management strategy and new technology', *Journal of Management Studies* 25 (3): 197–216. (Interesting discussion of the ways in which technology can affect the organization of work.)

* Berggren, C. (1992) *Alternatives to Lean Production: Work Organization in the Swedish Auto Industry*, Ithaca, NY: ILR Press. (Reviews the drawbacks of lean production [and related systems] and offers alternatives.)

* Braverman, H. (1974) *Labor and Monopoly Capital: The Degradation of Work in the Twentieth Century*, New York: Monthly Review Press. (Marked a revival of the Marxist notion and popularized the labour process perspective.)

* Brown, R.B. (1992) *Understanding Industrial Organizations, Theoretical Perspectives in Industrial Sociology*, London: Routledge. (Discusses organization design from a sociological perspective.)

* Burns, T. and Stalker, G.M. (1961) *The Management of Innovation*, London: Tavistock Publications. (Explores how organizations react to change. Many subsequent organization theory and related texts build upon this work.)

Cappelli, P., Bassi, L., Katz, H., Knoke, D., Osterman, P. and Useem, M. (1997) *Change at Work*, New York: Oxford University Press. (Presents and analyses data about the pressures for workplace transformation, particularly in the US.)

* Child, J. (1984) *Organization: A Guide to Problems and Practice*, 2nd edn, London: Harper & Row. (Discusses the major issues relating to organization design and organization theory.)

* Clawson, D. (1980) *Bureaucracy and the Labour Process: The Transformation of US Industry, 1860–1920*, New York: Monthly Review Press. (Reviews the major changes to US organizations from 1860–1920.)

* Dertouzos, M.L., Lester, R.K. and Solow, R.M. (1989) *Made in America, Regaining the Productive Edge*, New York: MIT Press. (Discusses the findings of a major US study of the sources of competitive success.)

Eaton, J. (2000) *Comparative Employment Relations*, Cambridge, UK: Polity Press. (Discuses whether work systems are converging on a Japanese model, and the implications for employment relations.)

* Farias, G. and Varma, A. (1998) 'High Performance work systems: what we know and what we need to know', *Human Resource Planning* 21 (2): 50–5. (Reviews studies of high performance work systems and concludes that such systems improve organisational performance.)

Gittleman, M., Horrigan, M. and Joyce, M. (1998) '"Flexible" workplace practices: evidence from a nationally representative survey', *Industrial and Labor Relations Review* 52 (1): 99–115. (Reviews the incidence of new work practices in the US and concludes that there is little evidence of a new 'best practice'.)

* Graversen, G. (1989) 'Social factors in the introduction of new technology: a Scandanavian case study', in G.J. Bamber and R.D. Lansbury (eds), *New Technology: International Perspectives on Human Resources and Industrial Relations*, London: Routledge. (Discusses perspectives to the introduction of new technology from a sociotechnial viewpoint.)

Grint, K. and Woolgar, S. (1997) *The Machine at Work: Technology, Work and Organization*, Cambridge, MA: Polity Press. (Overview of the effects of technological innovation on human-machine systems.)

* Heller, F. (1989) 'Human resource management and the socio-technical approach', in G.J. Bamber and R.D. Lansbury (eds), *New Technology: International Perspectives on Human Resources and Industrial Relations*, London: Routledge. (Discusses perspectives on the introduction of new technology from a socio-technical viewpoint.)

* Klein, J.A. (1989) 'The human costs of manufacturing reform', *Harvard Business Review* 60 (6). (Discusses the problems relating to the introduction of innovative work systems and related technology.)

* Lawrence, P.R. and Lorsch, J.W. (1967) *Organization and Environment*, Cambridge, MA: Harvard University Press. (An important book which shows how the characteristics of an organizsation's various sub-environments affect internal structure and behaviour.)

Lindbeck, A. and Snower, D. (2000) 'Multitask learning and the reorganisation of work: from Tayloristic to holistic organization', *Journal of Labor Economics* 18 (3): 353–76. (Discusses not only the impact of technological change but also the implications of employee preferences and human capital for the organization of work.)

* MacDuffie, J. (1995) 'Human resource bundles and manufacturing performance: organizational logic and flexible production systems in the world auto industry', *Industrial and Labor Relations Review* 48 (2): 197–221. (Highlights the importance of integrating bundles of innovative HR practices with manufacturing policies to improve organizational preformance.)

* Northcott, J., with Rogers, P., Knetsch, W. and de Lestapis, B. (1985) *Microelectronics in Industry, An International Comparison: Britain, Germany, France*, London: Policy Studies Institute. (An international comparison of the different implications relating to the introduction of new technology.)

* OECD (1992) *New Directions in Work Organisation: The Industrial Relations Response*, Paris: Organization for Economic Cooperation and Development. (An international perspective on the industrial relations issues associated with the introduction of innovative approaches to work organization.)

* Peters, T.J. and Waterman, R.H. (1982) *In Search of Excellence: Lessons from America's Best-Run Companies*, New York: Harper & Row. (Popular management book that ushered in a flood of related texts.)

* Roethlisberger, F.J. and Dickson, W.J. (1939) *Management and the Worker*, Cambridge, MA: Harvard University Press. (Text written by human relations advocates that discusses the experiments of the period.)

* Rose, M. (1975) *Industrial Behaviour: Theoretical Development Since Taylor*, London: Penguin. (A comprehensive overview of the different approaches to industrial organization since Taylor.)

* Shadur, M.A. and Bamber, G.J. (1994) 'Towards lean production? The transferability of Japanese management strategies to Australia', *International Executive* 36 (4): 343–64. (Analysis of the effectiveness of *Kaizen* in a non-Japanese setting.)

Simpson, H. (1999) 'Historical patterns of workplace organization: from mechanical to electronic control and beyond', *Current Sociology* 47 (29): 47–76. (Discusses the way in which electronic technology has removed the time and space constraints on work organization.)

* Taylor, F.W. (1911) *The Principles of Scientific Management*, New York: Harper & Row. (Classic work by the father of scientific management; introduced the concepts of scientific management to the world.)

* Thompson, P. and McHugh, D. (1990) *Work Organisations: A Critical Introduction*, London: Macmillan. (Reviews the different issues relating to work organization theory.)

* Trist, E.L., Higgin, G.W., Murray, H. and Pollock, A.B. (1963) *Organisational Choice*, London: Tavistock Publications. (Seminal work on the sociotechnical perspective.)

* Vogt, J.F. and Murrel, K.L. (1990) *Empowerment in Organisations*, San Diego, CA: University Associates. (Extols the benefits of the popular concept of empowerment.)

* Wagner, J.A. (1994) 'Participation's effects on performance and satisfaction: A reconsideration of the research evidence', *Academy of Management Review* 19 (2): 312–30. (A re-analysis of research on relationships between participation and performance or satisfaction suggests that participation can have statistically significant effects on performance and satisfaction, but the average size of these effects is small enough to raise concerns about the practical significance.)

* Williams, K., Haslam, C. and Williams, J. (1992) 'Ford versus "Fordism": The beginning of mass production', *Work Employment and Society* 6 (4): 517–55. (Provides historical data on Henry Ford's manufacturing operations and the beginning of mass production.)

* Womack, J.P., Jones, D.T. and Roos, D. (1990) *The Machine That Changed the World*, New York: Macmillan. (Popularized the lean production notion.)

Wood, S. (1999a) 'Human resource management and performance', *International Journal of Management Reviews* 1 (4): 367–413. (Reviews a number of empirical studies and concludes that the case for a single 'best practice' work organization has yet to be established.)

* Wood, S. (1999b) 'Getting the measure of the transformed high-performance organization', *British Journal of Industrial Relations* 37 (3): 391–417. (A statistical study into the extent to which various 'high performance' management practices co-exist in business enterprises.)

* Zuboff, S. (1988) *In the Age of the Smart Machine: The Future of Work and Power*, New York: Basic Books. (A critical review of the influence of new technology, especially information technology, on work organization and workers.)

See also: EMPOWERMENT; HUMAN RELATIONS; HUMAN RESOURCE MANAGEMENT; INDUSTRIAL CONFLICT; JAPANIZATION; MAYO, G.E.; ORGANIZATION TYPES; TAYLOR, F.W.; TECHNOLOGY AND ORGANIZATIONS

Workfare

Overview

The concept 'workfare' is commonly used today by labour market researchers to designate welfare schemes that seek to encourage or even compel people to search for a job rather than to rely on welfare transfers (Heikkilä 1999: 29). Although such schemes have a long history, they have been especially emphasized during the 1990s and have eventually become the leading ideology proposed by the European Commission in its current employment policy programme. According to Robert Solow workfare can generally be regarded as a set of policy 'efforts to ... eliminate as far as possible the passive receipt of transfer payments and replace it by a requirement to work, either as conditions for receiving benefits or as total substitute for receiving benefits' (Solow 1998: 6). More specifically, workfare most often refers to policies that introduce work requirements for claimants of public support: that is, claimants will have their benefits reduced or withdrawn if they are not willing to participate in work or training programmes (Heikkilä 1999: 29).

As we will see, workfare schemes are of many different kinds. Moreover, they also have widely different targets. Generally, we can trace two aims of using workfare which have different implications both for the individual and society. First, workfare can be aimed at decreasing the taxpayer's bill for the cost of unemployment relief. In order to achieve this goal the main method proposed is to create incentives for the individual to seek a job by, for example, withdrawing welfare payments or making them less generous. Secondly, workfare schemes can also be aimed at increasing the 'employability' of the indi-

vidual by means of vocational training, education, on-the-job training, etc. In this case the aim is rather to empower the unemployed person and make him or her more selfsufficient. In the short run, such schemes are costly and may not at all imply lower public spending on unemployment. However, in the longer run they may cut welfare payments by making the welfare recipients less reliant on transfers and more active in searching for a new job.

1 History

Systems for subsidising workers during periods of unemployment are as old as industrial society itself. In the early period, unemployment benefits were most often voluntarily provided by trade unions or other working class organizations. However, gradually during the twentieth century unemployment relief became part of a wide range of welfare programmes pursued by an ever more ambitious welfare state. The first unemployment insurance system was introduced in Great Britain in 1911 and was followed by many others. Perhaps the most influential architect of the modern welfare state – which developed in particular after the Second World War – was William Beveridge. He regarded full employment as the main political objective for the modern welfare state and unemployment benefits as a means to protect workers from income loss during cyclical and frictional periods of unemployment.

It was among northern European nations especially that the state became involved early on in unemployment insurance systems. In most countries today the state is at least involved to some extent in subsidising schemes of unemployment protection. In present day Europe Luxembourg is the only country where unemployment insurance is fully financed by the state, while in a majority of countries employers, employees and the state share the costs in different combinations.

However, unemployment insurance benefits are only one scheme to protect workers from unemployment. More active measures to keep people employed also have a long history in the industrial countries. Hence different forms of public involvement have often been utilized during the nineteenth and twentieth centuries, especially during periods of depression and unemployment crises. During the inter-war period John Maynard Keynes was a keen supporter of state-subsidized public work schemes (see KEYNES, J.M.). However, after the Second World War active measures have been part and parcel of many countries' labour market policies to protect workers from unemployment and make them more employable. Hence, during periods of unemployment, instead of receiving welfare people have been encouraged to acquire vocational training, etc. In this context the active labour market policy of Sweden and other Nordic countries has been of special significance.

2 Different policies

We may distinguish between three types of schemes utilized by modern states to protect workers from the hardships of unemployment: unemployment insurance benefit, additional social assistance and, lastly, active policies (workfare) to make the individual more employable and protect him or her from long-term unemployment or exclusion from the labour market.

Unemployment insurance benefits

Unemployment insurance benefits vary considerably from country to country, especially with regard to how generous they are. Generally, they are intended to compensate for the loss of income which unemployment causes. However, in principle it is possible to distinguish between a system which is based on the principle of income compensation and another which consists of a flat rate. In Europe only Britain and Ireland maintain a flat-rate system, most countries preferring to use a mixture of both systems. Moreover, the duration of benefit payments vary among countries. In certain countries the length of time

that benefit will be paid is affected by the length of the previous employment period (see EMPLOYMENT AND UNEMPLOYMENT, ECONOMICS OF).

Social assistance

In many countries social assistance is used as a protective measure, especially in cases where unemployment benefits are too small or not available. Hence, social assistance is often used in cases where the limit on the duration time for receiving unemployment relief has been reached or where the individual is an atypical worker and as such has no right to claim unemployment relief. As a consequence of the increase of part-time work and job insecurity during the 1990s, it is generally assumed that the number of the unemployed living on social assistance has increased. A problem for the individual in this context is that social assistance in general is less generous than unemployment benefit. In most countries assistance schemes are financed by the state. Generally they are flat rate and means tested.

Activating measures

Activating measures differ from place to place. Historically these measures have included extensive job training, counselling services, mobility bonuses, public sector relief work, youth programmes, measures for the disabled, vocational training, etc. during which the individual is subsidised. Perhaps the 'ideal type' in this context – as already mentioned – is the active labour market policy pursued in Sweden and other Nordic countries after the Second World War. In 1990 as much as 3 per cent of GDP was spent on government labour market programmes, and this level even increased during the following years when unemployment increased drastically. Certainly, the Nordic active labour market policies served several purposes. In Sweden in particular, its most important function was to bolster the political goal of full employment. Hence, active measures served as means to speed up structural change in the economy, to increase the flexibility of the labour market and create favourable conditions for individuals to find jobs that best suited to them. Another underlying argument was certainly the fact that passive measures such as unemployment benefits and social assistance create lock-in effects and increase the possibility of long-term unemployment and exclusion.

3 Neo-classical search theory

In a general sense, modern labour market economics – as formulated in current job search theory dominated by scholars such as Snower, Layard, Jackman, etc. – favours workfare instead of welfare. Hence, modern labour market search theory emphasizes the 'search effectiveness' of the individual in finding a new job (Layard *et al*. 1991: 216). Moreover, it is often assumed that such 'search effectiveness' has declined during the last decades because job vacancies have not fallen in proportion to the rise of unemployment: 'with more unemployed chasing fewer jobs the number of vacancies would be expected to fall' (Layard *et al*. 1991: 217). The blame for this decline in 'search effectivness' is mainly put on 'the unemployment benefit regime', that is unemployment benefits and unemployment protection legislation. According to such a view, generous welfare payments – which include employment benefits and social assistance – make the individual less interested in finding a new job. As his or her 'reservation wage' is conditioned by the level of unemployment benefits (plus additional search costs), the availability of unemployment benefits will determine the willingness of the individual to accept a job. Most certainly, a high reservation wage will be an important disincentive to search for work, and will create a rigid labour market characterized by wages that are downward. It is important to note that the reservation wage is not only influenced by the level of unemployment benefit and assistance but also by the possibility that when an individual accepts a new job other social benefits may perhaps be withdrawn. Moreover, if the length of time for which one can remain eligible for unemployment benefits is longer, the reservation wage will be higher. According to the logic of search theory, therefore, we should expect to find that various forms of unemployment benefits serve as disincentives to take a new job. In such cases individuals will be reluctant to take a low paid or less secure job.

The policy implications that follow from this theory are quite straightforward. In order to lower the level of unemployment a better incentive structure must be created which favours an active job search on the part of the unemployed. Among the most important distortions working against such market clearing, Layard *et al*. list the 'benefit system' as well as 'the system of wage determination, where decentralized unions and employers have incentives to set wages in a way that generates involuntary unemployment' (1991: 471). Their main conclusion with regard to increasing the effectiveness of the unemployed is twofold: 'the first is to take a tougher line on benefits, and the second is to offer active help in training and the provision of jobs' (Layard *et al*. 1991: 472).

In many respects, the job search theory model is a useful tool for understanding the realities of the labour market. However, it does not always provide strong empirical proof for its predictions. It is, for example, not self-evident that a steady number of vacancies when unemployment is rising can be explained by the benefit system. Instead this might be a consequence of an increased mismatch on the labour market (lock in) and/or it may be that many individuals in a period of mass unemployment believe it is hopeless trying to find a new job. Moreover, it is also difficult to find strong evidence for the existence of a casual relationship between different unemployment benefit regimes and the level and/or the duration of unemployment. Indeed, Layard *et al*. (1991) have presented data that show that in a number of countries there is a positive correlation between the length of individual unemployment periods and the benefit duration variable. Investigations carried out by the ILO and the European Commission, however, raise doubts about the extent to which the duration of benefit influences unemployment and job search activities. Moreover, when we try to measure the impact of the level of unemployment benefits on unemployment in different countries, it is difficult to find a positive correlation (European Commisson 1995; ILO 1995). As one critical observer, Anthony Atkinson, has pointed out, it is extremely difficult to assess the impact of different unemployment benefit schemes on job search, mainly because of the existence of 'important institutional features of real-world unemployment programs, features that may mitigate the disincentive effects of benefits' (Atkinson 1998: 15f). Hence, an individual may feel that going on to unemployment benefits – although they might be quite generous – is degrading and worse than taking a job with a wage that is lower than his or her implied reservation wage. Moreover, there might be stipulations in the unemployment schemes that are easy to overlook but that mean that in practice it is difficult to refuse a job offer that pays less than the reservation wage (Atkinson 1998: 10) (see COLLECTIVE BARGAINING; TRADE UNIONS).

Moreover, there might be benefits with (generous) unemployment regimes that are less easy to detect and even more difficult to measure. For example, a generous system of remuneration increases the welfare of the individual. However, a regime that does not force an individual to take any job that is available might lead to higher search effectiveness in the sense that it increases the likelihood of an individual finding a 'good job' (for example, in the modern high productivity sector). As Layard and others have shown, one of the most important causes behind the present high unemployment figures in Europe is an apparent mismatch between supply and demand on the labour market (Layard 1999). Hence, in order to obtain a job in the fast growing sector where demand is high, the individual must be prepared to move or to upgrade his or her skills. It is less likely that he or she will take such action if he or she feels that continuing training is prohibitively expensive or that the new job position will not be secure.

Lastly, as argued, to 'take a tougher line on benefits' might not help in a situation where mass unemployment occurs – a situation with which Western Europe has lived since the 1970s. In a situation where the unemployed feel it is more or less hopeless to get a new job (especially relevant for old, low skilled and perhaps also immigrant workers), less welfare will not make them more effective in their job search but rather may lead them to withdraw

from the labour market altogether. In such cases the main result might be that the participation rate in the economy is lowered (Freyssinet 1997).

4 A gospel for today?

Although there might be positive effects from generous unemployment benefit transfers and it is difficult to find robust evidence for search theory, the neo-classical perspective on unemployment has won overwhelming political support during the 1990s. For example, in the very influential OECD Job Study report of 1994 – which certainly sought to bolster the credibility of this theory – it is stated:

> Unemployment insurance and related benefit systems were originally designed to provide temporary income support to the unemployed during the process of finding a new job. With the growth of long-term, and repeated unemployment, these systems have drifted towards quasi-permanent income support in many countries, lowering work incentives. To limit disincentive effects – while facilitating labour market adjustments and providing a necessary minimum level of protection – countries should legislate for only moderate levels of benefits, maintain effective checks on eligibility, and guarantee places on active programmes as substitutes for paying passive income support indefinitely. Possibilities should be explored for making the transition from income support to work more financially attractive.
>
> (OECD 1994: 263f)

In a growing number of countries this view has become accepted as a undoubted truth. In America the welfare policy reform put forward by Bill Clinton in 1997 demonstrated a strong bias for workfare in its emphasis on putting pressure on passive welfare recipients in order that they should be stimulated to search for a job (Solow 1998). Moreover, among European welfare states during the 1990s a *de facto* policy shift can be detected from an emphasis on equity, freedom of choice and security of income towards various combinations of measures to increase the work incentive and to keep people in gainful employment. Hence, in a majority of countries we can detect a strategy to increase the participation rate in the labour market by means of activation measures. For example the Swedish government – with long experience of using measures in the name of an active labour market policy – has launched a plan to increase the labour force participation rate from 75 per cent to 80 per cent (in the 20–64 year age range) up until 2002. Other countries have presented plans of the same kind. In addition, an increase in labour force participation has become a major policy goal of the European Commission. Its common employment strategy, formulated at the Luxembourg summit in 1997, sets a target of increasing the participation rate in the European Union over the next five year period from 70 per cent to 75 per cent.

The main policies proposed to achieve this goal were also presented in the Luxembourg employment policy plan in the form of four pillars. Many of them touch upon the relationship between welfare and work, especially the policy suggestions in the 'employability pillar' section (Foden and Magnusson 1999). Moreover in 1997 a communication, 'Modernizing and improving social protection in the European Union' set forth the general strategy of making social protection more 'employment friendly'. This objective can only be achieved by two means: first, by increasing economic incentives through changes in the tax and social security system in order to increase the taking up of new jobs. Secondly, by activation measures and an active labour market policy. Therefore, the overall concern is to combat unemployment by emphasizing workfare rather than welfare. It is generally assumed that welfare schemes, including unemployment benefits and social assistance, create welfare entrapments and thus disincentives to job search effectiveness (Heikkilä 1999).

5 The problems of workfare

Workfare certainly introduces greater pressure on the welfare recipient, including the claimant of unemployment benefits, and thus also diminishes his/her freedom of choice. However, such measures are largely consid-

ered in order to avoid long-term unemployment and even the individual's exit from the long-term market. Hence, as Solow has pointed out there are many arguments that speak in favour of workfare. For one thing, a great deal of a person's identity, dignity and self-respect derives from having a job. Thus to earn one's own living is a sign of independence and as such is greatly heralded in Western culture. Secondly, taxpayers will probably be more willing to give money to welfare recipients if they feel that the unemployed are actively involved in job search and therefore that their 'altruism is not exploited' (Solow 1998: 5)

However, at the same time, there are a number of problems when moving from welfare to workfare. First, if the aim is to radically decrease unemployment and even increase the participation rate by means of workfare schemes, there will be an increased supply of labour on the labour market. If appropriate vacancies are not available, new jobs will have to be created. If this job creation is not possible in the private sector – which will be difficult in the short run – these new jobs must be provided by the public sector. Such public job creation in turn may entail public spending on a level that might cancel out the gains achieved by the decreasing number of welfare recipients.

Secondly, there is a danger that a stark increase in the supply of labour created by the shift from welfare to workfare will mean that, to quote Solow, 'ex-welfare recipients and their successors will drive down the wage for unqualified workers' (Solow 1998: 28). In cases where the purpose of workfare is only or mainly to drive down the level of unemployment benefits or withdraw social assistance, such downward pressure on wages at the low end of the labour market is certainly a most realistic scenario. However, this threat might be mitigated to the extent that workfare includes schemes to upgrade the skills of the individual. There are strong doubts, however, that most workfare schemes thus far suggested really will have such an effect. Moreover, there is a danger that such skills may not be rewarded by a labour market that must absorb a steady increase in the supply of more highly qualified workers.

Thirdly, and most importantly, it is possible that workfare may not be the right method for all unemployed and present recipients of welfare. For a number of people who are disabled, socially or in other ways, from finding and holding employment, cuts in welfare may not serve as an incentive to activate job search. Rather the opposite might happen: namely they may drop out altogether from the labour force. Hence for many persons the present policy of shifting from welfare to workfare may be a real threat, not only to their freedom of choice but also to their general welfare.

LARS MAGNUSSON
UPPSALA UNIVERSITY

Further reading

(References cited in the text marked *)

* Atkinson, A.B. (1998) *The Economic Consequenses of Rolling Back the Welfare State*, Cambridge, MA: MIT Press.
* European Commission (1995) *Social Protection in Europe*, Luxembourg: Office for Official Publications of the European Communities.
* Foden, D. and L. Magnusson (eds) (1999) *Entrepreneurship in the European Employment Strategy*, Brussels: ETUI.
* Freyssinet, J. (1997) 'Unemployment compensation and labour markets: a disincentive to work?', in A. Bosco and M. Hutsebaut (eds) *Social Protection in Europe*, Brussels: ETUI.
* Heikkilä, M. (1999) 'Brief introduction to the topic', Dublin: European Foundation for the Improvement of Living and Working Conditions, Linking Welfare and Work.
* ILO (1995) *World Employment*, Geneva: ILO.
* Layard, R. (1999) *Tackling Unemployment*, Basingstoke: Macmillan.
* Layard, R., S. Nickel and R. Jackman (1991) *Unemployment*, Oxford: Oxford University Press.
* OECD (1994) *Jobs Study: Facts, Analysis, Strategies*, Paris: OECD.
* Solow, R.M. (1998) 'Lecture I and II', in A. Gutman (ed.) *Work and Welfare*, Princeton: Princeton University Press.

See also: COLLECTIVE BARGAINING; EMPLOYMENT AND UNEMPLOYMENT, ECONOMICS OF; KEYNES, J.M.; LABOUR MARKETS; TRADE UNIONS; WEBB, B. AND WEBB, S.

Working capital management

Overview

Working capital management encompasses the financial management of short-term assets and liabilities. Gross working capital refers to current assets that a firm uses in its operations. Current assets generally include cash, accounts receivables, inventory and short-term securities. Net working capital refers to current assets less current liabilities. Current liabilities include accounts payable, accruals, and short-term debt with a maturity of one year or less. Working capital management involves setting policies for the management of short-term assets and liabilities and carrying out these policies on a daily basis. Overall working capital policies include the proper maturity matching for current assets and current liabilities and managing a firm's cash-to-cash cycle. A firm's cash-to-cash cycle is the number of days it takes for a firm to receive cash from the time it purchases and pays for purchases to the time it makes sales and receives cash for credit sales. This cycle is very important, because the longer the cycle, the more financing the firm requires from external sources to pay for net working capital.

Other policies for current assets include policies for: (1) the optimum amount of investment in current assets; (2) managing cash; (3) investing in marketable securities; (4) managing inventory; and (5) managing accounts receivables. Policies for managing current liabilities include: (1) the best type of financing for current assets; (2) estimating the cost for alternative types of short-term financing; and (3) timing and managing the payment of current liabilities. Working capital management for a corporation is part of the management of corporate treasury operations.

1 The importance of working capital management

Working capital management has always been important for firms since the sooner goods are sold and paid for by customers, the quicker an actual cash profit is produced. Similarly, the later that cash payments have to be made for inventory and other services used to produce goods, the more cash a firm will have available for profitable uses. Prior to the 1960s, however, cash management practices were not particularly widespread. Since interest rates were low in most countries in the 1940s and 1950s, firms generally had a low cost for financing working capital. They also had few investment opportunities for investing excess cash in the short term. In the 1960s and 1970s, widespread inflation and very high interest rates resulted in a very high opportunity cost for funds. Companies developed new policies to try to minimize the cost of financing working capital. They also developed policies to maximize the collection of cash, so cash could be invested immediately in marketable securities that offered high rates (see INTEREST RATE RISK).

Working capital management policies are particularly important for small firms that have limited sources of financing and a high cost of financing. The difference between a small firm surviving or failing often depends on the firm having sufficient liquidity available to make timely payments on debt and to finance new growth (see SMALL BUSINESS FINANCE). The globalization of businesses in the 1980s and 1990s increased the need for good working capital management policies. With international trade, the cash-to-cash cycle of a firm rises, since the receipt of payments and the time between purchasing goods abroad and making sales in another country takes considerable time. This delay creates new working capital management problems.

2 Managing a firm's cash-to-cash cycle

From an overall working capital management perspective, a firm needs to manage its overall days cash-to-cash cycle. This cycle represents the average number of days it takes from when: (1) a firm purchases raw materials, converts these goods into finished inventory and pays for this inventory; (2) the time it takes the firm to sell the inventory; and (3) the time it takes to collect payments for these sales. Hence, the days cash-to-cash cycle is approximately equal to a firm's average inventory period (days to sell inventory) plus its average collection period (days to collect on credit sales), less its average accounts payable period (days it takes to pay for inventory purchases):

Days cash-to-cash cycle =
Ave. inventory period + Ave. collection period − Ave. accounts payable period.

These respective periods can be calculated as:

Average inventory period = 365 /
(Cost of goods sold / Inventory)
Average collection period = 365 /
(Credit sales/Accounts receivable)
Average accounts payable period = 365 /
(Cost of goods sold / Accounts payable).

For example, suppose a firm had credit sales of $300,000 million, a cost of goods sold of $200,000 million, average inventory of $50,000 million, accounts receivables of $50,000 million, and average accounts payable of $30,000 million, its cash-to-cash cycle would be equal to:

Ave. inventory period = 365 /
(200,000/50,000) = 365/4 = 91 days
+ Ave collection period = 365 /
(300,000/50,000) = 61 days
− Ave. accounts payable period = 365 /
(200,000 / 30,000) = 55 days.
Cash-to-cash cycle = 61 days + 91 days
− 55 days = 97 days.

A firm's approximate average working capital loan needs for the year could be estimated as: Days cash-to-cash cycle × Average daily cost of goods sold.

For this firm, its approximate working capital loans would be equal to its average daily costs of good sold $547.95 ($200,000 million /365) times 97 days, its cash-to-cash cycle. Hence, the approximate working capital loan would be $53,151 million. If the firm's average interest rate on its loans was 10 per cent, this would represent an annual interest expense of:

$53,151 million × 0.10 = $5,315.10 million.

If the firm could reduce the days cash-to-cash cycle, it could reduce this expense. For instance, if it lowers its accounts receivables period to 20 days, its new cash-to-cash cycle would be only 56 days, and its interest expense would only be:

$547.95 million × 56 days = $30,685 million × 0.10 = $3,068.50 million.

This represents a saving of $2,246.58 million ($5,315.10 million − $3,068.50 million).

If a firm can develop policies to speed up the collection of accounts receivables or speed up the days to sell its inventory, or reduce the time it takes to pay its accounts payable, it can reduce its working capital financing needs and its interest expenses. Thus, firms are very concerned about managing respective accounts receivables, inventory management, and accounts payable policies to reduce their days cash-to-cash cycles and interest expense. Different industries by their nature have shorter and longer cash-to-cash cycles, but effective policies can help firms to reduce these cycles, subject to the particular nature of their businesses (see FINANCIAL RATIOS, MATHEMATICS IN FINANCE).

3 Overall working capital policies

Overall working capital policies include setting policies for target levels for each type of current asset and deciding how current assets will be financed. One ratio that is commonly used to evaluate a firm's liquidity and how its current assets are financed is its current ratio, which is equal to current assets divided by current liabilities. Often this ratio is refined by subtracting inventory from current assets and then dividing by current liabilities, which gives a quick ratio or acid test. The higher these ratios, particularly the quick ratio, which includes only the firm's most liquid assets, the better able the firm is to pay off its upcoming liabilities with current assets.

Current asset investment policy

A firm has a choice of alternative policies concerning the amount of current assets it will carry and how these current assets will be financed, which affects both the firm's liquidity and future profitability. Under a relaxed current asset investment policy a firm would carry large amounts of cash, marketable securities, and inventory and have a liberal credit sales policy stimulating a high level of accounts receivables.

Alternatively, under a restrictive current asset investment policy, a firm would have small levels of current assets, at the risk of potential stock-outs for inventory, or lower sales levels with a stringent policy for credit sales. The restrictive policy, however, would involve a faster cash-to-cash cycle and, hence, lower working capital financing and interest expense. This policy would be at the expense of perhaps greater sales under a more liberal current asset policy, which allows greater liquidity, more credit sales, and excess inventory available for potential unexpected sales that might occur. A compromise between the two policies would be a moderate current asset investment policy between the two extremes.

The type of current asset investment policy that a firm chooses will also depend on the certainty with which a firm can predict sales as well as costs, lead times in production or receiving inventory, and payment periods, among other factors. The better a firm can predict these factors, the less excess liquidity or excess current assets it needs to hold. For instance, with an improved inventory monitoring system, a firm has better information to determine the inventory that it will need and it can hold less. Similarly, if a firm has accurate sales forecasts, it can hold only the inventory

it needs. If technology improves the lead time to produce inventory, this would also reduce the safety stock that a firm needs to hold. Many firms have seasonal sales where they have higher inventory levels and accounts receivable periods during particular months during the year. Thus, their level of working capital fluctuates during the year, and they only need seasonal working capital loans for estimated sales during peak seasons which are paid off during the year as credit sales are collected (see SALES MANAGEMENT).

Holding more current assets is expensive. For example, inventory often has high storage and spoilage costs. Similarly, as accounts receivables get larger and age and are not collected, a firm has higher potential bad debt losses and collection costs. The trade-off between potential lost sales and the costs of holding excess current assets needs to be carefully considered, and the turnover of inventory and the average collection period (often called days sales outstanding) need to be carefully monitored.

Some firms have even moved towards a concept of zero working capital in terms of defining working capital as inventories plus receivables less payables. Under this concept, the majority of financing for inventories and receivables should be through supplies, i.e., accounts payable. For the average firm, working capital has an overall turnover ratio (revenues/working capital) of about 5 or about 20 cents of working capital per dollar of sales. Under a zero working capital concept, this cost per dollar would be reduced to increase a firm's profitability. A firm would try to produce and deliver its products or services faster and more efficiently than its competition under this goal. By doing this, it would reduce its need to hold inventory, for instance, reducing storage costs and obsolete inventory. Management of current assets would follow what is called demand flow, whereby a firm would have a goal for its production system to be both quick and efficient, reducing the need for working capital.

Current asset financing policies

In addition to current asset investment policies, firms have alternative current asset financing policies to choose from (see FINAN-CIAL ACCOUNTING). Under a permanent current asset financing policy, a firm would finance its level of current assets that always remain on the balance sheet with long-term debt, and its seasonal or temporary current assets above this level with short-term debt. This policy is often called a maturity matching or self-liquidating approach. This policy recognizes that the temporary current assets will convert to cash in the near future to pay for the short-term debt. Under a more conservative approach, some of the temporary current assets would be financed with long-term debt as well. An alternative aggressive financing approach would be to finance all current assets with short-term debt if short-term debt is cheaper than long-term debt. This strategy has higher risk, but the potential for higher profits. Short-term financing has the advantage of ease of financing and flexibility, but the risk of higher potential interest rates when it is refinanced and the possibility of not being able to be refinanced. Long-term, fixed-rate financing has the advantage of a stable interest expense, but the opportunity cost of having a lower interest expense if interest rates fall and if short-term financing is cheaper.

4 Cash management

Reasons for holding cash

Working capital management also involves individual polices for different types of current assets. Since cash is needed for transactions, and often with working capital loans banks require firms to hold compensating balances (deposit accounts that do not pay interest), firms need to hold cash. Similarly, firms hold cash for precautionary reasons, for unexpected liquidity needs, and for speculative reasons for opportunities that might come up. Often excess cash for precautionary or speculative reasons is held in short-term marketable securities that earn interest. Firms that hold larger percentages of cash face an opportunity cost in terms of lost income that they could earn by investing funds in long-term, more productive assets. Firms with greater short-term borrowing capacity can afford to hold less cash, since they can always borrow short-

term for these needs. However, they face greater risks of having to borrow at higher rates or not being able to borrow when they might need extra cash (see CAPITAL, COST OF).

The cash budget

One of the essential tools for estimating how much surplus cash a firm will have on hand to invest and/or how much of a cash deficit the firm will have in the future is the cash budget. Monthly cash budgets are often used for planning purposes and weekly or even daily cash budgets to keep track of and control cash receipts and disbursements. Basically, a cash budget estimates sales for each month and the percentage of sales for any month that will be collected that month and the following two months to arrive at total cash collections for each month. Similarly, total purchases of inventory are estimated for each month and the payment pattern for those purchases that month and the following months is estimated. Other variable cash payments, such as wages and salaries that may vary with sales, and fixed payments, such as rent and other expenses, are also estimated for each month to come up with total cash disbursements. The difference between cash collections and cash disbursements gives the firm an estimate of its monthly net cash flow. Thus, the cash manager can see when there will be a surplus or deficit of cash and the amount of cash that a firm will have to keep as an excess balance to cover deficits and/or borrow to meet expenses during months when a deficit occurs. Start-up firms often use a monthly cash budget to determine how much cash they need to have to start off to cover the highest monthly deficit during their first year. The cash budget can be elaborated to include a target cash balance and total cumulative borrowing needs including interest expense and principal repayments.

Cash management techniques

Cash management techniques attempt to speed up cash collections and slow down cash disbursements to maximize a firm's cash flow. The time between when a payment is made to a firm and the firm actually receives it and it is deposited in the firm's bank earning interest is often called collection float. Collection float includes mailing time, processing time, and cheque clearing time. One way to reduce this float and accelerate receipts is to develop a bank collection system, whereby customers are asked to send their payments to the firm's bank in their region. The bank sets up a lockbox arrangement whereby the bank picks up the firm's payments from a post office box several times a day, opens the envelopes, and deposits the cheques right away for the corporate customer. The bank provides the customer with a daily record of the receipts collected and often wires funds electronically to the firm's primary bank, so all new funds are available in a central location for the cash manager's use. Some firms are able to reduce collection float by requiring that payments be made by wire or automatic electronic debits.

Disbursement float is the time it takes from when the firm writes cheques to its suppliers to the time when the supplier receives the cheque, processes it, and the cheque is cleared and money is removed from the firm's account. Cash managers try to stretch disbursement float. However, at the same time, the firm does not want to alienate its suppliers or to lose discounts for paying bills on time. A firm's banking system can also help cash managers to increase disbursement float by electronically transferring funds for firms just in time to pay bills. Similarly, banks often engage in sweeping funds for firms from an interest-earning account to a zero balance chequing account to make disbursements. Funds are kept in the interest-earning account until the last moment, so firms can continue earning interest for as long as possible.

5 Inventory management techniques

Since inventory must be purchased prior to sales, establishing sales forecasts and target inventory levels are difficult but critical tasks in working capital management. Inventory managers have dual goals of making sure that sufficient inventory is available for sales, but also trying to minimize inventory carrying and ordering costs. Carrying costs for holding inventory include the interest cost to finance the inventory, the storage and handling costs,

insurance, property taxes, and depreciation and obsolescence. For the average manufacturing firm in the United States, carrying costs can be 25 per cent of inventory values. Ordering costs include the cost of placing orders including production and set-up costs, and shipping and handling costs. By minimizing inventory, carrying costs are reduced. However, with low inventory, ordering costs may rise and a firm may lose sales or customer goodwill if customer orders cannot be filled. Some companies have adopted just-in-time inventory systems, first developed by Japanese firms. Under a just-in-time system, inventory is delivered just when it is needed. To have such a system, a firm has to have an excellent relationship with its suppliers to coordinate the timing of the delivery of inventory and the quality of inventory. Other firms have adopted policies of producing inventory only after orders are received, again to minimize carrying costs.

Inventory control systems are also used with greater monitoring for more crucial items. Under an ABC approach, for instance, A items with greater monitoring are those that are a significant proportion of the total value of inventory. B items are items with average usage rates that are monitored less, and C items are items that not are used in total to a significant degree and require little monitoring. Companies also use computerized inventory control systems that contain an inventory count that is adjusted as inventory withdrawals are made. When the inventory reaches a certain minimum level, the computer automatically places a reorder for additional inventory. Changes in usage for different items should be monitored to determine the optimum reorder points and quantity of inventory to order.

A popular model for determining the optimal quantity of inventory to order to minimize carrying and ordering costs is the Economic Ordering Quantity Model (EOQ). Under this model, the optimum ordering quantity where total costs are minimized is equal to the square root of (two times the fixed cost per order times the total number of annual sales for the inventory item divided by the dollar carrying cost per unit). At this EOQ point, total carrying costs equal total ordering costs. Total inventory costs are equal to the carrying cost per unit times the average inventory held plus the fixed ordering cost times the number of orders made over the year. With this model adjustments need to be made for the firm's desired safety stock, quantity discounts, inflation and seasonal demand.

6 Receivables management

By offering lenient credit policies, sales can rise, but accounts receivables will rise as well. Accounts receivables have costs associated with them, including the financing cost of carrying accounts receivables. The dollar financing cost of carrying accounts receivables is equal to the level of accounts receivables times one minus the profit margin on sales (i.e., the variable cost ratio) times the interest rate on funds. Other credit-related costs include credit analysis and collection expenses, bad debt losses, and the discount offered for early payment of credit sales. A firm's optimal credit policy is one that maximizes a firm's net cash flows over time considering the risk that the firm assumes.

A firm's credit policy includes: (1) the credit period, the number of days before payment is due; (2) credit standards, which customers will receive credit; (3) collection policy, how collections will be handled; and (4) any discounts, including the discount amount and time period when a discount will be given (see CREDIT MANAGEMENT).

The credit period

An example of typical quoted credit terms is: 2/10, net 30 to all acceptable customers. The 2/10 implies that a 2 per cent discount will be given if the bill is paid in 10 days. If not, the payment is due in 30 days. Thus, a customer has a choice between receiving a 2 per cent discount by paying in 10 days or forfeiting that discount and receiving an additional 20 days of credit. A firm's average accounts receivables is a function of its average sales per day and its average collection period which is partly determined by its credit terms. By giving a discount for payment, the firm has an additional discount cost, but its average accounts receivables will decline as more cus-

tomers pay earlier. In effect, a firm's average account receivables is equal to its average sales per day times its average collection period, so any reduction in the average collection period will reduce the financial carrying costs of accounts receivables.

Credit standards

Firms have to be very careful in setting credit standards. They can only discriminate based on the risk of a particular customer. To avoid losing customers, they might want to set standards, such as payment in advance or half payment in advance for riskier customers. Sources of information to evaluate the credit experience of business customers include Dun and Bradstreet, which publishes business credit reports about six times a year, and regional and national directories providing credit evaluations for businesses. For consumer credit reports, TRW, Equifax and Trans Union provide reports in the United States. Other local credit groups have their own credit information agencies and credit interchanges. Firms can grant better credit terms to better rated firms and require cash on delivery or before delivery for customers that have credit risk.

Credit-scoring systems are also often used to evaluate both business and consumer customers. Such systems use statistical techniques using massive amounts of historic data to determine what factors help to identify which customers will be more likely not to repay their debt. Firms need to be careful that such systems do not violate consumer credit laws and that they have strong statistical validity.

Setting the collection policy

Firms need to develop procedures to follow in collecting past due accounts, such as first sending a letter when a bill is late. This procedure may be followed up by a more severe letter and/or a telephone call. After a certain amount of time, the account might be turned over to a collection agency. Collection managers realize that a certain amount of salesmanship is involved and a positive attitude to optimize collections. By being congenial and finding out why a customer has not paid a bill, such as an error in the bill or never receiving it, collections may be worked out more easily. Similarly, a careful billing process and making sure that bills are correct can help speed collections (see CREDIT RATINGS, INTERNATIONAL).

Other factors affecting credit policy

Other factors affecting credit policy include assessing the profit potential of additional sales that will occur by extending credit with the carrying costs associated with credit sales. Different credit instruments can also facilitate collections. A promissory note may be used if an order is large and there may be a potential problem in collecting a bill. With a promissory note a buyer is given a longer than usual time to pay for an order with interest charges built into the promissory note. A commercial draft is used often in international trade, whereby a seller draws up a draft which is a combination of a cheque and promissory note noting that the buyer must pay a specific amount to the seller by a certain date. The draft is sent to the buyer's bank along with shipping documents for possession of the goods. The bank then forwards the draft to the buyer which is signed and returned to the bank before the bank delivers the shipping documents to the customer who can then claim the goods. With a sight draft the buyer's bank withdraws funds from the buyer's account and forwards it to the selling firm upon delivery of the shipping documents and acceptance of the draft by the buyer. Time drafts in contrast specify payment on a future date. When the bank accepts this draft it amounts to a promissory note that the seller can hold for future payment and use as collateral for a loan. If the bank guarantees the draft, it becomes a banker's acceptance. The instrument can be sold at a discount below its face value and traded as a negotiable security prior to maturity. For more risky customers, a conditional sales contract may be drawn up where the seller retains legal ownership of goods until the buyer completes payment. Such a sales contract is more often used for large purchases that will be paid over a period of two to three years.

Analysing a proposed change in credit policy

To analyse a proposed change in credit policy, a firm needs to compare the change in sales with the change in policy less any change in discounts paid less any change in production costs or overhead associated with new sales. This gives the change in before-tax profit before credit costs. Then the change in credit-related costs needs to be estimated, including the change in the cost of carrying receivables, the change in credit analysis and collection expenses, and the change in bad debt losses. By subtracting the change in credit costs from the change in profits before these costs, the change in income can be estimated to determine if the change would be profitable.

Monitoring accounts receivables

Methods of monitoring accounts receivables include monitoring the average collection period; using an ageing schedule for accounts receivables; and looking at the payment pattern for accounts receivables.

Average collection period

The average collection period (ACP) can be estimated for a change in credit policy by taking the expected fraction of customers that will pay within the discount period plus the expected fraction of customers that will take the extra days of credit and pay later. For example, if credit terms are 2/10, net 30, and 70 per cent of customers are expected to pay in 10 days and 30 per cent to pay in 30 days, the weighted average collection period is $(0.70)(10 \text{ days}) + (0.30)(30 \text{ days})$ which equals 16 days. Hence the average expected accounts receivables would be equal to the average daily sales times 16 days. For instance, if sales per day are $300,000, then the expected average accounts receivables would be:

$$\$300,000 \times 16 \text{ days} = \$4,800,000.$$

For monitoring purposes, the ACP can be used to determine if the firm is failing to collect accounts receivables fast enough compared to industry peers or compared to past performance. However, on a monthly basis, if sales vary by month, a change in the ACP can simply reflect greater sales during that month versus any change in collection experience.

Ageing schedule

A similar problem occurs with ageing schedules when sales vary and comparisons are made on a monthly basis. However, for a static comparison ageing schedules are very helpful to judge the quality of accounts receivables. Thus, they are used by banks in evaluating accounts receivables as collateral for working capital loans. An ageing schedule basically classifies accounts receivables according to how long they have been outstanding. Firms often computerize their accounts receivables ledger, so they can easily see the age of each invoice and sort categories electronically by age, generating an ageing schedule. A simple sample ageing schedule would look like that shown in Table 1.

A large amount of older accounts receivables would indicate a greater probability of bad debt losses for the firm. A bank might also look at individual accounts; large accounts that are delinquent by one individual or firm could indicate a serious problem for the firm.

Payments pattern

In contrast to the ACP and ageing schedule, the payments pattern is a technique that can be used to monitor monthly changes in the management of accounts receivables without creating a bias based on monthly sales differences. The payments pattern approach simply measures the percentage of sales in a particular month that are paid that month, the percentage that are paid the following month, and the percentage that are paid the next month. For example, it may be that the firm has a typical payments pattern of 20 per cent being of sales being paid in the month of the

sale, 60 per cent in the month after, and the remaining 20 per cent the following month. The sales pattern for each month's sales can be calculated, and any changes in this pattern can alert the firm to any problem with sales collections for a particular month.

For June sales, for instance, if the pattern changed to 15 per cent paid the month of the sale, 30 per cent paid the month after the sale, and 55 per cent paid the next month, a problem with collections would be revealed.

Use of computers in receivables management

Just as with inventory management, computers are widely used in receivables management to record sales, send out bills, keep track of when payments are made, and to alert a credit manager when accounts are past due to ensure actions are taken. Payment histories of customers can also be summarized to help establish credit limits for customers and classes of customers, and the data on each account can be aggregated and used for the firm's accounts receivable monitoring system. Data can also be stored in the firm's database to use for studies related to any credit policy changes.

7 Managing the cost of current liabilities

To determine what type of current liabilities are optimal to finance current assets, the cost of different types of liabilities need to be estimated.

The cost of accounts payable

Generally, accounts payable or trade credit is the largest single category of short-term debt, representing approximately 40 per cent of all

Table 1

Age of accounts (days)	Value of accounts ($)	Percentage of total value
0–10 days	2,000,000	57
11–30 days	1,000,000	29
31–45 days	500,000	14
Total accounts receivables	3,500,000	100

current liabilities for the average business firm. Trade credit is often referred to as a spontaneous or operational source of financing since it arises automatically when firms charge purchases with suppliers. The credit terms quoted on accounts payable are the opposite side of the coin from the credit terms quoted on accounts receivables. For instance, credit terms from a supplier might be 2/20, net 50, whereby the firm gets a 2 per cent discount if the bill is paid in 20 days. Otherwise, the firm is expected to pay in 50 days. It is important to determine the additional 30 days of trade credit if the firm pays in 50 days. The cost in essence is the cost of the lost discount times the average number of times the extra days are taken during a year. Hence, the approximate annual cost of taking the additional 30 days is:

Annual percentage cost = (Discount per cent / 100 – Discount per cent) × (360 days / Extra days credit)

For the previous terms, the annual percentage opportunity cost of taking the extra 20 days would be:

$$(2 / 98) \times (360 / 30) = 2.041\% \times 12 = 24.49\%.$$

If a bank offered a lower rate than 24.49 per cent, the firm would be wise to take a bank loan instead of the extra 30 days credit to avoid the high opportunity cost of not taking the discount. The cost of trade credit rises with a rise in the discount per cent and falls with a rise in the number of extra days to pay beyond the discount payment period.

The average accounts payable for a firm is equal to its average purchased per day times its average payment period. The longer the payment period, the larger will be its accounts payable.

Cost and considerations in short-term bank loans

Short-term bank loans generally appear on the balance sheet as short-term notes payable. Working capital loans are often collateralized by accounts receivables and inventory. With asset-based lending rules of thumb are sometimes used, such as lending 40 to 60 per cent against raw materials and finished goods inventory which are easier to liquidate, and 50 to 80 per cent against accounts receivables depending on the ageing schedule and collection experience. Asset-based lending often necessitates costly monitoring for collateralized loans. Often banks require that a corporate borrower keeps a compensating balance (non-interest-earning demand deposits) with the bank in addition to the interest rate charged. This brings up the effective annual interest rate paid for the loan. The actual rate based on the actual money that the firm receives (the loan amount less the compensating balance) is equal to:

Effective annual rate =
Nominal rate charged /
(1 – Fraction compensating balance)

For example, if a 10 per cent compensating balance was required for a loan with a 10 per cent stated rate, the effective annual rate would be: 10% / (1 – 0.10) = 11.11%. Thus, the actual loan rate would be much higher than the stated rate.

Banks often offer lines of credit to businesses whereby they can borrow up to a certain limit. With an informal line of credit, borrowers can borrow up to a certain amount and repay the loan during the year, subject to any change in the borrower's financial condition. A revolving line of credit is a more formal arrangement that legally guarantees that funds will be available for the firm. In return for this guarantee, the bank charges an annual commitment fee, such as 0.25 per cent on the unused balance of the commitment as compensation for keeping funds available for the firm.

Another source of short-term financing is commercial paper, which is an unsecured promissory note issued by large, financially strong firms. In order to avoid required security registration, commercial paper is generally less than 270 days in maturity.

8 Conclusion

Working capital management entails skill on the part of managers in terms of trying to minimize the firm's costs for financing and holding working capital, but at the same time keeping sufficient working capital to maintain a firm's operations, keep customers happy, and provide liquidity. When the cost of funds is high, working capital management becomes particularly important, since firms have a high cost of financing current assets and a high opportunity cost for holding too much excess liquidity. New techniques have developed to make working capital management more efficient facilitated by new technology that allows firms to better monitor both inventory and accounts receivable. With better monitoring firms can hold less working capital and still be assured that the firm will meet customer's needs, minimizing the costs of holding working capital. Faster transfers of funds also allow the firms to collect on accounts more quickly and put funds to more profitable uses more quickly.

BETH COOPERMAN
UNIVERSITY OF COLORADO – DENVER

Further reading

Brigham, E.F., Gapenski, L.C. and Ehrhardt, M.C. (1999) *Financial Management: Theory and Practice,* 9th edn, Fort Worth, TX: Dryden Press (An excellent text on corporate financial management with chapters on managing working capital.)

Gardner, M.G., Mills, D.L. and Cooperman, E.S. (2000) *Managing Financial Institutions: An Asset/Liability Approach,* 4th edn, Fort Worth, TX: Dryden Press. (Discusses short-term financing from a financial institution perspective.)

Hill, N.C. and Sartoris, W.L. (1995) *Short-term Financial Management: Text and Cases*, 3rd edn, Englewood Cliffs, NJ: Prentice Hall. (A text on different aspects of working capital management with short cases for each area.)

Logue, D.E. (1995) *The WG&L Handbook of Short-term & Long-Term Financial Management*, Cincinnati, OH: Warren, Gorham & Lamont. (Contains theory and excellent reading lists on different management issues.)

Maness, T.S. and. Zietlow, J.T (1998) *Short-Term Financial Management*, Fort Worth, TX: The Dryden Press (Harcourt Brace College Publishers). (Text with problems and integrative cases on short-term financial management.)

Masson, D.J. and Wikoff, D.A. (1995) *Essentials of Cash Management,* 5th edn, Bethesda, Maryland: Treasury Management Association. (A practical primer on cash management.)

Osteryoung, J.S., Newman, D.L. and Davies, G.D. (1997) *Small Firm Finance: An Entrepreneurial Analysis*, Fort Worth, TX: The Dryden Press (Harcourt Brace College Publishers). (Paperback text that deals with different aspects of working capital management from the perspective of a small firm.)

Scherr, F.C. (1989) *Modern Working Capital Management: Text and Cases*, Englewood Cliffs, NJ: Prentice Hall. (A more detailed text on working capital management with cases for each aspect.)

Scott, D.F., Jr., Martin, J.D., Petty, J.W. and. Keown, A.J (1999) *Basic Financial Management, Eighth Edition*, Englewood Cliffs, NJ: Prentice Hall. (Financial management text with very good detailed chapters on working capital management.)

Smith, K.V. and Gallinger, G.W. (1988) *Readings on Short-term Financial Management*, 3rd edn, New York: West Publishing Company. (A book of readings on short-term financial management issues.)

Treasury Management Reader (1996–1998) Bethesda, MD: Treasury Management Association. (A collection of articles from the Treasury Management Association Journal (e-mail: *tma@tma-net.org*; website: *www.tma-net.org/treasury/*).)

[For more information, contact: TMA, 7315 Wisconsin Avenue, Suite 1250 W., Betheseda, Maryland 20814.]

See also: BANKING; CAPITAL, COST OF; CAPITAL MARKETS, REGULATION OF; CAPITAL STRUCTURE; CREDIT MANAGEMENT; FINANCIAL RATIOS; MONEY AND CAPITAL MARKETS, INTERNATIONAL

World Bank

Overview

Created at the Bretton Woods Conference in 1944, the World Bank is the leading multilateral organization providing development assistance to developing countries and countries in transition. It is an important source of finance, raising funds in capital markets and providing loans to governments for about US$30 billion per year at below market rates. Originally focusing on large-scale infrastructures, Bank funding has diversified and ranges from projects in health and education, to statewide reform programmes.

The World Bank is also the leading theorist and agenda-setter on development and poverty issues. Its own vision of development has evolved over the years, from capital intensive state-led development in the 1950s and 1960s, basic needs in the 1970s, macro economic stability and microeconomic efficiency in the 1980s to a comprehensive approach to poverty alleviation in the late 1990s.

Since the late 1960s, the evolutions of Bank strategies and of the international economy have been closely related. Among other things, Bank strategies respond to structural changes in the international economy and at the same time, given the Bank's influence, these strategies participate in shaping the evolution of national economies and the international system. By the late 1990s, the Bank was, with the International Monetary Fund (IMF) and the World Trade Organization (WTO) (see IMF and WTO); one of the three pillars of the system of global governance supporting the process of economic and financial globalization.

1 Structure and mission

The World Bank Group comprises five agencies:

- The International Bank for Reconstruction and Development (IBRD), commonly known as the World Bank, was established in 1945. As of 1999, it counted 181 members. Its sources of funds are paid-in capital, capital market borrowings, repayments on earlier loans, and retained earnings. It provides loans to middle-income countries and creditworthy poorer countries.
- The International Development Agency (IDA), established in 1960, is the Bank's concessional lending arm. It provides interest free loans to poor eligible countries. Sources of funds include contributions from government and transfers from IBRD profits.
- The International Financial Corporation (IFC) was established in 1956 to finance private sector investments and play a catalytic role with private investors by demonstrating the profitability of investments in poorer countries.
- The Multilateral Investment Guarantee Agency (MIGA), established in 1988, facilitates investment primarily by providing investment guarantees against non-commercial risks.
- The International Center for the Settlement of Investment Disputes (ICSID), created in 1966 to facilitate the settlement of investment disputes.

This entry focuses mainly on the IBRD and IDA.

The original mandate of the World Bank, as agreed in the Articles of Agreement of the Charter approved by Member States in the Bretton Woods Conference, is to: 'assist in the reconstruction and development of territories of members by facilitating the investment of capital for productive purposes' and to 'promote the long range balanced growth of international trade...by encouraging international investment...thereby assisting in raising productivity, the standard of living and conditions of labour'.

Importantly, Article IV stated that the Bank would make decisions on the sole basis of economic and financial justifications without making political considerations:

> The Bank and its officers shall not interfere in the political affairs of any member, nor shall they be influenced in their decisions by the political character of the member or members concerned. Only economic considerations shall be relevant to their decisions.

Project lending, a traditional Bank activity until recently, involves lending for projects for the extraction or use of natural resources, infrastructures such as dams, roads, powerplants. Sectorial lending is mostly aimed at the reform, restructuring and privatization of entire productive sectors, mainly the energy sector, one of the crucial components of every state's development and economic policy. A more recent instrument used by IDA and IBRD is the 'social safety net programme lending', the volume of which has substantially increased, together with the lending volume for structural adjustment programmes (SAPs) as a consequence of the financial crises that struck Asia and Latin America in the late 1990s. In the 1999 financial year, lending directly or indirectly connected to SAPs and Financial Rescue Packages accounted for 64 per cent of overall lending.

The private sector arms of the Bank, namely IFC and MIGA, lend not to governments but to companies. IFC participates in joint ventures to attract foreign capital and provide a seal of quality and reliability to the private investment. The surge of Foreign Direct Investment (FDI) on a global scale has been accompanied by a remarkable increase in volume of lending by IFC and MIGA, in line with the approach according to which the Bank's scarce resources should be used to 'catalyse' private sector flows, especially in countries out of the loop of FDI. MIGA in turn operates as an insurance agency to support private investments in countries with high political risk.

The International Center for the Settlement of Investment Disputes (ICSID) is an arbitration body to which companies can resort in case of violations of contractual agreements with governments and vice-versa. An institution almost unknown to the general public, ICSID was active in providing consultancy and know-how to OECD during the negotiations of the aborted Multilateral Agreement on Investments.

The World Bank governance structure is organized as follows: the Council of Governors gives general policy direction. It meets twice a year in spring and fall and is composed of the Ministers of Finance and Governors of Central Banks of member states. The implementation of the policy directions is the task of the Board of Directors, composed of 24 members. They represent either single member states (as is the case with the US, Japan, Canada, France, Germany, and the United Kingdom) or a constituency of states (Italy, for instance, represents a 'Mediterranean Constituency' with Italy, Portugal, Malta, Greece, Albania). The Head of the Board and President of the World Bank Group is always a US citizen, appointed by the US Administration. The current President, James Wolfensohn, is now serving his second five-year term.

2 A brief history: from bank to development agency

The International Bank for Reconstruction and Development (IBRD) was set up in 1944 at the Bretton Woods Conference, and opened its doors for business on 25 June 1946, in Washington DC. Under the impulse of the US Government, the Bank was created to provide loans for reconstruction and development to war-torn countries. Thirty-eight countries were members. Original capital subscriptions were small, and the Bank was dependent on private investors for funds, which underlined the importance of establishing its position on capital markets.

The Bank got off to a slow start. Demands for reconstruction loans quickly overstretched the capacity of the Bank to manage them properly, signalling that the needs for reconstruction funds had been largely underestimated. The Bank was a new and strange creature in the financial community and it took time to overcome Wall Street scepticism. The first years also witnessed a tense battle between the Bank management and the appointed governors. From 1948, the unfolding of the Cold War and the launch of US Marshall Plan Assistance (which dwarfed Bank efforts) entailed important changes in the external environment within which the Bank operated. Nevertheless, when Eugene Black took over the Presidency of the Bank in 1949, the foundations had been laid for its development.

The 1950s saw the Bank grow into a respected multilateral institution, the independence gained by its management protecting it from the Cold War frictions and the political strains induced by growing membership (67 members in 1958). The Bank also expanded organizationally, with the creation of its private-sector affiliate (IFC) in 1956 and of its soft-loan arm, the International Development Agency (IDA) in 1960. By the end of the decade, it had earned the stature of a triple A bond rating, and had become the fourth largest financier of international development projects. The Bank's recipe for success was conservative lending, a requirement for gaining the confidence of the international banking community. Loans went mainly for large infrastructure projects: power plants, railroad lines, highway networks and dams. These projects required investments that were too large and too uncertain, both politically and economically, to be attractive to private investors. World Bank historians suggest, however, that the availability of funds for these projects stimulated the philosophy that accorded a vital role to infrastructures in the development process, rather than the reverse.

The creation of the IDA manifested the recognition that development in former colonies was raising new challenges. Within the United Nations there was an ongoing struggle over the setting of a Special UN Fund for Economic Development (SUNFED) to provide support to newly independent countries that could not afford the loans at near to market rates that the Bank provided. At the same time the need for Bank operations in Europe and countries like Japan and Australia was diminishing. The

IDA was a response to these international changes and organizational needs.

The Bank took further steps towards becoming a development agency in the 1960s. This was a time of development optimism and belief in state leadership. Although the bulk of its loans remained for large-scale infrastructure projects and agriculture (in 1968 66 per cent of loans went to basic infrastructure), the Bank also supported five-year plans, and invested more and more resources in Technical Assistance (TA). The purpose of TA was to support governments with weak capacities to identify needs and develop project proposals that could be acceptable to the Bank. Bank operations were geographically concentrated from 1945 to 1970, with five countries – Colombia, Brazil, Pakistan, India and Thailand – receiving around 35 per cent of all lending.

The Presidency of Robert McNamara (1968–80) marked a new phase in the Bank's history. During a period of increasing development pessimism and tensions in North–South relations (the oil shocks of 1973 and 1979; the Vietnam War; UN discussions on the New International Economic Order), World Bank lending increased fourfold in real terms, and shifted its orientation radically towards addressing poverty. McNamara became convinced that the Bank should transform itself into a development agency: 'we believe economic progress remains precarious and sterile without corresponding social improvement. Fully human development requires attention to both. We intend, in the Bank, to give attention to both' (address to the Board of Governors in Copenhagen in 1970). This view marked a departure from belief in the 'trickle down effect' – the view that poverty alleviation indirectly but automatically stems from economic growth – and called for projects that would reach the poor directly. Changes in the Bank's structure of lending were significant. In the late 1970s, the share of lending to rural areas and agriculture doubled to 28 per cent, while the share of loans for basic infrastructures fell to 35 per cent. New areas in which the Bank got engaged include population issues (health and education), unemployment and the environment. It is under McNamara that the 'pressure to lend' became one of the key features of the Bank's institutional culture.

During that period the Bank also became more prominently engaged in development theory as a way of defining what it considered to be appropriate development strategies (see WORLD TRADE ORGANIZATION). Following the realization that institutional and policy parameters influenced the success of development projects the Bank increasingly took up the role of policy adviser and developed its research capacity in this domain. It launched the World Development Report in 1978 which, with an average distribution of 120,000, is by far the most widely read document in development economics.

The lending spree and poverty orientation of the McNamara years came to a sudden halt in the early 1980s. The debt crisis that unfolded after Mexico's default in 1982 revealed the mistakes in previous development strategies and led to the development of the Bank's structural adjustment lending. The Bank also became a main proponent of the new pro-market ideology of the time, bringing to the forefront of development discussions key neo-classical economic tenets like 'getting the prices right'.

Structural adjustment programmes (SAPs) provide loans tied to state and institutional reforms in line with the so-called 'Washington consensus' on the best ways to organize an economy. Reforms consisted of trade liberalization, de-regulation, and privatization. The priority was on rolling back the state and inserting the national economies into the Northern-dominated global economy, while little attention was given to the complementarity between the private and public spheres of the national economy. SAPs thus led to a systematic undermining of the capacity of states to pursue independent and innovative development strategies. Countries in Latin America were the first to embrace this path of reform, followed by Eastern European countries after 1989, and then Africa and Asia in the 1990s.

3 Criticism and response: projects, programmes and policies

The World Bank is often the target of criticisms, in particular from citizen groups based in industrialized and developing countries. The international campaign '50 years is enough' culminated in 1994 calling for the closure of the Bank.

Criticisms against the Bank are as various as its operations. Critics have focused in particular on the economic, social, and ecological impacts of projects financed by the Bank; the social and political consequences of its structural adjustment programmes; and its development strategies in general (see INTERNATIONAL MONETARY FUND).

Projects

Until the late 1970s the Bank enjoyed a high reputation in terms of project management. But that reputation soured in the 1980s. The Wapenhans Report, a major study by the Operations and Evaluation Department released in 1992, revealed that projects throughout the 1980s had not performed according to expectations in one-third of the cases, mainly because of poor economic analysis. This under-performance was particularly the case for its core-business operations, lending for large infrastructures.

While the Bank's projects were increasingly failing according to its own narrow economic criteria, the criteria themselves came under intense criticism. In particular the Bank became a prime target for critics who drew attention to the ecological, cultural, and social costs of large infrastructures like dams and resource-extraction activities. In the early 1990s under pressure of citizen organizations, the Bank was forced to pull out from the Narmada Dam project in India. Major international mobilization also targeted its support to power-generating projects because of the potential impact on climatic change, and the Chad-Cameroon oil pipeline. While the share of the Bank's loans is relatively small in the overall financial package of these large projects, the Bank's involvement is crucial to bring in private investors.

The Bank responded in a number of ways to these criticisms. In the 1990s, it changed its operational policies and directives. The assessment of the environmental impacts of projects has become more stringent; an operational directive sets special procedures for projects that affect indigenous peoples; it reviewed its disclosure policy to increase the information made publicly available.

In 1993, as a consequence of the findings of the Morse Commission Report – the internal report on the Narmada valley development project — the Board of Executive Directors created the Inspection Panel, a three-member non-judicial body that provides an independent forum to private citizens who believe that their rights or interests have been or could be directly harmed by a project financed by the Bank due to a failure of the Bank to follow its policies and procedures. Affected people bring their concerns to the attention of the Panel by filing a Request for Inspection. The Panel makes a preliminary review of the request, considers a response from the Management, and recommends to the Board whether the claims should be investigated. If the Board approves a recommendation to investigate, the Panel proceeds with the investigation.

Another response of the Bank has been to broaden consultation processes with citizen organizations. For instance, with the World Conservation Union (IUCN) it takes part in the World Commission on Dams, which attempts to mediate a major global controversy democratically – the building and impact of large dams.

Programmes

Since their inception, the World Bank's structural adjustment programmes (SAPs) have been the target of major criticism for their economic, social, and political implications. While officially aiming to restore macroeconomic stability in the aftermath of the debt crisis, they imposed on people living in poverty and in vulnerability the costs of adjustment by decreasing state services, reducing public subsidies on basic goods like food, or introducing fees for health and education services and water. Riots and public demonstrations took place in many countries where the programmes have been implemented.

The Comprehensive Development Framework (CDF) introduced by World Bank President James Wolfensohn in 1998 is the most significant response to these criticisms, and echoes McNamara's reorientation of the Bank strategy in the late 1960s:

> Development is not just about adjustment. Development is not just about sound budgets and fiscal management. Development is not just about education and health. Development is not just about technocratic fixes ... Development is about getting the macroeconomics right – yes; but it is also about building the roads, empowering the people, writing the laws, recognizing the women, eliminating the corruption, educating the girls, building the banking systems, protecting the environment, inoculating the children ... Development is about putting *all* the component parts in place – together and in harmony.
>
> (Wolfensohn's address to the Board of Governors, 6 October 1998)

Another criticism of SAPs is the way they have been imposed on cash-starved countries by the Bank and the IMF, with far-reaching political implications in breach of Article IV of its Articles of Agreement. Bank (and IMF) conditionalities integral to structural adjustment lending contain strong policy prescriptions to the borrowing government including cutting unproductive expenditures, supporting privatization and deregulation to attract foreign capitals, increasing labour market flexibility and increasing prices of key consumption goods such as gasoline. The political implications of these measures often go much beyond good management of the economy.

In part as a response to that criticism, in late 1999, the Bank replaced its 'Country Assistance Strategy' by 'Poverty Reduction Strategy Papers' (PRSPs). The intention is to highlight that poverty reduction, not adjustment, is the paramount new objective of the Bank; but also that country ownership of a poverty reduction strategy is paramount. However, Bank management retains significant control over these strategies by expressing to the Board a judgement on whether the policies prepared by the countries are economically sound, independently of the legitimacy of the process of preparation of these documents.

Policies

Structural adjustment programmes come with conditionalities in terms of economic policies. The same package of policies referred to as the 'Washington consensus' have been pushed in all countries undertaking SAPs, irrespective of the particular economic, political, social or environmental context. The emphasis of the policies and the development strategy they entail is on microeconomic efficiency and integration into the global economy by promoting exports and attracting foreign investments.

The interpretation of the sustained growth of the East Asian economies up to 1997 has been a major battlefield for rival development theories. In 1993 the World Bank published the influential 'The East Asian Miracle' report that interpreted the success in East Asia in terms of the key principles of the Washington consensus. But critics were quick to point to a different story, in particular to the importance of price distortion ('getting prices wrong') in stimulating economic growth and to state-designed export strategies instead of straightforward trade liberalization (see ECONOMY OF JAPAN).

Importantly the report failed to foresee the financial crisis that hit these countries in 1997 and revealed some structural weaknesses in their development strategies. At the same time, the very disappointing performance of the Russian economy revealed the limits of the Washington consensus, while the success of China continued to show the existence of alternative successful development paths (see CHINA, MANAGEMENT IN).

In 1999, Joseph Stiglitz, then chief economist of the World Bank, acknowledged publicly the limits of the Washington consensus in a series of speeches and academic articles (see STIGLITZ, J.). The main lesson he drew from Russia and the financial crisis in Asia was the key importance of adequate institutions to support the proper functioning of a market economy. The logical consequence of that point is the adoption of more gradualist approaches to adjustment to permit the required institutional development and change. This perspective led Stiglitz to voice strong criticisms against the conditionalities part of the IMF-led rescue packages offered to the Asian countries hit by the financial crisis and fully in line with the Washington consensus orthodoxy. While not following its chief economist entirely, the World Bank also distanced itself from the IMF on that occasion. Stiglitz's resignation from the World Bank in early 2000 has been attributed to his unorthodox position on the crises in Asia and Russia, and his departure leaves the future direction of World Bank development thinking uncertain.

4 New directions and further evolution

Since the late 1960s, the evolution of Bank strategies and of the international economy have been closely related. Bank strategies respond not only to internal organizational impulses and to the needs of its clients (national states) but also to structural changes in the international economy as a whole. Conversely, given the wide direct and indirect influence of the Bank, its strategies and policies participate in shaping the evolution of national and the international economies (see GLOBALIZATION).

Since the early 1980s the Bank has actively participated in promoting and shaping the process of economic globalization. In many developing countries, trade liberalization was not an outcome of negotiations within the frame of the General Agreement of Tariffs and Trade (GATT) but a result of reforms within the frame of SAPs. After the creation of the World Trade Organization in 1994, the Bank became, with the International Monetary Fund (IMF) and the WTO, one of the three pillars of the global economic governance system. Coordination between the three organizations is based on a shared belief in the benefits of trade and exchange liberalizations, complemented by various institutional mechanisms of consultation and co-ordination.

In this system, the role of the Bank is to provide funds, technical expertise, and political advice to compensate for the negative impacts of globalization on developing countries. The two new strategic directions introduced in the late 1990s – CDF and PRSPs – will take the Bank into a post-adjustment era. They are global responses to the increasing problems of social marginalization and the political risks it creates, which depart from the classic development view that these problems are best addressed as part of a strategy of nation building.

The challenges for the Bank will be numerous. It needs to convince its political masters that the strategy is sound at a time when many voices express criticism on the ever-increasing scale and scope of Bank operations and areas of responsibility. In the Metzler report released in the year 2000 a commission of the US Congress advocated a refocusing of the Bank mission. It will also need to retain the confidence of the financial markets from which it raises its resources at the same time as it increases lending in non-productive areas. It is more than likely that the Bank may be the victim of backlashes against globalization. Its current strategy to become a global safety net may eventually conflict with people's aspirations to regain democratic control over their destinies within the national space.

FRANCK AMALRIC
SOCIETY FOR INTERNATIONAL
DEVELOPMENT, ROME

FRANCESCO MARTONE
CAMPAGNA PER LA RIFORMA DELLA BANCA
MONDIALE, ROME

Further reading

(References cited in the text marked *)

Bello, W. (1994) *Dark Victory. The United States, the World Bank, and Global Poverty*, London: Polity Press. (A thorough analysis and criticism of structural adjustment programmes.)

Bergesen, H. O. and Lunde, L. (1999) *Dinosaurs or Dynamos? The United Nations and the World Bank at the Turn of the Century*, London: Earthscan. (Traces the history of the World Bank from a development bank to a development agency in comparison to changes within the UN system.)

Caufield, C. (1997) *Masters of Illusion. The World Bank and the Poverty of Nations*, New York: Henry Holt and Company. (An overall critical analysis of the World Bank's record in alleviating poverty.)

George, S. and Sabelli F. (1993) *Faith and Credit, The World Bank's Secular Empire*, Boulder, CO: Westview Press (An influential critical, sociological analysis of the World Bank.)

Kapur, D., Lewis J. P. and Webb, R. (eds) (1997) *The World Bank: Its First Half Century*, Washington DC: Brookings Institution Press. (Comprehensive compilation of texts on the World Bank.)

Mason, E. and Asher, R. (1973) *The World Bank since Bretton Woods*, Washington DC: Brookings Institution Press. (Official history of the first quarter-century of Bank operations.)

Rich, B. (1994) *Mortgaging the Earth, The World Bank, Environmental Impoverishment, and the Crisis of Development*, Boston, MA: Beacon Press. (A review of the Bank's environmental record.)

World Bank (various years) *World Development Report*, New York: Oxford University Press. (Main development policy documents produced by the World Bank.)

See also: EAST ASIAN ECONOMIES; ECONOMIC GROWTH; GROWTH THEORY; INTERNATIONAL FINANCIAL STABILITY; INTERNATIONAL MONETARY FUND; WORLD TRADE ORGANIZATION

World Trade Organization (WTO)

Overview

The World Trade Organization (WTO) was established on 1 January 1995. It is the umbrella organization governing the international trading system. It oversees international trade arrangements and it provides the secretariat for the General Agreement on Tariffs and Trade (GATT), which has been based in Geneva since its inception in 1948. The GATT undertook eight 'rounds' of multilateral trade negotiations which were successful in achieving major cuts in tariffs and (since the 1970s) some reductions in related non-tariff barriers to trade. The last GATT round, the Uruguay Round, took seven years as its agenda had broadened to include trade in services, trade in intellectual property and a revised system of dispute settlement mechanisms.

The WTO holds ministerial meetings every two years. At the Seattle ministerial meeting in December 1999 there were large protests by 10,000 members of non-governmental organizations (NGOs) joined by 40,000 US labour unionists in a coalition against the proposed launch of the Millennium Round.

The WTO has been a target for such anti-globalization protests. With a total of 500 employees and its modest role in global governance it may appear to be an unlikely target. Nevertheless, it is a symbol of trade and investment among nations and is therefore seen by activists as an imposing force oppressing the developing countries. The WTO basically serves as a committee room for the individual governments to propose and negotiate multilateral trade and investment liberalization measures. It also now serves as a legal dispute settlement body at which countries can litigate for trade remedies when other governments fail to abide by negotiated agreements. The work of the WTO is largely technical, sector specific, and limited by the powers devolved to it by its member governments. In this entry the origins, principles, operations and the agenda for a new round will be reviewed.

1 Origin

Contrary to popular belief, the WTO does not replace the GATT. An amended GATT remains as one of the legal pillars of the world's trade and, to a lesser extent, investment system (see INTERNATIONAL TRADE AND FOREIGN DIRECT INVESTMENT). The other pillars were set up in the Uruguay Round's Marrakesh agreement of 1994 and include the General Agreement on Trade in Services (GATS) and the Agreement on Trade-Related Aspects of Intellectual Property Rights (TRIPS). The membership of the WTO has increased from the 76 founding members of 1995 to 132 members in 1998. Members include virtually all the developed and most of the developing countries. The members of the WTO account for well over 90 per cent of the world's trade and virtually all of its foreign direct investment. A notable non-member of the WTO is the People's Republic of China, whose entry has been delayed, despite support by the United States and the European Union (EU), on the grounds that its economy is still not open enough, that intellectual property rights are not sufficiently protected, and that it is still demanding too long to bring its domestic institutions into line with its WTO commitments. However, this is not to say that China has not tried hard to become a member. It has been on a quest to join the WTO since 1987 and its membership has been fraught with delays and problems. On 15 November 1999, the United States and China signed a bilateral trade agreement in Beijing. The agreement with the USA overcomes the largest obstacle in China's quest for WTO membership. In the agreement, China agrees to lower barriers on American products; in return, the USA agrees to support China's quest to become a member of the WTO. Additionally, the US Congress has to approve this trade agreement. The trade deal promises greater access for the USA to China's markets and offers substantial concessions to lower trade barriers in areas ranging from telecommunications to insurance.

The origins of the WTO can be traced back to the Atlantic Charter of 1941 developed by US President Franklin Roosevelt and British Prime Minister Winston Churchill. In order to counter US isolationism, the principle of the Atlantic Charter was for an international trading system with equal access to trade for all nations. This was seen as a complement to an effective world political forum, the United Nations, established in 1946, with its permanent headquarters in New York City. The United States organized an international conference on trade and employment which resulted in the Havana Charter of 1948, in which it was proposed to establish the International Trade Organization (ITO). Concurrently, twenty-three countries agreed to a set of tariff cuts and these were ratified by the GATT, which was set up as a transition arrangement to be subsumed under the ITO. However, the ITO was never ratified and the GATT continued for forty-seven years until the WTO finally emerged in the last stages of the Uruguay Round to take on the powers originally designed for the ITO. The WTO now stands with the World Bank and the International Monetary Fund as the third leg of global governance for the world economic system (see INTERNATIONAL MONETARY FUND; WORLD BANK).

2 WTO principles

The WTO carries on the key GATT principle of non-discrimination, i.e. that any barrier to trade should be applied equally to all member countries. It also maintains the most favoured nation (MFN) principle, i.e. that any liberalization measures, with some exceptions, should also be granted to all members. To understand what these principles mean, it is fruitful to think of the WTO as a club whose membership rules require that all countries

receive the same treatment, and if one member rescinds a trade concession then other affected members can retaliate by withdrawing their reciprocal concessions, or else receive compensation to equivalent commercial effect. If trade disputes arise, they can be settled by the unified dispute settlement mechanism of the WTO, which can ensure timely compliance, in contrast to the basically voluntary procedures of the old GATT system. Now decisions of a WTO dispute panel can no longer be blocked by the disputant party, as was possible under the GATT. Panel findings can be subject to review by an Appellate Body of the WTO. There are now about a dozen such appeals a year, including the bananas, beef hormones and US export subsidies cases between the EU and the United States. In addition, the publication of trade policy reviews and the activities of the Trade Policy Review Body (which regularly monitors the trade policies of member countries) complement the WTO's dispute settlement activities by contributing significantly to enhanced transparency.

There are four important exceptions to the key GATT principle of non-discrimination: (1) developed countries can give tariff preference to developing countries; (2) countries entering into regional free trade agreements do not need to extend the preferences negotiated in this context on an MFN basis; (3) a country can invoke temporary 'safeguard' protection to one of its industries suffering serious injury due to a surge of imports; and (4) temporary quantitative restrictions can be invoked by a country with serious balance of payment problems. In the latter two cases, these measures are temporary exceptions to the member's commitment to the GATT and a public investigation has to be undertaken to allow for limited relief from GATT obligations.

Another important principle of the WTO, which is a significant improvement on the GATT, is the 'single undertaking'. WTO members must accept all of the obligations of the GATT, GATS, TRIPS and any other corollary agreements. This ends the 'free ride' of some developing countries under the old GATT when they could receive the benefits of some trade concessions without having to join in and undertake their full obligations. For most developed countries in North America and Western Europe the single undertaking was already being made and the WTO meant few new obligations.

3 Analysis of WTO operations

The major technical tensions within the WTO relate to the issues of agriculture, trade in services and trade-related investment measures. None of these issues were included in the original mandate of the GATT, which dealt with trade in goods. Agriculture is a sector subsidized by most governments and it was badly neglected in the fifty years of GATT. One technical advance which helps to increase the transparency of subsidies is the calculation of producers' subsidy equivalents. As a result, in the Uruguay Round some progress was made towards the future reduction of the most egregious agricultural subsidies through a process of 'tariffication', i.e. the translation of existing subsidies and other barriers to trade into tariff equivalents. Much work remains to be done in future rounds to liberalize agricultural trade.

Today, services account for 70 per cent of the employment and value added in advanced industrialized countries, and also for at least half the world's trade and investment (see GLOBALIZATION). The Uruguay Round started to address issues of trade in services with the establishment of GATS. Subsequently, some progress has been made in sector-specific liberalization, e.g. in the market-opening measures in telecommunications (although individual countries still closely regulate this sector). Trade-Related Investment Measures (TRIMS) were also considered and a substantive agreement that prohibits a number of investment requirements affecting cross-border trade in goods was reached, e.g. the TRIMS agreement restricted the imposition of export requirements on foreign investors. Future negotiations at the WTO (following upon the last Uruguay Round of the GATT) will need to develop a deeper and more comprehensive set of rules for multinational investment than in TRIMS. These may well be based upon the model of NAFTA (North American Free Trade Association), using the national treatment principle as the ba-

sic logic. National treatment states that foreign investors should not be discriminated against, but receive the same treatment as domestic firms in the application of domestic laws.

A future WTO round should attempt to build upon a multinational agreement on investment (MAI) which was partially negotiated by the Paris-based Organization for Economic Cooperation and Development (OECD) over the 1995–98 period. This would apply the principle of national treatment to foreign direct investment, but allow sensitive sectors (such as culture and transportation) to be exempted. Currently, investment issues are still being discussed at the WTO in the context of the Working Group on the Relationship between Trade and Investment, established with a two-year mandate at the 1996 ministerial meeting in Singapore, and subsequently continued. Another important Working Group established during the WTO Singapore meeting is the one examining the interaction between trade and competition policy.

4 The Millennium Round

At the regular two-yearly ministerial meeting of the WTO in Seattle in December 1999, an attempt was made to launch a new round of negotiations for multilateral trade and investment liberalization. This failed, partly because of protests by NGOs and US labour unions, but also because of a lack of US political leadership and consensus at the WTO itself. For another round to be launched a US President must be granted 'fast-track' authority by the US Congress. This did not occur at Seattle. The agenda for Seattle was to carry on with the unfinished business of the Uruguay Round, specifically issues involving trade in services, trade-related investment measures, intellectual property, competition policy, technical assistance, agriculture etc. There was also talk of dealing with some environmental and labour/human rights issues, although these are basically outside of the mandate of the WTO.

In addition there was really no consensus on the Seattle agenda by the major economic powers (the United States, the EU and Japan), while developing countries were also divided on the pace of trade and services liberalization, as well as concerned about its perceived unequal benefits. Despite this temporary setback, the work of the WTO continues in the technical committees. It is possible that a future round will be launched once a new US President has fast-track authority and the views of the more responsible NGOs are better reflected in the individual country agendas. The NGOs need to target their home countries rather than the WTO as the real negotiating positions and decisions are made by ministers, not WTO bureaucrats

5 Conclusion

Over a fifty-year period, the GATT has moved forward to the extent that today's new constitution for international trade, embodied in the WTO, includes an even fuller agenda of policy issues than envisaged by its pioneering founders. These issues include: further reduction of tariffs; a new set of rules for multinational investment and competition policy; and the development of increased linkages between trade and issues of social policy, such as the environment and labour policy. The hurdles to achieving these three sets of objectives are lowest for tariff cuts, higher for investment and highest of all for environmental and other social issues.

ALAN M RUGMAN
INDIANA UNIVERSITY AND
TEMPLETON COLLEGE
UNIVERSITY OF OXFORD

Further reading

Krueger, A.O. (1998) *The WTO as an International Organization*, Chicago: University of Chicago Press. (Leading US academics analyse the WTO as an institution and consider current policy issues.)

Ostry, S. (1997) *The Post-Cold War Trading System: Who's on First?*, Chicago: University of Chicago Press. (An analysis of the GATT and WTO by the world's leading scholar of international institutions.)

Ostry, S. (2001) 'The multilateral trading system', in A.M. Rugman and T. Brewer (eds), *The Oxford Handbook of International Business*, Oxford: Oxford University Press. (Contains the first objective analysis of the role and power of non-governmental organizations as the operated at Seattle and beyond.)

Qureshi, A.H. (1996) *The World Trade Organization: Implementing International Trade Norms*, Manchester: Manchester University Press and New York: St. Martin's Press. (Explains the legal framework of the WTO, how it works in practice and contains an appendix which reprints key selected documents.)

Rugman, A.M. (1996) *Multinationals and Trade Policy: Volume 2 of the Selected Scientific Papers of Alan M. Rugman*, Cheltenham, UK: Edward Elgar. (Contains research papers reporting tests of GATT-related dispute settlement procedures on countervail and anti-dumping, and on trade in services.)

Rugman, A.M. (2000) *The End of Globalization*, London: Random House Business Books. (Contains factual analysis of the nature of triad-based regionalism and the problems for the WTO created by misguided protesters against globalization.)

Rugman, A.M., Kirton, J. and Solway, J. (1999) *Environmental Regulations and Corporate Strategy*, Oxford: Oxford University Press. (Explores the broad spectrum of multilateral, regional and national environmental regulations and their impact on strategies of multinational enterprises.)

Schott, J.J. (1996) *WTO 2000: Setting the Course for World Trade*, Washington, DC: Institute for International Economics. (Discusses the challenges facing the WTO and the agenda for future trade negotiations.)

World Trade Organization (1995) *The Results of the Uruguay Round of Multilateral Trade Negotiations: The Legal Texts*, Geneva: WTO. (The actual legal texts of the last GATT round.)

World Trade Organization (1996) *Singapore Ministerial Declaration*, Document WT/MIN/(96)/DEC/W, Geneva: WTO. (Report of the first WTO ministerial meeting in December 1996, including the Working Groups on competition policy and on investment.)

World Trade Organization (2000) *Annual Report 2000*, Geneva: WTO. (Up-to-date information on the WTO available on the web at *http://www.wto.org.*)

Further resources

World Trade Organization website:
  http://www.wto.org
Independent Media Center. Includes news articles on the WTO protests worldwide.
  http://www.indymedia.org

See also: ECONOMIC INTEGRATION; INTERNA-
TIONAL; GLOBALIZATION; INTERNATIONAL
BUSINESS; INTERNATIONAL BUSINESS,
LEGAL DIMENSIONS OF; INTERNATIONAL
MONETARY FUND; INTERNATIONAL TRADE
AND FOREIGN DIRECT INVESTMENT;
KEYNES, J.M.; NORTH AMERICAN FREE-
TRADE AGREEMENT; RICARDO, D.; SMITH,
A.; WORLD BANK

World Wide Web (WWW)

Overview

The World Wide Web as a part of the Internet is increasingly becoming an international platform for information exchange and electronic commerce. This service is based on hypertext and hypermedia technologies that connect so-called HTML (HyperText Markup Language) documents. Mouse-sensitive objects like texts or graphics link to other paragraphs in the same document or in other documents or to other file types, such as graphics, audio or video files, or to other Internet services on the same or another Web server. This results in a network topology that gives its name to the service. The graphical user interface means wide acceptance and allows commercial usage. Companies use the World Wide Web as a further distribution channel for their products and services.

1   The history of the WWW

The beginning of the World Wide Web was in March 1989. Tim Berners-Lee of the European Particle Physics Laboratory in Geneva, Switzerland (CERN) had the idea of developing a hypertext system that integrated different workgroups with a simple tool so that they could work efficiently and effectively together. This idea was written down in the 'Proposal for a HyperText project':

> HyperText is a way to link and access information of various kinds as a web of nodes in which the user can browse at will. Potentially, HyperText provides a single user interface to many large classes of stored information such as reports, notes, databases, computer documentation and online systems help. We propose the implementation of a simple scheme to incorporate several different servers of a machine-stored information already available at CERN, including an analysis of the requirements for information access needs by experiments. ... At CERN, a variety of data is already available: reports, experiment data, personnel data, electronic mail address lists, computer documentation, experiment documentation, and many other sets of data are spinning around on computer discs continuously. It is however impossible to "jump" from one set to another in an automatic way: once you found out that the name of Joe Bloggs is listed in an incomplete description of some on-line software, it is not straightforward to find his current electronic mail address. Usually, you will have to use a different lookup-method on a different computer with a different user interface. Once you have located information, it is hard to keep a link to it or to make a private note about it that you will later be able to find quickly.
>
> (Berners-Lee and Cailliau 1989)

At the end of 1990, the first line-oriented browser was developed. This meant that hypertext and the integration of different media types were realized. The first network was developed and implemented in 1991 at CERN. The first browser was stored on an ftp server at CERN. Everybody who was able to use the Internet could download this browser onto his or her local computer. In 1992, the first graphical user interface was developed. In February 1993, the first version of the Mosaic browser was presented for the UNIX-platform X Windows. The World Wide Web consisted of 500 servers. In 1994, Netscape Communications Corp. was founded and at the end of that year the first version of the graphic browser Netscape Navigator was offered. Another graphic browser is Microsoft's Internet Explorer.

2 WWW as a part of the Internet

The Internet is an electronic information system that connects different institutions, universities, commercial corporations and other groups (see INTERNET AND BUSINESS). The basic idea is to connect existing networks to a single network. The Internet is not administrated by an organization; it consists of a large number of networks that are managed individually. The Internet is connected to other networks, e.g. networks of commercial network providers, several mailbox systems and local networks. Figure 1 shows the architecture and the Internet as a part of this structure.

There are three main functionalities of the Internet:

- to allow the exchange of data and software between different users,
- to present information, and
- to use computers around the world.

The beginning of the Internet was the introduction of the ARPANET (Advanced Research Projects Agency NET) by the US Department of Defense in 1968. The goal was to research and develop the network technology. The intention was to have very high availability of the system, even if parts of it

didn't work. Therefore a protocol that controls the addresses and the transmission of messages is necessary. The protocol is named Internet Protocol (IP). In 1982, the Transmission Control Protocol (TCP) was implemented. Together with the Internet Protocol, it was used to control data exchange in the ARPANET. The combination of these both protocols (TCP/IP) allows the connection of different networks.

Each computer must have an address in order to exchange data. The address is a sequence of four numbers. Each number is smaller than 256. The numbers are separated by points, e.g. 192.11.77.11. Data transmitted on the Internet are divided into segments containing from 1 to about 1,500 characters. These parts are called packets. The packets will be reunited by the Transmission Control Protocol (TCP). The TCP adds a control number to the message. So, the receiver can verify that it has received all the packets. If there is one missing, the sender will be requested to send it again.

Using the Internet address to communicate with other computers is not very comfortable, especially if you want to communicate with a large number of different computers. To make communication easier the Domain Network System (DNS) was developed. This means that each computer is given a name and the

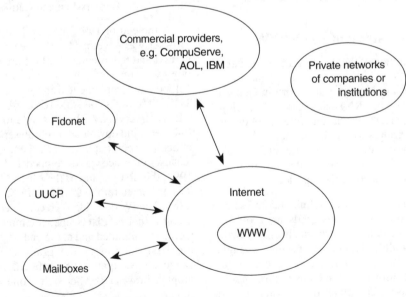

Figure 1 The Internet as a part of a large network

DNS administrates the names. Organizational or geographical names are used as domain names.

The Internet consists of a number of services such as electronic mail, newsgroups, telnet, ftp (file transfer protocol), archie, gopher, WAIS (Wide Area Information Service) and the WWW. Electronic mail is used to send electronic messages to other persons. Newsgroups are a location to discuss very different themes. There is a hierarchy with seven main groups in order to introduce some order into the proceedings. Telnet is a service that allows the user to log in and use the resources of a remote computer. To transfer files from one computer to another, the file transfer protocol is used. Archie is a database that contains all files stored on an ftp server and a short description of the files. The archie service is almost always used with a telnet session. Gopher is a service that was developed at the University of Minnesota. The aim is to sort information according to different criteria. The user doesn't know where the data are stored. Gopher uses the ftp and telnet services. The WAIS service allows full-text searches in text documents or in binary files.

3 The concepts of the WWW

The WWW is based on three fundamental characteristics: hypertext, hypermedia and the other Internet services. The browser integrates the different services and reacts like a client of the dedicated system.

Figure 2 shows how the browser integrates different services in the Internet. The browser is able to run special scripts, e.g. written in Perl, C, C++ or VBScript, to build connections to other servers in an intranet or in the Internet. To handle user inputs in a form, scripts are necessary to process the data.

Hypertext means the connection between two different texts. It is possible to jump from one text to another. The different texts may be in one or more documents. The connections are also called hyperlink Figure 3 shows the concept of hyperlinks. Hypermedia is an extension of hypertext by multimedia elements such as pictures, videos or music.

To realize such a system, it is necessary to use the following concepts:

- Client-server architecture: The server provides information, the client requests information.
- HTML (Hypertext Markup Language): This language is used to describe the presentation of information in hypertext documents. Hyperlinks allow connections to other documents and binary information like pictures, images, music, videos, and so on. HTML is based on SGML (Standard Generalized Markup Language) which is an ISO (International Standards Organization) standard to define structured document types.

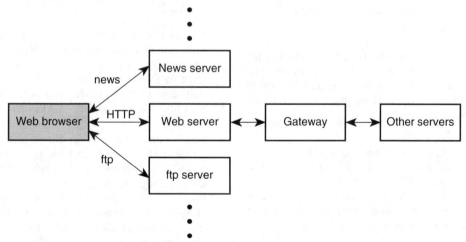

Figure 2 The browser as an interface to different Internet services

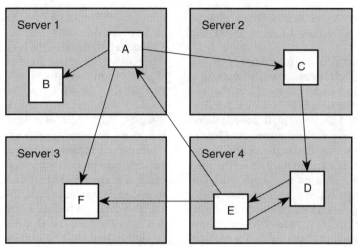

Figure 3 Example of hyperlinks between hypertext documents on different WWW servers

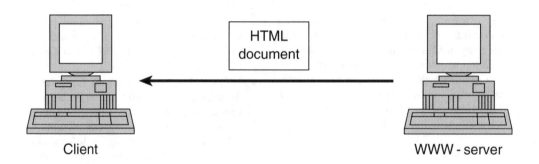

Figure 4 Hypertext Markup Language

Figure 4 shows the transmission of an HTML document from the server to the client. The HTML document is presented on the client's screen by the browser.

- HTTP (Hypertext Transfer Protocol): This protocol is used to control communication between the WWW server and the WWW client. A transaction consists of four steps:

  1 The client contacts the server to open a TCP/IP connection.
  2 The client sends a request to the server. Most of the requests contain a demand for an HTML document.
  3 The server responds if it is possible to send the document and sends it or if there is an error.

  4 After the transmission of the request and the response, the connection is closed.

- URL (Uniform Resource Locator): Hyperlinks are realized by using URLs. All Internet services are addressed by a uniform method. This means the user is not only able to read HTML documents but may also use ftp, gopher, WAIS or news services.

- Multimedia: The WWW allows picture, image, video and music files to be integrated. The browser usually cannot show these pictures or interpret video or music files. Therefore special viewer and player plug-ins are necessary. To play music files the computer needs a sound card. Video files are very large. A video of about 30 seconds means a file of more than 400 KB.

4 Further development in the World Wide Web

HTML documents describe static information in the World Wide Web. More interactive sites could be designed by integrating Java applets. Java is an object-oriented programming language developed by Sun Microsystems in Mountain View, California. Java is independent of hardware platforms. Java applets are small programs developed in the programming language Java. These programs are implemented in HTML documents. The program will be downloaded automatically at the request of an HTML document and runs on the client.

HTML 4.0 provides further possibilities for describing documents. A new table model has been implemented, it is more international, and style sheets and scripting are better supported. Style sheets allow style guides to be designed to enable a uniform appearance of a website. This allows, for example, companies to redo all their documents without changing the HTML. Nowadays a workgroup of the W3 Consortium develops XML (Extensible Markup Language) as a meta-language that allows, for example, the simplification of database connections. The PNG format is a new, bigger and better graphics format to replace the GIF format. Another goal is to solve internationalization problems such as different type settings and character sets.

The second trend is to have a higher security level to allow transactions such as financial transactions (see E-BANKING; INTERNET BANKING). Therefore the authenticity of transactions and the confidentiality of messages are necessary. Digital signatures are developed to allow legally effective contracts. Trust centres are established to guarantee the authenticity of digital signatures. Cryptographic methods are used to transmit confidential messages.

VRML (Virtual Reality Modelling Language) is a language to describe three-dimensional scenes, such as landscapes or buildings. Special viewers are integrated in some browsers to allow VRML documents to be visualized and to navigate in virtual space. The client needs a fast processor but it is not necessary to have a fast phone line. Because fast processors will be developed sooner than there will be fast phone lines to each household, three-dimensional sites may be available a long time before video (see E-COMMERCE).

JUERGEN SEITZ
VIADRINA UNIVERSITY

Further reading

(References cited in text marked*)

Berners-Lee, T. 'HyperText and CERN', *http://www.w3.org/HTandCERN.wn* (An explanation of hypertext, and why it is important for CERN. A background document explaining the ideas of the World Wide Web.)

Berners-Lee, T. 'Hypertext design issues', *http://www.w3.org/DesignIssues/Overview.html* (A detailed look at hypertext models and facilities, with a discussion of choices to be made in choosing or implementing a system.)

Berners-Lee, T. (1990) 'Information management: a proposal', *http://www.w3.org/History/1989/proposal.html* (A discussion of loss of information in complex evolving systems and a description of a solution based on a distributed hypertext system.)

Berners-Lee, T. (1996) 'The World Wide Web – past, present and future', *http://www.bcs.org.uk/news/timbl.htm* (An overview on the origins of the World Wide Web, and the present and future developments.)

* Berners-Lee, T. and Cailliau, R. (1989) 'Proposal for a HyperText project', *http://www.w3.org/Proposal.html* (Basic ideas of the World Wide Web.)

Booth, S. (1997) 'The World Wide Web: creating and organizing the digital library', *http://www.qcc.mass.edu/booth/students/www/www.htm.* (Explains the problems of information retrieval in the World Wide Web.)

Chaum, D. (1992) 'Achieving electronic privacy', *Scientific American*, August: 96–101. (An approach on anonymous digital money with blind signatures.)

Hammond, R. (1996) *Digital Business. Surviving and Thriving in an On-line World*, London: Hodder and Stoughton. (An explanation of transformation of traditional business models and approaches, and a practical guide for companies to exploit their potential.)

Moline, J. *et al.* (eds) (1990) *Proceedings of the Hypertext Standardization Workshop*, 16–18 January, National Institute of Standards and Technology, US Dept of Commerce. (Different approaches to hypertext standardization.)

Schneier, B. (1994) *Applied Cryptography – Protocols, Algorithms and Source Code in C*, 2nd edn, New York: John Wiley & Sons. (Overview on basic cryptographic methods and applications.)

Smish, J.B. and Weiss, S.F. (1988) 'An overview of hypertext', *Communications of the ACM* 31 (7). (General aspects and basic elements of hypertext.)

Sterling, B. (1993) 'Short history of the Internet', *http://www.forthnet.gr/forthnet/isoc/short.history.of.Internet* (An overview of the history of the Internet.)

Wayner, P. (1996) *Digital Cash – Commerce on the Net*, Chestnut Hill: Academic Press Professional. (An overview on digital payment systems and their consequences on commerce.)

Further resources

W3C World Wide Web Consortium
http://www.w3.org
Tim Berners-Lee
http://www.w3.org/people/Berners-Lee

See also: E-BUSINESS; E-COMMERCE; FIREWALL SYSTEMS; INTERNET AND BUSINESS; INTERNET BANKING; SECURITY AND INFORMATION SYSTEMS

Yang, Jerry (1968–)

Personal background

- born 1968 in Taiwan
- graduated from Stanford University in 1990 with a BS and MS in Electrical Engineering
- PhD student at Stanford
- launched Yahoo! with David Filo in 1995
- appointed to board of directors of Metricom Inc. in 1996
- in 1996, Yahoo!'s initial public offering of stock was the second most profitable ever
- in 2000, joins the board of Cisco Systems, Inc.
- in 2000, Yang was the world's youngest billionaire

1 Introduction

Jerry Yang was born in Taiwan in 1968. When he was two years old his father died. According to his mother, Lily, Jerry was precocious and started learning the Chinese alphabet by the age of three. In 1978 Yang, his younger brother Ken and his mother moved to San Jose, California, where Yang became a straight-A student (Plummer and Harrison 1995).

He graduated from Stanford University in 1990, earning both Bachelor of Science and Master of Science degrees in Electrical Engineering. Yang then entered the PhD engineering programme at Stanford after determining that the job market was not robust. As recently as 1994 he was a PhD student at Stanford University. He described himself as 'quasi retired at age 23 ... playing a lot of golf' (Plummer and Harrison 1995). That lifestyle changed in April 1995 when Yang and David Filo launched Yahoo! as a business. Now they 'can barely find the time to sleep and eat'

(Plummer and Harrison 1995). Yang married his girlfriend of several years (Akiko) in 1997 (1st Person Personal 2001).

Co-founder David Filo's father used to call Yang and him 'Yahoos', and Yang has become known as the Chief Yahoo. Officially, Yahoo! stands for 'Yet Another Hierarchical Officious Oracle' (Plummer and Harrison 1995). According to Jerry, the exclamation mark is 'pure marketing hype' (Stross 1998). Yang appears to enjoy the press and public relations aspects of his job. Perhaps most notable was his meeting with the US vice-president, Al Gore, to discuss the future of the Internet (Wylie 1997). In June 1996, Metricom Inc. appointed Yang to its board of directors (*PR Newswire* 1996c). In August 2000, Cisco Systems, Inc. named Yang to its board of directors (*Wall Street Journal* 2000).

Money does not seem to be an important motivator for Yang: 'To tell you the truth ... I don't even know how many shares I have. ... I mean I'm 28 – I don't need the money, I don't want the money, I don't want to pay taxes' (CNET 1997). He has an easygoing image and has been pictured working in T-shirts, jeans and without shoes (Wylie 1997). According to Yang, 'Yahoo! was my first job and, hopefully it's going to be my last' (*The Straits Times*, 2000).

2 Main contribution

Yahoo! was created in 1995 when two Stanford PhD students, Jerry Yang and David Filo, created a directory of their favorite Web sites. 'As a lark, they decided to offer their combined list to other WEB wanderers – and now Yang and Filo are on the verge of becoming as well-known, say, as Hewlett and Packard' (Plummer and Harrison 1995). By October 2000 their business had grown into an Internet empire with 780 million 'page views' per day (Hils-Cosgrove 2000) (see INTERNET). In 1997, while its revenues were low ($67 million), it had a market capitalization of $2.8 billion, putting it in the same league as Estée Lauder, the cosmetics giant (Stross 1998). By 2000, revenues had climbed to $296 million (Hils-Cosgrove 2000) and Yahoo! had 145 million users and 22 offices worldwide, making the firm the world's leading Web portal (*The Straits Times* 2000). Yahoo! Inc. is located in the Silicon Valley of California.

Yang is able to describe metaphorically the business intensity that he and the other employees at Yahoo! face on a daily basis. He says: 'There's this huge, fast moving train called the Internet. And we're just half a mile ahead laying tracks to make sure it doesn't go off the cliff. It's felt like that since the very beginning' (CNET 1997). According to Yang, 'you never, ever want to compete with Microsoft. And even if they want to compete with you, you run away and do something else' (Wylie 1997). He sees his role at Yahoo! Inc. as one of influence, not control or dominance (CNET 1997) (see LEADERSHIP).

From the beginning the strategy has been 'to make money through advertising and licensing fees from on-line services rather than charging for the service itself' (Plummer and Harrison 1995). The company has been developing a group of Yahoo! brand services, including Yahoo! Computing; Yahoo! Internet Life; Yahooligans – a web guide for kids; Yahoo! Japan; and Yahoo! Canada (*PR Newswire* 1996b). As of February 1998, Yahoo! offered its Internet directories in German, French, Japanese, Korean and three Nordic languages (Michelson 1998).

Yang spends his time primarily in business development. He has formed key partnerships in order to expand Yahoo! For example, he worked with Softbank to set up Yahoo! Japan and with Ziff-Davis Publishing Company to establish the interactive magazine Yahoo! Internet Life (CNET 1997). Yang stated in early 1996 that 'Yahoo! Internet Life has already established a new standard for in-depth, insightful, comparative reviews of Web sites' (*PR Newswire* 1996a). Yahoo! Internet Life is the largest and fastest-growing consumer magazine dedicated to the Internet and maintains its own separate Web site (*PR Newswire* 1996d). Among the services offered by Yahoo! is a free e-mail service (*http://www. yahoo.com*).

In 1996 Proctor and Gamble (P & G) contracted Yahoo! as an interactive advertiser to promote its brands and to direct interested Internet users to P&G Web sites. 'Yahoo! has run interactive promotions with leading companies like Citibank, NBC, NFL, Disney Online, Snapple and Southwest Airlines' (*PR Newswire* 1996c). In early 1998, *Autoweb.com,* an online car-buying service, coordinated a car giveaway with Yahoo! which gave 15 million Yahoo! users the opportunity to see Autoweb.com's promotion on Yahoo!'s home page (*Business Wire* 1998).

There is recent evidence to suggest that Yahoo! is beginning to take a more aggressive position in the marketplace: 'Yahoo! ... now aims to create communities on the net and compete with on-line service providers such as America Online as well as publishers' (Michelson 1998). In 1998, Yahoo! hoped not only to expand its search and directory service geographically, but to connect users online and to develop relationships with its users. In January 1998 Yahoo! entered into a marketing deal with MCI Telecommunications Corporation to provide 'a Yahoo! branded internet-access service' by the end of March 1998 (Stross 1998). Over the past several years Yang has been increasing Yahoo! market share overseas, e.g. Europe, Taiwan, China (Treanor 2000; Sorkin 2000).

3 Evaluation

What started as a hobby has in a very brief period of time grown into an important and trend-setting corporation (Wylie 1997). Yang and Filo did not have previous business experience (CNET 1997), but they did have the skills successfully to develop 'a computerized index system that catalogs the Web' (Plummer and Harrison 1995). Yahoo! has hired Tim Koogle, a Stanford-educated engineer with nine years' experience at Motorola, as chief executive officer (CEO) (Stross 1998). In an era of struggling 'dot.com' firms Yahoo! has been recognized for its '... remarkably stable team of managers, including its two founders ...' (Orr 2000).

According to Yang, 'Had we wanted to do it for money, we would have sold it very early on, because there was a lot of money dangling in front of us' (CNET 1997). Some key agreements early on were important. They received cash from a Menlo Park, California, venture capital firm, and Netscape lent them computers and Internet access lines in exchange for a Netscape advertisement that appeared whenever the Yahoo! Web site was accessed (Plummer and Harrison 1995). In early 1996, Yahoo! made history when its initial public offering (IPO) of stock was the second most profitable ever (*PR Newswire* 1996c). In 2000, Forbes listed Yang as the world's youngest billionaire ($5.7 billion) (*The Straits Times* 2000).

Jerry Yang has helped guide Yahoo! Inc. to respect simultaneously First Amendment free speech rights, the Communications Decency Act and the basic rights of advertisers. This, however, has not been easy as there have been legal challenges such as those involving *Yahoo.com* auction sites selling Nazi and Ku Klux Klan paraphernalia (Reuters 2000). Yahoo! has tried to be socially responsible by denying tobacco and hard alcohol manufacturers the right to advertise on Yahoo! sites (CNET 1997).

In October 2000, investors became concerned about Yahoo!s shrinking number of advertisers and shares fell to a year low of $77 per share (Hils-Cosgrove 2000). This situation worsened in early 2001 after two top international Yahoo! executives resigned and Yahoo! stock fell to $29 per share (Abrahams 2001). Given these recent events, it is unclear if Yahoo! will be able '…to preserve the company's independence, yet still keep their promise to provide anything to anyone on the WEB' (Heim 2000).

STEPHEN J. HAVLOVIC
UNIVERSITY OF WISCONSIN - WHITEWATER

Further reading

(References cited in the text marked *)

* 1st Person Personal (2001) 'Jerry Yang', *http://www.edmond.com/krt/computers/lpyang/html/1a.htm The Edmund SUN* (A brief listing of personal biographical information on Jerry Yang.)
* Abrahams, P. (2001) 'Yahoo! shares down 7% as another top executive resigns', *Financial Times*, 17–18 February: 24. (Article discusses the future of Yahoo! after recent resignations and drop in share value.)
* *Business Wire* (1998) 'Autoweb.com and Yahoo! partner to deliver biggest on-line promotion', *Business Wire*, 26 January. (News release.)
* CNET (1997) 'Yang: just for fun', *News.com – Newsmakers*. (An exclusive interview with Jerry Yang.)
* Heim, K. (2000) 'Yahoo! bucks merger trend, works to stay independent', *The Arizona Republic*, 20 April: D2. (The article discusses the independent streak of Yahoo! that has earned it the nickname of 'the Switzerland of the Internet'.)
* Hils-Cosgrove, M. (2000) 'Worth Shouting Yahoo! about? *The Scotsman*, 12 October: 4. (The article reviews Yahoo!'s performance and its shrinking pools of advertisers.)
* *http://www.yahoo.com* (Home of the Yahoo! World Wide Web directory.)
* Michelson, M. (1998) 'Yahoo! to offer services, eyes Spain', *Reuters*, 10 February. (News Release)
* Orr, A. (2000) 'Stable DOT-COMs review executive needs', *The Toronto Star*, 14 December: Section 'Business'. (A review of management teams among stable DOT-COMs such as Yahoo!.)
* Plummer, W. and Harrison, L. (1995) 'The world at their fingertips', *People*, 4 December. (Takes a look at Jerry Yang and David Filo.)
* *PR Newswire* (1996a) 'Ziff-Davis names Barry Golson editor-in-chief of Yahoo! Internet Life', *PR Newswire*, 15 February. (News release.)
* *PR Newswire* (1996b) 'Yahoo and Proctor & Gamble develop interactive traffic building promotion', *PR Newswire*, 8 May. (News release.)
* *PR Newswire* (1996c) 'Metricom announces Yahoo! co-founder and the CEO of World-Net Access join its board of directors', *PR Newswire*, 25 June. (News release.)
* *PR Newswire* (1996d) 'Cybercolumnist John Motavalli "scoops" for Yahoo! Internet Life', *PR Newswire*, 7 October. (News release.)
* Reuters (2000) 'Yahoo! won't remove Nazi memorabilia', *The Jerusalem Post*, 26 June: Section 'Jewish World' 6. (Yahoo! rejects French court order stating that it is technically impossible to scan the content of all its service sites for Nazi memorabilia.)
* Sorkin, A.R. (2000) 'Yahoo buys Taiwan Portal Company', *The New York Times*, 10 November: C6. (Announcement of Yahoo!'s purchase of Kimo.com to expand its internet offerings in Taiwan and China.)

* Stross, R.E. (1998) 'How Yahoo! won the search wars', *Fortune*, 2 March: 148–54. (Takes a look at Yahoo!'s growth and business performance.)

The Straits Times (2000) 'He gave up a PhD, but is worth billions', 28 June: Section 'Technology & Science' 52. (Review of Yang's transition from student to billionaire.)

Treanor, J.l (2000) 'Takeover trail: Yang takes Yahoo! into Europe', *The Guardian*, 16 June: Section 'Guardian City Pages': 32. (The article reviews Yahoo!'s acquisitions and expansion in Europe.)

* *Wall Street Journal* (2000) 'Who's news', 1 August: B14. (Executive updates.)

* Wylie, M. (1997) 'Barefoot millionaire boys', *News.com – Newsmakers*, 10 November. (Reviews the business successes of Jerry Yang and David Filo.)

Further resources

Yahoo! Web site
http://www.yahoo.com (Home of the Yahoo! World Wide Web directory.)

See also: E-BUSINESS; E-COMMERCE; GLOBALIZATION; INTERNET; LEADERSHIP; WORLD WIDE WEB

Yugoslavia, management in the former

Overview

Yugoslavia followed a distinctive path of economic development after the Second World War. It developed a system of economic management based on social ownership of property and decentralized decision making. This approach set it apart from the other countries of Central and Eastern Europe (CEE) which adopted the Soviet model of economic organization and management. Workers' self-management was a concept which appeared to many an alternative to both Soviet communism and capitalism.

Declining economic performance in the 1980s raised doubts about the efficacy of the Yugoslav economic system and of the way enterprises were run. With the collapse of communism and the subsequent break-up of the Yugoslav Federation, the successor states have established their own systems of economic organization, although developments have been affected by conflicts between the successor states. The relative homogeneity of management practices has begun to give way to approaches influenced by historical practices and traditions. Two major trends can be identified: in Croatia and Slovenia practice is being moulded by the legacy of the Austro-Hungarian Empire and aspirations to join the European Union; in the other successor states, because of the cultural legacy of the Orthodox variant of Christianity and of Ottoman rule, a generally autocratic model of economic organization and management is likely to become the norm.

1 Introduction

One of the tragedies of the collapse of communism in Central and Eastern Europe has been the implosion of Yugoslavia. During the Second World War (1939–45) Tito's communist partisans had played a key role in liberating Yugoslavia from Nazi occupation. After the end of the Second World War Yugoslavia established a communist regime based on the Soviet model of economic management. According to Blumberg (1968: 170) 'Yugoslavia developed more quickly along orthodox Stalinist lines than any other Communist state in Eastern Europe'. The central five-year plan of 1947 favoured the development of heavy industry, transportation and intensive rates of investment, which were to be achieved by constraining personal consumption. Prices of goods, wages and salaries and the appointment of enterprise directors were all decided centrally (see EASTERN EUROPE, MANAGEMENT IN).

Yugoslavia, however, refused to submit to the political hegemony of the Soviet Union under Stalin and in 1948 broke its links with Moscow. After this break the Soviet model of economic management was in the first instance criticized and subsequently replaced by a distinctive system of economic and enterprise management. Moreover, from the early 1950s Yugoslavia played a leading role among the nations that were aligned politically neither to the Soviet Union nor to the USA. The death of Tito in 1980 and the collapse of communism in 1989 plunged Yugoslavia into a state of internal conflict borne of nationalistic and ideological rivalries which reduced some areas of the former federal republic to 'garrison societies with little or no economic infrastructure' (Silber and Little 1995: 388) (see RUSSIA, MANAGEMENT IN).

The establishment of the Yugoslav state (initially called the Kingdom of the Serbs, Croats and Slovenes) in 1918 brought together a diverse group of Southern Slav peoples as well as non-Slav minorities such as

Albanians and Hungarians. Ethnic diversity went hand in hand with religious diversity: the Croats and Slovenians were predominantly Roman Catholic, the Serbs, Montenegrins and Macedonians were predominantly Greek Orthodox, while there was also a substantial community of Southern Slav and Albanian Muslims in the central and southern parts of the state.

Yugoslavia was therefore characterized by a high degree of internal diversity: ethnic, religious and economic (with different areas demonstrating widely diverging levels of economic wealth and development). While the Serbs were the largest ethnic group, they accounted for only somewhat more than one third of the total population.

2 The Yugoslav model

Numerous writers (for example Barratt Brown 1984), have described and analysed the Yugoslav model of socialism. Interest in the Yugoslav experience was based both on the fact that it diverged from the Soviet model and that it offered an economic model for developing countries (Zeffane 1988). The key characteristics of the Yugoslav model were social ownership of property, decentralization of decision-making, self-government and self-management of economic enterprises.

By a constitutional law of January 1953, state ownership of property was transferred to the population. This law was applied to economic enterprises and other institutions such as hospitals. These organizations were now owned and managed by various local authorities on behalf of society as a whole.

Social ownership in combination with the decentralization of government functions established a system which differed in substantial elements from the Soviet model which emphasized state ownership and control. Decentralization gave local authorities and individual organizations a key role in decision-making and the implementation of organizational plans.

With decentralized decision-making the national plan functioned as a coordinating framework for the activities of the totality of individual organizations. This aspect was fundamentally different from the Soviet model where the central plan was the starting point for the activities of individual enterprises which were each allocated production targets.

Decentralization was reinforced in the 1960s when 'ownership' of economic enterprises was transferred to the workers themselves. From the legal point of view nobody actually owned the enterprises, but in principle employees enjoyed the economic benefits of ownership. Furthermore in 1965, economic enterprises were opened up to world market forces as many import controls were removed. To a far greater degree than among the communist states of Central and Eastern Europe Yugoslav economic enterprises were subjected to the competition of Western companies and products and the free market system. A further dimension of the opening up of the Yugoslav economy was the permission given to Yugoslav workers to work abroad. Many were employed as guest workers (*Gastarbeiter*) in the Federal Republic of Germany. This latter practice benefited the Yugoslav economy in two ways: first it reduced the pressure on employment at home; second the remittances of the Yugoslav guest workers represented a valuable source of hard currency.

However, the aspect of the Yugoslav system of economic management which has possibly attracted most interest has been the concept of self-management as embodied in the worker-managed enterprise.

Self-management did not signify that workers managed the enterprise directly. In enterprises with at least 70 workers the total workforce elected a Workers' Council of at least 15 members. Members of the Workers' Council were elected for a two-year period, 50 per cent of members being renewed annually. The Workers' Council elected each year a Management Board as its executive body. The Management Board was then responsible for the appointment and dismissal of the General Director of the enterprise and for the senior managers. Appointment was normally for a four-year period and renewable. The system of self-management in Yugoslavia differed fundamentally from the Soviet model as practised in other CEE countries, where industrial organizations were in general run on a consensual basis by a combination of enterprise management, communist party and trades union.

In the early 1970s there was a further development of the concept of self-management. The so-called Basic Organizations of Associated Labour (BOAL) were introduced and became the basic unit of economic organization, a function previously fulfilled by the enterprise (Petkov and Thirkell 1991: 179). One aim of this change was to reduce the power of managers which had expanded as a result of the influence of market forces (Zeffane 1988: 413). The enterprise could in consequence be considered a federation of BOAL.

Under self-management, enterprises were involved in investment decisions, which were partly influenced by the overall plan as well as by the enterprise itself. Sources of investment funding could be either internal (by allocating part of the enterprise surplus to investment rather than wages and salaries) or external (by taking on bank loans). Interest rates for such loans were no more than nominal, never exceeding six per cent even when inflation began to soar.

Self-management may be regarded as having been successful in a number of ways (Heller *et al.* 1998): it encouraged and achieved high levels of worker participation in enterprise management, including longer-term decision making; it provided a mechanism for educating the workforce and training managers; it acted as a safety valve (participation did not eliminate conflict and Yugoslav enterprises were more prone to conflict than either British or Dutch companies [Industrial Democracy in Europe (IDE) 1981: 164]); it contributed to a substantial raising of gross national product (GNP), at the same time constraining the social pressures generally experienced under such conditions (see INDUSTRIAL DEMOCRACY).

3 Criticisms of the Yugoslav model

As well as arousing considerable interest the Yugoslav model has received a number of criticisms. Barratt Brown (1984: 65) describes the model as 'Utopian in its expectations'. In practice many workers were unwilling or ill-prepared to fulfil the role expected of them. Furthermore, the BOAL, as the basic unit of organization, tended to encourage the fragmentation of enterprises. In such circumstances enterprises and the participative organs within them tended to be dominated by managers and other professionals who deployed their superior knowledge and expertise as well as membership of the League of Communists to achieve the decisions and policies they desired. The macroeconomic benefits of self-management were also difficult to assess. While GNP had grown at an annual rate of 5.9 per cent in the 1960s and 5.4 per cent in the 1970s, this had declined to 1.2 per cent in the first half of the 1980s. Subsequently GNP actually declined in real terms. The 1980s were a decade of high and rising inflation and declining productivity. To quote Warner (1990: 23), 'What had been designed as a consensual mechanism, albeit imposed from the top, began to reveal its structural weakness!'.

4 After Yugoslavia

The early 1990s witnessed the collapse of the Yugoslav Federation. Slovenia was the first of the constituent republics to declare its independence in 1991. Subsequently Croatia, Macedonia and Bosnia-Hercegovina followed suit, leaving Serbia and Montenegro to retain the name of Yugoslavia. While the secession of Slovenia passed with limited open conflict, the 1990s saw open warfare between Croatia and Serbia as well as a civil war in Bosnia-Hercegovina (in which Croatia and Serbia also participated).

The dissolution of the Yugoslav Federation has served to accentuate the differences, including the economic differences, between the former constituent republics of Yugoslavia. The transition to independent statehood has been largely conflict-free in Slovenia and Macedonia. Bosnia-Hercegovina, on the other hand, has been ravaged by bitter warfare. Croatia (at least up to the mid 1990s) and Serbia/Montenegro have tended to focus more on issues of political sovereignty than on economic aspects of their changed circumstances. The situation in Serbia/Montenegro has been furthermore dominated by the ethnic agenda relating to the position of Serbs in Bosnia-Hercegovina and Croatia and the demands of the Albanians in the Serb region of Kosovo (which has an overwhelming Albanian majority). Economic developments have thus progressed relatively slowly in Croatia because of the conflict with Serbia and even more slowly in Serbia/Montenegro because of the preoccupation with military-territorial issues and the sanctions imposed by the international community on Serbia/Montenegro.

5 Privatization, small business and foreign direct investment

Privatization is one of the major issues facing governments engaged in the transformation of their economies and the development of market systems. In the successor states of former Yugoslavia the privatization debate has been heavily influenced by the legacy of enterprise self-management (Deškovicz 1995) (see PRIVATIZATION AND REGULATION).

The privatization scheme eventually adopted in, for example, Slovenia, is complex, the result of intense political debates. The 1992 Law on Ownership Transformation sought to prevent 'wild privatizations'. It combined the issue of certificates to citizens who could then use them to buy shares in their own or any other company that also included within its privatization programme a public offering of shares or invest them through investment funds. Proportions of shares were also reserved for internal buy-out or commercial privatization as well as for transfers to the national Pension Fund and Compensation Fund.

Croatia followed a similar approach to Slovenia, though at a slower pace and possibly with a greater degree of government control, as the Croatian government regarded the sale of enterprises as a source of income for financing unemployment and the repair of war damage (Bartlett and Bateman 1997). Parallel to the privatization of formerly socially owned enterprises governments have provided opportunities and assistance to new businesses. For example, both Croatia and Slovenia have witnessed a considerable expansion of the small business sector. This expansion has affected all sectors of the economy, but is partic-

ularly evident in trade, financial and business services and construction (Bartlett and Bateman 1997). This development has created a substantial group of business people who own and run their own companies and have a personal commitment to the market reforms.

By mid-1997 it was estimated that 50 per cent of Slovenia's and 55 per cent of Croatia's gross domestic product (GDP) originated in the private sector, a substantially lower proportion than in the Czech Republic and Hungary (European Bank for Reconstruction and Development [EBRD] 1998). The situation in the other states of former Yugoslavia is less clear although privatization is being pursued and in Macedonia too the private sector accounts for 50 per cent of GDP (EBRD 1998).

Foreign direct investment (FDI) has in many instances acted as a catalyst for privatization. Unless allocated vouchers at little or no cost, the domestic populations in CEE lack the financial resources to participate in the acquisition of companies or their shares. The volume of FDI can also be regarded as an indicator of the relative attractiveness of each country for foreign investors. Cumulative FDI inflows per head of population over the period 1989–97 amounted to US$543 for Slovenia, US$233 for Croatia and US$31 for Macedonia (EBRD 1998). FDI in the other former Yugoslav states has been minimal either because of the war situation or international sanctions.

6 From self-management to management

In the economic sphere the system of self-management has given way to the influence of system change, privatization and the development of a market economy. This transformation has been most evident in Slovenia, although Croatia, since the conclusion of hostilities, has accelerated the process. Developments in the other states of the former Yugoslavia have in general been relatively slow (in part because of the war situation, in part because of international responses, in part because of the level of economic development in the respective countries).

The situation in Slovenia can serve as an illustration of the changing situation although it needs to be borne in mind that Slovenia was the most economically advanced republic in Yugoslavia and had been in the forefront of introducing Western-style management development in CEE with the establishment of the Brdo Management School in 1986 (Warner 1990).

One survey (Bodenhöfer and Stanovnik 1992) of the views of Austrian investors underlined the relatively higher level of management abilities of Slovene managers, when compared to those of other communist economies and to those of managers in developing countries. A majority of respondents were of the opinion that the majority of Slovene managers in Austrian direct investment projects were as capable as managers in the Austrian company. Reasons cited for the relative superiority of Slovenian managers included the tradition of decentralized decision making and 'market socialism' which gave managers greater independence and responsibility for managing and developing companies and for marketing their products, in particular abroad.

Nevertheless a number of key weaknesses were also identified such as knowledge of and competence in marketing, general management and financial management. In this respect Slovene managers demonstrated similar deficiencies to those of managers throughout Central and Eastern Europe, though to a lesser degree (see MANAGEMENT EDUCATION IN CENTRAL AND EASTERN EUROPE).

In another investigation (Edwards and Lawrence 1995) senior Slovenian managers commented that the nature of managerial work had changed with the demise of self-management. One manager commented that self-management had been 'beautiful for those who had wanted to just put their feet up'! Considerable managerial time had been expended in attending various boards and committees and the initial impetus from self-management had soon dried up.

With the end of self-management managers enjoyed in general a lower intensity of work and also more discretion to exercise managerial prerogative. However, managers also indicated that external pressures had increased and there was generally more pressure on them.

7 The future

The former Yugoslavia was characterized by cultural, ethnic and economic diversity. The differences between the successor states are likely to persist. Diversity may become increasing divergence. The former economic system created a certain homogeneity of approach. This has now disappeared and two main lines of development seem to be emerging.

Slovenia and Croatia are strongly oriented to West European values and affiliations. Slovenia, together with the Czech Republic, Estonia, Hungary and Poland, is one of a first group of CEE countries to gain admission to the European Union (EU). Croatia is regarded as a possible candidate for a second group of EU aspirants, provided that it succeeds in establishing democratic institutions acceptable to existing EU members. Management in both Croatia and Slovenia therefore will become more integrated into Western European approaches and practices. In view of both countries' historical legacies and current aspirations, the development of Croatian and Slovenian management will tend towards practices in Germany and Austria.

The situation in the other successor states of former Yugoslavia is more difficult to ascertain. The future of these countries appears less certain because of general political instability and relative poverty. The respective legacies of the Orthodox Church and Ottoman rule would suggest, however, that management would tend to be autocratic (Hickson and Pugh 1995: 134). Somewhat paradoxically, the legacy of self-management will persist, albeit diluted in the form of codetermination translated from German practice, to a greater extent in Croatia and Slovenia than in the other successor states of Yugoslavia which hitherto have made less progress from the structures and practices of the former socialist federation.

VINCENT EDWARDS
BUCKINGHAMSHIRE CHILTERNS UNIVERSITY COLLEGE

Further reading

(References cited in the text marked *)

* Barratt Brown, M. (1984) *Models in Political Economy*, London: Penguin. (A presentation and discussion of models of capitalist and socialist economies, including the Yugoslav model.)
* Bartlett, W. and Bateman, M. (1997) 'The business culture in Croatia and Slovenia', in M. Bateman (ed.), *Business Cultures in Central and Eastern Europe*, Oxford: Butterworth-Heinemann, 88–127. (Traces the transformation process in a range of CEE countries, including Croatia and Slovenia.)
* Blumberg, P. (1968) *Industrial Democracy*, London: Constable. (Chapters 8 and 9 are devoted to workers' management in Yugoslavia and are particularly interesting for the account of the origins and early experience of self-management.)
* Bodenhöfer, H.-J. and Stanovnik, P. (eds) (1992) *Wirtschaftsreform in Slowenien und Wirtschaftskooperation Slowenien–Österreich*, Klagenfurt and Ljubljana. (Covers the transformation in Slovenia and aspects of cooperation with Austria.)
* Deškovicz, D. (1995) 'Corporate governance in Slovenia: Transformation from self-management to codetermination', in R. Culpan and B. Kumar (eds), *Transformation Management in Postcommunist Countries, Organizational Requirements for a Market Economy*, Westport CT: Quorum Books, 61–70. (The entry reviews developments in corporate governance in Slovenia. The book is a collection of entries on a broad variety of themes relating to company transformation.)
* EBRD (1998) *Annual Report 1997*, London: EBRD. (The annual report of the European Bank for Reconstruction and Development containing information and data on the EBRD's activities in CEE.)
* Edwards, V. and Lawrence, P. (1995) 'The transition to capitalism in Slovenia', Chalfont St Giles: Buckinghamshire Business School Research Paper 3/95. (An analysis of the economic transformation in Slovenia, with data obtained from interviews with senior managers in Slovene companies.)
* Granick, D. (1975) *Enterprise Guidance in Eastern Europe*, Princeton: Princeton University Press. (A study of enterprise management in East Germany, Hungary, Romania and Yugoslavia, based on field research conducted in 1970–71.)
* Heller, F., Pusi, E., Strauss, G. and Wilpert, B. (1998) *Organizational Participation*, Oxford: Oxford University Press. (Described as a valedictory volume, presenting and evaluating many years of research into participation in economic organizations, including self-management.)
* Hickson, D. and Pugh, D. (1995) *Management Worldwide*, London: Penguin. (A treatment of management from the viewpoint of national and regional cultures, with a chapter devoted to the East-Central Europeans.)
* IDE (1981) *Industrial Democracy in Europe*, Oxford: Clarendon Press. (The Industrial Democracy in Europe International Research Group findings on national schemes for employee participation. The project included Yugoslavia and involved Yugoslav academics. The IDE (1981) research was replicated ten years later and the findings were published in IDE (1993) *Industrial Democracy in Europe Revisited*, Oxford: Oxford University Press.)
* Petkov, K. and Thirkell, J. (1991) *Labour Relations in Eastern Europe*, London: Routledge. (Covers the development of labour relations in CEE in the period preceding and at the demise of communism.)
* Silber, L. and Little, A. (1995) *The Death of Yugoslavia*, London: Penguin/BBC. (A blow-by-blow account of the internecine strife in the former Yugoslavia up to mid-1994.)
* Warner, M. (1990) 'Management versus self-management in Yugoslavia', *Journal of General Management* 16: 20–38. (An assessment of the transition from self-management to more orthodox management approaches in Yugoslavia.)
* Zeffane, R. (1988) 'Participative management in centrally planned economies: Algeria and Yugoslavia', *Organization Studies* 9: 393–422. (A comparison of economic management in Yugoslavia and Algeria [both non-aligned nations].)

See also: ALGERIA, MANAGEMENT IN; CZECH AND SLOVAK REPUBLICS, MANAGEMENT IN THE; EASTERN EUROPE, MANAGEMENT IN; ECONOMIES OF CENTRAL AND EASTERN EUROPE, TRANSITION OF; EUROPE, MANAGEMENT IN; GLOBALIZATION; HUNGARY, MANAGEMENT IN; MANAGEMENT EDUCATION IN CENTRAL AND EASTERN EUROPE; POLAND, MANAGEMENT IN; PRIVATIZATION AND REGULATION; RUSSIA, MANAGEMENT IN; WORLD BANK

Z

zaibatsu: see KEIRETSU (ZAIBATSU)

Zambia, management in

Overview

Management in Zambia and the parastatal sector grew as a result of the nationalization policies which have existed since the 1970s. The overall economic policy evolved around a static command economy which allowed the government to provide financial and administrative capacities to manage commerce and industry. The economy in Zambia is unbalanced and heavily dependent on supplies and markets outside the country. The political system is trying to unite disparate peoples and to establish an orderly effective mechanism for governing and for directing development.

Zambia's economy is overwhelmingly dependent on copper mining. Over 92 per cent of the values of Zambian exports and 60 per cent of government revenue are directly derived from this industry. At the time of independence, virtually all of the transportation facilities and sources of power essential to Zambia's copper industry were located in territory controlled by white minority regimes. Political tensions between Zambia and these governments necessitated the heavy costs of developing alternative transportation routes and power supplies. Imbalances in Zambia's economy are not only related to copper. Very little development has taken place in the 290,000 square miles of Zambia except along the single existing railway line that runs north–south through the centre of the country.

The political and economic need of extending economic development to the rest of the country is a matter of the highest urgency.

1 Introduction

Zambia began its existence as an independent country when Northern Rhodesia, a British protectorate in central Africa, became the independent Republic of Zambia on 24 October 1964; this First Republic ended in December 1972. The independence constitution, which has allowed multi-party competition, was then amended to provide for a one party participatory democracy. The Second Republic was inaugurated and its government institutions elaborated during 1973.

Its existence as an independent country began with only 1200 citizens with secondary school certificates and 104 with college degrees. This number was hardly adequate to satisfy the demands for an improvement in the material conditions of living, to perform the non-development tasks of government and to operate the world's second most productive copper industry. Moreover, because of racial barriers to advancement during the colonial period, few Africans could claim any experience in a position of meaningful responsibility. In other words, experience did not compensate for a lack of formal training.

This entry charts the historical background of Zambia's colonial rule and analyses the emergence of the civil servants and parastatal companies in Zambia's bid to operate effectively in the world economy.

2 Colonial rule and its consequences

The BSA Company ruled Zambia from 1890 to 1924 for mainly economic reasons. It handed over its administrative role to the British Colonial office. Britain, although allowing local European settlers a progressively larger say in government, retained ultimate control of the territory until Independence. Britain did, however, permit the creation of the Central African Federation which united southern and northern Rhodesia with Nyasaland, under the control of predominantly southern Rhodesian whites.

In the 1930s, copper began to be exploited on a large scale. This led, on the one hand, to a rapid and large increase in the number of Europeans in the country, and, on the other, to the formation of the powerful African mine workers union in 1949.

Even before this, African protest against colonial rule had begun with the emergence of the Northern Rhodesian Colonial system in the first half of the nineteenth century. It not only shaped the nationalist movement – which emerged to oppose and eventually overthrow it – but has also had consuming consequences for Zambia since Independence. Northern Rhodesia Colonialism was an extension of white South Colonial rule, which involved the introduction into northern Rhodesia of European and Asian minorities. While the former monopolized managerial, professional and skilled artisan occupations, the latter (although much smaller) conducted much of the country's mid-range retail commerce. Both groups were deeply committed to a private enterprise economy, although at the same time few of them were prepared in 1964 to take out Zambian citizenship or to invest in long-term projects essential to the development of the economy.

Paradoxically their dominant position in the economic structure forced the UNIP (a non-racialist party) to draw a non-racialist policy. It was at this time that many of its African supporters deeply resented the wealth, exploitation, social exclusiveness and arrogance of these minorities. Citizenship policy and fears of 'Paper Zambians' were recurrent issues throughout the First and Second Republics.

The European minority also successfully institutionalized racialist practices against the African majority: wage discrimination, exclusion from many occupations and social facilities, segregated public services. While racialism created a convenient target for the nationalist movement, it also created a series of post-independence problems. Many Europeans left precipitately after 1963, before indigenous citizens had been trained to replace them. Perhaps most of all the continuing economic clearance between Africans and other racial groups has diverted popular attention from the evolving inter-African class formation which has taken place as independence paved the way to African entry into the private sector and domination of the public bureaucracy.

3 Government and administration: First and Second Republics

Industrial participatory democracy

Under the President Dr Kenneth Kaunda, the UNIP government issued the policy of Industrial Participatory Democracy. This policy decision was to actively involve workers in the management of industries (see INDUSTRIAL DEMOCRACY). The ideal version of the industrial participatory democracy stipulates that:

1 Workers and progressive managerial elements should seize 'power from a few who have organized to exploit the working people'.
2 Workers and progressive managers are charged with the responsibility of managing the seized industries.
3 Gaining the skills of production by workers represents the initial step towards equity in the distributing income.
4 Workers participation in industries also placed upon them the moral responsibility to promote the interests of the peasants.
5 Workers participation in industrial enterprises is essential for the realization of the moral goal and of promoting the interests of the common man (see Industrial Relations Act 1971 Part II: 98–9).

The more practical implementation of the industrial participatory democracy or the works council calls for the promotion of efficient participation of the workers in the affairs of industry for which the works council was established. It also envisages some considerable degree of influence by the workers in the management of industries.

The UNIP also introduced radical programmes of administrative decentralization in order to increase and widen the scope of liaison between local administration, the party, government administration and parastatal organizations. In operational terms, the policy of administrative decentralization followed in the wake of local government reforms which placed a cabinet minister at the head of each of Zambia's nine provinces with a permanent secretary who functions as Chief Civil Servant in the provinces to assist him. Industries in Zambia are either state-owned and controlled by the civil service or are parastatal companies, the interim stage of the country's privatization programme.

4 The civil service

In 1971, 'grass-root' participatory structures came into effect with the introduction of the Registration and Development of Villages Act. The functions of the village productivity committees, ward councils and ward committees serve as the basic units of local administration to the rural areas, responsible for:

1 maintenance of law and order, promotion of commercial services and community interests;
2 interpreting national electives and policies in terms of their applicability to local needs and to transmit local interests and aspirations to the national decision-making structures;
3 economically, to promote rural development and the spirit of self-reliance, including the employment of the institutions and faculties provided by the government to achieve this objective;
4 formation and implementation of rural development policies, assisting in the promotion of health and education, establishment and maintenance of local welfare services or amenities.

However, the Zambian civil service suffers from a number of internal weaknesses, including the lack of sufficient coordination and communication between ministries and their field staff, over-centralization, a bureaucratic structure and procedures, a lack of financial control, and cases of official corruption and accidents. The parastatal sector has also been criticized for financial indiscipline and inefficiency, which has led to its growing dependence on central government subsidies and grants.

Over-centralization and overburdening of the top level hierarchy have had serious effects on the civil service's ability to implement the second National Development Plan. Technical departments still had to be handled by expatriate officers recruited from overseas.

The morale of the civil service has been adversely affected not only by the poor quality of personnel management but also by the erosion of the principle of political neutrality. Top civil servants worry about job security whilst those below them wonder whether proved political loyalty will be a more important criterion for promotion than administrative or technical efficiency. In these circumstances, it is not surprising that many civil servants have either resigned from the service to join private companies or have transferred to the parastatal sector (see HUMAN RESOURCE MANAGEMENT IN THE EMERGING COUNTRIES).

5 Parastatal companies

Parastatal companies refer to those institutions created by government for implementing development programmes or for supplying essential services which by the nature and magnitude of the capital involved cannot be left to free enterprise. They are set up by Acts of Parliament and are an arm of the government. The Acts of Parliament set out their objectives, duties and powers, while policy matters and the day-to-day running of these enterprises is the concern of the Board of Directors. Parastatal companies are not supposed to be bound by civil service red tape and should be in a position to take major decisions by themselves within the scope of their powers but subject to certain safeguards in the national interest. In short, parastatal companies encompass state companies, state trading corporations, utility corporations, regulatory commissions and marketing boards.

The state companies, unlike statutory corporations, are established under the ordinary company law of Zambia and some shares may be in private hands. It is the form used when governments want to enter into partnership with foreign private investors.

The economic rationale for the creation of parastatal companies is in the assumption that:

1 Efficiency can be achieved to a higher degree than is possible if the enterprise is run by a government department or ministry.
2 There will be freedom of initiative, and the possibility of quick decisions and more flexible policies and methods.
3 As a result, the corporation will be in a position to run the enterprise at a profit.
4 As a government-run organization, the people are the ultimate owners of the enterprise. Thus the profits accrued from their operations are public money and can be fully utilized in the public interest, e.g. by reducing consumer prices for the products.
5 Although public corporations are expected to operate as a business and produce a profit, they are also expected to provide better employment opportunities for citizens. It is generally believed that the big expatriate-owned commercial and industrial enterprises in the country could employ more people and offer more generous conditions than at present if they were less profit-oriented. Thus, public corporations should be motivated by social welfare and profit at the same time.
6 Profits made by state-owned corporations, unlike those of private enterprises, could be ploughed back into the domestic economy while most of the profit made by foreign-owned enterprises, on average, benefit the expatriates. In other words, the income from public corporations can produce and multiply economic effects of the country and bring about economic development.

Mismanagement of parastatal companies

Since the inception of parastatal companies, the experience in Zambia has shown that very few of these economic expectations have been met. Numerous factors have characterized their operation, including staffing problems, the cost of equipment and quality of service, financial management, politics and trade unions.

Staffing

Over-staffing occurs when the staff strength of a corporation exceeds the volume of work which it is intended to cope with, and vice versa (see HUMAN RESOURCE MANAGEMENT; INDUSTRIAL AND LABOUR RELATIONS). The result is that corporations lose money through under utilization of capacity. The Zambian experience is dotted with perennial troubles arising from the threat of or actual mass retrenchments and from anxieties over delays in paying staff regular wages. Another aspect of this problem is having too much stable employment. Rather than hiring on a day-to-day basis or on a piecework basis, staff are given tenure, thus causing a perpetual burden on the funds of the corporation concerned. One of the results of this is that tenure tends to reduce alertness, dedication and diligence and therefore aggravates human obstacles.

Over-staffing not only reduces the profit margin of the enterprise concerned but also reduces the total output per person. The problems of over-staffing in Zambia have been necessitated through political patronage. Heads of parastatal companies were appointed by the President and cabinet ministers and felt an obligation to employ relatives of politicians.

Most parastatal companies follow the civil service tradition of hierarchical levels of personnel when in fact, these roles could be dispensed with and one or two persons could do the job more effectively.

The wage rate of parastatal companies in Zambia is higher than those of the government although total benefits, including job security, may compare unfavourably with those of the latter. Fringe benefits and conditions of service differ from one corporation to another. The problem here is that wage rates and fringe benefits are not determined by economic realities, such as the size of profits or output per worker, but fixed even before the corporations begin to operate.

High cost of equipment

Many parastatal companies have to import most, if not all their capital equipment. Costs are naturally high, especially since some are not exempt from large import duties. Expectations of profit must take into account heavy maintenance costs as well as the considerable time lag needed to offset the heavy sums initially invested.

Uncompetitive or low quality products and services

Most parastatal companies produce services rather than goods. In recent years there have been constant public complaints about the quality of service provided by parastatals. As far as goods are concerned, there has been the persistent impression that locally manufactured goods are inferior in quality and much higher in price than imported goods. The result is the continued importation of foreign brands.

6 Financial management

Another serious aspect of financial mismanagement is the over-pricing of contracts and the attendant kickbacks for top level personnel. The result is that large amounts of money earmarked for investment do not take the corporations as far as they were expected to do because only part of this money is actually invested.

Socio-political factors

The intervention of politics into the affairs of parastatal companies has been a major problem both in the First and Second Republics of Zambia. Unprofitable ideologies like Humanism in Zambia and the First National Development Plan were implemented unsuccessfully. Their failure is due to political interference in the running of the companies, especially through the politically influenced appointments of senior management staff. Other areas in which political intervention is manifested include the award of major contracts and determination of further investments.

7 Industrial relations and trade unions

The role of the trade unions is unclear. Labour relations are seen as merely working for the employees and working out what they can get from the corporations. Few if any assess the efficiency and productivity of workers as a basis for demands for higher pay and better working conditions. Cases have arisen where unions have put pressure on directors to recall workers dismissed for theft or those who have retired after reaching retrenchment age. Such frivolous or one-sided demands have resulted in a discipline problem and a workforce that is demotivated.

However, it is also important to state that labour organizations have helped in the development of public corporations generally. Unions often provide checks on board and management prone to tribalism, corruption or applying partisan political considerations in the running of the company. The extent to which they can continue to be constructive or destructive will depend on the opportunities provided at state and national levels and also on the education of trade union leadership (see HUMAN RESOURCE MANAGEMENT IN THE EMERGING COUNTRIES; INDUSTRIAL RELATIONS IN THE EMERGING COUNTRIES; TRADE UNIONS).

8 Conclusion

An efficient management is indispensable to the success of a public corporation, especially if it is expected to operate as a competitive business and make profits. Corporation management in Zambia is handicapped by the lack of sufficient management experience, as is seen in most developing countries.

The Movement for Multiparty Democracy (MMD), the ruling party in Zambia, have identified the parastatal sector as a primary obstacle to economic growth. They have indicated their intentions to relinquish the government's role in running business and revert back to its traditional role as a provider of services to the people – for example health, education, infrastructure and social welfare.

To ensure the Zambian economy does not collapse, a Structural Adjustment Programme has been embarked upon. Part of this programme of change is the introduction of the privatization policy and the establishment of the Zambia Privatisation Agency (ZPA). Through the privatization policy, the Zambian government intends to divest all the 150 parastatal companies except, possibly, a few public utilities.

VICTOR MUHANDU
ZAMBIA PRIVATISATION AGENCY

Further reading

(References cited in the text marked *)

Dado, R.H. (1971) *Unions, Parties and Political Development: A Study of Mineworkers Union in Zambia*, New Haven, CT and London: Yale University Press. (Useful study of trade unions and industrial relations in Zambia.)

Dresang, D.L. (1975) *The Zambia Civil Service: Entreprenuerialism and Development Administration*, Kenya: East African Publishing House. (Informative book on the emergence of the Zambian civil service and its introduction of policies and administration.)

* Industrial Relations Act No. 36 (1971) and its supplement Statutory Instrument no 206 (13/12/74) Zambia: Government Printers. (Contains Kenneth Kaunda's legal sanction of the IPD policy.)

Kaunda, K.D. (1987) *Humanism in Zambia and a Guide to its Implementation Part I*, Zambia: Zambia Information Services. (Kaunda's policy of humanism and its development into national policies.)

Makoba Wagona, J. (1998) *Government Policy and Public Enterprise Performance in Sub-Saharan Africa: The case studies of Tanzania and Zambia, 1964–1984*, New York: Edwin Mellen Press. (Investigates the impact of state development policies of nationalization, Africanization and import substitution industrialization (ISI) on the activities and performance of selected industrial public enterprises or parastatal organizations.)

Mphaisha, C.J.J. (1988) *State of National Politics and Government*, Zambia: Kenneth Kaunda Foundation. (Good primary source of information on the political development of Zambia.)

Mpuku, H.C. and Zyuulu, I. (1997) *Contemporary Issues in Socio-economic Reform in Zambia*, Aldershot: Ashgate Publishing Ltd. (This text examines the attempts and potential pitfalls of the reform programme and argues that while reform is a necessary condition for economic rebirth, it needs to ensure it has the desired socioeconomic impact on Zambian society.)

Ollas, P.E. (1979) *Participatory Democracy in Zambia: The Political Economy of National Development*, Devon: Arthur H. Stockwell Ltd. (Discusses the introduction of national development in Zambia and its implications for the political economy.)

Rweyemamu, A.H. and Goran, H. (1971) *A Decade of Public Administration*, Kenya: East African Literature Bureau. (Overview of the key events of public administration policies.)

Turok, B. (1979) *A Development in Zambia: A Reader*, London: Zed Press. (Provides a detailed account of the social and political evolution of Zambia.)

United National Independence Party (UNIP) *The National Policies for the Decade 1985-1995*, Zambia: Office of the Secretary General. (Aims and objectives of the Third Phase of the Party Programme.)

Zulu, J. B. (1970) *Zambia Humanism*, Zambia: National Education Company of Zambia, Ltd. (Discussion of the spiritual and economic challenges in Zambia.)

See also: BUSINESS CULTURES IN THE EMERGING COUNTRIES; HUMAN RESOURCE MANAGEMENT IN THE EMERGING COUNTRIES; INDUSTRIAL RELATIONS IN THE EMERGING COUNTRIES; MANAGEMENT EDUCATION IN THE EMERGING COUNTRIES; NIGERIA, MANAGEMENT IN; SOUTH AFRICA, MANAGEMENT IN; ZIMBABWE, MANAGEMENT IN

Zimbabwe, management in

1 Introduction
2 Context
3 Specific features
4 Conclusion

Overview

Contemporary business and management practices in Zimbabwe emerged during the 1960s and there has been gradual integration of the latest management styles and techniques ever since. Contemporary management approaches commonly found in the country are reflective of the long way the system has come. The new domestic economic scenario and globalization have also brought new dimensions and challenges to management in the country.

The management style in Zimbabwean organizations has been mainly inward looking and strongly defined by a top-down approach in decision making. However, over the past eight years there has been a gradual opening up, accompanied by a shift toward participative management.

1 Introduction

The current practice of management in Zimbabwe is mainly defined by the economic and political milestones of the past three decades. The changes brought a lot of uncertainties and sometimes anxiety to the process of management both in the private and public sector, thus at times rendering experiential knowledge redundant.

The 1966 imposition of sanctions by the United Nations led to the development of business and management practices premised on protectionist tendencies, reflected in policies such as import substitution, official foreign currency allocation and domestic-oriented management. This scenario moulded management that locked itself away from knowledge systems that were developing outside the national boundaries. The attainment of political independence in 1980 saw the opening up of the economy, giving a jolt to the domestic-oriented management; this opened the economy to international competition and management practices. However, this reorientation did not come into being until 1990 when the economy was forced to adopt an Economic Structural Adjustment programme. The adoption of the programme marked an important watershed in the practice of business and management, as the country shifted from a socialist orientation to a market-oriented economy. Management had to adapt quickly to the new dispensation or risk sinking.

2 Context

Labour and political change

Changes in the labour sector have seen a consolidation of growth in trade unionism over the past twenty years. In 1980, a trade union organization, the Zimbabwe Congress of Trade Unions, was formed to represent the interests of the national labour. Prior to the formation of the labour body, small fragmented groups had represented workers with subscriptions from a few thousand employees (see TRADE UNIONS). The main trade union body's membership has fluctuated quite significantly in the past few years, mainly exhibiting a downward trend due to closures and retrenchment. The Labour Relations Act (1985) sought to protect the worker and, in the process, made it virtually impossible for employers to dismiss or retrench some of the workers. The government, as part of its socialist philosophy, legislated minimum wages across the board. Further, the government strengthened the role of trade unions and works councils in the name of the welfare of the employee. Management in both the public and private sectors had to abide by stipulations of the legislation, to the detriment of productivity. Politically it became anathema to challenge the position of the legislature. Thus the government usurped the management decision-making function on fundamental corporate aspects such as wages and salaries determination, market prices and investment in capital goods.

The development of labour representation has, of course, led to fair employment practices, fair promotion practices, and a focusing of management on the needs of general employees. Participative decision making, especially on issues directly affecting labour, is now the new accepted culture. Since 1991 both employers and employees have had to learn negotiating skills very quickly as the government adopted market policies. Until 1998 trade unions were focused on bargaining for workers with employers. In 1999 they became politically active. The main trade union body formed a political party whose main support base is ordinary workers. The party is also supported by industry. This scenario has created a situation where government on one hand, and labour and industry on the other, now mistrust each other (see INDUSTRIAL RELATIONS IN THE EMERGING COUNTRIES).

Socio-economic factors

In late 1990, the government adopted Phase I of an Economic Structural Adjustment programme, backed by the IMF and World Bank, which remained in operation until 1996. The thrust of the structural adjustment programme was to open up the economy and introduce free market policies. It was therefore imperative for domestic firms to adapt and adjust management style to the new reality of external competition and removal of protectionist policies. It was necessary to upgrade the management resource base and modernize production systems. In response, management processes in most companies have witnessed an increase in strategic planning, corporate re-engineering, marketing re-orientation, and management training and development. Government, for its part, began the process of commercialization and privatization of public enterprises. In both cases there has been an apparent demand for professional and experienced managers in all sectors of the economy. Trends remain biased

towards Western management principles, reflecting an overlay of cultural and societal influences with respect to the conduct of managerial work. This has brought about a new management ethic with respect to leadership, competition and customer service (see AFRICA, MANAGEMENT IN; INTERNATIONAL MONETARY FUND; WORLD BANK).

Although economic growth has averaged no more than 2 per cent in the 1990s, population growth has been unsustainably high at between 2.8 and 3.1 per cent during the same period. Unemployment is officially estimated at 45 per cent. Whereas employment grew by 2.4 per cent on average during the period 1985–90, it decreased to about 0.6 per cent during the period 1990–5 (Kanyenze 1998). Although during the 1980s downsizing, particularly through retrenchment, was not a common feature, since adoption of structural adjustment in 1991 retrenchment has become one of the commonest strategies to improve or return companies to performance. During the early part of the structural adjustment programme, the retrenchments focused mainly on shop-floor workers. However, managerial-level employees soon got involved as companies attempted to make management structures leaner, flatter and more focused. This is also aimed at improving productivity of ordinary employees and managers. In some instances companies have gone to the extreme of completely dispensing with the middle management layer. Bahrami (1992) noted that: 'The de-layering and downsizing trend was initially triggered by the need to reduce costs. Increased use of information technologies ... has ... reduced the need for traditional middle management, whose role was to supervise others and collect, analyze, evaluate, and transmit information up, down, and across the organizational hierarchy'. The need for turnaround strategies has necessitated the replacement of top management. The dwindling of the domestic market, the intensification of competition from imports and the lack of new investment have now led to serious liquidations in sectors such as textiles and clothing. Large textile and clothing companies such as Cone Textiles and Fashion Enterprises had to close operations completely as competition intensified. This is coupled with the fact that by April 2000 inflation was 48.9 per cent, having come down from a high of 70 per cent in December 1999. Interest rates went up to 68 per cent and the local currency has depreciated by over 60 per cent since November 1997 when the country experienced a 75 per cent crash of the local currency. This has presented management with a complicated socio-economic scenario that has seen change management becoming a topical issue (Quinn 1980). In reality, change management has become a strategic reference point in itself. The turbulent environment that has been in the country since 1997 has also seen companies introduce highly innovative control measures reminiscent of the sanctions era to keep costs to the barest minimum. It has also forced companies to tighten tolerance levels with respect to deviation from both operational and strategic plans.

Structural factors

The economic influence of the corporate sector has been mainly concentrated in a few companies, although this is gradually changing. Companies such as TA Holdings, Delta Corporation, Anglo American, Lonrho and Old Mutual have been wielding a lot of economic power but that scenario has recently been changing with the introduction of the concept of 'indigenization'. For example, TA Holdings, one of the largest conglomerates in the country during the 1980s, has gone through three restructuring exercises within five years. At each stage the exercise has involved trimming off some business units to concentrate on core businesses. It is now under the control of black investors. Old Mutual undertook a de-mutualization process concluded in 1999 that left policyholders the local shareholders of the local subsidiary.

Managerial control, especially at director level, has recently seen new faces being brought in. The traditional situation was a closed system with a small number of people circulating around most of the boards. The situation is worse in public enterprises where political patronage determines appointment to boards. The Institute of Directors, a forum representing the interests of directors in both private and public enterprises, has been lobby-

ing its members to bring in new directors with new ideas. With changes in the racial composition of the top management of most highly rated companies, blacks are now also well represented at director level. However, there remains a serious lack of female representation at top management level, and especially at director level.

3 Specific features

Management styles in private companies

Management styles commonly found in Zimbabwe are a hybrid of Western approaches, the autocratic approaches of the socialist era, and the indigenous top-down approach (Khumalo 1999). The indigenous approaches mainly centre on paternalistic tendencies where seniority and good decision making are equated. This approach tends to create senior management who favour use of the top-down approach. Leadership is slowly shifting from a task-oriented approach to an employee-oriented approach. Change management has not been adopted easily, although some companies, such as Commercial Bank of Zimbabwe, Merspin, and Zimbabwe Spinners and Weavers have succeeded in turning around their huge organizations, moving from serious losses only a few years ago to acclaimed profit.

With high inflation, high interest rates, a depreciating currency, shortage of foreign currency, and at times shortage of fuel, management in Zimbabwe has been adopting new approaches mainly centred on high productivity and maximization of value for money (Thompson 2001). The unreliability of the domestic market has now made management outward-oriented. This has also been a result of globalization whose impact is now being felt by industry. The management style now commonly applied is participative management where workers – through the works councils – are expected to participate in major decisions. Management wants workers at all levels to feel they have ownership of major decisions in the company. Participative management has been observed to be a central attribute among Zimbabwe's top companies registered on the Zimbabwe Stock Exchange (Khumalo 1999). To some extent team building, with its pluralistic approach to problem solving, is becoming a widely used tool in some companies, especially high-tech companies in highly competitive sectors. Companies in the cellular phone business in Zimbabwe, i.e. Econet, Telecel and Net*One, have successfully been using the teamwork approach, although with varying degrees of success.

The organizational culture now widely prevalent in companies is defined by group cooperation where workers and employers are all of one vision (see ORGANIZATION CULTURE). This culture has grown stronger over the past decade as companies have liquidated due to economic hardships. Workers now feel just as responsible as management, for the survival of the company also means survival of their welfare and therefore they should participate in decision making. To strengthen the idea of ownership and responsibility, companies such as APEX Corporation now reward workers with stocks in the company.

Management training and development

Management training in Zimbabwe is grounded in Western concepts and the emphasis is on the gradual development of employees toward managerial positions as they attain seniority in the workplace (see MANAGEMENT EDUCATION IN THE EMERGING COUNTRIES). Although other, shorter routes to attaining managerial status are also in use, both in the private and public sectors, the emphasis on seniority is still highly important in Zimbabwe. Bates (1993: 70) notes that seniority in Zimbabwe has traditionally been a major consideration in the promotion of staff, especially in government and parastatal organizations. Shorter routes mainly involve employees who enter managerial positions through graduate trainee or cadet programmes. Such graduate trainees hold degrees in Business and Commerce. Recently, large commercial banks such as Standard Chartered Bank and Barclays Bank have recruited trainees at mid-career level. Such trainees go through an accelerated training for immediate deployment in responsible management positions. Employees with higher qualifications such as

MBA, MA or MSc are almost always recruited for the top posts. In the case of top posts, employers also demand a number of years of experience. Increasingly, managerial positions are now being filled by employees whose backgrounds are in disciplines such as engineering, psychology, and sometimes the hard sciences such as chemistry and biochemistry. In one such recruitment exercise the Posts and Telecommunications Corporation, which is in the process of commercialization with the eventual intention to privatize, has insisted on recruiting top managers with an MBA majoring in information technology.

Managerial positions are more or less equally shared on a 50:50 basis between blacks and whites in the private sector. In the public sector, blacks occupy no fewer than 80 per cent of the managerial positions. Women managers occupy 15–20 per cent of the positions in both the private and public sectors. Women in general only account for 16.5 per cent of waged employment in the country. A complex set of factors such as socio-cultural mores and behavioural expectations, as well as organizational policies and practices, influence women's opportunities to get into decision-making management positions (Dirasse 1991).

Companies in Zimbabwe have always tended to take two routes through which to develop their managers. First, managers have been sent into business schools for further training. Second, managers have been groomed internally through a career path that ensures their suitability, even though some may not be products of business schools. In business schools, managers are normally enrolled into MBAs or executive development programmes. The degrees are mainly awarded by any one of the four major universities in the country, i.e. University of Zimbabwe, National University of Science and Technology, Africa University and Solusi University. Seven new universities have just been established and they have also shown interest in offering training in management, especially at executive level. The University of Zimbabwe, which was the only university in the country until 1990, has trained about 1500 MBA graduates since 1986. Professional institutes such as Zimbabwe Institute of Management, Institute of Personnel Management, Chartered Institute of Secretaries and Administrators and the Institute of Chartered Accountants, which all offer certificates and diplomas, have also made a significant contribution to management training in the country. To promote human resource development, the government has also offered scholarships for training nationals in countries such as the USA, UK, Canada, Australia and others. At independence in 1980 a lot of managers who had been trained in former Eastern-bloc countries also entered both the private and the public sectors. The curriculum offered by business schools in the country is naturally biased towards Western management principles. However, there is an integration of these management principles with the political and socio-cultural traditional dimensions on aspects such as loyalty and leadership (see LEADERSHIP).

Companies in Zimbabwe spend on average 5–10 per cent of their human resources development budgets on management development. Although in Zimbabwe there is no forum that represents the interests of particular racial groups in management, blacks in management have moved up the ladder in relatively larger proportions than other groups. This is a result of intense lobbying by the government and Affirmative Action Group (a black empowerment group) in the country. For example, the Affirmative Action Group has so far forced multinationals in the country, such as Standard Chartered Bank, to identify potential understudies of the Chief Executive of the company. The tradition in major multinationals has been to appoint the chief executive from outside the ranks of local professionals. The argument of the Affirmative Action Group is that appointing the chief executive from outside means that no Zimbabwean will ever have the opportunity of heading the company. Other multinationals, such as Anglo American Corporation, have also come under intense scrutiny by lobby groups due to the tendency to fill chief executive posts with appointees from outside the country.

Management in public enterprises

The post-independence era witnessed an increase in the number of public enterprises as the government sought to strengthen its involvement in economic affairs and broaden accessibility to services offered by such enterprises. For those public enterprises that were already in operation, the exodus of white managers due to political uncertainty created a new challenge. It created a serious management skills vacuum in public enterprises. As a result, the new government appointed mainly inexperienced black managers into key management positions in these enterprises. In an effort to bridge the skills gap, the government also introduced staff training and development programmes, locally and abroad.

Management in public enterprises has no autonomy in determining policy and strategy, unlike the culture in the private sector, due to interference by politicians. Managers are involved more in programmed decisions than non-programmed decisions, irrespective of rank. The only material difference between one rank and the next is in the scope and depth of programmed decisions the manager can handle. Politicians influence aspects relating to work organization, purchase and supply (through a government-sanctioned tender system), corporate strategy, and the selection of top management. In most cases management ideas are considered to be at variance with the government interests and thus have often led to dismissal of managers. Thus companies such as Zimpapers, Zimbabwe Broadcasting Corporation, Zimbabwe Electricity Supply Authority, Zisco Steel, Posts and Telecommunications Corporation, etc., have lost good managers due to political meddling in managerial autonomy and decision making. Managers in public enterprises are sometimes rewarded, not for their managerial capability and entrepreneurial acumen, but rather for their capacity to adapt and enforce government policy. Internal control systems are also quite weak in public enterprises compared to the private sector. This has led to managers in public enterprises being involved in corrupt deals. Recently the entire top management of The National Oil Company of Zimbabwe was dismissed. Some of the managers have been arraigned on corruption charges. A similar situation has taken place at the Grain Marketing Board. In both instances weaknesses have been observed to lie in porous internal control systems and interference by politicians with corrupt intentions. Overall, the management philosophy in public enterprises has been a fusion of cultural and political factors that have sacrificed professionalism in many respects.

In view of this analysis, it is apparent that managers in public enterprises are recruited not to ensure profitability and high return to the shareholder – mainly the government – but to ensure government control. Top managers in public enterprises sometimes lack professional qualifications and have created a non-results-oriented management culture. This culture is evident in lack of accountability in most public enterprises.

4 Conclusion

The analysis above shows the fundamental shift in management styles and focus that has been necessitated by economic, political and corporate re-orientation. The new trends have been matched by the adoption of an outward orientation and an emphasis on professional management skills. Management philosophy in Zimbabwe is thus undergoing changes that seek to position organizations competitively in the global business environment.

The attendant trade sanctions era nurtured an inward-oriented management perspective. Thus, during this era, management was preoccupied with meeting domestic demand under a plethora of restrictive economic and political regulations. The execution of management tasks was bureaucratic, rule-driven and top-down, and most organizations were virtual monopolies. Ironically, the prevalent business environment to some extent forced management to be innovative in terms of survival, and in adaptation of obsolete plant and machinery and redundant technology. The key management principles revolved around centralization of decision making, formal control systems, and a paternalistic management–employee relationship that was not open to employee contribution in decision making.

In public enterprises, government has had total control over corporate policy and strategy. In contrast, the private sector has gradually filled managerial ranks with qualified and experienced management. In many ways, organization structures are still bureaucratic, with most decision making located at higher management levels. The prevalence of the top-down approach in high echelons of management reflects the inequitable distribution of power in the structures.

The adoption of the structural adjustment programme in 1990 exposed local business organizations to foreign and regional competition. At the same time, the government introduced dramatic changes by way of removing trade restrictions, foreign exchange control, subsidies, and privatization of state-owned enterprises. These changes required the adoption of competitive strategies in aligning with trends in the global business environment. As a result, competent management resources became a key success factor and organizations found themselves recruiting and developing requisite skills. Management in the private and public sectors now consciously realize the importance of recruiting, training and developing professional managerial and general staff in order to survive in the global competitive environment. In many ways, management principles and practices in Zimbabwe have undergone significant transformation over the past thirty years and should prepare for greater challenges in the new millennium.

ZIVANAYI TAMANGANI

ZORORO MURANDA
UNIVERSITY OF ZIMBABWE

Further reading

(References cited in the text marked*)

* Bahrami, H. (1992) 'The emerging flexible organization', *California Management Review* 34 (4): 33–52. (A paper discussing organizational restructuring including the concept of delayering.)
* Bates, A. (1993) *Personnel Management in Zimbabwe*, Harare: Jann Investments. (A text that extensively discusses personnel management practices in Zimbabwe.)
  Carrol, G.R. (1994) 'Organizations ... the smaller they get', *California Management Review* 37 (1): 28–41. (A comprehensive article that widely discusses the concept of downsizing in the American corporate world.)
* Dirasse, L. (1991) 'Reaching the top – women managers in Eastern and Southern Africa', *Women in Development/Women in Management Division* 4: 11. (A text discussing the current posi-

tion of women in corporate governance in Eastern and Southern Africa.)

* Kanyenze, G. (1998) 'Youth and Self-Employment: The Role of Trade Unions', paper presented at the ARLAC Regional Seminar on the Role of Labour Administration in Employment Promotion in Small Enterprises, Harare. (A seminar paper that discusses self-employment options for school dropouts and unemployment statistics in Zimbabwe.)

* Khumalo, R. (1999) 'Decision-making structures for successful management in Zimbabwe', *South African Journal of Business Management* 30 (1): 14. Database: Business Source Premier.

Montgomery, J.D. (1987) 'Probing managerial development: image and reality in Southern Africa', *World Development* 15 (7): 911–29. (A comprehensive article discussing behavioural tendencies of African administrators in the Southern Africa region.)

Mparutsa, A. (1987) 'Indigenous Leadership Styles: Shaping the Future', paper presented at the Institute of Personnel Management (Zimbabwe) National Convention, Harare. (A useful paper discussing leadership styles commonly observed among indigenous Zimbabweans.)

Nyangulu, M.N. (1992) 'An Analysis of the Issues, Concerns, and Problems being faced by Women in Management and in Development in Zimbabwe: The implications for WIM/WID Network objectives, Strategies, and Activities', paper prepared for the launch of Women in Development/Women in Management, Harare. (A paper outlining problems faced by women in management and development.)

* Quinn, J.B. (1980) *Strategies for Change – Logical incrementalism*, Irwin, Illinois. (A text on change management with an emphasis on incremental change.)

Rodrik, D. (1997) 'Has globalization gone too far?', *California Management Review* 39 (3): 29–53. (A comprehensive paper discussing implications of globalization on international trade relations.)

Smit, P.J. and Cronje, G.J. de J. (eds) (1992) *Management Principles – A Contemporary South African Edition*, Cape Town: Juta & Co. (A text on management based on South African experiences.)

* Thompson, J.L. (2001) *Strategic Management*, 4th edn, London: Thomson Learning. (Best-selling textbook on Strategic Management.)

Wild, V. (1997) *Profit Not for Profit's Sake: History and Business Culture of African Entrepreneurs in Zimbabwe*, Harare: Baobab Books. (An excellent overview of the manner in which the modern business sector is organized, with the inherited European economy on the one hand and the more complex African enterprise on the other.)

Further resources

Africa Online website. Useful focus on doing business in Zimbabwe:
http://www.africaonline. co.zw

See also: AFRICA, MANAGEMENT IN; GHANA, MANAGEMENT IN; MANAGEMENT EDUCATION IN SUB-SAHARAN AFRICA; MANAGEMENT EDUCATION IN THE EMERGING COUNTRIES; NIGERIA, MANAGEMENT IN; SOUTH AFRICA, MANAGEMENT IN; ZAMBIA, MANAGEMENT IN